SCRIBNER LIBRARY OF MODERN EUROPE

EUROPE
1789 TO 1914
ENCYCLOPEDIA OF THE
AGE OF INDUSTRY AND EMPIRE

SCRIBNER LIBRARY OF MODERN EUROPE

EUROPE
1789 TO 1914

ENCYCLOPEDIA OF THE
AGE OF INDUSTRY AND EMPIRE

Volume 4

Pacifism to Syphilis

John Merriman and Jay Winter

EDITORS IN CHIEF

CHARLES SCRIBNER'S SONS

An imprint of Thomson Gale, a part of The Thomson Corporation

Detroit • New York • San Francisco • San Diego • New Haven, Conn. • Waterville, Maine • London • Munich

Europe 1789 to 1914: Encyclopedia of the Age of Industry and Empire

John Merriman
Jay Winter
Editors in Chief

LIBRARY OF CONGRESS CATALOGING-IN-PUBLICATION DATA

Europe 1789 to 1914 : encyclopedia of the age of industry and empire / edited by John Merriman and Jay Winter.
　　p. cm. — (Scribner library of modern Europe)
　Includes bibliographical references and index.
　ISBN 0-684-31359-6 (set : alk. paper) — ISBN 0-684-31360-X (v. 1 : alk. paper) — ISBN 0-684-31361-8 (v. 2 : alk. paper) — ISBN 0-684-31362-6 (v. 3 : alk. paper) — ISBN 0-684-31363-4 (v. 4 : alk. paper) — ISBN 0-684-31364-2 (v. 5 : alk. paper) — ISBN 0-684-31496-7 (ebook)
　1. Europe–History–1789-1900–Encyclopedias. 2. Europe–History–1871-1918–Encyclopedias. 3. Europe–Civilization–19th century–Encyclopedias. 4. Europe–Civilization–20th century–Encyclopedias. I. Merriman, John M. II. Winter, J. M.
　D299.E735 2006
　940.2'8–dc22
　　　　　　　　　　　　　　　　　　　　　　　　　　　　　　　　　2006007335

This title is also available as an e-book and as a ten-volume set with
Europe since 1914: Encyclopedia of the Age of War and Reconstruction.
E-book ISBN 0-684-31496-7
Ten-volume set ISBN 0-684-31530-0
Contact your Gale sales representative for ordering information.

Printed in the United States of America
10 9 8 7 6 5 4 3 2 1

CONTENTS OF THIS VOLUME

CONTENTS OF OTHER VOLUMES

C

VOLUME 2

D

VOLUME 5

MAPS OF EUROPE, 1789 TO 1914

The maps on the following pages show the changes in European national boundaries from 1789 to 1914, including the unification of Italy and of Germany.

Europe, 1789

— International border

• City

0   100   200 mi.

0 100 200 km

Norwegian Sea

SWEDEN

FINLAND (Sweden)

Gulf of Bothnia

Faroe Islands

Shetland Islands

NORWAY (Denmark)

Helsingfors

• St. Petersburg

Gulf of Finland

• Christiania

• Stockholm

• Moscow

Orkney Islands

Scotland

• Edinburgh

North Sea

DENMARK

• Copenhagen

Königsberg

RUSSIA

Baltic Sea

Ireland

GREAT BRITAIN

• Dublin

PRUSSIA

POLAND

Hanover

• Berlin

• Warsaw

Wales **England**

Amsterdam

• Hanover

Saxony

GALICIA

NETH.

• London

Brussels

Austrian Netherlands

HOLY ROMAN EMPIRE

• Bohemia

Moravia

HABSBURG POSSESSIONS

Moldavia

ATLANTIC OCEAN

• Paris

Austria

• Vienna

• Buda • Pest

TRANSYLVANIA

Bavaria

Munich

HUNGARY

Bay of Biscay

SWISS CONFED.

Tyrol

Wallachia

Black Sea

FRANCE

Milan **VENICE**

PIEDMONT

Venice

Genoa

• Florence

VENICE

MONTENEGRO

• Constantinople

TUSCANY

PAPAL STATES

RAGUSA

Adriatic Sea

ANDORRA

Corsica (France)

• Rome

OTTOMAN EMPIRE

PORTUGAL

• Madrid

Minorca (Great Britain)

NAPLES

Naples

SPAIN

SARDINIA

Tyrrhenian Sea

• Athens

Lisbon

Majorca (Spain)

Iviza (Spain)

Ionian Sea

Sicily

• Algiers

Tunis

Malta

Crete (Ottoman Empire)

OTTOMAN EMPIRE

Mediterranean Sea

France in 1789

— International border
• City

GREAT
BRITAIN

English Channel

Flanders
• Lille

AUSTRIAN
NETHERLANDS

GERMAN
STATES

N

• Rouen

Île de
France

Seine River

Normandy

• Paris

• Nancy

Lorraine

Alsace

Rhine River

Brittany

Loire River

F R A N C E

Franche
Comté

NEUCHÂTEL

• Nantes

SWISS CONFEDERATION

*ATLANTIC
OCEAN*

Poitou

Burgundy

• La Rochelle

Geneva

Lyon

KINGDOM OF
SARDINIA

*Bay of
Biscay*

• Bordeaux

Garonne River

Rhône River

AVIGNON

NICE

REPUBLIC
OF GENOA

Guyenne
and
Gascony

Provence

Languedoc

• Toulouse

• Marseille

0   50   100 mi.
0   50   100 km

ANDORRA

Corsica

SPAIN

Mediterranean Sea

Europe, 1815

— Boundary of the German Confederation, 1815

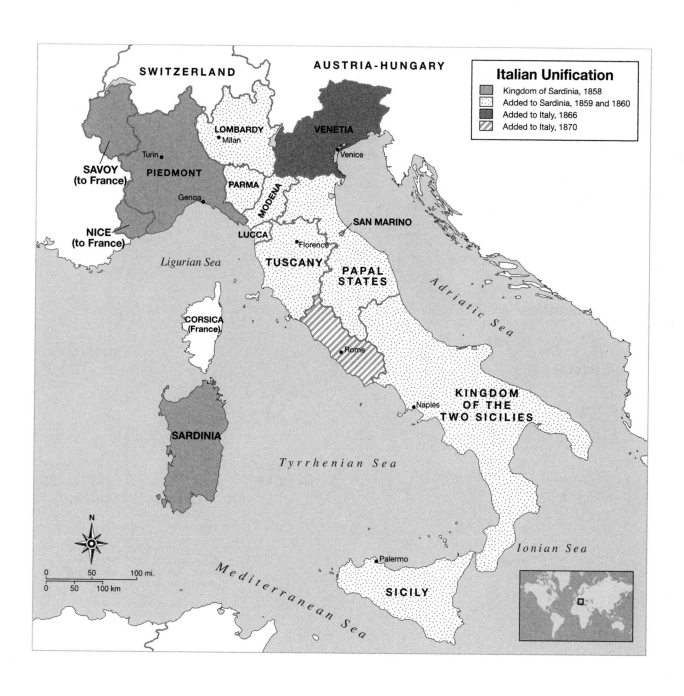

Italian Unification

- ▨ Kingdom of Sardinia, 1858
- ⬚ Added to Sardinia, 1859 and 1860
- ▨ Added to Italy, 1866
- ▨ Added to Italy, 1870

SWITZERLAND

AUSTRIA-HUNGARY

LOMBARDY
• Milan

VENETIA

• Venice

SAVOY
(to France)

Turin •

PIEDMONT

PARMA

Genoa •

MODENA

NICE
(to France)

LUCCA

SAN MARINO

Ligurian Sea

Florence •

TUSCANY

PAPAL
STATES

Adriatic Sea

CORSICA
(France)

• Rome

KINGDOM
OF THE
TWO SICILIES

Naples •

SARDINIA

Tyrrhenian Sea

N

Ionian Sea

0   50   100 mi.
0   50   100 km

Palermo •

Mediterranean Sea

SICILY

German Unification

	Prussia, 1865
	Added to Prussia, 1866
	Added to form North German Confederation, 1867
	Added to form German empire, 1871
	Boundary of German empire, 1871
	Route of Prussian armies in Austro-Prussian War
	Route of German armies in Franco-Prussian War
✳	Battle sites

0   50   100 mi.

0   50   100 km

Europe, 1914

International border

0 250 500 mi.
0 250 500 km

ICELAND

ATLANTIC OCEAN

NORWAY

SWEDEN

North Sea

Baltic Sea

DENMARK

RUSSIA

UNITED KINGDOM

NETH.

GERMANY

BELG.

LUX.

Caspian Sea

FRANCE

SWITZ.

AUSTRIA-HUNGARY

ROMANIA

Black Sea

ITALY

SERBIA

MONT.

BULGARIA

PORTUGAL

ANDORRA

SPAIN

ALBANIA

GREECE

OTTOMAN EMPIRE

PERSIA

Spanish Morocco

Tunisia (Fr.)

Morocco (Fr.)

Algeria (Fr.)

Mediterranean Sea

Libya (It.)

Egypt (Br.)

PACIFISM. Pacifism as the absolute refusal to bear arms or engage in violence, a doctrine derived from the strict construction of New Testament protocols, became a secularized ideology in the decades between the French Revolution and World War I. Its content was loosely defined depending on time, place, occasion, class, gender, and objective. When the French activist Emile Arnaud (1864–1921) first used the word in a 1901 article, he assured readers that pacifists were not "passive types," but active "peace makers," negotiators, and something more—believers in the rational application of peaceful methodologies to resolve conflicts that did not have to produce war. By the opening of the twentieth century, Arnaud's community of pacifists was composed of approximately 3,000 activists across a dozen European and North American nations, organized into local, national, and international groups—the Universal Peace Congress and the Interparliamentary Union. Members could be conservatives, liberals, socialists, feminists, international law specialists, diplomats, politicians, businessmen, union leaders, authors, journalists, philanthropists, salonnières, united in a belief that the future of civilized nations required civilized means of resolving conflicts.

An idea expressed in 1849 by Victor Hugo (1802–1885) at a peace congress held in Paris that anticipated a "United States of Europe" was understood in the late century to be a very distant objective. Its realization first required that nation-states learn to apply law to the international anar-chy just as governments had applied law to the feudal anarchy. Slow steps such as arbitration tribunals, mediation, leagues of neutrals, the estab-lishment of constitut ional regimes respecting basic civil rights, and the spread of international law to both commercial and political conflicts might need a century to evolve.

The movement that organized annual confer-ences from 1889 to 1914 was the culmination of a century-long evolution on the European continent. While peace societies were initially small, church-related Anglo-American groupings following the Napoleonic Wars, by 1840 there was enough of a base to convene an international congress in Lon-don—largely composed of people involved in the antislavery movement. A few years later in 1848–1852 when peace congresses assembled on the con-tinent and in Great Britain, attendees were drawn from a wider pool than the original Quaker-inspired voices. Peace activism increasingly attracted followers of liberal economic thinking—people such as Richard Cobden (1804–1865), Frédéric Bastiat (1801–1850), and Frédéric Passy (1822–1912), who were convinced that war was bad for business; peace-induced prosperity and free international trade opened the path toward the end of poverty. Hugo gave their economistic analysis a moral and humani-tarian vision. By mid-century, when intellectuals joined ministers in promoting peace congresses, the process of secularization was well established.

The nineteenth-century movement had an erra-tic history. The promising midcentury initiatives were overwhelmed by the tides of revolution and

Children holding a peace banner, London, 1898.
©HULTON-DEUTSCH COLLECTION/CORBIS

counterrevolution, but in 1867, a new set of voices appeared to try once again. Under the formal presidency of Giuseppe Garibaldi (1807–1882), a meeting convened in Geneva that brought together an amazing array of European progressive liberals, democrats, progressive revolutionaries, professors in exile from Napoleonic France, Saint-Simonians, and a few delegates from First International Socialist contingents. The resultant Ligue internationale de la paix et de la liberté and its long-running journal, *Les États-unis d'Europe,* was frankly democratic in orientation, committed to the notion that international peace required more than free trade—it demanded the end to absolutism, privilege, established religion, and social birthrights. In short, it wanted the realization of the French Revolution as the basis of human rights across Europe. This meeting included the first peace initiative where women raised independent voices and established separate organizational efforts, led by the Swiss activist Marie Goegg (1826–1899). The Ligue that followed had a heady

growth until the Franco-Prussian War, but it survived under the determined leadership of Charles Lemonnier (1806–1891), a Saint-Simonian democrat, and in the 1890s under Arnaud.

In 1889, on the centennial of the French Revolution when a huge exposition was to open in Paris, a group of English and French parliamentarians who had been in communication over the possibility of joint lobbying for an arbitration treaty, invited members of European parliaments to attend an organizational meeting. This produced the Interparliamentary Union (which still exists) and the decision to establish a central headquarters with a permanent secretariat. Simultaneously, citizen activists called a meeting to consider an organization to study and further international peace. This initiative created the Universal Peace Congress movement that opened a permanent headquarters in Bern (it still exists, but now in Geneva). Initially, there was no collaboration with the other international founded in 1889—the Socialist Second International—but in the following quarter century, individuals would work with peace parliamentarians and citizens in discreet national groups. By 1900, women drawn from the national councils of women, from the international associations of women suffrage organizations, and from societies of women teachers, as well as a few women lawyers and journalists, brought their voices into the international peace movement.

By and large, the late-century peace movement, often defined as liberal internationalism, de-emphasized disarmament as a provocative strategy that would elicit ridicule and cries of utopianism. Nor did they reject the right of self-defense, and indeed, their new definition of "just war" was contained in a doctrine of defense. A major exception to this cautious approach, however, arose from some feminist peace crusaders who campaigned against the arms race and tied its costs to the absence of social programs that they saw as crucial to democratic development. Thus, while liberal internationalism often confined itself to limited and presumably realistic objectives, by the opening of the twentieth century voices agitated for a more holistic anti-war approach. Just as the 1867 Ligue saw democratization as a first step toward peace, many feminist peace activists connected arms reduction to social justice and peace. Nonetheless, the establishment

Peace demonstration in London, May, 1914. As tensions between Great Britain and Germany escalated, pacifists in England became alarmed at the growing threat of open warfare, which indeed followed in August 1914. ©HULTON-DEUTSCH COLLECTION/CORBIS

core of the movement campaigned for objectives that seemed realistic for nineteenth-century bourgeois and progressive values: arbitration tribunals, international law codification, mediation, arbitration treaties between and among specific states. Despite this cautious approach, the moderate peace activists—such as the German Ludwig Quidde; the French Passy, Arnaud, and Gaston Moch; the Austrians Bertha von Suttner and Alfred Hermann Fried; the Italian Ernesto Teodoro Moneta; the Belgians Henri La Fontaine and Edouard Descamps; the English Sir William Randal Cremer, William Thomas Stead, and Hodgson Pratt; the Swiss Elie Ducommun and Charles Albert Gobat; the Dane Frederik Bajer—were subject to biting ridicule and denunciations ranging from antipatriotism to brainless utopianism. *Le Pacifisme* by Emile Faguet (1908) typified the assault from the nationalist, militarist, and masculinist point of view.

When the first Hague Conference called by the czar convened in 1899 to discuss the dangers of the arms race; when the peace prize established by Alfred Nobel (1833–1896) was first awarded in 1901; when the Russian Revolution of 1905 introduced a version of representative government in Europe's last remaining autocracy; and when the millionaire Andrew Carnegie (1835–1919) contributed an enormous fortune to the Endowment for International Peace as well as the structure to house the arbitration tribunal at The Hague, peace activists believed that their message was reaching the circles that counted and made political decisions. The Hague Convention of 1899 standardized procedures for convening arbitration tribunals when two powers agreed to adjudicate differences—the century-old ancestor of the twenty-first-century International Criminal Court and the standing World Court. Nations began to use arbitration to solve "minor" issues; Norway and Sweden separated and avoided the war that threatened; books such as von Suttner's *Die Waffen nieder!* (1889) and Norman Angell's *The Great Illusion* (1913) reached mass audiences; congresses addressing new forms of international law, issues of race, and women's rights multiplied and added peace proposals to their agendas. The centrist vision of the Socialist Second International strongly hinted that workers might call a general strike in the event of war, and the radical wings of the left, including anarchists, preached noncompliance and threatened barracks strikes in a variety of forms of antimilitarism. A major war had not been fought on European soil since Waterloo—and a sense of the vast dangers that a modern technological war would produce was captured in Jean de Bloch's six-volume 1898 study of the probable effects of modern warfare (originally in Russian, German, and French; only one volume in English). Peace activists clung to these signs of progress even in face of the imperial confrontations, escalating arms expenditures, and the increasingly violent language of nationalism that existed simultaneously. The struggle between the "old" and the "new" forces for Europe's soul, observed von Suttner who became the first woman to win the Nobel peace prize in 1905, was not settled, but at least a serious challenge had been made to the sovereign right of a government to declare war at will. Moreover, peace activists even began to debate what might be done to isolate a state that did declare war.

Obviously the twenty-five years of organizing and propagandizing, the constantly expanding membership base of peace societies, the millions of signatures assembled by women's groups in support of the Hague conferences, did not prevent the outbreak of that Great War that peace activists feared and tried to prevent. But when that war came, its initiators all insisted that it was a defensive and justifiable struggle, one for the survival of the nation and its civilization. Political, official discourse no longer allowed for aggressive warfare.

See also **Hague Conferences; International Law; Nobel, Alfred; Suttner, Bertha von; Tolstoy, Leo.**

BIBLIOGRAPHY

Brock, Peter. *Pacifism in Europe to 1914*. Princeton, N.J., 1971.

Caedel, Martin. *Thinking About Peace and War*. Oxford, U.K., 1987.

Chickering, Roger. *Imperial Germany and a World Without War: The Peace Movement and German Society, 1892–1914*. Princeton, N.J., 1975.

Cooper, Sandi E. *Patriotic Pacifism: Waging War on War in Europe, 1815–1914*. Oxford, U.K., 1991.

Grossi, Verdiana. *Le Pacifisme Européen 1889–1914*. Brussels, 1994.

Petrocoli, Marta, Donatella Cherubini, and Alessandra Anteghini, eds. *Les Etats-Unis d'Europe/The United States of Europe: Un Projet Pacifiste/A Pacifist Project*. Bern, 2004.

Van den Linden, W. H. *The International Peace Movement, 1815–1874*. Amsterdam, 1987.

SANDI E. COOPER

PAGANINI, NICCOLÒ (1782–1840), Italian violinist and composer.

Niccolò Paganini's astonishing bravura and compositional originality on the violin enabled him to carry out, in the years 1812–1834, the most successful concert career of any instrumentalist before him. He brought audiences all over Europe to frenzies of enthusiasm and earned numerous honors and titles. His twenty-four *Caprices* for solo violin, first published in 1820, have formed a central foundation of violin technique since the mid-nineteenth century.

Paganini was born in Genoa and spent his entire life in Italy until 1828. He received training in violin and composition from several musicians, among them Alessandro Rolla. From 1801 to 1809 he lived in Lucca, serving from 1805 in the orchestra of Prince Felice and Elisa Baciocchi. Here he first explored the possibilities of writing for the G-string alone, producing the *Sonata Napoleone.* Temperamentally unsuited to the restrictions of the court, he left Lucca, and from 1810 to 1827 led an itinerant life as a concert violinist, interspersed with periods of relative inactivity due to illness, amorous affairs, gambling, and dissipation. A series of concerts in Milan in 1813, featuring his new variations on *Le streghe,* established him as the leading violinist of his age. In the following years he developed a close association with Gioacchino Antonio Rossini (1792–1868), whose melodies he favored as themes for concert variations and whose opera *Matilde de Shabran* he conducted in 1821. In the early 1820s his health showed a precipitous decline, apparently from venereal disease, that plagued him the rest of his life and left his body emaciated. He nevertheless continued to concertize, often with his lover, the singer Antonia Bianchi, who gave birth to his son and only child, Achille, in 1825.

In 1828, armed with two newly written concertos, Paganini launched his legendary European tours with a wildly successful series of concerts in Vienna. Over the next six years he concertized constantly in Bohemia, the German Confederation, Poland, France, and England, accompanied only by his son, whom he adored and treated with immense affection, and occasionally by a travel companion who kept track of his books. He earned enormous sums of money. His concerts usually featured one of his lengthy concertos, one or two of his variation sets with orchestra, and an extended work for solo violin, intermingled with short orchestral fillers and arias by guest singers. His reclusive lifestyle, ravaged body, dark looks, and his unusual performing posture, together with the sometimes bizarre sounds he was able to call forth from the instrument, gave him a mysterious, demonic presence on stage that riveted audiences and led to a whole series of rumors about his past and personal life. Journalists steeped in the literary style of Romanticism, especially in Germany, invented fantastic tales and constructed his image as the protopyical Romantic virtuoso. An amorous scandal in England provoked Paganini to retreat from public concerts in 1835, and he remained between Italy and France until his death five years later. At Parma he reorganized and conducted the ducal orchestra for a short period, and in 1837 he tried to establish in Paris, together with an entrepreneurial friend, a "Casino Paganini," but it soon foundered.

Paganini's compositional output can be divided into three categories: the twenty-four *Caprices* for solo violin; concert pieces for violin and orchestra, including both concertos, variation sets, and solo violin pieces; and chamber music for strings and guitar or mandolin. The *Caprices,* dedicated "to the artists," constitute his main compositional legacy, although he considered them studies and did not play them in public. They are indispensable builders of technique for aspiring

Niccolò Paganini. Engraving from an 1825 drawing by Daniel Maclise. © BETTMANN/CORBIS

virtuosos, and as prototypical character pieces they influenced later composers such as Frédéric Chopin (1810–1849), Franz Liszt (1811–1886), Robert Schumann (1810–1856), Johannes Brahms (1833–1897), and Sergei Rachmaninov (1873–1943). The concert works feature an extremely high level of virtuosity and usually assign a minimal role to the orchestral part. The chamber pieces are mostly for amateurs and accordingly are light and pleasant in tone.

Paganini's playing combined the fire and virtuosity of the Italian virtuoso school with the elegance and melodic focus of the French violin school. His principal technical innovations in writing for the violin include the extensive use of harmonics (high-pitched tones produced by touching the strings lightly rather than pressing them against the fingerboard), left-hand pizzicato (plucked notes), the polyphonic mixture of pizzicato, legato, and harmonic tones in rapid alternation, composition for the G-string (the lowest-pitched one) alone, and a bowing technique that helped project a strongly impassioned or tragic melody. His legacy was taken up most explicitly by the violinists Ole Bull (1810–1880), Heinrich Wilhelm Ernst (1814–1865), and Henri Wieniawski (1835–1880).

See also **Liszt, Franz; Music; Opera; Romanticism; Rossini, Gioachino.**

BIBLIOGRAPHY

Courcy, Geraldine I. C. de. *Paganini, the Genoese.* 2 vols. Norman, Okla., 1957.

DANA GOOLEY

PAINE, THOMAS (1737–1809), political philosopher, pamphleteer.

Thomas Paine was one of the most colorful and successful political pamphleteers during the age of the American and French Revolutions. Born in Thetford, England, he emigrated to Pennsylvania when he was thirty-seven years old after pursuing a series of failed careers in making stays for women's corsets, teaching school, operating a general store, and collecting excise taxes. In Philadelphia, Paine wrote short pieces for such journals as the *Pennsylvania Magazine.* His first major pamphlet, *Common Sense* (1776), argued, for one of the first times in print, why the American colonies must immediately separate from England. During the Revolutionary War, he published several newspaper articles, later collected as the *American Crisis* series, to rally American courage and patriotism against overwhelming British military forces (the first essay included the famous inspiring words, "These are the times that try men's souls").

After the war, Paine spent much of his time writing against the establishment of a national bank and in designing a pierless iron bridge. Unsuccessful in having his bridge built across the Schuylkill River, he went to France in 1787 to seek investors who would fund its construction across the River Seine. Failing that, he moved to London to find financial supporters interested in seeing it span the Thames. There, he traveled throughout the Midlands with the British statesman and philosopher Sir Edmund Burke (1729–1797), his later nemesis, in search of iron suppliers.

Two years later, just after the French Revolution erupted in Paris, Paine returned to France, convinced that the democratic forces that had emerged in America in 1776 were now on the march in Europe. He wrote Burke about the political changes taking place in Paris and, as it turned out, unwittingly helped stimulate Burke's developing animosity against the Revolution. In November 1790, Burke published his famous antirevolutionary attack in *Reflections on the Revolution in France.* In February of the following year, Paine answered Burke in *Rights of Man* (part one). Burke vigorously attacked the revolutionaries' wholesale destruction of the French social and political order, especially the monarchy and aristocracy. In response, Paine railed against Burke by attacking these same two institutions because they enslaved human beings' minds and bodies.

One year later, Paine published part two of *Rights of Man,* one of the most radical expressions of social reform ever to appear. Totally ignoring Burke, Paine proposed a remarkably detailed government program that would ameliorate the living conditions of less fortunate citizens, including provisions for old-age retirement income, welfare payments for the impoverished, public education, and free funerals for poor people.

In 1792, after the fall of the monarchy, Paine was elected to the French National Convention, one of only two foreigners to receive this honor. With Marie-Jean de Caritat, marquis de Condorcet (1743–1794), and other notable figures, he served on the committee that was to draft a new republican constitution for France. At the time, Paine was allied with the moderate Girondin faction, which included the journalist Jacques-Pierre Brissot de Warville, Madame Roland (Jeanne Manon Philipon Roland de la Platiére) and her husband, Jean-Marie Roland de la Platiére, and Condorcet, against the radical Jacobin faction, led by Maxmilien Robespierre, Jean-Paul Marat, and Louis-Antoine de St. Just. Against the latter, Paine argued that King Louis XVI (r. 1774–1792) should be exiled and not executed, but he lost that battle when the king was condemned to death. Soon, Paine was arrested and imprisoned for eleven months in the Luxembourg prison during the Reign of Terror (1793–1794).

Just before his imprisonment, Paine had completed the first part of *The Age of Reason,* his attack on the superstitions of all organized religion. It appeared first in French in Paris in 1793 and in English a year later. The second part, a devastating critique of the Bible, appeared in 1795.

After the fall of Robespierre, Paine was reelected to the Convention, where he participated in the drafting of the Constitution of 1795, creating the government known as the Directory. In 1796 he published an open letter attacking the U.S. president George Washington, who, he claimed, had done nothing about his imprisonment. When the letter was published in America, Paine became extremely unpopular there. Although he retired from government after his service on the Convention, he remained in France, living with his journalist friend Nicolas de Bonneville from 1797 until his eventual return to the United States in 1802. In Paris, he wrote his last great work, *Agrarian Justice,* calling for heavy inheritance taxes on the wealthy to support social welfare programs.

Paine spent his last years in America viciously attacking the Federalists, especially John Adams, whose presidency had ended in 1801. By the time of his death in 1809, he was a largely ignored and forgotten man.

See also **French Revolution; Republicanism.**

BIBLIOGRAPHY

Claeys, Gregory. *Thomas Paine: Social and Political Thought.* Winchester, Mass., 1989.

Foner, Eric, ed. *The Writings of Thomas Paine.* New York, 1995.

Fruchtman, Jack, Jr. *Thomas Paine and the Religion of Nature.* Baltimore, Md., 1993.

———. *Thomas Paine: Apostle of Freedom.* New York, 1994.

Keane, John. *Tom Paine: A Political Life.* Boston, 1995.

JACK FRUCHTMAN JR.

PAINTING. Modern art really begins with the French Revolution. Breaking the ruling elite's grip on art and democratically restructuring its institutions, the French Republic lay the foundations for increased production by artists and a wider audience for their works. Modern and often politically charged subjects challenged the old regime of classical, mythological, and religious painting, with its claims to universality. Realistically represented, such new subjects also undermined the hallowed academic principles of idealizing, classical style based on antiquity and the Renaissance. From this point on, discussion of art became divided over the legitimacy of contemporary subjects and the forms of representation they entailed. The conflicts of the first part of the century reached a crisis around 1850 with the emergence of the avant-garde, leading to a now familiar state of constant critical opposition and renewal. From this crucible came impressionism and its aftermaths, which are often grouped under the general category of modernism. Paris was already the cultural center of Europe in the eighteenth century; the closely interrelated political, economic, and artistic events from 1789 to 1914 would transform Western art into something far closer to the art we know today. Other centers—Spain, Germany, England, and Italy—owed much to French art, whether adopting its modes or in opposition to them.

The arts of the nineteenth century were dominated by three overriding, but neither equivalent nor mutually exclusive concepts: Romantic individualism, naturalism, and modernism. The first two can be used generally to describe ideas or practices of both the past and the present, but which in the nineteenth century were elevated to the status of movements. The third has its seeds in the first two but is like neither, since it describes a tradition, mainly internal to artistic thinking, though necessarily supported by the art market, of critical responses to recent art in order to maintain a state of originality and successive innovation.

Romanticism is mistakenly called a style. It is, rather, a set of attitudes that prioritize individual creativity and inner emotion over learned rules and conventional morality. It is a mode of thinking and feeling manifested through a variety of aesthetics, ranging from neoclassicism (as the official style of the Revolution) to naturalism (as in Eugène Delacroix's evocation of the suffering of Greeks under Turkish rule). Naturalism is a mode of representation based primarily on observation rather than on predetermined recipes or ideals, and may also reveal a variety of attitudes, including, for example, a Romantic love of solitude in nature (as in the Barbizon School) or opposition to authoritarian regimes, whether political, artistic, or both (as in Gustave Courbet's realism). Often, but not always, Romanticism and naturalism contain something of one another. Modernism takes off from the Romantic emphasis on the individual and drew sustenance from realism, since the latter constituted a critical challenge to earlier convention. Thus, "early modernism" can be found in many places. When modernity became a value for its own sake, with the Industrial Revolution and the rise of capitalism, innovation became the driving force through which artists staked their claim within an art world in which entrepreneurial dealers, critics, and private collectors, more than government or academies, came to determine financial success and reputation.

THE AGE OF REVOLUTION

The French revolutionaries wanted to break not only with the politics of the past but also with the art they believed served such politics. Literally, a revolution (a full rotation) is a turning that is simultaneously forward and backward. Reformers prior to the Revolution urged that progress required a return to original principles, such as the heroic and just conduct of the ancients and the classical style of art that supposedly embodied their much revered morality. In Rome, sculptors from places as far-flung as Denmark (Bertel Thorvaldsen, 1768 or 1770–1844), England (John Flaxman, 1755–1826), and Italy (Antonio Canova, 1757–1822) had been pioneering evocations of ancient beauty and sublimity through statues of sleek beauty or imposing power. In a quest to replace the tired conventions of their predecessors and the perceived trivialities of rococo art, they tapped both historical knowledge and inner emotion to produce seductive and moving alternatives. Combining their stylistic rigor with his smoldering political activism, Jacques-Louis David (1748–1825) first painted potentially revolutionary themes from ancient Roman history. His *Oath of the Horatii* (1784) heralded patriotism as an overriding virtue. After 1789 he applied these artistic principles to repre-

sentations of Revolutionary events and heroes, such as *Marat Assassinated* (1793). At the same time, David was elected from the radical Jacobin party to the new legislature, which abolished the French Academy and its privileges. He organized public celebrations, using motifs from antiquity to suggest that the new regime had given rebirth to its noble ideals. The neoclassicism (literally new/renewed classicism), for which David's tautly linear, stripped-down, and highly finished style became the model, used significant elements of realism to create its powerful effects. When contemporary models such as the radical journalist Jean-Paul Marat became the basis for his painting, naturalism acquired a progressive, even politically radical dimension, often called realism.

From the Revolution onward, modern subjects and the degree to which artists based their work on observed models from reality versus those from the aesthetic repertoire of antiquity and old masters became the touchstone of artistic debate. Underlying both the neoclassicists of Rome and the politically motivated David had been the commitment to freedom from establishment constraints. Concurrent with the revolutionary rhetoric of liberty and individual rights that proved so explosive in America and France, two aesthetic theories accompanied artistic developments and set the stage for much that followed. First was the notion that artistic creativity came from within the self—from an intuitive basis called genius—which might, according to some, be enhanced through training, but which must never be subjugated by rules and formulas. Second was the ancient concept of the sublime, rearticulated in the eighteenth century by Edmund Burke (1729–1797), better-known for his political writings. The sublime offered the possibility of an aesthetic alternative to beauty, one rooted more in emotion than in reason, yet of equal value. Grand and even fearful works, whether of art or nature, might be morally uplifting as they reveal human limitations and the presence of a grander power—call it Nature or God. These ideas lay the foundation on the one hand for Romanticism, attuned to the individual and his or her feelings, and on the other for naturalism, which found value in aspects of the surrounding world.

Concurrent with the career of Jacques-Louis David, and a barometer of artistic developments from the 1780s to the 1820s, was that of Francisco José de Goya y Lucientes (1746–1828) in Spain. Goya evolved from being a court painter to a liberal inspired by the French Enlightenment, then to a patriot disgusted by the Napoleonic invasion of his country, and finally to a tormented exile grappling with fantasies. Spanish art always had a realist bent, linked as it was through Spain's history to the Netherlands and the Caravaggesque trends of southern Italy, absent the strong academic tradition of the French. Goya's democratic ideals were translated into his *Family of Charles IV* (1800). Although dressed in their uniforms and gowns, the royals are shown as everyday people, unidealized (some say caricatured, but studies for the painting show the opposite), in a space shared both by their employee, the artist, and with the ordinary viewer, thanks to the picture's construction of perspective. Having suffered an illness that left him deaf, yet at the summit of his career, by 1800 Goya enjoyed a kind of freedom that allowed him to follow his personal preoccupation with the inner nature of humankind. On the one hand, he explored themes of witchcraft and hallucination—the irrational; on the other, he recorded the many acts of violence and terror perpetrated by all sides during warfare. His political and intellectual ideals merged in a profoundly pessimistic yet humanitarian vision that is exemplified in his satirical *Los caprichos* series of prints in 1796 and his *Executions of May 3, 1808* (1815), which showed the fate of Spanish rebels.

Another artist who explored the depths of the human spirit was the Swiss-born Johann Heinrich Füssli (or Fuseli, 1741–1825), who made London his base and joined the Royal Academy. When Füssli drew on the classical tradition, he sometimes parodied it or selected themes that contradicted its ideals of beauty and reason. Seeking shock-value and originality, he explored erotic themes (including pornographic drawings of his wife) and the world of dreams and visions. His many paintings drawn from John Milton's *Paradise Lost* (1667, 1674) or from Germanic mythology reveal his search for alternatives to the sunny Mediterranean classics of those who hoped to rival France by imitation. His best-known painting, *The Nightmare* (1781), combines the erotic and the hallucinatory in a style that seems drawn more from Italian mannerism than from nature, and an expressive handling that defied his colleagues' focus on crispness and finish. His quip "Hang nature, she puts me out!" embodies one extreme of the Romantic quest for forms to embody the visions of the inner world with which he was obsessed.

ROMANTIC NATURALISM

While the mainstream of French painters were deeply engaged in the political aftermath of the Revolution and on the Napoleonic battlefield, both England and Germany were discovering nature as the place where they could pursue art peacefully and as a source both satisfying to their personal convictions and to the demands of an increasingly middle-class market. Caspar David Friedrich (1774–1840) observed his surroundings closely, but he put his studies together into landscape constructions that were intended to reveal the sublime scale of nature and the presence of God. Friedrich hated the French, whom he regarded as godless and imperialistic. His strong Protestant culture believed in searching for direct communion with the divine, in his case through the contemplation of nature, as inspired by the *Natur Philosophie* of August Wilhelm von Schegel (1767–1845) and Friedrich Wilhelm Joseph von Schelling (1775–1854). His *Monk by the Seashore* (1809–1810) strips landscape to its bare essentials in order to enhance its didactic impact (ironically, much as David had done in his history paintings). The scale of man to sea, sky, and heavens is minute; that the human figure wears a monk's habit specifies the religious reverence before such grandeur. One of Friedrich's students said the monk was a self-portrait, a statement not to be taken literally—the figure is too small to be identifiable, and Friedrich belonged to no monastery—but to mean that, for Friedrich, art was a vehicle for self-expression elevated to universal experience. This was one of the guiding principles of Romanticism.

In England, the two greatest proponents of landscape during the Romantic period were Joseph Mallord William Turner (1775–1851) and John Constable (1776–1837). Turner used the tradition of the sublime to transform his often narrative human subjects into the overarching theme of man's dependency on nature. He usually chose one meteorological extreme or the other for his

Peace—Burial at Sea. Painting by J. M. W. Turner, 1841. CLORE COLLECTION, TATE GALLERY, LONDON/ART RESOURCE, NY

setting, from lowly fishermen waiting for the wind to rise to the ancient Carthaginian invader (whose present imperialist successor was Napoleon) beset by howling gales in *Snow Storm: Hannibal and His Army Crossing the Alps* (1812). Turner's theme was always nature's dominance and the "Fallacies of Hope"—the title he gave to bombastic lines of poetry he wrote to accompany his pictures. With compositional structures that draw the viewer into

a vortex to be enveloped by sweeping strokes of paint and flayed by smears and gobs violently applied with the palette knife, Turner conveyed the physical experiences of intense sunlight or the ferocity of wind and rain.

Constable, on the other hand, eschewed bravado. In the eighteenth century, landed gentry fresh from tours of the Continent commissioned garden designs for their estates and paintings for their country houses that reminded them of Italy's glorious scenery as represented in seventeenth-century art. Eventually, they began to see beauty in their native surroundings, as the Industrial Revolution transformed British cities into sprawling urban nightmares. They developed a nostalgia for the agricultural past, which led Constable to believe there was room for a "natural painter," who could appreciate the beauty with which God endowed even ordinary places. For him, Salisbury Cathedral was the ideal subject, a symbol of God yet surrounded by lush grounds and ample vegetation on which even cattle could graze, unifying the material and spiritual realm. Constable justified his work on utilitarian grounds, claiming both that "painting is a science," but also that it "is a way of feeling." His rich paint surfaces and relatively loose handling made his closely observed trees and clouds appear spontaneously observed and directly available to the senses, seductive in their calm material amplitude rather than spewing, as in Turner, with tumultuous rage. Yet both regarded nature rather than human reason as the source of power and truth, and they appealed to body and soul through symbolic structures and their psychological impact rather than through the narratives of history painting.

While Britain and Germany gave impetus to the rise of landscape painting, the figure tradition still dominated Romanticism in France, which continued struggling with its convulsive politics following the defeat of Napoleon I (r. 1804–1814/15) and a powerful, if waning, academic influence. For Théodore Géricault (1791–1824) the theme of man versus the elements was articulated through a grand figure composition, *The Raft of the Medusa* (1818–1819), replete with references to historical tradition as well as to contemporary politics. (The ship ran aground and was abandoned by its incompetent captain, a Royalist appointee. Sound familiar?) His younger friend, Eugène Delacroix (1798–1863), gave new definition to Romanticism when in 1824 he exhibited *Scenes from the Massacres at Chios* (1822–1824, Musée du Louvre, Paris), a large and ostentatiously naturalistic painting about the cruelty of the Turkish rulers crushing the impoverished Greeks struggling for independence. Delacroix's painting appealed to its viewers' empathy for fellow Christians' suffering as well as

to political ideals of freedom. It was an unmistakable challenge to the new darling of the Academy, Jean-Auguste-Dominique Ingres (1780–1867), the former student of David recently returned in triumph from years of residence in Rome. Despite his youthful rebelliousness, Ingres became a professed classicist, whose style was based on first-hand study of the ancients and old masters, particularly Raphael (1483–1520). His *Vow of Louis XIII* (1824) displayed a respect for both political and artistic authority through its display of unity between church and monarchy (restored to power following Napoleon's defeat) based on traditional compositional and stylistic features—those taught by the Academy. Ingres became associated with a smooth, polished style based on expert drawing and crisp linearity, whereas Delacroix exemplified a looser, more spontaneous-looking style, based on masses of color modeled broadly with light and shade. Romanticism came to be linked with this freedom of execution and liberal politics, hence with feelings of thwarted aspirations to transform the present and transcend tradition; classicism with obstinate academic standards, official power, and the status quo. Ingres was welcomed by the Academy, which he prevented Delacroix from joining until Delacroix ultimately outlived him.

As France, following England, joined in the Industrial Revolution, middle-class patronage encouraged a host of artists to practice portraiture and landscape. The latter in particular, inspired in part by the British, fulfilled a growing need for images that combined both the fantasy of escape and the demand for naturalism. Artists toured the countryside, bringing back to the Parisian art market scenes of rural life and contemplative solitude that satisfied the urban myth of nature as a realm of innocence and purity. The farming village of Barbizon, near the Fontainebleau Forest about a day's travel from Paris, became a settlement for artists (Jean-Baptiste-Camille Corot, 1796–1875; Théodore Rousseau, 1812–1867; Jean-François Millet, 1814–1875), who exemplified rural virtue by their humble surroundings and unpretentious lifestyle while they catered to their patrons' vicarious yearning for a simpler, quieter life. In literature and politics, as well, a reaction to modernity was forming—a double-edged reaction in which looking backward became revolutionary once again. In the

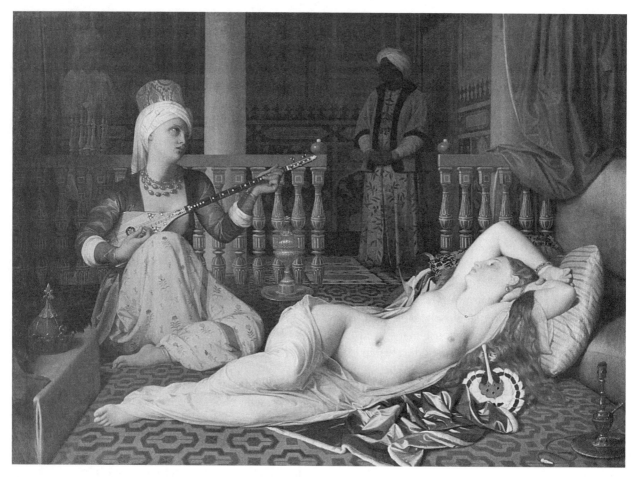

Odalisque with a Slave. Painting by Jean-Auguste-Dominique Ingres, 1839. ©BURSTEIN COLLECTION/CORBIS

writings of George Sand (Amandine Dudevant; 1804–1876) and Pierre-Joseph Proudhon (1809–1865), rural ways provided the basis for utopian thinking that showed up the injustices of the oligarchs who ruled France since the 1830s. It was from this crucible that socialism and anarchism were born, flaring in 1848 into the second overthrow of the French monarchy and various uprisings across Europe. It was from the same conditions that the artistic avant-garde emerged.

THE AVANT-GARDE

Gustave Courbet (1819–1877) seized public attention by embodying the 1848 revolution's violent rupture with the past. He became the first leader of the avant-garde. His images of common people from his home province (Franche-Comté, near Switzerland) lacked the veneer of nostalgia. His *Stonebreakers* (1848) were contemporary workers whose presence revealed that actual social and economic conditions in the countryside had little to do with the mythology of his Romantic Barbizon predecessors. The Second French Republic lasted briefly, however, ending in 1851 with Louis-Napoleon Bonaparte's coup d'état, which established him as Emperor Napoleon III (r. 1852–1871) and his regime as the Second Empire. Courbet's art was seen as a democratic challenge to this politics as well as to government dominance of the arts through official patronage. His *A Burial at Ornans* (1849–1850) dared treat the theme of death from an everyday, down-to-earth rather than religious point of view. To its insulted Parisian audience, it appeared crudely painted in a manner appropriate to its gawky subjects and to the workman-like painter they assumed Courbet to be. His *The Painter's Studio; A Real Allegory* (1855) placed the artist himself at the center of a crowd representing French society, claiming leadership in a revolution

Young Girl at Her Toilet. Painting by Jean-Baptiste-Camille Corot, c. 1860–1865. Corot celebrates the beauty and simplicity of an everyday scene. LOUVRE, PARIS, FRANCE/BRIDGEMAN ART LIBRARY/GIRAUDON

of consciousness—hence both political and artistic—for vision based on honest observation and independence from convention. He exhibited the painting at a self-funded pavilion, called Realism, set up across from the officially sponsored art shows of the Exposition Universelle. He published what is now called the Realist Manifesto, in which he stated that his aim was "to translate the customs, the ideas, the appearance of my epoch, according to my own estimation." The painting and its manifesto became a touchstone for the free artist of the avant-garde, establishing a tradition of questioning old shibboleths while self-consciously expressing one's own way of seeing.

At the same time, England was experiencing a minor artistic revolution. The Pre-Raphaelite Brotherhood, founded by some pious Catholic Oxford students in 1848 (William Holman Hunt, 1827–1910; John Everett Millais, 1829–1896; and Dante

Gabriel Rossetti, 1828–1882), was also a protest against authority and tradition. Yet its ideals were far more conservative than Courbet's. They paralleled the critic John Ruskin's (1819–1900) call for an art that would reveal the greatness of God through meticulous observation of nature. Ruskin had been writing about Turner in the 1840s; but the Pre-Raphaelites took inspiration from the religious art of the German Nazarenes and the moralizing social art of Ford Madox Brown (1821–1893). As exemplified by Hunt's *The Light of the World* (1853), they fused archaic quattrocento composition and simplification with the precision and ultraoptical naturalism of scientific studies. The result was a strange and stifling realism that quite effectively conveys Victorian society's alienating combination of materialism and high moral aspirations based on oppressive sensual self-denial.

The other artist who defined the early French avant-garde was Édouard Manet (1832–1883). Of very different origins from the reputedly coarse provincial Courbet, the elegant Parisian Manet represented his Parisian peers to become what in a famous essay his friend the poet and critic Charles Baudelaire (1821–1867) called "The Painter of Modern Life." Following Courbet's strategy of attracting public attention through controversy, Manet painted his *Déjeuner sur l'herbe* (1862; Picnic on the grass), which showed a naked woman staring out at the viewer while accompanied by two clothed men. Following protests when this and a number of other paintings were rejected by the Salon Jury of 1863, Emperor Napoleon III instituted a Salon des Refusés, in which Manet's painting starred. Reforms of the selection process for 1865 allowed Manet to exhibit an even more confrontational picture, his *Olympia* (1863). In it, a naked woman, visibly a prostitute with a servant from the colonies bringing an admirer's bouquet, is on display as if in a shop window. She is accompanied by her black cat, an animal celebrated in recent literature for its independence (as well as reputed promiscuity) and its companionship with poets and artists. Manet stripped away the seductive ideal of womanhood, which he now placed in the demimonde of Paris's thriving culture of courtesans and prostitutes. Through her gaze and Manet's palpable painting of her flesh, Manet reduced male fantasies of sexual conquest to a business transaction. At the same time, he flaunted a style of painting through broad strokes and patches of color, imposing a willful lack of finish that drew attention to a technical deliberateness that shattered the possibility of illusion. In defining this mode of painting, which gave rise to impressionism, Manet's admirer, the novelist Émile Zola (1840–1902), called art "a corner of nature seen through a temperament"—rephrasing Courbet's commitment to representing the observable world through his own way of seeing.

The impressionists were guided by this principle. But unlike Courbet and Manet, many of them concentrated on landscape, which in the early to mid 1870s they vowed to make a reflection of modern France. The best known are Claude Monet (1840–1926), Camille Pissarro (1830–1903), and Paul Cézanne (1839–1906). No longer would landscape painting offer a refuge in nature from the effects of modernity; it would celebrate the human impact on the landscape through cityscapes as well as the new economic and leisure activities in suburbs and countryside that signaled contemporary prosperity and optimism. Contemporary technology, such as train travel, made the countryside accessible and underlay expansion of the suburbs, while photography provided a new standard for naturalism and often documented modern industrial constructions such as train stations, new bridges, and the metallic framework of the architect Charles Garnier's new Opera House. The impressionists' utopia could be found, thus, in their own surroundings. One such place was *La Grenouillère* (1869), where Monet developed his characteristic style of broken, sketch-like brushwork, rather than in some solitary wooded glen or isolated province. That technique itself conveyed the spontaneity of direct observation associated with painting *en plein-air* (outdoors). It embodied both the artist's creative energies and the ever-changing world, which Baudelaire, in "The Painter of Modern Life," called the essence of modernity. At this formative time in their careers, the impressionists successfully followed up previous challenges to the art world with a series of eight independent exhibitions from 1874 to 1886. Following on the heels of the collapse the Second Empire under Prussian boots and the brief civil war of the Paris Commune (1871), these challenges linked the

Amazon. Portrait by Édouard Manet, 1882. Manet depicts a lesbian dressed elegantly in male attire. NIMATALLAH/ART RESOURCE, NY

impressionists to radical politics. Yet as they were discovered by Charles Durand-Ruel, a visionary art dealer willing to support them, and by notable collectors particularly from the business class, they were quickly assimilated to the mainstream, as so many avant-garde movements would be in the future.

Like Manet, the impressionists Pierre-Auguste Renoir (1841–1919) and Edgar Degas (1834–1917) were more interested in figure painting than landscape, but their subjects were taken from modern urban or suburban modernity, as well. Degas's more traditional technique eschewed the affectation of spontaneity, but he highlighted his own creative processes through arresting vantage points and orchestrated compositions, to which he found parallels in other art spectacles, most famously, the ballet. To emphasize the idea that even naturalism in art is a deliberate production rather than mechanical copying, Degas's *Musicians in the Orchestra* (c. 1870, reworked c. 1874–1876) shows the ballerinas taking bows before very broadly brushed theater flats, after the players in the foreground have completed their accompaniment. Renoir's own gregarious personality and his affection for women is reflected in his many superb portraits as well as in scenes of social gatherings, such as his *Le Moulin de la Galette* (1876). The location is an indoor-outdoor café-cabaret in the working-class Montmartre neighborhood where Renoir had his studio and from which he and his friends, some of whom are shown in the painting, recruited models. Here it appears transformed into an updated and urban rococo *fête-galante*.

MODERNISM

Postimpressionism is not a style but a term used to group a number of artists who responded critically to impressionism and thus constitute its aftermath. It led directly to the abstraction we associate with the founding of modern art. As impressionism's success turned it more toward bourgeois subjects, brightly decorative colors, and private dealers, the next generation looked toward a less ephemeral and what they considered a more democratic image of modernity. Georges Seurat's (1859–1891) *A Sunday Afternoon on the Island of La Grande Jatte* (1886) became the touchstone for neoimpressionism, which sought greater permanence by appearing to synthesize methodically a whole series of moments instead of catching a single moment candidly, as in the work of the previous generation. What is more, Seurat's mechanistic and impersonal pointillist recipe for style aimed at making art accessible to the widest number of practitioners whose quality of vision would not be affected by their varied skills at handwork. Finally, Seurat and his followers attempted to use color scientifically, again favoring objective method over impressionist intuition.

Vincent van Gogh (1853–1890) and Paul Gauguin (1848–1903) had very different responses to impressionism, but both emphasized personal expression over the kind of naturalism they associated with the latter. Van Gogh worked from nature, but insisted on going beyond surface appearances to deeper truths. Gauguin disparaged

L'Arlesienne (Madame Ginoux). Painting by Vincent van Gogh, 1888. METROPOLITAN MUSEUM OF ART, NEW YORK, USA/ BRIDGEMAN ART LIBRARY/LAUROS/GIRAUDON

direct observation in favor of recollections and mental images. Both used bold colors that often departed from observed reality, but van Gogh painted with powerful workman-like brushstrokes, as if to emphasize simultaneously the personal emotional content of his work and the physical effort of productivity underlying it. Gauguin, on the other hand, developed a style based on flat areas of color through which he emphasized the artifice of his process and a creative transformation of reality he hoped would conjure up heightened states of consciousness. He called the style synthetism for its combination of reality and imagination, the material and the spiritual. He traveled widely, first to Brittany, then to the Caribbean, finally to Tahiti, in search of a cultural purity and simplicity he associated with "primitive" peoples, whose artistic monuments and aesthetic creations often inspired him.

This cycle of self-conscious critical responses to previous art, responses that focus more on matters of aesthetic process and creative method than on the implications of subject matter or contemporary history, marks the advent of modernism. Although it of course has roots in previous generations, the latter's motivations were most often social and political, as well as artistic, whereas the avant-garde now became increasingly removed from mainstream culture, focusing more on its own artistic concerns. Cézanne's withdrawal from Paris to Aix-en-Provence in 1886 is characteristic of this move. Having at first essayed crude expressionistic paintings meant to shock his contemporaries, Cézanne had spent the decade of the 1870s assimilating impressionist attitudes regarding plein-air painting. Yet with Pissarro in the late 1870s and early 1880s, he became more concerned with the structure and unity of his pictures, realizing that impressionist spontaneity and focus on the specific moment must be tempered by the prior knowledge of objects and experience of space one brings to any empirical moment. Cézanne claimed to be seeking an art more permanent than impressionism, more "like the art of the museums," while nonetheless deploying impressionism's tactic of working from direct observation. Cézanne's mature paintings sum up the efforts of impressionism as well as those of the other postimpressionists. For example, his *Mont Sainte-Victoire, Seen from Bellevue* (c. 1882–1885) conveys both duration in time and the specifics of a directly observed scenery through its rigorous geometry and patchwork of color dabs. A construction derived from methodical observation of reality, the painting reveals a deeply contemplative consciousness at the same time as it displays the means through which that consciousness is given a physical presence on the canvas. That presence, combining its evidence of the exercise of human intellect with its reflection of the natural world, seems to clarify that world epistemologically. In this, it has often been discussed by philosophers of phenomenology, especially in the writings of Maurice Merleau-Ponty (1908–1961).

All through the realist and impressionist revolutions, academic painting continued to flourish, with great society portraitists such as Jacques-Émile Blanche (1861–1942) and Giovanni Boldini

(1845–1931) or figure painters like Adolphe-William Bougereau (1825–1905) and Pierre-Auguste Cot (1837–1883), as in the latter's *The Storm* (1880, The Metropolitan Museum of Art, New York). As avant-garde artists gained publicity and a serious critical audience, however, academic art lost its historical relevance and the avant-garde became international. Postimpressionism directly inspired the two dominant trends of the pre–World War I period, expressionism and cubism. The Catalàn native Pablo Picasso (1881–1973), combined Gauguin's "primitivism" with the faceted reconstructions of form he saw as a potential in Cézanne's late paintings. His revolutionary, though experimental and somewhat awkward early masterpiece, *Les demoiselles d'Avignon* (1907) showed the way toward the highly fragmented and abstracted forms of cubism he and his cohort Georges Braque (1882–1963) were practicing just prior to the outbreak of World War I. Collage, with its inclusion of everyday materials such as newspaper, in cubist compositions led to synthetic cubism, in which the image was not derived from observing a motif, as in analytic cubism, but rather appeared to be assembled out of parts, painted or otherwise, producing the artwork as a completely novel object. This concept emerged as Picasso experimented with sculpture, largely moribund during the nineteenth century, and gave it a new impetus based on this process of fusing pieces together into images that suggest or even parody real objects rather than describe them.

Whereas cubism was developed within the artistic hothouse of Paris, expressionism took various guises and was more or less pan-European. Gauguin and Van Gogh's use of bright colors and bold shapes led Henri Matisse (1869–1954) and his followers to paint so broadly and in such flat and simplified forms that critics called them *fauves* (wild beasts). In fact, Matisse's *Luxe, calme et volupté* (1904) combines both the classicizing and neoimpressionist strains of utopian landscape representation, revealing its roots both in impressionism's discovery of the French Riviera and in Gauguin's synthetist style perfected in Tahiti. The Norwegian Edvard Munch (1863–1944), used the stylistic simplifications he saw in French art, focusing on the core of human emotion in scenes of death, yearning, or anxiety. Wassily Kandinsky's (1866–

1944) early work seems related to fauvism, but its visionary imagery suggests memory and dreams layered over nostalgic yearnings for his native Russia. He founded a movement he called Der Blaue Reiter (The Blue Rider), referring to a figure on horseback who appeared in many of his expressionist works. A parallel movement based in Germany called Die Brücke (The Bridge) can be represented by Ernst Ludwig Kirchner (1880–1938), who used cubist fragmentation and angularity in *The Street, Berlin* (1913) as well as lurid color to suggest the inner psyche, oppressed by the urban culture of his times. Quite to the contrary, the Italian futurists, led by Umberto Boccioni (1882–1916), used cubist-inspired faceting but with expressionist colors and dynamism to herald the new age of the city and the machine. Truly, the first decade of the twentieth century was filled with experimentation that would have extraordinary consequences for the future of art. Yet its challenges to tradition would be readily assimilated by a market now eager to consume work associated with new ideas and progressive thinking.

See also **Avant-Garde; Cubism; Fauvism; Impressionism; Modernism; Realism and Naturalism; Romanticism.**

BIBLIOGRAPHY

Brettell, Richard. *Modern Art, 1851–1929: Capitalism and Representation*. Oxford, U.K., 1999.

Chu, Petra ten-Doesschate. *Nineteenth-Century European Art*. New York, 2003.

Eisenman, Stephen F., et al. *Nineteenth Century Art: A Critical History*. 2nd ed. New York, 2002.

Goldwater, Robert. *Symbolism*. New York, 1979.

Honour, Hugh. *Neo-Classicism*. Harmondsworth, U.K., 1968.

———. *Romanticism*. London, 1979.

Nochlin, Linda. *Realism*. Harmondsworth, U.K., 1971.

Rosenblum, Robert, and H. W. Janson. *19th-Century Art*. New York, 1984.

Rubin, James H. *Impressionism*. London, 1999.

JAMES H. RUBIN

PALACKÝ, FRANTIŠEK (1798–1876),

Czech historian and statesman, and the dominant figure in the Czech national movement of the nineteenth century.

Born to a Protestant family in northeastern Moravia in 1798, František Palacký attended the famous Evangelical Lyceum in Pressburg, Hungary (now Bratislava, Slovakia), where he discovered the exciting new trends of liberalism and nationalism that were sweeping Europe. In 1823 he went to Prague to work on the Czech national revival. Launched in the late eighteenth century by enlightened scholars who undertook to "defend" the Czech language and culture, which had been in decline for over a century, the revival was entering its second phase. Led by a new generation of scholars and writers, who were inspired by romantic notions of national destiny, the revival was moving beyond language reform to a broad-based program of cultural renewal. Securing employment as an archivist for the patriotic nobleman Count Francis Sternberg, Palacký became acquainted with the leading lights of the revival and worked in the organizations they had created to promote Czech life. He helped transform the Society for the Patriotic Museum of Bohemia, which had been founded in 1818 as a bilingual Czech-German institution, into a vehicle for Czech nationalism, using it to set up projects such as the *Matice česká* (Czech literary foundation), an association for publishing books in Czech.

His scholarly work and social connections brought Palacký to the attention of the Bohemian Diet, which commissioned him in 1827 to write a history of the province. The result was his monumental *History of the Czech Nation in Bohemia and Moravia* (in German, 1836–1867; in Czech, 1848–1876), a multivolume work chronicling Czech history from the arrival of the Slavs in the area until 1526, when the Habsburgs assumed rulership of the kingdom. Palacký's *History* articulated several themes that became fundamental to Czech nationalism, such as the notion that German overlords had destroyed the democratic and egalitarian structure of early Slavic society when they imposed feudalism on the area. He put special emphasis on the Hussite period, a Protestant interlude of some two hundred years that ended in 1620, when Habsburg forces reconquered the area for Catholicism. The Hussites had been condemned by the Counter-Reformation as dangerous heretics, but Palacký presented them as fighters for truth and freedom whose struggle was part of the age-old conflict between Germans and Czechs in the region.

The revolution of 1848 was a turning point in Palacký's career, when he emerged as the spokesperson for the Czech national program. His letter to the preparatory committee of the Frankfurt National Assembly rejecting their invitation to represent Bohemia at the gathering won him international renown. Claiming that as a "Czech of Slav descent" (my translation) he could not participate in the creation of a German national state, he defended the multinational Austrian Empire as a bulwark protecting the small nations of central Europe, arguing (my translation), "If the State of Austria had not already been in existence for centuries, we should be forced, in the interests of Europe and even of humanity, to create it" ("Psaní do Frankfurta" [Letter to Frankfurt], p. 20). In addition, he was a leading figure in the short-lived Pan-Slav Congress in Prague in 1848, which sought to unify the scattered Slavic populations of the empire behind a common program, an approach called "Austro-Slavism," and he also served as a delegate to the new imperial parliament (the Reichsrat), where he helped draft a constitution to reorganize the empire along ethnic lines.

After the revolution failed, Palacký retreated to scholarly work but returned to public life in 1860, when a new constitution revived political activity in the empire. As the leader of the Czech National Party, he fought for the autonomy of the Bohemian crown lands on the basis of historic state rights, and supported a tactical alliance with the conservative great landowners to achieve this goal. The aristocratic alliance, along with his support for Czech abstention from governmental bodies such as the imperial parliament, eventually caused the party to split between "Old Czechs," who supported his program, and "Young Czechs," who favored a more progressive program and activist stance. The promulgation of the 1867 Ausgleich (compromise), which created the new state of Austria-Hungary out of the old

empire, dealt a crushing blow to Palacký's efforts, and he warned as the negotiations for it got under way (my translation), "We were here before Austria and we will be here after it is gone" ("Idea státu Rakouského" [The meaning of the Austrian state], p. 266). Disillusioned by the repeated failure of Czech political efforts, he urged his countrymen to cultivate moral and cultural superiority over their enemies. He died in 1876, his reputation as the "father of the Czech nation" firmly established.

See also **Austria-Hungary; Bohemia, Moravia, and Silesia; Nationalism; Prague Slav Congress; Revolutions of 1848; Young Czechs and Old Czechs.**

BIBLIOGRAPHY

Primary Sources

Palacký, František. "Idea státu Rakouského." In *Spisy drobné*, edited by Bohuš Rieger. Prague [1898]. Vol. 1, 209–267.

———. "Psaní do Frankfurta dne 11. dubna 1848." In *Spisy drobné*, edited by Bohuš Rieger. Prague [1898]. Vol. 1, 16–22.

Secondary Sources

Kořalka, Jiří. *František Palacký, 1798–1876: Životopis.* Prague, 1998.

Morava, Georg J. *Franz Palacký: Eine frühe Vision von Mitteleuropa.* Vienna, 1990.

Pech, Stanley Z. *The Czech Revolution of 1848.* Chapel Hill, N.C., 1969.

Zacek, Joseph Frederick. *Palacký: The Historian as Scholar and Nationalist.* The Hague, Netherlands, 1970.

CLAIRE E. NOLTE

PALMERSTON, LORD (HENRY JOHN TEMPLE) (1784–1865), British politician.

Born in London on 20 October 1784, Palmerston inherited his Irish peerage in 1802 on the death of his father, Henry Temple, who had served as an English member of Parliament (MP) for forty years. Palmerston would soon enter politics as well, but not before completing what for an aristocrat was a remarkably solid education at Edinburgh University (1800–1803), where he studied with the moral philosopher Dugald Stewart, and also at Cambridge University (1803–1806), where he obtained important social connections and credentials. His first electoral victory for Horsham in 1806 was invalidated the following year, but he nevertheless gained a seat in 1807 for the pocket borough of Newport, Isle of Wight. Palmerston sat in the House of Commons for nearly fifty-eight years, a political career that only ended because of his death. During that long span, his political loyalties shifted from right to left; he began as a Tory, drifted to the Whigs, and ended up in the Liberal Party. He also held several offices, most notably foreign secretary (1830–1834, 1835–1841, 1846–1851) and prime minister (1855–1858, 1859–1865).

As foreign secretary, Palmerston successfully articulated a vision of Britain's place in the world that resonated loudly with a British public increasingly aware of its voice in national politics. The substance of this vision was relatively straightforward: Britain should serve as a model for, and align itself with, nations fighting for liberal, constitutional governments, but at the same time, Britain had to maintain its independence and the freedom to pursue and defend its own interests. In practice, of course, the resulting policies appeared contradictory. Palmerston actively secured an independent Greece and Belgium and forcefully promoted constitutionalism in Portugal and Spain. Yet, apart from moral support, he did little to assist rebelling Poles in the 1830s or Italians in 1848, and he backed the use of military force against China in the Opium Wars (1839–1842, 1856–1860), which expanded British trade far more than the sphere of liberty. Because Britain had, as Palmerston claimed, no permanent allies, only permanent interests, he pursued policies that were sometimes belligerent, sometimes conciliatory.

Palmerston papered over these apparent inconsistencies by skillfully courting favorable public opinion and shrewdly exploiting the press. In his famous June 1850 speech before the House of Commons, he defended his brash actions in the Don Pacifico affair, when he sent a naval fleet to Athens to back up the monetary claims of an aggrieved Gibraltar-born merchant. His strong appeals to British nationalism won over the public. Then when the government barred him from meeting with the exiled Hungarian revolutionary Lajos Kossuth in 1851, he met instead with a group of London radicals who presented an address fiercely condemning Kossuth's enemies, the Austrian and Russian emperors. On the surface, these were merely gestures, but Palmerston's blunt and blustery manner endeared him to the public at the same time as it irritated Queen Victoria (r. 1837–1901) and his parliamentary colleagues. Because of his ability to attract support from across the political spectrum with his patriotic vision of a morally superior and militarily strong nation, it is hardly surprising that he became prime minister when Britain experienced serious setbacks during the Crimean War (1854–1856). He managed to extract a peace and end the war on a victorious note.

Any assessment of Palmerston's political legacy must take into account his remarkable longevity. It has been argued that because he became prime minister at the age of seventy, he was out of touch with the changing times, a conservative who blocked the needed reforms that his brilliant chancellor of the Exchequer, William Ewart Gladstone, would eventually undertake as prime minister. Yet it has been argued more recently that because of his cultivation of public opinion, for example with forward-looking policies that attracted dissenters to the Liberal Party, Palmerston ushered in a mode of modern, democratic politics, which later politicians then expanded. Was Palmerston a genuinely progressive politician, or a regency rake who favored aristocratic dominance—as well as aristocratic dalliance, judging from his relations with women? Perhaps he was two politicians in one, a liberal in foreign policy and conservative in domestic policy. While the historiographical debate will continue, it will nevertheless remain true that Palmerston himself had little difficulty finding his way through two very different political worlds, one dominated by the French Revolution and the other by the Industrial Revolution. He was a consummate political survivor, having won an impressive electoral victory (July 1865) just a few months before he died.

See also **Gladstone, William; Great Britain.**

BIBLIOGRAPHY

Primary Sources

Bourne, Kenneth, ed. *The Letters of the Third Viscount Palmerston to Laurence and Elizabeth Sulivan, 1804–1863.* London, 1979.

Guedalla, Philip, ed. *The Palmerston Papers: Gladstone and Palmerston: Being the Correspondence of Lord Palmerston with Mr Gladstone, 1851–1865.* London, 1928.

Secondary Sources

Bourne, Kenneth. *Palmerston: The Early Years, 1784–1841.* New York, 1982. The definitive biography for that period.

Steele, E. D. *Palmerston and Liberalism, 1855–1865.* Cambridge, U.K., 1991. An important revisionist work.

ELISA R. MILKES

PANKHURST, EMMELINE, CHRISTABEL, AND SYLVIA.

Emmeline Goulden (1858–1928), born in Manchester, England, into a middle-class family, married Dr. Richard Pankhurst, a radical barrister, in 1879. Their children were brought up in a household where their parents supported advanced causes of the day, especially women's suffrage and socialism. Christabel Harriette (1880–1958), the eldest child and their mother's favorite, was the brightest and prettiest of the three daughters, which caused considerable rivalry with her two younger sisters, Estelle Sylvia (1882–1960) and Adela Constantia Mary (1885–1961).

When Richard died in 1898, the family was left in straitened circumstances. Further, Emmeline became increasingly disillusioned with the lukewarm attitude of the Independent Labour Party (ILP) toward women's suffrage. When she heard, some five years later, that the hall built in her husband's name was to be used by a branch of the ILP that would not admit women, she was so indignant that she founded, on 10 October 1903, the Women's Social and Political Union (WSPU) as a women-only organization that would campaign for the parliamentary vote for women on the same terms as men. Thus was born what has been termed a "militant" suffrage society that was to influence the Edwardian political landscape for the next eleven years until militancy was called to a halt on the outbreak of World War I. The daring deeds of the suffragettes involved not only constitutional protest, such as deputations to parliament and the assertive questioning of members of the government, but also, from 1912, activities that involved public disorder, such as setting fire to empty buildings and the large-scale smashing of plate glass windows in London's West End. Over one thousand suffragettes were imprisoned for their activism and, from 1909, forcibly fed when they went on hunger strike.

Throughout these years, the WSPU was led by the charismatic Emmeline, a powerful orator and a woman of enormous courage, and the clever, witty Christabel, the WSPU's chief organizer and key strategist. The artistic Sylvia never held any formal position, although she was an active WSPU member as well as a designer for many of its artifacts. In 1907, much to Sylvia's dismay, Emmeline and Christabel resigned from the ILP since they wished to unite all women as one independent force, free from any formal allegiance to any one political party. As a socialist feminist, Sylvia was often at odds with such women-centered policies. Emmeline and Christabel, who leaned much more to a radical feminist analysis, emphasized gender rather than class solidarity, the importance of a women-only movement, the power of men (even socialist men) over women in a male-defined world, and the commonalities that all women shared despite their class differences. Disillusioned, in 1912 Sylvia with her mother's agreement set up her own East London Federation of the Suffragettes, which functioned as a semi-independent grouping within the WSPU. However, contrary to WSPU policy, Sylvia sought to tie her Federation to socialism and worked with the socialist Herald League. The move angered Christabel and their mother, who expelled Sylvia from the WSPU in January 1914.

The tensions between the Pankhurst women deepened during World War I, which Emmeline and Christabel supported and Sylvia opposed. The later careers of the Pankhurst women followed divergent paths too. Christabel converted to Second Adventism in late 1918 and then, in the 1920s, moved to America, where she became a well-known preacher and successful writer about the Second Coming of Christ. For Sylvia, an agnostic like her father, such a religious turn was incomprehensible. Emmeline visited Russia in 1917, just before the revolution, and became very critical of Bolshevism, which she argued was undemocratic and nonrepresentative of the working class as a whole. She then went to North America, where she lectured for the Canadian National Council

Emmeline Pankhurst being arrested outside Buckingham Palace, May 1914. Pankhurst and other suffragists developed techniques for civil disobedience that were used in later liberation and civil rights movements. ©HULTON-DEUTSCH COLLECTION/CORBIS

for Combating Venereal Diseases, and returned to England just before Christmas 1925.

Sylvia, on the other hand, supported the Russian Revolution and moved further and further to the left, becoming a founding member of the British Communist Party. However, her constant criticisms of the Party led, in 1921, to her expulsion from its membership. When she heard, late in 1926, that her mother would be standing as a Conservative candidate in the next general election, Sylvia interpreted this change in political allegiance as the final betrayal of her father's ideals. Estranged from her mother and sister and now living with her Italian lover, Silvio Corio, she gave birth to a son in December 1927, an event known only to a few trusted friends and certainly not Emmeline. The "wayward" daughter made the news public through the press, however, in April 1928, when her mother was campaigning in her constituency. The aging and frail Emmeline never recovered from the shock and died a few months later, on 14 June 1928.

After Emmeline's death, Christabel continued to live in the United States, where in addition to her religious work she tended to the sick and dying. Sylvia took up the cause of antifascism, settling in Ethiopia, where she died in 1960. In 1953, after almost forty years of estrangement, Christabel initiated an affectionate correspondence with Sylvia that continued intermittently until her death in 1958.

See also **Feminism; Great Britain; Suffragism.**

BIBLIOGRAPHY

Crawford, Elizabeth. *The Women's Suffrage Movement: A Reference Guide, 1866–1928.* London, 1999.

Pankhurst, Christabel. *Unshackled: The Story of How We Won the Vote*. London, 1959.

Pankhurst, Emmeline. *My Own Story*. London, 1914.

Pankhurst, Estelle Sylvia. *The Suffragette Movement: An Intimate Account of Persons and Ideals*. London, 1931.

Pugh, Martin. *The Pankhursts*. London, 2001.

Purvis, June. *Emmeline Pankhurst: A Biography*. London and New York, 2002.

JUNE PURVIS

PAN-SLAVISM. Originating in the first half of the nineteenth century, Pan-Slavism was a current of thought envisioning the various Slavic peoples of east-central and eastern Europe uniting to promote their common interests. Its first proponents were intellectuals living in the Habsburg Monarchy. After a political brotherhood of Slavs failed to materialize in the Habsburg lands in 1848, support declined there, but during the last third of the century, it gained new life in Russia, where the Russians' role as a protector of the other Slavs became its main emphasis.

The idea of a Slavic unity can be traced to the creation of Old Church Slavonic, an invented language that could be understood by all the Slavic tribes and that was promulgated by St. Cyril and St. Methodius in the ninth century. As an ideology, however, Pan-Slavism emerged only at the beginning of the nineteenth century as a response to German nationalism. While German literary culture was already well developed, many Slavic languages had not yet been codified in their modern form, and their literatures were weak. The similarity of Slavic dialect made unifying the various Slav peoples in the Habsburg realms seem a plausible means to challenge German cultural dominance.

Pioneering work by the linguist Josef Dobrovský (1753–1829), who codified Czech after more than a century of neglect, made Czech the main candidate for a unifying language. But indicative of the attraction of bringing Slavs together, the most influential figures in Habsburg Pan-Slavism were two ethnic Slovaks. Jan Kollár (1793–1852) wrote the sonnet cycle *Daughter of Sláva* (1824), the greatest literary expression of the Pan-Slav idea. Meanwhile, Pavel Šafařík (1795–1861) gave a scholarly basis for Pan-Slavism with an ethnography of the Slavs published in 1842.

Despite Slavic intellectuals' attraction to Pan-Slavism, there were always tensions. Another Slovak, L'udovít Štúr (1815–1856), rejected Czech in favor of codifying a distinct Slovak tongue, and Ukrainians living in the Austrian Empire likewise defended the distinctiveness of their language. Kollár, however, advocated "Slavic reciprocity" such that would allow for common interest without threatening each group's individuality. This notion found its ultimate expression when a Slav congress convened in Prague on 2 June during the revolution of 1848. Shortly before, prominent Czechs, most notably the historian František Palacký (1798–1876), had rejected appeals to attend the German pre-parliament then meeting in Frankfurt, and ensuring the survival of the Habsburg Monarchy, albeit with a new constitutional structure, was an important goal of those at the Slav congress. Habsburg's traditional supporters overlooked that, and the gathering broke up prematurely when conservative pro-Habsburg forces bombarded Prague on 12 June.

Although negotiations during the conference suggest Slavic reciprocity was not necessarily an idle dream, in retrospect the differences between various groups stand out. Polish interest in reviving an independent Polish state undercut the Habsburg orientation of the Czech Pan-Slavs. The various groups also had different views of Russia, with Czechs seeing Russia as a relatively benign force, something Poles could not accept. Reconciling Galician Poles' and Ukrainians' interests also presented problems, while some Slovaks' protection of their own linguistic traditions also weakened the Pan-Slav project.

Reimposition of absolute rule in the Habsburg lands in 1851 reinforced these differences. Habsburg absolutist policies frustrated the ambitions of Czechs and Poles to play a greater role in government without their shared disappointment bringing the Poles and Czechs closer together. Meanwhile, threatened by Polish ambitions, Ukrainians viewed the reestablishment of absolutism more favorably, as did the Slovaks and Croatians who felt similarly threatened by Hungarian aspirations for independence. Šafařík rightly opined that the Habsburg Slavs would never unite again as they had in Prague.

In the Russian Empire, Pan-Slavism developed later. In 1846 the Brotherhood of Saints Cyril and Methodius, which included the Ukrainian poet Taras Shevchenko (1814–1861), was founded around the principle of unity among independent Slavic peoples, a stance similar to that of Kollár. The brotherhood did not participate in the Prague conference though; the only Russian figure of stature to attend was Mikhail Bakunin (1814–1876), who just happened to be in the vicinity. Before the brotherhood could promote its idea widely the Russian government cracked down in 1847. At the end of the 1860s, however, a new Pan-Slavism more acceptable to Russian authorities emerged. It emphasized the obligation of the Russians to protect their Orthodox Slav brothers living outside the empire. In this guise Pan-Slavism finally reached people beyond narrow intellectual circles for the first time, as became apparent during the Balkan crisis of the mid-1870s and at the outbreak of World War I. That belief reverberates to this day in Serbians' and Bulgarians' continued close cultural bonds with Russia.

See also **Nationalism; Palacký, František; Prague Slav Congress; Slavophiles.**

BIBLIOGRAPHY

Agnew, Hugh LeCaine. *Origins of the Czech National Renascence.* Pittsburgh, Pa., 1993.

Kirschbaum, Joseph M. *Pan-Slavism in Slovak Literature: Ján Kollár—Slovak Poet of Panslavism (1793–1852).* Cleveland, Ohio, 1966.

Kohn, Hans. *Pan-Slavism: Its History and Ideology.* 2nd ed. New York, 1960.

Milojkovic-Djuric, Jelena. *Panslavism and National Identity in Russia and the Balkans, 1830–1880.* Boulder, Colo., 1994.

Orton, Lawrence D. *The Prague Slav Congress of 1848.* Boulder, Colo., 1978.

Sydoruk, John P. *Ideology of Cyrillo-Methodians and Its Origin.* Winnipeg, Man., 1954.

Walicki, Andrzej. *The Slavophile Controversy: History of a Conservative Utopia in Nineteenth-Century Russian Thought.* Translated by Hilda Andrews-Rusiecka. Oxford, U.K., 1975. Reprint, with a new introduction, Notre Dame, Ind., 1989.

HUGO LANE

PAPACY. The nine popes from Pius VI (r. 1775–1799) to Benedict XV (r. 1914–1922)—more than half of whom chose the name Pius—had to confront the innumerable crises that rocked their world for more than a century. These figures were constrained to react to the French Revolution and the Napoleonic imperium, the upheavals troubling Europe from 1820 to 1848, industrialization, urbanization, and increased secularization, as well as liberal Catholicism, Italian and German unification, and the Kulturkampf. Four of these popes—Pius VI, Pius VII (r. 1800–1823), Pius IX (r. 1846–1878), and Leo XIII (r. 1878–1903)—pontificated for more than two decades, providing one third of the list of the twelve longest-reigning popes in the institution's two thousand–year history. They utilized their time to confront the ideological currents that challenged the spiritual authority of the papacy, even as political events threatened their temporal power. The effort only succeeded in part, for 1870 witnessed the collapse of the Papal State. The loss of the temporal power during the course of the Risorgimento, the movement for Italian unification, did not silence Rome's enemies.

Throughout much of the nineteenth century some loudly decried papal primacy and centralization in the Vatican, which seemed to increase as its political power was challenged. In response, the papacy remained neither silent nor passive, mounting an energetic counteroffensive. As early as 1775, Giovanni Angelo Braschi (Pius VI) condemned attacks on orthodoxy by the "monstrous desire of innovation." Despite these papal protests, dechristianization and secularization proceeded apace in the political arena and the broader society.

FRENCH REVOLUTION AND NAPOLEONIC IMPERIUM

The revolt of the American colonies from 1775 to 1781, justified by the broad precepts of the Enlightenment, did not threaten the Catholic Church or its head. The consequences of the French Revolution, however, proved far more dangerous for the papacy. Beginning with the confiscation of church property in 1789, followed by the Civil Constitution of the Clergy shortly thereafter (1790), the ensuing years witnessed a determined, often violent assault against the temporal and spiritual authority of the papacy, culminating with the spiriting of Pius VI from the eternal city and the proclamation of a republic in Rome. The worship of reason and the cult of the supreme being were proclaimed in France as alternatives to the traditional faith. Napoleon, who became first consul in 1799, questioned the prudence of this policy and sought some reconciliation with Rome. In 1801 he concluded with the Holy See a concordat that recognized Catholicism as the religion of the majority in France, provided for the reestablishment of public worship there, and ended the prospect of schism. The agreement did not prevent the emperor from occupying the Papal States in 1808, nor from annexing the territory in 1809.

Barnaba Gregorio Chiaramonti (Pius VII), like his predecessor, was dragged into exile by the French. As Napoleon's domination spread throughout Europe, the papacy once again appeared to be on the verge of collapse. Although Napoleon deemed the papal institution an important moral force whose military equivalence he compared to a "corps of 200,000 men," during these years Rome found itself politically and ideologically on the defensive. The threat posed by the French only dissipated with the dissolution of Napoleon's legions in Russia and the emperor's exile to St. Helena. Unlike Pius VI, Pius VII did not die in exile but, assisted by his secretary of state cardinal Ercole Consalvi, survived the Napoleonic ordeal and returned to Rome as spiritual ruler of the church and sovereign of his state.

THE RESTORATION ERA

The settlement of 1815 witnessed a reconstitution of the Papal State, the restoration of the Jesuits, the return of the Inquisition in Rome and Spain, and a renewed appreciation of the union of throne and altar in conservative circles. The monarchs who adhered to the principles of the "Holy Alliance," the product of the religious fervor of Tsar Alexander I of Russia (r. 1801–1825), promised to conduct their foreign relations in accordance with the precepts of holy religion. Writers such as Edmund Burke (1729–1797), Joseph-Marie de Maistre (1753–1821), Louis de Bonald (1754–1840), and Father Gioacchino Ventura (1792–1861), who

borrowed freely from them, saw a close nexus between religion and society. While Pius VII sought to adopt his secretary of state Consalvi's reformism in his 1816 program, which incorporated many French innovations, his moderation was counterbalanced by the intransigent *zelanti* (conservative intransigents) in the curia and by the traditionalists abroad who called for papal absolutism and shunned constitutionalism.

His successor, Annibale Francesco Clemente Melchiore Girolamo Nicola della Genga (Leo XII), who followed the *zelanti* agenda, dismissed Consalvi and issued decrees against liberalism and Freemasonry while restricting the Jews once again to the Roman ghetto. Francesco Saverio Castiglione, who followed as Pius VIII (r. 1829–1830), sought to overturn the more reactionary features of Leo's regime, but the opposition of the *zelanti*, combined with the shortness of his pontificate, aborted most of his reformist attempts. Thus, there was considerable discontent in the Papal State as Europe witnessed a new outburst of revolutionary upheaval in 1830. Not surprisingly, the revolutions of 1830, like those of 1848, were directed against the religious order that critics charged bolstered the prevailing power structure. The Camalolese monk Bartolomeo Alberto Cappellari, who became Pope Gregory XVI (r. 1831–1846), had to confront the revolutionary upheaval in Europe and in his own state, as well as the new ideological currents emerging not only in liberal circles, but in the Catholic camp.

REVOLUTIONS OF 1830 AND 1848

The revolutions of 1830, especially those in France and Belgium, encouraged the appearance of a liberal Catholic movement that sought to disassociate the church and the papacy from the moribund monarchical structure, giving rise to Hughes-Félicité-Robert de Lamennais's *Avenir* movement, which invoked a separation of church and state. At the same time the outbreak of revolution in the Papal State, suppressed only by Austrian intervention, prompted the drafting of a Memorandum of the Powers (1831) urging the pope to introduce reforms in his government, including the laicization of its administration. Pope Gregory XVI, who questioned Lamennais's support of the revolutions in Poland and Belgium, and his attempts to modernize the church, condemned the *Avenir* movement in his *Mirari vos* (1832). Resenting foreign interference in his state, Gregory shelved the reformist suggestions of the powers. Indeed, he continued to adhere to the position he had earlier outlined in his "Triumph of the Holy See and Church against the Assaults of Innovators" (1799). Critics charged that this pope virtually ignored the social and economic dislocation caused by the Industrial Revolution, as he focused on the religious and political consequences it provoked.

The thirty-two-year pontificate of Giovanni Maria Mastai-Ferretti (Pius IX or Pio Nono), the longest to date, opened on an optimistic note as the new pope, who was known to associate with liberals and called for a reform of the administration of the Papal State, was hailed as the figure who would reconcile liberty and Catholicism, and unite the Italian peninsula. Reformers and liberals applauded his political amnesty, the establishment of a consultative chamber and a constitution for the Papal State, and the prospect of his leadership in the national movement. This reformist image was shattered by his refusal to declare war against Catholic Austria, which provoked riot and rebellion toward the end of 1848. Subsequently, Pius IX concluded that the revolutionaries made demands to which he could not concede and that endangered the church he was elected to guide. Advised by Cardinal Giacomo Antonelli, he fled from his state and subjects, and from his exile in the Kingdom of Naples witnessed the toppling of the Papal State and its replacement by a Roman republic guided by Giuseppe Mazzini and defended by Giuseppe Garibaldi. The pope, who was restored to power in 1849 by the Catholic powers Austria, France, Spain, and Naples, judged that his position as supreme pontiff had been jeopardized by his brief flirtation with constitutionalism. Following his return to Rome (1850), Pius focused on his position as head of the faith, leaving the execution of political matters in the hands of his astute secretary of state, Antonelli.

PIUS IX'S CONSERVATIVE CRUSADE

Within the church, Pope Pius IX favored centralization by imposing the Roman liturgy seeking to reduce the autonomy of the bishops of the eastern churches united with Rome, while extending the scope of Roman jurisdiction, by prompting the bishops to make periodic or *ad limina* visits to Rome. Devoted to Mary, the mother of Jesus, Pius proclaimed the dogma of the Immaculate Conception (1854), which stipulated that she was born without the stain of original sin. Politically, Pius refused to reconcile himself to the loss of the bulk of his territory to the Kingdom of Italy (1861), which he refused to recognize. Following a Franco-Italian agreement (1864) to withdraw French troops from the remaining papal territory, which included Rome and its surroundings, Pius IX responded by issuing the encyclical *Quanta cura,* to which was appended a "Syllabus of Errors." First and foremost a denunciation of religious liberalism and the growing secularism of the age, it condemned naturalism, indifferentism (the belief that all religions beliefs were equally acceptable), and absolute rationalism, upsetting moderate and liberal Catholics. Even greater consternation was caused by his attack on liberalism, nationalism, and the separation of church and state. Critics charged the "Syllabus" reiterated the stance of Leo XII and Gregory XVI, putting the papacy in conflict with the modern world.

Pius was not deterred by the criticism and continued his crusade against the dangers he perceived in modern civilization. Mobilizing the forces of the church to bolster the position of the papacy, he convoked the Vatican Council in 1869, which in the following year proclaimed the primacy and infallibility of the pope. Opponents such as the Bavarian theologian Ignaz von Doellinger, among others, refused to recognize its validity, and his public opposition led to his excommunication by the bishop of Munich in 1871. He was not silenced, nor was the pope. The combative Pius refused to sanction the loss of Rome during the Franco-Prussian War (1870–1871), which ended the oldest sovereignty in Europe, nor would he accept the conditions imposed by the Italians in their Law of Papal Guarantees of 13 May 1871, thus provoking the Roman Question, which persisted until 1929. Pius IX was no more accommodating or willing to submit to the Kulturkampf in Otto von Bismarck's Germany or the Los von Rom movement in Austria, which sought freedom from Rome. Critics such as the archbishop of Rheims cited the need for some accommodation with the

Huge crowds gather in St. Peter's Square to receive a benediction by Pope Pius IX, 1860. ©HULTON-DEUTSCH COLLECTION/CORBIS

modern world. Pius, a crusader in a secular age, was not prepared to comply; his successor would make an attempt.

TURN OF THE CENTURY

At the turn of the century, Gioacchino Vincenzo Raffaele Luigi Pecci (Leo XIII) proved somewhat more diplomatic than his predecessor and sought to heal the rift between Rome and democratic governments such as existed in Republican France (the *Ralliement*) and to diffuse the Kulturkampf with Bismarck's Germany. He also showed himself to be more concerned about the tribulations of the working classes in the industrial age, citing the weaknesses of laissez-faire social indifferentism on the one hand, but condemning Marxism as a cure worse than the disease (*Rerum Novarum,* 15 May 1891). In *Graves*

de Communi (18 January 1901) Leo expressed his position on Christian democracy, emphasizing its moral rather than its political role. His diplomatic initiatives led him to arbitrate the dispute between Spain and Germany over the Caroline Islands, to reestablish relations with Spain, Mexico, and Colombia, and to secure the opening of a Russian embassy to the Vatican, while instituting diplomatic relations with imperial Japan. Leo's pontificate was perceived by some as a movement away from the intransigence of Gregory XVI and Pius IX, marking the first attempt of the papacy to reach an accommodation of sorts with the modern world. Nonetheless, Leo declared Anglican ordination invalid (1896) and would not condone Americanism.

Leo's successor, Giuseppe Melchiorre Sarto (Pius X, r. 1903–1914), proved to be more of a pastoral than a diplomatic pope. He denounced the modernist attempt to harmonize Catholic thought and theology with modern scientific and critical historical scholarship. In his decree *Lamentabili* of 1907, reinforced by his encyclical *Pascendi Dominici Gregis* of the same year, he denounced the attempt to alter Catholic doctrine to render it more palatable to the contemporary age. Furthermore, his intransigent defense of conservative causes and papal prerogatives contributed to the separation of church and state in France in 1905, and in Portugal in 1911, while neglecting the diplomatic role of the universal church. The next pope, Giacomo della Chiesa (Benedict XV), belonged to the diplomatic school of Leo rather than the pastoral one championed by his immediate predecessor, although he continued the missionary efforts of his predecessor. Much of Benedict's effort was directed to bringing the World War to a speedy conclusion and providing for a just peace.

Since the late nineteenth century scholars have denounced popes Leo XII, Gregory XVI, Pius IX, and Pius X for their alleged rejection of liberty, equality, and fraternity, and for supposedly fighting a rear-guard action against the contemporary world. Other scholars have focused on the reformism of Leo XIII and Benedict XV. Despite the continuing controversy and varied assessments of the papacy during this period, most concur that during these years, the Holy See had to face internal and external opposition, including the undermining of traditional forms of authority in the church as well as the society at large, and responded accordingly. All nine popes of this period rejected the ethics of a secular society including the collectivism of socialism and the selfish individualism of economic liberalism. In its place the Vatican pursued its own via media or third path in pursuit of social justice.

See also **Catholicism; Kulturkampf; Papal State; Pilgrimages; Pius IX; Protestantism; Secularization; Separation of Church and State (France, 1905).**

BIBLIOGRAPHY

Primary Sources

Atti del sommo pontefice Pio Nono felicemente regnante. Rome, 1857.

The Great Encyclicals of Pope Leo XIII. Edited by John J. Wynne. New York, 1903.

Romana beatificationis et canonisationis servi dei Pii Pape X. Rome, 1950.

Secondary Sources

Chadwick, Owen. *A History of the Popes, 1830–1914.* Oxford, U.K., 1998.

Coppa, Frank J. *The Modern Papacy since 1789.* London and New York, 1998.

Hales, Edward Elton Young. *Pio Nono: A Study in European Politics and Religion in the Nineteenth Century.* London, 1954.

O'Dwyer, Margaret M. *The Papacy in the Age of Napoleon and the Restoration: Pius VII, 1800–23.* Lanham, Md., 1985.

Pollard, John. *The Unknown Pope: Benedict XV (1914–1922) and the Pursuit of Peace.* London, 1999.

Reinerman, Alan J. *Austria and the Papacy in the Age of Metternich.* Washington, D.C., 1979.

Rinieri, Ilario. *La diplomazia pontificia nel XIX secolo.* 5 vols. Turin, 1901–1906.

Wallace, Lillian Parker. *Leo XIII and the Rise of Socialism.* Durham, N.C., 1966.

FRANK J. COPPA

PAPAL INFALLIBILITY.

Papal infallibility, for the exponents of the doctrine in the nineteenth century, referred to the inerrancy of official papal pronouncements and to the unfailing character of the papal teaching mission; the rock of Peter, it was claimed, would not succumb to the tide of doctrinal error that had engulfed the modern Western world. The promotion of this doctrine was bound up with the rise of ultramontanism from the late eighteenth century. Ultramontanism asserted the pope's absolute sovereignty over the Catholic Church, in opposition to Gallicanism, a tradition of the French church, and to German Febronianism (after "Febronius," pseudonym of Johann Nikolaus von Hontheim, assistant bishop of Trier [1701–1790]); these latter doctrines portrayed the leadership of the church in collegiate terms, as belonging to the body of the bishops, among whom the pope simply had primacy. Those who pressed for an official declaration of the doctrine of papal infallibility saw it as a precondition for a

"A MIDSUMMER NIGHT'S DREAM."

A Midsummer Night's Dream. Cartoon by Thomas Nast c. 1871. Nast depicts the pope as the comic character Bottom, who, in the Shakespeare play referred to in the title of the drawing, is transformed into an ass. The pope dreams that his doctrine of infallibility will restore the temporal power lost by the papacy during the preceeding decades. ©CORBIS

closing of ranks within the Catholic Church around the papacy, in the face of threats from liberalism and anticlericalism. The doctrine was primarily promoted initially by lower clergy and lay publicists and had widespread support among the Catholic faithful by the mid-nineteenth century; the attitudes of bishops, who often saw their own position as threatened, were mixed. It was a central issue of the First Vatican Council of 1869–1870, an assembly of bishops called by Pope Pius IX. His primary objective, following on from the notorious *Syllabus of Errors* of 1864 condemning liberalism and the principle of religious toleration, was to arm the church doctrinally in the face of the "errors" deriving from rationalism. Clergy, nuns, and the devout laity were mobilized by ultramontane zealots to petition the pope to have papal infallibility declared a church doctrine; the initiative did not really come from the Vatican in the first instance.

VATICAN I AND INFALLIBILITY

The council was divided between, on the one hand, an infallibilist "majority," led by the extremists Henry Edward Manning, archbishop of Westminster, and Ignaz von Senestrey, bishop of Regensberg in Bavaria, and, on the other hand, the "minority" opposed to a declaration of papal infallibility. Of the latter, some regarded the doctrine as positively false, but most asserted its declaration to be "inopportune," on account of its likely impact in the world at large; it would further alienate Protestants and Eastern Christians and would deepen the gulf between the church and the world of liberalism. They also feared a form of declaration that would strengthen the extreme ultramontane party. Leaders of the "minority" within the council were Félix Dupanloup, bishop of Orléans, Georges Darboy, archbishop of Paris, Wilhelm Emmanuel von Ketteler, archbishop of Mainz, Cardinal Friedrich von Schwarzenberg, archbishop of Prague, and the forceful Joseph Georg Strossmayer, bishop of Djakovo, a spokesman of the Slav minority in Hungary. Outside the council, Johann Joseph Ignaz von Döllinger, professor of church history at Munich, was the most combative opponent of infallibilism. His pupil the historian Lord John Acton played a key role in cementing the group of those opposed to an infallibilist definition, liaising between the bishops in Rome and exploiting his links with the government of William Gladstone in Britain and that of Prince Chlodwig zu Hohenlohe-Schillingsfürst in Bavaria. The British, French, Italian, and sundry German governments feared that it would be used to buttress theocratic claims to papal oversight over state affairs, while the Italian government was apprehensive that it would aggravate the developing "Roman question." Gladstone feared that it would jeopardize his policy of religious toleration in Ireland and provide fuel for Protestant intolerance in Britain. It was the liberal ministry of Hohenlohe in officially Catholic Bavaria that took the initiative, in liaison with Döllinger. On 9 April 1869 Hohenlohe sent a circular to all European governments suggesting joint intervention to prevent a conciliar declaration of papal infallibility, which, he claimed, would subject civil to ecclesiastical power and give a seal of approval to the *Syllabus.* The initiative was unsuccessful. The governments of France, Austria-Hungary, Baden, and Prussia, however much they shared Hohenlohe's concerns, declined to intervene with the papacy.

The clause on papal infallibility, in the fourth section of the constitution *Pastor aeternus* (The eternal pastor) of 18 July 1870, voted by the council after the committed anti-infallibilists had left, stated that when the pope declared a doctrine ex cathedra—that is, by virtue of his supreme apostolic authority—he exercised the infallibility that Christ had promised to the church and there was no appeal from his decision. This was an ambiguous formula that met the demands neither of the "minority" nor of the extreme infallibilists (including now Pius IX), who had wanted the pope to be declared to enjoy the privilege of infallibility independently of the body of the church. The extremists, however, presented it as a triumph, and pressure was exerted against liberal interpretations of the formula. The French bishops accepted the definition with varying degrees of alacrity, those with reservations being under strong pressure from lower clergy and militant laity. A strong anticonciliar reaction in Germany, spearheaded by Döllinger, provoked a closing of the ranks in favor of acceptance among the German bishops, under the leadership of Ketteler. Reservations were especially marked among Czech and Hungarian bishops. In Germany, anti-infallibilists, led by the layman Johann Friedrich von Schulte, professor of canon law at Prague, broke away to form the Old Catholic Church, founded at the Munich congress in September 1871, which recruited particularly among officials, academics, and the middle class generally.

GOVERNMENTAL REACTIONS TO THE DEFINITION

On 25 July 1870 the Habsburg government of Austria-Hungary abrogated the concordat it had signed with the papacy in 1855 and whereby it had relaxed state control over the church. Now it stated that the definition of its infallibility had made the papacy an institution different from the one with which it had contracted in 1855. Reactions in Italian governing circles were muted, and, in fact, the issue of papal infallibility was not used by the papacy to support its claims regarding its lost temporal power. In 1872 Otto von Bismarck, who, ironically, had opposed Bavarian calls for diplomatic intervention in 1869, used the pretext of the definition of papal infallibility to launch the *Kulturkampf* (war for culture) in Prussia, setting a model for governments of other German states. Doubtless he sought to exploit divisions among German Catholics and, in particular, those between liberal Catholic officials who favored a unified Germany and militant popular clericalists, who were often anti-Prussian. In the event, however, the *Kulturkampf* tended to provoke greater unity among German Catholics and a certain healing of divisions over the issue of papal infallibility.

See also **Catholicism; Kulturkampf; Manning, Henry; Papacy; Pius IX; Roman Question.**

BIBLIOGRAPHY

Aubert, Roger. "The Victory of Ultramontanism." In *The Church in the Age of Liberalism,* edited by Roger Aubert et al., 304–334. London, 1981.

Chadwick, Owen. *A History of the Popes, 1830–1914.* Oxford, U.K., 1998.

Tanner, Norman P., ed. *Decrees of the Ecumenical Councils.* Vol. 2: *Trent–Vatican II.* London, 1990.

OLIVER LOGAN

PAPAL STATE. The States of the Church (or Papal State from 1815) were the temporal domain of the papacy. They covered a large wedge of central Italy, basically the area of the modern provinces of Lazio, Umbria, Marche, and Emilia-Romagna, which roughly correspond to the old administrative areas of the Patrimonium Petri (Patrimony of Peter), closest to Rome, and of the Legations; Bologna was virtually a second capital after Rome. Although the papacy had held title to much of this area in the Middle Ages, in real terms the States of the Church were a creation of the period between the mid-fifteenth and late sixteenth centuries, as the papacy absorbed essentially independent fiefs, extended the boundary northward, and established administrative control over this formerly anarchic region. Cities, Rome included, had retained their municipal councils dominated by local elites, but these were subject to the control of papal governors, who, from the mid-sixteenth century, were always churchmen. The whole administration of these territories, indeed, became strongly clericalized (that is, run by clergy) from this time. From the mid-sixteenth century the States of the Church were exploited as a major source of revenue for the papacy. By the eighteenth century, however, the area was increasingly appearing as economically backward, in relative terms, and by the nineteenth century the papacy was in serious financial difficulties.

THE FRENCH DOMINATION

In the summer of 1796, French troops entered the States of the Church and, by the peace of Tolentino of 19 February 1797, the northern regions were ceded to French control, being annexed to the Cisalpine Republic. In January 1798 a French army moved south and received the capitulation of Rome on 10 February. On 15 January a movement of Roman citizens proclaimed the Roman Republic and the fall of the papal monarchy. The Republic lasted until the summer of 1799 under French auspices. The new pope, Pius VII (r. 1800–1823), elected in Venice in 1800, was installed in Rome by the Austrians. The French had withdrawn from Italy in late 1799, but reentered in 1800. In early 1808 they occupied Rome, and the States of the Church were annexed to the Napoleonic Kingdom of Italy. In July the uncooperative pope was arrested and taken into exile. The northern and Adriatic regions of the states of the church were annexed to the Napoleonic kingdom of Italy, while Umbria, the Patrimonium Petri, and also eventually Rome were annexed to the empire. With the crumbling of the Napoleonic kingdom in northern and central Italy in 1814, Napoleon's brother-in-law Joachim Murat, ruler of the Kingdom of Naples since 1808, attempted to take over the States of the Church as part of an independent policy of political survival. Napoleon riposted by restoring Pius VII to Rome in 1814. The Congress of Vienna in 1815 recognized the papal dominion in its old form, but with a more clearly monarchic title, due in part to the able diplomacy of Pius VII's secretary of state Cardinal Ercole Consalvi (1757–1824). Austria became an overweening protector of the restored regime.

RESTORATION AND REACTION

The papacy of Pius VII, like the Habsburg governments in Italy, recognized the value of the administrative and legal reforms of the Kingdom of Italy and sought to build on them. Consalvi embarked on a program to modernize and render more uniform the patchwork institutions of the Papal State and, with limited success, to stimulate its commerce and agriculture. The papacy, which in general followed a policy of moderation toward former supporters of the Napoleonic regime, appointed many of its administrators to such posts as were not reserved for churchmen.

Consalvi faced opposition from reactionary "zealots" within the Curia. The elections of Leo XII (1823), Pius VIII (1829), and Gregory XVI (1831), were victories for the zealot party, and Consalvi was dismissed on Leo's accession. Gregory XVI was impelled into reactionary and vindictive policies by the revolts of 1831–1832. From Leo XII's pontificate there was a clericalization of the upper levels of the administration of the Papal State, but, particularly under Gregory XVI, there was also an expansion of officialdom, not least on the technical side, which brought in many laymen from families of a developing commercial bourgeoisie.

TENSIONS AND UNREST

There was a growing resentment of Roman central control in the northern region of the state, particularly in the more economically advanced Emilia with its capital Bologna, where the old elites, on whom the papal administration relied, were being challenged by social newcomers. The administrative centralization and standardization, pursued especially under Pius VII and Gregory XVI, were alienating factors. Unrest was particularly marked in Emilia and Romagna. In the state more generally, an expanding educated middle class that included officials was intolerant of papal autocracy and of the political and administrative dominance of clergy. From the 1830s public opinion was being formed by a developing press, primarily in Rome and Bologna. The pressure of growing population on resources that were only slowly expanding made for popular misery. There were acute problems of administrative control and policing in the Papal State. After grumbling unrest in the 1820s, the wave of revolutions that swept western Europe from 1830 broke in the Papal State in 1831–1832. An autonomous republic was declared in Bologna, while the Romagna descended into anarchy. There were less serious outbreaks in the south of the state.

PIUS IX

There were great expectations of change when Giovanni Maria Mastai-Ferretti, the former bishop of Imola, was elected to succeed Gregory XVI as

Unseating the Pope. Cartoon by Thomas Nast, 1871. Nast depicts Victor Emmanuel II of Italy unceremoniously dethroning Pius IX, while a character representing U.S Catholics demonstrates allegiance by kissing the pope's foot. ©CORBIS

Pius IX in 1846. In 1847 the process of political liberalization began with the initiatives of Pius IX in the Papal State, perhaps precisely because of the exceptional problems of police control there. The early Pius IX should be seen less as a benign liberal than as a hesitant pragmatist seeking to canalize a movement for change that he certainly regarded as threatening. In March 1848 the pope conceded a constitution providing for a lower Chamber elected on an ill-defined but narrow franchise and for an upper house, the Council of State, nominated by the pope. These chambers were responsible for drafting legislation, while ultimate authority lay with the College of Cardinals as a senate. The Chamber that first met in April was composed mainly of liberal moderates with a sprinkling of radical democrats. Censorship of publications other than religious ones was relaxed and entrusted to boards of laymen.

Pius IX lost much of his popular support when he refused in the papal allocution of 29 April to commit the papal army to a nationalist war against Austria. This was exploited by radical-democrat agitators. Following the assassination of the prime minister Pellegrino Rossi on 15 November 1848, the pope fled to Neapolitan territory on 24 November. In Rome, radical democrats took control of the political process and proclaimed a Roman Republic on 9 February 1849.

The papal regime was restored by joint Austrian, Neapolitan, and French intervention in July 1849. The France of Louis-Napoleon Bonaparte now became the regime's main protector. Notwithstanding French, Piedmontese, and British urgings to continue liberalization, the pope abrogated the constitution of 1848. The decree of 12 September 1849 instituted an absolutist central government, while allowing significant autonomy to local administrative bodies. The restored regime became a by-word for obscurantism.

In 1859, following the defeat of the Austrian army by the Piedmontese at Magenta in June and the withdrawal of Austrian garrisons from the north of the state, cities there came out in revolt. Provisional governments handed control over to Piedmontese commissioners. In 1860, in order to block the advances of the Italian nationalist leader Giuseppe Garibaldi's Red-Shirt army, the Piedmontese army took over most of the remaining area of the Papal State, leaving to the papacy only Rome and part of the Patrimonium Petri. Notwithstanding the verdict of popular plebiscites, Pius IX refused to accept the annexation of his dominions to the new Kingdom of Italy and became increasingly intransigent. The papal enclave was protected by French garrisons, while the papacy recruited a supposedly international, but mainly French, army of volunteers, the Zouaves, to protect it.

Italian governments of the Right were initially concerned not so much to round off the unification process by annexing the remaining papal territory as to secure the removal of the French garrisons, whose presence gave Napoleon III an unwelcome leverage over Italian affairs. This objective was temporarily achieved by an Italo-French accord of 15 September 1864, but the invasion of the Patrimonium Petri by Garibaldian volunteers in 1867 provoked the embarkation of a new French force. In 1864 governing circles in Italy had hoped that the issue of the papal temporal power would be resolved with time: that the papacy would voluntarily liberalize its regime and bring the institutions of its residual state into line with those of the Italian kingdom, making some sort of fusion possible.

It was largely the papacy's refusal to modify its regime that made a radical solution inevitable. Ultimately, it was pressure from the opposition liberal Left and the growing weight of public opinion that impelled the government toward the final annexation. With the outbreak of the Franco-Prussian War in 1870, the French garrisons were withdrawn. Italian troops invaded the Patrimonium Petri and on 20 September conducted a ritual storming of the walls at Porta Pia, subsequently occupying the city. The papacy's temporal dominion was finally ended, to the joy of the strong liberal movement that had developed in Rome.

See also **Italy; Pius IX; Risorgimento (Italian Unification); Rome.**

BIBLIOGRAPHY

Caravale, Mario, and Alberto Caracciolo. *Lo Stato Pontificio da Martino V a Pio IX.* Turin, 1978. Fundamental.

Coppa, Frank J. *Cardinal Giacomo Antonelli and Papal Politics in European Affairs.* Albany, N.Y., 1990. A particularly useful study of the reign of Pius IX.

———. *The Modern Papacy since 1789.* London, 1998.

Kertzer, David I. *Prisoner of the Vatican: The Popes' Secret Plot to Capture Rome from the New Italian State.* Boston, Mass., 2004.

OLIVER LOGAN

PARIS. When the French king Louis XIV (r. 1643–1715) abandoned Paris for Versailles in 1682 the city drifted apart from the monarchy, following a destiny that would prove momentous for France. Although it was still governed by royal appointees, only the law courts, legal apparatus, and those who served them remained in the city. The rest of the government, the court, and a massive cohort of hangers-on and those who catered to the king and his courtiers, followed Louis XIV to his enormous, sumptuous, self-indulgent chateau, gorgeously decorated and furnished, with an elaborate iconography—worked out by the king and Charles-François Le Brun—that made the palace the principal shrine of monarchical idolatry.

Once Louis had left his capital he seldom returned for the remaining thirty-five years of his reign and never again lived in Paris. His great projects and buildings—the *grands boulevards* that replaced the razed city walls, two triumphal arches, Les Invalides army hospital and hospice, the Place Louis-le-Grand (later and still the Place Vendôme), among others—had no sequel in the last three decades of Louis's long reign or those of his successors. After his last great public work in Paris, the eastern facade of the Louvre (designed by Claude Perrault in the 1670s) the king lost interest in Paris, lavishing his money and attention on Versailles. The short-lived regency (1715–1723) returned to Paris but contributed little to the city, and when Louis XV (r. 1715–1774), the great-grandson of Louis XIV, achieved his majority, the monarchy definitively departed Paris. The steady stream of royal projects that had endowed the city over the centuries with so many great buildings, dried up. His two successors would add some important embellishments—most notably Jacques-Ange Gabriel's Place Louis XV (where the guillotine would soon stand, today the Place de la Concorde), the Hôtel de la Marine and the Hôtel Crillon that anchor it, Charles de Wailly's Odéon theater, and the École Militaire (the last royal project before the Revolution)—but Revolutionary Paris was not physically much different than it had been in Louis XIV's day.

PRE-REVOLUTIONARY PARIS

Despite its many neoclassical buildings Paris remained a medieval city. The tangle of twisted streets was shared and contested by pedestrians and horse-drawn vehicles; the few tallow lamps suspended by ropes cast the dimmest light; garbage, offal, and human waste were thrown regularly into the streets; mean hovels were attached like barnacles to the great buildings; the courtyard of the Louvre-Tuileries was filled with squatters and their animals; it was impossible to cross the city without navigating the patternless maze of streets; and an inadequate police force struggled to keep order. At midcentury (1749) Voltaire pleaded for urban renewal. He lamented the lack of public markets, fountains, regular intersections, and theaters, and he called for widening the "narrow and infected streets" and liberating the great buildings from the sprawl and squalor he contemptuously called "gothic." With his inimitable malicious wit he regretted that Paris had not had a fire like that of London in 1666, which would have cleared away the "dark, hideous" accretions of medieval Paris. Not until a century later would Voltaire's prayer for transformation be answered.

Population Any number of factors set Paris apart from the court and the kingdom. It was far and away the largest city in France and although no statistics from the *ancien régime* are either accurate or reliable, the city's population increased significantly in the eighteenth century. By 1789 its estimated population was between six and seven hundred thousand, and its surface area was three times greater than it had been in Louis XIV's reign.

Literacy rates were unusually high: 90 percent of men and 80 percent of women who made wills were able to sign them. Town criers no longer read out rulings of the law courts, they pasted them up on the walls for all to read. The elites no longer had a monopoly on written culture. By the mid-eighteenth century almost every parish had at least one free school for boys (half as many for girls), and most Paris children attended long enough to learn to read and write.

Paris was not a city of nobles, despite their domination of public life. A good modern guess is that two to six thousand noble families lived in the capital and made up about 3 percent of the population. They played an enormous role as cultural consumers, and theater, music, and art in Paris easily rivaled that patronized by Versailles. They also employed tens of thousands of domestic servants, another significant difference between Paris and its rival cities. This nobility too was changing from the old stereotype of proud ignorance and contempt for the charms of civilized domesticity that went beyond hunting and war. As the French Revolution approached, richly bound books began to appear in the background of noble portraits, displacing the heretofore dominant military accessories, and there were a growing number—well over a hundred—sizable noble libraries in Paris.

The overwhelming population, however, was working class, although it is difficult to find equivalent modern categories for the vast variety of jobs, skills, trades, and occupations. With the exception of the Marais area, where the elite of the legal system lived in splendid town houses, the east side of Paris was poor, the west side was rich. It is no accident that the great urban uprisings of the French Revolution came from the neighborhoods of St. Antoine and St. Marcel, on opposite sides of the Seine but in the eastern quadrant of Paris. From painstaking splicing of evidence we know the numbers of the poor were growing. The last great subsistence crisis in France was in 1709. Afterward mortality rates gradually fell, chances of survival improved for children, and life expectancy increased. In the Paris basin the population increased by 32 percent between 1750 and 1790, which meant in reality an enormous increase in the numbers of the poor. Between these extremes were the bourgeoisie of the eighteenth century, a middle class made up of professionals, rentiers (living on income from property and investments), and businessmen (both large and small), with a smattering of manufacturers.

Grandeur and misère Paris produced a unique new literature in the eighteenth century, one which would have a vigorous life until the present day: books about the city. Most notable was Louis-Sébastien Mercier's *Tableau de Paris* (1781–1789) and *Le nouveau Paris* (1793–1798), a sequel to the popular *Tableau*. These eighteen volumes contained, in no discernible order, the author's descriptions of the varied life of the city, contrasting the high and the low, the *grandeur* and the *misère* of the teeming capital—a theme that would be taken up by Honoré de Balzac in the next century—where walking was hazardous (there were more than twenty thousand carriages) and the mud of the unpaved streets was "filthy, black with grit," and stank with a "sulphurous" odor and the "tang of nitric acid" created by the domestic waste running in the streets. A "spot of this mud left on a coat will eat away the cloth," Mercier states.

What made Paris so volatile and unruly, so immune to control, was its size, the enormous difficulty of provisioning such a city, and the concentration of the poor and the working class in densely packed neighborhoods. The royal government (and then the Revolution) struggled to keep Paris fed with decent and affordable bread: the best recipe for riot was expensive and/or adulterated bread. The first riot of the Revolution began as small, spontaneous gatherings for self-defense and culminated in the attack on the Bastille. On 14 July 1789 the price of bread was the highest it had been in a century. The next important riot, the Women's March on Versailles (5–6 October 1789), which began as a market riot over bread prices, returned the king to Paris as a virtual prisoner and made the capital the epicenter of the Revolution. From then on Paris's central place and importance in France would be uncontested.

REVOLUTION AND EMPIRE

When Louis XIV left Paris it was an unwalled city with a population of less than five hundred thousand living on twenty-five hundred acres. When Louis XVI was brought to Paris in 1789 it was again walled—this time in wood with fifty-two booths for taxing everything that came into the city (the hated *octroi*)—and had a population of more than six hundred thousand spread over seventy-four hundred acres. The attack on the Bastille was the first urban insurrection of the Revolution and definitively yoked the Revolution to Paris and its unique problems. The dreaded prison was demolished and successor governments would strive to put their mark on the hallowed ground where the sinister building had stood. During the Revolution the space remained empty. Napoleon I tried to erect a fountain in the shape of an elephant, which collapsed before it could be cast in bronze. The July Monarchy ultimately built the July Column, which still stands and contains the remains of some who fell in the revolutions of 1830 and 1848.

Soon after the Bastille fell the National Assembly moved from Versailles to Paris, where the deputies would be under constant surveillance by the radical populace. The most characteristic aspects of the Revolution—the political clubs, the deliberations of the various elected assemblies, the organization of the city into forty-eight sections that represented local democracy, the urban mobs who overthrew the monarchy on 10 August 1792 and would continue to pressure and intimidate the new government—and some of its most famous acts—the prison massacres, the king's trial and execution, the purge of the Convention Assembly, and the Terror—were Parisian deeds. During its first years Paris and the Parisians directed the Revolution, shaped revolutionary politics, and provided the militancy that drove the Revolution on.

There was no time to build during the Revolution. The revolutionaries improvised, taking over abandoned palaces and ecclesiastical buildings for assemblies, committees, and bureaus. The radical Jacobins met in a former Dominican cloister, and the National Assembly met for a time in the royal riding academy in the Tuileries gardens. The Revolution planned to improve the capital and strip it of its royalist identity, but got only as far as toppling some statues, renaming some *places* and streets, and making the Plan des Artistes, a carefully drawn, accurate, and influential map of the city with radical proposals for new streets and an attack on the medieval tangle of Paris. This plan, the first such to consider the city as a whole, the first to propose cutting straight streets through Paris, the first to imagine a modern rather than a medieval city, would influence all the subsequent governments until the Second Empire, when a new plan superseded the Plan des Artistes.

Napoleon Bonaparte (later Napoleon I, r. 1804–1814/15), who seized power in a coup d'état (1799), had grand plans for his capital. Like everything else Napoleon did, his transformations of Paris fell far short of his sometimes fantastic dreams. He imagined a city of ten million (the approximate population of Paris and its suburbs in 2005). In fact the population of Paris was about the same under Napoleon, who took the first census, as it had been during the Revolution. (The population did not begin its steady upward climb until 1817.) On the same scale of grandeur, Napoleon envisioned a gigantic palace for his son, the king of Rome, which was never built. Nor were most of his grandiose schemes built. Curiously Napoleon had no overall plan for the city. The many urban projects he undertook seem to have been inspirations or improvisations of the moment. But if he built in fits and starts he built a great deal. There were monuments to his glory: the Arc de Triomphe (unfinished at his fall), the Vendôme Column, the elephant fountain where the Bastille had stood, and the arch of the Carrousel (Louvre-Tuileries courtyard). He built the Bourse du Commerce (the grain exchange), the Bourse (the stock market), and a temple of peace (which became the Madeleine Church), as well as the rue de Rivoli adjacent to the Tuileries, the first east-west straight street in Paris, with its stately, arcaded buildings (left unfinished). He enhanced the Louvre-Tuileries, which became the imperial court (he never liked Versailles), and elegantly decorated the Malmaison (his home with Josephine) and St. Cloud (his preferred residence in Paris, now destroyed). He built the Ourcq canal, which improved Paris's water supply, as well as the abattoirs, a wine market, and two bridges over the Seine: the *ponts* Austerlitz and Jena. He was also one of the great Paris vandals, razing a number of churches and ecclesiastical buildings. He did little or nothing to protect the city's small and precious legacy from the Middle Ages.

BOURBON RESTORATION AND SECOND EMPIRE

After Napoleon, the city fell on spare times. The Restoration of the Bourbons (1815–1830), constrained by an enormous war indemnity, added only one significant Paris building: the Expiatory Chapel to honor the guillotined king, Louis XVI. The sluggish economic revival of the July Monarchy (1830–1848) allowed some building but it was piecemeal. Again there was no comprehensive plan for urban renewal. The population reached a million around 1846, but the timid bourgeois government was parsimonious and narrow-minded: the idea and practice of deficit spending was not realized until the 1850s. However, the cholera epidemics, especially that of 1832, persuaded everyone that Paris had to be cleaned up. The July Monarchy cleared the slums around the Hôtel de Ville, but cut only one important street, the rue Rambuteau: it foreshadowed the future. It was the first broad street cut in the center of Paris, through the dense urban fabric (next to Les Halles, the great city markets), and it was lined with new, uniform buildings. The regime also put in place all the legislation needed to condemn property for urban renewal, along with elaborate building regulations, and it made Paris the hub of the French rail system, just then being built, thus ensuring Parisian predominance in France.

It was Louis-Napoleon Bonaparte, the nephew of Napoleon I, who as Emperor Napoleon III (r. 1852–1871) undertook the enormous task of transforming Paris. His authoritarian government, directed by a man worshipfully devoted to his uncle's every dream and ambition (both real and imagined) created the modern city in the spirit of the first Napoleon. The new emperor appointed Georges-Eugène Haussmann (1809–1891), a tough, egotistical, efficient, and arrogant career bureaucrat, as the Prefect of the Seine. Haussmann translated the emperor's vague desires into urban realities, and put tens of thousands to work reviving an economy recovering from the bad harvests and stock market catastrophes of the late 1840s.

Haussmannization The transformation of Paris was the largest urban renewal project in history, and so it remains. The street was the principle element and instrument of urban transformation, and a new word was coined: *haussmannization*

View to the east from the Pont Royal, Paris. Photograph by Gustave Le Gray c. 1856. In the foreground is the Pont du Carrousel, designed by Antoine-Rémy Polonceau and built in 1833, linking the Louvre with the Left Bank. Centre Canadien d'Architecture/Canadian Centre for Architecture, Montreal

roughly means urban renewal by demolition. All his projects, except those streets in unurbanized western Paris, involved massive demolition. He cut great thoroughfares through the city, like saber-thrusts in the novelist Émile Zola's graphic image, razing whole neighborhoods to do so. His most radical project was the Ile de la Cité, the original cradle of Paris. He destroyed virtually all the housing on the Ile—it had become a slum—and left standing only official buildings and the great cathedral of Notre-Dame. So it remains, a kind of urban ghost town at night.

After carefully making the first accurate topographical map of the city, Haussmann divided the work into three *réseau* or stages, depending on their priority. The first projects were concentrated in the center of the old city, where he began by cutting north-south and east-west axes through the urban fabric to make the so-called *grande croisée*.

All the work was financed by substantial grants from the national government and municipal income (mostly from the *octroi* or internal customs duty on everything entering Paris), but there was never enough money, and Haussmann adopted some unorthodox financial expedients—most importantly deficit spending, at that time a radically new idea. He also invented other expedients that were dubious and probably illegal. He forced city contractors, for example, to give the city an enormous security deposit, which he then used for other projects, and even issued bonds based on future revenues. The city's debt, amassed by Haussmann, was not retired until 1929.

The new city taking shape within the old—some of which, especially on the Left Bank, was left intact—was quickly becoming one of the wonders of the Western world. The regular, rectilinear boulevards, lined with chestnut trees and stately apartment buildings whose height, distance from the street, ornamentation, and balconies were regulated by law, had many partisans, and still do. As impressive as was Paris above ground, Paris underground was even more so. Haussmann built an enormous sewer system, its channels and chambers following the streets above. After a long polemical struggle with the advocates of drinking water from the polluted Seine, he also gave Paris a new water supply, carried to the city by more than one hundred miles of aqueduct. The emperor had become enamored of parks and residential squares from his exile in England. Haussmann dutifully built parks throughout the city. The two largest, the Bois de Boulogne (on the western edge of Paris) and the Bois de Vincennes (on the east) were described by Haussmann as the "lungs of the city."

Model city Although Haussmann has been much criticized for his banal taste, disregard for the poor, neglect of some public services (especially schools), and his contempt for the medieval parts of Paris, he was also a man of vision. In 1860 he incorporated the surrounding townships, the so-called *banlieue* into Paris, thus nearly doubling the size of the city and immensely increasing its population. It is precisely here that the greatest growth and expansion of Paris has taken place since his day. He also proposed the novel idea of moving the cemeteries out of the city and serving them with a new rail line. This suggestion was rejected.

Whatever judgments one makes about the man and his work, he completed the transformation of Paris from a medieval to a modern city. He proudly enumerates, in his *Mémoires,* the kilometers of sewer pipe laid, chestnut trees planted, and new streets cut. But Haussmann's Paris is more than stone, infrastructure, and population control—the boulevard Sébastopol effectively divided Paris into east and west, and in the eastern part of the city

(around the St. Martin Canal) he constructed one of his few strategic projects to quarantine street fighting. (Since the French Revolution street barricades had become the hallmark of urban insurrection.) Paris was, at least until the early twentieth century, the very type of a modern city, much imitated, much admired, and much visited.

Grumbling about the perpetual work site that Paris had become, resentment of the prefect's high-handed and callous manner and demolitions, and public complaints about the cost of the projects, brought Haussmann's dubious financial arrangements under attack. He was dismissed in 1870. Paris lived on and *haussmannisme* has remained the dominant form of urban planning until the present day.

The template of new streets and the architecture of the Beaux-Arts school lining those streets fixed the itineraries and the look of Paris well into the twentieth century. A few unique structures—the Eiffel Tower, for the World's Fair in 1889 (the centenary of the French Revolution) and the Sacre-Cœur church (1909), originally built as a political deal to placate both the Left and the Right in France—broke sharply with the recent past, but there would not be, could not be, another major transformation of Paris until there was land to build on. With the destruction of the last military wall around Paris, built in the 1840s, land finally became available (1919), but only on the outskirts of the city.

THIRD REPUBLIC

Haussmann's disgrace, followed some months later by the German victory at Sedan and the collapse of the Second Empire, brought all his projects to a halt. Despite the Prussian siege of Paris and the horrendous bloodletting of the Commune, and the passionate resentment of the empire, its works, and the humiliations it brought on France, a number of the projects of Haussmann's third *réseau* were soon resumed. The Paris Opéra of Charles Garnier (1825–1898), the single most expensive building of the Second Empire, was completed and opened in 1875. A number of Haussmann's boulevards were similarly completed. Indeed *haussmannisme* continued long after its creator's fall, even after his death. One of the last Haussmann boulevards to be finished, ironically enough, was the boulevard Haussmann, completed in 1926.

Walk down almost any of the new boulevards and it is difficult to distinguish the apartment houses of the Second Empire from those built thirty or forty years later. Young architects clamoring to be heard deplored the staid Paris of their fathers, the sclerosis of the Beaux Arts aesthetic, but *haussmannisme* held the city in thrall for decades. His legacy lived on.

It is striking that Haussmann's Paris, frozen in the old patterns and styles, should serve as the stage for some of the most innovative, daring, imaginative, and liberating art movements of the late nineteenth and early twentieth centuries. The impressionist painters celebrated the new city, with its distinctive boulevards and parks: Gustav Caillebotte painted his own neighborhood, around the new Opéra; Claude Monet painted the parc Monceau and the trains in the new Gare St. Lazare; Pierre-Auguste Renoir painted the boulevard des Capucines; Camille Pissarro did serial paintings of the boulevard Montmartre; Édouard Manet painted the new Opéra and the Gare St. Lazare. The brilliant efflorescence of the belle epoque unfolded in Haussmann's city: Marcel Proust's novels would be unimaginable without the Bois de Boulogne and the boulevards. Art nouveau, with its fantastic sinuosity, easily attached itself to Paris. The first Métro line was opened in 1900, on the Right Bank, and a number of Métro stations were designed by Hector-Germain Guimard (as well as a synagogue with an undulating facade, which still stands in the Marais), the father of the movement. Cubism, a contemporaneous development, did not contribute to urbanism or Paris street furniture.

By the turn of the new century, marked by the Paris World's Fair of 1900, the city had a population of nearly two-and-a-half million; the Third Republic had weathered, albeit desperately, the plague of political scandals and the Dreyfus affair; and the divisions in society, deep and poisonous, were engraved on the map of the city. The east end continued to be working-class neighborhoods, and would, with the surrounding communes, soon become known as the Red Belt, a voting bloc regularly supporting the French Communist Party. The *banlieue*, incorporated by Haussmann but largely undeveloped at the time, became another home of the working class, the poor, and left-wing

The flower and pet market on the Île de la Cité c. 1875. ©STAPLETON COLLECTION/CORBIS

politics. It was here that massive urbanization, industrialization, and population growth took place. The city had been deindustrialized by Haussmann, now this policy was reversed. This centrifugal movement away from the center of old Paris by the poor and the working classes had been encouraged by Haussmann, who razed so much poor and marginal housing in the core city. The movement continued, and Paris became a city with a prosperous center surrounded on three sides—the western suburbs are wealthy—by potentially antagonistic populations (the contrary of most American cities).

The flowering of cultural life from about 1880 to 1914 masked much of the urban misery and tensions. After World War I the belle epoque appeared even more attractive and was retrospectively mythologized. But life in Paris, except for the happy few, was difficult in the decades before the war. Class antagonisms, always present, now had representation in the Chamber of Deputies (Jean Jaurès, the great socialist leader and orator, was elected in 1885 and again in 1893). Tuberculosis had reached epidemic proportions, and the city identified a number of *îlots insalubres,* which were declared unfit for habitation and destined for destruction. A wave of strikes between 1904 and 1907, both nationally and in the reindustrialized capital, accentuated the economic and social crisis, and war was in the air as Europe stumbled from one international crisis to another. The city itself had built no significant housing for decades, and the expanding population put extraordinary burdens on Haussmann's city. Nor had public transportation caught up until Paris began constructing the Métro system (rather later than London).

By 1900 Paris lagged behind many of the great capitals of Europe. Bedazzled by the belle epoque, the city had avoided its problems. Only a generation after Haussmann's Paris had captured the world's imagination as the very ideal of a modern city, it was being surpassed. Charles-Maurice de Talleyrand's witty remark about the life of the privileged in the last years of the *ancien régime* comes to mind: "Anyone who did not live before the Revolution cannot understand the art of living." In the belle epoque, as during the *ancien régime,* Paris was elegantly poised on the edge of catastrophe.

See also **Berlin; Cities and Towns; Class and Social Relations; France; Haussmann, Georges-Eugène; Housing; London; Rome.**

BIBLIOGRAPHY

Chevalier, Louis. *The Assassination of Paris.* Translated by David P. Jordan. Chicago, 1994.

Everson, Norma. *Paris: A Century of Change, 1878–1978.* New Haven, Conn., 1979.

Favier, Jean. *Paris, deux mille ans d'histoire.* Paris, 1997.

Jordan, David P. *Transforming Paris: The Life and Labors of Baron Haussmann.* New York, 1995.

Marchand, Bernard. *Paris, histoire d'une ville, XIXe–XXe siècle.* Paris, 1993.

Sutcliff, Anthony. *Paris: An Architectural History.* New Haven, Conn., 1993.

DAVID P. JORDAN

PARIS COMMUNE. The Paris Commune of 1871 was the most important urban popular rising in Europe between the French Revolution of 1789 and the Russian Revolution of February 1917. It ended the series of Paris popular risings begun in July 1789 and continued in July 1830 and June 1848; it involved a popular revolutionary seizure of power in Continental Europe's premier city; and it inspired a legend of revolutionary government, heroic resistance, and tragic martyrdom that enjoyed a century's iconic status for the European Left.

ORIGINS

The reasons for the outbreak of the Paris Commune were many and complex. Paris was a quite exceptional city. Its population had risen from approximately 1.2 million in 1850 to nearly 2 million in 1870, a figure larger than that of the combined populations of the next fourteen most populous French cities. Rapid expansion reflected the city's status as France's most important industrial center and largest building site. More than one-fifth of all French urban workers lived in Paris and they tended to be highly skilled and literate. The rebuilding of Paris under Baron Georges-Eugène Haussmann (Prefect of the Seine, 1853–1869) in the interests of modernization, imperial prestige, security, and the bourgeoisie necessitated tax increases, involved authoritarian planning decisions, and attracted large numbers of construction workers and other migrants to the capital.

At the same time, workers and their families were displaced from the city center to outlying suburbs with virtually nonexistent public transport. Since Paris was the imperial capital, as well as the principal business center and urban resort of the rich in France, Paris workers were exposed to the extravagances and excesses of the court and of the wealthy elite in this "New Babylon." Moreover, Paris had a revolutionary tradition going back to 1789, renewed in the revolutions of 1830 and 1848, and demonstrated again in the resistance to Louis-Napoleon Bonaparte's (later Napoleon III; r. 1852–1871) coup d'état of 2 December 1851. Thereafter, election results and the plebiscite of May 1870 confirmed that Paris remained the center of opposition to the Second Empire. The liberalization of the regime during the 1860s simply facilitated the emergence of radical opposition leadership, for example, against state centralization, of opposition newspapers, and of opposition

ideologies (the Belleville Programme of 1869), aided by the law of 18 June 1868, which tolerated public meetings.

THE FRANCO-PRUSSIAN WAR

The political alienation of the Paris working class from the Second Empire did not mean that a revolutionary situation existed in Paris before July 1870. It took the Franco-Prussian War, the siege of Paris, and the decisions of the Thiers government to transform political alienation into violent revolution. The outbreak of the Franco-Prussian War on 19 July 1870 rapidly led to the defeat at Sedan on 2 September, when Napoleon III and approximately one hundred thousand French soldiers surrendered. The news of this catastrophe in turn led on 4 September to a crowd invasion of the Legislative Body (the lower house of the French parliament), the proclamation of the Third Republic at the Hôtel de Ville (the Paris city hall), and the formation of a Government of National Defense. The new French government included a radical, Léon-Michel Gambetta (1838–1882), as Minister of the Interior, but moderate republicans predominated. The moderate republicans wanted to make peace, but the demands of Otto von Bismarck (1815–1898) for a large indemnity and the cessation of Alsace and much of Lorraine were considered too high. The war therefore continued. By 19 September German forces had surrounded Paris, cutting it off from the rest of France. Paris had modern fortifications, consisting of a thirty-mile rampart and sixteen outlying forts; the city had numerous defenders, including both regular soldiers and members of the National Guard (a civilian militia), who were reasonably well supplied with weapons and ammunition; and the city initially had substantial food stocks. Consequently, the Germans decided not to try to capture the city by assault, while the Parisians were able to survive a prolonged siege.

The Government of National Defense (except Gambetta) wanted to end the war as quickly as possible and so neither introduced radical measures nor prosecuted the war vigorously. In contrast, most of those besieged in Paris, fired by political radicalism and patriotic republicanism, urged a total mobilization of national resources for the war effort and an aggressive military strategy against the Germans. The failure of sorties from Paris or of a relieving force from the provinces to end the siege, the German decision to begin an artillery bombardment of Paris from 5 January 1871, and, above all, the near-exhaustion of food supplies in Paris, led to the negotiation of an armistice on 28 January 1871.

By this date the siege had transformed the situation in Paris. A revolutionary leadership had emerged, partly through vigilance committees set up in each *arrondissement* or district. A popular revolutionary program had been developed, including the introduction of an elected city council or commune, the election of all public officials, and the replacement of the police and the regular army by the National Guard. The National Guard itself had been hugely expanded to more than 340,000 men, all of whom were paid one franc and thirty centimes per day and most of whom were issued with a uniform and military equipment. Recruitment was organized on a neighborhood basis and officers were elected. Much of the population of Paris had been radicalized by political clubs and newspapers; by the conservative and defeatist policies of the Government of National Defense; and by the whole traumatic experience of the siege, especially the desperate food situation, aggravated by the nonimplementation of an adequate food-rationing system.

THE VERSAILLES GOVERNMENT

One of the conditions of the armistice was that elections should be held as soon as possible for a National Assembly that would approve the final peace treaty between France and the newly proclaimed German Empire. The elections (8 February 1871) revealed the political division between Paris and the provinces. Nearly all the forty-three representatives elected in Paris were prowar radical republicans, whereas provincial voters returned more than four hundred conservatives but barely one hundred republicans. The National Assembly, meeting at Bordeaux on 17 February, chose Adolphe Thiers (1797–1877) as head of the executive. Unsurprisingly, Thiers and his new government pursued conservative policies, unsympathetic to Paris: a law of 15 February limited National Guard pay to those who could present an official certificate of dire pov-

Communard cannons at a barricade at the Porte de Saint Ouen in Paris, 1871. © ALINARI ARCHIVES/CORBIS

erty; the Germans were allowed to hold a military parade down the Champs Elysées on 1 March; a right-wing aristocrat, General de Paladines, was appointed on 3 March commander of the Paris National Guard; six radical Paris newspapers were suppressed; a military court condemned two radical leaders (Marie-Jean-Pierre Flourens [1838–1871] and Auguste Blanqui [1805–1881]) to death; the moratorium in Paris on the payment of rents and commercial bills of exchange was ended; and the National Assembly decided to meet at Versailles, former seat of absolute monarchy and recent setting for the proclamation of the German Empire (18 January 1871).

THE OUTBREAK OF THE PARIS COMMUNE

Finally, the Versailles government on 18 March sent troops to remove cannon parked in the working-class suburbs of Belleville and Montmartre. This attempt to deprive the National Guard of its most dangerous weapons is understandable, but so too is the Parisian response. Angry crowds of National Guards and civilians obstructed the troops, who refused to resist. Several officers were arrested and two generals, Claude Martin Lecomte (1817–1871), the commander of the troops at Montmartre, and Clément Thomas (1809–1871), the former commander-in-chief of the Paris National Guard, were executed.

A panicked Thiers, fearing that troops of the Paris garrison and civil servants would become prisoners of the insurgents, ordered all soldiers and government civil servants to withdraw to Versailles, thereby creating a power vacuum. The remaining representatives of authority in Paris, the mayors of the city's *arrondissements,* the National Assembly representatives of Paris, and the Central Committee of the National Guard all agreed that elections should be held on 26 March for a new commune or city council. Political radicalization during the siege, hatred of Thiers and the Versailles government, and the behavior of the bourgeoisie (who tended either to leave Paris or to boycott the elections) led to a sweeping left-wing victory: only nineteen moderates, as opposed to seventy-three members of the Left, were elected. The Paris Commune was formally proclaimed in a solemn ceremony on 28 March.

The military situation for the Paris Commune was hopeless from the start. The Paris National Guard lacked discipline and units were usually reluctant to fight outside the neighborhoods from which they had been recruited. Attempts to mount sorties against the well-entrenched Versailles troops all failed. Communes in Lyon, Marseille, Limoges, Toulouse, Narbonne, St. Étienne, and Le Creusot were soon suppressed, so no help came from provincial France. The German army remained encamped on the outskirts of Paris, ostensibly neutral but potentially hostile to the Commune. Bismarck released French prisoners of war to the Versailles government, which was able to build up forces of overwhelming strength and begin a steady assault on the city's defenses. The southwestern ramparts were penetrated on 21 May, although it took a week of sometimes intense fighting against insurgents defending buildings and street barricades before the Commune finally fell on 28 May.

THE CHARACTER OF THE PARIS COMMUNE
Despite its increasingly desperate military situation, the short-lived Paris Commune was remarkable for its social and political character. Most members of the Commune council belonged either to the lower middle class or to the working-class elite, at a time when upper-class elites dominated governments throughout Europe. Politically, Communards saw themselves as being republicans, revolutionaries, patriots, and Parisians. No organized political parties existed, although there were factions such as the Blanquists (revolutionaries) and the Jacobins (left-wing republicans). Although distorted by military demands and limited by lack of time, Communard priorities can be discerned. Communards believed in grassroots democracy and the election and public accountability of all officials. The National Guard, recruited from all able-bodied men, replaced the police and the regular army. The confiscation of church buildings, the destruction of religious symbols, the dismissal of religious personnel from their

jobs, and the planning of a secular educational system all featured in an anticlerical crusade. Women-friendly policies included equal pay for male and female teachers, support for women's committees and women's cooperatives, and pensions for common-law wives of National Guards killed in action.

Economic policy, though, was relatively conservative. Night-work in bakeries was banned and the price of bread was fixed. The moratorium on rents was reinstated and extended to objects pawned in the state pawnshops. However, property was not confiscated, except church property; and, until the last week of the Commune, property was not destroyed, again except church property and symbolically significant buildings and monuments, such as Thiers's townhouse and the Vendôme column. A decree of 16 April did provide for the confiscation of workshops, but only if they had been abandoned. Compensation was to be paid to their owners, and the decree was not put into practice. The Commune also promoted the establishment of producers' cooperatives.

THE DEFEAT OF THE PARIS COMMUNE
The final week of the Commune (21–28 May), "the Bloody Week," witnessed atrocities on both sides. Communards burnt prominent public buildings, such as the Hôtel de Ville and the Tuileries Palace, and executed hostages, including the Archbishop of Paris, Georges Darboy (1813–1871) on 24 May, and a group of fifty (mostly priests and policemen) on 26 May. The Versailles troops shot numerous prisoners, most notoriously in front of a wall in the Père Lachaise cemetery.

After final resistance had been overcome, nearly forty thousand suspects were rounded up, of whom approximately ten thousand were found guilty. In all, it is likely that as many as twenty-five thousand Parisians were executed, with notoriously radical neighbourhoods such as Belleville especially targeted. Four thousand people were transported to New Caledonia and the remainder were imprisoned. An amnesty was not granted until 1880.

THE LEGACY AND SIGNIFICANCE OF THE PARIS COMMUNE
The total military defeat of the Commune and the harsh treatment of suspected Communards vir-

Insurgents from the Paris Commune displayed in their coffins, 1871. ©BETTMANN/CORBIS

tually destroyed the radical Left in French politics for nearly a decade and massively discouraged any future resort to violent popular revolution in France. Under the leadership of Thiers until 1873, and then the Duc de Broglie (Albert, 1821–1901) and Marshal de Mac-Mahon (1808–1893) (commander of the troops who suppressed the Commune), the Third Republic emerged as a conservative regime. A monarchist restoration was avoided, but when republicans came to power from 1877 their radicalism was anticlerical rather than socialist. Paris lost its National Guard and mayor (the latter until 1977). The French parliament and president did not leave Versailles for Paris until 1879. Public buildings burnt by the Communards were rebuilt exactly as they had been, except for the Tuileries Palace. The basilica of Sacré Coeur was erected on the heights of Montmartre, where the Commune had begun and Generals Lecomte and Thomas had been executed. Altogether, the memory of the Commune was officially obliterated while conservatives portrayed the Communards as bloodthirsty savages and blamed the burning of public buildings on female incendiarists (*pétroleuses*).

In contrast, Karl Marx (1818–1883) hailed the Commune as a proletarian government that had destroyed the bourgeois bureaucratic machine and as "the glorious harbinger of a new society" that should serve as a model for future revolutionary governments. He did, however, criticize the Commune for failing to launch an immediate attack on Versailles and for failing to seize the gold reserves of the Bank of France. For the French Left, the Commune became a symbol of heroic resistance and martyrdom, annually commemorated at a ceremony at Pére Lachaise cemetery.

See also **Blanqui, Auguste; First International; France; Franco-Prussian War; Marx, Karl; Paris; Republicanism; Socialism.**

BIBLIOGRAPHY

Primary Sources

Marx, Karl. *The Civil War in France.* Peking, 1966.

Secondary Sources

Edwards, Stewart. *The Paris Commune 1871.* London, 1971.

Greenberg, Louis M. *Sisters of Liberty: Marseille, Lyon, Paris, and the Reaction to a Centralized State, 1868–1871.* Cambridge, Mass., 1971.

Rougerie, Jacques. *Paris libre, 1871.* Paris, 1971.

Shafer, David A. "*'Plus que des Ambulancières'*: Women in Articulation and Defence of Their Ideals during the Paris Commune (1871)." *French History* 7 (1993): 85–101.

Tombs, Robert. *The War against Paris, 1871.* Cambridge, U.K., 1981.

———. *The Paris Commune 1871.* Harlow, Essex, U.K., and New York, 1999.

WILLIAM FORTESCUE

PARKS. According to notable landscape librarian Theodora Kimball, it was a letter of complaint addressed to a Burgermeister in Magdeburg, Germany, in 1815 that instigated the municipal park movement in Europe. Writing in 1923, Kimball quoted the Magdeburgian grouser, who feared that the incursions of troops during the war had so badly damaged the environs, "there would soon be no rural enjoyment possible in the vicinity." The city council subsequently underwrote the transformation of certain municipal properties into the first parks created specifically for public enjoyment. While urban parks already existed in Europe by this point—Charles I (r. 1625–1649) had opened the royal preserve of Hyde Park to the public in 1637—the idea that a park might be built for and owned by the public, as opposed to being merely publicly accessible, was novel.

By the end of the nineteenth century, this *public* aspect of the urban park would itself be entirely natural, due in large part to British Parliamentary legislation regarding the sanitary conditions of the working classes and similar concern for creating what would be called "urban lungs" for the growing industrialized urban centers of France and Germany, especially evidenced by the comprehensive Parisian park system designed under Georges-Eugène Haussmann (1809–1891) and Jean-Charles Adolphe Alphand (1817–1891) in the 1850s and 1860s, and the German *Volksparks* from the end of the century.

Throughout the nineteenth century, many royal hunting grounds and country estates in England were opened, thereby exposing the public to the results of the previous century's debates over the picturesque and sublime that had established the reputations of such landscape designers as Lancelot "Capability" Brown (1715–1783) and Humphry Repton (1752–1818), father of the "Gardenesque" landscape movement. These Romantics, like their counterparts in France and Germany, sought to balance the natural and the scientific, carefully composing nature into a sublime tableau all the while artfully compensating for limitations of reality, such as property boundaries and views unto neighbors. The majority of public parks resulted not as much from the dissolution of these estates, however, as from British legislation, such as the Public Health Act of 1848, which recognized that public urban parks offered intertwined political and economic benefits. By improving air quality and providing space for recreation, the parks distracted the lower classes from their lives of drudgery and kept them out of the pubs, while improving their health and therefore their productivity. These public parks were simplified microcosms of the more elaborate picturesque gardens of the English Romantic movement.

Paralleling these parks aimed at ameliorating industrialized conditions in England's urban centers were pleasure parks, epitomized by the design of the Great Exhibition of 1851 held in Hyde Park. Joseph Paxton's (1801–1865) Crystal Palace was such a success at the Exhibition that after its close, the Palace was moved to Sydenham Hill in South London where it became the anchor of what could only be called a 200-acre Victorian theme park. Such attractions, like the public promenades of London, designed by John Claudius Loudon (1783–1843), were aimed less at providing health benefits than at creating a leisure landscape for the developing nineteenth-century urban bourgeoisie that emerged under industrialization.

Hyde Park, London. Illustration by R. Caton Woodville from the *Illustrated London News,* 1885. An outing in the park provided socialization as well as an opportunity to display the outward signs of prosperity. MARY EVANS PICTURE LIBRARY

In France, unlike England, the public parks that developed in the nineteenth century were situated primarily in the nation's capital and, furthermore, were less the result of industrialization than that of royal decree. While they helped to clean the city's air and provided nature for those who had neither time nor money to travel outside of Paris, these parks primarily provided a setting for the leisure of the bourgeoisie, as illustrated by Impressionist paintings such as those of the Parc Monceau by Claude Monet (1840–1926). Napoléon III (r. 1852–1871) provided Baron Haussmann, the Préfet de la Seine, with the power to transform Paris, cutting a Baroque network of monuments and parks into the city's dense medieval fabric. With the assistance of engineer Alphand, Haussmann created the first comprehensive urban park system. This network consisted of two large forests, the Bois de Boulogne to the west and the Bois de Vincennes to the east, as well as three primary interior parks: the Parc Monceau, the Parc de Montsouris, and the Parc des Buttes-Chaumont,

completed in 1863 in a working-class district on a site that had previously served as a gallows, a lime quarry, and even a waste dump. This final park is the most dramatic of all of Haussmann's interventions into Paris. Using dynamite, he blasted the quarry rock to create cliffs, a waterfall, and a 61-acre romantic park, complete with grotto, temple, and a suspension bridge. All three parks, along with the two forests, adopted the English Romantic style, although the Parisian examples retained a degree of control for which the French garden is famous: Rather than providing large spaces for informal recreation, Haussmann's parks emphasized the ordered—and carefully orchestrated—sequences of promenades for stylish strolling.

The roads that Haussmann cut through Paris, linking the city's many monuments in a dramatic Baroque web, gave an ordered elegance to a previously chaotic city, but were largely aimed at facilitating the movement of the emperor's troops through Paris. Haussmann and Alphand's generous

Le Jardin des Buttes-Chaumont. Nineteenth-century lithograph. ©Leonard de Selva/Corbis

parks, however, like the parks in England, were more purely aesthetic: while they certainly increased the value of land where they were inserted, they primarily provided the public with sites of leisure—especially for the strolls of the bourgeoisie—while simultaneously cleaning the city's foul air.

As in France, the English Romantic style influenced the German parks of this period as well. Peter Joseph Lenné (1789–1866), the landscape designer of the Klosterberg public gardens in Magdeberg, which were among the first manifestations of the pressure to preserve spaces for "rural enjoyment" after the ravages of the Napoleonic Wars, had traveled to London and had greatly admired Regent's Park by Repton and architect John Nash (1752–1835). In Berlin, Lenné was responsible for the designs of the Neuen Garten in Potsdam (1816) and Berlin's famous Tiergarten (1818), to the west, which were both designed in Loudon's "Gardenesque" manner.

The most original contribution that the Germans made to public park design, however, were not these beautiful Romantic gardens, but the more utilitarian *Volksparks*, or "people's parks," which proliferated especially at the beginning of the twentieth century. Functional in design, unpretentious in character, these parks were aimed at the working classes. The famous slogan for these parks was that they were places "where families can make a cup of coffee," which underscores that they were not sites of pomp and promenade, but rather open spaces designed for everyday use. They included restaurants, playing fields, and bathing areas, and were used for games, demonstrations, and workers' parades. Lenné designed Berlin's first Volkspark, the Friedrichshain, which was laid out by the city in 1840 to celebrate the centenary of Frederick the Great's (r. 1740–1786) accession to the throne. Later famous Volksparks include the Stadtpark in Hamburg, the Grüngürtel (Greenbelt) around Cologne, and the Jungfernheide in Berlin.

The Volkspark movement brought the development of the European municipal park full circle.

For while the great parks of the nineteenth century were Romantic exercises in designing sublime, elegant gardens in city centers that served as stage sets for the strolls of the developing middle class, ultimately both the impetus and the greatest benefactors of these green spaces were the working classes, whose grumblings at the beginning of the nineteenth century prompted the entirely new discipline of landscape architecture.

See also Berlin; Cities and Towns; Crystal Palace; Haussmann, Georges-Eugène; London; Paris.

BIBLIOGRAPHY

Alphand, Adolphe. Les Promenades de Paris. 2 vols. Paris, 1867–1873. Reprint, Princeton, N.J., 1984.

Chadwick, George F. The Park and the Town: Public Landscape in the 19th and 20th Centuries. London, 1966.

Cosgrove, Denis E. Social Formation and Symbolic Landscape. London, 1984.

Jellicoe, Geoffrey, and Susan Jellicoe. The Landscape of Man: Shaping the Environment from Prehistory to the Present Day. London: 1975. Reprint, London, 1987.

Kimball, Theodora, to Frederick Law Olmsted Jr., letter written in Richardson Hall, Harvard University, Cambridge, Mass. 1923. Concerning the early development of parks in Europe.

Limido, Luisa. L'Art des Jardins Sous Le Second Empire: Jean-Pierre Barillet-Dechamps. Seyssel, France, 2002.

Pregill, Philip, and Nancy Volkman. Landscapes in History: Design and Planning in the Western Tradition. New York, 1993.

SARAH WHITING

PARNELL, CHARLES STEWART

(1846–1891), Irish nationalist leader.

Charles Stewart Parnell came from an Anglican landed family yet established himself as the leader of a revolt by predominantly Catholic and nationalist tenants against his own class. Unfortunate educational experiences in Britain left him with abiding resentment of British contempt for the Irish, yet he retained a certain social distance from his plebeian followers.

In 1875 Parnell was elected to Parliament as a member of Isaac Butt's Home Rule Party, which advocated limited autonomy for Ireland. Parnell rapidly emerged as a powerful speaker and a prominent "obstructionist." (These were members of Parliament [MPs] who thought Butt insufficiently radical and tried to force Parliament to pay attention to Ireland by systematically disrupting debates with long speeches.) In 1879, as crop failure and falling agricultural prices led to renewed tenant farmer agitation against landlords, Parnell entered into the "New Departure," an alliance with the Land League (founded in 1879 by Michael Davitt) and Irish-American physical-force separatists represented by John Devoy. This increased Parnell's popular support, enabling him to strengthen his support within the Home Rule Party at the 1880 general election and to become its leader shortly afterward. Parnell, a man of few words and significant silences, allowed his new allies to presume his agreement with them while using them for his own political purposes; meanwhile, he recruited able young lieutenants (including William O'Brien, John Dillon, and Timothy Michael Healy).

Many British commentators blamed Parnell for the agrarian violence that accompanied the land agitation; in 1881, after denouncing land legislation passed by the government of Prime Minister William Ewart Gladstone as insufficient, he was interned with many other activists. The land agitation was sustained by the Ladies' Land League under Parnell's sister Anna. Violence continued, and in 1882 Parnell and his allies were released in return for his tacit agreement to control the radicals. (Parnell was also motivated by his developing relationship with Katharine O'Shea, the wife of a Home Rule MP, William Henry O'Shea.) This "Kilmainham Treaty" (called after Parnell's prison in Dublin) was limited by British revulsion at the subsequent assassination of a junior minister and a prominent civil servant in the Phoenix Park, Dublin, by members of a separatist splinter group. Parnell's initial reaction was panic over the possible consequences of his previous flirtations with the physical-force movement; but in the long run his position was strengthened by the flight to America of many radical activists. (His abrupt dissolution of the Ladies' Land League earned him Anna Parnell's enmity.)

In the following years Parnell built up a powerful, centrally controlled political organization, secured the support of the Catholic Church, and developed a personality cult through newspaper propaganda and carefully managed appearances. Parnell skillfully played conservatives and liberals against each other in 1884–1885; at the 1885 general election he monopolized the parliamentary representation of nationalist Ireland, electing eighty-six nationalist MPs (against eighteen conservative Irish Unionists) and acquiring a pivotal position within Parliament. Soon after the election it became known that Gladstone now favored the creation of a subordinate Irish Parliament.

The defeat of Gladstone's first Home Rule Bill (1886) by liberal Unionist defectors led to the formation of a pro-Union Conservative government with liberal Unionist support. While Gladstone sought British support for Home Rule by presenting the issue as a moral crusade, Parnell's lieutenants led a renewed land agitation in Ireland. Parnell himself was kept in the public eye by accusations that he had connived at the Phoenix Park murders (on the basis of letters subsequently revealed to have been forged by the journalist Richard Pigott). The government used an inquiry into these allegations to present the whole nationalist movement as a criminal conspiracy.

In 1890 Parnell's leadership was shattered by the public disclosure of his affair with Mrs. O'Shea, after her husband (who had previously connived at the relationship) sued for divorce. After Gladstone, pressured by Protestant zealots among his supporters, declared that he could not deliver Home Rule if Parnell remained leader, the majority of Home Rule MPs voted to depose him. Parnell (who had never forgiven Gladstone for imprisoning him in 1881–1882) and his supporters argued that the majority betrayed nationalist principles by accepting English dictation, and that Parnell remained the best-qualified leader. The bitter political conflict that followed did much to discredit Irish nationalism; Parnell made opportunistic appeals to separatism, while Healy (supported by the Irish Catholic bishops) subjected Parnell to unrelenting personal abuse as a lecherous, selfish, and generally un-Irish Protestant aristocrat. Parnell's frail health was undermined by unremitting campaigning, and on 6 October 1891 he died at Brighton (where he was living with Mrs. O'Shea, whom he had married after her divorce).

Parnell's followers saw him as a martyr, and the split between Parnellites and Anti-Parnellites continued until 1900. The failure of Gladstone to pass Home Rule in 1892–1893 and the weak and divided state of nationalism contributed to the growth of a Parnell legend; since he had skillfully maintained ambiguity about his ultimate aims, separatists and liberal Unionists as well as parliamentary nationalists could lay claim to him. (He is now often regarded as a conservative seeking to maintain a role for his class in a changing Ireland.) Writers such as James Joyce and William Butler Yeats saw him as the inspired hero destroyed by ungrateful and hypocritical philistines; the defeat of his campaign for Home Rule is one of the great might-have-beens of British and Irish history.

See also **Great Britain; Ireland; Nationalism.**

BIBLIOGRAPHY

Bew, Paul. *C. S. Parnell*. Dublin, 1980.

Callanan, Frank. *The Parnell Split, 1890–91*. Syracuse, N.Y., 1992.

Kee, Robert. *The Laurel and the Ivy: The Story of Charles Stewart Parnell and Irish Nationalism*. London, 1993.

Lyons, Francis Stewart Leland. *Charles Stewart Parnell*. New York, 1977.

O'Brien, Richard Barry. *Life of Charles Stewart Parnell, 1846–1891*. New York, 1898.

PATRICK MAUME

PASTEUR, LOUIS (1822–1895), French microbiologist.

The Pasteurian revolution may have been the final touch to an internal line of development in scientific thought and medical practice, but the most spectacular and far-reaching effects of Louis Pasteur's discoveries were in the field of public health. Pasteur the experimenter revolutionized public health by proving bacterial pollution, demonstrating pollution prevention through pasteurization, describing the microbial etiology of infectious diseases, and demonstrating that disease could be prevented through vaccination.

FIRST LESSONS: FROM CRYSTALS TO MICROBES

Louis Pasteur was born at Dole, France, into a modest family whose name had never shone in history. His father operated a tannery at Marmoz, Franche-Comté, where Pasteur spent his childhood. In October 1843 he entered the École Nationale in Paris and worked in the laboratory of Jérôme Balard. Pasteur built his first discovery on tartaric and para-tartaric acids: he showed that the two substances are identical but that their atomic positions are reversed. Pasteur defined what thirty-five years later Lord Kelvin (William Thomson), was to call chirality, from the Greek *kheir,* the hand, a symbol to designate a shape that cannot be superimposed on its mirror image.

This success led Pasteur to study the optical activity of a whole series of substances. At the University of Strasbourg, where he was appointed as professor of chemistry in January 1849, Pasteur examined meticulously diverse kinds of molecules and was intrigued by a strange finding: asymmetry, it appeared, had its limits. All the substances composed of asymmetrical molecules came from plant, human, or animal models. Conversely, chemical substances that do not deviate light and possess an axis of symmetry are all of mineral origin. Pasteur deduced that the molecules of life are asymmetrical. Applying this discovery to fermentation, he went on to consider it as a natural biological occurrence, not as an artificial chemical synthesis. To prove that the fermentation was a germ of life he switched from crystals to microbes, from chemistry to microbiology and immunology.

BACTERIAL POLLUTION AND PASTEURIZATION

Pasteur had begun his studies on fermentation in 1854 at the University of Lille, where he had been appointed dean of the science faculty two years earlier, and he soon turned his attention to incomplete distillation. He took a microscope to a beet sugar factory and spent days on end making alcohol. Looking through the eyepiece he watched the growth of the globules that were present as sugar was being turned into alcohol. Pasteur showed that minute organisms acted because they were alive and breathing. In holding his own against some of the greatest biochemical theories of the time, which maintained that fermentus was indispensable because of its capacity to disappear, Pasteur was going to give the germ its due importance in alcohol and lactic fermentation and then in the rotting process. Aerobic germs are necessary to the life cycle

since they take in oxygen and expel carbon dioxide, which is absorbed by plants. Building on this, he held that microorganisms, both parasitic and useful ones, must be everywhere—in the water, the air, the ground. This hypothesis from the outset was waged against one of the major philosophical and biological problems of the nineteenth century: the theory of spontaneous generation, which claimed that germs are born directly in mineral matter.

To show that such theory was wrong and that spontaneous generation does not occur, Pasteur first had to develop a new experimental strategy. At the École Normale Supérieure, where he had been appointed director of scientific studies in 1857, he invented an external device used to pump air from the school's garden and filter it through a fluff of cotton. Microbes could be detected when the cotton was washed on a watch glass. This debate on spontaneous generation was to turn into an analysis of air and the first epidemiological analyses of the presence of microorganisms in the environment. Pasteur showed that germs vary in relation to place and season depending on climatic conditions and hygiene.

In 1865, upon orders from Napoleon III, Pasteur went to work on wine diseases, using heat as a source of prevention. He adopted Nicolas Appert's procedure for food keeping and recommended a new method for conserving wine: heating between 60°C and 100°C in an air-free environment for one to two hours. The pasteurization method circled the globe.

From 1865 through 1869 he investigated the pebrine disease that had been devastating the production of raw silk. He discovered that silkworms were contaminated when hatched, as the butterfly was already sick because of a minuscule parasite. Pasteur demonstrated that healthy eggs could be seen under a microscope and hatched. His cellular system helped end the disease by 1875.

ASEPSIS AND ANTISEPSIS

In France, by the end of the Franco-Prussian War of 1870–1871, a surgeon named Alphonse Guérin began to accept that infection could be caused by the microbes described by Pasteur. By applying a cotton dressing, Guérin was able to avoid microbial overinfection.

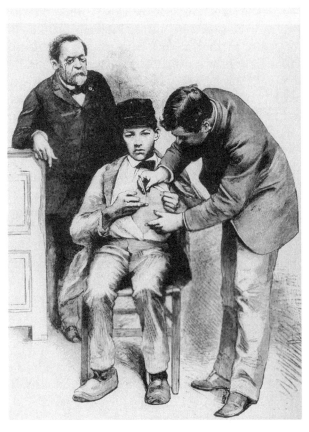

Louis Pasteur. Pasteur observes as a boy is innoculated against rabies in this 1885 print. ©BETTMAN/CORBIS

It was Joseph Lister from England, however, who was the first to officially apply Pasteur's discoveries to medicine. In 1865 Thomas Anderson, a chemistry professor in Glasgow, first showed Lister reports from Pasteur. Lister suddenly understood the link that might exist between the decomposition of organic matter and postoperative infections. He, like Pasteur, believed that the ambient air was one of the main pathways for the propagation of germs. He thought it would be possible to kill the germs using a substance that would not be toxic to human tissue but could prevent abscess formation, even in a nonsterile environment. In recounting the circumstances that convinced him of such hypothesis, Lister explained that he had been very impressed by a report on the remarkable effects of carbolic acid on sewer water. Understanding that carbolic acid not only removed the smells but also killed the germs, he discovered antisepsis.

Antisepsis (destruction of pathogenic microorganisms already present) was adopted before asep-

sis (prevention of such microorganisms from occurring); the latter only reached Paris toward the end of the 1870s and was not routinely used until the end of the 1880s. The application of asepsis progressed in parallel with hygiene.

THE MICROBIAL THEORY OF INFECTIOUS DISEASES

The debate on aspesis and antisepsis only provided indirect arguments on the pathogenic effect of germs. The absence of germs indeed prevented the diseases, but it did not confirm the cause-and-effect link. Direct evidence came from Pasteur's work on anthrax.

Anthrax is a redoubtable infectious disease that wipes out whole herds of cattle and flocks of sheep. Sick animals soon collapse in the field. Scientists before Pasteur, such as Casimir-Joseph Davaine in France and Robert Koch in Germany, felt that bacteria were the cause but had not been able to prove it.

To demonstrate that bacteria transmitted the disease, Pasteur performed a simple experiment. All he had to do was dilute a drop of anthrax-infected blood and simulate microbial proliferation. By leaving to the bacteria the time they needed to multiply, a bacterial culture could soon be obtained that was nearly pure. The only thing then left to do was to inject a drop into an animal and demonstrate that such inoculation was as lethal as the anthrax-infected blood.

In the summer of 1878 the Ministry of Agriculture gave him a new assignment. He was to carry out a survey among cattle producers to find out how anthrax invaded the herds. Pasteur approached the problem using two clearly observed facts: the disease was transmitted by bacteria, and it depended on the grazing zone. Once again, proof involved field observation. Pasteur noticed that sharp, cutting leaves or barley beard caused abrasions in the animals' mouths. His conclusion was that the disease inoculation occurred when the cow or sheep cut its mouth or when it swallowed contaminated herbage.

But there was an outstanding question: How do anthrax spores rise to the surface when the dead animals have been buried deeply underground? In a flash of genius, Pasteur found the missing link in his anthrax transmission chain. "The worms are the carriers of the spore. As they dig galleries underground, they move near the animal graves, then transport and spread the spores."

VACCINATIONS

For Pasteur, prevention was still the main therapy. Vaccination was soon to become one of the main concerns of his research.

Pasteur felt it would be possible to find a method of protection against each and every microbial strain. With the help of Émile Roux, in 1880, he applied his theory to chicken cholera. After a partly accidental discovery, Pasteur prepared a bacillus culture with attenuated virulence, which therefore offered protection against the fatal infection. Pasteur thus added a genuine biological reagent to Lister's antiseptic techniques. Such attenuated germs were not pathogenic but instead, acted as reagents to prevent the disease induced by virulent ones. It did not cause the disease but became a weapon to stimulate natural resistance.

By using the word *vaccinate* to mean inoculating the germ of attenuated virulence, Pasteur showed how much he owed to his predecessors, first and foremost the English physician Edward Jenner. However, Pasteurian vaccination is very different from Jenner's method of using a cow's udder because it includes biological experiments. Pasteur discovered the vaccine, not the vaccination. Indeed Jenner proposed a method to vaccinate against smallpox, but did not know how to make a vaccine. Pasteur did not discover the principle but instead described procedures to make vaccines, which, since then, have been applied with success.

Pasteur applied the vaccine to cattle diseases, chicken cholera, hog erysipelas, anthrax, and, although he used a different principle, to human rabies. These results automatically led the way to other vaccines, which were developed thereafter for numerous infectious diseases by many men and women of science and industry.

THE PASTEUR INSTITUTES

Pasteur's contribution to public health, from the rules of hygiene to knowledge of germs and the development of vaccines, was not limited to scientific experimentation. Pasteur wanted to apply his ideas himself. The need for a place to combine instruction and industry became clear and led to the opening of the Pasteur Institute on 14 November 1888. He was also desirous of having his research findings serve the most underprivileged countries, and several other Pasteur Institutes were funded overseas from Asia to Africa.

When he died in 1895, Pasteur was judged one of humanity's most important scientists. By opening the way to the rational analysis of the elements of disease prevention, he changed the lives of people around the globe.

See also **Chemistry; Disease; France; Jenner, Edward; Koch, Robert; Lister, Joseph; Wine.**

BIBLIOGRAPHY

Primary Sources

Pasteur, Louis. *Oeuvres de Pasteur réunies.* 7 vols. Paris, 1922–1939.

———. *Correspondance générale.* 4 vols. Paris, 1951.

Secondary Sources

Calmette, Albert. "Pasteur et les Instituts Pasteur." *Revue d'hygiène* 45 (1923).

Dagognet, François. *Méthodes et doctrine dans l'œuvre de Pasteur.* Paris, 1967.

———. *Pasteur sans la légende.* Le Plessis, 1994.

Debré, Patrice. *Louis Pasteur.* Paris, 1994.

Dubos, René. *Le Leçon de Pasteur.* Paris, 1988.

Geison, Gerald. "Pasteur." In *Dictionary of Scientific Biography,* edited by Charles Coulston Gillespie. Vol 1. New York, 1974.

Metchnikov, Elie. *Trois fondateurs de la médicine moderne: Pasteur, Lister, Koch.* Alcan, 1933.

Pasteur Vallery-Radot, Louis. "Les Instituts Pasteur d'Outre-Mer." *La Presse Médicale* 21 (1939).

Ramon, Gaston. "Ce que Pasteur doit aux vétérinaires et ce que le médecin vétérinaire doit à Pasteur." *Revue Médicale et Vétérinaire* 112 (1936).

Vallery-Radot, René. *La vie de Pasteur.* Paris, 1900.

PATRICE DEBRÉ

PATER, WALTER (1839–1894), English writer, critic, and aesthete.

In June 1858 Walter Horatio Pater matriculated at Queen's College, University of Oxford, where he read classics. Pater's earliest published review essays, "Coleridge's Writings" (1866) and "Winckelmann" (1867), expressed his unorthodox views on Christian religion and sexuality, as did two unpublished essays circulated in 1864, "Diaphaneite" and "Subjective Immortality." The latter essay stoked theological controversy among the high-church party at Oxford for its denial of an afterlife. In February 1864 Pater was elected to the first nonclerical fellowship in classics at Brasenose College, Oxford, where he resided until 1869.

Soon after, Pater published three anonymous articles for the *Westminster Review* on Samuel Taylor Coleridge, Johann Winckelmann, and William Morris. In particular, he attacked theological dogmatism, glowingly advertised Winckelmann's promotion of Hellenism and homoeroticism, and linked himself to his pre-Raphaelite contemporaries such as John Ruskin as well as to the style of "aesthetic poetry." Pater's Morris essay climaxed in a conclusion that presented life as a flux of sensory perceptions in which the noblest task for the observant eye was to identify and capture a momentarily stable and satisfying form, thereby extending life's "highest" moments. His approach openly esteemed the male form in art in the same measure as it appreciated the application of abstract reason and logic. His conclusion advocated the cultivation of "passion," defined as the "fruit of a quickened, multiplied consciousness." These views would mark the rest of Pater's career, to the delight of aesthetes and the consternation of Anglican clergy.

In 1869 Pater moved to north Oxford, living with his two sisters, and began to dress as a dandy. For the first time he published articles under his own name in the *Fortnightly Review*. The first, on Leonardo da Vinci (1869), included his famous invocation of the *Mona Lisa*: "She is as old as the rocks upon which she sits," the influence of which W. B. Yeats carried into the twentieth century when he printed this passage as the first poem in his *Oxford Book of English Verse* (1939). Studies of Botticelli, Pico della Mirandola, and Michelangelo followed. In 1872 he combined these with new essays, to produce *Studies in the History of the Renaissance* (1873). To this work he attached the "Conclusion" from the Morris essay, which proved highly controversial in its new context and was withdrawn in

the 1877 edition, only to be reinstated in 1888. Oscar Wilde, a former student, would praise *Studies* as the "golden book" of his youth, but the notoriety Pater's work attracted among traditionalists turned him away from publishing another book for twelve years.

In *Studies*, Pater redefined the Renaissance as a "tendency" in human civilization, rather than as a specific historical "moment"—a tendency that was born in ancient Greece and is characterized by the "desire for a more liberal and comely way of conceiving life." He would do the same to the terms "Romantic" and "classical" in an 1876 essay. The bold preface to his *Studies* overturned Matthew Arnold's call for an objective analysis of art by emphasizing instead the primacy of subjective responses. For Pater, the first task of any serious viewer is to recognize "one's own impression" of a work of art rather than the qualities of the object in itself.

His links to the "aesthetic school," with its practitioners' reputation for hedonism and "Greek love," and the discovery of letters exposing his intimacy with a young man at Brasenose threatened Pater with expulsion from Oxford. He was subsequently passed over for important university posts in the late 1870s and 1880s and rendered financially vulnerable. At this time he also experimented with a hybrid genre that fused biography, fiction, history, and criticism, which he labeled the "imaginary portrait." In 1882 he traveled to Rome and in 1883 resigned his Oxford tutorship. March 1885 saw the publication of his only finished novel, *Marius the Epicurean*, which Pater identified as an extended elaboration upon his infamous "Conclusion." Set in the Rome of Emperor Marcus Aurelius, the novel treats the problems of morality in a decadent pagan world where an ascetic Christianity is in the ascendant.

In the late 1880s Pater's productivity increased. His output included short stories, collected in *Imaginary Portraits* (1887), and criticism of modern French and English literature in *Appreciations: With an Essay on 'Style'* (1889). In 1893 Pater published his last book, *Plato and Platonism*, derived from lectures on ancient Greek philosophy, art, and archaeology.

Pater won little recognition in his lifetime. Modern scholars recognize Pater for having introduced a distinctively gay sensibility into English letters and for lending quiet inspiration to a generation of similarly inclined male writers, including J. A. Symonds, Edward Carpenter, Havelock Ellis, and Oscar Wilde. Critics are still divided as to whether Pater's ethereally refined prose style expresses the final bloom of late Romanticism or announces a nascent modernism.

See also **Arnold, Matthew; Carpenter, Edward; Decadence; Ellis, Havelock; Philhellenic Movement; Symonds, John Addington; Wilde, Oscar.**

BIBLIOGRAPHY

Brake, Laurel. *Walter Pater.* Edited by Isobel Armstrong. Plymouth, U.K., 1994.

Buckler, William E. *Walter Pater: The Critic as Artist of Ideas.* New York 1987.

Donoghue, Denis. *Walter Pater: Lover of Strange Souls.* New York, 1995.

Iser, Wolfgang. *Walter Pater: The Aesthetic Moment.* Translated by David Henry Wilson. Cambridge, U.K., and New York, 1987.

Wright, Thomas. *The Life of Walter Pater.* 2 vols. New York, 1969.

STEPHEN VELLA

PAUL I (in Russian, Pavel Petrovich; 1754–1801; ruled 1796–1801), emperor of Russia.

Officially, Paul was the son of Peter III (r. 1762) and Catherine II (the Great, r. 1762–1796), but it is likely that his real father was the Russian nobleman Sergei Saltykov. Paul never doubted his royal paternity and revered his father's memory, but he grew to hate his mother. The antipathy was mutual. Peter III had been groomed to succeed his aunt, Empress Elizabeth (r. 1741–1762), under the terms of a 1722 law requiring reigning monarchs to nominate their successors. Peter duly became emperor in January 1762 (December 1761, old style), but his policies and personality alienated powerful nobles and his reign and his life were cut short in July 1762 by a coup in favor of his wife. The astute Catherine, who had strong support in court and diplomatic circles, claimed to rule by popular acclaim. She resisted

In March 1801 conspirators broke into the bed-chamber of Emperor Paul I of Russia and placed him under arrest. "What have I done to you?" Paul asked. The answer came: "You have tortured us for four years!" Moments later Paul was dead. (Reminiscences of Count Levin Bennigsen)

suggestions that she serve as regent to Paul, who became painfully aware that his mother could legally disinherit him. For her part, Catherine feared the formation of factions around her son. Paul received a good education, but his mother kept him away from government. Official visits abroad, drilling his own guards on his barracks-like estate at Gatchina near St. Petersburg, and family life kept him occupied. In 1773 Paul was married off to Wilhelmina of Hesse-Darmstadt (known after conversion to Orthodoxy as Natalya Alexeyevna), who died giving birth in April 1776. Five months later he married Sophia Dorothea of Württemberg (Maria Fyodorovna), who bore him four sons and six daughters.

When Catherine II died from a stroke in November 1796, Paul had Peter III's remains exhumed and buried alongside her. Much of his activity thereafter aimed at reversing Catherine's policies and expunging her memory. In 1797 he introduced a new succession law based on male primogeniture. Never again would a woman rule Russia. A military atmosphere pervaded St. Petersburg, replacing the French refinement of Catherine's court. Paul outlawed French fashions, from hats to carriages, and banned the import of books. One of Paul's role models was his great-grandfather Peter I (the Great, r. 1682–1725). Paul deplored the erosion under Peter's successors of the principle that all nobles must serve the state for life. He ignored his mother's 1785 Charter to the Nobility. Nobles lost their exemption from corporal punishment, their provincial assemblies were abolished, and many were exiled or demoted on the emperor's whim. An edict of 1797 limiting the time spent by serfs working on their owners' land was probably inspired by Paul's dislike of "indolent" nobles rather than humanitarian concern for peasants.

Paul's reign coincided with the rise to power in France of Napoleon Bonaparte. Despite his antipathy toward the French, Paul initially abandoned the anti-French coalition that his mother had entered, but in 1798 joined the Second Coalition (with Austria, Britain, Naples, Portugal, and Turkey). The most memorable incident in Russia's campaigns was the heroic defeat of France in Italy led by Field Marshal Alexander Suvorov, who later was forced to evacuate his army across the Alps. In 1800 Paul broke off with Austria and Britain. The elite's dislike of Paul was exacerbated by the danger that his erratic policies and behavior apparently posed to Russia. His election in 1798 as grand master of the Catholic Order of Knights of the Hospital of St. John of Jerusalem (also known as knights of Malta) and an ill-conceived scheme to send Russian troops to India fueled further fears. Eventually, Paul's eldest son, Alexander (born 1777; ruled as Alexander I, 1801–1825), approved a plot masterminded by the governor-general of St. Petersburg, Count Peter von Pahlen, to force Paul to abdicate. When a group of army officers broke into Paul's bedchamber on the night of 23 March (11 March, old style) 1801, the emperor resisted and was murdered during a scuffle.

Historians long maintained that the obsessive and inconsistent Paul was mentally unstable, a "tsar madman." Revisionist historians have detected method in his apparent madness, arguing, for example, that Paul was motivated by deeply held moral principles and a strong sense of duty and order. He had good reason, for example, to cut back on his mother's expensive foreign policy and lavish court. By alienating the nobility, however, he fell victim to the fact that under an autocratic regime lacking representative higher institutions of government, assassination was sometimes the elite's only means of making its voice heard.

See also **Alexander I; Catherine II; Russia.**

BIBLIOGRAPHY

McGrew, Roderick E. *Paul I of Russia, 1754–1801*. Oxford, U.K., 1992.

Ragsdale, Hugh. *Tsar Paul and the Question of Madness: An Essay in History and Psychology*. New York, 1988.

Ragsdale, Hugh, ed. *Paul I: A Reassessment of His Life and Reign*. Pittsburgh, Pa., 1979.

LINDSEY HUGHES

PAVLOV, IVAN (1849–1936), Russian physiologist.

Born in Ryazan, central Russia, the son of a priest, Ivan Petrovich Pavlov was inspired by progressive ideas in the early 1870s to study the natural sciences, and he received a doctor of medicine degree from St. Petersburg University in 1883 for his thesis "The Centrifugal Nerves of the Heart." He then studied for two years in Germany, before becoming director of physiology at the St. Petersburg Institute for Experimental Medicine, where he stayed for many years.

Pavlov's research was groundbreaking and laid the foundations for the development of key branches of physiological psychology. His first set of research interests focused on mammalian digestion, where he determined three phases of absorption and confirmed that a specific hormone was responsible for pancreatic secretion. He also observed that gastric juices could be made to flow even when no food had entered the stomach of an animal. It was for this area of investigation, the results of which were published as "Lectures on the Function of the Principal Digestive Glands" of 1897, that Pavlov was awarded a Nobel prize in 1904. He was the first Russian scientist to be so honored. This work also involved innovative surgical techniques that enabled the continuous observation of organs. However, the area of research that he is more closely associated with, and through which he is linked by name—"Pavlov's dogs"—is conditioned reflexes, which he pursued from 1902 onward.

Developing his initial interest in what he called the psychic secretion of the digestive glands, Pavlov investigated how food inserted into the mouth of a dog produced a flow of gastric juices, this reaction being termed an "unconditioned reflex" or an inherited nervous response. But if a bell was sounded alongside the insertion of food, and this association was repeated, then eventually the dog would salivate on hearing the bell alone, this reaction being termed a "conditioned reflex" or a learned physiological response. This idea was first reported at a conference in Madrid in 1903, and the experiment was part of a larger study of the psychopathology of the living organism in its entirety. Although the popular conception of salivating canines being strapped into a testing frame is nowadays something of a visual pun, in fact Pavlov's work remains part of the contemporary approach to understanding the nature of animal learning, with terms such as "stimulus-response learning" and "classical (or Pavlovian) conditioning" enduring in the literature.

Moreover the results of Pavlov's experiments on dogs were used to provide a more general theory of higher nervous activity in which reflex actions were analyzed in terms of the underlying neural activity that generated them. An initial external stimulus was seen to progress through chains of neurons in the brain to certain muscles or glands in the body, causing the reflex action to occur. Further related enquiry revealed the laws governing the functioning of the cerebral hemispheres. However the notion that conditioning experiments on animals might be an important tool in explaining human behavior fell out of favor with the decline of mechanistic behaviorism in psychology, and the advent of the cognitive revolution focusing on mental processes at the end of the 1970s.

In historical terms, Pavlov's physiological researches before 1917 can be located in a broader "silver age" of Russian natural science culminating in the period of the belle epoque, viewed together with the contributions of other world-famous Russian scientists like Dmitri Mendeleev (1834–1907) on chemical periodicity and Nikolai Lobachevsky (1792–1856) on non-Euclidian geometry. Pavlov built directly on the contributions of older scientists like Ivan Sechenov (1829–1905), the father of Russian physiology, who published a paper on "Reflexes of the Brain" in 1863 that characterized thoughts as reflexes.

After 1917 Pavlov's life constituted a unique case. He was in no sense a Marxist and even criticized Soviet communism on some occasions; his international stature as a scientist gave him a license to be difficult. In 1921 Vladimir Lenin (1870–1924) signed a governmental decree implying that special dispensation should be given to Pavlov's "outstanding scientific services," and a new center

for his work was constructed in an area later named Pavlovo. Lenin's apparently admirable concern for scientific progress is however quickly diminished in light of the fact that Pavlov's work on conditioning was (at the time) seen to have propaganda application.

Perhaps as a consequence of such favorable treatment, and partly due to being singled out by the Communist Academy as refusing to cooperate with Soviet power, in the 1930s Pavlov publicly praised the Soviet government's emphasis on science and education, but henceforth remained silent about its political system. Pavlov was not targeted in the purges that occurred in the USSR throughout the 1930s and he died of natural causes in 1936, leaving a legacy of distinguished pupils and world-class physiological institutions.

See also **Science and Technology.**

BIBLIOGRAPHY

Babkin, Boris. *Pavlov: A Biography.* Chicago, 1949.

Graham, Loren. *Science and Philosophy in the Soviet Union.* London, 1973.

Parry, Albert. *The Russian Scientist.* New York, 1973.

Pavlov, Ivan. *Lectures on Conditioned Reflexes.* Translated by W. Horsley Gantt. London, 1929.

Todes, Daniel Philip. *Pavlov's Physiology Factory: Experiment, Interpretation, Laboratory Enterprise.* Baltimore, Md., 2002.

VINCENT BARNETT

PAVLOVA, ANNA (1881–1931), Russian dancer.

When Anna Pavlova first appeared in London in 1910, *The Daily Express* described her performance as an extraordinary success. Others agreed. Pavlova was considered one of the greatest dancers that London had ever seen. Although she also had detractors—critics in Berlin and Vienna, for example, objected to her thinness and fragile appearance—sixty years later, her biographer could still describe her as the best-known dancer of all time.

For all her fame, mystery surrounds Pavlova's origins. She was born on 12 February (31 January, old style), probably in 1881, because she entered the Imperial Ballet School in 1891 (ten being the usual age for admission). Her mother, a laundress, had married Matvei Pavlov, a peasant reserve soldier who died when Anna was two, but Pavlova rejected all association with him. Rumors of her illegitimacy circulated throughout her career.

Born two months prematurely, Pavlova was a sickly child. Her first teacher at the Imperial Ballet School, Yekaterina Vazem (1848–1937), feared the fragile girl could never handle a stage career, but Pavlova exhibited great determination. With the help of Pavel Gerdt (1844–1917), who recognized her lyrical gift, and Enrico Cecchetti (1850–1928), who strengthened her jumps and turns, Pavlova entered the Maryinsky Theater as a coryphée (one step above the usual entry point) in 1899. There she attracted the attention of the ballet master Marius Petipa (1818–1910). In 1902 Petipa cast her as Nikiya in *La Bayadère,* a ballerina role. In 1903 he gave her the title role in *Giselle,* a portrayal for which she became famous. Within an unusually short time—seven years—she achieved the formal rank of ballerina.

In this period, Pavlova often danced with the emerging choreographer Michel Fokine (1880–1942), who became a close friend and created the role for which she is best known, *The Dying Swan,* to music by Camille Saint-Saëns, in 1907. Like Fokine, Pavlova joined other dancers in protest against the theater management during the Revolution of 1905; and like Fokine, she began to find her artistic opportunities restricted when the protest ended. In 1908 she made her first foreign tour. She briefly participated in the Saisons Russes organized by Sergei Diaghilev (1872–1929) in Paris in 1909, but—in part because Pavlova disliked sharing the spotlight and in part because she received a lucrative offer to perform with her own troupe in London—she refused to return for a second season. In 1911 Victor Dandré, Pavlova's business manager and self-proclaimed husband, although there is little evidence that they ever married, was accused of diverting St. Petersburg city funds to support Pavlova. Dandré fled abroad rather than stand trial. In 1912 he and Pavlova bought Ivy House, in northwest London, where they lived until she died. Pavlova performed intermittently in Russia until 1914, but the outbreak of World War I brought her permanently to the West.

Anna Pavlova dancing *Swan Lake* c. 1910. ©BETTMANN/ CORBIS

Pavlova enjoyed great success in Britain and in the United States, which she visited regularly from 1910 on—the first European ballerina to tour North America since Fanny Elssler in the early 1840s. Her troupe brought classical ballet to Central and South America, South Africa, Australia, New Zealand, East and Southeast Asia, Egypt, and India. By some estimates, her touring company traveled 350,000 miles between 1910 and 1931. They gave ten performances a week in gymnasiums, music halls, warehouses, even bullfighting arenas, as well as theaters, on stages of varying quality and sometimes outdoors. For the first decade, Pavlova herself appeared twice daily, assisted by one other ballerina. Her stamina and work ethic were legendary. So was her temperament: tantrums, refusals to perform, and sudden dismissals alternated with lavish parties and unexpected generosity.

Although numerous photographs and several short films survive of Pavlova dancing, few of these convey the traits for which she was known.

Critics praised her unusual expressiveness, ability to sustain balance on pointe, airy jumps, and rapid turns. Her ballets showcased these qualities. She rarely staged full-length works, instead favoring short pieces depicting butterflies, dragonflies, flowers, or leaves. Only those choreographed by Fokine are still performed today. Her main impact on Western dance was through her audiences: the choreographer Frederick Ashton (1904–1988), among others, began to study dance because of Pavlova. Her students and performers did much to promote classical ballet in Britain.

Pavlova gave her last performance near her London home on 13 December 1930. A few weeks later, while on tour, she contracted pleurisy, perhaps exacerbated by overwork. She died in The Hague, Netherlands, on 23 January 1931, two weeks before her fiftieth birthday. That night, in tribute, the orchestra played Saint-Saëns's music while the stage stood empty.

See also **Diaghilev, Sergei.**

BIBLIOGRAPHY

Benois, Alexandre. *Reminiscences of the Russian Ballet.* Translated by Mary Britnieva. London, 1941. Reprint, New York, 1977.

Dandré, Victor. *Anna Pavlova.* London, 1932. Reprint, as *Anna Pavlova in Art and Life,* New York, 1972.

Fonteyn, Margot. *Pavlova: Portrait of a Dancer.* New York, 1984.

Kerensky, Oleg. *Anna Pavlova.* New York, 1973.

Krasovskaya, Vera. *Anna Pavlova: Stranitsy zhizni russkoi tantsovshchitsy.* Leningrad, 1964. Reprint, Moscow, 1999.

Roslavleva, Natalia. *Era of the Russian Ballet.* London, 1966. Reprint, New York, 1979.

Svetloff, Valerian. *Anna Pavlova.* Translated by A. Grey. New York, 1974. Includes Pavlova's memoirs, *Pages of My Life.*

CAROLYN J. POUNCY

PEASANTS. Until far into the nineteenth century, the greater part of the Europeans lived in rural areas, with peasants accounting for 78 percent of the population in 1800. Peasantry was an order of society whose condition by birth, in many areas of Europe, was servitude, the lack of personal freedom. For at least a part of the century, peasants remained dependent upon and subservient to those above them in the social structure, to whom they paid compulsory dues and services in cash, kind, and labor, and to whose legal jurisdiction they were subject.

Grain and livestock were the prime foods, and large tracts were devoted to the production of both through farming practices that had so many similarities in all European regions that they have come to be seen as a "system." Lands followed a rotation, most commonly a sequence of winter-sown grain, spring-sown crops, and a fallow year. Common-field farming and grazing in common after harvest persisted.

Country people's diet varied greatly: according to region bread was made from wheat, chestnut flour, oats, or rye. In pastoral areas, people ate fewer cereals and more nuts, meat, and dairy products. In the South, they drank wine, in the North ale, hopped beer, and vodkas made from grain or potatoes. In fruit-growing countries, they enjoyed cider; in dairying areas, milk and whey; in sugar-beet areas, *kvas*; and everywhere, herbs infused in water. They ate less meat (some 15 kilograms per person in 1800, but already 50 kilograms in industrial states by 1900, when pig breeding grew significantly), and more bread (approximately 300 kilograms yearly) and potatoes.

The peasant wardrobe contained woolens, linen, fleece, and hand-spun flax fiber garments; wooden clogs, and leather shoes that were beginning to be worn for everyday work.

Mortality was high, often as a result of serious epidemics, famines, and wars. The most widespread diseases—plague, tuberculosis, cholera, dysentery, smallpox, and leprosy—claimed more lives among poorly nourished rural populations, who lived in crowded villages. The 1846–1847 potato famine killed one in eight residents of Ireland, while others emigrated overseas. The dreadful famine winter of 1847–1848 left one-third of Europe's population totally impoverished.

Peasants lived in the village that often constituted their whole world—the Russian word *mir* signifies community, world, and peace, while the word for the peasant, *krestyanin* is almost identical to *kristyanin*, Christian, which elsewhere (Italian *cristiano*) stands for the human being in general. The village was a self-contained, self-maintained, self-reliant community of illiterate workers, who led a hard life on the margin of subsistence.

The exact number of Europe's villages is not known: by 1789 France had some 44,000; the twenty-two provinces of European Russia surveyed in the 1850s counted 100,348 rural settlements, from isolated farmsteads occupied by a single family to villages with more than five hundred homesteads. Most of Russia's villages contained fewer than three hundred people, England's one hundred to two hundred, and southern Italian rural towns had populations of eight hundred to one thousand.

Many villages had existed "from time immemorial," but new ones were continuously being established. There, egalitarianism was an exception, inequality and an accentuated stratification the rule. Even on lands of periodic redistribution, wealthy peasants were allotted more shares of communal land.

In 1800 only 43 percent of peasants were self-sufficient farmers and smallholders, while 35 percent were wage laborers, with only a scrap of land around their huts, or the landless, working as farmhands or servants and living in landholding peasants' households. On the eve of the French Revolution, 86 percent of peasant households in Picardy and 30 to 40 percent in Normandy were landless. Inequality and poverty increased during the century with the upsurge of population: landless peasants greatly outnumbered those with holdings, and parish poor relief in England grew from £700,000 in 1750 to £8,000,000 in 1818.

Almost all peasant families sought an external source of earning. In Scandinavia and in central Europe most households drew their livelihoods exclusively from their holdings, but in the rest of Europe, around 1850, some 70 percent of the rural household budget went for food purchases. Independent tradesmen and artisans accounted for 5 to 15 percent of the rural population. Smallholders had outside employment as farmhands and skilled artisans or migrant workers in mining, metallurgy, forest industries, and transport; each spring the roads came alive with thousands of peasants seeking work in distant places. They typically returned home in late autumn. All households were involved in cottage industries, usually spinning, weaving, and small metal production.

Village assemblies, held on Sundays and holidays, often in the open air, were usually composed only of landholding peasants, though in Hungary and Switzerland, smallholders could also vote, as could all adult males in prerevolutionary France. Women could sometimes represent a household, if their men were dead or absent. Frequency of meetings varied from one to three times per year in the Małopolska province of Poland to ten times per year in Romania and each Sunday in Denmark. Assemblies chose officials, the headmen (who in Ireland and Norway were known as "kings") for the day-to-day governance, for the intermediation between the village and its lord, and for the practice of periodic redistributions of village lands which although not universal were quite widespread. The mir was nearly universal in Russia (90 percent of land) until 1906, but repartitions of land were also practiced until late in the century in parts of Poland, Hungary, Eastern Galicia, and Moldavia; along the Moselle River; in Leon, the Spanish Galicia, the Aragonese slope of the Pyrenees and Estremadura; in most of Sardinia and Corsica; in Carinthia, Carciola, and Tyrol; in parts of Norway (until a royal decree forbade it in 1821), Ireland, the Rhine, and the Belgian Ardennes. In Scotland, groups of families rented land jointly, in Switzerland parts of common land were used to plant crops.

Peasant family typology included a nuclear or conjugal family that included servants; a stem family, where only one married son remained living with the parents; and a multiple family where all sons remained and tilled the land jointly. The size of the latter varied from ten to twelve people in the Papal States, to twenty to thirty, even eighty to one hundred family members among the Slavs of the Balkans, in Bohemia, Moravia, Silesia, Romania, Hungary, some regions of northern Italy, and western Europe. The daughters usually left.

The family often lived, ate, and slept in the same room. Boys and girls went into service for long hours, often spending days and months outside the home. Young children were the worst off among the members of the household, because

Irish peasants outside their peat house, c. 1890. MARY EVANS PICTURE LIBRARY

they were often considered unwelcome burdens and became victims of parental neglect. Infant death rates were very high (one in five died before the age of one), and the murder of unwanted children was frequent.

Europe's overall death rates dropped steeply from the 1750s on, with northwest Europe leading the trend, while the birthrates dropped only one hundred years later. This led to a veritable population explosion, from one hundred eighty-five million in 1800 to four hundred million in 1900.

Food requirements of the rising population forced the pace of agricultural change. Major effort was put into improving the productivity of staple foodstuffs, grain, and other high-starch-content foods, and livestock, and in promoting high-yielding crops such as buckwheat, potatoes, and maize. Sugar-beet cultivation spread widely during the Napoleonic Wars when the English naval blockade cut off supplies of sugarcane. Agricultural production entered a growth cycle in the 1830s and more than doubled in the next four decades. More intensive use of the soil led to the use of modern

chemical fertilizers. The old three-field system gave way to permanent crop rotation, but mechanization proceeded very slowly. These changes and a massive rural emigration to large cities caused the "depopulation of the countryside," a frequent subject for a growing number of sociological studies, such as Eugène Bonnemère's *Les paysans au XIXe siècle* (1846).

From the late eighteenth century, the pessimistic belief that Europe was a vast territory of poor farming and impoverished peasants helped to promote radical transformations in farming and spurred legal reforms. Agricultural improvers insisted upon transition from communalism to individualism (private property and freedom of action for individuals) and viewed constraints imposed by the community as a major hindrance to agricultural progress. Central governments entered the village to promote agricultural reforms and reinforce the impact of individualism and, in the process, encroached upon village autonomy. The French revolutionary government weakened the communes through legislation, the Helvetic Republic integrated them into new and larger political districts, Austria and Saxony (in 1849 and

1839 respectively)—into large townships. Only in Russia did the state support communalism as an insurance against social unrest. Whereas the German and Austrian serf-emancipation laws contemplated no role for the communes, the Russian 1861 law preserved a central position for the mir.

The transition from communal collectivism to individualism was swift in England, Scotland, Denmark, Sweden, and Norway—by the 1840s remaining open fields and the commons were divided and enclosed farms multiplied. Elsewhere, the transition was slower. Even when each household occupied a specific holding, the commune still supervised pastures, meadows, and other resources held in common. The village community was vanishing, but only slowly. The process could not go on, however, without a radical abolition of all forms of unfreedom.

In many lands, peasants were dependent upon and subject to the legal jurisdiction of the lords. Serfdom was the most common form of unfreedom. Usually serfs were bound to the soil, but in Russia and in Poland lords could sell, exchange, or move serfs from one land to another. The initiatives for reform came from sovereigns supported by sections of the nobility inspired by fear of peasant rebellion, economics, and idealism, or in some cases by military defeats (Prussia's in 1806, Russia's in the Crimean War).

The liberation of Europe's peasantry proceeded steadily for more than a century. In 1767 Maria Theresa's (r. 1740–1780) great code *Urbarium* regulated the lord-peasant relationship in Hungary (in eastern Hungary, the Ottomans had ruled with a lighter hand) and in 1771 a princely decree ended the feudal subservience of Savoyard peasants. Emperor Joseph II (r. 1764–1790) formally abolished serfdom in Austria in a series of legislations from 1781 to 1789. France's National Assembly declared all the seigneural rights to be null and void on 4 August 1789 and in 1793 abolished all feudal rights and made peasants into freeholders. Napoleon's (r. 1804–1814/15) conquest carried emancipation to the lands subject to French rule. In 1810–1811 Prussia granted ownership of land to peasants and did away with fundamental privileges of the nobility. But emancipation on German lands was not completed until the Revolutions of 1848, when the Frankfurt Parliament established a list of basic civil rights. The last acts of peasant emancipation in Europe were Russia's in 1861 and Romania's in 1864.

Everywhere, emancipation released the peasants from bondage and from manorial obligations; gave them civil rights; and guaranteed their personal freedom of movement, choice of vocation, and equality with all other subjects before the law; and abolished the hierarchical system of orders. Common lands were partitioned, scattered plots of arable land concentrated, and the collective system of farming dissolved. The emancipation heralded an unprecedented era of freedom in the history of the peasantry and led to a change in their public image.

Endemic rural unrest and everyday violence has always been an expression of the strong attachment of peasants to their own community as well as an attempt at resistance. Peasant revolts could be prompted by many factors, including cruel frustrations engendered by the greatest hopes. Peasants revolted against conscription; abuses by local lords; illegal imposition of excessive corvee or taxation; and especially the appropriation of common lands and customary rights to water, passages, grazing, gleaning, and wood-gathering.

Villagers usually had the right of self-defense with no police force present until later in the century, but their access to justice was limited, because the local nobility—in England, eastern Europe, and southern Europe—were also magistrates. Lawsuits started by the community against the landlords' usurpation of common rights could last for decades. Thus, peasants frequently resorted to the weapon of riot. As the catalog of offenses was similar in many regions, also the typology of peasant response was similar: smashing fences and walls, filling up ditches, tearing down hedges, and occupying "usurped" land. Peasants armed with scythes, pitchforks, and axes attacked lords and their officials, pillaged homes, and burned the (supposed) records of their submission. In the regions of pastoral economy, rural brigandage was widespread, which attracted novelists and painters of the Romantic age.

Frequent food riots were typical for the subsistence economy. The Great Hunger of 1846–1847 broke down the resistance of the small farmers throughout Europe, but the last famine of the century, in Russia in 1891, which was said to have cost seven hundred thousand lives and reduced thirty million to indigence, led to mass pillaging of barns on great estates.

The fear of peasant armies in revolt haunted governments and landlords, as was the case of the "Great Fear" in France in 1789. Their numbers were unknown. Yemelyan Pugachev's (1742–1775) army of Cossacks and Russian peasants, in the period from 1773 to 1775, was said to count around twenty thousand men, Cardinal Fabrizio Ruffo (1744–1827)—who led Calabrian peasants in a crusade against the French-imposed Neapolitan republic in 1799—never knew how many men he could count on every day. The risings in the French Vendée lasted from 1793 until 1833 but the peasant armies of the Vendée were mobilized for only a few days or a few weeks each time. Elsewhere, peasant revolts repeated the Vendée pattern on a smaller scale in 1798 to 1799: the Cudgel War in Luxembourg, the Peasants War in Limburg, the "war of shepherds' smocks" in the mountain cantons of Switzerland, the Santa Fede march of Calabrians, and the Viva Maria rising in the Tuscan Apennines near Arezzo.

A new "Great Fear" came in the period from 1846 to 1848, triggered by a large peasant uprising in Polish Galicia in February 1846, at the time when the Polish patriots, who were also the peasants' overlords, were preparing an insurrection against the Austrian yoke. The peasants, led by a small tenant farmer named Jakub Szela, frustrated by abuses and excessive corvée, turned their arms against the country nobility and townspeople, and, in one week of bloodshed, sacked four hundred mansions and killed twelve hundred nobles and their servants. In 1848–1849 many peasants revolted, in the French *Midi*, in the Pyrenees, in the Two Sicilies, against taxation or just in the hope of regaining their customary rights.

The political upheaval over, once again the resistance resumed its "normal" course with "Captain Swing" riots against threshing machines in England in 1830–1832, the Irish "Troubles" (1812–1822, 1830–1834), land agitations in Scotland in the 1860s, in Ireland again in 1878–1882, and in Andalusia in 1854, 1868, and 1871. In Russia, in the period from 1825 to 1854, from Nicholas I (r. 1825–1855) to the Crimean War,

the "ghost of Pugachev" was evoked with the average of twenty-three cases of rural revolt per year, and the serfs, emancipated by the statute of 1861, rioted again over the delays in instituting the statute.

One long-term effect of emancipation was the incorporation of peasants into the new liberal social and political order. Peasants had been enfranchised in Norway as early as 1814 and in Prussia and in France in 1848. In Switzerland the union government of 1848 integrated alpine peasants into a unified Switzerland with the introduction of single currency, unified postal service, and integrated army. Eventually, peasants also became political subjects throughout Europe and were wooed by political leaders. Their support was sought for a variety of different political views: the evangelical movements in Norway, conservatives, and the Catholic Church saw in them the heroes of the Vendée and the Santa Fede, while the Italian, French, and Spanish anarchists, followers of Mikhail Bakunin (1814–1876) and Peter Kropotkin (1842–1921), praised their revolutionary potential of the "powder box," and the Russian populists (*narodniki*) their egalitarian tradition. In 1851 in France the peasants voted massively for the Second Empire of Napoleon III (r. 1852–1871) that led Karl Marx (1818–1883) to refer disparagingly to them as "sacks of potatoes," while Léon Michel Gambetta (1838–1882) saw them as the potential basis for a democracy of small property-owners.

Peasants were also part of the discourse of nation-building in Ireland, Germany, southern Italy, Russia, and Poland. The Polish peasant Michał Drzymała became a patriotic symbol of the opposition to the Germanization of the soil, while the German nationalist Wilhelm Heinrich von Riehl (1823–1897) saw the peasant as the savior of Germany in 1848 and as "the future of the German nation."

Another effect of emancipation was the exposure of peasants to market mechanisms. After 1870 when grain poured into Europe from the Americas and livestock products began arriving in refrigerated ships, European peasants could not compete. The deep depression followed, from the mid-1870s to the 1890s: in favorably situated areas, peasants turned to specialized crops, such as citrus fruits, olives, and bergamot in the Mediterranean and vegetables and fruits in cities' hinterlands. Peasants emigrated in millions from other areas, in the greatest exodus from Europe ever experienced, mostly to the Americas.

The general crisis of the peasant economy gave rise to the formulation of the so-called peasant question (*Agrarfrage*). The Marxists, such as Friedrich Engels (1820–1895), Vladimir Lenin (1870–1924), and Karl Johann Kautsky (1854–1938), saw no future for peasant agriculture, and the inevitable triumph of capitalist, privatized, and rational large estates. The socialists considered it a duty to convince the peasants of the hopelessness of their situation: "capitalist mass production will trample over the impotent, antiquated small farm just as a train crushes a push cart." A dissenting voice was that of the Russian economist Alexander Chayanov (1888–1937), who saw a different rationality in the small peasant economy.

The systematic study of folklore that began in the nineteenth century focused exclusively on rural folk songs, fairy tales, folk music, local customs, material culture, and dialects. Two main tendencies emerged in these studies: a conservative idealization of the village and an enlightened critical approach.

The former idealized country life, in the tradition of pastoral poetry. The picturesque played a big role: merry country folk were observed dancing round maypoles, expressing their simple piety in pilgrimages or wayside shrines. The humane traditional village culture, the quintessential "community" (*Gemeinschaft*) was counterposed to the modern industrial anonymous "society" (*Gesellschaft*) of the "madding crowds." Change was sadly portrayed as a transition from the former to the latter, and—in the wave of the midcentury nostalgia—began to be perceived as an irreplaceable loss.

Many early folklorists were nationalists who saw the tenacious conservatism of village communities as the guarantor of their fidelity to the true national ethos. The Romantics were interested in *Volksgeist*, because they saw the *Volk* as a depository of ethnic purity. The Grimm brothers, Jacob Ludwig Carl (1785–1863) and Wilhelm Carl (1786–1859), collected peasant fairy tales in order to reconstruct the "Germanic mythology"; the

Norwegians sought to change the written language from the Bokmol to the folk Nynorsk.

A different tradition with roots in the Enlightenment saw the village and the peasant family as the matrix of authoritarian behavior. The socialists blamed Bonapartism on the natural antiliberalism of the peasants, on the "idiocy of rural life." Theodor Adorno (1903–1969) argued that it was "a duty to deprovincialize" the village society that was hindering its own emancipation and progress. Mid-nineteenth-century German and Danish studies of old German practices of "agrarian communism" led to the formulations of "universal laws" of social evolution that everywhere began with the communal ownership of land and equated communalism with the primitive. It would be a century later with the social anthropological approach of Robert Redfield and Eric Wolf when the view of the "peasant society" shifted, and was seen instead as a modern industrial society, market-oriented and assimilated into a political unit.

While most nineteenth-century social scholars were concerned with urbanization and industrialization, writers were fascinated by the peasant. The *romans rustiques* enjoyed great popularity, Irish peasant plays were performed at the Abbey Theatre, and Władysław Reymont (1867–1925) was awarded a Nobel prize for his novel *Chłopi* (Peasants; 1904–1909). After 1848 rural themes became even more present in poetry, songs, and novels.

This literature was realistic in its description of the peasant condition: Silas Marner in George Eliot's (Mary Ann Evans, 1819–1880) novel lived, worked, and slept in a single room; Nikolai Gogol's (1809–1852) peasants were ignorant, brutish and drunk. *La vie d'un simple* by Emile Guillaumin, Honoré de Balzac's (1799–1850) peasant novels, Giovanni Verga's (1840–1922) novellas, all showed the hardship of the everyday life. The memory of feudal oppression survived—in 1856 Alexis de Tocqueville (1805–1859) thought the bitterness of the French peasantry inextinguishable—and lived as late as 1890 in Jacques le Roy's novel *Jacquou le Croquant*. But there was also change and social mobility: Gustave Flaubert's eponymous protagonist Emma Bovary (1857), a daughter of a rich peasant, could read and write and marry a doctor.

The Romantic nostalgia for a way of life led the writers to romanticize and idealize peasants and their institutions and to celebrate them as the preservers of the special human quality, as in George Sand's (Amandine-Aurore-Lucile Dudevant, 1804–1876) novels and in Pierre Dupont's populist songs and poems.

After the midcentury the yearning for a rural world became a counterweight to the drastic alterations of society under the impact of rapid industrialization. People clung to comforting ideals of rusticity that derived their meaning from the opposition to the city, Thomas Hardy's (1840–1928) flight far from the "maddening crowds." The countryside stood for simplicity of the bucolic worlds free of the corruption of cities; for virtuous work in a direct relationship to animals and land, with no money, no organized labor, no slums, and no unemployment; for innocence, childhood, and arcadia; for timelessness; for instinct and freedom. In short, the countryside represented the primitive in the sense of the first and the original.

This nostalgia for the Golden Age of the preindustrial past gave the peasantry, in the years from 1875 to 1914, a popularity never before known. With Paul Gauguin's (1848–1903) "primitive" and "sauvage" Brittany, the myth of the lost paradise of preindustrial humanity assumed a new meaning, proclaiming the superiority of the rustics over sophisticated ladies of Paris. Filippo Palizzi's (1818–1899) *Contadinelle* or Camille Pisarro's (1830–1903) (a follower of Kropotkin) *Plowman* expressed ideas of health, honest labor, and dignity set against the pollution and degraded labor of the city.

In the wake of 1848 the peasants came to new political and cultural prominence and became a radical force in the society. New art celebrated the arrival of the "common man." The "peasant painter" Jean-Francois Millet's (1814–1875) *Winnower* (c. 1847) is a vigorous standing male shaking his basket, the embodiment of the spirit of 1848, and so is Gustave Courbet's (1819–1877) *Stonecutter* (1849). As Alexandre Dumas fils (1824–1895) wrote, this is no longer "the peasant of 1660, but the proletarian of 1859." Giuseppe Pellizza da Volpedo's (1868–1907) *The Fourth Estate* (1901) showed the peasants as a conscious class of distinct individuals, marching together for a common cause. Still, until 1914, lurking behind the arcadia and class consciousness, was the bestial and unthinking peasant brutalized and crushed by famine and starvation as portrayed in Sergei Ivanov's *The Death of the Settler*.

See also **Agricultural Revolution; Aristocracy; Bourgeoisie; Cities and Towns; Class and Social Relations; Emigration; Labor Movements.**

BIBLIOGRAPHY

Blum, Jerome. *The End of the Old Order in Rural Europe.* Princeton, N.J., 1978.

Herbert, Robert L. *From Millet to Léger: Essays in Social Art History.* New Haven, Conn., 2002.

Hobsbawm, E. J., et al., eds. *Peasants in History: Essays in Honour of Daniel Thorner.* Calcutta, 1980.

Jones, P. M. *Politics and Rural Society: The Southern Massif Central, c. 1750–1880.* Cambridge, U.K., and New York, 1985.

Parker, William N., and Eric L. Jones, eds. *European Peasants and Their Markets: Essays in Agrarian Economic History.* Princeton, N.J., 1975.

Williams, Raymond. *The Country and the City.* New York, 1973.

MARTA PETRUSEWICZ

PEEL, ROBERT (1788–1850), English politician.

Robert Peel was born in Bury, Lancashire, the son of Robert Peel, a wealthy calico manufacturer and landowner, and Ellen Yates. Peel spent his formative years in Lancashire before the family removed in 1796 to Tamworth, Staffordshire, where his father had purchased an estate and become the local member of Parliament (MP). Peel did well at school and in 1805 he became a student of Christ Church, Oxford. After three years he graduated with a double first in classics and mathematics.

At age twenty-one, Peel joined his father in Parliament as the MP for Cashel in Tipperary. Peel's entry into public life was accomplished in the familiar way for pre-Reform Britain: his father purchased the right to nominate the member for the seat in southern Ireland.

Peel accepted his first office, undersecretary for war and the colonies, a few months after becoming an MP, and in May 1812 he joined the administration of Lord Liverpool (1770–1828) as chief secretary for Ireland. Peel's six year tenure in the Irish post was marked by a protracted confrontation with the leading Catholic politician of the day, Daniel O'Connell (1775–1847), in opposition to the demand for Catholic emancipation; by his ardent support for the Protestant ascendancy in Parliament and through government patronage; and by his largely successful attempts to quell Irish unrest and maintain order that included the creation of a police force—a forerunner to the royal Irish constabulary—which became known colloquially as the "peelers."

Peel's hard-line attitude to Ireland made him the favorite of many Tories and earned him a new seat in Parliament as the representative of Oxford. Despite his success, he decided to return to the back-bench in 1818. Although he rejected numerous offers to return to the cabinet, Peel was not idle. In 1819, he chaired an enquiry into the Bank of England, which by 1823 had entirely reformed the currency system.

Early in 1822, Peel returned to Liverpool's cabinet as home secretary, a post he held (with a short interval) until 1830. As home secretary, Peel oversaw a wide-ranging program of reform in the administration of law and order. The central element was a consolidation of the criminal law and the repeal of a plethora of old statutes, as well as the creation of an effective police force for London whose members are known to this day as "bobbies."

The first major crisis of Peel's political life occurred over Catholic Emancipation. In 1827, he had resigned from the government—then headed by George Canning (1770–1827)—over the issue, only to be coaxed back to the Home Office as part of the cabinet of Arthur Wellesley, 1st Duke of Wellington (1769–1852) early in 1828. In the months that followed, Peel reversed his stance, steering a bill granting some of the privileges of citizenship to Catholics through the House of Commons. Peel's supporters defended his change of heart as an act of statesmanship, but many of his colleagues reacted bitterly. When he resigned from parliament to test the views of his constituents he lost his seat, only returning to the House a month later when a vacancy occurred at Westbury. It would not be last time that Peel would undergo a political conversion that lost him the support of many colleagues and divided his party.

In 1830, Peel succeeded to his father's baronetcy and became the member for Tamworth in his place. Following the defeat of Wellington's government, Peel became a member of the opposition. During the crisis that gripped the nation over reform of the House of Commons, Peel was a vehement defender of the existing system, including the so-called rotten boroughs that contained a handful of electors. His intransigence won him back the support of many Tories.

Following the resolution of the crisis and the election of the Whigs, Peel accepted the new system and set about rejuvenating his party, called Conservative for the first time in 1831, as a political force. Although he was out of office, his influence hardly diminished, and on numerous occasions during 1833–1834 he voted with the government, removing the need for them to seek support among the radicals and O'Connell's Irish members. With the resignation of Charles Grey (1764–1845) in 1834, Peel became prime minister. Without a majority in the House of Commons, he dissolved Parliament and at the subsequent election the ranks of the Tories were substantially increased. Peel still did not command a majority, however, and by April 1835 he resigned, returning to the opposition benches for the second time.

Peel's second opportunity for the premiership came after the resignation of the government of William Lamb, 2nd Viscount Melbourne (1779–1848) in 1839. Peel had the composition of his cabinet finalized but he stumbled when he sought to effect changes in the staff of the household of Victoria (r. 1837–1901). The young queen reacted strongly against Peel's suggestion that some of her ladies in waiting be replaced by those more favorable to the Tories, and what became known as the "bedchamber crisis" resulted in the return of Melbourne's government. Peel knew that he was right in constitutional terms, but he did not have a parliamentary majority to back him and he did not desire further confrontation with Victoria. On the contrary, over the coming months Peel and his associates devoted considerable effort to smoothing over the rift with the palace in anticipation of the day when they would command the floor of the House of Commons. He did not have long to wait. In 1841, Melbourne's Whig government again fell and at the subsequent general election Peel and the Conservative Party were swept to power with a substantial majority.

Peel faced many difficulties when coming to office, from war in China and Afghanistan to poverty and unrest throughout the British Isles. Over the next five years, Peel's government was renowned for facing the threats of Chartism and Irish Repeal; for introducing an income tax; for extensive reform of the Bank of England; and, preeminently, for repealing the Corn Laws. The regime that governed the importation of corn and other grain products had been established in 1815 in the aftermath of the French wars. The Corn and Provision Laws prohibited the importation of corn at a price below the very high price of the domestic product, thereby buttressing the political and social power of the landowning class with a guaranteed income.

From the beginning the system was unpopular with the majority of the people who paid for it in the form of higher bread prices. It was also increasingly unpopular with the growing middle class that derived its income from manufacturing. Industrialists, manufacturers, and merchants complained that their trade with Europe was being hampered by protectionist measures implemented in retaliation for the Corn Laws. Increasingly they called for free trade. Prohibition was replaced in 1828 by a sliding scale, but this had little practical effect and did little to silence the rising chorus of opposition. By the end of the 1830s, a nationwide campaign for the "total and immediate repeal" of the Corn Laws had been commenced.

Corn Law repeal was only one of a number of challenges that the failing Whig government was unable to meet. The Whigs clung doggedly to the sliding scale until 1841, when they opted for a fixed duty; the Tories remained committed to protection. After coming to government, Peel attempted to address the issue by introducing a revised sliding scale. His approach satisfied neither opponents nor supporters of the Corn Laws, and, although it bought him some time, within three years the revised system was overtaken by circum-

stances. In 1845 the potato blight plunged Ireland into famine. The extent to which Peel had already become convinced of the merits of free trade is a moot point; the national emergency in Ireland forced his hand.

Between October and December 1845, Peel sought unsuccessfully to convince his cabinet colleagues of the need to freely import grain to meet the food crisis, and on 9 December he resigned. This allowed a Whig government headed by John Russell (1792–1878) (who had committed himself to repeal a month previously) to briefly come to office. Peel resumed the prime ministership on 20 December, and in January 1846 he introduced a corn bill into the House and advocated free trade in a series of speeches. About 120 of Peel's Conservative colleagues supported his change of heart; the rest remained staunchly protectionist and assailed him as a traitor who had betrayed a foundational principle of the party. In June 1846, Peel resigned a few days after the House of Lords passed the bill repealing the Corn Laws. Over the next four years, Peel and his associates supported Russell's Whig administration.

Peel died in July 1850 following a riding accident. His actions in relation to the Corn Laws earned the ire of die-hard Tories, but were tremendously popular in the nation at large. After Peel's death, many monuments were erected to the memory of the man who had secured the people's bread. Peel's political career was marked by a determination to do what he felt was right regardless of its popularity or political ramifications. As a consequence, he both built and wrecked the Conservative Party as a political force during his public life. Peel was remembered for his political courage over the Corn Laws, but his reforms of the administration of justice and the introduction of an income tax in peace time had a far more lasting effect on the lives of Britons.

See also **Conservatism; Corn Laws, Repeal of; Great Britain; Tories.**

BIBLIOGRAPHY

Cowie, L. W. *Sir Robert Peel, 1788–1850: A Bibliography.* Westport, Conn., 1996.

Gash, Norman. *Mr. Secretary Peel: The Life of Sir Robert Peel to 1830.* London, 1961.

———. *Sir Robert Peel: The Life of Sir Robert Peel after 1830.* London, 1972.

Hilton, Boyd. "Peel: A Re-appraisal." *Historical Journal* 22 (1979): 585–614.

Peel, G. V. "Sir Robert Peel (1788–1850)." *Dictionary of National Biography*, Vol. 15, edited by Leslie Stephen and Sidney Lee, 655–668. London, 1972. Entry by Peel's grandson.

Prest, John. "Sir Robert Peel, Second Baronet (1788–1850), Prime Minister." *Oxford Dictionary of National Biography*, Vol. 43, edited by H. G. C. Matthew and Brian Harrison, 406–418. Oxford, U.K., 2004.

Read, Donald. *Peel and the Victorians.* Oxford, U.K., 1987.

PAUL A. PICKERING

PÉGUY, CHARLES (1873–1914), French writer and poet.

Charles-Pierre Péguy was born in Orléans on 7 January 1873. After losing his father at a very young age, he was raised in poverty by his mother, who instilled in him what he considered to be the true pride of the people—the love of a job well done, which he opposed to the "bourgeois" reign of "money." A hardworking student, he entered the École Normale Supérieure in 1894. After rejecting Catholicism in the name of the pursuit of an ideal of universal justice, he followed Jean Jaurès into the battle for socialism with his ever-present and highly characteristic ardor and intransigence. His first works, *Jeanne d'Arc* (1897; Joan of Arc) and *Marcel; La cité harmonieuse* (1898; Marcel; The harmonious city), both evoke this demand for a purity he held to be essential in the fight for justice, which explains why he was militantly pro-Dreyfus and easily exasperated by political compromises. Péguy sought to live "as a socialist" without conceding anything. He married Charlotte Baudouin in a civil ceremony, quit the École Normale Supérieure, and funneled the money he received from his in-laws into the launching of a socialist bookshop.

As the socialists became increasingly organized into a unified political party, the compromises attended by the process and the discipline necessary to unify it led Péguy increasingly to distance himself from Jaurès, who had become an ambitious political actor. To emphasize their split, Péguy founded the *Cahiers de la quinzaine* in January 1900, an independent publication where his compatriots could express themselves freely. From 1900 to 1914, the *Cahiers* were an important intellectual home for the likes of Romain Rolland (1866–1944), Julien Benda (1867–1956), Georges-Eugène Sorel (1847–1922), Jacques Maritain (1882–1973), Alain-Fournier (1886–1914), and others. The journal broached a number of burning questions, including the crisis in education, the defense of colonized peoples, and the Russian Revolution of 1905. Péguy himself published many polemical texts written in his characteristic style—replete with repetitions and digressions.

Under the increasingly predominant influence of the philosopher Henri-Louis Bergson (1859–1941), with whom he had become friends, Péguy began to decry with increasing harshness what he called from 1905 onward the "intellectual party," an alliance of the socialists with the anticlerical bourgeoisie and university scientists. His version of revolution was to become heavily steeped in tradition instead, an evolving perspective that began in 1905 with his signal work *Notre patrie* (Our fatherland).

In 1908 Péguy confided in a friend that he had returned to Catholicism, something he openly proclaimed in 1910 with his breathtaking book *Le mystère de la charité de Jeanne d'Arc*, in which he revisited the work he had accomplished in his younger days (*Jeanne d'Arc*), and reformulated in more Christian terms its spirit of rebellion. However the irregularity of his marital situation required Péguy to stand always at the threshold of the church, whose history and dogmas he nonetheless embraced with open arms. Firmly a Catholic, Péguy placed his still-intact rebelliousness under the patronage of the great figures of the Church of France—Joan of Arc (c. 1412–1431), Saint Geneviève (c. 422–c. 500), and Saint Louis (King Louis IX; 1214–1270)—all figures of purity and nonsubmissiveness.

Despite the strain of financial and family worries that threatened at times to overwhelm him, the works of poetry he published during this period, including *Porche du mystère de la deuxième vertu* (1911; The porch of the mystery of the second virtue), *Mystère des saints innocents* (1912), and *Eve* (1913), developed lengthy meditations on the theme of hope in its opposition to the modern idea of "progress," and incarnation as that which allows faith to become intertwined with earthly struggles:

> Car le spirituel est lui même charnel
> Et l'arbre de la grâce est raciné profond
> Et plonge dans le sol et cherche jusqu'au fond
> Et l'arbre de la race est lui-même éternel. (*Eve*)

> [For the Spiritual is itself Charnel
> And the Tree of Grace's roots grow deep
> And plunge deep into the soil and reach the bottom
> And the Tree of Race is itself Eternal.]

Péguy's friendships, and the struggles he waged (including his pro-Dreyfus stance), preclude us from attributing to him any kind of racism. For him a "race" is synonymous with a "people," and both signify the inscription of a struggle against political powers in an incarnated history.

In 1914 the general war mobilization forced him to interrupt the writing of his defense of Bergson against the attacks of Thomist Catholics. On 5 September 1914 Péguy was killed in Villeroy, while leading his regiment onto the field, thus leaving behind the work of a poet and a polemicist.

The various readings of Péguy primarily part company over the following question: Should his rejection of socialism and return to Catholicism be seen as a point of rupture? His heroic death, combined with a general lack of awareness of his early works, cemented his image as a nationalist. Nevertheless he exercised a considerable influence on the personalist movement founded in 1934, and more recent readings, made possible at last by the publication of his complete works by Gallimard in 1987, depict the unity of a life that pursued the same demand for justice from socialism to Catholicism.

See also **Bergson, Henri; Catholicism; Jaurès, Jean; Socialism.**

BIBLIOGRAPHY

Bastaire, J. *Péguy, l'inchrétien.* Paris, 1991.

Burac, Robert. *Péguy: La révolution et la grâce.* Paris, 1994.

Dumont, J.-N. *Péguy, l'axe de détresse.* Paris, 2005.

Finkelkraut, Alain. *Le mécontemporain: Péguy, lecteur du monde moderne.* Paris, 1991.

Robinet, André. *Péguy entre Jaurès, Bergson, et l'Église.* Paris, 1968.

JEAN-NOËL DUMONT

PELLETIER, MADELEINE (1874–1939), French feminist.

Madeleine Pelletier was a pioneering feminist and socialist, doctor, anthropologist, and psychologist, significant for her work as a feminist theoretician, which in the decade before World War I prefigured the insights of second-wave feminism.

Born on 18 May 1874 to a poor Parisian family, Pelletier obtained a science degree from the University of Paris and became an active member of the Paris Anthropological Society. In the early 1900s, she published a dozen major papers in the materialist craniometry then fashionable, but moved on (probably because the materialist paradigm led to the conclusion that women's intelligence was inferior to men's because their brains were smaller) to study medicine and then psychology, becoming the first woman psychiatric intern in France. In 1906, after a major battle, she obtained the right to sit the competitive examination to become a doctor of the state asylums, the equivalent of a psychiatrist today, but did not succeed. Subsequently she earned her living as a general practitioner.

Pelletier was a leading activist in a surprising variety of areas. In 1904, she was initiated into a mixed Freemasons' lodge, where she became a Venerable. Her campaign for women's entry into regular (i.e., male) Masonry made significant inroads before she was blocked in 1906. She was a founding member of the unified French Socialist Party (the Section Française de l'Internationale Ouvrière) in 1905. In 1906, she steered a strong resolution committing the party to women's suffrage through the national congress. In 1910 she became the first woman member of the party's central committee (the Commission Administrative Permanente) and represented the party at international socialist congresses before the war. She acted and dressed as a man insofar as possible, arguing that to act and dress as a woman was to accept "servility." She rejected mainstream feminists who sought to "remain feminine"; for her the task was "to virilize women."

Also in 1906, Pelletier became secretary of La Solidarité des Femmes (Women's Solidarity) and made of it the most radical feminist organization in France. She represented this group in the famous 1908 Hyde Park (London) demonstrations for women's suffrage and from 1909 until the war published a monthly feminist magazine, *La Suffragiste*. She was a major figure on the extreme left of the neo-Malthusian movement, as birth control was then known. Her 1911 book *L'émancipation sexuelle de la femme* (Woman's sexual emancipation) contained a chapter supporting the right to abortion, published as a separate brochure in 1913. She was the first French doctor to support abortion publicly and the first person to base the argument on women's equal right to sexual pleasure. Above all, she was the first to place abortion in the context of a woman's political rights.

After World War I Pelletier wrote and spoke extensively, playing a prominent role in Parisian left-wing intellectual circles. A founding member of the French Communist Party, she traveled to the Soviet Union in 1921. This led to disillusionment with the party and she did not challenge her expulsion as a Freemason in 1924. Subsequently, she was active in a debating forum, the Club du Faubourg. In 1939, she was prosecuted for practicing abortion. She was not tried but was committed to the asylum of Perray-Vaucluse, where she died on 29 December 1939.

Pelletier's outstanding achievement is as a theoretician. She analyzed for the first time the question of the gendered structure of society and the resulting construction of the individual's gendered identity (or "psychological sex," as she termed it). To explain these issues, she wrote countless brochures and articles, a dozen works of general socialist and feminist theory, several plays, an autobiographical novel, and a utopia.

La femme en lutte pour ses droits (1908; Woman's struggle for her rights) began her analysis of gender formation. The first chapter is entitled "The Sociological Factors in Feminine Psychology." Pelletier pursued these questions in *L'Emancipation sexuelle de la femme* (1911), where she argued against the nuclear family: men profited from marriage, but not women: "Instead of being served it is [women] who serve," she wrote. Marriage restrained women from fulfilling themselves: "The woman, for her part, does not live, she only watches her husband live."

Pelletier believed that women's struggle for political rights was burdened by the psychological devaluation of self of which they were victims. *L'éducation féministe des filles* (The feminist educa-

tion of girls), published in 1914, attempted to break the vicious circle. "It is the mother who begins to create the psychological sex," she stated. Feminist mothers should raise girls so that they attained a sense of self-development and aimed at making a mark in the "real world," not simply finding a marriage partner, for only through work could women improve their self-esteem, as she had long argued. In these analyses, she prefigured key ideas not to be voiced again until Simone de Beauvoir's *The Second Sex* (1949) or even second-wave feminism of the 1970s.

See also **Auclert, Hubertine; Feminism; Population, Control of; Suffragism.**

BIBLIOGRAPHY

Primary Sources

Pelletier, Madeleine. *L'éducation féministe des filles*, suivi de *Le droit à l'avortement; La femme en lutte pour ses droits, la tactique féministe; Le droit au travail pour la femme*. Paris, 1978.

———. *La femme vierge*. 1933. Reprint, Paris, 1996.

———. *Mon voyage aventureux en Russie communiste*. 1922. Reprint, Paris, 1996.

Secondary Sources

Bard, Christine, and Jean-Christophe Coffin, eds. *Madeleine Pelletier: Logique et infortunes d'un combat pour l'egalite*. Paris, 1992.

Gordon, Felicia. *The Integral Feminist—Madeleine Pelletier, 1874–1939: Feminism, Socialism, and Medicine*. Cambridge, U.K., 1990.

Scott, Joan Wallach. *Only Paradoxes to Offer: French Feminists and the Rights of Man*. Cambridge, Mass., 1996. See chapter 5

Sowerwine, Charles. *Sisters or Citizens? Women and Socialism in France since 1876*. New York, 1982. See chapter 5.

———. "Woman's Brain, Man's Brain: Feminism and Anthropology in Late Nineteenth-Century France." *Women's History Review* 12, no. 2 (2003): 311–329.

Sowerwine, Charles, and Claude Maignien. *Madeleine Pelletier, une féministe dans l'arène politique*. Paris, 1992.

CHARLES SOWERWINE

PENINSULAR WAR. The Peninsular War is the name that is traditionally given to the long struggle that raged in Spain and Portugal between

The trickery and utter lack of integrity evinced in his dealings with the King of Spain and his sons may be regarded as the most obvious cause of Bonaparte's ruin. From the moment when Savary, his faithful henchman and aide-de-camp, had deceived these princes by bringing them from Madrid to Bayonne under various specious pretexts...no-one in Europe ever again placed any confidence either in the emperor's word or his treaties....In the eyes of political observers, it was with the impious war against Spain that the fall of Bonaparte's colossal empire commenced.

Bertrand Barère. *Memoirs of Bertrand Barère, Chairman of the Committee of Public Safety during the Revolution.* Translated by De V. Payen-Payne. London, 1896. Vol. 3, pp. 142–143.

1808 and 1814. The origins of this conflict are to be found in Napoleon's decision to occupy Portugal in 1807 in order to seize that nation's fleet and subject it to his Continental System (also called the Continental Blockade). Thus, this move saw troops dispatched not just to Lisbon (from whence the Portuguese royal family and much of the governing elite were evacuated to Brazil by Britain's Royal Navy) but also to significant areas of northern Spain. Initially, the reason for this additional deployment was purely strategic in that Napoleon simply wanted to protect the communications of the troops sent to Portugal with France. At the same time he was acting with the full agreement of the Spanish government, which had been promised territorial acquisitions in Portugal in exchange for its cooperation; indeed, Spain was France's ally and had been fighting on France's side against Britain ever since 1796. Very soon, however, matters grew more complicated.

PRECIPITATING EVENTS

From the early 1790s onward, the Spanish court had been gripped by bitter factionalism that saw the king and queen, Charles IV and María Luisa, and their favorite, Manuel de Godoy, ranged against the heir to the throne, Ferdinand, and a clique of discontented aristocrats. Just as the French forces entered Spain, moreover, matters reached crisis point: in brief, Godoy accused Ferdinand of

plotting the overthrow of Charles IV and seeking the support of Napoleon to secure this goal. This brought a major change in the emperor's policy. Hitherto there had been no question in his mind of intervening at Madrid, but the chaos in the Spanish court caused him to fear that the British might somehow take advantage of the situation to get Charles IV to change sides (something that had already almost happened in 1806). Even as it was, Spain had proved less than satisfactory as an ally: with Spain gripped by a terrible social and economic crisis that was in part the result of war against Britain, neither the Spanish navy—in 1789 the third strongest in Europe—nor the Spanish army had made much of a showing. All this, Napoleon, believed, was the fruit either of backsliding and incompetence on the part of the regime or of the backwardness brought by the centuries-old dominance of the Catholic Church, and he therefore decided to take action. Exactly what this meant was initially unclear even to him, and he seems to have toyed with various alternatives: bringing in one of his brothers was certainly one option, but he also seriously considered the idea of putting Ferdinand on the throne as a puppet monarch. But whatever course he chose, one thing was clear: the Spanish government would have to be deprived of all capacity for independent action, and to this end late February 1808 saw the French forces in northern Spain—now heavily reinforced—ordered to seize all the Spanish border fortresses and march on Madrid.

As can be imagined, the sudden change in Napoleon's policy led to a renewed crisis in the Spanish capital. Unwilling to see Spain lose its independence and, still less, to accept his own downfall, Godoy desperately tried to organize resistance and secure the evacuation of the royal family to South America. But for Ferdinand and his supporters war with France was anathema, because in their view Napoleon was on their side. Aided by the fact that the royal guard hated Godoy on account of a series of reforms he had made to its structure, they therefore hastily organized a military coup. With the favorite under arrest, the king and queen were forced to abdicate and on 19 March 1808 Ferdinand took their place as Ferdinand VII. Over the next few weeks, the new monarch and his advisers spared no effort to win Napoleon's support, but it was not forthcoming. On the contrary, the emperor

Less than a year after the peace of Tilsit, the armies of Napoleon were sent to invade Portugal, and the house of Bragança was reduced to seeking a refuge in its American dominions. The throne of Spain was given by him to one of his brothers, and the Spanish branch of the house of Bourbon was imprisoned in France.... The consequences did not delay in making themselves felt most heavily.

Duc d'Audiffret-Pasquier, ed. *Mémoires du Chancelier Pasquier.* Paris, 1914. Vol. 1, p. 325.

was now set on getting rid of the Spanish Bourbons, and he therefore summoned the entire royal family to a conference at Bayonne, at which both Charles IV and Ferdinand VII abdicated their claim to the throne into the hands of Napoleon.

In many other states this démarche might have passed unremarked, but Spain was very much a special case. Long years of economic chaos had engendered a mood of bitter anger among the populace, and in recent years Ferdinand's supporters had been playing upon this in order to undermine Godoy. In a sustained propaganda campaign, then, they portrayed the crown prince as a savior who would set all to right and usher in a new golden age; as for the favorite, he was painted, almost literally, as a fiend in human shape. In consequence, the news that Ferdinand was not going to be king after all came as a bitter blow. Still worse, meanwhile, France's intervention was interpreted as the fruit of a devious plot on the part of Godoy, it being assumed that he had put himself forward as Napoleon's man in Spain. With the resultant air of crisis whipped up by misfortune—above all, a spontaneous riot in Madrid on 2 May that turned into a full-scale battle in which some four hundred Spaniards were killed—and the desire of a number of "out" groups to turn the situation to their own advantage, the result was that in the last week of May the whole of Spain rose in revolt, in which respect it was followed shortly afterward by Portugal. Unperturbed by this development, however, Napoleon proclaimed his elder brother, Joseph Bonaparte, to be king of Spain.

THE COURSE OF THE WAR

Thus began the Peninsular War. So far as the military history of this conflict is concerned, it began with a great French offensive. Although they had been taken by surprise, the invaders struck out in all directions from the bases that they had occupied—Madrid, Barcelona, and a few garrisons along the roads that linked these two cities with the French frontier. Many victories were obtained, but attacks on the cities of Valencia, Zaragoza (Saragossa), and Gerona were all turned back, while an entire French army was surrounded and forced to surrender at Bailén. As a result, the imperial forces in central Spain were all withdrawn to Navarre and the Basque provinces, while the garrison of Barcelona was left with no option but to barricade itself in the city and await relief. In Portugal, meanwhile, a British expeditionary force commanded, initially at least, by Sir Arthur Wellesley defeated the French garrison at Vimeiro and forced it to surrender, albeit on very generous terms. Under a new commander, Sir John Moore, the British then advanced into Spain to reinforce the Spaniards. Needless to say, Napoleon was unwilling to take all this lying down, and there now began the next phase of the war. Pouring reinforcements into Spain, the emperor came to take charge of operations in person, and in a brilliant campaign that lasted less than one month defeated the Spanish forces on the Ebro River and reoccupied Madrid. Elsewhere, meanwhile, Zaragoza was besieged once more, and the blockade of Barcelona broken. As for the British army, after a short-lived offensive in Old Castile, it was forced to cut and run. Pursued every step of the way by the French, Moore led his men to the sea at La Coruña. On 16 January 1809 there followed a sharp rearguard action in which Moore himself was killed, but the French were beaten off and the battered British forces got away by sea.

By the beginning of 1809, then, the military situation had more or less been restored to the position in which the fighting had started six months earlier: if the French had lost Portugal, they had gained Galicia in recompense. With matters in this state, there began the next phase in operations. Napoleon himself returned to France, but left his commanders in Spain with orders, as he saw it, to mop up Spanish and Portuguese resistance. This was easier said than done, but the next three years saw the French forces gradually gain the upper hand over the Allies. Two further invasions of Portugal were repelled by the Anglo-Portuguese forces of Wellesley (from August 1809 Lord Wellington), who, particularly through his construction of the "lines of Torres Vedras," showed himself to be a defensive strategist of the highest order. (Wellington is often referred to as Duke of Wellington, but this title was not awarded him until 1814, the title that he received in 1809 being that of Viscount.) But, even with British support, successive Allied counteroffensives in Spain were repelled, and the Spanish forces suffered very heavy losses. In the famous "little war," or *guerrilla,* a combination of "flying columns" of regular troops and bands of irregular volunteers, many of which steadily assumed a character that was ever more military, harassed the invaders incessantly, but their heroics made little difference to the overall picture, and, although the French were forced to evacuate Galicia in the summer of 1809, everywhere else they continued to advance. By the beginning of 1812, indeed, the only Spanish territory that remained unoccupied was Galicia, a small part of Catalonia, the area around Alicante, and the island city of Cádiz, which as the temporary capital had become the headquarters of a political revolution that in March 1812 gave Spain its first modern constitution.

With matters in this state, the war was very much poised in the balance, and it is highly probable that the French would have won the war if they had continued to receive the constant stream of reinforcements that had poured across the Pyrenees between 1808 and 1811. At the end of 1811, Napoleon decided on the invasion of Russia. Surprisingly few troops were withdrawn from the Iberian Peninsula, but no more fresh troops were forthcoming. As the emperor insisted that offensive operations continue in Spain, the result was the French position there was completely destabilized. Taking advantage of the situation, Wellington once more advanced across the Portuguese frontier, and this time achieved much greater success, most notably at the Battle of Salamanca (22 July 1812). In the autumn a French counteroffensive forced him back once more, but the campaign of 1812 had still cost the French fully half their Spanish conquests. In the course of the winter, Wellington

was heavily reinforced, moreover, and in May 1813 he struck deep into northern Spain. Outguessed and outmaneuvered, the French were heavily defeated at Vitoria on 21 June. Forced to retreat to the Pyrenees, they launched a series of fierce counterattacks in July and August, but these were repelled with heavy losses. In October there came the coup de grâce: Wellington invaded France and inflicted several more defeats on the French. At the other end of the Pyrenees a few imperial troops still clung onto Barcelona and a number of other towns, but the Spaniards had them under close blockade. The Catalan capital was still holding out when Napoleon abdicated in April 1814, but to all intents and purposes the Peninsular War was over.

THE WAR'S IMPACT

The long struggle that raged in Spain and Portugal between 1808 and 1814 is often argued to have been one of the chief factors in the defeat of Napoleon. As the Napoleonic Wars drew to their climax, with Napoleon's men caught up in a long war they could not win, the emperor found himself deprived of perhaps 250,000 veteran troops who might have tipped the balance in Russia and Germany. With French casualties mounting steadily, morale slumped both on the home front, which was assailed by ever-higher levels of conscription, and in the army. With the empire's prestige tarnished by a series of dramatic defeats, the powers of Europe were encouraged to resume a struggle that they might otherwise have abandoned. With the ports of Portugal, Spain, and Latin America open to British trade, the Continental System was outflanked. With the people of Portugal and Spain engaged in a heroic war of national resistance, the peoples of Russia, Germany, and Italy were galvanized to take up arms in turn, thereby confronting Napoleon with a force that even he could never have overcome. With its soldiers fighting heroically in the Peninsula—practically the only place where it had some hope of maintaining a permanent toehold on the Continent—Britain could no longer be accused of fighting to the last Austrian. And, finally, with the Pyrenees in the hands of a victorious enemy, in 1814 Napoleon's Grand Army found itself not just outnumbered but surrounded.

To reinforce the point, one can contrast all this with an imagined view of what might have happened had Napoleon not taken the disastrous step of overthrowing the ruling dynasty in Spain in 1808. Given that Spain's new king, Ferdinand VII, was the darling of the Spanish masses, there would have been no Spanish insurrection. Without a Spanish insurrection, there would have been either no Portuguese insurrection at all, or a rapid French victory that would simply have swelled Napoleon's prestige still further. With Lisbon in French hands, British control of the seas would have been gravely jeopardized (for the Portuguese capital played a massive part in Britain's naval calculations). With Spain a loyal ally, the wealth of the Americas would have started to flow into French coffers and thereby to have both boosted the French economy and reduced the pressure of taxation on the home front. With no soldiers needed in Spain, far fewer young Frenchmen would have had to be conscripted, thereby further consolidating the popularity of the empire. With no means of securing new markets or intervening on the Continent, Britain would have been bankrupted and left without the Continental allies that were its only hope of winning the war. And, finally, with a bigger and better Grand Army, Napoleon would have swept to victory in Russia in 1812, thereby forcing Britain to drop out of the war and enshrining the French imperium for good. Not for nothing, then, did a defeated emperor admit on St. Helena that the Peninsular War was his "Spanish ulcer" and, more than that, the central cause of his overthrow.

This is, however, an extremely problematic view of the events of 1808 to 1814. Flying in the face of a variety of historical realities as it does, it would not be going too far to say that it has obtained the popularity that it enjoys only because it has suited a wide variety of commentators and historians to take this view. Thus, for British scholars such as Sir Charles Oman (1860–1946) it was a useful means of both gilding the already legendary figure of the Duke of Wellington and maximizing the role Britain had played in saving Europe from the emperor, while for both Napoleon himself and the legions of his apologists and admirers it was a subtle way of reinforcing the link between the emperor and the cause of liberation and modernity. To elaborate, the Bonaparte kingdom of Spain stood for an assault upon the privileges of the Catholic Church and the nobility and for the abolition of the Inquisition; indeed, the Bonapartist line

has even on occasion been to argue that it was precisely to secure these objectives that France intervened in the Iberian Peninsula in the first place—that the overthrow of the Braganças (the Portuguese ruling family) and the Bourbons, in short, was the fruit of generous and altruistic missionary zeal. In Spain and Portugal, however, the ideas of the French Revolution met their match in the form of the Catholic Church. Determined to defend their status, the argument continues, the clergy whipped up a holy war by exploiting their hold over a superstitious and ignorant populace, and in the end not even Napoleon could prevail against them. What defeated Napoleon, then, was not just Spain and Portugal, but rather a combination of black reaction and his own warmth, benevolence, and love of liberty. To return to the impact of the Peninsular War, however, the fact that it suited a variety of interest groups to stress its role in Napoleon's downfall is neither here nor there. Strip away the political proclivities that have tended to dominate debate, and it is a very different story.

On many counts, the evidence against the traditional view is overwhelming. First, there is the issue of the veteran French troops tied up in Spain. Assume either that they had been used to augment the very large army that was deployed against Russia in 1812, or that they had taken the place of the roughly equivalent numbers of Germans, Italians, Dutchmen, Poles, and others whom the emperor was forced to employ in their stead. Fair enough, but how would they have helped? To have employed still more troops on the Russian front simply would have increased the scale of the logistical chaos that marked the French invasion—the fact was that the French war machine could barely sustain and make use of the troops that it did deploy against Russia—while there is little real evidence Napoleon's foreign auxiliaries fought any worse than their French counterparts.

In Russia, then, they would have made little difference, but what about in Germany in 1813 or France in 1814? Clearly, negotiating an end to the Peninsular War and bringing his forces back to France (as he in fact tried to do) would have greatly boosted Napoleon's position in the short term. But to what end? With ever increasing numbers of opponents arrayed against him, the French ruler's only real chance of survival was negotiating a compromise peace that would have secured him the throne and France its natural frontiers. Yet giving him more troops would not have helped at all in this respect, everything that is known about Napoleon suggesting that he would simply have been encouraged to pursue the futile and ultimately self-defeating chimera of total victory. And what of the impact on French morale? Certainly, the Peninsular War caused more men to be conscripted than would otherwise have been the case, but, apart from the crisis years of 1812 to 1814, the incidence of desertion and draft evasion was actually at its highest in the early years of the Napoleonic Wars. Equally, the fact that French soldiers suffered repeated defeats and heavy losses in Spain and Portugal seems to have had little impact on their willingness to sacrifice themselves on the battlefield in those countries, let alone anywhere else. And what, meanwhile, of the wider war? Here, too, there are problems. Except in the case of Austria (but even then only in 1809 rather than the more interesting case of 1813), Napoleon's problems in Iberia did not persuade any of the powers to fight France, while of national insurrections there appear nothing of the sort. Discounting the so-called revolts that took place in 1813 and 1814 in cities such as Hamburg and Milan that had temporarily or otherwise been evacuated by the French, and the wave of village riots that gripped northern Italy in 1809, the only serious popular insurrection that took place in Europe in the period from 1808 to 1814—the Tyrolean rebellion of 1809—was only marginally influenced by the Spanish example. And, last but not least, the Peninsular War did not make much difference to Britain even in economic terms: Britain may have gained direct access to the markets of Spain and Portugal, but in the circumstances that did not mean very much, while such was its control of the seas and the success its merchants enjoyed in smuggling their goods past Napoleon's Continental System, it is hard to believe that Britain would not have made up the same ground come what may. In the end, then, one must look elsewhere for an explanation of the defeat of Napoleon: to say that the Peninsular War played no part in Allied victory would be risible—it was, beyond doubt, a contributory factor in the collapse of the imperial regime in 1814—but this is not to say that the traditional view can be accepted at face value.

See also **Continental System; Ferdinand VII; France; French Revolutionary Wars and Napoleonic Wars; Napoleon; Napoleonic Empire; Portugal; Spain; Wellington, Duke of (Arthur Wellesley).**

BIBLIOGRAPHY

Esdaile, Charles. *The French Wars, 1792–1815.* London, 2001.

———. *The Peninsular War: A New History.* London, 2002.

Gates, David. *The Spanish Ulcer: A History of the Peninsular War.* London, 1986.

———. *The Napoleonic Wars, 1803–1815.* London, 1997.

Riley, J. P. *Napoleon and the World War of 1813: Lessons in Coalition Warfighting.* London, 2000.

CHARLES J. ESDAILE

PEOPLE'S WILL. The Party of the People's Will was a late-nineteenth-century conspiratorial revolutionary organization that assassinated the Russian emperor Alexander II and other high officials, with the aim of securing political liberties. The organization grew out of the intelligentsia's disillusionment with Russia's incomplete "Great Reforms" of the 1860s. Influenced by writings of (among others) Nikolai Chernyshevsky, Mikhail Bakunin, and Peter Lavrov, activists sought to remedy the poverty and oppression of the Russian peasantry through direct action. They hoped to steer Russia away from the perceived evils of capitalist development, toward a free socialist society resting upon the peasantry's communal traditions. In the "mad summer" of 1874 several thousand young people traveled through rural districts to spread ideas of social revolution. They found the peasants unreceptive and suspicious, and the police vigilant. Some sixteen hundred would-be propagandists ended up in police custody.

Those who avoided arrest adopted more conspiratorial tactics. The Land and Liberty group (Zemlya i Volya, 1876–1879) established secret hideouts, false identities, and clandestine printing presses. Its "disorganizing" efforts included jailbreaks and defensive or retaliatory terrorism, epitomized by Land and Liberty member Vera Zasulich's 1878 attempt to kill the military governor of

St. Petersburg, F. F. Trepov, after he ordered the flogging of a radical prisoner.

In the spring of 1879 exponents of terrorism began to reevaluate Land and Liberty's strategy and objectives, advocating instead that terror should be turned into an offensive weapon against the autocratic state. In one radical's words, "no activity aimed at the good of the people is possible, given the despotism and violence which here reign supreme. There is no freedom of speech or freedom of press, which would allow us to act by means of persuasion.... [Hence we] must put an end to the existing regime" (quoted in Venturi, p. 649). Leaders of this new faction were wary of "Jacobinism" and did not propose to take state power into their own hands. They argued that a direct attack against the state would promote creation of a free and socialistic society "from below." The militants formed a secret Executive Committee that functioned briefly within Land and Liberty and then, when the latter group split over the terrorists' agenda, took the name People's Will (Narodnaya Volya).

Over the next eighteen months the conspirators made a series of dramatic and bloody attempts to kill the emperor. The committee had barely a hundred adherents, but the mystique of a vast conspiracy created widespread panic. In response the Russian state tightened its police regime. Interior Minister M. T. Loris-Melikov recognized that repressive policies alone would not overcome the threat and urged Alexander II to seek broader popular support from the propertied classes through reforms and consultations. On 1 March 1881 (the day of his assassination) Alexander accepted these proposals, but they were later rejected by his successor.

The assassins prepared their attack with great care, monitoring the emperor's movements about St. Petersburg. They dug a tunnel under a main thoroughfare in order to blow up his sleigh when he passed by. When Alexander changed routes, two of the conspirators attacked him with hand-thrown bombs. Police soon apprehended the plotters. Five were executed, and the rest received long prison sentences. A few activists escaped abroad to a life of isolation and, for several, disillusionment. Instead of triggering a popular revolt, the emperor's assassination provoked pro-monarchist demonstrations, anti-Semitic riots, and an extended crackdown on all oppositionists.

After killing Alexander II, the remaining conspirators declared their political agenda in a public letter: They would abandon terrorism if the new monarch granted basic freedoms (of speech, assembly, and press) and transferred power to an elected assembly. Alexander III was unswayed. In July 1881 the surviving members of the People's Will denounced the murder of U.S. president James Garfield. Assassination, they declared, was a last resort in a tyrannical state such as Russia, but unacceptable in a free country.

Over the next decade several new groups tried to revive the People's Will. Some cooperated with Marxists and "propagandist" Populists, while others flirted with the idea of a revolutionary dictatorship. In 1887 five members of a new People's Will—including Alexander Ulyanov, older brother of Vladimir Lenin—were hanged for planning to murder Alexander III. In all, more than five thousand people were arrested in the 1880s for antistate activities.

Later generations remembered the People's Will as idealists, fanatics, and utopians. (Soviet historians underscored their petty-bourgeois origins and "voluntarist" conception of revolution.) The group's direct heirs were terrorists associated with the Socialist Revolutionary Party who carried out many assassinations between 1898 and 1918. More broadly, the terms of struggle laid down by the People's Will— centralized, conspiratorial, and uncompromising— became a shared legacy of other revolutionary factions, including the Bolshevik wing of Russian Social Democracy. The state's response, equally uncompromising, was to reject all constitutional proposals and treat all manner of critics as revolutionaries. Instead of bringing political liberty to Russia, the People's Will helped to polarize state and society and destroy the possibility of reform.

See also **Alexander II; Nechayev, Sergei; Populists; Zasulich, Vera.**

BIBLIOGRAPHY

Primary Sources

Figner, Vera. *Memoirs of a Revolutionist.* Authorized translation from the Russian; introduction by Richard Stites. DeKalb, Ill., 1991. Translation of *Zapechatlennyi trud* (1921).

Secondary Sources

Naimark, Norman M. *Terrorists and Social Democrats: The Russian Revolutionary Movement under Alexander III.* Cambridge, Mass., 1983.

Venturi, Franco. *Roots of Revolution: A History of the Populist and Socialist Movements in Nineteenth Century Russia.* Translated from the Italian by Francis Haskell. London, 1964. Translation of *Il Populismo Russo* (1952).

ROBERT E. JOHNSON

PHILHELLENIC MOVEMENT.

Classical or Greco-Roman antiquity is one of the foundations of European civilization as a whole, but a passionate admiration of the arts and civilization of ancient Greece, as distinct from those of Rome, is a more recent phenomenon. The philhellene creed was summed up by Percy Bysshe Shelley's declaration, in the preface to his drama *Hellas* (1822), that "We are all Greeks." All western civilization, on this account, derives from Greece, with Rome seen merely as the conduit through which this influence flowed. The origins of Hellenism lie in the mid-eighteenth century, in the shift of taste and attitudes that expressed itself aesthetically in a reaction against the baroque and the pursuit of simplicity; socially in the cult of the primitive, natural man, and the noble savage; and politically in the ideologies of the American and French revolutions. Johann Joachim Winckelmann (1717–1768), the founder of art history, characterized the qualities of Greek sculpture and literature as "a noble simplicity and a calm greatness." The critic and thinker Gotthold Ephraim Lessing (1729–1781), in his essay *Laocoon* (1766), accepted this account of sculpture but disagreed over literature, observing that Greek tragedy represented extreme emotional and physical suffering. These ideas were popularized by August Wilhelm von Schlegel (1767–1845) in his *Vorlesungen über dramatische Kunst und Literatur* (1809–1811) translated into English in 1815 as *Lectures on Dramatic Art and Literature*; translated into English in the first years of the nineteenth century, it had great influence in Britain. Such discourse commonly admired Greek civilization for being unlike that of the modern world and measured it against the present day through various contrasts: between past and present, South and North, classical and Romantic, sculpture and music, perfection within defined limits and a reaching for the infinite.

Meanwhile, an accurate knowledge of classical Greek architecture was made known to western Europe for the first time since antiquity through James Stuart and Nicholas Revett's *The Antiquities of Athens* (first volume, 1762; second volume, 1787). This made possible the Greek Revival, an architectural style that aimed at copying Greek forms as far as was practicably possible in modern conditions. It reached its zenith in the first decades of the nineteenth century but had a longer significance in establishing revivalism in architecture (that is, the faithful imitation of old forms as distinct from the adaptation of them to new aesthetic effects). The Greek Revival was Europe-wide but especially favored in Germany and Britain (above all in Scotland), in part because it was felt to embody a reaction against the Latinate or baroque culture of southern Europe. In the United States, comparably, it was seen as a plain, manly style, fit for a young nation that had thrown off the fripperies of the Old World.

The literature and thought of Greece was especially important to Germany at a time when it was emancipating itself from a sense of inferiority to France and Italy. One view was that there was a natural kinship between Greece and Germany; another view, exemplified in the poetry of Friedrich Hölderlin (1770–1843), saw ancient Greece as a distant, ideal aspiration. From either viewpoint the significance of Greece to the German spirit was profound. The architecture of Karl Friedrich Schinkel (1781–1841) made Greek forms seem the natural expression of modern German resurgence. Meanwhile, Germany was leading all of Europe in classical scholarship and philology. The work of Swiss historian Jacob Burckhardt (1819–1897) exercised a substantial influence on general culture; a more unorthodox figure was the self-taught Heinrich Schliemann (1822–1890), excavator of Troy and Mycenae, and still the most famous of all archaeologists, whose discoveries gave glamour to the material remains of the Greek world.

In parallel with these aesthetic and historical explorations came throughout Europe a shift in political attitudes: Athenian democracy, which had usually been regarded as an awful warning of the disastrous effects of giving power to the common people, now became an object of praise. Thomas Paine (1737–1809) was radical but a harbinger of the future when he declared that he found more to admire and less to censure in the Athenians than in any other form of political organization. At the same time, the modern Greek struggle for independence fired the imagination of idealists. (Often the term *philhellenism* is applied to an enthusiasm for modern Greece, with the term Hellenism applied to a love for ancient Greek culture.) When Lord Byron adopted the modern Greek cause, his international prestige gave it an added glamour, which was made all the more romantic by his death in Greece (of an illness, however, not in battle). Once the Greeks gained their freedom, western Europe largely lost interest in the modern nation, but a passion for ancient Greece continued through the nineteenth century. It provided an arena in which modern debates could be fought out: thus Christians saw Greek thought and culture as helping to prepare the ground for the coming of 0the Gospel (and it was not forgotten that the New Testament was written in Greek), while for agnostics and atheists Greece offered an alternative source of moral and spiritual values. The aesthetic movement of the later nineteenth century, both in France and Britain, celebrated ancient Greece for its worship of beauty and the supposed youthfulness and innocence of its culture; Walter Pater (1839–1894) was the most eloquent spokesman for this view. Pater also hints at the homoeroticism in Greek culture, a subject handled more overtly by other apologists for homosexuality. In Germany, however, a new kind of Hellenism appeared in Friedrich Nietzsche's *The Birth of Tragedy* (1872), which saw in the tragedians Aeschylus and Sophocles a tense equilibrium between the Apollonian and Dionysian impulses of the human psyche. These ideas were to influence Sigmund Freud's theory of the mind, and Freud also drew on Sophocles for his idea of the Oedipus complex. In contrast to earlier Hellenism, a sense that the Greeks explored the dark and irrational side of humanity was to be influential throughout the twentieth century.

See also **Burckhardt, Jacob; Byron, George Gordon; Greece; Hölderlin, Johann Christian Friedrich; Nietzsche, Friedrich; Pater, Walter; Schinkel, Karl Friedrich; Schlegel, August Wilhelm von; Shelley, Percy Bysshe.**

BIBLIOGRAPHY

Butler, E. M. *The Tyranny of Greece over Germany.* Cambridge, U.K., and New York, 1935.

Jenkyns, Richard. *The Victorians and Ancient Greece.* Cambridge, Mass., 1980.

Spencer, T. J. B. *Fair Greece! Sad Relic.* London, 1954.

RICHARD JENKYNS

PHOTOGRAPHY. Photography was presented as a new visual medium simultaneously in England and France in 1839. This invention had been preceded by a decade of experimentation. The aim was to fix a fragment of reality projected via a lens onto the ground glass of a camera obscura on a support sensitized to light with silver nitrate. The Frenchman Louis-Jacques-Mandé Daguerre (1789–1851), a theatrical designer for the Paris Opéra, partly in collaboration with Joseph-Nicéphore Niépce (1765–1833), developed a process whereby a single print could be recorded on a silvered copper plate. His invention, termed *daguerreotype*, was immediately acquired by the French government and used on a small scale in Europe and America throughout the 1840s primarily for portraits and the occasional city view and landscape. No prints could be made from daguerreotypes: they were unique objects. Around the same time in England, William Henry Fox Talbot (1800–1877) developed a negative-positive process, which he called the calotype. Using this process, multiple positive prints could be made from a paper negative. Talbot's invention of paper photography remained experimental into the 1840s, in part because Talbot obtained patents and then defended them vigorously. New inventions, in fact, improvements on Talbot's principle, surpassed the negative-positive method making possible modest printed editions. The most common method used, well into the nineteenth century, was the wet collodion process (developed by Frederick Scott Archer in 1851), by which prints on albumen paper were made from glass negatives.

A speech the physicist François Arago gave at the Académie des Sciences in Paris in 1839 reveal-

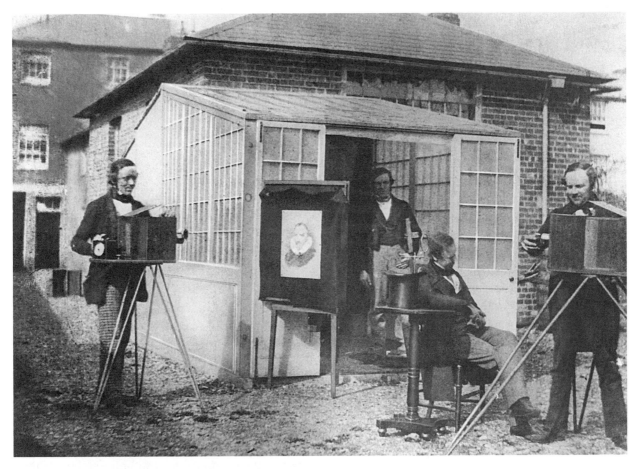

William Henry Fox Talbot (right) making a photograph. ©Hulton-Deutsch Collection/Corbis

ing the infinite possibilities of photography is famous: he claimed it could be applied in the arts, archaeology, and the sciences. In his now classic photo book *The Pencil of Nature* (1844–1846), Talbot also outlined the many objectives of photography: from the reproduction of art to the capturing of still lifes, landscapes, portraits, and architecture. In the early days the new art relied heavily on existing visual traditions, and photographers borrowed all manner of motifs and compositions from painting, drawing, and the graphic arts. The first photographers practiced this new branch of art as amateurs, often in and around their own homes. They purchased their camera and equipment in major cities such as London, Paris, and Berlin and were generally affluent. These enthusiasts were interested in experiments with chemistry and physics and eagerly studied the manuals that came onto the market. Artists, scientists, lithographers, and printers also tested the two methods, the daguerreotype and paper photography.

SPREAD OF PHOTOGRAPHY

The early photographers rapidly organized themselves in the form of associations and clubs, and went public with their photographic series at various important international exhibitions (London, 1851; London, 1852; Paris, 1855; Amsterdam, 1855; and Brussels, 1856). These same years witnessed the realization of several prestigious projects, some commissioned by governments or associations, the first one being the photographing of the Great Exhibition of 1851 in London, an idea launched by the British prince consort, Albert. He was also excited about the mission of Roger Fenton (1819–1869) to photograph the Crimean War in 1855. French photographers, including Gustave Le Gray (1820–1884), Henri Le Secq (1818–1882), and Édouard Baldus (1813–1882) were commissioned in 1851 to record the monuments in their country. The French photographers in particular raised the art to great heights. In the second half of the 1850s Baldus photographed the construction of the new Louvre and numerous railway projects; Le Gray made wonderful sea views; and Nadar (1820–1910) received writers, statesmen, and artists in his atelier on the Boulevard des Capucines. Handsome results were also achieved fairly early on farther afield: in Egypt and the Holy Land, as well as in the colonies in Asia. As an army photographer, Linnaeus Tripe (1822–1902) recorded monuments in India (1858), and Isidore van Kinsbergen (1821–1905) did the same in the Dutch East Indies a few years later for the Dutch government.

Europe experienced sweeping political, economic, and social changes in the middle of the nineteenth century. The eruption of the European revolutions of 1848 marked a turning point: it helped form new, larger nation-states, new consitutitions, and more democracy. Large-scale industrialization, which had emerged in Britain at the end of the eighteenth century, continued to gain momentum across Europe in this period. This development is aptly phrased in the motto "Mechanization takes command," which also pertained to the visual production in which mechanization (photography) gradually took over handwork (drawing and printmaking). After having been the province of princes, the elite, and the highest classes until the mid-1850s, photography became the new visual medium of the affluent bourgeoisie. The ascendancy of the bourgeoisie was directly linked to the rise and applications of photography as a visual medium for a broad, and increasingly affluent, public. The Paris photographer André-Adolphe-Eugène Disdéri (1819–1889) developed the *carte-de-visite* portrait in 1854. The first "mass media," this novelty along with stereophotography (developed by Sir David Brewster in 1849), boomed around 1860. People not only wanted to be eternalized in photographs, but they also wanted to own them for their own pleasure and for their travel albums. From that moment the occupation of photographer took on greater substance, and photographic studios were established in virtually every city. Thus, at this time the invention of photography was part and parcel of a technological development that seemed unstoppable, and it blossomed in a period of prosperity when the European public was eager to give evidence of its new status.

Book and print sellers also began dealing in photography, thereby effecting a widespread and international dissemination, as had been the case in the preceding centuries with prints. Photographs were affixed to preprinted sheets, a few of which were then combined in a cover (creating a fascicule) and sold directly or mailed. When the series was complete, the fascicules were bound together with the accompanying text. Photography rapidly became popular as a form of book illustration: initially entire editions were provided with manually inserted photographs: novels, poetry, scientific publications, catalogs, and series. Many now famous photographs were first part of a book, for instance Maxime Du Camp's photographs of Egypt (1849–1851), John Thomson's photographs of China (1873–1874), and Thomas Annan's images of the slums of Glasgow (1868–1877).

Photography was closely linked to the world of art, architecture, and culture. It led to a far greater accessibility of "realistic" imagery that formed a source of inspiration for painters, sculptors, and architects alike. Photography particularly suited such characteristics as atmosphere, naturalism, and *plein air* in nineteenth-century art. Photographic nudes, studies of architectural detail, landscape, and even street scenes were used by artists. Moreover, in the realm of science, photography was used for diagnostic purposes or as a means for astronomers to record their observations. In the 1870s and 1880s, photography and the study of motion came together in the experiments of Eadweard Muybridge (1830–1904) and Étienne-Jules Marey (1830–1904), culminating in the development of film at the beginning of the twentieth century.

THE TURN OF THE CENTURY

The new medium was first seen in retrospective in 1889, when photography celebrated its fiftieth anniversary. Historical surveys were organized for which the earliest photographs were brought together and exhibited at the World's Fair in Paris in that year. This moment coincided with the rise of the first international movement within photography, pictorialism, which was actually a reaction to the standardization in the studios of the professional photographers. Alfred Stieglitz (1864–1946), the American photographer born to German parents, was an important advocate of this direction, which propagated photography as art. European and American photographers interacted

Paris, 1858. Aerial photograph of the city taken from a balloon by French photographer Nadar. ©HULTON-DEUTSCH COLLECTION/CORBIS

in Stieglitz's gallery in New York and in his influential magazine *Camera Work* (1903–1917). The year 1889 was significant for other reasons as well. It marked the introduction in Europe of an American invention, namely the small, portable Kodak camera with a roll of film. Initially these cameras were used primarily by well-to-do amateur photographers, and in the following decades they gave an enormous boost to nonprofessional photography. Avid amateur photographers included artists such as the Frenchmen Pierre Bonnard and Edgar Degas, the Dutch painter George Hendrik Breitner, and Pablo Picasso. Their handling of the medium photography was quite fresh and unconventional. It was the prelude to the new vision fully explored by avant-garde photographers in the twentieth century.

The 1890s brought still more important changes. The printing business was increasingly employing photomechanical printing techniques to produce high-quality illustrations for art and architecture books. This allowed photographs in photolithography, photogravure, and collotype to be printed in ink. Around 1900 these techniques were used in book printing in all manner of variations. The invention of autotype with halftone printing of the image, moreover, made it possible to print both the photograph and the text during the same printing. Newspapers and magazines illustrated ever more photographs starting in the second half of the 1890s. The press in particular developed rapidly in the first decade of the twentieth century. Photographs increasingly came to determine the face of weekly magazines such as the *Illustrated London News, L'Illustration,* and the *Berliner Illustrirte Zeitung,* and the drawn illustrations in wood engraving faded into the background. The outbreak of World War I in 1914, not surprisingly, only

The sluice system of the Paris sewers. Photograph by Nadar, 1864–1865. Nadar's photographs of the Paris sewers, taken at the invitation of the city's chief water engineer following their reconstruction during the previous decade, demystified the system for Parisian citizens. These photographs were among the first to be taken with artificial light, and the lengthy exposure time necessitated the use of the mannequin seen here in a seat that would ordinarily be occupied by a man. ©HULTON-DEUTSCH COLLECTION/CORBIS

ing. Because of its realism, the photograph proved to be an appealing object both in the private realm and in numerous areas of the public domain.

See also **Atget, Eugène; Avant-Garde; Nadar, Félix; Paris.**

BIBLIOGRAPHY

Asser, Saskia, and Mattie Boom, eds. "Early Photography, 1839–1860: The Rijksmuseum, the Leiden Print Room, and Other Dutch Public Collections." Available at http://www.earlyphotography.nl.

Aubenas, Sylvie. *Gustave Le Gray, 1820–1884.* Edited by Gordon Baldwin. Los Angeles, 2002.

Boom, Mattie, and Hans Rooseboom, eds. *Een nieuwe kunst: Fotografie in de 19de eeuw; De nationale fotocollectie in het Rijksmuseum / A New Art: Photography in the 19th Century; The Photocollection of the Rijksmuseum.* Ghent, Belgium, 1996.

Dewitz, Bodo von, and Reinhard Matz, eds. *Silber und Salz: Zur Frühzeit der Photographie im deutschen Sprachraum, 1839–1860; Kataloghandbuch zur Jubiläumsausstellung 150 Jahre Photographie.* Cologne, West Germany, 1989.

Frizot, Michel, ed. *A New History of Photography.* Cologne, Germany, 1998. Translation of *Nouvelle histoire de la photographie.*

Haworth-Booth, Mark, ed. *The Golden Age of British Photography, 1839–1900: Photographs from the Victoria and Albert Museum, London, with Selections from the Philadelphia Museum of Art, Royal Archives, Windsor Castle, The Royal Photographic Society, Bath, Science Museum, London, Scottish National Portrait Gallery, Edinburgh.* New York, 1984.

Jammes, André, and Eugenia Parry Janis. *The Art of French Calotype: With a Critical Dictionary of Photographers, 1845–1870.* Princeton, N.J., 1983.

McCauley, Elizabeth Anne. *Industrial Madness: Commercial Photography in Paris, 1848–1871.* New Haven, Conn., 1994.

Pohlmann, Ulrich, and Johann Georg Prinz von Hohenzollern. *Eine neue Kunst? Eine andere Natur! Fotografie und Malerei im 19. Jahrhundert.* Munich, Germany, 2004.

Rosenblum, Naomi. *A World History of Photography.* 3rd ed. New York, 1997.

MATTIE BOOM

whetted the appetite for images, and the war years were formative for photojournalism. A vital technical development was the autochrome color process, presented in 1907 by the Lumière brothers (also responsible for introducing cinema photography in 1895). Primarily amateur photographers (with a talent for chemistry), but pictorialists too, now recorded the world in color for the first time.

The most striking feature of the invention of photography—with its technological development and long series of applications until the first decade of the twentieth century—is the remarkable swiftness with which this new visual medium penetrated all sectors of society. In little more than half a century, photography replaced both drawing and printmak-

PHRENOLOGY. Phrenology was a science of brain, mind, and human nature that began in the late eighteenth century and endured in modified forms into the mid-twentieth century. The modern name, *phrenology*, was adopted in Britain in the late 1810s in place of earlier names such as *craniology* or *the physiognomical system*. The name is derived from the Greek roots *phren*, meaning "mind," and *logos*, meaning "study/discourse."

Phrenology was the creation of the Viennese physician Franz Joseph Gall (1758–1828). In the early 1790s Gall became convinced that he had discovered localized regions or "organs" of the brain where innate mental faculties resided. He postulated twenty-seven faculties/organs from "impulse to propagation" to "mechanical skill" and "pride, arrogance, love of authority." The particular faculties of Gall's psychology and organology reflect the cases he witnessed in his patients and in local asylums, prisons, and hospitals. Each of these faculties/organs was given a number. Gall believed that the activity or power of a faculty must be due to the size of its cerebral organ, just as strength is proportional to the size of a muscle. Furthermore, Gall asserted that the shape of the skull followed the shape of the underlying brain. Therefore, Gall concluded, through an examination of the exterior of the head or skull of a person or animal it was possible to discover character, abilities, and so forth. Between 1805 and 1807 Gall conducted a highly successful lecture tour throughout Europe. In 1807 he settled permanently in Paris, where he continued to lecture and publish on his doctrine.

In 1813 Gall's longtime dissectionist and assistant, Johann Gaspar Spurzheim (1776–1832), left Gall to begin his own lecture tour in Britain. In Britain, Spurzheim represented himself as the co-originator of the doctrine in order to increase his own status. Even in the early twenty-first century phrenology in the English-speaking world is often described as the system of Drs. Gall and Spurzheim. Spurzheim introduced many significant changes to Gall's system, including renaming all of the organs/faculties to make them seem more benevolent and precise and arranging them in a hierarchical schema of orders and genera. Thus "impulse to propagation" became "Amativeness" and "murder" became "Destructiveness." Spurzheim also introduced several new organs/faculties. He presented the system as something that others should learn and practice themselves. He succeeded in making many converts in England and Scotland. Some of the most prominent of these were the

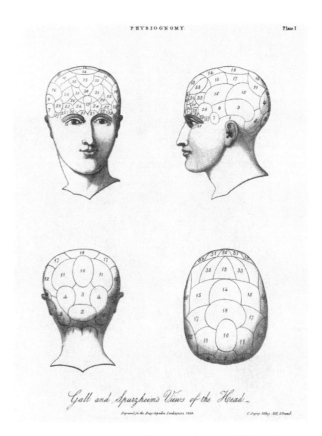

An illustration from the *Encyclopedia Londiniensis,* 1824, shows the various regions of the skull as delineated by phrenology. MARY EVANS PICTURE LIBRARY

Edinburgh lawyer George Combe (1788–1858), his brother the physician Andrew Combe (1797–1847), and the radical London physician John Elliotson (1791–1868).

In the hands of the new British advocates the science evolved almost as far away from Spurzheim's ideas as his had from Gall's. They melded Spurzheim's moralistic doctrine of brain and character with the culture of British scientific societies to create a quasi-institutional science of human nature with local societies such as the Edinburgh Phrenological Society (1820–1870) or the Lancaster Phrenological Society (1843) and later national societies such as the Phrenological Association (1838).

As the practice of phrenology diffused throughout Britain it also diversified. There was a widespread naturalistic branch led by George Combe, who presented his phrenologically inspired philosophy of natural laws in *The Constitution of Man* (1828), which became one of the most widely read and discussed books of the century. Christian

Consulting the phrenologist. Illustration by A. S. Hartrick from the *Daily Graphic,* January 1896. Parents look on as a phrenologist evaluates their son. MARY EVANS PICTURE LIBRARY

phrenologists combined their religion with phrenology and created their own societies and periodicals. Many prominent phrenologists in the period from the 1820s to the 1840s were also social reformers and offered phrenology as both a mechanism of social control and critique of existing society. Even more numerous were the "practical" phrenologists who earned money and a measure of authority and respect from curious multitudes who paid a few shillings to hear a lecture or have their heads read to discover their fortune.

British phrenology diffused to the United States, France, Germany, and other countries in the 1840s via itinerant lecturers or natives converted in Britain taking it back to their homelands. Phrenology in Germany never became the widespread phenomena it was in Britain. In France, only Paris saw much phrenological activity. Phrenologists in these countries continued to use the lists of thirty-

five or so organs/faculties and the white plaster busts demarcated with the organ locations that had been developed by British phrenologists. By the 1860s phrenology had mostly gone out of fashion in Britain and elsewhere. But in the 1870s the American Fowler family brought phrenology back to Britain and excited renewed interest in their own version of phrenology, derived from the earlier British phrenology. They established the British Phrenological Association in 1886. This final phrenological movement did not contain the same scientific pretensions as the earlier phrenology.

The phrenology movement had many consequences. It can be found in hundreds of works of literature from Charles Dickens to Edgar Allan Poe. Phrenology also accustomed many ordinary people to believe that natural laws had power over their own bodies. More visibly, phrenology made the localization of functions in the brain both notorious and suspect. Phrenology inspired later racial anthropologists to use head measurements, among others, to make racial comparisons and judgments.

See also **Crime; Gall, Franz Joseph; Lombroso, Cesare; Race and Racism; Science and Technology.**

BIBLIOGRAPHY

Cooter, Roger. *The Cultural Meaning of Popular Science: Phrenology and the Organization of Consent in Nineteenth-Century Britain.* Cambridge, U.K., 1984. The most comprehensive history of phrenology, with a strong social historical bent.

Wyhe, John, van. "The Authority of Human Nature: The Schädellehre of Franz Joseph Gall." *British Journal for the History of Science* (March 2002): 17–42. The beginnings of phrenology thoroughly outlined.

———. *Phrenology and the Origins of Victorian Scientific Naturalism.* Aldershot, U.K., 2004. Discussion of phrenology and its impact on Victorian naturalism.

———. "Was Phrenology a Reform Science?: Towards a New Generalization for Phrenology." *History of Science* 42 (2004): 313–331. A critique of a widespread misunderstanding of phrenology.

JOHN VAN WYHE

PHYLLOXERA. The railways inaugurated a "golden age" of wine production, providing cheap and easy access to urban consumers at a time when real incomes were rising. Per capita consumption in France rose from around 76 liters in 1850–1854 to 168 liters by 1900–1904. In the meantime, however, prosperity had been threatened by three "plagues"—oidium, mildew, and above all phylloxera. The first of these, a fungal parasite, devastated vineyards throughout southern Europe in the 1850s. French wine production fell from around 57 million hectoliters in 1863–1875 to some 31 million by 1879–1892. The solution was to dust the plants with sulphur. As in the case of the devastating potato disease in the 1840s, the cause was probably the import of infected plants from the Americas. Globalization was not without its dangers.

Phylloxera, an aphid-like insect, would represent an even greater danger to the vines. This tiny insect, difficult to observe with the naked eye, probably originated in the eastern United States. It fed on the vine, particularly on its roots, and in the process injected its poisonous saliva into the plants. Its presence became evident from the formation of galls on leaves and roots, followed by defoliation, reduced growth, a decline in grape yields and quality, and the eventual death of the vine as damaged plants also became more susceptible to fungi and the eating habits of other insects. The aphid spread more or less rapidly depending on the vine-type, soil structures, and climate. Vines growing in deep and well-drained soils were likely to survive longest. Following the first reported cases of a mysterious affliction affecting vines near Roquemaure in the Rhône valley in 1863, its spread accelerated throughout southern France, toward Bordeaux (1866), and up the valleys of the Rhône and Saône toward Burgundy (1878), Champagne (1890), and the Paris region (1900). Insect infestation also spread to Switzerland and Portugal (1872), Germany (1874), Austria (1875), Spain (1877), and Italy—reaching Lake Como in August 1879 and Sicily by the following spring. Reports of the appearance of the aphid were also coming from as far afield as the Crimea and Romania. By the end of the century, the insect had destroyed two-thirds of European vineyards.

Initially explanations of the catastrophe varied, with experts blaming "abnormal" climatic conditions, "degenerate" plants, or soil exhaustion. It took time and the development of an international network of investigators to detect the predator and identify causal links. Together with private organizations like the Société des Agriculteurs de France, large landowners, and the PLM Railway company, which had lost so much traffic, the French government sponsored research and offered prizes for a solution. Finally, the aphid was identified in July 1868 and its complex life cycle subsequently investigated by Jules-Emile Planchon (1823–1888), professor of botany at Montpellier. It was evident that the insect was capable of flight but more commonly spread through the soil, on cuttings or even laborers' boots. Planchon was also increasingly convinced that phylloxera had originated in North America and that its spread reflected the growing international traffic in plants, partly in response to the devastation wrought by oidium.

The cause identified, the search for remedies could proceed. However, in 1871, a pessimistic official French report insisted that in the meantime there was no alternative to uprooting and burning infested plants. Subsequent replanting would be accompanied by the application of insecticides that it was hoped would protect the vines. Moreover, following a visit to the United States in 1873, Planchon had insisted, in Darwinian language, that through "a process of natural selection" American vines had acquired resistance. Eventually, replanting would affect 2.5 million hectares. Desperate to avoid the uprooting of their vines, peasants often preferred denial, quack remedies, or prayer. Debts piled up, land was abandoned. Replanting was not only expensive in itself but would be followed by three years without a crop. Slowly the government accepted the need to proceed with compulsory inspection of vineyards suspected of harboring the pest, to offer subsidies (1878) and tax concessions (1887), followed by the abolition of the municipal octroi (entry tax) in 1900, but introduced nothing on the scale of the compulsory insurance against phylloxera and compensation schemes introduced in Switzerland. The favored alternatives to uprooting, the application of carbon bisulphide or potassium sulphocarbonate, appeared effective but the latter in particular depended on access to large volumes of water to get the chemicals to the roots. Only large estates producing expensive high-quality wines could hope to meet the cost of repeated treatment. Flooding to destroy the aphids was also possible, but only where soils were impermeable. It was also noted that sandy soils with high levels of silica were unfriendly to the aphids.

In 1878 and 1879, as the appearance of the mildew fungus added to the misery of growers, in despair French legislators decided to partially end the policy of frontier quarantine by permitting the import of American plants under license into those areas, especially in the Midi and the southwest, in which the vineyards had been devastated already. Replanting could begin on a massive scale, encouraged by the high prices resulting from reduced production. However, the last thing as-yet-unaffected regions wanted was further imports of American vines. Concern was also expressed about the impact on the quality and taste of wine. A more palatable solution emerged, favored by Planchon, which involved grafting European stems on to phylloxera-resistant American roots. It would, though, take time-consuming field trials to identify those American rootstocks that had developed resistance, and to determine which were the most appropriate to particular grape varieties, soils, and climatic conditions. Nevertheless, from the 1890s the practice spread.

As the ravages of the phylloxera insect had spread, as-yet-unaffected regions profited. Imports into France increased substantially, with "French" wines often blended with Algerian, Spanish, and Italian produce or manufactured from raisins and currants. British demand for claret had collapsed in response. In the south in particular, production recovered rapidly as new larger-scale vineyards replaced cereals on the plains. Wider gaps between the rows allowed for the passage of wagons and ploughs in an effort to increase productivity. Nevertheless, capital and labor costs were both substantially higher. Higher-yield grafted plants required more manure and frequent chemical treatment. Yet as imports and higher yields led to substantial growth in the supply of wine, a market glut ensued accompanied by a rapid collapse in prices—in the Midi for example, for *vin ordinaire*, from thirty francs per hectoliter in the 1880s to eight francs, and falling, by 1901. Phylloxera had merely postponed the onset of overproduction. Under pressure from peasant voters and following serious disorders in the Midi in 1907, the government began to act more decisively through the introduction of tariffs to reduce imports (from 1892) and prevent fraud. As a result,

Spanish exports to France fell from a peak of 9.7 million hectoliters in 1881 to 2.2 million by 1900, bringing to an end a period of exceptional prosperity. In 1905, the appellation system was introduced in an effort to protect the reputation of quality wines.

Few vine-growing areas had escaped entirely the devastation and all its costs. In France, pockets of old vines still survive occasionally. In Chile, wine production is based on rootstocks imported from France in the 1850s. Moreover, phylloxera did not disappear. The genetic evolution of both plants and aphids still periodically renews the threat.

See also **Agricultural Revolution; Wine.**

BIBLIOGRAPHY

Campbell, Christy. *Phylloxera: How Wine Was Saved for the World.* London, 2004.

Guy, Kolleen M. *When Champagne Became French: Wine and the Making of a National Identity.* Baltimore, Md., 2003

Lachiver, Marcel. *Vins, vignes et vignerons: Histoire du vignoble français.* Paris, 1988.

Loubère, Leo A. *The Red and the White: The History of Wine in France and Italy in the Nineteenth Century.* Albany, N.Y., 1978.

Paul, Harry W. *Science, Vine, and Wine in Modern France.* Cambridge, U.K., 1996.

Simpson, James. "Selling to Reluctant Drinkers: The British Wine Market, 1860–1914." *Economic History Review* 57 (2004): 80–108.

ROGER PRICE

PHYSICS. Physics is a systematic, organized, and ordered knowledge about the physical world. Concepts, theories, and laws of physics are obtained by experimental and mathematical reasoning.

Physics around 1914 was different from natural philosophy (as the study of the physical world was then known) around 1789. First, the community of physicists by 1914 was self-conscious and international, and consisted of trained professional physicists, whereas in 1789 natural philosophy was local and its community consisted of both professionals and amateurs. Second, the education of physicists in universities was systematic, whereas there was no such systematic education in natural philosophy. Third, research in physics was performed in university and national laboratories, whereas natural philosophy was practiced in private laboratories, theaters, salons, and even coffeehouses. Fourth, the tight linkage between mathematics and experimental data was emphasized in physics, whereas natural philosophy was largely experimental. Finally, research in physics was performed for its own sake or for the sake of technology and industries, whereas natural philosophy was more tig'htly coupled with religion and social philosophy.

EMERGENCE OF PHYSICS

In the mid-nineteenth century, scientists noticed the emergence of a scientific discipline that is now called physics. Around this same time, some physicists appeared who began to teach physics at physics departments in universities. Before then, mathematical physics, such as Newtonian mechanics, belonged to mathematics, and experimental fields, such as the study of electricity, magnetism, and heat, belonged to natural philosophy. These two different traditions—mathematics and experimental (Baconian) physics—had developed along different paths. Mathematical physics, such as mechanics, had existed since ancient times, and it underwent a radical, conceptual transformation during the scientific revolution of the seventeenth century. On the other hand, experimental physics, such as the study of electricity, magnetism, and heat, was born during the scientific revolution with Francis Bacon's emphasis on experiments, and these fields used such new instruments as the barometer, air pump, and microscope. These two different fields, that is, mathematical mechanics and the experimental sciences, merged into a single discipline called physics in the mid-nineteenth century.

The gap between the mathematical sciences and the Baconian sciences was wide during the eighteenth century. One can see this in the case of French *physique*. Throughout the eighteenth century in France, *physique* had consisted of two separate disciplines: *physique générale* (general physics) and *physique particulière* (particular physics). The former meant Newtonian mechanics, while the latter connoted experimental science in general, but sometimes meant specific studies in heat, light, sound, electricity, and magnetism. They were not considered to form a unified discipline.

FACTORS CONTRIBUTING TO PHYSICS'S FORMATION

One factor that contributed to the formation of the single discipline of physics was the mathematization of experimental fields. Since the last quarter of the eighteenth century, experimental fields were rapidly mathematized mainly by French physicists such as Charles-Augustin de Coulomb, Pierre-Simon de Laplace, Siméon-Denis Poisson, Augustin-Jean Fresnel, and Jean-Baptiste Biot. Because of this mathematization, several branches of physics now use the same mathematics and the same mathematical equations. The second factor was the principle of the conservation of energy. In the first half of the nineteenth century, scientists discovered that various forms of forces were converted into other forms. The Danish physicist Hans Christian Ørsted and the English chemist and physicist Michael Faraday discovered the mutual relation between electricity and magnetism; Faraday also discovered the connection between magnetism and light; and the English physicist James Joule discovered the conversion of mechanical motion into heat. Mechanical motions, heat, electricity, and magnetism could be converted into one other, which meant that something in the universe was being conserved. This something was then named energy, which became a common element among various studies that eventually merged into physics.

The germ of this unifying concept can be found in the Scottish natural philosopher John Robison. He had divided mechanical philosophy into four subdisciplines: astronomy, studies on the force of cohesion (involving the theory of machines, hydrostatics, hydraulics, and pneumatics), electricity and magnetism, and optics. Robison saw two links between these four subdisciplines. First, all concentrated on "forces" existing in nature: gravitation, cohesion, electrical and magnetic forces, as well as forces between light and material particles. Second, all concerned motions of bodies in one fashion or another. Newtonian mechanics and electricity and magnetism were classified into a single discipline. During the 1850s, the second law of thermodynamics, which states that the entropy of the universe is always increased, was established.

Laplace's *Celestial Mechanics* (1799–1825) provided a conceptual basis for mathematization. In it, Laplace examined two phenomena—capillary action and the refraction of light in air—by employing the assumption of short-range forces that act between material particles, and between material particles and imponderables. These forces took the form of mathematical equations. His work influenced such followers as Biot, Étienne-Louis Malus, and Poisson. Biot extensively studied voltaic electricity, the propagation of sound, and chromatic polarization; Malus worked on double refraction and polarization; and Poisson devised mathematical formula on electricity and magnetism by using Laplace's method. Their work comprises what is now called "Laplacian physics."

It is worth noting that Laplace's followers were all graduates from the École Polytechnique, which was a new educational institution established during the French Revolution. It opened its doors to all classes of people, not just to the upper class. Though it was a military engineering institution, it trained students not only in military and civil engineering but also in mathematics and physics, including experimental fields such as heat, optics, electricity, and magnetism. Biot and Malus, two full-fledged Laplacians, were among the first *polytechniciens*. Poisson and François Arago studied there, as did Fresnel, who was, however, not a Laplacian physicist. Fresnel suggested the wave theory of light in the mid-1810s, and with this he successfully refuted the most important part of the Laplacian program in optics. After Fresnel's success, the Laplacian program rapidly declined. Although it was short-lived, Laplacian physics has historical significance, because it provided a model for research in experimental physics. The Laplacian physicists devised mathematical formulas for electricity, light, heat, and magnetism, and combined these mathematical formulas with precise experimental data.

DISCOVERIES IN ELECTROMAGNETISM

During the nineteenth century, classical electromagnetism was fully developed. The Italian physicist Alessandro Volta invented the voltaic pile to generate continuous electrical currents in 1800. Twenty years after Volta's invention, Ørsted discovered that a small magnetic needle was affected by a current-carrying wire near it, which showed that a magnetic force exists in a circular way around a current-carrying wire. This phenomenon was theoretically explained by a French physicist and mathematician, André-Marie Ampère. He conjectured that there were many tiny atomic electrical currents in a magnetic needle, and explained the interaction that Ørsted noticed in terms of the interaction between macrocurrent and atomic currents. Based on this idea, he established a mathematical formula of this force, following the Newtonian tradition. Ampère's achievement was developed further by some German scientists of the nineteenth century.

Faraday, however, suggested a radically different approach to electrical phenomena. In the early 1830s he discovered that a moving magnetic field (or a moving conductor that cuts the magnetic field lines) will generate electric currents on a nearby conductor. Faraday suggested a unique theory to understand electrical and magnetic phenomena. His theory had several distinct features, one of which was that electric and magnetic actions occurred along the curved line of actions. He later called these curves "the lines of electric and magnetic force" and gradually believed that these lines exist as a physical reality in the medium. His idea of the lines of force was taken up by two eminent British physicists, William Thomson and James Clerk Maxwell, and was developed in mathematical terms into the field theory.

In particular, Maxwell's field theory predicted the existence of electromagnetic waves that propagate in the medium at the velocity of light. In other words, light became a special form of electromagnetic waves. Around 1888, German physicist, Heinrich Hertz, first succeeded in generating and detecting the electromagnetic waves that Maxwell had predicted. The Italian physicist Guglielmo Marconi soon transformed Hertz's laboratory experiment into commercial wireless telegraphy, which opened a new era of radio communication and eventually radio and television broadcasting in the twentieth century.

THE NEW PHYSICS

At the end of the nineteenth century, physicists began to feel that classical electromagnetism and thermodynamics did not fully or satisfactorily explain questions related to the microscopic world, such as blackbody radiation, the evasive ether, and the atomic structure. During the early twentieth century, new theories, such as Albert Einstein's special theory of relativity and quantum mechanics, began to replace the old physics. With this substitution, people gradually realized that there is a mysterious source of enormous energy inside the atom. Some scientists and writers dreamed about using this power for military or industrial purposes. Later, this dream came true with the discovery of atomic fission and chain reaction. The atomic bomb was the ultimate result of the power residing inside the atom.

See also **Chemistry; Einstein, Albert; Helmholtz, Hermann von; Hertz, Heinrich; Marconi, Guglielmo; Maxwell, James Clerk.**

BIBLIOGRAPHY

Buchwald, Jed Z., and Sungook Hong. "Physics." In *From Natural Philosophy to the Sciences: Writing the History of Nineteenth-Century Science,* edited by David Cahan, 163–195. Chicago, 2003.

Harman, P. M. *Energy, Force, and Matter: The Conceptual Development of Nineteenth-Century Physics.* Cambridge, U.K., 1982.

Purrington, Robert D. *Physics in the Nineteenth Century.* New Brunswick, N.J., 1997.

Warwick, Andrew. *Masters of Theory: Cambridge and the Rise of Mathematical Physics.* Chicago, 2003.

SUNGOOK HONG

PICASSO, PABLO (1881–1973), Spanish avant-garde painter.

Pablo Picasso is an undisputed giant of twentieth-century art. His formation as an avant-garde artist owed much to the fin-de-siècle artistic and literary culture of Barcelona and Paris. From the turn of the century through until 1914, his work evolved in response to far-reaching questions about the nature of art that were posed within that milieu. This development culminated in the invention of cubism, a towering intellectual and artistic achievement that irrevocably altered the course of European art by shattering the spatial field and reassembling its component parts from different angles.

EDUCATION AND EARLY CAREER

Pablo Ruiz y Picasso was born on 25 October 1881. His mother, María Picasso López, was of Italian descent; his father, José Ruiz Blasco, who came from a family of Córdoban landowners, was a painter and art teacher by profession. The adoption of his mother's family name (Picasso) has been seen as a portent of the later rejection of the academic heritage of his father. The family moved around a lot in his childhood: from Málaga, where Picasso was born, to Coruña in the far northwest of Spain, eventually settling in Barcelona. Among his earliest paintings and drawings are some charmingly observed images of doves and the bullfight, subjects that recur throughout his life, revealing the extent to which his outlook was imbued by his Spanish upbringing. The works from his youth that are housed at the Museu Picasso in Barcelona attest to a solid grounding in the technical craft of painting. In 1895 Picasso was admitted to the School of Fine Arts in Barcelona. A further stint at the San Fernando Academy in Madrid between October 1897 and June 1898 brought to an end this period of academic training as he gravitated toward *modernisme,* a local variant of the art nouveau and Jugendstil styles current in other European capitals that flourished in cosmopolitan Barcelona.

It is customary to periodize Picasso's work after this point on stylistic grounds. The Blue Period (1901–1904) ensued from his close association from 1900 with a circle of symbolist and decadent artists and writers who met at the café known as *Els Quatre Gats.* Picasso honed his skill as a caricaturist at this time in portraits of his friends, including a superb spoof of Jaime Sabartès (who in later life was Picasso's secretary) as a decadent poet. Henri de Toulouse-Lautrec's (1864–1901) acerbic depictions of Parisian nightlife were a source of inspiration. Isidro Nonell y Monturiol (1873–1911), a Catalan artist who specialized in portrayals of the poor, was another influence on Picasso during the Blue Period. The extent to which the beggars and other outcasts that populate the Blue Period pictures reflect the anarchist political views of his acquaintances is debatable. The pathetic blind figure in *The Old Guitarist* (1903), whose angular emaciated limbs recall the paintings of El Greco (Doménikos Theotokópoulos; 1541–1614), can be read as a cipher for the modern artist. The suicide in 1901 of the poet Carles Casagemas (who had accompanied Picasso on his first trip to Paris the year before) following an unhappy love affair provided raw material for a fin-de-siècle musing on death and sexuality. The picture known as *La vie* of 1903, which sums up and concludes the Blue Period, took this incident as its starting point, though in its final state both the setting and the allegorical meaning of the composition are rendered enigmatic.

PARIS

In 1904 Picasso made the inevitable move to Paris in pursuit of his artistic career. There he took up residence at Montmartre in the Bateau-Lavoir, a suitably ramshackle abode for a bohemian artist. He began an affair with Fernande Olivier, who was living at the Bateau-Lavoir and was an aspiring painter when he moved in. Her memoir, *Souvenirs intimes* (1988; written in the 1950s), reveals that he introduced her to smoking opium and stifled her artistic career. Also in 1904 Picasso met the poets André Salmon and Guillaume Apollinaire (1880–1918). The latter was a brilliantly erudite writer who became an indispensable ally and muse to Picasso until his untimely death from influenza in 1918. It was Apollinaire who instigated the cult of genius that surrounded Picasso. Reportedly, Picasso and Fernande would go as often as three or four times a week to the Cirque Médrano, where they sought out the company of circus entertainers. The clowns, jugglers, and acrobats became Picasso's new subjects. The *Family of Saltimbanques* of 1905, which epitomizes the wistful elegance of the short-lived Rose Period (1905–1906), draws together this retinue of characters in the largest composition he had yet painted. Under cover of a group of itinerant fairground performers, Picasso represents himself as harlequin (a self-identification that is found in other works of this period) along with other members of his troupe, including Apollinaire as a rotund jester.

In 1906 the already formidable variety of his sources expanded to include non-European art, the passion for which he shared with Apollinaire and Salmon, who were collectors of African and Oceanic objects. Recently excavated Iberian artifacts that had gone on display in the Louvre were a source for the mask-like stylization in the *Portrait of Gertrude Stein* (1906). Picasso met Stein (1874–1946) in 1905, and she soon became a trusted confidant as well as an important patron. With his interest in the primitive already primed, in early 1907 Picasso underwent an epiphany in the presence of African masks and statues in the Museum of Mankind in Paris. The experience occurred while he was midway through painting *Les demoiselles d'Avignon* (1907) and led him to repaint the faces of three of the figures as scarified masks. Picasso later described this radical and confrontational work, which even the French painter Georges Braque (1882–1963) found disturbing, as his first exorcism picture. The fact that he recognized an almost sacral power in African masks suggests that his interest was not only formal; indeed attempts have been made to correlate his valorization of the primitive with denunciations of European colonialism emanating from anarchist political circles. Added to the array of primitive influences on Picasso at this moment is his admiration for Henri Rousseau (known as Le Douanier; 1844–1910), a self-taught painter of imaginary jungle scenes inspired by weekend visits to the Jardin des Plantes, for whom Picasso held a legendary banquet at the Bateau-Lavoir in 1908.

Les demoiselles d'Avignon was a hugely ambitious work that was preceded by many hundreds of studies. It is replete with references to European art but exhibits a markedly iconoclastic attitude toward that tradition, bearing out Picasso's later claim that "Art is a sum of destructions." One of the main points of reference is Paul Cézanne (1839–1906), who had come to be seen as the most important recent painter. The late bather compositions of Cézanne only became known after his death in 1906, an event that also prompted a major reassessment of his legacy. The lack of a unitary viewpoint in Cézanne is pushed to such an extreme by Picasso that the picture looks disjointed. At the same time there is an odd congealment of interstitial space, which stems from El Greco as well as Cézanne. It is small wonder that contemporaries found the picture incomprehensible. The title of the work evidently refers to a well-known red light district in Barcelona. Shifting the Cézanne bathers indoors, so to speak, compounds the formal violations with a transgressive eroticism. Picasso, who was no stranger to such locales, apparently feared that he may have contracted syphilis from a prostitute. The still horrifying disfigurement of the women in the *Demoiselles* can perhaps be associated with the ravages of a disease that was

Les demoiselles d'Avignon. Painting by Pablo Picasso, 1907. AP/WIDE WORLD PHOTOS © 2006 ESTATE OF PABLO PICASSO/ ARTISTS RIGHTS SOCIETY (ARS), NEW YORK

then untreatable. Remarkably, the picture by Picasso that many now regard as the most important of the twentieth century lay rolled up in his studio for almost two decades after it was painted.

CUBISM

Les demoiselles d'Avignon was not yet a cubist picture though it points firmly in the direction of cubism. The ensuing couple of years were required in order to absorb its lessons. After 1908, Picasso tended to work on a smaller easel-scale, which permits a more serial and experimental mode of production. The overt eroticism and primitivism of 1907–1908 also receded. The works display a gradual subtraction of color and a growing emphasis on the analysis of form into simple geometric planes, which are heavily modeled but which articulate with each other in an ambiguous, reversible way. It has been suggested that Gertrude Stein who had studied psychology at Harvard may have introduced Picasso to William James's *Principles of Psychology* (1890), which illustrates various kinds of visual illusion. The deliberate incorporation of such ambiguities produces a flickering effect as the eye scans the image. It also becomes more difficult to identify objects, as the distinction between figure and ground is eroded in favor of a more homogeneous integrated surface. These trends are demonstrated in a series of nudes and landscapes painted in the summer of 1909, when Picasso and Fernande were on holiday in the isolated Spanish village of Horta de Ebro. Snapshots taken at the time show how far the paintings' cubic structure was inspired by the buildings themselves. Stein noted astutely that: "Cubism is part of the daily life in Spain, it is in Spanish architecture." There is a constant interplay between painting and sculpture in Picasso's work. On his return to Paris, Picasso made a bronze bust of Fernande, which transfers these cubist forms back into three dimensions.

Picasso was engaged in a close artistic dialogue with Braque by this stage, and although their relative contributions to the invention of cubism are hotly disputed by scholars, with the increasing convergence between them it can be difficult to tell the work of one from the other. Daniel-Henry Kahnweiler was the dealer for both artists up until the First World War. He signed exclusive contracts, agreeing to buy all their work, and in return discouraged them from exhibiting in the public salons. These business practices may have contributed to cubism's hermetic character; they certainly meant that the work of Picasso and Braque was largely invisible in the public arena. Picasso's *Portrait of Kahnweiler* (1910) is one of the masterpieces of high analytic cubism. A shorthand system of signs disposed on the main cubist scaffold is enough to indicate the main features of the sitter—Picasso's caricaturist eye for the telling detail is exploited here to the full. An overall crystalline transparency permeates the figure. The silvery, nocturnal lighting has a strongly lyrical quality. It is a common misconception that cubism offers a more objective or complete view of the world by surveying objects from several different angles. Picasso cautioned that the reality of cubist painting is elusive and impalpable, like a perfume (the choice of analogy was one favored by symbolist poets).

With the invention of collage, the character of cubism changed dramatically. Collage looks cheap and shabby by comparison with the extreme refinement of high analytic cubism. Collage made possible the incorporation of preformed elements of reality into the pictorial field. The frame of reference widened to include popular culture and even the world of consumerism and advertising—all that the modernist critic Clement Greenberg would later denounce as *kitsch*. The combination of word and image in cubist collage often depends on a punning relation between the various elements—not infrequently in the case of Picasso with a sexual innuendo—that seems to emulate the way adver-

tisements work. In 1912 Picasso made a sequence of *papiers collés* using newspaper cuttings that make insistent reference to war in the Balkan region as well as to antiwar protests. Here again the world of politics is like a base intrusion into a very spare pictorial field. The inclusion of mechanically reproduced imagery of various sorts relativizes the unique painterly gesture and prefigures, in this respect, the ready-mades of Marcel Duchamp (1887–1968), which sounded a death knell to painting. Unlike that other main claimant to the title of greatest twentieth-century artist, however, Picasso—despite the extreme iconoclasm of his work in this period—never abandoned his attachment to the craft of painting.

Picasso recalled waving farewell to Braque and the French painter André Derain (1880–1954) on the platform at Avignon at the outbreak of war. Their separation brought to a close one of the most extraordinarily inventive moments in Western art. By the age of thirty-three Picasso had produced some of the most astonishing paintings in the Western tradition; he had also dismantled that same tradition.

See also **Anarchism; Avant-Garde; Cézanne, Paul; Cubism; Modernism; Painting; Primitivism; Toulouse-Lautrec, Henri de.**

BIBLIOGRAPHY

Brown, Jonathan, ed. *Picasso and the Spanish Tradition.* New Haven, Conn., 1996.

Golding, John. *Cubism: A History and an Analysis, 1907–1914.* London, 1959.

Green, Christopher, ed. *Picasso's Les Demoiselles d'Avignon.* Cambridge, U.K., 2001.

McCully, Marilyn, ed. *Picasso—The Early Years, 1892–1906.* Exhibition catalog. Washington, D.C., 1997.

Richardson, John. *A Life of Picasso.* 2 vols. New York, 1991, 1996.

Rubin, William. *Picasso and Braque: Pioneering Cubism.* Exhibition catalog. New York, 1989.

DAVID LOMAS

PIEDMONT-SAVOY. The lands of Piedmont-Savoy formed an important European regional power in the late eighteenth and early nineteenth centuries. There is an irony surrounding

Piedmontese history in this period, however. The Savoyard realm was impossible to describe in terms of the modern nation-state, yet it played the pivotal role in the unification of Italy by the 1850s. It did not correspond to the modern prototype of a nation, yet was at the heart of a great nationalist movement from 1849 onward. By the 1850s, Piedmont was the most modernized, powerful state in Italy, and the motor of Italian unification.

THE NATURE OF THE SAVOYARD DOMAINS

Ruled over by the House of Savoy, one of the oldest and continuous ruling dynasties in Europe, this relatively small state in northwestern Italy was an ally much sought after by France and the Habsburgs. To remain useful, as much as to defend itself, the Savoyard state developed a small but formidable army in the eighteenth century, supported by a professional, highly trained bureaucracy and an efficient taxation system. It also had a distinguished, if largely technocratic university in its capital, Turin, and insisted that all its senior magistrates and civil servants have relevant degrees from it. Its public institutions, armed forces, and the dynasty itself were the chief binding elements in a state best described as territorially "composite" and politically "patrimonial," as its only real source of cohesion was the House of Savoy.

The core of the Savoyard lands was a collection of contiguous territories in northwestern Italy, east of the Alps and north of the Mediterranean Apennines, known for convenience as "the Principality of Savoy," although no such entity legally existed. It was a collection of former provinces and tiny city-states welded together by the House of Savoy since the sixteenth century with a population of roughly one million, most of whom spoke an Italian dialect that also had a developed literary form; the upper classes were bilingual in French and Tuscan Italian. Its capital, Turin, chosen because of its central position, was an artificial creation of the seventeenth century with a population of about ninety thousand. These territories provided the real heartland of the realm; its inhabitants—of all classes—were bound by loyalty to the dynasty and were governed by a uniform, centralized administration at the provincial, if not at the local, level.

However, the dynasty drew its name from its traditional heartland, the French-speaking Duchy of Savoy, which was separated from the core of the realm by the Alps. It was easily lost to France in 1790, and was regained in 1814 only to be lost again on the unification of Italy in 1860. The same diplomatic fate befell its other "French possession," the county of Nice, on the Mediterranean. Finally, the dynasty took its favored title, "Kings of Sardinia," from its possession of the island, acquired in 1720. Just as the "Kings of Prussia" had to draw their royal title from a peripheral territory outside the Holy Roman Empire—where no ruling house could claim kingship—so the Savoyards did the same. The poor, remote island was of little interest or value to them, save between 1801 and 1814, when the Court took refuge there, during the Napoleonic occupation. Ironically, this composite, heterogeneous character was actually accentuated after 1814, when the Congress of Vienna awarded the Savoyards the former Ligurian Republic, centered on Genoa. So opposed were the Genoese to this annexation, that they declared they would rather become part of France than be ruled from Turin. Relations between Liguria and the core of the realm were never easy in the early nineteenth century, so different were the political cultures of the absolute monarchy in Turin and the former merchant republic.

THE SAVOYARD STATE, 1773–1801

Thus, the realm of the House of Savoy continued to be seen as a viable state in its own right by the Great Powers, well into the nineteenth century. However, the strategic position of its core territories, guarding the Alpine passes between France and northern Italy, also made it prey to threats of annexation—and total oblivion as a state—for the same reasons that made it a valuable ally, and led the Congress of Vienna to reenforce it as a barrier to French expansion. It all but disappeared in the period 1801–1814, when Napoleon annexed its mainland areas directly to France, but reemerged in 1814 strengthened by the acquisition of the Ligurian Republic, which gave it the major port of Genoa and a large outlet to the sea for the first time. Even so, during the Congress, Savoyard diplomats had to use all their skills to save the state from Austrian plans to annex the state to its Italian possessions in Lombardy. This tense, conflicting relationship to the Great Powers dominates Piedmontese history in the period 1773–1861.

When Victor Amadeus II (Duke of Savoy as Victor Amadeus III, r. 1773–1796; king of Sardinia as Victor Amadeus II, r. 1773–1796) ascended the throne in 1773, he inherited a territorially stable state, on good terms with both major powers in the region, France and the Habsburg Monarchy. However, the last decades saw Piedmont racked by social and economic crises, stemming from population growth in poor, upland areas and the rack-renting, land hunger, and inflation this produced. This crisis was aggravated further by the decimation of the population of the eastern lowlands through the spread of rice cultivation, bringing with it disease and poverty, as independent farmers were transformed into laborers, or were displaced. The subsequent growth of banditry—always prevalent along the southern border—and general dislocation strained the powers of the absolutist state by his death in 1796.

The monarchy finally collapsed under the onslaught of Napoleon's first Italian campaign of 1796. With his army defeated, the new king, Charles Emmanuel II (Duke of Savoy as Charles Emmanuel IV, r. 1796–1798; king of Sardinia as Charles Emmanuel II, r. 1796–1802), fled to Sardinia in 1797, leaving the country under virtual French control. Napoleon established a short-lived provisional government under pro-French liberals, which had little popular support and was easily swept away in 1799, when the Austro-Russian armies briefly drove out the French. Napoleon's second Italian campaign of 1800 saw these "patriots" reestablished in power, but their weak position in so strategically vital an area led to Piedmont's incorporation into France, as five departments, in 1802. In exile in Sardinia, Charles Emmanuel II abdicated in favor of his nephew, Victor Emmanuel I (Duke of Aosta, Duke of Savoy, and king of Sardinia, r. 1802–1821).

THE FRENCH OCCUPATION, 1801–1814

The Piedmontese heartland was one of the non-French parts of Europe longest under Napoleonic rule; as such, Piedmontese society absorbed many key aspects of Napoleonic rule, and was transformed by the occupation. The French restored law and order, extirpating the large brigand bands by 1807, through the introduction of the Gendarmerie, a paramilitary police force, into the countryside. Taxation on the French model and the Napoleonic Code were also well established by the fall of the empire in 1814. Many aspects of French rule were hated, particularly conscription and the religious reforms of the Concordat, but a generation of Piedmontese were trained in French judicial and administrative norms, even if many, like the future prime minister, Cesare Balbo (1789–1853), detested the loss of independence.

THE RESTORATION, 1814–1849

Victor Emmanuel I returned from exile in Sardinia in 1814, restored by the allied powers who had defeated Napoleon, his realms swollen by the acquisition of Liguria and internally pacified by the French. He retained the Gendarmerie, changing its name to the *Carabiniere Reale,* and their taxation system, but nothing else. The period 1814–1821 was a disastrous attempt to reverse history, and culminated in a small revolt within the army in 1821, closely linked to similar risings in Naples and Spain. Victor Emmanuel I abdicated in favor of his uncle, Charles Felix (king of Sardinia-Piedmont, r. 1821–1831), who imposed a reactionary regime backed by Austria until his death in 1831. However, under his cousin, Charles Albert IV (king of Sardinia-Piedmont, r. 1831–1849), the essence of the Napoleonic Code and legal system was restored and the administration modernized. Politically and culturally, the regime remained repressive, but early in 1848 Charles Albert IV was forced to grant a limited constitution under pressure from liberals at home, especially in Genoa, and from the rising tide of revolution in France and Naples. This won him the backing he needed to invade Lombardy, ostensibly in the cause of Italian unification, but really reviving traditional Savoyard designs on expansion into Austrian-ruled Lombardy. He was defeated at the battle of Novara in March 1849, then abdicated in favor of his son, Victor Emmanuel II (king of Sardinia-Piedmont, r. 1849–1861).

The combination of constitutional government, a new king, and the defeat of the 1848 Italian revolutions ushered in a new era. Elections empowered the upper bourgeoisie, bringing to power progressives led by Count Cavour (Camillo Benso, 1810–1861) and Massimo Taparelli,

Marchese d'Azeglio (1798–1866), who initiated liberal economic policies that led to the growth of trade, railways, and industry. Defeated, dissident nationalists from elsewhere in Italy were sheltered in Turin, and transformed its political and intellectual life during the "miraculous decade" of the 1850s; Piedmontese participation in the Crimean War (1853–1856) won Cavour the friendship of Britain and France, which he needed to challenge Austria. Thus transformed, Piedmont-Savoy became the natural focus for the eventual unification of Italy in 1859–1861. The House of Savoy became Italy's dynasty, and Piedmontese political, legal, and administrative institutions were the templates for the new unitary state.

See also **Cavour, Count (Camillo Benso); Charles Albert; Italy; Risorgimento (Italian Unification); Roman Question; Victor Emmanuel II.**

BIBLIOGRAPHY

Primary Sources

D'Azeglio, Massimo, *Things I Remember*. Translated by E. R. Vincent. Oxford, U.K., 1966. Translation of *I miei ricordi*. 1866. The memoirs of one of the leading Piedmontese statesmen of the Restoration period.

Secondary Sources

Broers, Michael. *Napoleonic Imperialism and the Savoyard Monarchy, 1773–1821: State Building in Piedmont.* Lewiston N.Y., 1997.

———. "The Restoration in Piedmont-Sardinia, 1814–1848: Variations on Reaction." In *Napoleon's Legacy: Problems of Government in Restoration Europe,* edited by David Laven and Lucy Riall, 151–164. New York, 2000.

Hearder, Harry. *Italy in the Age of the Risorgimento, 1790–1870.* London, 1983. An older, but wide-ranging introduction, with good sections specifically on Piedmont.

Mack Smith, Denis. *Cavour.* New York, 1985. A highly critical, comprehensive life of the dominant figure in Piedmont post-1849.

MICHAEL BROERS

PILGRIMAGES. Since late antiquity Christians have made pilgrimages, journeys to sacred sites that were generally under the protection of a particular Catholic saint. Pilgrimages always have devotional significance, insofar as they affirm a bond between the pilgrim and the patron of the shrine. But devotion to saints and their shrines generally is coupled with some more practical agenda. Families and individuals sought cures, with some shrines and saints specializing in particular ailments. In exchange for a healing pilgrims made bargains with the saints, to come to their shrine annually on a pilgrimage, to leave an ex-voto (an offering of thanks), which might be money, a small replica of the body part that had been afflicted, crutches no longer needed, or a depiction of the miracle to display the power and kindness of the saint toward his or her devotees. Catholics in rural areas celebrated the Rogation days in the spring, a three-day period when pilgrims would visit shrines that marked the boundaries of the village. If bad weather threatened the crops, or disease struck, villagers and city-dwellers could make vows to visit a particular shrine each year, if the saint would help them. From the perspective of believers, pilgrimages were a way of appealing to the saints for protection in a time of need and thanking them for past favors. For historians, such practices are an important aspect of popular culture, insofar as shrines served as symbols of local identity and instruments for creating a sense of solidarity.

PILGRIMAGES AND POLITICS

While pilgrimages draw on a traditional reservoir of belief and practice, they also have changed over the centuries, reshaped to express the problems of a particular age. In the nineteenth century the official Church made a serious effort to be more accommodating toward pilgrimages and shrines. In encouraging such devotions the clergy were responding to rationalist attacks on belief in the supernatural and political efforts to control or eliminate Catholicism. The loyalty of lay Catholics to shrines that offered them health and healing provided a basis for the clergy to link such traditional concerns with contemporary political questions. The relationship between pilgrimages and politics emerged clearly during the French Revolution, when many shrines became sites of political resistance against a regime that perceived pilgrims as superstitious political reactionaries. In France, statues of Mary wept and bled in 1793 when pilgrimages were banned. In Italy, devotion to the numerous Marian shrines in northern Italy played an important role in the uprising of 1799 directed against the French occupiers. The popular appeal of pilgrimages during the revolutionary era helps explain why they became such an important element in the Catholic revival of the middle of the nineteenth century.

The pilgrimage to the Holy Shroud at Trier illustrates some of the characteristics of nineteenth-century pilgrimages. The shroud, reputed to be the garment in which Christ was buried, was not displayed between 1655 and 1810, when it was exposed with the approval of Napoleon to demonstrate that French administrators of this former episcopal state supported the revival of the Catholic Church. It was the pilgrimage orchestrated by Bishop Arnoldi in 1844, however, that drew the attention of the press in Germany and throughout Catholic Europe. During a fifty-day period as many as one million pilgrims came to Trier, a town of about 25,000, to venerate the relic, to ask for cures, and to express their loyalty to the church. Contemporary observers, both supporters and critics, were impressed with the careful organizational work conducted by the clergy. Coming just a few years after a major conflict over mixed marriages between Catholics and Protestants in the Prussian Rhineland had led to the imprisonment of the bishop of Cologne in 1837, the pilgrimage to Trier in 1844 demonstrated the vitality of Catholic belief and the ability of the clergy to mobilize the Catholic minority in Prussia. The shroud was exposed once again during the nineteenth century, in 1891, to celebrate the conclusion of the Kulturkampf, the battle between the German state and the Catholic Church that followed German unification in 1870.

MARIAN APPARITIONS AND SHRINES

The pilgrimage to Trier exemplifies the more sympathetic attitude toward pilgrimages adopted by the Catholic clergy in the nineteenth century, and the interest the church had in organizing such manifestations of popular piety. Even more typical of the nineteenth century were shrines established on the basis of Marian apparitions. Hundreds of such apparitions occurred, and while most faded in significance, several generated major pilgrimage shrines that were a distinctive element in nineteenth-century Catholicism. Apparitions occurred in Paris in 1830, when a medal was revealed to a Sister of Charity, Catherine Labouré, which became immensely popular during the cholera epidemic of 1832. In 1846 Mary appeared to two shepherd children, Mélanie Calvat and Maximin Giraud, at LaSalette in the French Alps in 1846, where she warned of a famine if the people did not attend Sunday mass and abstain from eating meat on Friday. Such messages combining threats and promises became a common element in subsequent apparitions, which have continued in the twentieth century, playing a central role in the devotion to Our Lady of Fatima in Portugal, established in 1917, and at the shrine of Medjugorje in Bosnia-Herzegovina, which has drawn a steady stream of pilgrims since 1981. Throughout the past two centuries Mary has generally appeared in rural settings, and addressed herself to children, mostly girls, and the poor. Her apparitions thus reinforced Catholic anxieties about the dangers of modern urban life, and appealed to the powerless, many of whom were drawn to her cult as a source of hope and consolation.

The single most famous shrine to emerge during the nineteenth century was based on a series of Marian apparitions in 1858 to Bernadette Soubirous, a fourteen-year-old girl from an impoverished family in the town of Lourdes in southern France. Mary appeared at a grotto just outside of Lourdes, continuing a tradition in which shrines are frequently situated at the periphery of a Catholic parish. In the course of the apparitions Mary revealed a spring, another feature common to older shrines, which produced water that soon gained a reputation for its miraculous properties. Within days of the original apparition thousands of pilgrims were gathering at the grotto to observe Bernadette, who fell into a trance-like state when Mary appeared to her, while remaining invisible to the crowd. Mary's declaration to Bernadette that "I am the Immaculate Conception" helped generate clerical support for the apparition, for the doctrine of the Immaculate Conception (which holds that Mary was conceived without Original Sin, a unique privilege distinguishing her from all other human beings) had been declared by Pope Pius IX in 1854. The apparition and the miraculous cures at the shrine thus seemed to provide supernatural support for the pope and the new doctrine. The shrine developed quickly after the bishop

The Grotto at Lourdes. Nineteenth-century illlustration by A. Deroy. The cave outside Lourdes, in southern France, where the Virgin Mary was thought to have appeared to a young girl, later St. Bernadette, became the most popular shrine in Europe in the nineteenth century. ©ARCHIVO ICONOGRAFICO, S.A./CORBIS

approved it in 1862. Pilgrimages were encouraged by the construction of a railroad link in 1866, the construction of an enormous basilica over the grotto in the 1870s, and the establishment of a Medical Bureau in 1883 to investigate the widely reported miraculous cures. Lourdes, along with other shrines throughout France, witnessed an enormous revival in the early 1870s, when pilgrimages provided a source of solidarity and hope after the defeat in the Franco-Prussian war. In 1908 over 400,000 pilgrims came on organized trips to celebrate the fiftieth anniversary of the apparitions, with tens of thousands more coming on their own. Catholic writers and journalists made Lourdes a central element in their defense of Catholicism, seeing in the miraculous cures proof for the truths preached by the Catholic Church and the power of its saints. Lourdes remains a major attrac-

tion for Catholics in the early twenty-first century, drawing over four million visitors a year.

The enormous publicity given to Lourdes helps explain subsequent apparitions, some of which also became major religious and political events. When Mary appeared to three young girls in Marpingen, Prussia, in 1876 the pilgrimage that resulted combined devotional fervor and a quest for miracles with a sense of frustration over an economic depression and the political persecution of the Catholic clergy during the the Kulturkampf of the 1870s. Although the church ultimately did not approve the apparitions at Marpingen, the popularity of the pilgrimage in the late 1870s confirms the close ties that could be forged between devotion to Mary and political support for the Catholic Church. Mary appeared at Knock in 1879 in County Mayo,

Ireland, to between fifteen and twenty villagers, in the midst of an agricultural crisis in which many tenants were being evicted from their land. Mary delivered no message at Knock, but some of the most forthright defenders of the apparitions in the press were also proponents of the Land League, seeking to defend the rights of the displaced. The Knock apparitions were eventually approved, and the site remains a major pilgrimage destination in the early twenty-first century.

The development of Marian shrines in the nineteenth century included not just new sites, such as Lourdes and Knock, but the renewal of interest in older ones, such as Our Lady of Czestochowa. Following the partition of Poland in the late eighteenth century this shrine in the Russian zone became a symbol of national identity. The shrine image, a Byzantine icon of the Virgin and Child, had drawn pilgrims since the fourteenth century and was associated with a miraculous victory over an invading Swedish army in 1655. As we have seen, Marian pilgrimages were associated with counter-revolutionary movements in France and Italy during the late eighteenth century, but in 1863 some of the Polish rebels in a failed insurrection against the Russian occupiers carried banners that bore the image of Our Lady of Czestochowa.

Catholic pilgrims in the nineteenth century continued to visit shrines when their health and security were threatened. But the traditional prayers and rituals were now regarded more favorably by many of the clergy, who sought to infuse pilgrimages with messages about the political, social, and doctrinal issues faced by Catholicism in the nineteenth century. The revival of pilgrimages in the nineteenth century is most clearly evident at Lourdes, where Marian apparitions became the basis for a shrine that offered healings, promoted the doctrine of the Immaculate Conception, and demonstrated the ability of Catholicism to mobilize a mass audience.

See also **Catholicism; Pius IX; Popular and Elite Culture; Secularization; Tourism.**

BIBLIOGRAPHY

Blackbourn, David. *Marpingen: Apparitions of the Virgin Mary in a Nineteenth-Century German Village.* New York, 1995. A model study with an excellent introductory chapter on apparitions in Europe throughout the nineteenth century.

Carroll, Michael P. *Madonnas That Maim: Popular Catholicism in Italy since the Fifteenth Century.* Baltimore, 1992. Proposes a Freudian analysis that is dubious, but summarizes a great deal of Italian scholarship.

Donnelly, James S. "The Marian Shrine of Knock: The First Decade." *Eire-Ireland* 28 (summer 1993): 54–99.

Harris, Ruth. *Lourdes: Body and Spirit in the Secular Age.* New York, 1999. The single best book on Lourdes.

Kselman, Thomas. *Miracles and Prophecies in Nineteenth-Century France.* New Brunswick, N.J., 1983.

Nolan, Mary Lee, and Nolan, Sidney. *Christian Pilgrimage in Modern Western Europe.* Chapel Hill, N.C., 1989. Includes much data on developments over the centuries.

THOMAS KSELMAN

PINEL, PHILIPPE (1745–1826), French physician.

Philippe Pinel was born on 20 April 1745 in a farmhouse at Roques in southwestern France and died as physician-in-chief of Salpêtrière Hospice in Paris on 25 October 1826. His life thus spans a brilliant, but turbulent, era in French history, from the late Enlightenment to the Revolution and Napoleonic Empire, ending in the Romantic era. He belonged to a group of outstanding French physicians who formed the "Paris School": the clinician Jean-Nicolas Corvisart des Marets, the investigator Marie-François-Xavier Bichat, the surgeon Jacques Tenon, the administrator Michel-Augustin Thouret, the philosopher Pierre-Jean-Georges Cabanis, and the chemist and minister of the interior Jean-Antoine Chaptal. Pinel's achievement was the reform of the diagnosis and treatment of what he called "mental alienation." That he freed his women patients from their shackles—the feat for which he is universally famous—was an incidental detail of his humane attitude toward the mentally ill.

Born into a modest family of country doctors, Pinel owed his mastery of Latin and his love of learning to the village teacher and a fine humanistic education as scholarship student to a Catholic teaching order, the Brothers of the Christian Doctrine.

He earned the M.D. degree in 1773 from the University of Toulouse. Judging this education mediocre, he moved to Montpellier where he spent four years reading, attending hospital rounds, and even presenting three papers on mathematics to the Montpellier Royal Academy of Sciences.

In 1778 he left for Paris where, for fifteen years, he eked out a living as translator, editor, and amateur researcher and author. The Revolution finally opened a career path commensurate with his talents. He was appointed as "physician of the infirmaries" at Bicêtre Hospice in 1793, then physician-in-chief of Salpêtrière Hospice in 1795. These two hospices were part of the so-called General Hospital created by King Louis XIV in the mid-seventeenth century to confine not only beggars, vagrants, and prisoners but also the destitute, ailing, and aged "deserving poor," including the mentally ill. Pinel lived and worked at the Salpêtrière for thirty-one years. Some four thousand women were confined there in his day, with about six hundred hospitalized at any one time, in the infirmary or on special mental wards. Pinel combined supervision of their care with teaching: he occupied the chair of internal medicine at the École de santé (the Paris Health School) starting in 1795, and he considered the training of young doctors essential. Another important step in his career was his election to the Academy of Sciences in 1803. But his fame derived from his writings and his teaching.

Pinel is usually credited with three books, the *Philosophic Nosography* (first published in 1798), the *Medico-Philosophical Treatise on Mental Alienation* (first published in 1800), and *Clinical Medicine* (first published in 1802). But he wrote much more, in particular long articles on key psychiatric concepts, published in the *Dictionnaire des sciences médicales* (Dictionary of the medical sciences). The book that brought him worldwide fame was the *Treatise*, unfortunately available in English only in one wretched translation.

At the Salpêtrière, Pinel created a clinical teaching service that the students prized. "With Corvisart we learned quickly," commented one of them, "with Pinel we really understood." Pinel focused on observation and diagnosis; on taking a careful patient history, knowing the natural history of the disease so as to arrive at a correct diagnosis and thus to make the right prognosis and establish the

appropriate therapeutic regimen. He maintained the traditional categories of mania, melancholia, dementia, and idiocy, but he focused on mania—particularly on what he called "periodic mania." Commentators as diverse as the psychiatrist Gladys Swain (1945–1993) and the philosopher Georg Wilhelm Friedrich Hegel (1770–1831) admired his emphasis on the intervals of sanity that permitted a therapist access to the healthy person who was only intermittently deranged.

Between 1802 and 1805 Pinel conducted what he called an "experiment," namely the careful study of every patient admitted. He wanted to establish all possible criteria for curability. He developed a detailed plan for housing, observing, guiding, and occupying convalescents, calling this "moral treatment." This notion has been widely debated and generally misunderstood. Pinel never defined it clearly, nor did he sufficiently explore the continuing role of the therapist. But the main cause of misunderstanding is that the French *moral* does not translate into the English "moral" with its judgmental overtones. *Traitement moral* contrasts with *traitement physique,* meaning bodily and medical—rather than psychological—therapies. Owing largely to Pinel's belief in the curability of mental illness, the numbers of mental patients seeking admission to the asylum grew tenfold in all Western countries in the nineteenth century. Thus Pinel wrestled with a severe future problem. Unfortunately he did not train enough successors: that task fell to his star pupil Jean-Étienne-Dominique Esquirol. Nor did Pinel, or anyone else in early-nineteenth-century Europe or America, train professional nurses to replace the religious sisters. As a result, the asylum remained woefully understaffed.

Pinel's main achievement was to bring the condition of the mentally ill into prominence and thus attract the attention of the medical profession to the study and cure of what he called "mental alienation." He thus founded a new medical specialty, psychiatry. Critics charge that he was but a symbol and that the French Revolution created a call for patient rights and equal treatment that any reformer could have used. Such an assessment discounts Pinel's personal qualities: as clinical teacher, as author of books and of magisterial articles that helped define the vocabulary of the new psychiatric medical specialty, and as director of the first large modern asylum. Pinel should be considered a major founder of psychiatry.

See also **Charcot, Jean-Martin; Nurses; Professions; Psychology.**

BIBLIOGRAPHY

Primary Sources

Pinel, Philippe. *Nosographie philosophique; ou, La méthode de l'analyse appliquée à la médecine.* 2 vols. Paris, 1798. Subsequent editions published in 3 vols. in 1802–1803, 1807, 1810, 1813, and 1818.

———. *Traité médico-philosophique sur l'aliénation mentale.* Paris, 1800. 2nd ed., 1809. English translation of 1st ed. as *A Treatise on Insanity,* translated by D. D. Davis, Sheffield, U.K., 1806. Critical version of 2nd ed., edited by Jean Garrabé and Dora B. Weiner, Paris, 2005.

———. *La médecine clinique rendue plus précise et plus exacte par l'application de l'analyse.* Paris, 1802. 2nd ed., 1804. 3rd ed., 1815.

———. *The Clinical Training of Doctors: An Essay of 1793.* Edited and translated, with an introductory essay by Dora B. Weiner. Baltimore, Md., 1980.

Weiner, Dora B. "The Apprenticeship of Philippe Pinel: A New Document, 'Observations of Citizen Pussin on the Insane.'" *American Journal of Psychiatry* 136, no. 9 (1979): 1128–1134.

———. "Philippe Pinel's 'Memoir on Madness' of December 11, 1794: A Fundamental Text of Modern Psychiatry." *American Journal of Psychiatry* 149, no. 6 (1992): 725–732.

Secondary Sources

Postel, Jacques. *Genèse de la psychiatrie: Les premiers écrits de Philippe Pinel.* Paris, 1981.

Swain, Gladys. *Le sujet de la folie: Naissance de la psychiatrie.* Toulouse, France, 1977.

Weiner, Dora B. *Comprendre et soigner: Philippe Pinel (1745–1826); La médecine de l'esprit.* Paris, 1999. English translation as *Observe and Heal: Philippe Pinel and the Birth of Psychiatry in the French Revolution.* Aldershot, U.K., forthcoming. Includes a 14-page bibliography of Pinel's writings.

DORA B. WEINER

PISSARRO, CAMILLE (1830–1903), French painter.

A key figure in both the impressionist and postimpressionist movements, Jacob-Abraham-Camille Pissarro is best known for his versatility as an artist and for his landscapes, his views of provincial towns and peasants at work, and his townscapes of Paris, Rouen, and other French cities. The only artist to participate in all eight impressionist exhibitions, he maintained relationships with artists of both movements and mentored younger artists, including Paul Cézanne (1839–1906) and Paul Gauguin (1848–1903). His political and social opinions were radical, and he openly sympathized with anarchism.

Pissarro was born on 10 July 1830 on St. Thomas in the Danish West Indies. His parents, Frédéric Pissarro and Rachel Petit, were of French Jewish origin and earned a comfortable income as merchants. Between 1842 and 1847, young Pissarro attended the Pension Savary in Passy, outside Paris. He received instruction in art and frequented the Louvre. Some contemporaries, including his friend Cézanne, and modern scholars contend that Pissarro's independence and originality as an artist stemmed in part from his lack of exposure to the Parisian art world or the Academy. Pissarro returned to St. Thomas in 1847 and worked unhappily in the family business until 1852. Meanwhile, he began sketching nearby scenes. Around 1850, he met the Danish artist Fritz Melbye (1826–1896), received more instruction, and decided to be an artist. Between 1852 and 1854, he lived in Caracas with Melbye and completed drawings, watercolors, and oils. Characteristic subjects included views of marketplaces, studies of females, landscapes, and genre scenes. After another year working in the family business, Pissarro departed for Paris in 1855 and began his artistic career.

In Paris, Pissarro continued his training and enjoyed initial success, including exhibiting eleven works at seven Salons between 1859 and 1870. He attended classes at the École des Beaux-Arts, copied paintings in the Louvre, and attended the Académie Suisse. He met Claude Monet (1840–1926), Cézanne, and other aspiring painters. Works from this period reflect the influence of the Barbizon painters, particularly Jean-Baptiste-Camille Corot (1796–1875), who advocated painting out-of-doors. Frequently on the move, Pissarro lived and worked both in Paris and a series of provincial towns, like Louveciennes and Pontoise, the latter the subject of important paintings. Landscapes, like *The Banks of Marne at Chennevières*

Avenue de l'Opéra: Sunshine, Winter Morning. Painting by Camille Pissarro, 1898. MUSÉE DES BEAUX-ARTS, REIMS, FRANCE

(1864–1865), provincial townscapes like *The Hill-sides of the Hermitage, Pontoise* (1867), and numerous views of Louveciennes illustrate how Pissarro developed an individual style. Works exhibited at the Salon won praise, particularly from novelist and critic Émile Zola (1840–1902). Pissarro joined Monet and other young artists in critiquing what they considered the stranglehold then held by the Salon on French art. Meanwhile he commenced a relationship with Julie Vellay, with whom he had eight children; the two did not marry until 1871.

After the Franco-Prussian War began in 1870, Pissarro left for London, where he joined Monet and met the art dealer Paul Durand-Ruel (1831–1922). He returned to France in 1871 and found that his house had been looted by Prussian soldiers, who had destroyed many paintings. Although he

lived mostly in Pontoise during the 1870s, he continued his practice of painting in a variety of locales, including Paris. It was there that Pissarro, in collaboration with Monet, Pierre-Auguste Renoir (1841–1919), and other painters discontent with the official salon, formed the "Société anonyme des artistes peintres, sculpteurs, graveurs, etc." and staged the first Impressionist Exhibition in 1874. He contributed five paintings, mostly of rural and provincial subjects, including *The Chestnut Trees at Osny* (1873). Pissarro helped organize the other seven impressionist exhibitions, and he exhibited in each of them, even as artists like Monet, Renoir, and Cézanne ceased to show and younger artists like Gauguin began participating. During the 1870s, Pissarro and Cézanne worked closely together and influenced each other's artistic development.

In 1884 the Pissarros moved to Eragny-sur-Epte, and his career took a new direction, one influenced by neo-impressionism and artists like Georges Seurat (1859–1891) and Paul Signac (1863–1935). He briefly experimented with pointillism. At the eighth and final Impressionist Exhibition (1886), he showed nine oils and a number of drawings and prints, including the pointillistic *View from My Window, Eragny* (1886–1888). Paintings from this decade include railway views, images of peasants at work, and depictions of provincial marketplaces.

During the 1890s, Pissarro undertook a series of urban paintings and expressed forcefully his long-held sympathy for anarchism. He subscribed to anarchist publications like Jean Grave's *La Révolte,* shared the anarchist's disdain for the state and its institutions, bourgeois society, organized religion, and exploitive capitalism, and expressed sympathy for the oppressed, the poor, and the outcast. There also is pictorial evidence, like *Apple Picking at Eragny-sur-Epte* (1889), that he valued the work of the rural peasant over that of the urban factory worker. Rarely, however, did Pissarro's political beliefs directly influence his art. An important exception is the *Turpitudes sociales* (Social turpitudes), a collection of sketches and anarchist texts he sent to his niece Esther Isaacson in about 1890. These images critiqued the greed of capitalism and depicted the oppression of workers and the poor. In 1892 a successful retrospective of Pissarro's work took place at the Durand-Ruel Gallery.

Beginning about 1892, Pissarro painted over three hundred urban scenes, especially the streets of Georges-Eugéne Haussmann's transformed Paris, the streets and harbor of Rouen, and harbor scenes of Dieppe and Le Havre. Pissarro often painted these scenes from an elevated viewpoint, perhaps because of his chronic eye disease or an aversion to urban noise and congestion. As paintings like *Avenue de l'Opéra: Sunshine, Winter Morning* (1898) or *The Boieldieu Bridge, Rouen, Damp Weather* (1896) make evident, Pissarro's treatment of urban topography and life is dispassionate and detached. Pissarro died in Paris on 13 November 1903, and he is buried with much of his family in the cemetery of Père Lachaise.

See also **Anarchism; Cézanne, Paul; Gauguin, Paul; Impressionism; Monet, Claude; Painting; Paris; Seurat, Georges.**

BIBLIOGRAPHY

Primary Sources

Bailly-Herzberg, Janine, ed. *Correspondance de Camille Pissarro.* 5 vols. 1980–1991. Available only in French.

Pissarro, Camille. *Camille Pissarro: Letters to His Son Lucien.* Edited John Rewald with Lucien Pissarro. 3rd ed., rev. and enlarged. Mamaroneck, N.Y., 1972.

Secondary Sources

Brettell, Richard R., with Joachim Pissarro. *Pissarro and Pontoise: The Painter in a Landscape.* New Haven, Conn., 1990. A pioneering scholarly study.

———. *The Impressionist and the City: Pissarro's Series Paintings.* Edited by MaryAnne Stevens. New Haven, Conn., 1992. Well-illustrated exhibition catalog.

Pissarro, Joachim. *Camille Pissarro.* New York, 1992. Beautifully illustrated account of his life and work.

Shikes, Ralph E., and Paula Harper. *Pissarro: His Life and Work.* New York, 1980. A comprehensive biography.

ROBERT W. BROWN

PIUS IX (Giovanni Maria Mastai-Ferretti; 1792–1878), pope (1846–1878).

Pius IX (in Italian, Pio Nono), the longest reigning pope, was a major protagonist in the ideological struggles of the nineteenth century. He commenced his pontificate as a prince who sought to modernize the Papal State (1846–1848), but following the revolutionary events of 1848 and the restoration of 1849–1850, he reigned as a priest determined to shield the church from the perils of the modern age. Although troubled by civil and religious controversy, he reorganized the papacy and reoriented the church, and had a profound impact in Europe and the world beyond. During his momentous pontificate, Pius IX shaped the character of the Catholic Church prior to the convocation of the Second Vatican Council (1962–1965), and the role of the papacy to the present. Forging dogmatic unity in the church and strengthening the position of the papacy, he provided some compensation for the collapse of the temporal power.

Pius IX, photographed c. 1870. ©HULTON-DEUTSCH COLLECTION/CORBIS

Pius IX had an impact on the diplomatic as well as the religious issues of the day, influencing the policies of the emperors Francis Joseph of Austria and Napoleon III of France, and of the German Empire under the chancellor Otto von Bismarck, and was especially embroiled in the affairs of the Italian peninsula. The ruler of the Papal States until their disappearance in 1870, and the head of the church from 1846 to 1878, he influenced the Risorgimento, which culminated in the unification of Italy, and the counter-Risorgimento, the bitter papal opposition to the creation of the Italian kingdom. Pius refused to accept the loss of his territory, which was incorporated into the unitary state, and rejected the concessions granted by the Italian government in the Law of Papal Guarantees (13 May 1871), declaring himself a prisoner in the Vatican and refusing to leave its palaces and grounds until his death on 7 February 1878. His intransigent opposition to the Italian kingdom provoked the Roman Question, or *dissidio*, which troubled relations between the Vatican and Italy until 1929.

Waging war against the secular philosophies of the modern world and the anticlerical policies he perceived they inspired, Pius responded by championing ultramontanism, which exalted the papacy by increasing centralization of authority in Rome. Among other things he defined the Immaculate Conception of Mary as born without original sin (1854); condemned the ideologies of liberalism, naturalism, nationalism, socialism, and communism (1864); and convoked the First Vatican Council (1869–1870) and encouraged it to proclaim papal infallibility (18 July 1870), fostering the structure of the modern, infallible papacy. He refused to bow to the anti-Catholic measures unleashed by Bismarck and his liberal allies in the Kulturkampf in the newly created German Empire and denounced the anticlerical course championed by the Third French Republic, which succeeded the Second Empire. His reach transcended Europe, and he almost became embroiled in the diplomacy of the Civil War in the United States.

EARLY LIFE AND CAREER

Born Giovanni Maria Mastai-Ferretti on 13 May 1792, in Senigallia near Ancona, the future pope received his early education from his mother, the former Caterina Solazzi, who was devoted to Mary. In 1803, at the age of eleven, he was sent to Saint Michael's school in Tuscany, but his studies there were interrupted by an attack of epilepsy in October 1809. He resumed his studies at the Roman College at the end of 1815. Determined to enter the priesthood, he was ordained in 1819, despite his malady, by special dispensation of Pius VII (r. 1800–1823), to whom he was devoted. His initial assignment was at the Roman orphanage of "Tata Giovanni," where he remained until 1823. From 1823 to 1825 he formed part of a papal diplomatic mission to Chile and Peru to explore the prospect of Rome's establishing relations with the former Spanish colonies; this made him the first person to become pope to have been to America. Upon his return to Rome, he became the director of the hospice of San Michele (1825–1827). Serving as archbishop of Spoleto from 1827 to 1832, he was appointed bishop of Imola in 1832, and cardinal by Gregory XVI (r. 1831–1846) in 1840. Both at Spoleto and Imola, Mastai-Ferretti was appreciated for his receptivity to some of the ideas of the nineteenth century, including aspects of liberalism and nationalism. On the other hand, he was conservative in his theological outlook, and thus had a wide appeal in the conclave convened following the death of Gregory XVI in 1846. He was elected pope on 16 June 1846, assuming the name Pius in honor of Pius VII, who had supported his ordination.

THE REFORMING POPE

Upon assuming the tiara, the new pope, recognizing that the papal regime confronted increasing discontent, championed a limited reformism and common-sense measures to prevent the outbreak of revolution. Although not a liberal, and indeed ultra-orthodox in religious matters, Mastai-Ferretti believed that conditions in his state could, and should, be better attuned to the needs of its people, and favored innovations such as the building of railways and the illumination of major avenues in Rome. He had earlier championed technical reforms in his "Thoughts on the Administration of the Papal States," which even invoked a collegiate body to advise and coordinate its administration. Committing himself to administrative, economic, and limited political changes, Pius promised to implement many of the reforms Gregory XVI had rejected when he shelved the Memorandum of 1831, in which France, Great Britain, Austria, Prussia, and Russia had suggested a degree of modernization to the Rome government.

Following the conservative, often autocratic course of Gregory XVI, Italians responded enthusiastically to Pius IX's limited reformism; some identified him with the pope-liberator prophesied by Vincenzo Gioberti in his *Del primato morale e civile degli italiani* (1843; On the civil and moral primacy of the Italians). Because he was perceived as a reformer as well as a patriot, Italians approved his appointment of Cardinal Pasquale Gizzi, considered a leading liberal, as his secretary of state, and his amnesty of political prisoners (16 July 1846). The amnesty aroused enthusiasm throughout the peninsula, leading the conservative Klemens von Metternich of Austria to quip that God pardons, but does not grant amnesties. The revised press law of 1846 permitted the publication of liberal and national sentiments and widely disseminated the innovations of the new pope. In 1847 Pius announced the formation of a *consulta*, or consultative chamber, to advise him on administrative and political matters and instituted a

council of ministers, permitted to discuss crucial administrative and political matters. These reforms led to the expectation that more would be forthcoming from the pope, who appeared to support liberal and national aspirations.

Adulation was not universal, as conservatives inside and outside Rome warned of the adverse consequences wrought on church and state by these changes. Pius, meanwhile, was torn between his obligation to protect the church and his desire to please his people. Consequently, he had reservations about creating a civil guard, granting his people a constitution and establishing a political league in Italy—but reconsidered his stance early in 1848, as revolution threatened Italy and Europe. The guard was created, a constitution was drafted for the Papal States, and talks were opened with the other Italian princes for the formation of a political league that transcended the tariff league the pope had originally intended. In March 1848 he announced the formation of the constitutional ministry headed by Cardinal Giacomo Antonelli and published a *statuto*, or constitution, that created two deliberative councils for the formation of law.

Despite massive demonstrations, Pius refused to secularize his administration, introduce constitutionalism into the church, accord equality to non-Catholics, or to wage war on Catholic Austria. The call for papal participation in a war of national liberation against Austria proved especially troubling, revealing the rift in his dual role as prince and priest. The papal refusal to enter the war, announced in an allocution of 19 April 1848, provoked the assassination of his minister Pellegrino Rossi (15 November 1848), followed by a revolutionary outburst in Rome. This led the pope to flee to Gaeta in the Kingdom of the Two Sicilies on 14 November 1848. His flight was followed by the proclamation of a republic in Rome later led by Giuseppe Mazzini and Giuseppe Garibaldi.

THE RESTORATION PAPACY

Pius IX and Cardinal Antonelli invoked the intervention of France, Austria, Spain, and the Kingdom of the Two Sicilies, and these Catholic powers overturned the Second Roman Republic in 1849, paving the way for the pope's return in 1850. These revolutionary events led Pius to question his reformism as well as constitutionalism. He complained that his efforts to introduce legitimate change had been subverted by calls for inadmissible innovations that threatened his spiritual and temporal power and deplored the fact that his refusal to wage an aggressive war against Catholic Austria had provoked revolution and necessitated his flight. During his exile, he had recognized the incompatibility between constitutionalism and the governance of the church.

Fearing religious incredulity and social dissolution, his restored government abandoned many of the liberal as well as national concessions of the prerevolutionary period. Among other things, Jews in the Papal State were again restricted in their movement, with the pontifical government stipulating that the Israelites should not be permitted to leave their usual residence without a permit from the Holy Office. Thus, the reformist pope of 1846–1848 turned into the conservative of the second restoration and was portrayed by some as the personification of reaction. The Piedmontese complained that he conspired with the Austrians to annul Turin's constitutional regime.

A priest first and a prince second, once back in Rome (1850) a chastened Pius concentrated on church affairs, focusing on the moral life of the rank and file of the clergy. He left much of the political responsibility, if not decisions, to his secretary of state and chief minister, Cardinal Giacomo Antonelli. Pius had previously restored the Latin patriarchate in Jerusalem in 1847, and reestablished the hierarchy in England in 1850 and in the Netherlands in 1853. His devotion to Mary led him to proclaim the Immaculate Conception (the dogma that Mary was free from original sin from the moment of her conception), and he remained convinced that she helped him and others escape injury when the floor of the convent of Sant'Agnese collapsed in April 1855. In gratitude, he visited her shrine at Loreto in 1857. Opposed to the "pernicious secularism of the age" and the "flagrant immorality associated with the modern philosophies," Pius sought solace in scripture and the consolation of religion, fostering centralization and uniformity in liturgical matters, which became the hallmark of his pontificate. Shunning theological innovation, he laid the foundation for neo-Scholasticism in church teaching. To facilitate centralization, Pius encouraged seminarians to study in Rome, founding a French seminary there

in 1853. This was followed by the inauguration of the North American College in 1859.

His strong religious fervor often conflicted with political expediency, perhaps most notably in his refusal in 1858 to return the Jewish boy Edgardo Levi Mortara, who had been secretly baptized by a Christian servant in Bologna and seized by papal forces, to his parents. The papal action in the "Mortara affair" outraged public opinion in liberal circles in Europe and America; alienated Napoleon III, who served as protector of the pope; and thus worked to undermine the Papal State, which was condemned as medieval and out of touch with the modern world. His intransigent stance facilitated the seizure of most of his territory or temporal power in 1859–1860, especially following the battle of Castelfidardo (18 September 1860). Following these events, Pius was left only with Rome and its immediate environs, protected by the troops of Napoleon III. When these forces withdrew during the Franco-Prussian War (1870–1871), Pius had to endure the loss of Rome as well. The pope perceived the criticism of his policies and the seizure of his state as integral parts of the broader attack on the church and its principles. He therefore proved unwilling to negotiate on the issue of the temporal power or accept its absorption into a united Italy, considering it essential for the preservation of the pope's spiritual power.

ASSESSMENT OF PIUS IX AND HIS PONTIFICATE

In the decade between his return to Rome, and the proclamation of the Kingdom of Italy (1861), Pius IX issued numerous condemnations of Count Cavour (Camillo Benso) and his colleagues, who were responsible for Italian unification and the seizure of his state. His encyclical *Jamdudum Cernimus* of 1861 denounced the modern philosophies and ideologies that the pope believed inspired the Piedmontese aggression. In September 1864 the French and Italians signed the September Convention, by which Napoleon III promised to withdraw his troops from Rome within two years, in return for a pledge from the Italian government to respect and protect the surviving Papal State from outside incursions.

Pius was appalled by the Convention, claiming it left the wolves to guard the sheep. He responded later that year (December 1864) in his encyclical *Quanta cura*, to which was appended the "Syllabus of Errors," which rejected the notion that the temporal power should be abolished, while denouncing liberalism, socialism, communism, nationalism, secret societies, and the separation of church and state. By his actions, Pius was seen to align the papacy and the church against contemporary developments. The papal counteroffensive was continued by the convocation of the Vatican Council, which, guided by Pius, culminated in the declaration of papal infallibility (18 July 1870), even as the Italians entered Rome (20 September 1870) and made it their capital. Both critics and admirers acknowledge that Pius played an important role in the Council and its proclamation of infallibility. The Powers responded negatively to the proclamation, but it was generally accepted by the Catholic laity, except for the "Old Catholic" minority movement.

Although he was heralded at his accession as a reformer, some claimed that Pius IX closed his pontificate as a reactionary. He was seen to range the church not only against the Risorgimento and Italian unification, but against much of the prevailing culture of the century. Furthermore, his opposition did not prevent Italian unification, and was seen to place the church on a collision course with the modern world. Rejecting the national faith of the age, his conflict with liberalism and nationalism contributed to the Roman Question in Italy and the Kulturkampf in Germany, and troubled relations with the French Republic that followed the collapse of Napoleon III's empire. Nonetheless, the Catholic masses in Europe and abroad admired his courage and tenacity in the face of adversity.

Although he lost his state, the ecclesiastical accomplishments of Pius IX were more substantial. He founded over two hundred new dioceses and erected thirty-three apostolic vicariates along with fifteen prefectures. His proclamation of the Immaculate Conception (8 December 1854) provided encouragement to the strong Marian movement in the nineteenth century, and the development of Marian devotion in the twentieth. His fervor for the missions led him to establish a special seminary for the training of missionary priests under the Congregation for the Propagation of the Faith, and encouraged missionary activity in the second half of the nineteenth century and into the early twentieth century. Following his death there was talk of Pius IX's beatification (the second step in the process toward sainthood), and his cause was opened in 1955 by Pius XII (r. 1939–1958). He was beatified by John Paul II (r. 1978–2005) in 2000, along with John XXIII (r. 1958–1963).

See also **Catholicism; Kulturkampf; Papal State; Roman Question.**

BIBLIOGRAPHY

Primary Sources

Atti del sommo pontefice Pio IX, felicemente regnante: Parte seconda che comprende I motu proprii, chirografi editti, notificazioni, ec. Per lo stato pontificio. 2 vols. Rome, 1857.

Blakiston, Noel, ed. *The Roman Question: Extracts from the Despatches of Odo Russell from Rome, 1858–1870.* London, 1962.

Franciscis, Pasquale de, ed. *Discorsi del sommo pontefice Pio IX prounziati in Vaticano ai fedeli di Roma e dell'orbe dal principio della sua prigionia fino al presente.* 4 vols. Rome, 1872–1878.

Stock, Leo Francis, ed. *Consular Relations between the United States and the Papal States: Instructions and Despatches.* Washington, D.C., 1945.

———. *United States Ministers to the Papal States: Instructions and Despatches, 1848–1868.* Washington, D.C., 1933.

Secondary Sources

Chadwick, Owen. *A History of the Popes, 1830–1914.* Oxford, U.K., and New York, 1998.

Coppa, Frank J. *Cardinal Giacomo Antonelli and Papal Politics in European Affairs.* Albany, N.Y., 1990.

———. *Pope Pius IX: Crusader in a Secular Age.* Boston, 1979.

Hales, Edward E. Y. *Pio Nono: A Study in European Politics and Religion in the Nineteenth Century.* New York, 1954.

Martina, Giacomo. *Pio IX.* 3 vols. Vatican City, 1974, 1986, 1990. The three volumes cover the time periods 1846–1850, 1851–1866, and 1867–1878.

Serafini, Alberto. *Pio Nono: Giovanni Maria Mastai-Ferretti, dalla giovinezza alla morte nei suoi scritti e discorsi editi e inediti.* Vol. 1. Vatican City, 1958.

FRANK J. COPPA

PLANCK, MAX (1858–1947), German theoretical physicist.

Max Karl Ernst Ludwig Planck, the initiator of a fundamental transformation in physics deeper even than the theory of relativity, was a revolutionary neither by background nor by temperament. He came from a line of pastors, theologians, and jurists and married the daughter of a banker. His father was a professor of law, first at Kiel, where Planck was born, and then in Munich, where he attended university.

As a student, Planck distinguished himself by breadth rather than brilliance. He toyed with making a career as a historian, musician (he played the piano at concert level), or mathematician. He decided on physics as a way of combining mathematics with earthier interests. But he stayed close to the abstract, developing his physical ideas without special assumptions about the structure of matter and without reference to the concerns of human beings. Whereas Albert Einstein's test for the goodness of a theory was whether God would like it, Planck's was whether a Martian could understand it.

The branch of physics that lent itself best to Planck's approach was thermodynamics. He took its principles as the subject of his doctoral thesis (1879) and pursued their applications as extraordinary professor of physics in Kiel and during his first decade in Berlin, where he became professor of theoretical physics in 1888. In the late 1890s, however, he found that he could not solve the problem he had set himself without recourse to an atomic model.

This problem, from which quantum theory emerged, was the derivation of the relative intensities $I(n)$ of the various frequencies n in the radiant heat within an oven maintained at a constant temperature T. This problem intrigued Planck because, on thermodynamic grounds, I should depend only on the quotient n/T and not at all on the material or shape of the oven. Thus he could picture the radiators in its walls as he pleased without compromising generality. He chose identical charged particles attached to perfectly elastic massless springs. To derive a formula that fit the measurements, he supposed, against his previous absolutism and in agreement with the statistical mechanics of Ludwig Boltzmann (1844–1906), that the entropy principle permitted exceptions. This supposition when applied to the oscillators underwrote late in 1900 a derivation that limited the energy possessed by an oscillator of frequency n to a multiple of hn, where h, "Planck's constant," came from fitting the formula to experimental results.

Planck delighted in his formula because of a second universal constant (besides h) that it contained; he called it k and named it after Boltzmann. Unlike h, k had a clear physical meaning. Through it Planck could calculate the electronic charge and other atomic constants. For the formula and the calculations, he almost received the Nobel prize in 1908. Before the Royal Swedish Academy of Sciences accepted him, however, it learned that energy quanta might not be compatible with sound physics. Planck did receive the physics prize, but not until 1919 (the reserved prize for 1918).

Planck came to regard the violation of ordinary ideas required by the acceptance of the quantum discontinuity as a good thing, a step toward the removal of human traces from physical science. For a similar reason—its rejection of ordinary ideas of space and time—Planck promoted relativity theory immediately after its publication in 1905. Later, his extraterrestrial epistemology enabled him to accept, while Einstein (1879–1955) rejected, wave mechanics and its probabilistic interpretation.

In 1912 Planck began the administrative career that would make him the most respected spokesman for German science. In that year he took office as a permanent secretary of the Prussian Academy of Sciences. He added service to and ultimately (in 1930) assumed the presidency of the Kaiser-Wilhelm-Gesellschaft (KWG), the most important organization for scientific research in Germany. His frequent lectures on the nature of science, science and values, science and religion, and the state of physics earned him a wide following between the wars. His standing during the postwar Weimar period was enhanced by his behavior during World War I. He was the only signatory to the infamous manifesto supporting the German army's actions in Belgium, *An die Kulturwelt!*, to repudiate it during the war. He had a deserved reputation for courage and probity. Even Einstein, whose religion, pacifism, and bohemian behavior separated him from most Germans, esteemed Planck for his human qualities. They were fast friends until the Nazis took power in 1933.

Planck visited Adolf Hitler in 1933 soon after the promulgation of the law cleansing the civil service—which, with some loopholes, discharged Jews from government jobs including university professorships. Planck protested that the measure would cripple German science. Hitler replied that he had nothing against Jews, only against communists, and that all Jews were communists. He then flew into such a rage that Planck could only creep away. Nevertheless, Planck retained his positions in the Academy and the KWG in hope of protecting their employees and for fear of being replaced by a party hack. This decision required him to give the Hitler salute, pay court to small-minded government and party officials, discharge some Jews to keep others, and make other demeaning concessions.

Planck decided to retain his offices well beyond retirement age (he was seventy-five in 1933) on the mistaken belief that he still possessed the sort of influence he had enjoyed in imperial and Weimar times. He found out just how little influence his compliance had earned him when, in 1944, he sought clemency for his son, an army officer implicated in the plot to kill Hitler. Planck could not even obtain a hearing; Erwin Planck was executed; and Planck lost the last of the four children who, along with his first wife, friends, work, and music, had made his life and home a joy before World War I. (His elder son was killed in the war; his wife died before it began, and his twin daughters at its end.)

At the end of World War II, Allied bombing drove Planck and his second wife out of Berlin and into the woods near Göttingen. Rescued by American troops, the old man (then eighty-seven) revived enough to attend, as the only German invited, the postponed celebration in London of the 300th anniversary of Isaac Newton's birth, and to serve as the figurehead president of the revived KWG. The American occupiers agreed to the revival on condition that the institution change its name. It prospers into the early twenty-first century as the Max Planck Society for the Advancement of Science.

See also **Physics; Science and Technology.**

BIBLIOGRAPHY

Primary Sources

Hentschel, Klaus, ed. *Physics and National Socialism: An Anthology of Primary Sources.* Translated by Ann M. Hentschel. Basel, 1996.

Planck, Max. *The Origin and Development of the Quantum Theory.* Translated by H. T. Clarke and L. Silberstein. Oxford, U.K., 1920. Planck's Nobel lecture.

———. *Scientific Autobiography, and Other Papers.* New York, 1949. Includes some of Planck's public lectures.

———. *Physikalische Abhandlungen und Vorträge.* 3 vols. Braunschweig, 1958.

———. *The New Science.* Translated by James Murphy and W. H. Johnston. New York, 1959.

Secondary Sources

Beyerchen, Alan D. *Scientists under Hitler.* New Haven, Conn., 1971.

Heilbron, J. L. *The Dilemmas of an Upright Man: Max Planck and the Fortunes of German Science.* 2nd ed. Cambridge, U.K., 2000.

Kuhn, Thomas S. *Black-body Theory and the Quantum Discontinuity, 1894–1912.* Chicago, 1978.

Macrakis, Christie. *Surviving the Swastika: Scientific Research in Nazi Germany.* New York, 1993.

J. L. HEILBRON

PLEKHANOV, GEORGY (1856–1918), Russian revolutionary and social philosopher.

Often called the "Father of Russian Marxism," Georgy Plekhanov was born into a minor gentry family on 11 December (29 November, old style) 1856, in Gudalovka, a village in Tambov Province. In 1873, after completing his studies at the Voronezh Military Academy, he enrolled in a St. Petersburg military school, with the intention of becoming an army officer. Affected by the vogue of science among Russia's engaged youth, he soon transferred to the St. Petersburg State Mining Institute. Before long he abandoned his studies to participate wholeheartedly in the burgeoning populist revolutionary movement. His military training and the allure of science undoubtedly helped shape his character.

In the period from 1875 to 1880 Plekhanov was active in the populist movement's efforts to foment a peasant uprising and thereby create an agrarian socialist society. Foreshadowing his future, his efforts happened to center on urban workers, and his writings exhibited unmistakable signs of Marxist influence. A leader of the populist Land and Liberty group for a while, he spearheaded opposition to its increasing resort to terrorism. The alternative group he formed, Black Repartition, did not endure, and in 1880 Plekhanov fled abroad to avoid arrest. He did not return to Russia until 1917.

In exile Plekhanov resided mostly in Geneva, Switzerland. In 1883, with a few friends, he established the Emancipation of Labor group, Russia's first Marxist revolutionary organization. In two major works, *Socialism and Political Struggle* (1883) and *Our Differences* (1885), he launched a destructive critique of populism and laid the ideological basis of Russian Marxism. Russia, he argued, had embarked on a capitalistic development that was creating the preconditions for the overthrow of Russian autocracy and the installation of a bourgeois-democratic regime. The Marxists must organize the emerging industrial proletariat for the struggle against autocracy. Thereafter, continuing capitalistic development would multiply the numbers of the proletariat, and, under social democratic leadership, the working class would ultimately carry out a socialist revolution. This two-phase revolutionary scheme was central to Russian Marxist thought for many years.

During the formative years of the labor movement in Russia, Plekhanov made influential contributions to debates within the Russian Social Democratic Labor Party (RSDLP) over both economic development *and* revolutionary strategy. Meanwhile, Plekhanov had continued his polemics against the populists. According to Vladimir Lenin, Plekhanov's opus *On the Development of the Monistic Conception of History* (1895) "reared a whole generation of Russian Marxists." He also produced tracts defending Marxist orthodoxy against the reformist revisionism of the German Social Democrat Eduard Bernstein, and a Russian tendency called "economism," which allegedly slighted political struggle, concentrating instead on the betterment of working conditions. These battles over theory and tactics were waged together with Lenin and others, who, in 1900, began publishing the militant journal *Iskra* (The spark).

A controversy over the character of the party split the second congress of the RSDLP into what became known as the Bolshevik and Menshevik factions. Plekhanov initially sided with Lenin, the Bolshevik leader, but soon after joined the Mensheviks in attacking Lenin's dictatorial tendencies. For the rest of his life, Plekhanov generally associated with the Mensheviks, while frequently criticizing them. As a prominent member of the Second International, Plekhanov assumed a "defeatist" stance toward his country in the Russo-Japanese War (1904–1905). By contrast, he supported the Triple Entente during World War I, as he feared that the victory of German militarism would spell disaster for Russia's workers.

The Revolution of 1905 tested the revolutionary scheme Plekhanov had devised and found it wanting. Key groups—the bourgeoisie, the peasants, and the proletariat—all acted contrary to his predictions. Yet Plekhanov did not modify his theory, and his political influence declined in the next decade. In the last two decades of his life, Plekhanov nevertheless produced significant philosophical, artistic, literary, and historical studies.

In 1917 Plekhanov greeted the February upheaval as the long-awaited bourgeois-democratic revolution. Returning to Russia, he urged continuation of the war to victory, but his pleas for soldier, peasant, and worker restraint fell on deaf ears. After the October Revolution, he harshly criticized the Bolsheviks' march to power and warned that a socialist revolution in socioeconomically backward Russia must end catastrophically. Overzealous Red Guards subsequently harassed him as "an enemy of the people," leading him to leave St. Petersburg. Plekhanov died on 30 May (17 May, old style) 1918 in Terioki, Finland.

See also **Bolsheviks; Lenin, Vladimir; Mensheviks; Revolution of 1905 (Russia).**

BIBLIOGRAPHY

Baron, Samuel H. *Plekhanov: The Father of Russian Marxism.* Stanford, Calif., 1963.

——. *Plekhanov in Russian History and Soviet Historiography.* Pittsburgh, Pa., 1995.

Plekhanov, Georgy. *Sochineniia.* 24 vols. Moscow, 1923–1927. The most complete edition of Plekhanov's works.

——. *History of Russian Social Thought.* Translated by Boris M. Bekkar and others. 1938. Reprint, New York, 1967.

——. *Selected Philosophical Works.* 2nd ed. 5 vols. Moscow, 1975–1981. Includes a number of his most important writings.

SAMUEL H. BARON

POGROMS. A pogrom is generally understood as an attack on a minority population, usually perpetrated by a quasi-military mob. While communal violence of this sort has been part of the human experience since the appearance of social organization in prehistoric times, the Russian word *pogrom* came into common usage in the late nineteenth and early twentieth centuries as Jews fleeing the late tsarist empire used the term to describe their experience with this anarchic form of violence. The term *pogrom* may be used with justification to describe violence against many ethnic groups, but it is more often than not associated specifically with anti-Semitic attacks. Pogroms are distinct from both spontaneous riots on the one hand and organized state attacks on the other, although they share elements of both types of aggression.

The paradigmatic pogrom takes place in an atmosphere of anarchy or of weakened state control, and is often preceded by a period of anticipation as rumors of an impending attack circulate—rumors that may in fact accelerate the process. Perpetrators, often unemployed men or migrant workers with little property to protect in the region, descend on a highly visible and usually semi-urban minority population for attacks that last for several days. Minority populations who live together in villages are often singled out for attacks, as they typically have fewer allies and resources in the surrounding area. Property damage, assault, and rape are common elements of pogrom attacks, and some even have elements of organized mass murder, but the basic motivation for such violence seems to be the desire for ill-gotten wealth, wine, and women.

A key element in pogrom violence is the identification of the victim as "the other." Historically, this otherness was based on religious, ethnic, or linguistic criteria; in the nineteenth century, nationality became a key determinant. Pogrom violence is often justified by appeal to some greater cause, and whereas the medieval victims were attacked because they were perceived as infidels or traitors to the throne, modern victims are often identified through their perceived threat to the political status quo. For example, medieval pogroms against Jews were often sparked by the charge of "blood libel," based on a myth that Jews drink the blood of crucified Christian children, whereas in the early twentieth century Jews were attacked for their perceived support of socialism.

Attack on a Jewish house in Konnovino, near Nijni-Novgorod, 7 June 1884. Sketch by Karazine from the French journal *L'Illustration*, 2 August 1884. PRIVATE COLLECTION/ BRIDGEMAN ART LIBRARY/ARCHIVES CHARMET

Pogroms are often a function of major social upheaval, as they tend to flourish when police authority declines. Other factors, such as the social and economic upheaval that accompanies rapid industrialization, contribute to the anarchic atmosphere that promotes such violence. Pogroms took place immediately after the French Revolution (1789), and persisted with some regularity in the German lands throughout the nineteenth century, including the so-called Hep, Hep pogroms of 1819. The defining period of pogroms, however, was the declining years of the tsarist empire.

The first major wave of Russian pogroms occurred after the assassination of Tsar Alexander II in 1881, when rumors circulated that the new tsar, Alexander III, had given permission to "beat the Jews for three days." These three days stretched into three years as much of the southwestern portions of the Russian Empire suffered periodic pogrom attacks, especially in the Ukrainian and Polish ethnolinguistic areas. Jewish activists at the time argued that these pogroms were somehow orchestrated by the government, perhaps in an

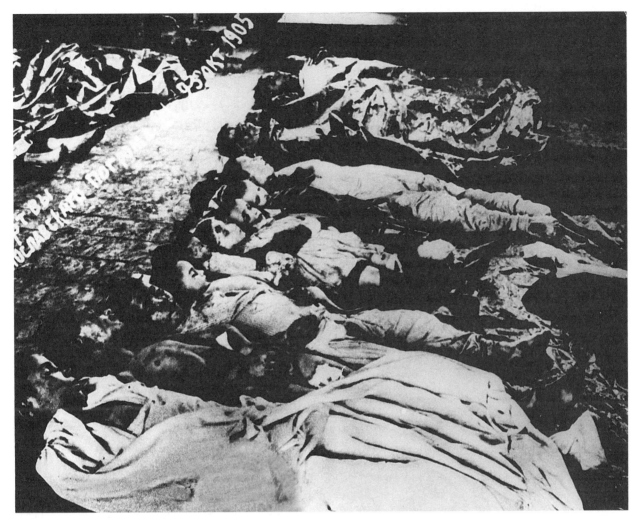

The bodies of Jews killed in a Russian pogrom, 1905. ©Hulton-Deutch Collection/Corbis

attempt to deflect social pressures from the ruling elite to the hapless Jewish minority, but archival researchers of the late twentieth century conclusively demonstrated that these attacks were the product of migrant workers, often following the rail lines from their temporary industrial jobs in cities such as Odessa to their villages in the Russian interior.

The subsequent tsar, Nicholas II (r. 1894–1917), had few qualms about anti-Semitic hooligans, and openly supported right-wing organizations such as the Black Hundreds and even gave 12,000 rubles to facilitate the publication of the notorious *Protocols of the Elders of Zion,* an anti-Semitic tract that claimed Jews were secretly planning to dominate the globe. Increasingly vicious pogroms occurred in 1903 and 1905 (coinciding with political upheaval) and the violence was steadily extended to several non-Russian groups such as Poles. With the outbreak of World War I in 1914, German-speaking populations were also victimized, especially in the newly renamed Petrograd. These pogroms, however, were completely overwhelmed by the attacks that accompanied the collapse of the tsarist empire during World War I. As several groups attempted to form a successor government to the Romanov dynasty, regions abandoned by the German forces fell into anarchic civil war, with several major factions (the Red Army, the anticommunist White Army, Ukrainian nationalists, and others) and bands of roving hooligans terrorizing minority populations at will. Deaths attributable to pogrom violence peaked in 1919, with reasonable estimates in the neighborhood of fifty thousand Jews and an unknown number of Poles and Mennonites killed.

While economic factors were the most significant reason some three million Jews left the Russian Empire after 1881 (principally for the United States), pogroms certainly accelerated that mass migration. Furthermore, the charge that Jews were communist sympathizers had the ironic result that many later joined the Red Army, which under Vladimir Lenin had gained a reputation for refraining from such attacks.

See also **Anti-Semitism; Jews and Judaism; Russia.**

BIBLIOGRAPHY

Abramson, Henry. *A Prayer for the Government: Ukrainians and Jews in Revolutionary Times.* Cambridge, Mass., 1999.

Aronson, I. Michael. *Troubled Waters: The Origins of the 1881 Anti-Jewish Pogroms in Russia.* Pittsburgh, Pa., 1990.

Berk, Stephen M. *Year of Crisis, Year of Hope: Russian Jewry and the Pogroms of 1881–1882.* Westport, Conn., 1985.

Charters, Wynn. *Workers, Strikes and Pogroms: The Donbass-Dnepr Bend in Late Imperial Russia 1870–1905.* Princeton, N.J., 1992.

Klier, John D., and Shlomo Lambroza, eds. *Pogroms: Anti-Jewish Violence in Modern Russian History.* Cambridge, U.K., 1992.

HENRY ABRAMSON

POINCARÉ, HENRI (1854–1912), French mathematician and scientist.

The son of a professor on the faculty of medicine in Nancy, France, Jules-Henri Poincaré (29 April 1854–17 July 1912) was a member of an influential family that included his cousin Raymond Poincaré (1860–1934), president of France during World War I, and his brother-in-law Étienne-Émile-Marie Boutroux (1845–1921), professor of philosophy at the Sorbonne. A graduate of the École Polytechnique, Poincaré quickly established his scientific credentials in the theory of functions and the qualitative theory of differential equations. His discovery in 1880 of the automorphic functions of one complex variable, which he used to solve second-order linear differential equations with algebraic coefficients, was widely hailed as a work of genius.

Starting in 1881 Poincaré taught mathematics at the University of Paris, becoming professor of mathematical physics in 1886 and a member of the Academy of Science in 1887. Two years later he was awarded the Grand Prize of Oscar II, king of Sweden (r. 1872–1907), for his study of a thorny question in celestial mechanics known as the "three-body problem": How do three masses behave under the influence of gravitation? A milestone in the history of both celestial mechanics and dynamics, Poincaré's prize paper contains the proof of Poincaré's Recurrence Theorem, which states (roughly) that a closed mechanical system with finite energy (like that of three planets gravitating in empty space according to Newton's law) will return periodically to a state very close to its initial state. It also contains the first mathematical description of what is now known as chaotic motion.

Both in this work in dynamics and others in group theory, multiple integrals, and the theory of functions, Poincaré would let the problem conditions vary continuously, and observe what happens, a method that leads directly to questions of topology. This branch of mathematics is concerned with properties of figures that are invariant under homeomorphisms (or bicontinuous one-to-one transformations). In algebraic topology, one such topological invariant is the Euler characteristic, which for a convex polyhedron is given by Euler's formula: Sum the numbers of faces and vertices, subtract the number of edges, and the result is always the same, $F - E + V = 2$. Starting in 1895, Poincaré laid the foundations of algebraic topology (then called analysis situs), defining "Betti numbers," and inventing a number of tools, which he used to generalize the Euler theorem for polyhedrons.

From the late 1880s Poincaré engaged with James Clerk Maxwell's theory of electrodynamics, and helped introduce this theory to Continental readers. In 1896 he relinquished his chair in mathematical physics for another in mathematical astronomy and celestial mechanics, but maintained a lively interest in the newly discovered phenomena of x-rays, gamma-rays, and electrons. Most notably, Poincaré pointed out in 1900 that in order for the principle of relative motion to hold (i.e., the principle according to which physical phenomena are insensible to uniform rectilinear motion), it was necessary to refer time measurements not to the "true time" of an observer at rest with respect to a universal, motionless carrier of electromagnetic waves known as the ether, but to a "local time" devised by the Dutch physicist Hendrik Antoon Lorentz (1853–1928) as a mathematical shortcut. For Poincaré, local time was the time read by the light-synchronized clocks of observers in common motion with respect to the ether, corrected by the light signal's time of flight, but ignoring the effect of motion on light propagation.

There was more to this exchange of light signals than the synchronization of clocks. The simultaneity of two events is not determined by objective considerations, Poincaré observed in 1898, but is a matter of definition. Measurements of distance suffer the same underdetermination, such that there is no true geometry of physical space in Poincaré's view. According to Poincaré's conventionalist philosophy, scientists are often confronted with open-ended situations requiring a choice between alternative definitions of their objects of study. In virtue of this freedom of choice, which marks the linguistic turn in philosophy of science, Poincaré was often thought to be upholding a variety of nominalism, an error he denounced with vigor. The choice scientists have to make, Poincaré explained, is not entirely free, as scientists are guided by experimental facts. In line with this understanding of scientific activity, Poincaré deplored the logicist program of Bertrand Russell (1872–1970), which sought an axiomatic foundation for mathematics.

Conventionalism gained greater recognition upon publication of *La science et l'hypothèse* (1902; *Science and Hypothesis*), whose readers included the young Albert Einstein (1879–1955). In the summer of 1905 Poincaré and Einstein independently proposed what was to be known as the special theory of relativity, and are generally considered to be the theory's cofounders (along with Lorentz), although the question of paternity continues to spark debate.

Poincaré was a phenomenally productive scientist, with more than five hundred scientific papers and twenty-five volumes of lectures to his name, spanning the major branches of mathematics, mathematical physics, celestial mechanics, astronomy, and philosophy of science. By 1900 he was widely acknowledged to be the world's foremost mathematician.

See also **Einstein, Albert; Science and Technology.**

BIBLIOGRAPHY

Primary Sources

Œuvres. 11 vols. Edited by Paul-Emile Appell et al. Paris, 1916–1956.

New Methods of Celestial Mechanics. Edited by Daniel L. Goroff. New York, 1992. Translation of *Les méthodes nouvelles de la mécanique céleste,* 3 vols. (1892–1899).

The Foundations of Science. Translated by George Bruce Halsted. Lancaster, Pa., 1913. Translation of *La science et l'hypothèse* (1902), *La valeur de la science* (1905), and *Science et méthode* (1908).

Secondary Sources

Barrow-Green, June. *Poincaré and the Three-Body Problem.* Providence, R.I., 1997.

Greffe, Jean-Louis, Gerhard Heinzmann, and Kuno Lorenz, eds. *Henri Poincaré: Science and Philosophy.* Berlin, 1996.

SCOTT WALTER

POINCARÉ, RAYMOND (1860–1934), French politician.

Born in Bar-le-Duc (Meuse) in Lorraine on 20 August 1860, Raymond Poincaré occupied the highest offices of the French state, including president of the republic, in a political career that ran from 1886 to 1934. Longevity and achievement made him one of the foremost statesmen of the French Third Republic. He played crucial roles in France's entry into World War I, the organization of the war effort, the peace settlement, the reparations question, the occupation of the Ruhr, and the reorganization of French finances in the 1920s.

Born into a solidly middle-class family, the eldest son of an engineer, Poincaré was educated at the lycées of Bar-le-Duc and Louis-le-Grand in Paris, and graduated from the Sorbonne with an arts and a law degree. He was called to the Paris bar in 1882. At an early age he displayed the intelligence and enormous capacity for work that were hallmarks of his political career.

Poincaré began his life in politics in 1886 as a councilor for the Meuse, a position he would retain until his death on 15 October 1934. In 1887, he was elected a member of the lower house of parliament for Meuse and sat on the center-left of the Chamber with the Progressists. His reputation for efficient committee work on legal and financial matters saw him appointed minister of education and culture (April–November 1893) at only thirty-two years of age. The following year he was finance minister (May 1894–January 1895), then education minister again (January–October 1895).

Throughout his political career, Poincaré always steered a middle course. A champion of secularism, he was no anticlerical. Although opposed to the more left-leaning Radicals, he was no reactionary, and often included them in the governments he later formed. Disillusioned with the radical turn in French politics from 1901, he withdrew from ministerial office (apart from a brief interlude as finance minister in 1906) and concentrated on his extremely successful legal practice. Politics were not abandoned altogether, as he was elected vice-president of the Chamber of Deputies in 1895 and remained a member of the lower house of parliament until his election to the Senate in 1903. During those wilderness years he produced a number of books and articles on politics, which helped secure his election to the Académie Française in 1909. Those years also saw him promote ideas far less associated with his austere legalistic image. He championed animal rights and antivivisectionism and promoted women's rights from the freedom to practice law to the vote.

Following the 1911 Franco-German Agadir crisis in Morocco, Poincaré was recalled to office as premier and foreign minister on 12 January 1912. He set about ensuring that diplomatically and militarily France was prepared for any eventuality. Although he did so by tightening up France's alliance and entente with Russia and Britain, he was careful not to adopt an aggressive policy toward Germany. Even when in January 1913 he was elected president of the Republic, he saw to it that governments were put in place that would continue his firm policy. This, combined with his Lorraine origins—supposedly synonymous with revanche—has been interpreted as meaning that he sought war. However, his role in the circumstances that led up to the outbreak of war in August 1914 was far more blameless than the myth of *Poincaré-la-guerre* would suggest. That myth was the result of postwar propaganda generated by Germany and Poincaré's political opponents at home. The former wished to contest the principle of German war guilt on which the payment of reparations was built by displacing some of the blame onto France; the latter were intent on blocking Poincaré's return to power in the 1920s. His greatest triumph was to ensure that the country entered the war united, symbolized by his famous *union sacrée* speech of 4 August 1914, following Germany's declaration of war on France the day before.

Poincaré and his policies have traditionally been associated with values that posterity has tended to view as unfashionable—order, stability, dignity, politeness, honesty, and thrift. His identification with the middle class, which claimed to incarnate those values and which historiography has not found exciting or treated kindly, has left Poincaré, if not one of the unsung heroes of modern French history, then one whose political stature has not received the recognition it deserves.

See also **Alliance System; France.**

BIBLIOGRAPHY

Keiger, John F. V. *Raymond Poincaré*. Cambridge, U.K., 1997.

Roth, François. *Raymond Poincaré: Un homme d'Etat républicain*. Paris, 2000.

J. F. V. KEIGER

POLAND. The Polish-Lithuanian Commonwealth, once the largest country in Europe, entered the era of revolution in a wounded and weakened state. The nobility, long the political class, had hindered the development of the cities and opposed the creation of a centralized state. For much of the eighteenth century, the Commonwealth was in effect a Russian protectorate. In 1764 Catherine the Great placed her former lover, Stanisław Poniatowski, on the Polish-Lithuanian throne. Polish-Lithuanian nobles responded by forming the Confederation of Bar, directed against both royal authority and Russian power. After some five hundred engagements, the rebels were defeated, their leaders dispatched to Siberia. Poland-Lithuania's neighbor Prussia seized the opportunity to propose a new territorial settlement to Russia and Austria. In 1772 the Polish-Lithuanian Commonwealth was partitioned, each of the

Commonwealth's three neighbors seizing a portion of its territory.

This external shock provided King Stanisław with an argument for reform. Despite demands for loyalty from Catherine and insistence on the status quo from much of the nobility, Stanisław forced through an impressive range of reforms over the next two decades. The Polish parliament, essentially dormant and decadent over the previous decades, began to act. Ministries of government met regularly in cabinet meetings, for the first time in living memory. Stanisław created a unified system of administration, created a royal army worthy of the name, schooled officers in a military academy (whose uniform he himself favored), rebuilt Warsaw and cleaned and lit its streets, and sponsored translations of European scientific literature. He stood behind a project to map his domains, naming some localities himself. His Commission on National Education was the first ministry of education in European history. Its final goal was to replace church schooling (supplanting the Jesuits) with a unified public school system, with Polish as the language of instruction.

These reforms created the beginnings of a civil society, in the form of educated civil servants and a growing urban population. The educated classes took an enthusiastic part in constitutional debates that began in parliament in 1789. The constitution approved by the parliament on 3 May 1791, the first written constitution in Europe since antiquity, would have radically advanced Stanisław's project of creating a reformed state. The Commonwealth would have been transformed from a republic of nobles to a constitutional monarchy. The nobility would have lost its traditional right to elect kings; dynasties rather than individuals would have been elected. This would have strengthened the connection of kings to the land they ruled. Nobles without land would have lost their political rights, while non-nobles with property would have entered the political community. The traditional problems of the political institutions, such as the right of veto by any noble voter and the right to confederate, would have been eliminated. Civil rights such as habeas corpus were extended to property owners and Jews. The Polish-Lithuanian Commonwealth, created in 1569 as the union of the Kingdom of Poland and the Grand Duchy of Lithuania, would have become a more unified state.

Noble opponents to reform, and above all noble lackeys of Russia, announced their opposition. They established the Confederation of Targowica and invited Russian military intervention; Russia explained that it would protect the traditional rights of the nobles. The Commonwealth was a multiconfessional country with a large Orthodox population; Russia justified its intervention as necessary to protect the Orthodox. The Polish parliament was forced to accept a second partition, this time by Russia and Prussia, in 1793. Whereas the first partition was a consequence of decadence, the second was a result of fears by neighbors that reform could succeed. In March 1794 Tadeusz Kościuszko began a national uprising, promising equal rights to burghers and land to peasants. He routed the Targowicans and won some engagements with the Prussian and Russian armies. Catherine the Great was able to turn the bulk of her forces from the Ottoman to the Polish front later that year, and crushed the uprising. In the third partition (1795), Russia, Austria, and Prussia seized the remainder of the territory of the Commonwealth, which ceased to exist. All in all, Russia had taken about 62 percent of its territory, Prussia, 20 percent, and Austria, 18 percent.

Whereas the impulse for a constitutional revolution in Poland was quelled by Poland's neighbors, the revolutionary French state succeeded in bending its own neighbors to its will. As Napoleon ranged his armies against the European powers, hopeful Poles perceived a natural ally. Because Poles had lost their state, theirs was the only political class that stood to gain from a radical transformation of the map of Europe. During the twenty years between the third partition in 1795 and the Congress of Vienna in 1815, the Polish question seemed open. Some prominent Poles, among them Adam Jerzy Czartoryski, allied themselves with the reforming Russian Tsar Alexander I, in the hopes that he would one day crown himself king of a united Poland. In the meantime, Czartoryski rose to a position of enormous influence in the Russian court, and carried out educational reforms that preserved and probably spread Polish culture in Lithuania and Belarus. Thousands of Polish exiles sided with Napoleon in his Italian wars of 1797 to 1801, hoping that they would be rewarded in a peace settlement. These hopes were dashed.

When France brought its power to the edge of Russia by defeating Prussia in 1807, Napoleon and Alexander jointly addressed the Polish question. Alexander agreed that Napoleon would establish a Grand Duchy of Warsaw on territories seized from Prussia. In 1809, after Napoleon defeated Austria, Cracow was added to the Grand Duchy of Warsaw. Although the Grand Duchy was one of the constellation of puppet kingdoms and duchies that constituted Napoleon's European empire, it was nevertheless a fruitful institution, in its own way. The introduction of Napoleonic civil and commercial codes created durable precedents and practices. The use of Polish as the effective language of administration, and the training of Polish civil servants and military officers, created the appearance of something like a Polish state. It also gave rise to hopes that Napoleon would recreate Poland after defeating Russia. In June 1812 Napoleon began his eastward march, with some thirty thousand Poles in his armies. He met crushing defeat. Russian troops reached Warsaw in February 1813. They would remain for more than a century.

As part of the general European peace settlement, the Congress of Vienna settled the Polish question. The three partitioning powers accepted a new distribution of the territories of the old Commonwealth. The Grand Duchy of Warsaw was liquidated. Poznań was returned to Prussia, where it was the capital of an autonomous Grand Duchy of Posen. Cracow was not restored to Austria, but made a free city under the common protection of the three powers. It became a tiny republic, uniting the city with three towns and some two hundred villages. Gdańsk, which had been a free city, was conceded to Prussia. Warsaw, which had been in Prussia before becoming the capital of the Grand Duchy, was added to Russia. Russia was now home to an absolute majority of the world's Poles. Since the old Commonwealth had been the center of Jewish life in Europe, the Russian Empire was also home to most of Europe's Jews. Austrian Galicia also was home to a large Jewish population.

After 1815 Warsaw became the center of a new kingdom of Poland, known as the Congress Kingdom, which Tsar Alexander was to rule as constitutional monarch. Here legislation was passed by a local parliament, the language of administration was Polish, and there was even a Polish military academy and army. The Congress Kingdom comprised only one-seventh of the territory and one-fifth of the population of the old Commonwealth, but between 1815 and 1830 it was nevertheless a reasonably close approximation of a Polish state. Precisely because it was a constitutional entity, it created expectations that, after the death of Alexander in 1825, were not met. The November Uprising of 1830 was intended to defend the Congress Kingdom's constitution. Because there was a Polish army at this time, of all the Polish uprisings this revolt most closely resembled a regular military campaign, and probably enjoyed the greatest chances of success. After Russia defeated the uprising in 1831, Tsar Nicholas I reestablished Russian rule in the Congress Kingdom on the basis of the Organic Statute of 1832. Further east, in historical Lithuania, the 1830s and 1840s saw the dissolution of remaining institutions of the old Commonwealth, such as the Uniate Church and the Lithuanian Statute.

The defeat of 1831 led to the Great Emigration, the departure of some ten thousand Poles from the Russian Empire to western Europe, especially France. The Great Emigration defined enduring trends of Polish intellectual and political life. Poles disagreed as to whether a monarchy or a republic would best shelter the nation, although a consensus emerged (among people who generally had lost their property) that some kind of land reform would be needed to bring the peasantry into the Polish nation. The monarchist trend was associated with Czartoryski, the republican with the historian Joachim Lelewel. The same period saw the development of Polish Romanticism, most fetchingly by Adam Mickiewicz and Juliusz Słowacki. Less well known but important at the time were the Polish national philosophers, often students at German universities who also were familiar with French thought. August Cieszkowski, known by his German colleagues as a Left Hegelian, developed a theory of action.

Of the lands of the former Commonwealth, it was the Prussian territory that in the 1840s offered the most freedom of action. Especially after the ascension of Frederick William IV to the Prussian throne in 1840, Poles in Posnania exploited a certain liberalism of German rule. Their slogan was "organic work," which meant a concentration of economic organization and educational attainment. Nevertheless, Poznań was also the center of planning for a general insurrection planned for all three partitions in 1846. After the Prussian police arrested the main organizers, sporadic and uncoordinated outbreaks followed. Polish rebels managed to defeat the Austrian garrison in Cracow and briefly hold the tiny republic. In Austria proper, the authorities exploited the hostility of the peasant population for Polish lords, and defeated the uprising. The Cracow Republic was annexed by Austria. Meanwhile, the trial of the Polish rebels in Prussia became a cause célèbre of German radicals, linking the Polish events of 1846 to the European revolutions of 1848. German liberals in 1848 were initially rather favorable to the demands of Poles, until they realized that Polish autonomy could lead to losses of German territory and would certainly provoke Russia. In the 1850s the distinct Grand Duchy of Posen was liquidated. Against the will of Poles, formerly Polish regions were incorporated into Otto von Bismarck's North German Confederation in 1867, and then into his German Empire in 1871. Poles had been a rather important population in Prussia; in a united Germany they were a small Catholic minority.

After the disaster of 1846, Polish nobles in Austrian Galicia were fairly easy to intimidate. The backward province was already proverbial in its misery. In its eastern half, the peasantry was not only alien to Polish nobles by social background but also by nationality and religion. Most of the population of eastern Galicia was Ruthenian and Uniate rather than Polish and Catholic. The European lesson of 1848, that the aims of liberal revolutionaries can be confounded by class and nation, had already been learned by Polish nobles in 1846, and a few reminders two years later was enough to teach them that other methods would be required to secure autonomy for Poles. Agenor Gołuchowski, the longtime governor of Galicia, was seen by many Poles as a traitor, but in fact he laid the foundations for important Polish gains in the province in the 1850s and 1860s. Like the Hungarian nobility, the Polish nobility exploited Austrian weakness after the military defeats of the 1860s to demand political concessions. Shortly after the Ausgleich of 1867 transformed the Habsburg domains into Austria-Hungary, Polish nobles secured for themselves de facto autonomy in

Galicia. The schools, the judiciary, and the administration became Polish. A local parliament functioned in Lwów. Yet this was rather autonomy for traditional elites—Polish nobles—than it was home rule for the population as a whole. The cause of social and economic reform was essentially set aside, because traditional Polish elites secured for themselves an excellent arrangement.

In the early 1860s, many Poles believed that a wave of reform in the Russian Empire could be turned to their advantage. The abolition of serfdom in 1861 sparked an intense discussion of the land question; as ever, Polish nobles were confronted with the choice between (perhaps) gaining the loyalty of peasants by conceding land or (perhaps) preserving their own social position by insisting on the status quo. This question was never answered to anyone's satisfaction, but Poles did agree that there was a chance to revive local institutions. Andrzej Zamoyski, a leader of the Agricultural Society and the leading voice in this debate, spoke of a moral revolution: if Poles could reform themselves, political change would follow. His rival Aleksander Wielopolski, the leading Polish administrator in the Congress Kingdom, began rather from the premise that any reform in Polish lands had to begin with an explicit endorsement from Russia. Wielopolski did gain the tsar's approval for an institute of higher education in Warsaw, and for civil equality for the Jews (whom he regarded as the "third estate" of Polish society). As Russia struggled with the abolition of serfdom and radical ideas flowed from the east (as well as from the emigration, and increasingly from Polish society), conservative reforms backed by Russian force seemed unsatisfactory.

Wielopolski was aware that he was opposed by Polish radicals known as "Reds"; he had some of them hanged. To forestall their revolutionary threat, he ordered their conscription into the Russian army. This forced the Reds to revolt without due preparation. The moderate reformers, known as Whites, then generally felt obliged to join them in the field. The revolutionaries of 1863 established a short-lived National Government. It promised land to the peasants, but had mixed success in recruiting them to the Polish cause. The January Uprising of 1863 to 1864 was the high point of Polish-Jewish cooperation; many Jews fought and died for the cause,

Russian troops occupy Warsaw after the January Insurrection of 1863–1864. ©Hulton-Deutsch Collection/Corbis

especially in Warsaw. Unlike the uprising of 1830, this movement had no real chance of success. Although in reality less threatening than Polish participation in Napoleon's campaign of 1812 or the uprising of 1830, the November Uprising of 1830–1831 brought the harshest Russian response yet. A Russian political class beginning to understand the world in national terms was shocked by Polish perfidy. The Russification that began in 1864, while consistent with the general trend of Russian policy in its western lands, was particularly harsh in Polish lands.

A few hundred or perhaps a few thousand participants in the uprising were executed; several thousand more were exiled to Siberia. More than three thousand noble estates were confiscated, their land generally given to tsarist officials. Polish landowners were required to pay a massive indemnity in historic Lithuania as well as in the former Congress Kingdom. The name "Kingdom of Poland" was actually abolished at this time; Russian officials began referring to

the "Vistula Land." From the 1870s the territories were ruled by governors-general with extensive executive and judicial powers; after 1879, for example, they could order that civilians be deported without trial. After 1831 these territories had lost the principle of constitutional rule; after 1864 they lost most of the institutional advantages they had enjoyed over the rest of the Russian Empire. The separate treasury and budget were eliminated, and the Polish Bank was subordinated to the Imperial Bank. Schooling was Russified. Basic reforms of the rest of the empire were not applied here. The former Congress Kingdom did not have trial by jury, for example, nor were its regions allowed to have local self-government by zemstvo. Land reform was carried out by the Russian state. Polish nobles had lost their chance to use this question to build a national community.

The failure of the January Uprising revealed the bankruptcy of Polish internationalism. Important political émigrés such as Czartoryski had tried for decades to exploit each international crisis to force the Polish question onto the negotiating table. His last real hope had been the Crimean War (1853–1856), which pitted the liberal powers of Britain and France against Russia, but the field of battle in the end was limited to Crimea itself. The Romantic poet Adam Mickiewicz died trying to raise a battalion of volunteers to fight against Russia. Mickiewicz invented messianism, and the Polish cause was in some sense a Roman Catholic one, but Polish rebels never enjoyed the support of the Catholic Church. To say that Mickiewicz's religious views were heretical drastically understates the matter, and in any case the Vatican had no wish to upset the partitioning empires by raising the Polish question. Even so, the Catholic Church was punished in Poland after the uprising; by 1870 not a single bishop of 1863 remained in his diocese. The only state that offered even verbal support for the Polish cause was France; this ceased later when France and Russia allied.

The complete fiasco, domestic and international, forced Polish patriots to reconsider traditional approaches to the national question. The third quarter of the nineteenth century was the great era of faith in science, and in the Vistula Land Polish students and journalists developed their own school of "positivism." Although they took the term from the French philosopher Auguste Comte, they were more influenced by the English sociologist Herbert Spencer, believing in the possibility of evolutionary (as opposed to revolutionary) progress. They also accepted the organic metaphors whose use was widespread in the Europe of the 1880s, which allowed them to regard the intelligentsia as both a social class and as the mind of the nation. In this way the traditional role of the nobility as the leading class of the nation was claimed by a generation of educated Poles largely of noble (though sometimes of Jewish) origin. Warsaw positivists hoped that Polish society could be made to function as a self-sufficient organism, even though it lacked a Polish state: they drew the same kinds of libertarian conclusions from the English naturalist Charles Darwin as the social Darwinists did, although in a very different political context. They counted on industrialization to create a new Polish middle class. Their leading light, Aleksander Świętochowski, spoke of "internal independence." When they spoke of society

they meant the nation. They believed, in a word, in progress.

Industrialization was a reality; the lands of the former Congress Kingdom were among the most developed of the Russian Empire. A middle class and a working class did indeed emerge, especially in Warsaw and Łódź. Yet progress was elusive. Russia could, and did, alter tariff and other economic policies in ways unfavorable to the Polish lands. New ideas presumed modern education, but Russian policies emphasized ancient languages and religion; for the natural sciences it was desirable and for the social sciences it was necessary to leave the Empire and study in western Europe. The most famous case of the resulting brain drain is Marie Curie (née Skłodowska), the Nobel Prize–winning physicist. Men and women who came of age in the 1890s developed the positivists' scientific approach to society, while rejecting their more optimistic beliefs. The National Democrats also accepted Spencerian ideas, but emphasized competition between groups rather than organic harmony. The National Democrats also emphasized the entirety of Polish society rather than simply the nobility. Rather than counting on changes in Russian policy or a rising tide of general enlightenment, they organized conspiratorial national education on the scale of the entire country, in all three partitions. The Marxists, meanwhile, accepted the overall idea of progress, while maintaining that progress could result only from conflict between classes. Most of the Polish Marxists were allied with Rosa Luxemburg, who believed that the national question was a distraction from the general European revolution.

The main current of Polish socialism, however, was that of Józef Piłsudski and his Polish Socialist Party. This party, although it included several Marxists and former Marxists, was essentially anti-ideological. Its leaders believed that national independence was a precondition for social justice, and generally that national independence was a good in itself. In the 1890s and the early part of the twentieth century, Piłsudski's socialists were the main rival of the National Democrats, who were led by Roman Dmowski. Where Piłsudski's party included many Jews and many Poles of eastern (Lithuanian, Belarusian, Ukrainian) background, Dmowski's party was more attractive to Poles from central

Jewish textile worker in Poland. Early-twentieth-century drawing. The artist comments on the exploitation of Jewish workers in Polish factories by depicting a vampire-like character drinking the worker's blood. ©CHRISTEL GERSTENBERG/CORBIS

and western Poland. While Piłsudski referred to the traditions of the former Commonwealth, Dmowski argued that excessive toleration had doomed that Polish-Lithuanian state. While Piłsudski believed that a future Poland would and should emerge as a federation of peoples between Germany and Russia, Dmowski advanced the ideal of a national state. Piłsudski and his followers treated the Russian Empire as the great threat to Poland; Dmowski placed Germans and increasingly Jews in this role. Piłsudski saw the competition with Russia as essentially political and military; Dmowski perceived the competition with Germans and Jews as social and economic. In this way among others Dmowski's ideas were innovative; his influential 1903 essay was titled "Thoughts of a Modern Pole."

In some sense the Russian Revolution of 1905 offered the same kind of opportunity to Polish patriots as the instability of the early 1860s, and it provoked the same kinds of disagreements. Piłsudski's socialists disagreed among themselves, some of them frightened that the mass character of the revolt of Polish workers had slipped free from their control, some wishing to push forward to revolution. Piłsudski himself hoped to exploit the Russo-Japanese War to destroy the Russian Empire: he traveled to Tokyo to offer the help of his socialists to the Japanese, only to find that Dmowski had come to Japan to thwart his designs. Piłsudski emerged from the revolution at the head of a new Revolutionary Fraction of the party, a group that had essentially abandoned politics in favor of military training in anticipation of a European war. Dmowski, by contrast, sought to play a role in the internal politics of Russia, and he and his National Democrats sought to play a role in the State Duma established by Tsar Nicholas II in 1905. Their only legislative victory was the return of the Polish language to Polish schools; this reform was rather soon undone. After 1907 Russian electoral law guaranteed the election of Dumas that were "Russian in spirit." Dmowski's bet on Russian reform failed, but his general program of education and agitation made his organization the most important Polish movement of the early twentieth century.

By the end of the nineteenth century, in all three partitions of Poland, the Polish question was posed as one of modern mass movements confronting more or less premodern political systems. In Austria, the free press and then (after 1907) suffrage for adult males created the conditions for an open political competition between Poles and Ukrainians. Polish nobles dominated the local administration, and democracy created threatening social movements, some of which were also national movements. In Germany the competition was between an industrializing state that wished to colonize its own eastern marches, and a strong Polish civil society that responded by its own initiatives. Bismarck's Kulturkampf of 1872 to 1887 was directed against the Roman Catholic Church, and thus de facto against most Poles who were German subjects. In 1872 German was made the only language of instruction in the Poznań region, and in 1876 the use of Polish was banned in the administration and the courts. In the 1880s and 1890s official policies encouraged German colonization of Germany's eastern marches; Poles responded by establishing their own land banks and credit unions.

The history of Poland in the nineteenth century is one of variety, continuity, and anticipation. Despite the partitions, there were elements of Polish rule in one place or another for most of the years between the French Revolution and World War I. Polish society was transformed importantly by the policies of each partitioning power. Politics in Russia was most revolutionary, in Austria most conservative, and in Germany most keyed to economic life. Communication between Polish lands, despite incompatibilities of rail lines and political hindrances, was far easier in 1914 than in 1789. In all three partitions, the number of people who identified themselves as Poles certainly increased radically during this period. The important political movements, on the right as on the left, wished to reach mass society while anticipating another radical transformation of Europe. When that transformation came, with World War I (1914–1918), the opportunity was seized by those who had anticipated it. An independent Poland drawn from territories of all three partitioning powers was established in 1918.

See also **Chopin, Frédéric; Czartoryski, Adam; Endecja; Mickiewicz, Adam; Polish National Movement; Russia; Ukraine.**

BIBLIOGRAPHY

Jedlicki, Jerzy. *A Suburb of Europe: Nineteenth-Century Polish Approaches to Western Civilization.* Budapest, Hungary, 1999.

Kieniewicz, Stefan. *Historia Polski, 1795–1918.* 8th ed. Warsaw, 1996.

Leslie, R. F., ed. *The History of Poland since 1863.* Cambridge, U.K., 1980.

Porter, Brian. *When Nationalism Began to Hate: Imagining Modern Politics in Nineteenth-Century Poland.* New York, 2000.

Snyder, Timothy. *The Reconstruction of Nations: Poland, Ukraine, Lithuania, Belarus, 1569–1999.* New Haven, Conn., 2003.

Walicki, Andrzej. *Philosophy and Romantic Nationalism: The Case of Poland.* Oxford, U.K., 1982.

Wandycz, Piotr S. *The Lands of Partitioned Poland, 1795–1918.* Seattle, Wash., 1974.

TIMOTHY SNYDER

POLICE AND POLICING. The nineteenth century witnessed significant developments in police institutions across Europe. The developments were driven by concerns about crime, public order, and the control of public space, but also by different bureaucratic and political imperatives related to the expanding state structures.

THE FRENCH MODEL

Under the Old Regime before the French Revolution, policing tended to depend upon municipalities or local institutions and powerful interests. At the close of the seventeenth century, however, the French monarchy had created a police executive for Paris with responsibility for a wide range of municipal services as well as for the suppression of crime and maintenance of public order. There was also a military body, the *maréchaussée*, charged with policing the main roads and small towns and villages of provincial France.

Under the revolution and Napoleon policing was considerably centralized and unified, though much still remained under local control. The *maréchaussée* was enlarged and renamed the Gendarmerie Nationale. After a brief period of municipal devolution during the 1790s, the police system of Paris was tightly unified under a government-appointed prefect of police. A *commissaire*, directly responsible to the prefect, was established in each of the city's forty-eight districts. In addition there were officers with remits that ran across the whole city, and in 1829, in an attempt to demonstrate government paternalism for the people of the capital, a force of uniformed patrolmen (*sergents de ville*) was created. Outside of Paris, legislation of 1791 enabled the election of a *commissaire de police* by any town that so wished. Under Napoleon these appointments were made centrally from a list of names prepared by the departmental prefect and were required for every town with a population in excess of five thousand. The men who were responsible to the *commissaire*, however, depended upon what the local municipality was prepared to pay for and recruit. Outside of the towns, and in addition to the gendarmes, there were other locally appointed, locally financed police who maintained surveillance of the villages, forests, and crops. With local variations these

The name *bobby* was derived from the diminutive of Sir Robert Peel's first name. The term *peeler* was also used, especially in Ireland, where, as chief secretary in 1814, Peel had established the precursor of the Royal Irish Constabulary. In working-class districts the police were often known by terms such as *crusher*. Similar disparaging terms were used elsewhere: *bulle* (Germany); *flic* (France); *sbirro* (Italy).

three broad types of police—the military, state-appointed gendarmes; the state-appointed civilian police; and the locally appointed and financed municipal police—became common across Europe over the nineteenth century. The French, however, did not provide the model for development in every case.

Gendarmes, who also had responsibility for policing the military, followed Napoleon's armies across Europe. They were established across the Napoleonic empire, and Napoleon encouraged his satellites and allies to create similar bodies. In addition to combating banditry and other forms of crime, the gendarmes were useful for ensuring that taxes were paid and delivered and that conscripts reached their muster points. While the name was often changed (to *carabinieri* in Italy and to *Landjäger* in parts of Germany), the gendarmerie model survived Napoleon's fall. Together with the roles of crime fighting and bringing in conscripts, gendarmes showed the national or imperial flag in rural areas and, by being available to provide assistance in times of natural disaster or epidemic, they partly fulfilled the expanding state's broader promise of protection for its citizens. Even Napoleon's most consistent enemies adopted the gendarmerie model when and where it suited them: Spain, with the Guardia Civil in 1844, and the Austrian Empire in 1849. The British considered that a form of gendarmerie was the best system for Ireland and, subsequently, for many parts of their empire. But, at home, the British were responsible for developing the most influential civilian police model of the nineteenth century.

THE BRITISH MODEL

London's Metropolitan Police was established by act of Parliament in 1829. The new force replaced the old parish watches. Sir Robert Peel, the home secretary responsible for the legislation, insisted that a unified policing structure for the city would provide a more efficient police. This, in turn, would stem the rise in crime and, ultimately, achieve economies for metropolitan taxpayers. Since there was a long-standing antipathy to the deployment of soldiers for the maintenance of public order in England, the Metropolitan Police was carefully designed to appear nonmilitary. The uniform was blue, as opposed to the scarlet tunics of the British infantry. Initially the men wore a top hat, as opposed to any form of military helmet, and they were armed only with a wooden truncheon. The new police constables were instructed that their first duty was the prevention of crime, and to achieve this they were required to make regular patrols of fixed beats to discourage offenders and to ensure that property owners took appropriate precautions, particularly at night, by locking their doors and windows. Similar civilian forces were established in the principal towns as part of the reform of municipal corporations in 1835, while enabling legislation of 1839 and 1840 permitted the creation of constabularies in the counties. The London model was not rigidly followed in the provinces, though senior officers for the municipalities were often recruited from the metropolitan force. Moreover, while the Metropolitan Police was answerable to the central government, the provincial forces, as was the case elsewhere in Europe, were answerable to local authorities.

London's Metropolitan Police became the model for liberal politicians across the European continent. The police were seen as contributing to Britain's avoidance of revolution in 1848; though troops were held in reserve, the major Chartist demonstrations of that year, and of earlier years, were handled by the police. The Great Exhibition of 1851 also contributed to the prestige of London's police when tens of thousands of people from all classes, from all parts of Britain, and even from overseas visited the city, policed only by the unarmed "bobbies," without any serious incident. Napoleon III reorganized the Paris police in the mid-1850s, drawing ideas from his experience as an exile in London. Some German

The Poor and the Police on a London Street at Night.
Engraving by Gustave Doré c. 1869–1871. Doré included
harrassment by police as one of the problems faced by the
poor of London in his famous series of etchings on the subject.
SNARK/ART RESOURCE, NY

states cherry-picked from the London model. The legislature of the new Italian state was also impressed by *il bobby inglese* but was concerned that its own population was not yet ready for a similar civilian force. The Italians, in consequence, maintained their carabinieri under the war ministry and established a new state police under the Ministry of the Interior that was armed and partly militarized, the Guardie di Pubblica Sicurezza (Public Security Guards).

The police system in England liked to boast of another difference from its continental counterparts, namely that it was not a political police. One reason for the uniform of London's Metropolitan Police in 1829 was to demonstrate that the constables were not spies. In addition to concerns about military policing, the English professed to dislike the idea of a police that investigated people's politics and attitudes. They perceived that idea as being French, conceived in the Old Regime and reaching fruition in Napoleon's Ministry of Police under Joseph Fouché. Concerns about men

acting in plain clothes inhibited the development of a detective branch in London for many years. But the threat from Fenian bombers in the 1860s and again in the 1880s led to the deployment of officers whose task was to investigate political suspects, and the interests of these officers rapidly spread beyond the investigation of Irish activists.

AIMS AND IMPACT OF POLICING

Elsewhere in Europe, at least from the period of the French Revolution, it was accepted though rarely popular that policing involved the surveillance of political dissidents, radicals, and labor activists. In Russia, from its origins, the gendarmerie was officially attached to the third section of the tsar's private Imperial Chancery, the political police. In Germany the first moves to bring together the police systems of individual states occurred during the early 1850s. They were coordinated by the head of the Berlin police, Karl von Hinckeldey, in an attempt to provide an effective system of surveillance over political suspects and to ensure the circulation of information relating to such suspects.

Political policing has an aura of sinister romance; however, most policing in the nineteenth century involved the surveillance of city streets and provincial roads and the enforcing and maintenance of new levels of decorum and order in public space. The principal targets of this police strategy were the working classes, who tended to take their leisure on the streets, as well as at fairs and other events in public space. At the same time, criminality was generally regarded as a problem situated in the lower strata of the working class. Thus the control of the working classes in public space could also be seen as a way of controlling the criminal or dangerous classes. Decorum in public space also meant the control of prostitution, and most European police forces had special units whose duties related specifically to the supervision and regulation of prostitutes—*la police des moeurs* in France, *die Sittenpolizei* in Germany, *polizia dei costumi* in Italy. Here again England was an exception. Police officers could apprehend women for soliciting but only in certain naval ports and garrison towns, and only from the mid-1860s to the mid-1880s under the Contagious Diseases Acts were certain police officers specifically delegated to the supervision of prostitutes.

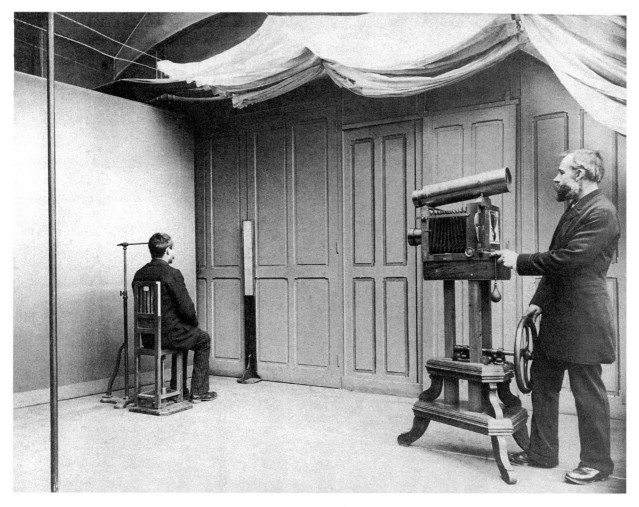

Alphonse Bertillon taking an anthropometrical photograph, late nineteenth century. The Bertillon system, officially adopted by French police in 1888, was an early attempt at identification of criminals through an extensive series of measurements and descriptions. It became a standard worldwide but was later replaced by fingerprint identification. Musée de la Préfecture de Police, Paris, France/Bridgeman Art Library

It is difficult to assess the impact of the new police institutions on levels of crime and disorder. Generally speaking the statistics of crime appear to have leveled off in most countries from the mid-nineteenth century. Probably the regular patrols of police officers had some impact on minor street crime. Most of the big city forces began to collect and exchange information on offenders. By the turn of the century the larger forces had photographic records and physical descriptions of offenders. They had the body measurements of offenders collected and cataloged under the system devised in Paris by Alphonse Bertillon, and there were also the beginnings of fingerprint archives. Yet it remains an open question as to how good police institutions were at retrieving such information and using it to solve

more serious crimes. A similar question arises regarding the application of some of the criminological theories that began to be taught in the Italian Scuola di Polizia Scientifica established by Salvatore Ottolenghi, a pupil of Cesare Lombroso.

The men who attended Ottolenghi's school were to be the leaders of the police, and they already had a significant degree of education. Most continental European forces recruited their senior officers, such as the *commissaire* in France and the *questore* in Italy, from the middle classes, from men with some education and social standing. In Britain, in contrast, all men except for the most senior commanders were expected to start as ordinary constables and work their way up. In the smaller British towns even head constables were known to have begun their police careers as bobbies on the beat. Generally speaking, policing in the nineteenth century was an unskilled or at best a semiskilled job. Patrolmen were usually recruited from the working class. In continental Europe they seem often to have been selected from former soldiers, usually noncommissioned officers; places were specifically reserved for army veterans in the Paris police. In Britain the decision of whether to recruit ex-soldiers appears usually to have been left to chief constables; some of these favored military men for their bearing, but some were concerned that army life fostered idleness and a fondness for drink.

The patrolmen were expected to be respectable and to ensure that their families were also respectable. Police service often meant some form of pension at the end of a man's career. Police pay, however, was rarely generous and, as with other working-class trades during the nineteenth century, police officers occasionally banded together to demand improvements in pay and conditions. Such behavior was rare among the gendarmeries, even though their trade papers voiced discontents. It was more common among the civilian forces, where strike activity was also known. By the outbreak of World War I Belgian, Dutch, French, and Scandinavian police officers had established trade unions, and a similar body was in embryo in Britain.

See also **Anarchism; Class and Social Relations; Crime; Fouché, Joseph.**

BIBLIOGRAPHY

Berlière, Jean-Marc. *Le monde des polices en France: XIXe–XXe siècles.* Brussels, 1996.

Emsley, Clive. *The English Police: A Political and Social History.* 2nd ed. London, 1996.

———. *Gendarmes and the State in Nineteenth-Century Europe.* Oxford, U.K., 1999.

Jensen, Richard Bach. "Police Reform and Social Reform: Italy from the Crisis of the 1890s to the Giolittian Era." *Criminal Justice History* 10 (1989): 179–200.

Spencer, Elaine Glovka. *Police and the Social Order in German Cities: The Düsseldorf District, 1848–1914.* De Kalb, Ill., 1992.

CLIVE EMSLEY

POLISH NATIONAL MOVEMENT.

The state formally known as "The Republic of the Kingdom of Poland and the Grand Duchy of Lithuania" (sometimes labeled the "Polish-Lithuanian Commonwealth" in English-language texts) was once one of the largest countries in Europe, but by the eighteenth century its decentralized political system was unable to resist the expansionist ambitions of its more absolutist neighbors. The polity's decline culminated in a series of diplomatic and military disasters known as the Partitions of Poland: three treaties (1772, 1793, and 1795) that carved up the country between Russia, Prussia, and Austria. After the third partition there was no longer a Polish state on the map, but in its place there had emerged a committed core of patriotic activists who were devoted to the restoration of independence.

Hardly had the post-partition boundaries been established when the Napoleonic Wars threw the entire international order into chaos. Many Polish national activists were enthusiastic about the transformative potential of the French Revolution, and a Polish legion was formed alongside the French army in 1797. Because of this, when Napoleon defeated Prussia in 1806 many hoped that he would sponsor a Polish restoration. This is not quite what happened. In 1807 he created a small, dependent puppet state called the Duchy of Warsaw, which encompassed only a fraction of the former republic's territory. For all its limitations, the Duchy did revitalize Polish political life, and made it difficult to return to the status quo ante after Napoleon's fall.

THE UPRISINGS

The Congress of Vienna (1814–1815) once again drew a space for Poland on the map, elevating its status to that of a "kingdom" with its own parliament, legal system, administrative autonomy, and army. But there was one stipulation: the Russian tsar would be ex officio king of Poland. This would ensure that Polish autonomy would be more nominal than real, and that the national movement would continue to grow. Under Alexander I (r. 1801–1825), the Polish kingdom did indeed enjoy some meaningful self-governance, but this quickly eroded under the more authoritarian

Nicholas I (r. 1825–1855). Opposition to his efforts to curtail Polish autonomy exploded in 1830 with the so-called November Uprising. The Polish parliament dethroned Nicholas and a brief war ensued, but the Poles stood little chance of success. After the suppression of the uprising, martial law was declared and Polish self-rule was effectively ended.

The defeat of the November Uprising forced thousands of Polish national activists to flee abroad in what came to be labeled the Great Emigration. Most of these exiles settled in France, where they continued to conspire against the partitioning powers. Many of the masterpieces of nineteenth-century Polish culture (nearly all of which were imbued with patriotic content) emerged from this context: the poetry of Adam Mickiewicz (1798–1855), Juliusz Słowacki (1809–1849), and Zygmunt Krasiński (1812–1859), and the music of Frédéric Chopin (1810–1849), just to name a few. In the hothouse atmosphere of the Great Emigration, an idealistic brand of Polish patriotism emerged, committed not only to another insurrection but also to the subsequent creation of a new, more perfect Poland in which the mundane injustices of nineteenth-century Europe would be resolved. A number of ephemeral conspiracies were organized by these émigrés in the 1830s and 1840s, and one significant revolt was attempted in Cracow (Kraków) in 1846, but all of these efforts failed. During the European-wide revolutionary year of 1848 the Russians managed to keep any unrest from breaking out in their partition, and although there were violent conflicts between Poles and Germans in the Prussian partition, nothing was accomplished to advance the Polish cause.

The culminating moment of conspiratorial Polish nationalism came with the January Uprising of 1863. After the reform-minded Alexander II became emperor in 1855, the restoration of some sort of Polish autonomy seemed possible. A handful of Polish aristocrats attempted to cooperate with the Russian authorities toward this end, but the pent-up ambitions and frustrations of the past decades soon exploded in a series of mass demonstrations. These were violently broken up by the Russians, which only further radicalized the Polish activists and spurred the development of an extensive patriotic conspiracy. On 22 January 1863 the leaders of this underground group launched a national uprising, and for more than a year a guerilla war raged throughout the Polish territories of the Russian Empire. Eventually this revolt failed as well, but not before thirty thousand rebels had been killed and thirty-eight thousand exiled to Siberia.

THE EMERGENCE OF MODERN NATIONALISM

In the aftermath of the January Uprising the tsarist authorities abolished all remnants of Polish autonomy and launched a campaign of Russification. A similar program was attempted in the newly created German Empire starting in the 1870s. Poles who advocated independence had long been targeted for repression in all three partitions, but there had been no real attempt to culturally transform the Poles into Germans or Russians. For the last third of the century, however, the Polish language was almost entirely pushed out of the educational system and the administrative structures of the German and Russian states. Only in Austria did the situation for the Poles improve: when the Habsburg Empire was reorganized with the Ausgleich (compromise) of 1867, the Poles gained nearly full autonomy within the province of Galicia.

After the crushing defeat of 1863 most Polish activists turned to what they called "organic work": a program of economic and cultural development combined with an explicit repudiation of political conspiracies. Only in the 1880s did a few small nationalist organizations begin to take shape once again. At the time few Polish activists saw any contradiction between socialism and nationalism, but gradually the two paths started to diverge. Some nationalists argued that social justice had to be subordinated to the need for national solidarity, and while few socialists actually repudiated the cause of independence they did insist that it had to be accompanied by a radically new social order. These divisions were solidified with the creation of two rival organizations, the Polish Socialist Party (founded in 1892) and the National Democratic Movement (or Endecja, founded in 1893). Both groups emerged as mass movements at the time of the Russian Revolution of 1905, and by then their hostility toward each other was almost as intense as their opposition to the partitions.

When World War I broke out in 1914, the "Polish question" was as much a factor in European politics as ever. The Polish national movement had met with repeated failures during that long century, and the cost in lives and material destruction was great. On the other hand, the very persistence of the movement inspired all sides during World War I to attempt to win Polish support with promises of autonomy and eventually independence. There were many debates among the Poles about which side to join during the war, but in the end it did not matter: all three of the partitioning powers were destroyed by the conflict, and Polish independence was proclaimed on the very day of the armistice: 11 November 1918.

See also **Endecja; Mickiewicz, Adam; Poland; Nationalism.**

BIBLIOGRAPHY

Hagen, William W. *Germans, Poles, and Jews: The Nationality Conflict in the Prussian East, 1772–1914.* Chicago, 1980.

Porter, Brian. *When Nationalism Began to Hate: Imagining Modern Politics in Nineteenth-Century Poland.* New York, 2000.

Walicki, Andrzej. *Philosophy and Romantic Nationalism: The Case of Poland.* Oxford, U.K., 1982.

Wandycz, Piotr S. *The Lands of Partitioned Poland, 1795–1918.* Seattle, 1974.

BRIAN PORTER

POLITICAL CATHOLICISM. *See* Catholicism, Political.

POOR LAW.

In Britain, the term *poor law* was commonly applied to various laws that provided for the sick, disabled, and unemployed. A body of legislation from the sixteenth, seventeenth, and eighteenth centuries was known collectively as the Poor Law or, after 1834, the Old Poor Law. In that year the old legislation was superseded by the Poor Law Amendment Act (1834), which became known as the New Poor Law.

Under the Old Poor Law, poor relief was managed at the parochial level by an annually appointed overseer of the poor. In the main, provisions consisted of what was called outdoor relief: supplemental payments made to individuals or families living in their homes, rather than in workhouses or debtors' prisons. The Old Poor Law also included a series of acts of settlement designed to prevent vagrants and other outsiders from receiving the aid of the parish. The most significant of these was the Settlement Act of 1662, which facilitated the eviction of paupers, who were to be returned to the parishes of their birth.

The Old Poor Law was clearly designed to accommodate a society of small villages and limited mobility. Its provisions were by and large successful in such an environment, and the poor in England were generally regarded as being better off than their counterparts in the rest of Europe. But with demographic and other change in England, especially in the second half of the eighteenth century, this increasingly failed to match reality.

In the face of inadequate wages and high food prices (exacerbated by the Napoleonic Wars), Speenhamland Parish in Berkshire experimented with a modified project of poor relief in 1795. The plan instituted a sliding-scale of outdoor relief, based on wages, number of dependents, and the current price of food. The scheme's intent was charitable, but an unfortunate (if hardly unforeseeable) consequence was that unscrupulous wage-payers could become even more ruthless, on the grounds that if wages were not adjusted to reflect living costs, the parish authorities would meet the difference. In spite of its shortcomings, some variant of the Speenhamland system, as it was called, quickly spread to most of the southern counties of England, and the amount English parishes paid for poor relief skyrocketed. In 1785, English parishes paid out about £2 million on poor relief. At its height, in 1818, English parishes provided £7,871,000 in poor relief, and in the last decade of the Old Poor Law, outdoor relief averaged around £7 million per year.

The abuses of the Speenhamland system, together with changing liberal attitudes regarding poverty and self-help, produced an environment that demanded reform. In 1832, the Whig government of Earl Grey (Charles Grey, 1764–1845) established a royal commission to investigate the workings of the Old Poor Law. Twenty-six commissioners visited about three thousand parishes, and filed their report in 1834. The government accepted its proposals and pushed through the Poor Law Amendment Act the same year. More commonly known simply as the New Poor Law, its major provisions included widespread establishment of workhouses and the curbing of outdoor relief. A workhouse was built for every parish or, in the case of small parishes, for a union of parishes. Outdoor relief was discontinued, so the able-bodied poor no longer received aid unless they agreed to live in the workhouses. To further discourage recourse to poor relief, workhouse inmates lived under extremely harsh conditions. (In the language of the Poor Law Amendment Act, conditions offered in a workhouse were to be "less desirable" than the poorest private dwelling.) A poor law commission was set up in London to supervise and support the work of parish poor law guardians, previously the sole responsibility of elected local officials.

In some respects, the New Poor Law was highly effective. From the point of view of expenditure, the poor rate dropped from about £7 million per year from 1830 to 1834 to between £4 and £5 million annually thereafter. Ratepayers and others who were convinced the poor were simply lazy and had brought their troubles on themselves could rest assured that the "less desirable" clause of the act guaranteed in most cases that only those truly in need would apply for aid. Moreover, meager and unappealing though it was, the diet provided in the workhouse was probably more nourishing than what many low-paid workers could have afforded.

Nonetheless, there was widespread opposition to the implementation of the New Poor Law. Under the Old Poor Law, the "deserving" poor—the aged, sick, handicapped, or widowed—and their dependents had come to expect relief in the comfort and dignity of their own homes. Similarly, the families of the "able-bodied" poor had come to rely on the Speenhamland system or other projects. But with the termination of outdoor relief, a pauper had to enter a workhouse to be eligible for aid, and many poor families suffered. Furthermore, workhouse inmates were housed by sex and age, so husbands, wives, and children were separated. As well as a stark and unappealing diet,

other "less desirable" conditions in a workhouse included harsh, menial, and monotonous tasks. The aloof oversight of the workhouses by the London-based Board of Guardians was another source of resentment.

Anger with the New Poor Law occasionally led to riots, abuse of poor law officials, and attacks on the workhouses, which were popularly derided as Bastilles, after the hated prison of pre-Revolutionary Paris. Probably the most famous contemporary critic of the provisions of the New Poor Law was the novelist Charles Dickens who, in *Oliver Twist* (1838), aimed to arouse middle-class consciences. Indeed, it is chiefly through Dickens that the workhouse and the plight of the poor in nineteenth-century England remains part of current vocabulary and imagination.

Although amended repeatedly throughout the nineteenth and early twentieth centuries, vestiges of the New Poor Law persisted until 1929, when Public Assistance Committees (PACs) replaced the Board of Guardians.

See also **Great Britain; Poverty; Welfare.**

BIBLIOGRAPHY

Brundage, Anthony. *The English Poor Laws, 1700–1930.* New York, 2002.

Kidd, Alan J. *State, Society, and the Poor in Nineteenth-Century England.* New York, 1999.

RICHARD FLOYD

POPULAR AND ELITE CULTURE.

The term *culture* is hard to define, and the difference (if any exists) between popular culture and elite culture is often controversial. Terms such as *elite culture* (or simply *culture*) have often been used to designate literature, the fine arts, and the performing arts, in contrast to a less refined and less educated mass (or popular) culture. The academic fields of social history and cultural history have greatly revised the perception of popular culture since the 1970s by exploring topics as diverse as material culture and department stores, nationalist culture and war monuments, folk culture and the *charivari* (rough music), or urban culture and the rise of spectator sports. This entry considers the above topics to be popular culture in contrast to traditional high culture (such as literature or opera) and it will discuss the relationship between popular and elite culture.

REGIONALISM AND CULTURAL DIVERSITY

Generalizations about popular culture in the nineteenth century must begin with the qualification that in many ways it remained local or regional, not shared across the Continent. The centrality of the *corrida* (bullfight) in Spanish culture, especially in regions such as Andalusia, its great theaters such as the Plaza de toros in Madrid (which held more than twelve thousand people), and its spectacular rituals of *banderillos* and *picadores* (secondary participants in bullfights who goad the bull) shaped a local popular culture for thousands, if not millions, of people. Yet this was utterly different from Nordic local culture, especially in regions such as Telemark, Norway, where the tradition of skiing shaped a culture old enough to have fascinated Procopius and to have roots in a pre-Christian cult of Uller, the god of winter, who walked on skis. When skiers in Telemark began competitive skiing in 1864, it remained quite unknown in the land of the matador.

Similarly, important differences existed between the popular culture of the town and the village. To some urban eyes, rural Europe was a country of savages, "as brutal as the bears it breeds," in the words of a French prefect in 1831 (Weber, p. 3). Centuries-old traditions continued to characterize the cultures of rural Europe. Many rural cultures (especially in Mediterranean regions) still lived by such time-honored behaviors as the vendetta, in which matters of individual or family honor were resolved outside of the law. Other communities still employed such collective action as the *charivari*, in which villagers would serenade an unpopular or misbehaving member of the community with loud and cacophonous sounds. The derision of the *charivari* might include such traditional symbolism as antlers to humiliate a cuckolded (or simply weak-willed) husband. In the German version, the community might remove the thatch roof from the home of a man who seemed to be dominated by his wife.

Yet a nuanced view of popular culture must also note similarities across regions or between urban and rural culture. For example, scholars such

as Eric Hobsbawm have explored the persistence of banditry, often sustained by family and community networks. Some regions, such as Sicily or Greece, became notorious for their culture of banditry, most famously the Mafiosi of southern Italy. Yet the image of the bandit flourished in northern societies too, as in the constantly retold sagas of Robin Hood and Dick Turpin in English popular culture or in the accounts of the bandit-hero Oleksa Dovbush in the Habsburg Empire. Social historians, cultural historians, and anthropologists continue to debate the extent to which highwaymen and brigands were seen as romantic heroes struggling against authority or as thugs who terrorized the countryside, but bandits (and popular tales about them) existed in most regions.

Similarly, networks of cultural support for criminal behavior also link the rural and urban worlds of nineteenth-century Europe. Early industrial outbursts of violence against machinery—from the Luddites in the English Midlands (1811–1813) to industrial sabotage in northern France (the word *sabotage* derives from the wooden shoes, or *sabots,* that workers threw into the machinery)—followed patterns that were similar to rural collective behavior. Both drew upon a community sense of a moral economy that heroic figures (from the fictitious Ned Ludd in early-nineteenth-century Britain to the real women who forced bakers to sell bread at the "just price," as French women did for centuries) might enforce; when such figures broke the law, they often received the support of the community, just as rural bandits did.

It should not be inferred from these examples that popular culture was chiefly grim or violent. Most regions of Europe retained a mixture of oral culture and folk tales; of song, village bands, and workers' music halls; of street and festival entertainment such as rope-walking, juggling, acrobatics, and marionettes; of itinerant magic lantern shows and theatrical groups.

The diversity of popular culture also included dramatic variation within a single country. Some historians of rural France have insisted upon the infinite diversity of the peasantry and the weakness of generalizations about them, leading to a tradition of scholarly studies based upon a single community or region. As late as 1863, government figures show that nearly one-fourth of the communes of France (8,381 out of 37,510) contained no one who even

May Day, 1869. Watercolor by Charles Green. Traditional May Day celebrations in nineteenth-century England included dancing around the Maypole and the appearance of Jack-in-the-Green, a man wearing a large conical framework of vegetation probably representing the Green Man of Christian iconography. HARRIS MUSEUM AND ART GALLERY, PRESTON, LANCASHIRE, UK/BRIDGEMAN ART LIBRARY

spoke French; more than 10 percent of all French schoolchildren spoke no French, and a remarkable 48.2 percent of schoolchildren age seven to thirteen could not write in French. The persistence of regional languages and local patois underscores the variation of subcultures.

EDUCATION AND THE TRANSFORMATION OF POPULAR CULTURE

The nineteenth century witnessed a transformation of popular culture as a world of superstition, witches, ghosts, fortune tellers, phantoms, and spells—counterbalanced by magic, amulets, talismans, and rituals—gradually yielded to a more educated and rational culture, a world of wider travel and broader experience. This did not mean the end of the supernatural in popular culture (Bram Stoker published *Dracula* in 1897), nor did it impede such fads in popular culture as mesmerism, phrenology, and spiritualism.

The foremost agent of this historic change was the spread of universal education and literacy. Although the data are sketchy, studies have found that 72 percent of the men who married in France in 1800 could not sign their name to their wedding certificate; by 1860, those signing with an X had declined to 30 percent (45 percent for women), and thereafter illiteracy rapidly disappeared, reaching 3 percent for men and 4 percent for women in France in 1910. Germany reached a similar level of literacy in 1890 and Britain in 1900. Many regions in Mediterranean and eastern Europe, without laws mandating education, had significantly higher levels of illiteracy.

The rising literacy rate had a far-reaching impact on popular culture. Books, newspapers, and periodicals had been relatively few and were limited to an educated elite in the eighteenth century. A newspaper with a large circulation printed five thousand copies in 1789; by 1900 major

Russian peasants in traditional dress demonstrate a folk dance c. 1890s. ©CORBIS

papers were printing one million copies. Technology (such as the rotary press and the linotype machine) drove prices down: whereas leading papers such as the *Times* of London cost seven pence at start of the century, by the 1860s the penny press put newspapers within the reach of almost all readers. Imaginative editors changed newspapers to attract a mass readership, giving birth to the woodcut (and then the photographic) illustration, the anecdotal feuilleton, the cartoon, the serialized novel, the telegraphic report, and the war correspondent. Writers such as Victor Hugo, Charles Dickens, and Arthur Conan Doyle attracted tens of thousands of readers.

In 1789 newspapers had been important attractions in cafés, libraries, and *cabinets de lecture* (reading rooms), but they played a limited role in mass culture; by the early twentieth century, great cities such as London and Paris published nearly one hundred newspapers each, specialized to suit a wide range of tastes and opinions. The combined circulation of papers in such cities passed five million. Provincial towns published their own papers on at least a weekly basis. Specialized interests sustained periodicals on such topics as agriculture, sports, or fashion.

Thus the nineteenth century saw the oral culture of rural society largely replaced by the written culture of urban society. This transformed popular culture in ways far beyond newspaper readership. The manufacturing and mercantile economy of the age responded to a literate popular culture. Advertising (in forms such as the poster) changed material culture by promoting new products and the mail-order catalog made those products available to the small town and village. Complex equipment and procedures—from the camera to bicycle repair to the application of the chemical industry's new fertilizers—became available to readers.

LEISURE AND THE TRANSFORMATION OF POPULAR CULTURE

Neither the rural nor the urban world of 1789 provided Europeans with significant amounts of leisure or the means to use such freedom. Market days and festivals, carnivals and fairs, birth and marriage celebrations, holidays and saints' days created a culture of occasional leisure; however, these events were limited in both time (they were infrequent) and space (they involved minimal travel). Both restrictions eased during the nineteenth century, transforming popular culture.

Leisure time remained limited for most Europeans in 1914: the forty-hour work week, the paid annual vacation, and retirement were accomplishments of the twentieth century. Nineteenth-century industrialization, however, resulted in a gradual reduction of the work week for the urban masses, shortening work days and creating a weekend. The ten-hour workday had become standard in Britain by the late 1840s; by the 1890s, coal miners had achieved a workweek of 42.5 to 55 hours and textile workers had achieved a 56-hour week (five and one-half days). By 1900 the typical worker in western and central Europe could expect a minimum of Sunday and half of Saturday free from work. An academic debate still rages concerning the extent to which this reduction in work was achieved through the success of the industrial economy or through the hard-fought battles of labor unions and militant workers, but the basic fact remains that the century saw many people win a certain amount of free time.

A large proportion of the urban population was dechristianized by 1900—only a minority attended church on Sunday. The upper classes of Victorian England were shocked to see proof of this in 1851, when a national survey of people in church on Sunday morning March 31 found only 24.2 percent of the population there. This trend, combined with the shrinking work week, greatly increased the popular culture of leisure activity.

Simultaneously, European technology conquered distance. The railroad, the steamship, and the bicycle opened tremendous new opportunities. Whereas leisure travel in the eighteenth century—such as the English gentleman's grand tour of the Continent—had been the prerogative of prosperous few, the nineteenth century saw working-class families able to spend a day at the beach in Brighton or Nice (or in the mountains, or even at a mineral spring) or to visit a world's fair in the capital. Cheap railway excursions (third class travel was available), Cook's tours (the first carried visitors to the Great Exhibition of 1851), and Baedeker's guidebooks had become important elements in popular culture by 1914. The bicycle reshaped work habits (it was no longer necessary to live within walking distance of a factory), mating habits (one could find a companion at a greater distance), gender relations (women achieved new mobility and freedom), and recreational habits (bicycle races were begun, such as the Tour de France in 1903).

Leisure and mobility sustained a variety of institutions and activities that characterized European culture in 1914. They permitted thousands of people to attend spectator sporting events and even to follow their team to nearby towns. European football (soccer) soon became a central element in popular culture. The British Football Association began a championship competition in 1871 with fifty clubs; in 1901 Britain had more than ten thousand football clubs and the F. A. Cup Final drew more than 110,000 spectators. Immensely popular clubs, such as Juventus of Milan (1893) or Real Madrid (1902), were established across the Continent.

Perhaps the most universal element of shared popular culture by 1914 was the cinema, which was born in France in 1895 although its ancestry stretched back to the magic lantern shows of the eighteenth century. In the twenty years after Auguste and Louis Lumière projected the first film (*Workers Leaving the Lumière Factory,* 1895), sophisticated film industries appeared in Italy, Russia, Germany, and Britain as well as in France. In 1909 London had ninety motion picture theaters; by 1912 the number had grown to four hundred.

THE BLENDING OF ELITE CULTURE AND POPULAR CULTURE

The great popularity of motion pictures suggests a reconsideration of the connections between popular culture and elite culture, because cinema became an important element in both. Most cultural historians argue that such connections had always been stronger than seems apparent from narrowly focused studies of high culture. Traveling drama companies had long brought Shakespeare to

32 — LUNA PARK. Le Scenic Railway. ND Phot.

The Luna Park Scenic Railway, Paris, c. 1914. Modeled after one of the amusement parks on Coney Island built just after the turn of the century, another Luna Park opened in Paris in 1909. Amusement parks were often derided for lowering the moral caliber of the middle and working classes, among whom they were hugely popular. PRIVATE COLLECTION/BRIDGEMAN ART LIBRARY/ ARCHIVES CHARMET

the English countryside, just as Viennese music halls had produced popular adaptations of Mozart's operas. Conversely, composers of symphonic music had great success transposing the themes of folk music to the orchestra hall, as Franz Liszt did in his *Hungarian Rhapsodies,* and many writers of elite culture prospered by adapting folk tales. The distinction disappears entirely in the age of the serialized novel, which made Charles Dickens an important figure of both elite and popular culture.

Nineteenth-century institutions, especially the public library and the public museum, did more to blend popular culture and elite culture. The first public art museum opened in Vienna in 1781, and French revolutionaries converted the Louvre into a museum in 1793; the National Gallery in London opened in 1823. The British Museum had opened in 1759, but at that date it still required visitors to write a letter seeking admission. These cultural institutions also remained inaccessible to the lower classes, sometimes due to admission charges or Sunday closing policies, but the world of painting and sculpture, architecture and artifacts, was no longer an exclusive element of elite culture.

THE PERSISTENCE OF TRADITION IN POPULAR CULTURE

It would be an error to conclude that these changes in European popular culture between 1789 and 1914 made that culture utterly different. A balanced understanding must also recognize continuity, even across the *longue durée*. Religion and nationalism provide good illustrations of this, because both were central features of European culture at the beginning of the nineteenth century and remained so in 1914.

Although it is true that the nineteenth century witnessed a significant diminution in Christianity's role in Europe, religion nonetheless remained central to European culture. The age of cathedral building may have passed centuries earlier, but the French constructed the basilica of Sacré Coeur in Paris between 1876 and 1914; the Germans consecrated the neo-Romanesque Kaiser Wilhelm Gedächtniskirche in the center of Berlin in 1895; and Antoni Gaudi began work on the astonishing neo-Gothic Templo de la Sagrada Familia in Barcelona in 1883. At the level of daily life, saints' days, patron saints, religious festivals, and religious ceremonies remained at the center of popular culture. Pilgrimages to Compostela or to sites such as the grotto at Lourdes remained popular.

Similarly, the patriotic nationalism that developed during and after the revolutionary and Napoleonic wars was even stronger in 1914. A century that began with soldiers singing Claude-Joseph Rouget de Lisle's *La Marseillaise* (1792) and Ernst Arndt's *Was ist des Deutschen Vaterland?* (1806) ended with the militaristic jingoism of *Germany and the Next War* (1912) and the naïve chauvinism of Rupert Brooke's *1914*. Indeed, nationalism so flourished during the nineteenth century that it spread across most of the forms of popular culture discussed in this essay, from newspapers to sports. Nationalism and leisure merged in the adoption of patriotic holidays, such as July 14 in France, and nationalism appeared in architecture in the form of war monuments in many European villages.

See also **Art Nouveau; Automobile; Cabarets; Cinema; Cities and Towns; Clothing, Dress, and Fashion; Decadence; Education; Impressionism; Libraries; Modernism; Press and Newspapers; Romanticism; Sports; Transportation and Communications.**

BIBLIOGRAPHY

Abel, Richard. *The Ciné Goes to Town: French Cinema, 1896–1914.* Berkeley, Calif., 1994.

Beck, Robert. *Histoire du dimanche: De 1700 à nos jours.* Paris, 1997.

Betts, Raymond F. *A History of Popular Culture: More of Everything, Faster and Brighter.* New York, 2004.

Birley, Derek. *Land of Sport and Glory: Sport and British Society, 1887–1910.* Manchester, U.K., 1995.

Burke, Peter. *Popular Culture in Early Modern Europe.* New York, 1978.

Cantor, Norman, and Michael S. Werthman, eds. *The History of Popular Culture.* New York, 1968.

Corbin, Alain. *The Foul and the Fragrant: Odor and the French Social Imagination.* Cambridge, Mass., 1986.

———. *Village Bells: Sound and Meaning in the Nineteenth-Century French Countryside.* Translated by Martin Thom. New York, 1998.

Corbin, Alain, ed. *L'Avènement des loisirs, 1850–1960.* Paris, 1995.

Crossick, Geoffrey, and Serge Jaumain, eds. *Cathedrals of Consumption: The European Department Store, 1850–1939.* Aldershot, U.K., 1999.

Darnton, Robert. *The Great Cat Massacre and Other Episodes in French Cultural History.* New York, 1984.

Dauncey, Hugh, and Geoff Hare, eds. *The Tour de France, 1903–2003: A Century of Sporting Structures, Meanings, and Values.* London, 2003.

Feifer, Maxine. *Tourism in History: From Imperial Rome to the Present.* New York, 1986.

Golby, J. M., and A. W. Purdue. *The Civilisation of the Crowd: Popular Culture in England, 1750–1900.* Phoenix Mill, U.K., 1999.

Harris, Tim, ed. *Popular Culture in England, c. 1500–1850.* New York, 1995.

Herlihy, David V. *Bicycle: The History.* New Haven, Conn., 2004.

Hobsbawm, E. J. *Primitive Rebels: Studies in Archaic Forms of Social Movement in the Nineteenth and Twentieth Centuries.* 3rd ed. Manchester, U.K., 1971.

Holt, Richard. *Sport and the British: A Modern History.* Oxford, U.K., 1989.

Kete, Kathleen. *The Beast in the Boudoir: Petkeeping in Nineteenth-Century Paris.* Berkeley, Calif., 1994.

Koshar, Rudy. *German Travel Cultures.* Oxford, U.K., 2000.

Koshar, Rudy, ed. *Histories of Leisure.* Oxford, U.K., 2002.

Perrot, Philippe. *Fashioning the Bourgeoisie: A History of Clothing in the Nineteenth Century.* Translated by Richard Bienvenu. Princeton, N.J., 1994.

Rauch, André. *Vacances en France: De 1830 à nos jours.* Paris, 1996.

Rhode, Eric. *A History of the Cinema: From Its Origins to 1970.* New York, 1976.

Ritvo, Harriet. *The Animal Estate: The English and Other Creatures in the Victorian Age.* Cambridge, Mass., 1987.

Roche, Daniel. *A History of Everyday Things: The Birth of Consumption in France, 1600–1800.* Translated by Brian Pearce. Cambridge, U.K., 2000.

Rybczynski, Witold. *Histoire du week-end.* Paris, 1992.

Thompson, E. P. *Customs in Common.* New York, 1993.

Vincent, David. *Literacy and Popular Culture: England, 1750–1914.* Cambridge, U.K., 1989.

Weber, Eugen. *Peasants into Frenchmen: The Modernization of Rural France, 1870–1914.* Stanford, Calif., 1976.

Williams, Rosalind. *Dream Worlds: Mass Consumption in Late Nineteenth-Century France.* Berkeley, Calif., 1982.

STEVEN C. HAUSE

POPULATION, CONTROL OF.

The population of Europe underwent two major shifts during the long nineteenth century. First, a population explosion occurred from about 1750 to 1850. During these decades moral reformers, especially in England and France, seeking to control the population of the poor, criticized women who had more children than they could afford, or who bore them out of wedlock. Then, starting around 1880, fertility declined as people sought to control their family size; at the same time, politicians in many countries decried alleged depopulation.

FERTILITY INCREASE: 1750–1850

The population of Europe expanded from 1750 to 1850 largely because of an increase in the birthrate. Religious moralists and economists, most notably Thomas Robert Malthus (1766–1834), believed that the population would expand in accord with the available supply of resources. He assumed that the population would be controlled by limited natural resources and a high age at marriage. But the natural ceiling on population growth did not materialize, and rapid population growth went hand in hand with changes in the economy and culture. Malthus, and the moral reformers in his wake, confined discussion of birth control to preaching abstinence.

The European birthrate increased, even though some men and women sought to control conception. With the lack of safe, efficacious, and affordable barrier contraception, abstinence and coitus interuptus were the main forms of birth control, but a man's withdrawal depended on his needs, his respect for the woman, and whether it was a companionate relationship. Although condoms had been known throughout the eighteenth century, not until after the vulcanization of rubber in 1844 did their use spread, mainly to prostitutes and their clients concerned about venereal disease.

Women tried their own means of contraception. Some inserted a sponge or pessary or douched with various herbs. These methods had limited success, with the vaginal sponge—reputedly used by noble women, the bourgeoisie, and prostitutes—being the most efficacious. Under church teaching, some relied on a woman's "safe period," miscalculated in midmonth, just between the menses. Abortion, although illegal, was the form of family planning of last resort. Abortion techniques were dangerous, and included tightly binding the abdomen, jumping from high places, taking hot baths, and ingesting particular herbs and chemicals. If noninvasive techniques failed, desperate women resorted to the insertion of a sharp instrument with the hopes that it would dislodge the contents of the uterus without perforation. They could try to do this themselves, with the help of a friend, an abortionist, or a midwife.

Some women attempted abortion before their fifth month of pregnancy, yet many attempted it later, after quickening (the sensation of fetal movement) when a woman might be sure she was pregnant; this was as true of nobility in England as it was of the poor shopwoman in France or the Italian peasant. If abortion failed, the truly desperate resorted to infanticide. Poor, single, unwed, or widowed women, alone in the cities or countryside, without community resources or networks, were those most often prosecuted for infanticide. There is no way of knowing how many infanticides actually occurred.

Late marriages had been another means of population control, and this marriage pattern prevailed in the north and west of Europe, across all socioeconomic levels, and decreased toward the southern and eastern regions of Europe. People delayed marriage until they could establish independent households. In northern and western Europe, the average age of first marriage for men was over twenty-six and that for women was over twenty-three years, giving a woman about twenty fertile years. In France, where population growth was not as high as in other countries, the average age of marriage was higher. Women's age of marriage was more significant than men's but would only control marital fertility and not nonmarital fertility or pregnancies that resulted in marriage. Russia did not follow the western European marriage typography. Women in Russian villages usually married before they turned twenty, resulting in more reproductive years.

A sound economic basis was expected for family formation, and in northern and western Europe this usually meant marriage was delayed until a man could obtain land or earn an independent living. Again, the pattern for Russia differed; sons did not separate from their fathers' households. They wed young, but a high mortality in part offset high fertility. These checks on population, whether by contraception, abstinence, or late marriage, were offset by better diets. A woman's fertility, in part, is based on the number of calories and types of nutrients she consumes in relation to her work.

Historians relate social and sexual practices resulting in more children to the transition to capitalism; but it is difficult to determine if an increase in the birthrate led to economic changes, or the reverse. Industrialization developed in different stages in various places in western Europe starting around the mid-eighteenth century. The relationship of family size to beginning industrialization is complex. Some historians argue that population pressure spurred industrial development, which in turn caused an increase in population. Families that engaged in some industrial production relied on their labor in manufacturing more than on obtaining land to farm. They tended to have a lower age at marriage; thus the woman could have more reproductive years within marriage and more children. Moreover, a family gaining most of its living from industry would benefit from more children, which meant more laborers. The major drawback to having many children was the life-cycle poverty that ensued when a woman had several young, nonproductive children at home.

Cultural, religious, and community factors also played a role in reducing the age of marriage and increasing the number of children per family. Ideas about the ideal number of children for a completed family, the birth intervals between children, and even breastfeeding may have changed, resulting in more children. There is some evidence that families wanted a certain number of children, depending on their economy, culture, and occupation; when families reached an ideal size, couples stopped having children. The ideal family size among certain groups of the population, such as those working in industry, may have increased. In some places, spacing childbirth every two years was pronounced biologically "natural." Women achieved this spacing by abstinence, miscarriages (induced or spontaneous), or by breastfeeding. Some cultures established taboos, such as prohibiting sexual intercourse when a mother was lactating. These cultural practices may have shifted, resulting in more births.

Although childbirth was supposed to follow marriage, conception often preceded it. When the family economy was predicated on the number of working hands, some families and communities tacitly condoned prebridal fertility. In small, endogamous, rural communities, kin and neighbors knew who was courting whom. When the woman became pregnant, community pressure could force a marriage. With development of the market economy and increased migration, especially of men, the ability of the family and community to enforce marriages broke down. Knowing he could escape marriage, a man might exercise less sexual restraint.

The number of births outside of legal marriage, generally called the illegitimacy rate, greatly increased during this time period, in some places more than others. The religion of an area was not generally a factor. In areas of high religiosity, a woman who was pregnant outside of marriage could go to a nearby city to have the baby, thus inflating urban statistics and showing few exnuptial births in a highly religious area. Historians have advanced several hypotheses to explain why an increasing proportion of women had babies outside of marriage. The most compelling explanation relates to change in the economy and community, as well as the increased vulnerability of women to men's advances and seduction. Increased male migration to commercial centers transformed what in the past might have been a prebridal pregnancy into an out-of-wedlock pregnancy. Single mothers maintained that the man had promised them marriage but then abandoned them as soon as they became pregnant. Men were freer to seduce and abandon or neglect coitus interruptus than they had been. Having a child out-of-wedlock was often a result of their traditional behavior in more modern times.

MORTALITY

Mortality was one form of population control; mortality rates throughout the century remained high, decreasing only at the end of that century, and even then mostly in western and northern Europe. Diseases and epidemics decimated large segments of the population, and until the end of the nineteenth century famine caused suffering and death in the rural regions of Europe, especially during "the hungry forties" of 1846 to 1848.

Infant and child mortality was especially high and did not significantly decline until the beginning of the twentieth century. One in four infants might have died before his first birthday, and one child in two before her fifth birthday. Yet, many women could have seen ten, or more, of their children live to adulthood. The underserved populations experienced a higher likelihood of infant and child mortality. In the mid-nineteenth century, the number of deaths of babies under one year was the lowest in France and the United Kingdom, where fewer than one in five babies born were expected to die. It was higher in Italy and Germany, where almost a quarter of all live births died. In Russia, almost a third of all babies born could be expected to die within their first year. Until the twentieth century, there was little medical protection against childhood diseases, and no cures either. Sending infants out to wet nurses was a largely unintended form of population control. Many women could not, or would not, keep their newborns, often sending them to wet nurses, where they had a higher mortality rate than among those who stayed with their mothers. Many destitute and unwed mothers (in France, Italy, Spain, Portugal, or Russia) abandoned their babies at a foundling shelter and authorities shipped them out to wet nurses. The mortality of abandoned children remained significantly higher than that of all other children. In England, in a system known as "baby farming," working mothers of ex-nuptial children paid another, nonlactating woman a fee to take their babies.

Mortality rates remained a measure of population control until the end of the nineteenth century because advances in medicine and modern ideas of public hygiene became known and accepted only then. These changes began in the northern and western areas of Europe, leaving high mortality in the eastern and southern regions.

FERTILITY DECLINE IN THE LATE NINETEENTH CENTURY

There is no historical certainty about why the fertility decline occurred. Some historians postulate that it began with the upper classes. Other evidence, however, disputes that diffusion theory and sees family limitation occurring in different communities at different times, according to community cultural norms and occupation-related concerns.

The term *fertility decline* indicates a decline in population *growth*, but not in total population. Nations, obsessed with economic and military competition, examined their numbers vis-à-vis those of other countries. French politicians, for example, looked at their own numbers in comparison with those of Germany. Whereas the population of France increased by 3 percent, that of Germany, since unification in 1871, increased by 20 percent. This meant that politicians were putting pressure on women to have more and healthier babies, for national strength. France had the greatest decline in both marital and nonmarital fertility, but the fertility decline occurred in all countries of western Europe starting around the 1880s. The decline in the number of births was only partly a result of delayed marriages or increased age in first marriage.

Technological innovations played only a small part in the fertility decline. In the 1880s condoms became more widespread, although they remained expensive and were associated with illicit sex. Other barrier contraceptions such as pessaries, diaphragms, cervical caps, suppositories, and sponges became efficacious and acceptable, especially among the middle and upper classes, spawning dissemination of birth control information. But it was only after 1920 that barrier contraception became affordable and available to all socioeconomic groups. Although men and women still practiced abstinence, coitus interruptus, and abortion, they increasingly sought barrier contraception. Except for the condom, all these technologies gave the woman control over conception, and their use speaks to women's increasing role in sexuality and family planning.

Contraception became a household word at the end of the nineteenth century, especially in England with the 1877 trial of Charles Bradlaugh and Annie Besant for publishing information about

French brochure against population control by Arthur Le Creps, 1895. Le Creps opposed the Malthusian idea of improving social conditions by controlling population growth, viewing it as a threat to the continuation of the French as a distinct cultural group. The cover presents an idealized picture of French families of earlier times. BIBLIOTHÈQUE DES ARTS DECORATIFS, PARIS, FRANCE/BRIDGEMAN ART LIBRARY/ ARCHIVES CHARMET

birth control. At the same time, the neo-Malthusian movement fostered family planning. Unlike Malthus, who advocated delayed marriages and moral restraint, the neo-Malthusians wanted to teach the poor how to use contraceptive devices. Neo-Malthusians were not necessarily arguing for women's choice; they generally lectured the poor on limiting their number of children to result in healthier workers.

New technologies for birth control did, however, contribute to family planning and the fertility decline, but families adopted birth control less because of new techniques and technologies, and more because of changing economic and social conditions. The shifting nature of industrialization to larger-scale industries requiring less child labor toward the end of the nineteenth century changed the economic value of children and favored small families among both the middle classes and the workers. The passage of effective child labor protection laws in the 1870s in England, France, and Germany, and the compulsory primary education laws of the 1880s in the same countries, also changed the economic value of children. According to one theory, since children could not work as many hours and had to attend school, they became economic liabilities rather than the economic assets they had been. Moreover, the depression of the same decades created economic uncertainty and material hardships, so parents who already had several children wanted to prevent more births.

The depression of 1880s, especially in England and France, along with the desire to maintain a certain quality of life despite an increased cost of living and diminished resources also led couples to limit the number of children. This was a middle-class rationale, based on the increasing cost of ensuring the educational, professional, and business success of their children. English and French parents believed that they could maintain their status and even secure a better life if they had fewer children. This was especially true in the rapidly growing urban areas. Furthermore, lower infant mortality led people to limit the number of children born, since each child would have a greater chance of survival.

Cultural changes toward the end of the century, including new concepts of motherhood, more affective parenting, and greater equality between husbands and wives may also have contributed to population control. Women, who bore the burden of childbirth and most of the burdens of childrearing, may have wanted most to limit family size, and were able to do so. The emphasis on the quality of nurturing that began with educated elites became culturally diffused. Having fewer children, and nurturing them, became the mark of civilization for all social groups. Evidence that working-class women emulated middle-class attitudes about family planning is sparser than evidence that they adopted family planning to fit their changing economic lives. Some families thought that having more than three children was immoral as well as materially unsound.

The development of feminism and the idea of women's individualism led to rhetoric about women's independence and led some women to take more control in family planning. Although few feminists advocated birth control, a rhetoric of family planning developed. Some male politicians and doctors condemned the nascent birth control movement, because they thought that birth control would lead to "female sexual excess" disrupting the social order and male control. In some countries where doctors adopted the "family planning" agenda, rather than use language about women's sexual freedom, they used terms that would give the men some aspect of control. In other areas, doctors eschewed the birth control movement and it remained subversive and against the national interests.

By 1914, in a merging of the public rhetoric and women's private lives, ideas of population control dominated the political-medical discourse. The history is complex and replete with paradoxes and contradictions, as traditional customs adapted to modern attitudes and practices, not without tension.

See also **Demography; Feminism; Malthus, Thomas Robert; Welfare.**

BIBLIOGRAPHY

Banks, Joseph Ambrose. *Prosperity and Parenthood: A Study of Family Planning among the Victorian Middle Classes.* London, 1954.

Banks, Joseph Ambrose, and Olive Banks. *Feminism and Family Planning in Victorian England.* New York, 1964.

Coale, Ansley J., and Susan Cotts Watkins, eds. *The Decline of Fertility in Europe.* Princeton, N.J., 1986.

Cole, Joshua. *The Power of Large Numbers: Population, Politics, and Gender in Nineteenth-Century France.* Ithaca, N.Y., 2000.

Dupâquier, Jacques, E. Helin, P. Laslett, et al., eds. *Marriage and Remarriage in Populations of the Past.* New York, 1981.

Gillis, John, Louise Tilly, and David Levine, eds. *The European Experience of Declining Fertility, 1850–1970: The Quiet Revolution.* Oxford, U.K., 1992.

Hajnal, John. "European Marriage Patterns in Perspective." In *Population in History: Essays in Historical Demography,* edited by David Victor Glass and David Edward Charles Eversley, 101–143. London, 1965.

Levine, David. *Reproducing Families: The Political Economy of English Population History.* Cambridge, U.K., 1987.

McLaren, Angus. *Sexuality and Social Order: The Debate over the Fertility of Women and Workers in France, 1770–1920.* New York, 1983.

Szreter, Simon. *Fertility, Class and Gender in Britain, 1860–1940.* Cambridge, U.K., 1996.

Tilly, Charles, ed. *Historical Studies of Changing Fertility.* Princeton, N.J., 1978.

RACHEL G. FUCHS

POPULISTS. Populism (*narodnichestvo*) has traditionally been defined as a peasant-oriented socialism, rooted in a utopian fantasy that Russia could avoid a capitalist stage of development by relying on the peasant commune. The movement to which this term refers emerged in response to the paternalism and compromise that—according to Russia's student radicals—nullified the freedoms promised in the emancipation reforms of 1861. Inspired by the teachings of Alexander Herzen (1812–1870) and Mikhail Bakunin (1814–1876), the *raznochintsy* (young men and women of "mixed ranks" who were educated beyond their inherited station in life) insisted that progress toward social equality be immediately manifest in the daily lives of its advocates. In the search for a link between lofty ideals and daily practice, Nikolai Chernyshevsky's 1863 novel *What Is to Be Done?* became a blueprint for action. Students in the 1860s formed egalitarian communes, devised "fictitious marriages" that freed young women from the constraints imposed by upper-class families, and supported Polish struggles for independence from Russia in 1863. Appropriating the traditional peasant rebel slogan "Land and Liberty" (Zemlya i Volya), a loosely structured student network organized cooperatives, Sunday schools to foster worker literacy, and, in one case, a summer school for young peasants.

Declaring themselves revolutionaries and socialists, radicals looked to the peasant commune (*mir*, or *obshchina*) as an alternative to the greedy individualism of western capitalist nations. In the 1870s, inspired by an ideal of service, a sometimes mystical faith in "the people," and a search for redemption through sharing and lightening the burdens of a cruelly exploited peasantry, thousands of young students went out to the countryside in a "movement to go to the people" (*khozhdenie v narod*). Seeking to learn from, to teach, and to incite peasants to revolution, they worked as laborers, shepherds, and village schoolteachers; young women like Vera Figner (1852–1942) abandoned their European medical training in order to provide peasants with health care.

However, it turned out that radicals operating in the Russian countryside under the hostile surveillance of landlords, government officials, and police informants could not convince peasants to rebel—the only exception was in Chigirin, where a forged manifesto from the tsar urging peasants to attack landlords triggered an uprising. In contrast, the government was quite successful in its campaign to hunt down, arrest, abuse, and imprison student radicals by the hundreds. In response to government-sponsored political trials of hundreds who participated in the movement to "go to the people," the student Vera Zasulich shot and wounded the governor-general of St. Petersburg in 1878, and the radical movement entered a more violent phase. A new organization, Narodnaya Volya (People's Will) set out to eradicate by terrorist means the political system that had decimated their grassroots efforts of the 1870s. In March 1881, the executive committee of Narodnaya Volya (a group that included the well-born Sofya Perovskaya, the peasant Stepan Khalturin, and the worker Andrei Zhelyabov) succeeded in assassinating Tsar Alexander II (r. 1855–1881).

Although the autocracy executed the Narodnaya Volya assassins, the spirit of the "movement to go to the people" persisted. After completing prison terms for dissident radical activity, many veterans of that movement emerged to direct and organize the massive zemstvo statistical investigations of the last third of the nineteenth century. (Elected, estate- and locally based, zemstvo institutions had been established in the 1860s and charged by the state to hire statisticians to collect fiscal data.) Able to continue their work because the government was so desperately in need of the statistics that they were hired to collect, radical zemstvo statisticians interviewed some 4.5 million peasant households between the 1870s and 1905. In their documentation and analysis of peasant testimony, they far exceeded the government's narrowly fiscal agenda. Their statistical findings enabled the economist Nikolai Danielson (1844–1918) to convince Karl Marx (1818–1883) that in Russia at least, the powerful force of capitalism had not yet rendered the peasant commune obsolete.

In the 1890s, the views of Danielson and the later writings of Marx were anathema to Peter Struve (1870–1944) and Vladimir Lenin (1870–1924), who were then engaged in a campaign to convince all and sundry that their brand of Marxism was infinitely different from and superior to all other traditions of Russian socialism. Their strategy of choice for discrediting political rivals was to denounce them as "populists" who ignorantly denied the existence of capitalism in Russia. In general, these accusations were false, and most of the accused denied that they were in fact populists. Yet, the notion that "populists" believed that Russia was "immune to capitalism" persisted for more than a century. Scholarly debates and disagreements over Marxism, populism, and the relationship between the two, would outlast both the imperial and soviet regimes.

See also **Alexander II; Herzen, Alexander; People's Will; Russia; Slavophiles.**

BIBLIOGRAPHY

Primary Sources

Figner, Vera. *Memoirs of a Revolutionist.* Authorized translation from the Russian; introduction by Richard Stites. DeKalb, Ill., 1991.

Kropotkin, Petr Alekseyevich. *Memoirs of a Revolutionist.* London, 1978.

Secondary Sources

Gleason, Abbott. *Young Russia: The Genesis of Russian Radicalism in the 1860s.* New York, 1980. Useful study of the "going to the people" movement.

Khoros, Vladimir. *Populism: Its Past, Present, and Future.* Translated from the Russian by Nadezhda Burova. Moscow, 1984. Balanced account of the pros and cons of Russian populism, considered in comparative historical perspective.

Kingston-Mann, Esther. "Deconstructing the Romance of the Bourgeoisie: A Russian Marxist Path Not Taken." *Review of International Political Economy* (2003): 93–117. Study of the Marxist-populist controversy as reflected in the work of Nikolai Danielson.

———. "Statistics, Social Change, and Social Justice: The Zemstvo Statisticians of Pre-Revolutionary Russia." In *Russia in the European Context, 1789–1914: A Member of the Family,* edited by Susan P. McCaffray and Michael Melancon. New York, 2005.

Pipes, Richard. "Narodnichestvo—A Semantic Inquiry." *Slavic Review* 23 (1964): 441–458.

———. *Struve: Liberal on the Left, 1870–1905.* Cambridge, Mass., 1970.

Venturi, Franco. *Roots of Revolution: A History of the Populist and Socialist Movements in Nineteenth-Century Russia.* Translated from the Italian by Francis Haskell. New York, 1960. Classic study of the origins and development of populism from the 1830s to 1881.

Walicki, Andrzej. *The Controversy over Capitalism: Studies in the Social Philosophy of the Russian Populists.* Oxford, U.K., 1969. Valuable critical analysis of populist thought

Wortman, Richard. *The Crisis of Russian Populism.* London, 1967. Influential critical study of the psychology of Russian populism.

ESTHER KINGSTON-MANN

PORNOGRAPHY. *Pornography* as a term meaning salacious art or literature emerged in the nineteenth century from *pornographos,* meaning "to write about whores." Its history is closely intertwined with the history of obscenity, an earlier term used by religious authorities and the state to condemn articles that would "offend, corrupt, and deprave," as it was commonly put. Walter Kendrick, a writer on the history of pornography, suggests that pornography was not eternal but named an argument, a "battlefield" about the legitimacy of sexual representations that emerged in the mid-nineteenth century. However, before there were great obscenity battles over works such as Émile Zola's *Nana* (1880) or James Joyce's *Ulysses* (1922), before there was pornography per se, there was salacious literature.

LIBERTINE LITERATURE

In the late eighteenth century and early nineteenth century, pornography owed a great deal to the libertine and Enlightenment traditions. The word *libertine* originally meant freethinker, but it began to take on connotations of sexual excess over the seventeenth and eighteenth centuries. Both the Enlightenment and libertinism arose out of a discomfort with established society, but where the first now signifies lofty literary and philosophic ideals, the other became grounded in base sexual practice. Despite this supposed chasm, libertine and Enlightenment claims overlapped, and some of the greatest freethinkers of the Enlightenment used the sexual body to discuss the corruption of the body politic including Honoré-Gabriel

Riquetti, comte de Mirabeau, who wrote *Erotika biblion* (1782), and Denis Diderot, who wrote *Les bijoux indescrets* (1748).

Furthermore, the French monarchy, by outlawing both pornography and philosophy, inadvertently tied the two together, as writers had little to lose from the most scurrilous allegations. Pornography criticized existing sexual mores and offered new sexual possibilities, often in the same work. Some works such as the libels against Marie-Antoinette (1755–1793) that detailed (falsely) her sexual profligacy, her tribadism (lesbianism), and her incestuous relationship with her son, allowed the French public an intimate if apocryphal glimpse into the Old Regime. Other works expounded on the sexual corruption of the Catholic Church, the sexual adventures of the aristocracy, and the problems of political tyranny from the view of the boudoir. Such works titillated readers with sexually detailed discussions, even as they called for the end of such practices and the social institutions that supposedly encouraged them.

In Britain as well, libertine works proliferated, although they tended to be less philosophical. John Cleland's *Memoirs of a Woman of Pleasure* (1748 or 1749), more popularly known as *Fanny Hill,* is the best-known libertine novel. The work, written as two long letters by the main character, Fanny Hill, explores the sexual culture of London through her personal adventures. The volume, criticizing traditional social relations and arguing for new patterns of relationships based on sexual freedom and personal inclination, became a best-seller throughout the eighteenth and nineteenth century, despite its continued ban.

Pornographic literature spread throughout Europe, with the same texts appearing in France, England, Switzerland, the Netherlands, Germany, and as far away as Russia, linked by itinerant printers, pirated texts, and smuggler networks. Free traders brought with them not only bootleg tea but also amorous novels such as *Fanny Hill.* And across Europe, states developed new obscenity codes, not only because of the political dangers that pornography brought, but also because of growing fears about the sexual and social corruption of the populace. In the German states in the early nineteenth century, for example, these obscenity codes focused less on a work's sexual explicitness than on the character's place in society. The works of Althing, the pseudonym for Christian August Fischer, including *Der Geliebte von Elftausend Mädchen* (The beloved of eleven thousand, 1804), for example, had little explicit sexual content, but were banned by the German states for showing a rootless individual in a sexually corrupt world.

Libertine pornography culminated, at least philosophically if not practically, in the works of Donatien-Alphonse-François, marquis de Sade. The marquis de Sade's novel *Justine; ou, Les malheurs de la vertu* (1791) was written three times. He completed and then lost the manuscript while a prisoner in the Bastille two years before the outbreak of the French Revolution. He published a second version in 1792 and then he reworked it to include the story of Juliette in 1797. In the work, Sade pointedly rewards vice and punishes virtue. This premise allows him to examine the logical result of an individual's freedom for personal gratification in an unplanned world; his characters find no limits to sexual gratification even to the extremes of child molestation, mutilation, and necrophilia. Libertine literature, or the pursuit of sexual liberty on philosophical grounds alone, has never quite recovered from Sade's bequest.

PORNOGRAPHY, POLITICS, AND CONSUMERISM

However, the link between pornography and politics continued well into the nineteenth century. Radical British pornographers, such as William Dugdale and George Cannon, churned out salacious, antigovernment texts during the Queen Caroline Affair (1812, 1818–1820) when George IV (r. 1820–1830) tried to divorce Caroline on the grounds of adultery. In the German states, political pornography also gained a foothold. Despite the relatively chaste language, the *Memoirs of Lola Montez* (1851) fit into this tradition by relating the problems of the Bavarian monarchy to a sexually chaotic world. Indeed, the relations of King Louis I (r. 1825–1848) with Lola Montez, an actress, and his desire to ennoble her contributed directly to the Revolution of 1848–1849, as the scurrilous *Memoirs* reminded readers.

In the latter half of the nineteenth century, the pleasures and dangers of sexuality became paramount both in terms of obscenity codes and pornographic content. While pornographers continuously republished the old "classics" in most European languages, newer works emphasized consumer pleasures and tended to excise philosophic and political considerations in favor of explorations of the pleasures of the flesh. Even in France, the epicenter of political pornography, pornography lost its political edge and concentrated instead on the sexually voracious woman or girl in the urban anonymous world. Across Europe, consumerism offered new opportunities for sexual exploration divorced from social repercussions. For instance, *My Secret Life* (1885–1890), a pornographic memoir, obsessively documents the male narrator's sexual experiences. The narrator's "real life" of family, community, and work are lost to the "secret life" of brothels, prostitutes, and voyeurism. The anonymous author documented consumer society through innumerable, impersonal exchanges. The narrator transforms his world into a "pornotopia," a word coined by the historian Steven Marcus to describe the ability to see the world entirely through sexuality.

The development of photography also gave a boost to pornographic consumerism. In 1839, the process of permanently "fixing" images began in two forms, the daguerreotype and the callotype. Pornographic daguerreotypes appeared by the 1840s, but the daguerreotype allowed only one image per exposure and therefore had limited circulation. Pornographic callotypes and later photographs began to circulate in earnest in the 1880s. Many photographs featured individual women or sexual intercourse; however, photographs of children, miscegenation, bestiality, and clerical corruption, as well as more prosaic vistas such as "foreign ladies" also appeared, widening the opportunities for consumers to broaden their sexual education. The new form of images was matched by new ways of visualizing sexuality including the close-up, the ejaculation or "money shot," and the keyhole, in which the image is bracketed by the shape of a skeleton keyhole making the viewer into a voyeur.

Pornographers expanded their consumer base by captioning photographs in as many as four languages, usually English, French, German, and Italian. While earlier libertine pornography had a

QUESTION D'ART
— Dans lequel qu'on aura l'plus d'femmes nues pour deux ronds ?

French schoolboys at a news kiosk. Lithograph by Grandjouan in *Le Rire*, 16 August 1902. The original caption reads: "Which one gives you the most naked women for two francs?" MARY EVANS PICTURE LIBRARY

diffuse social impact, the majority of the population did not have widespread access to these ideas. But a number of factors including rising literacy rates, increased wages, expanding city life and subsequent anonymity, and the opportunity for leisure fed the rise of consumer pornography in the late nineteenth century. Paperbacks, pamphlets, cheap magazines, postcards, and inexpensive photographs allowed greater opportunity for everyone to consume pornography. Access expanded beyond middle-class men, allowing all levels of society including the poor, the young, the colonized, and even women to view sexually explicit items.

The rapidly expanding empires of the 1870s–1890s also provided new opportunities for a popular, symbolic consumerism. Photographs, postcards, and illustrations from Asia, Central America, the Caribbean, and Africa flooded back to Europe, enabling all levels of European society to see images of nude imperial subjects. For example, images of Algerian women set in the harem became common across Europe, imported through France and then sold across the Continent. Despite crackdowns against obscenity, little was done to curtail the flood of imperial images because authorities believed that nudity was the natural state of "natives" and because of the amorphous line between science and pornography.

ATTEMPTS AT STATE INTERVENTION

The social sciences, such as anthropology, sociology, and history, were in the process of being formed as distinct disciplines over the course of the nineteenth century, and scholars who studied sexuality remained in danger of being accused of producing obscenity whether they wrote about the European or the imperial context. As a result, many wrote their works anonymously or pseudonymously. These authors wrote about sexual matters such as prostitution, aphrodisiacs, hermaphrodites, flagellation, domination, and intercourse. The scientific focus did not preclude these works from functioning as pornography, however.

As members of the Cannibal Club, the inner circle of the Anthropological Society of London, demonstrated, science and titillation often overlapped. The sexual and the intellectual realms reinforced each other; for example, the study of flagellation was often bolstered by a distinct personal preference for the practice. Furthermore, they used pornographers to publish their works and consumers bought scientific and salacious works in tandem.

Even the field of bibliography straddled this uneasy divide between the licentious and scientific realms as the great bibliographies of pornography were written during the late nineteenth century. The bibliographers insisted that their publications were in fact scientific endeavors that created order out of the literary world. Henry Spenser Ashbee published his three-volume bibliography of pornography in England—*Index Librorum Prohibitorum* in 1877, *Centuria Librorum Absconditorum* in 1879, and *Catena Librorum Tacendorum* in 1885—under the pseudonym of Pisanus Fraxi. In 1875 Hugo Hayn published *Bibliotheca Germanorum Erotica*, which was later expanded and then further supplemented between 1912 and 1929. Jules Gay's six-volume work entitled *Bibliographie des ouvrages relatifs à l'amour* was published in 1871–1873 and then supplemented by the publisher J. Lemonnyer between 1894–1900. These works on English, German, and French pornography, respectively, have formed the backbone for historical examinations of pornography even though the authors were understood as contributing to obscenity. Gay, for example, had his publishing license revoked because of it.

States across Europe passed laws against the "social evil" of pornography, which was conceptualized as the causal agent behind other types of sexual and social deviance. The broad growth of liberal governments insisted on a disciplined populace. Boosted by ideas of "respectability" and new interventions in social regulation by the middle class, the state tended to be more concerned with the sexual and social degeneration of the populace. Birth control information, abortion advertisements, and "how-to" manuals as well as more explicit materials came under obscenity legislation. Voluntary organizations and state agencies across Europe began to take part in international conferences regarding obscene publications by the 1910s and hoped to eradicate the trade at all levels.

In spite of increased attempts at state control, pornography flourished in many of the major cities of Europe. Paris, London, Amsterdam, Rotterdam, Budapest, Lyon, Milan, Barcelona, and Zurich constitute only some of the centers of trade. Pornographers produced works for the international as well as the national audience and no longer waited for a slow diffusion of their products throughout Europe and America. Instead, they functioned as petty entrepreneurs using an international mail-order system that included third-party shipping, dummy corporations, and front men and women who worked as go-betweens. The international traffic in pornography surpassed the boundaries of state control and state jurisdiction and international conferences could do little against the spread of pornography.

By World War I, pornography as a conceptual category and as an item for sale had matured; it had achieved a visual and literary form that many found compelling, it had made a market for itself that continued to expand, it absorbed new ideas of sexuality as they arose, and despite attempts to eradicate it, pornography continued to thrive.

See also **Popular and Elite Culture; Sexuality.**

BIBLIOGRAPHY

Alloula, Malek. *The Colonial Harem.* Translated by Myrna Godzich and Wlad Godzich. Minneapolis: University of Minnesota Press, 1986.

Darnton, Robert. *The Forbidden Bestsellers of Pre-Revolutionary France.* New York, 1996.

Hunt, Lynn, ed. *The Invention of Modern Pornography: Obscenity and the Origins of Modernity, 1500–1800.* New York, 1993.

Kearney, Patrick J. *A History of Erotic Literature.* London, 1982.

Kendrick, Walter. *The Secret Museum: Pornography in Modern Culture.* New York, 1987.

Marcus, Steven. *The Other Victorians: A Study of Sexuality and Pornography in Mid-Nineteenth Century England.* New York, 1966.

McCalman, Iain. *Radical Underworld: Prophets, Revolutionaries, and Pornographers in London, 1795–1840*. Cambridge, U.K., 1988.

Sigel, Lisa Z. *Governing Pleasures: Pornography and Social Change in England, 1815–1914*. New Brunswick, N.J., 2002.

———. *International Exposure: Perspectives on Modern European Pornography, 1800–2000*. New Brunswick, N.J., 2005.

Stevenson, David. *The Beggar's Benison: Sex Clubs of Enlightenment Scotland and Their Rituals*. East Lothian, Scotland, 2001.

LISA Z. SIGEL

PORTSMOUTH, TREATY OF. On 5 September 1905, in Portsmouth, New Hampshire, representatives of the Russian and Japanese governments signed the treaty ending the Russo-Japanese War. The war had occurred as the result of conflicting imperial ambitions between Russia and Japan in Manchuria and Korea. The Japanese had won all the major naval and land battles of the war and were therefore able to demand that their imperial preeminence in the region be acknowledged. Russia agreed in the Treaty of Portsmouth to recognize Japanese dominance in Korea, to sign over the leases of the Chinese ports of Port Arthur and Dalian (Dalny) to the Japanese, and to evacuate their troops from Manchuria in order to allow all the imperial powers to "develop" that region equally.

Still, the treaty was recognized nearly universally as a diplomatic success for Russia. Though the principal Russian negotiator, Count Sergei Witte, had been forced to accept the redivision of Asia to Russia's detriment, his mission was praised because he had made the Japanese blink on the next two most important issues: the disposition of Sakhalin Island, which Japanese forces had taken from Russia during the war, and the question of whether Russia would owe Japan a war indemnity. The indemnity question proved to be the thorniest one. Paying for the expenses of the winning party by the loser had become a tradition in recent years. Prussia had received one from France (after the Franco-Prussian War of 1870–1871), Japan had gotten one from China

(following the First Sino-Japanese War of 1894–1895), and even the Russians had expected to claim an indemnity in the event they had emerged militarily victorious over Japan. Each side was spending about a million dollars per day on the war, and each faced financial crisis. Witte had clear instructions from the tsar to reject any claim of indemnity, but the Japanese firmly desired monetary satisfaction.

At the last moment, with the Russian delegation's bags literally packed, the Japanese diplomats relented. Two factors tipped the scales. First, though the Russian military had been humiliated, it had not been destroyed, and a new wave of reinforcements was now making Russian military prospects look much brighter. The second factor was that Theodore Roosevelt, the American president who had agreed to host and mediate the conference, had quietly changed his mind. He had supported an indemnity at the outset, having admired the Japanese war effort and deplored Russian "mendacity" during the wave of Asian expansion. But a concerted public relations blitz by Witte in the United States had convinced important journalists and congressmen that Russia was right to reject the indemnity. Faced with the prospect of domestic political costs, Roosevelt pressured the Japanese to accept, pressure that gained added weight when New York financier Jacob Schiff telegraphed the Japanese delegation to inform them that they would be denied further loans in international markets if they allowed the conference to break up over the indemnity question. At this point, the Japanese leadership in Tokyo cabled their negotiators to accept the Russian offer, which included a compromise on Sakhalin that would divide the island in two. Roosevelt won the Nobel Peace Prize that year for his efforts.

The importance of the indemnity dispute, however, was not simply financial. Both sides understood that imperial status was the key issue at stake. Russia felt the need to recover some of the prestige it had lost on the battlefield by forthrightly rejecting the claims of an Asian state to demand war spoils, and Japan felt that it had to be able to press an indemnity claim on a European empire in order to be accepted into the club of Great Powers. It was this high-stakes contest that Witte had won. After the treaty was signed, the Russian delegation retired to its rooms to celebrate, while the Japanese delegation wept in their quarters. Their dismay was shared by Tokyo mobs, which rioted upon hearing the details of the treaty. The so-called Hibiya Riot resulted in seventeen deaths and demonstrated the public commitment to empire on the part of urban Japanese citizens. This manifestation of "imperial democracy" would have significant repercussions for Japanese politics in the following decades.

The Russians appeared to have maintained their Great Power status at the expense of their Japanese diplomatic counterparts. But more careful observers were not fooled. Japanese military success impressed the many neutral military observers posted to the Manchurian battlefields, and the Russian defeat caused deep concern for its allies and at home. The Russian military now focused on reform and attempted to keep out of Asian entanglements. The balance of power had clearly shifted in East Asia.

See also **Mukden, Battle of; Russia; Russo-Japanese War.**

BIBLIOGRAPHY

Primary Sources

Witte, Sergei. *The Memoirs of Count Witte.* Translated and edited by Sidney Harcave. Armonk, N.Y., 1990. Translation of *Vospominaniia.* Includes an invaluable but tendentious account of the conference and Witte's strategy.

Secondary Sources

Gordon, Andrew. *Labor and Imperial Democracy in Prewar Japan.* Berkeley, Calif., 1991.

Westwood, J. N. *Russia against Japan, 1904–1905: A New Look at the Russo-Japanese War.* Albany, N.Y., 1986.

JOSHUA SANBORN

PORTUGAL. Between the French Revolution and the onset of World War I, Portugal experienced both decline and revival in its overseas empire as well as in its economy and society. In politics, this small Iberian state underwent waves of revolutionary change. As of 1800, Portugal, with one of the largest contemporary overseas empires, was in a relatively stronger position vis-à-vis the other European imperial powers, than it was a century earlier or later. Following an imperial decline from 1580 to 1700, Portugal experienced a limited, imperial revival based largely on the resources of massive Brazil, its richly endowed but restive South American colony. Following French occupation of Portugal in 1807 and the opening of Brazil to foreign traders in 1808, Portugal's revival of imperial power and influence ended, its political system was destabilized, and its economy weakened. When Brazil declared its independence in 1822, Portugal confronted a crisis on the order of magnitude of the post-1580 decline; Portugal's very independence as a sovereign state seemed in peril.

FROM ABSOLUTE MONARCHY TO CONSTITUTIONAL MONARCHY AND CIVIL WAR (1789–1834)

The Peninsular Wars had a profound impact on Portugal and its people. After frustrating diplomatic skirmishing Napoleon (r. 1804–1814/15) sent French armies into Spain and Portugal. In vain Portugal tried to avoid involvement in the growing conflict between England and France. The first French invasion of Portugal in 1807–1808 precipitated the flight of the royal family and its retinue to Brazil, Portugal's jewel in the crown, transported and protected by an English fleet.

A major external factor was English intervention in Portuguese affairs. This reached a zenith during the nineteenth century and played a persistent role in both foreign and domestic affairs. Despite the fact that England defended Portugal from other foreign invaders on nearly a dozen occasions beginning in 1385, relations between the allies were uneasy. Sustained resistance to English intrusion became one key element in the psychology of Portuguese nationalism and imperialism as well as in Lisbon's efforts for a greater freedom of maneuver. The policies in dispute ranged from how to handle the suppression of the slave trade and slavery itself; questions of trade and industry; diplomacy connected to territorial claims; the maintenance of constitutional monarchy and the expansion of empire, and economic and financial issues.

Portugal's dogged push for a tropical African empire after 1822 was in part driven by resentment of a position of dependency under its oldest ally.

The relationship was troubled by English high-handedness and the disparity in power and status. England was the world's leading power while Portugal, especially after the loss of Brazil in 1822, slipped in importance as a power and became more dependent on Britain for defense. Indeed, in a standard diplomatic historical account of the 1960s, the former Portuguese prime minister Marcello Caetano (1906–1980) aptly described the nineteenth century of the Anglo-Portuguese Alliance as "The English Century," a period in which Portugal became, in effect, a dependent protectorate of its ally.

The French invaded Portugal on three occasions beginning in 1807 and their actions transformed Portugal's political system, endangered Portugal's hold on its empire, and brought greater English influence over Portugal. Yet again armed forces of Britain rescued an imperiled Portugal as the Duke of Wellington's (1769–1852) invading armies defeated and expelled the French and took the war across the frontier into Spain. By 1811 the French occupying forces had withdrawn but British officers governed the country until after the return of King John VI (r. 1816–1826) from Brazil in 1821.

In the meantime Portuguese constitutional liberals engineered a revolution in 1820 and demanded the king in Brazil return to Portugal and accept their constitution, a radical document that empowered parliament and stripped the constitutional monarch of most powers. The constitutional liberals called for an end to absolute monarchy, a reform of the economy, the end of noble privileges, and an abolition of entailed estates so that a rising middle class of non-nobles could own property. Ideas derived from the French Revolution, such as liberty, equality, and fraternity, were also discussed.

King John VI returned from Brazil in 1821 as a reluctant constitutionalist, and soon counterrevolutionary forces opposed the constitutional liberals' reform ideas and policies and abrogated the 1822 constitution. John's older son, Dom Pedro (1798–1834), remained in Brazil and helped engineer the declaration of independence for Brazil in 1822 and Brazil's secession from the Empire. There followed a struggle in Portugal, which lasted more than a decade, to determine if a constitutional monarchy system would prevail or if there would be return to an absolute monarchy, which eschewed any constitutional mandates or any social and economic reforms. The struggle reached another stage following the death of John VI in 1826.

Yet again an imperial question was at the center of a political sea change. The heir-presumptive, Pedro, was emperor of Brazil at the time and did not want the Portuguese throne for himself. Yet his brother, Miguel, who hankered after that throne, was a reactionary absolutist whose political values were in conflict with the liberal Pedro. Pedro was anxious, however, to restore political and family peace to Portugal. A compromise family agreement was reached, based on a new 1826 Charter or Constitution, designed by Pedro in Brazil and brought to Portugal, and on a family marriage agreement whereby Pedro's young daughter Maria Da Glória (r. 1834–1853), although only seven years old, eventually would wed Pedro's younger brother, Miguel (1802–1866), the darling of the Absolutist Monarchy party. The agreement collapsed when Miguel proclaimed himself king and refused to swear loyalty to the 1826 Charter. Beginning in 1828, Miguel's contested rule imposed reaction and repression on Portugal.

In 1831 Portugal's travail and Brazilian instability moved Pedro to abdicate as emperor of the Brazilian Empire, prepare an armed expedition, and return to Portugal to oppose Miguelite rule. Pedro's cause was supported initially by risings in the Azores Islands and in continental Portugal. In 1832 Pedro landed an army to fight in Portugal. There followed a civil war between the constitutionalists aligned with Pedro and the absolutists who supported Miguel, "The War of the Two Brothers," which lasted from 1832 to 1834.

CONSOLIDATING CONSTITUTIONAL MONARCHY AND THE REGENERATION (1834–1870)

The victory in 1834 of the constitutionalists over the absolutists in the War of the Two Brothers marked the end of one historical era and the beginning of another, and the beginning phase of the consolidation of Portugal's constitutional monarchy. The 1826 constitution, nicknamed "The Charter," born in Brazil but conceived in France, became the dominant constitutional instrument during much of the remainder of the constitutional monarchy. Its principal element was the monarch's "moderating power," a means of balancing the powers of different branches of government and providing stability and continuity when political dissension and inaction threatened good governance. Parliament consisted of two houses, the lower elected and the higher appointed.

The liberal constitutionalists who came to power in the years 1834 to 1836 passed key liberal legislation to institute basic reforms. To pay off large debts incurred during the wars fought between 1807 and 1834, the state confiscated the lands owned by the Catholic Church, abolished monasteries and convents, and put church lands up for sale. As these lands sold at auction, a new landed upper middle class emerged, part of the constitutional monarchist establishment. The land sales were intended to address the land distribution issue; most Portuguese who worked the land were landless and the middle and lower classes under the Old Regime could not legally own property. The new system, despite its good intentions, did not facilitate true land reform. Some aspects of liberal reform were successful: educational reforms, a standard system of currency, weights and measures, and a national transportation and communications system through the construction after 1850 of a railroad network and a telegraph system. In the 1860s entailed estates, key factors of the Old Regime, were finally abolished. The period of 1851 to 1870 was known as "The Regeneration," a time of new social and economic reforms and greater political stability.

Reform, however, was slow and radical reformers were frustrated. The so-called Generation of 1870 featured intellectuals who studied at Portugal's only full-fledged university of the time, the University of Coimbra, and who rebelled against conventional society and its political system which they saw as isolated, narrow-minded, ultraclerical, ignorant, and reactionary. These voices of reform included the novelist Jose Maria de Eça de Queirós (1845–1900), the poet Antero Tarquínio de Quental (1842–1891), and the economist Joquim Pedro de Oliveira Martins (1845–1894). They proposed radical land reform; the disestablishment of the Catholic Church; a secular educational system; and greater freedom of the press, of speech, and of assembly, but such reformist notions were in large part ignored or evaded.

ECONOMIC PROGRESS AND FAILURE IN POLITICAL REFORM (1870–1890)

While Portugal remained one of the poorest, least developed of western European states, after the failure of the radicals of the Generation of 1870 to institute their reforms, some economic progress continued. If the wolf of bankruptcy seemed always at the nation's door, Portugal's transportation and communications infrastructure experienced improvements. With assistance from foreign investors and engineers, especially from France, Belgium, and Britain, Portuguese railroads, trams, and telegraph systems were extended. In 1889 those "roads of iron" reached an important milestone: Portugal's rail system was connected at the frontier with Spain's. Now a traveler in Lisbon could take a train through Spain and across France to Paris and back.

For a resource-hungry country like Portugal, however, progress had its price and one cost of extending the railroad network was an increased foreign debt, a sensitive issue in a country where foreign investment could be judged as a prelude to foreign control. Earlier examples, when British or French armies ruled Portugal between the French invasions (1807–1811) and the return of King John VI from Brazil in 1821, were not easily forgotten. In 1890 Portugal's national finances were close to bankruptcy, which alarmed volatile politicians and worsened the national uproar over the "English ultimatum" crisis that began in January 1890. This crisis was based on a dispute between Britain and Portugal over Central African territory.

The tragedy of this troubled constitutional monarchy was not only institutional but also personal: the royal family sustained heavy losses in its efforts to adapt the monarchy to the new system. In 1834 the former emperor of Brazil, the exhausted Dom Pedro of Braganza, succumbed to tuberculosis at age thirty-six, only months after his forces triumphed in the Civil War. Following the death in 1853 of Queen Maria II in childbirth at age thirty-four Portugal was ruled by other courageous monarchs who also possessed special aptitudes. Young King Pedro V (r. 1853–1861), well educated and with prodigious intellectual gifts, began his brief reign with great promise, only to die of typhoid at age twenty-four. The brother who succeeded him, King Luis I (r. 1861–1889), was not as talented as Pedro but was a steady, conscientious leader during a long reign. His son, Carlos I (r. 1889–1908), who succeeded him, was more gifted than his father, but confronted a more challenging era, which began with a crisis after the English ultimatum incident of January 1890, when Britain humiliated Portugal and nearly declared war over disputed territory in Central Africa.

FROM MONARCHY TO REPUBLIC (1890–1910)

The ultimatum crisis produced an emotional, violent nationalistic response, weakened the monarchy, encouraged republicans and impelled Portugal finally to occupy and pacify larger portions of its tropical African empire. Riots broke out in Lisbon and in other towns. Despite the fact that there was little Portugal could have done so late in the scramble for Africa to thwart British action, the monarchy along with establishment politicians were discredited by the ultimatum and the idea of a republic that would bring "national salvation" and restore lost prestige attracted supporters. In January 1890 as Portuguese armed forces maneuvered in Central Africa, in what is now Malawi, Britain became aggressive toward its oldest ally and, in order to annex the area itself, demanded that Portugal withdraw all its forces. Humiliated but helpless before the threat of British naval action, a declaration of war, and an abrogation of the Anglo-Portuguese Alliance, Portugal ordered the withdrawal of its expedition from Central Africa and the Government resigned.

The political consequences of the English ultimatum crisis were significant. Although the immediate crisis dissipated when in January 1891 the government easily crushed an abortive military coup in Oporto, the crisis continued. The party system, although prodded by young King Carlos, failed to adopt genuine reform and remained corrupt. This era featured the increasing instability of governments that came and went rapidly, lack of administrative continuity, fractiousness of the political parties, and an increase in public violence, including the renewal of military rebellions. The

now-historic tradition of military insurrectionism, which began in Spain and Spanish America and emerged in Portugal as early as 1817, was revived after a hiatus of some decades (1860–1890) as republicans encouraged military rebellions in order to overthrow the monarchy.

The rise of republicanism after 1890 was encouraged, too, by secret or semisecret societies of militants, including well-educated Masonic orders as well as the *Carbonária,* a radical republican group, which advocated terrorist methods to achieve power. While some republican deputies managed to be elected to the parliament after 1900, a pattern restricted to Lisbon and Oporto, legal, peaceful ways of replacing the monarchists and gaining public office were blocked by the closed system, including rigged elections, heavy-handed police repression and press censorship. Urbanization burgeoned after 1890 and extremist elements, including anarchists and anarcho-syndicalists, grew more active. As conspiracies multiplied the government responded harshly to yet another republican coup plot in late 1907. By this time, the king, Carlos I, and his family had become fully identified with the failing system and he became a target of militants who in an age of political assassination believed in the anarchist-terrorist doctrine of the propaganda of the deed.

On 1 February 1908 in the streets of Lisbon, several republican Carbonária shot dead King Carlos and his eldest son, Luis Filipe, the heir presumptive, in their open carriage. A shocked, slightly wounded and unprepared young King Manuel II, at age eighteen deemed "The Unfortunate," succeeded to the throne, an orphan both personally and politically. Curiously, after the unexpected tragedy, which should have aroused sympathy for the ruling group, out of fear the government in office resigned. A republican-led military and civilian insurrection and an insurgent navy, beginning on 3 October 1910, neutralized the army. On 5 October a parliamentary republic was proclaimed from the balcony of Lisbon's city hall and a new political age began.

THE YOUNG REPUBLIC (1910–1914)

There was initial popular enthusiasm for the republic, but the country had inherited a deadly legacy from the monarchy. This included a largely rural, illiterate, peasant population, labor unrest among

Portuguese republican soldiers, 1910. Republican forces occupy the royal palace in Lisbon during the conflict that resulted in the abdication of Manuel II. ©HULTON-DEUTSCH COLLECTION/CORBIS

ill-paid, poor, repressed workers, a largely undeveloped, rebellious overseas empire in Africa and Asia, and heavy foreign and domestic debt. And how could this republic, only the third republic in a still largely monarchist Europe, bring genuine reform to a poor, isolated country, meet the expectations of classes that supported the republican revolution of 1910, and yet reconcile the passions of contending political forces?

The republic easily crushed armed incursions of monarchists from Spain in 1911 and 1912, but found that winning over and sustaining a broad range of supporters was more challenging. The republic's 1911 constitution, featuring parliamentary, not executive, power and the republican governing group with its assault on the Catholic Church alienated various classes of devout Catholics in a nation with an ancient Catholic tradition. Anticlerical legislation based largely on French legal models, for the first time separated church and state, expropriated all church

property, legalized divorce, expelled religious orders, restricted religious worship, and secularized education. The working classes, who expected much from promises made by republican leaders and from the initial legalization of strikes, were profoundly disappointed as the republic did too little to assist organized labor or the working classes.

The Democratic Party, which dominated elections for most of the first republic, favored immediate entry into World War I on the Allied side. This policy was controversial in Portugal, however, as other political parties as well as interest groups favored neutrality or only modest support for the Allies. Few Portuguese supported the Central Powers. In the summer and fall of 1914 the Portuguese parliament (Congress of Deputies and Senate) voted to join the Allied powers, but Portugal's oldest ally, Britain, requested Portugal not to join the war but to remain neutral. Portugal remained neutral for the time being, but late in 1914 German forces in German South West Africa (today Namibia) invaded Angola. This action did not bring Portugal into the war and only later, in March 1916, under new pressure from ally Britain to seize German ships in Portugal's harbors, did Portugal enter the war on the Allied side. As World War I deepened into the trench warfare stalemate, the novice republic had a bad press in Britain due to international controversies over the republicans' treatment of monarchist political prisoners and forced-labor practices in Portugal's African colonies. Even early in its history, the republic was beginning to suffer from the political instability, social turmoil, economic distress, and military insurrectionism that would help bring it down twelve years later.

See also **Colonies; Great Britain; Spain.**

BIBLIOGRAPHY

Costa Pinto, António, ed. *Modern Portugal.* Palo Alto, Calif., 1998. See early pages of chapters 1–3.

Eça de Queirós, Jose Maria. *The Maias.* Translated by Patricia McGowan Pinheiro and Ann Stevens. London, 1965. Classic nineteenth-century novel that portrays Portuguese society c. 1880, by Portugal's greatest modern novelist.

Feijó, Rui. *Liberal Revolution, Social Change, and Economic Development.* New York, 1993. See especially chapter 1, pp. 1–27.

Hammond, Richard James. *Portugal and Africa, 1815–1910.* Stanford, Calif., 1966.

Macauley, Neill. *Dom Pedro: The Struggle for Liberty in Brazil and Portugal, 1798–1834.* Durham, N.C., 1986.

Oliveira Marques, A. H. de. *History of Portugal.* 2nd ed. New York, 1976. See especially vol. 1, pp. 406–507, and vol. 2, pp. 1–137.

Wheeler, Douglas L. "The Portuguese Revolution of 1910." *Journal of Modern History* 44, no. 2 (June 1972): 172–194.

———. *Republican Portugal. A Political History (1910–1926).* Madison, Wis., 1978, See especially chapters 1–6.

DOUGLAS L. WHEELER

POSITIVISM. The fundamental axiom of positivism, the system of thought founded by Auguste Comte (1798–1857), is that everything, not only the natural world but also human morality and religion, should be ordered on the basis of science. The word *positive* (*positif* in French), deriving from the Latin *ponere* (to put or place) had been used in the sense of "relating to fact" from the sixteenth century and in opposition to "metaphysical" from the eighteenth century, when the encyclopedists had first begun attempting to synthesize human knowledge. Comte stands very much in the tradition of Denis Diderot (1713–1784) and his colleagues, attempting to ground political and social thought on the same rational basis as the natural sciences.

Another synonym for *positive*, in Comte's view, was *relative*, the Kantean belief that one can know nothing about things in themselves but only the relations between them. Positivism accordingly abandons the search for causes in favor of the laws of relation. All human conceptions, according to Comte's law of the three stages, pass from the theological through the metaphysical to the positive stage; from being seen as the result of supernatural agencies or abstract essences they are finally regarded as related to each other by fixed and invariable laws. This had long been recognized in the physical sciences; what was new in Comte was the attempt to devise a science of society, a social statics or order based on social dynamics or history. Comte attempted to give system and scientific rigor to the widespread contemporary confidence in a grand narrative of human progress.

Many of Comte's contemporaries were happy enough with his synthesis of the sciences, the *Cours de philosophie positive,* which appeared in six volumes from 1830 to 1842, but were less happy with the dictatorial tendencies that became all too evident in the second of his major works, the *Système de politique positive* (published from 1851 to 1854), setting out the details of his religion of humanity, on the basis of which society should be ordered. There is a continuing debate over the continuity between the two "halves" of Comte's career. There can be no doubt that Comte always intended positivism to provide a complete explanation of all phenomena, including the human sciences. The problem, at least for Comte's followers, was the detail with which Comte spelled out the way in which he believed society should be ordered.

Comte came to see the religion of humanity as the natural successor to Christianity. Much of his work is devoted to analyzing the merits and defects of Catholicism, which had provided the Middle Ages with a set of beliefs on which to base human morality. Those beliefs had gradually been eroded, however, by the Western Revolution, firstly under Protestantism and then under deism. Now, according to Comte, it was necessary to devise a new synthesis of knowledge on which to base human behavior, thus avoiding the anarchy and disorder that had been the result of the French Revolution (year one of the positivist calendar began in 1789). Positive morality was erected on the basis of the contemporary "science" of phrenology and faculty psychology, advocating the gradual strengthening of the altruistic instincts at the expense of the egoistic, a process involving an elaborate system of prayer and meditation based on "real" angels of the house (mothers, wives, and daughters).

Comte's French followers, historians of science such as Pierre Laffitte and Maximilien-Paul-Émile Littre, author of the famous dictionary of medicine, tended to play down the later Comte's attempted reconstruction of religion. Pioneering sociologists such as Émile Durkheim also drew more on the early work, helping to establish the new discipline of sociology on a genuinely scientific basis. This was also the case with Comte's most famous English disciple, John Stuart Mill, whose *System of Logic* (1843) culminated in the "Logic of the Moral Sciences." Mill advocated new sciences of the mind (psychology), of morals (ethology), and of society (sociology). In *Auguste Comte and Positivism* (1865) he distinguished clearly between the acceptable Comte of the *Cours* and the unacceptable high priest of humanity of the later work. His posthumously published *Three Essays on Religion* (1874), however, was surprisingly sympathetic toward the general aim of reorganizing religion on a humanist basis.

The most enthusiastic popularizer of Comte's philosophy of the sciences was George Henry Lewes, George Eliot's partner, whose widely read *Biographical History of Philosophy,* first published in 1845–1846, went through several editions, the third and fourth (1867 and 1871) displaying his continuing faith in their revised title, *The History of Philosophy from Thales to Comte.* Other prominent positivists, much read in their own time but now largely forgotten, included Frederic Harrison and

Edward Spencer Beesly, professor of history at University College London from 1860 to 1893. Both were actively involved in the development of working men's colleges and in the legitimization of the trade unions in the 1860s and 1870s. They saw to it that positivism was much discussed by politicians, historians, and theologians as well as by scientists in mid-to-late Victorian Britain. The official Positivist Society remained small in numbers, but everybody who was anybody in the world of late-Victorian Britain had to have a position on positivism as a general philosophy. Novelists such as George Eliot, Thomas Hardy, George Gissing (tutor to Harrison's children), and Mrs. Humphry Ward (Mary Augusta Ward) studied Comte carefully and developed their own views in relation to his.

Positivism made a particularly powerful impact in Latin America where intellectual elites considered it a tool for emancipating their nations from the economic backwardness, political and moral anarchy, and pre-scientific culture for which they blamed their former colonial powers. Under Julio de Castilhos, the first republican governor of the southern state of Rio Grande do Sul, positivism continued to guide state- and nation-building in Brazil over most of the twentieth century. The country's republican flag, with its motto of "order and progress," was reconfirmed after each regime change, and Brazil remains the only country worldwide that still has a positivist church.

The lasting legacy of positivism should probably be seen as the foundation of the new academic disciplines of sociology and the history of science. The logical positivists of the 1930s owed little to Comte, merely sharing his dislike of metaphysics. Modern humanism, attempting to gain recognition of the legitimacy of a lifestyle based entirely on human values, sees Comte himself as an embarrassment. His reputation has certainly not been enhanced by biographical studies focusing on his supposed madness and eccentricity. He can claim nevertheless to have articulated many of the basic assumptions of his time, albeit in an idiosyncratic and ultimately unacceptable manner.

See also **Comte, Auguste; Science and Technology; Secularization; Sociology.**

BIBLIOGRAPHY

Chadwick, Owen. *The Secularization of the European Mind in the Nineteenth Century.* Cambridge, U.K., and New York, 1975.

Hentschke, Jens R. *Positivism gaúcho-Style: Julio de Castilhos's Dictatorship and Its Impact on State and Nation-Building in Vargas's Brazil.* Berlin, 2004.

Kolakowski, Leszek. *Positivist Philosophy from Hume to the Vienna Circle.* Harmondsworth, U.K., 1972.

Simon, Walter Michael. *European Positivism in the Nineteenth Century: An Essay in Intellectual History.* Ithaca, N.Y., 1963.

Wright, Terence R. *The Religion of Humanity: The Impact of Comtean Positivism on Victorian Britain.* Cambridge, U.K., and New York, 1986.

T. R. WRIGHT

POSTERS.

In the modern era the poster became both a means of mass communication and a new artistic medium. The freedom to post bills was established in 1791 in France during the French Revolution; the poster was an important medium for nascent revolutionary political culture. Through much of the nineteenth century, however, political posters, subject to severe surveillance, were scarce in France and in much of Europe. On the other hand, commercial posters developed as part of the birth of mass consumer society. From the 1830s, places of consumption for the middle classes in Paris and London multiplied, prompting increasingly sophisticated advertising campaigns. London was the initial center of both poster and press advertising; English posters were exempt from special taxes, unlike in France. Posters were displayed on poster-carriages and construction fences lit at night. Charles Dickens (1812–1870) christened the droves of men carrying placards front and back "sandwichmen."

The pioneers of the illustrated poster were French. Jean-Alexis Rouchon (1794–1878) designed the first illustrated posters printed in color destined for the street from 1845. The fin de siècle marked the golden age of the illustrated poster, especially in France. Poster artists such as Jules Chéret (1836–1932) and Henri de Toulouse-Lautrec (1864–1901) were influential in both fine and commercial arts. Created by a designer, reproduced through modern technology, and widely displayed for the purpose of advertising, the illustrated poster was a locus of art, commerce, technology, and ideologies.

CHÉRET AND POSTERMANIA

Chéret was the most popular and prolific poster artist. He designed over one thousand posters by 1900, for subjects ranging from café-concerts, plays, novels, department stores, and exhibitions to countless consumer products. He transformed the poster when he introduced in 1869 a system of three-color lithographic printing. Until then, color was incidental to mainly black-and-white posters. The landmark French press law of 1881 endowed the freedom of the press and billposting and also allowed the use of white background in posters, previously reserved for official posters. This coincided with increased literacy. The popularity of poster art led to "postermania" from 1895 to 1900.

The illustrated poster transformed the way in which products were advertised, through the vast dissemination of images that decidedly targeted the consumer's visualizing capacity, eliciting desires and fantasies. The display of goods and commercial exchange had become subjects of modern art as well. *A Bar at the Folies Bergère* (1881–1882) by Edouard Manet (1832–1883) depicts a barmaid in a brasserie in which young women entertained male customers, a theme depicted in Chéret's 1875 poster for the same establishment. *Circus Parade* (1887–1888) and *Circus* (1891) by Georges Seurat (1859–1891) were clearly influenced by Chéret's circus posters. There was much cooperation among poster artists, fine artists, and literary figures. The journal *La Plume* (1889–1905) distributed poster panels and organized poster exhibitions. Contributors to *La Plume* included the artists Eugène Grasset (1845–1917), Georges de Feure (1868–1928), Pierre Bonnard (1867–1947), Toulouse-Lautrec, Theophile-Alexandre Steinlen (1859–1923), James Sydney Ensor (1860–1949), and the Symbolist poets Stephane Mallarmé (1842–1898) and Paul Verlaine (1844–1896).

THE IMPACT OF THE ILLUSTRATED POSTER

Poster art figured significantly in the debate over modernity and modern art and spurred debates as to its effectiveness as a commercial medium. Many

Advertising poster by Jules Chéret, 1889. A typical
"chérette"—a scantily clad woman who seems to float in the
air—adorns this poster for the Fairyland feature of the 1889
Paris exposition. ©HISTORICAL PICTURE ARCHIVE/CORBIS

contemporary critics embraced poster art as a truly
modern art that was transforming drab streets into
colorful outdoor galleries. The writer Joris-Karl
Huysmans (1848–1907) and others praised Chéret
for creating vital new art that revealed everyday
mores. Thought to be reviving French "gaiety,"
Chéret was called the "Watteau of the street." However, many advertising experts considered the illustrated poster an ineffective advertising method
compared to systematic "American" methods.
Others objected to the illustrated poster precisely
because it seemed to be effective at seducing the
public and inducing unnecessary consumption.

Poster images invariably depicted women.
Chéret's posters were populated with scantily clad
women called "chérettes," joyous figures who
seemed to float in the air. That images of women

predominated in posters signaled both the feminiza-
tion of consumption and the commodification of the
female form. Women were depicted as enjoying outdoor activities such as visiting exhibitions and fairs,
ice skating, bicycling, and traveling. The representation of women in posters can be seen as reflecting
both empowerment and dependency on appearances.
The illustrated poster also led to the intensification of
celebrity culture; the extraordinarily popular French
actress Sarah Bernhardt (1844–1923) and other stars
were frequent subjects of publicity campaigns and
were in turn hired to advertise products.

TOULOUSE-LAUTREC AND MUCHA

Toulouse-Lautrec became famous with his *Moulin
Rouge* poster of 1891. He was thought to turn poster
art into true fine art, through bold and striking compositions and expressive use of line. His main subject
was the world of Montmartre. The Czech artist
Alphonse Mucha (1860–1939) became an overnight
sensation in Paris in 1895 when he designed a poster
for Bernhardt. Mucha also designed theater decoration and jewelry for Bernhardt. His posters were filled
with Art Nouveau images of exotic and sensuous
women and symbolic and occult language. While
poster art was largely a French phenomenon, it was
also a cosmopolitan phenomenon fostering a great
deal of exchange of ideas. Postermania was embraced
by the international avant-garde and middle-class
aficionados. One of the most innovative poster artists
of the time was Thomas Theodor Heine (1867–
1948), whose images were strikingly modern and
simple.

POLITICAL POSTERS AND MEDIA
FOR BILLPOSTING

This period saw tens of millions of political posters
as well. During the intensive nationwide election
campaign by General Georges-Ernest-Jean-Marie
Boulanger (1837–1891), who threatened the
Republican system in France, billposters of rival
camps battled one another in the street and
employed long ladders to stick bills everywhere.
Posters were displayed on a large variety of media.
Besides walls and construction scaffoldings, in
France items of street furniture such as kiosks
and Morris columns were used—for commercial
posters only—as were vehicles and sandwichmen.
Posters were placed strategically according to the
geographic division of different classes.

REACTION AGAINST THE POSTER

After the turn of the century, the sheer inundation of streets by posters provoked a reaction from the public in many parts of Europe. Posters were seen as pollutants challenging the capacity of the human mind to absorb stimuli. Laws were passed to reduce the number and size of posters and preserve monuments and views of the countryside. At the same time advertising experts sought to adopt psychological theories into poster design. The poster art of the post–World War I period would be very different from the previous era, informed by such efforts as well as by trends in art.

See also **Art Nouveau; Bernhardt, Sarah; Dickens, Charles; Fin de Siècle; Manet, Édouard; Trade and Economic Growth.**

BIBLIOGRAPHY

Feinblatt, Ebria and Bruce Davis. *Toulouse-Lautrec and His Contemporaries: Posters of the Belle Epoque from the Wagner Collection.* Los Angeles, 1985.

Rennert, Jack. *Posters of the Belle Epoque: The Wine Spectator Collection.* New York, 1990.

Richards, Thomas. *The Commodity Culture of Victorian England: Advertising and Spectacle, 1851–1914.* Stanford, Calif., 1990.

Wischermann, Clemens, and Elliott Shore, eds. *Advertising and the European City: Historical Perspectives.* Aldershot, U.K., 2000.

HAZEL HAHN

POVERTY. In nineteenth-century Europe, the question of poverty presented itself in a double form. In the first, poverty was part of what various historians have termed a *moral economy,* that is, a public arena on a local scale, in which the initiative of the state remained in the background and the responsibility for the maintenance of the poor was part of the charitable practices of the aristocracy, following a model of paternalism that in times of crisis might become obligatory even for the ruling classes. Unrest over food supplies was not only a "spasmodic" reflex caused by a sudden surge in food prices, but also a means by which the poor could remind the aristocracy of their need to comply with this unwritten social pact. This moral economy translated a millennial cultural tradition into a civil and secular form. Whereas other religions of the Mediterranean basin (Judaism and Islam) prescribed a codified mandate of institutionalized solidarity with the poor in the form of a regular tax, Christian churches accentuated the spiritual value of poverty and charity, and did not invoke the collective sphere of social justice and responsibility: solidarity was an individual, abstract, and voluntary choice. Social harmony came to depend on this tradition, through practices and rituals involving the exchange of gifts and deference. Alongside free-market forms of exchange and the distributive authority of government, there was a place for relationships based on reciprocity, which built up and preserved symmetries and solidarity in the heart of the social organism.

The other face of poverty, however, belonged entirely to the political sphere. The governing of cities required means to control large numbers of beggars. Beginning in the sixteenth century, legislation began to appear throughout Europe ranging from the prohibition or repression of begging to the physical sequestration of healthy and idle paupers. The technical and legal principles that determined the classification of the poor were based on the ethos of work. Indigents who were elderly, sickly, or otherwise unfit for labor were "deserving poor," worthy of aid inasmuch as they were not culpable for their personal misfortunes. But beggars capable of work were an "undeserving poor" who infringed upon the social pact, contravened the law, and committed a crime. In the enlightened thought and the economic policies of the nineteenth century, these distinctions took their place alongside the negative preoccupation with police control of vagabonds, and the positive and laissez-faire philosophy of work as an instrument of social ascent. Missing from this conceptual framework was the typical *ancien régime* figure of the shamefaced poor: the disgraced noble who was secretly supported at home because he was still perceived to be the bearer of a social prestige independent of (and indeed contrary to) the obligation to work. While the definition of the poor that resulted from this cultural evolution presented infinite local variations, in all of Europe it did not diverge much from the canonical form elaborated by the English philosopher Jeremy Bentham: "poverty is the state of everyone who, in order to obtain subsistence, is forced to have recourse to labour.

A Beggar on the Path. Painting by Edward Thompson Davis, 1856. A sentimental but realistic portrayal of childhood poverty in Britain. HAMBURG KUNSTHALLE, HAMBURG, GERMANY/ BRIDGEMAN ART LIBRARY

Indigence is the state of him who, being destitute of property...is at the same time, either unable to labour, or unable, even for labour, to procure the supply of which he happens thus to be in want" (*Writings on the Poor Laws* [1796–1797], cited in Poynter, p. 119). On the basis of this generic definition, statistical data on the poor were compiled at more or less regular intervals in all of the greater European cities, in order to monitor a phenomenon that continued to preoccupy the ruling classes. Yet the methods of quantification were heterogeneous (records of poverty released by parishes, home visits by administrative officials, comprehensive censuses of familial economic conditions), and the classifications adopted varied greatly from one place to another and over time, to the point of making comparative studies extremely problematic.

England provides a good example of the evolution from a "moral economy" to the policing of the labor market. The old Poor Law, adopted in 1601 and kept in force until 1834, established a poor tax that was imposed at parish level, to which was added a self-correcting scale of wages (allowance system) linked to grain prices, formalized by the magistrates of Berkshire County assembled in 1795 at the Pelican Inn in Speenhamland. The English experience, therefore, took the form of a tax for the relief of poverty (typical of the non-Christian religions of the Mediterranean basin) distributed through a network of "outdoor relief" that did not restrict the free movement of the poor. In contrast, the new Poor Law, ratified in England in 1834, took up the idea of internment in workhouses, which was closely inspired by the principle of "less eligibility": of the lesser suitability of reclusion with respect to free labor (that is, the highest wage in the workhouse was lower than the lowest wage outside the workhouse on the free market). "Indoor relief" was substituted for "outdoor relief."

In many European countries, the period of Napoleonic domination had already witnessed the introduction of new institutions (*ateliers de charité* [charity workshops] and *dépôts de mendicité* [beggars' centers]) that united vocational training with the repellent physiognomy of the "total institution"—the gloomy image that Charles Dickens immortalized in *Oliver Twist* (1837–1839), and that the studies of the twentieth-century French philosopher Michel Foucault have shown to be a universal and divisive tendency in modern societies. A closer analysis of these institutions, however, reveals more articulated and complex realities. Superimposed over the initiatives of the authorities were the traditional networks of private beneficence and the improper use that the poor themselves were often able to make of the refuge offered in such institutions, by creating high rates of turnover and devising strategies for the temporary registration of family members too young or old to work. The sporadic data available (for the workhouses of London, Antwerp, and Florence) show that the average duration of reclusion was less than a year and that mortality rates were around 10 percent, with most deaths occurring among the very old. Even in the case of England, historians have questioned the effectiveness of the new Poor Law in practice, and a number of case studies document the continuation of the system of domestic subsidies before and after 1834, and with them the persistence of charitable practices foreign to the principle of internment. According to statistics from the United Kingdom in the second part of the nineteenth century, the proportion of "indoor paupers" remained constantly under ten per thousand, in the face of rates of overall demographic increase of 50 percent (from twenty-five million inhabitants in 1859 to thirty-eight million in 1900). The number of "outdoor paupers" in turn fell, both as a percentage of the total population and in absolute figures, though it always remained nearly triple that of the "indoor paupers."

All the same, the battle fought in England against the right of healthy paupers to receive assistance took on the character of a cultural divide, whose echo reverberated throughout the Continent. The criterion of "less eligibility" aimed at propelling the poor onto the free labor market, by reserving public aid exclusively for invalids. A new initiative for the management of poverty thus made headway by means of the mechanisms of free capitalist competition: social policy entered into the question of poverty. In 1842 Frederick William IV of Prussia approved, not without strong opposition, a law on poor relief—inspired by principles not dissimilar to those of the English reform—aiming at the free circulation of manual labor and at the unification of the labor market.

The revolutions of 1848 dramatically brought to light the other side of the coin. The mob, the "low population" of the principal European cities, gradually broke with the deferential ties of the moral economy and, perceiving the crisis of the old order, adopted new heroes and new banners. On the barricades of 1848 the urban poor again showed that it could be dangerous, but now no longer in the forms defined by the old and subaltern expedient of the grain riot, but rather by an adherence to political and national programs. Intent on defining the new revolutionary matrix by anchoring it firmly to the factory, manual labor, and class conscience, Karl Marx rigidly separated the proletariat from the subproletariat, relegating to the second category the varied world of the impoverished. Yet before Marx, for example in the sixth edition of the *Dictionary of the French Academy* (1832–1835), the definition of the proletariat closely resembled Bentham's concept of the

poor: those who, possessing neither capital nor property, lived from day to day on the fruit of their labors. Salaried work was usually an intermittent and precarious condition, not always sufficient to maintain a stable social position. Much more prevalent in the vocabulary of the democrats was the more generic and all-inclusive concept of the "people." This "people," defined by a sense of social inequality that had a vaguely evangelical tinge, encompassed the shadowy and typically urban world of the poor—a world that in the mid-nineteenth century became the focus of the new genre of "mystery" literature dedicated to the obscure underbelly of the great European metropolises. Small-time criminals, prostitutes, those who performed odd jobs—in a word the *misérables* of Victor Hugo's 1862 novel of that name—became the bearers of a "culture of poverty" that was radically foreign to prevailing concepts of legality and bourgeois morality; indelibly marked by precariousness, mistrust, and marginalization; and destined to propagate itself from generation to generation. The moral stigma reserved by the authorities for the undeserving poor in the *ancien régime* returned once more to prominence, and the idea of deviance overtook that of poverty. Early marriage, sexual promiscuity, drunkenness, heedlessness, apathy, blasphemy, and brutality henceforth defined the contours of the condition of poverty, adopting themes still current in modern sociology: absence of privacy, the chronological contraction of childhood, scarce faculties for economic planning, and fatalism.

The laissez-faire approach to employment, introduced by England's new Poor Law of 1834 as an aid in the struggle against poverty, came into collision, however, with the corporate protections that regulated access to skilled occupations and maintained an exclusive monopoly on charitable donations and pensions. Huge numbers of the poor continued to weigh on the cities. And the problem of urban misery was as a result separated from the problem of legislation designed to provide social security, which remained the privilege of recognized occupational groups who were already partially protected. Meanwhile, the task of providing assistance for the poor continued to be met on an emergency and temporary basis by local institutions and private beneficence. In no other century

London's Poor Sheltered under a Bridge. Engraving by Gustave Doré c. 1869–1871. Doré travelled to London in 1868 and afterward created a series of engravings documenting poverty and overcrowding in the city. SNARK/ART RESOURCE, NY

was "public beneficence" (where *public* stood for "directed at the public") written and talked about as much as in the nineteenth century: ten thousand volumes were published in the nineteenth century alone on this theme, many of which came to be best-sellers translated into several European languages and reprinted many times. In Italy, the *Saggi bibliografici di economia politica* (Annotated bibliography of political economy), compiled by Luigi Cossa at the end of the century, lists 151 studies on the theory of charitable donations for the period from 1800 to 1848, compared to 112 on the field of finance, 83 dedicated to problems of food supply, and 188 on money and credit.

The targets of the liberal polemic were twofold. On the one hand, the polemic aimed at all of those proposals—from the Declaration of the Rights of Man and of the Citizen put forth by the French Constituent Assembly in 1789 to the English formula of Speenhamland—that presented assistance

as a right and created fiscal levies specifically intended to finance initiatives on behalf of the needy; and on the other, at the typically European tradition of private charity, administered in a piecemeal, casual, disorganized manner and hence incapable of resolving the problem. In the wake of François Naville and Joseph Marie De Gérando, the need to devise forms of scientific and organized charity capable of overcoming the limits of individual generosity gained a growing place in European culture. In 1846 the Society of Charitable Economics was founded in Paris, and various authors lent their pens to the idea of a Christian reconciliation between laissez-faire policy and charity, which was to counter the socialist doctrines and the notion of "legislative charity" (charity made obligatory by law) that underpinned the English reform of 1834. In the course of the 1850s the municipal administration of Elberfeld, in the Rhineland, developed a full-fledged system for the adoption of poor families by richer citizens, who became jointly responsible for charity and social cohesion. This example of "familial morality" that was extended to become a form of governance enjoyed rapid success: it was widely followed in Germany, and served as a model in the following decade for the Charity Organization Society in London. Under the direction of an official in the Belgian government, Edouard Ducpétiaux—whose works were critically analyzed by Marx—the first international congress of these charitable organizations was convened in Brussels in 1856, and thereafter repeated annually in Frankfurt and London. The large majority of those who attended claimed no ideological or religious affiliations, and what brought them together was the growth in professional qualifications in the field of public assistance, and the shared goal of modernizing charitable activities on the principles of science, without jeopardizing the direct and reciprocal ties that existed between social classes. In short, "charitable economics" propagated a philosophy of labor and social mobility; public assistance was to be linked to civil progress and individual enterprise.

In its more radical and secular forms, the issue of poverty offered important benchmarks for new constitutional governments: the opportunity to achieve both a moral reform to restore to the people the right and duty to work, and a religious reform to resuscitate not an ecclesiastical but an interior and personal sense of the divine. In Bavaria in the 1830s and in Denmark in the 1860s, the volume of private donations—centralized and coordinated by this type of nongovernmental charitable association—greatly exceeded the expenditures earmarked for the poor by local administrations. A study on religious charities conducted in January 1863 by the Kingdom of Italy revealed that the influence of the Catholic Church was enormous, but not exclusive and perhaps not even predominant: roughly speaking, charitable enterprises run by the church made up 40 percent of the total. The report presented in parliament in 1887 reduced this figure further: out of 8,127 religious charities, only 2,195, or 27 percent, were under the "direct or indirect control" of the clergy. Even in the country of the Holy See, therefore, the majority of charitable foundations were part of a private and secular tradition of "public beneficence" that—in similar fashion to what occurred in the rest of Europe—contributed in various ways

to a common "paternalistic matrix." This matrix did not merely preserve an ancient tradition of charity and private beneficence, but was well adapted to modern times and revealed a surprising capacity to transform itself and evolve over time. Only in part did it recall the traditional philanthropic and paternalistic "ideology of dependence" that was colored by backward-looking rural and anti-industrial traits, and opposed to modernization, whose delays, compromises, and defects it highlighted. As occurred in England—where the local landowning aristocracy adapted to the reforming impulse of the state by adapting its charitable customs—so too in France, Italy, and Germany the paternalistic matrix adapted to progress, reflected on foreign examples, exorcised fears, and began to seek preventive measures against social disorder, in ways that often brought into the public sphere traditional private practices linked to the moral economy. The process of modernization, of state and nation building, did not negate these practices: alongside the centralizing impetus of government and politics, a deeper and more continuous dimension of welfare relations survived in which rich and poor continued to encounter each other and to exchange gifts in return for deference. This network of institutionalized social relations was not merely linked to a shadowy zone set apart from the modernizing initiative of the state but was also a valuable heritage of ancient and hallowed paternalistic initiatives on the part of the local elites that paved the way for successive developments not only by virtue of their simple capillary presence but also because they replicated enduring ways of approaching the social question. Cultural and technical concerns, for example, connected the forms of corporate paternalism that Italian entrepreneurs such as Alessandro Rossi and Paolo Camerini were developing in the Veneto at the turn of the twentieth century with the contemporary English experiences of welfare capitalism on a local level.

Historians writing in the "neo-laissez-faire" mood of the 1980s questioned the links between this tradition of private paternalism and the development of the modern welfare state, emphasizing the public function of the former as opposed to the bureaucratic and parasitic degeneration of the latter. The explicit target of these polemics was the model of modernization formulated in 1950 by the English sociologist Thomas H. Marshall that

The Sailor's Orphans; or, The Young Ladies' Subscription. Engraving by William Ward after a painting by William Redmore Bigg. Before the enactment of state policies to provide for the poor, it was considered a moral duty for the wealthy to do so, and well-bred young women often organized to help specific groups or classes of the needy. The relief thus provided was, however, minimal. FITZWILLIAM MUSEUM, UNIVERSITY OF CAMBRIDGE, UK/BRIDGEMAN ART LIBRARY

involved successive stages beginning with the conquest of civil rights in the great bourgeois revolutions of the seventeenth and eighteenth centuries; of political rights with the extension of the suffrage in the nineteenth and twentieth centuries; and finally of social rights that came over the course of the twentieth century with the reform of systems for public assistance and pensions. In fact the contrasts are overstated and when analyzed in localized contexts, the political and cultural origins of the welfare state reveal constant interactions between public and private, between paternalistic customs and popular associations, between the survival strategies of the poor and institutional reforms. The social state emerged, in other words, from negotiations conducted among numerous players,

while the state initiatives did not exhaust the politics of public assistance. There were also systems of welfare that embraced a wider social ambit, where modernization mixed with the maneuvers of local political elites and the centuries-old traditions of welfare relations inspired by charity and beneficence. These different variables gave rise to legislative processes in different national contexts that addressed the social question by adopting agendas based either on an English or a German model.

The English model embodied opposition to legislated charity, the "religion of freedom": every obligation mandated by law was seen as a threat to the sense of individual responsibility of rich and poor alike. Between 1833 and 1850, in response to pressure from the trade unions, limits were placed on the employment of children and women, an intervention protecting the social groups at greatest risk of poverty. Yet the traditions of local autonomy and the reform of 1834 enabled the English state to avoid direct intervention in the matter of poverty for a long time, with consequences that became public at the end of the century. Charles Booth's monumental study on the poor of London, based on years of house visits and published between 1892 and 1903, revealed that around a third of the urban population (of over four million inhabitants) lived in conditions of "casual labor" and "chronic want." On an inner circle of poor who lived on the margins of society (casual laborers, semicriminals, loafers), and amounted to 9 percent of the total, were superimposed concentric rings of the "very poor" (7.5 percent) and the poor (22.3 percent), all identified by low and irregular wages: of this million and more people only forty-five thousand were "indoor paupers" permanently supported inside the workhouses of the metropolis. For all the others, poverty was a permanent condition of life, bereft of potential avenues of escape and destined to propagate itself across the generations. Similar results were obtained through a contemporary inquiry conducted by B. Seebohm Rowntree on the smaller city of York (with a population of less than one hundred thousand): 10 percent of the populace lived in conditions of primary poverty (those permanently beneath the poverty line fixed by the minimum salary necessary for food and shelter sufficient to permit mere survival), while another 18 percent lived in secondary poverty (those liable to fall into the first category with any unforeseen or extraordinary expenditure). Poverty became a defining structural trait of the individual and familial cycle of life: the birth of children and their departure from home upon reaching adult age coincided with critical moments of income reduction to levels below the line of primary poverty. These were precisely the critical moments that determined the use made by the poor of the systems of indoor and outdoor relief, either by pressing for temporary aid in cash or by having the youngest and oldest members of the household shut up in workhouses.

During the nineteenth century poverty progressively lost its moralistic connotations and took on new economic overtones. From a vagabond and

Poster for a charity fundraiser. Lithograph by Jules Cheret, 1890. A graphic portrayal of a widow and orphan designed to generate sympathy and donations. PRIVATE COLLECTION/BRIDGEMAN ART LIBRARY/THE STAPLETON COLLECTION

marginalized member of society, the pauper became seen as the product of unemployment and underemployment, which were directly linked to the recessive phases of the economic cycle. Further, the connections between poverty and the cycle of life were seen to be related to historical constants that from the beginning to the end of the nineteenth century made the links between poverty and specific family circumstances permanent. The poor were composed of the solitary elderly, single women with children, and large families with one income. Even the reasons for decline from secondary to primary poverty described by Rowntree and Booth closely resembled those recorded in the more impressionistic inquiries from the beginning of the century: excessive family size, premature death of the head of family and breadwinner, and illnesses and invalidity among members of the household.

The great investigations-cum-denunciations of urban poverty by Booth and Rowntree set the English political world astir, and in 1897 the first law promoting voluntary accident insurance was passed. Considered over the long term, the English welfare system seems therefore to have followed a sort of pendular pattern: from privatization to state control after 1940 and then back again to privatization in the 1980s. This can be seen as a process of adaptation to the long-term trends of the capitalistic economy: the state retreated in step with expansive cycles and advanced under the threat of depression. It is also important to note that the notion of occupational risk remained outside the original scope of English social legislation: the early concern shown for women and children reflected a prevailing paternalistic and moralistic ethos rather than a general concern to regulate the workplace. By contrast, it was precisely the concept of risk that became the dominant feature in the German model—a concept that by definition reflected the progressive abandonment of a culture of poverty that paid no attention to the future and placed adversity in the magic world of the unforeseeable and uncontrollable calamities. This notion took shape in the wake of railroad accidents and the legal precedent that—beginning in Prussia in 1838—established the principles of the civic responsibility of a business enterprise for damages to personnel. It was from this earlier experience that in Bismarck's Germany the obligation to insure was seen as an economically rational response that was necessary to redistribute and reduce the overall costs of risk. Germany therefore followed a more politicized and rationalizing path: in contrast to England, poverty and social issues parted ways, and while the former remained the responsibility of municipal administrations, responsibility for the latter was forcefully assumed by the central state.

During the course of the nineteenth century, therefore, the problem of poverty shaped different aspects of the process of state building. England's new Poor Law of 1834 represented a model of governmental intervention designed to improve the functioning of the capitalist labor market, a model more or less closely imitated by nearly all the European countries. Yet modernization did not supplant private beneficence, which followed parallel models of rational self-organization that were driven by the activities of charitable institutions and by the survival strategies of the poor. From these different tendencies, various forms of the welfare state would emerge in the following century, from the universalist model based on individual rights that prevailed in southern Europe, to the particularist model financed by the contributions made by different groups of dependent workers that spread through northern Europe. Neither proved capable of providing any effective solutions to the problem of poverty, which continued in more or less severe forms as a result of economic downturns and of specific family situations unsuited to the conditions of the labor market (female heads of family, numerous dependent children, solitary and unproductive elderly), and through cases of social marginalization (depressed rural or mountainous zones, deindustrialized zones).

See also **Class and Social Relations; Demography; Economists, Classical; Poor Law; Statistics; Welfare.**

BIBLIOGRAPHY

Baldwin, Peter. *The Politics of Social Solidarity: Class Bases of the European Welfare State, 1875–1975.* Cambridge, U.K., 1990.

Barry, Jonathan, and Colin Jones, eds. *Medicine and Charity before the Welfare State.* London, 1991.

Booth, Charles. *Life and Labour of the People in London.* 17 vols. London, 1892–1903.

Boyer, George R. *An Economic History of the English Poor Law, 1750–1850.* Cambridge, U.K., 1990.

Chevalier, Louis. *Labouring Classes and Dangerous Classes in Paris during the First Half of the Nineteenth Century.* Translated by Frank Jellinek. London, 1973.

Cossa, Luigi. *Saggi bibliografici di economia politica.* Bologna, Italy, 1963. Includes reprints of articles published in the *Giornale degli Economisti* between 1891 and 1900.

Daunton, Martin, ed. *Charity, Self-Interest, and Welfare in the English Past.* London, 1996.

De Gérando, Joseph Marie. *Le Visiteur du Pauvre.* Paris, 1820.

Digby, Anne. *The Poor Law in Nineteenth-Century England and Wales.* London, 1982.

———. *British Welfare Policy: Workhouse to Workfare.* London, 1989.

Diver, Felix. *Power and Pauperism: The Workhouse System, 1834–1884.* Cambridge, U.K., 1993.

Finlayson, Geoffrey. *Citizen, State, and Social Welfare in Britain, 1830–1990*. Oxford, U.K., 1994.

Fraser, Derek. *The Evolution of the British Welfare State: A History of Social Policy since the Industrial Revolution.* 3rd ed. Houndmills, Basingstoke, U.K., 2003.

Gozzini, Giovanni. *Il segreto dell'elemosina: Poveri e carità legale a Firenze, 1800–1870.* Florence, Italy, 1993.

Grell, Ole Peter, Andrew Cunningham, and Bernd Roeck, eds. *Health Care and Poor Relief in Eighteenth and Nineteenth Century Southern Europe.* Aldershot, U.K., 2005.

Grell, Ole Peter, Andrew Cunningham, and Robert Jütte, eds. *Health Care and Poor Relief in Eighteenth and Nineteenth Century Northern Europe.* Aldershot, U.K., 2002.

Hennock, E. P. *British Social Reform and German Precedents: The Case of Social Insurance, 1880–1914.* Oxford, U.K., 1987.

Himmelfarb, Gertrude. *The Idea of Poverty: England in the Early Industrial Age.* New York, 1984.

———. *Poverty and Compassion: The Moral Imagination of the Late Victorians.* New York, 1991.

Joyce, Patrick. *Work, Society, and Politics: The Culture of the Factory in Later Victorian England.* Brighton, U.K., 1980.

Katz, Michael B., and Christoph Sachsse, eds. *The Mixed Economy of Social Welfare: Public/Private Relations in England, Germany, and the United States, the 1870s to the 1930s.* Baden-Baden, Germany, 1996.

Lees, Lynn Hollen. *The Solidarities of Strangers: The English Poor Laws and the People, 1700–1948.* Cambridge, U.K., 1998.

Mandler, Peter, ed. *The Uses of Charity: The Poor on Relief in the Nineteenth-Century Metropolis.* Philadelphia, 1990.

Marshall, Thomas H. *Citizenship and Social Class, and Other Essays.* Cambridge, U.K., 1950.

Melling, Joseph. "Welfare Capitalism and the Origins of Welfare States: British Industry, Workplace Welfare, and Social Reform, c. 1870–1914." *Social History* 17, no. 3 (1992): 453–478.

Naville, François. *De la charité légale, de ses effets, de ses causes.* 2 vols. Paris, 1836.

Oxley, Geoffrey W. *Poor Relief in England and Wales, 1601–1834.* Newton Abbot, U.K., 1974.

Poynter, J. R. *Society and Pauperism: English Ideas on Poor Relief, 1795–1834.* London, 1969.

Procacci, Giovanna. *Gouverner la misère: La question sociale en France, 1789–1848.* Paris, 1993.

Rimlinger, Gaston V. *Welfare Policy and Industrialization in Europe, North America, and Russia.* New York, 1971.

Ritter, Gerhard A. *Der Sozialstaat: Entstehung und Entwicklung im internazionale Vergleich.* 2nd ed. Munich, 1991.

Rose, Michael E. *The Relief of Poverty, 1834–1914.* 2nd ed. Basingstoke, U.K., 1986.

Rowntree, B. Seebohm. *Poverty: A Study of Town Life.* 2nd ed. London, 1902.

Rudé, George. *The Crowd in History: A Study of Popular Disturbances in France and England, 1730–1848.* Rev. ed. London, 1981.

Stedman Jones, Gareth. *Outcast London: A Study in the Relationship between Classes in Victorian Society.* Oxford, U.K., 1971.

Thomson, David. "Welfare and the Historians." In *The World We Have Gained: Histories of Population and Social Structure,* edited by Lloyd Bonfield, Richard M. Smith, and Keith Wrightston, 355–378. Oxford, U.K., 1986.

Williams, Karel. *From Pauperism to Poverty.* London, 1981.

Woolf, Stuart. *The Poor in Western Europe in the Eighteenth and Nineteenth Centuries.* London, 1986.

GIOVANNI GOZZINI

PRAGUE. Prague (Czech, *Praha*; German, *Prag*), the capital of Bohemia, the largest of the three provinces comprising the Bohemian lands of the Habsburg Monarchy, sits in a valley formed by the Vltava/Moldau River, which runs northeastward through the city. One of the largest cities in the Habsburg Monarchy, modern Prague was founded by imperial decree in 1784 during the centralizing and modernizing reign of the enlightened-absolutist emperor Joseph II (r. 1765–1790). The decree created a single administrative unit from four historic wards, Old Town (*Staré Město*) and New Town (*Nové Město*) on the east side of the Vltava, and Lesser Side (*Malá strana*) and *Hradčany* on the west. The newly united city had semi-independent governing bodies, including a municipal administration (*Magistrát*) and a city council (*Městský výbor*), as well as a mayor and two vice mayors. The *gubernium,* the highest level of state administration, acting as Vienna's agent, limited municipal activities and determined qualifications for and approved elected and appointed members. The *gubernium* was responsible for many of the modernizing improvements in Prague before 1848, including public parks and road works. Prague's early administration was a step toward nineteenth-century self-government. The municipal statute of Prague, of 1 May 1850, by which Prague was governed in the second half of the nineteenth century, was initially planned as a temporary measure, but it remained in effect with minor revisions until the dissolution of the Monarchy. The statute added a fifth ward to the city, Josefov (Josefstadt), whose boundaries coincided with Judenstadt, the former Jewish ghetto. It was named for Emperor Joseph II, who had reduced limitations on the Jews of the Monarchy with his Edicts of Toleration beginning in 1782. Three more wards were incorporated into Prague before 1914: Vyšehrad (1883), Holešovice-Bubna (1884), and Libeň (1901). The last two were among the industrial suburbs that grew up around Prague during the nineteenth century, expanding first through textile production and then machine industries. The other industrial suburbs were not united with the city until 1920, following the foundation of the First Czechoslovak Republic.

Prague's population grew rapidly during the nineteenth century, rising from 75,000 in 1800 to 118,000 in 1850. According to the last census of the Monarchy in 1910, Prague's population was 218,573, while the population of the metropolitan area had reached 600,000. By the middle of the nineteenth century, Prague was predominantly Czech, with a small, but influential, German minority and an even smaller, but also influential, and primarily German-speaking, Jewish minority. As elsewhere in the Bohemian lands, the Czech residents of Prague considered the Jews to be "German." Many Czechs conflated the Jews with their "national enemies," the Germans. According to the decennial censuses that the Monarchy began conducting in 1880, the declining percentage of Prague residents who employed German as their language of everyday use (*obcovacířeč / Umgangssprache*) was 17.5 percent in 1880, 14.7 percent in 1890, 8.6 percent in 1900, and 8.2 percent in 1910. Jews (identified by religion), constituted 9.27 percent of Prague's population in 1880,

9.19 percent in 1890, 8.62 percent in 1900, and 8.2 percent in 1910.

CONSTRUCTING CZECH PRAGUE

During the Revolutions of 1848 in the Habsburg Monarchy the municipalities received significant autonomy. Suspended in the 1850s during the semi-absolutist era of the minister of the interior Alexander von Bach, autonomy was reinstated in 1861. Like the limited male franchise of the Bohemian Provincial Diet (Český sněm/Böhmischer Landtag), the franchise that elected representatives to Prague's municipal government was based on education and property. Also like the provincial franchise but unlike the imperial franchise, which became increasingly democratic after the turn of the century, the municipal franchise remained restricted until the end of the Monarchy. Predominantly Czech Prague elected its first Czech mayor in 1861. From 8 October 1882, when the newly elected mayor spoke of "golden, Slavic Prague," and the city's five German aldermen first walked out, then demonstratively resigned their seats, Prague had only two German (-Jewish) aldermen, and from 1885, only one. After 1888 until the end of the Monarchy, Prague had no German aldermen at all. Czechs alone governed the mixed-nationality provincial capital.

The center of Czech artistic and intellectual life, Prague was also the center of Czech national life. It was home to the so-called Czech national revival (*národní obrození*) in the late eighteenth and early nineteenth century. Initially a linguistic-cultural movement, affecting mainly the nascent Czech intellectual elite, by the Revolutions of 1848, the national revival had become a political force. During the nineteenth century, many national organizations, among them the voluntary associations that were also a legacy of the Revolutions of 1848, were founded in the Bohemian capital. The most significant was the Sokol (Falcon), the Prague Gymnastics Association that two Czech patriots of German descent, Miroslav Tyrš (Friedrich Emanuel Tirsch) and Jindřich (Heinrich Fügner) established in 1862. With the slogan, "Every Czech a Sokol," this organization rapidly spread throughout the Bohemian lands. In contrast to many of its elite national predecessors, the Sokol, which promoted moral and physical health, was open to all Czechs. Sokol members soon became fixtures at Czech national ceremonies in the capital and elsewhere.

Prague, 1880. ©Alinari Archives/Corbis

During the 1860s and 1870s, Prague was home to the Máj School (after Karel Hynek Mácha's epic poem of the same name), which sought to create a new Czech literature. Exponents shared with the older generation of Czech writers the assumption that literature and nationality could not be separated. The authors Jan Neruda and Karolína Světlá were among its best-known adherents. While during the 1870s the almanac *Ruch* maintained the traditional Czech view of literature in service to the nation, those around the more cosmopolitan journal *Lumír* sought to introduce influences from world literature into Czech.

The development of urban infrastructure in the second half of the nineteenth century, in the form of telegraphs, telephones, expansion of tramlines, public lighting, and the installation of electricity, paralleled the growth of the capital. Between 1896 and 1912, the Prague city hall, in order to demonstrate that the Czech nation was not backward, but part of advanced civilization, undertook its most

ambitious urban renewal project: the thoroughgoing demolition and reconstruction of the city's former Jewish ghetto, located next to the Old Town in the center of the city. The poorest district in the capital, its population was by then majority Christian. Hundreds of buildings in Josefov and adjacent Old Town were demolished to make way for wider, straighter streets and luxury apartments and offices. Only six of nine public synagogues, the Jewish city hall, and part of the Jewish cemetery remained after its completion.

The Czechs of Prague also embarked on an energetic program of national building that provided the city with important new landmarks to complement the panoply of existing Gothic and baroque buildings that marked the city's skyline. Among the most important was the neo-renaissance National Theater (*Národní divadlo*), whose foundation stone was laid in March 1868. The building was funded with donations from Czechs throughout Bohemia. The motto on the proscenium, "The

Nation to Itself" (*Národ k sobě*), reflected the broad Czech national support that made the theater possible. Czech composer Bedřich Smetana's opera, *Libuše,* about the legendary female founder of Prague, was specially written for the theater and premiered at its opening in 1881. The building burned down shortly afterward, a new collection was taken, and the theater reopened in 1883, again with a performance of *Libuše.*

Another important effort of the Czech national revivalists was the foundation of the national cemetery, Vyšehrad, which opened on the grounds of the castle by the same name in 1869. The Prague architect Antonín Wiehl, the preeminent exponent of Czech neo-renaissance style, designed the cemetery's centerpiece, the famous Slavín monument, which was unveiled in 1893. This monument, crowned by a sarcophagus and a figure representing genius, stands above the communal grave of more than fifty famous Czech artists, including the painter-illustrator Alfons Mucha.

In 1893, street signs solely in the Czech language superseded bilingual ones, with the Czech colors white and red replacing the Austrian black-on-yellow on the signs. In the last decades of the Monarchy, other symbols of the Czech nation became part of the built environment. Construction of the art nouveau Municipal House (*Obecní dům*), paid for by the city government, began in 1905 and was completed in 1912. It was decorated with murals and stained glass windows by well-known Czech artists, among them Mucha. The Municipal House, located next to the Powder Tower (*Prašná brána/Pulver Turm*) at one end of *na Příkopech/Am Graben,* the most prestigious commercial street in the capital, constituted a national challenge, because the Germans' community building, the *Deutsches Haus,* better known as the German Casino, was located close to the middle of the six-hundred-foot-long street, which ended at Wenceslas Square (*Václavské náměstí/ Wenzelsplatz,* formerly the horse market). Shortly after the turn of the century, the Czech-language Charles University (founded in 1348 and the oldest university in central Europe north of the Alps, it was divided into independent Czech and German entities in 1882), which also attracted Ruthenian, Slovak, and South Slavic students, was almost twice as large as its German counterpart. The Czech

Charles University, together with the Municipal House and the National Theater, were among the most important built symbols of Czech Prague.

In addition, monuments to Czech national heroes were constructed. The most important was Ladislav Šaloun's art nouveau statue of the reforming Bohemian priest and Czech national hero Jan Hus, who was martyred in 1415. It shared the center of Old Town Square with the baroque Marian Column that the Habsburgs had unveiled in 1650 to commemorate their victory over the Swedes in the Thirty Years' War. The cornerstone of the Hus monument was laid amid much fanfare in 1903, and the completed monument was unveiled in 1915 on the four hundredth anniversary of Hus's death at the stake in Constance. Two more important national monuments in the center of Prague were Stanislav Sucharda's art nouveau monument of František Palacký, the leader of the Czech national revival, and Josef Václav Myslbek's equestrian statue of Saint Wenceslas at the top of the square that bore his name. Both were unveiled in 1912. The Palacký monument was among the largest in Prague. In addition to a huge granite statue of the great nineteenth-century Czech "national awakener" himself, it incorporated an allegory of the spiritual life of the Czech nation. The bronze figures around the base personified various phases of national life, including the physical and spiritual servitude of the Czech people. The equestrian statue stood before the neo-renaissance National Museum building that had been constructed between 1885 and 1890. These important symbols and institutions for nationhood that Czech leaders established in Prague's major public spaces during the second half of the nineteenth century both signaled the formation of the modern Czech nation and distanced the Czechs from the Germans.

The Bohemian capital, Prague, was host to a number of exhibitions and congresses at the turn of the century. The most important was the long-planned Provincial Jubilee Exhibition. Commemorating the centenary of the first industrial exhibition held in Bohemia (in honor of the coronation of the Habsburg emperor Leopold II [r. 1790–1792]), indeed in continental Europe, it opened in May 1891. Although it was originally conceived as a joint Czech-German project, the Germans had withdrawn the previous summer to protest Young

A street vendor sells marionettes, Prague, c. 1900. ©Scheufler Collection/Corbis

Czech opposition to the Bohemian Compromise in the imperial Parliament. Thus, the wildly successful exhibition became a display of Czech economic progress and the site of Slavic manifestations that highlighted Czech national cultural, economic, and political claims and achievements.

At the beginning of the twentieth century, predominantly Czech-speaking but cosmopolitan Prague was home to a circle of German-Jewish writers, the most famous of whom was Franz Kafka. Other important German-Jewish writers of that generation included Max Brod, Willy Haas, Egon Erwin Kisch, and Franz Werfel. They were part of a larger world of writers in German-speaking central Europe, and Brod espe-

cially played an important mediating role in helping make Czech literature better known in western Europe through translation into German.

NATIONALITY CONFLICT IN PRAGUE

The establishment of a republic in France in March 1848 had repercussions throughout the Habsburg Monarchy. Before 1848 Prague may have appeared to be a German city, but the revolutions that year demonstrated otherwise. Although Czech and German liberals made joint demands in March and April 1848, the language of the Slavic Congress, and the first open expression of Bohemian state rights (*české státní právo/Staatsrecht*) demonstrated the incompatibility of their aims.

The question of German unification was the largest issue dividing the Czechs and Germans during the revolutionary year, a division underscored by Palacký's refusal to participate in the planned Frankfurt Parliament to discuss that very subject. The Prague Slav Congress, to which all Slavic peoples of Austria were invited, was to be a symbolic counterpart to the Frankfurt Parliament. It opened on 31 May, the day the Frankfurt Parliament was meant to convene. Its 341 delegates from the Habsburg Monarchy sought to promote political cooperation among the Slavs, an idea that became known as Austro-Slavism. The revolution in Prague had national, political, and social aspects, as demonstrated by the worker unrest of April and May, which sometimes took an anti-Semitic character, as had earlier Czech worker protests in 1844. The return of Czech students from revolutionary Vienna in late May, together with increased military activity in Prague, increased tension until a student-led rebellion erupted on 12 June. The rebellion lasted five days, ending only when the rebels capitulated to the Austrian field marshal Prince Alfred Windischgrätz. This uprising was essentially a social one and separate from the Slavic Congress, although the Congress in Prague was precipitously closed in June when Windischgrätz declared martial law, which lasted until 1853.

Martial law would be declared in Prague four times after the revolutions of 1848: in 1868, 1893, 1897, and 1908. Residents of Prague supported the Monarchy during the Austro-Prussian War in 1866, sending declarations of support as well as the coronation jewels to Vienna. The war was a disaster for Austria, and shortly after its victory in the Battle of Königgrätz/Sadowa in northeastern Bohemia, the Prussian army occupied Prague, easily breaching the city's baroque fortifications. One result of Austria's defeat was the decision to reach a compromise (Ausgleich) with Hungary in February 1867, restoring the Magyars' historic rights. The failure of the Czechs to reach a similar agreement, despite their loyalty to Vienna in 1859 and 1866, resulted in both Czech political parties, the Young and the Old Czechs, boycotting the diet and the imperial parliament and led to demonstrations in Prague during 1867 and 1868. There were protests on 28 August 1867, when the Bohemian coronation jewels were returned from Vienna; in January 1868, when imperial ministers visited the city; on 14 June, the seventieth birthday of the historian-politician Palacký; and on 21 June, when Emperor Francis Joseph (r. 1848–1916) visited. The largest demonstration occurred on 14 May 1868, when the foundation stone was laid for the Czech National Theater. Paralleling the demonstrations in Prague were encampments (*tábory*, recalling the Czechs' Hussite legacy) at Czech historical sites throughout the Bohemian lands, in which thousands of Czechs participated. The imperial government declared martial law in Prague on 11 October 1868. It lasted for six months, during which time hundreds of Czechs were arrested, some patriotic associations were banned, and members of the Czech press—still headquartered mainly in Prague—were hounded.

Class-based demonstrations and protests in Prague, especially May Day celebrations, increased in size and intensity in concert with the growth of the organized working class. Although in November 1905 demonstrations for universal suffrage reached revolutionary proportions in Prague as well as in Vienna, bringing almost one hundred thousand workers into the streets of the Bohemian capital, there was no declaration of martial law. It was national conflict, sometimes containing a class component, that resulted in the declaration of martial law twice in the 1890s and once again in 1908. Beginning in 1891 there were street demonstrations in the capital in favor of universal suffrage. By 1893 they had taken on an antidynastic character, and the imperial government declared martial law. In its wake came the mass trial of the so-called *Omladina* (youth), in which Czechs were convicted of an alleged secret conspiracy against the state. The trial became a Czech national cause célèbre.

The 1897 and 1908 demonstrations, which included Czech attacks on both Germans and "Jew-Germans," reflecting persistent anti-Semitism in Prague, occurred within the context of Bohemia-wide, indeed, Cisleithania-wide national tensions. In April 1897 the imperial prime minister, the Polish count Kazimierz Badeni, proposed language ordinances calling for the equality of Czech and German in official usage among civil servants of Bohemia and Moravia, who would be required to demonstrate proficiency in both languages by June 1901. The proposal was met with eight months of protest throughout the Bohemian lands. Badeni's resulting resignation on 28 November precipitated violent clashes in Prague and its suburbs, after brawling erupted between Czech and German university students. Members of the Czech majority attacked German and Jewish property for four days, damaging German communal buildings and looting businesses and homes identified as German or Jewish in the city and its suburbs. A decade later, ongoing Czech-German tension throughout the Bohemian lands coalesced around the Diamond Jubilee celebration of the Habsburg emperor Francis Joseph's rule on 2 December 1908. They resulted in one more round of anti-German, anti-Semitic violence and the last declaration of martial law in Prague before 1914.

Following the outbreak of World War I, restrictions on the civilian population in Prague—political newspapers, many of which had their offices in the capital were censored or suspended; food and other commodities were rationed, and, increasingly unavailable—met little overt opposition prior to the abortive strike of Czech workers in Prague on 14 October 1918. When news that the Austrians had sued for an armistice on 27 October reached Prague the next day, hundreds of thousands of Czechs filled Wenceslas Square, and Czechoslovak independence was declared in Prague on 28 October 1918. Democratic interwar Czechoslovakia would provide ground as fertile for Czech-German national tension in Prague as had the Habsburg Monarchy, both because it was in fact a multinational state governed as a nation-state and because its legal system permitted a differently contoured, even an expanded, space for national opposition.

See also **Austria-Hungary; Austro-Prussian War; Bohemia, Moravia, and Silesia; Cities and Towns; Kafka, Franz; Nationalism; Palacký, František; Prague Slav Congress; Young Czechs and Old Czechs.**

BIBLIOGRAPHY

Demetz, Peter. *Prague in Black and Gold: Scenes from the Life of a European City.* New York, 1997. A thousand years of Prague cultural history.

Giustino, Cathleen M. *Tearing Down Prague's Jewish Town: Ghetto Clearance and the Legacy of Middle-Class Ethnic Politics around 1900.* Boulder, Colo., 2003. A pioneering study of middle-class politics in the Bohemian capital at the fin-de-siècle.

Hojda, Zdeněk, and Jiří Pokorný. *Pomníky a zapomníky.* 2nd ed. Prague, 1996. A fascinating, well-illustrated series of essays on the politics of national sculpture in Prague and elsewhere in Bohemia.

Ripellino, Angelo Maria. *Magic Prague.* Berkeley, Calif., 1994. The volume employs a blend of fact and fiction to examine the commingling of three peoples—Czech, German, and Jewish—who produced a city that continues to fascinate.

Vlcek, Toma. *Praha 1900.* Prague, 1986. This art and architectural history contains spectacular illustrations of the city.

NANCY M. WINGFIELD

PRAGUE SLAV CONGRESS. In early June 1848 an assembly of liberal intellectuals drawn from the various Slavic nationalities in central and east central Europe met in Prague to discuss civil rights and liberal constitutional reform for the Habsburg Monarchy. Nearly four hundred attended, and they were organized into three regional sections: (1) Czechs and Slovaks, (2) Poles and Ukrainians, and (3) South Slavs. The Russians who participated sat with the Polish-Ukrainian section.

In early spring 1848, Slavic intellectuals in central Europe grew concerned about German liberal efforts to create a large united Germany and the steps of Magyar liberal nationalists to establish Magyar-led self-government for Hungary. Speaking for Czech nationalists, the historian František Palacký rejected German liberals' invitation to participate in the Frankfurt parliament, and instead called for a reform of the Habsburg Monarchy to win civil rights and representative government for its Slavic peoples. Other liberal Slavic intellectuals in the monarchy took up this "Austro-Slav" policy. Writing in Ljudevit Gaj's Croatian newspaper, *Novine Dalmatinsko-Hervatsko-Slavonske* (The Dalmatian-Croatian-Slavonian news), Ivan Kukuljević-Sakcinski issued a call on 20 April for broader political cooperation among the Slavs and a meeting of their representatives to chart liberal reforms and counter the expansive nationalist initiatives of German and Magyar liberals. He proposed that such a conclave take place in Prague and include representatives from the Habsburg, Ottoman, and tsarist empires. At the same time Czech and Slovak liberals began discussions of a similar idea. By

FROM "THE MANIFESTO TO THE NATIONS OF EUROPE"

[The Slav] demands neither conquest nor dominion, but he asks for liberty for himself and all others: he demands that liberty shall be unconditionally recognized as the most sacred right that man possesses. Therefore we Slavs reject and hold in abhorrence all dominion based on main force and evasion of the law; we reject all privileges and prerogatives as well as all political differentiation of classes; we demand unconditional equality before the law, an equal measure of rights and duties for all . . . .

. . . [T]he German threatens many a Slavonic people with violence if it will not agree to assist in the upbuilding of the political greatness of Germany, and thus the Magyar is not ashamed to arrogate to himself exclusive national rights in Hungary. We Slavs utterly decry all such pretensions, and we reject them the more emphatically the more they are wrongfully disguised in the garb of freedom.

Source: English translation by William Beardmore, in *Slavonic and East European Review* 26, no. 67 (1948): 309–313.

30 April a preparatory committee for a Slavic congress had formed in Prague, and it approved an announcement for such a congress to convene on 30 May.

From the outset Palacký exercised a strong influence on the preparatory committee, and he emerged as the leading figure of the congress. The preparatory committee committed itself to advance Slavic interests through reform of the Habsburg Monarchy and to defend its territorial integrity from potential German or Russian ambitions. The organizers directed the call to participate primarily to representatives of the Slavic nationalities within the monarchy, but spokesmen of other Slavic groups outside the Habsburg realm were welcome to attend as guests. The committee's commitment to preserving the Habsburg Monarchy required that limits be placed on discussions of Polish nationalist aspirations. The organizers tried to reassure Habsburg authorities of their loyalty

and their desire to preserve the monarchy, but the ministers in Austria's new liberal cabinet, German liberals in Austria and Germany, and Habsburg military authorities were suspicious or openly hostile to what they feared was a Pan-Slav conspiracy to change the map of central Europe.

A total of 340 delegates came to Prague for the congress by the end of May: 61 in the Polish-Ukrainian section, 42 in the South Slav section, and 237 in the Czech-Slovak section. Forty-five additional guests and observers participated as well (Orton, 1978, p. 63). The participants met for discussions in plenary sessions and in loose roundtable sessions divided into the three regional sections. The congress convened on 2 June, and Palacký, as president, gave the opening speech, calling for the pursuit of equality and justice for the Slavic peoples and expressing respect for the Habsburg emperor. The formal proceedings were conducted in the various Slavic languages of the participants, although German journalists quickly spread the claim that German had to be used because of the multiplicity of languages represented.

The congress was cut short by the heavy street fighting that broke out in Prague between Habsburg imperial troops and Czech students and workers on Monday, 12 June. By that point, only one major document had been approved, "The Manifesto to the Nations of Europe." Some of the more radical congress participants, such as the Pole Karol Libelt and the Russian Mikhail Bakunin, advocated far-reaching democratic changes in central and east central Europe under a broad Slavic alliance; but the congress followed the moderate liberal course charted by the Czech leaders. The manifesto called for the recognition of individual liberty, freedom of speech and political action, and the development of nations and national interests as fundamental rights. It rejected authoritarian government and German and Magyar national domination of the Slavic nationalities; the Habsburg imperial state must be transformed fundamentally as a confederation of equal nations based on liberty and enlightened policies. The manifesto also condemned the partition of Poland and called for a general European congress of nations to take up all outstanding international questions. On 13 June 1848, the Habsburg military authorities began expelling congress delegates from Prague, and no new Slav congress was attempted again until the 1867 meeting in Moscow.

See also **Austria-Hungary; Bakunin, Mikhail; Bohemia, Moravia, and Silesia; Jelačić, Josip; Nationalism; Palacký, František.**

BIBLIOGRAPHY

Haselsteiner, Horst, ed. *The Prague Slav Congress 1848: Slavic Identities.* Boulder, Colo., and New York, 2000. Essays on important ideological and political aspects of the congress.

Klíma, Arnošt. "The Revolution of 1848 in Bohemia." In *The Opening of an Era: 1848,* edited by François Fejtö, 281–297. London, 1948. Reprint, New York, 1973. Classic short account of the 1848 revolution in Prague and Bohemia.

Kohn, Hans. *Pan-Slavism: Its History and Ideology.* 2nd ed., rev. New York, 1960. Classic study of the ideology and politics of Pan-Slav movement.

Kořalka, Jiří. *Frantisek Palacký (1798–1876).* Prague, 1998. Comprehensive biography by a leading Czech historian.

Orton, Lawrence D. "Did the Slavs Speak German at Their First Congress?" *Slavic Review* 33, no. 3 (1974): 515–521. Examines and refutes the old myth about the use of German at the congress.

———. *The Prague Slav Congress of 1848.* Boulder, Colo., and New York, 1978. Sound overview of the convening and proceedings of the congress.

———. "Palacký at the Slav Congress of 1848." *East European Quarterly* 15, no. 1 (spring 1981): 15–28. Thoughtful treatment of the role of Palacký in the congress.

Pech, Stanley Z. *The Czech Revolution of 1848.* Chapel Hill, N.C., 1969. Best full English-language account of Czech political activity in 1848.

Plaschka, Richard Georg. "Zur Einberufung des Slawenkongresses 1848." *Archiv für Österreichische Geschichte* 125 (1966): 196–207. Analyzes the preparations and convening of the congress.

Polišenský, Josef. *Aristocrats and the Crowd in the Revolutionary Year 1848: A Contribution to the History of Revolution and Counter-Revolution in Austria.* Albany, N.Y., 1980. Offers fresh insights into the actions of the proponents and opponents of the 1848 revolution in the Bohemian lands and Austria.

Urban, Otto. *Česká společnost, 1848–1918.* Prague, 1982; translated into German by Henning Schlegel as *Die tschechische Gesellschaft 1848 bis 1918.* Vienna, 1994. Excellent general treatment of Czech politics and society in the second half of the nineteenth century.

GARY B. COHEN

PRE-RAPHAELITE MOVEMENT.

The Pre-Raphaelite Brotherhood (PRB), founded in September 1848, is the most significant British artistic grouping of the nineteenth century. Its fundamental mission was to purify the art of its time by returning to the example of medieval and early Renaissance painting. Although the life of the brotherhood was short, the broad international movement it inspired, Pre-Raphaelitism, persisted into the twentieth century and profoundly influenced the aesthetic movement, symbolism, and the Arts and Crafts movement.

THE PRE-RAPHAELITE BROTHERHOOD

The PRB was founded by seven young men, three of whom became artists of major importance: William Holman Hunt, Dante Gabriel Rossetti, and John Everett Millais. All had studied at the Royal Academy Schools, where Millais's precocious talents had been recognized. The other founding members were the aspirant painters Charles Collinson and Frederic George Stephens, the sculptor Thomas Woolner, and the younger Rossetti brother, William Michael. A slightly older figure, Ford Madox Brown, was never a member of the group but shared many of its ideals.

The early days of the brotherhood were marked more by youthful exuberance than by a coherent program, but an admiration for art from the period before the High Renaissance (pre-Raphael) gave the group its name. The increased visibility of work from the fifteenth century in London collections, and notably the arrival of Jan van Eyck's *Arnolfini Marriage Portrait* (1434) at the National Gallery in 1842, prompted the young artists to turn against the old-master tradition propagated by the Royal Academy. Although there was never a single Pre-Raphaelite style, the earliest works to be exhibited with "P. R. B." appended to the artist's signature all bore the hallmarks of bright and brilliant color, sharp-edged draftsmanship, and an absence of the dark hues and carefully planned chiaroscuro of the typical academy product.

First to appear was Dante Gabriel Rossetti's *Girlhood of Mary Virgin* (1849), in which passages of striking naturalism were situated within a complex symbolic composition. Already a published poet, Rossetti inscribed verse on the frame of his painting. In the following year, Millais's *Christ in the House of His Parents* (1850) was exhibited at the Royal Academy to an outraged critical reception. The master of a brilliantly naturalistic technique, Millais represented biblical figures with closely observed portrayals of the features of real, imperfect models. In 1850 the Pre-Raphaelites also produced a literary and artistic magazine, the *Germ,* which was something of a manifesto for their artistic concerns and ran for only four issues.

From the first, the Pre-Raphaelites aspired to paint subjects from modern life. In *The Awakening Conscience* (1854), Hunt represented a kept woman realizing the error of her ways, and in 1852 Madox Brown began the most ambitious of all Pre-Raphaelite scenes from modern life, *Work* (1852–1865). Although the brotherhood included no women, Christina Rossetti, sister of Dante and William, pioneered a Pre-Raphaelite style in poetry, and Elizabeth Siddall—model, muse, and eventually wife of Dante Gabriel Rossetti—produced distinctive watercolors and drawings that went unrecognized in her lifetime but received critical attention after the advent of feminist art history in the late 1970s.

RUSKIN AND THE PRE-RAPHAELITES

The fortunes of the movement turned in 1851, when the most powerful critic of the era, John Ruskin, wrote to the *Times* (London) in defense of the young painters. Ruskin perceived in the Pre-Raphaelite work an echo of his publication of 1843, *Modern Painters* volume I, a manifesto favoring naturalistic landscape painting. He emphasized the realist rather than the revivalist elements in Pre-Raphaelitism, writing: "They intend to return to the early days in this one point only—that ... they will draw either what they see, or what they suppose might have been the actual facts of the scene they desire to represent, irrespective of any conventional rules of picture-making."

Under Ruskin's influence, outdoor painting from nature became a more central feature of Pre-Raphaelite work. Literary subjects, such as Millais's *Ophelia* (1852) and Hunt's *Valentine Rescuing Sylvia from Proteus* (1851), were painted in the open air with meticulous attention to natural detail. Ruskin commissioned a portrait of himself from Millais, painted in a landscape at Glenfinlas. Other early patrons of the movement included Thomas Combe, the superintendant of the Oxford University Press; Thomas Plint, a Leeds stockbroker; and Thomas Fairbairn, a major Manchester industrialist.

Under Ruskin's influence, a group of younger painters took up the challenge of Pre-Raphaelite landscape painting. John Brett and John William Inchbold were Ruskin's particular protégés, and their work (such as Brett's *Val d'Aosta,* 1858) achieved a seemingly miraculous level of detail in the representation of geology, flora, and meteorological conditions. This naturalistic trend in Pre-Raphaelitism was influential in the United States, where the journals the *Crayon* (1855–1861), edited by W. J. Stillman, and the *New Path* (1863–1865) publicized Ruskin's ideas. An exhibition of English Pre-Raphaelite paintings toured Boston and New York in 1857. The American followers of Pre-Raphaelitism included Thomas Farrer, William Trost Richards, and J. W. Hill.

PRE-RAPHAELITISM

The Brotherhood soon began to disperse. Collinson resigned in 1850, Woolner emigrated to Australia in 1852 (an event memorialized in Madox Brown's modern life painting *The Last of England,* 1852–1855), and it had effectively ceased to exist by the time of Holman Hunt's departure in search of religious subject matter in Palestine in 1854. The works produced from this trip—*The Scapegoat* (1855) and especially *The Finding of the Saviour in the Temple* (1860)—established Hunt as "the painter of the Christ." Millais moved to Scotland in 1856 and there created a series of poetic, lyrical works, including *Autumn Leaves* (1856), before turning to portraiture and more conventional forms of historical painting. Becoming a member of the Royal Academy in 1855, Millais soon joined the artistic establishment and ended his life as president of the academy; from PRB, as one wag put it, to PRA.

Rossetti abandoned oil painting for much of the 1850s and developed a more intimate visual vocabulary, creating small watercolors on medieval themes. It was this vein of Pre-Raphaelitism that inspired a second generation of artists and poets. Edward Burne-Jones and William Morris, under-

Portrait sketch by Gabriel Dante Rossetti, 1861.
©Stapleton Collection/Corbis

graduates at Oxford, met Rossetti in 1856 and joined him in an attempt to decorate the Oxford Union building with frescoes on Arthurian themes. The project foundered because the team of young painters had no knowledge of fresco technique. Among them were Arthur Hughes, John Rodham Spencer Stanhope, Simeon Solomon, and George Price Boyce, artists who constituted a second generation of Pre-Raphaelites. Of these, Solomon had the most distinctive voice. His exploration of Jewish and homoerotic themes marked a striking modification of Rossetti's idiom, but after his conviction for "gross indecency" in 1873 he was ostracized from Pre-Raphaelite circles.

Burne-Jones was to become the most important figure in later Pre-Raphaelitism. His early work espoused a Romantic medievalism, but in his maturity he created oil paintings on classical and literary subjects notable for their aesthetic refinement and distinctive poetic atmosphere. After the opening of the Grosvenor Gallery in 1877, Burne-Jones's work became known to a wider public and was central to the amorphous grouping known as the aesthetic movement. By this time, the realist commitment of the early Pre-Raphaelite Brotherhood had been completely abandoned. Burne-Jones

was an acknowledged influence on the European symbolist movement, from Pierre Puvis de Chavannes to Gustave Moreau and even Pablo Picasso.

Burne-Jones was also distinguished as a designer, especially of stained glass and book illustrations. He and his friend and lifelong collaborator William Morris were inspired by Ruskin's chapter "The Nature of Gothic" and attempted to revive both the aesthetics and working practices of medieval decorative art. Morris in particular excelled in the design of wallpapers, textiles, and hand-printed books. Their manufacturing company, Morris, Marshall, Faulkner, and Co., was founded in 1861 and found a small market for such products. Morris became a committed socialist in 1878 and became a primary influence on the founding of the Arts and Crafts movement, which emphasized the use of unadorned natural materials and hand crafting in the decorative arts and architecture.

CRITICAL FORTUNES

Vilified and then celebrated in its own time, Pre-Raphaelite painting fell from favor in the first decades of the twentieth century, and the triumph of French modernism in Roger Fry's post-impressionist exhibitions of 1910 and 1912 marked the beginning of a period of critical disapprobation, which lasted until the 1960s. The major figures left autobiographies or memoirs (notably Holman Hunt's *Pre-Raphaelitism and the Pre-Raphaelite Brotherhood*), and F. G. Stephens and W. M. Rossetti produced voluminous memoirs and collections of documents. It was not until the 1960s, however, that art historians paid serious attention to the movement—attention that culminated in the Tate Gallery's magisterial 1984 exhibition *The Pre-Raphaelites*. Revisionist scholarship in the 1980s began to re-examine the movement in terms of its sociohistorical importance, and feminist scholars examined the role of women Pre-Raphaelites. Since 1990 scholars have re-examined almost every major figure in the Pre-Raphaelite circle, and the popular standing of the Pre-Raphaelites has, perhaps, never been higher. Pre-Raphaelitism has come to be recognized as the highest achievement of Victorian art and a major contribution to European culture.

See also **Morris, William; Ruskin, John; Symbolism.**

BIBLIOGRAPHY

Primary Sources

Bryden, Inga, ed. *The Pre-Raphaelites: Writings and Sources.* 4 vols. London, 1998.

Hunt, William Holman, *Pre-Raphaelitism and the Pre-Raphaelite Brotherhood.* 2nd rev. ed. London, 1913.

Secondary Sources

Barringer, Tim. *Reading the Pre-Raphaelites.* New Haven, Conn., 1999.

Marsh, Jan, and Pamela Gerrish Nunn. *Pre-Raphaelite Women Artists.* New York, 1997.

Parris, Leslie, ed. *The Pre-Raphaelites.* London, 1984.

Prettejohn, Elizabeth. *Art of the Pre-Raphaelites.* Princeton, N.J., 2000.

TIM BARRINGER

PRESS AND NEWSPAPERS.

Newspapers, although vital to Europe's commercial and political culture well before 1789, underwent profound changes in the long nineteenth century. Technological, political, social, and communications revolutions transformed their audiences, appearance, content, journalistic style, and political significance. Once a preserve of elites, they were by 1914 a ubiquitous feature of working-class life, and played an important—if intangible—role in shaping the political destiny of Europe. A shift in the economics of newspaper production was central to these transformations, as newspapers—that is, regular, uniformly titled, dated, printed publications containing miscellaneous recent informational reports—evolved from small-scale enterprises into massive capital-intensive industries.

THE INDUSTRIALIZATION OF NEWSPAPERS

From 1500 to 1814, printing technology changed little. Press output depended on physical strength, employed in pulling a lever to press paper onto a page of set type. The process was labor-intensive, time consuming, and offered little opportunity for economies of scale. To increase production above 250 pages per hour required a new press, a new compositor to set the type, and new print-men. Thus when the London *Times* used the König steam press for the first time on 29 November 1814, it began a printing revolution. Friedrich König's machine could print 1,100 impressions per hour, but by 1830 improved machines could produce up to 4,000.

Early steam presses made impressions onto a flat bed and had significant limitations. They were costly to maintain and power, and quality of output was uneven. These problems were overcome by Richard Hoe's rotary press, first employed by the Parisian newspaper *La Patrie* in 1846. Shortly thereafter, the stereotype process, introduced by *La Presse* in 1852 and *The Times* in 1858, allowed multiple copies of the same page to be cast. This made it possible to imagine a single newspaper serving audiences of hundreds of thousands or even millions.

The realization of this dream depended on further developments. Web sheet feeders, pioneered in the United States, were introduced to Europe by *The Times* in 1868; cheap paper made from woodpulp rather than rags followed in the 1880s. The cost and speed of compositing were revolutionized in the 1860s by keyboard-based Hattersley machines, and again from the 1880s by "Linotype" machines—which cast new type at each use. However, the take-up of new printing technologies was slow, since local markets were often insufficient to justify purchasing them. In Sweden and other underpopulated countries, national dailies were produced on hand-presses several decades after 1814. From the 1830s and 1840s, investment in steam presses became more attractive. Newly built railways allowed metropolitan dailies to reach national audiences, and from the 1840s telegraph networks revolutionized the speed of news-gathering. Thereafter national newspapers could compete with regional rivals for stories from the provinces.

THE APPEARANCE OF NEWSPAPERS

The appearance of newspapers changed dramatically across the century. Eighteenth-century newspapers were not visually appealing. A page of newsprint usually comprised two or more columns of tightly cramped text, without headlines or illustrations, except, very occasionally, woodblock prints supplied by advertisers. Most newspapers were only four or eight pages long, and although many British papers appeared in folio-size editions, Continental papers often adopted smaller quarto or octavo formats. Before 1789, most serious Continental newspapers appeared in the traditional "gazette" format, reproducing stories verbatim from other sources under their dateline and place of origin, without editorial comment or gloss. This was true even of the *Gazette de Leyde,* Europe's most celebrated paper of the 1770s and 1780s, or the *Hamburgische Unpartheyische Correspondent* (Hamburg impartial correspondent), the continent's best-selling daily in the decade after 1800.

By 1900, newspapers were much more eye-catching, not least due to innovations pioneered by John Walter (1739–1812), founder of *The Times.* Realizing that newspaper readers wished to inform themselves quickly without wading through entire blocks of text, he introduced headlines so they could pick out stories that interested them. This innovation spread rapidly, and soon became universal. Walter also experimented with print sizes and fonts to develop a clearer typeface, "Times Roman," to enable readers to scan pages more rapidly.

Illustrations also began to appear. In the 1830s, the *Penny Magazine* pioneered the commercial use of Thomas Bewick's wood engraving process, and with the foundation of the weekly *London Illustrated News* in 1842, the technology spread to newspapers. Illustrated newspapers proliferated rapidly across Europe: Germany's *Leipziger Illustrierte Zeitung* and France's *L'Illustration* were founded as early as 1843. However, in the 1880s, the development of the halftone process for reproducing photographs sounded the death-knell for these papers. Cheaper and better adapted than woodblock prints to the demands of daily publication, halftone technology could illustrate stories in the quotidian press. By 1900, news photographs were a vital aspect of news reporting. As editors realized the emotional power of printed images, photographs increasingly determined both an item's newsworthiness and public reactions to stories.

Not all technical developments improved the look of newspapers. In particular, the introduction of wood pulp made for a poorer appearance and reduced durability. However, the low cost of wood pulp paper allowed for larger newspapers at a lesser price, and thereby pleased advertisers and readers alike.

ADVERTISING AND TAXES ON KNOWLEDGE

Two further developments made late-nineteenth-century newspapers more affordable. The first was the demise of "taxes on knowledge" and other provisions designed to prevent the lower orders from acquiring newspapers. In early-nineteenth-century Britain, where stamp duty and paper taxes were most burdensome, they inflated newspaper prices three or fourfold. At their height, *The Times* cost 7 pence per edition, perhaps a sixth of a London artisan's daily wage, and half that of a worker in the provinces. In addition, stamp duty on advertisements increased advertising costs by about 50 percent. High prices promoted the development of a vigorous, illegal, unstamped radical working-class press, and a vociferous campaign for the stamp duty's abolition, until it was substantially reduced in 1837, and finally scrapped in 1855. The paper tax survived until 1860.

An alternative method of pricing papers beyond working-class pockets—favored in France and Russia—was to insist that subscribers pay in advance. This was kinder on the pockets of the wealthy, while still preventing those without surplus cash from buying newspapers. Such measures were never fully effective, as entrepreneurial booksellers hired out newspapers by the hour, often illegally, and newspapers were available in coffee-houses, libraries, public reading rooms, and by joint subscriptions. Thus, by 1850, most governments had bowed to the inevitable and tolerated "boulevard sales" of individual copies of popular newspapers.

Newspaper prices also fell because growing commercialization, mass production, and expanding popular markets boosted advertising revenues. Eighteenth-century newspaper advertising targeted a small, wealthy elite, but late-nineteenth-century papers marketed cheap, branded goods to the lower bourgeoisie and wealthier urban workers, who increasingly depended on a market economy—rather than household manufacture—for products like soap, candles, clothes, and foodstuffs. As prices of manufactured goods fell, newspaper advertising helped to create a democratized commercial culture based on aspiration and emulation. Even in the underdeveloped economy of Russia, the major St. Petersburg and Moscow dailies dedicated around 30 percent of available space to advertising by 1900. By the mid-1840s, newspaper advertising was extensive enough to support specialized advertising agents in Britain, France, and the United States. Originally they sold column space, but from the 1870s American agencies began writing copy and planning advertising campaigns, and these practices quickly spread. By 1878 even Russia had an advertising agency, L. and M. Mettsl and Company. The scale of advertising varied between countries. Britain and France respectively boasted Europe's most and least commercialized presses. The Parisian daily *Petit Journal*, Europe's best-selling paper between the 1860s and 1900, derived only about 20 percent of its revenues from advertising. Hence French newspapers were dependent on other forms of finance.

CIRCULATION: THE COMING OF MASS READERSHIPS

Mass reading literacy was a further precondition for a mass-circulation press. While this was largely a nineteenth-century development, eighteenth-century literacy rates should not be underestimated. In much of England, Scotland, north-eastern France, the Netherlands, Germany, and Scandinavia, the majority of bridegrooms could sign a marriage register by 1800. In urban areas male signature-literacy rates often exceeded 80 percent. In contrast, signature-literacy was rare in Ireland, the Mediterranean basin, the Iberian peninsula, and central and eastern Europe. Moreover, the 1780s witnessed attempts to establish universal primary education in Baden, the Habsburg lands, and revolutionary France. The success of these projects was limited. Although in France, as in Britain, educational provision rose sharply from the 1830s, universal primary education was only secured in France by Jules Ferry's legislation in the 1880s, and in Britain by the Education Act of 1870. By the late nineteenth century even Russia had achieved widespread literacy, primarily by educating military conscripts. Thus significant increases in both basic literacy rates and the quality of literacy skills stimulated growth in nineteenth-century newspaper readerships.

The potential size of popular audiences was demonstrated by the *Penny Magazine*, launched in 1832 by the liberal philanthropic Society for the Diffusion of Useful Knowledge to educate the working classes and wean them from radical publications. Produced weekly, it soon achieved sales of over 213,000. A German imitator and namesake, the *Pfennigmagazin*, launched in 1833, reached over 100,000 subscribers. Within decades, popularly oriented, cheaply priced newspapers were achieving similar success: by the 1860s, the *Petit Journal*, with sales of 250,000, was the most successful paper yet seen. By 1900 it had become Europe's first million-seller, narrowly outselling London's *Daily Mail*. A decade later, London's quotidian press was printing over 4,500,000 copies daily. Elsewhere in Europe, sales figures for best-sellers were lower, but still impressive. In 1900, Italy's daily *La Tribuna* sold around 200,000, while Russia's *Novoe Vremya* sold about 60,000. Russian newspaper audiences expanded exponentially after the 1905 revolution, and in 1917, stimulated by war and further revolution, the Moscow-based *Russkoe Slovo* achieved sales of 1,000,000.

The extent of sales growth becomes apparent when these figures are compared with eighteenth-century circulations. Before 1800, individual editions seldom sold over 5,000 copies. At its most popular, during the American Revolution, the *Gazette de Leyde*'s sales peaked at 4,200 subscribers, while in the early 1800s, the *Hamburgische Unpartheyische Correspondent*'s print-run of 40,000 was unprecedented. Local weeklies with single editor-proprietors survived on circulations of two to three hundred well into the nineteenth century.

The rise in readership of individual titles cannot be attributed to press consolidation, since the number of periodicals of all sorts proliferated across the century, while total readerships grew massively. For example, in France in the early 1780s newspaper subscriptions totaled just 45,000, of which 15,000 were for foreign-produced international gazettes. During the Revolution the market for political news exploded: between 1789 and 1792 Parisian papers sold perhaps 300,000 copies daily. Contemporary sources and historians alike estimate that there were between four and ten readers per copy, although many readers read more than one paper. Assuming five readers per copy, the total audience for French newspapers expanded from perhaps 225,000 before the revolution to 1,500,000 thereafter, or from under 1 percent to just over 5 percent of the population. The revival of censorship, state-orchestrated market consolidation, and suppression of participatory political culture under Napoleon caused audiences to decline by 75 percent. Thus, by 1810 newspaper readership was only marginally higher than under the Old Regime. In contrast, in 1900 newspapers reached the majority of French households.

The growth of French newspaper audiences was probably near the middle of the European range. In regions with large, well-educated urban populations, especially northern Germany, the Netherlands, England, and Scotland, the social penetration of newspapers was already considerable by 1800. Stamp duty records for 1801 show that London newspapers (daily and otherwise) sold about 20,000 copies per day and provincial papers, which were mostly weeklies, a further 180,000 per week, suggesting total subscriptions numbered marginally over 200,000 and readership about 1,000,000, or 10 percent of the population. At the other end of the spectrum lay Russia, where newspaper readership was initially much lower and still largely restricted to urban areas prior to 1905.

CENSORSHIP AND PRESS FREEDOM

Early-nineteenth-century rulers were fearful of newsprint and attempted both to limit newspaper circulation and censor content. The case for tight government supervision appeared to be confirmed by the French Revolution of 1789, when budding politicians including Mirabeau; Jacques-Pierre Brissot de Warville; Camille Desmoulins; Jean-Paul Marat; and Maximilien Robespierre built power bases through journalism. Through their newspapers and new essay-style political journalism, these self-styled "tribunes of the people" did more than shape opinion. They also defined the significance of events. Thus the fall of the Bastille was transformed from an attack on a royal powder depot into the symbolic triumph of liberty over despotism. Jeremy Popkin has argued that the revolutionary press actually scripted the revolution, by promoting the nexus of tensions, suspicions, and recriminations that shaped popular actions, and calling for direct action against "enemies of the people." The prominence of journalists among the European revolutionaries of 1830 and 1848 only reinforced elite fears of the press. It is hardly surprising that Russia, Spain, postrevolutionary France, and many Italian and German states employed censorship systems deep into the nineteenth century, with mixed success.

Late-eighteenth-century Germany, for example, comprised a patchwork of states with varying censorship laws. Some were liberal in practice, if not theory, while others, such as Frederick II's Prussia, had rigorous laws but chaotic enforcement. This left loopholes for enterprising publishers and editors to exploit. However, under the Napoleonic occupation practices were standardized and legal or de facto press freedoms extinguished. After 1807 the only significant paper with any degree of autonomy was Johann Friedrich Cotta's *Allegemeine Zeitung*, but even it had to source political news from Napoleon's official *Moniteur*. Meanwhile, the *Hamburgische Unpartheyische Correspondent* declined rapidly after Napoleon commanded it to publish bilingually, thus halving its news coverage. Following the Vienna Settlement, hopes of a more liberal regime were scotched for several decades by the draconian Carlsbad Decrees of 1819, which exacerbated the damage done by Napoleon to the German press.

In Russia, the autocratic government maintained press controls until 1905. The press statute of 1865 offered a whiff of liberty, but this was neutralized by the simultaneous introduction of an arbitrarily administered system of censorship, warnings, and bans. A variety of sanctions existed for papers that displeased the authorities, including the prohibition of street sales. After three warnings a paper would be closed down. Despite these restrictions the Russian press blossomed in the late imperial period: between 1870 and 1894 some 1,400 periodicals were launched there, almost three times the total for the previous twenty-five years. Freedom of expression and an advanced capitalist economy were not necessary preconditions for a flourishing commercial press.

French censorship policy fluctuated wildly. Before 1789 the French domestic press was tightly licensed and censored, and political news had to be sourced from the official *Gazette de France*. Imported international gazettes, although freer, circulated through the post under license and so operated a rigorous self-censorship. The revolution of 1789 resulted briefly in a free press, guaranteed by the *Declaration of the Rights of Man*. Aborted by the Terror (1793–1794), press liberty was partially revived under the Directorial regime (1795–1799), despite sporadic clampdowns on

A Parricide. Cartoon from *Le Charivari*, 1850. French statesman Adolphe Thiers, a former journalist, is criticized for his advocacy of press censorship following the revolutions of 1848. BIBLIOTHÈQUE NATIONALE, PARIS, FRANCE/BRIDGEMAN ART LIBRARY/ARCHIVES CHARMET

Jacobin and Royalist papers. Press freedom was extinguished by Napoleon, who closed down most Parisian newspapers in January 1800 and only permitted publication of political news that had appeared in the *Moniteur.* The Constitutional Charter of 1814 restored a liberal press regime, but in 1830 infringements of that liberty by the Polignac ministry precipitated a journalist-led rebellion and change of dynasty. In the next five years radical journalism revived both in Paris and Lyon, where a vibrant workers' press and proto-feminist journals prospered. Press liberty was seriously curtailed again in 1835, reestablished following the revolution of 1848, and restricted once more under the Second Empire (1851–1870). Napoleon III's press regime liberalized in the 1860s, but censorship still existed at his fall in 1870 and was not finally abolished until the Press Law of 1881. The Third Republic was by then ten years old. Hence press liberty was not a necessary concomitant of democratic government.

However, democracy and a freer press often did go hand in hand, especially in Europe's newer nation-states, where the press played a role in nation-building. Liberals also argued for freedom of expression on pragmatic grounds, insisting that it would facilitate the generation and dissemination of socially useful ideas. They also insisted that the masses must be educated politically if experiments in representative government were to succeed and social revolution to be averted. Many contemporaries also linked Britain's commercial success and political stability to its constitution and free press. There thus appeared to be strong practical grounds for experimenting with press liberty. One such experiment occurred in postunification Italy, where liberal press freedoms introduced under the 1848 Piedmontese constitution were extended to the entire peninsula in 1859–1860. Together with Britain and France, late-nineteenth-century Italy enjoyed one of Europe's freest presses. At the same period, the laws of the newly unified Germany and of the Austrian Dual Monarchy allowed less freedom, but were considerably more generous than earlier in the century. The least free press in Christian Europe was in Russia, and even there some gains were made in 1865. In retrospect, the emergence of a freer press might appear almost inevitable, but such liberty was precarious and easily overturned.

THE "NEW JOURNALISM" AND THE NEW PUBLIC

Press freedom appeared more attractive as fears that democratization and a cheap popular press would radicalize the lower orders subsided. Such concerns declined for two main reasons. First, political democratization and progressive social legislation met or undercut radical demands. Simultaneously, falling newspaper prices promoted the growth of a cheap, commercially driven, mass-circulation press aimed at working-class readers, and the concomitant rise of the "New Journalism."

After 1870, this "New Journalism," developed in America, was exported to Europe. It catered for the cultural tastes of a newly literate mass audience, entertaining them with easily digestible coverage of sport, grisly crime, human interest stories, and fiction. This was very different from the sophisticated political and didactic role European liberals had hoped the press would play. Under the influence of the "New Journalism," the popular press tended to promote stereotypes, racial prejudice (as demonstrated in much European newspaper comment on the Dreyfus affair), and blinkered, jingoistic nationalism.

By 1900, the "New Journalism," industrialization, and commercialization had transformed successful newspapers into vast capital-intensive industries controlled by powerful capitalist interest groups. This process was accompanied by the consolidation of the newspaper industry in the hands of a few powerful individuals or conglomerates. In 1910, two-thirds of British metropolitan morning daily circulation and over four-fifths of evening daily sales were controlled by Alfred Charles William Harmsworth, Lord Northcliffe; Pearson; or the Morning Leader Group. Lord Northcliffe's *Daily Mail, Daily Mirror, Evening News,* and *The Times* alone sold over 1,500,000.

THE PROFESSIONALIZATION OF JOURNALISM

Alongside these developments, journalism emerged as a distinct profession with its own practices, career progression, established professional practices, and codes of ethics. This change resulted partly from an increase in editorial staff numbers and partly from greater journalistic contributions to reportage. Eighteenth-century newspapers had tiny editorial staffs. Often a single editor-proprietor compiled a newspaper by reproducing extracts from other papers, official publications, commercial correspondence, or other communications. Some international gazettes and enterprising metropolitan papers also paid newsmongers in foreign cities to supply regular newsletters. Comparison of different gazettes suggests that such writers seldom worked exclusively for one paper, and often wrote under the supervision of local political authorities. Thus, especially in continental Europe, many eighteenth-century "gazetteers" were compilers rather than true journalists.

Consequently, newspaper journalism was considered a lowly form of literary activity. Hence, in August 1791, the French revolutionary politician Brissot felt obliged to justify having worked on the *Courier de l'Europe* several years earlier:

> A career as a gazetteer, submitting to the censorship, was repugnant to my principles; but it would assure my independence...Bayle, I told myself, had been a teacher...Rousseau a lackey, and I

was blushing at the thought of being a gazetteer! I would honor this calling and it would not dishonor me.

In contrast, a century later, George Gissing's *New Grub Street* (1891) portrays the editorship of a newspaper or periodical as the ultimate prize for a literary hack. While Gissing's hapless, unworldly novelist Reardon expires in poverty, his friend and rival, the odious Jaspar Milvain, embraces the logic of the marketplace, secures the editorship of a periodical, makes his fortune, and marries Reardon's socially ambitious widow. To a large extent this portrayal mirrored social reality by the 1880s, when editors of large London dailies commanded salaries of between one and two thousand pounds and large staffs of journalists, each with specialized functions. They would include, for example, foreign correspondents. Such correspondents, first employed sporadically by London papers during the French revolution, became more common from the 1840s, as telegraph networks allowed reports to be lodged in real time. Increasingly, too, journalists chased stories and wrote their own copy, even when following up reports from news agencies like Reuters or national press associations, such as Agence France Presse (founded 1851) and the Press Association (founded 1868).

With greater professionalism, better pay, support from advertising, and mass audiences, journalists began to break free from political subsidy and articulate a set of professional standards. The later nineteenth century saw the emergence of journalistic ethics based on a set of ideological and moral claims, above all the assertion that newspapers "represented" (rather than created) "public opinion" and "the public interest." Ethical, that is reliable and hence superior, journalism rested on "objective" reporting and the rejection of political favor and subsidy. Although "public opinion," "the public interest," and "objectivity" are ideological constructs, these ideals developed a powerful hold over the Western psyche. In the public perception, public discourse, and some historical writing, newspapers became synonymous with "public opinion" throughout the twentieth century and beyond, while the appearance of "objectivity" supplied journalists with moral legitimacy, and a theoretical yardstick for judging reporting.

The practical improvement in journalistic ethics can be exaggerated. Early historians of the British press—some of them journalists themselves—offered a narrative in which corrupt, partisan, party-subsidized eighteenth-century newspapers evolved into heroic, impartial, organs of mid-nineteenth-century liberal public opinion. This Whiggish view dominated British historiography as late as Arthur Aspinall's monumental survey of *Politics and the Press, c. 1780–1850* (1950). This interpretation exaggerates the importance of political subsidy in late-eighteenth-century Britain. Government subsidies were meager and given primarily to reward support on individual issues. By the 1780s newspapers derived the vast bulk of revenues from advertisers and subscribers, and hence eschewed taking persistently unpopular editorial lines. Also, Whiggish newspaper history was developed before the emergence of the "New Journalism" and yellow press, whose journalistic practices fell short of the lofty ethics of the liberal press.

Moreover, especially in France, political subsidy continued for most of the nineteenth century. There were also serious financial scandals involving newspapers in late-nineteenth-century Italy and France, where papers were bribed not to reveal the Panama Company's precarious financial position. Other corrupt practices, including bribing journalists to puff products, offering inducements for endorsements, and hyping stocks for personal gain undoubtedly continued, although frowned on by more respectable papers. In France, the boulevard press continued time-honored customs such as blackmailing actresses, political figures, and minor celebrities, and accepting bribes from businesses to disparage rivals.

POLITICS AND THE PRESS

Contemporaries believed, and historians concur, that the political power of the press, increasingly described as "the Fourth Estate," grew across the nineteenth century. Nevertheless, while there are some spectacular examples of the pressure the press placed on individuals or governments, above all the 1830 revolution in France, it is more difficult to discern newspapers' day-to-day influence in shaping cultural and political life. Yet this influence was extensive. The press was, for example, undoubtedly instrumental in evoking "imagined national communities" based on a shared, media-mediated experience and culture, and in promoting greater

linguistic homogeneity within state borders. Moreover, the yellow press seems to have contributed significantly to the development of a distinctively working-class culture, filling the lower orders' leisure reading with a diet of sport, scandal, crime, sensation, and jingoistic nationalism.

Whiggish interpretations of newspaper history also suggest that the nineteenth-century liberal press played a key role in the emergence, formation, and leadership of public debate, although such claims are contentious. In the most suggestive treatment of the subject, Jürgen Habermas argues that the golden age of public debate was in fact the late eighteenth and early nineteenth centuries. At that stage, an educated, enlightened middle-class public opinion participated in genuine constructive rational-critical debate over issues of public policy in the print media and sociable institutions such as salons, coffeehouses, clubs, and reading rooms. The pronouncements of this autonomous limited "public" were soon invested with considerable moral authority, and hence able to influence state policy, even in absolutist states. However, during the nineteenth century, the twin processes of commercialization and democratization undermined the quality of public debate, as the rational and informed judgments of the elite were supplanted by ill-informed popular prejudice, largely shaped by the yellow press.

Habermas's claims have been influential, although it is unclear whether his account of the eighteenth-century press was intended as a description of reality or an ideal standard. Moreover, critics point out that eighteenth-century public debate was often partisan rather than consensual, especially after the French Revolution polarized Europeans ideologically. It was often characterized by irrationality and appeals to emotion, prejudice, or religious faith. Also, the audience for eighteenth-century newspapers was less thoroughly "bourgeois" and the press generally less autonomous of governments than Habermas supposed. Nor did newspapers provide an open forum for debate, or repository for opinion, save that of governments or powerful corporate bodies. Lacking much editorial opinion and drawing their information from official publications and public manifestos, they provided materials, rather than a forum, for political discussion.

Fewer critics have concentrated on Habermas's portrayal of the nineteenth-century decline of the liberal public sphere, which is overpessimistic. Certainly the hold of powerful commercial interests over the newspaper press was tightened, giving them control over the vital agenda-setting function of the media, by which it determines what subjects readers contemplate on a daily basis, if not how they actually think. However, the long nineteenth century also witnessed counterdevelopments including, in many countries, the establishment of constitutionally guaranteed freedom of expression; the spread of editorial content and a combative journalism of opinion; and the adoption of letters pages and columns that opened the range of political opinions on offer, even in partisan papers. Even yellow press journalism, which may be decried for thwarting liberal dreams of a didactic press educating the working classes, also operated as a valuable social control, helping to steer them away from violent social revolution. The press thus helped to smooth the transition to more representative forms of government in many states of Europe, even as it nurtured the militaristic nationalisms that so exacerbated the cataclysm of 1914–1918.

See also **Dickens, Charles; Jingoism; Literacy; Photography; Popular and Elite Culture; Trade and Economic Growth; Transportation and Communications; Zola, Émile.**

BIBLIOGRAPHY

Barker, Hannah. *Newspapers, Politics, and English Society, 1695–1855.* Harlow, U.K., 2000.

Barker, Hannah, and Simon Burrows, eds. *Press, Politics, and the Public Sphere in Europe and North America, 1760–1820.* Cambridge,U.K., 2002. The first attempt at an international survey of the press during this period in two hundred years.

Brennan, James. *The Reflection of the Dreyfus Affair in the European Press, 1897–1899.* New York, 1998. An impressively wide-ranging comparative study, offering useful, if uneven, summary background on the press in five different states.

Collins, Irene. *The Government and the Newspaper Press in France, 1814–1881.* London, 1959. Still useful survey of French government press policy from the Restoration to the end of censorship under the Third Republic.

Habermas, Jürgen. *The Structural Transformation of the Public Sphere: An Inquiry into a Category of Bourgeois Society.* Translated by Thomas Burger. Cambridge, Mass., 1989. First published in German in 1962, Habermas's comparative treatment of the public spheres of Germany, France, and Britain ranks among the most influential doctoral theses of all time and has an enduring heuristic value.

Lee, Alan J. *The Origins of the Popular Press in England, 1855–1914.* London, 1976. Still a valuable case study of the British context.

McReynolds, Louise. *The News under Russia's Old Regime: The Development of a Mass-Circulation Press.* Princeton, N.J., 1991. Impressive scholarly study of the coming of Russia's mass-circulation press covering 1855–1917.

O'Boyle, Lenore. "The Image of the Journalist in France, Germany and England, 1815–1848." *Comparative Studies in History and Society* 10 (1968): 290–317. Despite dated overemphasis on class issues, this remains a valuable and unique comparative essay.

Popkin, Jeremy D. *Revolutionary News: The Press in France, 1789–1799.* Durham, N.C., 1990. A thoughtful and stimulating treatment of the revolutionary press and its cultural significance.

Smith, Anthony. *The Newspaper: An International History.* London, 1979. Bold and readable attempt at an international synthesis, although it draws heavily on English and French examples. Aimed at a nonspecialist readership.

Stephens, Mitchell. *A History of News from the Drum to the Satellite.* New York, 1988. Aimed at a popular audience, but based on much fascinating material.

SIMON BURROWS

PRIMITIVISM. During the first decade of the twentieth century, primitivism became a cultural rage in Europe and influenced much of the avant-garde cultural production in the following decades. Its genealogy goes back to the concept of the "noble savage," which saw its first heyday during the eighteenth century when modernity and its antithesis evolved simultaneously. The concept of primitivism evokes the notion of the inferior primitive and savage, conveying both a sense of simplicity analogous to primitive lifestyle and technology as well as a life based on instincts, irrationality, and violence. But primitivism as a cultural construct conjures also the opposite: a belief in the superiority of the trouble-free and enviable primitive existence, a polar opposite to that under the corruption of modernity. It is this latter belief in the life of the "noble savage" that has made primitivism a mainstream worldview in art and literature since the beginning of the twentieth century.

This belief in humanity's natural goodness—evident in the contrast between a simple natural life and the deprivation of civilization—coexisted perilously close to the notion of the primitive and the savage as inferior. The romantic images of the Pacific islanders were coterminus with popular images of cannibals; Romanticism and racism both took the savage as their ultimate subject matter. Cannibalism and human sacrifice were common in European depiction of the native savage at least since the Renaissance and they would remain part of the mythologies of the savage. Historically, images of savages were also invoked closer to home; first represented by the peasants and later among the urban poor ("the nomadic races") who endured the expansion of the Industrial Revolution. *Primitives* was a closely related term, though during the nineteenth century it referred in art to Italian and northern schools (to the Pre-Raphaelites and the Flemish primitives) who were viewed as the infancy of modernity, and alternatively the term was used to describe antiquity in the sense of the early primitive Christian Church. The terms *primitive* and *savage* became more interchangeable early in the twentieth century.

The European search for the exotic led continuously during the nineteenth century to expanding explorations. Although not geographically linear, the orient, India, and China provided successive aesthetic foci for the alien and the exotic. Familiarity necessitated change and a continuous journeying—real and imaginary—that led to the prominence of Japonisme as a fashion in the last third of the nineteenth century. But when the influence of Japan became too pervasive (James Abbott McNeill Whistler [1834–1903], Edgar Degas [1834–1917], Henri de Toulouse-Lautrec [1864–1901], and Paul Gauguin [1848–1903] were just a few of the most prominent artists who depicted Japanese motifs), further explorations became necessary. The relatively rapid commodification of Japonisme induced the sophisticated explorer as well as the emerging avant-garde artists to shift their endeavor to discover a new source of primeval inspiration farther afield. This led to the South Seas and Africa. It was during the highest stage of imperi-

Contes Barbares. Painting by Paul Gauguin, 1902. Gauguin is among the most renowned of early primitivist painters, perhaps because his convictions about the superiority of less industrialized cultures led him to abandon his Parisian family and move to Tahiti, where he created many of his finest works. MUSEUM FOLKWANG, ESSEN, WEST GERMANY/BRIDGEMAN ART LIBRARY/GIRAUDON

alism late in the century that the duality of the primitive and the savage reached a crescendo enabling both the repression of non-Europeans, primarily in Africa, while employing the same images to liberate the imperialist agents and mind from the constraints of Victorian civilization.

Although primitivism evokes an appearance of reality that is mostly projected on societies in the Pacific and Africa, it does not refer to any external specific empirical phenomena but is rather a western constructed perception of the "other" representing an artistic creative movement. Primitivism, as a perpetual search for the exotic, never conveyed a particular style or aesthetic preference, nor a preference for the simple and peaceful or the savage and violent. Styles and subjects intertwined, and were best characterized by their opposition to modernity. This search for the exotic was closely related to imperialism and anthropology. Neither explicitly embraced primitivism, but each dominated and changed in distinct ways the world it considered primitive.

Beginning in the last third of the nineteenth century, the primitivist exchange intensified and expanded to include objects, people, and ideas. Europe was importing exotic objects—artifacts sent from military and scientific expeditions, travel engravings and photographs—and exporting colonial agents—including missionaries, explorers, and anthropologists—and providing an imaginary space into which the Victorian mind might escape. Three Europeans who illustrate this confusion of the seduction of imperialism entangled with racism and malice toward "the savage" were David Livingstone (1813–1873), Sir Richard Francis Burton (1821–1890), and Joseph Conrad (1857–1924). Livingstone, a missionary and an explorer who was seeking converts, desired an end to the slave trade, and hoped to penetrate Africa further than any previous European. He became a most popular national figure and perhaps the benevolent face of British imperialism. Distinctly more controversial was Burton, whose adventures, curiosity, racism, sexual proclivities, and even knowledge were mediated through engagement with the "other." An antecedent of the twentieth-century primitivists, Burton combined anthropology, science, religion, power, and sex to be everything the Victorians pretended they never were. His life, in hindsight, shows the extent of continuity between the Victorian period and modernism. This connection was even more pronounced in the work of Conrad, whose *Heart of Darkness* (1899) has become synonymous with the violence of imperialism. It is not insignificant that the book remained controversial, viewed by some as a classic foundational tale of the primitivist rejection of modernity, while others (most notably, Nigerian novelist Chinua Achebe) see it as the embodiment of European racism.

Much of the primitivist exchange took place in Europe itself, where most Europeans enjoyed the glamorous imperial domination through the various World Fairs that imported the world as a theme park, including "treasures," "artifacts," and flesh and blood "primitive" people and "villages." In addition to entertainment, the fairs provided justification for civilizing the globe out there, while providing raw material for exposing the contradictions of modernity. Social theorists pondered the limits of rationality (Max Weber [1864–1920]), solidarity (Emile Durkheim [1858–1917]), or how attractive primitive irrationality could be to a modern society (Lucien Lévy-Bruhl [1857–1939]). Anthropology projected a scientific discourse that postulated the polarized idea of "primitive" as a place of exoticism, eroticism, and virility.

It was in the shift from the social and political to the cultural and artistic that primitivism as we know it most contributed to modernism. If primitivism had an annus mirabilis, it must have been 1907, when Pablo Picasso (1881–1973) painted *Les Demoiselles d'Avignon,* which would prove to be a watershed in modern culture. Earlier artists, most famously Gauguin, eclectically combined "primitive" inspiration from medieval Europe to Polynesian Islands, as his images of the South Pacific fused conventions of French decadent art and colonialism. In Paris, beginning with the Fauves (the wild beasts), the best known of whom were André Derain (1880–1954) and Maurice Vlaminck (1876–1958), "wildness" became the rage. But it was Picasso's depiction of five naked prostitutes in a brothel, and the fusion of classical Greek influence with African masks, that most dramatically exhibited modernity as sexual savagery and launched "Cubism"—the epitome of the libertarian impulses of the European avant-garde ranging from sexual mores to form and content in art.

The Cubist African mask of modernism culminated the modernist revolution of beauty and art: primitive, simple, and even ugly became valorized high culture. The degree to which Gauguin, Picasso, and artists of their generation were influenced by anthropology and tribal art is significant to the dilemma of creativity and appropriation in modernism. While the issue will likely continue to be debated, there is no doubt that the exuberance of artistic primitivism led to a deeper scholarly interest in the subject. Primitives as the ultimate outsiders have always been represented by others in a distorted way. Often these misrepresentations are viewed as racist and exploitive. On other occasions, however, the depictions turn out to be inspiring and expansive, and to enrich human experiences. Primitivism as a component of modernism is precisely such an instance. Over time the "correctness" and "legitimacy" of these images have varied. While few will wish to argue that Burton's descriptions of Africa are acceptable in the twenty-first century, even fewer will contest Picasso's legitimacy to "distort" his subjects and to apply motives out of context.

Primitivism made it to center stage with the most evocative production of Igor Stravinsky's *Rites of Spring* (1913) staged by Sergei Diaghilev's Ballets Russes with its star dancer Vaslav Nijinsky. The combination of irrational "primitive" harmonic dissonances and explicit sexuality sent even the Parisian audience into frenzy that verged on a riot. The commotion began at once, and the audience, though accustomed to all of the components—disharmony, sexuality, primitivism—was seemingly shocked by the combination. The anxiety of primitivism would be replaced by aestheticization later on in the century, but not before the real savagery was about to unfold the following year, as the violence of modern warfare engulfed the continent.

See also **Conrad, Joseph; Cubism; Diaghilev, Sergei; Fauvism; Gauguin, Paul; Nietzsche, Friedrich; Picasso, Pablo.**

BIBLIOGRAPHY

Barkan, Elazar, and Ronald Bush, eds. *Prehistories of the Future: The Primitivist Project and the Culture of Modernism.* Stanford, Calif., 1995.

Goldwater, Robert. *Primitivism in Modern Art.* Rev. ed. New York, 1967.

Rubin, William, ed. *"Primitivism" in 20th Century Art: Affinity of the Tribal and the Modern.* New York, 1984.

ELAZAR BARKAN

PROFESSIONS. The word *profession* has become so imprecise by inflated usage that it needs to be defined so as to recover its historical meaning. From sports to hairdressing, all sorts of occupations have started to claim the adjective *professional* in order to suggest a degree of competence beyond the amateur level. Originally the English noun *profession* derived from the Latin verb *profiteri,* indicating the act of professing, that is, declaring something publicly. In contrast to a mere craft or trade, this linguistic derivation implies the pursuit of a livelihood that is based upon specialized knowledge beyond a mere skill and directed less toward private gain than toward rendering a public service. Through their transformation from learned guilds to modern self-governing associations, professions have come to be defined as special kinds of occupations based on higher learning, organized autonomously and dedicated to serving society.

TRAITS OF A PROFESSION

During the course of the nineteenth century the traditional "learned" occupations gradually became modern professions by acquiring such traits as specialized knowledge, rigorous examinations, independent associations, and autonomous practice. To begin with, the expertise of so-called professionals such as theologians, lawyers, and doctors rested on a broad liberal education in the classics, which endowed the holder with an aura of being a "gentleman." Increasingly, it went beyond scholarly information and included scientific training that made it possible for professionals not just to apply memorized rules of the craft but also to address problems creatively by researching new solutions. Nonetheless, there remained an important component of practical competence that codified the accumulated wisdom gathered from the actual practice of the profession in the past. This unique blend of cultivation, expertise, and experience set professionals apart from their predecessors and untrained competitors.

Professional expertise had to be learned during an extensive period of study that combined elements of apprenticeship with formal academic instruction. The polish of liberal education was generally acquired by boys in classical secondary schools such as boarding schools in Britain, *lycées* in France, or *Gymnasien* in Germany. Scholarly information was accumulated and scientific methods were assimilated subsequently during university study, whether at British colleges, French *hautes écoles,* or German *Universitäten.* Usually practical experience (*Berufswissen*) was gathered in some kind of apprenticeship as a probationary preacher at a church, as an intern in a law firm, or as a *famulus* helping an established physician. This lengthy process of training tended to be costly and could therefore be afforded only by members of the middle class.

In order to persuade a wary public of the proven expertise of professionals, a rigorous set of examinations was established so as to weed out the incompetent. While university access required some kind of demonstration of success at secondary school (A-levels, the *bac,* or the *Abitur*), the entry examinations into a profession, which were administered either by committees of experienced practitioners or by panels of government officials, tested both academic knowledge and practical competence. Public proof of passing was a degree that bestowed a title like *Herr Doktor,* certified in a diploma, which could be hung on the wall. Intended to keep charlatans from practicing on an unsuspecting public, this examination also served as social gate-keeping to bar undesirable elements and to restrict the number of newcomers in order to assure a comfortable living.

For the sake of sharing information and sociability, the practitioners of these elevated occupations tended to band together in so-called professional associations. Originally local, these societies gradually evolved into regional and national organizations so as to pursue their common interests more vigorously. To begin with, such groups merely provided social contacts that helped cushion competition between rival professionals. With time, lectures and congresses also made it possible to share in the further advancement of knowledge, especially important in the medical fields. More important yet were the efforts to promote the interests of the members by taking public positions, lobbying legislators, and influencing bureaucrats. During the nineteenth century, these initially social associations therefore increasingly transformed into vigorous professional interest groups.

In contrast to government servants or business people, professionals generally insisted on autonomy and on self-policing. Describing themselves as disinterested in material gain, the professions claimed to serve the public best when following the dictates of their expertise and not obeying bureaucratic orders. That meant that they

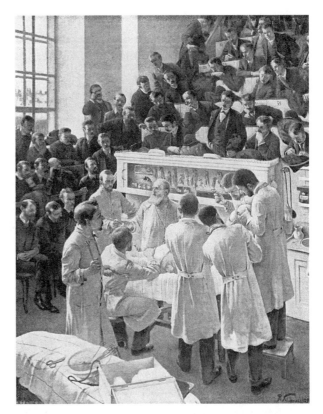

Professor Theodor Billroth Lectures at the General Hospital, Vienna, 1880. Engraving after the painting by Adelbert F. Seligmann. Billroth was the leading surgeon in Germany in the late nineteenth century. He influenced the development of the profession in particular through his advocacy of more extensive training for surgical students. MARY EVANS PICTURE LIBRARY

observed an independent standard of judgment, based on rational problem-solving rather than self-interest. In order to guard against an abuse of autonomy, the members elaborated extensive "codes of professional ethics" that defined what practitioners were allowed to do and imposed severe penalties in case of violations. Usually professional associations had ethics committees that possessed the power to punish errant members in order to reassure the public of the integrity of the remaining professionals. But since colleagues were often reluctant to censure each other, this arrangement worked only in really crass cases of malfeasance.

PROFESSIONALIZATION AS PROCESS

A product of this internal transformation, the process of professionalization led to the displacement of competitors, a gain in practical authority, and imitation by other occupations, which resulted in a rapid increase in the number of practitioners as well as of professional groups during the nineteenth century. As mentioned above, one central element in this success was the shift from practical experience to scholarly knowledge or scientific methods in the resolution of problems. This involved questioning traditional practices and supplanting them with new solutions that provided superior results. In the area of medicine this change was most dramatic, since the introduction of antibacterial and antiviral drugs triggered a quantum leap in successful cures and turned physicians from psychological advisors or recorders of death into effective healers of disease. Even if theologians or lawyers did not develop comparable advances in problem solving, they could also trade on the "scientific" aura that their advanced training provided.

As a result of being able to offer actual benefits based on their institutional education, professionals gradually succeeded in displacing their academically uneducated and nonlicensed rivals. For centuries, university-trained practitioners had been forced to compete with untutored lay preachers, uncertified legal advisors, and academically untrained midwives or other folk healers. Backed by scholarly instruction and academic examinations, professional organizations demanded a monopoly of practice for their respective trade, insisting on civil penalties for charlatans or amateurs. In most cases this lobbying effort was successful in reserving professional titles like "attorney" for the academically trained and in forbidding public advertising by their rivals. In churches, courts, and hospitals, professionals thereby erected a monopoly of practice, which claimed to protect the public from malpractice, but in effect also guaranteed an elevated standard of living to licensed practitioners.

Professionalization also meant that the professions succeeded in reversing the power relationship between patrons and practitioners. In the early modern period the nobility and wealthy members of the middle class condescended to employ the services of practitioners who were their social inferiors, firing them at will if the results did not please them. But during the nineteenth century, the claim of superior knowledge proved strong enough to endow the professional with unassailable authority, because he could now decide questions of life and death on the basis of scientific evidence. As a result, the erstwhile superior patron eventually became a supplicant client who had to compete for the services of prominent professionals and follow their instructions to the letter unless he wanted to risk dire consequences. This reversal of the power relationship raised the social standing of the professions in general.

Another facet of the transformation was the competition of newer occupations for elevation to the attractive status of a profession. Most of these pretenders came from the graduates of the arts and sciences faculty, such as the teachers of academic secondary schools, who campaigned tirelessly for acceptance among the ranks of the professions. Although not free practitioners like lawyers and doctors, university-trained educators wanted to gain control over their classrooms, obtain permission to organize, and achieve similar remuneration as their fellow graduates in other fields. In Germany, the *Gymnasium* teachers succeeded in getting nominal parity in the last decades before World War I, receiving a new title, *Studienrat,* which was modeled on the already existing designations *Konsistorialrat, Justizrat,* and *Medizinalrat.* But their elevation meant that primary schoolteachers would continue to be excluded from university training and superior rank. Another group of pretenders that had somewhat indifferent success were the graduates of new technical institutions, such as engineers.

The general increase in material prosperity created a rising demand for professional services that triggered an impressive expansion in the numbers of professionals throughout the nineteenth century. Whereas there were only a few thousand pastors, lawyers, and doctors in most countries during the early nineteenth century, one hundred years later their number had multiplied about tenfold. For instance in England the size of eight professions had risen to 191,384 by 1922, in France the number of liberal professionals and intellectuals reached 122,257 by 1906, and in Germany the increase reached 335,252 by 1933. While the number of theologians only modestly increased, the figure for lawyers and doctors multiplied steeply, and the share of practitioners in new professions such as teaching or engineering virtually exploded. This development also shifted the balance somewhat away from the traditional learned professions toward new white-collar callings in government and industry. In spite of the expansion, the overall share of the professions in the workforce remained rather limited, not surpassing 2 percent before World War I.

The rapid expansion was, however, not a linear success story, but rather a crisis-ridden process marked by cycles of oversupply of educated men. In central Europe the post-Napoleonic expansion reached a peak in the early 1830s, producing much-lamented unemployment of university graduates and impoverishment among beginning professionals. As a result, higher-education enrollments fell, and a deficit of professionals developed by the 1860s. This perceived lack of trained experts encouraged a second expansion cycle, which peaked in the late 1880s, triggering another overcrowding crisis and producing a veritable "academic proletariat." Government efforts to steer these academic cycles, demanded by the professions, were generally ineffectual, because restrictions, if they came too late, only exaggerated the deficits, and calls for higher enrollment added to the subsequent oversupply. Academic unemployment tended to have deleterious political consequences, since it fed into the unrest behind the Revolution of 1848 in France and into the radicalization of the intelligentsia in Russia.

As a result of their proliferation, the professions gradually transformed the face of the noneconomic middle class. In contrast to the financiers, industrialists, or merchants, professionals were not primarily interested in accumulating wealth, but rather propounded an ethos of public service. While they competed in a market of their own, this competition was regulated by barring rivals and insisting on ethical behavior. Unlike university trained bureaucrats, many professionals were not directly employed by the state either, and could therefore practice more freely, without having to obey political pressures or bureaucratic mandates. This intermediary position within the middle class, without a fixed salary but also without direct supervision, made professions an attractive calling, because they provided considerable freedom for personal choice. As a result, the professional ideal exerted a powerful pull on university graduates, since such a life promised to liberate them somewhat from the twin evils of the market and the government.

PATTERNS OF PROFESSIONALISM

Although the process of professionalization was universal in character, its institutional pattern varied considerably according to national context. Ironically, the British experience of the "self-governing professions," which is often taken as the classic case, was actually somewhat peculiar because of weak academic training and lack of state regulation. Until the middle of the nineteenth century, young professionals were essentially apprenticed to older practitioners at the Inns of Court or the Royal Colleges of Physicians and examined by "qualifying associations." Only in later decades could the development of the red-brick universities begin to shift more of the training back into higher education, but testing remained a prerogative of the professional organizations. Hence the strength of autonomy regulated by ethics and the freedom from bureaucratic control provided an inspiring model, but proved surprisingly unique.

In contrast, the French case of state supervision is more typical of the Continental pattern, albeit with a peculiar competitive twist. In its enthusiasm for *les carrières ouvertes aux talents* (careers open to talent), the French Revolution abolished the traditional self-governing corporations and introduced unrestricted competition that destroyed solidarity. Ironically, Napoleon I (r. 1804–1814/15) reestablished the professions under tight government control, allowing collective representation to the lawyers alone, leaving the rest fragmented. Only in the second half of the nineteenth century did French professionals manage to restore some of their associations and regain a measure of collective identity through a revitalization of university training and restrictions on competition. Lawyers in particular succeeded so much in politics that critics called the Third Republic a *République des avoués* (republic of lawyers). Less successful was the rapidly growing group of writers, artists, and journalists, dividing the educated therefore between professionals and intellectuals.

The German variant of the process, with strong state involvement and academic training, has been called "professionalization from above." From the late eighteenth century on, the introduction of a series of rigorous state examinations for clergymen, lawyers, doctors, and eventually also teachers created bureaucratically controlled academic occupations whose members were intensively trained at the universities. During the middle of the nineteenth century, liberal opinion forced the government to disestablish the medical (1869) and legal (1879) professions, allowing them to enter into free practice and to establish powerful professional associations. However, in the wake of the overcrowding crisis of the 1880s, many professionals gravitated toward establishing a kind of neocorporatism characterized by self-governing chambers with public authority that might restrict competition and reestablish a suitable income. The central European pattern therefore consisted of a mixture of practitioner self-assertion within a framework of bureaucratic control.

Although the state was strongest in Russia, a limited kind of professionalism emerged under the tsars as well. Initially, the weakness of primary and secondary schooling as well as the hierarchical structure of estate society and the heavy hand of the bureaucracy left little room for the emergence of independent professions. But in the wake of the reforms set in place by Alexander II (r. 1855–1881), academic practitioners began to band together, founded their first associations, and became active in the liberal *zemstvo* (local government) movement that tried to modernize Russian society from the bottom up. Frustrated by the slow pace of reform, the often unemployed higher-education graduates around the turn of the century began to join the radical intelligentsia instead, trying to promote revolutionary change.

In the smaller European countries, the pattern of professionalization tended to reflect the arrangements of the larger state that served as chief cultural reference point, modified somewhat by local tradition. The traditional model of corporate self-government of the professions survived longest in Italy. The British practitioner-control system was rare, except for a similar grassroots approach in Switzerland. The French mixture of state control and market freedom somewhat influenced the Belgian practice. The German example of professionalization from above could be found in Austria, the Netherlands, Scandinavia, and Greece. Finally, the Russian pattern of delayed professionalism coupled with a radical intelligentsia became typical of the emerging eastern European and Balkan countries. Beyond a basic similarity in the overall thrust of professionalization, cross-national comparison therefore reveals a bewildering variety of time sequences and institutional arrangements.

PROBLEMS OF PROFESSIONALIZATION

The spread of the modern professions throughout Europe should, however, not obscure the existence of a series of fundamental problems associated with the process of professionalization. One of the key conflicts concerned the tension between professed altruism and practiced self-interest. Especially in treating legal or medical clients, individual practitioners faced many choices between rational reasoning or personal gain, which could not be governed by codes of ethics. When trying to get public approval for expanding their prerogatives, following their advice, or undertaking social reforms, the professions collectively resorted to arguments that claimed service to society through better justice, health, or technology. However, behind these unselfish protestations often lurked material considerations of barring competition, raising fees, or carving out new areas of practice. The discrepancy between pious protestations and crass abuses time and again tarnished the image of professions so that they could be ridiculed in satire.

Another area of contestation was the loss of public accountability in the face of expert authority. No doubt, the switch from oral tradition to a scholarly knowledge base and from old wives' tales to scientific medicines, just to pick one example, was on the whole beneficial. But the displacement of unlicensed competitors also made advice in matters of religion, law, or medicine unavailable to the working masses, who could not afford to pay for professional counsel. Moreover, the rise of academic medicine also ruptured traditions of folk-healing, not all of which were ineffective, as the recent rediscovery of herbal medicine shows. Instead of being responsible for its own decisions, part of the public became accustomed to deferring to the opinions of professionals also in matters where they were hardly any better informed. Already around the turn of the twentieth century critics, especially life-reformers, began to rail against excesses of "medicalization" and against similar losses of independence in law and education.

Cartoon of a widow and her lawyer. From the series People of Justice by Honoré Daumier, first published in *Charivari*, 27 April 1848. The original caption read: "You lost your suit, it's true . . . but you must have taken great pleasure in hearing me plead your case." GALERIE DANIEL MALINGUE, PARIS/THE BRIDGEMAN ART LIBRARY

The politics of professionalization were also not unproblematic, since the general promotion of liberalization tended to give way to restrictive responses in moments of crisis. No doubt, the advancement of professionalism was generally associated with the rise of liberalism in the nineteenth century, since many of the leaders of liberal parties were lawyers, doctors, or educators. Aspiring professionals bought into the broader project of lifting the heavy hand of state so as to allow the emergence of a self-governing civil society, because they wanted to carve out an area of free practice for themselves. However, they did not envisage totally free competition, but rather preferred a regulated kind of freedom in which the state would protect their monopoly, guarantee a suitable standard of living, and follow their professional advice in questions of public policy. When threatened by overcrowding, assault on their privileges, or general impoverishment, the professions often entered alliances with conservative forces in order to protect their hard-won prerogatives.

A drastic case in point is the struggle over the admission of outsiders such as proletarians, Jews, or women, in which insiders used social prejudices and legal prohibitions to prevent their entry. As they could not be kept completely out, "undesirable" newcomers from the lower orders tended to be channeled into peripheral and subordinate positions. Jews had to overcome much social prejudice in western Europe, and they were forced to congregate in law and medicine in central Europe, because they were largely barred from state employment. In the more restrictive eastern Europe they had even less of a chance. The so-called weaker sex was excluded from the professions until the turn of the twentieth century by inferior secondary schooling that did not permit admission to university study and therefore prevented graduation. When social reformers managed to open higher education (in Prussia as late as 1907–1908), heated battles ensued over the acceptance of women into the professions, even if they had managed to acquire the right kind of credentials. Eventually the barriers were breached, especially in areas that seemed suited to the talents of "social mothering" such as in nursing or primary school teaching.

ATTRACTIONS OF PROFESSIONALISM

In spite of its attendant problems, the rise of the professions in the nineteenth century profoundly reshaped the lives of the educated middle class. All across Europe the traditional learned pursuits began to formalize academic training, tightened up entrance examinations, improved the standards of practice, founded associations, and struggled for greater autonomy. In short, they refashioned themselves into modern professions: in England the free professions became the dominant form of the noneconomic middle class; in France professionalized officials vied with the intellectual literati; in the German speaking countries, the *akademische Berufsstände* (academically trained pursuits) reorganized themselves along professional lines; in the Slavic societies national and liberal professionals competed with the radical intelligentsia. While the specific institutional arrangements varied drastically, the general thrust of professional development therefore transformed the non-economic middle class.

The professional social ideal proved so attractive because it suggested a fulfilling lifestyle, free from the constraints of the market and from the dictates of the bureaucracy. The academic knowledge base provided a superior competence that could outflank various rivals; the autonomy of practice allowed an independent existence that was able to follow its own preferences; the association of like-minded individuals offered a sense of community and an instrument for pursuing collective interests. Compared with other occupations in the economy and government, these were powerful advantages, even if professional life contained its own risks of intellectual failure, economic insecurity, and personal ostracism. Most powerful for many was, however, the ideal of service to the public that justified personal exertion and collective privileges. The novels of the British writer Archibald Joseph Cronin (1896–1981) describe this professional ideal as a kind of secular faith in the bettering of humanity that required personal sacrifice.

The success of professionalization therefore rested on persuasive public representations of the idealism of some practitioners and the provision of superior services. In speeches at their congresses and the pages of their journals, the professional associations conveyed a positive self-image to the public that stressed the altruism as well as the real benefits of their practice. Journalistic portrayals made the dedication of famous researchers like Louis Pasteur (1822–1895) or Rudolf Virchow (1821–1902) into "culture heroes" whose contributions were more constructive than those of poets or musicians, because they helped solve social problems. Graphic descriptions of the proliferation of new technologies based on chemistry, electronics, or the internal combustion engine also pointed to concrete advances that improved the lives of many people. With such powerful arguments, professionals could therefore claim that in the conduct of research, the growth of economies, the solution of social problems, and the governing of states the contributions of competent experts were becoming indispensable.

See also **Bourgeoisie; Education; Engineers; Intellectuals; Intelligentsia; Nurses;**

BIBLIOGRAPHY

Burrage, Michael, and Rolf Thorstendahl, eds. *The Professions in Theory and History: Rethinking the Study of the Professions.* 2 vols. London, 1990.

Charle, Christophe. *Les intellectuals en Europe au XIXe siècle: Essai d'histoire comparée.* Paris, 1996.

Cocks, Geoffrey, and Konrad H. Jarausch, eds. *The German Professions, 1800–1950.* New York, 1990.

Cohen, Gary. *Education and Middle Class Society in Imperial Austria, 1848–1918.* West Lafayette, Ind., 1996.

Geison, Gerald, ed. *Professions and the French.* Philadelphia, 1984.

Jarausch, Konrad H. *The Transformation of Higher Learning, 1860–1930: Expansion, Diversification, Social Opening, and Professionalization in England, Germany, Russia, and the United States.* Stuttgart, 1983.

———. *The Unfree Professions: German Lawyers, Teachers, and Engineers, 1900–1950.* New York, 1990.

Kassow, Samuel D. *Students, Professors, and the State in Tsarist Russia.* Berkeley, Calif., 1989.

Kovács, Mária M. *Liberal Professions and Illiberal Politics: Hungary from the Habsburgs to the Holocaust.* Washington, D.C., 1994.

Malatesta, Maria, ed. *Society and the Professions in Italy, 1860–1914,* Cambridge, U.K., 1995.

Mazón, Patricia, M. *Gender and the Modern Research University: The Admission of Women to German Higher Education, 1865–1914.* Stanford, Calif., 2003.

McClelland, Charles E. *The German Experience of Professionalization: Modern Learned Professions and Their Organizations from the Early Nineteenth Century to the Hitler Era.* Cambridge, U.K., 1991.

McClelland, Charles E., Stephen Merl, and Hannes Siegrist, eds. *Professions in Modern Eastern Europe.* Berlin, 1995.

Perkin, Harold, *The Rise of Professional Society: England since 1880.* London, 1989.

Rüegg, Walter, ed. *A History of the University in Europe.* Vol. 3: *Universities in the Nineteenth and Early Twentieth Centuries.* Cambridge, U.K., 2004.

Siegrist, Hannes. *Advokat, Bürger, und Staat: Sozialgeschichte der Rechtsanwälte in Deutschland, Italien und der Schweiz (18.–20. Jh.).* Frankfurt, 1996.

KONRAD H. JARAUSCH

PROSTITUTION. Prostitution was perceived as a serious and expanding social problem in nineteenth-century Europe. The dominant symbol of female disorder and immorality, the prostitute became the subject of lively debate, medical and sociological inquiry, and government legislation. Throughout Europe, politicians, doctors, criminologists, journalists, and feminists argued passionately about the causes, extent, and consequences of prostitution. Despite such intense controversy, however, few nineteenth-century documents offer a rigorous definition of prostitution. They focus on lower-class women and ignore altogether the male prostitute. While some experts admitted that upper-class concubines and mistresses should be classified as prostitutes, they nevertheless concentrated their anxiety on the poor as potential fonts of moral contamination and venereal disease. Rather than being strictly defined as the exchange of sex for money, prostitution became a general metaphor in nineteenth-century debate for any female behavior that defied the norms of bourgeois sexual respectability. Thus working-class women throughout Europe were subject to arrest simply for walking on public streets at night or appearing flirtatious.

The causes of this "moral panic" over prostitution lay more in general social and economic developments of nineteenth-century Europe than in an actual increase in the numbers of prostitutes. In a century of intense demographic growth, young women migrated to the burgeoning cities in search of work. Rather than emigrating to foreign lands, like many young men, women tended to move shorter distances to the nearest urban area. Unskilled and often uneducated, they usually found work in domestic service or other low-paid and often precarious jobs. Some women supplemented this work with prostitution, although reliable statistics on working prostitutes are difficult to obtain. Their numbers, however, never reached the inflated proportions imagined by middle-class observers, who tended to identify any poor woman living alone or without family as a prostitute. The emergence of the movement for women's emancipation intensified fears that increasing numbers of women were escaping the control of fathers and husbands only to sow social degeneration that might contribute to national decline.

PUBLIC POLICY ON PROSTITUTION

Two legal approaches to prostitution—regulation and abolition—dominated policy debates. Throughout the nineteenth century most European nations had some sort of regulationist policy that legalized the practice of prostitution and placed it under the strict control of police and health authorities. While many medieval and early modern cities had also tolerated prostitution, the modern model of regulation dates back to the Napoleonic era, when many cities began to subject prostitutes to periodic health examinations in an attempt to protect the civilian population—and even more the army—from venereal disease. Carried abroad by Napoleonic administrators, the French policy of regulation was copied after 1815 by many Restoration regimes and subsequent liberal governments.

The popularity of regulation lay in its claim to rationality and modernity. Its supporters championed regulation as secular and practical in opposition to traditional policies of the old regime that had tried to prohibit prostitution as immoral and sinful. Regulationists argued instead for enlightened acknowledgement that prostitution would never disappear. Society needed prostitutes to serve as an outlet for the natural and imperious male sex drive that might otherwise threaten chaste girls and respectable women. Acknowledged as a social necessity, prostitution nevertheless posed a danger to public morality, order, and health and required surveillance by police. Yet regulationists, drawn mainly from the liberal and professional middle classes, defended their policy as enlightened rather than repressive because of the benefits to public health promised by the periodic vaginal examinations of prostitutes.

As regulation spread across Europe and became the dominant policy on prostitution, opposition arose in the form of the "abolitionist" movement. Dedicated to abolishing regulationist laws, abolitionists came mostly from the ranks of the democratic Left or the nascent movement for female emancipation. They criticized regulationist laws for violating the civil rights of prostitutes by subjecting them to police and medical control. More fundamentally, they rejected the double standard that held men blameless for their sexual behavior; abolitionism instead preached chastity before marriage and monogamy afterward for both sexes. Rather than a social necessity, prostitution was considered by abolitionists to constitute a transitory evil that would disappear when women gained equality with men in access to work and fair wages.

The abolitionist campaign against regulation was led by the Englishwoman Josephine Butler (1828–1906), who founded the International Abolitionist Federation in 1876. With its headquarters in Geneva and branches throughout Europe and North America, the Federation issued a journal and held periodic congresses to promote its cause. Defending the plight of poor women who lacked economic alternatives to prostitution, the Federation denied the efficacy of the regulationist health policy by pointing out the illogic of subjecting only female prostitutes and not their male clients to medical examination and treatment. Anxiety about the "white slave trade," the international traffic in prostitutes, strengthened the abolitionist ranks since regulated brothels were seen as integral to a wider network that victimized defenseless girls and women. While recent research has found only limited evidence of a white slave trade in nineteenth-century Europe, sensationalist accounts flooded newspapers of the time and fueled popular perceptions that prostitution was a large and growing problem.

A series of excellent studies have analyzed the implementation of regulation and abolition in different nations during the nineteenth century. The majority of European countries, especially on the Continent, adopted some form of regulation on the French model. The popularity of regulation was boosted by the publication in 1836 of the first serious inquiry on prostitution, conducted by the French doctor Alexandre-Jean-Baptiste Parent-Duchâtelet (1790–1836). Entitled *De la prostitution dans la ville de Paris* (Prostitution in the city of Paris), his two-volume book offered not only a social profile of Parisian prostitutes but also a ringing endorsement of regulation as the appropriate government response. He emphasized the importance of concentrating prostitution in "closed houses," the official brothels patrolled by police, and of discouraging "clandestine" prostitution by unregistered women. Claiming to have applied scientific methods to deflate myths and discover facts, Parent-Duchâtelet's book appealed to the middle-class professionals and bureaucrats searching for a modern response to prostitution.

While regulation invariably required prostitutes to register with police, undergo periodic health examinations, and report to lock hospitals if diagnosed with venereal disease, legislation varied in scope among European nations. Most countries—including France, Germany, and Belgium—regulated prostitution through municipal laws on the assumption that prostitution was mainly an urban problem. Italy was one of the few countries to erect a national system of regulation administered by the Minister of the Interior in Rome and theoretically uniform across urban and rural areas. As in France, however, only the larger Italian cities had a "morals police" dedicated to the registration of prostitutes and surveillance over legalized brothels. Russia's system of registration fell between the municipal and national models. Imperial legislation passed in 1851 and 1903—requiring that prostitutes carry special health licenses known as "yellow tickets"—provided a guideline for the drafting of more specific local laws.

Regulation was less successful in England, where a strong and vocal abolitionist movement forced repeal. Never national in scope, English regulation was instituted in the major garrison and port towns by a series of "Contagious Diseases Acts" in 1864, 1866, and 1869. These "CD Acts" provoked opposition from an unusual coalition of feminists, Protestant ministers, and working-class men. Each group emphasized different threats posed by regulation to society: to gender equality for feminists; to Christian morality for Protestants; and to the daughters of the working class, whose virtue was sacrificed in the closed houses to meet the sexual needs of middle-class men. Aided by the press, this coalition forced parliament to repeal the CD Acts in 1886. This defeat of regulation, however, was rare despite the international network of abolitionists throughout Europe. More limited reform characterized nations like France and Italy, which closed the special lock hospitals for prostitutes and replaced them with venereal-disease clinics for both sexes.

SOCIAL PROFILE OF PROSTITUTES

A similar social profile united prostitutes across nineteenth-century Europe. Most were young, entering the trade in their mid- to late teens and leaving in their mid- to late twenties. This pattern echoed the age at which girls entered other kinds of work (and then often left to marry and have children) and argues against the popular nineteenth-century

Prostitutes in a bordello on the Rue de Londres, Paris. Nineteenth-century photograph. The decor mirrors that of a bourgeois salon. MUSÉE CARNAVALET, PARIS, FRANCE/BRIDGEMAN ART LIBRARY

notion that an international network of white slavers were preying on innocent children under the age of sixteen. As would be expected from their youth, most prostitutes were single, although some married women supplemented their income with part-time prostitution. That a significant number of prostitutes left the trade for marriage before the age of thirty indicates that lower-class opinion understood prostitution as a type of female work rather than a stigmatizing form of sexual deviancy.

As work, prostitution most often fell to unskilled migrants from the countryside rather than urban workers who dominated the more prestigious and remunerative factory jobs. Exhibiting higher rates of illiteracy than women in general, prostitutes were highly restricted in their options for employment, with domestic service usually offering the only alternative. Shunning the low pay and strict control typical of life as a live-in servant, some young women preferred the imag-

ined freedom and potentially high wages of prostitution, although neither was often realized by inmates of the closed houses. At best, madams in the tolerated brothels claimed half of prostitutes' earnings while many purposely kept their employees perpetually in debt for food and clothing to prevent them from fleeing.

Prostitutes' freedom was also circumscribed by surveillance by police and medical authorities. Regulationist laws typically required that prostitutes register with police when arriving in a new town, carry a special identification card, and request permission to move to another city or leave the profession. Identification cards certified that each woman had undergone periodic vaginal examination, usually by a state physician. If diagnosed with symptoms of venereal disease, she was forcibly admitted to a lock hospital, which resembled a prison more than a health facility. Forbidden to leave until they no longer showed symptoms of the disease, patients often had to work as a measure of reform. Such work emphasized "female" skills such as sewing, knitting, or doing laundry. Regulationists refused to admit the limited effectiveness of this health surveillance in an age when venereal disease was difficult to diagnose and impossible to cure.

PREVENTION AND REFORM

Regulationists and abolitionists agreed on the immorality of prostitution and therefore supported efforts to prevent women from "falling" into sin and to redeem them once fallen. Feminists and religious organizations were the most active in prevention and reform, although they often worked on the basis of different assumptions. Feminists, who provided the backbone of the early abolitionist movement, called for equality between the sexes to bring women's levels of education and wages up to the level achieved by men. They promoted the legalization of paternity suits in order to discourage men from seducing innocent girls with promises of marriage. Several refuges for "endangered" girls, like the Mariuccia Shelter in Milan, were established on feminist principles to mold "new women" endowed with a sound education, modern job skills, and self-confidence.

More institutions of rescue, however, were founded by religious organizations, both Catholic and Protestant. In England, for example, the religious revival of the mid-nineteenth century as well as the growing "social purity" movement inspired a proliferation of reformatories for prostitutes. One study estimates that by the end of the century there were fifty-three penitentiaries linked to the Church of England; 320 Magdalene homes established by the Evangelical Church; and various other refuges founded by the Salvation Army, the Church Army, and the Jewish Ladies' Association. In Catholic countries, charitable orders of nuns like the Sisters of the Good Shepherd staffed an international network of reform institutions. Religious institutions stressed moral reform and training in traditional female skills as preparation for marriage or domestic service.

HISTORIOGRAPHY

Research on prostitution has grown steadily since the early 1980s but does not yet encompass all European nations. Broad agreement exists on the social background of European prostitutes: that they tended to be young, single, poor, illiterate, immigrants from the countryside, and often domestic servants. Most studies stress that nineteenth-century European women were not forced into prostitution but made a choice among limited and not very appealing alternatives. Debate exists, however, over the quality of life for prostitutes. Some historians portray prostitutes as miserable victims of poverty and disease who had little opportunity to return to "normal" life. More widespread is the picture of prostitution as a phase in the lives of many young women that, while not highly remunerative, nevertheless ended frequently in marriage or return to their families. From this point of view, the repression of police and censure of middle-class society was partially offset for the prostitute by lower-class acceptance of her work as a necessary means of economic survival, especially if she was alone or supporting parents and children.

The most recent historiographical trend emphasizes the relationship between prostitution policies in European nations and their colonies. According to work by Philippa Levine, the Contagious Diseases Acts were promulgated first in Hong Kong (1857) and other colonies before being enacted in England itself. By 1870 regulation characterized prostitution policy in more than twelve British colonies. That the CD Acts applied only to brothels with European clients revealed that their intention had always been to protect the health of men—and in this case white men—rather than that of women or the population in general. Future studies of colonial policy by other European nations will further illuminate the gender and racial anxieties and ideologies that fueled the nineteenth-century moral panic about prostitution.

See also **Body; Butler, Josephine; Cities and Towns; Feminism; Poverty; Public Health; Sexuality.**

BIBLIOGRAPHY

Bartley, Paula. *Prostitution: Prevention and Reform in England, 1860–1914.* London, 2000.

Bernstein, Laurie. *Sonia's Daughters: Prostitutes and Their Regulation in Imperial Russia.* Berkeley, Calif., and London, 1995.

Corbin, Alain. *Women for Hire: Prostitution and Sexuality in France after 1850.* Cambridge, Mass., 1990.

Evans, Richard J. "Prostitution, State, and Society in Imperial Germany." *Past and Present* 70 (1976): 106–129.

Finnegan, Frances. *Poverty and Prostitution: A Study of Victorian Prostitutes in York.* Cambridge, U.K., 1979.

Gibson, Mary. *Prostitution and the State in Italy, 1860–1915.* New Brunswick, N.J., 1986. 2nd ed., Columbus, Ohio, 1995.

Harsin, Jill. *Policing Prostitution in Nineteenth-Century Paris.* Princeton, N.J., 1985.

Levine, Philippa. *Prostitution, Race, and Politics: Policing Venereal Disease in the British Empire.* New York and London, 2003.

Mahood, Linda. *The Magdalenes: Prostitution in the Nineteenth Century.* London, 1990.

Walkowitz, Judith R. *Prostitution and Victorian Society: Women, Class, and the State.* Cambridge, U.K., and New York, 1980.

MARY GIBSON

PROTECTIONISM.

By and large, protectionist trade policies prevailed in nineteenth-century Europe, although this protection was mild compared with that of the 1930s or the 1950s. The short interlude in the 1860s and 1870s and the free-trade policies of the United Kingdom and some smaller countries are exceptions, but ones that seem to confirm the rule. These protectionist practices contrasted with the almost unanimous opinion of professional economists, who regard free trade as highly beneficial.

FREE TRADE AND PROTECTION IN THEORY

This gap between theory and practice started to open in the eighteenth century. Until then, with very few exceptions such as Henry Martyn (1665–1721), it was believed that the wealth of a nation depended on its stock of gold, which had to be accumulated by running a positive trade balance, that is, by exporting more than importing. This mercantilist ideology was seriously challenged only in the 1750s and 1760s. Enlightenment thinkers such as the Italian Ferdinando Galliani (1728–1787) or the French Physiocrats advocated freedom in grain trade, and Adam Smith (1723–1790) made a compelling case for overall liberalization in his *Wealth of Nations* (1776). Free trade, according to Smith, is first and foremost a straightforward extension of the principle of the invisible hand—the market knows better than the state how to allocate resources. Furthermore, free trade increases the size of the market and hence the scope for the division of labor and specialization, which in Smith's view is the source of long-term economic growth.

David Ricardo (1772–1823), author of *Principles of Political Economy and Taxation* (1817), and other "classical" economists such as James Mill (1773–1836) and Robert Torrens (1780–1864) sharpened Smith's argument. They held that specialization is not driven by absolute advantage (i.e., by the comparison of costs between domestic and foreign producers) but by comparative advantage (i.e., by the comparison of production costs among alternative uses of available factors). A country can gain from trade even if it could produce the imported good at a lower cost, provided that it could produce something else at an even lower relative cost. Therefore, all countries have something to gain from free trade. The principle of comparative advantage is still the cornerstone of trade theory.

Economists later found some exceptions, such as Torrens's terms of trade argument for duties by large countries, Frank Graham's external economies argument for protection of industries with increasing returns, and Barbara J. Spencer and James A. Brander's strategic trade argument for export subsidies. These exceptions, however, hold true only under very special circumstances: in almost all cases, free trade would deliver the optimal allocation of existing resources, given the available technology.

In contrast, most arguments for protection focus on its alleged dynamic benefits. Advocates of protectionism hold that short-term losses from protection can be outweighed by long-term economic and/or geopolitical gains. The economic gains can include the full development of the potential of the country. Alexander Hamilton (1755–1804), the first U.S. secretary of the treasury, and John Stuart Mill (1806–1873), the most famous British economist (and a staunch protrader), argued that a limited period of protection could be necessary to start potentially suitable productions (the infant industry argument). Such industries need some time to acquire the necessary technical and organizational capabilities, to train the necessary workforce, and so on before they will be able to withstand the foreign competition. The geopolitical argument for protection assumes that an independent state could not pursue its foreign policy without military capabilities, which must be built up even at the cost of welfare losses. A great power should be able to produce all goods necessary to wage a victorious war, including of course its food. In this case, unlike in the infant industry argument, protection could be permanent. This line of reasoning can be traced back to Friedrich List (1789–1846), author of *The National System of Political Economy* (1841). The geopolitical argument was quite popular among nationalistic writers of the nineteenth and early twentieth centuries.

These "dynamic" arguments for protection were and still are fairly diffused among the lay public, but by and large they have failed to persuade economists. The latter doubt that protection could ever be temporary and stress that competition from imports is a powerful stimulus for improving the efficiency of domestic producers.

FREE TRADE AND PROTECTION IN PRACTICE

How is it possible to account for the gap between theory and practice? Why has protectionism been so often adopted if it is harmful to the overall welfare? One can suggest three possible answers: the need for state revenue, the state of international relations, and pressure from producers' lobbies.

Duties can be a sizable source of revenue only if imports do not fall, that is, if imports are not replaced by domestic production. This is the case with duties on goods that cannot be produced at home, such as wine in the United Kingdom. These duties were allegedly instituted only for fiscal purposes—although they could also guarantee some protection to domestic producers of competing goods (such as beer). But openly protective duties could also yield substantial revenue if domestic production is insufficient for the desired consumption at the prevailing price, inclusive of the duty. This fiscal motivation was particularly important in the nineteenth century, because, before the introduction of personal taxation, custom duties were in fact major sources of revenues. On the eve of World War I, they accounted for

about 10 to 15 percent of total revenues and up to 45 percent for federal states, such as Germany. Thus, the need for revenues could be invoked to justify otherwise unpalatable increases in protection. This happened in Italy in 1894, when the duty on wheat was increased by 50 percent during a budget crisis. In the following decade, duty on wheat provided between 3 and 4 percent of the total revenues of Italy.

The prevalence of protectionist policies may be associated with the lack of a "hegemonic" power, such as the United States after 1950. A hegemonic power would force other countries to adopt the trade policy that best fits its interests—that is, almost always, to open their markets to its own exports. In this vein, one might explain the liberalization in the first half of the nineteenth century with the waxing of British political hegemony and the return to protection toward the end of the century with its waning. But Peter T. Marsh strongly plays down the British role in the establishment of the network of trade treaties that was instrumental in the liberalization of the 1860s (if any country played the leading role, it was France). Similarly, it is difficult to attribute the return to protection in the late 1870s to the lack of a hegemonic power. If it had any effect at all, the system of international relations dampened the protectionist reaction via the network of trade treaties and the most favored nation (MFN) clause. Foreign policy motivations sometimes did influence negotiations for treaties, either speeding them up (Great Powers had some clout versus smaller countries) or retarding them (for instance, the breakdown of negotiations between France and Italy in 1887 was a step in a long-term realignment of Italian alliances toward Germany). In the overwhelming majority of cases, however, trade treaties were determined by the demands of domestic exporters. They needed access to foreign markets, which could only be gained through reciprocal concessions for other trading partners.

The lobbying by domestic producers of import-competing goods (the political economy of tariffs) is the most frequently given reason for protection. Interests can organize by sector (the iron and steel industry, wheat growing) or by factor (land, labor, capital). In the former, most common, case, the lobby allegedly represents all employees of the sector. Political action is nevertheless subject to the risk of free riding (i.e., shirking by potential members, who can profit from the lobby's activity without committing themselves). Thus, all other things being equal, the smaller the number of potential members, the easier the lobby is to organize and the more effective it will be. Consequently, organizations of consumers, potentially interested in free trade, have long been weak relative to producers' lobbies. Indeed there were no associations of consumers in nineteenth-century Europe, whereas producers lobbies, such as the German Bund der Landwirte (Agrarian League, established in 1893), were quite well organized and influential. According to a well-established tradition in many Continental countries, some producers' lobbies literally dictated the trade policy, at the expense of consumers and of other, weaker producers. The return to protection in the 1880s in Germany and Italy was the outcome of a bargain between cereal-growing Junkers and heavy industry. Wilhelmian Germany was called the "empire of rye and iron," although small-scale livestock producers also gained from protection. France followed this pattern, although bureaucrats had more power in the implementations of guidelines and, most crucially, in the negotiations of treaties than in Italy or Germany.

The United Kingdom is the paramount example of the alternative model of organization of interests. Parties represented factors of production, such as land (Tories), capital (Whigs), and labor (Labour), and thus trade policies were part of their agendas. The issue played a major political role on two occasions. In the early 1840s the Anti–Corn Law League, organized and funded by Manchester cotton industrialists, waged a strong campaign against the duty on wheat. It succeeded because the Tories split on the issue and lost power for a long period. Trade policy resurfaced as a major political issue in the late 1890s, when the movement for fair trade campaigned for reciprocity (i.e., the raising of duties on imports from countries that taxed British imports). This proposal became the main point in the Tory manifesto for the 1906 elections, but the party was clearly defeated.

Daniel Verdier argues that these differences among countries in the organization of interests reflect the features of the political systems, such as the loyalty of parliamentarians to their own party and the interest of voters in trade policy. Nevertheless, these characteristics, especially the latter, depend on economic features, most notably the mobility of factors among sectors. A specialized worker has little scope for changing sectors, and is thus more likely than an unskilled worker to join an industry lobby. Vice versa, sectorally mobile factors would more likely gather in major parties.

It is thus likely that all three factors—international relations, the need for revenue, and lobbying—contributed to shape trade policy in the nineteenth century. Their relative importance changed among countries and over time. More work, both with in-depth case studies and comparative statistical analysis, is needed to assess which cause prevailed.

See also **Trade and Economic Growth.**

BIBLIOGRAPHY

Bairoch, Paul. "European Trade Policy, 1815–1914." In *Cambridge Economic History of Europe,* edited by Peter Mathias and Sidney Pollard, vol. 8, pp. 1–160. Cambridge, U.K., 1989.

Gerschenkron, Alexander. *Bread and Democracy in Germany.* 1943. Reprint, with a new foreword by Charles S. Maier, Ithaca, N.Y., 1989.

Irwin, Douglas A. *Against the Tide: An Intellectual History of Free Trade.* Princeton, N.J., 1996.

Kitchen, Martin. *The Political Economy of Germany, 1815–1914.* London, 1978.

Lake, David A. *Power, Protection, and Free Trade: International Sources of U.S. Commercial Strategy, 1887–1939.* Ithaca, N.Y., 1988.

List, Friedrich. *The National System of Political Economy.* Translated by W. O. Henderson. London and Totowa, N.J., 1975. Originally published, 1841.

Marsh, Peter T. *Bargaining on Europe: Britain and the First Common Market, 1860–1892.* New Haven, Conn., 1999.

Olson, Mancur. *The Logic of Collective Action: Public Goods and the Theory of Groups.* Cambridge, Mass., 1971.

Ricardo, David. *Principles of Political Economy and Taxation.* London, 1817. Reprint, as volume 1 of *The Works and Correspondence of David Ricardo.* Cambridge, U.K., 1951.

Smith, Adam. *An Enquiry into the Nature and Causes of the Wealth of Nations.* 1776. Reprint, New York, 1965.

Smith, Michael Stephen. *Tariff Reform in France, 1860–1900.* Ithaca, N.Y., 1980.

Verdier, Daniel. *Democracy and International Trade: Britain, France, and the United States, 1860–1990.* Princeton, N.J., 1994.

Webb, Steven B. "Agricultural Protection in Wilhelminian Germany: Forging an Empire with Pork and Rye." *Journal of Economic History* 42, no. 2 (1982): 309–326.

GIOVANNI FEDERICO

TABLE 1

Regions of Europe with Protestant majority populations (Nominal Protestants as identified in national census)

Denmark (1880)	99.6%
Finland (1888)	98.1%
Germany	
Bremen (1910)	91.6%
Hamburg (1910)	92.6%
Hanover (1861)	95.7%
Hesse-Cassel (1866)	83.1%
Mecklenburg (1860)	99.3%
Oldenburg (1861)	74.6%
Prussia (1885)	64.4%
Saxony (1861)	89.1%
Saxe-Coburg-Gotha (1910)	97.8%
Netherlands (1879)	61.6%
Sweden and Norway (1875)	99.9%
Switzerland (1888)	59.0%
United Kingdom	
England and Wales (1887)	95.6%
Scotland (1887)	91.8%

PROTESTANTISM. Protestantism was one of the three varieties of Christianity in nineteenth-century Europe, along with Catholicism and Orthodox Christianity. The name originally referred to the protest made by Lutheran leaders at the Diet of Speyer in 1529, and in central Europe the term *Protestant* was still used as a synonym for Lutherans, but in general usage the term had come to include all Christians who rejected the authority of the pope and insisted upon the primacy of the Bible.

Protestantism was the dominant religion of northern Europe in the nineteenth century. The states of northern Germany and Scandinavia plus England, Wales, and Scotland all reported on national censuses that more than 90 percent of the population was Protestant. A majority of the population in Switzerland and the Netherlands was also Protestant, although such figures counted nominal Protestants (by birth and baptism, but not by practice). In addition, large Protestant minorities (20 percent of the population or more) existed in some of the states of southern Germany (including Baden and Bavaria), plus Hungary and Ireland.

Across southern Europe (which was overwhelmingly Catholic) and in most of eastern Europe (where the dominant faith might be Catholicism, Orthodox Christianity, or Islam in a few regions of the Balkans), Protestantism included but a tiny portion of society. It is also noteworthy that some countries with small Protestant minorities such as Catholic France (1.8 percent after the loss of Alsace and part of Lorraine to Germany in 1871) or Orthodox Russia (2.6 percent), the Protestant minority sometimes exercised a disproportionate influence, as members of the Calvinist *Église Reformée* (Reformed Church) did in France and the Baltic Lutheran population did in imperial Russia. But in many Catholic countries, especially Portugal, Spain, and Italy, the Protestant community was especially tiny (0.01 percent of the population of Portugal) and exercised extremely little influence. The Spanish census of 1884 identified 32,435 priests and 14,592 nuns but only 6,654 Protestants. Indeed, the Spanish constitution of 1876 still restricted freedom of religion for Protestants, who were allowed to worship, but only in private; any public announcement of Protestant worship was illegal. And the Vatican still held, as Pope Pius IX underscored in the *Syllabus of Errors* (1864), that it was wrong to believe that "Protestantism is nothing more than another form of the same true Christian religion, in which form it is given to please God equally as in the Catholic Church."

The Protestant population of nineteenth-century Europe belonged to a large variety of different churches. The three principal varieties of Protestantism were (1) Lutheranism, concentrated in Germanic central Europe and Scandinavia, where more than 90 percent of the population was typically Lutheran; (2) the Reformed Churches, which derived chiefly from the teachings of John Calvin, notably the Dutch Reformed Church, the Église Reformée in France and Switzerland, and the Presbyterian Church in Scotland; and (3) the Anglican churches of the British Isles. Significant Calvinist minorities had been scattered around Europe by the Huguenot diaspora of the sixteenth and seventeenth centuries (in Piedmont, Prussia, and especially Hungary), but few Anglicans were found on the Continent.

Small minorities of other Protestant churches existed in many countries. Baptist Churches (which also dated back to the Reformation), for example, reported in 1905 that they had 200 members in Spain, 1,400 in Italy, 2,300 in France, 9,800 in Austria-Hungary, 24,000 in Russia, 32,500 in Germany, and 427,000 in the United Kingdom. Methodist Churches (founded in Britain in the eighteenth century as an Arminian-Calvinist derivative of Anglicanism aimed at the poorer classes) reported similar numbers in 1908 (1,700 in France, 3,700 in Italy, 24,900 in Germany, and 521,000 in Britain). Even smaller populations of other Protestant churches had local strengths.

THEOLOGICAL AND ECCLESIASTIC PROTESTANTISM

The existence of so many varieties of European Protestantism means that there was no single or simple Protestant theology, nor any universal ecclesiastic organization. Instead, many individual confessions (or professions) of the faith existed, and churches were often still identified by the name of their confession—such as the Augsburg Confession of Lutherans or the La Rochelle Confession of Calvinists. In general, however, Protestant churches stressed the centrality of the Bible (the doctrine of *sola scriptura* [by scripture alone]), which individuals were expected to read and study for themselves and in whose message they must have absolute faith. Faith was the basis of salvation (the doctrine of *sola fide* [by faith alone]), and this produced significant differences between Protestant and Catholic subcultures.

Protestant emphasis upon reading the Bible in order to be saved led to noteworthy differences between Protestant and Catholic communities. In order to read, Protestants typically placed greater stress upon universal education and literacy. In France, for example, there had long been a tradition of excellent schools run by the Catholic Church, and both the French Revolution and Napoleon had done much to systematize these schools. But this school system served only a minor-

TABLE 2

Regions of Europe with Protestant minority populations	
Austria-Hungary	
Austria (1880)	1.8%
Hungary (1880)	20.2%
Belgium (1889)	0.2%
France (1881)	1.8%
Germany	
Alsace-Lorraine (1885)	20.0%
Baden (1885)	35.4%
Bavaria (1885)	28.1%
Ireland (1881)	23.4%
Italy (1881)	0.2%
Luxembourg (1885)	1.1%
Portugal (1881)	0.01%
Rumania (1887)	0.3%
Russia (1886)	2.6%
Serbia (1884)	0.04%
Spain (1887)	0.04%

ity of the population, and many Catholics opposed the creation of a public system of mandatory, universal education; consequently, the officials at the Ministry of Public Instruction who created the French school system under the Ferry laws of the 1879 and 1885 were predominantly Protestants. An important corollary to the Protestant insistence upon universal education was that Protestant communities were typically more insistent upon the education of girls, thereby contributing significantly (if unintentionally) to the rise of nineteenth-century feminism.

The Bible-based faith of Protestants produced other noteworthy differences. Many Protestants argued that Christian beliefs not found in the Bible were papal inventions with no true basis in the faith. Thus many Protestant churches rejected the cult of the saints that had evolved with Christianity, and many specifically rejected the centuries of Catholic Mariology (favoring a doctrine of *solus Christus* [Christ alone]). When Pope Pius IX promulgated, in the papal bull *Ineffabilis Deus* of 1854, the dogma of the Immaculate Conception (that Mary was, from the moment of her conception, without the stain of original sin) and insisted that this must be "steadfastly believed by all the faithful," many Protestants scorned the doctrine. While Anglicans concluded that the Immaculate Conception was "a legitimate development of early church teaching," Calvinists flatly rejected it.

In matters of ecclesiastic structure, most Protestants rejected the hierarchical structure of Catholicism, starting with the authority of the pope; the

TABLE 3

Lutheran populations of northern Germany compared with other religions

Hamburg (1910 census)

Lutherans	930,071 (92.6%)
Calvinists	3,942
Catholics	51,036
Jews	19,472

Hanover (1861 census)

Lutherans	1,555,448 (82.4%)
Calvinists	97,018
Catholics	221,576
Jews	12,085

Hesse-Cassel (1866 census)

Lutherans	236,290 (32.2%)
Calvinists	373,595
Catholics	107,695
Jews	16,358

Mecklenburg-Schwerin (1860 census)

Lutherans	537,986 (99.5%)
Calvinists	168
Catholics	882
Jews	1,413

Oldenburg (1861 census)

Lutherans	191,877 (65.4%)
Calvinists	1,369
United Evangelicals	25,916
Catholics	72,939
Jews	1,497

Saxony (1861 census)

Lutherans	2,175,392 (97.9%)
Calvinists	4,515
Catholics	41,363
Jews	1,555

Note: The Prussian data for 1861 combined Lutherans and Calvinists into 11 million Protestants, although 27,000 "other Christians" (chiefly Mennonites) were noted. Prussia was slightly more than one-third Catholic, because of the annexation of Polish territories.

Protestant authority was the Bible, and it did not mention a pope. Protestants who most accepted hierarchical governance (such as Anglicans) adopted an episcopal system that recognized the authority of a bishop; more Protestants favored a presbyterian system governed by an elected church council (or consistory), in some cases supplemented by the periodic assembly of an elected synod; those Protestants least agreeable to hierarchical authority favored a congregational system, in which the members of a congregation essentially governed themselves.

The combination of Biblical authority and limited church authority created distinctive developments in nineteenth-century European Protestantism.

Some Protestants concluded that individuals could find salvation through Bible study without the assistance a priesthood, such as the doctrine of *libre examen* held by many Continental Calvinists. Others, especially in Germany, turned this private study of the Bible into the scholarly field of Biblical criticism, producing some of the most controversial books of the century such as the French philosopher and historian Ernest Renan's *Life of Jesus* (1863). Protestants who were most resistant to ecclesiastic authority, such as the Calvinistic Methodists in England and Wales, put the control of the church pulpit in the hands of deacons, who engaged a preacher for a number of Sundays (often less than half of the year) and employed others on an individual basis. Some Methodists still preferred the itinerant preaching of the church's origins and hired no pastor.

The consequences of such distinctions between Protestantism and Catholicism have provoked a number of striking (and often controversial) interpretations of the historical impact of Protestantism. Scholars have linked Protestantism to the rise of European individualism, elective government, democracy, and feminism.

Two of the most debated arguments about Protestantism appeared in the early years of the twentieth century. Max Weber, a German sociologist, launched the "Weber thesis," asserting a strong correlation between Protestantism and the rise of capitalism, in a 1904 work titled *Die protestantische Ethik und der Geist der Kapitalismus* (The Protestant ethic and the spirit of capitalism). Weber argued that the "intramundane asceticism" of Protestantism, which forbade luxury and material self-indulgence, plus a "Protestant ethic" that stressed the virtues of hard work, resulted in great accumulation of capital and hence the dawning of an age of capitalism, which Protestants in government and business encouraged by removing historic barriers to economic development.

Élie Halévy, a French political scientist, produced similar controversy with a 1906 essay, "La naissance du Méthodisme en Angleterre" (The birth of Methodism in England). Halévy argued that the evangelical and fundamentalist Protestant churches (especially the Methodist Church), which won significant popularity with the lower classes in the late eighteenth and early nineteenth centuries, taught an ethic of the acceptance of the authority of the state and deference to the upper classes so effectively that it explains why Karl Marx's expectations of class warfare were not fulfilled by the British working class.

DECHRISTIANIZATION AND SECULARIZATION

Analyses such as the Weber and Halévy theses underscore the continuing importance of Protestantism in European civilization in 1914. Nonetheless, Protestantism (and Christianity in general) became significantly less central to European society during the nineteenth century. This decline continued a trend that was already well-established in the eighteenth century and that accelerated dramatically during the twentieth century. Historians have used two terms (both controversial) to describe this trend: *dechristianization* and *secularization*. By any name, religion became less central in both private and public life during the nineteenth century. This trend was clear to religious leaders who spoke of a need to "rechristianize" Europe. Although the best illustration of this concern among Christian leaders came from a pope (Pope Pius X, in his 1907 decree condemning "modernism," *Lamentabili Sane Exitu* [On a deplorable outcome] lamenting that Europe "rejects the legacy of the human race"), there is no doubt that Protestant pastors shared this concern.

The dechristianization of a significant portion of the educated upper classes of Europe during the Enlightenment—many of whom adopted a "modern paganism," choosing deism, theism, and open religious skepticism or agnosticism—was the prelude to trends accelerated by the French Revolution and industrialization. The term *dechristianization* (more widely used in French than in English) has been adopted to analyze the "revolution against the church" during the 1790s, an experience that had profound effects on the Protestant communities of Languedoc, Alsace, and the Franche-Comté in France, but was also transported by French armies to the Protestant populations of Holland, western Germany, and Switzerland.

The vast social transformations that accompanied Europe's industrialization during the nineteenth century led to another form of dechristianization, in which a significant portion of the urban working class—uprooted from the bonds of traditional rural

society and often living in demoralizing conditions of poverty—abandoned religious participation. These populations were most concentrated (as Weber observed) in predominantly Protestant societies such as Britain and Germany.

Those who abandoned Christian practice and church participation are often seen as lapsed, or nominal, Christians who retained some degree of belief within a secular life, and it is important to recall that Protestant theology generally understood salvation to be contingent upon faith and the Bible, not church attendance. Yet something startling was happening within Protestant communities in nineteenth-century Europe. Whereas church attendance had once been virtually mandatory in many societies, a majority of the population no longer attended (or contributed to) churches.

This startling fact received dramatic public proof in 1851 when the British conducted a survey of church attendance in England, Wales, and Scotland—all societies understood to be more than 90 percent Protestant. The data collected by the churches on Sunday, 31 March 1851, were controversial at the time, and remain so in scholarly debate in the early twenty-first century—only 24.2 percent of the population of England and Wales attended any religious service that morning. Total participating Protestants, from Quakers (14,016) and Unitarians (27,612) to the Church of England (2,371,732), represented just 22.9 percent of the population of England and Wales (not the 95.6 percent claimed). Even if one combined attendance at all church sittings during the day (many churches had three sittings), assuming that no one attended both morning and evening services, only 35 percent of the population participated (34 percent Protestant, 1 percent Catholic).

Church attendance in Scotland was higher (32.7 percent of the population), but still less than one-third of the population. The Scots repeated this survey across the remainder of the century with more alarming results: attendance at religious worship declined steadily, hitting 19.2 percent in 1891 (for all denominations combined); Protestant attendance represented 17.8 percent of the population. Although churches did not sort attendance data by gender, it was also becoming clear that the nonparticipation of large portions of the working

TABLE 4

Christian church attendance in Britain (1851) (Actual attendance in England and Wales on Sunday morning, 30 March 1851)		
Church	Attendance	% of population
Church of England (Anglican)	2,371,732	13.2%
Dissenters		
Methodists (six sects)	679,122	3.8%
Congregationalists	515,071	2.9%
Baptists	353,061	2.0%
Presbyterians (two sects)	126,473	0.7%
Unitarians	27,612	0.2%
Quakers	14,016	0.1%
Other dissenting Protestants	14,655	0.1%
Total Dissenters	1,730,010	9.6%
Total Protestants	4,101,742	22.9%
Catholic	240,792	1.3%
Total Christian	4,342,534	24.2%

SOURCE: "Report on the 1851 Census of Religious Worship," *Parliamentary Papers* (1852–1853), vol. LXXXIX, Table A, pp. clxxvii–clxxix. Reprinted in Chris Cook and Brendan Keith, eds., *British Historical Facts, 1830–1900* (London, 1975), p. 220.

class was disproportionately nonparticipation by men. The churches, despite their notoriously patriarchal structure, leadership, and teachings, were steadily becoming feminized.

A third aspect of the nineteenth-century pattern of dechristianization was the gradual secularization of the rites of passage in life, from civil marriages to unbaptized children and then to civil burial. The entire culture of these life stages was changing, leading even to "the dechristianization of death" (in historian Thomas Kselman's provocative phrase). In 1844 only 2.6 percent of the marriages in England and Wales were civil ceremonies; but the popularity of civil marriage increased sharply in every decade of the century, and by 1901 there were four times as many civil marriages as Catholic marriages, with civil marriages accounting for 15.8 percent of all unions. As late as 1855, there were only nine civil marriages in Scotland during the year; by 1901, the number stood at 1,952 and was doubling every decade. At the other end of life, the Christian doctrine of the resurrection of the body long blocked the adoption of cremation of the deceased, but by the first years of the twentieth century there were active crema-

tion societies in most of the nominally Protestant societies—Britain, Holland, Switzerland, Germany, Denmark, and Sweden. (There were also important cremation societies in France and Italy.)

Discussions of this nineteenth-century pattern of the secularization and dechristianization of daily life often stress the decline of church-based sociability. The urban civilization emerging in Europe provided many competing centers of sociability (such as cafés and music halls); industrial society led many to choose occupational alternatives at the center of their lives, notably trade unions; an age of mass culture produced new enthusiasms in competition with churches for Sunday time, from spectator sports to weekend excursions; the age of representative governments replaced the historic alliance of throne and altar with a world of secular schools, secular daily newspapers, and passionate secular politics (in which the churches were often considered an opponent rather than an ally).

PROTESTANT VITALITY: THE AWAKENING

Signs of the secularization of society reveal only part of the past, however, and a balanced understanding must recognize contrary indications of Protestant vitality. Perhaps the most important sign of the vigor of Protestantism in nineteenth-century Europe was the phenomenon known as "the awakening" (*le réveil* in French-speaking lands and *der Erweckung* to Germans). There had been several "awakenings" in the eighteenth century (such as the Baptist "Great Awakening" in England, 1740–1743). The awakening of the late eighteenth and early nineteenth centuries, like its predecessors, was a period of earnest Evangelicalism, stressing personal piety, Bible study, campaigns for public morality, and dedicated internal missions to convince others of this program.

The foremost examples of the Protestant awakening were Pietism, which originated in Germany and spread to neighboring countries, and Methodism, which began in England and crossed the channel to western Europe. Pietism (c. 1770–1850) began as a reaction against Enlightenment rationalism (especially within the church, in opposition to university-trained enlightened theologians) and free-thinking individualism; it gained further momentum in reaction to the dechristianization of the revolutionary age. The lay preachers who spread Pietism (and the similar Moravianism) did not seek to create new Protestant churches, but to create a new Lutheranism of Evangelical enthusiasm and Christian revival. By the 1850s, thousands of people (chiefly Protestants, but not exclusively) had converted to the faith of the awakening, reinvigorating churches across Germany and Scandinavia.

Similarly, Methodism began within the Anglican faith, among students at Oxford University led by John Wesley (1703–1791). Wesley, who remained closely attached to the doctrines of Anglicanism (although the churches were closed to his preaching), sought a revival of personal religion based on scripture. He spread this evangelistic faith through meetings in the open and traveling lay preachers. (As late as 1909, British Methodist churches employed 2,454 ministers while relying on 19,826 lay preachers.) Several varieties of the Methodist awakening emerged, some more Episcopal, others more deeply Calvinist, and others blending their Calvinist austerity with Arminianism (rejecting the Calvinist doctrine of predestination). In the immediate aftermath of the Napoleonic Wars, Methodist missionaries spread the awakening to western Europe, especially among French and Swiss Protestants.

Missionary zeal became one of the hallmarks of the Protestant awakening. At the height of the French Revolution's campaign of dechristianization, Protestant missionary societies were being founded across western Europe. In Britain, the Methodist Missionary Society (founded 1786), the Baptist Missionary Society (1792), the London (Congregationalist) Missionary Society (1795), and the Anglican Church Missionary Society (1799) were all active during the first French Republic, as was the Netherlands Missionary Society (1797). The transformation of the Wesleyan awakening into the French *réveil* after the battle of Waterloo (1815) led to the creation of the Société Biblique at Paris (1818) and the Société des Missions Evangélique (1822), both authorized by King Louis XVIII.

PROTESTANTISM AND THE STATE

In 1789 Protestant churches in northern Europe were typically closely linked to the state as the established state religion. Although Britain adopted acts of toleration in 1689, 1778, and 1791, the law required that the monarch be Anglican, forbidden to marry outside the faith. By the Test Acts (reformed in 1829), Nonconformist Protestants, Catholics, Jews, and nonbelievers could not take a seat in parliament, attend Oxford or Cambridge University (until 1871), nor hold public office. Twenty-six Anglican bishoprics and archbishoprics bore ex officio membership in the House of Lords. The British extended the same principle to Ireland, establishing a Church of Ireland and thereby excluding Irish Catholics from most aspects of public life. The Roman Catholic Emancipation Act of 1829 and the disestablishment of the Church of Ireland (1869, with enforcement beginning in 1871) changed this intimate bond between church and state, but the Church of England remained the established church throughout the century.

In northern Germany and Scandinavia, the Lutheran Church similarly remained the established state church in 1789. Prussia adopted a program of religious toleration in the eighteenth century, but Lutheranism remained an established religion across the region. In one famous illustration of the importance of established religion, Karl Marx's father (the descendant of a rabbinical Jewish family) was obliged to convert to Lutheranism in order to be admitted to the practice of law. An especially strict Lutheran establishmentarianism was maintained in Denmark and Sweden until the disestablishments of 1848 and 1860.

Conversely, in countries where the Protestant population was a minority and faced similar discrimination (especially Spain and Italy), Protestants typically became leading proponents of the principle of separation of church and state. The Swiss Protestant theologian Alexandre Vinet (1797–1847) became the leading advocate of this principle. Many French Protestants, often influenced by Vinet, founded new churches (the *églises libres*, or "free churches") outside of the national system of churches linked to the state that Napoleon had founded. Pastors from the *églises libres*, such as Edmond de Pressensé (1824–1891), became champions of the separation of church and state; de Pressensé's son, Francis, subsequently became one of the principal authors of the 1905 law separating church and state in France.

Protestant concerns about the relationship between churches and the state intensified after the papal bull *Pastor Aeternus* (1870) proclaimed the doctrine of papal infallibility. Liberal and conservative Protestants alike worried that citizens of the state would have conflicting loyalties. William E. Gladstone, the British prime minister, published a critical pamphlet in 1874 titled *The Vatican Decrees in Their Bearing on Civil Allegiance,* arguing that followers of a religion who must obey their spiritual leader rather than the government had put their loyalty in doubt. Otto von Bismarck, the German chancellor, carried the issue of a conflict between church and state much further. During the Kulturkampf of the 1870s, Bismarck won the adoption of three sets of May Laws (1873–1875), which put churches under strict state supervision.

It was in this climate of opinion that much of the secularization of the nineteenth century occurred. Governments took over historic church roles, creating state-run systems of public schools (often closing church schools) and beginning state-run welfare systems, from public hospitals to state-funded poor relief. Protestants were prominent leaders of these campaigns. In Britain, the Dissenters (non-Anglican Protestants) championed secular schools instead of schools run by the established church. In Germany, Bismarck pioneered the welfare state in the late 1880s. In both France and Germany, one of the most influential voices advocating a welfare system was the Alsatian pastor Johann Friedrich Oberlin (1740–1826).

PROTESTANTS AND REFORM CAMPAIGNS
Protestants, especially evangelical Protestants of the awakening, played noteworthy political roles in nineteenth-century Europe by providing a large portion of the leadership and membership of the morality campaigns in European politics. The antislavery, antiprostitution, and antialcohol movements each owed much to evangelical fervor. While noteworthy members of these campaigns certainly came from Catholic, Jewish, and freethinking Europe, a striking characteristic of each campaign was the role of Protestants.

The campaign against the European slave trade had no leader more ardent and influential than William Wilberforce. Wilberforce was drawn to Methodism in his youth and used his family wealth to help found an evangelical newspaper, the Church Missionary Society, and the Bible Society. His greatest effort, however, came as a founder of the antislavery movement and the member of Parliament (1780–1825) who led the struggle in the House of Commons to abolish the slave trade. Wilberforce's friendship with his Cambridge classmate, William Pitt the Younger, put the antislavery program on the government agenda, and Wilberforce's bill was adopted in 1807 by a vote of 283 to 16.

Similarly, the campaign against legal and regulated prostitution in nineteenth-century Europe had no more effective leader than Josephine Butler. Butler was raised in evangelicalism by her mother and subsequently married an Anglican clergyman. After several years of social work among prostitutes in Liverpool, Butler assumed the leadership of the Ladies National Association for the Repeal of the Contagious Diseases Acts (the laws regulating prostitution) in 1869. Five years later, she toured continental Europe, forming the International Society Against State Regulated Vice to expand her campaign to all countries that legalized prostitution. Butler finally won repeal in Britain in 1886.

A third morality campaign to which many Protestants devoted themselves with exceptional fervor was that against alcohol, whether the campaign was called antialcoholism, temperance, or teetotalism. Many prominent Catholics supported this campaign, such as Cardinal Manning, but Protestants were drawn to the battle in dramatic numbers. Many churches (especially Methodists and Baptists) adopted temperance as church doctrine. And when the National Temperance League in Britain (founded 1842) organized to demand that Parliament act, 13,584 Protestant clergymen signed the petition to Parliament.

Protestants in other countries organized parallel campaigns. Protestants founded temperance societies in Norway in 1836 and in Sweden in 1837. The Swiss Croix bleue (Blue Cross) became a model for Protestant temperance movements in French-speaking Europe. By the eve of World War I, there were five temperance societies in Denmark, six each in Holland and Sweden, and twelve in Germany.

See also **Catholicism; Jews and Judaism; Secularization.**

BIBLIOGRAPHY

Baubérot, Jean. *Le retour des Huguenots: La vitalité protestante, XIXe—XXe siècle.* Paris, 1985.

Bigler, Robert M. *The Politics of German Protestantism: The Rise of the Protestant Church Elite in Prussia, 1815–1848.* Berkeley and Los Angeles, 1972.

Brown, Callum G. *The Death of Christian Britain: Understanding Secularisation, 1800–2000*. London, 2001.

Encrevé, André. *Les protestants en France de 1800 à nos jours: Histoire d'une réintégration*. Paris, 1985.

Gilbert, Alan D. *Religion and Society in Industrial England: Church, Chapel, and Social Change, 1740–1914*. London, 1976.

Green, S. J. D. *Religion in the Age of Decline: Organisation and Experience in Industrial Yorkshire, 1870–1920*. Cambridge, U.K., 1996.

Hilton, Boyd. *The Age of Atonement: The Influence of Evangelicalism on Social and Economic Thought, 1785–1865*. Oxford, U.K., 1988.

Hope, Nicholas. *German and Scandinavian Protestantism, 1700–1918*. Oxford, U.K., 1995.

Inglis, Kenneth Stanley. "Patterns of Religious Worship in 1851." *Journal of Ecclesiastical History* 11 (1960): 74–86.

———. *Churches and the Working Class in Victorian England*. London, 1963.

McGrath, Alister E., and Darren C. Marks, eds. *The Blackwell Companion to Protestantism*. Malden, Mass., 2004.

McLeod, Hugh. *Religion and the People of Western Europe, 1789–1989*. 2nd ed. Oxford, U.K., 1997.

McLeod, Hugh, ed. *European Religion in the Age of the Great Cities, 1830–1930*. London, 1995.

McLeod, Hugh, and Werner Ustorf, eds. *The Decline of Christendom in Western Europe, 1750–2000*. Cambridge, U.K., 2003.

Rémond, René. *Religion and Society in Modern Europe*. Translated by Antonia Nevill. Oxford, U.K., 1999.

Shanahan, William O. *German Protestants Face the Social Question*. Notre Dame, Ind., 1954.

Snell, K. D. M., and Paul S. Ell. *Rival Jerusalems: The Geography of Victorian Religion*. Cambridge, U.K., 2000.

Watts, Michael R. *The Dissenters*. 2 vols. Oxford, U.K., 1979–1995.

Wintle, Michael. *Pillars of Piety: Religion in the Netherlands in the Nineteenth Century, 1813–1901*. Hull, U.K., 1987.

STEVEN C. HAUSE

PROUDHON, PIERRE-JOSEPH (1809–1865), French journalist and socialist.

Pierre-Joseph Proudhon became famous in 1840 when his book *Q'est-ce que la propriété?* (What is property?) attacked property and embraced anarchism. From this date until his death in 1865,

Proudhon was a highly visible participant in debates about religion, morals, economics, and politics. Never effective in the public sphere, Proudhon is best known for his writings, which are voluminous. As one observer noted, when Proudhon found himself with pen in hand, he seemed to have a fit of eloquence.

Proudhon was born in Battant, a modest *quartier* in the city of Besançon, bordering the River Doubs. He was proud of his humble origins, reminding people throughout his life that he was (as he put it in 1855) "raised in the customs, the mores, and the thought of the proletariat." Proudhon attended the Collège Royale de Besançon on a scholarship while an adolescent, and as a young man received an award that allowed him to spend several years (1838–1841) studying in Paris and attending the lectures of prominent intellectuals such as Jules Michelet and the economist Jérôme-Adolphe Blanqui. He always insisted, however, that his real education took place in the workshop, where both manual and mental skills were learned. As a young man he worked as a printer, and for several years (1836–1843) operated with some friends a printing house that lost money and left him heavily in debt. He also spent a number of years (1843–1847) working for a shipping firm in Lyon, which exposed him to various aspects of business and manufacturing.

Proudhon's notoriety resulted from his published writings, which trenchantly analyzed socioeconomic inequities and stridently criticized the selfish egoism of the wealthy classes. His engaging satires of governments and the wealthy came from a characteristic leftist moralism, what Jean Maitron has called a "native sensibility to injustice." Proudhon believed in an immanent morality that combined a secularized version of Christian morality and a modified version of republican virtue. When Proudhon adopted the label "anarchist" in 1840, he insisted that society be governed by a social morality that would lead men to recognize the dignity of their fellow citizens and to put aside their personal interests for the larger social good.

To the provocative question posed by the title of his 1840 book, "What is property?" Proudhon famously responded: "It is theft!" His position was, in fact, not as radical as this readily recalled

Pierre-Joseph Proudhon and His Children in 1853. Painting by Gustave Courbet, 1865. Musée de la Ville de Paris, Musée du Petit-Palais, France/Bridgeman Art Library

epigram might suggest. What Proudhon attacked was property that provided an income without requiring any labor; the kind of property that gave the unproductive "idle class" income in the form of interest and rent. Proudhon carefully distinguished this "property" from "possessions," by which he meant the land, dwelling, and tools necessary for day-to-day existence. For this latter type of ownership, Proudhon had the highest respect.

Proudhon's attack on property was part of his more wide-ranging proposal to create "progressive associations" for the educational and economic benefit of workers, and for the more general transformation of society. He believed that these associations would promote fraternal ties among workers by combining work and education in the workshop. He also believed that these associations would lead to a peaceful socioeconomic transformation:

they would push aside the idle property owners who inappropriately skimmed off profits; they would introduce a "fair" evaluation of goods (not based on the "arbitrary" system of supply and demand); and they would stimulate workers to be more productive because they would be working for themselves. Unlike other associative socialists of his generation, however, Proudhon insisted that these associations must avoid community, by which he meant government ownership of property and centralized control of economic and social decision-making. In 1846, Proudhon referred to this formula for socioeconomic justice as "mutualism." And since this time, "mutualist anarchism" has been a shorthand label for the antistatist position that calls for education and socioeconomic reform within the context of workers' associations and that recommends the avoidance of revolution and other forms of violent confrontation.

Proudhon's commitment to mutualist anarchism was tested during the French Second Republic. Proudhon participated in the Paris uprising of February 1848, composed what he termed the "first republican proclamation" of the new Republic, and was elected to the Constituent Assembly in June 1848. He quickly became disenchanted with the political reforms advocated by the new government, however, arguing that socioeconomic reform was more important and should be given priority. He proposed, more concretely, the establishment of a new bank to provide credit at very low interest and to issue "exchange notes" that would circulate in lieu of money based on gold. In early 1849, he established a Bank of the People to put this reform into action, but it quickly failed. He was more successful in his journalism. The masthead of one of his papers, *Le Représentant du Peuple,* stated his goal succinctly: "What is the producer in actual society? Nothing. What should he be? Everything."

Proudhon was shocked by the violence of the June Days (1848). He blamed the forces of reaction for the uprising, but he did not approve of the violent nature of the insurrection. His journalism was unrelentingly critical of both the Jacobin Left and the government. In March 1849, he was prosecuted for his newspaper attacks on the new president of the Republic, Louis-Napoleon Bonaparte, and sentenced to three years in prison. He published four books while in prison, and continued to write extensively during the 1850s and early 1860s. The books of these years built upon his vision of mutualist anarchism, but expanded to include support for regional organizations and federalism in what was, in effect, a geographical extension of his ideals.

Proudhon's elegant satires of the idle rich and his mordant criticisms of the expanding, intruding, and controlling state were widely influential before World War I. Opponents of Karl Marx in the First International; Italian, Spanish, and Swiss anarchists of the late nineteenth century struggling to gain benefits for workers; and federalists, regionalists, and syndicalists in France and beyond; all responded favorably to Proudhon's indignant attacks of coercive, bureaucratic, authoritarian institutions and his nonviolent proposals for socioeconomic reform.

See also **Anarchism; First International; France; Socialism.**

BIBLIOGRAPHY

Ansart, Pierre. *Naissance de l'anarchisme: Esquisse d'une explication sociologique du proudhonisme.* Paris, 1970.

Haubtmann, Pierre. *Pierre-Joseph Proudhon: Genèse d'un antithéiste.* Paris, 1969.

———. *Pierre-Joseph Proudhon: Sa vie et sa pensée, 1809–1849.* Paris, 1982.

Hoffman, Robert. *Revolutionary Justice: The Social and Political Theory of P.-J. Proudhon.* Urbana, Ill., 1972.

Ritter, Alan. *The Political Thought of Pierre-Joseph Proudhon.* Princeton, N.J., 1969.

Vincent, K. Steven. *Pierre-Joseph Proudhon and the Rise of French Republican Socialism.* New York, 1984.

Voyenne, Bernard. *Le fédéralisme de P. J. Proudhon.* Paris, 1973.

K. STEVEN VINCENT

PRUSSIA. The kingdom of Prussia encompassed the ensemble of lands ruled from Berlin by the Hohenzollern dynasty. With the invasion of Silesia in 1740 and its retention through three wars, Prussia Challenged the hegemony of the Austrian Habsburgs in German Europe and emerged as a major Continental power. The expansion of French power under the emperor Napoleon I (r. 1804–1814/15) led to a catastrophic defeat in 1806, but Prussia was one of the chief beneficiaries of the territorial settlements agreed at the Congress of Vienna in 1814–1815. In the 1860s, it was Prussia that drove the unification of the German states (excluding Austria) and the foundation of the German Empire of 1871. With the collapse of the Hohenzollern monarchy in 1918, Prussia survived as one of the *Länder* (federal states) of the Weimar Republic, but its autonomy was severely curtailed in 1932, when a conservative coup deposed the Prussian administration. The state of Prussia was formally abolished by order of the Allied Control Council in Berlin on 25 February 1947.

FROM THE FRENCH REVOLUTION TO THE CONGRESS OF VIENNA

Prussian foreign policy during the Revolutionary era was dominated by the quest for territorial gains. Having initially welcomed the news of upheaval in Paris, Prussia joined Austria in invading France in 1792. When the coalition forces were stopped in their tracks at the Battle of Valmy (20 September 1792), however, the Prussians lost interest in fighting France and focused instead on securing territorial gains at Poland's expense. Under the Prusso-Russian agreement known as the Second Partition of Poland (23 January 1793), Prussia annexed the commercially important cities of Danzig and Thorn and a triangle of territory plugging the cleft between Silesia and East Prussia. The Third Partition (agreed between Austria, Russia, and Prussia on 24 October 1795) extinguished what remained of the Polish Commonwealth and brought Berlin a further tranche of territory including the ancient capital of Warsaw. With these gains secured, the Prussians signed the Peace of Basel with the French Directory on 5 April 1795.

Prussia benefited from the territorial restructuring imposed by France on the German lands in 1797–1803, acquiring a brace of secularized bishoprics. In 1806, however, King Frederick William III (r. 1797–1840) allowed himself to be goaded by Napoleon into declaring war on France without first securing the support of another major power. At the Battles of Jena and Auerstedt (14 October 1806), Prussia suffered a shattering defeat. Napoleon imposed a weighty war indemnity and reduced the kingdom to a territorial rump: Brandenburg, Pomerania (excluding the Swedish part), Silesia, and East Prussia, plus the corridor of land that had been acquired by Frederick the Great (r. 1740–1786) in the course of the First Partition of Poland (1772).

In the aftermath of 1806, a new generation of reforming bureaucrats emboldened by the scale of the defeat took the helm and transformed virtually every branch of the Prussian state. The two dominant figures were Heinrich Friedrich Karl vom und zum Stein and Karl August von Hardenberg, both non-Prussians by birth, but the support of the king, Frederick William III, was also crucial. Thematic ministries replaced the chaotic departmental system of the old regime state; new educational institutions were established at the primary, secondary, and tertiary levels; the system of subject rural tenures was abolished, so that peasants were transformed from subjects of their noble landlords into "free citizens of the state" (though elements of the old "feudal" system, such as manorial jurisdictions, survived until 1848); restrictions on the purchase and sale of land and on the practice of skilled trades were dismantled. Prussia's Jews, a minority of rightless aliens subject to special levies and restrictions, were emancipated (though the right to occupy public office was as yet withheld). There were also important changes to the structure of the army, including the introduction of a more meritocratic system of promotions, the creation of a citizens' militia to serve alongside units of the line, and the development of a better coordinated and more flexible command structure. Some of these innovations proved immensely influential. Nineteenth-century British and American educators took an interest in Prussia's reformed school system, which produced literacy levels unmatched in most of the Western world. The general staff system pioneered by the military reformers was later widely emulated, and the Friedrich-Wilhelms-Universität established by Wilhelm von Humboldt in Berlin in 1810 was an influential prototype of the modern humanist university. In contrast, King Frederick William III did not honor his undertaking, reiterated at various points during the struggle against Napoleon, to create a unified territorial assembly. This unredeemed pledge was later a focal point for liberal dissent.

In the Wars of Liberation (1813–1815), the Prussians joined Russia and Austria in ousting Napoleon from Germany. Eager to restore their reputation and earn a generous share of the victors' spoils, the Prussians were the most active and aggressive element within the composite Allied command. In the decisive summer battles of 15–18 June 1815, they played a crucial role, bearing the brunt of the French attack at Ligny on 15 June and arriving at Waterloo on 18 June in time to open up the French rear at Plancenoit and stabilize the Duke of Wellington's crumbling left flank. At the Congress of Vienna (1814–1815), Prussia secured the duchy of Posen/Poznań (though the other Polish lands sequestered in the second and third partitions were lost), the northern half of the kingdom of Saxony, the Swedish-ruled rump of western Pomerania, and a vast tract of Rhenish and Westphalian territory reaching from Hanover in the east to the Netherlands and France in the west.

FROM RESTORATION TO REVOLUTION

Throughout this period, Prussia was one of thirty-nine member states of the "German Confederation" (Deutscher Bund), a loose association of independent states with the minimum in central institutions. The Hohenzollern kingdom was now a colossus that stretched across the north of Germany, broken only by one gap, forty kilometers wide at its narrowest point, where the territories of Hanover, Brunswick, and Hesse-Cassel separated the Prussian "Province of Saxony" from the Prussian "Province of Westphalia." The consequences for Prussia's (and Germany's) nineteenth-century political and economic development were momentous.

The Rhineland was destined to become one of the powerhouses of European industrialization and economic growth, a development entirely unforeseen by the negotiators at Vienna, who assigned little weight to economic factors when they redrew the map of Germany. The divided structure of the new Prussia, with its two large territorial blocks in east and west, meant that Berlin was bound to work toward the political and commercial integration of the German states. Finally, Prussia's massive presence in the Rhineland meant that it carried responsibility for the defense of western Germany against France. The lesser states of the south— Baden, Württemberg, and Bavaria—thus tended to look to Berlin for security during the intermittent French invasion panics of the post-Napoleonic era. None of these factors made it inevitable that Prussia would come to dominate a unified Germany, but in combination they tilted the scale in Berlin's favor.

The political leaders in Berlin did not pursue a pro-unification policy as such after 1815, but they consistently sought to extend Prussian influence in Germany and thereby qualify Austria's hegemonic position within the Confederation. The most successful initiative of this kind was the German Customs Union (Zollverein) that came into effect on 1 January 1834. The fruit of years of painstaking Prussian diplomacy, the Union incorporated the majority of Germans outside Austria, which was excluded from membership. The Union did not contribute in any direct sense to German unification—it was never an effective tool for the exercise of Prussian political influence over the lesser states. Nevertheless, it played an important formative role in the evolution of Berlin's "German policy," encouraging ministers and officials to think in an authentically German compass and to

combine the pursuit of specifically Prussian benefits with the building of consensus and the mediation of interests among the other German states.

On the domestic political scene, the postwar years brought a conservative crackdown. The Carlsbad Decrees, issued in 1819 after the sensational political assassination by a radical student of the dramatist August Friedrich Ferdinand von Kotzebue in Mannheim, imposed stringent censorship and surveillance measures. A number of prominent nationalist and liberal "demagogues" were arrested. The conservatives found it impossible, however, to halt or reverse the processes of change that had gained momentum during the upheavals of the Napoleonic Era. The acquisition of the Rhenish provinces brought an element of turmoil and dissent that altered the kingdom's political chemistry. Censorship proved inadequate in the face of a massive expansion in critical print and utterance. At the heart of liberal dissent was the demand for the parliament and constitution promised in 1815. Religion was another area where dissent and fragmentation were especially pronounced. The acquisition of the Rhenish lands brought a greatly enlarged Catholic minority under the authority of the Protestant administration in Berlin. There was a bitter dispute between the Prussian authorities and the Catholic Church over Catholic-Protestant mixed marriages in 1838–1840 and determined resistance in Silesia to the imposition of a new liturgy for the territorial Protestant church (known as the Church of the Prussian Union). In the 1840s these concerns were amplified by the deepening economic malaise associated with the "Social Question." Food riots multiplied, and in 1844 the brutal suppression by the military of a revolt by weavers in Silesia sent shock waves across the kingdom.

Like most other continental European states, Prussia experienced violent unrest during the revolutions of 1848. The highpoint was reached on the night of 18 March, when over three hundred citizens were killed in clashes with troops in Berlin. The king, Frederick William IV (r. 1840–1861), responded by ordering the army to leave the capital—a highly controversial decision at the time— and expressing his solidarity with the aims of the revolution. Leading liberals were appointed to ministerial posts and the new administration began work on a liberal constitution. The victory of the liberals was short-lived, however. Fighting on the streets continued into the summer, as the liberals attempted to stabilize their gains in the face of calls for a more radical "social" revolution. Collaboration between the monarch and his "March ministers" became increasingly difficult. On 9 November 1848, the national assembly in Berlin was adjourned by order of the king and transferred to the city of Brandenburg, where it was formally dissolved on 5 December. On the same day, in an astute move designed to neutralize opposition, the government announced the promulgation of a new constitution.

Often seen as a failure, the revolution of 1848 in fact produced a new point of departure for Prussia. The kingdom now had a constitution, which would remain in force (with various amendments) until 1918. It also had a territorial legislature. The reform-conservative governments of the 1850s introduced many of the changes the liberals had been calling for since the 1840s, such as the removal of restrictions on banking and investment, the modernization of the tax system, public infrastructural investment, and the abolition of manorial jurisdictions. The 1850s also witnessed a steep rise in industrial investment and production, especially in the Rhineland and the manufacturing zone around Berlin.

GERMAN UNIFICATION

During the upheavals of 1848, the Prussian government made tentative efforts to consolidate Prussian leadership within a more cohesive union of German states. Frederick William IV refused to accept the German national crown offered to him by the Frankfurt Parliament in April 1849. At the same time, however, he supported the creation of a short-lived Prussian-dominated association of twenty-six German states known as the "Erfurt Union" (because deputies elected in the member territories formed a parliament that convened in the city of Erfurt). Russia and France supported Austria in opposing this initiative and the Prussians abandoned the union project in November 1850, promising, in an agreement known as the "Punctation of Olmütz," to work together with the Austrians in rebuilding the German Confederation. For some contemporaries—including Otto von Bismarck—

Olmütz brought the realization that the German national question would only be resolved through armed conflict.

The plausibility of this view was reinforced in 1859 by the first Italian War of Unification, when the Piedmontese succeeded (with French help) in defeating the Austrians and uniting most of the Italian peninsula. After a mobilization in the Rhineland (to deter opportunist incursions by Emperor Napoleon III [r. 1852–1871]) revealed inadequacies in the Prussian military establishment, Prince William (standing in as regent for his incapacitated older brother) and the army chiefs Helmuth Karl Bernhard von Moltke and Albrecht Theodor Emil von Roon resolved to launch a program of military reforms. These were opposed by the parliament on financial and constitutional grounds and as the political crisis deepened, Otto von Bismarck was called in as Prussian minister president on 23 September 1862. Having tried without success to divide and win over the opposition, Bismarck opted for a program of head-on confrontation. In February 1864 he took Prussia into war (at Austria's side) against Denmark over Schleswig and Holstein without securing war credits from the parliament.

In the aftermath of the Danish war, Bismarck exploited disagreements over the military occupation of Schleswig and Holstein to engineer a war against Austria and its German allies in the summer of 1866. Prussia's success—sealed at the Battle of Königgrätz/Sadowa on 3 July 1866 and the Peace of Prague on 23 August—was greeted with elation by the Prussian public and did much to mollify the liberal opposition. Prussia annexed Schleswig and Holstein, along with part of Hesse-Darmstadt and the entirety of Hanover, Hesse-Cassel, Nassau, and the city of Frankfurt, all of which had sided with Austria in the war of 1866. The German Confederation was dissolved to make way for the Prussian-dominated "North German Confederation," whose parliamentary constitution went into operation on 1 July 1867. Prussia now emerged as the clear victor in the century-long struggle for hegemony in German Europe.

Exactly when and how Bismarck planned to integrate the still-independent southern German states remains controversial. He seems always to have been aware that the threat of war with France would awaken fears of invasion in the south and thereby undermine their objections to union with the north. Tensions with France over a German candidacy for the vacant throne of Spain provided him with the opportunity he needed. Having allowed the resulting crisis to escalate to the point where the French issued a declaration of war (19 July 1870), Bismarck exploited the mood of solidarity generated by a highly successful German campaign to secure first alliances and later treaties of union with the southern states. The new German Empire, incorporating all the German states except Austria, was proclaimed at Versailles on 18 January 1871.

PRUSSIA IN THE GERMAN EMPIRE

The German imperial constitution of 16 April 1871 was devolved in character. There was no national government and no national army. Sovereignty was vested in the federal council, comprising representatives of the governments of the individual member states. In reality, however, Prussia emerged as the dominant state within the system. It occupied about three-fifths of the empire's territory. Its king, William I (r. 1861–1888), was also the German emperor (r. 1871–1888). Its minister-president, Otto von Bismarck, was also imperial chancellor (even after Bismarck's resignation in 1890, the two offices were generally held by the same man). Its army set the tone for all the military contingents of the empire and the Prussian king was also, in wartime, "supreme warlord" of Germany's armed forces. Yet the lesser states—especially in the south—retained their own courts, parliaments, and administrations and were jealous guardians of their autonomy within the imperial system.

The foundation of the empire transformed the tone of politics within the kingdom of Prussia. During the 1870s, the Bismarck government mounted a campaign of unprecedented scale and radicality against the Catholic Church, which was seen as a supporter of Austria, an opponent of national unity, and an obstacle to further integration. The "struggle of cultures" (Kulturkampf) that resulted merely reinforced the political solidarity of the Catholics. The same can be said for Bismarck's campaign against the Social Democrats in the 1880s, which failed to prevent the movement's spectacular electoral success. Prussian policy vis-à-vis the Polish minority in Posen/Poznań also changed in conformity with the priorities of the new nation-state, as the administration switched to an abrasive and ultimately futile policy of "Germanization." After 1878, when the liberal majority in the Prussian parliament collapsed, the conservatives succeeded in using Prussia's obsolete three-class franchise to perpetuate their own dominance within the state. Prussia thus became, as Bismarck had intended it should, the "conservative anchor" within the German system.

The relationship between Prussia and the rest of Germany after 1871 was fluid and remains difficult to characterize. The Prussian foreign office, for example, controlled German foreign policy, but after 1890 some of its most important posts were held by Germans from elsewhere in the empire. By 1914 almost one-quarter of officers in the "Prussian" army were non-Prussians. The efforts of the last Prussian king, William II (r. 1888–1918) to integrate the German polity by developing the imperial dimension of the Prussian-German crown met with mixed success. Some Germans regretted the "Prussianization" of the empire. Some Prussians, conversely, regretted the "imperialization" of Prussia and the dilution of the kingdom's traditional values of modesty, austerity, self-discipline, and thrift.

See also **Austro-Prussian War; Bismarck, Otto von; Concert of Europe; Congress of Vienna; Franco-Prussian War; Frederick William III; Frederick William IV; Germany; Hardenberg, Karl August von; Nationalism; Stein, Heinrich Friedrich Karl vom und zum; William I; William II.**

BIBLIOGRAPHY

Bahners, Patrick, and Gerd Roellecke, eds. *Preussische Stile: Ein Staat als Kunststück.* Stuttgart, Germany, 2001.

Büsch, Otto, and Wolfgang Neugebauer, eds. *Handbuch der preußischen Geschichte.* 3 vols. Berlin, 1992–2000.

Clark, Christopher. *Iron Kingdom: The Rise and Downfall of Prussia, 1600–1947.* London, 2006.

Dwyer, Philip G., ed. *Modern Prussian History, 1830–1947.* Harlow, U.K., and New York, 2001.

———. *The Rise of Prussia, 1700–1830.* Harlow, U.K., and New York, 2001.

Feuchtwanger, Edgar J. *Prussia: Myth and Reality: The Role of Prussia in German History.* Chicago, 1970.

Heinrich, Gerd. *Geschichte Preußens: Staat und Dynastie.* Berlin, 1984.

Koselleck, Reinhart. *Preußen zwischen Reform und Revolution: Allgemeines Landrecht, Verwaltung und soziale Bewegung von 1791 bis 1848*. Stuttgart, Germany, 1967.

CHRISTOPHER CLARK

PSYCHOANALYSIS. In an encyclopedia article published in 1924, its founder Sigmund Freud (1856–1939) defined psychoanalysis as "the name (1) of a procedure for the investigation of mental processes which are almost inaccessible in any other way, (2) of a method (based upon that investigation) for the treatment of neurotic disorders and (3) of a collection of psychological information obtained along those lines, which is gradually being accumulated into a new scientific discipline." Within the theory there were four fundamental concepts on which the entire intellectual edifice was built: (1) the unconscious as a domain or a property of ideas (representations); (2) repression (and more generally a range of defenses that define the mind as a field of dynamic conflict); (3) the drives (or instincts), the basic elements that motivate the mind; (4) transference—the repetition or reenactment of early intense experiences, such as the "Oedipus complex," the ambivalent relation of the child to its parents—as the fundamental discovery and distinguishing feature of its therapeutic practice.

Freud was born on 6 May 1856 in Freiberg (now Príbor) in Moravia, a small town at the eastern end of what was then the Austro-Hungarian Empire and is now the Czech Republic, not far from the Polish and Slovakian borders. Freud's family moved when he was three to Vienna, where he would live until he was forced by the unification of Austria and Germany in 1938 to emigrate to London that year; he died there three weeks after Britain's declaration of war on Germany. An outstanding student at school and later at the University of Vienna, Freud trained as a doctor; he was enamored of Darwinism, positivism, and the grand ambitions of experimental science in the 1870s, but was also a serious student of philosophy, taking courses with Franz Brentano (1838–1917), to whom key developments in twentieth-century logic and phenomenology can be traced. Freud's scientific training made him an exemplary exponent of experimental laboratory science and the histological study of the brain, under the leadership of Theodor Meynert (1833–1892), one of the most important brain anatomists of the period. Freud's intention to pursue a research career in brain science was, however, deflected when he met, fell in love with, and quickly became engaged to Martha Bernays in 1882. By 1884 he knew that he would have to go into general medical practice if he wished to marry in the near future. Envisaging a career specializing in the nervous diseases, in 1885–1886 he spent four and a half months on a scholarship to Paris, working with the world-famous neurologist Jean-Martin Charcot (1825–1893). He opened his medical practice in April 1886, married in September, and over the next nine years Martha gave birth to six children, the last of whom, Anna (1895–1982), would become her father's nurse, the protector of her father's work, and a great psychoanalyst in her own right.

Freud encountered Charcot when his work on the rehabilitation of hysteria employing hypnosis was at its height; Freud joined the large numbers of European and American physicians intent on finding psychological cures for the common nervous diseases, at times employing hypnotic suggestion. It was certainly Charcot who, perhaps inadvertently, turned Freud away from his anatomo-physiological orientation toward the psychological, where he would thereafter remain. But an old friend and colleague in Vienna, Josef Breuer (1842–1925), supplied Freud with his distinctive starting point: Breuer's exhaustive eighteen-month treatment of Bertha Pappenheim (1859–1936, called "Anna O." in Freud's writings) in 1880–1882. The therapy Bertha invented, her "talking cure," consisted of tracing, in speech and in a cathartic reliving, the numerous occasions of the appearance of her symptoms. In 1893, Breuer and Freud put forward the thesis that "hysterics suffer mainly from reminiscences"; they developed this argument in *Studies on Hysteria* of 1895, affirming the psychological causation of the neuroses and the efficacy of Freud's method of exhuming the past through the technique of "free association": the instruction to the patient to say whatever entered her mind. Throughout the 1890s, Freud sought the underlying causes of the disposition to neurosis, becoming convinced that he would find them in the domain of sexuality and the traumas of early life;

this did not prevent him from elaborating materialistic brain-based models of the neuroses, which, when transposed into mentalistic language, would constitute his high-level theory.

Psychoanalysis came fully into existence with the publication in late 1899 of Freud's most important book, *Die Traumdeutung* (The interpretation of dreams), the fruit of several years of the practice of interpreting his own and his patients' dreams as part of a search for the fundamental mechanisms of unconscious mental activity and the sources of the repressed memories that led to neurotic symptoms. It was dream analysis that became the model for "self-analysis" and the extension of his theories to normal mental life. Freud set out the key theses of his work: the distinction between "latent" and "manifest" in mental life, particularly in dreams; the principle of psychic determinism, for Freud the guarantee of the possibility of a properly scientific study of the mind; the distinction between the unconscious, the preconscious, and the conscious, with the related distinction between primary and secondary modes of psychic functioning; the significance of early experience and memories for all aspects of mental life, and in particular the all-pervasiveness of sexuality, including childhood sexual experience, as causal factors in psychopathology.

In 1905 Freud published three major works: a case history ("Fragment of an Analysis of a Case of Hysteria: 'Dora'"), *Jokes and their Relation to the Unconscious,* and the fundamental *Three Essays on the Theory of Sexuality,* in which he outlined the theory of infantile sexuality that underpinned his account of the variety of forms of human sexuality and of the causality of neuroses. As he acquired an audience and followers in the ensuing years, he produced major works in the anthropology of kinship and religion, psychobiography (on Leonardo da Vinci), sociology and social psychology, alongside clinical and theoretical studies of the neuroses and the structure of the normal and abnormal mind. It was undoubtedly the fluency, cogency, and sheer variety of Freud's writing that made him and his movement so influential, both within professional circles and for the mass readership that he, like others such as Thomas Mann (1875–1955) and H. G. Wells (1866–1946), created in the postwar era. From very early on, Freud had a

wide readership outside professional circles; but it was within professional circles that he would begin to build a visible movement.

The first of Freud's followers were outsiders—independent-mindedly Jewish physicians like him. However, from 1904 on, Freud was contacted by the respected psychiatrist Eugen Bleuler (1857–1939) and his young assistant, Carl Jung (1875–1961), at the famous Burghölzli Hospital, Zurich, who were interested in his dream theories, his claims about the meaningfulness of psychical symptoms, and the possibility of using the psychoanalytic method of treatment as both therapy and research tool. From this contact with the world of psychiatry in 1907–1908 came some of Freud's most important and enduring younger disciples: Karl Abraham (1877–1925), later the founder of psychoanalysis in Berlin; Max Eitingon (1881–1953), later also based in Berlin and a crucial figure in the institutional development of psychoanalytic clinical training in the 1920s; Abraham Arden Brill (1874–1948), a young American psychiatrist who would become the linchpin of psychoanalysis in New York; and Ernest Jones (1879–1958), who helped found psychoanalysis in North America and then became the key figure in its institutional development in the United Kingdom from 1912 to the 1940s. These younger men, in particular Jung, became belligerent proponents of Freud's views in heated debates among German-speaking neurologists and psychiatrists in the period from 1907 on. In the years before World War I, Freud's psychoanalytic movement founded branch societies in Vienna, Zurich, and Berlin, set up an International Psychoanalytic Association (IPA) in 1910 and was riven by internal strife, with the departure of Alfred Adler (1870–1937), Wilhelm Stekel (1868–1940), and finally Jung himself, the president of the IPA.

Before 1914, psychoanalysis had already become a cause célèbre for modernists, Bohemians, and progressive professionals concerned with reforming sexual mores; undertaking the inner journey that would result in the literary modernism of Marcel Proust (1871–1922), Virginia Woolf (1882–1941), and James Joyce (1882–1941); and in applying these insights to the nervous diseases. Its impact on artistic and literary figures as well as "progressive" scientists and doctors was already considerable in the principal cities of Central Europe and in addition in circumscribed circles in New York and London.

The First World War unexpectedly became the turning-point for the expansion and reception of psychoanalysis, in two principal modes: firstly, a growing number of the mobilized physicians treating the tens of thousands of cases of "war neuroses" or "shell shock" became sympathetic to Freudian views concerning the psychogenic nature of these cases, and the use of psychoanalytic methods among other psychological therapies in their treatment. Secondly, the catastrophe of the war led to a sea change in cultural sensibility with which key psychoanalytic themes were resonant: its emphasis on the overwhelming power of instinctual forces and on the irrational forces determining human action. Psychoanalysis offered a powerful theory and therapy, alongside other psychotherapies that developed in the period, for doctors and other clinicians to deploy; it offered individuals—scientists, artists, politicians, ordinarily unhappy citizens—a description of the forces at work in the irrational mind that resonated with the times; and it offered a promise of a science of the mind, in reach of everyone, that could match the miseries and mysteries of a whole life and its history. The early 1920s became, in Germany, Britain, and the United States, the era of great new scientific discoveries, chief among which, alongside the theory of relativity, was psychoanalysis.

With psychoanalysis all the rage among modernist artists and with an expanding clientele of patients, the 1920s saw its professionalization: across Europe, following the model of Berlin, training institutes and clinics were established, centered on the obligatory training analysis; these training systems were independent of both universities and medical schools. They were also, in Europe, open to nonmedical ("lay") students. What was a movement before the First World War was rapidly becoming in addition an independent profession. But its independence—of academia, of medical schools—was both strength and weakness. Alliances between psychoanalysis and other disciplines drawn to its challenging and powerful ideas were manifold, often undisciplined, yet overall fitful. Psychoanalysis was taken up by maverick sociologists and anthropologists, relatively few academic psychologists, writers, and artists, some medical

scientists (for instance, in psychosomatic medicine and general practice) in addition to its considerable (though exceedingly variable from country to country) influence on psychiatry in the mid-twentieth-century. A full consideration of the complex developments and manifold influences of psychoanalysis belongs to a history of the twentieth century rather than the long nineteenth century; but psychoanalysis was undoubtedly a product of that long nineteenth century, a part of the emergence of psychology as a discipline and practice, a part of the emergence of positivist science and Darwinist critiques of religion that accompanied the development of the novel profession of scientist. Nor was the emergence of psychoanalysis conceivable without the social transformations of groups that constituted its core clientele and practitioners: the Jews who, since the opening up of the Central European ghettos and their emigration westward to Vienna, Berlin, and the New World, were becoming a significant proportion of the medical, scientific, and professional sectors; and the emancipated New Woman, for whom psychoanalysis, with its emphasis on the significance of sexuality and the rigors of the emotional life of the private sphere, would provide both ideology and novel professional practice. For these groups and many others, psychoanalysis offered a secular scientific alternative to traditional religious and ethical doctrines.

See also **Adler, Alfred; Brentano, Franz; Darwin, Charles; Freud, Sigmund; Jews and Judaism; Jung, Carl Gustav; Modernism; Rank, Otto; Vienna.**

BIBLIOGRAPHY

Primary Sources

Freud, Sigmund. *The Standard Edition of the Complete Psychological Works of Sigmund Freud.* Edited by James Strachey in collaboration with Anna Freud, assisted by Alix Strachey and Alan Tyson. 24 vols. London, 1953–1974.

Secondary Sources

Appignanesi, Lisa, and John Forrester. *Freud's Women.* New York, 1992.

Ellenberger, Henri F. *The Discovery of the Unconscious: The History and Evolution of Dynamic Psychiatry.* London, 1970. A monumental historical survey.

Gay, Peter. *Freud. A Life for Our Time.* London, 1988. A superbly researched and finely judged biography.

Roudinesco, Élisabeth. *Jacques Lacan & Co:. A History of Psychoanalysis in France, 1925–1985.* Translated by Jeffrey Mehlman. London, 1990.

Roudinesco, Élisabeth, and Michel Plon. *Dictionnaire de la Psychanalyse.* Paris, 1997. The most reliable and comprehensive starting-point for all researches in the history of psychoanalysis.

Schorske, Carl E. *Fin de Siècle Vienna: Politics and Culture.* New York, 1979.

JOHN FORRESTER

PSYCHOLOGY. Psychology, in a general sense, is age-old, extending back across all cultures to the beginnings of recorded time. The healing arts of ancient doctors and the conceptual musings of ancient sages often pointed toward factors that would be considered psychological today. Nevertheless, psychology in its specifically modern sense dates from the second half of the nineteenth century, when a self-consciously scientific, academic, professional discipline took shape in Europe and North America. This multiplex discipline grew and flourished in particular in the United States, where more than forty experimental laboratories, associated programs of research and study, and institutionalized means of communication, certification, and application were established, or at least initiated, in the last two decades of the nineteenth century. But even in the United States, where unique social and historical conditions facilitated it, the development of psychology depended on a common philosophical background and various traditions of research that had evolved in Europe.

COMMON PHILOSOPHICAL BACKGROUND

The common background provided by philosophers reflected both religiously grounded rationalism and scientifically inspired empiricism. Mindful of the achievements of Isaac Newton (1642–1727), John Locke (1632–1704) popularized the belief that the mind is a receptacle within which atomistic sensations, images, and ideas are drawn to one another by certain "laws of association." His *Essay Concerning Human Understanding* (1690) stimulated a long line of thinkers who modified these laws according to their own experience and reflection. Alexander Bain (1818–1903) and Herbert Spencer (1820–1903) were important nineteenth-century representatives of this tradition, which was incorporated into the new scientific psychology. Bain's journal *Mind* (founded in 1876) served as a major publication outlet for work in this tradition.

Meanwhile, the philosophical works of René Descartes (1596–1650) emphasized the distinction between mind and body, thus driving a sharp wedge between rational analyses of thought and language, on the one hand, and mechanistic interpretations of bodily action, on the other. The former analyses were consonant with religious beliefs about the soul. The latter interpretations foreshadowed, in some respects, the later transformation of Locke's association of ideas into an association of physical stimuli with reflexological responses. Over the coming centuries many theorists drew from both associationism and reflexology, while others continued to produce theories about the nature and functions of the mind based primarily on rational considerations.

The great French *Encyclopedia* of the mid-eighteenth century expressed this common background in the dualistic terminology of Christian Wolff (1679–1754), who contended that there are two kinds of psychology, epitomized in his *Empirical Psychology* (1732) and *Rational Psychology* (1734). At the end of the century, Immanuel Kant (1724–1804) accepted this distinction and argued that empirical psychology, though pragmatically useful, would remain forever fallible, while rational psychology, contrary to Wolff and others, would never reach the level of apodictic, or certain, truth. In defining the parameters of a "true science," however, Kant provided a road map for subsequent thinkers who developed the conceptual framework of psychology while making it increasingly mathematical and experimental. Meanwhile, the more rational side of psychology was further developed by followers of Georg Wilhelm Friedrich Hegel (1770–1831), leading eventually to the phenomenological psychology inspired by Edmund Husserl (1859–1938). Though buttressed by empirical and even experimental evidence, social and personality psychology still bears the impress of this side of the common background. The French journal *L'Année psychologique* (established by Alfred Binet in 1894) supported these developments.

DIVERSE EUROPEAN RESEARCH TRADITIONS

Against this common background, various national traditions provided other elements that are now embedded within modern psychology. Although instances of each tradition existed in other European countries, it is useful to highlight the naturalistic tradition of Britain, the experimental tradition of Germany, the psychiatric tradition of France, and the physiological tradition of Russia.

In Britain, Charles Darwin (1809–1882) brought the tradition of naturalistic observation to bear upon the development of evolutionary theory. In *On the Origin of Species by Means of Natural Selection* (1859), he established the basis for a comparative understanding of human and animal behavior within the context of physical and biological environments. His focus on the advantages and disadvantages of random variations among individuals within any given species encouraged his cousin, Francis Galton (1822–1911), to undertake a systematic study of human variation, which in turn spurred further investigation of individual differences with regard to various attributes and talents. In later works, Darwin himself applied evolutionary principles to the human situation, thus strengthening the foundation for comparative psychology. George Romanes (1848–1894) and C. Lloyd Morgan (1852–1936), among others, advanced this area of human and animal psychology, relying in part on assumptions from Lockean associationism.

The distinctive German contribution was the development of an experimental tradition in psychology. Wilhelm Wundt (1832–1920) has been given primary credit for this, though he and others depended upon previous experimental work in physiology by such individuals as Johannes Müller (1801–1858) and Hermann von Helmholtz (1821–1894), as well as upon the institutional support provided for experimental research by many German universities. Illustrating the international nature of what was occurring, Wundt too drew theoretical assumptions from Lockean associationism. With the publication of his *Principles of Physiological Psychology* (1873–1874) and the establishment of his psychological laboratory at Leipzig (1879), he began to attract students from other countries, including the United States. The quantity of work done in his lab warranted the founding of an influential journal, *Philosophische Studien,* in 1883.

In France, the discovery of hypnosis and the development of neurology were each reflected in the emergence of a distinctive tradition of psychiatry. Stimulated by the work of clinicians and researchers who followed up on the discoveries of Franz Anton Mesmer (1734–1815) and the conjectures of Franz Joseph Gall (1758–1828), Jean-Martin Charcot (1825–1893) and Pierre Janet (1859–1947) studied alternative states of consciousness and speculated about the possible neurological bases for these states, including various kinds of mental disease. Charcot's *Lectures on the Diseases of the Nervous System* (1889) was a major outcome of this work. The therapeutic insights and practices that evolved from this line of research had a profound influence on the development of psychoanalysis by the Austrian psychiatrist Sigmund Freud (1856–1939) and the articulation of alternative psychotherapeutic insights by the American psychologist William James (1842–1910), both of whom attended the first International Congress of Psychology in Paris (1889), over which Charcot presided.

The distinctive Russian developments, leading eventually to the Nobel award-winning work of Ivan Pavlov (1849–1936), involved physiological research that was conceptualized in terms of reflexology, first by Ivan Sechenov (1829–1905) and then by Vladimir Bekhterev (1857–1927). This line of research, especially the terminology of Bekhterev's *Objective Psychology* (1907–1912), inspired the American John B. Watson (1878–1958) to postulate that all behavior is ultimately reducible to concatenated reflexes, whether innate or learned. Watson's formulation of "behaviorism" in the second decade of the twentieth century influenced a wide range of psychological theory and practice, in Europe as well as the United States, though European psychologists never rejected mentalism to the extent that many American psychologists did over the next half century.

OVERLAPS AND DISJUNCTIONS

No short overview of psychology in the nineteenth century can convey the number and complex interactions of relevant figures, works, traditions, and developments. For instance, there were important non-British comparative naturalists like the German Ernst Haeckel (1834–1919), major non-German experimentalists like the Dutch F. C. Donders (1818–1889), groundbreaking non-French psychiatrists like the British Henry Maudsley (1834–1918), and significant non-Russian physiologists like the Spaniard Santiago Ramón y Cajal (1852–1934). While most researchers focused on the psychology of the white, adult male, presuming that their findings would reveal universal laws, some—including Darwin and Wilhelm Preyer (1841–1897)—pioneered the empirical study of child development, and others—often associated with "psychical research"—began studying females, then thought to be more susceptible to emotion, suggestion, and other conditions, thus suggesting lower levels of rationality. Meanwhile, the emergence of national and ethnic identities and the continuance of social unrest throughout the nineteenth century drew attention to the nature and processes of social identity and behavior. Wundt's ten-volume *Folk Psychology* (1900–1920) and the work of Gabriel Tarde (1843–1904) and Gustave LeBon (1841–1931) on imitation and crowd behavior contributed to knowledge in this area.

Some lines of research, like the psychophysics proposed by Gustav Theodor Fechner (1801–1887), were developed in relative isolation and have continued in the same basic form into the twenty-first century. More typical, however, have been changes and discontinuities that have kept psychology from becoming a completely unified discipline. Especially since applied psychology emerged more strongly in the early twentieth century in clinical, school, industrial, wartime, and policy-related settings "psychology" has covered a vast array of differing theories and practices. In addition, jurisdictional disputes with other sciences and tendencies toward disciplinary fragmentation have been apparent since the late nineteenth century, as psychologists have addressed a host of issues, ranging from the minutely physiological to the broadly cultural.

See also **Charcot, Jean-Martin; Darwin, Charles; Freud, Sigmund; Gall, Franz Joseph; Helmholtz, Hermann; LeBon, Gustave; Mesmer, Franz Anton; Pavlov, Ivan; Psychoanalysis; Wundt, Wilhelm.**

BIBLIOGRAPHY

Boakes, Robert. *From Darwin to Behaviourism: Psychology and the Minds of Animals.* New York, 1984.

Danziger, Kurt. *Constructing the Subject: Historical Origins of Psychological Research.* New York, 1990.

Finger, Stanley. *Origins of Neuroscience: A History of Explorations into Brain Function.* New York, 1994.

Koch, Sigmund, and David E. Leary, eds. *A Century of Psychology as Science.* 2nd rev. ed. Washington, D.C., 1992.

Smith, Roger. *The Norton History of the Human Sciences.* New York, 1997.

Woodward, William R., and Mitchell G. Ash, eds. *The Problematic Science: Psychology in Nineteenth-Century Thought.* New York, 1982.

DAVID E. LEARY

PUBLIC HEALTH. In 1793 the French Revolution invented health citizenship when the National Convention's Committee on Salubrity added health to the democratic state's obligations to its citizens. The Committee believed this could be achieved by establishing a network of rural health officers who, while trained in clinical medicine, would also become responsible for reporting on the health of communities and monitoring epidemics among both humans and farm animals. The citizen's charter of health, however, was double-sided. The idéologue Constantin-François Chasseboeuf, comte de Volney (1757–1820), raised the issue of citizens' responsibility to maintain their own health for the benefit of the state. In the new social order the individual was a political and economic unit of a collective whole. It was a citizen's duty to keep healthy through temperance, both in the consumption of pleasure and the exercise of passions, and through cleanliness.

This dialectical relationship of health citizenship, entitlements, and responsibilities was subsequently expressed in the political and social development of public health systems and practices up to the twenty-first century. The relative roles of the state and its citizenry in achieving population health, however, oscillated and changed focus throughout the period.

In the nineteenth century, new sciences of socio-medical inquiry were developed in Europe, which expanded the possibilities for investigating the health of populations.

FRANCE

France led the development of public hygiene as an academic discipline in the first half of the nineteenth century. The "birth of the clinic" in Paris following the end of the Napoleonic Wars was matched by the birth of a public hygiene movement. But unlike clinical medicine, preventive medicine remained largely an intellectual pursuit focusing on the analysis of social conditions and the way in which they influenced the spread of disease. The translation of public hygiene theory into public policy was restricted in France by a commitment to a liberal political-economic philosophy that was shared by politicians, public servants, the medical profession, and the "partie d'hygiene." Social analysis of health conditions did not translate into the construction of a state-apparatus of disease prevention as it did in England. Instead the central state relied on old structures of health surveillance set up under the *ancien régime* and left reform to local initiative. Local physicians were appointed as "health officers" to coordinate state action during epidemics, but full-time salaried employment of doctors by the state was limited to medical relief for the poor. Medical relief reached only a fraction of the population in need. Most provincial districts instituted few health reforms, but a local prefect could make a difference.

The Paris Health Council was the most active public health body in France in the early nineteenth century. The Paris prefect of police was responsible for the control of pollution, the inspection of markets and slaughterhouses, street and sewer cleaning, public lighting, monitoring and authorizing industrial establishments, the supervision of animal slaughter, maintaining the salubrity of public places, and the control of quackery. Health ordinances were issued by the prefect but, as the Health Council *Reports* demonstrate, few of these powers were ever enforced. From 1802 the Paris Health Council compiled medical statistics and mortality tables and produced reports on epidemics, rivers, cemeteries, slaughterhouses, refuse dumps, dissection rooms, and public baths. When

it was expanded in the 1830s, some of the major figures of the hygiene movement, such as Louis-René Villermé and Parant du Chatelet, were appointed to it and undertook innovative research into social and sanitary conditions within the city. But the Council remained an advisory body only, and many of its recommendations were never taken up by the Paris political administration because they were costly and they challenged an ideological allegiance to economic liberalism. Numerous programs proposed by the Health Council were never adopted, such as the creation of new municipal drainage and systematic refuse-removal systems. Nevertheless the Council was able to have some effect on industrial development in Paris through its power to authorize commercial establishments, and after 1848 it gained the power to regulate the salubrity of private dwellings.

BRITAIN

While France developed the academic discipline of public hygiene, the midcentury British state translated its premises into public policy, creating a national system of public health administration by the early 1870s. Despite the pervasive rhetoric of liberal individualism, the promotion of the economic ideology of laissez-faire and the reliance on voluntary effort to provide social services to those in need, the British Victorian state nevertheless continued to expand and become increasingly interventionist. Expansion was justified by utilitarian beliefs that the profitable operations of a market economy could be maximized if it was protected by a political, legal system that created the best conditions for its freedom. Nowhere were the contradictory tensions of Victorian political and economic philosophies more obviously reflected than in the growth of public health intervention. Public health policy in Britain exemplified the growth of a bureaucratic system within the liberal democratic state. The British state sought solutions to the epidemic costs of economic expansion through the creation of an interventionist bureaucratic system of health administration. Initially the role of the state was to "enable" local authorities to intervene to protect their environments. But the grammar of public health legislation increasingly adopted the syntax of compulsion. The architects of state intervention justified it by assuming that a large proportion of poverty and destitution—and

DIPHTHERIA.   SCROFULA.   CHOLERA.

FATHER THAMES INTRODUCING HIS OFFSPRING TO THE FAIR CITY OF LONDON
(A Design for a Fresco in the New Houses of Parliament.)

Father Thames Introducing His Offspring to the Fair City of London. Cartoon, possibly by John Leech, from *Punch*, 3 July 1858. By 1858, the quality of Thames River water had become a source of major concern, particularly after the horrible smell forced the closure of Parliament. The cartoonist here comments both on the overwhelming nature of the problem and the reluctance of city officials to enact meaningful legislation. MARY EVANS PICTURE LIBRARY

its costs on solvent individuals, industry, and society in general—could be reduced by preventing premature mortality of breadwinners caused by epidemic disease.

In Britain the initiative for public health intervention was driven by the actions of central government but relied on local government for its practical application. In this respect public health provision continued to be open to a degree of local government discretion and accessible to public participation in local democratic processes. However, the opponents of public health intervention in

Britain perceived it as a massive threat to local government autonomy and an unacceptable intervention by the central state in their affairs. Public health intervention was perceived by early Victorians as the most infamous growth of authoritarian, paternalist power of central government on the one hand and the growth of the despotic influence of a particular profession—the medical profession—on the other.

Industrialization in Britain exponentially multiplied environmental threats to health primarily through the massive growth of towns. For example, London had 800,000 people in 1801 and there were only 13 towns with populations of over 25,000. By 1841 London's population rose by one million and 42 towns contained over 25,000 people. By 1861 six British cities contained more than a quarter million inhabitants. In the early 1800s approximately 20 percent of the population of England and Wales lived in towns of over 5,000; by 1851 over half the population did so; and by 1901 almost 80 percent. By contrast in rural areas some counties contained less population in 1901 than they did in 1851.

DEMOGRAPHIC EXPLOSION

These patterns were repeated in Europe as industrialization gathered momentum. No urban development could accommodate such a demographic explosion, which resulted in mass overcrowding, inadequate housing, dramatic accumulation of human, animal, and industrial waste products together with rising levels of industrial and domestic atmospheric pollution, and deadly pollution of insufficient potable water supply. In Britain and on the Continent the grotesquely squalid conditions imposed on the slum-dwelling proletariat were revealed by a host of observers, from social reformers to investigative journalists, and soon produced dramatic rises in infant mortality, rising levels of epidemic diseases, such as "fever"—both typhoid and typhus—and rising levels of dependency created through sickness. The physical expansion of cities could not keep pace with population migration and growth. Existing building stock became grossly overcrowded with huge densities of people. The amenities designed for vastly smaller numbers were totally inadequate. The need for new housing led to building methods that sacrificed quality for speed. Sanitary facilities designed for less dense levels of population were the most serious failure. Traditional methods of waste disposal such as cesspits and middens served more sparsely distributed populations adequately but became dangerously overburdened under these new conditions. Cesspools turned into manure swamps and seeped into the local water supplies and wells. Dry middens and their consequent dung heaps turned into mountains infested with flies and vermin. Existing levels of intermittent water supply could not possibly serve the expansion of demand. The traditional life of market towns became fatally hazardous under

these new pressures. The defining feature of the heavily overstressed industrialized towns throughout nineteenth-century Europe was their stench, encouraging the popularity of an atmospheric theory, miasmatism, which identified a general etiology of disease through nonspecific contamination of the atmosphere by gaseous material given off by putrefying, decomposing, organic matter.

By the early 1840s sanitary reformers in Britain such as the Poor Law Commissioner, Edwin Chadwick, were convinced that the construction of massive new drainage and sewage removal systems was the primary means of preventing epidemic diseases such as typhoid, typhus, and cholera. Chadwick, in particular, believed that existing square-bricked sewers with large tunnel pipes that did not flush or empty should be replaced by small egg shaped sewers lined with glazed brick and connected by small earthenware pipes that would be constantly flushed by high-pressurized water. Liquid sewage could be recycled as manure fertilizer to outlying farming districts. Street widening, the removal of cesspools and all other noxious nuisances together with an end to intermittent drinking water were fundamental. With sanitary reforms such as these as its goal, the first British Public Health Act was passed in Britain in 1848. While comprehensive, it remained permissive. The Act created a central authority, the General Board of Health, with Anthony Ashley Cooper, the seventh Earl of Shaftesbury as its president and Chadwick as its secretary. The Act encouraged the appointment of local boards of health and local medical officers of health which became a national compulsory system under the later Public Health Act of 1872.

REFORM ON THE CONTINENT

The British model was intermittently reproduced throughout Europe in the latter half of the nineteenth and first half of the twentieth century, but different routes were taken in each national context. Although early-nineteenth-century French politics were dominated by economic and philosophical liberalism, France was the breeding ground for socialist theory in the 1830s and the Saint-Simonians incorporated public health reform into their critique of economic individualism and their belief in a new industrial order based on brotherhood.

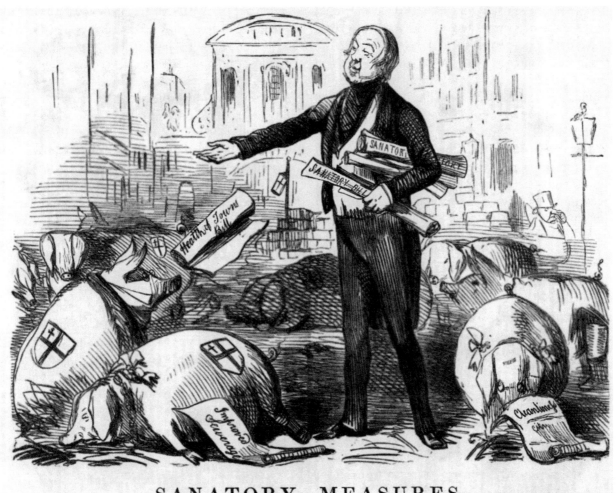

SANATORY MEASURES.

Lord Morpeth Throwing Pearls before ——— Aldermen.

Sanatory Measures: Lord Morpeth Throwing Pearls before—Aldermen. Cartoon from *Punch,* 1848. George Howard, Lord Morpeth, was the member of Parliament who introduced the bill that eventually became the British Public Health Act of 1848. The cartoonist represents opponents of the legislation as swine. MARY EVANS PICTURE LIBRARY

Revolutionaries in 1848 identified a new social and political role for medicine when the editor of the *Gazette médicale de Paris,* Jules Guérin, promoted a "brotherhood of physicians" dedicated to "social medicine." Guérin believed it was time for medicine to participate in government itself through the establishment of a Ministry of Public Health. The radicalism of 1848 matched that of the 1789 revolution but withered as the revolution failed. The emperor Napoleon III (r. 1852–1871) suppressed the Left after 1851. While he liberalized trade and took a new interest in alleviating the conditions of poverty, the central state continued to remain largely inactive in terms of health reform.

German states Similar health radicalism that wanted medicine to play a role in national government emerged within the German states during the 1848 revolutions. Within Prussia a philosophy comparable to Guérin's was outlined by the physician who became the founder of cellular pathology and a liberal politician, Rudolph Virchow. Following an investigation in 1848 of typhus in Upper Silesia, Virchow identified insanitary conditions as the cause of the epidemic. He developed what he called a "socio-logical" epidemiology, which led him to conclude that the strength of the disease among the Upper Silesians was due to their subjugated political state. The impoverished conditions and levels of squalor in which they lived would never have been tolerated by citizens living in a "free-democracy with general self-government." Therefore, Virchow concluded that "Free and unlimited democracy" was the only way to prevent typhus. A well-fed and politically emancipated population would produce a society in which both capital and labor had the same rights to health. Within this context Virchow outlined a political role for the physician as an ambassador for the poor, with the responsibility of identifying and recording sickness and devising measures to prevent it.

The revolutions of 1848 failed, but the political role of medicine in the state regulation of health expanded within the German states albeit incrementally and largely on a localized basis. Virchow encouraged Berlin to build sanitary infrastructures to supply pure water and remove sewage and refuse by the end of the 1860s. In Munich reform was led by the first German professor of public hygiene, Max Josef von Pettenkofer. Pettenkofer was a major figure both in the development of the academic study of public hygiene and sanitary reform in the nineteenth century. Pettenkofer was made professor of hygiene in 1865 and persuaded the Bavarian government to create an Institute of Hygiene in Munich in 1878 under his direction. His allegiance to a contingent-contagionist theory of disease transmission based on chemical fermentation led Pettenkofer to oppose the direct interventionist policies of the contagionists and support a broad-based agenda for disease prevention. In the 1870s he pushed the Munich authorities into acquiring a fresh mountain-water supply and to installing a modern sewage-removal system. He believed that whatever the medium of disease transmission, it required favorable local conditions to be effective, including climate and soil quality. Thus he thought that sewage must be removed down river in order to preserve the purity of the local soil from contamination. He argued that quarantine was a useless measure against epidemic invasion and advocated instead, improved housing and education of the population in healthy diet, exercise, and temperance. Pettenkofer's influence over policy continued until it was overtaken by Robert Koch, the champion of the new discipline of bacteriology, who, based in Berlin, was

embraced by the Prussian state's power within the Second Reich of unified Germany. Bacteriology facilitated a new administrative centralization of public health but with a less economic interventionist approach focusing instead on the isolation of infectious individuals and disinfection of effects. Prussia established full-time medical officers of health in 1899 but the replacement of part-time state doctors throughout Germany took place over a long period. Various municipalities such as Berlin, Charlottenburg, Schöneberg, and Neukölln soon created full-time medical departments. As in other European states, bacteriology was succeeded by the Darwinian inspired science of eugenics, which aimed to explain disease and biological degeneration by understanding the mechanisms of heredity. Eugenics inspired the creation of two new movements in Germany, social hygiene and racial hygiene. The rise to prominence of social hygiene along with new concerns over social assistance and health insurance demonstrated the level of political importance that population health had reached in Germany by the end of the nineteenth century.

France In the late nineteenth century public hygiene began to take on a new profile in France when the Third Republic, established in 1870, made an ideological commitment to the health of the people. Although the republic continued to prioritize the political rights of private property, socialists and moderate republican progressives all believed that public health programs would help sustain social stability. Bacteriology provided renewed ideological legitimation for public hygiene stimulated by the impact of Louis Pasteur's discoveries and his political influence within French society. Responsibility for the disparate features of health policy was brought together in a new Bureau of Public Health and Hygiene created within the Ministry of the Interior. This brought medical assistance and public health control under one administration headed by a Pasteurian-minded politician Léon-Victor-Auguste Bourgeois. In addition, the Consultative Committee on Public Health (CCHP), which maintained jurisdiction over quarantine, headed by the dean of the Paris Medical Faculty, Paul Brouardel, was moved from the Commerce Ministry to the Ministry of the Interior. The CCHP promoted new legislation making vaccination, notification of infectious disease, and death registration compulsory and making disinfection services and pure water supply universally available. No national system of public health administration was created comparable to that developed in England by the 1875 Public Health Act, but three-quarters of the regional *départements* had active health councils even though they still remained advisory bodies to the prefect. In 1884 France battled cholera with systematic environmental improvement and the closure of places of public congregation. By the time of the 1892 epidemic individual patients were isolated and their surroundings decontaminated.

Within a new context of political collectivism, represented not only by socialism but also by solidarism, new liberalism, and enthusiasm for social insurance, support for state health care provision expanded in Europe from the end of the nineteenth century up to the outset of World War I. In Germany in the 1880s statutory social security against the misfortunes created by sickness, disability, old age, and unemployment was established under the Health Insurance Law of 1883, and state support for old age and disability was established by a further statute in 1889. Together this legislation allowed the Reich chancellor, Otto von Bismarck, to create a model of social insurance that was subsequently reproduced throughout the industrializing European community, as both liberals and socialists feared the rising industrial and social strength of the unified German state with its state-supported systems of comprehensive health and welfare provision. In the 1890s and 1910s new laws were introduced that revived the 1789 principles of rights and obligations of health citizenship, transferring medical assistance from poor relief into a system of national insurance in Britain, France, the Netherlands, and Scandinavia.

See also **Cholera; Cities and Towns; Disease; Prostitution; Tuberculosis.**

BIBLIOGRAPHY

Porter, Dorothy. *Health, Civilisation, and the State: A History of Public Health from Ancient to Modern Times.* London and New York, 1999.

Virchow, Rudolf. *Gesammelte Abhandlungen aus dem Gebiete der öffentlichen Medicin und der Seuchenlehre: Collected Essays on Public Health and Epidemiology.* Edited and with a foreword by L. J. Rather. Canton, Mass., 1985.

DOROTHY PORTER

PUCCINI, GIACOMO (1858–1924), Italian operatic composer.

Giacomo Puccini's popular operas were long dismissed as "ear candy," in contrast to the work of contemporaries perceived to be more serious, such as Giuseppe Verdi and Richard Wagner. Almost a century after his death, Puccini is now widely recognized as a meticulous musical craftsman of the first rank.

Born on 22 December in Lucca, the sixth child and first son of Michele Puccini and Albina Maggi, Puccini was heir to a family tradition of church musicians and composers. His father died on 23 January 1864, when Puccini was five years old. His father's job of *maestro di cappella* and organist in the parish church was held in trust for the boy until he was old enough to assume the office. At the time of his father's death he was the only male in a family of six females, until three months later when his brother Michele was born. Puccini would be a dedicated womanizer throughout his life, a characteristic that many critics see as influential in his musical career.

After he composed several pieces of religious music, he was admitted to the conservatory in Milan in autumn 1880. His first operatic effort was *Le willis*, a one-act "opera-ballet" ghost story, written for a competition that he failed to win (perhaps due to his illegible handwriting). The opera, expanded to two acts and its title changed to *Le villi*, was performed the following year, and its success won him a contract with Giulio Ricordi (of Ricordi and Sons), who would remain his publisher, friend, and sometime collaborator. In 1884 his strong-willed mother, Albina, died, and Puccini eloped with his pupil, a married woman, the equally strong-willed Elvira Gemignani. The couple, whose relationship was stormy, had one son, Antonio, and married in 1904, after the death of Gemignani's husband.

PUCCINI'S OPERAS

Le villi, libretto by Ferdinando Fontana. Premier: Turin, Teatro Regio, 26 December 1884. A one-act version had its premier in Milan, Teatro dal Verme, 31 May 1884.

Edgar, libretto by Ferdinando Fontana. Premier: Milan, La Scala, 21 April 1889.

Manon Lescaut, libretto by Marco Praga, Domenico Oliva, Luigi Illica, and Giuseppe Giacosa. Premier: Turin, Teatro Reggio, 1 February 1893.

La Bohème, libretto by Giuseppe Giacosa and Luigi Illica. Premier: Turin, Teatro Reggio, 1 February 1896.

Tosca, libretto by Giuseppe Giacosa and Luigi Illica. Premier: Rome, Teatro Costanzi, 14 January 1900.

Madama Butterfly, libretto by Giuseppe Giacosa and Luigi Illica. Premier: Milan, La Scala, 17 February 1904; a revised version had its premier in Brescia, Teatro Grande, 28 May 1904.

La fanciulla del west, libretto by Guelfo Civinini and Carlo Zangari. Premier: New York, Metropolitan Opera House, 10 December 1910.

La rondine, libretto by Giuseppe Adami. Premier: Monte Carlo, Monte Carlo Opera, 27 March 1917.

Il trittico: Il tabarro, libretto by Giuseppe Adami; *Suor Angelica,* libretto by Giovacchino Foranza; *Gianni Schicchi,* libretto by Giovacchino Foranza. Premier: New York, Metropolitan Opera House, 14 December 1918.

Turandot, libretto by Giuseppe Adami and Renato Simoni; completed after Puccini's death by Franco Alfano. Premier: Milan, La Scala, 25 April 1926.

In the summer of 1891 Puccini moved to Torre del Lago, which would be his home for most of the rest of his life. His first enduring hit, *Manon Lescaut* (1893), based on the novel by Abbé Prévost, was an immediate sensation. By the end of 1893 Puccini set to work on an adaptation of Henri Murger's *Scènes de la vie de Bohème,* an episodic collection of sketches of love among the desperately poor "Bohemians" of early-nineteenth-century Paris. In Puccini's hands, Murger's stark tales become a paean to the bittersweet joys of youth. *La Bohème* (1896) would be the first of his trio of greatest hits (with *Madama Butterfly* and *Tosca*).

As early as spring of 1889 he had resolved to set Victorien Sardou's lurid melodrama *La Tosca* to music. It would be more than ten years before the project reached fruition in his powerful depiction of love and death in Napoleonic Rome, *Tosca* (1900).

The following year he turned to an "American" subject, based on David Belasco's dramatization of a Luther Long story. *Madama Butterfly* (1904) was the only one of his operas to meet with substantial initial hostility, but a revised, three-act version soon joined his other operas in the standard repertoire of opera houses around the world.

With fame and prosperity assured, he struggled for several years to find the right subject for his next opera. He considered several, including a version of Victor Hugo's *Hunchback of Notre Dame* and an opera about the trial and execution of Marie-Antoinette, but finally settled on another Belasco play, *Girl of the Golden West,* which became his seventh opera, *La fanciulla del west* (1910).

In 1914, as the world stumbled into a war that he would substantially ignore, Puccini turned to *La rondine.* More of an operetta in the Viennese style than an opera, this proved to be the least popular of his mature works.

He had long considered composing a trilogy, and as early as 1915 he had begun work on the tragedy *Il tabarro,* which would become one of three one-act operas to make up his *Trittico* (1919). The other two are *Suor Angelica* (a romance) and *Gianni Schicchi* (a comedy).

His last—and many believe his greatest—opera, *Turandot,* first appears in his letters early in

1920; it was complete except for the last scene when the composer died of throat cancer, on 29 November 1924.

Puccini's operas are characterized by strong melodic lines, meticulous musical craftsmanship, and plots that usually include a sadomasochistic undercurrent typical of the fin de siècle. His operas are much beloved by audiences and figure prominently in any list of the most popular operas of all time.

See also **Fin de Siècle; Music; Opera; Verdi, Giuseppe; Wagner, Richard.**

BIBLIOGRAPHY

Ashbrook, William. *The Operas of Puccini.* New York, 1968. Based on his study of the autograph scores as well as the literary sources of the operas.

Carner, Mosco. *Puccini: A Critical Biography.* 1st U.S. ed. New York, 1959. Still the standard biography of the composer, presenting a complete if sometimes excessively Freudian interpretation of his life and work.

Gara, Eugenio. *Carteggi pucciniani.* Milan, 1958. The most complete collection of Puccini papers, including more than nine hundred items to, from, and about Puccini.

Hopkinson, Cecil. *A Bibliograpy of the Works of Giacomo Puccini, 1858–1924.* New York, 1968. A detailed list of published Puccini scores, including nonoperatic works.

Marek, George Richard. *Puccini.* London, 1952. An earlier, and still valuable, biography.

Weaver, William, and Simonetta Puccini, eds. *The Puccini Companion.* New York, 1994. Essays on all things Puccinian, including two valuable bibliographic essays.

SUSAN VANDIVER NICASSIO

PUGIN, AUGUSTUS WELBY (1812–1852), English architect, designer, and theorist.

Augustus Welby Northmore Pugin grew up with Gothic architecture; his father, the French émigré architect and draftsman Augustus-Charles Pugin (1762–1832), had earned fame as the illustrator of books on Gothic architecture, furniture, and ornaments. Pugin's architectural training consisted of traveling with his father around England and France, assisting in the measurement and drawing of medieval buildings. He provided many of the illustrations for his father's last book (*Examples of Gothic Architecture,* 1831), proving himself a gifted draftsman.

Pugin's architectural career started in 1835 with the construction of his own house (St. Marie's Grange, Salisbury) and his first work for Sir Charles Barry (1795–1860)—the design of furniture and ornamental details for the King Edward VI Grammar School in Birmingham. In the same year Pugin converted to Roman Catholicism and began writing his first and most influential book, *Contrasts; or, A Parallel Between the Noble Edifices of the Middle Ages and Corresponding Buildings of the Present Day, Shewing the Present Decay of Taste.*

Published in 1841, *Contrasts* was the first serious polemic of the Gothic Revival movement. Juxtaposing illustrations of medieval buildings with those of his own time, Pugin compared the beauty and harmony of the Middle Ages with the squalor and ugliness of the contemporary world. It was a contrast Pugin attributed to the relative decline in religious faith and the abandonment of the Gothic style after the Reformation. In a bold synthesis of his religious views and love of Gothic design, Pugin argued that Gothic was not merely a "style": it had moral value as the true architectural embodiment of Christian belief, whereas other styles were "pagan" in origin, and therefore un-Christian. It was a turning point. Previously Gothic had been admired for its picturesque and ornamental qualities; now Pugin gave it a moral and symbolic value. It was an argument he developed further in *The True Principles of Pointed or Christian Architecture* (1841). Pugin's ideas were to be an influence on later Gothic Revival theorists including John Ruskin (1819–1900), who wrote *Seven Lamps of Architecture* (1849), and Eugène-Emmanuel Viollet-le-Duc (1814–1879).

Contrasts was published at a time of religious revival. In 1818, Parliament had called for the construction of six hundred new churches to serve Britain's expanding cities. The Oxford Movement, which sought the revival of Roman Catholic ideals and rituals in the Church of England, was gaining momentum through the 1830s and 1840s. Pugin's arguments appealed especially to Catholic patrons, and he began to receive commissions from prominent members of the Catholic community, particularly Charles Scarisbrick (Scarisbrick Hall, Lancashire, 1837–1845) and John Talbot, Earl of Shrewsbury (Alton Towers and Alton Castle, Staffordshire, 1837–1852). But of greater significance was the series of more than thirty churches and religious buildings that Pugin designed. The most notable of the early works was St. Marie's, Derby (1837–1839), where Pugin achieved a sense of soaring verticality in the interior through the use of scale and an exaggerated proportion between height and width, accentuated by tall arcades of bare stonework. A similar verticality can be seen in St. Chad's, Birmingham (1839–1840)—Pugin's first cathedral, and the first Roman Catholic cathedral to be built in England since the Reformation. In the 1840s, through the patronage of the Earl of Shrewsbury, Pugin was able to build the church that most clearly fulfilled his architectural manifesto—St. Giles', Cheadle (1840–1846). Huge in scale, opulent but restrained, in the year of its opening St. Giles was described by John Henry Newman (1801–1890), leader of the Oxford Movement, as "The most splendid building I ever saw."

Pugin's best-known work is the Houses of Parliament (from 1836), which he worked on throughout his career. Sir Charles Barry won the competition to design a new building in 1835, but it is now widely accepted that Pugin was involved in the design, especially in the decorative details. Pugin had never restricted himself to architecture but from the earliest days of his career had designed furniture, ceramics, textiles, wallpaper, and metalwork, collaborating with the manufacturers John Gregory Crace, Herbert Minton, and John Hardman. His work in the interior of the Houses of Parliament presented the opportunity to bring all these aspects together into a Gothic whole. From chandeliers to inkwells, Pugin designed every detail and the result was arguably the finest Gothic Revival interior of the nineteenth century.

See also **Barry, Charles; Nash, John; Romanticism; Viollet-le-Duc, Eugène.**

BIBLIOGRAPHY

Atterbury, Paul, ed. *A. W. N. Pugin: Master of Gothic Revival.* New Haven, Conn., 1995.

Clark, Kenneth. *The Gothic Revival: An Essay on the History of Taste,* 3rd ed. London, 1962.

Stanton, Phoebe. *Pugin.* London, 1971.

MARK FOLEY

PUSHKIN, ALEXANDER (1799–1837), Russian poet.

Alexander Sergeyevich Pushkin, who is generally recognized as Russia's greatest national poet, was born in Moscow on 6 June (26 May, old style) 1799. The Pushkins were descended from an old boyar family and could trace their lineage back for centuries. The future poet's maternal great-grandfather, Abram Hannibal, had been born in Africa and in 1705 had been brought to Russia from the court of the Turkish sultan by a Russian envoy as a gift to Peter the Great, who had the boy baptized as his godson. Hannibal lived a long and tumultuous life, eventually rising to the rank of general. Pushkin was proud of his forebears' role in Russian history and incorporated them into his works. Pushkin's parents, Sergei Lvovich and Nadezhda Osipovna Pushkin, were very much of a piece with their age. His mother, a moody society belle nicknamed "the beautiful Creole" for her African heritage, was cold toward her son, and his father was a poor estate manager who squandered money on gambling and social pursuits. As a child, Pushkin was introduced to literature and literary circles through his father's library of French literature and through the contacts of his uncle, the minor poet Vasily Lvovich Pushkin.

THE BEGINNINGS OF PUSHKIN'S POETIC CAREER

In June 1811 Pushkin was sent to boarding school at the lyceum at Tsarskoye Selo, outside of St. Petersburg. Pushkin was in the first class of the school, which was designed to train the sons of the nobility for government service. He made close and lifelong friendships there, and it is a measure of Pushkin's devotion to the lyceum and his classmates that the poet continued to write poems commemorating 19 October, the day the Tsarskoye Selo lyceum officially opened, throughout his life. Pushkin gained recognition as an extraordinary poetic talent while still in school, publishing his first poem in 1814.

After he graduated from the lyceum in 1817, Pushkin was awarded the rank of collegiate secretary in the civil service and took up a position in the ministry of foreign affairs. Pushkin, who had been accepted into one of the foremost literary groupings of his day—Arzamas—while still a lyceum student, continued his involvement in its successor, the Green Lamp. Discussions of literature and radical politics were the stock in trade of the society's meetings. In the spring of 1820 Pushkin scored a major literary success, and significantly advanced his poetic reputation, with the completion of his first lengthy narrative poem, *Ruslan and Lyudmila,* a comic work inspired by the Russian epic and folkloric traditions. At the same time, Pushkin found himself compromised politically for caustic epigrams he had authored at the expense of Tsar Alexander I himself. While retaining his civil service commission, he was sent into exile to Yekaterinoslav in what is now Ukraine. He was almost immediately given leave to travel to the Crimea with the family of his recent acquaintance, General Nikolai Rayevsky. During the trip, the general's son Alexander introduced Pushkin to the poetry of Lord Byron, which exercised a powerful influence over the poet's work of the period. By the time of his return from his travels in September, the chancellery to which he was assigned had been transferred to Kishinev in what is now Moldova. In July 1823 Pushkin was transferred to Odessa, where he remained for a year until, in July 1824, he was dismissed from the civil service and sent into exile in earnest at the family estate at Mikhailovskoye, ostensibly for professing atheism in a private letter, but most probably because he was having an affair with his superior's wife. The narrative poems Pushkin wrote during his southern exile—most notably *The Prisoner of the Caucasus, The Fountain of Bakhchisarai,* and *The Gypsies* (the latter of which he completed at Mikhailovskoye)—bear the imprint of his exposure to the heritage and peoples of the region as well as of his attraction to and eventual rejection of Byronism. Most notably, while still in the south Pushkin began writing *Eugene Onegin,* a "novel in verse" that would take him eight years to complete and would clinch his reputation as Russia's national poet.

While in exile at Mikhailovskoye, Pushkin continued work on *Eugene Onegin* and, under the inspiration of William Shakespeare, wrote the historical drama *Boris Godunov,* which would later serve as a basis for the Modest Mussorgsky opera of the same name. On 26 December (14 December, O.S.) 1825, in the wake of the death of Alexander I and as the succession to the Russian throne was being decided, a group of army officers, many of whom had been brought into touch with western European political views during their service in the Napoleonic Wars, staged what came to be known as the Decembrist revolt on Senate Square in St. Petersburg. The rebellion, which called for a constitutional monarchy, was quickly put down and the five ringleaders hanged. A number of the rebels were close friends of Pushkin's, and many were found to possess inflammatory poems by him, although the poet was never taken into the conspirators' confidence. In September 1826 Pushkin was brought out of exile to meet with the newly crowned Tsar Nicholas I, who, in a gesture apparently calculated to counter the bloody beginning of his reign, pardoned Pushkin and offered to supervise personally the censorship of the poet's works.

Pushkin's return to St. Petersburg marked the beginning of the final, increasingly troubled period of his life. Despite his privileged relationship with the tsar, he found it harder and harder to publish his works and, in the 1830s, his reputation began to decline, as he came to be considered an outmoded relic of the past. Increasingly he turned to prose, beginning in 1827 with the ultimately unfinished novel, *The Blackamoor of Peter the Great,* a fictionalized biography of his African great-grandfather. This was followed by a collection of short stories, *Tales of Belkin* (1830); the short story (1834) that inspired Peter Tchaikovsky's opera *The Queen of Spades;* and a travel sketch, *A Journey to Erzurum* (1836). Pushkin continued his experiments with dramatic form in the "little tragedies"—*The Covetous Knight, Mozart and Salieri, The Stone Guest,* and *Feast in Time of the Plague*—written, as were *Tales of Belkin,* during the productive autumn Pushkin spent at his Boldino estate in 1830. Pushkin also wrote some of his greatest poetic masterpieces in the 1830s, most notably the narrative poem *The Bronze Horseman* (1833) and his poetic testament titled "I Have Raised Myself a Monument Not Made by Hands" (1836). A new departure in Pushkin's work in this last period was the writing of history, most notably *The History of the Pugachev Rebellion* (1834), a subject he was to revisit in historical fiction in his only completed novel, *The Captain's Daughter,* published in 1836 in Pushkin's own journal, *The Contemporary,* which had come into existence in the same year.

On 2 March (18 February, O.S.) 1831 Pushkin married the society beauty Natalya Goncharova, who was thirteen years his junior. The marriage complicated Pushkin's already fraught relations with the tsar. Nicholas I, in order to keep Goncharova at the court, bestowed on Pushkin in 1833 the rank of Kammerjunker, which the poet found humiliating because it was usually held by much younger men. Moreover, the expense of court life placed a heavy burden on the family's finances, yet the tsar turned down Pushkin's repeated requests to retire to the country in the interests of economy. In 1836 the situation became unbearable when Goncharova was caught up in a flirtation with an émigré French officer, Georges d'Anthès. Despite repeated attempts by Pushkin's friends to defuse the situation, it came to a head on 8 February (27 January, O.S.) 1837, when Pushkin challenged d'Anthès to a duel. The poet was fatally wounded and died two days later.

Pushkin's legacy as the progenitor of the grand tradition of Russian literature, creator of the Russian literary language, and initiator of the canonic aesthetic paradigms of both Russian poetry and prose remains largely unchallenged. In the course of the past two centuries, the Pushkin cult has evolved into a powerful cultural and political force in Russia. Even before the poet's death, the writer Nikolai Gogol heralded him as the Russian of the future. From there Pushkin evolved into a metaphor for Russia's imperial aspirations, and anniversaries of his birth and death have been exploited by the tsarist, Soviet, and post-Soviet Russian governments—most recently during the celebration of the bicentennial of his birth in 1999—as a source of political legitimacy.

See also **Alexander I; Gogol, Nikolai; Romanticism; Russia.**

BIBLIOGRAPHY

Primary Sources

Pushkin, Alexander. *Eugene Onegin: A Novel in Verse.* Translated by James E. Falen. Oxford, U.K., 1995.

Secondary Sources

Bethea, David M. *Realizing Metaphors: Alexander Pushkin and the Life of the Poet.* Madison, Wis., 1998.

Sandler, Stephanie. *Distant Pleasures: Alexander Pushkin and the Writing of Exile.* Stanford, Calif., 1989.

CATHARINE THEIMER NEPOMNYASHCHY

QUETELET, LAMBERT ADOLPHE JACQUES (1796–1874), Belgian astronomer and statistician.

Adolphe Quetelet, prominent in his own time and since for work on social science and statistics, was trained in mathematics and began his scientific career in astronomy. In 1823 he persuaded the government of the Netherlands, which from 1815 to 1830 included Belgium, to construct in Brussels an observatory, of which he should be the first director. To this end he was authorized to travel to Paris and spend a season at the observatory there learning the ropes. The observatory in Brussels had a rocky start, for just as construction was nearing completion the 1830 revolution broke out in Belgium, and for a time the observatory was occupied by soldiers. But it endured, and Quetelet's whole career was framed by sciences of the observatory.

These sciences included not just astronomy, but geodesy (measurements concerning the shape and curvature of the earth), meteorology, and the study of tides, terrestrial magnetism, and other quantifiable phenomena such as blooming times of plants. As a leader of the Brussels Academy of Science, Quetelet aspired to organize its members into a single collaboration devoted to the study of periodic phenomena. This was work that required extensive, detailed observation, and for which scientific cooperation was essential. Although he could not control the careers of all his associates, he helped to create an international network devoted to quantitative natural history. His vast correspondence documents this important mid-nineteenth-century scientific movement, in which he took a central role.

Statistics, too, was for Quetelet a science of the observatory. From the 1820s until the end of the nineteenth century, "statistics" meant an empirical social science, the science of human collectives and of mass observation. Although it attained at least marginal status in the scientific academies, it was more often a bureaucratic study than an academic one. The statistical movement of the 1830s and 1840s was linked to new government bureaus that conducted censuses, registered births and deaths, and kept tabs on crime, trade, and schooling. Quetelet had an important role in the bureaucratic organization of statistics in his home country. Still more significant was his leadership of the International Statistical Congresses, which met more or less every second year for almost three decades beginning with the Brussels meeting of 1853. His great ambition, which proved very difficult in practice, was to harmonize statistical categories so that numbers could be compared across national boundaries. On this basis, he hoped, statistics would reveal the causes of crime, poverty, and disease, and show how to combat them.

Among the statisticians, Quetelet was unusual for his commitment to abstract science and to mathematics. He had in fact learned the methods for analyzing and managing error during his visit to the Paris Observatory, and he was very free in offering advice to his fellow statisticians about the indispensable role of probability theory for calculating the precision of rates and averages. In practice this was not easy in his time, because representative or random samples of the sort assumed by basic probability theory were hard to come by. In practice, Quetelet devoted himself above all to interpreting and popularizing the "laws" of statistics, the uniformity in the annual numbers of births, deaths, crimes, and the like. These regularities, especially of crime, had been shocking when Quetelet first noticed them in 1829 in a volume of French judicial statistics. For more than half a century, European moralists worried that human behavior, including moral behavior, appeared to be controlled by statistical law, leaving no room for personal freedom. Quetelet aimed to be conciliatory, emphasizing that lawlike behavior at the level of society still left room for a degree of freedom at the level of individuals.

This principle, that one could anticipate mass regularities even when individual causes were quite unknown, became a model for statistical reasoning in a range of sciences. In the 1860s the physicists James Clerk Maxwell and Ludwig Boltzmann invoked it as support for a statistical theory of gases, and Francis Galton drew on it for his statistical studies of heredity. Quetelet added one more crucial element to this mix, the idea that variability in nature and society was often governed by the astronomer's "error curve," known now as the bell curve or normal distribution. He was famous for his confidence in mean values, personified by his celebrated "average man," and for him, the bell curve gave evidence that departures from the mean were essentially error. But for his scientific descendants, the analysis of variation became fundamental to the emerging mathematical field of statistics.

See also **Crime; Science and Technology; Sociology; Statistics.**

BIBLIOGRAPHY

Primary Sources

Quetelet, L. A. J. *On Man and the Development of his Faculties; or, Essay on Social Physics.* London, 1842. Translation of *Sur l'homme et le développement de ses facultés.* Paris, 1835.

———. *Letters . . . on the Theory of Probabilities, as Applied to the Moral and Political Sciences.* London, 1849. Translation of *Lettres sur la théorie des probabilités, appliquée aux sciences morales et politiques.* Brussels, 1846.

Secondary Sources

Desrosières, Alain. *The Politics of Large Numbers: A History of Statistical Reasoning.* Translated by Camille Naish. Cambridge, Mass., 1998.

Lottin, Joseph. *Quetelet: Statisticien et sociologue.* Louvain, 1912.

Porter, Theodore M. *The Rise of Statistical Thinking, 1820–1900.* Princeton, N.J., 1986.

Stigler, Stephen M. *The History of Statistics: The Measurement of Uncertainty before 1900.* Cambridge, Mass., 1986.

THEODORE M. PORTER

R

RACE AND RACISM. Ideas about race, so commonplace in the early twenty-first century, emerged in very specific historical settings. Concepts of race changed remarkably over time, and from place to place. The use of the word *race* began to appear in English in the sixteenth century, but its usage was unusual and infrequent, and even then might refer to all kinds of groups. It is widely accepted that modern concepts of race derived essentially from the years of Enlightenment thinking in the eighteenth century. Ideas about racism (largely a twentieth-century phenomenon) were similarly prone to change and variation across time and place.

EIGHTEENTH-CENTURY DEBATES
Although theories about race flowered, and became most influential, in the nineteenth century, their origins are to be found in the previous century, and in the varied efforts to comprehend the origins of humankind. What gave the eighteenth-century debates such a sharp edge was their relevance for Europe's dealings with the wider world. Indeed it was the encounters with an obviously amazing variety of human types, societies, and people as Europeans traveled, traded, and colonized that formed the basis both for the inspiration and the data for the debate and writing about the nature of humankind. There had been observations about the distinctions between people in any number of historical settings. But it is really only since the early nineteenth century that Europeans (and then Americans) turned to the concept of race as the key concept for the categorization of human beings.

There were a number of major themes to eighteenth-century discussions of race. First, a race was seen to have a fixed set of characteristics that remained unchanged by outside conditions. Second, it was argued that a key feature of this racial typology was mental/intellectual, and that these features were not the same from one race to another (that is, some races were more intelligent or brighter than others). Third, it was argued that intellectual capacity revealed itself by outward physical characteristics: it was possible to tell, by physical appearance, the nature (and limitations) of a person's (or a group's) intellectual capacities. Thus were complex arguments about race simplified, over the eighteenth and nineteenth centuries, into relatively simple rules of thumb that gained remarkably widespread acceptance (through print and formal education) to become popular ideas that had a potency of their own. Thus did abstract literary and intellectual debates of the eighteenth century pass directly (if clumsily) into popular politics of the early twentieth century.

The early polarity of division, between Christians and pagans, gave way to ever more complicated divisions of humans, partly because the complexities of humanity were revealed as Europeans encroached on distant peoples, and partly as European intellectual traditions of philosophy and natural science also changed. The "discoveries" of the world's varied peoples pushed scholars toward new taxonomies (classifications). Inevitably, Western scholars inherited a powerful biblical tradition that explained the origins of humankind in relatively simple terms (via Adam and Eve). Inevitably too, these early analysts sought to strike a balance between the simple biblical explanation of human origins, and the geographic complexity of the world currently unfolding before them. In the process a string of new classifications emerged—most notably from the Swedish botanist Linnaeus (Carl von Linné; 1707–1778), and the German zoologist and anthropologist Johann Friedrich Blumenbach (1752–1840)—that were inherited and used by subsequent scholars. But the core belief was that environment shaped human differences, whatever term was used to describe those differences. Different climatic regions produced different human types, which in their turn created very different social forms and structures. More troubling, because of its obvious theological consequences, was the emergence of polygenism; that is, the idea that humanity did *not* spring from a single point of creation. But to promote such a case was to confront the biblical argument of the origins of humans through Adam.

All commentators on the origins of humankind had to wrestle with the extraordinary diversity and geographic spread of humanity. How had humankind spread itself so widely across the surface of the earth? Perhaps the most influential writer who tackled the origins of humankind was Georges-Louis Leclerc, comte de Buffon (1707–1788), whose massive work (running to forty-four volumes) sought to explain human features (color, appearance, size) in terms of environment. Transplant people around the globe and they would, he argued, adapt to local physical conditions. The problem however was that there was a growing volume of data that simply refuted such claims. There were for example sizable black minorities in Europe by the mid-eighteenth century that simply did not grow paler the longer they stayed in northern Europe. Equally, whites migrating to the tropics did not (if they survived) take on the physical features of local peoples. The clear problem was how to explain the diversity of humankind. For all Buffon's intellectual influence (a string of notable authors picked up and expanded his ideas), the human and anthropological evidence simply contradicted his case. A number of scholars wrestled with the concept of the human diversity, and by the late eighteenth century a number of scholars had begun to use the word *race* to describe the different groups they claimed to have identified.

The Different Human Races. Color plate from *Naturgeschicte des Teirreichs* (*Natural History of the Animal Kingdom*) by Gotthilf Heinrich von Schubert, 1861. Private Collection/The Bridgeman Art Library

RACE AS A DOMINANT CATEGORY OF CLASSIFICATION

From the late eighteenth century the idea of "race" emerged as a dominant category in the classification of humankind. Science, medicine, and early anthropology (not fully developed until the nineteenth century) turned to race. But it also spilled over into popular usage and custom, both as part of the popular spoken vernacular and as an expression of popular opinion.

Atlantic slave empires One critical element in this convergence of intellectual and popular usage of race stemmed directly from the emergence and significance of the Atlantic slave empires. From the mid-sixteenth century onward, especially after the development of the sugar plantations in Brazil and then the Caribbean, Europeans turned to Africa for slave labor. This in itself was a curiosity: why shift boatloads of Africans across the Atlantic to produce tropical staples for distant societies in western Europe? Moreover it was doubly curious in that slavery in Europe had effectively ended at the very period Europeans turned to Africa for slaves. Unable to persuade indigenous Indians to work in their new settlements, and incapable of securing adequate supplies of European settlers (free or indentured), colonists and their metropolitan backers turned to Africa. African slaves were already being used in the newly settled Atlantic islands. It seemed a natural step to transplant African slave labor into the Americas. The initial trickle became a flood after the establishment of the sugar plantations.

By the late eighteenth century, the Atlantic slave trade (now dominated by the British) ferried tens of thousands of Africans across the Atlantic every year. It is now known that some twelve million Africans were loaded onto the Atlantic slave ships, and about ten and half million landed in the Americas. Slavery was not, of course, unique to these newly created societies in the Americas. But what distinguished them—what made them unique—was their racial basis. At the height of the slave empires, to be black was to be a slave: to be a slave was to be black. Moreover this form of slavery hinged on the reduction of the African to the status of object/thing/chattel. Black humanity was, via the Atlantic slave trade, reduced to the level of thing.

Objectifying the African This may, at first sight appear to be simply an accidental consequence of trade and colonization. In fact the reduction of one branch of humanity—African— to the status of property was consciously and deliberately shaped and orchestrated by metropolitan commercial and political interests. British laws, for example, specifically designated Africans as things in acts of Parliament governing the slave trade. Colonial legislation regulating government in the slave colonies, even English courts, designated Africans as items of trade—as things. As early as 1677 the English solicitor-general declared that "Negroes ought to be esteemed goods and commodities within the Acts of Trade and Navigation."

There were numerous occasions when English law and lawyers confirmed the property status of black people. In 1749 Philip Yorke, Lord Hardwicke, declared that slaves in England were "as much property as any other thing." Thus even before the intellectual debate about lack of humanity had begun to focus on race as a category, colonizing nations had created a special category for Africans and their descendants: The black was a thing, a nonhuman.

Implications for ideas of race There was, of course, an abundance of evidence to the contrary. And the very idea of the black as a thing posed a serious intellectual challenge to a broadly based cultural acceptance of the African as *Homo sapiens.* Equally, there were powerful voices, growing in numbers and stridency by the late eighteenth century, that spoke out against the relegation of the black to the level of thing. Yet the critical fact remains indisputable. In order to tap the prosperity of the Americas, and to enhance the well-being both of the colonizing peoples and of their metropolitan nations, Europeans had created a special status for millions of humans. They had created a new form of slavery for their economic self-interest: a highly racialized form of slavery. Not surprisingly, this peculiar institution—so fundamental to life across swathes of the Americas until the mid-nineteenth century—had far-reaching consequences for the emergence of the debate about race, and for the development of a racism that had recognizably modern features. Stated simply, white society treated and viewed black humanity as a deeply inferior subset of humankind. The practical, intellectual, and popular consequences of black slavery were ubiquitous and pervasive.

What is odd is how this central fact—with consequences for four continents over more than four centuries—has rarely been recognized as a critical issue in the evolution of attitudes toward race in these years. It is worth asking the simple question: is it remotely possible that so prolonged a process of dehumanization for so many people (and scattered over such huge expanses of the globe) could *not* have shaped attitudes about race? The fundamental inspiration behind the Atlantic slave system was economic of course. But it came to be authorized and justified, in law, economic custom, and popular convention—and eventually in popular culture—in racial terms. Only black people could be slaves in the Atlantic system.

As part of the process of justification, commentators began to attribute to blacks "slavish" characteristics: ignorance, sloth, stupidity, duplicity, and mendacity—these and other vices were imputed to blacks as basic racial features that only the constraints of slavery could overcome. Without slavery, blacks would simply revert to their "natural" African vices and would prove of no value to society. Thus did slavery and all its punitive habits come to be explained and justified in terms of race. Blacks were of no economic use unless marshaled, regulated, and controlled by the repressions of slavery. What slavery did was to mark out millions of human beings (blacks) for special categorization. And in the process there was a marked slippage in definitions. The simple process of describing all black people as a type—a race—changed into something quite different: an explanation of human behavior by reference to race. What Atlantic slavery achieved was to lay the secure foundations for a form of racism. And that racism was to flourish, in changed and quite different circumstances, long after slavery itself had been abolished.

THE SPREAD OF "RACISM"

This relegation of black humanity to a deeply inferior level was confirmed by a range of popular cultural expressions: cartoons, prints, newspapers, tracts—all and more described black humanity in grotesque, often animal-like, terms. What compounded this tradition was the work of men closely linked to the slave system, notably the planters and their hired scribes intent on maintaining the slave as an item of property and keen to deflect any hint of black equality. And it was at this point—in the increasingly frenetic late-eighteenth-century debate about black humanity (prompted by the early abolitionist movement), that the pro-slavery lobby began to speak of blacks as a "race." Until roughly 1750 race had been used simply as a classification—a type. But the abolitionist-plutocratic debate was crucial in shifting the meaning of the word. Henceforth *race* came to mean a group of people whose differences lay in their physical features—their skin, color, shapes. It was possible henceforth to spot a person's race simply by looking at them (though it is also true that an increasing trend toward human mixing,

as peoples moved and settled around the globe, confused this pattern still further).

How this view of race spread and was made popular is a complex story, bound up with the emergence of a new culture of print, the transformation of urban life and the emergence, eventually, of widespread literacy. Equally, the establishment of popular education, in western Europe and North America, confirmed and extended the popular and scientific views of race by entering the classroom. Racism in a recognizably modern sense began to make itself felt both as an intellectual typology and as a popular concept.

Slavery left a distinct racial legacy. It was based on the proposition (however obviously flawed) that black people were things: chattels and objects of trade. Abolitionists' first task was to establish the humanity of slaves ("Am I not a man and a brother?"). But the theme persisted well into the nineteenth century. In the confused and widening debate about slavery (and the justifications for and against) the blackness of humanity was a central issue. But what made the older views about black inequality even more virulent was the emergence of new sciences that sought to discover categories of humans, and to provide a new scientific basis for that categorization.

The scientific urge to seek distinctions among humans concentrated not merely on color of course: shape, size, outward physical features (notably of the head), all and more were recruited to the task. But color remained the most obvious and immutable distinction. It was a protracted and confused process, but the outcome was a clear school of science, promoted by early anthropology and later social sciences, that claimed to explain human differences in racial terms. Not surprisingly, it led to a league table of humanity—with whites at the top. Blacks—inheriting the status endured by slaves in earlier centuries—were consigned to the lowest reaches of humankind.

There were also other forces at work, notably the emergence of powerful, popular attachments to racial feeling. Propagated by different but converging forces, popular racism equally consigned black humanity to the lowest rungs of humanity. One key explanation was the disappointment felt with the results of abolition. The high expectations of abolitionists, in the Caribbean and North America, that freed slaves would quickly take their place as a free and prospering peasantry, were soon disappointed. The poverty and continuing deprivation of former slaves in the Caribbean islands and in the U.S. South (in both cases, they were generally denied access to the land, education, and facilities required to improve themselves) confirmed the worst accusations of the pro-slavery lobby that blacks could never rise from the humblest of stations. They were, in effect, doomed to exist as the simple helots or serfs of superior peoples. Even in South America, where there had long been a powerful tradition of racial mixing, new waves of European immigration saw a hardening of local racial distinctions, and especially of the separation of black and white, in order to enhance and preserve the status of the more recently arrived white immigrants.

The language of race became hugely popular and widespread. Indeed it was so pervasive that it was applied, by the late nineteenth century, to much wider areas of society than previously. "Race" was thought a suitable category to describe a host of contemporary social structures. The British for example used *race* in the most casual and commonplace fashion: they called themselves "an island race" and even the lower orders of the British people (poor, urban, and industrial) were described as a "race" or a "race apart." In Europe as a whole, by the end of the nineteenth century, race had taken on an entirely new and more pervasive meaning. Germans viewed themselves as a national race, and scientists wrestled with the idea that Europeans might best be divided into racial groupings. What is remarkable about all this is the speed with which race became the widely and popularly accepted means of social categorizing and description. Race was no longer simply a tool used by social and natural scientists. It had taken on an entrenched and popular dimension.

It was greatly assisted by the rise of two related issues: mass education and literacy, and the urge to empire. The creation of modern empires (especially in Africa), the political debate in Europe about empire, and the classroom discussion of empire and of the wider world confirmed many of these new and simplistic views of race. What better way

of confirming the superiority of the white person than pointing to the imperial maps in European classrooms and letting the evidence speak for itself? Maps seemed to confirm that the white world had triumphed easily and swiftly over the nonwhite world, and offered positive proof, it was argued, of the superiority/inferiority that lay at the heart of the whole process.

Such views were embedded at the heart of the literature to which generations of schoolchildren were exposed before 1914. Textbooks, maps, and lessons from teachers who were themselves steeped in the rhetoric of race became the basic educational diet of millions of schoolchildren. The lessons of history, geography, and even literature were harnessed to the task of expounding a racial view of the world that saw white society at the top and black society at the bottom (wherever one looked). It was furthermore a view confirmed by popular culture: by the hugely influential popular newspapers and print culture of the late nineteenth century. Children's books, comics, and magazines extolled the virtues of empire, and of the bravery of white men bringing the benefits of empire to the less developed corners of the globe. Even the contemporary cult of popular games (the very games that dominate the social landscape to this day) had a role in this process: they were training grounds for the perfection of imperial and military qualities, and physical expressions of the very process of racial/national superiority. No one thought—or imagined—that one day (not far hence) those very games would be usurped by the subject people to whom they were introduced, and those same people one day might even beat their masters at their own games. What happened to the old theories of superiority when black men beat white men at football, cricket, boxing, and track and field?

The strength of popular racism can be seen in most forms of early twentieth century popular culture: in print, of course, and in cartoons and music—especially in music halls and vaudeville (where "blacking-up" was a peculiar variant of the wider theme). It passed directly from this tradition into the early day of cinema and silent movies. Thus did the racism of the few—of "scientists"—become disseminated among millions of people, on both sides of the Atlantic in the years before World War I.

ASSESSMENT

This account is, inevitably, a shortened account of what is a hugely complex and confusing story. But the basic point is simple enough. On the eve of World War I millions of people, throughout Europe and North America (and even wider afield) believed (and expressed) views about race that had, not long before, been the preserve of a small educated minority. The racism of the early twentieth century was a unique phenomenon. It was not, like the racial views of the era of slavery, a debate among relatively small numbers of interested parties and observers. It had become enormously popular and pervasive. It also had the potential to become a major political force. And that is exactly what happened. Scientific ideas about race were used by political groups, from the late nineteenth century onward, to develop a political case that hinged on concepts of racial superiority. This was transformed, in the 1920s and 1930s into its most virulent form, in the rise of fascism: a highly racialized philosophy that was to convulse Europe until 1945.

The line of descent between racial views in the eighteenth century and the ideological conflicts of twentieth century Europe may seem tenuous. In fact they were direct and unbroken. Views about race, and the emergence of modern racism, passed from the world of the slaveholder to the architects of twentieth century racial superiority. Naturally enough, the process, spread over such a long period (years marked by unprecedented social, economic, and demographic change) was complex and confusing. Yet there are recognizable elements from beginning to end. The categorization of humankind into racial groups, identified by outward appearances (color most notably) was perhaps the most striking and immutable legacy that passed from the world of racialized slavery in the eighteenth century to the twentieth century. At one level, the fact that racism, in all its varied and fluctuating forms, survives, is an indirect testimony to the persistence and durability of the ideas that underpinned the slave system in a long-distant era. It is as if the sins of the fathers continue to trouble descendants down to the present day.

See also **Anti-Semitism; Chamberlain, Houston Stewart; Civilization, Concept of; Eugenics; Evolution; Imperialism; Slavery.**

BIBLIOGRAPHY

Augstein, Hannah Franziska, ed. *Race: The Origins of an Idea, 1760–1850.* Bristol, U.K., 1996.

Back, Les, and John Solomos, eds. *Theories of Race and Racism: A Reader.* London, 2000.

Bulmer, Martin, and John Solomos, eds. *Racism.* Oxford, U.K., 1999.

Chaplin, Joyce E. "Race." In *The British Atlantic World, 1500–1800,* edited by David Armitage and Michael J. Braddick, 154–172. Houndmills, Basingstoke, Hampshire, U.K., 2002.

JAMES WALVIN

RADICALISM. In the late nineteenth century French Radical republicanism constituted an established political tradition and a new political enterprise. Radicals claimed the heritage of the French Revolution and pledged to complete transformations begun in 1789 and 1793. They participated in a distinctive political culture, which took shape in the 1860s in opposition to the Second Empire. Radicals were principal actors in the audacious project to create a republic in a major European state after 1870. By the first decade of the twentieth century Radicals dominated the Chamber of Deputies and led French governments. While such popularity and authority were not duplicated elsewhere in Europe, smaller Radical groups and parties could be found in Spain and Italy.

RADICAL POLITICAL CULTURE

In general Radical politicians emerged from the professional bourgeoisie. They were men with lycée and university education—lawyers, physicians, and journalists. They were trained in classical rhetoric and had a passion for words. Politicians were expected to present endless extemporaneous speeches, and their supporters devoured newspapers devoted to parliamentary intrigue, foreign affairs, and serialized novels. Parliamentary deputies mixed with the Parisian avant-garde and frequented popular music halls. Rank-and-file Radicals inhabited small-town provincial France. Especially in the south, teachers, pharmacists, and café owners served as local militants.

Radical political culture was profoundly masculine. Radicals always spoke of "universal suffrage," when they meant universal male suffrage. The citizen was assumed to be a man. Radicalism developed at a moment of extreme gender segregation within the bourgeoisie. Radical politicians inhabited exclusively male environments—the lycée, the university, the law courts, newspaper offices, and the Chamber of Deputies. By the late nineteenth century, women were entering the political arena. Feminists were demanding civil and political rights. A few Radicals, following the logic of their own political beliefs, supported them. Other women passionately and vociferously defended the Catholic Church and denounced Radical anticlericalism. The majority of Radicals became even more convinced of the need to exclude women from political life.

Among the defining tenets of Radical political culture, secularism was paramount. Radical republicans viewed themselves as embattled opponents of an obscurantist and militant Catholic Church. They claimed to defend Enlightenment principles of science and reason. Religion must be excluded from public life. Radicalism drew on and in turn energized the organizations of Freemasons and Free Thinkers. Positivism with its insistence on a knowable objective world was a major philosophical support of this secularism. Kantian moral imperatives and liberal Protestantism tempered this scientism.

Equally central to Radical beliefs was a deep commitment to representative government created and legitimated by universal male suffrage. The authority of the state could only function when based on a fully democratic electoral process. Such a state could only take the form of a republic. Immediately after the establishment of the Third Republic intransigent Radicals condemned the parliamentary institutions inherited from successive nineteenth-century monarchies, viewing them as obstacles to popular sovereignty. However, being ambitious politicians, the Radicals came to terms with parliamentary structures and by 1910 were the dominant force in both the Chamber of Deputies and the Senate. By the first decade of the twentieth century their critics decried Radicals as consummate parliamentarians steeped in pomposity, corruption, and immobility.

The Radicals' republicanism called for active citizens who were bound together by fervent patriotism and whose rights were protected by the state. Steeped in an antiaristocratic tradition, Radicals were suspicious of any privilege. Citizens' independence could be hampered not only by clerical interference but also by economic dependence. Radicals proposed and supported legislation to limit economic privilege and safeguard the ability of workers to function as citizens. They decried class divisions as antithetical to the Republic. They collaborated with socialists on labor reform legislation. They called for a progressive income tax as a measure to support egalitarianism.

The high point of French Radicalism occurred between 1899 and 1910. The Radicals were the unanticipated victors in the aftermath of the Dreyfus affair, the scandal over the Army condemnation of a Jewish officer, Alfred Dreyfus, for espionage. A few idiosyncratic Radicals had been prominent supporters of Dreyfus. As a group, however, Radical politicians had long hesitated to take a position. By 1900 following legislative elections and the formation of a government of "republican defense" the political tilt was clearly in the Dreyfusard direction. Radicals and Dreyfusards shared the same opponents—rightwing nationalists, conservatives, the church, and the military. Radicals seized this opportunity to extend their anticlerical campaign and to promote a more republican political and social life. In 1901 most Radicals, although not all, organized the Radical and Radical-Socialist Party, the first formal party in France. Although a step to greater unity, the party's composite name suggests the continuing diversity within Radicalism.

AGENDA

The Radical Party collaborated with Socialists and a few moderate republicans in a parliamentary coalition. The 1902 and 1906 legislative and municipal elections were victories for this coalition and Radical-led governments were formed. Their agenda was continuing secularization, moderate social reforms, and further republicanization of French society. Anticlerical measures were enacted that severely constrained the existence of religious congregations and the ability of their members to teach. These were condemned as sectarian attacks on religious freedom, but they had the enthusiastic support of the Radical rank and file. Church and state were formally separated in 1905, and France became the only secular polity in Europe. By 1907 however the government encountered ever more determined and popular Catholic resistance to its efforts to limit church influence and presence. Quietly the state retreated and relaxed the implementation of the most contested laws.

While Radicals called for social reforms, the accomplishments were small. Legislation on obligatory old-age pensions had been debated for years and remained blocked in the Senate. The progressive income tax made little progress. The French working class was increasingly organized and militant. Major strikes demanding legislation for an eight-hour day received little response. Efforts to unionize postal workers alarmed Radicals. The revolutionary antimilitarism of some unions enraged patriotic Radicals. The powerful alliance of the left between Radicals and Socialists unraveled and in 1905 the Socialists withdrew. Finally among the Radicals themselves, never a homogeneous group, tensions increased. Parliamentarians ignored the progressive programs endorsed by party militants at annual congresses. Some Radicals viewed Socialists as dangerous "collectivists"; others saw them and their working-class constituents as natural allies. These differences reflected the persistent tension within Radicalism between efforts to promote the equality of all citizens and the commitment to protect the independent, autonomous individual.

Although still a powerful electoral and parliamentary force in the years immediately preceding World War I, Radicals no longer dominated governments, nor did they set the parliamentary agenda. Their goals had encountered considerable obstacles, perhaps inescapable in a society composed of contending classes, sharply distinguished genders, and diverse cultures. The politics of interest, class, and war invaded their ranks and overwhelmed their agendas. Nonetheless, the political significance of Radicalism and the assumptions of its political culture continued to be influential through the interwar years.

See also **Dreyfus Affair; Liberalism; Separation of Church and State (France, 1905); Socialism.**

BIBLIOGRAPHY

Berstein, Serge. *Histoire du parti radical.* 2 vols. Paris, 1980–1982.

Mayeur, Jean-Marie, and Madeleine Rebérioux. *The Third Republic from Its Origins to the Great War, 1871–1914.* Translated by J. R. Foster. Cambridge, U.K., 1984. (This work originally appeared as two separate volumes in French: Jean-Marie Mayeur, *Les débuts de la Troisième République, 1871–1898,* Paris, 1973; and Madeleine Rebérioux, *La république radicale? 1898–1914,* Paris, 1975.)

Nord, Philip. *The Republican Moment: Struggles for Democracy in Nineteenth-Century France.* Cambridge, Mass., 1995.

Stone, Judith F. *Sons of the Revolution: Radical Democrats in France, 1862–1914.* Baton Rouge, La., 1996.

JUDITH F. STONE

RAILROADS. To those who witnessed its construction the railroad was a symbol of the progress of human civilization. Historians too traditionally assumed that the new mode of transport had a revolutionary impact. According to W. W. Rostow the railway was undoubtedly "the most powerful single initiator of [economic] take-off" (p. 302). Doubts were provoked, however, by the counterfactual approach adopted by Robert Fogel in *Railroads and American Economic Growth: Essays in Econometric History* (1964). On the basis of some very questionable assumptions, the Nobel prize–winning economist attempted to calculate the cost to the economy if the railways had not existed. His conclusion was that "no single innovation was vital for economic growth in the nineteenth century." This really quite unexceptional insight was subsequently applied to most European countries. In accordance with Fogel's approach, the calculations in table 1 subsequently emerged, purporting to show the relatively small amount of "social saving" that resulted from the transport of freight by rail, rather than the alternatives, in Europe.

However, the theoretical and statistical model-building engaged in by the econometricians abstracts out of existence variables that cannot be quantified and tends to make simplistic and static assumptions concerning quantifiable elements. Furthermore the statistical information available is itself fragmentary and the subsequent calculations impossible to verify. Thus, and in spite of the claims made concerning

TABLE 1

Social saving derived from use of railways		
Countries	Date	Social saving expressed as a percentage of GNP
England and Wales	1865	4.1
England and Wales	1890	11.0
Belgium	1865	2.5
Belgium	1912	4.5
France	1872	5.8
Germany	1890s	5.0
Russia	1907	4.6
Spain	1878	11.8
Spain	1912	18.5

SOURCE: Patrick O'Brien, ed., *Railways and the Economic Development of Western Europe* (London, 1983).

greater intellectual rigor, the results are no more nor less than suggestive pointers to questions that ought to be asked by more empirically minded social and economic historians interested in the perceptions and behavior of the historical actors themselves rather than in assumptions concerning the "rational" actions of the *homo economicus* beloved of classical economic theory. Furthermore, the assertion that much of the capital invested in railways might have been more profitably employed elsewhere, while valid for underused portions of the rail networks, ignores the intense pressure on governments to ensure construction coming from localities that otherwise would have been excluded from the benefits of "modern civilization." The calculations also tend to underestimate the impact of forward (to markets) and backward (to industry) linkages, as well as the complex interactions between technical systems. In comparison with previous transport technologies, in terms of the resources necessary for its construction as well as the linkages that developed, it still makes sense to claim that the railways promoted a "transport revolution" even if it has become unfashionable to use the term. Nevertheless Fogel's revisionism has had a significant outcome in promoting an important change of emphasis in the assessment of the characteristics of technological innovation and its social impact. It has become more clearly evident that the evolution of the railway as a technical system becomes explicable only in relation to specific economic, technological, and additionally sociocultural and political contexts.

CONSTRUCTION

Transport facilities developed in response to perceptions of the need to reduce the cost and increase the efficiency of movement of people, goods, and information. Throughout the eighteenth century political economists such as Adam Smith (1723–1790) in Britain and administrators like Anne-Robert-Jacques Turgot (1727–1781) in France insisted with growing force on the close association between improved transport and greater prosperity. Merchants and manufacturers were only too aware of the practical impact of bottlenecks within existing communications networks. From around the 1740s, substantial investment followed in roads, canals, and port facilities. Success in achieving efficiency gains stimulated further innovation. In all of this, Britain, the first to experience the pressures of industrialization, took the lead. The application of steam power to haulage on the wagon-ways linking coal mines to waterways, on which rails had already been laid in order to reduce friction between wagon and surface and increase the pulling power of horses, represented the injection of a complex new technology into the existing road and water transport system, initially piecemeal and as a means of overcoming the shortcomings of existing modes of transport. It was followed by the construction of the first major-purpose-built railway from Liverpool to Manchester, opened on 15 September 1830. Although much of Britain already possessed efficient waterborne transport, there was substantial demand for railway construction. Moreover, throughout northwestern Europe, in relatively advanced societies the capital and skills necessary to build and operate the new networks already existed, while an increasingly widely shared culture of consumption encouraged international technology transfer and the adaptation of best practice to local circumstances. Enthusiasm for the new railway spread relatively rapidly within the more economically dynamic and densely populated areas of western Europe and then more gradually into regions likely to generate less traffic and toward the European periphery where capital and technical expertise were less plentiful.

Investment in rail had come to be seen as a technological imperative, an economic necessity, and additionally a means of promoting political integration. Space-time perceptions were fundamentally

The Rocket. Engraving depicting the steam locomotive developed by English engineer George Stephenson in 1829. After winning the contest to determine which engine was best suited for the job, it was Stephenson's Rocket that powered the the first major purpose-built railway, from Liverpool to Manchester, which opened on 15 September 1830. PRIVATE COLLECTION/BRIDGEMAN ART LIBRARY

altered. Indeed space appeared to have shrunk. Although in Britain rail construction was essentially left to private companies, on the Continent mixed regimes were the norm, reflecting particular legal and administrative traditions, concerns about public safety, and military-strategic interests. Decisions were the outcome of negotiations between ministers, senior civil servants, politicians representing the socioeconomic elites, and bankers. In France, the provisions of an 1842 law represented a compromise following a highly politicized debate between liberals like Louis-Adolphe Thiers (1797–1877) convinced of the superiority of the market in the allocation of resources and proponents of state intervention concerned to prevent the development of monopoly and protect the public service functions of the new mode of transport. It was agreed that the engineers of the state's Corps des Ponts et Chaussées should plan the layout of the primary network with its tracks, reflecting a political/administrative conception of space, radiating out from Paris and largely following the existing major lines of communication and of economic activity. While the state would finance construction of the roadbed, concessionary companies would accept responsibility for providing the superstructure and rolling stock. The unprecedented financial burden was thus shared.

Typically, in the case of a new technology construction costs would generally prove to be much higher than suggested by overoptimistic estimates. The construction process had a substantial impact on financial markets. In France rail investment amounted to 10 to 15 percent of gross domestic capital formation between 1845 and 1884. Fluctuations in investment by the railway companies inevitably had a significant influence on the business cycle. The provision of capital through the auspices of private banks, with the Rothschilds to the fore, and the subsequent sale of bonds and shares spread the habit of purchasing financial assets. A speculative boom was followed by the collapse of concessionary companies during the lengthy midcentury crisis, and briefly, following the Revolution of 1848, complete nationalization was considered. Instead the establishment of authoritarian government following Louis-Napoleon Bonaparte's coup d'état in December 1851 was followed by efforts to restore business confidence by extending the length of concessions and encouraging amalgamations to create financially stronger regional companies. Public pressure to be linked to the only means of cheap and rapid transport ensured that further construction remained a political imperative, and from 1859 a series of conventions that provided for state guarantees of dividends stimulated further extension of the network. This culminated in the laying of narrow-gauge lines and local tramways at the beginning of the twentieth century.

Elsewhere the situation varied, ranging from a mixture of state and private companies to complete state control in Belgium as a means of reinforcing the independence of the recently created state while at the same time integrating its economy into that of Western Europe. In the various German states, Italy, and Austria-Hungary the balance between state and private companies was increasingly altered by the nationalization of failing companies. External investment of capital and construction skills, initially by Britain and subsequently France, was substantial. For the Austrian Empire the railways appeared to offer an opportunity to secure the political and financial dominance of Vienna and to promote an economic modernization based upon the more intense industrialization of the Czech lands and the commercialization of Hungarian agriculture. In the case of Russia, where the state itself prioritized defense expenditure, there were two major periods of rail construction, in the 1870s and 1890s. In addition to the stimulus afforded to agriculture, the railways also provided efficient links between coal and iron deposits promoting heavy industry in the Donets Basin in Ukraine and engineering in St. Petersburg and stimulating the further development of the established industrial regions around Moscow and the Baltic, and in Warsaw and Łodz in tsarist Poland. While the impact of rail construction varied considerably within countries, in general it was the major urban centers, the lowlands, and major river valleys in which population and economic activity were already concentrated and which had been well placed within the pre-rail water/road networks that especially benefited. Unfavorable topography, particularly in the uplands, could add considerably to both construction costs and, as a result of high fuel costs and low speed, to subsequent operating expenses, while limited utilization in economically less dynamic regions inevitably meant that fixed costs were distributed over a low level of traffic. Along the Scandinavian coasts seaborne transport continued to be preferred.

Progress would be slowest where low levels of economic activity and governmental instability discouraged outside investors. As a result, in Italy the existing disparities between the north (Turin, Milan, Genoa) and the south became even more pronounced. Outside the Po valley, where the major lines had been constructed even before the establishment of national unity in 1861, the trunk routes were primarily of political and strategic importance. A rugged terrain ensured high operating costs. In more "peripheral" areas of the Iberian Peninsula and the Balkans, rail construction would in particular facilitate the development of agriculture and mineral extraction. Designed to support the export of raw materials, the configuration of the Spanish network typically took on a quasi-colonial shape.

Various forms of state subsidy sought to reduce the uncertainties in order to accelerate the process of "modernization." Nevertheless, even where private companies predominated, the establishment of freight and passenger tariffs involved constant negotiation. While the companies were anxious to

TABLE 2

Length of railway track and use, 1913

Country	Track length (km)	Track (km) per 1,000 sq. km	Metric ton/km of freight (millions)	Index of use made of lines
Austria-Hungary	22,981	36.8	17,287	0.399
Belgium	4,676	153.3	5,729	1.224
France	40,770	76.0	25,200	0.622
Germany	63,378	117.2	67,700	1.106
Great Britain	32,623	139.5	—	—
Greece	1,584	24.4	50	0.032
Italy	18,873	65.9	7,070	0.391
Norway	3,085	9.5	401	0.135
Russia	70,156	—	76,800	—
Spain	15,088	29.8	3,179	0.217

SOURCE: Data from B. R. Mitchell, *International Historical Statistics: Europe 1750–2000* (Houndmills, U.K., 2003) and Norman J. G. Pounds, *An Historical Geography of Europe* (Cambridge, U.K., and New York, 1985), pp. 496–497.

maximize their returns and adapt charges to the diversity of demand, government officials were concerned about the quasi-monopoly powers enjoyed by railway companies on most of their routes. The commercial flexibility of the companies was thus restricted. Direct state ownership, on the other hand, tended to result in higher charges designed to supplement the public revenue. Even so, substantial and repeated reductions in transport costs undoubtedly stimulated economic growth and increased traffic. In Germany freight rates by 1900 were one-quarter of their 1845 level; in Belgium they fell from 10.8 centimes per metric ton-kilometer in 1845 to 3.6 by 1913.

Historians have generally focused on the "big" innovations and neglected the incremental impact of smaller changes. Technologies tend to be improved as part of the process of diffusion. The reduction in freight rates and passenger fares achieved by the railways was thus not a once-and-for-all achievement. Over time, as traffic built up and the shortcomings of the earlier lines became evident, considerable improvements were made in their operating efficiency. This was achieved as a result of improved mechanical and civil engineering that involved most notably the replacement of iron with steel in the construction of more durable steel engine boilers and production of rails capable of carrying heavier trains. The development of more powerful and fuel-efficient compound engines ensured that in France, whereas the typical Crampton goods engine had weighed 125 kilograms for every horsepower generated in the 1870s, by 1913 this had been reduced to 50 kilograms. The intro-

duction of continuous brakes (from 1869) and electric signals (from 1885) represented responses to safety concerns and to the congestion evident on most major lines from the 1870s. With traffic generally exceeding expectations, passenger stations, goods yards, and engineering workshops were all rapidly in need of enlargement. In Britain rail freight amounted to some 38 million tons in 1850 and 1.996 billion (expressed in U.S. figures) by 1875. In France traffic increased by around 4 percent per annum between 1851 and 1913, with 70 percent of all freight being moved by rail. More bureaucratic and systematic business procedures and accounting practices also contributed to the efficient utilization of equipment and labor. Major stations like Frankfurt, with a staff of over one thousand in 1904, were vital hubs of activity. Military-style regulations were imposed on the labor force in the interests of both safety and efficiency. Efforts were also made through complex bonus systems and pensions to instill a sense of pride and loyalty within a labor force that in Britain had grown to 600,000 and in France to 355,000 on the eve of World War I.

LINKAGES

The broader impact of rail construction has generally been discussed in terms of "backward" and "forward" linkages. The most profound effect of improved communications was to reduce market fragmentation. As markets were widened many enterprises experienced a crisis of adaptation as new opportunities for profit were created but within more competitive markets—a situation

Royal Albert Bridge, Saltash, England, 1869. Designed by noted transportation engineer Isambard Kingdom Brunel and completed in 1857, the Royal Albert bridge spans the Tamar River and thus extended the English railway system westward from Plymouth to Cornwall. GETTY IMAGES

that promoted technical and organizational innovation. The reduction in transport costs and, in effect, of the cost of the final product for consumers, as well as the more rapid diffusion of marketplace information, was especially significant for products of low value in relation to weight such as coal, iron ore, building materials, and agricultural produce and for the finished products of the metallurgical, engineering, chemicals, and textiles industries. Falling prices stimulated the growth in demand for a wide range of products, further stimulating the creation of a mass market. This was particularly evident in regions lacking efficient waterborne communication, as in Germany, where fragmentation of economic space due to the lack of east-west river links had been particularly evident.

In the case of backward linkages, a massive stimulus was afforded to metallurgy and engineering. Demand for rails and rolling stock accounted for 13 to 18 percent of iron and steel orders in France during the height of the railway boom between 1845 and 1884 as well as for 12 to 18 percent of building materials, although subsequently demand was increasingly restricted to extensions to the network and replacement. The needs of the railway, together with competitive pressure, provided a vital stimulus to innovation designed to increase both the volume and quality of production. In metallurgy this involved the transition from small charcoal-based to large coke-using furnaces and the development of the refining, puddling, and rolling processes. Initial dependence on imports and on technological borrowing from

Britain and Belgium was short-lived. Thus by the mid-1850s Germany had already achieved self-sufficiency in locomotive production, and companies like Borsig in Berlin were already looking for export markets. The supply of coal was also substantially increased as falling transport costs for domestically produced coal and rising demand from industry and the railways themselves encouraged increased production and in areas like the Ruhr or northern France led to the emergence of coal-based technical systems. Coal producers in an area like the Loire basin, which had previously dominated regional markets due to its position within the waterway network, now however faced competition from more efficient mines in the north, the owners of which themselves complained about the competitive threat from Belgian and from seaborne British coal, penetrating inland as a result of rail company efforts to generate traffic from the ports serving their networks. Improved transport not only increased the elasticity of supply of coal and other raw materials and reduced their cost, but by providing for the greater regularity of supply also ensured that industry was less susceptible to price fluctuations, as well as allowing the reduction of stocks, which had previously tied up substantial capital.

The railways thus served as a "leading sector" stimulating the modernization of key sectors of the industrial and commercial economy and also the development of agriculture. Thus the equalization of regional and then of international grain prices substantially reduced the age-old association between climatic conditions and food prices and considerably increased food security. By the 1880s half the Russian wheat harvest was being transported to western Europe from rapidly developing ports like Odessa. Cereals from the Hungarian plains increasingly met Austrian needs. The bulk transport of wine and livestock, as well as of perishables like meat, fruit, vegetables, and dairy products, encouraged agricultural specialization and modified dietary practices. The more intensive commercialization of farming sustained a growing demand for inputs including chemical fertilizers as well as for manufactured goods at the same time, however, that the concentration and increased scale of industrial production effected a rapid decline in dispersed rural manufacture and the deindustrialization of many regions. Furthermore, competition

from large industrial flour mills at the ports sounded the death knell for numerous rural mills, while the construction of railways outside Europe and particularly in North America, together with falling maritime freight rates, promoted a process of globalization and heralded the onset of the "great depression" in European agriculture. It was hardly surprising, as import penetration increased, that both rail freight rates and tariff protection would become major political issues.

As well as promoting the concentration of industrial and commercial activity and thus the increased concentration of population, the railways made possible the massive transportation of the building materials needed for urbanization. The construction and then reconstruction of passenger stations with train sheds made of iron and glass behind more traditional facades, and of extensive goods yards, was in itself a central feature of the redevelopment of city centers. By the end of the century Paris had eight rail termini and Berlin seven. Their construction fundamentally affected land use and the flows of traffic and people. City centers were increasingly clogged by vast numbers of horse-drawn carriages, buses, trams, and carts. While the areas inhabited by the better-off classes were largely spared, large numbers of poorer people were displaced by the construction of lines, bridges, viaducts, and stations, and even if the relatively impoverished were increasingly likely to travel by train or tram it was the middle classes who were best placed to enjoy the suburban living that cheap mass transport made possible. In countless small towns and rural areas too the station offered a new hub for economic activity, ever more closely focused on provisioning the growing urban centers. Road traffic, which had been displaced from routes parallel to the railways, grew substantially for relatively short-distance movement to the nearest railway station. Migration too was made easier, whether to the city or to the ports and on, across the Atlantic. Construction of the Trans-Siberian Railroad from 1905 eased the movement of around 250,000 people each year from western Russia in search of a better life.

In addition to facilitating the movement of goods and people the railways, together with the electric telegraph (introduced by the Great Western Railway in Britain in 1839 and in France from 1845), combined to considerably increase the

TABLE 3

Country	Passenger kilometers (in millions)	Index
Austria-Hungary	8,321	0.193
Belgium	6,242	1.334
France	19,300	0.477
Germany	41,400	0.676
Greece	297	0.188
Italy	5,000	0.276
Norway	462	0.155
Spain	2,139	0.146
Russia	25,200	

Passenger traffic, 1913

SOURCE: Data from B. R. Mitchell, *International Historical Statistics: Europe 1750–2000* (Houndmills, U.K., 2003) and Norman J. G. Pounds, *An Historical Geography of Europe* (Cambridge, U.K., and New York, 1985).

speed and volume of information diffusion. The latter had initially served as an "enabling technology," constructed alongside the railway as a means of controlling traffic and then spreading outward. The number of telegrams dispatched rose in France from 500,000 in 1858 to 51 million in 1913. The first transatlantic cable entered service in 1866, heralding a growing globalization reinforced by the development of more efficient rail-borne postal services and of mass-circulation newspapers. In France the number of items sent through the post rose from 254 million in 1850 to 3.724 billion in 1913; in Germany the rate of increase was even more rapid, from 85.9 million to 7.024 billion during the same period. As well as reinforcing trends toward market integration, rail and telegraph also brought political centralization closer by increasing the efficiency of administrative reporting systems and the potential for central control over the provinces. The telephone represented further technical innovation to provide a more flexible means of communication in the office and home and became increasingly attractive as more extensive networks developed. There were 12,000 telephones in use in France in 1889 and 310,000 by 1913. In that year 430 million calls were made. In Germany the corresponding figures were 37,000 rising to 1,428,000, with the number of calls reaching 2,518 million. As well as stimulating business and personal contacts, improved communications also had substantial military implications, both for internal security and the waging of war.

In 1846 Prussian troops were transported to Kraków to suppress a Polish revolt; in order to achieve concentration for the 1859 campaign against Austria fought in northern Italy, the French moved substantial numbers of men and horses by rail. The experience of the Franco-Prussian war in 1870 and of mobilization in 1914, however, revealed that, on the one hand, incompetent planning could result in chaos, and on the other, that sustained efforts to remedy deficiencies might result in the rigidities associated with the Schlieffen Plan (Germany's early-twentieth-century military deployment plan). Moreover, movement away from railheads continued to be on foot or dependent on horse transport.

CONCLUSION

The railway might be viewed as a means of easing transport bottlenecks in an advanced economy (Britain, Belgium) or else as a leading sector promoting broader economic development (France, Germany, Russia). Nevertheless, even if the impact of railway construction, and that of the improvements in information diffusion it stimulated, varied between regions, there can be little doubt that it was everywhere considerable. The economic and social geography of Europe was modified substantially. In spite of continuities, the construction of national rail networks, followed by the development of international links, contributed to rising levels of productivity in both agriculture and industry. Even if the benefits were shared unequally, widespread and substantial improvements in living standards were evident. The development of coal-based technological systems also, however, substantially increased the capacity of states to wage destructive military campaigns and to sustain the war effort over long periods. In the last analysis, the impact of the railway, and of any technology, thus has to be assessed to a considerable degree in relation to the perceived interests of those who controlled its development and subsequent use.

See also **Coal Mining; Industrial Revolution, First; Industrial Revolution, Second; Science and Technology; Transportation and Communications.**

BIBLIOGRAPHY

Caron, François. *Histoire des chemins de fer en France, 1740–1883.* Paris, 1997.

Cohen, Jon S., and Giovanni Federico. *The Growth of the Italian Economy 1820–1960.* Cambridge, U.K., and New York, 2001.

Mitchell, Allan. *The Great Train Race: Railways and the Franco-German Rivalry.* New York, 2000.

O'Brien, Patrick, ed. *Railways and the Economic Development of Western Europe, 1830–1914.* London, 1983.

Pierenkemper, Tony, and Richard Tilly. *The German Economy during the Nineteenth Century.* New York, 2004.

Price, Roger. *The Modernization of Rural France: Communications Networks and Agricultural Market Structures in Nineteenth-Century France.* London, 1983.

Rostow, W. W. *The Stages of Economic Growth.* Cambridge, Mass., 1960.

Roth, Ralf, and Marie-Noëlle Polino, eds. *The City and the Railway in Europe.* Aldershot, U.K., 2003.

Schram, Albert. *Railways and the Formation of the Italian State in the Nineteenth Century.* Cambridge, U.K., 1997.

Szostak, Rick. *The Role of Transportation in the Industrial Revolution: A Comparison of England and France.* Montreal, 1991.

Teich, Mikulus, and Roy Porter, eds. *The Industrial Revolution in National Context.* Cambridge, U.K., and New York, 1996.

Ville, Simon P. *Transport and the Development of the European Economy, 1750–1918.* London, 1990.

ROGER PRICE

RANK, OTTO (1884–1939), Austrian psychologist and philosopher.

Otto Rank was born Otto Rosenfeld to a poor family in Vienna. A self-educated polymath, he was schooled to become a locksmith but meanwhile read extensively in art, literature, music, philosophy, anthropology, history, and science. Rank's diary, begun at age eighteen, reveals a number of intellectual forebears, notably Johann Wolfgang von Goethe, Arthur Schopenhauer, Henrik Ibsen, and Friedrich Nietzsche.

In 1905, at age twenty-one, Rank made contact with Sigmund Freud, twenty-eight years his senior, who became his employer, sponsor, and virtual foster father. Freud encouraged him to continue his education at the University of Vienna. By the time he earned his Ph.D. in 1912 with a psychoanalytic thesis on Lohengrin, he had already published three books: *The Artist* (*Der Künstler,*

1907), *The Myth of the Birth of the Hero* (*Der Mythus von der Gerburt des Helden,* 1909), and *The Incest Motif in Literature and Legend* (*Das Inzest-Motiv in Dichtung und Sage,* 1912). As secretary of the Vienna Psychoanalytic Society from 1906 and a member of the Committee or Ring of Seven in Freud's inner circle, Rank remained Freud's closest associate for the next twenty years, the foundational period of the psychoanalytic movement. His name appeared on editions four through seven (1911–1922) of Freud's *Interpretation of Dreams* as contributor of two chapters. The most prolific psychoanalytic writer next to Freud himself, Rank became a central figure in the psychological revolution of these years. Rank wrote poetry and philosophical aphorisms, loved the art and music of Vienna, and admired Freud greatly. He hoped his independent contributions would enrich Freud's discoveries but encountered resistance from his mentor even after initial encouragement of some innovations after 1918. Rank viewed Oedipus as a social construct—a tragic hero and poetic symbol as much or more than a template of family dynamics. His differences with Freudian psychoanalysis came to include an egalitarian focus in therapy, interest in pre-Oedipal development and the nurturing role of the mother, and the importance of conscious will (not just wish and drive) in therapy, creativity, ethics, and psychology generally. The year 1924 marked Rank's break with psychoanalysis. Returning to Vienna after a visit to the United States, where he had been made an honorary member of the American Psychoanalytic Association, Rank encountered hostility from Freudians for the ideas he had developed on the mother-child relationship, separation, and the actual engagement in therapy, expressed in two books he published that year. *The Development of Psychoanalysis* (*Entzwicklungsziele der Psychoanalyse*), written with Sándor Ferenczi, proposed a form of psychotherapy that was more active and less authoritarian than that practiced by the Freudians, while *The Trauma of Birth* (*Das Trauma der Geburt*) presented a theory of anxiety that diverged from the father-centered focus of psychoanalytic thought by emphasizing separation from the mother. Though Freud's response to *The Trauma of Birth* was initially very positive, he later rejected Rank's new work, leading to a final break between the two men.

In 1926 Rank moved to Paris with his psycho-analyst wife, Beata, and their daughter, Helene. One of his patients there was Anaïs Nin, who wrote about her therapy with Rank, their love affair, and his rivalry with Henry Miller. Rank immigrated to the United States in 1935. Though his work continued to be spurned in orthodox Freudian circles, he lectured, taught at the University of Pennsylvania School of Social Work, and prac-ticed psychotherapy in New York. His ideas also became better known in the United States through English translations of works published by Knopf as *Art and Artist* (1932), *Modern Education* (1932), *Truth and Reality* (1936), and *Will Therapy* (1936). In 1939, having by then been divorced and remarried, Rank died of an adverse reaction to a sulfanomide treatment of a systemic infection at age fifty-five. Rank's work has attracted a new audience not only in the field of psychotherapy, where some of his once radical ideas have become mainstream, but also among students of philosophy, humanistic psychology, feminism, and the arts. His insights on the soul, will, fear of life, fear of death, myth, and reli-gion, to name but a few, make him one of the major twentieth-century innovators of interper-sonal and existential psychotherapy.

See also **Adler, Alfred; Freud, Sigmund; Jung, Carl Gustav; Psychoanalysis; Psychology.**

BIBLIOGRAPHY

Primary Sources

Rank, Otto. *A Psychology of Difference: The American Lectures.* Edited by Robert Kramer. Princeton, N.J., 1996. Annotated collection of lectures given between 1924 and 1935, some of which are the only English versions of articles and book chapters.

———. *Art and Artist: Creative Urge and Personality Development.* Translated by Charles Francis Atkinson. Giessen, Germany, 1997. The introduction from the original 1932 English edition is by Ludwig Lewisohn and is important. The book addresses all the arts, and creativity, in light of history, culture, philosophy, and psychology.

———. *Psychology and the Soul.* Translated by Gregory C. Richter and E. James Lieberman; introduction by E. James Lieberman. Baltimore, Md., 1998. A com-bined history of soul and will, psychology and reli-gion, from animism to psychoanalysis, incorporating anthropology, philosophy, Shakespeare, myth, and physics.

Secondary Sources

Halliwell, Martin. *Romantic Science and the Experience of Self: Transatlantic Crosscurrents from William James to Oliver Sacks.* Aldershot, U.K., 1999. Includes Otto Rank, Ludwig Binswanger, and Erik Erikson.

Lieberman, E. James. *Acts of Will: The Life and Work of Otto Rank.* Rev. ed. Amherst, Mass., 1993.

Roland, Alan, Barry Ulanov, and Claude Barbre. *Creative Dissent: Psychoanalysis in Evolution.* Westport, Conn., 2003. A collection of twenty-two essays in honor of the Rankian psychologist Esther Menaker with her afterword.

E. JAMES LIEBERMAN

RANKE, LEOPOLD VON (1785–1886), German historian.

Leopold von Ranke was one of the most important historians of the modern era, whose work became the model of professional historical writing for the modern academic discipline in Germany and abroad, especially the United States and Britain. Ranke was remarkable for aspiring to dispassionate treatment of past eras; for attempting to understand them on their own terms, without the imposition of anachronistic ideologies; for assessing their significance in the broadest possible chronological and geographic frame of reference; for focusing on political his-tory; and for insisting on critical use of original written sources as the foundation of professional historical writing.

Born on 20 December 1795 in Wiehe, Thu-ringia/Saxony, Ranke came from an educated Lutheran family. His paternal grandfather was a pastor, and his father, Gottlob Israel Ranke, began his studies in theology before switching to law. At age eighteen Ranke himself went to the University of Leipzig, where he studied theology and classical philology from 1814 to 1817. He gradually decided to become a historian, but with his perso-nal piety undiminished. He received his initial appointment at the University of Berlin in 1825 and became professor of history there in 1834, making the Prussian capital his home until his death on 23 May 1886. In the fall of 1827 he began a research trip that took him to Vienna, Venice, Florence, and Rome. Returning to Berlin in the spring of 1831, he produced a succession of ambitious works over the next half century including *Geschichte der romanischen und germanischen Völker von 1494 bis 1535* (1824; History of the Latin and Germanic peoples from 1494 to 1535), *Die römischen Päpste. Ihre Kirche und ihr Staat im 16. und 17. Jahrhundert* (1834–1836; The Popes: Their church and state in the sixteenth and seventeenth centuries), *Deutsche Geschichte im Zeitalter der Reformation* (1839–1847; German history in the age of the Reformation), *Französische Geschichte* (1852–1856; French history), *Englische Geschichte* (1859–1868; English history), and *Weltgeschichte* (1881–1888; World history). His graduate seminar, which turned out generations of professional historians, contributed to the outstanding reputation of Germany's historical profession.

Ranke's conception of history was inseparable from his political conservatism. He was hostile to the democratic political movements that had challenged the traditional European order since 1789 and thought of the political actors in the moderate French Revolution of 1830 as a "mob"; for his model of government he looked to monarchs and statesmen like Frederick William IV, king of Prussia (r. 1840–1861), Maximilian II, king of Bavaria (r. 1848–1864), and Otto von Bismarck (1815–1898), all of whom admired his work. He tried to further a pragmatic conservatism that respected historical institutions while accommodating innovation. The historian Friedrich Meinecke interpreted his approach to nationalism as typical for his politics: he argued for maintaining the individual German states, and in particular Prussia with its conservative social order, in a larger German nation-state—which was in fact the goal Bismarck realized by 1871.

Ranke's history had the parallel aim of furthering his readers' insight into past historical eras. He was dismissive of theories of progress that made the past into a means to a final historical end. Instead he asserted in his private lectures for Maximilian II that "every era is next to God; its value depends not at all on what emerges from it, but on its own existence, its own self"(Ranke, 1979, p. 17). He particularly objected to what he considered G. W. F. Hegel's empty scholasticism for draining past eras of their individuality and meaning. Instead

he was fascinated by the task of an impartial, dispassionate discovery of the specific structure of different historical eras, which could be recovered by means of intensive research in written sources. Not that Ranke believed the facts spoke for themselves: The famous statement (in the preface to the *History of the Latin and Germanic Peoples*) that he wished to write history "*wie es eigentlich gewesen*" ("as it really was"), was a protest against imposing ahistorical schemas on the past (Ranke, 1867–1890, vol. 33, p. vii). Taken out of context it belies the complexity of his efforts to understand previous times in an age of accelerating change. As George Iggers has noted, Ranke was not a narrow fact-mongerer, even if some of his American and German followers chose to interpret him in this way. Far from letting the facts speak for themselves, he selected and narrated with great artistic skill and readily employed concepts like "nation" and "state" as organizing principles. His histories were never chosen for their local interest, but had the high drama, as he related them, of chapters within a universal history of humankind, its meaning never wholly clear, its future unpredictable, but nonetheless in retrospect a meaningful story of ever richer political, religious and cultural life.

Ranke has been criticized by Wolfgang J. Mommsen and other historians for hiding conservative politics beneath an ideology of objectivity and contributing to the generally antidemocratic politics of the German historical profession before 1945. Peter Burke has argued that many varieties of social history flourished in the eighteenth century only to be excluded by Ranke's narrow preoccupation with diplomatic and political history. Rudolf Vierhaus has analyzed how Ranke's political conservatism made it impossible for him to come to terms with the class society and proletarian politics undermining the traditional social order, a limitation that carried over into his historical writing, which failed to conceptualize the novel social history of his own time. His narratives lack anything comparable to Karl Marx's analyses of capitalism or Alexis de Tocqueville's grappling with democracy in America. A distinctive feature of Ranke's work, however, is its cosmopolitanism. He published a history of Serbia, wrote about Turkish diplomacy, and immersed himself in French and English history; although he wrote about individual nations and states he strove to establish their significance, as Leonard Krieger has emphasized, within a unified world history. His works remain timely for their synthesis of sympathetic imagination and dedication to empirical accuracy, qualities that make them enduring classics for the historical profession.

See also **Bismarck, Otto von; Germany; Hegel, Georg Wilhelm Friedrich; History; Mommsen, Theodor; Nietzsche, Friedrich.**

BIBLIOGRAPHY

Primary Sources

Ranke, Leopold von. *Das Briefwerk*. Edited and with an introduction by Walther Peter Fuchs. Hamburg, 1949.

————— *Über die Epochen der Neueren Geschichte* and *Das Politische Gespräch und Andere Schriften Zur Wissenschaftslehre*. New York, 1979.

————— *Sämmtliche Werke*, 3rd ed. Leipzig, 1867–1890.

Secondary Sources

Dove, Alfred. "Ranke, Leopold v." *Allgemeine Deutsche Biographie* (1875–1912), vol. 27, 242–269. Reprint, Berlin, 1967–1971.

Iggers, Georg G., and James M. Powell, eds. *Leopold von Ranke and the Shaping of the Historical Discipline*. Syracuse, N.Y., 1990.

Krieger, Leonard. *Ranke: The Meaning of History*. Chicago, 1977.

Liebersohn, Harry. "German Historical Thought from Ranke to Weber: The Primacy of Politics." In *A Companion to Western Historical Thought*, edited by Lloyd Kramer and Sarah Maza, 166–184. Oxford, U.K., 2002.

Meinecke, Friedrich. *Cosmopolitanism and the National State*. Translated by Robert B. Kimber. Introduction by Felix Gilbert. Princeton, N.J., 1970.

Mommsen, Wolfgang J., ed. *Leopold von Ranke und die moderne Geschichtswissenschaft*. Stuttgart, 1988.

Vierhaus, Rudolf. *Ranke und die Soziale Welt*. Münster/Westfalen, 1957.

HARRY LIEBERSOHN

RAVACHOL (FRANÇOIS CLAUDIUS KOENIGSTEIN-RAVACHOL)

(1859–1892), French anarchist.

François Claudius Koenigstein-Ravachol was born into gnawing poverty in the small town of Saint-Chamond near the French industrial city of Saint-Étienne in 1859. His father was a Dutch mill hand who abandoned his French wife and four children. Ravachol's mother worked in a silk-throwing factory. With three siblings, the boy was handed over at age eight to a succession of farmers, for whom he worked caring for their animals. Until he was eleven, Ravachol attended primary school, where he was embarrassed by having clothes so shabby that he looked like a small beggar. He went to church in what remained a region of relative fidelity to the Catholic Church, receiving his first communion at the age of eleven.

As a boy and then a young man, Ravachol worked here and there where he could find employment, in a mine and in textile workshops, once joining other workers on strike. He refused to work again for one employer to whom he had complained that the pressure to keep on the job constantly left him no time to eat or to go to the bathroom. He went to Lyon in search of work and joined a study group that read socialist and anarchist newspapers and brochures and listened to speakers. Gradually he became an activist, and then a brawler. He was now eighteen. After reading Eugène Sue's *The Wandering Jew,* a popular novel published in 1844–1845 about the poor neighborhoods of Paris, Ravachol lost his religious faith and joined some of his friends at a socialist gathering. But socialists believed in political participation, and Ravachol turned toward anarchism, convinced that political participation only propped up the corrupt, oppressive state. After an arrest (for having helped a young woman exact horrible revenge on a lover by providing the sulfuric acid she threw into his eyes) Ravachol turned to the illegal sale of alcohol, grave robbing, and counterfeiting in order to obtain money for his sick mother. And finally he became a murderer: in 1891 he killed a hermit reputed to have a fortune hidden in his strange house. Ravachol fell under suspicion and was arrested but managed to escape the police in Saint-Étienne as he was being taken to prison.

Ravachol fled to Paris in July 1891. In the capital, the name of the Russian anarchist Mikhail Bakunin (1814–1876) still resounded and the writing of another Russian, Peter Kropotkin (1842–1921), a man of peace who had coined

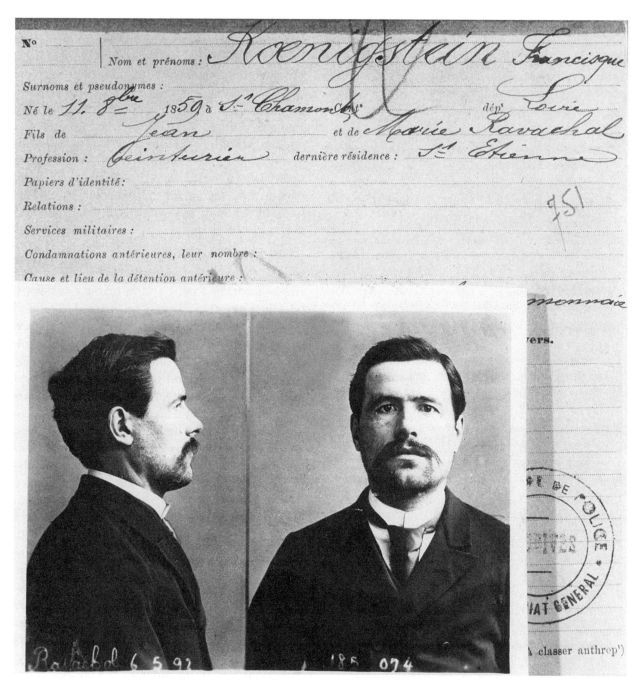

Documents from Ravachol's 1892 arrest for murder in Paris. Musée de la Prefecture de Police, Paris, France/Bridgeman Art Library/ Archives Charmet

the chilling phrase of strategy "Propaganda by the Deed," was well known. Ravachol lived with a couple in the industrial suburb of Saint-Denis and took an alias. They introduced him to anarchists. Police had recently fired on anarchists demonstrating on the Boulevard Clichy on the western edge of the city. Several had been wounded, three put on trial, and two condemned to long prison sentences. Ravachol decided to blow up a police office and in March 1892 constructed a bomb of dynamite and pieces of iron. But he was unsuccessful. And so Ravachol decided to kill a magistrate involved in the trial of the anarchists, but, here too, he was foiled by being unable to get

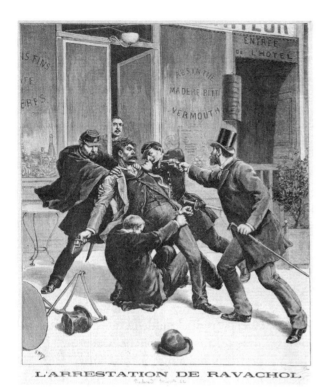

The arrest of Ravachol. Cover of the French publication *Le Petit Journal*, 16 April 1892. BIBLIOTHÈQUE NATIONALE, PARIS, FRANCE/BRIDGEMAN ART LIBRARY/ LAUROS/GIRAUDON

into the building on the Boulevard Saint-Germain. Next, he targeted another magistrate from the trial and this time was successful. The bomb he placed on the Rue de Clichy on 27 March wounded seven people. On the way home, Ravachol stopped in a restaurant called Le Véry, on the Boulevard Magenta. He engaged a waiter in conversation about anarchism, and the employee remembered the scar Ravachol had on his left hand. Three days later, he was arrested, although hardly with ease. It took ten policemen to subdue the brawler from the Loire.

Condemned to death for the murder of the hermit near Saint-Étienne, as well as for several other killings he probably did not commit, Ravachol went to the guillotine on 11 July 1892. He turned to the crowd of onlookers and shouted "Long live anarchy!" Several days later, a bomb destroyed Le Véry, giving rise to the pun that served as an anarchist signature: *Vérification*.

After his death, some sympathizers began to compare their martyr Ravachol to Jesus Christ. Anarchists sang "La Ravachole" to the tune of a song of the left during the French Revolution, "Ça ira" (It will be):

> In the Great City of Paris
> Live the well-fed bourgeois
> And the destitute who have empty stomachs
> But they have long teeth.
> Dance the Ravachol.
> Long live the sound of explosions!
> So it will be

Dynamite became the symbol of these anarchists.

> Let's dance the Ravachol, Long live the sound,
> Let's dance the Ravachol, long live the sound of
>   the explosion!
> It will be, it will be,
> All the bourgeois will taste the bomb,
> It will be, it will be
> These bourgeois, these bourgeois, we'll blow
>   them up!

In his "Eulogy for Ravachol," Paul Adam, an anarchist editor, warned that "the murder of Ravachol will open an era." And it did. Among other attacks, an anarchist stabbed a Serbian minister visiting Paris. One anarchist writer outraged public opinion by provocatively stating, "What do the victims matter if the gesture is beautiful?" Parisian anarchists hotly debated the strategy of "Propaganda by the Deed." Émile Henry on 12 February 1894 tossed a bomb into the Café Terminus next to the Gare St. Lazare, horribly wounding a number of clients. He, too, went on trial for his life and was guillotined several months later. When an Italian anarchist stabbed President Sadi Carnot to death that same year in Lyon, the killer proudly proclaimed the act as vengeance for the execution of Ravachol. Gradually, however, anarchist attacks subsided. Some workers and radicals favored syndicalism, others political contention-through reform socialist or revolutionary socialist parties.

See also **Anarchism; Anarchosyndicalism; Bakunin, Mikhail; Kropotkin, Peter.**

BIBLIOGRAPHY

Joll, James. *Anarchists.* London, 1979.

Maitron, Jean. *Histoire du movement anarchiste en France (1880–1914).* Paris, 1951.

———. *Ravachol et les anarchistes.* Paris, 1964.

Salmon, Andre. *La terreur noire: Chronique du mouvement libertaire.* Paris, 1959.

Sonn, Richard D. *Anarchism and Cultural Politics in Fin-de-Siecle France.* Lincoln, Neb., 1989.

Varias, Alexander. *Paris and the Anarchists: Aesthetes and Subversives during the Fin de Siècle.* New York, 1996.

Woodcock, George. *Anarchism: A History of Libertarian Ideas and Movements.* New York, 1962.

JOHN MERRIMAN

RAVEL, MAURICE (1875–1937), French composer.

Maurice Ravel was one of the most original figures in early twentieth-century French music. Though he clearly benefited from the revolutionary changes wrought by Claude Debussy (1862–1918), Ravel was nonetheless able to create his own musical idiom very early on, successfully combining a love of traditional forms with great inventiveness, retrospective elements with modern harmony, and this in many genres.

Born to a Basque mother and a Swiss father, Ravel trained in Paris beginning in 1889. At the Conservatoire he studied piano, counterpoint, and composition in turn. His first works were shot through with fin-de-siècle symbolist culture and musical impressionism. Like Debussy, Ravel employed parallel uninverted triads, sequences of refined dissonant chords, and abrupt modulations. Some of his compositions quickly earned him a solid celebrity, among them *Pavane pour une infante défunte* (1899; Pavane for a dead princess), *Jeux d'eau* (1901; Water games), String Quartet in F (1902–1903), *Sonatine* (1903–1905), and *Miroirs* (1904–1905).

Despite a promising second place in the Prix de Rome in 1901, Ravel failed repeatedly to win the prize in subsequent years. Much played up by the press, this rejection was clearly motivated by prejudice, and in 1905 the matter was dubbed the "Ravel affair." At this time Ravel belonged to the avant-garde group of writers and composers called the "Apaches" and occupied a peripheral position relative to the formal musical world. In 1906 Ravel composed a song cycle, based on the play *Histoires Naturelles* (1896) by Jules Renard (1864–1910), that used a vocal style that hewed fast to the rhythms of speech. His *Mother Goose* (1908) revealed his sensitivity to the world of childhood.

In 1909 Ravel was one of the founders of the Independent Musical Society—another way of marking his distance from the National Society, which was dominated by the most conservative musicians. In the following years he wrote *Rapsodie espagnole* (1908; Spanish rhapsody); *L'heure espagnole* (1911; The Spanish hour), based on a play by Franc-Nohain (1873–1934); and *Valses nobles et sentimentales* (Noble and sentimental waltzes; piano, 1911, orchestral version, 1912).

Daphnis and Chloé, a "choreographic symphony" for the Ballets Russes (1909–1912), was a "musical fresco" loyal to "the Greece of his dreams"—albeit more in the spirit of the eighteenth century than in that of the ancient world. Ravel was very close now to the international avant-gardes. The influence of Arnold Schoenberg (1874–1951) was discernible in his musical adaptation of three poems by Stéphane Mallarmé (1842–1898) for voice and nine instruments (1913). In the same year he worked with Igor Stravinsky (1882–1971) on the orchestration of a lyrical work by Modest Mussorgsky (1839–1881).

World War I precipitated a distinct break in Ravel's work, sending him back to a more classical aesthetic, as witnessed in his Piano Trio in A Minor (1914) and Piano Concerto in G (1929–1931), composed after the fashion of Wolfgang Amadeus Mozart (1756–1791). In quest of the true spirit of French music, Ravel looked, on the one hand, to the eighteenth century—as in his *Le Tombeau de Couperin* (Couperin's tomb; piano, 1917, orchestral version, 1918–1919), composed in memory of seven friends killed in the war—and, on the other hand, to the Renaissance. He cultivated archaic formal features: parallel fifths and octaves, melodies based on church modes and "gapped" scales, or ornaments borrowed from baroque music.

Ever an independent spirit, Ravel declined induction into the Legion of Honor in 1920 and led a secluded life while constructing a public image for himself as a dandy. The formal perfection of his work (Stravinsky caricatured him as "a Swiss clockmaker"), with its obsession with clarity and attachment to tonal functions, caused Ravel to be rejected by the new generation (Darius Milhaud [1892–1974], Francis-Jean-Marcel Poulenc [1899–1963], Georges Auric [1899–1983]). Among his works of the 1920s were *Waltz* (1920) for Sergei

Maurice Ravel (right) with Vaslav Nijinsky, 1912. ©BETTMANN/CORBIS

Diaghilev (1872–1929); a Duo for Piano and Cello in memory of Debussy (1922); *Tzigane* (1924); the opera *L'Enfant et les sortilèges* (1925; The child and the spells), with a libretto by Colette (1873–1954); and *Chansons madécasses* (1925–1926; Madagascan songs), the sensuality of whose exoticism was combined with anticolonialist themes.

Ravel's most celebrated composition was *Bolero* (1928), in which he achieved an incantatory effect through a rhythmic ostinato and two melodic ostinatos produced by the gradual introduction of more and more instruments leading up to a fortissimo. This work points up two very typical aspects of Ravel's music: its straight rhythms and the great richness of its orchestration. The composer was interested in dance not only for its structure but also for its rhythmic creativity and its expression of joie de vivre, and dance inspired a wide array of musical forms in his work.

In the late 1920s, Ravel's tours of Scandinavia, the United States, and Canada secured him a worldwide reputation. His Concerto in D Major for the Left Hand (1929–1930), composed for the pianist Paul Wittgenstein (1887–1961) who had lost his right hand in the war, developed new pianistic ideas and employed many effects borrowed from jazz. Ravel also wrote three songs, *Don Quichotte à Dulcinée* (1932; Don Quixote to Dulcinea), for a projected Russian film. He died in 1937; he had no disciples.

See also **Music.**

BIBLIOGRAPHY

Bruyr, José. *Maurice Ravel ou le lyrisme et les sortileges.* Paris, 1950.

Cahiers Maurice Ravel. Paris, 1985–. Annual journal.

Jankélévitch, V. *Maurice Ravel.* Paris, 1939. Rev. ed., Paris, 1995.

Larner, Gerald. *Maurice Ravel*. London, 1996.

Lesure, François, and Jean Michel Nectoux. *Exposition Maurice Ravel*. Paris, 1975.

Maule, M. de, ed. *Ravel par lui-même et par ses amis*. Paris, 1987.

"Maurice Ravel hier et aujourd'hui." *Revue internationale de musique française* 24 (1987).

Ravel, Maurice. *Lettres, écrits, entretiens*. Edited by A. Orensteil and J. Touzelet. Paris, 1989.

SOPHIE LETERRIER

REALISM AND NATURALISM.

Realism was a mid-nineteenth-century, primarily French, movement in literature and art. To realists, the arts did not exist for their own sake (*l'art pour l'art*), as they had for the Romantics, but served the cause of mankind (*l'art pour l'homme*) by exposing political and social evils. Realism as a broad movement in art and literature survived until the end of the nineteenth century, but it changed in the 1870s, when the artist Jules Bastien-Lepage (1848–1884) introduced a form of painting that today is generally referred to as *naturalism*, though in the nineteenth century that term was often used interchangeably with realism.

REALISM

Realism was based on the idea that writers and artists must focus on the here and now. *Il faut être de son temps*—"one must be of one's own time," was the current phrase that summed up this central idea of the movement succinctly. Realism was both an outgrowth of and a form of rebellion against Romanticism. While it rejected much of late Romantic art for its historic, exotic, or imaginary subject matter, it embraced one of the main tenets of early Romanticism, which held that art should be involved with the present. Or, as the Romantic critic and theorist Stendhal (pseudonym of Marie-Henri Beyle, 1783–1842) had written in 1824, "the '*romantic*' in all the arts is that which shows the men of today." But while to Stendhal showing the "men of today" meant to represent important men engaged in consequential acts, the realists focused on the trivial doings of ordinary people. In a now famous section of his review of the 1846

Paris Salon, the poet Charles Baudelaire (1821–1867) called for artists to depict "private subjects" and to open their eyes to the "thousands of floating existences … which drift about in the underworld of a great city."

Realism may also be seen as an artistic response to the social and political climate of the late 1830s and 1840s and its culmination in the explosive revolution of 1848. This new climate was marked by a growing awareness of the enormous gap between rich and poor that the Industrial Revolution had caused. Intellectuals, especially, became concerned with the abominable working and living conditions of factory workers, peasants, and the urban proletariat. Some developed fantastic utopian schemes aimed at bettering the lives of the lower classes and eliminating the excesses of wealth and poverty. Others felt that nothing but a war between rich and poor could bring about the wholesale change or revolution that was needed. In 1847 the German journalist Karl Marx (1818–1883), recently exiled from Paris to Brussels, and his friend Friedrich Engels (1820–1895) wrote a short text entitled *The Communist Manifesto*, in which they encouraged the "proletarians" to rise up and break the chains that bound them to their miserable fate. Even before the manifesto was published in 1848, Paris had become the scene of a violent revolution, aimed at radical political and social change.

Many young artists who lived through the Revolution of 1848 and the short-lived Second French Republic that followed it responded by redirecting their choice of subject matter to the lives of the lower classes—peasants, manual workers, beggars, and the like. It is not that such subjects had not been painted before but, while the older generation of painters, working during the 1830s and 1840s, had for the most part sentimentalized and trivialized low-class scenes, typically painting them in miniature formats, the young artists who emerged in the 1850s set out to depict them in a monumental, dignified, and honest manner. The Salon of 1850–1851—called by one critic a historic exhibition that marked the victory of "the feeling or at least the search for the truth"—would include several works that defined the realist movement. Among them were *The Stonebreakers* (1849) and *A Burial at Ornans* (1849–1850) by Gustave

Courbet (1819–1877); *The Sower* (1850) by Jean-François Millet (1814–1875); *Hunger* (1848), a painting of a starving family, by Jules Breton (1827–1906); and *School for Orphan Girls* (1850) by François Bonvin (1817–1887). Common characteristics of these works were their focus on contemporary life and their engagement with the daily labor, ritual activities, and miserable conditions of ordinary people—manual laborers, rural bourgeois, peasants, the urban poor, and their abandoned children. Courbet's *Stonebreakers,* for example, shows two men, one old, the other young, engaged in the manual breaking up of field stones into gravel used to pave the roads. Both are dressed in patched and torn hand-me-downs, which seem emblematic of the miserable lives that fate has handed them.

In referring to the works of Courbet, Bonvin, Breton, or Millet, both advocates and detractors used words like *honesty, truth, naivety,* and *from life,* but while to the former these attributes signaled the beginning of a new, progressive, and democratic art, to the latter they signified the abomination, even the end of art and the specter of a new "socialist" order in which beauty, culture, style, and sophistication no longer had a place. *Realism* became the signature term to refer to the works of the new artists. Courbet, who more than any of his contemporaries realized the importance of being part, and preferably even the leader, of the new artistic movement that would replace "outmoded" Romanticism, was quick to adopt the term as a banner for his art. In 1855, organizing a private exhibition of his paintings on the grounds of the first International Exposition in Paris, he referred to his exhibition building as the Pavillon du Réalisme. And as a preface to the small printed catalog of the exhibition he wrote a statement titled "Le Réalisme." Admitting that the title of "realist" was thrust upon him just as "the title of Romantic was imposed upon the men of 1830," and drawing into doubt the suitability of a term "nobody . . . can really be expected to understand," Courbet went on to explain what it meant to him:

> I have studied outside of any system and without prejudice, the art of the ancients and the art of the moderns. I no more wanted to imitate the former than copy the latter; nor, furthermore, was it my intention to attain the trivial goal of *art for art's sake.* No! I simply wanted to draw forth from a complete acquaintance with tradition the reasoned and independent sense of my own individuality.
>
> Knowing as a means of being able [to create], that was my idea. To be in a position to translate the customs, the ideas, the appearance of my epoch as I see it, to be not only a painter but also a human being, in a word, to make living art, that is my goal. (Author's translation)

To Courbet, then, Realism entailed the creation of a visual record of his epoch in a style that was his own individual distillation of the lessons he had learned from the art of the past. His art was based on his personal vision and understanding of his time, hence Courbet called it "living," as it was rooted in his own life experience.

Unlike *Romanticism* or *impressionism, realism* was not a new term in art criticism. As a term qualifying a mode of representation in paintings and sculptures, it had been used at least since the beginning of art criticism in the eighteenth century. Often used interchangeably with *naturalism,* it was applied to art works—paintings or sculptures—that closely copied reality rather than "improved on" it. Realism thus was the opposite of idealism: an artistic practice aimed at enhancing the "imperfect" forms found in reality in order to create art forms of absolute beauty. Rooted in classical antiquity, idealism was exemplified in Greek sculpture of the fifth and fourth centuries B.C.E. and their Roman imitations of early Imperial period. The idealist practice was revived in the Renaissance and survived throughout the baroque period to be given its theoretical foundation in the neoclassical period of the eighteenth century.

NATURALISM

While naturalism, like realism, aimed at the truthful representation of ordinary life, preferably of the lower classes and especially the peasantry, it differed from realism in three important ways. First, it lacked the political overtones of the works of the realists who, especially early in their careers, were keen to communicate a sense of social concern. Instead, naturalist artists were out to capture the true character of the scenes they chose to paint, rendering them with the scientific accuracy and detachment of the ethnographer. Second, while realist painters drew heavily on past art and often acknowledged this practice (see Courbet's quote above), the naturalists placed a premium on the direct observation of reality. Many of them had received an academic training (unlike the realists, who were mostly self-taught) and had learned to carefully record their visual expressions in detailed preliminary drawings and oil sketches. Some naturalists, such as Pascal-Adolphe-Jean Dagnan-Bouveret (1852–1929) and Jules-Alexis Muenier (1863–1942), also used photography as an important intermediary process in the creation of their paintings. Lastly, unlike their academic teachers, the naturalists were drawn to *plein-air* painting and often posed their models in the open air, like the impressionists. They did not, however, adopt the "broken" brushwork of the impressionists.

While realism had been at first a French movement, naturalism became an important international style with practitioners across Europe and the United States. British painters George Clausen (1852–1944) and Herbert Henry La Thangue (1859–1929), Americans Thomas Alexander Harrison (known as Alexander, 1853–1930) and Birge Harrison (1854–1929) and Gari Melchers 1860–1932), Scandinavians Albert Edelfelt (1854–1905) and Anders Leonard Zorn (1860–1920), Hungarian Károly Ferenczy (1863–1917), and Belgians Léon Frédéric (1856–1940) and Theodoor Verstraete (1850–1907) all practiced naturalism well into the twentieth century, after modernist movements like expressionism, cubism, and futurism had already been introduced.

See also **Balzac, Honoré de; Baudelaire, Charles; Corot, Jean-Baptiste-Camille; Courbet, Gustave; Flaubert, Gustave; Marx, Karl; Painting; Positivism; Revolutions of 1848; Romanticism; Zola, Émile.**

BIBLIOGRAPHY

Boas, George. "Il faut être de son temps." *Journal of Aesthetics* 1 (1941): 52–65.

Clark, T. J. *The Absolute Bourgeois: Artists and Politics in France, 1848–1851.* London: Thames and Hudson, 1973.

———. *Image of the People: Gustave Courbet and the Second French Republic, 1848–1851.* London, 1973.

Galassi, Peter, ed. *Before Photography: Painting and the Invention of Photography.* New York, 1981. Exhibition catalog.

Nochlin, Linda. *Realism.* New York, 1971. Reprint, New York, 1993.

Weinberg, Bernard. *French Realism: The Critical Reaction, 1830–1870.* New York, 1937.

Weisberg, Gabriel P. *Beyond Impressionism: The Naturalist Impulse in European Art, 1860–1905.* New York, 1992.

Weisberg, Gabriel P., ed. *The Realist Tradition: French Painting and Drawing, 1830–1900.* Cleveland, Ohio, 1980. Exhibition catalog.

PETRA TEN-DOESSCHATE CHU

RED CROSS. Five Genevan philanthropists founded the Red Cross in 1863 in order to prevent needless suffering during war. The Red Cross promoted international agreements regulating warfare and encouraged the creation of national committees that would prepare volunteer nurses to treat wounded and sick soldiers during war. Despite its successes, the Red Cross's close relationship with national governments sometimes compromised its humanitarian goals. The organization's treatment of noncombatants and position on pacifism also remained ambiguous.

FOUNDATIONS

Genevan businessman Jean-Henri Dunant (1828–1910) provided the inspiration for the Red Cross after witnessing French and Italian allies fight the Austrians in the battle of Solferino on 24 June 1859. He was appalled that thousands of wounded soldiers were left to suffer on the battlefield without treatment. In 1862 he published an account of his observations and a call for action in *Un Souvenir de Solférino* (Memory of Solferino). The following year, four Protestant Genevan philanthropists joined Dunant to form the International Committee for Assistance to Sick and Wounded Soldiers (known as the International Committee of the Red Cross, or ICRC, by 1884). Lawyer Gustave Moynier (1826–1910) in particular worked hard to make Dunant's inspiration a reality.

On 22 August 1864 the ICRC achieved its first international victory when twelve nations signed the first Geneva Convention. This convention protected the neutrality of wounded or sick soldiers, those who tended them, and any place where they

Should the sight of these young invalids, deprived of an arm or a leg, who return sadly to their homes, not stir in us remorse or regret? ... What is needed, therefore, are male and female volunteer nurses, who are diligent, prepared, and ready for this work, and who, recognized by army leaders during a campaign, are facilitated and supported in their mission. ... In an era when one speaks so much of progress and civilization, and since unfortunately wars cannot always be avoided, is it not urgent in the spirit of humanity and true civilization to try to forestall it, or at least to soften its horrors? (author's translation)

Henry Dunant, *Memory of Solferino* (1862), pp. 108–109, 110, 113.

were sheltered. The convention, however, did not mention volunteer associations, as many states viewed these associations as potential threats to their authority. The convention adopted the symbol of a red cross on a white field as a means of identification. Later, the Ottoman Society (founded 1868) adopted the symbol of the Red Crescent, to distance itself from the Christian symbolism of the cross.

ORGANIZATION AND VOLUNTEERS

National committees began to form in 1864, and by 1899 thirty-seven committees had been established in countries throughout the world, including Peru (1879) and Japan (1886). National committees raised money, gathered resources, and organized and trained volunteers for service in case of war. Upper-class notables dominated many of these committees, which often formed separate "ladies' committees" run by aristocratic women. The committees varied in the amount of training they provided and generally did not prepare volunteers to become professional nurses. Some organizers claimed that women were natural nurses who required very little training.

The ICRC was initially intended to serve only as a link between the national committees, through the *Bulletin* (regularly appearing since 1869). However, the ICRC first sent its own volunteers into the field during the First Balkan War (1912).

The ICRC was composed solely of male Genevan Protestants until 1918.

IN PRINCIPLE AND IN PRACTICE

The Geneva Convention was first applied during the Austro-Prussian War (1866), but the Franco-Prussian War (1870–1871) was the first conflict in which both sides had signed the convention and formed national committees. Whereas German committees proved organized and prepared, the French committee had to improvise ambulances. The French and German committees tended to thousands of sick and wounded, which demonstrated the effectiveness of the Red Cross. But many officers and soldiers on both sides were unfamiliar with the Geneva Convention, and scavengers took advantage of the Red Cross armband in order to rob wounded soldiers. The ICRC did not become involved in fieldwork, but instead formed an agency in Basel, Switzerland, as a liaison between the national committees and between wounded prisoners of war and their families. The ICRC furthermore established a semi-independent agency under the sign of the green cross that sent aid to nonwounded prisoners of war and compiled lists of prisoners. This agency opened the way for an expansion of the Red Cross mandate.

The Red Cross's policy on the treatment of civilians and nonwounded prisoners of war remained unclear through 1914. During the Russo-Turkish War (1877–1878), the ICRC helped civilian war victims. During the Boer War (1899–1902), however, neither the ICRC nor the British Red Cross assisted Boer civilians or Black Africans caught in the British campaign to stamp out Boer resistance. In the *Bulletin,* the ICRC did not mention the concentration camps in which 26,000 Boer civilians died. In 1914 the ICRC formed the International Prisoners of War Agency, although the Geneva Convention did not address the treatment of prisoners of war until 1929. National Red Cross committees and the ICRC eventually also provided aid and volunteers during non-war-related emergencies, such as the Messina earthquake in Italy (1908).

The Red Cross organizations hoped to alleviate suffering, but did not oppose war itself. Both Dunant and Moynier advocated the establishment of an international arbitration tribunal. The ICRC

The Red Cross transporting injured Russians on skis. Illustration from the French publication *Le Petit Journal,* c. 1904. Conducted in often-remote and mountainous regions of Korea and Manchuria, the Russo-Japanese War of 1904–1905 provided great challenges for Red Cross volunteers. PRIVATE COLLECTION/BRIDGEMAN ART LIBRARY/ARCHIVES CHARMET

lobbied to place limits on warfare at international peace conferences in Brussels (1874) and at The Hague (1899 and 1907). The first Hague conference extended the Geneva Convention to include naval warfare, but a 1906 revision of the convention restricted the wartime activities of committees from neutral countries. Many Red Cross volunteers were more interested in social functions and military heroism than in tackling thorny issues of international law and working toward durable peace. Over the years, national committees became more closely tied to their national armies and thus seemed to serve national, rather than humanitarian, interests. Yet the ICRC maintained its independence from state governance. Despite these contradictions, Dunant shared the first Nobel Peace Prize, awarded in 1901.

See also **Geneva Convention; Nightingale, Florence; Switzerland.**

BIBLIOGRAPHY

Primary Source

Dunant, Jean-Henri. *Un Souvenir de Solférino.* Geneva, 1862.

Secondary Sources

Harouel, Véronique. *Histoire de la Croix-Rouge.* Paris, 1999.

Hutchinson, John F. *Champions of Charity: War and the Rise of the Red Cross.* Boulder, Colo., 1996.

Moorehead, Caroline. *Dunant's Dream: War, Switzerland, and the History of the Red Cross.* London, 1998.

RACHEL CHRASTIL

REIGN OF TERROR. The term *Reign of Terror* is an interesting and somewhat misleading label. It might suggest, in one view, that revolutionary terror was so pervasive in France during this period as to have been virtually inescapable, yet in many areas of the country there were few, if any, executions in 1793 and 1794. Alternatively, the label might be taken to refer to the dictatorial power of the Committee of Public Safety, the group of twelve deputies who assumed executive authority during the Terror, or to Maximilien Robespierre, who was accused by his opponents of aspiring to dictatorial power. Yet, the Terror, for all of its ferocity and its many victims, was a legal policy, and those condemned to die on the guillotine or by other means were, in the majority, charged with specific crimes and convicted by official tribunals. Those who instituted the Terror did so, at least in part, with the goal of curbing popular violence.

Terror became the "order of the day" in Revolutionary France in the fall of 1793, following an uprising in Paris on 4 and 5 September that occurred in response to escalating food prices and news that the city of Toulon, on the Mediterranean coast of France, had fallen to the British. Some would mark the Terror as beginning, however, with the execution of King Louis XVI in January 1793, or with the creation of the Revolutionary Tribunal in March 1793, or with the consolidation of the power of the Committee of Public Safety in July 1793. The end of the Reign of Terror is easier to designate—it came with the fall of Robespierre on 9 Thermidor Year II (27 July 1794).

GOVERNMENT BY TERROR

Government by terror was imposed in response to two perceived dangers: public panic and popular violence provoked by food shortages and rising prices; and the threat posed by traitors at a time when both war and civil war confronted the nation. As early as May 1793 the National Convention imposed price controls on grain and bread in an effort to ensure an adequate food supply. In September 1793 price controls were extended to other staple consumer goods, and the *armées révolutionnaires* were created to enforce these price controls and coerce peasants to deliver grain to the markets. Some of these revolutionary armies patrolled the provinces with ambulatory guillotines, prepared to administer revolutionary justice on the spot to those who hoarded grain or manipulated market prices. Parisians had seen their city dangerously undersupplied in the summer of 1793, but other large

cities, too, felt vulnerable to grain shortages and the popular unrest that generally accompanied them.

The Terror was most severe in areas of civil war and counterrevolution, and in some of the frontier departments. In approximately one-third of the eighty-three departments the Terror claimed fewer than ten victims. Seventy percent of the death sentences were handed down in just five departments. In some areas the Terror was particularly harsh. In Nantes, near the center of the Vendée rebellion and also a city sympathetic to the federalist revolt, Jean-Baptiste Carrier and local militants ordered the drowning of three thousand suspected counterrevolutionaries. In Lyon, a city with a reputation for royalist sympathies and also a federalist center, nearly two thousand were executed, some by guillotine and others shot down by cannon. Toulon, Marseille, and Bordeaux—cities that resisted the National Convention in the summer of 1793—all suffered three hundred or more executions during the Terror.

LAW OF SUSPECTS

The Law of Suspects, passed in September 1793, empowered local committees of surveillance to draw up lists of suspects and order their arrest. Those subject to arrests included anyone suspected of being an enemy of liberty, an advocate of tyranny, or a supporter of federalism; those who had emigrated illegally since the beginning of the Revolution; and ex-aristocrats who had not shown support for the Revolution. Some seventy thousand people were arrested under this law, roughly 0.5 percent of the population. The best estimates of historians suggest that forty thousand were executed during the Terror, but if one includes those who died in the repression of the Vendée the death toll mounts considerably higher.

The most salient images of the Reign of Terror, however, come from Paris, where the most dramatic "show trials" of the Revolution took place. The Revolutionary Tribunal in Paris was created in March 1793 on the proposal, ironically, of Carrier, who would later be sentenced to death by the tribunal he had helped bring into being. In April 1793 Antoine-Quentin Fouquier-Tinville was named public prosecutor attached to the Revolutionary Tribunal, a post he would occupy until 9 Thermidor. In September 1793, when Terror became the order of the day, the Revolutionary Tribunal was expanded so that four courts might operate concurrently. The procedures of the Revolutionary Tribunal also grew increasingly streamlined over time. During the trial of the Girondins, in October 1793, the National Convention decreed that juries might restrict trials to three days if they were convinced of the guilt of the accused. The Law of 22 Prairial (10 June 1794), passed following an alleged assassination attempt against Robespierre, eliminated defense counsel and cross-examination, decreed that moral evidence as well as material evidence might justify a conviction, and restricted juries to two possible verdicts: acquittal or death. This law ushered in the most active period of the Revolutionary Tribunal's existence, even though the threat from war abroad and from rebellion within France had substantially abated by this time.

SHOW TRIALS

The show trials of the Year II (September 1793–September 1794) claimed victims on both the left and the right of the revolutionary political spectrum. The first of these was in October 1793, when the Girondin deputies, led by the great orator Pierre-Victurnien Vergniaud, were tried and executed. Later that month Marie-Antoinette ascended the scaffold. In March 1794 Jacques-René Hébert and a number of his supporters on the extreme left were tried before the Revolutionary Tribunal, found guilty, and executed. Barely a week later Georges Danton and the Indulgents, accused of advocating leniency toward the enemies of the Revolution, suffered the same fate. As he rode to the guillotine Danton gestured toward the residence of Robespierre, promising his former ally that one day he would follow him along that same route. As suggested above, political threats to the Jacobin republic abated in the late spring of 1794, but the Terror had developed a momentum of its own—nearly 60 percent of those sentenced to death by the Revolutionary Tribunal in Paris were executed in June and July 1794. This escalation of revolutionary justice led to the fall of Robespierre on 9 Thermidor Year II (27 July 1794) and his execution the next day. Among the final victims of the Revolutionary Tribunal was Fouquier-Tinville himself.

Historians have long debated the meaning of the Reign of Terror. Some see it as an inevitable outcome of the ideology of the Jacobin clubs or the thought of Jean-Jacques Rousseau, while others interpret the Terror as an unfortunate, but understandable, response to the circumstances of war and counterrevolution. Supporters of the Revolution tend to downplay the scope of the Terror, whereas its opponents tend to exaggerate its scope. Some view the French Terror as the precursor of the much bloodier revolutionary terrors of the twentieth century. For virtually all who study the French Revolution, however, the ideals of 1789 are tarnished by the violence of the Reign of Terror.

See also **Danton, Georges-Jacques; Federalist Revolt; French Revolution; Girondins; Jacobins; Louis XVI; Marie-Antoinette; Republicanism; Robespierre, Maximilien.**

BIBLIOGRAPHY

Arasse, Daniel. *The Guillotine and the Terror*. Translated by Christopher Miller. London, 1989. Translation of *La guillotine et l'imaginaire de la Terreur*.

Baker, Keith Michael, ed. *The Terror*. Vol. 4 of *The French Revolution and the Creation of Modern Political Culture*. Oxford, U.K., 1994.

Gough, Hugh. *The Terror in the French Revolution*. New York, 1998.

Greer, Donald. *The Incidence of the Terror during the French Revolution: A Statistical Interpretation*. Cambridge, Mass., 1935.

Gross, Jean-Pierre. *Fair Shares for All: Jacobin Egalitarianism in Practice*. Cambridge, U.K., 1997.

Lucas, Colin. *The Structure of the Terror: The Example of Javogues and the Loire*. London, 1973.

PAUL R. HANSON

RELIGION. *See* **Catholicism; Jews and Judaism; Protestantism; Russian Orthodox Church.**

RENAN, ERNEST (1823–1892), French philologist and historian of religion.

The work of Ernest Renan can be fully understood only in light of the religious crisis that marked his life as well as those of many of his contemporaries. In his autobiography, *Souvenirs d'enfance et de jeunesse* (1883; *Memories of Childhood and Youth*), he relates how discoveries in the natural sciences and rational criticism of the Bible shook his belief in Christian dogma when he was a young seminary student at the Grand Séminaire de Saint-Sulpice in Paris. In 1845, convinced of the incompatibility of Catholic orthodoxy and the demands modern rationalism, Renan gave up on the priesthood in order to study classical languages and philosophy. A member of the Académie des Inscriptions et Belles-Lettres from 1856 on, he was granted the Hebrew chair at the Collège de France in 1862. But he was suspended after his inaugural lecture, in which he implicitly denied the divinity of Jesus by describing him as "an incomparable human being." Several months later, the success of his bestseller *Vie de Jésus* (1863; *The Life of Jesus*) assured Renan's reputation. He became a major intellectual voice for the generation that came to political power and gained control of the reformed university system after 1870 under the Third Republic, a regime that heaped honors upon him. Reinstalled in his position at the Collège de France, he became its administrator in 1883. In 1878, he was elected a member of the Académie Française, and he was given a state funeral at his death in 1892.

In the early twenty-first century Renan is most often remembered for his definition of a nation in terms of a free political choice. This definition, given in *Qu'est-ce qu'une nation?* (1882; *What Is a Nation?*), was opposed to that of most German thinkers. But in his own time, during which political debate was obsessed with the question of secularism even while thousands of pilgrims flocked to Lourdes, Renan became famous primarily as a spokesperson for the rational approach to religion. His intellectual project crystallized around 1848. In *L'Avenir de la science* (*The Future of Science*; a manifesto written in 1848 but published in 1890), he outlined a history of the human spirit that was inspired by Georg Wilhelm Friedrich Hegel but borrowed its methodology from the positive sciences, scholarly historical criticism, and comparative philology. Considered an "embryogeny of the human spirit" (*De l'origine du langage*, 1848; *On the Origin of Language*), Renan's historical project focuses on the manifestations of spirit—language and religion—throughout time. Thus it is

divided into two main parts, a study of Semitic languages and a history of Christianity.

Renan's works, like those of John Stuart Mill and Émile Littré, illustrate the diversity of nineteenth-century positivism. *The Future of Science* advocated a science that would bring humanity to a rational consciousness of itself. On this basis, Renan constructed a philosophy of history that differentiated the three stages of syncretism, analysis, and synthesis. The first stage is that of a poetic and religious intuitive apprehension of the world in its totality. The second stage is that of modern scientific rationality, which only produces a fragmentary consciousness of reality. This will then give way to the stage of synthesis, at which a fully mature science will rationally reconstitute the lost sense of totality. Even though the embryogeny of the spirit and the model of the three stages may call to mind Auguste Comte's sociology and law of the three states, Renan nevertheless made a distinction between his own ideas and Comte's. His stages were not precisely datable temporal eras, but moments of the spirit that, allowing for recurrences, could in fact coincide; meanwhile, Comtean sociology is primarily concerned with society in its current state, while Renan's "embryogeny" investigates the moment of origin, seeking to isolate the principle of the spirit's development.

Renan was an apostle of rationalism, but not the radical proponent of scientism that a hasty reading of *The Future of Science* might suggest. His life and work were marked by a tension between the demands of reason and a nostalgia for the comforting beliefs of his youth. Indeed, Renan appealed to rationality as a principle unique to scholarly studies. He took the natural sciences as his model, and the expression "embryogeny of the human spirit" harks back to the work of contemporary anatomists. But his intellectual ambition was to reconcile science and religion. *The Future of Science* looks forward to a time when science will reconstitute a sense of the totality of the universe, which will merge with the impression of the universe that syncretic metaphysical thought forms intuitively. *The Life of Jesus* attempts this reconciliation in a specific case: in that work, Renan provides a rational explanation for miracles without negating the historical reality of Christ. Like that of Comte,

Renan's work thus exemplifies the complex relations between positivism and religion in the nineteenth century.

See also Comte, Auguste; France; Mill, John Stuart; Nationalism; Positivism.

BIBLIOGRAPHY

Primary Sources

Renan, Ernest. *Oeuvres complètes d'Ernest Renan, édition définitive établie par Henriette Psichari.* 10 vols. Paris, 1947–1961.

Secondary Sources

Burrow, John W. *The Crisis of Reason: European Thought, 1848–1914.* New Haven, Conn., and London, 2000.

Lee, David C. J. *Ernest Renan. In the Shadow of Faith.* London, 1996.

Petit, Annie. "Le prétendu positivisme d'Ernest Renan." *Revue d'histoire des sciences humaines* 8 (2003): 73–101.

Pholien, Georges. *Les deux "Vie de Jésus" de Renan.* Paris, 1983.

Retat, Laudyce. *Religion et imagination religieuse: leurs formes et leurs rapports dans l'oeuvre d'Ernest Renan.* Paris, 1977.

Richard, Nathalie. "La Vie de Jésus de Renan: un historien face à la question des miracles." In *Religion et mentalités au Moyen Âge. Mélanges en l'honneur d'Hervé Martin,* 87–99. Rennes, 2003.

———. "Analogies naturalistes: Taine et Renan." *Espaces Temps* , nos. 84–85–86, (2004): 76–90.

NATHALIE RICHARD

RENOIR, PIERRE-AUGUSTE (1841–1919), French impressionist painter.

The son of a tailor, Léonard Renoir (1799–1874), and a dressmaker, Marguerite Merlet (1807–1896), Pierre-Auguste Renoir was born in Limoges, France. His family moved to Paris in 1844.

Although he would gain real fame as a painter, his early training was in decorative arts, and it left its mark on his mature style. He was apprenticed to a porcelain painter and also took lessons from the sculptor Callouette in Paris. In the late 1850s Renoir was painting fans and heraldic designs and began working as a decorator for a manufacturer of blinds. He began copying paintings in the Louvre (a common practice for art students at the time), studied painting with the renowned studio professor Charles Gleyre (1808–1874), and was admitted to the École des Beaux-Arts, the official art school of the French Academy.

In the early 1860s Renoir painted in the Forest of Fontainebleau alongside a group of landscape painters who were gradually transforming landscape painting away from the cerebral and highly structured approach to the historiated landscape, or landscape with historical subject, sanctioned by the Academy. The Barbizon painters, as they were known, painted more intimate views of highly particularized patches of terrain in the outdoors, and Renoir joined them. His landscapes of the 1860s have a lighter palette than some of the other Barbizon artists' canvases, but his approach to value (light to dark tones) in these early paintings is still fairly traditional. He had his first painting accepted to the Salon in 1864.

By the late 1860s Renoir was friends with Claude Monet (1840–1926), Alfred Sisley (1839–1899), and Jean-Frédéric Bazille (1841–1870). These painters were increasingly disillusioned with their frequent rejections from the Salon, and they were inspired by the suave and sketchlike manner of painting of Édouard Manet (1832–1883), his engagement with modernity, and the social and artistic controversies that swirled around paintings such as *Olympia* (1863). When Monet began to paint a series of sketches at La Grenouillère, a swimming and open-air dining establishment on the Ile de Croissy, near Bougival, Renoir followed suit with his own suite of paintings. Monet's paintings done there in 1869 would, within the span of a few years, suggest to him a new way of painting that was more sketch-like and more responsive to transitory effects of light and weather. Monet and the painters around him (including Renoir, Bazille, and Sisley) would begin to search for a more optical form of naturalist painting. These artists began to represent light and shadow in terms of color rather than value. Renoir's paintings at La Grenouillère demonstrate his use of blue (in addition to black) for shadow, as well as his interest in the reflection of the trees and foliage beyond

La Loge. Painting by Pierre-Auguste Renoir, 1874. SAMUEL COURTAULD TRUST, COURTAULD INSTITUTE OF ART GALLERY/BRIDGEMAN ART LIBRARY

La Grenouillère in his lively representation of ripples on the surface of the Seine.

In 1874 Renoir was one of a group of artists, including Paul Cézanne (1839–1906), Edgar Degas (1834–1917), Monet, Berthe Morisot (1841–1895), and Camille Pissarro (1830–1903), who organized an exhibition independent of the Academy-controlled Salon. The first Impressionist Exhibition was held in the studio of the portrait photographer Félix Nadar (1820–1910), and Renoir showed six paintings and one pastel, including *La Loge* (1874). The poet Stéphane Mallarmé (1842–1898) referred indirectly to *La Loge* when he wrote in 1876 of "a box at a theatre, its gaily-dressed inmates, the women with their flesh tints heightened and displaced by rouge and rice powder, a complication of effects of light." Many critics, however, reacted harshly to Renoir's painting *The Swing* (1876), in the third Impressionist Exhibition of 1877; they singled out the excess of blue, as well as the blotches of sunlight on the figures' clothing that looked like stains, or

that created the effect of a disorder of the eye. *Ball at the Moulin de la Galette,* also from 1876 and shown in the same exhibition, features a similar effect of dappled sunlight on the figures. Renoir's friend Georges Rivière, who also wrote a biography of the artist, claimed that the entire painting was executed at the outdoor Montmartre dance hall, although its large size probably necessitated some reworking in the painter's nearby studio.

Despite the critics' hostility to the early impressionist exhibitions, Renoir achieved commercial success as a portrait painter in such works as *Madame Charpentier and Her Children* (1878). Georges Charpentier was Émile Zola's publisher, and he and his wife were important figures in Parisian society. The work was praised at the Salon of 1879, and this success led to other portrait commissions. Although Renoir continued to engage with modern-life themes as did the other impressionists, he frequently did so with more sentimentality than colleagues such as Degas and Pissarro. At the same time, he was a great admirer of the music of Richard Wagner (1813–1883), and he sought to achieve complex chromatic effects in his paintings that resembled Wagner's "color-music."

His experience painting *Madame Charpentier and Her Children* not only led to more portraits but also played a role in his move toward greater definition of figures in modern-life genre paintings such as the *Luncheon of the Boating Party* (1880–1881). Although this painting is quite anecdotal, with its muscular boaters, couples chatting, and woman playing with her toy dog, it also demonstrates that Renoir remained committed to the painting of effects of sunlight on the figure group. At the same time, in comparison with *Ball at the Moulin de la Galette,* the figures in the *Luncheon* no longer dissolve into disparate spots of color and light. Many of the figures are identifiable as friends of the artist who pose on the terrace of the Restaurant Fournaise in Chatou.

Renoir continued to focus on the human figure, as can be seen in a series of works representing dancing couples such as *Dance at Bougival* (1882–1883); a highly classicized painting of bathing women known as *Bathers* (1887); and an anecdotal series of paintings of *Young Girls at the Piano*

(1892). *Bathers* represents something of a radical departure from his impressionist style, as the figures are sharply defined by emphatic drawing. Renoir's later work frequently featured bathing women, often with ample figures; he also did sculptures, including a relief medallion of the head of his youngest son, Claude, in 1907, and several sculptures in bronze of nude women, sometimes taken from mythology. He had severe arthritis by 1910 and was only able to execute sculptures with the aid of assistants; he did, however, continue to paint, sometimes with a brush tied to his arm.

Renoir married the milliner Aline Charigot in 1890; they had three sons: Pierre, Jean (the renowned filmmaker), and Claude. He died of lung congestion in 1919 in Cagnes, France.

See also **Cézanne, Paul; Degas, Edgar; Impressionism; Monet, Claude; Morisot, Berthe; Pissarro, Camille.**

BIBLIOGRAPHY

Daulte, François. *Auguste Renoir. Catalogue raisonné de l'oeuvre peint.* Lausanne, France, 1971.

House, John, et al. *Renoir.* London, 1985. Exhibition catalog.

Moffett, Charles S., et al. *The New Painting: Impressionism 1874–1886.* Washington, D.C., 1986. Exhibition catalog.

Monneret, Sophie. *L'Impressionisme et son époque.* Paris, 1978–1979.

Rivière, Georges. *Renoir et ses amis.* Paris, 1921.

White, Barbara Ehrlich. *Renoir, His Life, Art, and Letters.* New York, 1984.

NANCY LOCKE

REPIN, ILYA (1844–1930), Russian realist painter.

Ilya Yefimovich Repin was Russia's foremost realist painter and a pivotal figure in winning Russian realism a long-lasting recognition as the national school of art. Repin was born in 1844, before the emancipation of the serfs, into a peasant family in the village of Chuguyev, near Kharkov (now Ukraine). In 1863, after receiving some training from itinerant icon painters, he set out for St. Petersburg to attend the Imperial Academy of Arts, graduating in 1871 as a recipient of the academy's Major Gold Medal. The same year the young artist gained public attention with a canvas on a nonacademic topic, *Barge Haulers on the Volga.* At the time, this depiction of eleven toiling peasants—never before presented in such monumental proportions and with such serious intent—struck an original chord and a significant note. The liberal, populist-minded intelligentsia hailed the painting as an inspiring image that demonstrated the latent, renovating power of the Russian people (*narod*).

Repin's *Barge Haulers* represents a key canvas in the formation of Russian realism, much as Gustave Courbet's *The Stone Breakers* (1849) is considered a defining work of realism in France. In Russia, the autocratic government with its ubiquitous censorship imbued Russian realism with an intense political-moral partisanship. The agrarian character of the country and the intelligentsia's infatuation with the peasantry gave Russian realism a strong rural and antiurban bias. Finally, its goal was to instruct with content rather than to delight with color or light. These extra-painterly goals stressing content over technique underwent an evolution: the 1870s and early 1880s were marked by a liberal and open-minded outlook. But by 1890, due in part to the Russification program promoted by Alexander III, Russian realism was fashioned into a national school of painting with strong chauvinist, anti-Western overtones.

Repin's works and their reception illustrate the formation and development of Russian realism. In 1878, after a three-year Imperial Academy fellowship spent in Paris, where he much admired the art of Édouard Manet and the impressionists, Repin joined the Association of Traveling Art Exhibits. This first independent professional artists' organization in Russia, formed in 1870 to challenge the monopolistic controls exercised by the Imperial Academy, the court, and the state, favored realist art depicting the country's problems and scenes. Once part of the association, Repin easily gave up his infatuation with the advanced French art (an infatuation that could be detected in his impressionist-like painting of an outdoor family outing, *On the Turf Bench,* 1876) and adopted the ethos of the Wanderers (or *Peredvizhniki* in Russian), as members of the association were called. According to Ivan Kramskoy,

Barge Haulers on the Volga. Painting by Ilya Repin, 1870–1872. ©THE STATE RUSSIAN MUSEUM/CORBIS

the philosopher of the group, Russian artists were not "free as birds" to paint what struck their fancy but were obliged to "serve society" by commenting on public issues.

Repin's canvases, invariably the center of attention at the association's annual exhibits, managed to combine spirited technique and great talent with some public message that was expected by the critics and the public. His portraits of individual peasants endowed that underprivileged class with character and dignity, an attitude in keeping with the preoccupations of the populist intelligentsia. His most ambitious painting in this genre, *Religious Procession in Kursk Province* (1880–1883), was a group portrait that depicted the post-emancipation socio-economic differentiation in the countryside. Repin's portraits of outstanding cultural figures, many marked by rough brushwork and temperamental rendition, have given the Russians permanent images of their literary and musical giants, including Leo Tolstoy (1887), Vladimir Stasov (1883), Modest Mussorgsky (1881), Alexander Glazunov (1887), and Anton Rubinstein (1881). Repin's historical canvases often had some contemporary association, as was the case with *Ivan the Terrible and His Son Ivan* (1885), painted soon after the assassination of Tsar Alexander II and the execution

of the plotters, with its emphasis on the theme of repentance and forgiveness. Repin is also remembered for commemorating the contemporary revolutionary movement, of which *They Did Not Expect Him* (1884–1888), depicting the unexpected return of a political exile and the mixed reception by his family, is generally recognized as a masterpiece. By modeling his composition, in part, on Rembrandt's etchings of scenes from the life of Christ, Repin elevated these topics from anecdotal storytelling to high art.

In the early 1890s, Repin's career and oeuvre lost much of their initial anti-official and political edge. He helped reform the Imperial Academy and joined it in 1893, a move seen as an apostasy by many older Wanderers but welcomed by the younger generation. In the late 1890s, Repin cooperated briefly with Sergei Diaghilev, the founder of the journal *World of Art* (*Mir iskusstva*), because at the time Repin also advocated art for art's sake and a rapprochement with the Western art scene to end the parochial isolation that prevailed in Russia. He soon quarreled, however, with Diaghilev and from 1900 became an intolerant critic of post-realist trends, branding everything that departed from strict figurative art as "decadent" and "alien" to Russian traditions. As a result, he became in the eyes of the *World of Art* aesthetes, as well as of the emergent avant-garde, the personification of ossified, Russophile opinions.

That reputation persisted during the 1920s, when, after the Bolshevik Revolution, the leftists dominated the Soviet artistic scene. But with the onset of Stalinization Repin's stature and reputation experienced a spectacular reversal. Beginning in 1934, with the imposition of Socialist Realism as the officially prescribed style for all the Soviet arts, the painter (who had died in obscurity in Finland four years earlier) was refashioned into a model for the politically committed and state-serving art of the Soviet Union.

See also **Painting; Realism and Naturalism.**

BIBLIOGRAPHY

Ilya Repin: Painting, Graphic Arts. Introduction by Grigory Sternin. Catalog and biographical outline by Maria Karpenko, Yelena Kirillina, Galina Pribulskaya, and Natalia Vatenina. Leningrad, 1985.

Liaskovskaya, Olga Antonovna. *Ilya Efimovich Repin.* 3rd ed. Moscow, 1982. A full and good biography in Russian.

Repin, Ilya Y. *Dalekoe blizkoe.* Edited by K. Chukovsky. Moscow, 1961. Repin's autobiography—very vivid and informative.

Valkenier, Elizabeth Kridl. *Ilya Repin and the World of Russian Art.* New York, 1990.

ELIZABETH KRIDL VALKENIER

REPUBLICANISM.

The French Revolution created the modern European republican tradition. The broadest and most general definition of a nineteenth-century republican was someone who aspired to liberty, equality, and fraternity, the triad of revolutionary virtues. Republicanism was complex and creative because its adherents had to resolve the inherent tensions between these revolutionary ideals while simultaneously defending the problematic legacy of the Revolution. The specificity of European republicanism lay in its unequivocal embrace of democracy. The Anglo-American, or Atlantic, republican tradition contrasted the republic, a mixed form of government, with democracy, a simple form. This opposition made no sense in modern European republicanism. In consequence of this development European republicanism distanced itself from an entire canon of early modern republican theory, a body of work that stretched from Niccolò Machiavelli's (1469–1527) commentaries on Livy to *The Federalist Papers,* based on precisely this distinction between republic and democracy. European republicanism was a curious ideology, one that developed as a continuous tradition of interpretation of an event, rather than a set of texts. Unlike competing nineteenth-century political ideals such as socialism, liberalism or even conservatism, republicanism had no founding mothers or fathers. Republicanism was the continuing project of instituting revolutionary democracy, of achieving the French Revolution, while debating the nature of that very democracy and the legacy of the Revolution.

ANCIENTS AND MODERNS

A republic, for most early modern people, was any lawful state. Classical republicanism, or the neo-Roman theory of a free state, in Quentin Skinner's phrase, was a theory of the best kind of lawful state, which thinkers from Machiavelli to James Harrington (1611–1677) and beyond asserted was one in which the citizens governed themselves. Antimonarchical republicanism was a particular argument, generated after the execution of Charles I (r. 1625–1649) of England in 1649, that citizens could not govern themselves under a monarchy. The thrust of classical republicanism was to identify the qualities necessary for a citizenry to be self-governing, a set of qualities loosely organized under the term virtue. Virtue was the capacity to prefer the public good to one's own interests, or at least to recognize that the two were identical. The consensus among theorists as different as the Abbé Mably (1709–1785) and Thomas Paine (1737–1809) was that the main condition of virtue was material independence. Slaves, wage earners, children, women—indeed, anyone who relied on another—could not exercise virtue. In effect this restricted citizenship to property-owning male heads of households. The developing economies of the Atlantic world generated an interesting debate internal to republicanism, the luxury debate, which turned on the political consequences of the increase in non-landed property in a commercial society. Antique republicans argued that only landed property fostered virtuous independence while modern, or commercial, republicans criticized the martial tenor of the antique virtues and argued for a new set of polite or civil virtues generated from commercial society. In all cases the central problems of republican theory were to identify the persons who could exercise virtue and to design a constitution that would allow them to exercise power.

French revolutionary republicanism turned the republican debate on its head. During the Revolution the republican problem became to identify the institutions that would allow everyone to achieve virtue and so participate in political life as a citizen, rather than to find the virtuous citizens who already existed in the population. The universality of this aspiration could be inspiring. The French Republic restored Jews and colonial slaves to equality and liberty. The Jacobin constitution of 1793, which was ratified but never put into force, comprised a breathtaking aspiration to participation in the political process. Any law might be overturned by a reviewing process that could be initiated by local citizens. The Jacobins also generated new sets of rights claims, particularly the right to education and to welfare. Radical Jacobins went even further and argued for a right to work. The ideal had effects in realms outside the classically political: Philippe Pinel (1745–1826) transformed the treatment of the mentally ill as chief "alienist" in the Salpêtrière hospital in Paris by releasing them from incarceration and developing courses of treatment based on conversation, in the hope of restoring fellow citizens to their places in the republic.

All these claims were based on the republican idea that citizens had to be able to participate in public life on an equal footing if a modern society was to flourish. This complex position was not first arrived at as a theoretical reflection but was worked out in the complex conditions of revolutionary politics. In the context of the Revolution this notion of citizenship was a limited, moderate position on an ideological spectrum that went from the Marquis de Sade's (1740–1814) libertarianism to the revolutionary conservatism of Joseph de Maistre (1753–1821). Republicanism argued that the equality enjoyed in political citizenship could stabilize and compensate for the inequalities generated by difference in the economy, society,

and the arts. The politics of the Republic would reconcile self-asserting and self-interested modern people to one another and generate a social ethic appropriate to a modern commercial society. The consequence was that other spheres, such as the family, property relations, and education did not need to be revolutionized directly. The strict principles of democracy were to be limited to citizenship; other forms of authority were appropriate in other spheres. Democracy in the state and individualism in society were to be reconciled by *moeurs,* common values or culture. Republican institutions, such as schools, hospitals, theaters, festivals, and the military were to be schools of *moeurs.* The Republic comprised an institutional form, democracy, and an ethical aspiration to a limited kind of moral equality. The big problem within republicanism was identifying the boundary between politics and ethics, between the institutions that citizens used to represent themselves, such as suffrage, and the institutions that allowed them to know themselves as citizens, such as literacy.

THE RIGHTS OF MAN

The French Revolution did not begin as a republican revolt. A republic was an unthinkable regime in 1789, largely because France was understood to be too unequal to tolerate universal citizenship. Political thinkers interpreted contemporary France through the lens of ancient Rome and argued a republic would provoke a civil war between patricians and plebeians. The republic became a necessity because the monarch, Louis XVI (r. 1774–1792), could not accommodate his throne to the new realities. The failure of the monarchy demanded an alternative to be found if the country was not to descend into anarchy. The most important element of the three-year legacy of revolution was the language of rights. The Declaration of the Rights of Man and the Citizen, debated by the National Assembly between 20 and 26 August 1789, was not a republican text. It was created to set the terms of legitimacy for the new regime, to set a baseline for the exercise of power. Its specific provisions, such as rights to religious expression and the presumption of innocence in legal procedures, were not consistent derivations from a coherent theory of rights but compromises that reflected the complexity of French historical experience. The first five articles however, asserting the equality of rights and the goal of government as the protection of rights and identifying the primordial rights as liberty, property, security, and resistance to oppression, were to define the Revolution and consequently republicanism. The Republic, declared in September 1792 after mismanagement of war had fatally discredited the monarchy, inherited these aspirations and had to accommodate itself to them. All citizens would have to enjoy all rights, the principle of universality was incontestable, and if citizenship demanded virtue then virtue would have to be universal also.

Republicanism has never fully mastered the conditions of its birth. A battery of thinkers such as Etienne Clavière (1735–1793), Jacques-Pierre Brissot (1754–1793), the Marquis de Condorcet (1743–1794), and Camille Desmoulins (1760–1794) offered inspiration on what universal virtue demanded and how it might be achieved. The politics of 1792 and 1793 overshadowed these efforts and generated its own images and archetypes of mobilized virtuous citizenship such as the sans-culotte, the canonical popular revolutionary identified by his trousers rather than elite knee-breeches, or the far-left radically egalitarian *enragé*. These figures represented political virtue as the willingness to act directly to represent the people against its representatives or the state. This version of virtue identified republicanism with revolutionary energy and made commitment to continuing the Revolution an end in itself. It identified republicanism, and particularly the right to resist oppression, with the right to bear arms and to insurrection. One meaning of fraternity came to be the bond between volunteers fighting together against the enemy, be they internal or external. This strand of republicanism also promoted a citizen army and eventually demanded universal male conscription, initiated in the *levée en masse* of 1793. The Parisian radical storming the Tuileries and the soldier of the republic fighting across the Rhine were both versions of the people in arms. The nation, the state, and the people were all possible forms for the sovereign and each promoted its version of the citizen in arms: national guardsman, soldier, and sans-culotte.

The repertoire of insurrectionary republicanism was elaborated from 1792 to 1795. The only new element that would be added to insurrection by nineteenth-century republican rebels would be the barricade, and it is arguable that the barricade represented a retreat from the claim to represent the people to representing, and defending, a people, be it of a *quartier* or the working class. A particular feature of the culture of insurrectionary republicanism was exemplary defeat and moral victory through death. This could take the form of the *Girondins*, who opposed the centralizing Jacobins around Maximilien Robespierre, singing republican songs in the tumbrel on their way to the guillotine, or the heroic suicide of the *Prairial* martyrs stabbing themselves with a dagger and then passing it to a comrade while in the dock for rebellion. The most advanced form was the cult of the martyrs, such as Lepeletier de Saint Fargeau (1760–1793), Jean-Paul Marat (1743–1793), and Joseph Bara, a drummer boy in the army of the West put to death by Vendean counterrevolutionaries. Each of these was memorialized in paintings by Jacques-Louis David (1748–1825), although only the *Death of Marat* (1793) survives in finished form and is the best illustration of the moral authority claimed by the republican rebel.

The brother in arms, dead or alive, was not the only, or even the major, version of universal citizenship. From 1792 to 1799 administrators, political leaders, and political thinkers struggled with the interrelated problems of pragmatically making a democratic republic function and conceptually working out on what basis it should function. It has been argued that the division between *Montagnard* (the radical delegates who sat in the highest seats, or *Montagne* [Mountain], of the Convention) and *Girondin*, crucial to the politics of the Convention, was based on two different ideas of the republic, classical and commercial. This position is very difficult to sustain. Marie-Jean Hérault de Séchelles (1759–1794) was the principal author of the radical 1793 constitution and so strongly aligned with the *Montagne*, and also a dandified lawyer whose intellectual background was indistinguishable from that of the Brissot circle. The focus on institutions was shared by such radicals as Louis-Antoine-Léon de Saint-Just (1767–1794) and moderates such as the Marquis de Condorcet (1743–1794). Debates between factions in the Convention took place within a shared conceptual language. That language was elaborated by groups of reflective public actors, such as the

Cercle sociale, a prototypical think tank and publisher organized around the constitutional bishop Claude Fauchet (1744–1793). After 1794 the most important such unit developing republican thought and practice was the group contributing to the weekly journal *La décade philosophique.* The problem of generating insight into a new kind of regime, the modern, democratic, commercial republic, was so rich that it spun out a series of innovations. The second section of the *Institut,* a research body for the human sciences founded in 1795, can reasonably be seen as the birthplace of the modern social sciences: psychology, sociology, and anthropology, all disciplines that sought to understand the citizen of this new entity. One of the most successful areas of reflection was political economy. Jean-Baptiste Say (1767–1832), a member of the *Décade* coterie, developed Adam Smith's (1723–1790) ideas on labor value to generate a republican political economy, one that imagined the market as one of the institutions that taught the republican virtues of self-command and love of the public good to the citizenry.

Between the end of the Terror in 1794 and the rise of Napoleon Bonaparte (r. 1804–1814/15) in 1799 republicans had the opportunity to experiment with these ideas. During Thermidor and the Directory an alternative model of universal virtue emerged, one that saw citizenship as a feature of everyday life in a commercial republic rather than as an extraordinary capacity for direct action maintained by the people. Modern republicans argued that the most characteristic features of a modern commercial society, the industriousness of the population and communication in print culture, created republican *moeurs.* They argued that the role of a republican state was to ensure that there were outlets for industriousness and that every citizen could participate in print culture. Their first institutional innovation was a republican political economy that turned on the critique of monopoly, an endorsement of free trade, and an embrace of national development strategies. Industriousness was the basis of citizenship; therefore anything that hampered work was a political evil. The critique of monopoly in turn produced a preference for small units of production, particularly for owner-occupier farming. The second characteristic commitment was the embrace of right to education.

Every citizen should be capable of participating in public debate and the duty of the community was to equip them to do so. These economic and educational policies were to be reprised by the Third Republic as were some of the characteristic features of the public culture of the commercial republic, especially anticlericism and a penchant for celebrating national anniversaries with industrial exhibitions. The first industrial exhibition was set up as the Festival of the Republic at the Champs de Mars in 1798. By 1799 elections were beginning to become another important entry in the inventory of institutions that fostered republican virtue. However, it would take a century for republicanism to embrace the suffrage as a superior kind of political activity to insurrection and republicans have never abandoned the principle that in the last analysis the population retain the right to assert themselves directly. The relationship between the two wings of republicanism, insurrectionary and modern, remained unpredictable throughout the nineteenth century.

EXCLUSIONS

Republicans argued that rights were political, and so limited in scope, but that the social sphere should be organized in a manner that allowed citizens to assert their political rights. This distinction, but not disjunction, between politics and society allowed republicanism enormous flexibility. It allowed republicanism to recognize differences without having to inscribe those differences at the level of political identity. It was this flexibility that allowed for the easy integration of German- and Occitan-speaking areas of the country in an ideal "one and indivisible" republic, but it also denied that any purchase to any particularity in political identity. The Republic would be unfriendly to Occitan even as the peasantry of Southern France became one of its social bases. Managing the relationships between political and social identities was difficult and often as unsuccessful in theory as it was in practice. This was nowhere more evident than in the relationship of republicanism to women.

Clear thinkers condemned the exclusion of women from political rights from the very outset of the Revolution. Condorcet, who was later to embrace republicanism, published his plea for inclusion of women in the political nation in the *Journal de la société de 1789* in July 1790 arguing that "either no individual of the human species has genuine rights, or all have the same rights; and he who votes against the rights of another, whatever that person's religion, color or sex, thereby foregoes his own rights." Yet the arguments of Condorcet, Mary Wollstonecraft (1759–1797), Olympe de Gouges (1748–1793), and Etta Palm (1743–1799), all feminist theorists active in the Revolution, were all ignored and sexual difference was the only social distinction inscribed as essential to political life. The reasons for this particular exclusion are still debated. A body of scholarship argues that the very notion of universality appealed to by republicans has masculine assumptions built into it and that the Republic was inherently committed to excluding women from public life. Another line of interpretation argues that the exclusion was a failure to overcome the cultural context and points to the adaptation of republican ideals by women as different as Sophie de Grouchy (1764–1822), the theorist of feminism and moral sentiment, and Louise Michel (1830–1905), the Communard fighter and working-class organizer at the end of the century, to support the idea that republicanism held genuine universal promise.

What is undoubted is the complexity and contradiction of this particular zone of engagement. A particular, odd idea of female autonomy was embraced by republicans. Directly after the declaration of the Republic in 1792 the Convention passed a law allowing for no-fault divorce. This was on the grounds that women had the same right to self-realization and autonomy as men. However, women were confined to the private or domestic sphere, and in consequence they could only pursue their happiness in this limited sphere. Divorce compensated for the limitations of femininity by releasing women from particular situations and allowing them to pursue their self-realization. This central paradox of acknowledging women as autonomous beings by limiting the scope of that autonomy also characterized other republican measures such as the provisions mandating female inheritance in the Civil Code. Republicanism would continue to be contradictory in its attitude to female citizens right through the period.

REVOLUTIONARY AFTERMATHS
The problematic legacy of the Revolution to republicanism comprised three distinct elements.

The Republic had concentrated power in the hands of the Committee of Public Safety, which relied on the cooperation of Jacobins and sans-culottes to exercise a dictatorship. The committee had ruled through Terror and had justified that Terror as the lawful will of the people. Finally, the Republic's doctrine of popular sovereignty was as intolerant of all national difference as it was of political difference and had unleashed a destabilizing general war. Republicans reflecting on the revolutionary experience had to explain how citizenship and popular sovereignty did not threaten civilized life with dictatorship, terror, and destruction of the international system.

This particular debate remains current and is constitutive of the continuing legacy of the French Revolution. Conservative thinkers, drawing on the work of Edmund Burke (1729–1797) or Georg Wilhelm Friedrich Hegel (1770–1831), have contrasted the irrationality of popular will with either the reason of the legal tradition incarnated in the state or the trust created between individuals in the local and specific interactions of social life. Liberals from Constant to François Furet (1927–1997) have argued that citizenship has to be interpreted within constitutional constraints if it is not to offend against liberty. Socialists beginning with Charles Fourier (1772–1837) have denounced the republican embrace of political citizenship as a sham, an illusion distracting from the real forces of the economy and technology operating in modern life. Political theory has interacted with historical interpretation. The Third Republic evaded the instability that had plagued the earlier incarnations, but the regime cannot be taken for an unproblematic example of a successful republic. A vibrant tradition of historical interpretation has argued that the eventual triumph of the Third Republic in France after 1871 masked the transformation of republicanism into French liberalism in the hard school of the Second Empire.

In the aftermath of the Revolution French republicans identified the political community as "le peuple" rather than "la nation." The French historian Jules Michelet's (1798–1874) 1846 book using the title was the most visible example of the celebration of a moral community with a definite character that preexisted political constitution. What the people demanded and the nature of the people could be differently interpreted within the republican tradition and these contrasting ideas reflected the continuing division between insurrectionary and commercial republicanism. One strand argued that the conditions for the advent of the people had to be brought about by a conspiratorial elite. Louis-Auguste Blanqui (1805–1881) gave his name, Blanquism, to this tendency in France. Blanqui developed the strategy of revolutionary will, the public uprising of an armed vanguard as a catalyst to a general rebellion, and carried it through in the failed Paris uprising of May 1839, the model for the barricade scenes in Victor Hugo's (1802–1885) *Les Misérables* (1862). The majority tradition, led in the 1840s by parliamentary orators and journalists such as François Arago (1786–1853) and Alexandre-Auguste Ledru-Rollin (1807–1874), saw the task of republicans to be to gain their rights for the people, notably the suffrage. The end of privilege, understood as the monopolization of rights by an elite, would reveal the true moral nature of the population to express itself. Republicans developed an impressive array of public manifestations, such as subscription banquets and political funerals, designed to illustrate their popular support while evading legal restrictions on political assembly. A strong republican press, best represented by *Le National* and *La Réforme,* allowed republicans to develop their ideas and to communicate them to their constituency. The two traditions coalesced in the 1848 February revolution in Paris. Republicans such as Alphonse-Marie-Louis de Prat Lamartine (1790–1869) and Ledru-Rollin worked to dispel the fear of the Republic by such measures as the repeal of the death penalty and the renunciation of all territorial ambitions. The compromise between the wings of republicanism unraveled in the uprisings by the poorer districts in June. The June revolts were interpreted, particularly by Karl Marx (1818–1883), as an illustration of the bankruptcy of republicanism in the face of the demands of mass, class-divided societies.

Republicanism outside France enjoyed its apogee in 1848. The argument that legitimacy lay with "the people" was equally attractive to reformers in England and nationalists in Hungary and Italy. The notion that industriousness was a characteristic of citizenship was central to the claims of the Chartists. One of the leaders of the Chartists, Feargus O'Connor (1796–1855), was the grandnephew by marriage of Condorcet and Sophie de Grouchy, and both his father and uncle had been republican rebels in Ireland in 1798. His ideas were in direct continuity with the Jacobin revolutionaries, and his "land plan" in particular was inspired by the republican preference for independent labor over wages. Italian republicanism was bifurcated in exactly the same way as French republicanism; the insurrectionary and social strands were represented by Giuseppe Garibaldi (1807–1882) and Giuseppe Mazzini (1805–1872) respectively. The commercial republicans' emphasis on industriousness was a core ideal for Lajos Kossuth (1802–1894) in Hungary as he sought to disassociate national sentiment from the caste privilege of the Magyars. A modern Hungarian nation would be a commercial society rather than an ethnic group dominating a subject population by appeal to the ancient constitution. Republicanism infused the revolutionary outbreaks of that year but their failure in turn generated its greatest crisis.

The manner in which republicanism would survive as a real political option after the debacle of 1848 was indicated by the republic that was least influenced by French experience: Switzerland. Béla Kaposy has argued convincingly that an independent Swiss commercial republicanism had developed from the 1750s and that by the 1860s it had arrived at a clear notion of a modern commercial republic, one in which the republic guaranteed the welfare of the citizens. The Swiss extended commercial republicanism to welfare, to insuring the citizens against the risks generated in modern capitalist society. Swiss republicanism also embraced the language and practice of civil society and argued that a dense associative life was a positive political good. Welfare and civil society were to be the animating ideas of French republicanism as it recovered from the disaster of 1848. The diversity of republican thought that exploited this opening is striking. On the left Léon-Michel Gambetta's (1838–1882) Belleville programme of 1868 laid out an array of social rights that the Republic would defend. Maximilien-Paul-Émile Littré (1801–1881) was an unabashed elitist, but he argued that the political health of the Republic depended on trade unions, a free press, and widespread participation in political clubs. All of these measures would be passed into law by the Third Republic. They complemented the creation of universal primary education, through the Ferry Laws, and industrial planning, such as the Freycinet Plan, which were already inherent in commercial republicanism. Under the Third Republic republicanism rearmed itself with a political movement, radicalism, a social base, particularly among the small-holders of the south, the *Midi rouge*, a new doctrine that illuminated the movement, solidarism, and finally embraced suffrage as the basis of the citizen's public commitment.

The division between revolutionary and commercial or social republicanism was not entirely healed by the Third Republic. The Communards were pardoned in 1880, but the memory of the Parisian revolutionary tradition could not be effaced. Georges Clemenceau (1841–1929), for example, flirted with the appeal of direct action in his support for General Georges-Ernest-Jean-Marie Boulanger (1837–1891) in 1889. But the alliance that sought justice for Alfred Dreyfus (1859–1935) aligned the two in the 1890s, and the appeal to the nation in arms would again be deployed in 1914 in support of the institutions of the existing republic and not its revolutionary twin. Elsewhere revolutionary republicanism retained its capacity to encourage direct action. Kossuth's commercial republicanism was the paradoxical inspiration for the founding of the Irish Republican Party, Sinn Féin, and in 1916 this vanguard of the people would express itself in Dublin. Republicanism continued to suggest criteria of legitimacy that could not be fully represented by a state.

Nineteenth-century European republicanism was dominated by the French experience. The ideals were forged in the Revolution, undermined in 1848, renewed and institutionalized in the Third Republic. Elsewhere republican influence was more sporadic and derivative. Republican ideals could be found in unexpected places, however. In the aftermath of the failure of Chartism in England, working-class radicals in London experimented with republican ideals. William James Linton (1812–1897) founded the Bethnal Green Republican Propagandist Society and published *The English Republic,* which sustained the continuity of English republicanism into the later part of the century. These kinds of movements were always vulnerable to events in France and the English republican movement collapsed in the aftermath of the Paris Commune. In France the political

culture eventually learned how to comprise the repertoire of republican political action, to accommodate direct action without threatening the system of governance. Elsewhere, in such countries as Italy, Spain, and Ireland republicanism in 1914 remained a revolutionary faith.

See also **Blanqui, Auguste; Chartism; Citizenship; Clemenceau, Georges; Conservatism; French Revolution; Garibaldi, Giuseppe; Girondins; Gouges, Olympe de; Jacobins; Kossuth, Lajos; Lamartine, Alphonse; Ledru-Rollin, Alexandre-Auguste; Levée en Masse; Liberalism; Mazzini, Giuseppe; Nationalism; O'Connor, Feargus; Paine, Thomas; Socialism; Wollstonecraft, Mary.**

BIBLIOGRAPHY

Higonnet, Patrice L. R. *Goodness beyond Virtue: Jacobins during the French Revolution.* Cambridge, Mass., 1998.

Livesey, James. *Making Democracy in the French Revolution.* Cambridge, Mass., 2001.

Nicolet, Claude. *L'idée républicaine en France (1789–1924).* Paris, 1982.

Nord, Philip. *The Republican Moment: Struggles for Democracy in Nineteenth-Century France.* Cambridge, Mass., 1995.

Rosanvallon, Pierre. *Le sacre du citoyen.* Paris, 1992.

Skinner, Quentin. *Liberty before Liberalism.* Cambridge, U.K., and New York, 1997.

Stone, Judith F. *Sons of the Revolution: Radical Democrats in France, 1862–1914.* Baton Rouge, La., 1996.

JAMES LIVESEY

RESTAURANTS. The word *restaurant* comes from the French verb *restaurer* ("to restore or refresh"), and for much of the nineteenth century restaurants were a phenomenon specific to French urban life. This does not mean that everywhere else, all food was eaten at home. Inns and taverns had existed for centuries; caterers prepared holiday and banquet meals; and cafés/coffeehouses had been common in parts of Europe since the mid- to late seventeenth century. But none of these establishments shared the features that had made restaurants into a recognizable cultural institution by the early 1800s.

The first self-styled restaurateurs went into business in Paris in the 1760s, serving a limited menu of "restorative" dishes (bouillons, broths,

Men in a restaurant. Illustration by DuMaurier from *Punch*, 1875. The excesses of restaurant dining are caricatured. MARY EVANS PICTURE LIBRARY

rice puddings, etc.). If they had innovated only in the foods they sold, their popularity would not have outlasted the faddish medicalized sensitivity of which they took advantage. The first restaurateurs also introduced new forms of service, however, which contributed to a sense of social and cultural distinction that became among the hallmarks of restaurant life. Whereas customers at an inn expected to eat either in their own rooms or, more likely, at a large table with other travelers (the *table d'hôte* or "ordinary"), restaurant patrons were seated at separate tables within a large dining room. Guests at a *table d'hôte* shared dishes, but restaurant customers were, from the 1770s onward, presented with a printed menu from which they made their own choices. Seated at their own table, ordering their own foods, restaurant clients created their own temporarily private spaces within a restaurant's public room. Going to a restaurant made it possible to make a public show of private good taste.

In the aftermath of the French Revolution of 1789, visitors to Paris tried to identify its effects on daily life. Many writers mistakenly included restaurants in this category, claiming that their opulently mirrored interiors, heavy silverware, fine china, and extensive wine lists made it possible for commoners to dine like a king. Antoine Beauvilliers (1754–1817), former pastry chef to the king's brother, did in fact open a well-known restaurant, but he did so before 1789 and much of his fame derived from a cookbook, *L'Art du cuisinier* (The cook's art), which he published in 1814. Jean Anthelme Brillat-Savarin (1755–1826) described Beauvilliers in his *Physiology of Taste* (1826), one of the best-known works to treat restaurants as an example of the Revolution's democratization of aristocratic privilege. For radical republicans and socialists, however, the spread of restaurant culture proved only that money had replaced birth as a new, but equally pernicious, form of privilege.

A CHEAP RESTAURANT.

Russian restaurant c. 1885. Illustration from *Harper's Monthly*. Peasants in Nizhny Novgorod are shown at a rudimentary outdoor restaurant. MARY EVANS PICTURE LIBRARY

By the early 1800s, restaurants such as the Grand Véfour, the Restaurant Véry, the Rocher de Cancale, the Maison Dorée, and Aux Trois Frères Provençaux were fixtures in any description of fashionable Paris, but comparable establishments were uncommon in other parts of France and even rarer elsewhere. As late as the 1850s, American and British visitors to Paris remarked on how strange it felt to be offered the choice of so many different dishes and then to eat those dishes in an ornate dining room surrounded by groups of both men and women. Many of London's exclusive gentlemen's clubs had famous chefs (such as Alexis Soyer [1809–1858] at the Reform Club) but these clubs, restricted to members and forbidden to women,

were not the same as restaurants. For members of the Victorian middle class in Britain, domestic comfort played a central part in defining their own national, social, and gender identities. They therefore looked askance at Paris restaurants as offering proof that the French were promiscuous and incurably attracted to publicity. In contrast, the famous late-nineteenth-century London steak restaurant, Simpson's in the Strand, had separate dining rooms for men and women.

In the last third of the nineteenth century, the Paris restaurant was imitated across much of Europe. The word *restaurant* was widely adopted (*ristorante* in Italian, *restauracja* in Polish) and eateries were named after the most famous bygone establishments of the French capital. (For example, in 1909, there was a Restaurant Verry in London, a Café de Paris in Brussels, and a Maison Dorée in Barcelona, but the originals were no longer in business.) Many of the most famous restaurants of this period were found in the grand luxury hotels that became such important features of the urban landscape after railways and steamships transformed international travel. Across western Europe and North America, notionally "French" cuisine dominated in these hotel restaurants, thanks to the comparatively early professionalization of French chefs and the dominance of work practices developed by Georges Auguste Escoffier (1846–1935), a chef who worked closely with the hotel entrepreneur César Ritz (1848–1918). "International" hotel cuisine in luxury hotels across the world referred to "French" food. Cookery, nonetheless, was one of the ways that Europeans brought their empires home. After the success of the food pavilions at the World's Fairs, several ostensibly Chinese and Indian restaurants opened in London and Paris in the 1880s and 1890s.

Throughout the nineteenth century, restaurant going was for most Europeans a highly mysterious affair. Restaurants, after all, were urban institutions, and Europe was predominantly rural. Guidebooks, beginning with Alexandre-Balthasar-Laurent Grimod de la Reynière's *Almanach des gourmands* (1803–1812), promised to instruct the uninitiated, but if they could tell the novice where to dine, they could not tell him (restaurant guides presumed a male readership) how to eat. Social distinction, and a sort of legitimate licentiousness, remained key features of restaurant culture. If, in the 1830s and 1840s, movements for political reform often took the form of banquets, this was because the table was so closely identified with innocuous frivolity that no government thought it necessary to ban them.

See also **Cabarets; Diet and Nutrition; Popular and Elite Culture; Wine.**

BIBLIOGRAPHY

Mennell, Stephen. *All Manners of Food: Eating and Taste in England and France from the Middle Ages to the Present.* Oxford, U.K., 1985.

Spang, Rebecca L. *The Invention of the Restaurant: Paris and Modern Gastronomic Culture.* Cambridge, Mass., 2000.

Trubek, Amy B. *Haute Cuisine: How the French Invented the Culinary Profession.* Philadelphia, 2000.

REBECCA L. SPANG

RESTORATION.

Restoration is the term that historians have adopted to describe the political settlement that reigned in Europe between the abdication of Napoleon in 1815 and the Revolutions of 1830. Yet in reality "restoration" was only one of a range of options available to the allies who met at the Congress of Vienna and to individual regimes as they emerged from the turmoil of the Revolution and the Napoleonic Wars. The states that wholly rejected the experience of the Revolutionary era and sought determinedly to put the clock back and restore Christian monarchy (the cases of Spain and Piedmont-Savoy in 1814, for example) were, in fact, the exception rather the rule.

The majority of regimes sought to compromise in one way or another with the political changes of the Revolutionary era, whether by adopting limited constitutions (such as in France, or in the states of southern Germany), or by preserving the advances made in administration under Napoleon, while rejecting constitutional government (as in Prussia and Austria). The agreement finally signed at the Congress of Vienna in 1815 did not support the radical, counterrevolutionary aspirations of those hoping for a restoration. In fact, it produced a territorial settlement that both acknowledged many legacies of the Revolutionary period and sowed the seeds for future revolution. Yet the wish for a Restoration was very powerful right after 1815 and it would take more than a decade of experimenting with counterrevolution before even its staunchest defenders would abandon it in 1830 in favor of other more effective and less incendiary tactics for shoring up a conservative political order in Europe.

THE IDEA OF RESTORATION, IN THEORY AND IN PRACTICE

Many of the key concepts of Restoration philosophy emerged in the last decades of the eighteenth century, when writers such as Edmund Burke (*Reflections on the Revolution in France,* 1790), Joseph de Maistre (*Considerations sur la France,* 1796), and Novalis (*Christenheit oder Europa,* 1799) launched an assault on the Enlightenment and its seemingly destructive and sinful cult of abstract reason. Against the necessarily dangerous and violent consequences that for them stemmed ineluctably from the presumptuously optimistic belief that rational individuals could form the basis of a political system born of their own design and consent, these counterrevolutionary philosophers hearkened to an idyllic and peaceful Old Regime characterized by tradition, respect for hierarchy, and humility before Providence. While English conservatives (chief among them Burke) remained committed to Lockean individualism and an idea of representative government, Continental Restoration philosophers upheld traditions over rights, saw families and communities rather than individuals as constitutive of human society, and yearned for the social organicism and political authoritarianism that reigned supreme in the Old Regime. More than attempting a restoration of eighteenth-century monarchy, these Continental thinkers strove to revive the social and political order as it existed before a century of enlightened reform had whittled away at the power and prestige of the church, the monarchy, and the nobility.

As revolutionary ideals and institutions spread across Europe during the Napoleonic wars, more voices joined this late-eighteenth-century chorus, and when Napoleon I (r. 1804–1814/15) was finally defeated in 1815 they found an audience receptive to their ideas and eager to seize the opportunity to put them into practice. Most enthusiastic among those desiring a return to the Old Regime order of things were the noblemen, clergymen, and monarchs forced out of power and into exile during the Revolution and the Napoleonic Wars. De Maistre (1753–1821) and Louis de Bonald (1754–1840), for example, returning émigrés, writers, and politicians who served the regime of the restored Bourbon monarchs, spent their lives trying to transform the ideal of Restoration into a reality in France. Ridiculing the rationalist pretensions of the eighteenth century, interpreting the violence of the Revolution, the Terror, and the Napoleonic Wars as divine punishment for

the crime of unbelief, these writers espoused divine right monarchy and the renewed power of the pope across Europe; they lent their support to Louis XVIII (r. 1814–1815, 1815–1824), and later to Charles X (r. 1824–1830), in the hopes that they might lead the Continent back into the hands of Providence. Such a view allowed for no compromise or negotiation with the revolutionary legacy; the people of France had to be returned to Christ, the legal system and bureaucracy consolidated under Napoleon had to be dismantled, any idea of founding monarchy on the basis of a man-made constitution had to be abandoned. For as de Maistre explained, "[Man] can no doubt plant a pip, grow a tree, improve it by grafting, and prune it in countless different ways, but he has never imagined that he had the power to make a tree; how then can he have supposed he had the power to make a constitution?"

During the fifteen years that the Bourbon monarchs ruled in France in the nineteenth century (1815–1830) a religious revival, supported by powerful nobles and clergymen, translated these radical, counterrevolutionary Restoration ideas into practice. Missionaries traveled to all corners of the kingdom to reintroduce French subjects to the catechism and to deliver the sacraments. They organized autos-da-fé of Enlightenment texts (especially those of Voltaire [François-Marie Arouet, 1694–1778] and Jean-Jacques Rousseau [1712–1778]), and denounced from their pulpits the selling of church lands during the Revolution (*biens nationaux*) and the killing of Louis XVI (r. 1774–1792) and Marie-Antoinette (1755–1793). Their six-week-long revivals culminated in spectacular processions in which tens of thousands of followers were enjoined to expiate for the sins of the Revolution, a ritual crowned by the planting of a mission cross, an enormous crucifix adorned with the Bourbon royal lily, representing the reconsecration of the French nation to God, Church, and King. While Louis XVIII officially sanctioned this religious revival, he did not lend it his public support. In contrast, when his more religious, and ultrareactionary brother, Charles X, ascended the throne, he not only participated in the missionaries' spectacles (as for the Papal Jubilee in 1826), he also passed a series of laws defining sacrilege and indemnifying nobles for the *biens nationaux.* His regime also favored nobles with lucrative positions in the administration and the clergy; churchmen actively campaigned for ultra-royalist candidates from their pulpits. In short, it appeared as if the ideal of a restoration of Christian monarchy had been translated into reality in France (at least after 1825).

Similar enactments of the Restoration ideal took place in Spain and in Italy after 1814. In Spain, when Ferdinand VII (r. 1808, 1814–1833) was released from captivity by Napoleon and restored as an absolute monarch, religious orders were welcomed back, the Inquisition was reinstated, and many nurtured hopes that the power and privileges gradually taken away from the nobles and the church by the enlightened Bourbon monarchs of the eighteenth century would be restored. All over Italy sovereigns proclaimed the renewed alliance between altar and throne after 1815, but King Victor Emmanuel I (r. 1802–1821) of the Kingdom of Sardinia-Piedmont distinguished himself in the early days of the Restoration by the zeal with which he brought back into force both the letter and the spirit of the Old Regime. Abolishing Napoleonic legislation in a single decree, he also purged the administration, judiciary, and army of those who served under the previous regime.

In each of these cases—in France, Spain, and Italy—this counterrevolutionary enactment of the Restoration ideal provoked unrest and ultimately revolution. In France, Charles X's elaborate Old Regime–style coronation at Reims, his participation in the papal jubilee, and the Passage of the Sacrilege Law aroused growing suspicion and eventually a broad anticlerical movement against the monarch suspected by many of being a "Jesuit-king." Theater riots around Molière's (Jean-Baptiste Polquelin, 1622–1673) anticlerical comedy, *Tartuffe* (1667), and seditious writings and songs publicizing the dangers of the regime's clericalism escalated into violent assaults on the emblems of Christian monarchy, the mission crosses planted all over the kingdom. By 1830 a full-fledged revolution broke out, and the Bourbon Charles X was deposed in favor of the less religious, more moderate constitutional monarch, the Orleanist, Louis-Philippe (r. 1830–1848). In Spain in 1820 a military revolt against Ferdinand VII led to a proclamation of the constitution of 1812, a document issued by

Donoso Cortes (Juan Francisco María de la Salud, 1809–1853) during the fight against Napoleon, saturated with liberal and even democratic ideals, which had been revoked in 1814. In Piedmont Victor Emmanuel I was driven to abdicate in the face of a revolution in 1821. Put down by the Habsburgs, the revolution produced a successor, Charles Felix (r. 1821–1831), who continued to pursue a restoration strategy, granting a powerful role to the church in political life, working for administrative decentralization and the restoration of noble prerogatives, clerical privileges, and local autonomies. These are precisely the issues that would arouse continuous protest and unrest during the 1820s. It would take another revolution, and the reformist efforts of Charles Albert (r. 1831–1849), to move beyond the dynamic of counterrevolution and revolution that defined Piedmont in this post-Napoleonic era.

A closer look at even these most reactionary and counterrevolutionary regimes illustrates that restoration was not only a dangerous and potentially inflammatory goal but also one that was never fully embraced by any of the rulers in this period. If Charles X came to the throne in 1825 and moved in a direction that seemed to favor the ultraroyalists seeking a restoration of the Old Regime, his predecessor, Louis XVIII, had ruled for eight years before him at the head of a bureaucracy and on the basic of a legal code inherited from Napoleon. While he represented himself as a monarch by virtue of birth and tradition, he ruled on the basis of the Charter of 1814, which included protection for basic freedoms (of expression, of worship), and a representative government (with one appointed Chamber of Peers and one elected Chamber of Representatives, based on a very limited franchise). If even Louis moved in a reactionary direction after 1820 in the wake of the Duke de Berri's assassination, he still presided over a nation with a Charter he promised to respect. While he purged the bureaucracy of one-third of its Napoleonic staff (although only after the Hundred Days), and while nobles certainly moved back into the administration over the course of the Restoration, recruitment continued on the principle of merit and talent, rather than birth and privilege, and Napoleonic educational institutions, such as the École Polytechnique, continued to furnish this new elite.

Similarly, while the Catholic Church was favored in this period (religious orders were allowed to return and clergymen and religious institutions in general became notoriously richer), the basic subjugation of the church to the state that had taken place over the eighteenth century and that had been consolidated by the Revolution and Napoleon's Concordat (of 1802), was not undone. The *biens nationaux* were not restored; the church hierarchy was appointed and paid for by the government; while Catholicism was recognized as the religion of the state, freedom of worship for Protestants and Catholics was protected by law. Even Charles X, when faced with outright opposition to his blatant clericalism, relied upon this bureaucracy and legal framework to bring peace to the nation. The police did not clamp down on protestors nor punish anyone under the unpopular Sacrilege Law (which would have involved cutting off their hands, before marching them to the town square for public execution); rather his civil officials enjoined missionaries to stay inside their temples, mission crosses were quietly removed from public squares, and sermons were checked for incendiary attacks on *biens nationaux* or other revolutionary legacies that were protected by law in France.

In Spain, far from restoring the power of the church to its glory days of the Spanish Inquisition, King Ferdinand VII did not relinquish the gains of his eighteenth-century predecessors. He refused to give back the ecclesiastical estates sold off during the war with Napoleon, and he found new ways to plunder the church's revenues. He appointed more than sixty new bishops and blatantly used the church as a weapon of political control. The radical hopes of churchmen and nobles alike were frustrated by the continued regalism of the king. Struggles regarding the legacies of the eighteenth-century kings, the Napoleonic innovations, and the limited Restoration after 1814 (and again after 1823) sparked unrest and revolution well into the 1830s. In Italy the Napoleonic regime had not offered the full, democratic participation in government with which France experimented during the Revolution, but the Napoleonic state did offer a secularized and egalitarian government that reformed society from above and left room for the emergence of liberal political discussion.

In spite of the appearance of a restoration of the power and privilege of the church and state, which predated these innovations, governments up and down the peninsula retained significant elements of the Napoleonic legacy. This was true in the Kingdom of Lombard-Venetia, in the Duchies of Parma and Modena and in the Kingdom of the Two Sicilies, in the Grand Duchy of Tuscany, and in the principality of Lucca; it even took place in the Papal States, and, within a few years, in the Kingdom of Sardinia-Piedmont, where the most thoroughgoing Restoration seemed to have been achieved. Everywhere in Italy subjects remained fundamentally equal before uniform legal codes, a Napoleonic innovation not undone by any of the restored monarchs. Neither aristocratic title nor ecclesiastical office brought with it fiscal or judicial immunities or privileges. While it is true that the purge of the bureaucracy (as in Sardinia-Piedmont) left room for many nobles to fill vacant positions, they remained cogs in a machine over which they had no control, and which gave them no particular advantage. As a result, within ten to fifteen years many of these nobles withdrew from their posts in disappointment.

RESTORATION IN THE INTERNATIONAL ARENA

At the international level the eastern monarchies (Russia, Austria, and Prussia), most often led by Alexander I (r. 1801–1825), tried to push the Allies who had defeated France in 1814 (and especially in 1815 after Napoleon's return in the Hundred Days) down the path of restoration and counterrevolution. Certainly the Holy Alliance proffered by Alexander I in 1815 expressed a desire to unify Europeans around the wish for Christian monarchy and a renunciation of all of the liberal legacies of the Revolution. The Foreign Secretary, Viscount Castelreagh (Robert Stewart, 1769–1822), the British representative at Vienna in 1815, refused to have anything to do with this alliance. The text that he did agree to sign, the Treaty of the Quadruple Alliance (20 November 1815), which established the territorial settlement and the diplomatic architecture of Europe that would reign for the next few decades, was much more modest and moderate in its goals. The principle of legitimism inscribed in the treaty bore no trace of the divine-right monarchy desired by the signatories of the Holy Alliance. Rather, this term, invented by Charles-Maurice de Talleyrand-Périgord (1754–1838), was used to mean that the rights of pre-Napoleonic rulers of European states should be respected and their thrones restored to them if they lost them in the course of the wars. Likewise, the determination to ensure a stable "balance of power" was not predicated on any specific agenda to undo the domestic or international legacies of the past decades. Rather it was based on two pillars: first, that Austria, Prussia, Russia, and Britain agreed to maintain, by armed force, the exclusion of the Bonaparte dynasty from France for twenty years; and second, that the Allies were to "renew their meetings at fixed periods" for the purpose of consulting upon their common interests, and to take such action as was necessary for "the maintenance of the peace of Europe."

Between 1815 and 1823 the Russians tried repeatedly, with the support of Austria and Prussia, to broaden the terms of this initial treaty, and to interpret the "peace of Europe" or the "balance of power" as being dependent on putting down any and all changes brought about by revolutionary action. This was the spirit of a memorandum signed by Austria, Prussia, and Russia at the Congress of October 1820 in reaction to a succession of revolutionary uprisings in Spain and Italy. Castelreagh refused to go to Troppau or to adhere to the so-called Troppau Protocol. Indeed he responded with a famous memorandum denouncing the blanket counterrevolutionary goals of his allies: "The Principle of one state interfering in the internal affairs of another in order to enforce obedience to the governing authority is always a question of the greatest moral, as well as political delicacy. ... to generalize such a principle, to think of reducing it to a system or to impose it as a blanket obligation, is a scheme utterly unpracticable and objectionable."

Individual monarchs acted on behalf of the principles of Restoration and counterrevolution although these tenets were not adopted as the official policy of the Concert of Europe. The repressive Carlsbad Decrees, adopted in the German Confederacy at the urging of the Austrian chancellor Clemens von Metternich (1773–1859) in 1819, represent an important moment in which at least the eastern allies tried to enforce counterrevolution and prohibit the more liberal German states in the south and west from consolidating constitutional governments. In 1821 the Habsburgs intervened militarily and put down the revolutions in Italy; in 1823 the French Bourbon monarchy sent a hundred thousand troops to put down the revolution in Spain. In both cases this was done with the express sanction of those continuing to meet at regular congresses. But Britain increasingly refused to attend or send representatives to these congresses, and so the practice of meeting regularly to maintain a Concert of Europe broke down by 1823, precisely over the question of how committed to Restoration and counterrevolution the Concert of Europe should be.

CONSERVATIVE ALTERNATIVES TO RESTORATION

The case of France serves as one example of a conservative alternative to Restoration worked out over the period between 1815 and 1830. Ultraroyalists launched a full-scale attack on the liberal legacy of the eighteenth century and rejected all compromises in the form of man-made constitutions defining the sovereignty of the monarch, limiting the power or authority of the church, or depriving the nobility of their natural and traditional right to rule. Yet they met with staunch opposition from liberals, also known as Doctrinaires, who were committed to retaining many of the political and material legacies of the Revolution while avoiding its excesses. They defended, above all, the Charter, which ensured basic freedoms (especially of the press and of religious expression) and limited representative government. But it was necessary to bolster this limited constitutional government with traditions and habits of deference that would assure social peace even as liberty was being expanded. Hence, Pierre-Paul Royer-Collard (1763–1845), a chief spokesman for the Doctrinaires continued to support the monarchy and the hereditary Chamber of Peers as necessary counterweights to the elective Chamber of Deputies. François Guizot (1787–1874), who led the fight against the ultraroyalists in the 1820s, espoused constitutional government, but, unlike his radical predecessors in the eighteenth century, denounced popular sovereignty as leading ineluctably to tyranny. He believed in the sovereignty of reason, but it was not something that could be determined by the majority, but rather by those elites capable of knowing what would ensure the greatest happiness for all. This limited liberal constitutional program was complemented by a conservative social and cultural agenda with which many ultra-royalists agreed, such as giving the church the right to educate the young, and therefore instill habits of deference and obedience, or enacting legal reforms to shore up the family, such as the abolition of divorce.

A second conservative alternative to Restoration was forged in Prussia in these years. The history of the German Confederation, to which Prussia belonged, beautifully captures the complexity of real political settlements after 1815 and the degree to which this period was marked not only by a return to what was, or a reconciling to some changes, but also by innovations and important legacies of its own. The very existence of the German Confederation in 1815 is testimony to the willingness of the signatories at Vienna not to go back to the world of the Old Regime. Rather than restore the more than three hundred states that existed before the Revolution and Napoleonic Wars, the German Confederation was composed of about three dozen states. Furthermore, each member state was required by the terms of the treaty to establish a constitution for the assembly of its estates. In the south and in the west, some leaders of German states, such as the Grand Duke of Saxe-Weimar and the rulers of Bavaria, Württemburg, Baden, and Hesse-Darmstadt took advantage of this opportunity and granted very liberal constitutions.

Prussia adopted a very different course. In much the way that Italian monarchs maintained and modified the structure of the Napoleonic bureaucracy and legal code, Prussia built on the efficient corps of highly trained, well-educated civil servants that came out of the Napoleonic period and used it both to institute reforms from above, and through its police functions, to ensure absolute obedience to an increasingly powerful state. King Frederick William III (r. 1797–1840) expanded universal education and made Prussian universities among the best and best-funded in the world; he pursued economic liberalization (taking on the Junkers and serfdom, pushing for the Zollverein, or a free-market zone for the German states).

These "progressive" changes that one could clearly describe as legacies of the eighteenth century and the Napoleonic period were balanced by measures to ensure stability and the power of the state. Constitutional, representative institutions did exist, but they were always subordinate to the state, and for decades remained powerless. The Carlsbad Decrees of 1819, which extended state surveillance and control over the educational system, the press, and all political activity, ensured that calls for political liberty and real constitutional government could easily be thwarted. This was extended throughout the German Confederation by 1820, and so the authoritarian, repressive influence of Prussia reached some of the more liberal, constitutional states to the South and West as well. King Frederick William III also innovated in the realm of church-state politics. In 1817 he created a new (Protestant) Church of the Prussian Union and over the 1820s he used it to pursue an aggressive confessional statism; in particular he used it against Catholic minorities who had been added to Prussia by the settlement of Vienna.

1830: THE ABANDONMENT OF RESTORATION AND THE RISE OF A CONSERVATIVE CONSENSUS

After the trauma and violence of the Revolution, the Terror, and the Napoleonic Wars both international and domestic politics were motivated above all by a desire to ensure peace and stability in Europe. Yet how that was to be achieved was far from clear in 1815. For the ultrareactionaries this required nothing less than a frontal assault on all changes brought about during the entire eighteenth century. Monarchs needed to be put back on their thrones, established churches needed to be restored to their full power and glory, the radical spirit of the Enlightenment, and all of the evils to which it had given rise, had to be expunged and actively prevented from reemerging in Europe. Powerful figures espoused this radical Restoration philosophy at the Congress of Vienna in 1815 and were in a position to enforce it in many parts of Europe in the years that followed. Yet, nowhere in Europe was a real restoration of the Old Regime realized; too much had changed and too many people were invested in those changes. This was clear everywhere monarchs, nobles, and clergymen tried to stage such a restoration. More importantly, efforts to do so proved to be quite destabilizing, producing (as in Spain and northern Italy by 1820, and France after 1825) popular revolts. By 1830 Russia, Prussia, and Austria accepted changes to the original territorial settlement from Vienna and acknowledged the independence of Greece and Belgium, even though national independence had been won by revolution, in the name of liberal constitutionalism. These countries still pursued counterrevolutionary policies, putting down revolutions (for example in Poland, Germany, and Italy in 1830). But as a general policy, Restoration was progressively abandoned by 1830, even by the signatories of the original Holy Alliance.

By 1830 the idea of a Restoration proved to be impossible, even dangerous, and this is one reason it was scuttled; but another reason it was abandoned was that over the past decade and a half regimes had developed new strategies for containing the disorder and the uncertainty of the Revolutionary period using many of the tools that came out of that era. In France the Doctrinaires led the way toward a more moderate constitutional monarchy: using the bureaucracy and legal structure inherited from Napoleon, they fought not for popular sovereignty and a perfect liberal polity, but rather for a mixture of institutions and traditions from the Old Regime and the Revolution that would allow them to avoid the worst excesses of the Revolutionary period. In Prussia, the administrative centralization and empowerment of the state that was the primary consequence of the Napoleonic era was not undone; rather it was used to institute a wide range of reforms and to create an economically liberal, but politically and socially authoritarian state that would find many emulators in decades to follow. What one sees across the political spectrum during the period known as the Restoration (including most liberal England) is the abandonment of the most radical hopes and wishes that were at the heart of the Enlightenment—that society and politics could be organized on rational principles and the idea that the freedom and enlightenment of every individual was absolutely essential for the prosperity and happiness of all. For men like Adam Smith (1723–1790) and Marie-Jean-Antoine-Nicolas de Condorcet (1743–1794) the reasoning power of every man and woman was a necessary bulwark against the tyranny

of powerful and established institutions of all kinds (the church, the monarchy, monopolies). But two decades of political violence and turmoil led the leaders of Restoration Europe to turn back to those powerful and established institutions and reconsider how they might be used to provide stability and security, and very few of them talked about the price for that shift. Leaders in the period between 1815 and 1830 did not succeed in restoring the Old Regime and abolishing the rational spirit of the Enlightenment and liberalism entirely, but they did preside over a world that saw the return of faith in religion, in political authority, in tradition, and in hierarchy and a profound loss of faith in the project of freedom and liberty for all.

See also **Charles X; Concert of Europe; Congress of Vienna; Ferdinand VII; Francis I; Frederick William III; Greece; Guizot, François; Lafayette, Marquis de; Louis XVIII; Metternich, Clemens von; Ottoman Empire; Revolutions of 1820; Revolutions of 1830.**

BIBLIOGRAPHY

Alexander, Robert. *Re-writing the French Revolutionary Tradition: Liberal Opposition and the Fall of the Bourbon Monarchy.* Cambridge, U.K., and New York, 2003.

Berdahl, Robert M. *The Politics of the Prussian Nobility: The Development of a Conservative Ideology, 1770–1848.* Princeton, N.J., 1988.

Bertier de Sauvigny, Guillaume de. *The Bourbon Restoration.* Philadelphia, 1966. Standard work on the French Restoration, with detailed attention to the political controversies defining the reigns of Louis XVIII and Charles X.

Boime, Albert. *Art in an Age of Counterrevolution: 1815–1848.* Chicago, 2004.

Broers, Michael. *Europe after Napoleon: Revolution, Reaction, and Romanticism, 1814–1848.* Manchester, U.K., 1996. Excellent overview of the range of political settlements negotiated in Europe among a specific generation.

Callahan, William J. *Church, Politics, and Society in Spain, 1750–1874.* Cambridge, Mass., 1984.

Di Scala, Spencer M., and Salvo Mastellone. *European Political Thought, 1815–1989.* Boulder, Colo.: Westview Press, 1998.

Fitzpatrick, Brian. *Catholic Royalism in the Department of the Gard, 1815–1832.* Cambridge, U.K., 1983.

Gibson, Ralph. *A Social History of French Catholicism, 1789–1914.* London, 1989.

Higgs, David. *Ultraroyalism in Toulouse: From Its Origins to the Revolution of 1830*. Baltimore, Md., 1973.

Jardin, André, and André Jean Tudesq. *Restoration and Reaction: 1815–1848*. Translated by Elborg Forster. Cambridge, U.K., 1983.

Kroen, Sheryl. *Politics and Theater: The Crisis of Legitimacy in Restoration France (1815–1830)*. Berkeley, Calif., 2000. On the ideal of Restoration as enacted by the missionaries as opposed to the moderate, conciliatory policies of the regimes; also considers popular reactions to both.

Laven, David, and Lucy Riall, eds. *Napoleon's Legacy*. Oxford, U.K., 2000. Superb series of articles representing a new generation of scholarship exploring the complexities of negotiating the Napoleonic period in the years right after 1814. Absolutely indispensable.

MacMahon, Darrin. *Enemies of the Enlightenment: The French Counter-Enlightenment and the Making of Modernity*. Oxford, U.K., 2001.

Matthews, Andrew. *Revolution and Reaction, Europe, 1789–1849*. Cambridge, U.K., 2001.

Pilbeam, Pamela. *Themes in Modern European History, 1780–1830*. London, 1995. Excellent, lively overview, with good detail on France.

Rosanvallon, Pierre. *La Monarchie Impossible: Les Chartes de 1814 et de 1830*. Paris, 1994.

Rothschild, Emma. *Economic Sentiments: Adam Smith, Condorcet, and the Enlightenment*. Cambridge, Mass., 2001. Beautiful treatment of the economic and political liberalism at the heart of Smith and Condorcet; how and why the Revolutionary and Napoleonic period severed the connection between economic and political freedom, and left a world where economic liberalism would be coupled to social and political conservatism for almost two centuries.

Sevrin, Ernest. *Les Missions religieuses en France sous la Restauration, 1815–1830*. Vol. 1: *Le Missionnaire et la mission*. St. Maudé, France, 1948. Vol. 2: *Les Missions, 1815–1820*. Paris, 1959.

Sheehan, James J. *German History, 1770–1866*. Oxford, U.K., 1989.

Sperber, Jonathan. *Popular Catholicism in Nineteenth-Century Germany*. Princeton, N.J., 1984.

Weiss, John. *Conservatism in Europe, 1770–1945: Traditionalism, Reaction, and Counter-revolution*. London, 1977.

Woloch, Isser. *The New Regime: Transformations of the French Civic Order, 1789–1820s*. London, 1994.

SHERYL KROEN

REVOLUTIONARY WARS. *See* French Revolutionary and Napoleonic Wars.

REVOLUTION OF 1789. *See* French Revolution.

REVOLUTION OF 1905 (RUSSIA).

Russia's first twentieth-century revolution began on 22 January (9 January, old style) 1905. In October a general strike paralyzed the country. The tsar responded by granting an elected parliament (the State Duma) with limited powers. This partial victory did not, however, put an end to the mutinies, unrest, and widespread lawlessness, which continued into 1906. Intensifying the level of repression, the regime continued to mistrust the newly legalized political parties. The first and second sessions of the Duma, despite their restricted franchise, proved more radical than the tsar and his advisors had hoped. On 16 June (3 June, O.S.) 1907 the Second Duma was dissolved by imperial fiat, and the electoral laws were altered to guarantee a more docile assembly. The Russian Revolution of 1905 thus ended in a coup d'état.

Once the Bolsheviks came to power, they celebrated 1905 as a link in the chain of revolutionary inevitability. Vladimir Lenin called it the "dress rehearsal" for October 1917. Leon Trotsky called it the "majestic prologue." While the experience of 1905 influenced participants and leaders in the next crisis, the political settlement offered statesmen and moderate public figures the chance to establish common ground. The autocracy's fate was not yet sealed. On both sides of the barricades, however, the spirit of intransigence prevailed. The tsar resented the concessions he had been forced to make and chose ministers who endorsed his attachment to outmoded autocratic principles. The Duma deputies, for their part, lacked parliamentary decorum and had little taste for compromise.

In retrospect 1905 seemed a milestone in the process of decline, but it can also be viewed as a product of the regime's positive achievements. The state had itself created the conditions for social and economic progress that its shortsightedness then undermined. The alliance of disgruntled entrepreneurs and professionals with exploited workers and impoverished peasants reflected the country's variegated social landscape. The movement that challenged the absolutist state relied, however, on modern forms of transport and communication—railroads, newspapers, and telegraph. Its leaders used the tools of modern political life—parties, programs, and propaganda.

GREAT REFORMS

When Tsar Alexander II (r. 1855–1881) instituted the Great Reforms (1861–1874), he opened the door to economic and social advancement. The abolition of serfdom spurred the growth of wage labor and stimulated entrepreneurial activity. The creation of organs of local self-administration (the zemstvos), composed of elected representatives of the different social classes, provided experience in civic responsibility. The loosening of censorship and encouragement of scientific training promoted the emergence of a professional elite. Judicial reform introduced notions of due process and respect for the law that contradicted the principles of absolute rule embodied in the monarch. Military reforms stressed the importance of education and expertise in equipping the empire's armed forces to fight successfully in the modern age.

The Great Reforms were designed to remedy the underdevelopment so painfully manifested by Russia's defeat in the Crimean War (1853–1856). To the same end, the government also sponsored railroads and manufacture. In 1891 a devastating famine prompted ever more peasants to leave the villages for factories and towns. Along with poverty, slums, prostitution, and crime, the growing cities developed a western-style public culture: parks, movie theaters, department stores, and a boulevard press.

The reforms were important not only for their results but also for the process involved in their shaping and implementation. The gentry were allowed—indeed obliged—to take part, along with farsighted bureaucrats and statesmen, in committees that helped reshape the empire's legal and social foundation. These committees were not secret: Alexander II also introduced *glasnost*

(greater openness, a slogan of that era as well as of the late twentieth century). The elites were disappointed, however, when Alexander finally refused to "crown the zemstvo edifice," as the saying went, with empire-wide political institutions. Political parties (not to speak of trade unions or strikes) were illegal—indeed, there was no context in which they could function. Even professional gatherings were monitored by the police. In this institutional vacuum, the zemstvo became the seedbed of a movement for moderate political reform based in local gentry circles.

FORCES FOR CHANGE

The dangers of change were underscored by another consequence of the reforms. The expansion of the universities in the 1860s, connected to the need for a technically literate elite, brought young men of nonaristocratic background into the lecture halls along with the sons of gentlemen (women were excluded from the universities in this period). While men of the older generation became contentious liberals, the students yearned for more radical change. Dreaming of a new social order, young men and women "went to the people," hoping the villages would rise in revolt. Their attempts failed, but the generation of the 1860s laid the ground for a radical culture that tried mightily for almost half a century to connect its vision of social transformation to the social animosities of the laboring poor. Frustrated and impatient, the radicals acted on their own, with dubious results. The assassination of Alexander II by the conspiratorial People's Will in 1881 ended the era of reform and ushered in the reigns of Alexander III (r. 1881–1894) and Nicholas II (r. 1894–1917), resolute enemies of compromise and progress.

The Revolution of 1905 emerged from the confluence of these forces: a growing class of literate or semiliterate, urban or semiurban laborers; a politically dissatisfied urban elite; a disjuncture between the expectations raised by the reforms and their institutional outcomes; the growth of an ideologically driven social formation known as the intelligentsia determined to provoke social conflict, unleash violence, and destroy existing institutions; and an empire weakly governed from the center and arbitrary in its manner of rule. The Revolution of 1905 was at once a triumph of solidarity—the simultaneous revolt of almost all social forces against the principles and representatives of the state; and an expression of deep social division— the emerging incompatibility of interests among the varied allies.

REVOLUTIONARY MODEL

The revolution, as Lenin and Trotsky claimed, established precedents for 1917. On the one hand, 1905 produced the State Duma and legalized political parties. Among the latter were the liberal parties central to the Provisional Government of early 1917. On the other hand, the revolution also created a new political formation, the soviets (councils) of workers' deputies, which were to confront the moderates in 1917 across the barrier of class and ideological conviction. The soviets constituted the other face of "dual power" in 1917, the organizational stalemate that opened the door to Bolshevik success. The events of 1905 also strengthened the myth of revolution as a glorious exercise in collective self-assertion and self-sacrifice.

In fact, radical leaders played almost no role in starting the conflict of 1905. The Marxist-inspired Russian Social-Democratic Workers' Party, formed in 1898, was weakened by arrests; the Socialist Revolutionary Party (heir to nineteenth-century Populism) had emerged only in 1901. Their efforts to gain a foothold in the factories had met with limited success. Many leaders were in exile. Lenin, for example, spent 1900 to November 1905 in Europe.

The Revolution of 1905 began not at the bottom but at the top of the social hierarchy. In 1899 the students of St. Petersburg University protested official interference in university life. A group of liberal intellectuals founded the journal *Osvobozhdenie* (Liberation) in 1902. Two years later ill-considered expansionism drew Russia into war with Japan. When the war led to defeat and national humiliation, patriotic enthusiasm waned. The autocracy had again failed the test of military competence.

ESCALATING UNREST

It was the regime itself that stimulated action from below. Worried by the spontaneous labor protests of the 1890s and wishing to counteract the lure of radical ideas, it instituted police-sponsored trade unions. The experiment backfired. Georgy Gapon, a socially minded Orthodox priest, had started such an organization in St. Petersburg. Hoping to interest the tsar in the workers' cause, Gapon led his followers on a humble procession to the Winter Palace. Trudging through the snow on 22 January 1905, the petitioners were met by gunfire. More than one hundred marchers were killed, and at least three hundred more were wounded.

The shock of Bloody Sunday galvanized an array of social forces burdened by diverse grievances. Workers left their benches, demanding better conditions. Radical activists (Socialist Revolutionaries and Social Democrats, the latter now divided into factions: Lenin's Bolsheviks and the more cautious Mensheviks) were taken by surprise, but eager to gain some influence over the movement. Some of the most volatile episodes were linked only indirectly to labor issues. Some parts of the Caucasus, where Marxists enjoyed a certain degree of success, had been in revolt against Russian domination since 1903. Inhabitants of the Polish kingdom acquired by Russia after the Napoleonic Wars had twice risen against imperial rule in the nineteenth century. Strikes and protests mobilized all classes of the Polish population throughout 1905. Protests mixing economic and cultural resentments swept through the Baltic provinces and Finland. Meanwhile, peasants of the Russian heartland, following their own timetable, turned their wrath against the landowners.

Throughout the spring and summer of 1905, the regime attempted to defuse the crisis with half-hearted measures. A commission to solve the labor problem was disbanded without results. It left the worker delegates feeling both frustrated and self-important—a volatile mix. A proposed legislative assembly with minimal powers pleased no one. Educated society sympathized with the workers and mimicked their forms of association: teachers, agronomists, lawyers, and doctors joined in the Union of Unions. The soldiers and sailors mobilized in the distant war were affected by the political ideas of their junior officers. They were troubled by news of unrest at home. In June the sailors of the Black Sea Fleet seized control of the warship *Potemkin* (a mutiny that became the subject of Sergei Eisenstein's 1925 film, *The Battleship Potemkin*).

First Blood in the Revolution. Painting by H. W. Kockkock for the *Illustrated London News,* 1905. Kockkock depicts the events of 9 January 1905, also known as Bloody Sunday. THE ILLUSTRATED LONDON NEWS PICTURE LIBRARY, LONDON, UK/BRIDGEMAN ART LIBRARY

If the outbreak of war had contributed to popular discontent, its conclusion in August, with the Treaty of Portsmouth, did not calm the waters. In September new labor contracts were drawn up, workers returned to their shops, students returned to the lecture halls, and the strike movement resumed its course. The strikes rarely followed the direction of radical leaders, but they generated organizations that suited the radicals' plans. Thus, in Moscow, the neighborhoods and factories elected deputies who formed local councils (in Russian, *soviets*). By October the various strikes spurred by trade-specific problems (of bakers, printers, cigarette makers, and so on) had converged into an empire-wide movement.

GENERAL STRIKE

The participation of railroad and communications workers was decisive in bringing the economy to a halt. The trams stopped, the lights went out, shops closed. Liberals and radicals differed in their goals, but they rallied behind the mass movement. A kind of organizational fever seized the population: waiters, nurses, even peasants, formed and joined organizations. In St. Petersburg, the Mensheviks had the notion of consolidating the various strike committees into a citywide Soviet of Workers' Deputies: this was the prototype of what in 1917 became the symbol and instrument of revolutionary governance. It was understood by its organizers and participants in 1905 (among them Trotsky) as an organ of grassroots democracy.

The general strike was not, however, an exercise in saintly self-restraint and ideological high-mindedness on the part of the masses. On the one side, violence was inflicted by the police, Cossacks, and troops sent to impose order. Violence also emanated from pro-monarchist mobs, egged on by right-wing organizations, which attacked intellectuals and Jews. On the other side, strike recruitment was often coercive: workers from one factory would threaten those next door or rough them up; foremen were treated without ceremony; workers sometimes combined anger at the bosses with anger at the Jews. The Socialist Revolutionaries observed the populist tradition of political assassination: having eliminated Vyacheslav Plehve, the minister of internal affairs, in July 1904, they dispatched the reactionary Grand Duke Sergei Alexandrovich in February 1905. More generally, the revolution unleashed a flood of unfocused violence: laws were ignored, crime flourished, the streets became dangerous. Ordinary inhabitants felt not only exhilaration and hope but also anxiety and fear.

OCTOBER MANIFESTO

Reluctantly, Nicholas II heeded the counsel of his prime minister, Count Sergei Witte. As minister of finance in the 1890s Witte had promoted railroads and manufacture. He now believed the revolution could be checked only by serious concessions. On 30 October (17 October, O.S.) 1905 Nicholas issued a manifesto establishing the State Duma and promising the future extension of civil and political rights.

The October Manifesto brought an end to the general strike and gave rise to widespread rejoicing—the so-called Days of Freedom. While moderates hastened to form political parties, radicals at both extremes refused to abjure violence. Monarchist mobs, encouraged by the police, staged anti-Jewish pogroms. In early November the sailors of the Kronstadt naval base went from indiscipline to riot; in November the Black Sea Fleet mutinied once again, as did the troops returning from Manchuria. In December, as strikes escalated, radical leaders agitated for insurrection. Workers in sections of Moscow built makeshift barricades and traded shots with the troops summoned to stop them. The insurrection was crushed by artillery fire that left many dead. Arrests and executions followed.

ANTICLIMAX: 1906

The events of the year 1905 unfolded with an attractive symmetry: beginning with Bloody Sunday in St. Petersburg and ending with insurrection in Moscow. It seemed in the new year as though political life had acquired a new moderation. In March trade unions were legalized and workers flocked to join. The Duma met in session from 10 May to 22 July. Its opening was clouded, however, by the government's enactment of the Fundamental Laws, alterable only by the monarch. The laws reaffirmed the tsar's autocratic power, guaranteed only limited civil liberties, and confirmed the endowment of the partially appointed State Council with legislative rights equal to those of the Duma. Liberals were disappointed by the conservative character of the constitutional settlement, yet peasants took advantage of the new institution to petition the deputies on the principal cause of their discontent: land shortage.

The deputies, however, demonstrated a pattern of mutual intolerance and political impatience. Their sense of grievance was stoked when police raided private homes, dispersed public meetings, fired schoolteachers, and harassed the press. When Peter Stolypin became minister of internal affairs in May 1906, the popular movement was far from exhausted: rural unrest reached a climax in the summer months. Mutiny in the armed forces was endemic. The Socialist Revolutionaries continued to target officials, including Stolypin himself. The minister responded with intensified repression. Prisons throughout the empire overflowed, as the authorities made mass arrests. Punitive expeditions staged public hangings, floggings, and random shootings. Officials themselves encouraged mob action: the Bialystok pogrom in June 1906 left eighty-two Jews dead and seven hundred injured. The tsar himself applauded pro-monarchist vigilantes.

When the Second Duma, which opened on 5 March (20 February, O.S.) 1907, proved as intractable as the first, the tsar ordered its dissolution and redefined the electoral laws to further restrict the franchise. Doing so violated the provisions of the Fundamental Laws, and therefore the decree of 16 June (3 June, O.S.) 1907 was considered a coup d'état. Stolypin had the premises locked and radical deputies arrested. At the same time, he instituted a series of agrarian reforms. Designed to instill respect for private property and promote rural prosperity, the reforms encouraged ambitious peasants to separate from the commune.

Both Witte and Stolypin, the most capable of the tsar's ministers, believed modernization was crucial to imperial survival. Their model was a managed modernity under old-style political control. The concessions promulgated by Witte were entirely pragmatic. Stolypin did not hesitate to violate the letter and spirit of the October Manifesto, which Nicholas himself disdained. Yet the Duma was not abolished. Combined with relaxed censorship and expanded freedom of association, it provided the public and the masses with new opportunities for political participation. The Revolution of 1905 in the end had a constructive result. But it also served as a stepping-stone to October 1917 rather than as a salutary jolt that might have saved the autocracy from its own worst instincts.

See also **Great Reforms (Russia); Nicholas II; Russia; Stolypin, Peter; Witte, Sergei.**

BIBLIOGRAPHY

Primary Sources

Bely, Andrei. *Petersburg.* Translated, annotated, and introduced by Robert A. Maguire and John E. Malmstad. Bloomington, Ind., 1978. Originally published serially, 1913–1914. Symbolist novel set during the revolution.

Gorky, Maxim. *Mother: A Novel in Two Parts.* Translated by Margaret Wettlin. New York, 1962. Translation of *Mat'* (1906). Socialist realism–style novel with a worker-hero, set in 1905.

Luxemburg, Rosa. *The Mass Strike, the Political Party, and the Trade Unions.* New York, 1971. Translation of *Massenstreik, Partei, und Gewerkschaften* (1906). Luxemburg's polemic with Lenin about popular revolution.

Trotsky, Leon. *1905.* Translated by Anya Bostock. New York, 1971. Translation of *Tysiacha deviat' sot piaty* (1922). Participant's Marxist account.

Weber, Max. *The Russian Revolutions.* Translated and edited by Gordon C. Wells and Peter Baehr. Ithaca, N.Y., 1995. Translation of *Zur Lage der bürgerlichen Demokratie in Russland* (1906) and *Russlands Übergang zum Scheinkonstitutionalismus* (1906). Famous sociologist's analysis of current events.

Secondary Sources

Ascher, Abraham. *The Revolution of 1905.* 2 vols. Stanford, Calif., 1988–1992. The best scholarly account.

Blobaum, Robert E. *Rewolucja: Russian Poland, 1904–1907.* Ithaca, N.Y., 1995.

Bushnell, John. *Mutiny amid Repression: Russian Soldiers in the Revolution of 1905–1906.* Bloomington, Ind., 1985.

Engelstein, Laura. *Moscow, 1905: Working-Class Organization and Political Conflict.* Stanford, Calif., 1982.

Surh, Gerald D. *1905 in St. Petersburg: Labor, Society, and Revolution.* Stanford, Calif., 1989.

Weinberg, Robert. *The Revolution of 1905 in Odessa: Blood on the Steps.* Bloomington, Ind., 1993.

LAURA ENGELSTEIN

REVOLUTIONS OF 1820.

The revolutions of 1820 were the first challenge to the conservative order of Europe established after the fall of Napoleon I in 1815. Though most ended in failure, they demonstrated the rising strength of the liberal-nationalist movement that would eventually sweep away the conservative order.

BACKGROUND

The years following 1815 were generally quiet. Most Europeans were satisfied to see peace and order restored after years of revolution and war. But the liberal-nationalist minority, deeply discontented, organized secret societies dedicated to overthrowing the existing order. The most important was the Carbonari, which played a key role in the 1820 revolutions.

REVOLUTION IN SPAIN

The revolutions began in Spain, where King Ferdinand VII followed a firmly reactionary policy. Moreover, his determination to restore Spanish rule over its rebellious American colonies was proving costly in lives and money and seemed increasingly hopeless. On 1 January 1820 the liberal officers of a regiment destined to sail for South America rose in revolt and marched on Madrid, demanding a constitution. Decisive action by the king might have stopped them, because they had little popular support, but his indecision and incompetence allowed the revolt to gain headway. In March the rebels entered Madrid. Ferdinand was forced to grant a constitution, but secretly appealed to the conservative powers to aid him in overthrowing it.

The powers were alarmed by the reappearance of revolution, but divided in their response. Alexander I, tsar of Russia, urged a joint intervention by the Quintuple Alliance, the union of great powers set up after the Napoleonic wars to keep the

DIA 10. DE MARZO DE 1820. EN CADIZ.
Plaza de S.ⁿ Antonio, hoy de la Constitucion.

The Tenth of March, 1820, in Cadiz. Nineteenth-century engraving. The uprising that forced Ferdinand VII of Spain to accept a constitutional monarchy began in Cadiz when soldiers, angry over lack of pay, rebelled. © Archivo Iconografico, S.A./Corbis

peace. The British foreign secretary, Lord Castlereagh, rejected his suggestion, arguing that the alliance had no right to intervene against revolution unless it threatened other states. France was indecisive. The Austrian chancellor, Prince Clemens von Metternich, although generally hostile to revolution, opposed intervention. He did not wish to alienate Britain and perhaps drive it from the alliance, and in any case, Spain was too distant to be a threat to Austria. In the face of this opposition, the tsar temporarily dropped his proposal.

REVOLUTION IN ITALY

Metternich's attitude quickly changed, however, when the Spanish example provoked imitation in Italy. In July 1820, liberal army officers, members of the Carbonari, revolted against Ferdinand I, the reactionary king of the Two Sicilies, demanding a constitution. This revolt too succeeded mainly because of the incompetence and cowardice of the king, who, in fear of his life, on 13 July 1820 promised a constitution. The new government won some support from moderate liberals among the landowners, but they were soon alarmed at the radical demands of the Carbonari, and quarreling between the two factions broke out. The revolutionary regime was further distracted by revolt in Sicily, which had long resented rule from Naples and demanded autonomy. The Neapolitan government decided to suppress the Sicilians, and this too weakened the revolution.

It was not these internal quarrels, however, that caused the revolution to fail, but Austrian intervention. Metternich could not ignore the revolt in Naples as he had that in Spain, for it threatened one of the pillars of Austria's international position, its predominance in Italy. A liberal Naples would surely reject Austrian tutelage; moreover, the example of its success would inspire imitation elsewhere in Italy. The Austrian army could easily suppress the revolution, but there were international complications. Castlereagh had no objections to Austrian intervention, but insisted that it must intervene unilaterally, not in the name of the alliance, whose general right of intervention he could no more accept in Italy than in Spain. France, an old rival of Austria for predominance in Italy, was inclined to support the revolutionary regime as a means of replacing Austrian influence at Naples with its own. Though the tsar agreed that the revolution must be suppressed, he was unwilling to give Austria a free hand, insisting that it could intervene only in the name of the alliance and under its supervision. He demanded a conference of the powers to work out terms on which intervention could take place. He also insisted that before the intervention could take place, mediation with Naples be undertaken that might avert the need for intervention, perhaps by an agreement that a more conservative constitution be adopted.

Because Russia, with its massive military power, could make Austrian intervention impossible if it chose, Metternich agreed to a conference at Troppau in October 1820. At the tsar's insistence, and at the risk of alienating Castlereagh, Metternich agreed to sign the Troppau Protocol, which proclaimed a general right of the alliance to intervene against revolution. Having thus won the tsar's agreement for intervention, he proceeded to deflect the tsar's other demands by a series of brilliant maneuvers at another conference at Laibach in early 1821. At Laibach, Metternich won full support for an intervention with no strings attached—there would be no mediation and no constitution. Now at last the Austrian army could move south. In March 1821 Austria defeated the Neapolitan army at Rieti, and easily suppressed the revolutionary regime.

Meanwhile, another revolution had been brewing in the Kingdom of Sardinia (or Piedmont-Sardinia) and the Austrian province of Lombardy. In these regions, a conspiracy was organized to drive out the Austrians and form a constitutional Kingdom of Northern Italy. The conspiracy in Lombardy was checked by the arrest of its leaders in October 1820, but in Piedmont liberal army officers rose in revolt on 10 March 1821 and demanded that the king lead them against Austria. The king refused, the powers at Laibach condemned the revolt, and loyal Piedmontese troops, aided by an Austrian contingent, quickly suppressed the rebels.

END OF THE SPANISH REVOLUTION

Attention now reverted to Spain. Though an unsuccessful royalist coup in 1822 left the liberals still in control of the king, a rival absolutist government was set up near the French border, which declared itself a regency for the king and appealed to the powers for intervention. Britain still opposed intervention, but the tsar strongly supported it, urging France to intervene on behalf of the alliance. Metternich, fearing that intervention would drive Britain from the alliance, but unwilling to offend the tsar, sought to arrange a compromise. The French, however, rejected both his compromise and a mandate from the powers, believing that unilateral intervention would win them greater prestige. France declared war and in April 1823 invaded Spain. They easily overcame all resistance, and restored Ferdinand to his throne.

THE GREEK REVOLUTION

The Spanish and Italian revolts had failed because they had little popular support, and because the powers were united against them. Neither of those factors weakened the Greek Revolution. Greece, like all the Balkans, had long been under Turkish rule, but revolution was not inevitable. Greeks held a privileged position in the Ottoman Empire: they were generally allowed to manage their own affairs, many held high positions in the administration, and they enjoyed a near-monopoly of trade. Moreover, the Orthodox patriarch of Constantinople preached submission to the sultan.

The revolution came because the new idea of nationalism had begun to influence many educated Greeks, especially those living outside the Ottoman Empire. A small but active secret society, the Philike Hetairia (Society of Friends), had grown up since 1814, dedicated to Greek independence. The crisis began in March 1821 when Alexander Ypsilanti, leader of the Hetairia and a Russian general, proclaimed a revolt in Moldavia. Both his timing and his target were poor. He hoped for the support of the tsar, but Alexander was still at Laibach, under the counterrevolutionary influence of Metternich; he quickly condemned the revolt. Moreover, the Romanian inhabitants of Moldavia hated the Greeks, who governed them in the name of the sultan, and refused to rise.

Ypsilanti's revolt quickly collapsed, but not before it touched off a true revolution in Greece itself. There, Orthodox Christian Greeks and Muslim Turks lived in mutual hostility, deeply divided by religion, customs, and legal standing. The revolt that broke out in April spread with elemental fury, driven more by religion than by nationalism. Within a month, Turkish forces had been driven from southern Greece, and most of its Muslim population had been massacred. The Turks responded with their own atrocities, and on Easter Sunday, 1821, the Orthodox patriarch of Constantinople was hanged before the door of his own cathedral.

This was a direct challenge to Russia, which claimed a right to protect the Orthodox Church, and war seemed inevitable. Everything pushed Alexander toward war: popular religious sentiment in Russia demanded it, his foreign minister, the Greek Count John Capodistrias, urged it, the long Russian tradition of southward expansion would be served by it. But Alexander hesitated. His commitment to the counterrevolutionary cause was still great, as was his commitment to the alliance, which war might destroy, for Austria and Britain would surely oppose it. Both those powers wished to preserve the Ottoman Empire as a bulwark against Russian expansion and revolutionary Balkan nationalism. Metternich and Castlereagh used all their influence to persuade the tsar to keep the peace; and at last, in June 1822, the tsar dismissed Capodistrias and agreed to refrain from war. He kept his word until his death in 1825.

Metternich was hopeful that if he could restrain Russia, the revolt would eventually collapse. But the revolt went on, and the European situation began to change. A groundswell of popular opinion known as philhellenism developed throughout Europe. To a generation brought up on the classics, a Greek revolt had enormous emotional appeal, and when in 1824 the most famous writer in Europe, Lord Byron, died while fighting for Greece, popular pressure on Britain and France became irresistible. Moreover, the new tsar, Nicholas I, felt that Russia's failure to aid the Greeks had diminished its prestige. In 1827 he persuaded Britain and France to aid him in bringing pressure on the sultan by sending their fleets to Greece. In October 1827 their fleets destroyed the Turkish navy at Navarino. In April 1828 the tsar declared war on the sultan, and the peace signed in 1829 assured Greece its independence.

The Greek Revolution, the first break in the status quo of 1815, began a new era. As Metternich had feared, Greek victory encouraged liberal-nationalists everywhere, and marked the beginning of the end for the conservative order of Europe.

See also **Concert of Europe; Greece; Italy; Metternich, Clemens von; Restoration.**

BIBLIOGRAPHY

Acton, Harold. *The Last Bourbons of Naples.* London, 1961.

Clogg, Richard, ed. *The Struggle for Greek Independence.* Hamden, Conn., 1973.

Dakin, Douglas. *The Greek Struggle for Independence, 1821–1833.* Berkeley, 1973.

Martínez, Rafael Bañón, and Thomas M. Barker, eds. *Armed Forces and Society in Spain Past and Present.* Boulder, Colo., 1988.

Romani, George T. *The Neapolitan Revolution of 1820–1821.* Evanston, Ill., 1950.

Schroeder, Paul W. *Metternich's Diplomacy at Its Zenith, 1820–1823.* Austin, Tex., 1962.

ALAN J. REINERMAN

REVOLUTIONS OF 1830. The revolutions of 1830 were a lengthy continent-wide crisis involving many forms of political change as well as outright revolution. On a more significant scale than 1820, these separate but interrelated outbreaks were a real turning point, ending the French Restoration and modernizing European politics.

Yet historians have often ignored or undervalued them. They have been seen simply as isolated, and often half-hearted, outbreaks in just a few states. And 1830 has been interpreted in simplistic terms of mechanical responses to the July Days, of conspiracies, or of the rise of the industrial bourgeoisie. In fact it had variegated causes and dynamics, reflecting differing conditions in individual countries.

ORIGINS

The revolts were encouraged by the Parisian July Days, which breached the dam holding back separate and varying local grievances, both political and socioeconomic. They had roots in open political opposition, usually among liberal professionals (not capitalist entrepreneurs), to the increasingly reactionary policies of many restoration regimes. The latter's ignoring of aspirations for voice and ineffectual attempts at repression were crucial in Belgium, Switzerland, France, Portugal, and Italy, often turning moderates into opponents.

The economic crisis in the late 1820s was a reinforcing factor. A cyclical downturn and bad winters combined with surging population growth to produce rising food prices, falling wages, and declining consumer spending on artisanal goods. The resulting depression provided combustible material that was fired when elites were forced into direct action.

DYNAMICS

The outbreaks were initially driven by responses to government mistakes, whether political, as in Switzerland and Bologna, or military, as in Paris and Brussels, or by related liberal national aspirations, as in Warsaw. Such political responses to government provocation, often led by the press, stimulated spontaneous social explosions in the French provinces, Belgium, and Warsaw. With the middle classes able to make common cause with solid artisans, in a way not seen in 1820, revolts grew. Belgium and Switzerland thus did not need, or receive, French infiltration.

The shedding of blood, as in Paris and Brussels, helped to stimulate national fervor, while military conflict also intensified the crises. Unfounded beliefs that France would either aid revolutionary movements or force nonintervention on the conservative powers encouraged more radical developments than the initial desires for the open politics of the Napoleonic era. Social distress and domestic political ambitions carried things forward until success, fears of anarchy, or external intervention brought them to an end.

PRELUDES

Despite the defeats of 1820 new troubles appeared late in the decade as the economic situation deteriorated, with rural disturbances in France, Ireland, and Wallonia. Politically there were organized liberal electoral victories in France, pressures for constitutional reform in Swiss cantons, and unions of oppositions in Belgium, Britain, and Brunswick. In Portugal there was armed resistance to the reactionary Dom Miguel.

It was not until the spring of 1830, however, that the real crisis broke. Its first phase saw conflict developing well beyond Paris following the very rapid change of regime there. Partial consolidation of these outbreaks followed in the winter of 1830–1831, but, in the following spring and summer, the movement began to run down. There was a long and painful aftermath.

OUTBREAK

The first signs of change came in Switzerland where the Ticinese government broke with its conservative leader and sponsored constitutional reform. Then, in May 1830, worried by mass petitions, the government of Vaud preemptively introduced a restrictive reform. This was badly received and raised the political temperature. There were also riots in Saxony and Greece.

The conflict between French liberals and Charles X then came to a head. The opposition had demanded the dismissal of Jules-Armand de Polignac, Charles's unpopular premier, on 16 March. Charles refused and called new elections only to lose more seats. Hence, in late July he issued the Four Ordinances, thereby dissolving the new Chamber of Deputies, calling further elections on a reduced franchise, and curbing the press.

These inflammatory changes led journalists and printers to protest and businessmen to shut shops and factories. Early disturbances were easily quelled, but when, on Tuesday, 27 July, police attempted to close newspapers they were resisted. The tricolor was flown, royal insignia torn down, and skirmishing started. The next day, faced with barricades throughout the city, the detested Marshal Marmont declared martial law and tried to use his troops to reassert control. Understrength, unprepared, and unhappy, his columns suffered heavy losses before finding themselves under sniper fire back in the Louvre. With morale falling, the army broke up as it retreated in disorder on St. Cloud.

This left Paris in the hands of a makeshift committee of deputies and others. They proved unwilling and unable to negotiate with Charles's new premier. The vacuum was filled by activists pushing Louis-Philippe, duc d'Orléans. Coming to Paris on Saturday, 31 July, he won popular approval to act as lieutenant general. Then, after Charles abdicated, Louis-Philippe was invited to take the throne. The Charter of 1814, by which the country was governed, was rapidly revised and, on 9 August, he took the oath as "king of the French." His unopposed regime rapidly secured its position in Paris.

DEVELOPMENT

The sudden change of regime in Paris had far-reaching effects. In France it prompted a wave of local unrest in cities and the countryside, leading to tax cuts and food subsidies. These troubles were echoed in Belgium and the Rhineland. In Switzerland there was a fever of protest against the constitutional dominance of urban aristocrats, while in Britain the first Whig government in fifty years emerged.

In Belgium news from Paris put the authorities on alert given long-running arguments about the discriminatory rule of William I, king of the Netherlands, and the maintenance of food taxes to pay for royal birthday fireworks. Nevertheless when, on 25 August, a middle-class demonstration, following an opera, degenerated into antiestablishment riots, the authorities failed to respond. Local burghers had to create a civic guard and negotiate, unsuccessfully, with William for administrative separation from the Netherlands.

Simultaneously radicals took control of affairs in Brussels. So, fearing anarchy, some middle-class elements appealed to the Dutch. Unfortunately when their forces entered the town on 23 September they encountered not burgher support but popular resistance for which they were unprepared. They thus found themselves under intermittent siege in the royal park until they decided to withdraw on 27 September. The shedding of blood led to a nationalist seizure of power throughout the country. William's acceptance of separation came too late to prevent this, and the use of artillery in Antwerp killed hopes of reconciliation.

Elsewhere Spanish exiles created a provisional government in Bayonne, while dissent flourished in Poland and central Italy. Several German rulers were either ejected or forced to concede constitutional change. In Brunswick the duke fled after crowds burned his palace. With England experiencing the beginning of the Swing Riots, by autumn the crisis had spread throughout western Europe.

CONSOLIDATION

From then on into early in 1831, many movements built on their initial breakthroughs. In Switzerland continuing popular mobilization, often threatening violence, forced Zurich, Vaud, Aargau, and other cantons to call constituent assemblies to rewrite their constitutions, giving more rights and influence to rural areas. The Swiss diet encouraged this "regeneration" by recognizing the right to change. In central Germany limited reforms went ahead in Brunswick, Hesse-Cassel, and Saxony, while there were liberal election victories in the south.

In Belgium a parliamentary congress declared the country independent, deposed William I, and began drafting a new constitution. This caused friction with the diplomatic conference called to discuss the Belgian situation. The limited frontiers offered at the conference led to a patriotic mobilization. Nonetheless, by the late spring a deal was done and the crown offered to Leopold of Saxe-Coburg-Saalfeld (Leopold I).

This might not have been possible because on 17 October 1830 Tsar Nicholas, whose daughter was married to the Dutch heir, had ordered the Russo-Polish army to be mobilized for a western intervention in December. So patriotic young Polish officers, already planning a rising for January, staged their putsch in Warsaw on 29 November. Although it took the local populace to rescue this uprising, the Russian Grand Duke Constantine and his garrison withdrew rather than risk confrontation. This prevented any Russian intervention in Belgium and allowed radicalism to flourish. By late January a parliament in Warsaw had deposed Nicholas and created a national "dictatorship." And the next month Polish forces checked an initial Russian push on Warsaw in battles at Grochów and elsewhere.

This was part of the way revolt expanded into the peripheries of Europe. Thus Hanover began to consider political change, and exiled liberals staged several desperately unsuccessful forays into Spain. More significantly, a liberal conspiracy in central Italy, partly encouraged by the unlikely Francis IV of Modena, finally led to an assault on the city in early February. Although this was easily repelled, Francis fled, allowing a revolutionary regime to emerge. It was soon loosely linked to Parma where a similar body had developed. Trouble also spread to Bologna in the Papal States where the calling of a committee of notables by the local pro-legate, or deputy governor, encouraged the creation of a provisional government. This became the hub of the United Provinces of Italy as Rome's northern territories threw off their allegiance. There were also signs of dissent in Greece and the Balkans.

DECLINE

Few of these new regimes were to be very long lasting because the revolutionary impetus was increasingly lost. In central Italy, Austrian troops were called in, and their defeat of an Italian sortie in early March 1831 forced the revolutionaries to evacuate Modena. A few days later Parma was also reoccupied. The remaining revolutionary forces then fell back on Bologna, only to be interned in the hope that this would avert foreign intervention. In fact, despite an Italian attempt to march on Rome, the Austrian advance continued, forcing a government retreat southward. At the end of March, a capitulation was arranged to prevent more bloodshed, as realization grew that France would not help. Alarmed by rising radicalism, Louis-Philippe had, that month, brought in a conservative ministry to reassure the powers. The French could then send a relief force into Belgium to stop a successful invasion by the aggrieved Dutch, forcing the weakened Belgians to agree to a treaty regularizing their position.

The collapse of the Polish revolt was more dramatic. The Poles suffered a major defeat at Ostrołęka in May, allowing Russian forces to attack Warsaw from the west. When, in mid-August, the Polish army withdrew into the city and did not oppose the Russians, indignant gentry radicals and the populace revolted against the moderate government. This made it easier for the Russians to take

the city. By mid-October the whole country was in Russian hands, forcing thousands of Poles to flee abroad as resistance faded with the peasantry refusing to rally to the cause.

The Swiss reform movement ran into often-violent resistance in Basle, Neuchâtel, and Schwyz. In Schleswig-Holstein demands for a united diet were rejected by the Danes. Many concessions made in Germany were also revoked later in 1831. In Britain, the parliamentary reform movement, facing opposition in the House of Lords, had to resort to civil disobedience to help secure its ends.

AFTERMATH

All this left radicals unsatisfied and conservatives worried. So dissent and repression continued for some years. Seven liberal Swiss cantons felt they had to unite to defend their gains, prompting first a counterleague of reactionary cantons and then unsuccessful onslaughts on the dissident regions of Schwyz and Basle. The diet was able to negotiate acceptable deals and to dissolve the leagues but not to revise the confederal charter. The Reform Act, however, went through in Britain in June 1832. In Germany agitation for change continued, leading to the Hambach rally for national unification in May 1832 and, a year later, an attack on the diet. Thereafter the German Confederation imposed harsh controls on liberalism. These were underwritten at Münchengrätz in 1833 through a new alliance among the conservative powers of Austria, Prussia, and Russia.

Poland and Italy were more harshly treated. Poland was Russified, losing much of its old autonomy. In Modena conspirators were executed or interned by Austria. In the Papal States the new pope, Gregory XVI, refused to accept reforms urged on him by the Great Powers, preferring to create a new army, which, in January 1832, sacked his own cities of Cesena and Forli, until the French intervened. Repression and Austrian occupation were common elsewhere. In France the new regime found itself faced with worker risings in Lyon, republican attacks in Paris, and an abortive royalist rising in the west. In Portugal Dom Pedro seized Oporto in June 1832 but needed British help to win the resulting civil war. The final territorial deal over Belgium had to wait until 1838–1839 for acceptance by William, military success in 1831 having emboldened him to hold out for better terms. So the effects of the revolutions lingered on.

ACHIEVEMENTS AND FAILURES

Despite some defeats, the revolutions of 1830 did have significant outcomes. They partly blocked the emerging swing back to reactionary politics. Absolute monarchy was ultimately overthrown in Portugal and undermined in Spain. Liberal constitutional monarchy was established in France and the new state of Belgium. Political reform was successful in Finland, Germany, Switzerland, and, notably, the United Kingdom. The independence of Greece and Serbia was also confirmed. Socially the crisis facilitated mobility and, in Switzerland and Germany, peasant emancipation. It also encouraged industrial growth, as in Belgium.

The reason why things did not go as far as many had hoped lay, first, in the limitations of the revolutionaries. They were unprepared and could only respond to mistakes made by the authorities. Rarely did they have the time, resources, or vision to launch a successful move. And they could be naive about the ease with which domestic and foreign reaction could be overcome. In Iberia civil war proved necessary before liberalism could triumph. The fact that, as in Poland and Belgium, people were able only to agree on opposition to the existing order added to their problems.

Second, the international situation was unhelpful. French desires to avert a new Holy Alliance of autocratic powers made its leaders cautious especially as the eastern powers were largely untouched by the crisis. Equally, British support for change was limited. Hence nothing was done to block Austrian and Russian intervention. Nonetheless, the settlement of Europe achieved by the 1815 Congress of Vienna was weakened.

POLITICAL IMPACT

Moreover, 1830 had longer-term political effects. It encouraged new demands for unity in Germany and Italy. There were also Romantic national reawakenings in Poland and Switzerland. On the peripheries nationalism was more linguistic than political, as it was in Flanders and the Balkans.

The events of 1830 also aided the press and normal politics. Radicals had to rethink their way to revolutionary change, looking for new support—whether from friendly monarchies, from the popular involvement urged by the Italian nationalist Giuseppe Mazzini, or by relying on class and socialism. As a result middle-class fears of revolt often grew. Yet, though conservatives came to realize that revolution still threatened, they failed to learn the lessons of 1830.

So new vistas opened up. And more people explored them. Hence 1830 encouraged the modernization of political life and debate. This was to become clear in 1848, when another and more extensive revolutionary wave coursed across Europe.

See also **Belgium; Captain Swing; Charles X; Holy Alliance; Leopold I; Louis-Philippe; Mazzini, Giuseppe; Münchengrätz, Treaty of; Poland; Restoration; Revolutions of 1820.**

BIBLIOGRAPHY

Birmingham, David. *A Concise History of Portugal.* 2nd ed. Cambridge, U.K., 2003.

Church, Clive H. *Europe in 1830.* London, 1983.

Davies, Norman. *God's Playground: A History of Poland.* 2 vols. Oxford, 1981.

Di Scala, Spencer M. *Italy from Revolution to Republic.* 3rd ed. Boulder, Colo., 2004.

Longworth, Philip. *The Making of Eastern Europe.* Basingstoke, U.K., 1992.

Luck, James Murray. *A History of Switzerland.* Palo Alto, Calif., 1985.

Merriman, John M., ed. *1830 in France.* New York, 1975.

Pierson, Peter. *The History of Spain.* Westport, Conn., 1999.

Pilbeam, Pamela. *The 1830 Revolution in France.* London, 1991.

Pinkney, David H. *The French Revolution of 1830.* Princeton, N.J., 1972.

Sperber, Jonathan. *Revolutionary Europe, 1780–1850.* Harlow, U.K., 2000.

Waller, Bruce, ed. *Themes in Modern European History, 1830–1890.* London, 1990.

Witte, Els, and Jan Craeybeckx. *La Belgique politique de 1830 à nos jours.* Brussels, 1987.

CLIVE H. CHURCH

REVOLUTIONS OF 1848.

REVOLUTIONS OF 1848. Of the major waves of revolution in modern European history—1789 to 1799, 1848 to 1851, 1917 to 1923, and 1989 to 1991—those of the mid-nineteenth century extended across the largest territory and among the greatest diversity of political and socioeconomic regimes. The 1848 revolutions occurred in lands from the Atlantic to Ukraine, and from the Baltic to the Black Sea, including France, Prussia, Austria, Bavaria, as well as the smaller and midsized German states; the Kingdoms of the Two Sicilies and the Kingdom of Piedmont-Sardinia, the Papal States, and the smaller Italian states; and, in the far southeastern corner of Europe, the Danubian Principalities of Moldavia and Walachia. The revolutionary movement had a strong effect on the Scandinavian lands and the Low Countries, with major mass movements in Norway, and important reforms in Denmark, Belgium, and the Netherlands. The states of the Iberian Peninsula and the two peripheral Great Powers, the Russian and British Empires, were the only parts of Europe not directly affected in their domestic politics.

The 1848 revolutions were directed against absolutist regimes, such as the Italian states, the Austrian Empire, and the Prussian kingdom, and against constitutional monarchies in France or in a number of the smaller German states. If one includes the Swiss civil war of 1847, seen by contemporaries as the beginning of the midcentury revolutions, then they affected one of the very few republican governments in Europe. There was a similar diversity in socioeconomic settings and issues in the 1848 revolutions. Abolition of serfdom was central to events in the Austrian Empire and in the Danubian principalities, while in northern France, western Germany, Saxony, and large cities across Europe, trade unions, cooperatives, and workers' associations were formed, whose members raised socialist demands.

This diversity contrasts with previous and subsequent revolutionary events. The revolutionary wave of 1789 to 1799 was largely a French affair, and the Revolution was brought to other parts of Europe primarily by invading French armies. The post-1917 revolutions occurred among the defeated powers of World War I, and those of 1989 to 1991 against communist regimes.

This description by Carl Schurz (1829–1906), of the democratic club in the German university town of Bonn during the revolution of 1848, demonstrates the growing radicalism of revolutionary activists and the powerful example of the French Revolution of 1789.

> Our democratic club was composed in almost equal parts of students and citizens. . . . At first the establishment of a constitutional monarchy with universal suffrage and well-secured civil rights would have been quite satisfactory to us. But the reaction, the threatened rise of which we were observing, gradually made many of us believe that there was no safety for popular liberty except in a republic. From this belief there was only one step to the further conclusion that in a republic, and only in a republic, could all evils of the social body be cured and the solution of all the political problems be possible. . . . the history of the French Revolution satisfied us that a republic could be created in Germany and could maintain its existence in the European system of states. In that history we found striking examples of the possibility of accomplishing the seemingly impossible, if only the whole energy existing in a great nation were awakened and directed with unflinching boldness. Most of us, indeed, recoiled from the wild excesses, which had stained with streams of innocent blood the national uprising in France during the Reign of Terror; but we hoped to stir up the national energies without such terrorism. At any rate, the history of the French Revolution furnished to us models in plenty that mightily excited our imagination.

Source: Carl Schurz, *The Reminiscences of Carl Schurz.* 3 vols. (New York, 1908), vol. 1, p. 137.

Another difference from previous and successor waves of revolutions was that the 1848 revolutions did not lead to new regimes. Instead, the revolutionary governments established in the spring of 1848 were short-lived and gave way, generally within a year and a half, to counterrevolutionary successors, closely related to the regimes overthrown in 1848. Important nationalist projects of the 1848 revolutions—the national unification of Italy or Germany, the liberation of Poland, the reorganization or outright destruction of the multinational Habsburg Monarchy along national lines—were not accomplished. Many of the social and economic questions raised in the revolution were not resolved and organizational initiatives were suppressed. A full consideration of the 1848 revolutions must take into account these opposing features—the wide spread of the mid-nineteenth century revolutions and the remarkable political mobilizations accompanying them, but also their ultimate failure.

ORIGINS AND BACKGROUND

The crisis years from 1845 to 1847, leading up to the 1848 revolutions, showed, in extreme form, political, social, and economic tensions that had been mounting for decades. Population growth, increasing across Europe since the 1750s, placed pressure on existing resources. The size of average agricultural landholdings declined, and the number of totally landless rural families increased substantially. Ever more urban craftsmen and shopkeepers were competing for a customer base with, at best, constant purchasing power, as real wages fell. Even university graduates in the Italian and German states as well as the Austrian Empire—less so in France—had difficulty finding employment, because there were too many of them for the available positions.

The ultimate response to these difficulties, already apparent in Great Britain, and practiced in continental Europe on a wide scale after 1850, would be the growth of mechanized industry and the spread of a more productive and specialized agriculture, both of these developments made possible by the construction of a rail network. Although, particularly in the 1840s, the regionally scattered beginnings of industrialization in western and central Europe, as well as the first steps in rail construction had occurred, the chief measures taken before 1850 to increase output tended to sharpen social pressures. Increasing grain production, by introducing new systems of crop rotation and dividing common lands, worsened the prospects of villagers with little or no property, who depended on the commons to feed their animals or to gather wood. Expansion of nonfarm production occurred primarily via the spread of outworking, which subjected nominally independent master craftsmen to the control of merchant contractors.

If these measures to expand the market created social conflicts in the pre-1848 decades, so did institutions restricting the market, such as serfdom and seignorialism, still widely practiced in central and eastern Europe, whose burdens were increasingly resented by the peasantry, and the guild system, which made life difficult for journeymen artisans, excluded from the guilds, dominated by master craftsmen.

The difficulties of this economic situation were exacerbated by the way European states increased their claims on the population—raising taxes, imposing customs duties, drafting young men into the army, garrisoning or quartering soldiers, imposing rules on the use of forestlands—when the lower classes were having a hard time making ends meet. While demanding more from their subjects, most Continental states lacked a police force to establish their authority and, in crisis situations, had to depend on soldiers, the use of which to restore order was provocative and created more disorder.

Opposing the existing regimes were scattered and informally organized groups of activists, "the party of movement" as contemporaries said. Supporters of this trend advocated the creation of constitutional governments, whose charters would guarantee basic civil liberties and the powers of an elected legislature. They favored the equality of all (male) citizens before the law, took aim at privileges of the nobility, and called for an end to religious discrimination—if sometimes reluctantly, when it came to the Jews. Particularly in western Europe, although to a certain extent elsewhere, this party of movement was divided into radicals, demanding a democratic republic, and moderates, who advocated a constitutional monarchy. Also primarily in western Europe, there existed a current of socialist or communist thought, popularized in vague phrases such as the French socialist Louis Blanc's "organization of labor," containing elements of democratic ideals, heterodox forms of Christianity, visions of women's emancipation, and artisans' desires for a revival of the guilds.

An ideology central to the party of movement was nationalism, the doctrine that nations should be the basis of individuals' political loyalty, and that national groups should be free to create their own nation-state. Conservatives of the 1840s, supporting

PAINTING

S. Giorgio Maggiore, Early Morning. J. M. W. Turner, 1819. Turner developed a revolutionary approach to landscape painting early in the nineteenth century, anticipating and influencing the impressionists' interest in luminosity and the depiction of subtle atmospheric phenomena. Turner's approach, however, differs in its essentially Romantic origin; his goal was not to record scientific facts but to create evocative, often symbolic scenes. CLORE COLLECTION, TATE GALLERY, LONDON/ART RESOURCE, NY

RIGHT: *The Death of Sardanapalus.* By Eugène Delacroix, 1827. The most skilled exponent of the Romantic school, Delacroix is also recognized as one of the greatest colorists in French painting. Here he illustrates the tragedy depicted in the ancient story of Sardanapalus, a king who, facing defeat at the hands of an enemy, orders his slaves to kill him and all members of his household and to destroy his palace and possessions. © PHILADELPHIA MUSEUM OF ART/CORBIS

BELOW: *The Gleaners.* By Jean-François Millet, 1857. Millet's scenes of rustic life, depicting the hardships of farm labor while celebrating the strength and nobility of peasants, distinguished him as one of the principal exponents of the French realist school of painters. RÉUNION DES MUSÉES NATIONAUX/ART RESOURCE, NY

LEFT: *The Cradle.* By Berthe Morisot, 1872. The sole female member of the core group of impressionists, Morisot chose her subjects primarily from the domestic sphere. Here she depicts her sister, Edma, with her child. RÉUNION DES MUSÉES NATIONAUX/ART RESOURCE, NY

BELOW: *Remembrance of Montefontaine.* By Jean-Baptiste-Camille Corot, 1864. Regarded as the most influential French landscape painter of the first half of the nineteenth century, Corot departed from traditional models in his more poetic celebrations of the beauty of the French countryside. RÉUNION DES MUSÉES NATIONAUX/ART RESOURCE, NY

TOP: *Paris, a Rainy Day.* By Gustave Caillebotte, 1877. In this study for one of his acknowledged masterpieces, the impressionist Caillebotte depicts the anomie engendered by Haussman's wide, uniform boulevards. MUSÉE MARMOTTAN, PARIS, FRANCE/BRIDGEMAN ART LIBRARY

MIDDLE: *Impression: Sunrise.* By Claude Monet, 1872. Shown at the renowned 1874 exhibition of Impressionist works, Monet's painting of the harbor at Le Havre gave the movement its name. © ARCHIVO ICONOGRAFICO, S.A./CORBIS

BOTTOM: *The Gare St.-Lazare.* By Claude Monet, 1877. The series of paintings depicting the Paris train station at different times of day and in different weather conditions ranks among Monet's most celebrated works. Here he reveals the beauty of the interplay of steam and light. MUSÉE D'ORSAY, PARIS, FRANCE/BRIDGEMAN ART LIBRARY

TOP: *Starry Night.* By Vincent van Gogh, 1889. Van Gogh used color and brushwork to create emotional content in his works. He thus provided inspiration for later artistic movements that proposed the further manipulation of form in service of emotional or symbolic ends. Museum of Modern Art, New York City. Lillie P. Bliss Bequest. The Art Archive/Album /Joseph Martin.

BOTTOM: *White Horse.* By Paul Gauguin, 1898. Allied with other postimpressionist artists in his use of strong colors and manipulation of form, Gauguin was unique in his absolute rejection of Western civilization, and his finest works were those drawn from his experience of Tahitian life and culture. Erich Lessing/Art Resource, NY

TOP RIGHT, THIS PAGE: *The Scream.* By Edvard Munch, 1893. Munch's highly emotional works are regarded, along with those of van Gogh, as a primary force in the development of expressionism during the first decade of the twentieth century. NASJONALGALLERIET, OSLO, NORWAY/BRIDGEMAN ART LIBRARY, LONDON/NEW YORK. © 1999 THE MUNCH MUSEUM/THE MUNCH-ELLINGSEN GROUP/ARTISTS RIGHTS SOCIETY (ARS), NEW YORK

BOTTOM RIGHT, THIS PAGE: *The Lighthouse at Collioure.* By André Derain, 1905. Derain was a prominent member of the fauvist painters, who were distinguished primarily by their use of intense colors, building upon the examples of van Gogh and Gauguin. GIRAUDON/ART RESOURCE, NY. © 2005 ARTISTS RIGHTS SOCIETY (ARS), NEW YORK/ ADAGP, PARIS

OPPOSITE PAGE, TOP LEFT: *First Day of the Russian Revolution, 9 January 1905.* By Vladimir Makovsky, 1905. Makovsky's realism is in marked contrast to the increasing abstraction of western European art of the period. © Archivo Iconografico, S.A./Corbis

OPPOSITE PAGE, BOTTOM LEFT: *Judith II (Salome).* By Gustav Klimt, 1909. The modernism of Klimt's Austrian *Sezession* style, a variation of art nouveau, derives from the blending of figures with purely decorative and symbolic elements. MUSEO D'ARTE MODERNA, VENICE, ITALY/BRIDGEMAN ART LIBRARY/CAMERA-PHOTO ARTE VENEZIEA

OPPOSITE PAGE, TOP RIGHT: *Woman with a Madras Headdress and Oranges.* By Henri Matisse, 1907. Matisse was the most prominent of the fauvist painters; his masterly use of pure, expressive color and decorative abstraction marks him as one of the most influential painters of the twentieth century. THE BARNES FOUNDATION, MERION, PENNSYLVANIA, USA/BRIDGEMAN ART LIBRARY. © SUCCESSION H. MATISSE, PARIS/ARTISTS RIGHTS SOCIETY (ARS), NY

OPPOSITE PAGE, BOTTOM RIGHT: *Two Female Nudes.* By Egon Schiele, 1912. Schiele was a disciple of Gustav Klimt and built upon the older artist's use of the human form as a vehicle for expressionist distortions of color and form. © GEOFFREY CLEMENTS/CORBIS

Dynamism of a Cyclist. By Umberto Boccioni, 1913. Boccioni was the preeminent futurist painter, seeking to reflect the movement and vital force of modern life in his canvases. The futurists' belief that movement actually fragmented physical structures resulted in great similarity between futurist works and those of the cubists. © Archivo Iconografico, S.A./Corbis

Polish insurgents. Nineteenth-century engraving. In 1846, Polish insurgents in Kraków unsuccessfully rebelled against Austrian rule. The city remained part of the Austro-Hungarian Empire until 1919. ©CORBIS

the linked principles of dynastic legitimacy and the political significance of revealed religion, strongly condemned nationalism. They perceived, correctly, the potential disruption and warfare that would come from trying to apply nationalist principles to the many German or Italian states, the multinational Austrian Empire, or the Poles, divided by the eighteenth-century partitions among Prussia and the Austrian and Russian Empires.

The party of movement was not a modern political party, since such organizations were generally illegal in pre-1848 Europe, and limitations on communication and transportation would have made them hard to create in any event. Rather, supporters of political change worked through the expanding network of organizations of civil society: the press (often heavily censored or otherwise restricted), public meetings, when allowed, and, above all, voluntary associations. Political ideas were propagated in social clubs, popular among the middle class; or in learned and literary societies, and gymnastics, sharpshooting, and choral societies, intellectual and popular reservoirs of nationalism, respectively. Where constitutional regimes existed—in France, the Low Countries, and most midsized German states—such efforts had ties to the law-making and oratorical efforts of parliamentarians. They also extended to the underground world of conspiratorial secret societies. The insurrections launched by these groups were all failures, but their sometimes-substantial membership (Giuseppe Mazzini's "Young Italy" movement may have had as many as fifty thousand members by 1834) helped spread oppositional political ideals.

The crisis years from 1845 to 1847 began with the potato blight of 1845 and the failed grain harvest of 1846, which led to a doubling of food prices and near-famine conditions. Although mass starvation was avoided (except in Ireland), real wages and standards of living plummeted, culminating a two-decade-long trend; demand collapsed; and 1847 saw a credit crisis, widespread bankruptcies, and a severe recession. There were hundreds, probably thousands, of bread riots and other subsistence disturbances in Europe, as well as more widespread disorders, such as the famous 1844 rising of the outworking Silesian weavers against the merchant contractors who employed them. Declining tax receipts put state budgets under stress, particularly that of the Austrian Empire, whose chancellor, Prince Metternich, had led the fight against revolution in Europe for three decades, but whose government now teetered on the edge of bankruptcy.

At the same time, supporters of the party of movement launched a political offensive in many parts of Europe. Best known are the banquet campaigns of the French opposition, mass meetings, thinly disguised as public meals, where speakers demanded a more democratic franchise. The election of the reputedly liberal bishop of Imola as Pope Pius IX in 1846 raised hopes among Italian liberals for constitutional governments and a union of the states of the peninsula. The victory of the opposition in elections to the 1847 Hungarian Diet, the clash between the king of Prussia and the liberal majority in the United Diet of that year (which reminded contemporaries of the Estates-General in France in 1789), and the confrontations between liberals and their erstwhile hero Pius IX in the consultative assembly he summoned for the Papal States, were all evidence of growing political tensions. Finally, the Swiss civil war of 1847, pitting the more left-wing and Protestant cantons against the conservative and Catholic ones, and resulting in a very quick victory of the radicals, suggested that violent change was on the agenda. Financial difficulties prevented a unilateral Austrian intervention; Metternich's inability to create a coalition of Great Powers to rescue the Swiss conservatives was striking evidence that the post-1815 order was crumbling.

THE OUTBREAK AND SPREAD OF REVOLUTION

The first six months of 1848 saw a chain of revolutionary uprisings across the European continent. They began in mid-January in Palermo, chief city of Sicily, then spread at the end of the month to the Italian mainland with barricade fighting in Naples, capital of the southern Italian Kingdom of the Two Sicilies. The insurgents were victorious and King Ferdinand II agreed to grant a constitution and appoint new, liberal government ministers. The following month, participants in the banquet campaign poured into the streets of Paris, clashed with police and the army, and began building barricades—a signature feature of urban street fighting in 1848. Three days of barricade fighting, 22–24 February 1848, with the National Guard either neutral or joining the insurgents, and the regular army distinctly reluctant to fight, ended with the flight of King Louis-Philippe to London, and the proclamation of a republic.

This dramatic news encouraged supporters of the party of movement in many countries to hold large public meetings, on the model of the Parisian banquet campaign. Participants demonstrated, clashed with soldiers, and built barricades: in Munich, 4 March; in Vienna, 13 March; Budapest, two days later; Venice and Kraków, two days after that; and, on the 18th, in Milan and Berlin. News of each uprising encouraged the next, and their outcomes were the same: withdrawal of increasingly unreliable troops; dismissal of the old, conservative government ministers and naming of liberal replacements; the creation of national committees or the proclamation of national unity; and either the granting of a constitution or the agreement to call a constituent assembly to write one.

In most of the midsized German and Italian states, as well as in the Netherlands and Denmark, large-scale demonstrations, or just the threat of them, sufficed for governments to make similar concessions without risking a trial of strength on the barricades. After repelling an invasion staged from northern France by Belgian radicals at the end of March, the Belgian government proceeded to expand the franchise and introduce other reforms. Young Romanians, studying in Paris, returned to their homes in the Principalities of Moldavia and Walachia, after participating in the barricade fighting of February 1848, and launched similar banquet campaigns and demonstrations in April and May 1848. Suppressed by the prince in Moldavia but leading in June to a revolutionary government in Walachia, they concluded, at the southeastern end of the Continent in Bucharest, the initial wave of revolution.

The major exceptions to this initial wave were the British and Russian Empires. A mass demonstration by the radical opposition in the United Kingdom, the Chartists, in London on 10 April, inspired by events on the Continent, was met with an overwhelming show of force as over 100,000 police, soldiers, and volunteer "special constables" ensured that the demonstration would not take a revolutionary turn. There were no visible manifestations of political opposition in the absolutist tsarist empire, just a small revolutionary secret society, the "Petrashevtsy," whose members were arrested and sent to Siberia. Both Great Powers lacked the preconditions for revolution present in the rest of Europe, albeit for different reasons. The United Kingdom (except for Ireland, whose inhabitants were too busy in 1848 starving to death or fleeing the island to think of revolution) had, by the 1840s, made the transition to a more productive economy, based on factory industry and efficient agriculture, with rising standards of living. In Russia, there was little in the way of a civil society—almost no voluntary associations, not much of a press, indeed very few people who were literate—in which opposition to the government could form.

POSSIBILITIES AND PROBLEMS

The victories of the insurgents and the coming to power of new liberal regimes unleashed an enormous potential for democratic activity and political participation. This very potential also led to conflicts and increasingly violent clashes that would weaken and ultimately destroy the revolution.

There were two characteristic and largely spontaneous responses to the new regimes' coming to power. One was a wave of festivity, with parades, nocturnal illuminations, plantings of trees of liberty, and church services of thanksgiving, in euphoric celebration of the end of decades of oppression—later dubbed the "springtime of the peoples." Another was the violent actions of the lower classes to resolve their long-held social and economic grievances. In regions of serfdom and seignorialism, from southwestern Germany to the Banat in southern Hungary, peasants attacked castles of their lords and destroyed charters of feudal privileges. Peasants assaulted their creditors (in some places, this developed into attacks on the Jewish population, identified with moneylenders); they reappropriated divided common lands and seized wood from the forests. Artisans and outworkers attacked the merchant capitalists who had exploited them; there were several spectacular instances of machine breaking, involving the destruction of factories, railroads, or steamships. The lower classes, both rural and urban, destroyed tax-collection offices and customs stations, and assaulted the officials who staffed them. The perpetrators saw these actions as part of the celebrations of freedom, waving tricolor flags and chanting revolutionary slogans as they performed them.

From the late spring of 1848 through the spring of 1849, these spontaneous actions gave way to more systematic and planned ones. The numbers and circulation of newspapers expanded five- to tenfold throughout revolutionary Europe, and readership reached parts of the rural, lower-class, and female populations. Equally impressive was the creation and growth of political clubs. First formed in large cities, and lacking specific political profiles, they spread from there to smaller towns and the countryside, and divided along lines of political orientation, while combining in provincial and national federations. Most common in the German states, where their membership may have been as much as 10 percent of the adult male population, the clubs were also prevalent in France, Italy, and, to a lesser extent, or supplemented by nationalist societies, in much of the Austrian Empire. Clubs held regular meetings and sponsored political debates, organized rallies with hundreds or thousands of participants, sent petitions and addresses to parliaments, and, in times of crisis, mobilized members for revolutionary or counterrevolutionary actions.

Workers' associations, consumer and producer cooperatives—national federations of these existed in France and Germany—and, to a lesser extent, trade unions were founded throughout western and central Europe. Elementary and secondary schoolteachers mobilized to improve their position, often with an anticlerical hostility to church control of public education. Protestant, Catholic, and Orthodox clergy and laymen organized in turn, to preserve or improve the position of their respective churches vis-à-vis the government, or to attempt (usually unsuccessfully) to change their churches' hierarchy and governance. In 1848–1849, women

Our Motion Is Carried! Lithograph after the paintig by Antal Gorosy. The Hungarian Parliament votes to create an army to oppose Habsburg rule. PRIVATE COLLECTION/BRIDGEMAN ART LIBRARY/ARCHIVES CHARMET

emerged vigorously into public life. Most women's activity was devoted to assisting men, sewing flags for national guards, and forming associations—there were two in Prague alone—to promote the use of "national" languages and national costumes, or to support political prisoners and their families. There were also women's newspapers, and women formed their own clubs to debate political issues and, primarily in Paris (to some extent in other large cities, including Berlin and Vienna), to promote women's rights, including public employment for unemployed women, and woman suffrage.

This same explosion of public political participation created two kinds of potentially violent conflicts that would undermine the revolution. One involved the practice of democracy itself. Elections held in April and May 1848 to constituent assemblies or parliaments, under a broad franchise, with relatively little preparation or organization, were dominated by locally influential men, including

the clergy (who were very active), the nobility, and other substantial property-owners; moderate and conservative outcomes were the result. A clash between such moderate parliaments and the radicalized masses of capital cities, with their newly formed political clubs, would duly occur.

The second and perhaps most important source of conflict came from the attempt to create unified nation-states. The 1848 revolution in Italy was dominated by warfare aimed at driving the foreign, Austrian rulers out of their two northern Italian provinces as a step toward a united Italy. The effort to create a German nation-state was in part peaceful, via the election of the Frankfurt National Assembly, charged with writing a constitution for a united Germany. Violent conflicts arose, however, over the question of the national status of territories previously under dynastic rule. Was the Prussian province of Posen (in Polish, Poznań) part of a Polish nation-state, as the revolutionary national committee formed there in March 1848 asserted, or would it be part of a German nation-state, as the province's German-speaking minority insisted, backed by the Prussian army? Were the duchies of Schleswig and Holstein—mostly German-speaking but with a Danish-speaking minority, and before 1848 provinces of the Danish crown—part of a German nation-state, as German nationalist insurgents asserted, with the support of the Prussian army, or was Schleswig part of a Danish nation-state, as the new liberal government in Copenhagen saw it?

The most complex and violent clashes between nationalists occurred in the multinational Austrian Empire. Should the empire—and, if so, which part of it—join a German nation-state? German nationalists thought the provinces of Bohemia and Moravia were part of Germany; Czech nationalists did not. The Polish National Committee in Kraków, like its counterpart in Posen, saw the Austrian province of Galicia as part of a Polish nation-state, while the Supreme Ruthenian Council in Lviv (in German, Lemberg) laid a contrasting national claim to the province. The nationalities conflict was strongest in the Hungarian provinces, which the newly constituted Hungarian National Assembly wanted to unite into a Hungarian nation-state, basically independent of the empire, while Croatian, Serb, Slovak, and Romanian nationalists wanted their own nation-states, or at least autonomous national areas, independent of Hungary.

CONFRONTATIONS AND DECISIONS

The midcentury revolutions were marked by two periods of conflict: in the second half of 1848, and in the spring and summer of 1849. The first conflicts would reveal the discords beneath the surface of the springtime of the peoples, the second would reflect the process of organization and mobilization occurring during the revolution itself; the struggles would shift from the capital cities to the provinces, from urban populations to those of small towns and the countryside.

The first period of conflict was marked by a wave of counterrevolution spreading across Europe, paralleling the preceding wave of revolution. This counterrevolution took three forms. One involved a monarch using his armed forces to reassert control over elected assemblies. The crushing

of the parliament of the Kingdom of the Two Sicilies by troops of King Ferdinand II in May 1848 began the period of counterrevolution. A very similar action occurred toward its end in November, when the king of Prussia sent fifty thousand soldiers into Berlin to dissolve the Prussian Constituent Assembly. In both cases, the capital cities were quiet, but there were demonstrations and uprisings in the provinces against the royal coups. A variant on this form occurred in September in the Principality of Walachia, where Turkish and Russian armies of intervention restored the authority of the ruling prince.

The central event of the counterrevolution, like that of the revolution, occurred in Paris. There, a confused situation involved differences among a governmental executive composed of an uneasy alliance of moderate liberals and militant republicans; a constituent national assembly, most of whose members wanted a restoration of a monarchy; increasingly radical political clubs; and an active labor movement, with strikes, cooperatives, and the "national workshops," a giant public-works project providing jobs for 100,000 unemployed, promoted as a socialist experiment. This volatile situation led to repeated clashes between demonstrators and the authorities, culminating in the so-called June Days, four days of bitter barricade fighting on 23–26 June. After much fiercer combat than in the overthrow of the monarchy in February, the insurgents were defeated, leaving five thousand dead, the radical clubs closed and dissolved, the labor movement in tatters, and the government, if still officially republican, increasingly conservative. The landslide victory of Louis-Napoleon Bonaparte, nephew of the great emperor Napoleon, in the December 1848 French presidential election made the future of the republic look much less republican.

The third feature of this wave of counterrevolution was its relationship to the clash of nationalist movements. In July, Austrian forces, commanded by General Joseph Radetzky, defeated the army of the Italian Kingdom of Sardinia at the battle of Custoza and quickly reconquered Austria's northern Italian provinces, except the island city of Venice. The following month, the Prussian government, under heavy pressure from the tsar, agreed to an armistice with Denmark, abandoning the

German insurgents in Schleswig and Holstein. Protesting this betrayal of the nationalist cause, radical demonstrators stormed the Frankfurt National Assembly (which had endorsed the armistice) the following month. There was street fighting in Frankfurt, and the insurrection was suppressed by Prussian and Hessian troops.

The main aspect of this phase of counterrevolution was the exploitation of rivalries between different nationalist movements by Austrian soldiers and government officials to return the empire to authoritarian rule. In June, Habsburg troops crushed a Czech radical-nationalist insurrection in Prague, to the applause of German nationalists; at the end of October, they crushed a German nationalist-radical insurrection in Vienna, to the applause of Czech nationalists. There was violent and bloody street fighting in both cities.

The opposition of Serbian and Romanian nationalists to the authority of the Hungarian National Assembly intersected with struggles between lords and serfs, because the serfs of the Banat and Transylvania were mostly Serbian- and Romanian-speaking, whereas the local representatives of the Hungarian government that had, among its reforms, officially abolished serfdom, were Hungarian noble landlords, reluctant to give up their feudal privileges. In these struggles that left tens of thousands dead, and at times approached ethnic cleansing, Austrian officials and officers tacitly and openly supported the anti-Hungarian nationalists.

Most importantly, the Austrian government ministers and the imperial court encouraged the ban (provincial governor) of Croatia, Josip Jelačić, colonel in the border regiments, to oppose Hungarian authority and, in September 1848, to lead his troops, many of whose officers were sympathetic to Croatian nationalism, into war with the government of Hungary. The Hungarian National Assembly responded with a revolutionary war, turning over power to the nationalist leader Lajos Kossuth, but its forces were steadily forced back and by December had to evacuate Budapest.

At the end of 1848, the initial revolutionary movement had been largely suppressed. A second round of struggles in the spring of 1849 showed that the revolutionary movement had spread beyond its original centers of the previous year.

One locus of the new wave of revolution was in central Italy. At the end of 1848, radical insurgents, working from the network of democratic clubs that had been established, overthrew the governments of the Papal States and of the grand duke of Tuscany, replacing them with revolutionary regimes, dedicated to Italian national unity and a resumption of the war with Austria. Elections in the Kingdom of Sardinia produced a victory for the democrats and a swing of royal policy in the direction of resuming the nationalist war.

A second locus was in central Europe. In March 1849 the Frankfurt National Assembly completed a constitution for a German nation-state, creating a constitutional monarchy with democratic features, such as legislative elections under universal manhood suffrage. Because the Austrian government, by then under counterrevolutionary rule, rejected any connection with the subversive ideas of nationalism, the result was, as contemporaries said, a "little German" nation-state, without the Germans of Austria. The Frankfurt parliamentarians proposed to make the king of Prussia, head of Austria's central European military and diplomatic rival, the emperor of their German nation-state.

A third locus was in France, where radicals, democrats, and socialists, reeling from their defeats in the streets and at the ballot box in the second half of 1848, united around the defense of the republican form of government. Their candidates did surprisingly well in the legislative elections of May 1849, emerging as the single largest caucus, albeit outnumbered by the different monarchist groups.

Finally, the Hungarian forces rallied in the winter of 1848–1849, defeating Austrian troops on three different fronts, recapturing Budapest, and marching menacingly on Vienna. The Austrian government lacked the funds to continue the war; its efforts to conscript fresh soldiers were met with recruiting riots, organized by democratic activists.

This second round of revolutionary confrontation was resolved with military means. The Austrian General Radetzky once again defeated the Piedmontese forces of the Kingdom of Piedmont-Sardinia, bringing the war in northern Italy to a quick end. The revolutionary regime in Tuscany collapsed and the grand duke returned; Austrian troops reconquered

Venice. French intervention destroyed the Roman Republic and restored the rule of the pope.

The Prussian king rejected the constitution of the Frankfurt National Assembly, and democrats throughout Germany launched a movement to support it. Mass demonstrations, organized by the political clubs, culminated in the storming of arsenals, uprisings, and the creation of revolutionary governments in Saxony, Baden, and the Bavarian Palatinate. These governments were overthrown by Prussian soldiers, in a brief civil war occurring from May to June 1849.

While the Austrian government was unable to deal with the Hungarians on its own, it received assistance in the form of Russian military intervention. By August 1849 Russian and Habsburg troops had defeated the Hungarian forces and restored the authority of the imperial government over the entire territory of the monarchy.

In France, a June 1849 demonstration in Paris, organized by radical parliamentary deputies against the French intervention in Italy, was a fiasco, resulting in the arrest or flight of most of the radical leaders and an increasing rightward direction in French politics. Yet from mid-1849 through 1851, the remaining left-wing activists organized a network of some seven hundred secret societies, successors to the legal democratic political clubs, mostly in villages and towns of central and southeastern France. When, in December 1851, President Louis-Napoleon launched a coup to overthrow the republic and make himself emperor, Paris was quiet, but at least 100,000 insurgents, led by the secret societies, rose up against him, reiterating the political and social demands of the French left. Their defeat by the French army marked the end of the second wave of revolution and of the mid-nineteenth-century revolutions altogether.

STRUGGLES AND ACCOMPLISHMENTS

Reasons for the failures of the 1848 revolutions were already being debated in 1850, and historians have done so ever since. Paradoxically, the revolutions' failures came from their successes. The massive increase in political participation following the insurrections of January–March 1848 allowed different political tendencies to emerge. Radicals and socialists clashed with moderates, especially in France, but also in Germany and Italy. The different nationalist movements in central and eastern Europe battled each other very bitterly. Unlike France after 1789, radicals in 1848 were never able to gain control of a Great Power and launch a revolutionary war. In contrast to 1917 or 1989, existing governmental structures had not completely collapsed in 1848, and their proponents could still be active after the initial wave of revolution. While different elements of the party of movement were fighting each other, conservatives were able to rally supporters, regroup the armed forces under their control, exploit differences of opinion among their opponents, and regain control—although only after fierce struggles, from June to December 1848 and from May to August 1849, with a final outburst in France, two and a half years later.

If unsuccessful at installing new regimes, the 1848 revolutions nonetheless had important long-term effects. The revolutionary abolition of serfdom and seignorialism in the Austrian Empire and the German states remained, even after the triumph of counterrevolution. Constitutional governments became the norm; by the 1860s, they would exist everywhere in Europe except for the tsar's empire. The national unification of Germany and Italy between 1859 and 1871 and the compromise of 1867 creating an autonomous Hungarian nation-state within the Austrian Empire, all stemmed from initiatives first taken in 1848. Europe's socialist and feminist activists of the third quarter of the nineteenth century began their political career in the 1848 revolutions, as did the leaders of the Catholic political movement developing at that time.

Most of all, the 1848 revolutions involved an explosion of political participation. Although there would certainly be examples of mass politics in subsequent decades, it was only in the 1890s—after a substantial expansion of communication and transportation networks—that as great a proportion of the population would take part in public life as had been the case in the years 1848 and 1849.

See also **Austria-Hungary; Berlin; Blanqui, Auguste; Bohemia, Moravia, and Silesia; Bonapartism; France; Francis Joseph; Frederick William IV; Garibaldi, Giuseppe; Germany; Italy; Kossuth, Lajos;**

Lamartine, Alphonse; Ledru-Rollin, Alexandre-Auguste; Liberalism; Marx, Karl; Metternich, Clemens von; Napoleon III; Paris; Pius IX; Prague Slav Congress; Rome; Socialism; Vienna; William I.

BIBLIOGRAPHY

Primary Sources

Price, Roger, ed. *Documents on the French Revolution of 1848*. Rev. ed. New York, 1996. A very useful collection of documents.

Schurz, Carl. *The Reminiscences of Carl Schurz*. 3 vols. New York, 1907–1908. Contains a lively account of events in Germany by a radical political activist, who later went on to a distinguished career in American politics.

Secondary Sources

Agulhon, Maurice. *The Republic in the Village: The People of the Var from the French Revolution to the Second Republic*. Translated by Janet Lloyd. Cambridge, U.K., 1982. A famous regional study that has set the terms for the modern history of the 1848 revolutions, in France and more broadly in Europe.

———. *The Republican Experiment, 1848–1852*. Translated by Janet Lloyd. Cambridge, U.K., 1983. A classic history of the 1848 revolution in France.

Deák, István. *The Lawful Revolution: Louis Kossuth and the Hungarians, 1848–1849*. New York, 1979. Far and away, the best English-language book on the 1848 revolutions in the Austrian Empire, especially in the empire's Hungarian lands.

Dowe, Dieter, Heinz-Gerhard Haupt, Dieter Langewiesche, and Jonathan Sperber, eds. *Europe in 1848: Revolution and Reform*. Translated by David Higgins. New York, 2001. A massive collection of essays on all aspects of the 1848 revolutions, throughout Europe, including essays on events in the smaller countries, and on women and peasants, as well as a very extensive bibliography.

Evans, R. J. W., and Hartmut Pogge von Strandmann, eds. *The Revolutions in Europe, 1848–1849: From Reform to Reaction*. Oxford, U.K., 2000. Not as extensive as the Dowe et al. collection of essays, but a useful supplement to it, especially the articles on Russian and U.S. responses to the 1848 revolutions.

Ginsborg, Paul. *Daniele Manin and the Venetian Revolution of 1848–49*. Cambridge, U.K., 1979. The best English-language work on the 1848 revolutions in Italy.

Margadant, Ted W. *French Peasants in Revolt: The Insurrection of 1851*. Princeton, N.J., 1979.

Merriman, John M. *The Agony of the Republic: The Repression of the Left in Revolutionary France, 1848–1851*. New Haven, Conn., 1978. An excellent monographic study, particularly illuminating on events outside of Paris and during the often-neglected years 1849–1851.

Robertson, Priscilla. *The Revolutions of 1848: A Social History*. Princeton, N.J., 1952. A general history whose scholarship is outdated but still makes for charming reading. The bibliography contains a very helpful and extensive list of memoirs by participants in the 1848 revolutions.

Siemann, Wolfram. *The German Revolution of 1848–49*. Translated by Christiane Banerji. New York, 1998. The best English-language general history of the 1848 revolution in central Europe.

Sperber, Jonathan. *Rhineland Radicals: The Democratic Movement and the Revolution of 1848–1849*. Princeton, N.J., 1991. A regional study emphasizing the relationship of the revolutionary movement to pre-1848 social, economic, political, and religious conflicts.

———. *The European Revolutions, 1848–1851*. 2nd ed. Cambridge, U.K., 2005. The most up-to-date general history of the 1848 revolutions.

Vick, Brian E. *Defining Germany: The 1848 Frankfurt Parliamentarians and National Identity*. Cambridge, Mass., 2002. A careful study of a crucial aspect of the German revolution of 1848 and also an unusually helpful account of the phenomenon of nationalism in the mid-nineteenth century.

JONATHAN SPERBER

RHODES, CECIL (1853–1902), British mining magnate, politician, and imperialist.

Cecil John Rhodes was born in Hertfordshire and brought up in modest circumstances as the son of an English clergyman. He migrated from Britain in 1870 to join his farmer brother, Herbert, in South Africa, a part of the British Empire about which he knew virtually nothing. After little more than a year in rural Natal, he moved on to the mineral fields of the northern Cape town of Kimberley, where diamonds had been discovered in 1867. A confident and grasping figure, Rhodes thrived in the coarse and edgy environment of early industrial colonial capitalism, advancing from being a speculative digger to forming the De Beers Mining Company and De Beers Consolidated Mines in the 1880s.

By the end of a decade of ruthless acquisitions, Rhodes and his mining associates controlled over 90 percent of world diamond production. In the course of making his pile from the Kimberley monopoly, he acquired a buccaneering business reputation that he was subsequently never able to shake off. Rhodes's ambitions as a mining magnate did not stop there. Following the discovery of gold on the Witwatersrand, he soon acquired a stake in the new gold mines of the Transvaal, establishing the Gold Fields of South Africa Company in the late 1880s and forging ever-closer ties with influential members of the London financial elite, such as Lord Nathan Rothschild (1840–1915).

A perpetually scheming figure, obsessed with asserting his influence over Southern African affairs, Rhodes lost no time in hitching his rising financial wealth to political ambition, assiduously using that wealth to cultivate favor and preferment. Within three years of being elected to the Cape colonial parliament at the age of twenty-seven, he had wormed his way into the Cabinet. By 1890, this formidable embodiment of imperial capitalism had become prime minister of the Cape Colony, a vaulting politician determined to dash creeping German and Transvaal Boer influence in the region, and bent upon keeping open a great road to the north for a further burst of British territorial expansion.

To cap it all, Rhodes secured a royal charter for the predatory operations of his British South Africa Company (BSAC), giving him virtually unfettered rights of land acquisition and plunder northward from the Limpopo to well beyond the Zambezi river. In the early 1890s, his company troops and agents either swindled or blasted their way through African resistance and laid the foundations for the exploitation of the colony he named, with customary modesty, Rhodesia. Viewed largely as his personal fiefdom, the settler territories were left to a notably unsavory and callous administration.

An imperialist with towering faith in his own powers, Rhodes declared repeatedly that he valued wealth not for its own sake but for the idealism and strength it gave him to extend the British Empire. In this, however, he finally overreached himself in the mid-1890s. An armed plot that he sponsored to overthrow the Transvaal government of Paul Kruger (1825–1904) to force the Boer republicans (with their massive gold deposits) to amalgamate with the British colonies was bungled. The 1895 Jameson Raid was easily squashed by the Boers, leaving Rhodes with egg on his face for having implicated Britain in a grubby conspiracy against an independent white Christian state. The debacle dented him

politically, forcing his resignation from the Cape premiership as well as from the board of his own BSAC.

Slinking off to Rhodesia, Rhodes regained his forceful company influence there and threw himself into imposing colonial authority, advancing settler interests, and dreaming of building a railway from the Cape to Cairo. He died in 1902 in Muizenberg, South Africa.

At his peak, his huge fortunes from diamond- and goldmining made Rhodes one of the world's wealthiest men. Against the background of the "Scramble for Africa," he acted as a freelance titan of capitalist imperialism, a single individual who was decisive in shaping the destiny of Southern Africa and for whom personal gain was indistinguishable from the imperial mission. Rhodes always believed that Britons were divinely chosen for world supremacy, and fantasized that the consummation of their empire would be the recovery and absorption of the United States and the sealing of Anglo-German fraternity. This, he concluded, would end all war. With these beliefs went racial contempt for Africans in Southern Africa. Rhodes's trumpeted 1898 promise of "equal rights for every civilized man south of the Zambesi" had little meaning, given his record of smothering black economic and political rights.

Much of his lavish philanthropic legacy from 1903 was educational, including the endowment of hundreds of Rhodes Scholarships at Oxford University to train male students from the white self-governing colonies and America for leadership of the imperial world to which he had devoted himself.

See also **Africa; Boer War; Civilization, Concept of; Imperialism; South Africa.**

BIBLIOGRAPHY

Flint, John E. *Cecil Rhodes.* Boston, 1974.

Galbraith, John S. *Crown and Charter: The Early Years of the British South Africa Company.* Berkeley, Calif., 1974.

Rotberg, Robert I., with Miles F. Shore. *The Founder: Cecil Rhodes and the Pursuit of Power.* New York, 1988.

Worger, William H. *South Africa's City of Diamonds: Mine Workers and Monopoly Capitalism in Kimberley, 1867–1895.* New Haven, Conn., 1987.

BILL NASSON

RICHER, LÉON (1824–1911), French pioneer of feminism.

In the 1860s Léon Richer quit his job of eleven years as a notary's clerk for the Orleans Railroad in order to become a full-time activist on behalf of liberal republicanism, anticlericalism, and, especially, feminism. An energetic Freemason and journalist, Richer initially wrote a controversial anticlerical column for Adolphe Guéroult's *L'opinion nationale*. Controversial, too, were the philosophical conferences that Richer organized at the Masonic Grand Orient in 1866, a series that, over objections from fellow Freemasons, afforded women the opportunity to speak in public. Among these women was one in particular, Maria Deraismes (1828–1894), with whom Richer worked closely during the years to follow as he came more and more to focus his activism on women's emancipation. In 1869, Deraismes backed the launching of Richer's journal, *Le droit des femmes* (The right of women), and then a year later joined him in founding the Société pour l'amélioration du sort de la femme.

Shortly thereafter, however, these initial feminist efforts by Richer and Deraismes fell victim to the Franco-Prussian War (1870–1871), the collapse of the Second French Empire (1870), the Paris Commune (1871), and the bitter political infighting of the first years of the Third French Republic (1870–1940). Indeed, in the early 1870s, conservatives forced Richer to drop the word *droit* from the title of his journal, which he retitled *L'avenir des femmes* (The future of women), and then, in 1875, ordered the disbandment of L'Amélioration. In the meantime, Richer published *Le divorce* (1873), which later influenced the text of Alfred Naquet's 1884 law reestablishing the right to divorce, but had to await the republican resurgence that followed the *seize mai* (16 May) crisis of 1877 in order to begin rebuilding the feminist movement. From 1878 to 1883, Richer took advantage of the improved political climate to host with Deraismes the first French Congrès international du droit des femmes (1878), regain L'Amélioration's official authorization, restore his journal's title to *Le droit des femmes*, establish the Ligue française pour le droit des femmes (1882), and write *Le code des femmes* (1883). In 1889 Richer and Deraismes hosted the second Congrès français et international du droit des femmes.

In his pursuit of women's rights, Richer adhered closely to the moderate strategy of the *politique de la brèche*, a strategy aimed at lifting women's civil disabilities through temperate appeals to public opinion and quiet lobbying, hoping to "breach" the wall of masculine domination one reform at a time. Consistently, he railed against Hubertine Auclert (1884–1914) and her suffragist allies for employing the *politque de l'assaut*, a strategy bent on "assaulting" the wall of masculine privilege all at once through securing women's right to vote. To Richer, the partisans of the *politique de l'assaut* not only weakened the feminist movement by dividing it into competing wings and alienating many potential supporters, but also placed the newly won republic in mortal danger. Because "the feminine mind was still too crushed by the yoke of the Church," Richer charged, the Third Republic would not last six months if women were to vote. Out of the nine million women prospectively eligible to vote, Richer reckoned, no more than a few thousand possessed the independence requisite for casting a ballot responsibly; the remainder would take their orders from the confessional. Hence, Richer barred Auclert from addressing the issue of women's suffrage at the 1878 and 1889 women's rights congresses and, in spite of fierce criticism from within the movement, urged indefinite postponement of women's enfranchisement until all French women had undergone a thorough republican reeducation.

Richer thus imparted a mixed message to the embryonic French feminist movement. On the one side, he drew public attention to women's civil disabilities, provided the movement with an organizational structure, and helped secure several specific reforms. On the other side, his vehement opposition to women's suffrage provided opponents of women's right to vote with an authoritative "feminist" voice on which to base their arguments. Richer retired from the movement in 1891, by which time his *Le droit des femmes* had become the longest-lived of any nineteenth-century feminist publication in France. His Ligue française pour le droit des femmes still exists in the early twenty-first century. Other men also followed his lead in becoming feminist activists, but never again did a Frenchman play so pivotal a role in exercising dominance over the movement's organizational structure or by imparting to its ideology a vision so exclusively limited to the pursuit of civil, but not political, rights for women.

See also **Auclert, Hubertine; Deraismes, Maria; Feminism; Suffragism.**

BIBLIOGRAPHY

Bidelman, Patrick Kay. *Pariahs Stand Up!: The Founding of the Liberal Feminist Movement in France, 1858–1889.* Westport, Conn., 1982.

Hause, Steven C., with Anne R. Kenney. *Women's Suffrage and Social Politics in the French Third Republic.* Princeton, N.J., 1984.

Klejman, Laurence, and Florence Rochefort. *L'Égalité en marche: Le féminisme sous la Troisième République.* Paris, 1989.

Moses, Claire G. *French Feminism in the Nineteenth Century.* Albany, N.Y., 1984.

Rabaut, Jean. *Histoire des féminismes français.* Paris, 1978.

PATRICK KAY BIDELMAN

RIMSKY-KORSAKOV, NIKOLAI (1844–1908), Russian composer and conservatory pedagogue.

Nikolai Andreyevich Rimsky-Korsakov began his career during the 1860s as one of the composers of the "Mighty Handful," a group that sought to establish a Russian national style in music. (The other members were Modest Mussorgsky, Alexander Borodin, César Cui, and the leader Mily Balakirev.) Outside Russia, Rimsky-Korsakov's most celebrated works are the symphonic suite *Scheherazade,* the *Russian Easter Festival* overture, and the orchestral showpiece *Capriccio espagnol,* but he also produced fifteen operas, nearly ninety songs, about twenty other orchestral works (including three symphonies), fifteen chamber works, and more. He completed several unfinished works by his colleagues in the "Handful," and more controversially he revised Mussorgsky's finished opera *Boris Godunov.* A profoundly influential pedagogue, he wrote textbooks on harmony and orchestration and taught at the St. Petersburg Conservatory from 1871 until his death in 1908, with a brief hiatus in 1905.

Born on 18 March (6 March, old style) 1844 in Tikhvin, near Novgorod, Russia, Rimsky-Korsakov demonstrated an interest in music as a child but was educated for a career as a naval officer at the St. Petersburg Naval Academy. In 1861, while still a student, he met Balakirev and began composition lessons with him. Balakirev was himself self-taught and did not value systematic conservatory instruction. Instead he taught his pupils by playing great music with them at the piano, all the while explaining, examining, and criticizing each work piecemeal. He then put his students to work writing their own pieces, dissected their music the same way, and sent them off to implement necessary changes. In such fashion Rimsky-Korsakov completed four sizable orchestral works, several songs, and the opera *The Maid of Pskov* within just ten years.

On the strength of this catalog, Rimsky-Korsakov was offered a post as professor of composition at the St. Petersburg Conservatory in 1871, which he accepted. Profoundly embarrassed at the gaps in his own training, he then began an intensive program of self-education. Over the next few years he acquired a disciplined technique, which he immediately put to use in several new orchestral works, revisions of old works, and two new operas, *May Night* and *The Snow Maiden.* First produced in 1882, *The Snow Maiden* is still regarded as a pivotal work in Rimsky-Korsakov's development.

After Mussorgsky's death in 1881, Rimsky-Korsakov volunteered to prepare his friend's legacy for publication, beginning with the unfinished opera *Khovanshchina.* In all his editions of Mussorgsky, Rimsky-Korsakov corrected passages that he thought were technically flawed, a procedure for which subsequent generations have severely criticized him. After Borodin's death in 1887, he and Alexander Glazunov completed that composer's opera *Prince Igor.* Then in 1887 and 1888 he wrote the colorfully orchestrated symphonic works that made him famous in Europe—*Capriccio espagnol, Scheherazade,* and the *Russian Easter Festival* overture. The fantastic opera-ballet *Mlada,* written under the spell of Richard Wagner's *Ring of the Nibelung,* was completed in 1890 and first performed in 1892. It marked the beginning of an even more sophisticated style of orchestration.

The early 1890s were a fallow period in Rimsky-Korsakov's creative work, which ended only with the composition of the opera *Christmas Eve* (1894–1895). He then worked energetically until his death in Lyubensk on 21 June (8 June, old style) 1908, completing ten more operas, many fine songs, a few minor orchestral works, a set of memoirs, and an orchestration textbook. Foremost among the late operas are *Sadko*, *The Tsar's Bride* (a lyrical work and his most popular opera in Russia), *The Tale of Tsar Saltan* (from which "The Flight of the Bumble Bee" is extracted), and *The Legend of the Invisible City of Kitezh and the Maiden Fevronia*. His final opera, *Le coq d'or* (The golden cockerel), is a satire of the tsarist bureaucracy and the only one of his operas that he did not live to hear—the censor delayed its production. It also is his only opera to have at least a modest foothold in the repertoire in the West, mainly because of the lavish production given to it by Sergei Diaghilev in Paris in 1914.

Rimsky-Korsakov's music is known for its brilliant orchestration and its systematic exploration of the harmonic resources of two synthetic scales, one consisting of consecutive whole steps, the other of alternating whole steps and half steps. His operas illustrate two categories that recur often in nineteenth-century Russian opera: works based on subjects from Russian history (*The Maid of Pskov*, *The Tsar's Bride*) and works based in Russian folklore and fairy tale (*The Snow Maiden, Mlada, Sadko, Tsar Saltan, Kitezh, Le coq d'or*). The symphonic suite *Scheherazade* extends the Russian "oriental" idiom found in Balakirev (*Tamara*) and several others. The popular *Russian Easter Festival* overture uses liturgical melodies in a glittering evocation of the Russian Orthodox Easter service. Rimsky-Korsakov's influence as a teacher extends throughout twentieth-century Russian music because many major figures—including Igor Stravinsky, Sergei Prokofiev, and Dmitri Shostakovich—were taught by him or one of his pupils.

See also **Mussorgsky, Modest; Opera; Wagner, Richard.**

BIBLIOGRAPHY

Primary Sources

Rimsky-Korsakov, Nikolay Andreyevich. *My Musical Life*. Translated by Judah A. Joffe. Edited by Carl Van Vechten. New York, 1942. Translation of *Letopis moyey muzykalnoy zhizni* (1909).

Yastrebtsev, V. V. *Reminiscences of Rimsky-Korsakov*. Edited and translated by Florence Jonas. New York, 1985.

Translation and abridgement of *Nikolai Andreyevich Rimsky-Korsakov: Vospominaniya* (1959–1960).

Secondary Sources

Abraham, Gerald. *Rimsky-Korsakov: A Short Biography*. London, 1945. Reprint, New York, 1976.

Seaman, Gerald R. *Nikolai Andreevich Rimsky-Korsakov: A Guide to Research*. New York, 1988.

ROBERT WILLIAM OLDANI

RISORGIMENTO (ITALIAN UNIFICATION).

Risorgimento, meaning "resurrection," was the term used as early as the 1840s to describe the aspirations to Italian independence that would finally be achieved between 1859 and 1870. For centuries Italy's political geography had been shaped by rivalries between major European dynastic powers, but it was not until the nineteenth century that demands for political change within the individual Italian states began to be linked to broader projects for political independence or unification. However, the two were never the same and there was strong support for alternative federal solutions. But in the event, the political outcome of the political struggles in Italy was determined as much by external as internal forces.

ITALY IN THE REVOLUTIONARY AND NAPOLEONIC ERA

By the end of the eighteenth century Habsburg Austria was the dominant foreign power on the Italian peninsula. Austria ruled only the prosperous northern province of Lombardy, but the grand duke of Tuscany was a Habsburg and the two Spanish Bourbon rulers—the duke of Parma and the king of the Two Sicilies—were close allies of Vienna. So was the pope, who ruled as a king over the Papal State that covered much of central Italy. As well as numerous lesser principalities, the remaining Italian states included the former mercantile republics of Venice and Genoa, but the only Italian dynasty that enjoyed real autonomy was the house of Savoy, the hereditary rulers of Piedmont, Savoy, and Nice whose royal title had come from the more recent acquisition of Sardinia.

The Revolutionary Wars gave the European powers an opportunity to resume their old rivalries and resulted in France taking Austria's place in Italy. When the French invaded northern Italy in 1796, Napoleon's victories forced the Austrians to abandon Lombardy (Treaty of Campoformio, October 1797). As the French advanced, numerous Italian republics were created, the last being the Roman Republic (February 1798) and the Neapolitan Republic (January 1799). In the spring of 1799 the Italian republics collapsed amid popular counterrevolution and royalist purges when the Directory withdrew its troops from Italy. Although short-lived, the republics marked the first brief moment of freedom of speech in modern Italian history and, among many other political projects, provided the first occasion in which proposals for Italian independence and unity were publicly debated.

The political climate was very different when Napoleon returned with another French army to Italy in 1800, and after the coup of Brumaire (November 1799) France's new first consul wanted nothing to do with the Italian Jacobins. Napoleon's victory over the Austrians at Marengo (June 1800) ended Austrian power in Italy, and the Italian Republic that was established in 1802 with its capital in Milan became the cornerstone of French domination. Following the proclamation of the French Empire in 1805 it was renamed the Kingdom of Italy.

Napoleon's stepson, Eugène de Beauharnais, was nominated viceroy, but the kingdom was ruled from Paris. It was the largest and most important of France's imperial satellites and at its height included the former Venetian Republic and the northern provinces of the Papal State south of the Po River. But French rule deliberately accentuated existing political differences and added new ones. The Kingdom of Italy was cut in two by the duchy of Parma while Piedmont was annexed to France and the former Genoese Republic and Tuscany became French protectorates. In 1806 a French army placed the emperor's brother Joseph on the throne of Naples, and he was replaced two years later by the emperor's brother-in-law Joachim Murat. In 1808 Tuscany was annexed and the Papal State was occupied, and a year later pope Pius VII became Napoleon's prisoner.

By 1809 all of Italy except for Sicily and Sardinia were under direct or indirect French rule. The imperial administrators consolidated reforms begun by the Italian princes in the late eighteenth century and won the support of the propertied classes by rescuing the creditors of the former monarchies and selling off the lands of the monasteries. But the costs of empire were heavy. Conscription and taxes were the main causes of popular unrest and revolts, but the subordination of the Italian states to the needs of empire also provoked opposition among sections of the elites. In 1814, on the eve of the empire's collapse, Napoleon's former chief of police, Joseph Fouché, reported that nationalism was the most powerful political force on the peninsula. But although the Allies and Joachim Murat tried to exploit these aspirations to independence, they had little political focus or cohesion.

RESTORATION ITALY

The principal concern of the European statesmen at the Congress of Vienna (1814–1815) was to ensure that France would never regain a foothold on the Italian peninsula, which was placed exclusively under Austria's control. Although it ruled directly only in the newly created northern Kingdom of Lombardy-Venetia, Austria was the power behind every Italian throne, and when the Italian princes were threatened by revolution—as happened in Naples and Sicily in 1820, in Piedmont in 1821, and in the Papal State in 1831—Austrian bayonets kept them in power.

The principal cause of political unrest in Italy was not nationalism but opposition to the reactionary Restoration autocracies. Since Austria kept the legitimist rulers in power it became the common enemy of all those who favored political change within the individual states. But that did not create a common program, and aspirations to greater political freedom gave rise to different and often conflicting political projects. Since censorship and police surveillance made any form of open political debate impossible, literature, painting, and music were evocative vehicles for nationalist aspirations, but as soon as these were translated into specific political programs it became clear that nationalism was more likely to divide than unite Italians.

In the early years of the Restoration the secret societies mobilized demands for constitutional government, but they were denounced by Giuseppe Mazzini (1805–1872), who founded Young Italy in 1831 with the specific aim of creating a single nationalist movement devoted to the overthrow of the existing Italian rulers and the creation of an independent Italian republic. Mazzini's proposals were anathema to conservatives and moderates, who preferred to think that Italy's independence could be achieved without political upheaval through a confederation of the existing rulers. But democrats like the Lombard economist Carlo Cattaneo also rejected Mazzini's ideas, arguing that only a federal solution along Swiss or American lines would accommodate the diversity of the Italian states.

The examples of the July monarchy in France (1830) and Britain's Great Reform Act (1832) persuaded many conservatives that gradual political change was the best antidote to social unrest. But the Italian rulers refused either to make political concessions or adopt more liberal economic measures, and as economic conditions deteriorated throughout Europe in the early 1840s popular unrest and political apprehensions in Italy grew. The revolutionaries took this as an opportunity to incite insurrections, but like the attempt by the Venetian Bandiera brothers to start a revolt in Calabria in 1844 these were unsuccessful. As tensions rose, the moderates for the first time broke cover and appealed to the rulers to take initiatives to stave off the threat of revolution. One appeal that aroused great attention came from a former Mazzinian, the abbé Vincenzo Gioberti, whose clandestinely published treatise on *Del primato morale e civile degli italiani* (1843; On the moral and civil primacy of the Italians) called for the papacy to revive the political leadership it had given in the Middle Ages. This improbable proposal aroused great enthusiasm but alarmed the supporters of the Piedmontese monarchy, who argued that only a secular prince could provide leadership for the establishment of an independent confederation of Italian rulers, a role that the king of Piedmont, Charles Albert (1798–1849; r. 1831–1849), was admirably qualified to fulfill. But in 1846 the champions of the house of Savoy were upstaged by the election of a new pope, Pius IX, who for no very good reason was believed to be sympathetic to reform.

THE ITALIAN REVOLUTIONS, 1848–1849

The election of Pius IX heightened expectations throughout Italy, and in the Papal State the new government quickly lost control. Political demonstrations and the clandestine press spread into neighboring Tuscany, forcing the grand duke to make political concessions in the fall of 1847. It only needed a riot during the festivities of Palermo's patron saint, Santa Rosalia, for the city to become the theater for the first of the European revolutions in January 1848. Hoping to contain the political protests that quickly spread to the mainland, the king of Naples conceded a constitution (29 January), a lead followed by the grand duke of Tuscany (11 February), the king of Piedmont (5 March), and finally by the pope (14 March). But the situation took a new turn when Vienna was overwhelmed by revolution in March. Faced by militant protests in Venice and then by a popular insurrection in Milan that lasted five days (18–22 March) the Austrian forces made a tactical retreat.

With the Austrians temporarily gone, the conflicting aims of the Italian rulers and nationalists quickly became apparent. In March Piedmont declared war on Austria to liberate Lombardy, but many Lombards feared this was just an excuse for the expansionist ambitions of King Charles Albert. In April the unlikely idea that the pope might lead the nationalist cause collapsed when Pius IX denounced the war against Austria. Then on 15 May the king of the Two Sicilies, Ferdinand II, ordered his army to fire on the delegates that were gathered for the opening of the new parliament in Naples and suspended the constitution.

Events took a more radical turn when in July an Austrian army defeated Charles Albert at Custoza. Mazzini called for a war of the people to take over from the war of the princes, but there was little response. Daniele Manin, the moderate leader of the republican government in Venice, shared none of Mazzini's aims, which found little support until more leaders came to power in Tuscany and Piedmont. But the republicans' best opportunity came in November when the moderate provisional government set up by Pius IX in Rome collapsed. Disguised as a woman the pope fled (24 November), appealing to the Catholic powers for help.

Republicans and radicals from all over Italy now headed for Rome, where a republic was proclaimed in February 1849. Mazzini was a member of the new government which introduced some important welfare measures. However not only the rulers of Naples and Spain but also the government of the French Republic had already dispatched armies to restore the pope to his capital.

The city's defense was organized by Giuseppe Garibaldi (1807–1882), and after a long siege the French finally occupied Rome on 3 July.

ITALY AND EUROPEAN POLITICS, 1849–1859

The revolutions were over. In the spring of 1849 Austrians returned in force. After suffering a second shattering defeat (at Novara, 23 March), Charles Albert abdicated in favor of his son Victor Emmanuel II (1820–1878). In Tuscany the grand duke was restored and after a long siege and an aerial bombardment Venice capitulated in August. In the south, the Bourbon army regained control of Palermo in May. By summer constitutional government survived only in Piedmont, and for the next decade Turin became a haven for political refugees from all over Italy. Under the leadership of Count Cavour (Camillo Benso; 1810–1861), liberal reforms were introduced that made Piedmont attractive to foreign investors.

Victor Emmanuel grudgingly conceded some power to parliament, mainly because the liberals supported his expansionist ambitions while the Piedmontese conservatives and the church were pro-Austrian. But Victor Emmanuel's cynical exploitation of the nationalist cause paid rich dividends, and when the Crimean War (1854–1856) revealed the weakness of the Austrians the Piedmontese government set out to exploit the expansionist ambitions of the new French emperor, Louis-Napoleon Bonaparte (Napoleon III).

The French army that had restored Pius IX in 1849 was still in Rome, but Louis-Napoleon understood that backing the Piedmontese monarchy against Austria offered important opportunities for expanding France's political influence on the Italian peninsula. An attempt on Louis-Napoleon's life by the Italian nationalist Felice Orsini in January 1858 marked the beginning of diplomatic contacts between Turin and Paris that resulted in a secret meeting between the French emperor and Cavour at the lakeside resort of Plombières in July 1858. A joint war against Austria was planned, after which Italy would be divided into four states. In January 1859 the French and Piedmontese rulers signed a secret treaty, and in April, Cavour finally provoked the Austrians into issuing an ultimatum. After three very bloody battles—Magenta (4 June), Solferino, and San Martino (both 24 June)—that were fought mainly by French troops, Louis-Napoleon abruptly ended the war without consulting his ally when the Austrians agreed to abandon Lombardy.

The Peace of Villafranca (11 July) outraged the Italian nationalists because the Veneto remained under Austrian control. Cavour's supporters, who in 1857 founded the Italian National Society, had in the meantime been busy staging fake revolutions in Tuscany, the central duchies, and the northern parts of the Papal State in order to create a legitimate pretext for plebiscites in favor of annexation to Piedmont. But the situation was very confused, not least because Britain now also intervened to ensure that France made no territorial gains in Italy.

THE SOUTH AND UNIFICATION

Cavour had resigned after Villafranca but returned to office in January 1860. In March a plebiscite approving annexation to Piedmont won overwhelming support in Tuscany, but in April the government announced that France was to receive Nice and Savoy. The nationalists were outraged, but when it was learned that an insurrection against Bourbon rule had broken out in Palermo the radicals and democrats seized the opportunity to relaunch the project for the unification of the whole peninsula and overturn the monarchist solution worked out by Cavour and Victor Emmanuel in the north. The hopes of the radicals rode therefore on the ramshackle steamboats that in May carried Garibaldi's famous thousand volunteers to Sicily, where they disembarked at Marsala. Garibaldi's defeat of a small Bourbon force at Calatafimi was the signal for peasant insurrections throughout the island, which threatened the lines of communication of the Bourbon army and forced a retreat. In August, Garibaldi crossed to the mainland, where the landowners abandoned the Bourbon monarchy and were taking control of local government. The young king of Naples, Francis II, decided to make a stand north of the capital, and on 7 September, Garibaldi entered Naples unopposed.

From Turin, Cavour followed events with growing alarm. He had tried unsuccessfully to regain the political initiative in Sicily and then to organize a moderate coup in Naples to forestall Garibaldi. Cavour's aim was to prevent the radicals from gaining control of the south and to prevent Garibaldi from attempting to liberate Rome, which might easily lead to war with France since Louis-Napoleon had guaranteed the pope's safety and still had an army in Rome. To avoid both eventualities Cavour acted decisively. In September 1860 a Piedmontese army headed by Victor Emmanuel invaded the Papal State ostensibly to protect the pope but in reality to block Garibaldi's advance. With Garibaldi's Redshirts in front of them and the Piedmontese army in their rear, the Bourbon army sued for terms. In what would later become one of the most celebrated scenes of the Risorgimento, Garibaldi and Victor Emmanuel met on horseback at Teano on 26 October, and Garibaldi loyally surrendered his command to the king. The danger that the Piedmontese forces would clash with the nationalists had been averted, and after hurriedly organized plebiscites, the southern provinces and Sicily, as well as the former papal provinces of Umbria and the Marche, voted for annexation (October–November 1860).

THE AFTERMATH

In 1861 Victor Emmanuel II was proclaimed king of a new Italy that was far from complete. The pope still held Rome and was under the protection of Louis-Napoleon. Venice remained under Austrian rule until Prussia's victory at the Battle of Sadowa in 1866. In the south unification was followed by violent rural insurrections, and in the operations against so-called brigandage in the southern provinces and in Sicily that followed, more troops were engaged and more lives lost than in all the Italian wars of liberation. In 1862 Garibaldi attempted to revive the campaign to liberate Rome but was stopped and wounded by Piedmontese troops at Aspromonte in Calabria. In 1866 Italy acquired the Venetian province, but other Italian speaking territories—notably the South Tyrol and Trieste—remained under Austrian government. In 1867 Garibaldi made another attempt to free Rome which ended in disaster at Mentana, and it was only after Louis-Napoleon's defeat by the Prussians at the battle of Sedan that Italian troops could finally enter the Eternal City on 20 September 1870.

Italy's unexpected unification was a direct consequence of the decline of the Habsburg monarchy and the rise of the new German Reich. Italian nationalists, not surprisingly, saw things differently: the new Italy, they claimed, was the realization of the aspirations of the Italian people to freedom and independence. The Italian people, however, had played little direct part in the Risorgimento and had little part in the new kingdom since fewer than 2 percent of the population met the literacy or property requirements needed to vote in 1861. The elites were also divided. Until the end of his life in 1872, Mazzini—who believed the triumph of the Piedmontese monarchy to be a travesty of the ideals of the Risorgimento—was under sentence of death for treason while Pope Pius IX had declared himself the prisoner of the Vatican, denounced the new state as the negation of God, and forbade practicing Catholics from voting or holding public office.

Long after unification, the Risorgimento was the battlefield on which Italians fought out their national and political identities. Unification proved to be a point of departure, not arrival, and the task of creating of an independent nation-state imposed heavy burdens on a country whose unity was recent and fragile and whose economic resources were slender. It was made more difficult by the changes that accompanied the emergence of mass society and intensified rivalries among the leading industrial states. When Italy's parliamentary democracy collapsed after World War I it was often claimed that fascism was a consequence of the defects of the Risorgimento, but twenty-first-century historians are wary of the retrospective logic and determinist assumptions that lie behind such a judgment. The burdens of independence were heavy, but the differences between Italy and its western European neighbors in the nineteenth century have been frequently exaggerated, and, although in many ways an accidental outcome of the Risorgimento, Italy's unification has proved remarkably resilient.

See also **Cavour, Count (Camillo Benso); Charles Albert; Garibaldi, Giuseppe; Italy; Kingdom of the Two Sicilies; Mazzini, Giuseppe; Milan; Papal State; Piedmont-Savoy; Rome; Venice; Victor Emmanuel II.**

BIBLIOGRAPHY

Davis, John A., ed. *Italy in the Nineteenth Century.* Oxford, U.K., 2000.

Mack Smith, Denis. *Cavour.* London, 1985.

——. *Mazzini.* New Haven, Conn., 1994.

Woolf, Stuart. *A History of Italy 1700–1860: The Social Constraints of Political Change.* London, 1979.

JOHN A. DAVIS

ROBESPIERRE, MAXIMILIEN (1758–1794), French revolutionist.

Maximilien Robespierre's life before 1789, like so many other revolutionaries, was unexceptional and showed no hints of the future Jacobin. He was born on 6 May 1758 in Arras, France, the capital of the old province of Artois, four months after his parents married. His mother died when Maximilien-François-Marie-Isidore (to give him his full name) was six. Two years later his father abandoned his law practice and his children, who were raised by relatives.

Robespierre showed early intellectual aptitude and entered the *collège* of Arras with the support of charitable foundations. At eleven he won a much-coveted scholarship to Louis-le-Grand in Paris, one of the best schools in France. There he was lonely and studious, and performed brilliantly, winning several academic prizes. His accomplishments in Latin earned him the sobriquet the Roman, and he was chosen to deliver an address in that learned language to Louis XVI and his queen as they returned from coronation ceremonies at Reims Cathedral (1775). Robespierre graduated from Louis-le-Grand with a gift of 600 livres from the school's board, in recognition of "good conduct during twelve years ... and in his examination in philosophy and law." He returned to his natal town to open a law practice and look after his brother, Augustin, and his sister Charlotte.

The turbulent 1780s passed tranquilly for Robespierre in Arras. He enjoyed modest success in his practice, the high point coming in 1783 with a case involving the installation of one of the first lightning rods in the province. Robespierre defended modern science against superstition, and the case brought him some small renown. The views expressed in his other cases were enlightened, moderately advanced, but by no means radical. He was considered a solid citizen and member of the bar of regular habits, with literary tastes—he wrote some mediocre verse and contributed to an essay contest—and a devotion to the care of his siblings. He turned thirty in 1788, the fateful year in which the Estates-General were summoned.

REVOLUTIONARY TRANSFORMATION

The Revolution transformed Robespierre. He published a political pamphlet (*À la nation artésienne* [To the nation of Artois]) stumped for a seat in the Third Estate, to which he was elected, and was active in helping a local guild prepare its *cahiers de doléances* (list of grievances). He left for Versailles with his two worn suits, a few shirts, and some shabby culottes, and printed copies of his briefs and the unexceptional bland pamphlet on representation he had written in 1788.

The obscure deputy first addressed the Third Estate on 18 May 1789, two weeks after it assembled in Versailles. From then on he spoke regularly. He defended the people, equality, and democracy; opposed any property qualification for voting; distrusted the rich, the nobility, the church hierarchy, and the court; and made frequent references to himself. He supported the Declaration of the Rights of Man and of the Citizen of July 1789, opposed giving the king a veto over legislation, and was on the democratic side of virtually all the issues of the day. He also condemned the death penalty as unworthy of an enlightened people, an opinion that would come back to embarrass him. These views isolated him in the National (Constituent) Assembly and earned him a reputation for democratic radicalism.

As an orator he had a high and weak voice, his gestures at the podium were restrained and even stiff, and he almost always read from a carefully prepared manuscript. His foes accused him of "speaking out the window" rather than to the assembled deputies—one of his many democratic instincts—and attributed his self-references to vanity. This last point needs nuance. Robespierre identified himself completely with the Revolution. He would later say that he was no more than an instrument of the Revolution and the people, who spoke through him. He insisted he was the embodiment of the Revolution. Even his health vibrated to revolutionary politics. He was often ill at times of crisis and returned to the struggle strengthened.

Perhaps his most brilliant speech and intervention in the Constituent Assembly (13–15 May 1791) was against slavery, and he also championed citizenship for Jews. Judged by his ability to persuade his colleagues, Robespierre was a parliamentary failure. Only one of the causes he supported in the Constituent Assembly was carried: barring deputies from sitting in the new Legislative Assembly. But his dogged consistency, intense conviction, and austere eloquence won praise from no less a figure than the comte de Mirabeau, the first parliamentary leader of the revolution. At the close of the Constituent Assembly when the new constitution was signed (September 1791), the Parisians embraced him and his then friend and ally Jérôme Pétion as popular champions. His reception in Arras was equally enthusiastic.

Out of office Robespierre turned to journalism and the Jacobins as an outlet for his ideas. He published two newspapers in 1792. The first of these, *La défenseur de la constitution* (The defender of the constitution), took the line proclaimed in its title: he advocated a strict adherence to France's first constitution as the true revolutionary course. He was converted to the need for another revolution only on the eve of 10 August 1792, when an insurrection overthrew the monarchy. His second newspaper, *Lettres à ses commenttans* (Letters to his constituents), began appearing after his election to the National Convention and continued until April 1793. In it he carefully published his major speeches, again with his democratic instincts reaching out for an audience beyond the walls of the Convention.

At the Paris Jacobins Robespierre rebuilt the club, disrupted after the marquis de Lafayette and his associates left during the Constituent Assembly. It is important to note that the most significant debates on whether or not to declare war took place at the Jacobins not in the Legislative Assembly. Robespierre, increasingly isolated, argued against an expansionist and messianic war on Europe before the gains of the Revolution were solidified at home. War was declared on 20 April 1792. Robespierre's opponents, who would become the so-called Girondist faction, left the Jacobins.

NATIONAL CONVENTION AND THE COMMITTEE OF PUBLIC SAFETY

Once the monarchy was gone Robespierre soon became the interpreter of the insurrection and the voice of the new republic. He was overwhelmingly elected to the Paris delegation of the National Convention. He quickly emerged as the spokesman for Paris, for his deputation (the most radical in the Convention), and for the Jacobins. He fended off personal attacks, called for a veil of oblivion to be drawn over the ghastly September Massacres when

Maximilien Robespierre. Anonymous portrait, c. 1792. © ARCHIVO ICONOGRAFICO, S.A./CORBIS

half the prison population was slaughtered, and led the regicide attack against Louis XVI. He shared with his young disciple Louis de Saint-Just the extremist view that the king should be summarily executed and not tried. Despite his importance he held no appointment in the National Convention and sat on no committees until he was elected one of the twelve members of the Committee of Public Safety on 27 July 1793, a position he would hold for precisely a year.

In appearance and demeanor he was a man of the *ancien régime*. His personal habits were austere and thought "republican," his ideas were radically democratic, but he dressed simply in the old style, and his exquisite manners were remarked. His taste in literature ran to the dramatic poets of the seventeenth century and Jean-Jacques Rousseau (one of the powerful influences on his ideas as for so many other revolutionaries), and his only personal indulgence seems to have been a fondness for oranges. He was dubbed the Incorruptible, a sobriquet he did not himself use but that pleased him. The word carries not only the political connotation of a man above corruption and self-interest, but also suggests chastity. Both qualities are appropriate to Robespierre. The Jacobin Club, now shaped in his political image, became, with the Convention and the Committee of Public Safety, one of the synapses of Robespierre's power. He sat at the confluence of popular politics (mediated by the Jacobins) and the revolutionary government (dominated by the committee), receiving political energy from the popular movement in Paris, directing it to the National Convention and the committee via the Jacobins, and also reversing the flow.

Robespierre defended virtually all the radical measures taken by the Convention, and he was one of the instrumental figures in purging that body (31 May–2 June 1793) of the Girondists. Although personally aloof and formal he inspired passionate personal attachments and ideologically dominated the Committee of Public Safety and the Jacobins during the Year II (September 1793–September 1794 in the revolutionary calendar). His Manichean cast of mind gave his opinions certainty, and his distrustful nature made him at first wary and ultimately unreasonably suspicious. In addition to his instinctive understanding of the mechanisms of democratic politics, he had a gift for ideology, able to fit the complex flood of events of the Revolution into persuasive patterns of meaning and political action.

Of all the revolutionary work he did, his colleagues never forgave him for purging the Convention and eventually attacking Georges Danton and his friends. He is intimately associated with (and unfairly blamed for) the Terror. He did not invent the Terror nor was he himself a bloodthirsty man. But he did provide the year of Terror (declared the order of the day on 10 October 1793) with a philosophical pedigree in his *Rapport sur les principes de morale politique qui doivent guider la Convention nationale* ... (Report on the moral principles that must guide the National Convention ... ; February 1794). Hitherto the idea of virtue (*virtù*) had meant civic responsibility and was considered by the theorist Montesquieu (in *The Spirit of Laws*, 1748) to be the essence of a republic. Robespierre quite originally and chillingly wed virtue to Terror, sought to create a Republic of Virtue through Terror, and never turned aside from the bloody course of revolutionary politics he advocated.

His personal and political popularity, based on his ability to articulate the ideology of the Revolution as it unfolded and on his personal rectitude, which he often mentioned, remained intact until the spring of 1794. In March he successfully attacked the popular leaders of the Parisian sans-culottes, and in the first week of April he turned on Danton and his friends. Ironically, the elimination of these enemies and rivals isolated Robespierre and the Jacobins from the source of their political authority: the *menu peuple,* the Parisian sans-culottes. Although a brilliant political tactician, Robespierre was apparently unaware of how vulnerable he had now become. His colleague Saint-Just, however, said the "revolution was frozen."

Long opposed to the atheists whose dechristianizing zeal often turned to vandalism against churches as well as bullying priests and the pious, Robespierre countered with his least-characteristic and -popular political innovation: the cult of the Supreme Being. In a huge festival on the Champ-de-Mars (8 June 1794), orchestrated by the great Jacobin painter Jacques-Louis David, Robespierre declared the existence of the Supreme Being and offered the cult as a civic religion to replace Christianity and trump atheism. Based on the ideas of Rousseau and the Deist traditions of the century, it proved unpopular and a bit ridiculous. To all who thought the Revolution was anti-Christian, and there were many, Robespierre became anathema.

FALL FROM POWER AND EXECUTION

His fall came about because it was the only means of ending the Terror that most of the deputies could agree upon. Robespierre was unaccountably absent from the Committee of Public Safety for some weeks in late June 1794, at the height of the Terror. When he returned he delivered his last speech to the Convention, on 26 July, in which he threatened more Terror to root out those currently in the government who sought to destroy the Revolution. The following day (9 Thermidor, Year II) he was shouted down by the Convention, declared an outlaw, and took refuge in the Hôtel de Ville (City Hall). The expected Paris uprising to rescue Robespierre and his friends did not come off. As the police burst into the Hôtel de Ville he shot himself in the jaw, but he survived the suicide attempt. He was executed the next day, and more than a hundred of his followers were hunted down and guillotined.

From the time of his death to the present he has remained the most controversial figure of the French Revolution. There is no statue or street in Paris dedicated to Robespierre, and only in the 1980s was a new Métro subway station named for him. He is, in many ways, the most representative Jacobin and has thus become the epicenter for all the passionate debates on the Revolution.

See also **Danton, Georges-Jacques; French Revolution; Jacobins; Reign of Terror.**

BIBLIOGRAPHY

Primary Sources

Société des Études Robespierristes. *Œuvres complètes de Maximilien Robespierre.* 10 vols. Paris, 1910–1967.

Secondary Sources

Gallo, Max. *Robespierre the Incorruptible: A Psycho-biography.* Translated by Raymond Rudorff. New York, 1971.

Jordan, David P. *The Revolutionary Career of Maximilien Robespierre.* New York, 1985.

Thompson, J. M. *Robespierre.* 2 vols. Oxford, U.K., 1935. Reprint, Oxford, U.K., 1988.

DAVID P. JORDAN

RODIN, AUGUSTE (1840–1917), French sculptor.

François-Auguste Rodin was born on 12 November 1840, in Paris. He was introduced to drawing at the age of fourteen. In 1860, in hope of becoming a sculptor, he vowed to enter the reputed School of Fine Arts but was refused three times. To make a living, he undertook rather tiresome decorative work as a mason, an ornamental decorator, and a chiseler, while attending at night a course on sculpture.

In 1863, Rodin met Rose Beuret, a young seamstress who became his life-long companion and bore him a son. In 1864, having studied ancient Roman heads, he submitted to the Paris Salon a work entitled *The Man with a Broken Nose,* which was refused under its original title but later accepted

The subject matter of *The Gates of Hell* is drawn from *Les fleurs du mal* by French symbolist poet Charles Baudelaire and from Dante's *Divine Comedy* through Gustave Doré's illustrations and William Blake's engravings. The design was inspired by both Ghiberti's *Paradise Gate* for the Florence Bapistry and Leonardo da Vinci's *Last Judgment* in the Sistine Chapel. The work provides the viewer with a suggestive and deliberately frenzied chaos of tormented, anguished figures. Those figures show an important aspect of Rodin's art: his opposition to the accepted academic insistence on the noble image of humanity. Instead he focused on the distress and anxiety of the human condition while at the same time celebrating human heroism in the face of sorrow.

as *Portrait of a Roman.* Between 1864 and 1870, Rodin set up his first studio in an abandoned stable while still working full-time as a decorator. In 1875, Rodin visited Italy where he encountered the works of Donatello and Michelangelo, effecting his separation from academism. While most of his contemporaries were still convinced that the block had to be skillfully sculpted to represent a commemorative figure or a precise event following the aesthetics of illusionist naturalism that had borne witness since the Italian Renaissance to principles of mimetic representation, Rodin deemed such ideas both outmoded and inadequate.

Two years later, in 1877, confirming his new anti-academic stance, Rodin began working on his first independent major work, a free-standing sculpture of a man, originally titled *The Vanquished,* which would be exhibited as *The Age of Bronze.* Despite its degree of realism, the work's reflecting quasi-impressionist, vibrant surfaces, which are formed in large part by the sculptor's most intimate thoughts and beliefs on the dilemma of the private human being in modern society, give evidence to the fact that Rodin wanted to express a new sensitive reality through the human body, and to expose it as a vehicle of unabashed sensuality. But it is that work's lifelike quality rendered through Rodin's novel modeling and his accurate depiction of proportion or anatomy, as well as his rendering of movement, that caused a violent controversy. In 1878, Rodin was accused of having cast it directly from the living model but an investigative committee cleared him of the charge.

RODIN'S MATURE STYLE

During the period between 1879 and 1890, embarking upon a vigorous confrontation with modern life, Rodin tried to create a new type of sculpture by using fragments to portray specific facets of life or partial depictions of the whole. In 1878, he completed two masterful works of expressive power, *The Walking Man* and *Saint John the Baptist Preaching,* the latter bringing him his first official honor from the Paris Salon, a third-prize medal. The French government awarded him a studio in the state marble depository. In 1883, Rodin began a tumultuous love affair with young Camille Claudel (1864–1943), a student of modeling who became his inspiration, lover, model, apprentice, and collaborator until 1893. After receiving a state commission for a large sculptured portal for the new Museum of Decorative Arts, in 1883 Rodin started working on his greatest masterpiece, *The Gates of Hell,* and for some thirty-odd years he worked on as many as 182 free-standing figures and figure combinations adapted from it. The emotional and violent content of *The Gates* set out to denounce the moral issue of Rodin's era. Thus, to reveal conditions of distress, anxiety, convulsive revolt, and striving, Rodin gave some parts of the portal a delicate finish, while leaving other parts undeveloped, and multiplied surface accidents and shadowy effects that arrest the gaze of the viewer.

In these works, as a way of dealing with problems of three-dimensional spatial relations or compositions, against the static heritage of classical sculpture with its mimetic norms and ways, Rodin addressed the question of an autonomous sculptural object, a nonacademic concept involving the significant interplay of nonrepresentational sculptural components or variables. Combining literary and symbolic themes with pure sculptural form, this mature artistic style was mainly characterized by a newly expressionist aesthetic that was based in the beliefs that the flesh is the sign of the spirit and that emotions are deeply rooted in the soul.

In that sense, through his use of suggestive emotion or feeling, symbolic distortion, suggestions of volume and movement, and through his amazing utilization of fragments, Rodin showed a very modern preoccupation with posturing, surface interactions and effects, nonrhetorical or nonallegorical gestures, an absence of ornamentation or allegorical attributes, and a vivid description of the subject combined with a newly found liberty of interpretation of its materiality.

While opening up new avenues for the sculptor and viewers alike, such experimentation drew a torrent of adverse criticism and aroused a great deal of controversy. Therefore *The Gates of Hell,* as well as most of Rodin's other public commissions, were deemed unsuitable by an opposition that could not make sense of his stylistic ideas. As a result, many of Rodin's mature works were left unfinished, or were never erected as planned, as only a few of his monuments went beyond the stage of sketches or models.

Besides working on *The Gates* and on related figures, between 1883 and 1900 Rodin created a series of busts of important people and artists. Also, in 1884, he completed *The Thinker.* That same year, he began a monumental sculpture for the city of Calais entitled *The Burghers of Calais* (1884–1886), which was only erected ten years after its completion and not according to Rodin's original design. Other great works followed: *The Kiss,* in 1886; a state-commissioned monument to French novelist Victor Hugo (1802–1885) for the Pantheon produced between 1889 and 1896; and a statue of French novelist Honoré de Balzac (1799–1850), arguably Rodin's most mature work, completed in 1898.

FAME AND FORTUNE

In 1889, in recognition for his work, Rodin received the French Legion of Honor. Four years later, the French state selected three sculptures by Rodin for Chicago's World Columbian Exhibition. From 1897 onward, while pursuing numerous liaisons with female students and benefactors, Rodin settled in the Villa des Brillants in Meudon with Rose Beuret, whom he eventually married in January 1917, near the end of his life. After the turn of the century, Rodin attained international fame in Europe and in America, and acquired considerable

The Burghers of Calais. Sculpture by Auguste Rodin, 1886, commemorating the sacrifice of six leading citizens of Calais who offered themselves as hostages to Edward III of England in exchange for an end to his seige of their city in 1347. VANNI/ART RESOURCE, NY

wealth through his full-length portraits and busts of the eminent personalities of the time. In 1900, at his own expense, he organized a complete retrospective of his work for the Paris World's Fair.

Before World War I, Rodin completed innumerable small-scale sculptures, drawings, and watercolors of nude women, dancers, and heads, but did not undertake a new large-scale commission. Inspired by the art of the dance, Rodin excelled at portraying movement and anatomical details through modeling and composition in his statuettes. In 1913, seven drawings by Rodin were shown at the Armory Show and two years later he participated in San Francisco's Panama Pacific International Exposition. Rodin died in Meudon on 17 November 1917.

THE LEGACY, THE SCHOLARSHIP

After his death, Rodin's influence on the next generation of sculptors was profound, even though many critics violently denounced his innovative sculptural ideas. Because of his singular combination of realistic characterization and fragmented modeling, Romanticism and modernity, they could not appreciate these seemingly contradictory aesthetic preferences.

To that extent, between 1910 and 1940, during the heyday of avant-garde European modernist sculpture with its emphasis on purely geometrized sculptural form, because of its literary and symbolic existential references, Rodin's art was seen as not in line with contemporary artistic trends. But beginning after World War II and through the 1970s, art historian Albert E. Elsen and influential American art critics such as Clement Greenberg, Rosalind E. Krauss, and especially Leo Steinberg showed a renewed interest in Rodin's experiments with fragmentation and with three-dimensional spatial composition. They recognized that Rodin addressed the issue of non-iconic, self-referential visual and plastic surface components in sculpture, thereby putting forth a new idiom that dominated twentieth-century sculpture until the advent of postmodernist art-making in the 1970s.

See also **Balzac, Honoré de; Degas, Edgar; Hugo, Victor; Realism and Naturalism; Romanticism.**

BIBLIOGRAPHY

Primary Sources

Bartlett, Truman H., ed. "August Rodin, Sculptor." *American Architect and Building News* 25 (1889): 687–703. These conversations between American sculptor Truman H. Bartlett and Rodin resulted from Bartlett's numerous visits to the sculptor's Parisian studio in 1888–1889.

Dujardin-Beaumetz, Henri, ed. *Entretiens avec Rodin.* Paris, 1913. In these conversations the aging artist looked back on his life and times.

Gsell, Paul, ed. *On Art and Artists.* Translated by Mrs. Romilly Fedden. New York, 1957. Shortly before Rodin's death, French critic Paul Gsell compiled this collection of the artist's writings.

Rodin, Auguste. "To the Venus of Milo." *Camera Work* 34–35 (April–July 1911). Translation of "À la Vénus de Milo." Rodin's first attempt at expressing his ideas on art.

———. *Les Cathédrales de France.* Paris, 1914. In this book published in Paris thirty-seven years after his first encounter with the Gothic cathedrals of France, Rodin explained his fascination for the size, scope, effect, and splendor of these monuments.

———. *Rodin on Art and Artists.* New York, 1984. Sculptor's wide-ranging comments on the meaning of art and on the relations of sculpture to painting, poetry, and music.

Secondary Sources

Butler, Ruth. *Rodin in Perspective.* Englewood Cliffs, N.J., 1980. Sets the stage for Rodin and his contemporaries. Contains historical articles and critical essays by Rodin himself, fellow artists, art critics, and specialists.

Cladel, Judith. *Rodin: The Man and His Art, with Leaves from His Notebook.* Translated by S. K. Star. New York, 1917. Early laudatory monograph of Rodin that dealt mainly with his love affairs and overrated their importance on his creative energy and impulse.

Elsen, Albert E. *Rodin.* London, 1963. In this thoroughly researched study of Rodin's life and art, the author set the standard in English for all future scholarship.

Grunfeld, Frederic V. *Rodin: A Biography.* New York, 1987. Well-documented popular biography on the life and times of Rodin.

Jarrassé, Dominique. *Rodin: A Passion for Movement.* Translated by Jean-Marie Clarke. London, 1995. Explores Rodin's major works through three basic dimensions of his art: movement, light and shade, and the fragmented figure.

Krauss, Rosalind E. *Passages in Modern Sculpture.* New York, 1977. The author discusses at length the modernity of *The Gates of Hell,* and documents its specific influence on twentieth-century sculpture.

Steinberg, Leo. "Rodin." In *Other Criteria: Confrontations with Twentieth Century Art,* 322–403. New York, 1972. First-rate critical reevaluation of Rodin's mature style, and use of fragments, by one of America's leading contemporary art critics.

MARIE CARANI

ROENTGEN, WILHELM (1845–1923), Prussian scientist, discoverer of x-rays.

Wilhelm Conrad Roentgen was born on 27 March 1845 in Lennep, Prussia (now Remscheid, Germany). During the Revolution of 1848, the family moved to Apeldoorn, Netherlands, Roentgen's home until 1870. He then returned to Germany, dying in Munich on 10 February 1923.

After earning a doctorate in physics from the University of Zurich in 1869, Roentgen worked at various German universities before becoming, in 1879, professor and chair of physics at the Hessian Ludwigs University in Giessen. There, he became increasingly well-known for research into the effect of electricity on gases and crystals, an investigative area that was revealing a relationship between electricity, light rays, and magnetism. In 1888, Roentgen provided experimental proof of the Faraday-Maxwell theory of electrodynamic power, which earned him an invitation to head the Physics Institute at the Julius Maximilians University in Wurzburg. He remained there until 1900, becoming president of the university in

1894, then moved to Munich to direct the Physics Institute at the Ludwig Maximilians University, retiring in 1920.

During his early years at Wurzburg, Roentgen focused his research on the effect of pressure on water and other liquids. In mid-1894, however, his interest was piqued by progress in the study of cathode rays, a surge of electrons produced when electricity passes through a vacuum tube. In order to familiarize himself with recent research in that area, Roentgen began repeating experiments reported by other physicists. It was the work of Philipp Lenard that led him to his groundbreaking discovery of x-rays on 8 November 1895.

An invention by Lenard allowed scientists to study cathode rays flowing out of a vacuum tube, in addition to rays confined inside one. In air, the rays caused a board coated with barium platino-cyanide to fluoresce, but since they faded quickly, the board had to stand inches from the equipment. Preparing to witness this phenomenon for himself, Roentgen switched on the electricity activating the tube but accidentally left the board propped some feet away. To his surprise, it was nevertheless glowing. Since cathode rays could not be present at that distance, the vacuum tube must also have been emitting another form of radiation. Unable to identify that, Roentgen himself dubbed it an "x-ray."

Over the next few weeks, Roentgen spent most of his waking hours studying x-rays. After determining that they traveled farther in air than any ray yet known to science, he wondered whether they would pass through solid objects. Earlier, the German physicist Hermann von Helmholtz had argued that very-short-wave light rays should do so. X-rays proved this theory correct, penetrating even metal, except for lead. Objects held in front of the vacuum tube caused shadowy marks within the fluorescence, and it was while testing a piece of lead that Roentgen saw the shape of his own finger bones, a chilling observation that temporarily made him doubt his own sanity. Would anyone believe him? Other scientists would need to see such a sight for themselves. Again, Roentgen drew inspiration from Lenard, who had reported that fluorescence from cathode rays darkened a photographic plate. The photographs Roentgen made to document his discovery of x-rays were sensational: the best known of them shows the bones in Mrs. Roentgen's hand.

In late December, Roentgen communicated his findings to the Physical-Medical Society of Wurzburg, which published his paper in its last journal issue for 1895. By the first week of January, the news was already spreading around the world. Roentgen's discovery sparked a revolution in both medicine and physics. So simple was the technology involved that the first diagnostic use of x-rays occurred on 7 January 1896, and physicians were soon also using them to treat skin diseases and tumors. The discovery also inspired other physicists investigating radiation: the atomic age was just around the corner.

Roentgen became a celebrity, receiving innumerable awards, including the first Nobel Prize for physics in 1901. Some people thought the honors more properly belonged to Lenard and other cathode ray researchers, whose work had led directly to the discovery. The Nobel Prize committee was struck, however, not only by Roentgen's actual identification of x-rays but also by the scope of his consequent gift to humanity. His observations had generated successful treatments for hitherto fatal or crippling diseases and injuries. "Roentgen's discovery has already brought so much benefit to mankind," said the presenter at the award ceremony, "that to reward it with the Nobel Prize fulfils the intention of the testator [Alfred Nobel] to a very high degree."

See also **Body; Nobel, Alfred; Science and Technology.**

BIBLIOGRAPHY

Gherman, Beverly. *The Mysterious Rays of Dr. Röntgen.* Illustrated by Stephen Marchesi. New York, 1994. For younger readers.

Glasser, Otto. *Wilhelm Conrad Röntgen and the Early History of the Röntgen Rays.* Edited by Jessie C. Tucker. Springfield, Ill., 1934. Translation of *Wilhelm Conrad Roentgen und die Geschichte der Roentgenstrahlen* (1931). Primarily concentrates on technology. Contains the text of Roentgen's three papers on x-rays, and a chapter of reminiscences by Margret Boveri, a Roentgen family friend.

Mould, Richard F. *A Century of X-rays and Radioactivity in Medicine: With Emphasis on Photographic Records of the Early Years.* Bristol, U.K., and Philadelphia, 1993. Contains an extensive and entertaining collection of illustrations.

Nitske, W. Robert. *The Life of Wilhelm Conrad Röntgen: Discoverer of the X Ray.* Tucson, Ariz., 1971. Includes a chapter on claims by others to have discovered x-rays.

"The Nobel Prize in Physics 1901." Available from http://nobelprize.org/physics/laureates/1901/press.html

L. Margaret Barnett

ROLAND, PAULINE (1805–1852), French feminist and socialist.

Pauline Roland was born in Falaise, in northern France. Her widowed mother, the town's postmistress, worked hard to give her two daughters a good education. Introduced to Saint-Simonian socialism by her tutor at the age of twenty-two, Roland embraced its dedication to "the largest and poorest class." She also welcomed its belief in women's "liberty" and its controversial claim that "the flesh" was sacred, not sinful. Roland moved to Paris in November 1832 to join the Saint-Simonian movement. She wrote for its *Tribune des femmes* (Women's tribune), the first newspaper produced by working-class women.

The Saint-Simonians' call for "the rehabilitation of the flesh" divided the organization and saw its leaders prosecuted for immorality. But Roland embraced the belief that women could use their sexuality to heal and moralize men. The two men who benefited from her ministrations fathered her four children, born between 1835 and 1845. Roland assumed sole responsibility for her children, asserting her independence despite her precarious finances. She wrote articles on history and geography for the *Encyclopédie nouvelle* (New encyclopedia) and the *Revue indépendante* (Independent review) and reported on women and children in the coal mines (1842). She also published histories of France and England and a series of articles on the history of women in France (1846–1847).

In 1847 Roland joined Pierre Leroux's socialist community at Boussac, where she ran the school and wrote for Leroux's *Revue sociale* (Social review). Absent from Paris in February 1848, she was not involved in the revolution or its feminist activities.

Woman is a free being, equal to man whose sister she is. Like him she must fulfil duties towards herself by maintaining her personal dignity beyond all reproach, by developing in virtue, by making her life, not from the work or love or intelligence of another but from her own work....Like the man she must fulfil family duties which are the sweetest recompense of other labours, but which cannot completely absorb her....Finally, woman is a citizen by right, if not in fact, and as such she needs to become involved in life outside the home, in social life, which will not be a healthy one until the whole family is represented there.

Letter from Pauline Roland to Emile de Girardin, April 1851, in Felicia Gordon and Máire Cross, *Early French Feminisms, 1830–1940: A Passion for Liberty* (Brookfield, Vt., 1996), p. 90.

But she attempted (unsuccessfully) to vote in the Boussac municipal elections. Returning to Paris in December 1848 she helped organize an association of republican schoolteachers. She was then involved in Jeanne Deroin's "organization of workers' associations," which aimed to reorganize the economy along cooperative lines. The government prosecuted the organization for conspiracy and for promoting dangerous ideas like female equality. Roland served six months in jail in 1851, publishing a defense of women's personal liberty from her prison cell.

Five months after Roland was released, a coup d'état effectively ended the Second Republic (2 December 1851). Although not involved in resistance to the coup, Roland was arrested on 6 February 1852. She admitted sympathizing with the resisters and was convicted and deported to Algeria. She was treated as a recalcitrant prisoner because she refused to admit guilt or plead for mercy. Her case received much publicity and she was released in November 1852. But her six-day sea voyage to Marseilles, exposed to winter weather on the open deck, proved fatal. She died at Lyons on her way back to Paris, on 15 December.

Roland's life epitomized the radical currents of her age. Her idealism reflected its romantic spirit.

Like many of her contemporaries, her socialism was imbued with religiosity and a commitment to women's rights. Roland's life also revealed a fundamental dilemma facing nineteenth-century women: legal marriage meant subordination to a husband, but motherhood without marriage presented major economic and moral difficulties. Roland came to believe that her choice of single motherhood was a mistake. But she never abandoned the view that one should put one's beliefs into practice and accept the consequences.

See also **Deroin, Jeanne; Feminism; Revolutions of 1848; Saint-Simon, Henri de; Socialism.**

BIBLIOGRAPHY

Primary Sources

Bell, Susan Groag, and Karen M. Offen, eds. *Women, the Family and Freedom: The Debate in Documents.* 2 vols. Stanford, Calif., 1983. Major collection of documents in English by women, including the Saint-Simonians.

Gordon, Felicia, and Máire Cross. *Early French Feminisms, 1830–1940: A Passion for Liberty.* Brookfield, Vt., 1996. Letters and articles in English by Pauline Roland and other nineteenth-century feminists, with contextual essays.

Moses, Claire Goldberg, and Lesley Wahl Rabine, eds. *Feminism, Socialism, and French Romanticism.* Bloomington and Indianapolis, Ind., 1993. Documents in English by Pauline Roland and other Saint-Simonian women, with contextual essays.

Secondary Sources

Barry, David. *Women and Political Insurgency: France in the Mid-Nineteenth Century.* Houndmills, U.K., and New York, 1996.

Berenson, Edward. *Populist Religion and Left-Wing Politics in France, 1830–1852.* Princeton, N.J., 1984.

Carlisle, Robert B. *The Proffered Crown: Saint-Simonianism and the Doctrine of Hope.* Baltimore and London, 1987.

Foley, Susan Kathleen. *Women in France since 1789: The Meanings of Difference.* Houndmills, U.K., 2004.

Grogan, Susan Kathleen. *French Socialism and Sexual Difference: Women in the New Society, 1803–1844.* Houndmills, U.K., and New York, 1992.

Moses, Claire Goldberg. *French Feminism in the 19th Century.* Albany, N.Y., 1984.

Offen, Karen M. *European Feminisms 1700–1950: A Political History.* Stanford, Calif., 2000.

Strumingher, Laura S. "Women of 1848 and the Revolutionary Heritage of 1789." In *Women and Politics in the Age of the Democratic Revolutions,* edited by Harriet S. Applewhite and Darline S. Levy. Ann Arbor, Mich., 1989.

Thibert, Marguerite. *Le Féminisme dans le socialisme français de 1830 à 1850.* Paris, 1926. This study remains invaluable on the relations between feminism and socialism.

Thomas, Edith. *Pauline Roland: Socialisme et féminisme au XIXe siècle.* Paris, 1956. The essential study of Roland's life.

SUSAN K. FOLEY

ROLLAND, ROMAIN (1866–1944), French novelist and dramatist.

Romain Rolland was born in Clamecy (Nièvre), France. His life spanned two centuries and he played a notable part in the history of his time, involving himself frequently in public debate.

Rolland's family left Clamecy in 1880 so that he could study in Paris. There he attended Lycée Saint-Louis (1880–1882) and Lycée Louis-le-Grand (1882–1886) and went on to earn his bachelor of arts degree and pass the *agrégation* in history at the École Normale Supérieure (1886–1889). He attended the École Française in Rome (1889–1891) and obtained his doctorate from Paris University in 1895, where he wrote a thesis on *Les Origines du théâtre lyrique moderne* (The origins of modern lyric theater).

Although resigned to a life of teaching, Rolland was always determined to write. His hope was that his work would express his vision of the world as summed up as early as 1888 in the declaration of faith, or "Credo quia verum": arising from nothingness, he asserted, Man partook of Being, of which he was but a fragment; his earthly life was merely a dream and true life lay elsewhere—beyond death. But how were these two realities to be reconciled?

As a professor at the École Normale, and later (1903–1910) at the Sorbonne, Rolland hewed fast to his literary ambitions, even as he taught the history of music. He began as a playwright, choosing subjects from the classical world (*Empedocles, Niobe, Caligula*) or writing what he called "tragedies of faith" (*The Siege of Mantua, Saint*

Louis, Jeanne de Piennes). None of these plays were produced.

Repelled by the literary and political atmosphere of the times, which he considered to be decadent, disillusioned, and in search of a faith, Rolland was drawn to socialism, which he felt held out the promise of renewal. He anticipated an era of revolutions but feared the violence that these upheavals were liable to precipitate. In 1897 he began a play on this subject, *Les Vaincus* (The defeated), which was never completed but which summed up his eternal dilemma: he was attracted by the heroic faith of revolutionaries, yet he could not embrace their violence. His enthusiasm nevertheless led him to write a cycle of plays highlighting the great moments of the French Revolution: *Les Loups* (1898; The wolves), *Le Triomphe de la Raison* (1899; The triumph of reason), *Danton* (1900), *Le Quatorze juillet* (1902; The fourteenth of July), and *Le Temps viendra* (1903; The Time will come).

Impressed by the productions of Maurice Pottecher's Théâtre du Peuple (People's Theater) in Bussang (Vosges), Rolland lent his energies to this attempt to create a theater that would serve as a "tool of social struggle." But these efforts came to naught, and after setting forth his thoughts on this experience in *Le Théâtre du Peuple* (1903), Rolland abandoned drama at least temporarily and turned his full attention to a project that he had been dreaming about for years: a novel for which he had already amassed copious notes.

It was Charles Péguy who made it possible for Rolland to embark on his great roman-fleuve, *Jean-Christophe,* by agreeing to serialize it in the pages of his fortnightly paper, *Les Cahiers de la Quinzaine,* which had already published the revolutionary dramas and the highly successful *La Vie de Beethoven* (1903)—the second of Rolland's "lives of famous men" (the first being *Millet,* 1902).

The ten volumes of *Jean-Christophe* appeared between 1904 and 1912. The first installment, *Dawn,* opens with a birth, and the series closes with *New Day*—the titles underlining the theme of the cyclical nature of life, of never-ending renewal as represented in the novel by the presence of the Rhine. By calling his German hero Krafft (strength), Rolland meant him to epitomize the power of life, which, though marked by much suffering, ends, echoing Beethoven, with a hymn to joy. From this point of view, *Jean-Christophe* may be considered a novel of education. But the work has another dimension, too, for Rolland placed his hero squarely in the Europe of the time: although German, Krafft visits France, Switzerland, and Italy in the course of the narrative. The author was thus able to paint a portrait of his era, and indeed a politically committed portrait. Predicting, in effect, the catastrophe then in the making, which emerged as World War I, the novel denounced the evil tendencies at work in each nation and constituted a last-minute appeal for European reconciliation. The novel's form was new. This was the first great roman-fleuve, tracing the entire course of the protagonist's life. Ultimately, however, it addressed the heart rather than the intelligence of the reader, playing above all on the emotions. Rolland himself saw the work as a poem—the poem of a life, or of Life itself—rather than a novel.

During these same years, Rolland completed his series of "heroic lives" with volumes on Michaelangelo (1906) and Leo Tolstoy (1911). His musicological work was represented by articles collected in *Musiciens d'autrefois* (1908; Musicians of yesterday) and *Musiciens d'aujourd'hui* (1908; Musicians of today). A study of Handel appeared in 1910 and *Voyage musical au pays du passé* (Musical voyage to the country of the past) in 1919.

Rolland's literary success (he was awarded the Vie Heureuse prize in 1905 and the Grand Prix of the Académie Française in 1913) won him international renown and allowed him to live by his writing alone. After two years on leave, he resigned his teaching post in 1912 and set to work on a new novel, different both in conception and in form from *Jean-Christophe.* This was *Colas Breugnon,* published only after the war, in 1919.

The coming of war in 1914 changed everything in Europe, and Rolland's life and work likewise took a new course. From Switzerland, he returned to the political struggles informing *Jean-Christophe.* In *Au-dessus de la mêlée* (Above the battle), a collection of articles published in 1915, he condemned the war, called for the belligerents to settle their differences peacefully, and became the voice of a passionate pacifism. His influence thereafter was substantial. In the same year, he received the Nobel prize in literature.

See also **France; Pacifism; Péguy, Charles.**

BIBLIOGRAPHY

Primary Sources

Rolland, Romain. *Jean-Christophe.* Paris, 1912. Reprint, Paris, 1966. The 1966 edition is definitive.

———. *Colas Breugnon.* 1919. Reprint, Paris, 1978.

Secondary Sources

Duchatelet, Bernard. *Romain Rolland tel qu'en lui-même.* Paris, 2002.

Fisher, David James. *Romain Rolland and the Politics Intellectual Engagement.* Berkeley, Calif., 1998.

Francis, Richard. *Romain Rolland.* New York, 1999.

March, Harold. *Romain Rolland.* New York, 1971.

Starr, William T. *A Critical Bibliography of the Published Writings of Romain Rolland.* Evanston, Ill., 1950.

———. *Romain Rolland: One Against All: A Biography.* The Hague and Paris, 1971.

BERNARD DUCHATELET

ROMANIA. Between the French Revolution and World War I, two major issues confronted Romanian elites: political independence and unification, and Europeanization. In a little over a century, Romanians united the principalities of Moldavia and Walachia, which formed the nucleus of the Greater Romania that emerged from World War I, and they gained independence for the new state. It was a century of great expectations: Romanians endowed the country with a constitution and parliamentary institutions based on Western models; they embarked upon industrialization and expanded their participation in international commerce; they experienced the rise of a native bourgeoisie, which assumed political and economic leadership; and they absorbed the intellectual and cultural heritage of the West and engaged in a wide-ranging debate about national identity and paths of development.

THE ROMANIAN CORE

At the end of the eighteenth century and in the early decades of the nineteenth, Moldavia and Walachia were under Ottoman Turkish suzerainty, as they had been since the fifteenth century. Unlike the lands south of the Danube, however, they had never been occupied by the Ottoman army and had preserved their own political institutions and social and economic structures intact. The War of Greek Independence beginning in 1821 and the Russo-Turkish War of 1828–1829 effectively ended Ottoman domination. A Russian protectorate, instituted by the Treaty of Adrianople (1829) and lasting until 1848, promoted political and social change, but at the same time aroused anti-Russian sentiments.

Intellectuals and politicians in the 1840s and 1850s were absorbed by the struggle to unite the principalities and free them from foreign domination. Educated in German and French universities and drawing inspiration from social thought and political movements in the West, these "forty-eighters," as they were known, shared the enthusiasm of Young Europe in 1848 for liberal and national causes and showed an unquestioning faith in the power of ideas to reform the old regime. But they badly misjudged the pace of historical change, and, in the end, they were overcome by Russian and Ottoman armies and conservative *boiers* (nobles) at home.

The discouragement of the reformers was only temporary; within a decade they had achieved union and virtual independence. Outsiders helped, if unwittingly. The Crimean War replaced Russian political predominance and nominal Ottoman sovereignty with a collective guarantee of autonomy by the Western Great Powers. Although the Powers insisted that the principalities remain separate, the Romanians elected the same man as prince of both in 1859, thereby bringing about union in fact. Prince Alexandru Ion Cuza (r. 1859–1866), a forty-eighter, oversaw the merging of institutions and in 1861 declared administrative union complete. The term *Romania* became the common designation for the "United Principalities." Cuza introduced legal and agrarian reforms and new electoral and education laws, but his authoritarian ways alienated key elements of the elite, who forced him to abdicate.

The arrival of Charles of Hohenzollern-Sigmaringen (Carol I [r. as prince, 1866–1881; as king, 1881–1914]) as Cuza's successor in the new capital of Bucharest in 1866 inaugurated a half-century of nation-building that determined the direction Romania would take down to World War II. Carol I played a decisive role in domestic politics and foreign policy. Eager to transform his new country into a modern state based on the Prussian model, he found it difficult at first to work within the political system created by the Constitution of 1866, which, drawing on the Belgian constitution of 1831, accorded primacy to the legislature over the executive. He also had to accommodate himself to the give-and-take of party politics and to the scarcity of resources of an underdeveloped country. In time, he and the leaders of the main political parties overcame their mutual distrust and developed a working relationship that ensured stability at home and an enhanced position in regional international relations.

At no other time perhaps was their cooperation so crucial as during the Eastern Crisis of 1875–1878, when a fundamental realignment of forces occurred in Southeastern Europe. Carol I and the Romanian party leaders joined Russia in war against the Ottoman Empire in 1877–1878, and were rewarded with the formal recognition of independence by the powers at the Congress of Berlin (1878) and the acquisition of the Ottoman province of Dobrudja. Nonetheless, Carol I and the political elite were reminded once again of how little Romania counted on the international stage: at the Congress they were merely petitioners, and they were forced to cede southern Bessarabia, which had been recovered from Russia at the end of the Crimean War, back to their erstwhile ally. Yet they gained sufficient self-confidence from the episode to proclaim their country a kingdom in 1881.

During Carol I's reign only two political parties counted—the Conservative, which defended the interests of the large landowners, and the Liberal, which represented the growing urban business and professional classes. It became customary after 1881 for the two parties to "rotate" in office; the king appointed the new prime minister, who then "organized" elections for a new parliament. No government thus appointed by the king was ever disappointed at the polls. It was government by oligarchy, as the mass of peasants and members of the incipient industrial working class were excluded from direct participation in the political process by high income requirements. Neither the Social Democratic Party, founded in 1893, nor any peasant party of the time became significant players. Yet a remarkable freedom of the press and right of assembly reinforced democratic ideals.

On fundamental issues of foreign policy, Liberals and Conservatives were in general agreement. To enhance the country's security and pursue its international goals successfully, the king and leading politicians brought about Romania's adherence to the Triple Alliance (between Germany, Austria-Hungary, and Italy) in 1883, mainly because of their admiration for Germany's military and economic strength. But Romania's relations with Austria-Hungary were never close, as the status of the Romanians in Transylvania and Bukovina, trade, and Balkan problems constantly caused friction. Relations warmed with France, for whom most Romanians had a strong sentimental attachment, and Russia, and in 1914 Romania chose neutrality rather than war on the side of her nominal allies, the Central Powers.

The new Romania experienced significant demographic changes. The total population rose from 3,917,541 in 1860 to 7,160,682 in 1912. The great majority was rural (82 percent in 1912), but the urban population grew steadily from 17.6 percent in 1860 to 18.8 percent in 1899, mainly as a result of migration from the countryside. Bucharest (381,000 in 1916) became the chief industrial as well as political, financial, and cultural center of the country. From an ethnic and religious standpoint, Romania was remarkably homogeneous. In 1899, 92 percent of the population was Romanian and 91.5 percent was Orthodox, most of them Romanian. Jews, who were generally treated as foreigners, were the only significant minority, numbering about 240,000 or 3.3 percent of the population in 1912, but forming 14.6 percent of urban dwellers.

Romania's economy was based on agriculture. The majority of the population depended on it for a living, and as of 1900 agriculture supplied two-thirds of the country's gross national product and three-quarters of its exports. Grain production for the international market became predominant, and by 1910 Romania was the world's third largest exporter of corn and fourth largest exporter of wheat. The majority of peasants, who provided

Postcard lithograph of Romanian shepherd c. 1906.
PRIVATE COLLECTION/BRIDGEMAN ART LIBRARY/ ARCHIVES CHARMET

the labor on large estates and their own small plots, did not share in the growing prosperity and rose up massively in 1907, but substantial agrarian reforms came only after 1918. As for industry, it expanded in the latter decades of the nineteenth century, but it was still mainly linked to the processing of agricultural products. Western investments spurred the growth of certain industries, notably oil and gas, electricity, and metallurgy, and contributed significantly to the development of a modern banking system and railroads. The Liberal Party, which sought to create a Western-style capitalist economy, strongly supported industrialization, but insisted that Romanians be in charge.

Economic change combined with growing Western influence in all areas of public life intensified the debate among intellectuals about national identity and models of development. Many, like the philosopher Titu Maiorescu (1840–1917), complained that the Romanians had borrowed wholesale from the West and thus had jeopardized the country's development by putting form ahead of substance. Others, the Europeanizers, insisted that

Romania had no other destiny but to follow the same course of industrialization and urbanization as the West, while their opponents, the traditionalists, argued that Romanians must remain true to their agrarian and rural heritage. Yet all were united in their determination to create a strong nation-state.

THE ROMANIANS OF THE HABSBURG MONARCHY

Substantial numbers of Romanians lived outside the core of Greater Romania. The largest community was in Transylvania (including here the provinces of Banat, Crishana, and Maramuresh), a part of Hungary after the Austro-Hungarian Compromise of 1867. In 1910, the Romanians in the region numbered 2,827,419 (53.7 percent of the population of Transylvania and 16.2 percent of the population of Hungary, excluding Croatia). They were Orthodox (34.3 percent) and Greek Catholic (23.7 percent). The overwhelming majority (85.9 percent) depended on agriculture for a living and were smallholders (78 percent had less than ten hectares). The Romanian middle class, though growing, was still small in 1910. Priests and schoolteachers formed the largest contingent, followed by members of the civil service and liberal professions; entrepreneurs engaged in large-scale manufacturing, commerce, and banking were few. Not surprisingly, the Romanians formed only a relatively small proportion of the urban population.

Romanian political life between the end of the eighteenth century and 1914 was animated by the struggle to secure rights equal to those of the Magyars, Szeklers, and Saxons, who were predominant politically and economically. Lacking political institutions of their own and recognition as a distinct ethnic community, the Romanians relied at first on their Orthodox and Greek Catholic churches to provide leadership and protection. Initially, Romanian leaders, mainly clergy, emphasized Roman origins and claims to be the oldest inhabitants of Transylvania as justification for equality. But in a monumental petition to Habsburg Emperor Leopold II (r. 1790–1792) in 1791, the Supplex Libellus Valachorum, they demanded rights because the Romanians were more numerous and contributed more to the general welfare than any other ethnic group.

Salutări din România.

Postcard depicting hay-making in Romania, 1909. Private Collection/Bridgeman Art Library/ Archives Charmet

By 1848, lay intellectuals had largely taken over leadership from the clergy. These forty-eighters were imbued with the liberal and national political ideals of the period and were determined to achieve full autonomy within the Habsburg Monarchy. They contemplated a possible union with Moldavia and Walachia, but they were realists who saw no immediate chance of success. Their reliance on the Habsburgs proved to be misplaced, and their movement, isolated and weak, disintegrated as the old regime was restored.

Romanian interests were ignored again in 1867, when the Austrian-Germans and Magyars divided the empire between them and made Transylvania a part of Hungary. By the 1880s the Romanians felt their very existence threatened as the government sought to transform multi-national Hungary into a Magyar national state. Romanian leaders—no longer the priests and intellectuals of earlier times, but lawyers, bankers, and businessmen—responded to the danger by founding the Romanian National Party in 1881 and organizing the Memorandum Movement in 1892 and a Congress of Nationalities

in 1895 to protest government restrictions on the use of the Romanian language and curtailment of the autonomy of the Orthodox and Greek Catholic churches and schools. They also turned to Vienna for support and cultivated relations with Archduke Francis Ferdinand (1863–1914), the heir to the Habsburg throne, in the hope that he would promote a federalist solution to the monarchy's nationality problem. They even negotiated with the Hungarian government, but on the eve of World War I neither side would compromise on matters they judged crucial to national survival.

In certain respects the Romanians of Bukovina, a province Austria had seized from Moldavia in 1774, resembled the Romanians of Transylvania. They were primarily rural and depended on agriculture for a living, almost all families making do with less than five hectares. The number of urban dwellers was small, and the middle class, consequently, was weak. Yet, on the whole, the Romanians of Bukovina were in a more precarious position than those in Transylvania. After 1880 they were no longer the largest ethnic group: 190,005 (33 percent of the total population) to the Ruthenians' 239,690 (42 percent), a gap that remained constant down to 1914. They were confronted also by significant Jewish (13.1 percent) and Polish (6 percent) communities, and the Austrian-German administration. Although the Orthodox Church strongly supported Romanian education and culture, it could not be the Romanian national institution that it was in Transylvania because the Ruthenians claimed it as their church, too. Intellectuals promoted Romanian language and history at the University of Czernowitz, the capital, but the multiculturalism of the province tended to dilute national cultures.

Romanian political activity in Bukovina never reached the same intensity and cohesion as in Transylvania. *Boiers* and intellectuals, who formed the elite, were few in number and divided, and only in 1892 did they establish a National Party. A strong national movement eluded them. Nationalists were anxious to strengthen the Romanians' position and railed against the continued immigration of Ruthenians from Austrian Galicia, while moderates urged cooperation with other nationalities and focused on improving the lot of the peasants. Few advocated union with Romania before 1916, a position largely due to the relative integrity of the Austrian bureaucracy and its recognition, in some degree, of ethnic individuality.

THE ROMANIANS OF BESSARABIA

From an ethnic standpoint, the Romanians of Bessarabia faced a more uncertain future than their brothers in the Habsburg monarchy. In 1812 Russia annexed this province of Moldavia between the Prut and Dniester rivers, and from then until 1917 it subjected its inhabitants to two of the main elements of tsarism: political centralization and cultural Russification. As the Moldavians lost control of their province they offered no effective resistance because they lacked adequate leadership. The majority of the *boiers* were pro-Russian, and as time passed they were assimilated to the upper classes of Russian society. The Moldavian Orthodox clergy was unable to maintain the Moldavian character of their church and use it to promote national interests because they were subject to the Holy Synod in St. Petersburg and were led by Russian or pro-Russian hierarchs. A Moldavian middle class hardly existed; Moldavians formed only a small percentage

of the urban population, and few belonged to the liberal professions or merchant organizations. The great majority were peasants who were poor and illiterate.

The consequences of Russian rule for Moldavians were striking. The ethnic character of the province changed under the continuous immigration of Ukrainians, Russians, and Jews. By 1912 Moldavians constituted only 48 percent of the population, down from 86 percent in 1817. In cultural life the Moldavian (Romanian) language was sorely neglected, and literary life all but disappeared. Education in the countryside suffered a serious decline, because of the lack of funds and the use of Russian as the language of instruction; only 18.2 percent of men and 4 percent of women in 1897 could read and write. Sporadic efforts by a handful of intellectuals to organize a national cultural life failed, and the main center of religious and cultural life became the rural parish, where some sense of Moldavian identity was preserved. A national movement of any dimensions was impossible until the Russian Revolution of 1905, when a brief period of liberalism enabled a few intellectuals to demand political and cultural rights for Moldavians. Nothing significant came of their initiative until the collapse of the Russian Empire in 1917.

See also **Austria-Hungary; Nationalism; Ottoman Empire.**

BIBLIOGRAPHY

Boia, Lucian. *History and Myth in Romanian Consciousness.* Budapest, 2001. A stimulating and controversial critique of Romanian historical thought.

Bolovan, Sorina Paula, and Ioan Bolovan. *Transylvania in the Modern Era: Demographic Aspects.* Cluj-Napoca, Romania, 2003. An indispensable investigation covering the period 1850 to 1914.

Dutu, Alexandru. *European Intellectual Movements and Modernization in Romanian Culture.* Translated by Adriana Ionescu-Parau. Bucharest, 1981. A subtle analysis of the Romanians' place in Europe.

Georgescu, Vlad. *Political Ideas and Enlightenment in the Romanian Principalities, 1750–1831.* Boulder, Colo., 1971. A valuable guide to Romanian thought in the early period of Europeanization.

Hitchins, Keith. *Rumania, 1866–1947.* Oxford, U.K., 1994. An investigation of modern nation-building.

———. *The Romanians, 1774–1866.* Oxford, U.K., 1996. A survey of the political, economic, social, and intellectual transition from Eastern to Western forms.

———. *A Nation Affirmed: The Romanian National Movement in Transylvania, 1860–1914.* Bucharest, 1999. An examination of the many sides of modern nationalism.

———. *A Nation Discovered: Romanian Intellectuals in Transylvania and the Idea of Nation, 1700–1848.* Bucharest, 1999. A study of the passage from a religious to an ethnic consciousness.

Jelavich, Barbara. *Russia and the Formation of the Romanian National State, 1821–1878.* Cambridge, U.K., 1984. A reliable guide to a controversial subject.

Michelson, Paul. *Romanian Politics, 1859–1871: From Prince Cuza to Prince Carol.* Iasi, Romania, 1998. A judicious survey accompanied by an exhaustive bibliographical essay.

Mitu, Sorin. *National Identity of Romanians in Transylvania.* New York, 2001. A model of analysis and synthesis.

Riker, Thad W. *The Making of Roumania: A Study of an International Problem, 1856–1866.* London, 1931. A fundamental work on the role of the Great Powers.

KEITH HITCHINS

Romanies pose for a photograph with their caravan, London, 1877. © HULTON-DEUTSCH COLLECTION/CORBIS

ROMANIES (GYPSIES).

The nineteenth century was of particular significance in European Romani history. Although the quest began during the Enlightenment to provide a legitimate history and identity for that population, ironically the same period saw the establishment of the romantic "Gypsy" image that remains so firmly in place into the twenty-first century. At the same time, the mid-nineteenth century saw the abolition of Romani slavery and the exodus of thousands of Romanies from the newly created state of Romania out into the rest of Europe and to the Americas, as well as the emergence of scientific racism that led ultimately to the attempted destruction of the Romani people in Adolf Hitler's Third Reich.

Romanies had arrived in the Balkans from Asia by 1300 C.E., and within two centuries had fanned out into almost every European country. In Ottoman-controlled territories their artisan skills, particularly in metalworking and weaponry, ensured a place for them in the economy, a status that by the fifteenth century had become institutionalized slavery in the principalities of Moldavia and Walachia. Elsewhere in Europe their foreign appearance and behavior, together with their being associated with the Islamic threat to Christendom, lay the foundation for an enduring anti-gypsyism, which was to emerge so virulently in postcommunist Europe at the end of the twentieth century and trigger a new migration to the West. Yet another factor was the lack of an identifiable homeland. In 1810 the German nationalist Friedrich Ludwig Jahn (1778–1852) wrote that "a *Volk* without a state is nothing, a bodiless, airless phantom, like the Gypsies and the Jews." Nonterritoriality marked both peoples as asocials, populations that did not belong. Even Charles Darwin (1809–1882), writing in 1871, contrasted Gypsies with "the *territorially settled* and culturally advanced Nordic Aryan race."

When the Romanies first arrived in Europe they were able to tell people that they had come there from India; but this did not become general knowledge and in time was forgotten by the Romanies themselves. At the popular level various hypotheses spread, some quite bizarre; they were thought to be survivors of a prehistoric race, dwellers emerging from the hollow Earth, visitors from space, or simply a population recruited from the fringes of European society that artificially dyed its skin and spoke a concocted jargon for purposes of criminal activity. Never referred to by their self-ascription *Romanies* (from an Indic root meaning "person"), many other names were given to them, most commonly *Gypsies, Gitanos, Gitans* (i.e., Egyptians), and *Zigeuner, Tsiganes* and *Cingaros* (all from a Greek word meaning "untouchables," from their perceived aloofness from the non-Romani populations). Stealing became associated very early on with the Romanies who, forbidden by law from taking up residence in a township, and refused service by shopkeepers, resorted to subsistence theft in order to survive. Measures taken to keep Romanies at a distance, even to destroy their existence, were sometimes surprisingly harsh; in 1830 the Nordhausen city council attempted to bring about the eventual eradication of the Romani population by taking children away from their parents for permanent placement with German families. A Rhineland hunter's diary from 1835 recorded the murder of "a Gypsy woman and her suckling baby" for sport in his list of kills, and whole forests were set ablaze during the same period to drive out Romanies camped there.

In the mid-eighteenth century, a student at a Dutch university observed that words in the Romani language (some of which he had learned from laborers on his family's estate in Hungary) resembled Indian words. This fact eventually found its way into a Vienna newspaper, and by the 1780s the first full-length book on the subject, Heinrich Grellmann's *Die Zigeuner,* was published. This coincided with Sir William Jones's famous lecture on the genetic (rather than random) relatedness of languages, which initiated the eventual emergence of linguistics as a scientific discipline. Because European scholars gave special status to the "classical" languages, and because Sanskrit was one of these, and because Romani was demonstrably descended from Sanskrit, ascertaining the precise origins of the Romani people and their language occupied a number of scholars throughout the nineteenth century. The prevailing theory regards Romanies as being descendants of a mixed

ethnolinguistic Indian population who were assembled as a military force to resist, but who were ultimately defeated by, the eleventh century Ghaznavid invasions, captives who were in turn appropriated by the Seljuks, who defeated the Ghaznavids in 1038 and who went on to occupy Armenia in 1071 using, inter alia, those same Indian troops to establish the Sultanate of Rum in the region of modern Turkey. Here, under influence of Byzantine Greek language and culture and through in-marriage, the formerly occupationally defined population became an ethnic one and their military lingua franca crystallized into the Romani language.

The nineteenth-century European domination of its overseas colonies and the prevailing urge to convert "heathen" peoples to Christianity led to notions of the biological and developmental superiority of Europeans over other human groups. Combining these socially motivated attitudes with the models provided by the new sciences of botany and zoology, a hierarchy of "races" emerged along with ideas of "racial purity." Race mixing was seen as necessarily debilitating. At the same time, it was recognized that the Romani gene pool included a considerable European component, and that the number of "True Romanies"—as the literature of the day referred to them, meaning individuals of presumed pristine Asian descent—was small. In the early twenty-first century there are no Romanies anywhere of unmixed Indian genetic ancestry; those criteria were mainly based upon physical appearance and way of life.

The ubiquitous Gypsy image was a consequence of the Industrial Revolution. By the mid-nineteenth century, social changes had scarred the land with coal mines and railways, and had populated the cities with an underclass of urban poor, grimly described in the novels of Charles Dickens (1812–1870) and others of that period. Artists and writers began to idealize the simpler, cleaner preindustrial days, and farmyards, meadows, and shepherdesses became artistic themes. Gypsies were increasingly being portrayed in the literature as having been unaffected by industrial blight, living as they always had in the countryside, subsisting on nuts and berries and the occasional stolen rabbit or chicken, mischievous but harmless and colorful children of nature. Being a closed, nonliterate society, the Romani population

Les camps-volants: Census of Bohemians in France.
Engraving by Henri Mayer from *Le Petit Journal*, 5 May 1895.
Always concerned about the presence of Romanies in Europe,
officials attempted to conduct surveys of their numbers in the
nineteenth century. PRIVATE COLLECTION/BRIDGEMAN ART LIBRARY/
GIRAUDON

western Europeans, were regarded as degenerate "half breeds" contaminating Europe. It allowed a non-existent category of "real" Romanies while justifying negative attitudes toward their mixed offspring who were, in fact, the actual population. In 1835, Theodor Tetzner referred in print to Romanies as "the excrement of humanity," while in 1850 Robert Knox, in his *Races of Men,* described Romanies as the "refuse of the human race." In 1863, Richard Liebich described them as "worthless life," a phrase which was applied to them by Richard Kulemann six years later, and which was to have ominous significance in Hitler's Germany.

Basing his ideas on Darwin, Cesare Lombroso published his influential work *L'uomo deliquente* in 1876; the work contained a lengthy chapter on the genetically criminal character of the Romanies, whom he described as "a living example of a whole *race* of criminals." In the United States, immigration policies dated 1883 and 1885 forbade the entry of Romanies into the country.

In 1886, a directive issued by Chancellor Otto von Bismarck (1815–1898) led to the creation of policies designed to deport non-German-born Romanies. In the early 1890s, the Swabian parliament organized a conference on the "Gypsy Scum" where the military was empowered to control their movements. In 1899, Houston Chamberlain published *The Foundations of the Nineteenth Century* supporting the German philosophy of its own racial superiority and arguing for a "newly shaped" and "especially deserving Aryan race." This was regarded as complete academic justification for actions directed at the Romani minority throughout the German-speaking territories. An information agency was established in Munich under the direction of Alfred Dillmann to consolidate reports on the movement of Romanies throughout German lands, and a register of all Gypsies over the age of six began to be compiled. This led in turn to the appearance of Dillmann's *Zigeuner-Buch* (the "Gypsy Book") in 1905, which laid the groundwork for what was to come twenty-eight years later. It maintained that the German people were "suffering" from a "plague" of Gypsies, who were "a pest against which society must unflaggingly defend itself," and who were to be "controlled by the police most severely," being "ruthlessly punished" whenever necessary. The notion of the particular dangers of a mixed Romani

itself remained unaware of this, and was not easily infiltrated by inquisitive outsiders, who as a result relied heavily upon their own imaginations to supplement what they wrote. Few people were in a position to refute the portrayal of Romanies by such writers as George Henry Borrow (1803–1881) or Charles Godfrey Leland (1824–1903), and thus the fictional stereotype became entrenched. This has grown to become so much a part of the contemporary popular image of Gypsies that it now constitutes a serious barrier to the recognition of legitimate Romani civil and political effort.

While the elusive "True Romany" was taking on a life of his own in the pages of various Victorian publications, the actual Romanies, numbering at this time some three million throughout Europe and most of whom differed little physically from and white gene pool, which Dillmann considered to characterize almost the entire Gypsy population, resurfaced in Nazi Germany, leading to Heinrich Himmler's (1900–1945) 1938 directive referring to the *endgültige Lösung der Zigeunerfrage*—the Final Solution of the Gypsy Question.

See also **Jews and Judaism; Minorities; Nationalism; Race and Racism.**

BIBLIOGRAPHY

Crowe, David. *A History of the Gypsies of Eastern Europe and Russia.* New York, 1994.

Fraser, Angus. *The Gypsies.* Oxford, U.K., 1992.

Guy, Will, ed. *Between Past and Future: The Roma of Central and Eastern Europe.* Hatfield, U.K., 2001.

Hancock, Ian. *We Are the Romani People.* Hatfield, U.K., 2002.

Liegeois, Jean-Pierre. *Gypsies: An Illustrated History.* Translated by Tony Berrett. London, 1983.

Marsh, Adrian, and Elin Strand, eds. *Contextual, Constructed and Contested: Gypsies and the Problem of Identities.* Malmö, Sweden, and Istanbul, 2004.

IAN HANCOCK

ROMAN QUESTION. The term *Roman Question* is applied to the long-running dispute, originating under Pope Pius IX (1792–1878), between the papacy (or Holy See in diplomatic language) and the Italian state. It refers to the problems arising from the latter's annexation of most of the old Papal State in 1860–1861 and of Rome with its adjacent area in 1870. However, it also refers to a wider range of issues, notably the official (but not altogether effective) abolition of religious orders and other ecclesiastical corporations and seizure of their assets, first under Piedmontese legislation in 1855 and then by the extension of this legislation to the Kingdom of Italy in 1866–1867. It was yet further extended to Rome in 1873, contrary to the original intentions of the government, but because of the bureaucracy's and the army's need for accommodation and in the face of pressure from Roman liberals and radicals. The Papal University of the Sapienza and the Jesuit Collegio Romano were turned into state institutions. The papal palace of the Quirinale became the royal residence. In more general terms, the secularization of the Holy City—that is, the former papal capital—whose strongly religious and clerical tone was now much diminished, was a painful issue.

The papacy refused to accept the annexations of its former territories. The core of its case was that a temporal dominion was essential to its independence and it evidently believed that the system of concordats, which it had established with various states, was now jeopardized. Pius IX condemned the first phase of annexations by the encyclical *Jamdudum cernimus* ("We have long perceived …") of 1861. The Law of Guarantees of 1871 stipulated the pope's autonomous position at law and the inviolability of the Vatican area, but did not accord the pope sovereign status. In other words, it treated his position as a purely internal matter, whereas the papacy was to insist that any settlement between itself and the Italian state must have international status. The papacy asserted that the guarantees under the aforementioned law were valueless and refused to accept the annual revenue, in compensation for its own territorial losses, for which the legislation made provision. Pius IX assumed the posture of "Prisoner in the Vatican" and deployed a barrage of Old Testament vituperation against the liberal Italian state.

Between 1868 and 1871 Vatican officials declared with increasing precision, albeit without strong publicity initially, that it was "not expedient" for Catholics to be electors or candidates in political, that is national, elections. The so-called *non expedit* became a firm policy. Catholics were, however, positively encouraged to participate in administrative elections—that is, to municipal and regional councils. Rowdy and sometimes violent anticlerical manifestations from the 1870s were cited by exponents of the papal line as proof that the Law of Guarantees was inefficacious.

PROLONGATION OF THE DISPUTE

The rationale of the *non expedit* shifted in due course. At the time of its initiation, it was believed in the Vatican that the new Italian state faced imminent collapse and it was probably considered that the *non expedit,* as an indication of refusal to recognize this state, would assist the process. However, it became increasingly obvious that the new Italy was there to stay.

By the time of the intransigent Pius IX's death and the accession of the more flexible Leo XIII (r. 1878–1903) in 1878, a pragmatic "middle party" had gained ascendancy in the Vatican and it was widely accepted in its upper levels that the *non expedit*, which was not rigorously observed by Catholics anyway, should be relaxed. A tentative process of détente with the Italian state indeed took place up to 1887. The pope hinted that he would be satisfied with territorial sovereignty over a small area in central Rome.

Negotiations collapsed in the summer of 1887 when the veteran anticlerical Francesco Crispi (1819–1901) became prime minister and the papacy moved toward a more intransigent line; Leo XIII had maintained a certain balance in his counsels between conciliators and intransigents, and the balance now swung rather more toward the latter. The rationale of the *non expedit* was now preparation in abstention, that is, through the build-up of Catholic lay organization, to form committed Catholics as a disciplined body of potential electors whose votes could be strategically employed to favor liberal candidates who were respectful of the Church interest and to thereby condition the policies of liberal governments toward the Church. Any premature relaxation of the *non expedit* might undermine such a strategy. A national Catholic lay organization, the Opera dei Congressi (that is, the institution organizing congresses of the Catholic laity), had been formed in 1874. It coordinated pressure groups drumming up support for the "Prisoner in the Vatican," collecting funds from the faithful to support him in his "august penury," and campaigning for Catholic values in society. It was also associated with social organizations, particularly mutual insurance associations and rural credit banks. Its strength was mainly in the "white provinces" of Venetia and Lombardy. From the 1880s, the Opera attempted to provide coordination at the national level for strategies in administrative elections. It was perceived that its social organizations could help to build a Catholic electorate.

A LIMITED DÉTENTE, 1904–1914

From the mid-1870s, the Church authorities and leading Catholic laymen had become increasingly concerned at the advances of the extreme left—that is, radicals, republicans, and socialists, who were strongly secularist and anticlerical, and who, by the early twentieth century, were pressing for a divorce law and for the abolition of religious instruction in schools. Following the unrest of 1898 and the government crackdown, which involved closure of the offices of the Opera dei Congressi, Catholics were particularly concerned to rebut accusations that they were subversive. Urgings by liberal moderates to allow Catholic votes to be freed to release support for candidates of order and exclude subversives on the extreme left were now received with more sympathy.

Pope Pius X (r. 1903–1914) succeeded Leo XIII in 1903; although a strong disciplinarian and theological hardliner within the church, Pius X was more accommodating politically than his predecessor. As Bishop of Mantua and Patriarch of Venice, he had established good working relations with the state authorities and with liberals. In 1904 he gave the first papal sanction to a breach of the *non expedit*, yielding to the pleas of Bergamese Catholic electoral managers that the faithful be allowed to vote in a closely contested political election. In 1904 he suspended the Opera dei Congressi, which had been plagued by disputes between somewhat radical Christian democrats and the old guard, and in 1907 replaced it by the Popular Union, in due course referred to as "Catholic Action," which was controlled by the bishops. Its lay leaders were clerico-moderates, disposed toward alliance with liberal moderates and a conciliatory stance toward liberal governments. The organization included an Electoral Union to coordinate electoral strategies, in local polls in the first instance. Giovanni Giolitti (1842–1928), the dominant figure in national politics between 1902 and 1914, dispensed favors to Catholic lay organizations in return for Catholic votes for government candidates. In 1913, Count Ottorino Gentiloni (1863–1916), president of the Electoral Union, concluded an agreement with the Giolitti ministry whereby Catholics would vote for government candidates who gave certain guarantees of respect for the Church interest. The Catholic vote was extensively deployed in the national election of 1913, to the advantage mainly of liberal moderates.

Under Pius X there was, perhaps, not so much a détente in Church-state relations as a growing conservative consensus in the face of disorder and the advances of the extreme left, a consensus within which committed Catholics and liberal moderates were moving closer together. Pius X, like Leo XIII, had avoided extremist postures on the Roman Question, but it remained unresolved. Hard-line clericalists, notably the Jesuit writers of the journal *La Civiltà Cattolica*, were determined to keep the issue alive. They raised the specter that if the extreme left came to power, the Law of Guarantees would not protect the papacy.

See also **Crispi, Francesco; Italy; Leo XIII; Papal State; Pius IX.**

BIBLIOGRAPHY

Coppa, Frank J. *The Modern Papacy Since 1789.* London, 1998.

Jemolo, Arturo Carlo. *Church and State in Italy 1850–1950.* Translated by David Moore. Oxford, U.K., 1960. Translation of *Chiesa e Stato in Italia dal Risorgimeto a oggi.* Turin, 1955.

OLIVER LOGAN

ROMANTICISM. Coming on the heels of the French Revolution and the enormous political turmoil that event entailed, the European Romantic movement of the first half of the nineteenth century was in many ways a reaction against the methods and ideals of the preceding eighteenth-century Enlightenment. Whereas the Anglo-French Enlightenment displayed considerable coherence and consistency in its basic ideas, however, Romanticism often appears a loose collection of diffuse characteristics, if not a mass of contradictions. The movement had no institutional locus, or organizational identity, or central publishing project. It was "Romantic" to exalt individual subjectivity but also to champion *le peuple* and the *Volk*. It was "Romantic" both to reject neoclassical formalism and to hark back nostalgically to Greco-Roman art and mythology. Romantics embraced the abstract and the infinite as well as the particular and the singular. What the thinkers and artists of the Europe-wide Romantic era did share was a rejection of the Enlightenment's secular, skeptical rationalism. The early Romantic German composer Franz Schubert (1797–1828) thus begged "imagination" to free him from the scourge of the preceding "Age of Reason," that "empty skeleton without flesh or blood." A survey of Romantic ideas reveals a shared emphasis on a desire for mystery, intensity, and profundity, reinforced by a fascination with individual subjectivity in all its forms. Ironically, this feature was itself derived at least in part from the individualism of the Enlightenment ideal of free and independent intellectual inquiry.

Chronologically, the French philosophe Jean-Jacques Rousseau (1712–1778) predates Romanticism. (The movement is generally agreed to range from the 1780s to the 1840s, although its manifestations in the fields of music and architecture extended well into the late nineteenth century.) Yet Rousseau's valorizing of the psychological Self—"I may not be better, but at least I am different," the "pre-Romantic" author wrote in the opening paragraph of his autobiographical *Confessions* (1782)—his communion with the world of nature, his defense of the "common man," and his rejection of the pretentious city life of his fellow philosophes all announced the birth of a new model of thought and apprehension. Romantics spoke of the Self and its creative resources in powerful, at times ecstatic, terms. Whereas Enlightenment thought tended to emphasize the physical and intellectual mastery of the natural world, Romantic garden and landscape designs brought out nature's wildness, beauty, and inspirational qualities. Whereas the mid-eighteenth-century French thinker Denis Diderot (1713–1784) defined love as "the rubbing together of two membranes," Romantics sought the mystery and magic of sexuality in an extensive "cult of love."

THE ENLIGHTENMENT/ROMANTICISM DICHOTOMY

No generational dialectic in cultural history is more fundamental than the Enlightenment/Romanticism dichotomy. The historic divide pits head against heart. If in his influential *Discourse on Method* (1637) the philosopher-geometrician René Descartes (1596–1650) had famously quipped "I think therefore I am," thereby centering rational cognition as the quintessential human faculty, the Romantic retort might well have been "I feel therefore I am." Romantics preferred to imagine and emote rather than to analyze and quantify. Whether the Enlightenment was really as sterile and hyperrationalistic as some Romantics claimed, or this vision was a self-serving ideological construction against which a subsequent generation defined itself, remains an open question. Whatever its nature, the "Romantic rebellion against reason" was perhaps the most salient characteristic of the movement, one of the few features shared by nearly all its followers. Romantics were intrigued by mental and emotional states that transcended the orbit of reason—dreams, horror, fantasy, the passions, madness, death—or what the Swiss painter Henry Fuseli (1741–1825) called "the dark side of life." Scholars debate whether Romantic antirationality represented an actual rejection of reason per se or rather a plea to explore a wider spectrum of emotional experience. Present-day psychologists have gone so far as to contend that the Enlightenment and Romantic styles of sensibility map onto two fundamentally different personality types. But, for all its familiarity and convenience, this division was not absolute and can be overstated, especially in the German-speaking cultural world: in their lives and work, titans like Immanuel Kant (1724–1804) in metaphysics, Ludwig van Beethoven (1770–1827) in music, and Johann Wolfgang von Goethe (1749–1832) in letters traversed both periods and simultaneously display "Romantic" and "Classical" traits.

In keeping with this dialectic, the Romantic period witnessed the early formation of the so-called two cultures. After cohabitating comfortably in antiquity, the Renaissance, and the eighteenth century, art and science began to go their separate ways in the Romantic era. With its exaggerated intellectual claims and its drive to mathematize all human knowledge, science, British literary Romantics claimed, represented a set of methods, activities, and ideologies antagonistic to art. Thus William Wordsworth's charge that the meddling scientific intellect "Misshapens the beauteous forms of things / We murder to dissect;" William Blake's drawing of a godlike Sir Isaac Newton (1642–1727) methodically reducing the cosmos to geometry; and Samuel Taylor Coleridge's assertion that "Poetry is not the proper antithesis to prose, but to science." Yet on this point, too, there were exceptions: Johann Wolfgang Goethe, who created the weepy, proto-Romantic protagonist Werther in the mid-1770s, later published entire treatises on plants and optics informed by the best science of his day. To similar effect, the gifted, young British poet John Keats (1795–1821) was trained medically, and the French Romantic novelist Victor Hugo (1802–1885) hailed science as progressive.

THE ROMANTIC MIND AND THE EMOTIONAL SELF

As these examples imply, the "Romantic mind" is perhaps best manifested in the artistic works of the period; these are astonishingly rich and varied. In contrast to the formalistic neoclassical spirit with its academically mandated methods and standards, Romantic art brims with free-flowing, emotive motifs. Thus, the brilliant landscapes and seascapes by painters as diverse as England's J. M. W. Turner (1775–1851), France's Eugène Delacroix (1798–1863), and Germany's Caspar David Friedrich (1774–1840); the melodic and instrumental extravagances of Richard Wagner's operas; and the nature-based emphasis on intimate affective experience in the poetry of Coleridge, Wordsworth, Keats, and Percy Bysshe Shelley (1792–1822). The search for idioms of art that enhanced emotional expression generated entire new forms of music and poetry. The most original and affecting examples of these experiments in form occurred in symphonic and instrumental music: the rhapsody, nocturne, fantasy, prelude, impromptu, ballad, intermezzo, and tone poem were all compositional genres for orchestra or keyboard pioneered by Romantic composers such as Johannes Brahms (1833–1897), Franz Schubert (1797–1828), Robert Schumann (1810–1856), Frédéric Chopin (1810–1849), and Franz Liszt (1811–1886). Romantic songs for solo voice deploy a greater range of tones and harmonies than ever before in music history. In the world of painting, color and light rather than line and form, the eighteenth-century preoccupations, became all important. And in literature, Romantic aesthetic ideology deemed poetry to have greater expressive appeal than the "rationalistic" prose of the age of Alexander Pope (1688–1744) and Samuel Johnson (1709–1784). The ode became the Romantic literary form par excellence. Emotion, in the Romantic ideal, should be captured by the poet, composer, and painter; but it was also to be experienced by the reader, listener, or viewer.

Percy Bysshe Shelley. Posthumous portrait by Joseph Severn, 1845. A respected painter and member of the Romantic circle in London, Severn is often remembered as the friend who accompanied John Keats to Italy to nurse him during his final illness. KEATS-SHELLEY MEMORIAL HOUSE, ROME, ITALY/BRIDGEMAN ART LIBRARY

Along these same lines, the exploration of the emotional Self became a Romantic preoccupation. Literary "ego-documents"—autobiographies, memoirs, confessions, autobiographical novels, compilations of letters—cascaded from the European press during the Romantic decades. Fictional writings betray a sharp increase in the use of the first-person "I." The Romantic cult of the Self extended to the visual arts, too: the portrait as a genre of painting flourished under Romanticism, with a subject's individuality mattering more than their social standing or occupational identity. The Enlightenment, including its most important political documents, had spoken grandly and abstractly of "Man"; *Homo Romanticus* was above all a singular individual.

Of all the emotional states the Romantics lavished their attention on, two emerged as recurrent themes: melancholy and love. In France, the literary productions of François-René Chateaubriand (1768–1848), Alfred Musset (1810–1857), and Alfred de Vigny (1797–1863) feature tearful and introspective protagonists, typically males, who suffer from a vague disenchantment with life and the world. This was the style of the French *mal du siècle*, which presages mid-twentieth-century existentialism. *Weltschmerz*, or "world pain," the German literary counterpart, tracked back to Goethe's tragic lovesick hero Werther of the 1770s. This gloomy side of Romanticism reached its highest philosophical expression in Arthur Schopenhauer (1788–1860), the anti-idealist "philosopher of pessimism" whose monumental *World as Will and Representation* appeared in 1819.

Not surprisingly, in light of the movement's name, love was a second cherished Romantic affliction. *La grande passion,* as they called it. But whereas the Enlightenment construed love primarily as fleeting sexual titillation—not coincidentally, pornography as a genre originates in eighteenth-century France—Romantic-era writers probed the countless permutations of love: Platonic love, unrequited love, love between friends, love between siblings, doomed love, the love of god. For them, love was not only an extraordinary, enigmatic force but also an artistic inspiration. Prominent romantic liaisons among artists—John Keats and Fanny Brawne, Chopin and George Sand (Amandine Dudevant; 1804–1876)—characterize the period. Published love letters proliferated, and Schubert and Schumann elevated the love song arguably to its highest musical level. Here the generic and historical meanings of the word *romantic* (lower case) and *Romantic* (upper case) merge.

At the same time, Romanticism was not an ideology of feminism. The Romantic idealization of women excluded a vision of political and legal equality for the female half of the population. As scholars have shown, the best-known Romantic artists, overwhelmingly male, sought to embrace what they perceived to be the specifically feminine modalities of intuition and sensibility in their search for heightened creative capacities. Yet artistic and intellectual genius remained wholly masculine, in their view. Romanticism was gendered male, but as a newly feminized version of masculinity. Furthermore, the creative roles played by women in certain male Romantic careers—for instance, the personal and artistic interplay between William Wordsworth and his sister Dorothy (1771–1855) and between Robert Schumann and his wife, Clara (1819–1896)—were often striking. Mary Shelley's (1797–1851) ever-popular novel *Frankenstein* (1818) is a protofeminist Romantic critique of modern science's destructive pretensions to self-sufficient masculine creativity. The movement's most substantial challenge to the traditional norms of gender identity was probably its fascination with the intermixture of masculine and feminine elements in history, culture, and biography—"Romantic androgyny," as one scholar has called it.

NATURE MYSTICISM

Another feature of Romanticism was nature mysticism. The Enlightenment world had been centered in the cities; it was nothing if not cosmopolitan, and its most characteristic organization had been the group salon. In contrast, self-styled Romantics preferred the country to the city. This was the age of the rural walking tour. Emblematically, Rousseau, in a much-discussed episode, abandoned Paris, the epicenter of the Enlightenment with its overcivilized *salonnières,* and retreated to an island in Lake Geneva. There he undertook his "reveries of a solitary walker." In Britain, the literary return to nature is best exemplified by Wordsworth, who in 1799 settled at Grasmere in the Lake District of the northwest of England. He and his fellow Romantics Coleridge and Robert Southey (1774–1843), who lived nearby, became known as the Lake Poets. From Dove Cottage, Grasmere, Wordsworth took long daily walks through the lovely, rolling countryside, poetizing upon returning home. (The poet's *Guide to the Lakes* of 1810 chronicles his countless outings.) This immersion in the natural world, Romantics insisted, was not just for its beauty; nature also served as a direct source of spiritual solace and artistic inspiration. The American counterpart of course is Henry David Thoreau's (1817–1862) extended experiment of living at Walden Pond, which in 1854 occasioned the most important Romantic prose work from the New World.

Appropriately, the Romantic exaltation of nature reached it highest expression in landscape painting. John Constable (1776–1837) and J. M. W. Turner, both Britons, depicted the natural world in two different moods: in canvases like *The Hay Wain* of 1821, Constable captured soothing, arcadian scenes of the English summertime, with its cottony cumulus clouds puffing across a rustic landscape. Turner's oeuvre was a good deal less tranquil. The most prolific of the Romantic painters and Britain's finest painter ever, Turner was powerfully drawn to "the Romantic sublime." In his famous sunsets, sea squalls, snowstorms, and shipwreck scenes, nature appears at its most awesome and destructive. Turner's and Constable's German contemporary was Caspar David Friedrich, whose empty, expansive landscapes at dusk and in the snow are often populated by only a solitary tree or person. They are highly evocative images.

For these artists, the neoclassical paintings of the previous 150 years, with their idealized forms and moralizing messages, ceased to appeal.

ROMANTIC MEDIEVALISM

The Romantic turning away from neoclassicism also ushered in a renewed interest in the European medieval period (which had been cast contemptuously by eighteenth-century intellectuals as "the Dark Ages"). In the field of architecture, a spirited "Gothic Revival" characterized the day. Remarkably, architects in the Romantic era applied a late medieval Christian/Catholic building style of tall spires, ribbed vaults, pointed arches, and decorative tracery to notably secular monuments in largely Protestant countries. Charles Barry's (1795–1860) and Augustus Welby Pugin's (1812–1852) Houses of Parliament, built along the River Thames in London during the 1840s, 1850s, and 1860s, is the best known example; the Oxford Museum (1851) and Manchester Town Hall (1877) are equally fine expressions. In France, an ambitious program to record, recover, and restore the nation's medieval heritage, foremostly Notre Dame Cathedral in central Paris, was supervised by Eugène-Emmanuel Viollet-le-Duc (1814–1879). Later in the century, the "mad" King Louis II of Bavaria (r. 1864–1886) had royal architects construct the spectacularly sited, fairytale castle Neuschwanstein (1869–1886) deep in the Bavarian Alps. Romantic neo-gothic style eventually reached rather kitsch proportions. In Britain, wealthy and eccentric landowners built pseudo-gothic "ruins" on their property, and extravagant private estates like Strawberry Hill, where the politician Sir Robert Walpole lived, and Fonthill Abbey were anything but livable. Neuschwanstein became the model for the original Disneyland castle in the United States.

New interest in the Middle Ages was not limited to architecture. Wordsworth chose the remains of Tintern Abbey, a twelfth-century Cisterian church in Wales, as the subject of his most famous poem. Neo-gothic elements also crop up time and again in such hugely popular literary works as Walter Scott's *Waverly* (1814) and Victor Hugo's *Hunchback of Notre Dame* (1831). The "gothic novel" emerged. The medieval legend of Faust in particular inspired not only Goethe's poetic masterpiece by that name (1832) but a symphony by Hector Berlioz (1803–1869), a tone poem by Liszt, and an opera by Gounod. In this same cultural atmosphere, medieval historical scholarship flourished, and the first accurate translations into English, French, and German of the great late medieval Italian poet Dante Alighieri (1265–1321) appeared.

SPIRITUALITY AND RELIGIOUS EXPERIENCE

Romantic medievalism points to a further feature of the movement: the return to spirituality and religious experience. Many Europeans who had left the church during the materialistic and anticlerical Enlightenment returned in the post-Revolutionary period. Voltaire's (François-Marie Arouet; 1694–1778) cultural standing declined. Nonetheless, the eighteenth-century scorn for religious dogma and church hierarchies by and large remained intact throughout the early decades of the 1800s. What typically interested Romantic Christian worshipers was the emotional and spiritual core of religious experience, including a direct relationship with the divine. Early in the new century, the German Protestant theologian Friedrich Schleiermacher (1768–1834) introduced a highly subjective "Theology of Feeling" that emphasized the presence of god within each one of us. More personalized, interiorized versions of religious experience came to the fore, including eccentric, individualized faiths like the English poet William Blake's prophetic, symbolic mythology. In figures such as the early German Romantic philosopher Johann Gottfried von Herder (and, for that matter, the American Ralph Waldo Emerson), philosophical pantheism integrated the worship of nature and the new religiosity; for them, physical nature itself incarnated a divine life-force. In France, a spirited Catholic Revival, abetted by Napoleon Bonaparte's Papal Concordat of 1801, marked the post-Revolutionary period and finds its most massive illustration in Chateaubriand's multivolume *Genius of Christianity* (1802)—"The Bible of Romanticism," as it has been called. But, once again, there are exceptions in this age of individualism: Schopenhauer's philosophy was overtly atheistic, and Shelley's no-holds-barred "The Necessity of Atheism" (1811) got the poet expelled from Oxford.

In Germanic central Europe, the Romantic spiritualist impulse even found its way into the new philosophy of the age. The metaphysician

Georg Wilhelm Friedrich Hegel's concepts of a "World-Spirit" and "the Absolute" potentially offered a version of God that was active in the very unfolding of history—or rather, "History"—in marked contrast to the distant and unknowable entity favored by Enlightenment deism. Hegel's concept of the "world-historical" event and hero, presented in his influential *Lectures on the Philosophy of History* of the 1820s, was part of a Romantic fascination with and reverence for historical geniuses. These larger-than-life figures were alternately political/military (Hannibal, Caesar, Napoleon) and cultural/artistic (Leonardo, Beethoven, Wagner, Hegel himself). The musical virtuoso, along the lines of the Hungarian pianist Liszt and the Italian violinist Niccolò Paganini (1782–1840), attracted swooning crowds who envisioned the performers as demigods. Hegel's contemporary in German philosophy Friedrich Wilhelm Joseph von Schelling (1775–1854) produced a theory that glorified the process of artistic creation itself.

"POLITICAL ROMANTICISM"

No dimension of Romanticism proves more difficult to determine than the political. Scholars have spoken of a "Romanticism of the left" and a "Romanticism of the right." Shelley rhapsodized in "Ode to Liberty" (1820). In 1823–1824, the British poet George Gordon Byron (1788–1824) perished famously in Greece during the War for Independence against the Ottoman Turks (although the cause of his death was unrelated to the war). And Delacroix's painting *Liberty Leading the People* (1830) and François Rude's sculpture relief *Departure of the Volunteers, 1792* (1833–1835) are quintessential visual representations of heroic republicanism in France. In parallel fashion, the pre-Marxist ideas of French social thinkers like Henri de Saint-Simon (1760–1825) and Charles Fourier (1772–1837) are sometimes labeled "Romantic Socialism." To a significant degree, the end of Romanticism corresponds with the failed democratic uprisings of 1848 in many European cities.

At the same time, however, both Wordsworth in Britain and the statesman and man of letters Alphonse Lamartine (1790–1869) in France moved rightward politically during their lives, and in the culture wars of the Napoleonic and Restora-tion periods, Chateaubriand believed that the Catholic Church was the greatest source of French national identity and stability. Edmund Burke (1729–1797), the Anglo-Irish critic of the French Revolution and defender of church and throne, is often dubbed a political Romantic, although the label applies as much to Burke's flowery, impassioned style as to his political ideology. Correspondingly, Hegel regarded the state as the greatest expression of the world-spirit, and the Hegel-inspired cult of the messianic leader surely conduced to nondemocratic governance, so much so that some mid-twentieth-century Cold War commentators tracked the origins of totalitarianism back to the Romantic era. This seems far-fetched, but there is little doubt that in central and eastern Europe, as well as in Italy, the Romantic period brought a great upsurge of cultural nationalism, which later in European history fed less benign nationalistic sentiments and activities.

RESISTING DEFINITION

Coleridge once neatly summarized the Romantic desire for new and intense experience when he wrote to his fellow poet Wordsworth that "the rationally educated" could not comprehend life's deeper dimensions. It was above all the quest for these more profound levels of experience that united the Romantic project. Inevitably, the vagueness and generality of this type of cultural consciousness leaves abundant room for confusion and contradiction. Decades ago, the historian of ideas Arthur Lovejoy recommended speaking not of one but of several "Romanticisms." The sheer diversity and multiplicity of the strands of Romanticism are themselves pertinent descriptive features of the period. Rejecting the Enlightenment belief that empirical and rational inquiry, patterned on the physical sciences, would lead to a single, complete, and universal "truth," the European Romantics generated an age of intense experience that deliberately sought to cultivate diversity and resist definition.

So what finally is the "meaning" of Romanticism? Observers have been posing the question for nearly two centuries. In its essence, should Romanticism be seen as a kind of Counter-Enlightenment? Or was the Romantic phenomenon, as chronology might suggest, the cultural and artistic working out of French revolutionary ideals? Or perhaps above all it was a reaction in the realm of philosophy and the arts to the rise of material, industrial civilization with its values of capitalist production and consumption. Does Romanticism represent the first inklings of our own age's postmodernism? And did it bring a salutary reintegration of the emotional and spiritual aspects of human nature or a dangerous collapse into mass irrationalism? Similarly, is Romantic emotionality fated to end in mawkish sentimentality and self-indulgent narcissism? Inevitably, these attempts at totalized interpretation all flounder in the face of the movement's endless internal variety. Regardless of these multiple readings, this much is certain: the Romantic movement of the years 1780 to 1850 was the richest and most far-reaching period in European cultural achievement between the Italian Renaissance and the cultural transformation of modernism.

See also **Barry, Charles; Beethoven, Ludwig van; Berlioz, Hector; Blake, William; Brahms, Johannes; Burke, Edmund; Byron, George Gordon; Carlyle, Thomas; Chateaubriand, François-René; Chopin, Frédéric; Coleridge, Samuel Taylor; Constable, John; David, Jacques-Louis; Delacroix, Eugène; Fichte, Johann Gottlieb; French Revolution; Friedrich, Caspar David; Gender; Géricault, Théodore; Goethe, Johann Wolfgang von; Goya, Francisco; Hegel, Georg Wilhelm Friedrich; Herder, Johann Gottfried; History; Hugo, Victor; Industrial Revolution, First; Lamartine, Alphonse; Liszt, Franz; Louis II; Michelet, Jules; Music; Napoleon; Nationalism; Paganini, Niccolò; Pugin, Augustus Welby; Revolutions of 1848; Rude, François; Sand, George; Schelling, Friedrich von; Schlegel, August Wilhelm von; Schopenhauer, Arthur; Schubert, Franz; Scott, Walter; Shelley, Mary; Shelley, Percy Bysshe; Turner, J. M. W.; Viollet-le-Duc, Eugène; Wagner, Richard; Wordsworth, William.**

BIBLIOGRAPHY

Abrams, Meyer H. *Natural Supernaturalism: Tradition and Revolution in Romantic Literature.* New York, 1971.

Barzun, Jacques. *Classic, Romantic, and Modern.* New York, 1956.

Bénichou, Paul. *Romantismes français.* 2 vols. Paris, 2004.

Berlin, Isaiah. "The Counter-Enlightenment." In his *Against the Currrent: Essays in the History of Ideas*, 1–24. Middlesex, U.K., and New York, 1979.

———. *The Roots of Romanticism*, edited by Henry Hardy. Princeton, N.J., 1999.

Bloom, Harold. *Romanticism and Consciousness: Essays in Criticism.* New York, 1970.

Brooks, Chris, *The Gothic Revival.* London, 1999.

Brown, David Blayney. *Romanticism.* London, 2001.

Christiansen, Rupert. *Romantic Attitudes: Portraits of an Age, 1780–1830.* New York, 1988.

Ferris, David S. *Silent Urns: Romanticism, Hellenism, Modernity.* Stanford, Calif., 2000.

Frank, Manfred. *The Philosophical Foundations of Early German Romanticism.* Translated by Elizabeth Millán-Zaubert. Albany, N.Y., 2004.

Heffernan, James A. W. *The Re-Creation of Landscape: A Study of Wordsworth, Coleridge, Constable, and Turner.* Hanover, N.H., 1985.

Hoeveler, Diane Long. *Romantic Androgyny: The Women Within.* University Park, Pa., 1990.

Honour, Hugh. *Romanticism.* New York, 1979.

Izenberg, Gerald. *Impossible Individuality: Romanticism, Revolution, and the Origins of Modern Selfhood, 1787–1802.* Princeton, N.J., 1992.

Jackson, James Robert de Jager. *Romantic Poetry by Women: A Bibliography, 1770–1835.* Oxford, U.K., 1993.

Larrissy, Edward, ed. *Romanticism and Postmodernism.* Cambridge, U.K., and New York, 1999.

Lovejoy, Arthur O. "On the Discrimination of Romanticisms." In his *Essays in the History of Ideas*, 228–253. New York, 1948.

Mellor, Anne K. *Romanticism and Gender.* New York, 1993.

Paulson, Ronald. *Representations of Revolution, 1789–1820.* New Haven, Conn., 1980.

Priestman, Martin. *Romantic Atheism: Poetry and Free Thought, 1780–1830.* Cambridge, U.K., and New York, 1999.

Rosen, Charles. *The Romantic Generation.* Cambridge, Mass., 1995.

Schenk, Hans G. *The Mind of the European Romantics: An Essay in Cultural History.* Oxford, U.K., and New York, 1979.

Stelzig, Eugene L. *The Romantic Subject in Autobiography: Rousseau and Goethe.* Charlottesville, Va., 2000.

Toman, Rolf, ed. *Neoclassicism and Romanticism: Architecture, Sculpture, Painting, Drawings, 1750–1848.* Translation from the German by Paul Aston, Peter Barton, and Eileen Martin in association with Cambridge Publishing Management. Cologne, Germany, 2000.

Williamson, George S. *The Longing for Myth in Germany: Religion and Aesthetic Culture from Romanticism to Nietzsche.* Chicago, 2004.

MARK S. MICALE

ROME. In the century between the French Revolution and World War I, Rome experienced changes as great as any in its long and adventurous history. From its beginning as the seat of the bishop of Rome, the Eternal City became the residence of the supreme pontiff of the Catholic world and in the eighth century became the capital of the pope's temporal dominions in central Italy (the Papal State). Over the centuries the city had become the architectural embodiment of papal power, but when the new kingdom of Italy was created in the mid-nineteenth century, Rome acquired a new secular vocation as Italy's new capital. In September 1870 Italian troops occupied the city, and the pope's temporal powers came to an end. A spiritual but no longer a secular ruler, the pope withdrew across the river Tiber to become a self-imposed "prisoner" with his cardinals in the Vatican City; and in the decades that followed, Rome's appearance, social structure, and functions changed radically. It never became an industrial city like Turin, Milan, Genoa, or Florence, but the city had always held an irresistible symbolic meaning for Italian nationalists. The city's new and often deeply contradictory Italian identities had still to contend, however, with its past.

ROME AND THE FRENCH REVOLUTION

Papal Rome had long been the center of the Catholic world, but in the eighteenth century the city found a new place on the itineraries of the grand tour and acquired a reputation as one of Europe's best party towns. Wealthy travelers mingled with the faithful to admire the city's monuments and art treasures and to enjoy its unparalleled public spectacles and festivals, notably the carnival. Although papal Rome could never be a center of the Enlightenment, in the final decades of the century numerous reform projects were initiated by Pope Pius VI (r. 1775–1799).

The revolution in France and the wars that followed brought all this to an end, and for Rome the immediate consequences were economic recession, invasion, and foreign occupation. A French army occupied the city in February 1798, set up a republican government, and carried Pope Pius VI off into exile, where he died a year later. So did the Republic, but when French armies returned to Italy in 1800 Rome initially maintained a precarious independence until 1808, when it was again occupied and a year later annexed to France.

Napoleon never visited Rome, but he dreamed of making it the second city of the empire. Joseph Valadier was commissioned to design a grandiose imperial forum around the Porta del Popolo, where a magnificent royal villa was to be surrounded by the "Gardens of the Great Caesar" on the Pincio. But when Napoleon's empire collapsed in 1814 work had barely begun, and the costs of French imperial rule had been heavy. The city's art treasures were plundered and its economy was devastated by economic recession and the Continental Blockade: between 1789 and 1814 the city's population had fallen from 185,000 to 135,000.

PAPAL ROME, 1814–1870: POLITICAL CHANGE

In 1814 the Congress of Vienna restored Pope Pius VII (r. 1800–1823) to his former title as king of the Papal State, which as well as Rome included the central Italian provinces of Emilia, Romagna, the Marche, and Lazio. But after the Restoration, Rome would never regain its eighteenth-century exuberance. Pius VII's successor, Pope Leo XII (r. 1823–1829) closed the city's cafés and theaters and banned the carnival. Foreign tourists stayed away, and even the British diplomatic envoy left the city because there was nothing to do. The pope's death in 1829 was greeted with celebrations, but things changed little under his successor Gregory XVI (r. 1831–1846).

Then in 1831 and 1832 the Papal State was the theater for major insurrections. Those were quickly suppressed by an Austrian army, but it was evident that papal rule was bitterly resented in central Italy, where sympathy for the Italian nationalist movement was strong. This was not the case in Rome, which enjoyed many privileges as the seat of papal government. But that did not lessen the expectations, when in 1846 a pope who was believed to sympathize with the liberal

A view of Rome taken from the Pincian Hill in the late nineteenth century. ©Michael Maslan Historic Photograph/Corbis

nationalist program was elected as Pius IX. As a result, when revolutions broke out in other parts of Italy at the beginning of 1848 Rome was soon at the forefront of events.

Pope Pius IX (r. 1846–1878) quickly disappointed the nationalists, however, and in April refused to take part in the war against Austria. The government's failure to introduce reforms also provoked unrest in Rome and when Rosolino Pilo, the moderate leader appointed by the pope, was assassinated in November, Pius IX took the opportunity to flee the city in a closed carriage, disguised as a woman. Followed by his cardinals he took refuge in the Kingdom of Naples and appealed to the Catholic rulers to restore him to his capital.

In Rome, meanwhile, the Roman Republic was formally declared on 9 February 1849 and began to implement radical reforms. But the flight of the pope had caused serious unemployment, and the city was now threatened by the armies of the Catholic rulers of Naples and Spain and of the new French Republic that had responded to the pope's appeal for help. On 30 April, nine thousand French troops commanded by General Charles Oudinot laid siege to the city, whose defense was organized by Giuseppe Garibaldi. The French finally overcame the heroic resistance and occupied the city on 3 July, but thanks to Garibaldi's skillful retreat many of the defenders escaped.

After the heroic fall of the Roman Republic, "Rome or Death" became the battle cry that rallied nationalists throughout Italy. But Rome was now occupied by a French army that remained on the pretext of protecting the pope, which enabled the French emperor Napoleon III (r. 1852–1871) to play a key role in the politics of Italian unification. When in 1860 the pope lost most of his temporal dominions, French support enabled Pius IX to hold on to Rome. Garibaldi made two attempts to liberate the city, but both ended in disaster:

the first at Aspromonte in 1862 and the second at Mentana, on the city's periphery, in 1867. But when in September 1870 Napoleon III was defeated by the Prussians at the battle of Sedan, the city's fate was sealed: on 20 September 1870 Italian *bersaglieri* (light infantry) breached the city walls near the Porta Pia and papal Rome finally made way for the capital of the new Italy, which was proclaimed a year later.

PAPAL ROME, 1814–1870: ECONOMY AND SOCIETY

In 1814 Rome was the third largest city in Italy, after Naples (450,000) and Palermo (180,000). It was still a walled city whose gates were shut at night, and inside the city walls there was still a great deal of farmland. The population lived concentrated along the banks of the river Tiber, which frequently flooded. Over four thousand Romans worked as agricultural laborers, and the other main sources of employment were domestic and other service activities. There were no industries except for home-based textile spinning and weaving and the state-run tobacco factory that was opened in Trastevere in the 1850s.

The population lived in extreme poverty, supported by the large number of convents and religious orders that were concentrated in the poorest districts—Monti, Trevi, Pigna, and Trastevere. In 1871 a third of the population was estimated to be permanently dependent on welfare, and among the poorest were the inhabitants of the Jewish ghetto. At the beginning of the century the French had abolished the regulations forbidding the Jews from leaving the ghetto, but these were reinstated after the Restoration, and in 1825 Pope Leo XII ordered the ghetto to be enlarged. In 1847 Pius IX ordered that the walls of the ghetto be destroyed, but this was revoked in 1850 and the Jews were again deprived of civil liberties.

Rome was primarily a city of priests, prelates, and the religious. They accounted for 5 percent of the population in the 1850s and together with the city's six hundred churches and convents were the principal consumers of the goods that were landed at the two busy ports on the Tiber: the Ripagrande and the Porto di Ripetta. Visitors also played an important part in the city's economy. In papal Jubilee years their numbers might reach one hundred thousand, and there was always a steady traffic of clerics on ecclesiastical business. The city was also a magnet for an ever-growing stream of international travelers, art-lovers, artists, and tourists, to cater for whom Rome could offer 30 hotels, 14 inns, 31 restaurants, 712 hostelries, and 217 cafés—more than any other Italian city in the mid-nineteenth century.

Down to the time of unification, agriculture continued to be the mainstay of the city's economy. To the immediate south the Pontine Marshes were infested by malarial swamps, but the rest of the vast plain surrounding the city was divided into huge estates known as *latifundia*. Two-fifths of property in the city and one-third of the rural estates were owned by religious foundations, while most of the rest belonged to a small number of very wealthy aristocratic families—the Borghese, the Chigi, and the Sforza Cesarini.

Except for the small number of agents who managed the estates of the great noble families and a few wealthy bankers like the Torlonia, papal Rome had no commercial middle class while public administration and education was controlled exclusively by the clergy. Nonetheless, ecclesiastical ritual, wealthy private patrons, and foreign tourists created a strong demand for a variety of luxury trades. The census of 1866 listed over 1,500 goldsmiths and jewelers, dozens of *botteghe* specializing in making mosaics or works in bronze or marble, and dealers in antiques and artworks of every kind.

ROME, 1870–1914: URBAN TRANSFORMATION

In the decades after 1870 Rome's physical appearance and social composition changed rapidly. Despite serious cholera outbreaks (in 1837, 1854/5, and 1867) immigration had already caused the population to rise to 220,000 by the time of unification, but over the next thirty years it more than doubled, jumping to 300,000 in 1880 and then to 460,000 by 1900.

In the 1850s the Belgian cardinal Frederick Xavier de Mérode had made the first attempt to devise an urban development project, but the papal government had no means to fund this. As a result, in 1870 Rome was still a city "without sewers, without street lighting, without any wide boulevards or wholesale markets, with few manufacturers, no

Rome, photographed in the 1890s. A man fishes in the Tiber River; the Castel Sant'Angelo is in the background at right and the dome of St. Peter's Basilica is visible behind the bridge. ©BETTMANN/CORBIS

industries and no industrial working class districts" (quoted in Vidotto, p. 129).

Rebuilding the capital was one of the new government's main priorities, but it too was very short of money. Developing a city that contained some of the finest architecture in Europe also raised major technical and artistic issues, but the greatest obstacles were municipal political rivalries, which meant that most of the development took place without any planning or regulation. The German historian Ferdinand Gregorovius described the speed with which former monasteries and convents were commandeered for the new ministries and public buildings while housing projects began to spring up everywhere. But these were insufficient to cater to the thousands of immigrants who were drawn to the city in search of work, so that conditions in

the already overcrowded working-class districts like Trastevere and Testaccio deteriorated even further.

In 1883 an urban development plan was finally approved. It provided for a new central thoroughfare (the Via Nazionale, linking the Termini Station to the Piazza Venezia) and new arterial roads to be named after Count Cavour (Camillo Benso; 1810–1861) and Victor Emmanuel II (1820–1878). New residential districts (Flaminio and Prati) were also projected for the army of white-collar workers needed to staff the new government offices, and the more crowded districts of the *centro storico* (city center) and the ghetto were to be demolished. The immediate consequence, however, was a speculative building boom that quickly spiraled out of control. When this burst in 1887 the crash nearly brought down the entire Italian banking system, and Rome's economy did not recover for over a decade. That was not the only damage, however, and one English observer sadly concluded that "twenty-two years of Piedmontese government have done more to destroy Rome than all the invasions of the Goths and the Vandals" (Hare, p. 12).

ROME'S CONTESTED IDENTITIES

Except for the new elevated embankments to protect the city from the recurrent flooding of the Tiber, government funds went mainly to prestigious projects designed to impose an Italian identity on the old papal city. Among the most important of the new ministries was the monumental Palace of Justice and the no-less-grandiose memorial to King Victor Emmanuel II (r. 1861–1878) that dominates the heart of the city today.

Parliament voted the funds for the monument to Italy's first king shortly after his death in 1878, but it was not completed until 1906. From the start the project was surrounded by controversy. By no means did all Italians recognize the monarch to be the nation's principal representative. Its siting between the Campidoglio, the Roman Forum, and the Ara Coeli convent was intended to stress continuities with the past, but every aspect of its design was fraught with polemic and financial problems that caused endless delay.

Republicans, democrats, monarchists, and Catholics rehearsed the same symbolic battles over every public ceremony, the naming of every street and piazza, and the erection of every statue. The decision to bury King Victor Emmanuel II in the Pantheon in 1878 pleased republicans but infuriated Catholics and the dynasty's Piedmontese loyalists. Attempts to bury Pius IX in 1881 provoked an anticlerical riot that nearly caused the pope's bier to finish in the Tiber. The inauguration of the statue to the philosopher Giordano Bruno (1548–1600) in the Campo dei Fiori in 1889 and of the equestrian memorial to Garibaldi on the Janiculum in 1895—provocatively overlooking St. Peter's—were both aggressive and officially endorsed anticlerical provocations. But the church never relinquished its hold on the city, and the revival of the papal Jubilee celebrations in 1900 marked the start of a concerted counteroffensive that was reinforced by popular new Marian cults and powerful lay Catholic organizations.

ROME BEFORE WORLD WAR I

After 1900 the city's economy recovered, thanks in part to increased trade, tourism, and above all the expansion of public administration: 20 percent of the active population were by now state employees. The government finally made special funds available for urban development, and in 1907 an energetic anticlerical administration headed by Ernesto Nathan (1845–1921), the son of a Jewish family of Italian descent born in London, came to power. As in many other Italian and European cities at this time, measures were taken to promote public services, municipal transport, establish primary schools, improve public hygiene, and enforce development regulations. But in 1914 Nathan's administration was decisively defeated by a conservative and clerical alliance that remained firmly in control of the nation's capital as Italy entered World War I. A newfound sense of national solidarity was reflected in closer rapprochement between church and state, and the monument to Victor Emmanuel II was renamed the Altar of the Fatherland. The solidarity did not outlive the war, but that did not lessen Rome's symbolic attraction, which was why Benito Mussolini (1883–1945) chose it as the setting for the fascist seizure of power in October 1922.

See also **Crispi, Francesco; Garibaldi, Giuseppe; Papacy; Pius IX; Risorgimento (Italian Unification); Roman Question; Victor Emmanuel II.**

BIBLIOGRAPHY

Primary Sources

Dickens, Charles. *Pictures from Italy*. London, 1846.

Gregorovius, Ferdinand. *The Roman Journals of Ferdinand Gregorovius, 1852–1874*. Edited by Friedrich Althaus, translated by Mrs. Gustavus W. Hamilton. London, 1907.

Hare, Augustus. *Walks in Rome*. London, 1903.

Secondary Sources

Bartoccini, Fiorella. *Roma nell'Ottocento: Il tramonto della città santa e la nascita di una capitale*. 2 vols. Bologna, 1988.

Brice, Catherine. *Monumentalité publique et politique à Rome: Le Vittoriano*. Rome, 1998.

Ciucci, Giorgio, ed. *Roma Moderna: Storia di Roma dall'Antichità a Oggi*. Rome, 2002.

Kertzer, David. *The Prisoner of the Vatican: The Pope's Secret Plot to Capture Rome from the New Italian State*. Boston, 2004.

Tobia, Bruno. *L'altare della patria*. Bologna, 1997.

Vidotto, V., ed. *Roma Capitale: Storia di Roma dall'Antichità a Oggi*. Rome, 2002.

JOHN A. DAVIS

ROSSINI, GIOACHINO (1792–1868), Italian operatic composer.

Gioachino Rossini was the most popular composer of the first half of the nineteenth century, capturing the ardent admiration of audiences throughout Europe with his thirty-nine serious, semiserious, and comic operas. Although this period of music history is now commonly referred to as the "Age of Beethoven," a far more accurate label for the era would list Rossini's name directly alongside that of his German contemporary.

Rossini was born on 29 February 1792 in Pesaro, Italy, to a family of musicians. His father was a trumpet and horn player, his mother a soprano who achieved moderate successes in comic operas. As a child, Rossini's talents were nurtured carefully by his parents, as well as by Canon Giuseppe Malerbi, who gave him lessons in composition. By age twelve, Rossini was singing professionally, and at age thirteen he appeared as Adolfo in Ferdinando Paer's *Camilla* (Teatro del Corso, Bologna). His compositional career began in 1810 with the premiere of his one-act *farsa La cambiale di matrimonio* (The bill of marriage) at the Teatro San Moisè, Venice, a debut that compelled the theater to commission from him four more one-act operas between 1812 and 1813. During these years, Rossini also composed his first full-length works, including *Tancredi* (Venice, 1813), *L'italiana in Algeri* (Venice, 1813; The Italian girl in Algiers), and *Il turco in Italia* (Milan, 1814; The Turk in Italy), all of which became international sensations. From this time forward Rossini was a household name, his life characterized by a continual stream of commissions that he fulfilled at an extraordinary speed, completing some operas in as few as three weeks.

Between 1815 and 1822, Rossini composed nine operas for the Teatro San Carlo in Naples, and nine others for theaters in Rome, Milan, and Venice. Among the products of this flurry of activity were *Elisabetta regina d'Inghilterra* (Naples, 1815; Elizabeth, queen of England), *Il barbiere di Siviglia* (Rome, 1816; The Barber of Seville), *Otello* (Naples, 1816; Othello), *La Cenerentola* (Rome, 1817; Cinderella), *La gazza ladra* (Milan, 1817; The thieving magpie), *Mosè in Egitto* (Naples, 1818; Moses in Egypt), *La donna del lago* (Naples, 1819; The lady of the lake), *Maometto II* (Naples, 1820), and *Zelmira* (Naples, 1822). The last opera he composed for an Italian theater was *Semiramide* (Venice, 1823), following which he and his first wife—the celebrated soprano Isabella Colbran (1785–1845)—traveled to London and then settled in Paris. In the French capital, Rossini became director of the Théâtre-Italien, where he supervised rehearsals of his own operas, as well as those of younger colleagues including Gaetano Donizetti (1797–1848) and Vincenzo Bellini (1801–1835). The first opera he composed specially for Paris was *Il viaggio a Reims* (1825; The journey to Reims) in celebration of the coronation of Charles X. He then he reworked two of his best Neapolitan operas for the French public: *Maometto II* became *Le siège de Corinthe* (1826; The siege of Corinth), and *Mosè in Egitto* became *Moïse* (1827). Over the next two years, he wrote two more original works for Paris—*Le comte Ory* (1828; Count Ory) and *Guillaume Tell* (1829; William Tell)—following which he retired from the hectic and complicated world of operatic composition. He was thirty-seven years old.

The next two and a half decades of Rossini's life were plagued with a series of morbid illnesses that were probably responsible, at least in part, for his compositional silence. During these years, he lived in Bologna, nursed by his mistress, Olympe Pélissier, who later became his second wife. In 1855 the Rossinis moved back to France, where he recovered and began to compose once again, though not opera. In his final decade, he produced over 150 piano pieces, songs, and works for small ensemble, and the *Petit messe solennelle* (Small solemn mass). Much of this music was written for and performed at the famous *samedi soirs,* weekly salons presided over by Rossini and featuring the most accomplished singers, instrumentalists, and composers working in Europe at the time. Rossini died in Passy, near Paris, on 13 November 1868.

It is impossible to exaggerate the impact Rossini's music had on spectators and composers throughout the nineteenth century. Although his operas began to fall out of fashion a few decades following his "retirement," his musical style and standardized forms were imitated by all of his successors up through and including Giuseppe Verdi (1813–1901). Between 1850 and 1950, the only Rossini opera to maintain a permanent position in the repertory was *The Barber of Seville,* and thus, for most of the twentieth century, he was recognized exclusively as a purveyor of comic farce. Beginning in the 1960s, however, this perception shifted dramatically, as all of his operas—comic and serious—witnessed a renaissance. In the early twenty-first century, it is possible to enjoy professional recordings of most of Rossini's operas and to watch them live in opera houses throughout the world, their vibrancy and energy emanating as fully as when they first appeared on the stage nearly two centuries ago.

See also **Music; Opera; Verdi, Giuseppe.**

BIBLIOGRAPHY

Gossett, Philip. "History and Works that Have No History: Reviving Rossini's Neapolitan Operas." In *Disciplining Music: Musicology and Its Canons,* edited by Katherine Bergeron and Philip V. Bohlman, 95–115. Chicago, 1992.

Senici, Emanuele, ed. *The Cambridge Companion to Rossini.* Cambridge, U.K., 2004.

Stendhal. *Life of Rossini.* Translated by Richard N. Coe. Rev. ed. London, 1985. Originally published in 1824.

HILARY PORISS

ROTHSCHILDS. The Rothschild bank was the largest and most powerful financial institution of the nineteenth century. Although owned and run until the late twentieth century as a private family partnership, principally concerned with the management of the family's own capital, the firm's ability to handle large-scale transactions in numerous different markets and in multiple financial centers set it apart from its competitors.

The original "house" of M. A. Rothschild was founded in Frankfurt by Mayer Amschel Rothschild (1744–1812) in the 1790s. Originally a dealer in coins and antiques, Mayer Amschel became a broker and later an investment manager to the court of William IX, the wealthy prince (later elector) of Hesse-Kassel. By 1797 Rothschild had already accumulated capital of around £10,000 and was extending credit to a wide range of German clients. When the elector quarreled with Napoleon I (r. 1804–1814/15) and was driven into exile, Mayer Amschel continued to help him manage his fortune, running the risk of arrest by the French authorities.

None of this was exceptional: Mayer Amschel was just one among many German-Jewish *Hoffaktoren* (sometimes known as "court Jews") offering financial services to petty princes. Nor was his decision unusual to send a representative—his third son Nathan (1777–1836)—to England in 1799. The rapid growth of industrial textile manufacturing in England attracted numerous German merchants, all eager to purchase the new Lancashire fabrics for the Continental market.

Even Nathan Rothschild's decision in 1811 to become involved in British war finance was unoriginal. Since the late seventeenth century, British government borrowing—both long-term through the Stock Exchange, and short-term from the money market—had attracted foreign financiers to the City of London. The Rothschilds' mobilization of their Continental credit network to relay bullion to the British armies in the field in France in 1814 and 1815, as well as to transfer subsidies to Britain's Continental allies, was remarkable only for its scale. The risks were commensurate: contrary to legend, Nathan and his five brothers were brought to the brink of insolvency by the news that Napoleon had been defeated at Waterloo, since they had accumulated large gold reserves in the expectation of a prolonged war. Nathan's immense and speculative purchases of British government bonds in the aftermath of Waterloo not only salvaged the situation but also reaped a huge profit. By 1818 the Rothschilds' combined capital amounted to nearly £1.8 million, an immense sum at that time.

Until this point, the Rothschilds' mode of operation had been crude. Their bookkeeping was chaotic. Their correspondence was often intercepted and, although written in *Judendeutsch* (German transliterated into Hebrew characters), deciphered by the Austrian authorities. However, under Nathan Rothschild's mercurial leadership, and on the basis of the funds they had accumulated during the war, the family now began to play a more innovative role, specifically in the integration of the European bond markets.

The system whereby European states funded their budget deficits by selling long-term interest-bearing bonds to an elite of investors through financial intermediaries was well established by 1818. But the loan of that year issued by the Rothschilds on behalf of the Prussian crown was novel in that it was issued simultaneously in multiple markets. The interest was also payable in the market of issue. This corresponded to the unusual form of the Rothschild bank itself. Although it remained a family firm—structured as a partnership between adult male family members—the Rothschild bank took on a multinational character, in that the five brothers were now based in five major European financial and political centers: Frankfurt, Vienna, London, Naples, and Paris.

The success of the Prussian loan and similar transactions for the other great European powers in the 1820s rapidly established the Rothschilds as the dominant force in European financial markets. In terms of capital, they dwarfed their nearest rivals, the Barings. The Rothschilds' operations extended far beyond the European bond markets, however, embracing a whole range of financial services including bullion and commodity broking, the discounting of commercial bills, insurance, and even private banking for an elite of aristocratic clients, selected according to their political influence.

Nevertheless, bond issuance and trading remained the Rothschilds' core business. In particular, their multinational structure and the sheer scale of their resources allowed them to conduct a huge and profitable arbitrage business. The acute sensitivity of the bond markets to political events— particularly intimations of revolution or war, both of which implied financial dislocation and an increased default risk—gave the Rothschilds an intense interest in the acquisition and rapid communication of political news. A network of salaried agents and correspondents spread rapidly outward from Europe to all the major financial centers of the Old and New World. Their function was as much to transmit news to the partners in Europe as to engage in commercial transactions. Even so,

the Rothschilds were surprised by the 1830 and 1848 revolutions and suffered heavy losses.

Declining public-sector deficits in the mid-nineteenth century and defaults by major borrowers in America and Iberia encouraged the Rothschilds to diversify into industrial investment. Mainly at the instigation of James de Rothschild (1792–1868), they acquired major stakes in Austrian, French, Belgian, and Italian railways, mercury mines in Spain, and the ironworks of Witkowitz (Vitkovic) in Moravia.

In absolute terms, the Rothschilds reached their zenith in 1899, when their combined capital (more than £41 million) exceeded that of the five biggest German joint-stock banks put together. In relative terms, however, they were in decline. In part, this reflected the diminishing returns of endogamy: the fourth generation evinced only mediocre financial acumen and was exceedingly risk-averse. But the economic and political environment had also become less favorable. The spread of joint-stock banking eventually created comparably large concentrations of capital; more importantly, joint-stock banks were more willing to accept deposits, whereas the Rothschilds persisted in acting more like an investment trust, managing the capital of the Rothschild family alone (and doing so very conservatively). At the same time, the advent of the telegraph and commercial news agencies eroded the advantage the Rothschilds had derived from their information network of private agents and couriers. Finally, the unifications of Italy and Germany shifted political power away from Naples, Vienna, and Frankfurt.

In the 1840s the Rothschilds had all but monopolized the markets for French and Belgian government bonds. By the 1890s there were only a few countries in a similar position of near-dependence, notably Brazil and Egypt. Increasingly, the Great Powers found themselves able to sell long-term bonds directly to the public or via rival intermediaries such as post offices, savings banks, or consortia of joint-stock banks. Even Russia—which relied heavily on the Paris market— was never wholly dependent on the Rothschilds.

By the end of the nineteenth century the extent of the Rothschilds' business empire remained impressive, ranging from Indian railways to South

African diamond mines to Caucasian oil fields. They continued to be a crucial part of the "international financial architecture" of the gold-standard era, often acting as intermediaries between the major central banks and the bullion market. Their political power was, however, in decline—a reality belied by the family's increasingly conspicuous consumption and investment, especially in art and real estate, and their acquisition of aristocratic titles and sons-in-law. As amateur diplomats, the Rothschilds worked in vain to avert a military clash between Britain and Germany. The ensuing First World War exposed their strategic Achilles heel: the absence of a full-fledged Rothschild house in New York. Heavy losses in the financial crises of 1914 and 1931 (the latter largely arising from the collapse and costly rescue of the Rothschild-founded Creditanstalt) drastically reduced the scale of the family's resources. At the same time, the formal ties between the remaining Rothschild houses in London, Paris and Vienna were dissolved.

The Depression, the rise of National Socialism, and the outbreak of World War II brought the Rothschilds to the nadir of their fortunes. The Vienna house was wound up following the Nazi *Anschluss* of Austria in 1938; the French Rothschilds had to flee Paris after the debacle of 1940; the London office was fortunate to survive the Blitz more or less unscathed. The Nazi war on European Jewry was worse than a return to the days when the family had been incarcerated in the Frankfurt ghetto; now those Rothschilds who fell into the hands of the Nazis risked losing their lives. Yet the family—grotesquely caricatured in the German propaganda film *Die Rothschilds* (1940)—had grown accustomed to vilification. In the wake of their spectacular rise to preeminence in European finance during the later Napoleonic Wars, there had been innumerable attacks on them, not just by avowed anti-Semites but also by conservative aristocrats, radical democrats, populists, and socialists—even Zionists. The image recurs in numerous publications of a vast spider's web of money, with the Rothschilds at its center, and politicians, kings, and even popes entangled round its edges. Recent scholarship, however, has produced a more balanced depiction of their political role.

The Rothschilds were able to achieve a partial—although very far from complete—restoration of their fortunes after 1945. Although the Paris house was nationalized by the government of François Mitterrand in 1981, it has since been reconstituted. Only the original London house of N. M. Rothschild & Sons has survived without interruption. In the early twenty-first century it forms part of a complex network of Rothschild-controlled companies.

See also **Banks and Banking; Jews and Judaism.**

BIBLIOGRAPHY

Corti, Count Egon Caesar. *The Reign of the House of Rothschild*. Translated by Brian and Beatrix Lunn. New York, 1928.

———. *The Rise of the House of Rothschild*. Translated by Brian and Beatrix Lunn. New York, 1928.

Ferguson, Niall. *The World's Banker: The History of the House of Rothschild*. London, 1998.

Gille, Bertrand. *Histoire de la maison Rothschild*. 2 vols. Geneva, 1965, 1967.

NIALL FERGUSON

ROUSSEL, NELLY (1878–1922), French feminist.

Feminist, advocate of birth control, and pacifist, Frenchwoman Nelly Roussel disseminated her various doctrines through public speaking, journalism, and acting. She dazzled her audiences with her stunning beauty, charismatic speaking style, powerful logic, and disarming wit. One of her friends accurately labeled her a "contemporary of the future"; far more modern than feminists of her era, Roussel anticipated "second-wave" feminism of the 1970s in claiming for women the right to have complete control over their own bodies. She devoted her career to transforming attitudes about female pain, especially in childbirth, by seeking to dislodge both religious and secular beliefs that pain in labor was the necessary and redemptive consequence of female sexuality. Roussel insisted that women should be able to free themselves of pain through birth control and medicalized childbirth. She linked sovereignty over one's own body to the potential for full human development and to the capacity for citizenship at a time when women were still denied civil and political rights. Full self-possession also meant the right to sexual pleasure as an end in itself.

Born into a bourgeois Parisian family and raised a devout Catholic, Roussel felt the injustice of sexual inequality by the time she was a teenager because she was prohibited from continuing her education and pursuing an acting career. At age twenty, she married Henri Godet, a sculptor, free-thinker, and feminist. They had three children, one of whom died in infancy. Roussel's painful experiences with childbirth further committed her to emancipating women from repeated and unwanted pregnancies. Over the course of her career, she traveled alone by train throughout France and five other European countries where she presented almost 250 lectures, often to audiences that numbered more than two thousand. She also wrote, performed, and sold several allegorical plays, one of which was translated into Russian and Portuguese. Her reach extended beyond the tens of thousands who heard her speak; forty-six Parisian and provincial newspapers summarized her lectures and published more than two hundred articles she wrote.

Most feminists of Roussel's era did not believe female sexual pleasure to be an important element of feminine identity. Moreover, they thought the separation of sexuality from reproduction would render women sexual objects and deprive motherhood of dignity. Roussel also differed from most other feminists because she made a deliberate effort to reach working-class women, and traveled into the provinces to do so. In observing the material conditions of their lives, and particularly those of single mothers, Roussel argued that maternal labor, "like other work, and even more than other work ... [should] ensure the independence and the well-being of all those who perform it, [but it] has so far been only a source of slavery and inferiority! ... Of all the social functions, the ... most magnificent, most painful, and the most necessary is the only one which has never received wages" ("She Who Is Always Sacrificed," pp. 23–24). She demanded that women be paid for their maternal labor and called for a "strike of wombs."

Roussel's speaking and writing career slowed after 1910 as she suffered increasingly poor health. She died from tuberculosis in 1922, shortly before her forty-fifth birthday. It was not only her health, however, that slowed her public career. Her views caused particular controversy in France because of the nation's sharp decline in birthrates, a demographic phenomenon that had ominous implications for military strength at a time of growing international tensions. Thus she was considered by many to be not only immoral but also unpatriotic and even treasonous in advocating women's right to contraception. In reaction to the campaign for birth control, as well as to the huge population losses suffered in World War I, the National Assembly passed a law in 1920 that prohibited the advertisement, sale, and public discussion of all birth control (except condoms to prevent venereal disease) and stiffened penalties for abortion. Even prior to the passage of this law—which remained in place until 1967—the political climate in pre–World War I France prevented Roussel from gaining a large following and certainly made institutional support impossible.

But Roussel did win the hearts and minds of numerous individuals who heard her speak or who read her published lectures and plays. Some of them—especially her daughter, Mireille Godet—kept her memory alive. Evidence suggests Roussel influenced the thinking of Simone de Beauvoir, who developed similar views about women and motherhood. Moreover, Roussel helped force public attention to the plight of mothers, a cause that mainstream feminists fully adopted and that ultimately resulted in government-sponsored child care and family allocations.

See also **Feminism.**

BIBLIOGRAPHY

Primary Sources

Roussel, Nelly. "She Who Is Always Sacrificed," "The Freedom of Motherhood," and "Let Us Create the Female Citizen." In *Feminisms of the Belle Epoque: A Historical and Literary Anthology*, edited by Jennifer Waelti-Walters and Steven C. Hause, 18–41, 242–251, and 278–291. Lincoln, Nebr., 1994.

Secondary Sources

Accampo, Elinor A. "The Rhetoric of Reproduction and the Reconfiguration of Womanhood in the French Birth Control Movement, 1890–1920." *Journal of Family History: Studies in Family, Kinship, and Demography* 21, no. 3 (1996): 351–371.

———. "Private Life, Public Image: Motherhood and Militancy in the Self-Construction of Nelly Roussel, 1900–1922." In *The New Biography: Performing Femininity in Nineteenth-Century France*, edited by Jo Burr Margadant, 218–261. Berkeley, Calif., 2000.

———. *Blessed Motherhood, Bitter Fruit: Nelly Roussel and the Politics of Female Pain in Third Republic France*. Baltimore, Md., 2006.

Albistur, Maïté, and Daniel Armogathe. Preface, notes, and commentaries to *L'éternelle sacrifiée*, by Nelly Roussel. Paris, 1979.

Cova, Anne. "Féminisme et natalité: Nelly Roussel (1878–1922)." *History of European Ideas* 15, nos. 4–6 (1992): 663–672.

Klejman, Laurence, and Florence Rochefort. *L'égalité en marche: Le féminisme sous la Troisième Rèpubliique*. Paris, 1989.

Offen, Karen. *European Feminisms, 1700–1950: A Political History*. Stanford, Calif., 2000.

Waelti-Walters, Jennifer, and Steven C. Hause, eds. *Feminisms of the Belle Epoque: A Historical and Literary Anthology*. Translated by Jennifer Waelti-Walters, Jette Kjaer, and Lydia Willis. Lincoln, Nebr., 1994.

ELINOR ACCAMPO

RUDE, FRANÇOIS (1784–1855), French sculptor.

Best known as creator of the iconic *Departure of the Volunteers in 1792* on the Arc de Triomphe, François Rude exemplifies the moral seriousness of monumental sculpture in mid-nineteenth-century France. An important figure in the burgeoning trend for commemorative statuary, Rude played a seminal role in the period's obsessive glorification of national heroes.

François Rude was born in Dijon on 4 January 1784, the son of a locksmith and stovemaker. Apprenticed to his father before training under the painter François Desvosges, Rude left for Paris in 1807, thanks to the help of a local tax inspector, Louis Frémiet, who was not only his earliest patron but who also adopted the young man when he was orphaned in 1805. Through an introduction to Dominique Vivant Denon, Napoleon's powerful director of the arts, Rude found work in Paris on the Vendôme column under the sculptor Edme Gaulle. Soon after, Rude signaled his artistic ambitions by entering the studio of Pierre Cartellier and registering as a student at the Ecole des Beaux-Arts. In 1809 he competed for the first time for the Prix de Rome, the school's most prestigious prize, which rewarded winners with a five-year stay at the academy's school in the Villa Medici. Although successful in 1812, Rude was denied the opportunity to study in Rome, since the authorities lacked available funds. As a result, the sculptor gained first-hand experience of Italy only in 1843. At a time when the authority of the antique remained central to sculptural practice, this missed opportunity set Rude apart from contemporaries such as David d'Angers, Pradier, and Ramey, whose success in the Prix de Rome was properly recompensed.

Rude's career was further disrupted in 1815 when his benefactor Frémiet, who had rallied to the Bonapartist cause during the Hundred Days, fled to Brussels following Napoleon's defeat at Waterloo. The sculptor, himself a fervent Bonapartist, accompanied his adoptive family and in 1821 married Frémiet's daughter Sophie, an accomplished artist in her own right. Rude's years in Brussels were busy, but did little to advance his reputation, and in 1827 he returned to France, where he enjoyed his first success at the Salon exhibition with *Mercury Attaching His Wings*. In 1831, his fame increased with the wildly successful *Neapolitan Fisherboy*, a genre work of a naked infant playing with a tortoise that spawned many imitators and countless reproductions.

It was, however, the commission for one of the colossal relief sculptures to decorate the Arc de Triomphe, a monument begun during the empire but completed only in 1836, that sealed Rude's reputation. The *Departure of the Volunteers in 1792*, popularly known as *La Marseillaise*, overshadows the other decorative groups, by Antoine Etex and Jean-Pierre Cortot, which recount the defense of the First Republic, and the triumph and subsequent defeat of the empire. Dominated by a compelling, dynamic allegory of Liberty, Rude's compact band of warriors and the monument's nationalist élan evokes a vast popular force rooted in the mythic struggles of ancient Gaul. During the Restoration, Rude had accepted a commission to eulogize the armies of the crown on Jean François Térèse Chalgrin's arch, and under the July Monarchy he produced statues of

The Marseillaise; or, the Departure of the Volunteers in 1792. Relief sculpture on the Arc de Triomphe, Paris, by François Rude, 1832–1835. BRIDGEMAN-GIRAUDON/ART RESOURCE, NY

the Maréchal de Saxe for the Musée historique in Versailles (1836–1838) and of the infant Louis XIII for the duc de Luynes's château at Dampierre (1840–1842). It is, however, works like the monuments to the Napoleonic general Henri-Gratien Bertrand (Châteauroux, 1850–1854) and Marshal Ney (Paris, 1853), and to the emperor himself, with the extraordinary *Napoleon Awaking to Immortality* (Fixin, 1845–1847), that seem closest to the sculptor's own sympathies.

Increasingly neglected by the authorities, frequently absent from the Salon, and snubbed by the academy, Rude focused on teaching during the 1840s and displayed sympathies with the republican Left with his haunting tomb to Godefroy Cavaignac (Paris, 1845–1847). A self-professed "radical democrat" in 1848, Rude produced a colossal allegory of the republic for the Pantheon, a monument that perished during the June uprising. Rude's final years

were dominated by two projects for his birthplace, Dijon. *Hebe and the Eagle of Jupiter* and *Love Ruling the World,* regarded by Rude as his "artistic testament," return to a classical idiom he had largely abandoned since the early 1830s. Though it is for works that reveal more contemporary, politically charged affiliations that he is best known, these large-scale marbles, still incomplete at his death on 3 November 1855, point to a tension between tradition and innovation that characterizes Rude's career as a whole.

See also **France; French Revolution; Napoleon.**

BIBLIOGRAPHY

Butler, Ruth. "Long Live the Revolution, the Republic, and Especially the Emperor! The Political Sculpture of Rude." In *Art and Architecture in the Service of Politics,* edited by Henry Millon and Linda Nochlin, 92–107. Cambridge, Mass. 1978.

Calmette, Joseph. *François Rude.* Paris, 1920.

Fourcaud, Louis de. *François Rude, sculpteur: ses oeuvres et son temps (1784–1855).* Paris, 1904.

NEIL MCWILLIAM

RUDOLF, CROWN PRINCE OF AUSTRIA (1858–1889).

Rudolf, crown prince of Austria, was born 21 August 1858 in Vienna and died 30 January 1889 in Mayerling. Rudolf was the only son of Emperor Francis Joseph I of Austria and Empress Elisabeth (originally of Bavaria). During his lifetime regarded as either the liberal hope of the Habsburgs, or as a wayward radical and dissolute, Rudolf is best known to posterity as the central figure of the legendary murder-suicide of Mayerling.

Due to his mother's influence, Rudolf received a liberal education from an array of highly respected liberal academics. This upbringing influenced Rudolf to be much more progressive in his thinking than his father. Relations between the emperor and his heir were strained from early on, with Francis Joseph denying Rudolf's wish when a teenager for a higher education in science. Francis Joseph insisted that Rudolf enter the military, for which Rudolf's sensitive personality and delicate constitution were not well suited. Rudolf was in his own way very loyal to his father, and tried his best, at least in his public life, to live and work within the limits set for him. These included marriage to the Belgian princess Stephanie in 1881 and pursuit of his career in the military, where in 1888 he was appointed general inspector of the infantry. This was, however, a title with little actual power, and the emperor in practice excluded his son from any major position of influence.

Rudolf therefore found ways to operate outside these public limits and spent much of his life working for his progressive goals, largely in secret, against the policies of his father's government. One very public form of engagement was his large-scale publishing project, *Österreich-Ungarn in Wort und Bild* (Austria-Hungary in words and pictures). Started in 1884, this illustrated guide-cum-encyclopedia of the monarchy, eventually twenty-four volumes, was intended to unite the public in a sense of the rich diversity of the shared realm. This reflected Rudolf's wish to create a liberal version of the old Habsburg "Austrian idea," in which the nationalities of the empire would live together in progressive harmony with each other, united by a supranational and liberal monarch (himself).

Rudolf's political aim was to create a liberal coalition that spanned the Monarchy's national fault lines. He shared this goal with his ideological ally and friend, the Jewish editor of the *Neues Wiener Tagblatt*, Moritz Szeps, with whom he collaborated under strict secrecy from 1881 onward. Rudolf's supranational liberalism made him popular with many of Austria's Jews, and, although he was critical of their nationalistic Magyarizing policies, Rudolf's approach also made him an ally of the Magyar liberal leadership. Political trends, at home and abroad, were not, however, moving in Rudolf's direction. The conservative, federalizing policies of the Taaffe government were counter to Rudolf's plans, and the rise of ethno-nationalism, also among Austrian Germans, prevented the emergence of a transnational liberal alliance; the associated rise of anti-Semitism also led to Rudolf being seen as a "servant of the Jews" because of his many Jewish friends.

Abroad, the death of his relative and ally, Louis II of Bavaria in 1886, followed by the death in 1888 of the Prussian king Frederick III, a liberal, and the succession of William II, whom Rudolf both detested and feared as a reactionary, left Rudolf's hopes for a band of progressive, liberal monarchs in central Europe in tatters. His efforts to strengthen Austria-Hungary's ties with liberal France also proved vain. Instead, as an open letter to his father in 1888, under the pseudonym Julius Felix, illustrates, he feared the results of the Dual Alliance with Prussia, warning Francis Joseph about involvement in Bosnia, which he presciently described as "one foot in the grave."

With all of his hopes seemingly dashed, Rudolf became deeply depressed, and he became ever more dissolute. Suffering from gonorrhea picked up from one of his many sexual liaisons, Rudolf retreated into a world of alcohol, drugs, and sex, and from autumn 1888 was clearly thinking of suicide, admittedly with the "romantic" twist that he should die together with a lover. It appears that Baroness Mary Vetsera agreed to his plan, and on 30 January at Mayerling, Rudolf shot first Vetsera and then himself. The subsequent attempts at a cover-up by the Habsburgs led to various conspiracy theories, feeding the Mayerling legend. One irony of Rudolf's death was that Francis Joseph's love for his son and the dignity of the Habsburgs overcame his strict Catholic faith, so that he had Rudolf declared insane at the time of his suicide, hence allowing the suicide-murderer to be buried in the family crypt in the Church of the Capuchins.

See also **Austria-Hungary; Francis Joseph.**

BIBLIOGRAPHY

Beller, Steven. *Francis Joseph*. London and New York, 1996.

Hamann, Brigitte. *Rudolf: Kronprinz und Rebell*. Vienna and Munich, 1978.

Kronprinz Rudolf. *Majestät, ich warne Sie: Geheime und private Schriften*. Edited by Brigitte Hamann. Vienna, 1979.

STEVEN BELLER

RUSKIN, JOHN

RUSKIN, JOHN (1819–1900), major British critic of art and architecture and influential political writer.

John Ruskin was born in London on 8 February 1819, the only child of Scottish parents who had settled in London and made good. His parents were powerful influences, for good and ill, in his life. His mother was an evangelical Christian who destined her son for a career in the Church of England, and from infancy he was made to read and memorize the Bible with this formidable and extremely narrow matriarch. Margaret Ruskin adored her son, but she smothered him emotionally, and many of the sexual and psychological problems that dogged his later life can reasonably be seen as having their roots in her unwise treatment of him.

Ruskin's father, John James Ruskin, was very different. An extremely wealthy wine merchant and typical Victorian self-made man, John James was widely read in the literature of his young manhood (especially Sir Walter Scott [1771–1832] and Lord Byron [George Gordon Byron, 1788–1824]), and he was a willing patron of the arts; by the 1860s his collection of paintings by Joseph Mallord William Turner (1775–1851) was the most important in the world. John James Ruskin acted in effect as John Ruskin's editor and literary agent, eagerly promoting his brilliant son's writing, paying for publication of his work, and in a sense acting as his son's personal assistant. John James's death in 1864 removed an essential prop from Ruskin's life. Margaret's death in 1871, by contrast, removed an impediment. Only when he was rid of her could Ruskin, now a very rich man, set up his own home, at Brantwood on Lake Coniston, where he spent the happiest periods of what remained of his very troubled life.

As a parvenu and tradesman, John James was determined to buy social status for his son by sending him to Christ Church, Oxford, as a "gentleman commoner" (a status normally reserved for aristocrats). John Ruskin's social radicalism, which came to dominate his work after 1860, may be said to date back to his judgments on the manners and morals of these arrogant young men from the ruling class who were his familiars at Oxford.

In 1843 Ruskin, aged only twenty-four, became famous with the publication of first volume of *Modern Painters: Their Superiority in the Art of Landscape Painting to All the Ancient Masters.* This huge study, published in five volumes between 1843 and 1860, proclaimed itself from its opening pages as the work of a young lion determined to sweep away established attitudes to, and preferences for, painting. Turner's late paintings were misunderstood by reviewers in the early 1840s, and the strength of Ruskin's work was to argue that Turner's work displayed the natural world *as God had made it.* This appeal to creationist theology gave Ruskin's revolution irresistible authority in the eyes of the new middle class (people like his father) who had the money to buy art. Turner's reputation and fortune were made by Ruskin, and within a few years the careers of the Pre-Raphaelite painters (Dante Gabriel Rossetti [1828–1882], Holman Hunt [1827–1910], and John Everett Millais [1829–1896]) were also established in effect by Ruskin's hugely influential advocacy.

With *The Seven Lamps of Architecture* (1849) and *The Stones of Venice* (1851–1853), Ruskin became as powerful a critic of architecture as he was of painting. The central argument was, again, couched in an appeal to Christian authority: the Gothic style was the style of the early, humble, Christian world, and was therefore the right style for any building which wished to be taken seriously. The point of Gothic architecture for Ruskin was that it was democratic, flexible, and universal. He also managed to argue that it was instinctively "Protestant," despite the fact that the great exemplar of the form, medieval Venice, was, obviously, rooted in Catholic Europe. He arrived at this position on Venetian Gothic by a historical sleight-of-hand: because Venice of the twelfth to fourteenth centuries was a republic and politically independent of the papacy, it could be seen in this argument as the forerunner of the Protestant resistance to Rome that developed in northern Europe in the sixteenth and seventeenth centuries. An extraordinary example of Ruskinian Gothic is the Oxford University Museum, created by Ruskin's friend Henry Acland (1815–1900, Regius Professor of Medicine at Oxford) in the 1850s. Ruskin's arguments ensured that a building based on the style of medieval structures devoted to Christianity was considered the obvious, and ideal, place for the study of geology, medicine, and the natural sciences, despite the fact that in the eyes of Oxford Movement theologians (such as Edward Bouverie Pusey [1800–1882]) science was the mortal enemy of religion.

In 1858 Ruskin lost his faith. He underwent what he called an "unconversion" in Turin, and from 1860 onward he devoted himself substantially to politics, especially in his brilliant and provocative essays published as *Unto This Last* (1861), which famously contains his anticapitalist battle-cry "There is no Wealth but Life." Ruskin followed this with his grand political project published serially from 1871 until the 1880s (with interruptions), called *Fors Clavigera: Letters to the Workmen and Labourers of Great Britain*. Concurrently with these political and social writings he created his own utopia in the Guild of St. George, a medieval-style agrarian society designed to offer a radical alternative to the hard and aggressive competitiveness of mainstream Victorian capitalism. He also served as the first Slade Professor of Fine Art at Oxford from 1869 to 1878 and again from 1883 to 1885.

Ruskin's personal life was notoriously unhappy. His marriage to Effie Gray in 1848 was annulled on the grounds of nonconsummation in 1854, and Effie then married Ruskin's former friend and protégé Millais (Millais went on to huge commercial fame and success, and he and Effie had eight children). His intense friendship with Rossetti was cruelly disappointing; Ruskin lavished money and affection on Rossetti, who responded with what is reasonable to regard as callous ingratitude and insensitivity. Later he was to lavish similar patronage on Edward Coley Burne-Jones (1833–1898), who was more responsive (and greatly benefited from Ruskin's support). In the late 1850s Ruskin fell in love with a little girl, Rose La Touche (she was ten years old), for whom he nurtured a consuming passion until Rose's early death in 1875. He suffered a period of complete insanity in 1878 and thereafter seems to have suffered bipolar disorder punctuated by periods of raving and violent derangement. His cousin Joan Severn became his companion and, when he was really mad, custodian, in these later years. Despite his illness, Ruskin wrote his magnificent and indispensable autobiography, *Praeterita* (1885–1889). This was his last work: he was silent for the last ten years of his life and died at Brantwood in 1900.

The opposition to capitalism set out in *Unto This Last* and *Fors Clavigera* made Ruskin hugely popular with late Victorian socialists, especially his disciple William Morris (1834–1896). Through Morris, Ruskin's work came to be seen in the 1890s as a bible of modern socialism. Ruskin was the central Victorian philanthropist, a man who could not find happiness for himself but passionately believed that it could be available to others. His influence is still seen in Victorian painting and architecture, and felt in the policies of successive socialist governments from the early days of the British Labour Party (the first Labour MPs named Ruskin as their leading influence). His intellectual and political heirs worldwide included Leo Tolstoy (1828–1910), Marcel Proust (1871–1922), and Mohandas Gandhi (1869–1948).

See also **Morris, William; Pre-Raphaelite Movement; Turner, J. M. W.**

BIBLIOGRAPHY

Batchelor, John. *John Ruskin: No Wealth but Life*. London, 2000.

Birch, Dinah. *Ruskin's Myths*. Oxford, U.K., 1988.

———. *Ruskin on Turner*. London, 1990.

Blau, Eve. *Ruskinian Gothic: The Architecture of Deane and Woodward, 1845–1861*. Princeton, N.J., 1982.

Hewison, Robert. *John Ruskin: The Argument of the Eye*. Princeton, N.J., 1976.

Hilton, Tim. *John Ruskin*. 2 vols. New Haven, Conn., 1985, 2000.

Wheeler, Michael. *Ruskin's God*. Cambridge, U.K., 1999.

JOHN BATCHELOR

RUSSIA. The outbreak of revolution in France in 1789 posed dilemmas for the imperial Russian state that persisted until the downfall of the Romanov dynasty in 1917. Empress Catherine II had succeeded to the Russian throne in 1762 and prided herself on her learning and her links with educated and progressive European society. Catherine the Great cultivated her ties with thinkers such as Voltaire and Denis Diderot, corresponding with them and portraying herself as a liberal and enlightened ruler. The French Revolution put Catherine's ideals to the test: the theories of liberty and individual rights that she had discussed were now being put into practice in France itself.

For Catherine, however, there was no question of relaxing her rule over the Russian Empire and letting western European ideas influence Russian government. She believed that Russia was a very different state from France and the rest of Europe, and that the theories that were inspiring revolution in France should remain purely a matter of intellectual curiosity and debate among a select few in Russia itself. Catherine had acted firmly to put down the Pugachev rebellion in Russia during the 1770s, and, while she liked to be seen in the tradition of "enlightened absolutism," her policies concentrated on strengthening the Russian monarchy and maintaining tight control over the population. Catherine refused to contemplate emancipating the peasant serf population, believing that it was more important to be able to exercise firm control over her subjects. The Russian state faced this problem right through the nineteenth century: how far could it make reform without endangering the authority of the monarchy? Successive Russian rulers tried to balance the conflicting demands of reform and of the autocracy itself, while the example of the French Revolution of 1789 inspired tsarism's opponents and spurred on generations of Russian revolutionaries to try to overthrow the regime.

The impact of 1789 ran much deeper, however, for Russia. It brought into sharp focus the relationship between Europe and Russia and raised questions about the way in which Russia should develop. At the beginning of the eighteenth century, Peter the Great (r. 1682–1725) had opened Russia's "window on the West," both literally through his foundation of the new capital of St. Petersburg at the eastern end of the Baltic Sea, and less tangibly through his promotion of Western culture and technology to develop Russia's economy and society. Peter had shown that he believed Russia must follow the model of the West if it was to progress and cast off its mantle of backwardness.

This approach did not find universal favor in Russia. There was a strong current of opinion that believed that Russia should hold true to its own historical path and that it should not merely seek to ape the West. The events of the French Revolution brought this debate to the fore and set the tone for much of Russian political thought during the nineteenth century. The Slavophile movement that emerged during the 1830s and 1840s argued that Russia had its own particular path of development and that Russia should remain true to the characteristics that distinguished it from the West. Count Sergei Uvarov, minister of education from 1833 until 1849, formulated the concept of Official Nationality that encapsulated Russia's unique nature. This suggested that the heart of Russia's identity lay in the fusion of its political system, its religion, and its nationhood. "Autocracy, Orthodoxy, and Nationality" formed the triad of beliefs that sustained Russia and that made it distinct from every other state in Europe. The Russian tradition identified by conservative Slavophiles held that Russia must remain an autocracy, because its unruly people needed strong government. The Orthodox Church was an essential element of Russia's identity, and Orthodoxy also proclaimed Russian distinctiveness. Finally, the concept of Russian nationality had an almost mystical quality to it, suggesting that Russia was superior to other nationalities and that the non-Russian peoples of the empire should be assimilated into Russia proper. Slavophile ideas found wide sympathy, including from the great novelist Fyodor Dostoyevsky (1821–1881), who was profoundly nationalistic in outlook.

But the example of the French Revolution and the progress that Western states were making gave added impetus to the Petrine model of development. "Westernizers" argued that Russia was self-evidently backward in economic, social, and political terms and that if Russia was to be able to retain its authority in Europe, it had to cast off some of its historical traditions and follow the pattern of development that had proved so successful in the West. This argument gained greater strength from the mid-nineteenth century onward, as Russia's military power appeared to be on the wane. The defeat of Napoleon I in 1812 in Russia and Tsar Alexander I's triumphal entry into Paris in 1814 had suggested that Russian power was immense and that the policies followed particularly by Catherine the Great were bearing fruit. The Crimean War (1853–1856), however, represented a severe setback for Russia, as its troops were defeated on home soil by British and French armies. This experience of military defeat again raised the question of how Russia could progress. The view of the Westernizers informed the series of Great Reforms that Alexander

II implemented in the 1860s and early 1870s, as Russia freed its serfs, established a proper legal system, and laid the basis for a civil society. This outlook also shaped the views of people who were opposed to the tsarist regime. The revolutionaries who formed the Russian Social Democratic Labor Party in the 1890s drew their inspiration from Karl Marx's theories, developed in the context of industrial western Europe. Vladimir Lenin and his fellow Bolsheviks explicitly wanted to see Russia follow the Western path of industrial capitalism and to become a socialist society. There was no consensus about the best way for Russia to progress. As Lenin was proclaiming the need for a socialist revolution in Russia, Tsar Nicholas II celebrated the tercentenary of Romanov rule in 1913 by appearing in the traditional costume of his seventeenth-century ancestors. On the eve of war and revolution, the debate was still raging.

REFORM AND REACTION

The tsar stood at the head of the Russian state, ordained to his position by God, and with the unrestricted power to make whatever dispositions he wanted. This was not just a theoretical position, because no institutions had developed that could provide any sort of check to the tsar's authority. It was not law that guided the activities of the state, but the conscience and, indeed, whims of the monarchs themselves. The tsars who ruled Russia between 1789 and 1914 were able to impose very different styles of government and to implement dramatic shifts in policy without having to gain the consent of any formal body. In 1802 a system of ministerial government was introduced in Russia to replace the haphazard structures that dated from the time of Peter the Great. These new ministries dealt with the traditional concerns of central government: finance, foreign affairs, justice, and the like, but there was no institution that coordinated their work. Individual ministers reported directly to the tsar, so that the monarch in effect acted as his own prime minister. The overall policy of the Russian government was, therefore, rarely formally discussed by the government as a whole and there was little consideration of the impact of one ministry's policies on the activities of other parts of the government.

The coordination of the work of the Russian government was achieved solely through the person of the monarch, but Russian tsars hardly possessed a personal staff to support them in this task and to organize the complex work of governing the empire. The views and abilities of the monarch were critical, therefore, not just in setting the overall tone for the government but also in determining how efficiently the day-to-day work of governing the empire was carried out. The personal qualities of the tsar became especially significant at times when the Russian state was faced with crises or difficult decisions. Whereas Alexander II was prepared to grasp the nettle of serfdom in the late 1850s and to persevere to push through the long and complicated process of emancipation, Nicholas II found it difficult to act decisively and equivocated when considering making substantial reforms to cope with the waves of discontent that swept the Russian Empire during his reign.

Catherine II died in 1796 and was succeeded by her son, Paul I (r. 1796–1801). Paul's reign was short-lived, as his attempts to impose an extreme form of absolutism on Russia met with great disfavor from elements of the noble elite. He was murdered in his own bedroom by a group of nobles, and his son, Alexander I, succeeded to the throne, promising to rule "in the mind and heart" of his grandmother, Catherine II. Alexander I's reign (1801–1825) saw Russia establish itself as the greatest military power in Europe, but the tsar was unsure about taking advantage of this authority to make reform at home. During the first part of Alexander's reign, he encouraged the development of projects to transform Russian government. The "Unofficial Committee" of the tsar's friends that met between 1801 and 1803 discussed how the rule of law could be implemented in Russia, but its deliberations came to naught. In 1809 the tsar's advisor Mikhail Speransky proposed the transformation of Russia into a constitutional state with a legislature whose members would be selected by the tsar from lists prepared by provincial authorities. Speransky's plans involved a clear limitation on the powers of the monarch and resurrected the idea of law becoming supreme, but Alexander I could not be persuaded to accept them. The tsar was fundamentally ambivalent about implementing a constitution for Russia, even though the idea was again discussed in the early 1820s. In the end, however, Alexander followed the pattern set by Catherine II and declared that constitutions were suitable only for sophisticated peoples and enlightened nations. The attractions of autocracy proved too strong for Alexander, and in the last years of his reign he rejected plans to free the serfs, instead agreeing to experiment with the establishment of "military colonies" to try to create a more educated and useful class of peasantry. Some 750,000 people were forced into these colonies by Alexei Arakcheyev, one of Alexander's trusted advisors, but the colonies proved to be extremely unpopular and were kept running only by the use of force.

Alexander I died in December 1825, but the succession was unclear. As Alexander had no surviving children, his elder brother Constantine was next in line to succeed. Constantine, however, had entered into a morganatic marriage and had secretly renounced the throne, with Alexander making a secret commitment that the succession should pass instead to his younger brother Nicholas. Alexander's death was followed by great confusion. Nicholas initially swore allegiance to Constantine, and it was only when Constantine made a public renunciation of the throne that Nicholas sought to take power. This period of uncertainty provided the opportunity for secret societies to stage a rebellion in favor of Constantine and the implementation of a constitution. Thousands of soldiers were marched onto Senate Square on a freezing December day by their officers, but there was no sustained attempt to stage a coup d'état, and forces loyal to Nicholas were able to open fire on the rebels and quell the uprising. The Decembrist revolt has been heralded as the first Russian revolution, and it marked an important shift from both the elemental peasant rebellions and the palace revolutions that had threatened the tsarist regime during the seventeenth and eighteenth centuries. For the first time, a group of radical thinkers had developed a program for change and had attempted to put it into practice, albeit with almost no popular support.

The Decembrist revolt set the stage for the reign of Nicholas I by reinforcing the new tsar's deep conservatism and making him extremely resistant to any proposals for reform that originated outside the government. Nicholas personally supervised the investigations into the conspiracy: its ringleaders were executed, and more than 120 were exiled to Siberia for long periods. The thirty years of Nicholas I's reign represented a period when substantive political reform was never on the regime's agenda. The constitutional ideas that had peppered his brother's reign disappeared from open discussion, and while Nicholas did examine the question of serfdom and make some reforms to the condition of the state peasantry, Russia's politics stagnated. The most significant result of this was to make open discussion of political and social questions difficult and to promote the formation of an intelligentsia that was fundamentally unsympathetic to the regime. The tsar's severe treatment of the Decembrist rebels alienated a significant element of the Russian nobility and provoked some of its members to take extreme views. Peter Chaadayev's "First Philosophical Letter" (written 1828, published 1836) portrayed Russia as deeply backward and in need of a radical change of direction; the reaction of the authorities was to declare him to be mad. Opposition to the regime also came from other parts of society. Literary criticism was one way in which political and social opinion could be voiced obliquely, and it became an important vehicle for critical views to be aired. Vissarion Belinsky, the son of a poor rural doctor, wrote literary criticism that had a sharp political edge to it, and during the 1840s literary politics came to act almost as a substitute for the real political life that Nicholas I disliked so much. The impact of these intellectuals was, however, very limited. The great majority of the Russian people were illiterate and had no access to the journals and magazines in which the intelligentsia propagated their views, so there was no wide audience for such views. During Nicholas I's reign, the intelligentsia largely confined themselves to abstract discussion and made no attempt to turn their criticisms of the regime into anything more practical.

The absence of any active domestic political opposition to Nicholas I meant that the only threat to his regime could come from outside. Even this looked unlikely, because Russian power appeared assured in post-Napoleonic Europe. Russia's foreign policy since Peter the Great had been to expand its boundaries where it encountered weak neighbors. Catherine the Great's final years had witnessed the partitions of Poland, with Russia gaining the lion's share of the Polish lands. The French Revolution and the rise of Napoleon threatened the European balance of power, and Russia was drawn into wars between 1805 and 1814 to counter the French threat. The famous defeat that Napoleon suffered in the frozen winter of 1812 as he marched on Moscow secured Russia's position in Europe and allowed the Russian state to concentrate on expanding its empire in the Caucasus and in Central Asia. The Crimean War (1853–1856), however, dealt a crushing blow to Russian prestige and power. Russia was defeated on its own territory by Britain and France, and, in the middle of the war, Nicholas I died from pneumonia, probably contracted when he insisted on inspecting troops on a freezing February day in 1855.

The death of Nicholas I marked a turning point. His successor, Alexander II, was entirely different in outlook. Defeat in the Crimean War provoked intense reflection about the reasons for the severe change in fortunes that Russia had suffered since the nation had been instrumental in defeating Napoleon. Alexander II accepted that Russia's military weakness was a symptom of a deeper malaise and that it reflected Russian backwardness in a variety of areas. A sizable group of "enlightened bureaucrats" were instrumental in preparing a major series of reforms that were implemented during the 1860s and early 1870s. The most important of these was the 1861 emancipation of the serfs, but these Great Reforms touched almost every aspect of Russian life.

In 1864 Alexander II took the important step of introducing elected local councils (zemstvos) into most of the provinces and districts of European Russia. These councils were elected on a narrow franchise and were dominated by the nobility. The councils were given rather general responsibilities: to deal with matters such as health, education, the maintenance of roads and bridges, and local economic affairs. Their involvement in local affairs grew substantially, and their expenditures grew sevenfold by 1914. This allowed councils to employ substantial numbers of teachers, doctors, agricultural experts and the like who came to play a prominent part in the life of provincial Russia. These professionals acquired a reputation as radicals, partly because their frequent and close contact with the rural population resulted in their making demands for social reform and improvements in living conditions in the countryside.

Local councils also represented an autonomous source of authority in imperial Russia, able to implement policies that did not necessarily coincide with those of the central government. Furthermore, once the principle of self-government had been conceded at the local level, the more liberal of the local councils argued that there was no reason why the same principle should not play a part in the national administration of the state. The activities of local councils provoked considerable disquiet within the central government, especially after the accession of Alexander III to the throne in 1881. In 1890 the councils' power to levy taxation was restricted, and provincial governors were given the right to veto any appointments the councils made.

The same attitudes had been true of the Russian judicial system during the nineteenth century, and Russian courts were notorious for their corruption, delay, and inefficiency. But the change in the status of the peasantry brought about by the emancipation of the serfs in 1861 and the emergence of each previously enserfed peasant as a legal entity, free from the ownership of the landlords, meant that they had to be granted access to the law. This prompted a fundamental review of the whole imperial legal structure. In 1864 a system of civil and criminal courts based on Western models was introduced, with clear lines of appeal and staffed by a judiciary whose independence was assured through good salaries, thus obviating the need to take bribes, and by their irremovability from office. Judges could no longer be dismissed for handing down verdicts that displeased the government. Furthermore, jury trials were introduced for the first time in criminal cases, thus adding another element outside the control of the government into the administration of justice. During the 1860s and 1870s an independent and articulate legal profession came into existence, encouraged by the new freedoms that lawyers had gained under the reform, and the courtroom became a focus for challenges to the authority and style of government of the autocracy. Lawyers came to be viewed by the regime as being in the same category as the zemstvo professionals—a source of autonomous opposition to the government—and the government made attempts to restrict their freedom.

Reform extended more widely. The education system was reformed in the early 1860s, giving greater autonomy to universities and introducing a wider and more modern curriculum into schools. Censorship was relaxed, giving authors and editors more latitude in what could be published after the rigid controls imposed by Nicholas I. The army underwent major reform in 1874, when Dmitri Milyutin, the minister of war, abolished what was in effect lifetime service in the army for conscripts and replaced it with a system of universal liability to conscription for a fixed period of six years, followed by nine years in the reserves. This reform recognized that the peasantry was now equal in legal status to the other parts of the population, and opened the way for military service to be a burden that was spread more equitably across Russian men.

REVOLUTIONARIES

For some Russians the autocratic state itself was beyond reform. Revolutionaries in Russia in the nineteenth century made up a tiny proportion of the population. As few as two thousand people took part in the attempts in 1873 and 1874 to take the revolutionary message into the countryside by "going to the people." The People's Will (*Narodnaya volya*), the organization that succeeded in assassinating Alexander II in 1881, had only five hundred members along with several thousand more sympathizers. Nonetheless, these groups did have an influence on Russia that was wholly disproportionate to their size, partly through their terrorist activities and partly through the largely illegal circulation of pamphlets and newspapers. The assassination of the emperor in 1881 had been but the latest in a series of attempts on his life, and despite the regime's efforts to restrict the flow of information through censorship and customs controls on publications from abroad, clandestinely produced works reached deep into Russian educated society.

Russian revolutionary thinking until the mid-1880s was centered around two basic positions. The most common belief of those who promoted revolution in Russia was that the Russian peasantry should form the basis of the new society that would emerge after the destruction of the tsarist regime. The early 1860s saw appeals such as "Young Russia" calling for a federal-republican Russia, based on peasant communes, and the establishment of the Land and Liberty (*Zemlya i volya*) group, which demanded a genuine peasant reform in the wake of

the 1861 emancipation of the serfs. Nikolai Chernyshevsky, the author of the tendentious novel *What Is to Be Done?* (1863) who was exiled to Siberia for twenty years starting in 1864, argued that change was needed in Russia and wanted to see the establishment of a society based on cooperatives in the new Russia. These rather isolated expressions of opinion were the forerunners, however, of the much broader populist movement during the 1870s; it tried to move from the theoretical musings produced by a myriad of individuals and small groups to practical action to realize its aims. Populist thinkers believed that humankind was inherently good but that the Russian state had repressed its population to such an extent that this prevented the emergence of any type of just or fruitful society. The Russian peasantry, in the populists' view, bore the brunt of oppression and it would be these same peasants who would form the basis of a new and equitable society. The peasant commune, already in existence in Russia, would lie at the heart of the postrevolutionary Russian state, and the communal structure could be extended to transform Russia into a federal state arranged around these socialized and self-governing units. The populists saw this as marking Russia out as being able to pursue a social and economic path that was different from the vigorous industrialization that had gripped western Europe by the 1870s. The price they saw the West paying for industrial growth was one that the Russian populists believed to be too high. They felt that Russia's relatively low level of industrial development meant that the opportunity existed for Russia to avoid capitalism altogether and to move directly to an agrarian socialism.

The second element of revolutionary thinking was related to the means through which revolution could actually be achieved in Russia. A debate raged in the Russian revolutionary intelligentsia about the role of the revolutionary elite and to what extent the ordinary people of the Russian Empire had to make their own revolution. The activities and writings of Sergei Nechayev and Peter Tkachev were important in developing this tradition. Nechayev set out elaborate plans for staging a revolution in Russia and emphasized the absolute commitment that must be demonstrated by those leading the process.

Execution of conspirators in the assassination of Alexander II. Nineteenth-century engraving. Five Russian nihilists found guilty of planning the 1881 assassination of Alexander II were executed by hanging in St. Petersburg. The actual bomber, a Polish dissident, was killed during the attack on the tsar; a sixth conspirator, who was pregnant at the time, was exiled to Siberia. ©CORBIS

For Tkachev the revolution had to be undertaken exclusively by this small group of committed revolutionaries, and power would be seized through some form of terrorist conspiracy. This trend was accentuated by the failure of the movement to draw the Russian peasantry onto its side in the early 1870s. A small number of radicals—mainly students and former students—fanned out into villages in most of the provinces of European Russia in the summer of 1874, but found the peasants unsympathetic to their cause. Instead of proving to be the naive and pliant material that the populists had envisaged, the Russian peasantry turned out to be highly resistant to condoning attacks on authority, demonstrating instead a solid faith in the tsar. Nearly eight hundred of these agitators were arrested during the summer,

but what most disturbed the government was the effect they had, not on the peasantry, but in inculcating radical views into the rural gentry and local officials.

The inability of the populists to gain popular support in the mid-1870s was repeated in 1881 when the murder of the emperor by revolutionary terrorists failed to result in any form of popular uprising. Revolutionaries faced a crisis in the 1880s and had to embark on a fundamental reassessment of their strategy. This was made the more urgent by the deeply conservative and repressive regime of Alexander III. The police were increasingly active against revolutionaries during the 1880s, infiltrating their organizations and acting quickly to preempt conspiracies. In 1887 a plot to kill the new tsar was uncovered, leading to the swift execution of five of its leaders, including Alexander Ulyanov, a trauma that was to have a decisive impact on his then seventeen-year-old brother Vladimir, soon to become better known under his revolutionary pseudonym of Lenin. In addition, the fundamental populist belief that Russia could avoid the process of industrialization and develop along a different path was being undermined by the growth of Russian industry and the way in which Russia was increasingly becoming integrated into the European industrial economy. The nature of opposition to the autocratic regime therefore underwent substantial changes during the 1880s and 1890s. Some of the chief proponents of agrarian socialism in Russia, such as Nikolai Mikhailovsky and Vasily Vorontsov, continued to believe that Russia need not experience capitalism, and these "legal populists" suggested that a policy of "small deeds" was the way forward instead of revolution. This meant using the institutions of the Russian state to bring about the greatest possible improvement in the life of the Russian people, in the belief that the state itself would gradually come to appreciate the benefits of a socialized economy.

Marxist ideas, which had been gaining currency among west European radicals, found a ready audience in Russia. Marx's work had been known in Russia since the mid-1870s, and in the wake of the failure of Russian radicals to enlist the support of the peasantry, Marx's emphasis on the role that would be played by the proletariat in initiating revolution was very welcome. Georgy Plekhanov, the "father of Russian Marxism," had begun his radical career as a populist, but in the 1880s he moved sharply away from peasant-centered politics. In 1898 the Russian Social Democratic Labor Party was founded, and the young Lenin played a key role in turning the party into a disciplined and well-organized group. Russian Marxism attracted relatively few adherents before 1914, hampered both by official oppression and by its concentration on an industrial working class that represented only a very small minority of the Russian people. Many Marxist leaders spent time in exile, both in Siberia and outside Russia, but while this also made it more difficult for the party to expand its support, it did allow the leadership to debate policy and strategy vigorously and openly.

THE ROAD TO DISASTER

The accession of Alexander III to the throne in 1881 marked the beginning of a period of reaction. He wanted to curb the revolutionary movement that had been responsible for the murder of his father, and believed that reform had served only to stimulate popular discontent. After 1881, much of the empire was ruled under emergency legislation and the "Russification" of the empire was a priority, as the Russian language and the Orthodox religion were imposed on non-Russians. Alexander III did make a radical departure in Russia's foreign policy, however. He drew away from alliances with Germany and Austria, the conservative monarchies that had been Russia's traditional allies for much of the nineteenth century. Instead, Russia moved toward friendship with France, motivated partly by economic reasons. During the 1890s, Sergei Witte, the minister of finance, pursued policies to attract foreign investment in Russian industry. It was important to demonstrate that Russia was politically stable and that investors could have confidence in the security of their funds. At the same time, France was a vital source of investment and was also in search of an ally in the wake of its defeat in the Franco-Prussian War (1870–1871). Both Russia and France saw advantages in drawing closer, and in 1894 they signed a formal alliance, designed to offer protection to both countries in case they were attacked by Germany. This had the desired effect of encouraging French investment in Russia, but it also helped to set in stone the alliance systems that were to contribute to the outbreak of war in 1914.

Alexander III died shortly after concluding this alliance and was succeeded by his son Nicholas II. Nicholas was temperamentally unsuited to rule Russia at a time of crisis. He was a weak ruler, but determined to pass on his inheritance intact to his heir. Nicholas found it particularly difficult to deal with strong-minded ministers, and although he could be persuaded into agreeing with policies, he often resented the pressure that had been placed upon him and tried to reverse decisions after they had been taken. In the years between 1894 and the outbreak of World War I, the Russian government swung sharply and frequently between reaction and reform. The assassination of Dmitri Sipiagin, minister of internal affairs, in April 1902 and the appointment of Vyacheslav Plehve in his place brought about an increase in the role of the police in the Russian Empire as the regime intensified its attempts to eliminate opposition and to consolidate its position in the face of widespread discontent. Finland, part of the Russian Empire since 1809, was severely affected by measures designed to reduce its autonomy, while anti-Jewish pogroms, especially the 1903 Kishinev massacre, produced only a muted response from the authorities. These authoritarian policies did not meet with wholehearted approval inside the government: Plehve's replacement as interior minister was Peter Svyatolpolk-Mirsky, a man of liberal opinions, but his period in office lasted only five months before he was in turn replaced.

During the 1890s the liberal elements of Russian society had begun to make a resurgence after the constraints placed upon their local government power base. The famine and cholera epidemic that struck Russia in 1891 and 1892, leaving four hundred thousand people dead, and the government's inadequate response to these disasters spurred liberal opinion to action. A small number of senior local council activists began to meet secretly from 1898 in a group that became known as *Beseda* and that was the basis of a liberal constitutional movement. Russian liberalism included a very wide range of opinions, and its leaders, such as Pavel Milyukov and Ivan Petrunkevich, had to take pains to make their program as inclusive as possible. The original 1902 program published in the illegal newspaper *Osvobozhdenie* (Liberation) steered clear of controversy by avoiding calls for a constitution or a parliament by name, although it included an explicit demand for a representative legislative body. The radical intelligentsia succeeded in moving the liberal movement to the left, so that when the Union of Liberation was formally established in 1903 it was intended as an underground organization, aimed at promoting revolution. This shift had come about as liberals had realized that the local councils where the movement had originated were unlikely to become motors of successful change in Russia and that more direct action was needed if reforms were to be achieved. During 1904 liberal calls for change were made more openly, more loudly, and more frequently than at any time previously.

Russian liberals lacked sufficient strength to bring about change by themselves, and revolution and reform took place in 1905 only as a result of pressure from a wider spectrum of society. Student demonstrations had become more frequent in the cities of the empire since 1899 with a much-publicized gathering taking place in St. Petersburg in 1901 to commemorate the fortieth anniversary of the emancipation of the serfs. The screw was tightened further on the Russian state by defeat in battle. In early February 1904 Russia and Japan went to war over their competing ambitions in the Far East. The Russian military performance was uniformly disastrous: the initial Japanese attack dealt a severe blow to the Russian Far Eastern navy; by May the main Russian base at Port Arthur was besieged, and it surrendered in January 1905. The Battle of Mukden (February–March 1905) was a Japanese triumph. The Japanese delivered a shattering blow to the Russian navy in May 1905 in the Tsushima Strait by destroying the fleet sent from Europe to rescue Russian fortunes, and in August 1905 both sides accepted the United States' proposal of peace negotiations. The continuing defeats Russia suffered caused a severe crisis of confidence in the tsarist regime and demonstrated the weakness of the autocracy more clearly than anything else.

At a time when the tsarist regime was already under severe stress, it was faced with an unprecedented upsurge in popular discontent. On 22 January (9 January, old style) 1905 a mass demonstration by striking St. Petersburg workers, marching into the center of the city to try to present a petition to the tsar, was met by troops who fired indiscriminately into the crowds, killing 130 people and wounding over 400 more. The events of "Bloody Sunday" brought about mass disillusionment with the government and rendered useless the very tentative steps the regime had been taking toward meeting some of the demands articulated by the liberal opposition. A few weeks earlier the regime had promised some concessions, such as easing press censorship and allowing greater freedom of religion, but Nicholas II, acting on the advice of Witte, the former minister of finance, had rejected granting members of local councils any form of participation in the work of central government.

The strike movement spread very quickly through Russia in January 1905 as working people expressed their anger at the events in St. Petersburg. More than four hundred thousand people

Russian peasants receive food, 1892. An estimated 400,000 people died during the catastrophic famine of 1892. ©CORBIS

took part in strikes during January and February, and they were joined in their protests by students at most of the empire's higher education institutions. The industrial unrest continued throughout the year, subsiding at the height of the summer, but reemerging with renewed vigor during the autumn so that during October 1905 nearly half a million people stopped work. These strikes were motivated by both economic and political concerns, and their very varied motivation made it extremely difficult for the authorities to take any sort of action, other than pure coercion, that would solve the problem. Discontent was not confined to the factories, for an unparalleled wave of rural disturbances also hit the empire. During 1905 there were more than three thousand instances of peasant rebellion, affecting Russia acutely during the spring and early summer and reaching a peak of ferocity at the end of the year. These uprisings frequently involved the burning and destruction of landowners' estates, along with strikes by agricultural laborers and the seizure of pastureland and meadows.

The concessions the regime agreed to during 1905 were wrested from it grudgingly. There was considerable debate inside the government about the best way of dealing with the revolution that threatened to engulf it; the policies of repression the Russian state had relied upon were called into question by Witte who argued that instead of dealing with the symptoms of discontent the government should address itself to the real causes of the strikes and rural uprisings. Little by little the regime moved toward granting a constitution; in February the government announced that it would allow "elected representatives of the people to take place in preliminary discussion of legislation," but when the details of the scheme were revealed in August its limitations were made clear. The State Duma, the national representative body, was to be only a consultative institution, and elections were to be indirect with the franchise heavily skewed toward large landowners and the peasantry, excluding workers and most urban inhabitants. The huge and renewed upsurge in discontent during the autumn forced the government to acknowledge that a consultative assembly was insufficient to satisfy its critics, and Nicholas II accepted, albeit with severe reservations, that the Duma should be transformed into a legislative body. The October Manifesto that announced this change of heart also declared that the new Duma would be elected on a wider franchise than originally planned and that the Russian people should be granted basic civil rights, including freedom of speech, conscience, assembly, and association.

The issuing of the October Manifesto did not put an end to popular unrest. On the contrary, violence intensified in the cities of the empire, and Jews suffered particularly from more than six hundred anti-Jewish pogroms. The climax of rural disturbances came in November, and the unrest was noticeably more violent than earlier in the year. More dangerously for the regime, mutinies began to break out in the army and navy. During the last ten weeks of 1905 there were more than two hundred instances of rebellion in the armed forces. The ability of the government to exert control over the population of the empire was seriously in doubt in the late autumn of 1905. Regaining the loyalty of troops was vital if the autocracy was to survive; conditions of service were improved in the armed forces, and the government demonstrated its determination to deal firmly with mutineers. Reform was not the only weapon the regime used to reassert its authority.

The Russian state was not prepared to abandon its traditional policies of repression, and the police and troops used considerable force to restore order. From 1905 until 1917 the relationship between reform and repression in the Russian state was exceptionally complex. After October 1905 the tsar increasingly resented that he had been compelled to concede a legislative parliament that limited his autocratic power. No longer could the emperor act precisely as he wanted, for now legislation had to be approved by the Duma before it could become law. The government moved to limit the effect of this concession as soon as it seemed that order was being successfully restored to the empire in the spring of 1906. New Fundamental Laws for the empire were issued in April 1906. The State Council was reformed to become the second chamber in the legislative process, to be composed of both members appointed by the tsar and representatives elected by corporate bodies in the empire. This arrangement guaranteed that the State Council would be solidly conservative in outlook and able to block bills passed by the Duma, while the legislative process was capped by making the tsar's approval the final condition for the enactment of a law. The Fundamental Laws continued to describe the monarch as an "autocrat," and he could issue emergency legislation when the Duma and State Council were in recess.

Although the franchise for the first elections to the Duma was limited and had been devised with the intention that a conservative peasantry would cast its votes for candidates who would support the tsarist regime, this judgment proved to be very wide of the mark. The First Duma, which convened in May 1906, was dominated by the Kadets (the Constitutional Democratic Party), the embodiment of the liberal movement, and the Trudoviki, a largely peasant party more radical than the liberal Kadets. Government and Duma found themselves wholly at loggerheads and after less than three months the Duma was dissolved and an interval of more than six months interposed before the Second Duma was to meet. These new elections produced a body little different from its predecessor and the situation of deadlock was repeated. After little more than three months the Duma was again dissolved, but this time the government took more radical action to ensure that the composition of the Duma would be more in line with its own thinking. On 16 June (3 June, old style) 1907, the day after the Second Duma had been dissolved, the government illegally altered the franchise to reduce peasant participation and increase the representation given to landowners and urban property owners. This had a profound effect on the results of the elections for the Third Duma, which resulted in the representation of the Left being dramatically reduced so that the Kadets and Trudoviki together made up only 15 percent of the deputies. The largest single group in the new Duma was the Octobrists, a center party that took its name from the October Manifesto of 1905 that had set up the legislative Duma, and that the government hoped would be a reliable ally. Parties on the right also gained substantial support, taking one-third of the seats.

Caricature of Tsar Nicholas II and his wife. From the Hungarian satirical journal *Kakas Márton*, 29 July 1906. Frequently viewed as a weak and ineffective sovereign, Nicholas II is here depicted as terrified of the newly formed Russian parliament. PRIVATE COLLECTION/BRIDGEMAN ART LIBRARY. ©2005 HUNGART, BUDAPEST/ ARTISTS RIGHTS SOCIETY (ARS), NEW YORK.

While the Russian regime was concerned to ensure a pliant Duma and was also busy during 1906 and 1907 continuing its policies of repression, the government was also committed to making fundamental reforms. The constitutional changes of 1905 also brought about for the first time the establishment of proper cabinet government, with the Council of Ministers transformed into a forum for the discussion of policy and its chairman taking the role of prime minister. Between 1906 and 1911 this post was occupied by Peter Stolypin who pursued a policy of "pacification and renewal" for Russia. He believed that the two parts of this policy had to run parallel, for to relax the fight against terrorism would result

in such havoc that reform could not be implemented, while to abandon reform would be to cease the attempt at removing the causes of the discontent that fed the revolutionary fervor. In 1906 and 1907 the government introduced a whole series of proposals into the Duma: a major agrarian reform; bills to extend civil rights; the reform of local government; changes to the education system; the reform of emergency powers; and a bill to reform local justice. Stolypin intended to alter Russia fundamentally through his reform program. He believed that "renewal must begin at the bottom" and declared that his reforms were predicated on the creation of "a wealthy, well-to-do peasantry, for where there is prosperity there is also, of course, enlightenment and real freedom." The transformation of Russia Stolypin envisaged would bring into being a class of independent peasant landowners, freed from the shackles of the peasant commune. In addition, Stolypin argued that the Russian state itself had to be transformed so that the ethos of arbitrary government was swept away and replaced with a commitment by the state to being itself governed by law. These twin areas of reform were designed to remove the underlying causes of discontent and to establish the tsarist state as a strong and modern institution.

Stolypin's plans for reform resulted in little real change. Most of his reform program got bogged down in the Duma and the State Council. His peasant reform required a long period of implementation, and, once rebellion was quashed across Russia, many on the right questioned the need for any sort of reform. Stolypin was assassinated in 1911, and this put an end to any hope of real reform in Russia. His successor as prime minister, Vladimir Kokovtsov, was a cautious bureaucrat who wanted only to maintain stability.

By 1914, many elements of Russian political opinion were warning that the country stood on the edge of disaster. Alexander Guchkov, leader of the moderate Octobrist Party, spoke in 1913 of the "inevitable and grave catastrophe" that Russia was heading toward. He believed that the government was so detached from popular opinion that it was doomed to collapse, but his gloom was such that he could not foresee any positive outcome from this, rather just a "period of protracted, chronic anarchy." At the other end of the political spectrum, Peter Durnovo, a deeply conservative former minister, foresaw the likelihood of war between Russia and Germany and predicted that it would lead to social revolution in both countries. Durnovo's views, expressed in a long memorandum of February 1914, showed remarkable foresight. The Russian regime had failed to make real reform during the nineteenth century, and the gulf between state and society had widened as the autocratic regime grew increasingly distant from its people. The tsarist state had failed to learn lessons from other European monarchies that had been destroyed by revolution, and the seeds of its downfall were sown long before revolution eventually struck in 1917.

See also **Alexander I; Alexander II; Alexander III; Anti-Semitism; Belinsky, Vissarion; Bolsheviks; Catherine II; Chaadayev, Peter; Cossacks; Crimean War; French Revolutionary Wars and Napoleonic Wars; Great Reforms (Russia); Intelligentsia; Lenin, Vladimir; Napoleonic Empire; Nicholas I; Nicholas II; Plekhanov, Georgy; Populists; Revolution of 1905 (Russia); Russo-Japanese War; Russo-Turkish War; Serfs, Emancipation of; Slavophiles; Speransky, Mikhail; Stolypin, Peter; Westernizers; Witte, Sergei.**

BIBLIOGRAPHY

Ascher, Abraham. *The Revolution of 1905.* 2 vols. Stanford, Calif., 1988–1992.

Crisp, Olga, and Linda Edmondson, eds. *Civil Rights in Imperial Russia.* Oxford, U.K., 1989.

Eklof, Ben, John Bushnell, and Larissa Zakharova. *Russia's Great Reforms, 1855–1881.* Bloomington, Ind., 1994.

Geifman, Anna, ed. *Russia under the Last Tsar: Opposition and Subversion, 1894–1917.* Oxford, U.K., 1999.

Hartley, Janet M. *Alexander I.* London, 1994.

Lieven, Dominic. *Nicholas II: Emperor of All the Russias.* London, 1993.

Lincoln, W. Bruce. *Nicholas I: Emperor and Autocrat of All the Russias.* Bloomington, Ind., 1978. Reprint, DeKalb, Ill., 1989.

Mazour, Anatole G. *The First Russian Revolution, 1825: The Decembrist Movement, Its Origins, Development, and Significance.* Berkeley, Calif., 1937. Reprint, Stanford, Calif., 1961.

McGrew, Roderick E. *Paul I of Russia, 1754–1801.* Oxford, U.K., 1992.

Naimark, Norman M. *Terrorists and Social Democrats: The Russian Revolutionary Movement under Alexander III.* Cambridge, Mass., 1983.

Raeff, Marc. *Michael Speransky: Statesman of Imperial Russia, 1772–1839.* 2nd ed. The Hague, Netherlands, 1969.

Raleigh, Donald J., ed. *The Emperors and Empresses of Russia: Rediscovering the Romanovs.* Armonk, N.Y., 1996.

Riasanovsky, Nicholas V. *Nicholas I and Official Nationality in Russia, 1825–1855.* Berkeley and Los Angeles, 1959.

Rogger, Hans. *Russia in the Age of Modernisation and Revolution, 1881–1917.* London, 1983.

Saunders, David. *Russia in the Age of Reaction and Reform, 1801–1881.* London, 1992.

Thaden, Edward C. *Conservative Nationalism in Nineteenth-Century Russia.* Seattle, Wash., 1964.

Venturi, Franco. *Roots of Revolution: A History of the Populist and Socialist Movements in Nineteenth-Century Russia.* Translated by Francis Haskell. London, 1960.

Waldron, Peter. *Between Two Revolutions: Stolypin and the Politics of Renewal in Russia.* London, 1998.

Wortman, Richard S. *Scenarios of Power: Myth and Ceremony in Russian Monarchy.* 2 vols. Princeton, N.J., 1995–2000.

Zaionchkovsky, Peter A. *The Russian Autocracy under Alexander III.* Edited and translated by David R. Jones. Gulf Breeze, Fla., 1976.

PETER WALDRON

RUSSIAN ORTHODOX CHURCH.

A bedrock institution in medieval Russia, the Russian Orthodox Church remained an important component of the political order and popular culture in imperial Russia. Despite the reforms of Peter the Great (r. 1689–1725) and the secularization of church property under Catherine the Great in 1764, the church remained distinct from the state, with its own administration and law, hereditary caste of servitors, and deep sense of special privilege and rights. Greater challenges, however, were to come in the nineteenth century—not only from unbelievers and other confessions but also from a secular state and lay believers intent on pressing their own respective interests. By the early twentieth century, the church was in the throes of profound crisis and openly acknowledged the urgent need of reform. During the final years of the old regime, however, it failed to resolve these problems and, as the country plunged into war and revolution, found itself ill-prepared to combat the new Bolshevik regime seeking to dismantle the church (as "counterrevolutionary") and to excoriate popular belief ("superstition").

ORTHODOXY IN THE LATE EIGHTEENTH CENTURY

Despite attempts by eighteenth-century rulers to restrict the church's power, it remained juridically, economically, and socially separate. Peter the Great sought both to tame the church (by replacing the unruly patriarchate with a "spiritual college," soon renamed the Holy Synod) and to make it into an instrument of cultural change. More dramatic still was the decision in 1764 to sequester the church's lands and peasants, a step that greatly diminished its resources and power. Nevertheless, the church retained its operational autonomy, contested further encroachments, and defended its traditional prerogatives and privileges.

Indeed, the eighteenth-century incursions actually helped the church to enhance its functional role in the strictly spiritual domain. Thus, consonant with the Petrine reforms, the church attended increasingly to the religious needs of the folk, sought to instruct and enlighten, and enforced canons on such important spheres as marriage and divorce. Ironically, whatever the motive for the secularization of church property in 1764 (with the state's fiscal greed doubtless playing a major role), it freed the church from this-worldly administration of estates and enabled it to concentrate on the purely religious mission. Over the subsequent decades, the church expanded its administrative system, intensified efforts to "Christianize" a believing but ignorant folk, and sought to redefine and secure the place of Orthodoxy in a changing society and culture.

INSTITUTIONAL ORTHODOXY IN THE NINETEENTH CENTURY

While the eighteenth-century rulers significantly altered the status of the church, the major assault of ecclesiastical privilege actually did not come until the nineteenth century. Only then did the chief procurator (a state official charged with overseeing the ecclesiastical domain) build a large apparatus and greatly expand his role in church decision-making and administration. In the judgment of ranking prelates, moreover, he did so in an effort to serve the interests of the state, not the church. Nor was he alone: state officials, in general, showed a growing sensitivity to the multi-confessional character of the empire and hence were less willing to uphold the special status of the church. That was especially apparent in the issue of religious freedom; on purely practical grounds, state officials showed a growing willingness to ameliorate the plight of religious minorities, especially those deemed politically loyal. Rebuffing the church's demand that apostates be prosecuted and punished, leading officials blamed such disaffection on the church's own shortcomings and argued that the clergy should rely only on suasion, not coercion, to combat the challenge of dissent and other confessions.

The church did indeed become more active, and aggressive, in defending and propagating Orthodoxy. By the late eighteenth century, it had significantly improved central and diocesan administration, achieving a marked increase in the volume and quality of its paperwork and documentation. The church gave tightened supervision over diocesan administration and systematized procedural rules for consistories (*Ustav dukhovnykh konsistorii*, 1841). As a result, the church substantially increased its control over religious life and, most notably, in such vital secular spheres as marriage and divorce. The church established an elaborate system of ecclesiastical schools, seminaries, and academies to train and "professionalize" the clergy. It succeeded in obtaining some state funding for parishes (initially for "poor" parishes, later for those in borderland provinces, and eventually for other areas as well) and for parish schools to serve the needs of the laity.

That institutional development brought significant changes in the clergy itself. The episcopate not only increased in size (accompanying the establishment of smaller, more manageable dioceses) but also changed in its social complexion. Drawn almost exclusively from the offspring of the parish clergy, it initially consisted mainly of "learned monks" but by the late nineteenth century promoted men with a more "practical" profile (as educators, missionaries, and widowed parish priests). Whatever their origin, these bishops had served in various dioceses across the empire and hence gained a close familiarity with the diverse problems facing the church in different parts of this far-flung realm. While radical priests were wont to castigate bishops as "bureaucrats in cassocks," most prelates were not only efficient administrators but also men fervently devoted to the church, its traditions, and its interests.

Catherine's secularization of ecclesiastical land and peasants not only expropriated the vast wealth of monasteries but also brought a massive reduction in the number of monasteries and monastic clergy. Monasticism languished for several decades (with strict obstacles to the tonsure of new monastics and opening of new institutions) but finally began to grow again in the 1830s and 1840s and, by 1914, had even recovered its pre-sequestration level. More important, the social profile of monasticism also underwent a significant translation, with much of the increase being concentrated in female monasticism. No less important was a spiritual renaissance, reflected most dramatically in the phenomenon of "elderhood" (*starchestvo*), whereby individual monks acquired extraordinary fame and influence for their spiritual power and guidance. This revival of monasticism—intellectual, spiritual, economic—naturally provoked a rise in anti-monastic sentiment, not only among the secular intelligentsia but also among married white (secular) clergy.

The secular clergy (composed of priests, deacons, and sacristans) manned the forty thousand parishes that dotted the Russian landscape. Required (by custom, not canon) to marry prior to ordination, the priesthood thus had a substantial population that demanded material support (in contrast to the celibate Catholic clergy), including a plethora of male offspring who naturally tended to follow in the footsteps of their fathers. In the eighteenth century that predilection turned into a rigid caste-like order, with virtually no outsiders gaining entry to the clergy, for three main reasons: state policy (above all, a poll tax that impeded the transfer of townspeople and peasants to the tax-exempt clergy), specialized ecclesiastical education in schools open only to the clergy's sons, and the clergy's own vested interest in ensuring positions for their own sons. While this hereditary status ensured a steady rise in the educational qualification of ordinands (with virtually all new ordinands in the mid-nineteenth century holding a

seminary degree), it produced far too many candidates (for a parish system that grew only marginally) and too few with a genuine sense of vocation (with many becoming priests out of inertia, not choice). To rejuvenate the secular clergy, the Great Reforms of the 1860s sought to facilitate the education and recruitment of male youths from other social estates. The reforms, however, served mainly to promote the exodus of priests' sons and did little to attract qualified ordinands from other social groups—in large measure, because of the failure to improve the social and material status of secular clergy. As a result, by the late nineteenth century the church faced a shortage of qualified candidates and had to ordain candidates with an incomplete seminary education.

POPULAR ORTHODOXY

The post-Petrine church sought to carry out an "Orthodox reformation"—that is, to standardize parish religious practice, raise the believers' comprehension of Orthodoxy, and combat superstition and heresy. In part, the church relied on better administrative control at the central, diocesan, and local levels to identify and combat religious deviance. But no less important was the vision of "enlightened Orthodoxy," whereby the church (in emulation of the German *Aufklärung*) endeavored not only to regulate but also to instruct and thereby help the faithful to understand, not merely blindly believe. It therefore expanded the publication of religious literature (sermons and catechisms) and intensified demands that parish clergy preach and catechize. To be sure, even zealous priests met with such obstacles as irregular attendance (because of the difficulties of attending distant churches in bad weather and because of distractions during peak times in the agricultural cycle), lack of public and parish schools, and the cultural gulf between the well-educated priest and his illiterate flock. Nonetheless, the church gradually made headway, first in the towns and eventually in the villages, after the expansion of schools to rural areas in the second half of the nineteenth century. While the local deans and bishops still bewailed the ignorance of the pious folk, they increasingly attested to signs of substantial improvement.

The Russian Orthodox Church also reported phenomenally high rates of religious observance.

St. Basil's Cathedral, Moscow. Photograph c. 1875. ©HULTON-DEUTSCH COLLECTION/CORBIS

Most impressive were the official statistics on confession and communion, an annual obligation that provided a common (if crude) measure of religious practice. Although such data may tell more about conformity than piety, they do indicate the willingness of the laity to perform—or flout—these two key sacraments. And, compared to western Europe, where such indices plummeted in the course of the nineteenth century, the rates for Russia remained extraordinarily high and showed no significant decline even in the tumultuous decades leading up to the revolution of 1905–1907, with the vast majority—well over 80 percent for men as well as women—continuing to perform these annual rites.

To be sure, the clergy did discern signs of dissent and disbelief. The erosion of piety seemed particularly evident among the young and, above all, migrant laborers. As the latter left their villages to work, seasonally or permanently in the ever

growing complex of factories and plants, they often left their "local Orthodoxy" behind and proved highly susceptible to the new mores and religious indifference of the city. No less important was the surge in religious dissent: not only disbelief, but also other faiths came to pose an ever growing challenge. In addition to the growing population of Old Believers (schismatics who rejected the seventeenth-century liturgical reforms and the official church that embraced them), the church now also had to combat a plethora of sects—from the infamous self-castrators (*skoptsy*) to various evangelical sects. In that sense, Russia was undergoing not so much a "secularization" as "sectarianization"— the formation of vigorous, energetic movements seeking not to inculcate Unbelief but rather New Belief and Old Belief.

Significantly, however, the challenge to the Orthodox Church also emanated from its own ranks of stalwart lay believers, who, especially from the mid-nineteenth century, became increasingly restive and intent upon asserting their own rights and prerogatives. Over the previous century or so, the church had gradually established tight control over the parish, claiming the right not only to regulate religious practice but also to appoint clergy and to siphon off parish assets for "general" church needs. The issue of parish finance was particularly intense: as the church diverted parish revenues to finance the church's bureaucracy and clerical seminaries, it deprived the laity of an opportunity to renovate their church and to appoint extra clergy—steps that, for the laity, were critical in enhancing the aesthetics of the liturgy. In the new atmosphere that emerged after serf emancipation in 1861, parishioners—like others in society—became increasingly assertive in claiming their rights and resisting traditional authority.

ORTHODOXY IN AN AGE OF REVOLUTION

By the early twentieth century, the Orthodox Church—like the rest of imperial Russia—found itself in the throes of profound crisis. The strains in church-state relations reached a new level of intensity under the chief procurator, Konstantin Pobedonostsev (1880–1905); attempts by the last emperor, Nicholas II (r. 1894–1917), to reinforce the eroding foundations of autocracy with religion (most notably, in the controversial canonization of Serafim of Sarov in 1903) only deepened clerical resentment. The final blow came amid the revolution of 1905–1907: the imperial manifesto of 17 April 1905 (Old Style), granting freedom of conscience and decriminalizing conversion from Orthodoxy, shattered any remaining illusions about the willingness of the secular state to defend the vital interests of the church. The Duma monarchy (a hybrid of monarchy and parliamentarianism) that emerged in 1906 only aggravated resentment and distrust among prelates and priests; it did nothing to address key issues and enable reform in the church. After 1914, as the country plunged into war and revolution, the church suffered a sharp fall in its administrative control, material resources, and popular confidence. In 1917, after the overthrow of the Romanov dynasty, the church council made a desperate attempt to embark on reform and convoke a church council

to address a broad range of issues. But it was too late: a new—Bolshevik—regime would soon come to power and wage a relentless campaign against "reactionary" clergy and "superstitious" folk.

See also **Catholicism; Jews and Judaism; Protestantism; Russia.**

BIBLIOGRAPHY

Primary Sources

Belliustin, Ioann S. *Description of the Clergy in Rural Russia: The Memoir of a Nineteenth-Century Parish Priest.* Edited and translated by Gregory L. Freeze. Ithaca, N.Y., 1985.

Hauptmann, Peter, and G. Stricker, eds. *Die Orthodoxe Kirche in Russland: Dokumente ihrer Geschichte (860–1980).* Göttingen, Germany, 1988.

Secondary Sources

Freeze, Gregory L. *The Parish Clergy in Nineteenth-Century Russia: Crisis, Reform, Counter-Reform.* Princeton, N.J., 1983.

———. "Policing Piety: The Church and Popular Religion in Russia, 1750–1850." In *Rethinking Imperial Russia*, edited by David L. Ransel and Jane Burbank, 210–249. Bloomington, Ind., 1998.

———. "A Pious Folk? Religious Observance in Vladimir Diocese, 1900–1914." *Jarbücher für Geschichte Osteuropas* 52, no. 3 (2004): 323–340.

Kivelson, Valerie A., and Robert H. Greene, eds. *Orthodox Russia: Belief and Practice under the Tsars.* University Park, Pa., 2003.

Smolitsch, Igor. *Geschichte der russischen Kirche, 1700–1917.* 2 vols. Leiden, Netherlands, and Berlin, 1964–1991.

GREGORY L. FREEZE

RUSSO-JAPANESE WAR. The first great-power conflict of the twentieth century, the Russo-Japanese War of 1904 to 1905 foreshadowed many of the political, military, and cultural trends of succeeding decades. Its outcome made Japan the undisputed hegemon of East Asia, swung Russian attention back to European issues, and brought the United States and Japan onto a collision course for war.

THE BACKGROUND

Throughout the eighteenth and nineteenth centuries, Russia colonized Siberia, and its interest in the Pacific maritime region eventually brought it into contact with Japan, then ruled by feudal lords, the most powerful of which, the Tokugawa family, set up a government called the shogunate and acted as a national hegemon. Starting in the 1790s, Russian explorers and adventurers began reaching the Japanese isles. Adam Laxman, a Swede in Russian service, encountered a land with tightly controlled foreign relations when he arrived in 1792. Since the 1630s, Japanese had been prohibited on pain of death from leaving or reentering the home islands. Of Westerners, only the Dutch were allowed a trading presence on the southern port of Nagasaki. Laxman was refused permission to trade, as were later visitors, such as Nikolai Rezanov in 1804 and Vasily Golovnin in 1811. Golovnin, in fact, was captured by Japanese forces, sparking a brief crisis between the two nations.

By the 1850s, Russia was determined not to be left behind in any commercial agreements being signed between Japan and Western powers such as the United States and Great Britain. Though as yet possessing little trade potential, Russia had watched Britain's expansion into China after the first Opium War (1839–1842), and in response approved expeditions deep into Siberia, reaching Sakhalin Island in 1852, and eventually resulting in the founding of Vladivostok, on the Sea of Japan, in 1860. Russia signed a commercial treaty with Japan in August 1858, though its trading presence was limited to the northern port of Hakodate.

Japan perceived Russia as a territorial threat, rather than an economic one. By the 1880s, Korea was the main strategic concern of the new imperial Meiji government. Both Ch'ing China and tsarist Russia threatened to control the peninsula. Russia in particular moved forward with its plans for the Chinese Eastern and South Manchurian Railroads, part of the Trans-Siberian network. Clashing over influence at the Korean court, Japan attacked China in 1894, inaugurating the Sino-Japanese War. Despite its victory, Tokyo was forced by Russia, France, and Germany to return its territorial gains in what was known as the Triple Intervention of 1895. In the years after the war Russia increased its influence in Korea, and as part of the Allied intervention against the Boxer Rebellion in 1900, dispatched 175,000 troops to Manchuria.

Repeated diplomatic wrangling failed to produce a solution, despite Japan's clear desire to

Russian prisoners of war, Mitsuhama, Japan, 1904–1905.
©HULTON-DEUTSCH COLLECTION/CORBIS

recognize Manchuria as Russia's sphere of influence in return for a reciprocal acknowledgement of its Korean interests. Russia continued to build naval bases in northern China and even in southern Korea. This intransigence generated anti-Russian popular movements in Japan and pushed Tokyo to pursue an agreement with Great Britain, namely the Anglo-Japanese Alliance, announced in January 1902. The Russian government remained unresponsive to Japanese proposals during 1902 and 1903, and by the end of that year, Japan had decided upon war.

THE FIGHTING

The war began with a Japanese surprise attack on the Russian Pacific Fleet at Port Arthur (now called Lüshun), located on the Liaodong Peninsula in northern China, in early February 1904. Japanese naval action during the first months of the war focused on bottling up and attempting to destroy the Russian fleet at Port Arthur. The Japanese, led by Admiral Heihachiro Togo, maintained a blockade of the port, and in mid-April their mines destroyed the Russian flagship *Petropavlovsk*, killing the Russian naval commander, Vice Admiral Stepan Osipovich Makarov. In mid-May, however, the Japanese in turn lost two of their six battleships to mines, leading to a naval stalemate and an increased focus on land warfare.

During February and March 1904, the Japanese First Army landed in Korea, occupying Pyongyang and other major cities. On 30 April, three Japanese divisions defeated the Russians, commanded by Alexei Kuropatkin, former war minister, at the Yalu River, thereby breaking Russia's defensive line into Manchuria and proving their ingenuity at hauling heavy howitzers over difficult terrain, among the first times it had been done in large-scale fighting. The battle of the Yalu River removed the Russian threat to Korea, which was the strategic objective of the war, and put at risk the Russian headquarters at Liaoyang, north of the Liaodong Peninsula. Equally important, it marked the first defeat of a European army by an Asian one, and was a correspondingly decisive military and psychological blow to the Russians.

The Russian Fleet remained at Port Arthur, although bottled up, and the Japanese landed the Second Army on the Kwantung Peninsula, an extension of the Liaodong Peninsula, in early May. After a month of heavy fighting around Nanshan, the Russians retreated south to Port Arthur, and the Japanese took control of strategically important Dalian (Dalny) on Dalian Bay. This gave them a superior vantage point from which to attack Port Arthur. The Japanese besieged the fortress from August through January 1905, led by General Maresuke Nogi, who had captured it from the Chinese in 1894. The months of fighting, the nature of which in many ways prefigured World War I, claimed over 30,000 Russian and 60,000 Japanese casualties.

As the campaign progressed, the Russians increasingly found themselves hampered by the logistics of an 8,000-kilometer (5,000-mile) supply line. Kuropatkin was also unable to reinforce his troops quickly enough to match the Japanese buildup, because fresh formations had to travel from western Russia by the Trans-Siberian Railroad. After advancing on Liaoyang during June and July 1904, the Japanese fought a pitched battle from 23 August to 3 September. The victory, purchased with heavy losses, was incomplete, for the bulk of the Russian army escaped north to their main headquarters at Mukden (now called Shenyang). The Japanese followed in pursuit, but both armies went into winter quarters—a vestige of earlier, more measured war making. Not till February 1905 did the armies clash once more. At a cost of nearly 16,000 killed and 60,000 wounded, the Japanese under Field Marshal Iwao Oyama destroyed Kuropatkin's forces, inflicting 70,000 casualties including 20,000 killed or missing. With the capture of Mukden, the land war came to an end.

The final act of the war was a naval battle in the Tsushima Strait, located between Japan and Korea. As part of the plan to relieve the then-blockaded Russian forces at Port Arthur, St. Petersburg ordered the Baltic Fleet to sail 33,300 kilometers (18,000 nautical miles) to the theater of war. Commanded by Rear Admiral Zinovi Rozhdestvenski, the fleet departed in October 1904 and reached the strait, intending to continue on to Vladivostok, in late May 1905. On 27 May, nearly the entire fleet was destroyed by the Japanese navy, which had been lying in wait off the coast of Korea.

THE PEACE

The destruction of the Baltic Fleet marked the end of hostilities. U.S. President Theodore Roosevelt, upon urging from Japanese diplomats, offered to mediate a peace settlement. The Russians were represented by Sergei Witte, former finance minister, and the Japanese by Baron Jutaro Komura. The two sides met during August and September, signing a treaty in Portsmouth, New Hampshire, on 5 September. The treaty gave Japan unfettered influence in Korea, and it ceded to Tokyo the southern section of the Manchurian Railroad, the southern half of Sakhalin Island, and the Russian lease on the Liaotung Peninsula, including Port Arthur. Nevertheless, the refusal of Russia to pay any indemnity and the joint agreement to withdraw troops from Manchuria led to popular riots in Tokyo against the treaty. Roosevelt won the Nobel Peace Prize for his mediating efforts.

THE EFFECT

Japan's victory made it the hegemon of East Asia. It took control over Korea as a protectorate in

Russian soldiers at a mass grave, c. 1905. Fighting far from bases of supply and in rough mountainous terrain, Russian forces sustained very heavy losses in the Russo-Japanese War. ©CORBIS

1905, and formally annexed it in 1910. Russian ambitions in Asia were destroyed, and popular riots against the tsar broke out in St. Petersburg and Odessa. More generally, the defeat of a European Great Power by an Asian nation seemed a harbinger of the end of Western colonialism, and gave rise to nationalist sentiments in colonized lands. It also engendered public riots in both Japan and Russia, exposing the increasing role of public opinion in foreign affairs. Finally, it made the United States and Japan the sole contenders for power in East Asia, and thus brought them closer to conflict.

Militarily, the war highlighted the role of technology and foreshadowed the type of fighting that would mark World War I. Mass infantry attacks, trench warfare, the extensive use of machine guns and heavy artillery on land,

and the comprehensive employment of steam-powered armored warships armed with big guns made the Russo-Japanese War the first modern war. Military observers from many nations took the lessons of the war with them into battle in 1914.

See also **Mukden, Battle of; Portsmouth, Treaty of; Revolution of 1905 (Russia).**

BIBLIOGRAPHY

Connaughton, R. M. *Rising Sun and Tumbling Bear: Russia's War with Japan.* Rev. ed. London, 2003.

Steinberg, John W., Bruce W. Menning, David Schimmel-penninck van der Oye, David Wolff, and Shinji Yokote, eds. *The Russo-Japanese War in Global Perspective: World War Zero.* Leiden, Netherlands, 2005.

MICHAEL R. AUSLIN

RUSSO-TURKISH WAR.

One of nine wars in which the principal combatants were imperial Russia and Ottoman Turkey, the Russo-Turkish War of 1877 to 1878 erupted over the status and rights of Orthodox Slavs in the Balkans. After the Crimean War (1853–1856), the Treaty of Paris had made protection of Balkan Christians a collective responsibility of the European Great Powers. Subsequently, St. Petersburg supported friendly contacts between Russians and the Orthodox and Slavic peoples of the Balkans. During the late 1860s and early 1870s, Russia also assumed an increasingly assertive formal role in advocating and defending the interests of Slavic nationalists, especially in Serbia and Bulgaria. These policies both accorded with rising Pan-Slav sentiment in Russia and afforded some political leverage against Turkey and the Great Powers. When peasant uprisings in Bosnia-Herzegovina during 1875 and in Bulgaria during 1876 elicited harsh Turkish countermeasures, Pan-Slavists in Russia pressed for direct intervention. Even as Chancellor Alexander M. Gorchakov, the tsarist foreign minister, worked for a diplomatic resolution of the crisis, Russian volunteers and contributions flowed to the anti-Turkish cause in Serbia. However, the collapse of Russian-led Serbian forces during the summer of 1876 caused Russia to impose an armistice on Turkey in October, backed by a partial Russian mobilization in November. During December, emissaries of the major European powers met at Constantinople to broker a compromise program of administrative reforms for the Balkans. When Turkey rejected this compromise in early 1877, diplomacy had reached a dead end. In the absence of other guarantors for the defense of Balkan Slavs, Russia assumed that role on behalf of the European powers. In anticipation of possible war between Russia and Turkey, the Budapest Convention (January 1877) between Austria-Hungary and Russia provided for Austrian neutrality in exchange for Russian acquiescence to the Austrian occupation of Bosnia-Herzegovina. Following a second Russian partial mobilization, a convention with Romania prior to the actual Russian declaration of war against Turkey on 24 April 1877 provided for passage of Russian troops through Romania in exchange for Russian assurances of Romanian territorial integrity.

RUSSIAN CALCULATIONS FOR WAR

Tsar Alexander II of Russia would later blame the rising tide of domestic Pan-Slav sentiment for his decision to go to war. The situation, however, was actually more complex. On the one hand Russia was not ready for war; on the other hand Russia was now presented with the opportunity to expand its influence in the Balkans while unilaterally resolving the "Eastern Question" (the fate of the Ottoman Empire and its holdings) on terms favorable to Russia, including unfettered access to the Turkish Straits. Hard realities suggested that Russia was in no position to go to war in 1877: the era of the Great Reforms with their emphasis on domestic preoccupations was still under way, the precarious state of the ruble and the imperial treasury afforded little financial flexibility, the army was still undergoing reorganization and rearmament, and Russian naval forces were practically nonexistent on the Black Sea. Accordingly, Gorchakov and Mikhail Reutern, the finance minister, preached moderation and accommodation within the framework of existing international processes and agreements. Others, including most notably Dmitri A. Milyutin, the war minister, held that the time was now ripe to revise the Crimean settlement and realize Russian interest by force of arms. The tsar vacillated in the face of conflicting counsel and the momentum of events, but over the winter of 1876 to 1877, he would clearly opt for war.

The sirenlike promise inherent in Russian war planning played a prominent role in the tsar's calculations. Through Milyutin, General Nikolai N. Obruchev of the Russian General Staff proposed a lightning land campaign aimed directly at Constantinople, the Ottoman heart. Obruchev would mobilize 250,000 troops in Bessarabia, march across Romania to force a crossing of the Danube south of Bucharest, erect defensive cordons facing east and west to cover a race for the Balkan divide, and then press Russian forces through the mountains to threaten the Turkish capital directly. A secondary theater in the Caucasus would tie down additional Turkish forces. With an intent to achieve the war's objectives within roughly two months after the onset of hostilities, the plan envisioned a rapid conclusion to forestall Great Power interference.

The realities of execution, however, precluded full implementation of Obruchev's plan. First, two partial mobilizations failed to provide adequate military manpower for all the war's phases, circumstances, and locales. Second, wet spring weather and a poor Romanian transportation network slowed the initial Russian movement into the Balkans. Third, the widespread assimilation of breech-loading shoulder weaponry accorded superiority to defensive tactics over the offensive. Fourth, distances and terrain aggravated supply shortages that stemmed from an inadequate Russian logistics system. Finally, lapses in Russian leadership both sapped resolve at key moments and let fleeting advantages escape the grasp of rapidly advancing Russian detachments. As a result the war dragged on for forty-seven weeks.

THE WAR'S CAMPAIGNS

In loose accordance with Obruchev's concept, the Russians deployed forces for offensives in the two major theaters of war. The decisive Balkan campaign against Turkey unfolded over three distinct phases: the initial Russian advance across Romania and into northern Bulgaria (24 April to 17 July 1877); operations in northern Bulgaria, including a series of costly assaults and a siege against Turkish positions at Plevna (present-day Pleven) (18 July to 24 December 1877); and trans-Balkan operations against Adrianople and Constantinople (25 December 1877 to 3 March 1878). In contrast, the campaign in the Caucasus was essentially an economy of force effort. During the first phase (24 April to 21 June 1877), four Russian detachments initially advanced against Turkish strongholds at Batumi, Ardahan, Kars, and Bayazid. The second phase involved the unanticipated containment of a Turkish counteroffensive and a subsequent Russian reinforcement (22 June to 1 October 1877). The third phase (2 October 1877 to 3 March 1878) witnessed a renewed Russian offensive to capture Kars, followed by a Russian advance as far west as Erzurum.

Despite bad weather and an agonizingly slow buildup, the Russian offensive in the Balkan theater at first promised to make good on Obruchev's original plan. Four Russian corps (260,000 troops) under Grand Duke Nicholas Nikolayevich marched across Romania, and by late June General Mikhail I. Dragomirov had wrested a suitable bridgehead across the Danube. In mid-July, as follow-on Russian forces assembled in northern Bulgaria, General Joseph V. Gurko's 12,000-man advance-

guard detachment even briefly penetrated the Balkan passes. The Russian high command suddenly grew cautious, however, calling a halt to await reinforcements and the full deployment of blocking detachments to cover the now-extended Russian flanks. This pause permitted 16,000 Turkish troops (subsequently reinforced to 40,000) under Osman Nuri Pasha to occupy strong defensive positions at Plevna, a key road junction one day's traverse south of the Danube that guarded access to the north Balkan slope. After three bloody and unsuccessful assaults (20 July, 30 July, and 11–12 September) on Plevna, the Russians settled down to a siege-style investment operation that forced Osman's capitulation on 10 December 1877.

With Plevna behind them, the Russians regained the initiative and pressed three strong detachments through the Balkan passes during the height of winter. On 4 January 1878 Gurko occupied Sofia. That same day converging Russian columns under Generals Mikhail D. Skobelev, Nikolai I. Sviatopolk-Mirsky, and Fedor F. Radetsky met at Shipka-Sheinovo to launch a battle of encirclement that crushed Vessil Pasha's 30,000-man army. Gurko then marched to Philippopolis (present-day Plovdiv), where in mid-January he routed a second Turkish army under Suleiman Pasha, thus opening the way to Adrianople. With Turkish defenses south of the Balkans now broken, and with the Ottoman government asking for terms, Grand Duke Nicholas Nikolayevich drove the Russian advance to the outskirts of Constantinople. The seizure of the Turkish capital, however, was now out of the question, because on 15 February a British fleet had steamed into the Sea of Marmara to signify possible Great Power intercession on the Turkish side. Russian and Turkish emissaries entered into peace negotiations at San Stefano.

In the Caucasus, meanwhile, the tempo of Russian operations mimicked those in the Balkan theater. Grand Duke Michael Nikolayevich had opened the campaign with 100,000 troops split into four detachments to assault four widely separated Turkish objectives. Although Bayazid and Ardahan fell in quick succession, Russian advances beyond Bayazid and against Kars and Batumi stalled, thanks to Turkish defensive skills and insufficient Russian manpower. Under pressure of a Turkish counteroffensive, the Russian operational pause over the

Evacuating the wounded. Nineteenth-century illustration. Wounded Turkish soldiers are evacuated through the Shipka Pass, Bulgaria, in September of 1877. ©HULTON-DEUTSCH COLLECTION/CORBIS

summer of 1877 soon turned into a partial Russian withdrawal. By fall, however, the arrival of fresh troops and a new chief of staff, General Obruchev, sparked a renewed Russian offensive. In early October, Obruchev devised a plan to turn the Turkish covering army at Kars out of its position, followed by an advance to besiege the fortress itself. On 17–18 November, after several feints, the Russians took Kars by storm. Subsequently, General Vasily A. Heimann's detachment advanced to besiege Erzurum, but the Turks held out until conclusion of the Treaty of San Stefano on 3 March 1878.

AFTERMATH

British naval power might have saved Constantinople, but it could not prevent the immediate imposition of harsh Russian peace terms. Although Russia did not press its demands for special rights with regard to the Turkish Straits, the treaty provided for a large and autonomous Bulgaria under substantial Russian influence. Serbia, Montenegro, and Romania were to attain full independence, while Russia received substantial Turkish territory in Transcaucasia and Asia Minor, along with southern Bessarabia from Romania in exchange for Dobruja. England and Austria-Hungary objected to these terms and obliged Russia to discuss their revision at a general conference of the European powers during the summer of 1878. Because Russia was now diplomatically isolated and verging on financial and military exhaustion, there was no realistic possibility for resistance. The resulting Congress of Berlin between 13 June and 13 July 1878 substantially amended the Treaty of San Stefano, especially by diminishing and dividing Bulgaria and by permitting Austria-Hungary to occupy and govern Bosnia-Herzegovina. These and other adjustments pleased almost no one, with the result that the seeds of future conflict were sown. In Russia especially, the Congress of Berlin was viewed as a severe defeat, despite its formal recognition of many Russian gains. Russia has supported Prussia against France in 1870–1871, and now sentiment within Russian governing circles held that Bismarck's united Germany had failed to reciprocate at the Congress of Berlin. Meanwhile, Russian distrust for Austria-Hungary, born during the earlier Crimean War, became more intractable.

See also **Alexander II; Congress of Berlin; Eastern Question; Ottoman Empire; Russia; San Stefano, Treaty of.**

BIBLIOGRAPHY

Fuller, William C., Jr. *Strategy and Power in Russia, 1600–1914.* New York, 1992.

Jelavich, Barbara. *St. Petersburg and Moscow: Tsarist and Soviet Foreign Policy, 1814–1974.* Bloomington, Ind., 1974.

Menning, Bruce W. *Bayonets before Bullets: The Imperial Russian Army, 1861–1914.* Bloomington, Ind., 1992.

Rich, David Alan. *The Tsar's Colonels: Professionalism, Strategy, and Subversion in Late Imperial Russia.* Cambridge, Mass., 1998.

BRUCE W. MENNING

RUTHERFORD, ERNEST (1871–1937), New Zealand-born scientist.

Ernest Rutherford's experimental work was essential to early-twentieth-century revolutionary developments in atomic physics. Born in New Zealand, Rutherford came to the Cavendish Laboratory at Cambridge University, England, in 1896 to study with Joseph John Thomson shortly after earning the M.A. degree at Canterbury College, Christchurch, New Zealand. He and Thomson studied the ability of X-rays (recently discovered by the German Wilhelm Conrad Roentgen) to "ionize" gases into positively and negatively charged particles and thus increase the ability of the gases to conduct electricity. Soon turning to investigations of radioactivity, which Antoine-Henri Becquerel (1852–1908) had just discovered, Rutherford applied the technique of quantitatively assessing ionization effects in air surrounding radioactive substances—he was able to identify two components of emissions from radioactive substances: *alpha* was easily absorbed by a thin foil, while *beta* penetrated the foil.

In 1898, Rutherford was appointed professor of physics at McGill University in Montreal, Canada. He and the chemist Frederick Soddy undertook monumental studies of radioactivity, combining chemical analyses with investigations of ionization effects. By 1902 they were convinced that radioactivity involved transmutations of atoms of one element into atoms of another element. In the following year, Rutherford hypothesized that radioactive emission occurs at the instant that an atom changes its elemental identity. By now recognizing that three major components could constitute these emissions—alpha, beta, and gamma—he was dedicated to identifying them. Beta seemed clearly to be fast-moving electrons (the subatomic, negatively charged particles that Thomson had identified in 1896 in studies of electrical effects in gases at very low pressures). Gamma appeared to be high-energy electromagnetic radiation. Alpha, Rutherford speculated, was a stream of positively charged helium ions.

By 1908, a year after moving to the University of Manchester in England, Rutherford was exploiting the alpha emission in a new experimental direction. Puzzled by effects seeming to indicate that air molecules slightly diverted alpha particles from their original directions, he embarked on a systematic investigation of this "scattering" by orienting alpha particle streams at very thin metal foils and determining how interaction with atoms in the foil affected the direction of the alpha particles' motions. By 1911 this work indicated that one out of eight thousand alpha particles was deflected ninety degrees or greater by the very thin foil. Rutherford's conclusion: atoms in the foil must be mostly empty space, with a tiny volume occupied by a massive and highly charged "nucleus." By 1913, combined speculations of Rutherford and the Dane Niels Bohr (1885–1962) had identified the nucleus as: (1) the positively charged component of an atom whose total charge determines the atom's elemental identity, and (2) the site of radioactivity (the origin of alpha, beta, and gamma emissions).

The impacts of Rutherford's work up to 1914 were enormous. He had determined what radioactivity was and had revealed essential aspects of the atom's structure. His findings furnished impressive evidence that atoms exist and helped resolve a long-standing tension in physical science between the concepts of *atom* and *element* by tying elemental identity to the constitution of the atomic nucleus. Moreover, his recognition that the energy involved in radioactive (nuclear) transformations far exceeded energy produced in chemical reactions had ramifications beyond physical science. It provided a means to surmount what had been one of the most imposing barriers to acceptance of Charles Darwin's evolutionary theory—that with the sun and earth presumed cooling over time, the earth could not sustain temperatures supporting life for a time long enough to have produced all the changes evident in the fossil record via Darwinian evolution. Rutherford himself estimated as early as 1904 that the significant amount of heat generated by radioactivity in the earth's crust would extend the earth's age much longer than previously believed. Presuming radioactive sources of solar and terrestrial energy opened the way for the revival of Darwin's theory of natural selection by the 1920s.

Rutherford remained at Manchester until 1919, when he succeeded Thomson as the head of the Cavendish Laboratory at Cambridge. There he was increasingly occupied with studies of artificial disintegration of atomic nuclei—changes in nuclear structure induced by high-energy particulate streams. Rutherford had initiated this branch of research with his discovery in 1918 that alpha-particle bombardment of nitrogen gas gener-ated hydrogen nuclei; he concluded a year later that the alpha particle's interaction with the nitrogen nucleus ejected a hydrogen nucleus from the nitrogen nucleus. This work led inexorably to the developments in nuclear physics of the 1920s and 1930s that culminated with the discovery of nuclear fission in 1938, followed by the feverish effort to exploit this militarily.

Rutherford's periods at McGill (1898–1907), Manchester (1907–1919), and Cambridge (1919–1937) corresponded to phases of a scientific career that contributed incisive understandings of radioactivity (McGill), atomic physics (Manchester), and nuclear physics (Cambridge). His health was robust when he died as a result of an accident in 1937.

See also **Physics; Science and Technology.**

BIBLIOGRAPHY

Badash, Lawrence. "Ernest Rutherford." In *Dictionary of Scientific Biography*, vol. 12, pp. 25–36. New York, 1975.

Campbell, John. *Rutherford: Scientist Supreme*. Christchurch, New Zealand, 1999.

DeKosky, Robert K. "Ernest Rutherford." In *Research Guide to European Historical Biography, 1450–Present*, edited by James A. Moncure, 4470–4481. Washington, D.C., 1993.

Heilbron, John L. *Ernest Rutherford and the Explosion of Atoms*. New York, 2003.

ROBERT K. DEKOSKY

SADE, DONATIEN-ALPHONSE-FRANÇOIS DE (1740–1814), French libertine and writer.

For a long time the work of Donatien-Alphonse-François de Sade (better known as Marquis de Sade) has been discredited through its association with the turbulent and diabolical life of its author. The writings of Sade reflect the extravagant adventures of the libertine marquis whose name gave birth to a common noun: *sadism.*

The House of Sade is one of the oldest in Provence, and in the Comtat Venaissin of southeastern France, dating back to the thirteenth century and distinguishing itself through the centuries in the service of both the state and the church. The father of the marquis, the count Jean-Baptiste de Sade (1702–1779), left the land of his ancestors during the regency of Philippe d'Orléans and sought his fortune at the court. He led the life of a gentleman libertine, squandering the family fortune and going so far as to marry the lady-in-waiting to the Princess de Condé, just so he could more readily seduce the latter. This loveless marriage produced a son, Donatien-Alphonse-François, on 2 June 1740, a year after the passing of their first-born, a two-year-old girl. Until the age of four the young marquis was raised in the Condé entourage by his mother, then was sent to his uncle's home in Provence. His father maintained high ambitions for his son and, when he was ten years old, sent to him to Paris to study at the Jesuit-run College Louis-le-Grand, a school attended by the sons of the high nobility. At age fourteen, his father pulled him from the college in order to place him in the army. Through nepotism, the young marquis rapidly rose in rank and, at age eighteen, became captain of the cavalry. Then came a marriage, negotiated by the count, to a young heiress, Renée-Pélagie Cordier de Montreuil, on 17 May 1763. After the death of a firstborn child in 1764, the young wife produced a son, Louis-Marie, in 1767, the same year that the Comte de Sade died. Two other children would follow, a son in 1769 and a daughter in 1771.

However, neither marriage nor parenthood restrained the libertine character and scandalous ways of the marquis. He was seen with actresses who became his mistresses while he consorted with young girls and frequented public houses. He brought young prostitutes, both male and female, to rented houses where he obliged them to satisfy his fantasies. In 1768 a woman, either a prostitute or a beggar, lodged a complaint, accusing him of having confined, then whipped, her before applying drops of hot wax in her wounds. The marquis was arrested and put in prison, while public opinion used the affair to condemn the degenerate morals of the aristocracy. His in-laws had him freed and forced him to stay in the château of La Coste, the birthplace of the de Sade family. He had a calm stay at the side of his wife and satisfied his passion for the theater. He also commenced an incestuous relationship with his sister-in-law, an affair that caused his strong willed mother-in-law, Madame de Montreuil, to develop an implacable hatred of him. This was exacerbated after the marquis was implicated in a new affair in Marseille in which a prostitute made a complaint that he sodomized and tried to poison her. Arrested again, Donatien was sent to the citadel near Chambéry, from which he soon escaped, fleeing first to Italy, then returning to La Coste. He remained there for some time, in retreat from the world, but having taken the precaution (with his wife's agreement) to surround himself with young domestics, both male and female, whose job was to satisfy his most perverse desires. These desires rapidly manifested themselves on the bodies of the children, scarred by blows from a rod and by incisions. The rumor mill worked overtime, and the scandals grew. The parents lodged a complaint, and Madame de Montreuil tried by all the means at her disposal to have her son-in-law institutionalized. No longer feeling himself protected, Donatien left La Coste on 17 July 1775 for Italy. There he traveled under a false identity for a year, accumulating notes and observations for the purpose of writing an account of his voyage.

In February 1777 he returned to Paris where he was greeted with a lettre de cachet (a document condemning him to prison) and was locked up in the dungeon at Vincennes. He began his literary career there and, according to the expression of Simone de Beauvoir (1908–1986), "entered prison a man and left a writer." The prison space nourished a diverse, long-winded, and wordy ode to liberty in which imprisonment figured throughout. In 1784 the prison at Vincennes was closed and the marquis was transferred to the Bastille, where he continued writing novels, all the while maintaining important correspondences, principally with his notary and his wife. Renée-Pélagie had not abandoned her husband and always fought for his freedom. But, tired of his character and his caprices, she chose never to see him after his liberation on 2 April 1790.

Though Sade was freed during the French Revolution, the storming of the Bastille had destroyed a portion of his manuscripts. Out of both conviction and necessity he supported the events of 1789, presenting himself as a victim of *ancien régime* justice and declaring himself to be a man of letters. In 1791 he anonymously published *Justine; or, the Misfortunes of Virtue,* a licentious novel in which Sade overstepped the boundaries of erotic discourse. Above all, though, he wrote theatrical works, increasing the number of plays he wrote and actively seeking to have them performed. In addition, he put his literary skills in the service of the nation and actively got involved in the sectional meetings of his district. However, on 8 December 1793, he was again arrested, this time for his atheistic convictions, his pornographic writings (though published anonymously, *Justine* was readily attributable to him), and his aristocratic lineage. He remained incarcerated for ten and one-half months before leaving prison after the fall of Maximilien Robespierre (1758–1794) on 29 July 1794.

His theatrical career having failed, Sade turned to writing novels: *Aline et Valcour* (1795) and *Philosophy in the Bedroom* (1795). He also continued to write unbridled pornography, producing *The New Justine; or, the Misfortunes of Virtue* (1797). But, as his biographer has indicated, his books only postponed the misery to which he seemed doomed. In March 1801 he was again arrested; the First Consul (Napoleon Bonaparte) was not a fan of his libertine writings. In order to cover up the illegality of the arrest, Sade was rapidly dispatched to Charenton, an old prison that had housed him during the first months of the Revolution but that had, since 1797, again become an insane asylum. He lived there until his death on 2 December 1814, in a condition of privileged incarceration, where he indulged his passion for theatrical staging with inmates serving as actors; except for the lack of freedom, he was deprived of nothing.

In terms of history and literature, Sade is for some a revolutionary, a genius of the imaginary, and a beacon of liberty; for others, he is an immoral and debauched individual and an advocate of criminality. Regardless of which character one sees him as, he cultivated a legend for himself that endures into the early twenty-first century.

See also **Body; Gender; Homosexuality and Lesbianism; Napoleon; Pornography; Sexuality.**

BIBLIOGRAPHY

Beauvoir, Simone de. *Faut-il brûler Sade?* Paris, 1972. First published in 1955 under the title *Privilèges.*

Lever, Maurice. *Donatien Alphonse François, Marquis de Sade.* Paris, 1991.

Michael, Colette Verger. *The Marquis de Sade: The Man, His Works, and His Critics: An Annotated Bibliography*. New York, 1986.

Pauvert, Jean-Jacques. *Sade Vivant*. 3 vols. Paris, 1986–1990.

PASCAL DUPUY

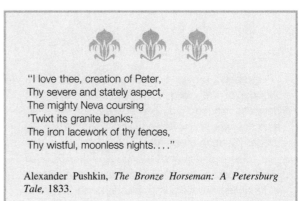

"I love thee, creation of Peter,
Thy severe and stately aspect,
The mighty Neva coursing
'Twixt its granite banks;
The iron lacework of thy fences,
Thy wistful, moonless nights...."

Alexander Pushkin, *The Bronze Horseman: A Petersburg Tale*, 1833.

ST. PETERSBURG.

Europe's "long nineteenth century" witnessed both the apogee of the Russian Empire and the beginnings of its collapse. Sharing the empire's fate in every major respect was its capital, St. Petersburg. Founded in 1703 by Peter the Great as a naval base and trading post, St. Petersburg had become, by 1914, the empire's largest city as well as its administrative headquarters, a bustling Baltic seaport and booming industrial site, an international center of art and fashion, and the crucible of a revolution that many historians would judge the single most important event of the ensuing twentieth century.

FOUNDATIONS

No major city of the modern world is more closely connected with its founder than St. Petersburg is with Peter I (known as Peter the Great), tsar and first Russian emperor (r. 1682–1725), whose patron saint is commemorated in the city's very name. Many of St. Petersburg's extant buildings date directly from Peter's time, including the central fortress and its church, where he is interred; his *domik*, or the little house that was his first home in the city; the Summer Palace, built for him from 1710 to 1714 by the city's first architect, Domenico Trezzini; and suburban Peterhof, as Peter called it, the complex of palaces and parks overlooking the Finnish Gulf that was his favorite retreat. The origins of numerous other important buildings, if not always their present structures, also go back to Peter's time: the Winter Palace; the Admiralty; the Academy of Sciences; the Kunstkamera, or natural history museum; the Menshikov Palace, residence of the region's first governor; the Alexander Nevsky Monastery, burial place of Russian heroes; and the Building of the Twelve Colleges, erected to house the administrative offices—of war, justice, foreign affairs, and so on—created in conjunction with Peter's drastic reorganization of Russia's central government and now, like Peterhof, part of St. Petersburg State University. Countless other mementos of Russia's first emperor are to be found in the city as well—museum exhibits, historic sites, shop signs, street names, and monumental statues, including, most famously, the statue of Peter known as the Bronze Horseman, which was dedicated in 1782 by Catherine II (known as Catherine the Great) and later celebrated in a long poem of that name by Alexander Pushkin (1799–1837), who is often called Russia's greatest poet. Even the popular nickname in Russian for St. Petersburg, "Piter," from the Dutch form of his name that he liked to use when corresponding with his close companions, evokes the sailor-tsar. These elements of St. Petersburg today all constitute tangible links with Peter the Great; all are enduring reminders of his life and reign. Yet more, in both its inception and its subsequent history, St. Petersburg embodies the revolution in Russia's government, culture, and international standing that was engineered by his regime. The whole city has an abiding historical significance, in other words, that goes well beyond its connections with the person of its founder.

Russia before Peter's reign was a vast yet sparsely populated kingdom centered in medieval Moscow, its sole city of any significant size and accessible from the centers of either European or Asian civilization only by a very long and perilous journey. Muscovite Russia's relative isolation was thus cultural as well as geographical: a "rude and barbarous kingdom," in the words of a later

"Petersbourg may with reason be looked upon as a Wonder of the World, considering its magnificent palaces, sixty odd thousand houses, and the short time that was employed in the building of it." (F. C. Weber [German diplomat], 1720)

"The richness and splendour of the Russian court surpasses description. It retains many traces of its antient Asiatic pomp, blended with European refinement. An immense retinue of courtiers always preceded and followed the empress [Catherine II]; the costliness and glare of their apparel, and a profusion of precious stones, created a splendour, of which the magnificence of other courts can give us only a faint idea." (Dr. William Coxe [English visitor], 1784)

"The prevailing taste here is the brilliant and the striking: spires, gilded and tapering like electric conductors; porticoes, the bases of which almost disappear under the water; squares, ornamented with columns which seem lost in the immense space that surrounds them; antique statues, the character and attire of which so ill accord with the aspect of this country, the tint of the sky, the costumes and manners of the inhabitants, as to suggest captive heroes in a hostile land. . . ."
(Marquis de Custine [French visitor], 1839)

"Is there anything more buoyant, more brilliant, more resplendent than this beautiful street of our capital? . . . The gay carriages, the handsome men, the beautiful women—all lend it a carnival air, an air that you can almost inhale the moment you set foot on Nevsky Prospect!" (Nikolai Gogol [Ukrainian-Russian writer], 1842)

"Petersburg lived a restless, cold, satiated, semi-nocturnal life. Phosphorescent, crazy, voluptuous summer nights; green tables and the clink of gold; music, whirling couples behind windows, galloping troikas, gypsies, duels at daybreak, ceremonial military parades marching to the whistling of icy winds and the squealing of fifes before the Byzantine gaze of the Emperor—such was the life of the city . . . in 1914." (Alexei Tolstoy, *The Road to Calvary*, 1921)

sixteenth-century English visitor; its capital, in those of a later seventeenth-century German resident, "built without any architectural order or art." Thus from the outset St. Petersburg's elegant parks and public buildings, broad boulevards, and symmetrical layout sharply distinguished its architecture from that of cloistered, cluttered, picturesque old Moscow (or any other Russian town). Even its very location, where the Neva River empties into the Baltic Sea's Gulf of Finland, at the extreme western edge of Russia—in fact, on land recently conquered from Sweden and aboriginally inhabited by Finns—is indicative of Peter's determination to make his city the capital of a cosmopolitan European empire.

And so it progressively became. Between 1703 and Peter's death in 1725 anywhere from ten thousand to thirty thousand workers labored annually on the construction of the city, their efforts directed by the thousand or more architects, masons, and interior decorators recruited for the purpose in Italy, Germany, Holland, and France. The architects included, besides Trezzini, a Swiss-Italian lured from the Danish king's service in 1703, Alexandre Le Blond, hired by the tsar's agents in Paris in 1716; Andreas Schlüter, a sculptor and architect famous for his work in Poland and Prussia; Niccolò Michetti, recruited in Rome; and Mikhail Zemtsov, the ablest of their Russian pupils. Almost as important were the first engineers, hired in England and the Netherlands, who built the sluices, canals, and dikes needed to tame the Neva delta on which the new city arose. The diverse skills and nationalities of these and the other first builders of St. Petersburg imparted to its architecture a distinctive baroque style, one that combined with its canalized seaboard site to produce, as it was soon said, a "second Amsterdam" or "another Venice." St. Petersburg's first builders also made the city the architectural trendsetter of the Russian Empire. Right down to the empire's demise in 1917, new construction even in Moscow would replicate the successive European architectural styles—baroque, neoclassical, empire, modernist—dominant in the capital by the Baltic.

Indeed, it was as the new cultural capital of Russia that St. Petersburg best embodied the Petrine revolution. The first systematic training in Russia in modern (post-Renaissance) European painting and sculpture as well as in architecture and the graphic arts was instituted in St. Petersburg, a development that culminated in the foundation by Peter's daughter, Empress Elizabeth, of the Imperial Academy of Fine Arts (1757). The St. Petersburg Academy of Sciences, after its founding in 1724,

Kazan Cathedral, St. Petersburg, c. 1870. Designed by architect Andrei Voronikhin and constructed 1801–1811, the Cathedral of Our Lady of Kazan was modelled after St. Peter's Basilica in Rome, particularly in its twin colonnades, which closely resemble those designed by Bernini for St. Peter's in the seventeenth century. ©Austrian Archives/Corbis

rapidly became the institutional hub for the development of mathematics and the natural sciences in Russia. The academy was the home, too, of Russia's first law professors, historians, archaeologists, ethnographers, and modern literary specialists. Equally critical was St. Petersburg's function, from its founder's time, as the wellspring in Russia of modern European music and dance as well as the visual arts, all of which would flourish brilliantly in the new capital until reaching their climax in the "Silver Age" of the decades before 1917, an age associated with such masters as Vasily Kandinsky in painting, Igor Stravinsky in music, and Sergei Diaghilev in dance.

APOGEE

St. Petersburg's international prestige, like that of the empire itself, reached its apogee in the century or so that elapsed between the accession of Catherine II in 1762 and the death of Nicholas I in 1855. Catherine especially left her mark on the

city. To Empress Elizabeth's colossal, flamboyantly baroque Winter Palace (designed by Bartolomeo Rastrelli) Catherine added a more intimate if still palatial "Hermitage," the first of three such additions (successively designated the Small Hermitage, Large Hermitage, and New Hermitage), together with an elegant court theater, which was subsequently also attached to the Winter Palace complex and named the Hermitage Theater. Giacomo Quarenghi built the theater in the restrained neoclassical style that Catherine favored, and he alone designed forty-five buildings in the city, mostly aristocratic palaces but also a splendid new home for the Academy of Sciences and another for what later became the Imperial State Bank. Other distinguished architects, Russian and foreign, designed the magnificent Imperial Academy of Fine Arts, the Marble Palace, and the Taurida Palace, each built for a leading court favorite, and the Smolny Institute, a school founded by Catherine for the education of noblewomen, which the Bolsheviks under Vladimir Lenin took over as their headquarters in 1917. Equally if not more important for St. Petersburg's future were the massive granite embankments built on Catherine's orders to restrain the turbulent Neva River and its tributaries, thereby providing protection from the recurrent floods that inundated the city. At Catherine's death in 1796 St. Petersburg's population had risen to more than two hundred thousand, up from forty thousand in 1725; its amenities rivaled those of any great city in Europe; and visitors had begun to call it, evoking the fabled metropolis of the ancient Middle East, the Palmyra of the North.

The similarly long reigns of Catherine's grandsons Alexander I (1801–1825) and Nicholas I (1825–1855) confirmed St. Petersburg's status as the seat of a mighty empire, an empire that by 1815 had defeated, more so than any other land power in Europe, the empire of Napoleon. This great victory was variously commemorated in the Russian capital, most notably by the erection of the huge Alexander Column in the immense square adjoining the Winter Palace. Two enormous churches were also built to affirm, if not loudly proclaim, Russia's arrival as a great European power. The first, completed under Alexander I, was a sternly neoclassical edifice called the Cathedral of Our Lady of Kazan (after a revered icon of that name) and prominently located on St. Petersburg's central thoroughfare, the Nevsky Prospect, whose perpetual throngs of every rank and nationality testified to the empire's vast size, multiethnic character, and international importance. A second, even grander church, constructed in a late neoclassical style of the most opulent materials available, arose under Nicholas I, whose reactionary policies at home and abroad earned him the nickname "the Gendarme of Europe." The Cathedral of St. Isaac, as it was called, was much less a church than a magnificent, Roman-style imperial monument. Its dome, the third largest in the world, provided a new focal point for Russia's increasingly sumptuous if not overbearing capital.

Numerous other major buildings, also still standing, were put up in St. Petersburg under Alexander I and Nicholas I in the empire style—the new or rebuilt Admiralty, Ministries of War and Foreign Affairs, offices of the Senate and Holy Synod (administering church affairs), General Staff Headquarters, and Stock Exchange—along with several

The Stock Exchange in St. Petersburg. Painting by Aleksandr Karlovich Beggrov, 1891. The stock exchange in St. Petersburg was designed by French architect Thomas de Tomon in the neoclassical style and built on Vasilievsky Island, 1805–1810. The two flanking columns, studded with ships' prows, served as navigation beacons in the nineteenth century. TRETYAKOV GALLERY, MOSCOW, RUSSIA/BRIDGEMAN ART LIBRARY

theaters, a ballet school, and still more military barracks, triumphal arches, and hero statues. Vast new parade grounds for staging the elaborate military exercises much favored by both emperors were laid out. Following grandmother Catherine's example, both rulers also made important additions to the Winter Palace complex, known today as the State Hermitage Museum. Simultaneously a major architectural monument and world-class art collection, the Hermitage remains the most impressive of St. Petersburg's many memorials to its imperial past.

INDUSTRIALIZATION AND REVOLUTION

St. Petersburg's Palace Square, adjacent to the Winter Palace and site of the Alexander Column, was also the site of "Bloody Sunday," as the massacre by imperial troops of demonstrating workers one Sunday in January 1905 was quickly dubbed. The city's population had grown enormously in the half-century or so since the death of Nicholas I: from an estimated five hundred thousand inhabitants in 1857, of whom the great majority were either officials, soldiers, or servants and their families, to nearly one and a quarter million in 1900, of whom roughly a third were industrial workers and their dependents. St. Petersburg had always been the center of the empire's carriage trade, catering to the official-noble elite and innumerable foreign visitors, as witness the famous jewelry shop founded by Carl Fabergé (1846–1920). But by 1900 the opulent core city was surrounded by a rapidly growing belt of factories, among which the giant Putilov metalworks alone employed some thirteen thousand men. Heavy industry prevailed, with attendant environmental pollution; worker slums had sprung up; and streetcars, telegraph and then telephone wires, massive apartment blocks and department stores, and all the other appurtenances of industrial modernity had penetrated even the city's central districts. Rising crime rates, worker strikes, and other manifestations of popular unrest had been quick to follow, culminating in the Revolution of 1905. The revolution ushered in Russia's brief period of quasi-constitutional government (1906–1916), during which the lower legislative chamber, the Imperial Duma, met in the Taurida Palace built by Catherine II for Prince Grigory Potemkin, conqueror of the Crimea (or Taurida). In the summer of 1917 the same palace housed the All-Russian Congress of Soviets (worker, peasant, and soldier councils), in whose name, in October of that year, Lenin would seize power from the Provisional Government that had taken office the previous February and was meeting in the Winter Palace.

By the early twentieth century, in other words, the majestic imperial capital of Pushkin's poems had been transformed into the turbulent metropolis depicted in Andrei Bely's allegorical novel *Petersburg,* first published in serial form in 1913, and in Alexei Tolstoy's darkly evocative *The Road to Calvary* (a trilogy, the first part of which was published in 1921). Nicholas II, Russia's last emperor, who came to the throne in 1894 and abdicated in February 1917, never liked the city that St. Petersburg had become, much preferring to live instead in the peace and quiet of his suburban palace-estate. He and his family also spent unprecedented amounts of time in the old capital, Moscow, in specially renovated apartments in the Kremlin. Picturesque old Moscow had once more become, in an age of rampant nationalism, the *national* capital of Russia, the sentimental heart of the Russian nation, an attitude that paid little heed to the realities of the multiethnic empire. Nicholas II was scarcely alone among Russians in experiencing the emotional pull of the old capital and in doing his part to promote a revival of traditional Muscovite forms in art, architecture, and decoration. The revivalist movement even succeeded in planting, in the heart of St. Petersburg itself, a gigantic edifice built in neo-Muscovite style, the Church of the Resurrection, which opened in 1907 (and is also known as the Church of the Savior on the Spilled Blood, in recognition of its location on the site where Alexander II was assassinated by revolutionary terrorists in 1881). The soaring cupolas and rich ornamentation of the Church of the Resurrection, restored in the late twentieth century after decades of Soviet neglect, stand in utmost architectural contrast to the austere, horizontal classicism of the surrounding buildings. Also highly indicative of the nationalist movement in late imperial Russia was the renaming of the capital itself, when war against Germany broke out in 1914, from the Germanic "St. Petersburg" of Peter the Great, now felt to be unacceptably foreign, to the more purely Russian "Petrograd."

It was as Petrograd that St. Petersburg witnessed the trauma of World War I and the Revolution of 1917. And it was the revolutionary government of Lenin and his Bolsheviks that in 1918, fearful of a German conquest, moved Russia's capital back to Moscow, where it remains. In 1924, following Lenin's death, Petrograd was renamed Leningrad in a transparent attempt to replace the aura of Peter and all it stood for with that of the founder of the Soviet Union. It was as Leningrad that the city endured the subsequent decades of Soviet rule and underwent the terrible German siege of World War II. Yet Leningraders, living amid innumerable mementos of their city's cosmopolitan past, never forgot St. Petersburg; in 1991 they voted to restore the city's original name. Russia's "Window on Europe," as it was first called (by an Italian visitor) in 1739, had been reopened.

See also **Cities and Towns; Moscow; Pushkin, Alexander; Russia.**

BIBLIOGRAPHY

Bater, James H. *St. Petersburg: Industrialization and Change.* Montreal, 1976.

Bely, Andrei. *Petersburg.* Translated by Robert A. Maguire and John E. Malmstad. Bloomington, Ind., 1978.

Buckler, Julie A. *Mapping St. Petersburg: Imperial Text and Cityshape.* Princeton, N.J., 2005. Nineteenth-century St. Petersburg as a "living cultural system."

Clark, Katerina. *Petersburg: Crucible of Cultural Revolution.* Cambridge, Mass., 1995. Cultural developments in the early twentieth century.

Cracraft, James. *The Petrine Revolution in Russian Architecture.* Chicago, 1988. Chapters 6 and 7 focus on the building and early history of St. Petersburg.

Cross, Anthony, ed. *St. Petersburg, 1703–1825.* Houndmills, Basingstoke, U.K., 2003. A collection of essays published to commemorate the city's tercentenary.

Kaganov, Grigory. *Images of Space: St. Petersburg in the Visual and Verbal Arts.* Translated by Sidney Monas. Stanford, Calif., 1997.

Lincoln, W. Bruce. *Sunlight at Midnight: St. Petersburg and the Rise of Modern Russia.* New York, 2000.

Norman, Geraldine. *The Hermitage: The Biography of a Great Museum.* New York, 1998.

Shvidkovsky, Dmitri. *St. Petersburg: Architecture of the Tsars.* Translated by John Goodman. New York, 1996.

Volkov, Solomon. *St. Petersburg: A Cultural History.* Translated by Antonina W. Bouis. New York, 1995.

JAMES CRACRAFT

SAINT-SIMON, HENRI DE (1760–1825), French social theorist.

Henri de Saint-Simon was one of the most idiosyncratic and unclassifiable thinkers of the immediate postrevolutionary era in France. He was also one of the most original and influential. He has variously been regarded as a founder of socialism and as a prophet of organized capitalism, as a romantic and as a technocrat. Some have seen him as an apologist for the managerial state, whereas others have interpreted him as a fore-runner of anarchism who anticipated the withering away of the state. In the nineteenth century the publication of his collected works was financed by a famous banking family, the Pereires, who also provided for the care of his grave, but his name also features on the "Obelisk to the Fighters for Freedom" in Red Square in Moscow.

Born into an impoverished branch of a famous noble family, Saint-Simon had little formal education and in 1778 entered the army as a commissioned officer, in which capacity he served under Lafayette in the War of American Independence. Disgusted by the experience of war, he subsequently left the army and was drawn into various speculative engineering projects, including the building of a Panama canal. But it was the French Revolution that enabled his entrepreneurial activities to thrive, and he made a small fortune by speculating on the "national property" confiscated from the church and émigré nobles. He survived imprisonment during the Terror, and was to thrive again, economically and politically, under the Directory. Under the Consulate he set himself up as a patron of the natural sciences, but overreached himself and squandered much of the fortune he had acquired. But it was his contacts with the scientists of the École Polytechnique and the École de Médecine that helped launch him on the career as a social theorist in which he would make his enduring reputation.

WORKS

Saint-Simon published nothing until he was past forty, but was prolific in the last two decades or so of his life. Early sketches of his ideas included the *Lettres d'un habitant de Genève à ses contemporains* (1803; Letters from a resident of Geneva to his contemporaries), *Introduction aux travaux scientifiques du XIXe siècle* (1808; Introduction to scientific works of the eighteenth century), and the manuscript *Mémoire sur la science de l'homme* (1813; Memoir on the science of man). But these works were notoriously chaotic, and had he died in 1813 Saint-Simon would probably have been remembered only as a quixotic and idiosyncratic nobleman. What made his reputation was his period of collaboration with two gifted secretaries, the future historian Augustin Thierry and the embryonic positivist Auguste Comte. With Thierry's help he published *De la réorganisation de la société européenne* (1814; On the reorganization of European society), which envisaged the unification of Europe under the leadership of Britain and according to the principles of a beneficent liberal capitalism. During this Anglophile phase Saint-Simon was a mainstream liberal proponent of constitutionalism. But the period of collaboration with Comte saw Saint-Simon react against constitutional liberalism, which he came to see as a purely negative doctrine that lacked constructive capacity. The central concept in his thought was that of "industry," by which he meant not factory production but any goal-oriented activity. Industry, he argued, was pacific and cooperative and bound men together in society: hence, in a society geared to industry rather than to war, the "government of men" would give way to the "administration of things." He expounded these ideas in *Du système industriel* (1821; On the industrial system) and in his *Catéchisme des industriels* (1823–1824; Catechism of the industrialists). He and Comte also came under the influence of the theocrats Louis de Bonald and Joseph-Marie de Maistre, for whom there could be no social order without a recognized moral and intellectual authority. Saint-Simon now returned to a doctrine he first adumbrated in 1813, and assigned a crucial role to a scientifically educated elite, which would take the lead in forging a new spiritual consensus that would be the functional equivalent of Catholic doctrine in medieval Europe. In a final phase, after his break with Comte, his interest turned more explicitly toward the cause of the spiritual regeneration of modern society, which he expounded in *Le nouveau christianisme* (1825; The new Christianity).

SAINT-SIMONISM

What really made Saint-Simon's reputation was the small group of gifted and dedicated disciples that formed at the end of his life, notably Olinde Rodrigues, Prosper Enfantin, and Amand Bazard, who organized a series of lectures in Paris in 1828 to propound Saint-Simonian ideas. These were published under the title *Exposition de la doctrine de Saint-Simon* (1829; Exposition on the doctrine of Saint-Simon). It was these Saint-Simonians who interpreted their master's ideas in such a way as to recruit him posthumously to the incipient socialist movement. They were also fervent advocates of the emancipation of women, and Rodrigues attributed

to the dying Saint-Simon the enigmatic pronouncement that "man and woman together constitute the social individual." For a time, in and around the Revolution of 1830, Saint-Simonism seemed to be the creed of the future, and its influence reached Thomas Carlyle and John Stuart Mill in Britain and Heinrich Marx (Karl's father) and the poet Heinrich Heine in Germany. In the *Communist Manifesto*, Karl Marx and Friedrich Engels identified Saint-Simon, along with Charles Fourier and Robert Owen, as an exponent of the kind of utopian socialism that their own "scientific" socialism was destined to supplant.

In 1832, two intrepid Saint-Simonian missionaries landed in England, a land ripe, they thought, for conversion. They were to be disappointed, and in France too the movement dissipated in the disappointing aftermath of the Revolution of 1830. Thereafter Saint-Simon's reputation suffered an eclipse, and Comte—whose influence in his lifetime was limited—came to be seen as the formative influence on the positivist tradition. The revival of Saint-Simon's influence occurred at the end of the nineteenth century: the path was cleared with the work of Paul Janet (1878), and in the 1890s there was a flurry of interest in him as a pioneer of socialism. Georges Weill and Émile Durkheim both took this line, which was echoed by Henry Michel in his classic *L'idée de l'état* (1898; The idea of the state). In the first two thirds of the twentieth century there was consistent scholarly interest in Saint-Simon. English-language editions of his selected writings appeared in 1952, 1975, and 1976, but nothing has appeared since then. A flurry of postwar publications on Saint-Simon and the Saint-Simonians largely petered out in the late 1970s, along with the waning of the kind of technocratic corporatism, which he has been seen as anticipating. But given the protean shape of Saint-Simon's social and political thought, a puzzle still remains. He has not yet, for instance, been rediscovered as a prophet of globalization. Even advocates of European integration, who have rarely missed a chance to recruit posthumous supporters, have largely failed to turn their attention toward Saint-Simon. One exception to this contemporary neglect is worth comment. In 1985 François Furet, Pierre Rosanvallon, and their allies chose the name "Fondation Saint-Simon" for a think-tank they established, which was finally wound up shortly after Furet's death in 1999. Given the neoliberal affinities of this group, the prophet of corporatism might seem an unlikely hero. But Saint-Simon appealed nicely to their project of ideological convergence.

ASSESSMENT

Saint-Simon is best understood as one of those thinkers who sought to "close" the French Revolution. For him the Revolution, like the Enlightenment that gave birth to it, was an essentially destructive process that was to be welcomed insofar as it put an end to the world of feudalism, but that must yield to a new "organizing" force. His "socialism" should be seen in this light. He wrote at a time when socialism was usually divorced from the revolutionary tradition, and was instead associated with a quasi-religious zeal for spiritual renewal. His "new Christianity" was an appropriate culmination of his intellectual odyssey, and probably makes him a more sympathetic figure than the soulless technocrat.

See also **Bonald, Louis de; Comte, Auguste; France; Maistre, Joseph de; Utopian Socialism.**

BIBLIOGRAPHY

Carlisle, Robert B. *The Proffered Crown: Saint-Simonianism and the Doctrine of Hope.* Baltimore and London, 1987.

Ionescu, Ghita, ed. *The Political Thought of Saint-Simon.* Oxford, U.K., 1976.

Manuel, Frank E. *The New World of Henri St. Simon.* Cambridge, Mass., 1956.

Simon, W. M. "History for Utopia: Saint-Simon and the Idea of Progress." *Journal of the History of Ideas* 17 (1956): 311–331.

H. S. JONES

SALVATION ARMY. In 1865, the Reverend William Booth (1829–1912), an ordained minister in the Methodist New Connexion (a group that had seceded from the Wesleyans), began an urban home mission in London's East End. In 1861, Booth had left the New Connexion for a successful itinerant evangelism in Cornwall and the English Midlands. But his call to London's slums was primarily due to his wife's success as an evangelist. Catherine Mumford Booth's (1829–1890) preaching in South and West London, and William's lack of engagements, caused her to ask him to bring their six children from Leeds to London to be cared for by her mother. The Booths' eldest son, Bramwell, termed this period his father's wilderness years. The best William could do was to fill in for an evangelist in an East London Quaker cemetery. As he became comfortable preaching to the "heathen masses," he organized a mission (1865–1879) that he renamed a "salvation army" in the years 1878 and 1879.

Reflecting this military theme, in 1879, William Booth changed his title from the Christian Mission's general superintendent to simply general and shortly after his lay evangelists became officers. Booth called war councils to announce strategy, and abolished the mission's Methodist conference system. Governance became autocratic, with Booth as sole arbiter of doctrine, policy, and appointments. Booth's model was the British Volunteers, a popular military organization among working-class men in 1879. The Volunteers held military exercises, including street parades. The Salvation Army adopted their uniforms, parades, bands, flags, and jargon as other groups were doing—including temperance crusaders, Boys' and Girls' Brigades, Boy Scouts, Girl Guides—to proclaim a "muscular Christianity."

As a militant evangelical mission, the Salvation Army grew into an international Christian imperium. Before 1879, lay missioners had set up stations in other parts of London, Scotland, Wales, Ireland, and even North America in 1872. In the 1880s, Booth standardized operations with Orders and Regulations patterned after the British Army. He sent his representative commissioners to lead "invasions" of Europe, North America, Australasia, Africa, and South America. In chronological order, the Army "attacked" France, India, Switzerland, Sweden, Sri Lanka, South Africa, New Zealand, the Isle of Man, Pakistan, St. Helena, Newfoundland, Italy, Denmark, Holland, Jamaica, Norway, Belgium, and Finland. It mimicked other churches in tying its growth to the expansion of Britain's imperial realm, as well as to European and American commercial and political expansion.

As the Army became international, it was dying at its urban core. The "heathen masses" it claimed as its primary constituents were resisting its evangelical gospel. Many European cities were absorbing rural and foreign immigrants who had no interest in Booth's form of Christianity. Rather than convert to abstinence and Protestantism, many formed mobs to attack the Army's drum, flag, and soldiers. Wisely, Booth ordered his street preachers and writers to stop attacking Roman Catholic dogma in 1883.

As the Army diminished as an urban mission in the 1880s, it grew in the Midlands and on the outskirts of its empire. Critics, including Anglican clergy, asked whether Booth was a unique failure in urban slums. In the late 1880s, Booth responded with social reform programs he termed *Wholesale Salvation*. Hungry souls had no time for spiritual conversion; they needed food, employment, housing, and clothes. In 1890, the Army published a social manifesto: *In Darkest England, and the Way Out*.

Since Booth was no social reformer, the book was a joint effort. Frank Smith was its intellectual and operational father and first commissioner of the Social Reform Wing. Major Susie Swift compiled Smith's notes into a book outline. William Thomas Stead (1849–1912), a leading journalist, wrote the final copy. As editor of the *Review of Reviews*, he named it the book of the year. William and Bramwell Booth oversaw each stage of composition as Catherine Booth was dying of cancer. Smith left the Army in 1891 in a dispute over Booth's refusal to separate the social and spiritual wings' funds. He became a socialist member of the London County Council and of Parliament. In 1897, Swift became a Dominican nun. Stead died on the *Titanic* in 1912. Their social program evolved into the Army's premier ministry.

After 1890, most Europeans knew Salvationists for their social rather than their spiritual emphases on holiness, abstinence, and female ministry. By 1919, the Army had grown in northern Europe where Protestantism predominated (mainly Scandinavia). After the High Council deposed Bramwell Booth as general in 1929, generals were elected rather than appointed by their predecessor.

See also **Missions; Poverty; Protestantism; Religion.**

BIBLIOGRAPHY

Primary Sources

Booth, William. *In Darkest England, and the Way Out.* London, 1890.

Secondary Sources

Murdoch, Norman H. *Origins of the Salvation Army.* Knoxville, Tenn., 1994.

Scott, Carolyn. *The Heavenly Witch: The Story of the Maréchale.* London, 1981.

Walker, Pamela J. *Pulling the Devil's Kingdom Down: The Salvation Army in Victorian Britain.* Berkeley, Calif., 2001.

Norman H. Murdoch

SAND, GEORGE (1804–1876), French novelist.

The greatest woman writer of nineteenth-century France, George Sand was born Amantine Aurore Lucile Dupin of "mixed" parentage. Her father was the illegitimate grandson of Maurice de Saxe (himself the illegitimate son of Augustus II, king of Poland) and her mother of proletarian background. Sand makes much of this double heritage in her autobiography, *Histoire de ma vie* (1854–1855; *Story of My Life*), and ascribes her penchant for celebrating rustic and proletarian life, in novels such as *Le compagnon du tour de France* (1840; *The Journeyman Joiner* or *The Companion of the Tour of France*), *Horace* (1842), *Jeanne* (1844), *La Mare au diable* (1846; *The Haunted Pool*), *François le champi* (1848), and *La petite Fadette* (1849; *Little Fadette*), to her maternal roots.

She burst onto the Parisian literary scene in 1832 with a novel entitled *Indiana*, an instant best-seller, which she signed G. Sand. It was only a year later, with the publication of *Lélia*, a work of dark lyric power, that she used the full-fledged pseudonym by which she became (and continues to be) known. At the time, *Lélia* caused a scandal for its daring depiction of female sexuality. In the early twenty-first century, it is considered one of Sand's masterpieces, along with *Consuelo* (1842–1843) and *La comtesse de Rudolstadt* (1843–1844; *The Countess of Rudolstadt*). The latter two works together constitute a great feminine bildungsroman, a historical saga, and a vast novel with a utopian message.

While *Lélia* and the *Consuelo* cycle stand as Sand's two great fictional achievements, representing her Romantic period and her politically engaged decade, they must not overshadow the fact that Sand wrote more than ninety novels during a period spanning more than four decades. She wrote regularly every day throughout her life. At her death, she left an unfinished novel, *Albine Fiori,* published posthumously and reissued in 1997. She also produced a large body of autobiographical writings; a substantial number of plays; a large number of critical articles on literary, artistic, cultural, and political subjects; and a vast correspondence (twenty-six volumes) with virtually every writer, politician, and cultural personality of her day. Georges Lubin, who devoted half a century to the compilation of her letters, estimates that she had more than two thousand addressees. The letters that Sand exchanged with Gustave Flaubert from 1862 until her death constitute one of the great literary correspondences of the century.

But ultimately it is her novels that matter. After falling out of favor for more than a century, Sand's fictional oeuvre is being widely rediscovered and read. In addition to the titles already cited, many other works are worthy of mention: *Spiridion* (1839), *Gabriel* (1840), *Isidora* (1846), *Le Péché de Monsieur Antoine* (1847; *The Sin of Monsieur Antoine*), *Le marquis de Villemer* (1861), *Antonia* (1863), *La Confession d'une jeune fille* (1865; Confession of a young girl), *Nanon* (1872). Unfortunately, English speakers may find it difficult to find good translations—indeed, to find translations at all in many cases. There is, for example, no full-scale translation of *Lélia* into English as of 2006. Her style is difficult to translate as she frequently employs some of the longest sentences in the French language after Marcel Proust. Unlike him, however, Sand has yet to be graced with the translators she deserves.

In her century, Sand was routinely discussed as Honoré de Balzac's equal, her idealism contrasted to his realism, an opposition that she herself addresses in *Histoire de ma vie* and *Le compagnon du tour de France.* Yet Sand's reputation steadily declined after her death, especially compared to the other great French nineteenth-century novelists. In the age of naturalism, her novels were criticized by Émile Zola and his followers who detested Romanticism and favored the realists. In the early twentieth century, her works were largely disdained, if not reviled, by the likes of Charles Maurras and Léon Daudet who found in her the epitome of what they called "the stupid nineteenth century," Even while abroad, though writers such as Fyodor Dostoevsky, Henry

George Sand. Photographed by Nadar in 1864. GETTY IMAGES

James, and George Eliot paid her homage, Sand was increasingly marginalized in France. Only her rustic novels were deemed worthy of attention, and these were relegated to the margins of the canon, classified as regional or children's literature.

Her fascinating life, her eccentric lifestyle (male dress and cigars), her famous lovers and friends (Delacroix, Balzac, Flaubert, Franz Liszt, and Frédéric Chopin, among others) exerted more fascination on the public than her works. As a result, many more biographies exist than critical works. The French have obsessed over her affair with the poet Alfred de Musset, with particular emphasis on their escapade to Venice that was a fiasco. This tragic affair has prompted dozens of accounts over the years, following their own original versions, his in *La Confession d'un enfant du siècle* (1836; *Confession of a Child of the Century*), and hers in *Elle et lui* (1859; *She and He*). Americans prefer to dwell on her nine-year liaison with Chopin. Critics have tended to judge Sand harshly, citing the fact that after they parted, she refused to see him again, even as he lay dying. That the composer produced a large portion of his best work in her care is less often acknowledged.

In the post–World War II era, the efforts of scholars such as Georges Lubin, Léon Cellier, and biographers such as André Maurois revived interest in Sand's work. The centennial of her death in 1976 provided an occasion for both academics and feminists to turn their attention to her, especially in the United States. Despite her renewed fortune, it is striking how easily she still provokes negative reactions in the early twenty-first century. Some feminists fault her for not being feminist enough, particularly for disassociating herself from women's political groups in 1848. Some biographers condemn her as a bad mother, a bad lover, a bad friend. Some critics, echoing Charles Baudelaire's scornful and sexist remarks, still dismiss her as a second-rate writer. Two hundred years after her birth Sand's reputation remains unsettled. The traditional view has not been wholly dislodged. But this is not surprising since taking Sand's writing into full consideration entails seeing nineteenth-century French literature in a radically new light. That is only a question of time.

See also **Chopin, Frédéric; Feminism; France; Gender; Liszt, Franz.**

BIBLIOGRAPHY

Primary Sources

Sand, George. *Correspondance.* 25 vols. Edited by Georges Lubin. Paris, 1964–1991; Vol. 26 (*Suppléments*), Tusson, 1995.

———. *Oeuvres complètes.* 35 vols. Geneva, 1979–1980. Reprint of C. Lévy, 1863–1926.

———. *Story of My Life: The Autobiography of George Sand.* Edited by Thelma Jurgrau. Albany, N.Y., 1991. Translation of *Histoire de ma vie* (1854–1855).

Steegmuller, Francis, ed. and trans. *Flaubert-Sand: The Correspondence.* New York, 1993. Translation based on the edition by Alphonse Jacobs (1981).

Secondary Sources

Didier, Béatrice. *George Sand, écrivain: "Un grand fleuve d'Amérique."* Paris, 1998.

Harlan, Elizabeth, *George Sand,* New Haven, Conn., and London, 2004.

Hecquet, Michèle. *Poétique de la parabole: les romans socialistes de George Sand, 1840–1845.* Paris, 1992.

Mallet, Francine. *George Sand.* Paris, 1976.

Mozet, Nicole. *George Sand: écrivain de romans.* Saint-Cyr-sur-Loire, 1997.

Naginski, Isabelle Hoog. *George Sand: Writing for Her Life.* New Brunswick, N.J., and London, 1991.

Powell, David A. *George Sand.* Boston, 1990.

Schor, Naomi. *George Sand and Idealism.* New York, 1993.

ISABELLE HOOG NAGINSKI

SAN STEFANO, TREATY OF. The Treaty of San Stefano was the agreement marking formal conclusion of the Russo-Turkish War of 1877–1878. With Turkish forces soundly beaten in the field by the beginning of 1878, the two sides agreed to an armistice at Adrianople on 31 January, followed by formal peace negotiations at San Stefano, a settlement close to Constantinople. There, on 3 March 1878, representatives of Tsar Alexander II (N. P. Ignatiev and A. I. Nelidov) and Sultan Abdul Hamid II (Safvet Pasha and Sadullah Bey, with Mehmet Ali assisting) concluded a peace treaty that heavily favored the victorious Russians.

According to its terms, Montenegro, Serbia, and Romania received their full independence, along with substantial territorial cessions, including northern Dobruja for Romania. Bosnia and Herzegovina were granted autonomy, while a greatly enlarged Bulgaria (with a seaboard on the Aegean) became an autonomous principality, with the right to elect its own ruler, who would be considered a vassal of the sultan. Turkish troops were to be withdrawn from Bulgaria, while fifty thousand Russians remained for at least two years. In the event of future hostilities, neutral commercial vessels retained the right of free trade through the Turkish Straits. Russia received the right to transit ten warships annually through the Turkish Straits. Bessarabia, which had been ceded to Turkish-dominated Romania according to the Treaty of Paris in 1856, reverted to Russian control, while a series of locales along the Black Sea coast and in Asia Minor, including Batumi, Ardahan, Bayazid, and Kars, also went to the Russians. Finally, the San Stefano agreement obliged the sultan to pay an indemnity of 510 million rubles to Russia, to reform Armenian administration, and to grant self-government on the model of Crete to Albania, Epirus, and Thessaly.

This treaty greatly expanded and solidified Russian influence in the Balkans, especially after the creation of an enlarged Bulgaria with a substantial Russian presence. Conditions were now ripe to assure future Russian control over the Ottoman Empire, an eventuality that neither England nor Austria-Hungary was prepared to accept. Moreover, because San Stefano appeared to violate previous international agreements over the Turkish Straits and the fate of "Europe's sick man" (as the Ottoman Empire was called), other European powers, including France, Germany, and Italy, saw their interests and the precarious Balkan balance at stake. Russia, diplomatically isolated and financially exhausted, now faced the prospect of contending with a gathering hostile European coalition. The result was Russian acquiescence to a great-power review of San Stefano's provisions at the Congress of Berlin in June–July 1878, during which the more significant elements of Russia's wartime gains and dictated settlement were nullified. A tenuous peace ensued, but the arrangement outraged Russian and Balkan nationalists of various stripes, fostered mutual Russian-German distrust, and led indirectly to the secret Austro-German Dual Alliance of 1879.

See also **Armies; Congress of Berlin; Russo-Turkish War.**

BIBLIOGRAPHY

Jelavich, Barbara. *St. Petersburg and Moscow: Tsarist and Soviet Foreign Policy, 1814–1974.* Bloomington, Ind., 1974.

Sumner, Benedict Humphrey. *Russia and the Balkans, 1870–1880.* Oxford, U.K., 1937.

BRUCE W. MENNING

SATIE, ERIK (1866–1925), French composer.

One of most influential and problematical composers of the twentieth century, Erik-Alfred-Leslie Satie was born on 17 May 1866 in the town of Honfleur, France, whose seascapes figure in many an impressionist painting. The family moved to Paris when he was four, but, after his mother's death in 1872, Erik and his brother were sent back to their grandparents in Honfleur. Erik was an unruly student but showed some predilection for music. When he was twelve, he rejoined his father in Paris, and his formal schooling was never resumed. Within several months, his father remarried a pianist and salon composer, Eugénie Barnetche, who was determined that her stepson study piano at the Paris Conservatoire. Satie impressed his teachers with his fine tone, weak sight-reading, and general laziness. In fall 1882 he was dropped from his class for insufficient progress. A second stint (1885–1886), undertaken with a view to reducing his term of military service, was no more successful. But his father had meanwhile set up shop as a music publisher and sometime composer of popular songs and facile piano music. Erik soon followed his father's example, writing piano waltzes and songs that may have benefited from his stepmother's polishing. These began to be published in 1887, a crucial year that witnessed Satie's first works of importance (because of their pathbreaking harmonic language), the *Trois Sarabandes*. Later that year, Satie left home and began frequenting the artists' cabarets and cafés-concerts of Montmartre. After having himself announced as a *gymnopédiste* in the Chat Noir, he wrote *Trois Gymnopédies* (1888), the haunting slow waltzes by which he is best known today.

The bohemian world of the Montmartre cabarets deeply affected Satie's aesthetic priorities, which ran toward the esoteric and outrageous. His penchants for odd titles, notational puzzles, extravagant calligraphy, bizarre performance instructions, and harmonic schemes that had little to do with traditional tonality were manifest nearly from the start. He associated briefly (1891–1892) with the writer Joséphin Péladan and wrote some pieces for Péladan's Rosicrucian sect based on an ancient Greek scale. Soon Satie was imitating Péladan's zanier pretensions, submitting himself (thrice) as a candidate to the Académie des Beaux-Arts, founding his own "church," and publishing crackpot tracts. He also befriended Claude Debussy, who called him a "gentle, medieval musician wandered into this century for the joy of his friend" (Whiting, p. 111). The relationship was hardly an easy one, but it lasted until Debussy's death. Off and on until 1909, Satie worked as a cabaret pianist and composer, writing songs for two prominent entertainers of the day, the satirist Vincent Hyspa and the chanteuse Paulette Darty. His work for Hyspa left an enduring mark on his compositional strategies, which perennially relied on parodic allusion. His work for Darty brought him into contact with the idiom of ragtime that was imported from the United States after 1900. A stylistic résumé is provided by the *Trois morceaux en forme de poire* (1890–1903; Three pieces in the shape of a pear), a seven-movement anthology of short pieces drawn from his Rosicrucian and cabaret music.

In 1905 the determined autodidact entered the Schola Cantorum to study counterpoint. During the ensuing years, Satie honed his piano writing into a lean-textured, dissonant, but still whimsical style. In January 1911 sponsorship by Maurice Ravel drew him out of bohemian obscurity and into the limelight, a position Satie maintained for the rest of his career. While attention first attached to the harmonic audacity of his early works (the sobriquet "precursor of genius" would come to haunt him), the public soon caught up with the humoristic piano suites he was now writing. The *Descriptions automatiques* (1913; Automatic descriptions) and *Embryons desséchés* (1913; Desiccated embryos) rely on techniques of parodic distortion of familiar musical materials learned in the cabarets, with a narrative overlay of fragmentary stories, which were not, however, to be read aloud in performance. The *Sports et divertissements* (1914; Sports and diversions) pose a daunting complex of musical, verbal, and visual imagery—for they add illustrations by Charles Martin and Satie's calligraphy to the mix—a complex that challenges the very notion of the musical "work." Satie became no less active as a writer of musical journalism, whimsical autobiography, and even an absurdist play, *Le piège de Méduse* (1913; Medusa's trap).

In 1915 the poet Jean Cocteau took Satie under his wing. The high point of their several collaborations was surely the ballet *Parade,* which involved Pablo Picasso as set and costume designer, Léonide Massine as choreographer, and Sergei Diaghilev as producer. At its premiere in May 1917, *Parade* caused a stir (though not quite the riot touched off three years earlier by *Le sacre du printemps* [The rite of spring]). The noise-making instruments (sirens, typewriter, pistols) added to the orchestra made Satie notorious, even though they were Cocteau's idea. Satie soon found himself at the head of a new "school" of young French composers (which included Darius Milhaud, Francis

Poulenc, Arthur Honegger, and Georges Auric) dubbed *les six* (by comparison with the Russian Five). *Parade* led to a string of further projects for Diaghilev's Ballets Russes and Rolf de Maré's Ballets Suédois, for whom he wrote his last work, *Relâche* (1924; No show today), with its cinematic interlude filmed by René Clair. In these last projects, the solidity of Satie's musical structure is in marked contrast to the absurdist scenarios. To those who bemoan Satie's studied avoidance of the "serious," one may recommend the "symphonic drama" *Socrate* (1918) and the gravely serene *Nocturnes* for piano (1919). Satie died on 1 July 1925 in Paris.

See also **Avant-Garde; Debussy, Claude; Diaghilev, Sergei; Fin de Siècle; France; Picasso, Pablo; Ravel, Maurice.**

BIBLIOGRAPHY

Orledge, Robert. *Satie the Composer.* Cambridge, U.K., 1990.

Shattuck, Roger. *The Banquet Years: The Arts in France, 1885–1918.* New York, 1958. Rev. ed., published as *The Banquet Years: The Origins of the Avant-Garde in France, 1885 to World War I.* New York, 1968.

Volta, Ornella, ed. *Satie Seen through His Letters.* Translated by Michael Bullock. London, 1989.

Whiting, Steven Moore. *Satie the Bohemian: From Cabaret to Concert Hall.* Oxford, U.K., 1999.

                                    STEVEN M. WHITING

SCHELLING, FRIEDRICH VON
(1775–1854), German Romantic philosopher.

Although he never developed a finished system of thought, Friedrich von Schelling exercised a considerable influence on early-nineteenth-century intellectual life, leaving a mark on fields as diverse as art, medicine, theology, mythology, philology, and political philosophy.

The son of a Protestant pastor and Old Testament scholar, Schelling was born in the Württemberg town of Leonberg. As a young boy he demonstrated remarkable academic gifts, and at the age of fifteen he enrolled in the Tübingen seminary (*Stift*). There Schelling befriended his older classmates Georg Wilhelm Friedrich Hegel and Friedrich Hölderlin, while drinking in the spirit of radical Enlightenment inspired by the French Revolution. Schelling seemed destined for a career in theology until 1793, when he encountered the philosophy of Johann Gottlieb Fichte (1762–1814). Just as the French Revolution had overthrown political tyranny, Fichte's system of transcendental idealism seemed to throw off the tyrannies of God and the empirical world, establishing the free conscious subject as sovereign and absolute. Inspired by this vision, Schelling published a series of studies on transcendental idealism, in some cases pushing the system in directions its creator had not intended. In particular, he located the absolute not in the realm of consciousness but in a prior, preconscious unity of thought and being. In addition, he turned to the study of nature, which, in a sharp break from prior mechanistic theories, he described as "unconscious mind." Schelling's *Ideas for a Philosophy of Nature* (*Ideen zu einer Philosophie der Natur,* 1797), written when he was just twenty-two, became a founding text of *Naturphilosophie,* influencing research and teaching in faculties of medicine and establishing his reputation in Germany and abroad.

In 1798 Schelling received an appointment as extraordinary professor of philosophy at the University of Jena. There he came into contact with the literary luminaries Johann Wolfgang von Goethe and Johann Christoph Friedrich von Schiller, as well as with some of the key figures of the emerging Romantic movement—the critics Friedrich and August Wilhelm von Schlegel and the poet Friedrich von Hardenberg (Novalis). Schelling's relationship with the Romantics was always tense, and it broke down completely in 1802 when he began an affair with August Wilhelm's wife, Caroline (they married the next year). Nonetheless, their interchanges left him with a renewed appreciation for the revelatory powers of art. In *System of Transcendental Idealism* (*System des transcendentalen Idealismus,* 1800), *Lectures on the Method of Academic Study* (*Vorlesungen über die Methode des akademischen Studiums,* 1803), and the unpublished *Philosophy of Art* (*Philosophie der Kunst,* 1802–1803), Schelling argued that art represented a union of finite and infinite, conscious and unconscious, that was the highest manifesta-

tion of the absolute. He also suggested that a new and higher art—a "new mythology"—might serve as the foundation for a renewed aesthetic, religious, and political order in Europe, healing the fragmentation and alienation of modern life.

A series of personal disputes and political squabbles caused Schelling to leave Jena in 1803, accepting positions first in Würzburg and then, three years later, in Munich. The change in locale coincided with a fundamental shift in Schelling's thinking, which became both more Christian and more conservative as he lost confidence in the French Revolution and came into contact with Catholic thinkers like Franz von Baader. At the heart of Schelling's late philosophy was an insistence on the real personality of God, who existed prior to and independently of his creation. In a massive series of lectures, most of which remained unpublished in his lifetime, he narrated the story of creation, humanity's fall from grace, the evolution of mythology from primitive star worship to Greek polytheism, and the final revelation in Christianity of the nature of freedom and the promise of a personal relationship with the triune God. Schelling's insistence on the primacy of personality (both human and divine) reinforced the restorationist defense of monarchy, influencing such conservative thinkers as Friedrich Julius Stahl (1802–1861). At the same time, it constituted a powerful critique of Hegel's "pantheism of reason," which by the 1820s had attained considerable influence in Germany, especially Prussia.

In 1841 Schelling was called by Frederick William IV (king of Prussia; r. 1840–1861) to the chair of philosophy in Berlin, where he was given the charge of wiping out the "scourge of Hegelian pantheism." His opening lecture in a series of lectures on *Philosophy of Revelation* (*Philosophieder Offenbarung*) was a public spectacle, attended by Søren Kierkegaard, Friedrich Engels, Leopold von Ranke, Ferdinand Lassalle, and Mikhail Bakunin, among others. Yet the difficult, obscure, and—many felt—overly mystical dimensions of Schelling's doctrine left most in his audience cold. The *Philosophy of Revelation* was dismissed as a reactionary relic of the Romantic era, and the philosopher soon retreated from public life. Despite their scorn for Schelling, however, the critiques by Kierkegaard and Ludwig Feuerbach of Hegelian idealism would follow along lines first traced by Schelling. Throughout the nineteenth century and well into the twentieth, Schelling's philosophy would serve as a resource for thinkers (including Friedrich Nietzsche [1844–1900], Franz Rosenzweig [1886–1929], and Martin Heidegger [1889–1976]) who sought an alternative to the rationalist tendencies of the nineteenth century and a sustained examination of the darker, prerational aspects of nature, history, and humanity.

See also **Fichte, Johann Gottlieb; Germany; Hegel, Georg Wilhelm Friedrich.**

BIBLIOGRAPHY

Bowie, Andrew. *Schelling and Modern European Philosophy: An Introduction*. London and New York, 1993.

Frank, Manfred. *Der unendliche Mangel am Sein: Schellings Hegelkritik und die Anfänge der Marxschen Dialektik*. 2nd ed. Munich, 1992.

Gulyga, Arsenij. *Schelling: Leben und Werk*. Translated by Elke Kirsten. Stuttgart, 1989.

O'Meara, Thomas. *Romantic Idealism and Roman Catholicism: Schelling and the Theologians*. Notre Dame, Ind., 1982.

Richards, Robert J. *The Romantic Conception of Life: Science and Philosophy in the Age of Goethe*. Chicago, 2002.

GEORGE S. WILLIAMSON

SCHIELE, EGON (1890–1918), Austrian painter.

At the time of his death at age twenty-eight, Egon Schiele was considered Austria's preeminent artist. In 1910 a collector of Schiele's works observed that his "powerful originality at first repels, all the more later to captivate." His paintings and drawings of explicitly erotic nudes, including children, still have the power to disturb. An exhibition of his works was censored in the United States as recently as 1960.

Schiele's father, Adolf, of German Protestant background, served as stationmaster of a major railway junction at Tulln, eighteen miles outside of Vienna. Egon's mother, Marie Soukup Schiele, was educated in a Viennese convent. Adolf contracted syphilis from a prostitute at about the time of his marriage. Marie's first three children were stillborn,

probably as a result of the disease, but eventually she gave birth to two healthy girls and a boy, Egon. (A third daughter, Elvira, died at age ten.) Adolf, who refused to seek medical treatment, entered the terminal stages of syphilis in 1902, when Egon was twelve, developing hallucinations and becoming so irrational that he burned the family's railroad bonds. His death marked the young Egon, who came to view love and death as inexorably intertwined.

Schiele showed a great gift for drawing at an early age. Despite the disapproval of his family, he spent hours outside drawing from nature, neglecting his academic studies. He could capture the essence of an object extremely quickly, in a few deft strokes, and took pencil and paper everywhere. He gained admittance to the Academy of Fine Arts in Vienna at age sixteen, the youngest student ever admitted. Schiele found study at the academy rigid and withdrew three years later.

In about 1907 Schiele met Gustav Klimt. The older artist encouraged Schiele's career, and for a time the younger artist borrowed motifs from Klimt's oeuvre. After a few years Schiele forsook Klimt's art nouveau style in favor of expressionism, which emphasized the artist's emotional reaction to his subject. He used unnatural colors to express emotional content in such paintings as *Self-Portrait with Hand to Cheek* (1910). Schiele portrayed himself, often naked, in many exaggerated self-portraits. His masterful use of line to portray a subject's character is evident in his minimalist watercolor portraits of this period.

With the decline in public commissions in Vienna, artists were forced to court a few wealthy patrons. Indeed Schiele had several such patrons, but their support was sporadic. As a result he faced financial hardship, often unable to purchase canvas, paper, or paint.

At the end of 1910 Schiele withdrew from the art scene in Vienna. Influenced by the symbolists, including Arthur Rimbaud and Rainer Maria Rilke, his works became more allegorical. He again painted many self-portraits, this time with multiple images. He also depicted frail, autumnal tree trunks against a hostile void.

In the spring of 1911 Schiele moved to a small town with seventeen-year-old Valerie Neuzil, nicknamed "Wally," who served as his principal model.

Self-Portrait with Black Clay Vase and Spread Fingers. Painting by Egon Schiele, 1911. ©ARCHIVO ICONOGRAFICO S.A./CORBIS

In 1913 a one-man show was held in Munich, but it met with little success. He now portrayed cloaked religious figures in works such as *The Hermits* (1912) and *Agony* (1912), which suggests a cubist influence.

In 1912 Schiele experienced what proved to be a pivotal experience: he was charged with exposing minors to pornography. His real sin seems to have been using nude child models in a provincial town. He served twenty-four days for the crime and found the experience of imprisonment shattering. Following incarceration, his art became less self-centered, more mature and empathetic. His portrayals of women were less erotic. He again created many works with religious themes, including *Self Portrait as St. Sebastian* (1914), *Holy Family* (1913), and *Resurrection* (1913), which perhaps referred to his period of imprisonment.

In November 1914 Schiele's beloved sister Gerti, the subject of many portraits, married Anton Peschka, a painter friend of Schiele's. Egon himself began thinking of marriage and began courting Edith Harms, a seventeen-year-old girl from a middle-class family, using Wally as a chaperone. (Wally later volunteered as a Red Cross nurse in World War I and died in Dalmatia in 1917.) Schiele's somber oil entitled *Death and Maiden* (1915) is thought to be a portrayal of his break with Wally.

Schiele married Edith Harms on 17 June 1915. At first exempted from the draft due to a weak heart, he was later declared fit for service. He reported for military service in Prague four days after his wedding. Like other Austrian artists, Schiele obtained a series of noncombat assignments. His first, digging trenches in Vienna, allowed him time to paint a portrait of his wife, whom he portrayed as awkward, stiff, and expressionless. Afraid of being sent to the front, Schiele sought a post as "war painter" or assignment to the Army Museum. Instead he was sent to a rural post outside of Vienna. Schiele painted some poignant portraits of Russian prisoners of war, but overall 1916 was not a productive year. *Die Aktion*, a leading left-wing Berlin magazine, devoted an entire issue to his work.

In early 1917 Schiele was transferred back to Vienna. He developed a new style—more empathetic and objective and less self-referential. His portraits of women depicted his subjects as thoughtful and intelligent. *The Family* (1918) is an allegory in which Man (Schiele) watches over a pensive wife and baby. The artist was asked to organize a Secession exhibition in Vienna that prominently displayed his works, all of which were sold. Schiele was recognized as the leading painter of his generation, and commissions began to pour in. With Klimt's sudden death from a stroke, Schiele acquired the mantle of Austria's foremost artist.

In April 1918 Schiele was at last assigned to the Army Museum in Vienna, where he organized exhibitions. In the same month, Edith became pregnant. As the war ground to its inevitable conclusion, food shortages, lack of fuel, and finally, the Spanish influenza pandemic, made life in Vienna precarious. Edith became ill with the flu and died on 28 October. Schiele succumbed three days later. His professional career had lasted only ten years.

See also **Art Nouveau; Klimt, Gustav; Modernism; Vienna.**

BIBLIOGRAPHY

Comini, Alessandra. *Nudes: Egon Schiele.* New York, 1994.

Kallir, Jane. *Egon Schiele: Life and Work.* New York, 1990.

Schröder, Klaus Albrecht, and Harold Szeemann, eds. *Egon Schiele and His Contemporaries: Austrian Painting and Drawing from 1900 to 1930 from the Leopold Collection, Vienna.* Munich, Germany, 1989.

Whitford, Frank. *Egon Schiele.* New York and Toronto, 1981.

CAROL P. MERRIMAN

SCHINKEL, KARL FRIEDRICH
(1781–1841), German architect.

Karl Friedrich Schinkel was the leading architect in Berlin during the first half of the nineteenth century, one of the most productive and innovative artistic minds of his era, and arguably one of the founders of the modern tradition in architecture as such. Schinkel's importance as a teacher and role model for architecture is as important as his work as designer and builder of several monumental structures in Berlin and in Prussia generally. He established a distinctive style of design and construction that combined earlier traditions of building, especially from classical antiquity and from the gothic Middle Ages, but also in several instances introduced a programmatically modernist design that in function and in materials points ahead to central features of twentieth-century architecture. Schinkel's reputation and his influence remain widespread, as does a universal respect and admiration for his life, his personality, and his work in general.

Schinkel was born in the town of Neuruppen, located in the region of Brandenburg, north of Berlin. Several years after the death of his father in a fire that broke out in his home town when Karl Friedrich was only seven, he moved with his mother and several siblings to Berlin (in 1794), where he attended the "Zum grauen Kloster" gymnasium, the leading school of the city, which he left in 1798. Schinkel's interest in architecture was aroused through contact with David Gilly (1748–1808), in particular in response to a design for a memorial for Frederick the Great designed by Gilly's son Friedrich (1772–1800) and exhibited in 1797. The monument was never built and the younger Gilly, who had become a close friend of Schinkel, died in 1800, the same year in which Schinkel's mother also died. Schinkel's apprenticeship years included an extended trip to Italy (1803–1805). Schinkel produced a number of monumental landscape paintings during these early years, which attracted wide interest. Usually located in an imaginary medieval setting with ornate gothic castles, cathedrals, and cities, these paintings demonstrate a distinct architectural vision. The pervasive influence of Romanticism is everywhere apparent.

EARLY CAREER

Following the defeat of Prussia at the hands of the emperor Napoleon I (r. 1804–1814/15) in 1806 and the subsequent occupation of Berlin by the French army, Schinkel had little opportunity to practice the craft of architecture. For the next decade he supported himself primarily through his painting and through set designs for the theater, where he achieved remarkable success. His designs for a production of Mozart's *Magic Flute* in the opera house Unter den Linden in 1815 remain perhaps the most famous ever conceived for that work. In 1809 he married Susanne Berger (1782–1861), who subsequently gave birth to three daughters and a son (Marie, 1810; Susanne, 1811; Raphael, 1813; and Elisabeth, 1822). Schinkel's work as a painter and theater designer quickly attracted the interest of the Prussian court, where he was appointed an architectural consultant (*Oberbauassessor*) as early as 1810, and in the following year he became a member of the Academy of Arts.

ARCHITECTURE

Schinkel's breakthrough as an architect occurred soon after the final defeat of Napoleon in 1815, when he was commissioned by the Prussian king Frederick William III (r. 1797–1840) to design a New Guardhouse (Neue Wache) on Unter den Linden, adjacent to the newly opened university. This modest, yet elegant classical structure adapted the model of a Roman Castrum with an entry consisting of six Doric columns. The building has seen various uses over the years, especially during the Nazi and communist eras, but in the early twenty-first century serves as a memorial for all the victims of political oppression and the destruction of wars, with an open inner space containing the powerful Pieta by Käthe Kollwitz (1867–1945).

Largely in response to the success of this first public building, Schinkel was appointed privy counsellor for public works and professor of architecture. The great era of his career as the leading architect of Berlin extended through the following two decades. His most significant monumental designs were the new Royal Theater (Schauspielhaus) on the Gendarmenmarkt, built on the ruins of the preceding structure, which burned to the

ground in 1817 (completed in 1821), and the Museum of Art (now called the Altes Museum), located at the northern end of the Royal Gardens (Lustgarten) opposite the great baroque city castle designed in the seventeenth century by Andreas Schlüter (1664–1714). Schinkel's museum combined several classical elements—including a long row of Ionic columns along the front of the building, a staircase with open landing ascending to the second level (where the collection of paintings was housed), and a central rotunda modeled on the Pantheon in Rome, where the collection of antique sculptures was arranged in a circle around the periphery of the hall. These two monuments of high culture—theater and museum—established the distinctive profile of Schinkel's plan for Berlin as an Athens on the Spree River.

A number of other projects by Schinkel demonstrate innovative construction techniques and a protomodernist functional style. He designed the monument to the Wars of Liberation from Napoleon on Kreuzberg, using cast iron with a distinct gothic design (1814). He designed the bridge (Schlossbrücke) from the boulevard Unter den Linden to the island where the royal castle was located, placed with sculptures on either side commemorating heroic figures in the arms of mythological divinities (1821–1824). Schinkel also redesigned the estate in Tegel of Wilhelm von Humboldt, the founder of the university in 1810 and the chief proponent of a neoclassical architectural style modeled on ancient Greece. The design of Schloss Tegel (1820–1824), however, demonstrates Schinkel's skill at combining traditional architectural features, including the grace of Italian villas, with a simplicity and symmetry of form that looked ahead to his modernist tendencies. Even more striking in simplicity and elegance is the pavilion (now called the Schinkel Pavilion, 1825–1830), located next to the Charlottenburg Palace, intended as a quiet retreat for the royal residents from that much more monumental structure. At the king's request it was modeled on the Villa Reale Chiatamone in Naples. The pavilion constitutes a perfect cube with rooms and balconies arranged in a symmetrical placement around the inner space on two levels in balanced proportions. Even today this building seems astonishing in its simplicity and elegance of design.

A view of the Altes Museum, Berlin. Aquatint by Johann Daniel Laurens after a drawing by Karl Friedrich Schinkel, 1831.
BILDARCHIV PREUSSISCHER KULTURBESITZ/ART RESOURCE, NY

The Friedrichswerder Church is perhaps Schinkel's most successful blending of the gothic revival and modern functional style of all the several churches he designed. It still stands and now functions as a museum in celebration of Schinkel's career and the culture of his time in Berlin. The Academy of Architecture (Bauakademie, 1832–1835) deserves to be celebrated as the most perfect fulfillment of Schinkel's modernist tendencies—a four-story, square ground plan that also constituted a perfect cube with an external facade consisting of industrially produced terracotta tiles. The inner rooms were arranged around a central courtyard with a variety of uses indicated for the instruction and training of future architects, as also for the offices of the central building authority (*Oberbaudeputation*). Schinkel himself occupied the top floor as atelier and residence, and after his death his drawings and writings were preserved there in his memory as a museum, subsequently moved several times until finally located in the new Kupferstichkabinett. In 1960, although the Bauakademie survived the bombings quite intact and was being renovated, the East German regime dynamited and removed it. In the early twenty-first century there is some hope that the Bauakademie may be reconstructed to honor Schinkel's memory.

DESIGN POSSIBILITIES

Schinkel's importance as a teacher and source of innovation in architecture is also measured by the plans and designs he prepared for buildings never built and for hypothetical architectural possibilities. He published these designs at various intervals during his career (from 1819 to 1840) under the title *Sammlung architektonischer Entwürfe* (*Collection of Architectural Designs*). Schinkel also drafted a comprehensive plan for the inner city of Berlin, which remained uncompleted for lack of funding from the king and the Prussian court. Issues of funding plagued Schinkel throughout his career and led to compromise and the abandonment of many projects. Nonetheless his designs in themselves provide a sense of his unique vision and the ambition for building that he brought to his career. Schinkel also designed a great diversity of furniture and decorative objects and domestic crafts, which supplement his architectural vision of a classical modernism. A project for a comprehensive textbook of architecture (*Architektonisches Lehrbuch*), which Schinkel worked on for many years, remained uncompleted at his death. Since many of the buildings and decorative objects designed by Schinkel do not survive, the documentary record provided by his drawings and engravings is all the more important for evaluating his achievement.

In the final phase of his career Schinkel was commissioned to build and renovate several buildings and royal residences in and near Potsdam, especially Schloss Charlottenhof, along with the court gardener's house and roman baths (1826–1829), the cavalier house on the Pfaueninsel (1824–1826), and Schloss Glienecke and Schloss Babelsberg (1834–1849; completed after Schinkel's death). Finally, Schinkel prepared elaborate plans with detailed illustrations for two projects that extended far beyond the limits of the possible and remain as utopian visions of an architectural grandeur symbolizing Schinkel's genius: the Royal Palace on the Acropolis in Athens, Greece (1834), and Orianda Castle on Yalta in the Crimea for the Prussian king Frederick William III's daughter, who was married to Tsar Nicholas I (r. 1825–1855) of Russia (1838).

In 1840 Schinkel collapsed into an unconscious state that lasted for more than a year until his death on 9 October 1841. His funeral procession and burial in the Dorotheenstrasse cemetery were attended by thousands of devoted followers. The legacy of this artistic genius remains unique in the annals of architecture, both in practice and in theory. His achievement in various fields of artistic endeavor is impressive, and the importance of the buildings he designed is acknowledged universally after nearly two centuries. The distinctive cultural style of the Romantic era in Berlin is almost entirely the legacy of Schinkel, despite the destruction and catastrophes of the twentieth century. Karl Friedrich

Schinkel fully deserves his reputation as the central precursor of modern architecture and as one of the most important architects who ever lived.

See also **Berlin; Prussia; Romanticism.**

BIBLIOGRAPHY

Ohff, Heinz. *Karl Friedrich Schinkel oder die Schönheit in Preußen.* Munich, 1997.

Pundt, Hermann G. *Schinkel's Berlin: A Study in Environmental Planning.* Cambridge, Mass., 1972.

Snodin, Michael. *Karl Friedrich Schinkel: A Universal Man.* New Haven, Conn., 1991.

Steffens, Martin. *K. F. Schinkel, 1781–1841: An Architect in the Service of Beauty.* Cologne and Los Angeles, 2003.

CYRUS HAMLIN

SCHLEGEL, AUGUST WILHELM VON

SCHLEGEL, AUGUST WILHELM VON (1767–1845), German literary critic and scholar.

August Wilhelm von Schlegel, older brother of the now more famous Friedrich von Schlegel (1772–1829), was the most learned and wide-ranging literary critic and scholar of the Romantic period in Germany. The journal *Athenaeum,* edited by both brothers from 1798 to 1800, served as a vehicle for their shared ideas about Romantic art and literature. Subsequently, in public lectures delivered over the course of his long career, August Wilhelm von Schlegel, more than any other writer of the time, disseminated the new ideas about literature that came to be identified with Romanticism. In addition, combining an unusual facility for other languages with a precise sense of literary form and style, Schlegel published verse translations of a number of important writers from European literature—most notably William Shakespeare (1564–1616)—that established a standard for accuracy, thoroughness, and poetic sensitivity unsurpassed to this day.

Schlegel was born in Hannover and attended the University of Göttingen (1786–1791), where he studied philology under the classical scholar Christian Gottlieb Heyne (1729–1812) and worked closely with the poet Gottfried August Bürger (1747–1794). Already as a student he published important reviews of new books in the *Göttinger Gelehrte Anzeigen,* including works by Johann

Wolfgang von Goethe (1749–1832) and Johann Christian Friedrich von Schiller (1759–1805), and he began an extended essay on Dante's *Divine Comedy,* translating selected cantos into verse. Together with Bürger he also translated, though did not yet publish, Shakespeare's *Midsummer Night's Dream.* After several years in Amsterdam as a private tutor, Schlegel moved to Jena in 1794, where he worked with Schiller as co-editor of the literary journal *Die Horen* (The Graces, 1795–1797).

In 1796, Schlegel married Caroline Böhmer (née Michaelis), who established a literary salon in their home, where the group of young Romantics gathered in the final years of the century (including Friedrich von Schlegel and his companion Dorothea Veit, Novalis [1772–1801], Ludwig Tieck [1773–1853], Friedrich Ernst Daniel Schleiermacher [1768–1834], Friedrich Wilhelm Joseph von Schelling [1175–1854], and others), as vividly depicted in Friedrich von Schlegel's *Dialogue on Poetry* (published in the *Athenaeum,* 1800). During these years in Jena, Schlegel published a great many reviews in the *Jena Allgemeine Literaturzeitung* and a number of important essays on literature and poetic form, including a program piece in *Die Horen* entitled "Something on William Shakespeare upon the Occasion of *Wilhelm Meister*" (1796), a response to the discussion of *Hamlet* in Goethe's novel *Wilhelm Meister's Apprenticeship* (1795–1796). Schlegel's translations of Shakespeare commenced at this time, including such plays as *Romeo and Juliet, Julius Caesar, The Merchant of Venice, As You Like It, The Tempest,* several of the later history plays, and, above all, his masterpiece, *Hamlet* (1797–1800).

In 1801, Schlegel moved to Berlin, where he began a series of lectures on the history of classical and romantic (i.e., medieval) literature, extending through three consecutive winters, in which a coherent critical perspective on European letters and culture was developed. He single-handedly revived the sonnet as poetic form in German after a century and a half of neglect, publishing several collections of his poems, which, though formally perfect, are generally facile and superficial; he adapted Euripides' play *Ion* into German, which was performed in Berlin and Weimar, though with only limited success; he began serious scholarly

work on the medieval German epic *Das Nibelungenlied,* planning an edition with commentary that was never completed; he continued his activities as a translator, publishing two volumes of plays by the seventeenth-century Spanish dramatist Pedro Calderon de la Barca (1600–1681) in 1803 and 1809; and he published a volume of poems translated from Provencal, Italian, Spanish, and Portugese, under the title *Blumensträuße* (1804).

In 1803, having divorced his wife Caroline, who subsequently married the philosopher Schelling, Schlegel attached himself to Madame Anne-Louise-Germaine de Staël (1766–1817). He met de Staël when she visited Berlin in the same year, became tutor to her children, and moved with her to her château in Coppet on Lake Geneva. There he remained, apart from intermittent travels with her to Italy, to Vienna, to Sweden, and to England during the years of upheaval due to the Napoleonic Wars, until her death in 1817. In 1808, when Schlegel visited Vienna with de Staël, he delivered a course of public lectures titled *On Dramatic Art and Literature* (published in three volumes, 1809–1811, and quickly translated into several languages, French, English, and Italian, among others). In addition to brilliant interpretations of Greek tragedy and Shakespearean drama, Schlegel also formulates at the outset his central conviction that criticism consists of a balanced mixture of theory, history, and interpretation. These lectures, along with the major work by de Staël, *De l'Allemagne* (1815)—which is arguably a direct product of her close collaboration with Schlegel—spread the ideas of German Romanticism throughout Europe. Schlegel also wrote a great deal in French during these years, which established his reputation as a scholar in France.

The final stage in Schlegel's career began with his appointment as Professor of Literature and Art History at the newly founded University of Bonn in 1818. In 1816–1817 in Paris, Schlegel had devoted himself intensively to the study of Sanskrit, and during the 1820s he published in nine volumes his *Indische Bibliothek,* containing editions and translations of such works as the Bhagavad Gita, the Ramayana and the *Hitopadesa,* with essays and commentary (much of it in Latin). Schlegel continued to write on a wide range of topics, to lecture on many aspects of literature and the arts, and to engage in frequent exchanges, many polemical, with contemporaries on an enormous diversity of subjects. In 1841 he was appointed to a chair at the University of Berlin by the newly inaugurated Prussian King, Frederick William IV (r. 1840–1861), but he soon returned to Bonn, where he continued to write until his death in 1845. His final publication was an edition of his essays in French, *Essais litteraires et historiques* (1842).

Schlegel was often criticized for a certain pedantry in his manner, and he has been unfavorably contrasted to his brother Friedrich on the question of originality and theoretical brilliance. Yet August Wilhelm von Schlegel, more than any other scholar of his time, established a model for the academic study of literature with an international, indeed almost global scope. His critical essays are often remarkable for their practical insights, and his translations are always painstakingly close to the originals in style and poetic form. Few scholars of literature have ever equaled Schlegel in range, diversity, linguistic finesse, critical insight, and consistent methodological expertise. He should be regarded as one of the greatest literary critics of all time.

See also **Romanticism; Schelling, Friedrich von; Staël, Germaine de.**

BIBLIOGRAPHY

Primary Sources

Körner, Josef, ed. *Briefe von und an August Wilhelm Schlegel,* 2 vols. Zurich, 1930. By the leading scholar of Schlegel in the first half of the twentieth century.

Schlegel, August Wilhelm von. *Oeuvres ecrites en francais,* 3 vols. Edited by Eduard Böcking. Leipzig, 1846.

———. *Sämtliche Werke,* 12 vols. Edited by Eduard Böcking. Leipzig, 1846–1847.

———. *Deutsche Litteraturdenkmale des 18. und 19. Jahrhunderts,* 3 vols. Edited by Jacob Minor. Heilbronn, 1884. The Berlin lectures of 1801–1803.

———. *Kritische Schriften,* 7 vols. Edited by Emil Staiger. Zurich, 1962.

Schlegel, August Wilhelm von, and Friedrich von Schlegel. *Charakteristiken und Kritiken,* 2 vols. Leipzig, 1801. Collections of his essays.

Secondary Sources

Atkinson, Margaret E. *August Wilhelm Schlegel as a Translator of Shakespeare.* Oxford, U.K., 1958.

Becker, Claudia. *"Naturgeschichte der Kunst": August Wilhelm Schlegel's ästhetischer Ansatz im Schnittpunkt zwischen Aufklärung, Klassik und Frühromantik.* Munich, 1998.

Haym, Rudolf. *Die romantische Schule.* Berlin, 1870. Still the best historical assessment of Schlegel's early work.

Höltenschmidt, Edith. *Die Mittelalter-Rezeption der Brüder Schlegel.* Paderborn, 2000.

Körner, Josef. *Romantiker und Klassiker.* Berlin, 1924. Valuable monograph dealing with the relations of the brothers Schlegel to Schiller and Goethe.

———. *Die Botschaft der deutschen Romantik an Europa.* Augsburg, 1929. Monograph on the European reception of the Vienna lectures on drama.

———. *Krisenjahre der Frühromantik; Briefe aus dem Schlegelkreis,* 3 vols. Brünn, 1936–1958.

Wellek, Rene. "August Wilhelm Schlegel." In *History of Modern Criticism, 1750–1950,* vol. 2: *The Romantic Age,* 36–73. New Haven, Conn., 1955. The first serious assessment of Schlegel's achievement in English.

CYRUS HAMLIN

SCHLEIERMACHER, FRIEDRICH
(1768–1834), German theologian.

Friedrich Daniel Ernst Schleiermacher was born in Breslau, Silesia (in present-day Poland) on 21 November 1768 into a family of the Reformed (Calvinist) tradition. Commonly known as the "father of modern Protestant theology," he is also recognized as an original ethical thinker, an influential preacher, a pioneering figure in modern hermeneutics (interpretation theory), the first classic translator of Plato's work into German, a cofounder of the University of Berlin, a statesman, and a leader in church and educational reform.

Schleiermacher's early formal education took place in institutions of the Moravian Brethren (Herrnhuter), a pietistic sect whose experiential form of religious life had impressed his father when he was stationed near their community as a chaplain in the Prussian army. Although doctrinal doubts eventually resulted in his move to the University of Halle (1787–1789), Schleiermacher retained from his Moravian education a strong sense of religious life and an appreciation for the Greek and Roman classics. At Halle, Schleiermacher studied theology, the Greek classics, and philosophy, focusing especially on the works of Immanuel Kant (1724–1804).

After passing his theological exams in 1790, Schleiermacher served as a private tutor in East Prussia from 1790–1793. In 1794 he was ordained and appointed assistant pastor in Landsberg. Schleiermacher moved to Berlin in 1796 to become chaplain of the Charité hospital, and soon entered the circle of German Romantics through a friendship with their intellectual leader, the philologist and literary historian Friedrich von Schlegel (1772–1829). Schlegel and Schleiermacher shared an appreciation for Greek literature and philosophy as well as a critical attitude toward the excesses of Kant's ethical understanding of freedom, and the two embarked on a fruitful if short-lived period of collaboration. Schleiermacher contributed to the literary journal *Athenaeum* published by Friedrich von Schlegel and his brother August Wilhelm from 1798 to 1800. Their mutually developed philosophical, ethical, and aesthetic views made their way into a protofeminist analysis of contemporary writings. Among Schleiermacher's contributions to this topic were two *Athenaeum* pieces, "Idea for a Catechism of Reason for Noble Ladies" (1798) and a review of Kant's *Anthropology from a Pragmatic Point of View* (1799), as well as a defense of Friedrich von Schlegel's controversial novel *Lucinde* (1799), published anonymously in 1800.

At the encouragement of his Berlin friends, Schleiermacher produced *On Religion: Speeches to Its Cultured Despisers* (1799; rev. ed. 1806, 1821). In this work, which brought him national fame at age thirty, Schleiermacher defended religion against Enlightenment critics who rendered it a dispensable servant of ethics or natural philosophy, and he defined the religious self-consciousness in such a way that his friends could recognize their own affinity for religion as a "sense and taste for the infinite" in and through the finite. In 1800, he published *Monologen* (Soliloquies), which, as an ethical counterpart to his *Speeches,* opposed a Kantian universalistic ethics with a view of true human freedom as the development of unique individuality in community with other unique selves.

In 1802 Schleiermacher left Berlin to serve as court-preacher in Stolpe. Here he continued his ethical reflection with the publication of *Outlines of a Critique of Previous Ethical Theory* (1803). He also published his first of many volumes of Plato

translations, part of a larger project initially undertaken with Friedrich von Schlegel but completed alone between 1804 and 1828. Accepting a call from the crown in 1804 to become professor of theology and university chaplain in Halle, Schleiermacher began lecturing on dogmatics, ethics, and the New Testament, subjects that he would continue to teach throughout his career. Also at Halle, he gave the first of many lectures on hermeneutics and published *Christmas Eve: A Dialogue* (1806), a literary piece offering significant insight into the development of his theology and religious ethics.

In 1806 Napoleon's troops occupied Halle, and the university was closed. Schleiermacher returned to Berlin in 1807 and, with a new political consciousness, worked both from the pulpit and as a statesman to encourage Prussian resistance. Holding a post in the Department of the Interior from 1808 to 1814, he helped restructure Prussian public education and to establish the new University of Berlin. In 1809 he married the widow Henriette von Willich, finally starting the family life that was so much a part of his ethical theory even as it broadened to include active participation in public spheres. In 1809 he became pastor of Trinity Church in Berlin, and in 1810 professor of theology at the University of Berlin, positions he would hold the rest of his life. He preached nearly every Sunday until his death, and taught an impressive array of subjects, not only in religion, hermeneutics, and ethics, but in aesthetics, dialectics, psychology, pedagogy, and history of philosophy. His major publications during this period were the *Brief Outline of the Study of Theology* (1811), and *The Christian Faith* (1821–1822; rev. ed. 1831), a systematic interpretation of Christian dogmatics considered to be one of the great masterpieces of Protestant theology.

Schleiermacher's death in Februrary 1834 brought about a massive outpouring of grief in Berlin, as evidenced by reports of between twenty and thirty thousand people attending his funeral procession, among them the Prussian king Frederick William III (r. 1797–1840). His influence was eclipsed momentarily between 1925 and 1955 with attacks on the cultural accommodation of religion by neoorthodox theologians such as Karl Barth (1886–1968) and Emil Brunner (1889–1966). With the waning of this movement, and with the availability of more of his unpublished or out-of-print writings and lecture notes in the new critical editions of his work (first volumes published in 1984), Schleiermacher's innovative views, especially on religion, ethics, hermeneutics, and translation theory, have received renewed attention and appreciation.

See also **Berlin; Protestantism; Romanticism; Schlegel, August Wilhelm von.**

BIBLIOGRAPHY

Blackwell, Albert L. *Schleiermacher's Early Philosophy of Life: Determinism, Freedom, and Phantasy.* Chico, Calif., 1981.

Brandt, James M. *All Things New: Reform of Church and Society in Schleiermacher's Christian Ethics.* Louisville, Ky., 2001.

Guenther-Gleason, Patricia E. *On Schleiermacher and Gender Politics.* Harrisburg, Pa., 1997.

Niebuhr, Richard R. *Schleiermacher on Christ and Religion.* New York, 1964.

Redeker, Martin. *Schleiermacher: Life and Thought.* Translated by John Wallhausser. Philadelphia, 1973.

Richardson, Ruth Drucilla. *The Role of Women in the Life and Thought of the Early Schleiermacher (1768–1806): An Historical Overview.* New York, 1991.

PATRICIA E. GUENTHER-GLEASON

SCHLIEFFEN PLAN.

The so-called Schlieffen Plan, Germany's infamous military deployment plan of the early twentieth century, took its name from Count Alfred von Schlieffen, chief of the German General Staff from 1891 to 1905. Its genesis and the reasoning behind it are best explained against the background of international developments in Europe at the beginning of the twentieth century.

INTERNATIONAL BACKGROUND TO SCHLIEFFEN'S MILITARY PLANNING

The Entente Cordiale (1904) between Britain and France had just been successfully tested during the First Moroccan Crisis (1905–1906), and Germany began to feel the full consequences of its own expansionist foreign policy. To Germany, British involvement in a future war now seemed almost certain, and consequently Italy, allied to Germany

and Austria since 1882, became a less reliable ally, because it would be unable to defend its long coastlines from Britain and might therefore opt to stay neutral in a future war. The international events of 1905 and 1906 marked the beginning of Germany's perceived "encirclement" by alliances of possible future enemies. Between this time and the outbreak of war in 1914, the General Staff became increasingly concerned about the growing military strength of Germany's enemies.

As a result of the Russo-Japanese War (1904–1905) Russia was eliminated as a serious threat to the European status quo for the foreseeable future. It would first of all have to recover from a lost war and revolution. For Germany's military leaders who feared Russia as a potential future enemy, this was a perfect time to consider "preventive war," because Germany still had a chance to defeat Russia. In the not too distant future, Germany's military planners predicted, Russia would become invincible. The Schlieffen Plan was developed against this background and designed primarily as a war against France (and Britain) in 1905 and 1906.

SCHLIEFFEN'S STRATEGY

Schlieffen saw Germany's best chance of victory in a swift offensive against France, while in the east the German army was initially to be on the defensive. Russia would be dealt with after France had been defeated. In effect, Schlieffen aimed to turn the threatening two-front war into two one-front wars. The plan further entailed that Germany would have to attack France while avoiding the heavy fortifications along the Franco-German border. Instead of a "head-on" engagement, which would lead to interminable position warfare, the opponent should be enveloped and its armies attacked on the flanks and rear. Moving through Switzerland would have been impractical, whereas in the north the terrain was easier to negotiate and the necessary railway lines existed that would ensure a swift German deployment. In addition, Luxembourg, the Netherlands, and Belgium were not expected to put up much resistance. With these considerations in mind, Schlieffen decided to concentrate all effort on the right wing of the German advancing armies. The plan involved violating the neutrality of Luxembourg, the Netherlands, and Belgium, but Schlieffen and his colleagues in the General Staff considered the political ramifications of this act of aggression insignificant.

In his planning, Schlieffen counted on two things—that German victory in the west would be quick, and that Russian mobilization would be slow—so that a small German force would suffice to hold back Russia until France was beaten. After a swift victory in the west, the full force of the German army would be directed eastward, and Russia beaten in turn.

This scheme was the result of years of planning and strategic exercises designed to find the best solution to the problem of a two-front war. Schlieffen put this version on paper in December 1905 in a memorandum written on the eve of his retirement (this document is usually referred to as the "Schlieffen Plan"). In subsequent years, the plan was adapted to changing international circumstances by his successor, the younger Helmuth von Moltke. Nevertheless, the underlying principles—trying to fight two wars on one front, wanting to fight against France before attempting to defeat Russia, and attempting to envelop the opponent—remained the same until August 1914, when Germany's deployment plan (now significantly revised) was put into action.

In 1914 the plan (more aptly called the "Moltke Plan" at this point) imposed severe restrictions on the possibility of finding a diplomatic solution to the "July crisis," particularly because of its narrow time frame for the initial deployment of troops into Luxembourg, Belgium, and France (the neutrality of the Netherlands was spared by this time). The escalation of the crisis to full-scale war was in no small measure due to Germany's offensive war plans.

THE MYTH OF THE SCHLIEFFEN PLAN
After the war was lost, Germany's military leaders initially attempted to keep details of the plan a secret, not least because they might have underlined the war guilt allegations made by the victors against Germany. Official document collections omitted Schlieffen's memorandum of 1905, although in private correspondence and in their memoirs, contemporaries frequently referred to Schlieffen's "recipe for victory," which had, in their opinion, been squandered by his successor. Details of the memorandum did not become public until

after World War II, when the German historian Gerhard Ritter published this and other documents. His study of the Schlieffen Plan, and his subsequent publications, blamed German militarism for the outbreak of war.

More recently, however, it has been argued by the American historian Terence Zuber that there never was a Schlieffen Plan. His contention is that the famous 1905 memorandum did not amount to a military plan. Other historians have suggested that it would be more appropriate to use the term *Moltke Plan* when referring to the outbreak of war in 1914, because by then Schlieffen's own plan had been superseded by that of his successor. Zuber's thesis has provoked much debate (see, for example, the journal *War in History* where much of this debate has taken place), but he has largely failed to convince his critics that there was no Schlieffen Plan. His apologetic interpretation that Germany did not have an offensive war plan in 1914 has similarly found few supporters.

The debate has, however, reemphasized what others had already stressed: that there never existed a guaranteed recipe for victory that Schlieffen's hapless successor adulterated, and that it would be prudent to think carefully about the terminology used to describe Germany's prewar military plans. The term *Schlieffen Plan* as a convenient way of summarizing German military intentions is perhaps not accurate enough; by 1914, when Germany put its offensive war plan into action, Schlieffen had long ceased to have any influence on Germany's military planning. The responsibility for the plans that were put into practice in August 1914 lay with his successor, Helmuth von Moltke, who had adapted Schlieffen's ideas to changing international and domestic conditions.

See also **Armies; Germany; Moltke, Helmuth von; Moroccan Crises.**

BIBLIOGRAPHY

Bucholz, Arden. *Moltke, Schlieffen, and Prussian War Planning.* New York, 1991.

Ehlert, Hans, Michael Epkenhans, and Gerhard P. Gross, eds. *Der Schlieffenplan: Anlayse und Dokumente.* Munich, 2006.

Foley, Robert T., trans. and ed. *Alfred von Schlieffen's Military Writings.* London, 2003.

Mombauer, Annika. *Helmuth von Moltke and the Origins of the First World War.* Cambridge, U.K., 2001.

Ritter, Gerhard. *The Schlieffen Plan: Critique of a Myth.* Translated by Andrew and Eva Wilson. London, 1958. Translation of *Der Schlieffenplan: Kritik eine Mythos.*

Zuber, Terence. *Inventing the Schlieffen Plan: German War Planning, 1871–1914.* Oxford, U.K., 2002.

ANNIKA MOMBAUER

SCHNITZLER, ARTHUR (1862–1931), Austrian playwright and novelist.

Arthur Schnitzler was a Viennese writer very popular before World War I for his "decadent" linkage of love, sexuality, and death. Some historians regard him as a voice of prewar culture at a peak of supposedly peaceful bourgeois creativity. Literary critics tend to set him aside as a marginal figure of emergent modernism, notable for some stream-of-consciousness narration (the novellas *Lieutenant Gustl,* 1900, and *Fraülein Else,* 1924; translated as *Viennese Novellettes,* 1931) and for allegedly Freudian treatment of the unconscious. Some feminists have admired his works for showing women who dream of erotic love only to be sexually used and discarded by men. Promiscuity of both sexes is another of his themes, most notorious in the play *Round Dance* (1900; Reigen), in which a circle of changing partners in compulsive coition enacted on stage—whore with a soldier at the outset, whore with a count at the end—shows love as bodies in a monotonous *Totentanz,* a dance of death.

Schnitzler also picked apart concepts of nationalism, both German and Jewish, in such works as the play *Professor Bernhardi* (1912) and the novel *The Way to the Open* (1908; *Der Weg ins Freie,*). His portrayals of manly violence, especially in dueling but also in war—particularly in *Young Medardus* (1910; *Der Junge Medardus*), a historical drama of Austria in the Napoleonic era—mocked the idea that honor finds exalted expression in combat, one on one or en masse. In World War I industrialized slaughter disillusioned multitudes of belief in such exaltation; Schnitzler's works gave prewar audiences a slightly subversive anticipation of such disillusionment. The fictive quality of collective entities that summon men to war—*das Volk* (the people), race, nation, fatherland—is emphasized in his private writings but only hinted in his public dramas and stories.

Schnitzler's father was a poor Jew who migrated from Hungary to Vienna, capital of the Habsburg Empire, abandoned the Yiddish and Magyar languages in favor of German, became a physician, and worked his way to a peak position in laryngology, treating actors and singers and harboring frustrated ambitions as a writer. Arthur too became a laryngologist, even working for a time in his father's clinic, and developed the use of hypnosis in treating speech problems that were psychological, without apparent organic cause. Father-son rivalry helped to make Arthur, the pampered son of a self-made magnate, disapprove his way of life as a womanizing playboy and to fear that he was a dilettante in medicine and in writing. That experience generated plays and stories that far surpassed the fame of a grudging father. Many readers, including the psychologist Theodor Reik and Sigmund Freud himself, have noted an affinity with Freudian ideas in Schnitzler's writing. Schnitzler disapproved their claim of affinity, or rather of scientific support for the writer's intuitive insights. "I have told Reik," he wrote to an inquirer, "that the Freudian methods of interpretation—from however deep a knowledge of human nature they may have emerged in their basic insights—will sometime signify to him not the one and the only saving way, but one among others, one that leads into the mystery of the writer's creativity, but also time and again leads past that into vagueness and error" (quoted in Sherman, pp. 201–202).

In *My Youth in Vienna* (*Jugend in Wien*), an autobiography written for posthumous publication, Schnitzler set apart the homeland (*Heimat*) that he loved—Vienna and environs—from the fatherland (*Vaterland*) of nationalist striving for one big German state, which he deplored. He clung nostalgically to the multinational coexistence that Habsburg Austria tried to maintain against German chauvinists and small-state nationalists, each against all, hastening the Habsburg collapse and the eruption of total war. He sympathized with the pacifist Bertha von Suttner, who won the Nobel Peace Prize in 1905 for writing against the arms race that portended war, but Schnitzler sympathized in private, smiling at her impractical-ity. His resistance to the anti-Semitism that attended nationalist politics was publicly expressed in *Professor Bernhardi* (banned in Vienna for its anti-Catholic passages) and in *The Way to the Open,* which has a pioneering diversity of Jewish characters instead of traditional stereotypes.

World War I made his works seem superficial, dated entertainments of a bygone time and place. Moviemakers have contributed to that reputation by occasional use of his style of linking prurience with mystery, to show love as sex and soul-searching in the absence of soul. In *Youth in Vienna,* Schnitzler took note of his reputation—"I am conscious of being an artist not of the first rank"—as he asked posterity to read his autobiography as a document of the age, and arguments of that sort persist among critics striving in his behalf. Stanley Elkin, for example, introduces an American selection of his work with condescension: "His plays remain chiefly, well, charming and conventional....What we're talking about *finally* is melodramatics, soap opera, the peculiar pulled punches of all distinctly social art forms" (Elkin, foreword to *Plays and Stories,* pp. xi–xii). Similarly, the German critic Friedrich Torberg's afterword to Schnitzler's autobiography essentially characterizes him as entertainer who did transient service to a bygone social order. Torberg is somewhat defensive in comparing Schnitzler's achievement to Chekov's. Schnitzler, Torberg argues, does not belong with the great modernists who expressed profound revulsion toward the culture of "Crapland" ("Kakania," Robert Musil's sardonic name for the Habsburg Dual Monarchy), but the ephemeral amusements he catered to may show the global future of art more than one would like to imagine.

See also **Freud, Sigmund; Hofmannsthal, Hugo von; Modernism; Vienna.**

BIBLIOGRAPHY

Primary Sources

Schnitzler, Arthur. *Viennese Novelettes.* New York, 1931.

———. *Jugend in Wien: Eine Autobiographie.* Edited by Friedrich Torberg. Vienna, 1968.

———. *My Youth in Vienna.* Translated by Catherine Hutter. Foreword by A. J. P. Taylor. London, 1971.

———. *The Road to the Open.* Translated by Horace Samuel. Forward by William M. Johnston. Evanston, Ill., 1991; and Berkeley, Calif., 1992.

———. *Plays and Stories.* Edited by Egon Schwarz. Foreword by Stanley Elkin. Vol. 55 of *The German Library* series. New York, 1998.

Secondary Sources

Farese, Guiseppe. *Arthur Schnitzler: Ein Lieben in Wien, 1862–1931.* Munich, 1999.

Fliedl, Konstanze. *Arthur Schnitzler: Poetik der Erinnerung.* Vienna, 1997.

Gay, Peter. *Schnitzler's Century: The Making of Middle-Class Culture, 1815–1914.* New York, 2002.

Lindren, Irène. *"Seh'n Sie, das Berühmtwerden ist doch nich so leicht!" Arthur Schnitzler über sein literarisches Schaffen.* Frankfurt am Main, 2002.

Sherman, Murray H. "Reik, Schnitzler, Freud, and 'The Murderer': The Limits of Insight in Psychoanalysis." *Modern Austrian Literature* 10, no. 3/4 (1977), 195–216.

Swales, Martin. *Arthur Schnitzler: A Critical Study.* Oxford, U.K., 1971.

Thompson, Bruce. *Schnitzler's Vienna: Image of a Society.* London, 1990.

DAVID JORAVSKY

SCHOENBERG, ARNOLD (1874–1951), Austrian composer.

Arnold Schoenberg was one of the greatest composers, theorists, and teachers of the twentieth century. Even had he not survived World War I—and thus without regard for his major innovation of the twelve-tone method, which he unveiled in 1923—his musical achievements up to 1914 alone would have caused him to be numbered among the most significant composers. But he is also one of the most controversial, and from very early in his career to the early twenty-first century, performances of his works have been met with incomprehension and even riot. The so-called Skandalkonzert of 1913 ended in brawls that involved the police and subsequent legal proceedings. Such opposition was frequently highlighted by Schoenberg as well as by his later champions, such as the philosopher Theodor Adorno (1903–1969), who made Schoenberg's isolation and difficulty an article of faith. But there is an increasing awareness that Schoenberg had a much more complex and ambivalent stance toward the public and popularity, evident in the considerable number of successful performances he had, as well as in the continuing attraction of his music to those willing to listen through, and to, its difficulties.

Born in 1874 into a Viennese Jewish family of modest means, Schoenberg's formal education ended at age sixteen when he began working in a bank following his father's death. He started composing when he was eight and taught himself violin and cello. His musical education was limited to informal studies with Alexander von Zemlinsky (1872–1942), who also introduced Schoenberg to the circle around Gustav Mahler (1860–1911). In 1895 Schoenberg left the bank and survived by orchestrating operettas and by composing and conducting for several workers' choruses.

An early String Quartet in D Major (1897), which showed the influence of Johannes Brahms (1833–1897) and Antonin Dvorak (1841–1904), marked his first major public performance. The following year, as with many Viennese Jews who sought a musical career, he converted, though atypically becoming a Lutheran. He did not reconvert to Judaism until 1933. In a number of songs as well as with the programmatic string sextet *Verklärte Nacht* (Transfigured night, composed 1899), he was inspired by the naturalistic poetry of Richard Dehmel (1863–1925), to whom he wrote, "from you we learned the ability to listen to our inner selves." He began work on the massive Wagnerian choral cantata *Gurrelieder* in 1900, though it was not completed until 1911. Zemlinsky's sister Mathilde became Schoenberg's first wife in 1901 (they had two children by 1906). The same year saw his first move to Berlin, where he taught theory and conducted at Ernst Ludwig von Wolzogen's "Buntes Theater," for which he wrote his *Brettl-Lieder* cabaret songs. He returned to Vienna in 1903.

Although Schoenberg had hundreds of students, his two most important were Anton von Webern (1883–1945) and Alban Berg (1885–1935), who both started lessons in 1904. The three composers were later known as the Second Viennese School, in reference to the earlier Viennese School of Wolfgang Amadeus Mozart (1756–1791), Franz Joseph Haydn (1732–1809), and Ludwig van Beethoven (1770–1827), and thus emphasizing their claim to represent the musical mainstream. Also in 1904 Schoenberg undertook with Zemlinsky the first of many initiatives to further the performance of modern music with his Society of Creative Musicians. The major compositions of these years were extended single-movement forms modeled on the tone poems of Franz Liszt (1811–1886) and Richard Strauss (1864–1949), including *Pelleas und Melisande,* op. 5 (1903) based on drama by Maurice Maeterlinck (1862–1949); the First String Quartet, op. 7 (1905); and the Chamber Symphony no. 1 (1906), which he later described as marking the end of his first period. These works are still tonal, but use extremely chromatic harmony, intricate counterpoint, and exemplify Schoenberg's idea of developing variation through which the melody evolves continually with little repetition.

In 1907 and 1908 he composed the Second String Quartet, op. 10; Schoenberg wrote of its two vocal movements, based on poems by Stefan George (1868–1933): "the overwhelming multitude of dissonances cannot be counterbalanced any longer by occasional returns to such tonal triads as represent a key." This was followed by a remarkable series of atonal works, including the songcycle *The Book of the Hanging Gardens,* op. 15 (1908–1909), also based on Stefan George; *The Three Pieces for Piano,* op. 11 (1909); the programmatic *Five Pieces for Orchestra,* op. 16 (1909); and the monodrama *Erwartung* (Expectation, 1909), libretto by Marie Pappenheim, in which he pursued an ideal of composition as the direct representation of the constantly changing and irrational unconscious. Writing to the painter Wassily Kandinsky (1866–1944) in 1911, he proclaimed the "elimination of the conscious will in art" to preserve what was "inborn and instinctive." Accordingly, Schoenberg composed very rapidly and with an avoidance of traditional structural devices. The brevity of many of the atonal works reflects his remark in a letter to musician Ferruccio Benvenuto Busoni (1866–1924), "My music must be *brief.* Concise! In two notes: not built, but '*expressed*!!'" Scholars have linked these works to the artistic movement of expressionism, a range of contemporary psychological theories by Sigmund Freud (1856–1939) and others, and the emotional aftermath of a traumatic affair in 1908 between Schoenberg's wife and the painter Richard Gerstl (1883–1908). Coming to terms with the atonal compositions has been a major project of music theory, and while there have been significant insights from "pitch class set theory," there are still disagreements about how best to understand and hear these works.

Despite his achievements, the feelings of liberation soon gave way to anxiety and doubt as the difficulty of living up to his creative ideal emerged, coinciding with a sharp reduction in his compositional output. In 1910 he started work on the opera *Die glückliche Hand* (The lucky [or fateful] hand), op. 18, which features elaborate staging with colored lights coordinated to the action; he did not complete it until 1913. Along with another move back to Berlin, 1911 saw the completion of only two small works, the *Six Little Piano Pieces,* op. 19, and *Herzgewächse* (Foliage of the heart), op. 20. Together with his compositional difficulties, Schoenberg experienced a profound crisis of faith in himself and his music. One manifestation of this was the *Harmonielehre* (Theory of harmony; 1910–1911), which served both to demonstrate his competence to the critics and to try to make things clear to himself; another was his interest in painting, which in the years 1910 and 1911 served as a major creative outlet.

The cycle of twenty-one short pieces for chamber ensemble and the half-sung, half spoken "Sprechstimme" in *Pierrot Lunaire,* op. 21 (1912), pointed to a new direction in his development marked by a return to more conscious control and traditional compositional techniques, evident as well in *Die glückliche Hand.* In May 1914, while working on a never-completed choral symphony, he sketched a theme using all twelve-notes, an idea he had already experimented with *Die glückliche Hand.* He later identified this as the "first step" in the path to twelve-tone composition, a development that would occupy much of his energy until his death in 1951.

See also **Mahler, Gustav; Modernism; Music; Vienna.**

BIBLIOGRAPHY

Primary Sources

Schoenberg, Arnold. *Theory of Harmony.* Translated by Roy E. Carter. Berkeley, Calif., 1978.

———.*Style and Idea: Selected Writings of Arnold Schoenberg.* Edited by Leonard Stein, translated by Leo Black. Berkeley, Calif., 1984.

Secondary Sources

Arnold Schönberg Center. Archive and library. Available at http://www.schoenberg.at. A huge range of archival materials housed at the in Vienna center are available online.

Auner, Joseph. *A Schoenberg Reader: Documents of a Life.* New Haven, Conn., 2003.

Frisch, Walter. *The Early Works of Arnold Schoenberg, 1893–1908.* Berkeley, Calif., 1993.

Shawn, Allen. *Arnold Schoenberg's Journey.* New York, 2002.

Simms, Bryan R. *The Atonal Music of Arnold Schoenberg, 1908–1923.* Oxford, U.K., 2000.

JOSEPH AUNER

SCHOPENHAUER, ARTHUR (1788–1860), German philosopher.

Arthur Schopenhauer produced a system of metaphysics, ethics, and aesthetics centered around the notion of the will. His works became influential on European philosophers, artists, and other intellectuals in the latter half of the nineteenth century.

LIFE AND WORKS

Schopenhauer was born in Danzig, the son of a wealthy merchant of cosmopolitan outlook and a mother who was to make her career as a popular novelist and patron of the arts. Though originally destined for a career in business, Schopenhauer struck out on his own in 1809 and attended university in Göttingen and Berlin. His first philosophical work, published in 1814, was a doctoral dissertation entitled *On the Fourfold Root of the Principle of Sufficient Reason,* an original analysis of different forms of explanation that he continued to regard as integral to his philosophy. In 1819 after a short but intense period of writing and synthesis of various sources (chiefly Kant, Plato, and the *Upanishads*) Schopenhauer produced the major work of his life, *The World as Will and Representation.* A second edition appeared in 1844 with some revisions and a new second volume of explanatory essays. This two-volume work is the central standard work on which his reputation chiefly rests.

Schopenhauer had tried and failed to establish a lecturing career for himself in Berlin. Despite or perhaps because of this, he was contemptuous of university philosophy, especially for its falling under the influence of Friedrich Hegel and the German idealists. The second edition of *The World as Will and Representation* and other works published in the 1840s are peppered with vitriolic attacks on Hegel and his legacy (which by then was past its peak). Among Schopenhauer's other works, two essays on ethics are especially notable: *On the Freedom of the Will* and *On the Basis of Morality,* which he published together under the title *Two Fundamental Problems of Ethics* in 1841. In 1833 Schopenhauer had settled in Frankfurt am Main, and spent his last three decades there, living a comfortable if essentially solitary life. Another two-volume work, *Parerga and Paralipomena,* appeared in 1851, consisting of "aphorisms on the wisdom of life" and many extended essays, some profound, some scholarly, and some opinionated, including a misogynistic essay "On Women." *Parerga* attracted some readership, and Schopenhauer enjoyed correspondence and visits during his last years that gave some evidence of growing, if belated, recognition. He died in Frankfurt in 1860.

In 1877 Wilhelm Wundt called Schopenhauer the "born leader of non-academic philosophy in Germany." Schopenhauer never had any systematic following, but his pessimism and his aesthetic theory were especially influential and continue to be the most discussed parts of his philosophy. Most important among those whom he influenced were Richard Wagner and Friedrich Nietzsche. Thomas Mann and Ludwig Wittgenstein were among a later generation to fall under his pervasive influence, and Sigmund Freud's theories of the unconscious and the centrality of sexuality were partially enabled by Schopenhauer's doctrine of the will.

WILL AND REPRESENTATION

Schopenhauer takes from Immanuel Kant the distinction between representation (*Vorstellung*) and thing-in-itself, the former comprising the objects presented to the mind in experience, the latter a reality that transcends our capacity for experience. Schopenhauer argues that Kant left the thing-in-itself a "riddle" that surpasses human knowledge, and offers to solve the riddle by showing that the reality underlying both the material world and the self is *will.* The single

world therefore has two aspects: it is human representation, but beyond that it is will. Schopenhauer's theory combines idealism—saying that the material world of objects in space and time does not exist independently of the subject's experience—with a metaphysical account of the fundamental essence of reality as will, a principle of striving without consciousness or purpose.

Schopenhauer reaches this conclusion from an initial consideration of self-consciousness. Individuals have an "inner" experience of themselves as agents, in which a subjective mental state of willing realizes itself as a moving of the physical body in space. The intimate awareness individuals have of themselves in action not only undermines any dualist picture of the relation of mind and body, but, Schopenhauer argues, also provides the key to understanding the relation of inner and outer in the world as a whole. The self is a microcosm analogous to the macrocosm, and what appear as external material bodies in space and time all have the same inner essence as ourselves, that is, they are will.

This core notion of the will gives rise to considerable philosophical difficulties. If it is the thing-in-itself, then it should be unknowable, yet Schopenhauer claims knowledge of it. Some interpreters have attempted to remove this inconsistency by arguing that Schopenhauer's position has greater complexity than he sometimes acknowledges, and that will is simply the one common essence of all experiencable objects, while the world considered truly in itself remains unknowable. But even with this modification it is hard to grasp the nature of Schopenhauer's will. It is called will because it corresponds to the human will known in self-consciousness, but Schopenhauer offers assurance that the will in nature is without intention, rationality, or concept and is neither a conscious nor even a mental force.

The influence of Schopenhauer's doctrine of the will stems not from its technical qualities as an exercise in metaphysics, but from the powerful vision of the character of the world and the human individual that he hangs around it. The world has no plan or purpose and is not rationally constructed. The single world-will endlessly tears itself apart through the multiplicity of individuals as which it manifests itself. Sexual instinct is

Arthur Schopenhauer. SNARK/ART RESOURCE, NY

the focus of the will in the human body and psyche. Human beings, like all organic nature, are primarily expressions of will to life, an unconsciously existing drive to survival and reproduction that dominates their psychology and pushes them on independently of all choice or reason and subjects them to inevitable and unredeemed suffering.

ETHICS, AESTHETICS, AND THE MEANING OF LIFE

Driven thus by the will, which is the underlying essence of the human character, individuals are predominately egoistic for Schopenhauer. Yet he believes that in each person there is at least a germ of compassion, the incentive that opposes egoism and seeks the well-being of others rather than one's own. Compassion is the foundation of morality. One cannot teach someone to be moral, because

the composition of their character is inborn and unchangeable; moral principles, laws, and constraints can only channel behavior into less deleterious forms. The deeper significance of compassion for Schopenhauer is that it diminishes the influence of the individual's will and hints at the more profound truth that individuality is really illusory. To commit wrong is to encroach upon the will of another individual; the good person does this as little as possible because he or she places less of an absolute division between individuals, and has the intuition that at the level of the thing-in-itself individuals are all the same will.

A prominent feature of Schopenhauer's system is his aesthetic theory. He regards aesthetic experience as a disinterested contemplative consciousness in which the will of the individual is temporarily suspended. Aesthetic experience is valuable for him because it is a respite from the round of desire and suffering to which humans are condemned by their nature as willing beings. But in addition he argues that it enables a timeless knowledge of universals in nature, which he calls Platonic Ideas, and which are inaccessible to ordinary empirical consciousness. The subject of aesthetic experience transcends its own embodiment as a willing individual, and the contemplated object is elevated to an Idea rather than a mere empirical object. In addition to this general theory of aesthetic experience Schopenhauer gives an account of the value of the different art forms, suggesting that some offer predominantly the peace of will-less experience, others knowledge of universals in human life, tragedy being the prime case of the latter. Finally Schopenhauer gives an account of music, which he regards as a uniquely important art form because it provides a direct copy of the movements of the will itself and replicates the whole range of manifestations of will in the world of human experience.

Schopenhauer's philosophy culminates with an account of salvation, which despite his atheism has affinities with parts of Christianity, Hinduism, and Buddhism. Salvation is needed because the world is full of unredeemed suffering and humanity's essence as will is to blame for the human predicament. Schopenhauer argues that if everyone properly understood the nature of their existence, they would judge that nonexistence would have been preferable. It is only if one's attachment to life and individual embodiment wanes, and the will to life within one turns and denies itself, that one can be free of the curse of unfulfilled willing and suffering. Schopenhauer is usually accounted a pessimist. The emphasis he places on mystical selflessness can be defended as a positive counter to pessimism, but is itself a fundamental negation of the value of human existence as an individual subject of will. The influence of this negation on Nietzsche was particularly pronounced.

See also **Hegel, Georg Wilhelm Friedrich; Nietzsche, Friedrich.**

BIBLIOGRAPHY

Primary Sources

Schopenhauer, Arthur. *The World as Will and Representation.* Translated by E. F. J. Payne. 2 vols. New York: 1969.

———. *On the Basis of Morality.* Translated by E. F. J. Payne. Oxford, U.K., 1995.

Secondary Sources

Gardiner, Patrick. *Schopenhauer.* Harmondsworth, U.K., 1967. Reprint, Bristol, 1997.

Janaway, Christopher. *Schopenhauer: A Very Short Introduction.* Oxford, U.K., and New York, 2002.

Janaway, Christopher, ed. *The Cambridge Companion to Schopenhauer.* Cambridge, U.K., and New York, 1999.

Magee, Bryan, *The Philosophy of Schopenhauer.* Rev. ed., Oxford, U.K., and New York: 1997.

CHRISTOPHER JANAWAY

SCHUBERT, FRANZ (1797–1828), Austrian composer.

Unlike most of the celebrated composers associated with Vienna, the city of music, Franz Peter Schubert was born there, in the Himmelpfortgrund suburb not far from the city walls, on 31 January 1797. He was the thirteenth child of a successful educator who ran a school where Schubert and his brothers studied and eventually taught. Domestic music making and activities at the parish church in Lichtental provided his first musical experiences. At age eleven, Schubert won an audition to join the choir of the Imperial Court Chapel and with it a scholarship to an elite private school. It was there that he formed friendships that lasted for the rest of his life. He was also given the opportunity to study with Antonio Salieri (1750–1825), court Kapellmeister and a leading figure in the Viennese musical scene. Friends encouraged his interest in literature and his inclination to set poetry to music. Even as a teenager Schubert experimented writing a wide range of music, including keyboard, chamber, sacred, dramatic, and orchestral pieces, but he won his first fame with smaller domestic genres, especially songs, part-songs, dances, and four-hand piano works. This intimate music was often performed at private homes in events that came to be known as Schubertiades. The poetry of Johann Wolfgang von Goethe (1749–1832) inspired Schubert's initial masterpieces at age seventeen and eighteen, specifically the songs "Gretchen am Spinnrade" and "Erlkönig." The public premiere of the latter in 1821, and its publication that year as Op. 1 (by which time Schubert had written hundreds of songs), marked a turning point in his career.

During the next seven years, before his death at age thirty-one, Schubert published more than a hundred lieder and became widely recognized for raising the stature of this nascent Romantic genre. In total, Schubert wrote more than six hundred lieder, setting to music the work of some one hundred different poets, ranging from friends to William Shakespeare (1564–1616), Johann Christoph Friedrich von Schiller (1759–1805), and Goethe. His ambitions in large-scale works faced obstacles in a city dominated by the instrumental music of Ludwig van Beethoven (1770–1827) and the operas of Gioachino Rossini (1792–1868). Schubert tried to succeed with German opera, with works such as *Alfonso und Estrella* (1822) and *Fierrabras* (1823), but these major efforts went unperformed. Focusing on instrumental music, he found greater success with piano sonatas and chamber music, which where performed and published by musicians and firms associated with Beethoven, the composer Schubert revered above all others. Some of his most famous instrumental works, such as the "Trout" Quintet, "Death and the Maiden" String Quartet, and "Wanderer" Fantasy are based in part on earlier songs.

Late in 1822, around the time of the "Unfinished Symphony," Schubert apparently contracted syphilis and was seriously ill for some time. (He is said to have written part of his song cycle *Die schöne Müllerin* while in the hospital in 1823.) Although he was better by 1825, Schubert feared he would never fully regain his health. The quantity of his song output significantly decreased as he spent more time working on formidable chamber music projects that he planned would "pave the way to a grand symphony." He wrote the so-called Great C Major Symphony in 1825, and probably revised it in 1828. That same year, on 26 March, the first anniversary of Beethoven's death, Schubert gave the lone public concert devoted entirely to his own music, which earned an enthusiastic response.

The twenty months that separate Schubert's death from Beethoven's saw a phenomenal outpouring of masterpieces. He wrote the "Drei Klavierstücke," the Mass in E-flat Major, the fourteen songs published as *Schwanengesang*, the String Quintet in C, three magnificent piano duets (including the Fantasy in F Minor), and the last three piano sonatas, as well as various brief sacred works, part-songs, dances, lieder, and some remarkable sketches for a "Tenth Symphony" (D936a). Many of these works, as well as significant earlier ones, were unknown for decades, which led the critic Eduard Hanslick to observe in his classic study of Viennese concert life (1869): "If Schubert's contemporaries rightly gazed astonished at his creative power, what shall we, who come after him, say, as we incessantly discover new works of his? For thirty years the master has been dead, and in spite of this it seems as if he goes on working invisibly—it is impossible to follow him" (Deutsch 1951, pp. 202–203).

Schubert, who traveled little, never married, and worked continuously, remains an elusive figure biographically. Less than a hundred of his letters survive, along with a few pages of an early diary. Information about his life comes primarily from his family and friends, most often from accounts written long after his premature death in November 1828 following a brief illness. The epitaph on his grave, written by Franz Grillparzer (1791–1872), Austria's leading writer and a friend of the composer, captures the sense of loss

and expectation, as well as a limited understanding of what he had in fact accomplished: "The Art of Music Here Entombed a Rich Possession, but Even Far Fairer Hopes." As the true extent of that accomplishment gradually became known during the following decades, his achievement was recognized as extending well beyond the lied and profoundly influenced Robert Schumann (1810–1856), Johannes Brahms (1833–1897), Gustav Mahler (1860–1911), and other later Romantics.

See also **Music; Romanticism.**

BIBLIOGRAPHY

Deutsch, Otto Erich. "The Reception of Schubert's Works in England." *Monthly Musical Record* 81 (1951): 202–203.

Deutsch, Otto Erich, ed. *Schubert: A Documentary Biography.* Translated by Eric Blom. London, 1946.

———.*Schubert: Memoirs by His Friends.* Translated by Rosamond Ley and John Nowell. London, 1958.

Gibbs, Christopher H. *The Life of Schubert.* Cambridge, U.K., 2000.

Gibbs, Christopher H., ed. *The Cambridge Companion to Schubert.* Cambridge, U.K., 1997.

McKay, Elizabeth Norman. *Franz Schubert: A Biography.* New York, 1996.

Newbould, Brian. *Schubert: The Music and the Man.* Berkeley, Calif., 1997.

CHRISTOPHER H. GIBBS

SCIENCE AND TECHNOLOGY. The view that science somehow leads to technology through the model known oddly as the "linear model" fared poorly in the late twentieth century. The linear model has it that in the past, pure science led to applied science, applied science to technology, and from there the path led to engineering and production. Among late-twentieth- and early-twenty-first-century scholars, however, there is consensus: first, that technology drove science at least as much as the reverse; second, that scientific understanding—whatever that precisely means—is neither a necessary nor a sufficient condition for technological progress; and third, that both are deeply influenced by a host of cultural, social, and economic factors too numerous and in dispute to list here. There is a danger that in their haste to criticize the highly simplified and schematic model, critics will end up without an appreciation of the importance of scientific knowledge in the process of technological and economic development between 1780 and 1914. Every technique has an "epistemic base"—that is, knowledge about natural regularities and phenomena—on which it rests. At times this basis is very narrow or barely even exists; in those cases, the technique in question works, but nobody is quite sure how and why. In other instances, some minimum has to be known before the technique can be realized.

THE INTERPLAY BETWEEN TECHNOLOGY AND SCIENCE

Perhaps the safest generalization one can make is that there was no single model or straightforward relationship between scientific knowledge and technological practice. Each industry and each practice differed in its need to rely on the formalized knowledge that was still known as "natural philosophy" in 1780. In the ensuing "long nineteenth century" (1789–1914), a large number of important inventions were made that owed little to science. This would include most breakthroughs in the textile industry; some of the canonical inventions that revolutionized the cotton industry were tricky mechanical problems that took mechanical ingenuity to solve, but "science" as such had little to do with their solution. Similarly, the invention of barbed wire by Joseph Farwell Glidden (1813–1906) in 1874, while of substantial significance to the American agricultural economy, owed nothing to science. A common story is that science discovers some phenomenon that can be exploited. The technique that emerges subsequently serves as a focusing device that makes scientists take a closer look, and as they begin to understand the underlying natural processes better and better, they can improve the technique and adapt it to new uses.

The paradigmatic example is of course steam power. By 1780 steam power was on its way to assume a central role in the industrialization and transportation revolution. The "science" behind it was nontrivial: to build an atmospheric engine, one had to know at least that the earth's surface was at the bottom of an atmosphere, whose pressure could be

Michael Faraday's inductor. Faraday used this device in 1831 to establish the principle of electromagnetic induction. THE ROYAL INSTITUTION, LONDON, UK/BRIDGEMAN ART LIBRARY

exploited. James Watt's (1736–1819) improvements to Thomas Newcomen's (1663–1729) steam engine depended in part on the further realization, due to his fellow Scotsman William Cullen (1710–1790), that in a vacuum water boils at much lower, even tepid, temperatures, releasing steam that would ruin the vacuum in a cylinder. Yet "understanding" steam power in a way that would conform to our notions of science was still many decades off: in the 1820s and 1830s, the best theorists of steam power still regarded it as a vapor engine rather than recognizing it for the heat engine it was. Inspired and focused by the steam engines they observed, the great theorists of thermodynamics such as Sadi Carnot (1796–1832) and James Prescott Joule (1818–1889) finally formulated the science of thermodynamics. Technology did not "depend" on science, but better science could improve it to the point where the productivity growth due to continuous improvements drove economic growth.

Another example is the electromagnetic tele-graph, one of the truly transforming inventions of the nineteenth century. Here, too, *some* science was necessary to make it possible. In this case, it was the discovery that electricity and magnetism were related after all (something that had been in serious doubt). In 1819 a Danish physicist, Hans Christian Oersted (1777–1851), brought a compass needle near a wire through which a current was passing. It forced the needle to point at a right angle to the current. A number of scientists put their mind to the problem, and by the mid-1830s Joseph Henry (1797–1878) and others realized that an electro-magnetic telegraph was possible, and by 1837 the device was shown to work.

Yet the epistemic base was still quite narrow, and it took the genius and energy of William Thomson (1824–1907, later Lord Kelvin) to work out the principles governing the relation between the signal and the resistance, inductive capacity, and length, and to compute the resistivity of cop-per and the inductive capacity of gutta-percha, the insulating material. He used his knowledge to invent a special galvanometer, a siphon recorder (which automatically registered signals), and a technique of sending short reverse pulses immedi-ately following the main pulse to sharpen the sig-nal. These inventions were based on best-practice mathematical physics, and although the epistemic base was far from complete (Kelvin resisted the electromagnetics of James Clerk Maxwell [1831–1879] and held on to the notion of ether, believed to be the weightless medium for the transmission of electromagnetic waves), they improved the tele-graph in every direction.

A third example of the subtle interplay between science and technology in the nineteenth century is found in soil chemistry. Since antiquity, farmers had realized that they could improve agricultural output by adding certain substances to the soil. Among those substances, animal manure and marl were widely used. Nobody, of course, quite under-stood how and why these procedures worked, and as a result progress in agricultural productivity was limited when judged by the standards of later development. By 1800 agricultural writers were busy cataloging what kind of substances worked on which soils and for what crops, but the epis-temic base this practice remained rather narrow and

consisted mostly of empirical patterns that these writers thought they were observing. However, the closing decades of the eighteenth century saw the rise of modern chemistry, and by the 1820s and 1830s, German chemists led by Friedrich Wöhler (1800–1882) and Justus von Liebig (1803–1873) discovered what today is called organic chemistry and realized that it helped them understand why certain substances such as phosphates and nitrates improved agricultural productivity. By midcentury, the important role of various chemical substances was better understood, and European farmers began to apply potash and nitrates to their soils. The greatest triumph of science was beyond ques-tion the distillation of ammonia from the atmo-sphere: nitrates were recognized as an essential ingredient in both fertilizers and explosives, yet although most of the atmosphere consists of nitro-gen, it was not known how to extract it. Fritz Haber (1868–1934) and Carl Bosch (1874–1940) solved this problem around 1910. Both were highly trained professional chemists, yet their process still relied on a great deal of trial-and-error research.

Perhaps nowhere are the complexities of the relation between science and technology better illustrated than in medical technology. The growth of medical science was unusually slow. It is not an exaggeration to point out that by 1800, medical science had developed little beyond the great medical writers of antiquity. Theories of disease were confused and mutually contradictory, and the ability of science to prevent, let alone cure, often-fatal infectious diseases was negligible. This started to change in the early nineteenth century due to two major developments. The first is the recognition that relatively poorly understood natural phenomena can be analyzed by means of statistical data. On that account, for instance, it became clear through the research of the French physician Pierre-Charles-Alexandre Louis (1787–1872) around 1840 that bleeding ill patients did little to improve their health, and (through the work of British physicians such as John Snow [1813–1858] and William Budd [1811–1880] in the 1850s) that water that appeared and tasted clean could still transmit deadly diseases. As a result, a great deal of effort was directed toward filtering the water supply and separating drinking

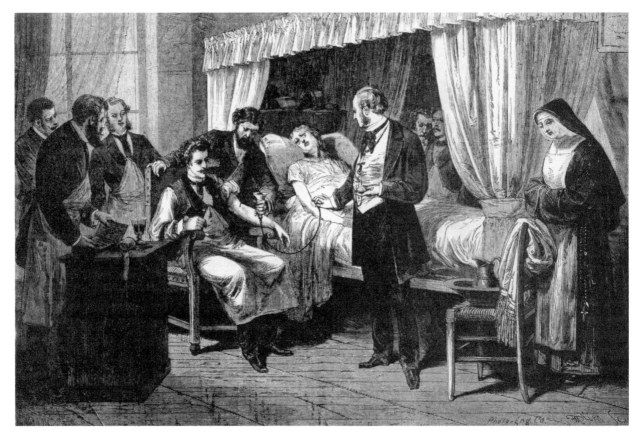

Illustration of blood transfusion from the *American Scientist* magazine, 5 September 1874. The technique of blood transfusion developed significantly during the nineteenth century. After the first successful transfusions beginning in 1818, doctors experimented with various techniques, including the use of milk as a substitute for blood. Joseph Lister's 1867 discovery of the efficacy of antiseptics to prevent infection during the procedure was of particular importance. PRIVATE COLLECTION/BRIDGEMAN ART LIBRARY

water from waste decades before the actual epistemic base of infectious diseases was established by Louis Pasteur (1822–1895) and Robert Koch (1843–1910) in the 1860s and 1870s. Following Pasteur and Koch, however, it not only became clear how and why Louis and Snow had been correct, but also how to apply this knowledge to further advance private and public health through preventive medicine. Pasteur's science helped change and improve the technology of surgery as much as it improved that of food canning—even if both had existed before his work.

DRIVERS AND INCENTIVES IN KNOWLEDGE PRODUCTION

The model that scientific knowledge somehow "leads" to technology is an oversimplification for another reason as well. Science is more than just the formal and consensual knowledge famil-

iar to the twenty-first century. The heritage of the eighteenth century to the modern age and the taproot of technological progress and economic growth was a radically different view of why and how science should be practiced. Curiosity and "wisdom" had to make room for another set of motives—namely, the growing conviction that understanding nature was the key to controlling it, and that controlling nature was in turn the key to technological and economic progress.

This attitude, often traced back to Francis Bacon (1561–1626), became more and more influential in the eighteenth century. It involved the separation of scientific practice from religion, the belief that nature was orderly, and that natural laws, once properly formulated, were universal with no exceptions (i.e., magic). It involved major cultural changes, above all the practice of "open science" (that is, placing scientific findings in the public realm), that had emerged during the Renaissance but only became unequivocally established during the second half of the seventeenth century. Open science did two things. First, it made scientific knowledge available to those who might be able to use it. Second, it increased the credibility of scientific knowledge by exposing it to the scrutiny and criticism of other experts. It was widely believed—often somewhat over-optimistically—that once scientific claims had been exposed to the rest of the world, those that survived must be correct. Scientists were rewarded by fame, prestige, and at times comfortable and secure positions, but they sought credit, not profit.

By 1780 the realm of useful knowledge had bifurcated into knowledge that was "propositional" (including science, mathematics, geography, and a catalog of successful techniques) in that it stated discoveries about nature and placed them in the public realm, and knowledge that was "prescriptive," that is, provided the actual instructions on how to produce. The latter kind of knowledge was increasingly driven by profit motives, and for it to keep expanding, it needed to secure a way of compensating inventors for their efforts and investments. This could be (and was) done in a variety of ways. One was to secure intellectual property rights in the form of patents, which would place the knowledge in the public realm but prohibit its exploitation without the permission of the patentee. The second was to keep the invention secret, a strategy that could work at best only if the innovation could not be reverse-engineered. The third was to reward the inventor through some formal government body that assessed the value to society of this knowledge and paid the inventor from the public treasury. Finally, a few inventors simply relied on the advantage of being the first mover; they knew they would be imitated but hoped to make enough money simply by getting there first.

ACCESS AND PROGRESS

In any event, the central factor in the growth of technology in the period from 1780 to 1914 was the continuous improvement in the access to useful knowledge. Knowledge meant both power and prosperity, but only if it could be accessed by those best able to exploit it. At times, of course, scientists rolled up their sleeves and applied their knowledge to new techniques themselves. The modern-age specialization between ivory-tower theorists and practically minded engineers and inventors (more of a stereotype than a reality even in the twenty-first century) was comparatively rare in the period of the First Industrial Revolution. Many theorists and experimentalists became interested in and solved applied production problems. The great chemist Humphry Davy (1778–1829), to cite one example, invented the mining safety lamp, wrote a textbook on agricultural chemistry, and discovered that a tropical plant named catechu was a useful additive to tanning. His colleague Benjamin Thompson (Count Rumford, 1753–1814) was most famous for the proof that heat is not a liquid (known as "caloric") that flows in and out of substances. Yet Rumford was deeply interested in technology, helped establish the first steam engines in Bavaria, and invented (among other things) the drip percolator coffeemaker, a smokeless-chimney Rumford stove, and an improved oil lamp. In the later nineteenth century, the physicist Joseph Henry (1797–1878) probably can make a good claim to being the inventor of the electromagnetic telegraph, and Lord Kelvin owned dozens of patents.

Communication between scientists and manufacturers became a matter of routine in the late eighteenth and nineteenth centuries. Such access is essential if the growth in useful knowledge is to have economic consequences. Early on, such contact often took place in meeting places and scientific societies that became typical of Enlightenment Europe. Of those, most famous were the Birmingham Lunar Society, in which manufacturers such as Josiah Wedgwood (1730–1795) and Matthew Boulton (1728–1809) picked the brains of scientists such as Joseph Priestley (1733–1804) and Erasmus Darwin (1731–1802), and the London Chapter Coffee House, which boasted a similarly distinguished clientele. The Royal Institution, founded in 1800, provided public lectures for the general public.

During the nineteenth century, the number of forums in which manufacturers and engineers could meet and communicate with scientists increased rapidly. Scientists were often retained as consultants and inventors. The German chemical

Orrery designed by Thomas Blunt c. 1808. Avid interest in astronomical knowledge during the nineteenth century was manifested in numerous mechanical models of the solar system, or orreries. The first was developed in England by George Graham during the early years of the eighteenth century and named for his patron, the Earl of Orrery. PRIVATE COLLECTION/BRIDGEMAN ART LIBRARY

and electrical firms, which carried out a substantial amount of the research and development that created the Second Industrial Revolution, often retained university professors who practiced a "revolving door" kind of career between their academic and industrial jobs. Thomas Edison (1847–1931), whose knowledge of science was intuitive rather than formal, employed a number of highly trained scientists with whom he consulted, though at times he wisely chose to ignore their advice. Yet what has to be realized is that personal contact was only necessary insofar that knowledge could not be codified—that is, described and depicted in words or pictures.

The proliferation of scientific and technological literature in the nineteenth century was simply enormous. This proliferation took the form of encyclopedias, textbooks, manuals, as well as scientific periodicals of many varieties. Libraries sprang up everywhere and the declining real price of books and printed matter made for an ever-growing accessibility of scientific and mathematical knowledge to those who could make use of it. Equally important, engineering education became increasingly science-based. In the French *grandes écoles* and in the German universities, mining academies, and technical colleges, formal science became part of the education of even midlevel technicians.

Inventing remained, as it is in the twenty-first century, open to "tinkerers" such as Sir Henry Bessemer (1813–1898), Sidney Gilchrist Thomas (1850–1885), and Edison. Yet their inventions, no matter how brilliant, only worked because they were subsequently refined and improved by people well trained in the relevant science.

Of course, some classic inventions originally were simply mechanical. The zipper (patented in 1893 by Whitcomb Judson) and paper clips (introduced by the Gem company in Britain in the 1890s) were much like barbed wire, simple and useful ideas that needed no science. But even in many cases of simple inventions, knowledge of the finer details of metallurgy, electricity, or mass production engineering was needed for further development.

FEEDBACK FROM TECHNOLOGY TO SCIENCE

The interplay of science and technology in the nineteenth century was bidirectional and can be viewed as positive feedback in the sense that technology helped science just as science helped technology. Such positive feedback mechanisms often lead to unstable systems that never converge to a given position. While such a view may be unsettling to scholars who like to think of the world as inherently stable and predictable, it is perhaps not an inappropriate way of viewing the historical process of technological change from 1780 to 1914, a period that displays continuous unpredictable change as its most enduring feature.

The ways in which technology affected science can be viewed in three broad categories. First, as already been shown, technological practices directed and focused the interests of researchers to discover how and why they worked. The search for the deep nature of electricity spurred the work of such scientists as Svante August Arrhenius (1859–1927), George Johnstone Stoney (1826–1911), and Sir Joseph John Thomson (1856–1940), leading to the discovery of the electron. It is almost comical to contemplate Thomson's alleged toast at an event celebrating his Nobel Prize in physics: "Here's to the electron, may no one ever find a use for it." By that time, of course, electrical lighting and appliances were ubiquitous. The practice of food canning, invented by Nicolas Appert (1749–1841) in 1795, stimulated Pasteur into his famous studies of putrefaction.

Or consider geology: the need to develop a better method to prospect for coal inspired William Smith (1769–1839) toward a growing understanding of geology and the ability to identify and describe strata on the basis of the fossils found in them. The idea (already widely diffused on the Continent but unknown to Smith) that there were strong natural regularities in the way geological strata were layered led to the first geological maps, including Smith's celebrated *Geologic Map of England and Wales with Part of Scotland* (1815), a "map that changed the world." It increased the epistemic base on which mining and prospecting for coal rested. One can track with precision where and through which institutions this interaction between propositional and prescriptive knowledge took place and the institutional environment that made them possible. Although the marriage between geology and mining took a long time to yield results, the widening epistemic base in nineteenth-century mining technology surely was the reason that the many alarms that Britain was exhausting its coal supplies turned out to be false.

Technology also stimulated science by allowing it to carry out new research. The extent to which science was constrained by instruments and tools is rarely fully appreciated. Astronomy, it has often been observed, entered a new age the day that Galileo Galilei (1564–1642) aimed his brand-new telescope toward the sky. Microscopy had a similar effect on the world of microorganisms. The invention of the modern compound microscope by Joseph Jackson Lister (1786–1869, father of the surgeon) in 1830 serves as another good example. Lister was an amateur optician, whose revolutionary method of grinding lenses greatly improved image resolution by eliminating spherical aberrations. His invention changed microscopy from an amusing diversion to a serious scientific endeavor and eventually allowed Pasteur, Koch, and their disciples to refute spontaneous generation and to establish the germ theory. The chemical revolution initiated by Antoine Laurent Lavoisier (1743–1794) and his French collaborators might not have achieved such a triumph had he not been equipped with unusually precise instruments. The famous mathematician Pierre-Simon de Laplace (1749–1827) was also a skilled designer of equipment and helped to build the calorimeter that resulted in the celebrated *Memoir on Heat* by Laplace and Lavoisier (1783), in which respiration was identified as analogous to burning. Much of the late-eighteenth-century chemical revolution was made possible by new instruments such as Alessandro Volta's (1745–1827) eudiometer, a glass container with two electrodes intended to measure the content of air, used by Henry Cavendish (1731–1810) to show the nature of water as a compound.

Perhaps the classic case of an invention that enabled scientific progress was the Voltaic Pile, the first battery that produced continuous current, invented by Volta in 1800. Through the new tool of electrolysis, pioneered by William Nicholson (1753–1815) and Davy, chemists were able to isolate element after element and fill in much of the detail in the maps whose rough contours had been sketched by Lavoisier and John Dalton (1766–1844). Volta's pile, as Davy put it, acted as an "alarm bell to experimenters in every part of Europe." Electrochemistry became the tool with which much of the chemical revolution was placed on a firm and systematic footing. For instance, Davy established that chlorine, the miraculous bleaching substance that played such a major role in the new cotton industry, was an element and not a compound.

Finally, technology often made it possible to verify and test scientific hypotheses and to decide scientific controversies. Much science is the subject of endless debate, and nothing will settle a scientific debate as effectively as a demonstrable useful application. The success of Koch and his followers in identifying a host of bacterial pathogens and the subsequent advances in public and private health helped wipe out whatever doubt there remained about the validity of the germ theory. Heinrich Rudolph Hertz's (1857–1894) work on oscillating sparks in the 1880s and the subsequent development of wireless communications by Sir Oliver Joseph Lodge (1851–1940) confirmed Maxwell's purely theoretical work on electromagnetic fields.

Most decisively, the success of the Wright brothers at Kitty Hawk in 1903 resolved the dispute among physicists on whether heavier-than-air machines were feasible. In 1901 the astronomer and mathematician Simon Newcomb (1835–1909, the first American since Benjamin Franklin [1706–1790] to be elected to the Institute of France) had still opined that flight carrying any-

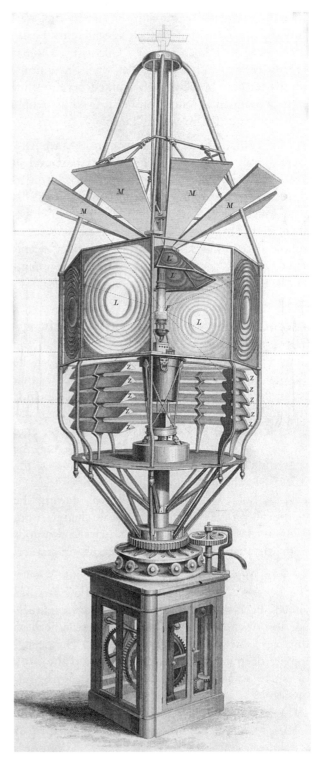

Revolving dioptric apparatus for a lighthouse.
Illustration from the *Cyclopaedia of Useful Arts and Manufactures*, edited by Charles Tomlinson, 1852. A celebration of midcentury technology, Tomlinson's cyclopaedia was published to coincide with the London Exhibition of 1851. PRIVATE COLLECTION/BRIDGEMAN ART LIBRARY/KEN WELSH

thing more than "an insect" would be impossible. Here, too, theory and practice worked cheek-by-jowl. The Wright brothers worked closely with Octave Chanute (1832–1910), the leading aeronautical engineer of the age. Yet it was only following their successful flight that Ludwig Prandtl (1875–1953) published his magisterial work on how to compute airplane lift and drag using rigorous methods.

COULD ECONOMIC GROWTH HAVE TAKEN PLACE WITHOUT SCIENCE?

It is often argued that the First Industrial Revolution (1760–1830) owed little to formal science. Most of the pathbreaking inventions such as Sir Richard Arkwright's (1732–1792) throstle (1769) or Henry Cort's (1740–1800) puddling and rolling technique (1785) were independent of the scientific advances of the age. While it is easy to show scientific progress during the Industrial Revolution, it is not easy to come up with many mechanical inventions that required advanced scientific knowledge as such. There are, of course, a few such instances, but before the middle of the nineteenth century they were not the rule.

In other words, scientific knowledge before 1850 was an input in innovation, but its importance was not decisive. Perhaps the best way of thinking about it is to realize that in addition to science affecting technology and vice versa, *both* were affected by a culture of growing material rationalism associated with the Industrial Enlightenment. It is interesting, however, to note that the major inventors of the time increasingly felt that they needed science and scientists to help them. Watt's milieu of scientists in Glasgow (and later Birmingham), Wedgwood's prodding of scientists (including Lavoisier himself) for advice on the technical problems that came up with his pottery, or the obsession of Leeds woolen manufacturer Benjamin Gott (1762–1840) with scientific experiment and chemistry demonstrate that such beliefs were widespread, at least in the circles that counted most.

As the nineteenth century advanced, such expectations were increasingly realized. One of the less well-known consequences of the chemical revolution is the work of the French chemist Michel-Eugène Chevreul (1786–1889), who discovered in the 1820s the nature of fatty acids and turned the manufacture of soap and candles from an art into a science. As director of dyeing at the Manufacture des Gobelins, he had a direct interest in the chemistry of dyes and colors. The original work on the chemistry of dyeing had been carried out by his predecessor at the Gobelins, Claude-Louis Berthollet (1748–1822, famous for the discovery of the bleaching properties of chlorine), but his work had been cut short by his political activities and it fell to Chevreul to realize his program.

The progress of steel, one of the truly central inventions that heralded in the Second Industrial Revolution, too, depended on science more than the usual story of the invention of the Bessemer process suggests. The epistemic base of steelmaking at the time was larger than Sir Henry Bessemer's (1813–1898) knowledge. This was demonstrated when an experienced and trained metallurgist named Robert Forester Mushet (1811–1891) showed that Bessemer steel contained excess oxygen, a problem that could be remedied by adding a decarburizer consisting of a mixture of manganese, carbon, and iron. In the years following Bessemer and Mushet's work, the Siemens Martin steelmaking process was perfected, and Henry Clifton Sorby (1826–1908) discovered the changes in crystals in iron upon hardening and related the trace quantities of carbon and other constituents to the qualities and hardness of steel. Steelmaking may not have been "scientific" in the modern sense of the word, but without the growing science of metallurgy, its advance eventually would have been stunted.

Economic growth can take place in the absence of advances in knowledge, but when it does so, it usually is more vulnerable and harder to sustain over long periods and large areas. When it is based on advances in knowledge, it is much less likely to be reversed. The twentieth century made a serious attempt to return to barbarism and to undo the advances of the years from 1780 to 1914, but in the end progress was resumed and has led to the stupefying growth in riches of the post-1950 decades.

The "Great Synergy," as Vaclav Smil has referred to it, between science and technology (or perhaps between propositional and prescriptive knowledge) is the central event of modern European history. It led to sustained and irreversible gains in productivity and quality of life, to the doubling of life expectancy, and to the realization of lifestyles that in 1780 must have seemed unimaginable in their material comfort and opulence.

See also **Agricultural Revolution; Industrial Revolution, Second.**

BIBLIOGRAPHY

Headrick, Daniel R. *When Information Came of Age: Technologies of Knowledge in the Age of Reason and Revolution, 1700–1850.* Oxford, U.K., 2000.

Jacob, Margaret C. *Scientific Culture and the Making of the Industrial West.* New York, 1997.

Jacob, Margaret C., and Larry Stewart. *Practical Matter: Newton's Science in the Service of Industry and Empire, 1687–1851.* Cambridge, Mass., 2004.

Mokyr, Joel. *The Lever of Riches: Technological Creativity and Economic Progress.* New York, 1990.

———. *The Gifts of Athena: Historical Origins of the Knowledge Economy.* Princeton, N.J., 2002.

———. "The Intellectual Origins of Modern Economic Growth." *Journal of Economic History* 65, no. 2 (2005): 285–351.

Musson, A. E., and Eric Robinson. *Science and Technology in the Industrial Revolution.* Manchester, U.K., 1969.

Petrosky, Henry. *Invention by Design: How Engineers Get from Thought to Thing.* Cambridge, Mass., 1996.

Rosenberg, Nathan. *Perspectives on Technology.* Cambridge, U.K., 1976.

———. "How Exogenous Is Science?" In his *Inside the Black Box: Technology and Economics.* Cambridge, U.K., 1982.

Smil, Vaclav. *Creating the Twentieth Century: Technical Innovations of 1867–1914 and Their Lasting Impact.* New York, 2005.

Smith, Crosbie, and M. Norton Wise. *Energy and Empire: A Biographical Study of Lord Kelvin.* Cambridge, U.K., 1989.

Winchester, Simon. *The Map That Changed the World: The Tale of William Smith and the Birth of a New Science.* London, 2001.

JOEL MOKYR

SCOTLAND. During a century of remarkable change, Scotland underwent some of the most profound social, economic, and political transform-ations found anywhere in Europe. In 1789 it was still primarily a rural society and an agrarian economy, existing politically in the shadow of its English neighbor. Yet it was separate and different in important ways, and rapid change was already underway. Scotland was a European leader in the fields of agriculture and commerce, with established coalmining and a developing textile-based industrial sector; its philosophers were changing the face of European thought; its inhabitants saw themselves as Scots, but also as Britons; its people, practices, and ideas were beginning to leave a stamp on the whole British, European, and Atlantic world. By 1914 Scotland was one of the most urbanized and industrialized countries in Europe, possessing an influential political voice within Britain and substantial wealth as well. Its people spanned the globe as traders, imperial administrators, sailors, and soldiers.

In 1789 Scotland and England shared a monarchy, parliament, empire, and an island, yet they were in many ways very different countries. The most obvious difference between Scotland and England lay in rural social structure. Scotland's rural population generally lived in dispersed farm settlements more reminiscent of Scandinavia than the nucleated villages of England. Landownership was concentrated in the hands of a few great lords and Scottish rural society was quasi-feudal. Except in some limited regions, there was no real equivalent of the English yeoman farmer. Underway since the seventeenth century in the Lothians (the most agriculturally precocious area of Scotland, thanks to its proximity to Edinburgh, the largest city until around 1790 when Glasgow took over), consolidation of tenancies and the removal of subtenants accelerated rapidly across Scotland from the 1780s. By the 1820s Lowland society had become polarized between landowners, tenants, and landless laborers, most subtenants and many smaller tenants having been swept from the land. In the Lothians, the laborers were mostly married men paid largely in kind. Elsewhere in Scotland (such as the northeast), single servants (both living-in and housed in bothies, or huts) and small-holders provided the labor that in England came from workers hired by the day. In Scotland, where mixed agriculture was less seasonal than that of much of England, females, children, and

The Highland Shepherd. Painting by Rosa Bonheur, 1859. HAMBURG KUNSTHALLE, HAMBURG, GERMANY/BRIDGEMAN ART LIBRARY

(for the arable Lowlands) migrant workers from the Highlands met additional labor needs.

ECONOMIC CHANGES

Aristocrats and gentry (called lairds in Scotland) dominated economic, political, and cultural life, for the rural middle class in Scotland was small. In contrast, a bourgeoisie flourished in the blossoming "New Towns" of the late eighteenth and early nineteenth century. Built on the profits of law, medicine, and commerce, Edinburgh's New Town is the most famous, but comparably extensive late-Georgian developments in the neoclassical style of London and Bath can be found in Glasgow (where wealth came primarily from the tobacco trade). Later Victorian suburbs bulked out the middle-class housing stock of these and other major towns such as Aberdeen, Perth, and Dundee.

If the middle class had been made prior to 1832, new sources of wealth enhanced its importance as the century progressed. Heavy industry began to expand from the 1830s and Scotland became a world-class industrial country. The chemical complex at St. Rollox in Glasgow was the largest manufactory in the world. The thread-making firms of J. & P. Coats and Clarks of Paisley merged in 1896 to become the largest manufacturing firm in Britain (and fifth largest in the world). Coal output rose dramatically to meet the new industrial and domestic demand, to the benefit of Scotland's economy and the detriment of its environment. Scotland became an urbanized and industrialized country in the second half of the nineteenth century. Agriculture employed two-thirds of the male labor force around 1789, 30 percent in 1851, and just 13 percent in 1911.

POLITICS

The economic changes that created a middle class of merchants, tradesmen, and professionals early in the nineteenth century were eventually reflected in political developments. From 1707, with the Union of Parliaments, until 2000, Scotland had no representative assembly but shared its government with its larger English neighbor. Eighteenth-century Scotland was effectively managed, with little interference from London, by a system of aristocratic patronage. Scotland was able to make its own place in the British polity.

Yet the Hanoverian political consensus was being destabilized before Catholic Emancipation (1829) and the Reform Bill (1832) put an end to it. Until 1832 Scotland's parliamentary franchise was far more restricted than in England. In the 1780s Scotland had just 3,000 county electors in a population of perhaps 1.5 million (0.2 percent), whereas the English electorate may have been as large as a third of a million in a population of about 7.5 million people (4 percent). The burgh (urban) franchise was confined to town councils: Edinburgh's member of Parliament (MP) at Westminster was elected by just thirty-three men prior to 1832. The electorate in England increased by 80 percent from the pre-Reform figure; in Scotland the change was 1,400 percent. That meant 13 percent of Scotland's male population could vote compared with about 20 percent of England's. By 1867, the proportion of males enfranchised was approximately equal in Scotland and England at about one third, and in 1884 the franchise was homogenized across Britain. Women had to wait until 1918 before they, too, could participate.

However, convergence is not the whole story, for Scotland showed distinctive political values. Notable is the enduring strength of Whiggism or Liberalism from 1832 to 1914 (England was more consistently Conservative), epitomized in the Midlothian Campaign speeches (1879) of British Prime Minister William Ewert Gladstone (1809–1898). Additionally, the Union of 1707 allowed for Scottish control over the major establishments of civil society: the law, the church, and education. These peculiarly Scottish institutions provided a continuing basis for national allegiances, and this was strengthened in 1885 with the founding of the Scottish Office, which acted as a symbol of an independent Scotland.

Reformed burgh councils (from 1833) acted as a focus of local and regional independence. Reform of county government did not come until 1889 when representative county councils were established. This allowed the continuation of aristocratic influence over county politics and administration throughout the nineteenth century—and far into the twentieth. Indeed it was conservative unionism, rooted in long-established loyalty to the houses of Hanover and Windsor, which would dominate twentieth-century Scottish politics.

RELIGION

The Hanoverian political consensus had been based partly on the fiction of unity in religion. Scotland had indeed been officially Protestant since the sixteenth century, yet the religious history of the eighteenth and nineteenth century is of schisms within the church. The early nineteenth century saw a wave of religious revival movements, coupled with a broadly based drift away from the established church, principally because of opposition to patronage (appointment of clergy by other than the flock). This ended in the Disruption of 1843 and the establishment of the Free Church of Scotland.

The religious consequences of the fragmentation of Protestantism were, on balance, positive. There was a surge in church- and school-building after the Disruption by the three main Protestant churches: Church of Scotland, Free Church, and United Presbyterian Church. Further, confessional pluralism allowed a further expansion of religious participation. Religion remained central to everyday life in Victorian Scotland, dominating organized leisure, the formation of social policy, and the moral values of temperance and self-help. Irish immigrants eventually created a coherent Roman Catholicism and a strong cultural identity, especially in the towns of west-central Scotland.

Yet there was also a negative effect. Diverging values and widening social differences were fragmenting Highland and Lowland societies in the eighteenth and nineteenth centuries. The religious schism of 1843 was linked to emerging class differences, and theological disputes were taken very seriously by Scots in ways perhaps unthinkable in the twenty-first century. Protestant fragmentation and Catholic consolidation after 1829 combined with a legacy of post-Reformation anti-Catholicism to create chronic sectarian rivalries.

SOCIAL ISSUES

In addition to their cultural implications, and when coupled with radical socioeconomic change, religious divisions also affected the structure of civil society because of the church's importance to poor relief. While the Poor Law (Scotland) Act of 1845 marked a convergence with English practice, differences nevertheless persisted, notably the lack of formal institutions for the poor, which the Scots had never favored, and a preference for (cheaper) outdoor relief. In 1906, 14 percent of Scotland's pauper population received indoor relief, compared with 32 percent in England. Furthermore, Scotland's poor relief (and many other aspects of its governance), remained less centralized than in England.

Despite the reorganization of relief and growing British prosperity, Scots endured a standard of living much below their English neighbors. In 1867, 70 percent of "productive persons" earned less than thirty pounds per annum, while the top 10 percent gobbled up half the national income. Wealth polarization was especially pronounced in towns. In 1911, over half the Scottish population lived in one- or two-roomed homes (usually apartments in the towns), and in Glasgow and Dundee the figure was over 60 percent. Overcrowding was the result, with nearly 56 percent of Glaswegians living more than two to a room. The urban poor moved into the central homes the middle class vacated on their way to "New Towns," and also the newly (but badly) built "tenements" (apartment buildings) that housed the industrial labor force of mushrooming towns like Paisley.

EDUCATION

Other social problems were addressed more successfully, at least in the long term. For example, social and economic change quickly outdated the (very successful) eighteenth-century education system. Early nineteenth-century studies showed large numbers of children excluded from education through the necessity of earning a living to help their impoverished families. Surveys also showed that, while the majority of male adults could read, very few could write, and female literacy was even less. Legislation in the 1870s and 1880s allowed

A street in Glasgow. Photograph from the series *Old Closes and Streets of Glasgow* by Thomas Annan, 1868–1877. Dramatic population growth in Glasgow during the early decades of the nineteenth century led to crowded and unhealthy living conditions in many parts of the city. In 1866, photographer Thomas Annan was commissioned by Glasgow officials to document such conditions as part of a plan of urban renewal. ©HISTORICAL PICTURE ARCHIVE/CORBIS

Scottish literacy to regain its relative standing, and by 1910–1911 Scotland had more children in the age group of five to fourteen attending school than all other northwest European countries except France.

In higher education, Scotland remained a leader. Around 1790, Scotland had the highest ratio of universities per million inhabitants in Europe (3.3 per million; the figure was 0.2 for England and Wales [and Ireland], 0.9 for France). The social distribution of university students was broader in nineteenth-century Scotland than in England—at least among males, for no woman was allowed to matriculate at any of Scotland's five universities until 1892. Scotland's universities produced nine out of ten British medical graduates around 1800 and, while they lacked mid-century dynamism, they were successfully reformed in the last quarter of the nineteenth century. Scottish law, medical expertise, and its very university system were all successfully exported to the wider world by missionaries, migrants, and imperial bureaucrats.

The universities had been the crucible of the eighteenth-century Scottish Enlightenment, which left a deep and lasting influence on the ideas and practices of the English-speaking world. Bound together by a shared faith in the improvability of individual and society through education, reason, and discussion, men like Adam Smith (1723–1790), the founder of laissez-faire, the concept that lay at the heart of nineteenth-century economics; Adam Ferguson (1723–1816); and David Hume (1711–1776) celebrated and promoted commercial change by arguing that economic cooperation and exchange would promote sociability, refinement, and "taste." The effect of these ideas pervaded nineteenth-century Scottish society and they help to explain the lower levels of popular protest there than in England. The radical working and middle classes were much influenced by ideas that stressed the importance of reason and argument over violence and irrationality.

A shared faith in the value of education (whatever its actual achievements) and in the improvability of civil society made Scotland's people more interested in treading a positive and peaceful path toward betterment. This is not to say that the Scots were a quiescent people: rather they coped better with change than some. Coupled with this was a darker force ensuring passivity: the power of paternalistic landlords and capitalists to shape individual lives and to break organized labor. Harsh brands of evangelical Protestantism also counseled quiescence.

HIGHLANDS VERSUS LOWLANDS

Not all of rural Scotland was as prosperous and peaceful as the Lowlands. Highland agriculture had long been geared to providing subsistence rather than growing productivity and Highlanders were affected by famine in the 1840s, though less severely than the Irish. Highland society had long been very different from Lowland. The great landowners left estate management to middlemen, who rented to subtenants and then to crofters. Highland society too underwent change as the landlords' priorities shifted during the eighteenth century.

They effectively repudiated centuries of being not just landlords, but also chiefs in charge of clans built on the bonds created by kinship (real or fictive), feuding, and feasting. Leaving the land was thus a far more traumatic process in the Highlands.

Initially landowners responded to population growth, economic shifts, and their own changing priorities by trying to redistribute labor supply, as their power enabled them to do. However, over time they resorted to wholesale evictions, plantations in overcrowded and economically marginal fishing villages, or to industrial enterprises that lacked staying power (like harvesting kelp from the sea to make fertilizer), and later by emigration schemes. Highland Scotland was progressively stripped of people. The empty landscape was filled by deer forests, which by 1884 covered two million acres or one tenth of the area of Scotland. The changes in landholding and the forcible clearance of sections of the peasantry from the land fomented collective resistance, which reached its apogee in the Crofters' Wars of the 1880s, and left a legacy of betrayal that had no Lowland equivalent. The nineteenth-century Highlands experienced social upheavals that, in their depth and breadth, were without parallel anywhere in Europe.

During the nineteenth century, distinctions between Highland and Lowland Scotland became increasingly blurred. The 1872 Education Act banned school lessons from being taught in Gaelic, but Highlanders were already won over to the benefits of English as a result of seasonal migration to the Lowlands and imperial service in the British army. Never the majority language (most Scots spoke a variation of English), Gaelic was the first tongue of just a fifth of Scots in 1806 and a tenth in 1900. Levels of literacy in the Highlands were much lower than in the Lowlands throughout the nineteenth century.

DEMOGRAPHIC CHANGE

Such important cultural changes as the decline of Gaelic stemmed partly from demographic forces. Population trebled to 4.5 million inhabitants between 1789 and 1911, a modest rate of growth that disguises the massive redistributions of people that came out of agrarian change. As late as 1789 just under half of Scotland's people lived north of an imaginary "Highland Line." By 1911 this had

Farmers plant potatoes on the Island of Skye, Scotland, c. 1899. Skye is the largest of the Inner Hebrides Islands, which lie off the western coast of the Scottish mainland. The traditional agricultural system, called crofting in Scotland, was a system of tenant farming which provided little income for farmers and, as in other areas of Great Britain, led to political unrest in the late nineteenth century. ©SEAN SEXTON COLLECTION/CORBIS

fallen to just a sixth. One Scot in eight lived in a large town in 1790, one in three by 1831, and three out of five in 1911, by which date Scotland was the most urbanized country in Europe after England. In the 1890s, a quarter of the adult population of Glasgow—then a city of 700,000 people—had been born in the Highlands and another quarter in Ireland.

In addition to redistribution and Irish immigration, emigration accelerated in the nineteenth century, when nearly two million people left Britain from Scottish ports. The majority went to North America (28 percent to Canada, 44 percent to the United States) and 25 percent to the Antipodes (Australia and New Zealand). One sort of migrant came from those dispossessed by the Highland clearances, but Lowland (disproportionately urban and industrial) emigration was every bit as significant as Highland (rural agrarian). Indeed, most nineteenth-century emigrants from

Scotland were not escaping a backward rural economy, but were voluntary exiles from a vital, industrializing and urbanizing society with plenty of employment opportunities and an improving standard of living.

Despite this, narratives of Highland dispossession dominate conventional understandings of Scottish migration, just as Highland images play a disproportionate part in modern conceptions of Scotland's past. In fact, the association of the material aspects of Highland life and regional identity—heather and thistles, bagpipes and tartan—with the symbols of being Scottish was invented during the Romantic period by the great Tory and monarchist, Sir Walter Scott (1771–1832), and perpetuated by George IV (r. 1820–1830) and Queen Victoria (r. 1837–1901). In reality, Highlanders between 1789 and 1914 were feared, romanticized, misunderstood, and then denigrated by the majority Lowlanders. A more representative symbol of late-nineteenth-century Scotland's people and its industrial success is the Forth Rail Bridge of 1890.

It is no myth that Scots were among the most mobile people of Europe. They had other demographic peculiarities. Mortality remained high and disease-dominated, but it was falling. Smallpox was conquered by the early nineteenth century, but typhus and cholera continued to decimate urban populations until mid-century and influenza until 1918. Infant mortality rates were lower in Scotland than England but still alarmingly high, and they did not fall as they did in England from the 1890s. Of those born around 1871, a quarter would not live to the age of five. The fertility regime was distinctive. Women married exceptionally late by European standards (a fifth did not marry at all), but, once married, fertility was high. This changed in the late nineteenth century, when Scotland participated in the fertility decline that characterized all of western Europe. The introduction of widespread knowledge and/or use of family limitation techniques produced a pronounced fall in family size. Two-fifths of marriages made in the 1870s produced more than six children, compared with less than 2 percent for 1920s marriages. Scotland's illegitimacy was among the highest in Europe, and in one part of rural northeast Scotland, four-fifths of women marrying in the late nineteenth century had their first child before, or within three months after, marriage. Throughout the nineteenth century, Scotland's was a young society: a third of its people were aged fourteen years or under and just 5 percent were sixty-five and over.

By 1911, the overall balance of the Scottish economy replicated the economic pattern found in the rest of Britain, mixing industrial, textile, and service industries. The first years of the twentieth century marked the zenith of power and influence of Scottish capitalists, who—despite comprising only 10 percent of Britain's gross domestic product—controlled the biggest concentration of heavy industry in Britain and exerted substantial political influence. Their wealth, nestling in a separate Scottish banking system, enabled them to invest in shipping lines, railway companies, mining ventures, and vast expanses of farmland in North and South America, Australia, and South Africa. At no time before or since had

Scotland been so closely integrated into the power structures of the empire it had helped to make and run. At no other time had it been so economically important. The society was peaceful. But there remained problems. Scotland had some of the worst slums in Britain. Social alignments and political allegiances were changing too. The stability produced by industrial expansion and benevolent paternalism was being replaced by the tensions of class and nation. Coupled with a harsher economic climate after World War I, these forces would create a very different twentieth-century Scotland.

See also **Great Britain; Ireland; Wales.**

BIBLIOGRAPHY

Anderson, Robert D. *Education and the Scottish People, 1750–1918.* Oxford, U.K., 1995. Mostly about institutions, but the definitive study.

Brown, Callum G. *Religion and Society in Scotland Since 1707.* Edinburgh, 1997. Does the same for religion.

Devine, Thomas M. *The Scottish Nation, 1700–2000.* London, 1999. A good overview, best on economic and political topics.

Devine, Thomas M., and Rosalind Mitchison, eds. *People and Society in Scotland,* 3 vols. Edinburgh, 1988. A wide-ranging edited collection.

Harper, Marjorie. *Adventurers and Exiles: The Great Scottish Exodus.* London, 2003. Lively and readable account of emigration, full of human detail.

Houston, Robert A., and W. W. J. Knox, eds. *The New Penguin History of Scotland.* London, 2001. A comprehensive and readable overview, which replaces all earlier texts.

Hutchison, Ian G. C. *A Political History of Scotland 1832–1914: Parties, Elections, and Issues.* Edinburgh, 1986. The basic work.

Tranter, Neil L. *Population and Society, 1750–1940: Contrasts in Population Growth.* London, 1985. A useful if dry overview.

Whatley, Christopher A. *The Industrial Revolution in Scotland.* Cambridge, U.K., 1997. A worthy overview.

R. A. HOUSTON

SCOTT, WALTER (1771–1832), Scottish poet and novelist.

If no longer lauded as "Scotland's Shakespeare," in the twenty-first century Walter Scott is recognized as a writer of immense talent, energy, and cultivation who single-handedly laid the way for the later glories of Victorian fiction. He was the founding genius of the British historical novel (and, via Victor Hugo, Alessandro Manzoni, and James Fenimore Cooper, those of France, Italy, and the United States).

Scott was born in Edinburgh's "Old Town" in 1771 (probably—he was never quite sure of his birth date), the third surviving son of a solicitor, or attorney, and the grandson on his mother's side of a professor of medicine at the city's university. His lineage, as he loved to recall, could be traced nobly back to the Scottish Middle Ages, but intellectually Scott was a mature product of the Scottish Enlightenment—that unique fusion of national, international, vernacular, and neoclassical cultures that made Edinburgh, for a few years, the "Athens of the North."

Scott was made lame, in his second year, by polio and was sent to recuperate at his paternal grandfather's farm, on the outskirts of Edinburgh. Here he picked up the rich folk-culture (legend, ballad, and border dialect) that underpinned his later creative writing. It was not, however, as a creative writer that he was trained. His father prudently enrolled him as an apprentice solicitor. After studying at Edinburgh's high school and university, young Walter rebelled against the "old trade" and struck out, in 1792, as an advocate, or barrister. His "infirmity" precluded him from the military career he yearned for. During the 1790s he was also writing and collecting ballads: something that would bear fruit in his monumental, three-volume, *Minstrelsy of the Scottish Border* (1802).

Scott married Charlotte Charpentier, a French woman with noble English connections, in 1797. The couple and their growing family occupied a number of town and country houses, culminating in the construction of his magnificent (and ruinously expensive) baronial pile, Abbotsford, near Melrose and Scott's beloved River Tweed. Over these years, Scott secured himself a series of semi-sinecurial legal posts, which set him up financially. He also formed a business relationship with the printers John and James Ballantyne. Literary fame came with the long poem, *Lay of the Last Minstrel* (1805). It was followed by others, equally popular, culminating in *The Lady of the Lake* (1810), a work that glamorized, forever, the Scottish highlands and its Celtic heritage (Scott was, as he proudly asserted, a lowland "Saxon"). Over these years—in which his literary, journalistic, and scholarly production was prodigious—Scott formed another partnership with the dynamic publisher, Archibald Constable.

Scott gave up poetry when trumped by Lord Byron's *Childe Harold's Pilgrimage,* in 1812. He outdid even Byron, however, with his first historical romance, *Waverley; or, 'tis Sixty Years Since* (1814). There followed a spate of anonymously authored, hugely best-selling, romances. The first phase of his work contains the admired "Scottish Novels": *Guy Mannering* (1815), *The Antiquary* (1816), *Rob Roy* (1818), and *The Heart of Midlothian* (1818). In 1820, Scott struck into English history, with *Ivanhoe*—a tale set during the reign of Richard the Lionheart.

In 1818 Scott, whose politics were staunchly Tory and Unionist, accepted a baronetcy from the prince regent. On the regent's accession as George IV (r. 1820–1830), Scott supervised the monarch's visit to Scotland in 1822. Throughout the early 1820s he was producing fiction at an astonishing rate. The quality was palpably declining, but romances such as *The Fortunes of Nigel* (1822) and *Quentin Durward* (1823) sustained his reputation.

In 1826 Scott, together with his business partners the Ballantynes and Constable, was ruined in the disastrous crash that rocked the British publishing industry. Scott's last years—during which he was widowed and suffered a series of crippling strokes—were devoted to clearing his massive debts, and his honor, with his pen. His last great work was the multivolume *Life of Napoleon* (1827). He died at Abbotsford in 1832. His death was an occasion for national mourning in Scotland.

See also **Great Britain; Romanticism; Scotland.**

BIBLIOGRAPHY

Johnson, Edgar. *Sir Walter Scott: The Great Unknown.* New York, 1970.

Lockhart, John Gibson. *Memoirs of the Life of Sir Walter Scott.* London, 1837–1838.

Rubenstein, Jill. *Sir Walter Scott: A Reference Guide.* Boston, 1978.

Sutherland, John. *The Life of Walter Scott: A Critical Biography.* Oxford, U.K., 1995.

JOHN SUTHERLAND

SEASIDE RESORTS.

SEASIDE RESORTS. Seaside resorts developed first in Britain, during the early to mid-1700s, when the practice of taking the waters, hitherto confined to inland mineral spas, was extended to the coast. Doctors, inspired to examine the benefits of seawater by their observation of popular sea bathing and the tough constitution of fisherpeople, as well as the example of the ancients (Seneca and Pliny recorded cold bathing in their time), prescribed immersion in seawater as a treatment for conditions as varied as rabies, gout, melancholy, and hysteria. They imposed strict rules on bathing, with invalids submitting to rigorous, supervised, and timed dunking sessions over a period of days or weeks. This was not swimming as it is known today, nor was it meant to be pleasurable, although it would eventually become so for many.

The growing fashion for therapeutic bathing was not enough on its own to guarantee the development of seaside resorts. The 1700s and early 1800s brought a new appreciation of nature, in particular of the coasts and mountains, arising out of a convergence of scientific and intellectual discoveries. New theories about landscape formation encouraged natural theologians, poets, and artists to find beauty in wild, untamed landscapes, where hitherto only ugliness and waste had been seen. The sea, once regarded as the remnant of the Flood, a sign of God's wrath, and thus something to be shunned, came increasingly to be appreciated as impressive and dramatic, and the shore a site of spiritual enlightenment, and later—for the Romantics—self-discovery. Their ideas resonated with an educated public, and with urban growth and industrialization taking their toll on the lives of city-dwellers, visiting the seashore became an opportunity to clear the mind, purify the body, and reacquaint oneself with nature.

RESORT DEVELOPMENT

The number of cure-seeking bathers increased rapidly in the second half of the eighteenth century in Britain, and inhabitants of coastal towns adapted to new demands, expanding and improving accommodation, transportation, and related services: thus, the first seaside resorts emerged out of preexisting settlements. By 1789 sea bathing was firmly established in Britain in places like Brighton, Margate, and Scarborough, and the fashion was beginning to attract adherents across the Channel. Local entrepreneurs, municipal and occasionally national government bodies, and outside investors like railway companies came together in various configurations to drive the construction of bathing facilities, hotels, casinos, public gardens, piers, and fun parks. An "architecture of pleasure" developed, with fanciful villas and public buildings creating unique urban environments, particularly along the prized seafront; the view, of course, was paramount.

The Revolutionary and Napoleonic Wars put a stop to most Continental resort development between 1789 and 1815, although in Germany the resorts of Doberan on the Baltic and Norderney on the North Sea emerged in 1794 and 1797. Over this period the British tended to frequent their own coastline, or took their Grand Tour further afield, to Greece—although this was in search of antiquities rather than bathing experiences—and Portugal, for example. After Waterloo (1815), Europeans could travel more freely, and there followed a surge in the number of mainland European seaside resorts, with the 1820s and 1830s a turning-point in France and Spain. The Duchesse de Berry is often credited with having relaunched the fashion for the seaside in 1824, with her famous swim at Dieppe in Amazonian dress.

BRAVING THE WATERS

Bathing practices varied according to region, but in many places men bathed naked, at least until the mid-1800s, while bourgeois women were expected to wear long gowns and pantaloons to preserve their modesty when they entered the water. Bathers feared the effects of sunlight, so exposure was kept to a minimum, with hats, veils, and parasols. Bathing machines—wooden huts or canvas tents on wheels designed to protect the bather's privacy—appeared in the 1730s in Britain, and soon spread elsewhere, though not to all resorts. The machine was towed by horsepower into the shallow water, and the bather, hidden from curious eyes, was immersed by a guide behind the cart. A simpler system was offered in some resorts: a rope, attached to dry land and extending across the beach into the water, to which fearful bathers could cling as they went under the waves. Changing tents and cabins also sprang up on beaches, though not all bathers were reassured: one nobleman complained that the interior of flimsy cabins on Arcachon's beach, on France's Atlantic Coast, resembled "a slab in the morgue"!

Manuals on bathing procedure proliferated in the 1800s, and the medical profession flourished in resorts, advertising in guidebooks and developing property. But the doctors' grip on bathing could never be complete. Their highly controlling approach coexisted uneasily with freer local practices, and as their patients became less fearful of the sea, pleasure took the upper hand. Many seaside municipalities tried to regulate behavior with bylaws prohibiting mixed and nude bathing, especially from the 1840s onward. At this time, sea bathing was attracting ever-increasing numbers of people from the middle and working classes, who did not always obey doctors' orders. Regulation would have limited success, however, because the beach, a liminal and ever-shifting zone, often overcrowded in summer, was notoriously difficult to police.

Bathing was never the only activity enjoyed (or endured) by the sea. Seaside resorts initially followed the design principles of inland spa towns, encouraging cultivated leisure in libraries, aquariums, games rooms, and (in larger resorts) attending the theater or casino, but outdoor pastimes triumphed: strolling on the sand and the pier, collecting shells, watching fisherpeople at work, riding, sailing, hunting and fishing, and socializing.

A distinctive feature of resort life was the coming together of different social groups on the beach, particularly as the number of people with the means to take vacations increased. Even resorts with an identifiable "tone" were never entirely monocultural. The shore was the site of unexpected, exciting, and for some, threatening, exposure to people one would never meet at home. This became increasingly problematic for status-conscious upper-class and bourgeois resort-goers, as working hours dropped and paid holidays were extended to more

and more professions and trades in the late 1800s, leading to a more mixed social scene.

HOW TO CHOOSE A RESORT

In the nineteenth century, colder northern waters were preferred to the Mediterranean Sea, as doctors considered the sharp shock of immersion and bracing air to be most beneficial. For this reason, Ostend in Belgium, Scheveningen in Holland, and the Normandy, Brittany, and Atlantic coastal resorts in France (Dinard, Dieppe, Biarritz, Royan, and La Teste-Arcachon, to name a few) prospered before their southern counterparts. In Germany, Travemünde drew bathers from 1800 (about which Thomas Mann wrote his *Buddenbrooks,* a century later), and Swinemünde in 1822. San Sebastian and Santander on the Gulf of Gascony were the first successful Spanish resorts, flourishing from the 1830s, long before the Costa Brava. Air quality (mild or bracing), water temperature, and surrounding landscape determined a resort's appeal, with the most successful able to offer both winter and summer seasons.

The villages on the French and Italian Riviera, though long on the Grand Tour itinerary, were considered pestilential in summer, so Nice, Cannes, and San Remo became winter retreats, drawing British and Russian visitors. Rough roads and political instability kept large numbers from coming to this region, ensuring its exclusivity for a wealthy clientele, at least until the arrival of the railway from Marseilles in the 1860s. Even though this stimulated growth, the Mediterranean coast remained a haven for the rich until the 1920s. Wealthy Parisians increasingly adopted the seaside resorts of the Norman coast, painted by the impressionists, and Adriatic and Amalfi resorts developed as well.

Improvements in transport were an important factor in resort growth. The building of a new road or railway could turn a small fishing village into a crowded coastal metropolis in summer. This often led to a change in the social fabric of resorts, as the wealthy, who had more time and money, would travel further afield in search of tranquility. For example, the British royal family abandoned Brighton in 1841, in part because the railway brought a new breed of bather in large numbers.

Beach Scene. Painting by Edgar Degas c. 1876–1877. Degas captures the sensual pleasure of a day spent at the beach. NATIONAL GALLERY, LONDON, UK/BRIDGEMAN ART LIBRARY

Royal patronage could ensure a resort's success or rediscovery. For example, the linking of the British royals to Brighton, the Spanish king and queen to San Sebastian, the king of Prussia to Swinemünde, and the empress Eugénie to Biarritz, boosted the public image of these towns, allowing them to draw on a wider potential visitor base than other resorts. Other promotional techniques included railway posters and cheap return Sunday fares (which catered to poorer bathers, who came in the thousands and became known in Britain as "day-trippers"), collectible postcard series, and locally sponsored guidebooks.

Newcomers attached therapeutic and moral values to an existing, communal work space, and their expectation of cleanliness, fresh air, uncluttered spaces, and "respectable" behavior changed the beach forever. This "reinvention" of the shore was not achieved without a struggle, however, for even if the morphology of the site satisfied the medical ideal (softly sloping fine sand and gentle waves), the continued occupation of the shore by fishing communities repairing their nets and touting for business, combined with the behavior of unruly day-trippers, tended to undermine the wished-for paradise.

World War I closed many resorts temporarily, with hotels converted to military hospitals, the shore a no-go zone, and leisure pursuits considered inappropriate, but with peace restored, seaside tourism resumed in unprecedented fashion, with the suntan and skimpier swimsuits appearing, and bathing for pleasure overtaking the medical model once and for all.

See also **Bourgeoisie; Leisure; Popular and Elite Culture; Railroads; Tourism.**

BIBLIOGRAPHY

Corbin, Alain. *The Lure of the Sea: The Discovery of the Sea in the Western World, 1750–1840.* Translated by Jocelyn Phelps. Cambridge, U.K., 1994. A groundbreaking history of Europeans' changing attitudes toward the sea.

Garner, Alice. *A Shifting Shore: Locals, Outsiders, and the Transformation of a French Fishing Town, 1823–2000.* Ithaca, N.Y., 2005. An analysis of conflicting understandings of the seaside in a fishing community-turned-resort.

Herbert, Robert L. *Monet on the Normandy Coast: Tourism and Painting, 1867–1886.* New Haven, Conn., 1994.

Towner, John. *An Historical Geography of Recreation and Tourism in the Western World, 1540–1940.* Chichester, U.K., 1996.

Urbain, Jean-Didier. *At the Beach.* Translated by Catherine Porter. Minneapolis, 2003. An innovative sociological study of the reinvention of the European beach over the nineteenth and twentieth centuries.

Walton, John K. *The English Seaside Resort: A Social History, 1750–1914.* Leicester, U.K., 1983. Walton is a pioneer in the history of seaside resorts; see also his work on Spain.

———. "The Seaside Resorts of Western Europe, 1750–1939." In *Recreation and the Sea,* edited by Stephen Fisher. Exeter, U.K., 1997. A useful overview.

ALICE GARNER

SECOND INTERNATIONAL. Socialists from several parts of the world, but mostly from Europe, gathered in Paris in 1889 to hold an international socialist congress, one of seventy international congresses held in conjunction with the Paris World's Fair celebrating the centennial of the revolution (Joll, p. 33). Eight more socialist congresses followed, with the last held in 1913, and although it had no permanent organization until 1900, when the International Socialist Bureau was formed, these congresses and their enduring organization came to be known as the Second International. This name reflected a popular, if somewhat confused, reference to the International Working Men's Association (i.e., the First International, after 1889) often associated with Karl Marx (1818–1883), and thus from the very beginning, the Second International seemed to constitute a continuation of Marx's view of the proper forms and realms of activity of the international workers' movement. In its origins, the Second International was seen by many, including and especially Friedrich Engels (1820–1895), as a revival of the spirit of the First International if not its specific content. This view was at least superficially reinforced by the prominent role played in the founding of the Second International by French participants most closely identified with Marx (including his son-in-law Paul Lafargue and Jules Guesde) and by the enduring importance of theo-

reticians and politicians closely associated with Marx and Engels, especially among the German, Austrian, and Russian activists (e.g., Wilhelm Liebknecht, Karl Kautsky, August Bebel, Victor Adler, Georgy Plekhanov).

In fact, however, most of the history of the Second International belied this close connection. The parties that made up its membership were anything but uniformly influenced by Marx and his writings. Even the dominant party of the organization, the German Social Democrats (*Sozialdemokratische Partei Deutschland*; SPD) could only be considered Marxist in the loosest interpretation of that label. Many elements of the German party were much more heavily influenced by the Lassallean traditions of Germany or were even, as in the case of the trade-union elements of the German movement, hostile to any theoretical orientation. While the Austrian and some of the Russian participants in the Second International might have been considered Marxist to some extent, the French, Italian, Belgian, and northern European parties that comprised significant elements of the organization were largely influenced by other than Marxist traditions. The more far-flung participants, including those from Asia, Africa, South America, and Australia–New Zealand, were similarly little influenced by Marx.

In retrospect, the great achievement of the Second International was the drawing together of a disparate group of socialist, trade-union, and other working-class elements into a body that transcended national, cultural, racial, and ethnic boundaries to form a body that could, without embarrassment or apology, claim to constitute an international organization at a time when national and imperialist conflicts characterized the world situation. The symbolic importance of having representatives from the United States and Spain embracing at a congress of the International during the Spanish-American War and Russian and Japanese delegates similarly expressing solidarity during the Russo-Japanese War of 1905, while easy enough to discount as hollow platitudes in the aftermath of 1914, was, at the time, a powerful beacon of hope in a world plagued by war. That, in the end, the Second International proved incapable of stopping the fearful slaughter that came with World War I is less a measure of its weakness than of the incredible strength of the forces against which it was working.

Historian James Joll has argued that opposition to war "became almost the reason for existence of the Socialist International" (p. 70). However, this is based on a perspective heavily influenced by the doubtless enormous impact of World War I and the Cold War years. Since the collapse of the Soviet Union, it might be more reasonable to focus on another aspect of the Second International, namely, its character as precursor of the united Europe that has followed from World War II, the Common Market, and the European Union. The Swiss chairman of the 1893 congress of the Second International that met in Zurich opened the meeting by declaring "that the Congress was 'a little blueprint (*Vorbild*) of the United States of Europe and the future world republic'" (p. 71). Now that it is known what came of Europe in the twentieth and into the twenty-first centuries, it might make more sense to emphasize this admittedly idealistic view of the promise of the Second International.

Nine congresses were held between the founding in 1889 and 1913 (the last was a much truncated emergency congress; a congress scheduled for 1914 in Vienna never happened because of the war). Besides being much occupied in the early congresses with just who could be seated as delegates (anarchist and reformist elements struggled to gain recognition until the turn of the century), questions of what sort of political behavior should be pursued on an international level garnered the most attention at the meetings. Again and again, the caution that characterized the most respected and successful participant in the Second International, the German Social Democratic Party, restrained the organization as a whole from adopting aggressive positions. The German party was by far the largest at the time and, it must be emphasized, the most admired. Because they had the most to lose if radical steps failed, the Germans vetoed almost all efforts to have the International take such positions. This was true with regard to having May Day celebrated as an international protest by the workers of the world (the Germans feared retribution by the state and employers), endorsement of the mass, general strike in response to threats of war (the

same concern), and, ultimately, calling for any form of action not based on the particular national conditions of the member parties. This caution lead the great French socialist, Jean Jaurès, to denounce the political impotence of the Germans at home as a restraint on the international movement at the 1904 Amsterdam congress.

All this was doubtless true in the context of the time, but it is very difficult to see how giving greater reign to the virtually impotent parties of France, Italy, Austria, the Netherlands, Belgium, and northern Europe (to say nothing of the far less significant parties of the rest of the world) could have yielded much of value. The last three gatherings of the Second International (Stuttgart, 1907; Copenhagen, 1910; and Basle, 1913) were devoted almost exclusively to attempting to counteract the growing threat of war on the Continent, but when the crisis came in 1914, none of the member parties could mount effective opposition to war. The assassination of the staunchest and ablest of the antiwar forces in the International, Jaurès, at the very outset was at the same time a blow to the chances to avert war and a symbol of the impotence of socialists to stop the madness.

Despite the almost immediate disappearance of the Second International in 1914, its legacy was carried on for some time. Feeble efforts to resurrect the old body, which yielded a brief-lived so-called Two-and-a-Half International, produced little of importance. The communist movement that emerged during and after the war formed its own International (called the Third in conscious reference to the preceding two) in 1919, but this became little more than an arm of Soviet foreign policy, though its pseudo-internationalist qualities were much trumpeted by its leadership and press. When Leon Trotsky eventually broke with Joseph Stalin and the Soviet Union, he too established an International of sorts, calling it the Fourth, and for a time, especially in Spain during the civil war, it managed to attract some following. Of the successor bodies only the Third survived for long (until World War II); it was replaced by the Communist Information Bureau in 1947, which lasted until de-Stalinization began in 1956.

While there was some overlap in terms of personnel among the several Internationals, especially between the Second and Third and the Third and

Fourth, the demise of the Second brought such fundamental changes in form and content that continuity is difficult to detect. However powerful the influence of the SPD had been in the Second International, this paled in comparison to the almost total domination of the Third by the Soviet communists, who brooked no deviation from centrally defined organizational structures and policies. Thus the legacy of the Second International must ultimately be found in the gradually emerging unity of Europe in the aftermath of World War II. Socialists who had had ties with the Second International frequently played prominent roles in postwar governments, and the survival of the spirit of international cooperation served the end of European unity well. Once the SPD returned to its former level of influence in Germany and the French socialists became more prominent in their country, the most serious obstacle to European unity, namely, German-French enmity, was at least in part tamed by the old traditions of the Second International.

See also **Engels, Friedrich; First International; Guesde, Jules; Jaurès, Jean; Kautsky, Karl; Lassalle, Ferdinand; Marx, Karl; Plekhanov, Georgy; Socialism.**

BIBLIOGRAPHY

Braunthal, Julius. *History of the International.* Vol. 1. Translated by Henry Collins and Kenneth Mitchell. London, 1966. Translation of *Geschichte der Internationale.*

Drachkovitch, Milorad, ed. *The Revolutionary Internationals, 1864-1943.* Stanford, Calif., 1966.

Joll, James. *The Second International, 1889–1914.* London, 1955.

GARY P. STEENSON

SECRET SOCIETIES.

Secret societies played a sustained, sometimes dramatic role in the revolutionary movement in nineteenth-century Europe. Though sectarian, widely scattered, and ephemeral, they provided the principal channel for the transmission of nationalist, republican, and democratic ideas during the era from 1815 to 1848, a time when the resurgent dynastic monarchies of Europe set strict limits on political opposition.

The formation of secret societies in this conservative era was inspired by the memory of the French Revolution, the transforming event of the late eighteenth century, in which a new politics was born. The work of constitutional reform and the experiment with republican government had been carried out by well-educated elites. But these projects had been made possible by the intervention of ordinary people in imposing crowds that pressured the revolutionary government to move in a more radical direction. The coming of Napoleon's rule (1799–1814/15) marked a retreat from the republican ideals of the Revolution's most radical phase (1792–1794). But the memory of the rising of the people served as an inspiring legend for the nineteenth-century revolutionary tradition, not only in France but throughout Europe. Radical reformers looked back to the unfinished agenda of the French Revolution for guidance. Echoes of its "revolutionary days" in the popular uprisings of the nineteenth century kept alive their faith that its experiment in republican democracy could be renewed in popular upheavals yet to come. In the minds of reformers on the extreme left, popular insurrection and democratic reform were inextricably allied. Their task, they believed, was to rekindle the latent revolutionary will of the people. In an era of limited outlets for legal opposition to monarchical authority, the secret society seemed the best vehicle for directing popular unrest. It was a romantic notion, in keeping with the nostalgia of idealistic reformers who came of age in the politically reactionary 1820s. So too was the notion that society might be transformed through a political coup d'état made possible by the support of insurrectionary crowds.

SECRET SOCIETIES IN ITALY AND FRANCE
The most famous secret society of the Revolutionary era was the Conspiracy of Equals, early communist ideologues who plotted the overthrow of the irresolute and politically corrupt Directory (1795–1999). Its leader, Gracchus (François Noël) Babeuf, was captured, tried, and executed in 1797, though his comrade-in-arms, Filippo Buonarroti, survived to conspire another day. He became the personal link between the radical sects of the Revolution and the incipient secret societies in France and Italy over the following decades. In 1828 he

published a memoir about the martyred Babeuf and so invented a myth of origins for the nineteenth-century revolutionary tradition.

The first secret societies of the revolutionary tradition appeared not in France but in Italy. The most famous was the Carboneria, formed about 1808 to oppose Napoleon's puppet regime in Naples. It continued its clandestine intrigues against its successor, the Bourbon Kingdom of the Two Sicilies, and won constitutional concessions in the revolution of 1820. Fascination with this subversive organization grew throughout Italy during the following decade, as popular resentment mounted against regional rulers beholden to the foreign monarchies in Spain and Austria. Cells affiliated with the Carboneria were established in a number of Italian cities and in France and Spain as well. To friends and enemies alike, the secret societies appeared to be coalescing into an international movement.

Though connected only in tenuous ways through personal contacts, the secret societies of the Restoration era adopted organizational principles that were much the same wherever they were founded. They were modeled on the hierarchical structure of the Masonic societies, popular during the eighteenth century as a vehicle for spreading the ideas of the Enlightenment. Like the Masonic lodge, each society was a pyramid of cells situated within a chain of command. Each cell was self-contained and the identity of its members their own shared secret. Recruits were initiated through elaborate rituals. They knew one another only by pseudonyms and spoke in coded language. They minimized written communication to avoid detection by governmental spies. They promised obedience to the society's directives. The historian Eric Hobsbawm, who has studied the origins of these societies, emphasizes their quasi-religious nature. Their new faith may have been in future-oriented ideologies, but their rituals were reminiscent of religious brotherhoods out of the past and they were given to millenarian expectations. Their most celebrated leaders—men such as Buonarotti, Auguste Blanqui, and Giuseppe Mazzini—served as models for a lifestyle of personal sacrifice and ascetic devotion to the cause.

The composition of the secret societies was diverse. Not surprisingly, many members were army officers, veterans from both sides of the Napoleonic Wars who had imbibed patriotic ideas during their service. Students, congregating in the burgeoning schools and universities of Europe during the 1820s, were also important recruits. Whatever their background, members tended to be young, youth having become a self-conscious cohort, reinforced by the camaraderie of student life or the shared hardships of military campaigns. The romantic idea of alienated youth played into a longing for revolt against an older generation content to live under an oppressive political order. In these early secret societies, workers were only a tiny minority. These were projects of idealistic aristocrats and the progressive-minded middle class.

Despite the loyalty demanded by the secret societies, their tenure was usually short-lived. Even the Carboneria in its far-flung network was active for less than a decade. Outlawed and harassed by the political police in countries across western Europe, secret societies dissolved and reshuffled their cadres under new organizational names. Members moved in and out of these organizations, as their leaders were imprisoned or fell to quarreling among themselves. The most dedicated leaders formed new groups with fresh recruits, of which there was a plentiful supply. There was also a loose network of exiled leaders who found sanctuary in neutral cities such as Brussels, Geneva, or London. But these professional revolutionaries were the exception. Tired of the risks and demands, most participants turned to less dangerous forms of political opposition or retreated into more conventional private lives.

The secret societies found little success in their direct efforts to foment insurrection. Their early goals were modest, focusing on constitutional reform. The Carboneria played a certain role in the revolution of 1820 in Naples, which won constitutional reforms later rescinded. But in Turin and Milan, conspirators plotting insurrections were arrested before they could act. Some Neapolitan conspirators took refuge in Spain but were thwarted there as well. The cause they championed, however, had some affinities with the revolt against Spain in South America during that era.

During the early 1820s the Carbonari, a French offshoot, won notoriety for a series of assassinations, plots, and failed insurrections in various parts of France. Publicity about these subversive activities contributed to the ferment that drove the Bourbons from power in the Revolution of 1830, though the direct influence of the secret societies themselves is difficult to assess in the web of economic, social, and political factors that led to this popular insurrection. While some militants helped overthrow the old order, they were shunted aside by moderates more adept at gaining leadership roles in the new regime. Their counterparts in Italy experienced similar disappointments. The popular insurrections they helped to instigate in 1831 in Parma, Modena, and the Papal States led to the formation of provisional governments, but these were soon turned out by the Austrian army.

Such failures did not weaken the resolve of the most resourceful leaders of the secret societies. In France during the July Monarchy (1830–1848), Armand Barbès and Blanqui rededicated themselves to the conspiratorial cause and formed new secret societies on the old model. This time, however, they emphasized socialist and egalitarian goals. They broadened their base by recruiting workers, and their discussions were enlivened by a mix of utopian socialist and communist theories—Saint-Simonian, Fourieriste, Babouviste, and Cabetiste—all informed by a romantic desire to turn the existing social world upside down. Absorbed in their own secret plotting, they overestimated the depth of their popular support. The spectacular attempt at a coup d'état led by Blanqui, Barbès, and their conspiratorial entourage in 1839 was easily routed. The conspirators were sentenced to long prison terms.

The futility of abortive coups, together with a growing disenchantment with the unrealistic methods of the secret societies, led some militants to try alternative strategies. In Italy, where national unification was the overriding goal, Giuseppe Mazzini turned to more open forms of political opposition. In 1831 he founded Young Italy to build a consensus among republicans beyond the secret societies. Paradoxically, the concept of national liberation served as the ideological bond that linked autonomous revolutionary movements across Europe in the 1830s and 1840s. As nationalist movements emerged in Italy, Ireland, Hungary, and the Germanies to challenge the dynastic monarchies, they sensed that they were contributing to a common cause. Mazzini quixotically dreamed of founding Young Europe to coordinate these ventures, though the proposed alliance, more sentimental than substantive, never materialized. Still, the consciousness-raising to which he contributed prepared the way for the Europe-wide revolutions of 1848. In France, secret societies, particularly in the south, began to organize in 1850–1851 in response to the repression of the Left orchestrated by the government of Louis-Napoleon Bonaparte. Following the coup d'état of 2 December 1851, they sparked the largest national insurrection in nineteenth-century France, having sworn to defeat *"la belle,"* the politically compromised republic.

SECRET SOCIETIES FROM MIDCENTURY

From mid-century, radical reformers increasingly spurned the sectarian subterfuge of the secret societies altogether. By the 1850s science had become the watchword of progress, and hard-headed political theorists sought to bring the projects of the romantic revolutionaries down to earth through more realistic agencies of change. The social theorist Joseph Proudhon pinned his hopes on the organization of labor, building solidarity around shared skills and mutual support. Karl Marx and Friedrich Engels ridiculed the romantic illusions of the secret societies and pointed instead to the self-destructive logic of capitalism as the prelude to the coming of an egalitarian society. The task of the revolutionary vanguard, they argued, was to help workers to understand the process through which the revolution would be ushered in, not to lure them into clandestine intrigue. Followers of Marx and Proudhon built the First Workingmen's International (1864–1878) on these new conceptual foundations.

Still, those who favored secret societies persevered. In France during the 1860s, Blanqui inspired radical students of a younger generation to found a secret society bent on bringing down the Second Empire. Even more doctrinaire than their predecessors, these aspiring revolutionaries worked openly with the atheist free thought movement to undermine confidence in the regime, while secretly recruiting workers to join them in the political underground. As participants in the broadening republican opposition to the regime, the Blanquists played a significant role in the popular insurrection of 4 September 1870 that toppled it and in the following insurrectionary Paris Commune (1871).

The Commune too was short-lived, and the Blanquists spent the following decade in prison or in exile. During the 1880s they found consolation in a politics calculated to build a mass following by commemorating the sacred days of the revolutionary tradition. But workers and reformers had by then become voters and had more immediate interests to advance. The revolutionary cause had passed to the socialist movement, which was willing to work gradually toward long-range objectives. The steady democratization of politics over the course of the nineteenth century in western and central Europe had rendered secret societies obsolete. Only in countries that had not yet escaped the tutelage of the old regime did they still have a role, such as the Fenians in Ireland, the Populists in Russia, and the Black Hand in Serbia.

The secret revolutionary societies of Europe filled a political need in their time in history. They fashioned a new instrument for political opposition in the transit from the primitive politics of aristocratic intrigue and clan feuds (Hobsbawm notes their organizational and ritual affinities with the Mafia) toward the modern politics of broad-based parties seeking the support of mass electorates. The revolutionary politics of the secret societies might be thought of as the shadow side of the drive for progressive reform sustained through the nineteenth century by more moderate politicians. Because they were isolated from politics at large, secret societies exaggerated their power to shape the course of events and so succumbed to the delusions that led them into so many failed ventures.

See also **Black Hand; Blanqui, Auguste; Carbonari; Italy; Mazzini, Giuseppe; Populists; Republicanism; Revolutions of 1820; Revolutions of 1830; Spain; Young Italy.**

BIBLIOGRAPHY

Eisenstein, Elizabeth L. *The First Professional Revolutionist: Filippo Michele Buonarroti (1761–1837)*. Cambridge, Mass., 1959.

Hales, Edward E. *Mazzini and the Secret Societies: The Making of a Myth*. New York, 1956.

Hobsbawm, Eric J. *Primitive Rebels: Studies in Archaic Forms of Social Movement in the 19th and 20th Centuries*. New York, 1959.

Hutton, Patrick H. *The Cult of the Revolutionary Tradition: The Blanquists in French Politics, 1864–1893*. Berkeley, Calif., 1981.

Johnston, Robert M. *The Napoleonic Empire in Southern Italy and the Rise of the Secret Societies*. 2 vols. London, 1904.

La Hodde, Lucien de. *The Cradle of Rebellions: A History of the Secret Societies of France*. New York, 1864.

Margadant, Ted W. *French Peasants in Revolt: The Insurrection of 1851*. Princeton, N.J., 1979.

Merriman, John. *The Agony of the Republic: The Repression of the Left in Revolutionary France, 1848–1851*. New Haven, Conn., 1978.

Perreux, Gabriel. *Au temps des sociétés secrètes: La propagande républicaine au début de la Monarchie de Juillet (1830–1835)*. Paris, 1931.

Spitzer, Alan B. *Old Hatreds and Young Hopes: The French Carbonari against the Bourbon Restoration*. Cambridge, Mass., 1971.

Tchernoff, Iouda. *Le parti républicain sous la Monarchie de Juillet*. Paris, 1901.

Weill, Georges. *Histoire du parti républicain en France (1814–1870)*. Paris, 1928.

PATRICK H. HUTTON

SECULARIZATION. Understood as a retreat of the sacred under the onslaught of the profane, and as the relaxation of religious control in face of the widening reach of the state, secularization manifested itself before 1789. But it was the French Revolution, and above all the Declaration of the Rights of Man and of the Citizen, published on 26 August 1789, that initiated a period, lasting until the outbreak of the First World War in 1914, during which the process of secularization accelerated and touched every corner of European societies. It affected the churches by radically transforming the role of religion, which lost ground in public life and was increasingly confined to private life.

Article 10 of the Declaration is indeed an essential starting point for understanding the nature of secularizing tendencies in the nineteenth century. "No one," it states, "shall be disquieted on account of his opinions, including his religious views, provided their manifestation does not disturb the public order established by law." The change implied by this Article was tantamount to a Copernican revolution. It meant that religion, hitherto the central reference point of civilization, became a mere matter of opinion, a function of the free exercise of individual consciousness. State religion, by extension, was destined to disappear.

THREE PHASES OF SECULARIZATION

Over the course of the "long nineteenth century," secularization went through three main phases. The first coincided with the Romantic generation. The Revolution, especially its antireligious violence, was severely criticized by some (Edmund Burke, Louis de Bonald) who sought to rehabilitate Christianity and what François-René de Chateaubriand (1768–1848) called its "genius" as the creator of civilization. In Germany, Novalis (Friedrich Leopold von Hardenberg; 1772–1801), Johann Wolfgang von Goethe (1749–1832), and Johann Christoph Friedrich von Schiller (1759–1805) exalted experience, including religious experience, as opposed to the reason acclaimed by the Enlightenment.

This reaction in its turn precipitated a second phase, influenced by a radical criticism of religion epitomized by Ludwig Andreas Feuerbach's *Das Wesen des Christentums* (1841; *The Essence of Christianity*), a work that opened the way to Karl Marx (1818–1883) and atheist materialism. At the end of the century Friedrich Wilhelm Nietzsche (1844–1900) went so far as to announce "the death of God" while the anarchists, following the recommendation of Mikhail Bakunin (1814–1876), declared their intention to "have done with God." To such philosophical and political challenges were added the development of positivism (Auguste Comte; 1798–1857) and of "scientism" (Joseph-Ernest Renan's *L'avenir de la science*, 1890; *The Future of Science*), according to which religion must give way to reason and science.

In a third phase, between 1890 and 1914, the certainties of the proponents of scientism were contested by philosophers such as Henri-Louis Bergson (1859–1941) and Edmund Husserl (1859–1938; in his 1913 *Ideen zu einer reinen Phänomenologie*; English translation, *Ideas: General Introduction to Pure Phenomenology*, 1931) and by a number of intellectuals, among them Maurice-Édouard Blondel (1861–1949), all of whom were concerned to restore faith and spirituality as well as experience and action to the religious sphere.

THREE MAIN AREAS OF SECULARIZATION

During the period with which we are concerned, secularization may be said to have occurred in three main areas: in social life, in the relations between the churches and the state, and in the sphere of intellectual and artistic activity.

Traditional religious authority over social life was eroded by the combined forces of technological progress, urbanization, and scientific advance. Meanwhile, the creationist theory of the scriptures was cast into doubt, first by Charles Lyell (1797–1875) and then by Charles Darwin (1809–1882).

As for the relationship between the churches and the state, secularization took the form of a long confrontation with two aspects: on the one hand, states gradually disentangled themselves from religious control in the name of civil rights and freedom of thought; on the other, they sought to impose their own authority on the religious institutions, as in the case of the established churches of the United Kingdom, Prussia, and Scandinavia. A cardinal shift was the channeling of religious fervor into patriotism, into a kind of secular religion committed to the service of the nation.

In the cultural realm, the newly emerging social sciences lent secularization a dimension that was deeply troubling to the main European religions. In the wake of the German historian Leopold von Ranke (1795–1886), a historicist approach intruded on fields such as scriptural exegesis and sacred history, hitherto considered the preserve of religious teaching. A tendency of German origin, represented by the French Catholic priest Alfred-Firmin Loisy (1857–1940), promoted the reading of the Bible, and especially the New Testament, with the methods of critical history, going so far as to separate a historical Jesus Christ from the Christian one. Sociology, meanwhile, from John Stuart Mill (1806–1873) to Émile Durkheim (1858–1917), acknowledged religion's importance as a social phenomenon but announced its ineluctable relegation to the realm of private life, as one form of cultural identity among others. Such changing attitudes were intimated in Gustave Courbet's realist painting *A Burial at Ornans* (1849–1850), a work deemed scandalous in 1851.

REACTIONS

Threatened, the Catholic Church reacted to these challenges either by condemning or by looking for new ways to reconcile religious traditions with modernity. In 1791 Pope Pius VI (r. 1775–1799) vigorously rejected the principles of the Declaration of the Rights of Man and of the Citizen, denouncing the very idea of liberty—especially the freedom to choose one's religion or to do without one—and the retreat of the divine right of kings in face of electoral democracy. God alone had rights, according to the pope; man had only duties. This was the foundation of Roman Catholic intransigentism, a posture upheld subsequently by the popes Pius IX (r. 1846–1878), Leo XIII (r. 1878–1903), and Pius X (r. 1903–1914), reflected by the doctrine of papal infallibility, declared by the Vatican Council I (1869–1870).

Another religious response to secularization was the clinging of the faithful to the rites and practices surrounding the most important events of life (birth, marriage, burial), or likewise to the tradition of pilgrimage. The manifest advances of social secularization in no way ruled out the survival of traditional expressions of faith, often reinforced by conversions or by collective outpourings of piety (as in Germany and Italy on the great liturgical feast days). For some scholars such survivals represented a process of re-Christianization driven forward by women, by dissident movements (Revivalism or English nonconformism), and by such enthusiasms as that attending the mystical experience of Thérèse de Lisieux (1873–1897).

Despite its extent, then, secularization in Europe was not a linear process. Though it provoked serious conflicts in the nineteenth century, especially those between church and state, it was continually subject to reverse tendencies and movements of resistance. This was as true of Protestants and Jews as of Catholics, especially when modernization, in conjunction with national unification and pressure for assimilation into new forms of collective life, gave the faithful cause to fear for their identity.

See also **Bergson, Henri; Catholicism; Chateaubriand, François-René; Comte, Auguste; Darwin, Charles; French Revolution; Marx, Karl; Nietzsche, Friedrich; Religion; Renan, Ernest; Young Hegelians.**

BIBLIOGRAPHY

Baumer, Franklin L. *Religion and the Rise of Scepticism.* New York, 1960.

Chadwick, Owen. *The Secularization of the European Mind in the Nineteenth Century.* Cambridge, U.K., and New York, 1975.

McLeod, Hugh. *Religion and the People of Western Europe, 1789–1970.* Oxford, U.K., and New York, 1981.

McLeod, Hugh, ed. *European Religion in the Age of the Great Cities, 1830–1930.* London and New York, 1995.

Miller, J. Hillis. *The Disappearance of God: Five Nineteenth-Century Writers.* Cambridge, Mass., 1963.

Tackett, Timothy. *Religion, Revolution, and Regional Culture in Eighteenth-Century France: The Ecclesiastical Oath of 1791.* Princeton, N.J., 1986.

Wagar, Warren W. *The Secular Mind: Transformations of Faith in Modern Europe: Essays Presented to Franklin L. Baumer, Randolph W. Townsend Professor of History, Yale University.* New York, 1982.

Wilson, A. N. *God's Funeral.* New York, 1999.

B. DELPAL

SEMMELWEIS, IGNAC (1818–1865), Austrian physician.

Born in the Hungarian capital of Buda, Ignac Semmelweis received his medical degree from the University of Vienna in 1844. While training as an obstetrician at the university's teaching hospital, the Allgemeine Krankenhaus, he became increasingly intrigued by the puzzle of childbed, or puerperal, fever, which at the time claimed the lives of some 15 percent of the mothers who delivered in the major hospitals of Europe. Although numerous theories existed to explain childbed fever's cause, none of them satisfied Semmelweis, especially because the preventive measures based on them were having no effect on incidence or mortality.

Relying on extensive autopsy studies, careful clinical observations, and a review of hospital records, Semmelweis determined that the disease was being spread by the unwashed hands of physicians, who began each day with the postmortem dissection of women who had died during the past twenty-four hours. The doctors' contaminated fingers, he asserted, were inoculating what he called "invisible cadaver particles" into the genital passages of women in labor. In May 1847 he instituted the policy that all students and physicians working on the ward under his direction must clean under their fingernails and wash carefully in a chlorine solution before examining patients. In the first full year of the program, the maternal mortality rate dropped to 1.2 percent, a figure astonishingly low for its time.

Semmelweis's theory indicted the very professors of obstetrics who throughout their careers had been struggling with, and failing to find a solution for, the tragedy of dying young mothers. These men, who were much senior to Semmelweis and owed their positions to powerful government connections, were threatened by the astuteness of a thesis that grew out of new discoveries in pathological anatomy, a discipline in which they were untrained. The theory became a battleground: they resisted the incursions of the younger clinical scientists, of whom Semmelweis was only one, while the younger clinicians approached medical problems with a form of investigative reasoning of which the older doctors were incapable.

It was at this point that Semmelweis committed a series of blunders that would in time destroy his career and ensure the rejection of his theory. The first of these was his failure to carry out the confirmatory laboratory experiments and microscopic studies that would have provided scientific rather than only clinical confirmation to his thesis. The second was his stubborn refusal, in spite of the urging of supportive and scientifically minded young colleagues, to publish his findings in a medical journal. And the third was his confrontational approach to his seniors, never hesitating to accuse them of continuing to murder their patients by ignoring his findings.

All of this resulted in the authorities refusing to renew Semmelweis's hospital appointment when it came up for review in 1850. Distraught, he returned to Hungary where he consoled himself with an appointment as professor of obstetrics at the University of Pest. Although his preventive measures were as successful there as they had been in Vienna, he became increasingly embroiled in personal disputes with colleagues and in acrimonious institutional battles in which he was the central figure. All of the frustrations and rages of the years were vented in the book he finally published in 1861, *The Etiology, the Concept, and the Prophylaxis of Childbed Fever*, a volume in which he tortuously explicated the details of his discovery and heaped insults on the leading obstetricians who had failed to appreciate its value. He followed this publication with a series of open letters to some of the most prominent European professors of obstetrics, castigating them for continuing their "murderous deeds" and "arrogant ignoring of my doctrine."

By this time it was becoming apparent that Semmelweis was showing signs of mental instability. As his deterioration progressed, he began to exhibit bizarre behavior and was finally admitted, in July 1865, to a mental institution, where he died two weeks later, probably at the hands of orderlies attempting to restrain him.

Two years after these tragic events, Joseph Lister of Glasgow began to publish the series of papers that, combined with the work of Louis Pasteur and Robert Koch, would establish the germ theory of disease, vindicating Semmelweis and in time rehabilitating his reputation. The key moment in this course of events took place in 1879, when Pasteur demonstrated the presence of streptococci in the blood and vaginal secretions of women who had died of childbed fever. These were the "invisible cadaver particles" that had been hypothesized by Semmelweis three decades earlier.

In time, Ignac Semmelweis became a Hungarian national hero, the subject of adulatory essays and biographies and the namesake of the nation's leading medical school. His childhood home is now the Semmelweis Museum of Medical History.

See also **Koch, Robert; Lister, Joseph; Pasteur, Louis.**

BIBLIOGRAPHY

Primary Sources

Semmelweis, Ignac. *The Etiology, Concept, and Prophylaxis of Childbed Fever.* Translated by K. Codell Carter. Madison, Wis., 1983. Translation of *Die Aetiologie, der Begriff, und die Prophylaxis des Kindbettfiebers,* 1861.

Secondary Sources

Lesky, Erna. *The Vienna Medical School of the Nineteenth Century.* Baltimore, Md., 1976.

Loudon, Irvine. *The Tragedy of Childbed Fever.* New York, 2000.

Nuland, Sherwin B. *The Doctors' Plague: Germs, Childbed Fever, and the Strange Story of Ignac Semmelweis.* New York, 2003.

SHERWIN NULAND

SEPARATION OF CHURCH AND STATE (FRANCE, 1905).

The separation of church and state requires the disestablishment of any religion with formal connections to the government. In the case of France in 1905, the term refers to the abrogation of the Concordat of 1801 between France and the Vatican and the abolition of the Ministry of Religion (*Ministère des cultes*).

SEPARATION AND THE FRENCH REVOLUTION

In 1789 the relationship between the Catholic Church and the government of France was defined by the Concordat of 1516, a treaty negotiated at the beginning of the reformation by Francis I of France (r. 1515–1547) and Pope Leo X (r. 1513–1521). The concordat recognized Catholicism as the sole religion of France and gave the nomination of all bishoprics, abbeys, and priories to the king rather than the pope.

The conflict between the French Revolution and the Catholic Church over such issues as the abolition of the tithe (August 1789), the nationalization of church lands (November 1789), and the Civil Constitution of the Clergy (July 1790) resulted in the supremacy of the state. All clerics were required to swear "to maintain with all their power the constitution decreed by the National Assembly." After increasing dechristianization in the years 1792 to 1794, the revolutionary government separated church and state on 21 February 1795 in a decree proclaiming freedom for all religions but renouncing state financial support. This decree (which paradoxically led to the reopening of many churches) formed the model for the nineteenth-century discussion of separation.

THE NAPOLEONIC CONCORDAT, 1801–1905

Napoleon Bonaparte (later Napoleon I, r. 1804–1814/15) held few religious convictions but he saw pragmatic reasons to restore church-state relations. Less than two years after his coup of 1799, Napoleon negotiated a new concordat (July 1801) recognizing that "the Roman, catholic, and apostolic religion is the religion of the great majority of the French citizens." Bonaparte granted similar Organic Articles for Protestants in 1802 and Jews in 1804. All religions were obliged to accept the changes wrought by the revolution and freedom of religion.

This concordat linked church and state throughout the nineteenth century. A restored *Ministère des cultes* provided upkeep for church structures and paid clerical salaries. The Ministry was typically headed by a Catholic, supported by a Protestant undersecretary heading a division of "*cultes non-catholiques.*"

THE CAMPAIGN FOR THE SEPARATION OF CHURCH AND STATE

Two strong voices kept the theory of separation alive: republicans, inspired by the revolution, and Protestants, seeking independence from a Catholic-dominated government. Republicans did not separate church and state during the short-lived Second Republic of 1848. Indeed, Chapter Two of the Constitution of that year reiterated the constitutional connection of church and state. For the remainder of the century, separation was a central feature of programs of radical republicans but postponed by moderates. Léon Gambetta (1838–1882) stressed separation in his Belleville Manifesto of 1869 and Georges Clemenceau (1841–1929) did the same in his Radical Manifesto of 1885.

Many Protestants did not wait for politicians to legislate separation. Inspired by the Evangelical revival known as the "awakening" (*le réveil*) and by the teaching of theologians such as Alexandre Vinet (1797–1847), Protestants founded "free churches" (*églises libres*) outside of the concordat system. These *églises libres* were self-financed and outside of state regulation. Prominent congregations, such as the Église Taitbout in Paris, led for much of the century by Pastor Edmond Dehault de Pressensé (1824–1891), became religious centers of the campaign for the separation of church and state.

SEPARATION AND THE THIRD REPUBLIC

Radicals did not have a parliamentary majority in the early years of the Third Republic, but a republican majority agreed upon an indirect form of separation. Beginning in the 1880s republicans voted to reduce the annual budget for religion, forcing churches to fund more of their activities. The budget for clerical salaries was cut by nearly 20 percent between 1880 and 1894.

The election of a parliamentary majority favoring separation was a consequence of the 1894 Dreyfus affair, in which a Jewish army captain, Alfred Dreyfus, was falsely accused of treason. Conservative defenders of the concordat were mostly anti-Dreyfusards, and the elections of 1898 and 1902 sent to office a majority of Dreyfusards. By 1902 a coalition of moderate republicans, Radicals, and socialists supported the government of Émile Combes (1835–1921) in readopting separation. Moderates were persuaded by the role of the Catholic Church in the Dreyfus affair; socialists were eager to get past the religious question and focus on social welfare.

A bill separating church and state was developed under the direction of Aristide Briand (1862–1932), the reporter of a committee studying the question. It was largely drafted by Francis de Pressensé (1853–1914), the son of Pastor de Pressensé and a Socialist deputy. The law of separation was promulgated, amid general Catholic opposition and Protestant enthusiasm, in December 1905. The contentious, and often bitterly resisted, inventories of churches followed the next year.

See also **Anticlericalism; Catholicism; Concordat of 1801; Dreyfus Affair; France.**

BIBLIOGRAPHY

Galton, Arthur Howard. *Church and State in France, 1300–1907.* London, 1907.

Larkin, Maurice. *Church and State after the Dreyfus Affair: The Separation Issue in France.* London, 1974.

Mayeur, Jean-Marie. *La Séparation de l'église et de l'état, 1905.* Paris, 1966.

McManners, John. *Church and State in France, 1870–1914.* New York, 1972.

Méjean, Louis. *La Séparation des églises et de l'état.* Paris, 1959.

Partin, Malcom O. *Waldeck-Rousseau, Combes, and the Church: The Politics of Anticlericalism, 1899–1905.* Durham, N.C., 1969.

STEVEN C. HAUSE

SEPOY MUTINY. The Sepoy Mutiny was a widespread and ultimately ineffective uprising against British imperial rule in India led by members of the Bengal army. Beginning in Meerut on 10 May 1857, the rebellion spread throughout north and central India to such cities as Delhi, Agra, Cawnpore, Gwalior, and Lucknow before the British reconquered these territories and officially declared peace on 8 July 1858. The Mutiny proved to be the greatest internal challenge to the British Empire in the nineteenth century and included the cooperation of civilians from many strata of Indian society.

Participation came mainly from the East India Company's army units, whose South Asian recruits were known as sepoys, an Anglo-Indian term derived from the Persian word *sipahi* (soldier). The vast majority of soldiers who served in the Indian army were native South Asians. This disparity existed in the eighteenth century but by 1856 the number of Europeans in the East India Company's army of 300,000 had fallen below 15 percent.

The East India Company's military forces were composed of the three armies raised from its separate presidencies, or administrative districts: Bengal, Madras, and Bombay. The Bengal army constituted the largest of the three and a significant portion of its regiments were stationed in north and central India as well as the Punjab. The Bombay and Madras armies remained loyal to the British, as did troops in Bengal and the Punjab. In addition, some 23,000 troops from the Queen's army were positioned in India at the time, providing additional support to beleaguered British garrisons. Above all, it was the support from the recently recruited Sikhs of the Punjab, carefully cultivated by the British since the end of the Anglo-Sikh wars of the 1840s, which proved decisive to Britain's ultimate victory. So, too, was the disinclination of the Bengali intelligentsia to throw in their lot with what they considered a backward revolt by landowning gentry. Overall, mutineers suffered from a lack of cohesion and a viable vision for the future; they were not self-conscious nationalists.

Led primarily by the old nobility and petty landlords, the popular insurrection received support from the lower orders of Indian society. Peasants destroyed any property that represented the authority of the East India Company: prisons, factories, police posts, railway stations, European bungalows, and law courts. They also sought revenge upon indigenous moneylenders and local magnates who had purchased land at government auctions and were seen as benefiting from Company rule. The rebels appealed to bonds of local community and village solidarity, frequently invoking religious sentiments. They did not seek to upset traditional hierarchies of caste or religion and sought the support of higher authorities, such as that of Mughal Emperor Bahadur Shah II (also known as Bahadur Shah Zafar, 1775–1862).

CAUSES

The Sepoy Mutiny erupted from a controversy surrounding the new Enfield rifles issued to Indian soldiers in January 1857 at Meerut. To load the rifle, the end of the cartridge containing the powder had to be bitten off so that the charge would ignite. To allow for easier passage in India's warm climate, the paper of which the cartridge was composed was heavily greased with tallow, rather than wax or vegetable oil. Rumors spread among soldiers that the grease used was derived from pig and cow fat, and therefore offensive to the religious tenets of Muslims and Hindus, respectively.

In April 1857, members of the 3rd Light Cavalry, a native regiment, refused to attend a firing drill with the new Enfield rifles. As a result, a court-martial convicted and sentenced eighty-five of these soldiers to imprisonment with hard labor for ten years. On 9 May 1857 all of the troops at Meerut were assembled on a parade ground to witness the 3rd Light Cavalry's humiliating march off to jail in shackles.

On Sunday, 10 May, during church services, the mutineers struck out in Meerut and killed about fifty European men, women, and children. Shocked European officers and troops, outnumbered by their South Asian counterparts, quickly

found themselves powerless to stop the movement. Sufficient warning could not be sent to Delhi or Agra, as the newly laid telegraph lines from Meerut had been cut.

The Sepoy Mutiny's immediate trigger was the cartridge crisis, but it also grew out of a larger context of quietly mounting fears and grievances directed against the political, economic, social, and religious policies and practices of British rule. One of the most alarming of these to Indians was Governor-General Dalhousie's (1848–1856) Doctrine of Lapse. This policy applied to those parts of the subcontinent that were still governed by nominally autonomous Indian princes, who were often financially and militarily dependent upon their British ally. Dalhousie believed India's princely states were corrupt, an affront to English standards of justice and an impediment to the consolidation of British power. His policy enabled the company to annex territories whenever they could be shown to be misgoverned or if a government-sanctioned male heir was not produced.

Following the annexation of Satara (1848), the Doctrine of Lapse was then applied against the dynastic houses of Sambalpur (1849), Bithoor (1853), Jhansi (1853), Nagpur (1854), Carnatic (1854), and Tanjore (1855).

The most important and unpopular annexation of all, however, was that of Awadh (1856), ruled by Nawab Wajid Ali Shah. Dirges were recited and religious men rushed to Lucknow to denounce the annexation. The Bengal army's recruits were mainly high-caste Hindus from Awadh, and its dynasty's lapse was a great blow to them, not least because they had received extra pay (known as "batta") while serving outside the Company's territories. Now that it belonged to the Company, the extra pay was withheld. Sikhs from the Punjab also now enlisted in native regiments of the Bengal army, to the disgust and anger of many Awadh sepoys who saw Sikhs as unclean. Sepoys, whose loyalty was divided between the Company and the native states from which they were recruited, regarded recent British setbacks in the Afghan and Crimean Wars as proof that the Company was not invincible.

By the 1840s East India Company officials had come to view India's landed aristocracies as

Two Scenes of the Indian Mutiny in 1857. Lithograph by George Franklin Atkinson. Atkinson was a captain in the Bengal Engineers who wrote and illustrated works based on his experiences in India at the time of the Sepoy Mutiny. Here he shows the discontented Indian soldiers (above), and an English agent extracting recompense from Indian princes. ÉCOLE NATIONALE DES LANGUES ORIENTALES, PARIS, FRANCE/BRIDGEMAN ART LIBRARY/ARCHIVES CHARMET anachronisms. The imperial government decided to collect taxes directly from peasants, displacing the landed nobles as intermediaries. Disarming the landed nobility threw the retainers and militia of the notables into unemployment. The Company's new system of land settlement dispossessed the old gentry and eroded peasant rights, enhancing the power of moneylenders. The Company also transferred judicial authority to an administration insulated from the indigenous social hierarchy.

With railways, the electric telegraph, and the steam-vessel, the Company used modern science and technology to make India easier to manage from a distance. The social effects of modernization and economic reform were often seen as a threat to religious tradition. The banning of the practice of *sati* (self-immolation by Hindu widows), permission of widows to remarry, and a law that enabled a son who had changed his religion to inherit his father's property all added to the sense of religious siege. Since evangelization had been made legal in India in 1813, missionaries spoke openly of the day when all men would embrace Christianity and turn against "heathen gods."

Fear of forcible conversion to Christianity became stronger than ever in the army in 1856 with the passing of the General Service Enlistment Act, which stipulated that all recruits to the Bengal army must agree to serve overseas if required to do so. Previously, only six battalions of the Bengal army had been available for foreign service. It was considered impossible for a faithful Hindu to go to sea as he could not, in a wooden ship, have his own fire to cook his food, which his faith obliged him to do himself; nor could he properly perform the prescribed rituals of daily ablution. The act supposedly applied only to new recruits, but it was feared these provisions might one day extend to cover all sepoys.

CONSEQUENCES

The Mutiny was countered with brutal vengeance. British forces and rebel militias had fought for nearly two years over several thousand square miles. Villages were captured and torched, while rebels were tied to cannons and blown to bits to teach Indians a lesson in power. Delhi fell to the British in September 1857; Lucknow in March 1858. After killing his sons and grandson in cold blood, the British exiled Emperor Bahadur Shah II to Burma, where he died in 1858. Most other rebel leaders were either killed in battle or executed.

The Queen's Proclamation, read by Governor-General Charles John Canning (1812–1862) at Allahabad on 1 November 1858, marked an official end of the rebellion. The speech made clear Britain's newly stated intention to respect, even embrace, traditional religious, social, and cultural practices on the subcontinent in the name of toleration. However, missionary activity increased after 1857, most of all in women's missions, which promoted English middle-class domestic ideals through extended house visitations. And despite official declarations, a hardening of attitudes against untrustworthy "orientals" had set in among most European colonialists.

The Mughal dynasty was not the only regime to end with the Mutiny. The East India Company was also dissolved, as the British crown took over direct rule of India for the first time. By making the Company the symbol of blame and the transgressor of the ideal of trusteeship in which India was to be held, the crown and British Parliament finally terminated the life of the merchant state that the philosopher and parliamentarian Edmund Burke (1729–1797) had criticized at the end of the eighteenth century.

The 1857 rebellion exposed the fundamental inadequacies of the information colonial authorities, evangelicals, and reformers had thus far relied upon. Enthusiastic modernizers now began to address with renewed urgency the demands for relevant and reliable local information. Traditional India and caste took on greater importance for colonialists as a way of understanding their Indian "others." This renewed need for practical knowledge was abetted by the rapid expansion of the communications network, the establishment of educational institutions, printing presses, and libraries by an English-educated elite. Yet these changes also promoted the development of indigenous forms of information that would help give rise to India's political independence movement.

See also **Colonies; East India Company; Great Britain; Imperialism; India.**

BIBLIOGRAPHY

Chakravarty, Gautam. *The Indian Mutiny and the British Imagination.* Cambridge, U.K., and New York, 2005.

David, Saul. *The Indian Mutiny: 1857.* London, 2002.

Embree, Ainslie Thomas, ed. *1857 in India: Mutiny or War of Independence?* Boston, 1963.

———, ed. *India in 1857: The Revolt Against Foreign Rule.* Delhi, 1987.

Hibbert, Christopher. *The Great Mutiny: India 1857.* London, 1978.

Metcalf, Thomas R. *The Aftermath of Revolt; India, 1857–1870.* Princeton, N.J., 1965.

Stokes, Eric. *The Peasant and the Raj: Studies in Agrarian Society and Peasant Rebellion in Colonial India.* Cambridge, U.K., 1978.

———. *The Peasant Armed: The Indian Revolt of 1857.* Edited by C. A. Bayly. Oxford, U.K., 1986.

Ward, Andrew. *Our Bones Are Scattered: The Cawnpore Massacres and the Indian Mutiny of 1857.* New York, 1996.

STEPHEN VELLA

SERBIA. The fully independent Kingdom of Serbia that went to war in 1914 entered the nineteenth century as an Ottoman territory called the Pashalik of Belgrade. During the course of its struggle for national independence, which began with the Serbian Revolution in 1804, Serbia underwent significant political, social, cultural, and, to a lesser degree, economic transformation.

THE SERBIAN REVOLUTION

The Serbian Revolution did not begin as an independence movement. In fact, most Serbs were content with their condition under Ottoman rule. In the Ottoman feudal system, the Serbian peasant was not a serf. Serbs did have to pay taxes, including a tithe in kind and a head tax on Christian males. But they owned their own land from which they could move and which they could manage as they pleased. The Serbian population lived in villages in the countryside. The villages were composed of *zadrugas,* households of two or more closely related families that communally owned, produced, and consumed their livelihood. This system allowed greater economic production through division of labor, and greater economic and personal security. The villages were organized into districts under the leadership of a *knez,* who collected taxes for the Ottoman feudal landlords (*sipahis*), who resided in the towns. Thus, the Serbian community had a degree of autonomy under their own notables, who were either elected or appointed from among the wealthier peasants, and only limited contact with Ottoman authorities during rent collection or inspection times. The church or district leaders also had jurisdiction over Serbs for all crimes that did not involve a Muslim or the Ottoman state. In 1793 and 1794 the Ottoman sultan passed a series of reforms granting Serbs greater self-government and limited Ottoman interference in their affairs. He also allowed the Serbs to construct new churches and gave Serbian *knezes* the exclusive right to collect taxes.

Several changes in the conditions of the Ottoman Empire in the eighteenth century had paved the way for national revolution, most significantly the disintegration of the Ottoman feudal system, internal opposition to the sultan by the elite Janissary corps of the army, and increasing secularization. As Ottoman central authority weakened and the Porte (Ottoman government) increasingly failed to maintain discipline in its ranks, this system of rule began to collapse. Defying the rule of the pasha of Belgrade, the sultan's direct representative in the pashalik, *sipahis* became increasingly corrupt. Furthermore, unruly Janissaries went to the countryside and seized lands from the Serbian peasants and took rent in addition to what the Serbs already paid to their landlords. They essentially forced Serbian free, landowning peasants into the position of serfs. Thus it was not against the sultan that the Serbs revolted, but against the corrupt and coercive local Ottoman authorities who threatened to divest the Serbs of rights that the sultan had granted them. In fact, the Serbs and the sultan had a common enemy in the Janissaries, who had transformed from an elite fighting unit into an undisciplined, defiant group of mercenaries over which the Porte could no longer effectively exert authority. In fact, the Janissaries who were present in the Pashalik of Belgrade had been sent there by the sultan in his effort to distance their opposition from the capital of Istanbul.

In response to Serbian calls for help, the sultan sent a new pasha to Belgrade, Hadži Mustafa. He was so beloved by the Serbs that they called him the "Mother of the Serbs." In 1797, when the Janissaries went on the offensive, Hadži Mustafa, financially supported the raising of a popular Serbian militia of fifteen thousand Serbian men commanded by Serbian officers. This policy of using Christians to combat unruly Janissaries was wildly unpopular among Muslims. The Janissaries also found a patron, Osman Pasvan-Oglu, Pasha of Vidin, whose support helped them conquer Belgrade and drive out Hadži Mustafa, whom they beheaded for supporting the Serbs. Following their victory, four Janissaries rose to power and called themselves the *dahi* (the title for Janissary officers). The *dahi* regime revoked all of the Serbs' autonomous rights. The Serbs planned to revolt against this new regime, and in order to prevent an uprising, the *dahis* carried out a massacre of Serbian leaders in 1804. This event, which has come to be known as "the slaughter of the *knezes*," precipitated a general uprising of the Serbian masses. The Serbs formed military units and chose as their leader one of the *knezes* who had escaped slaughter, Djordje (George) Petrović, known as Karadjordje (Black George) because of his swarthy complexion. Karadjordje was a man of the people, even though he was a wealthy swine trader. He had gained military experience fighting in a regiment of Serb volunteers in the Austrian military unit, the Freicorps (Free Corps), during the Austro-Turkish War of 1788–1791. Karadjordje led the First Serbian Uprising, which was the first phase of the Serbian Revolution and lasted from 1804 to 1813. As the revolt progressed, Karadjordje increasingly called for autonomy from the Ottomans and proclaimed himself as the hereditary supreme leader of Serbia. Largely because of an unfavorable international climate, however, the Serbs were defeated, with this first phase of the Serbian Revolution ending when Ottoman forces recaptured Belgrade in 1813. At the end of the uprising, Karadjordje fled to Habsburg lands.

The Second Uprising began in 1814, and was led by another wealthy peasant, Miloš Obrenović. After a year of fighting, Miloš succeeded in securing a degree of autonomy from the Porte in 1815, even though full autonomy would not be gained until 1830. First, he was recognized as "supreme *knez* of Serbia." Second, it was granted that Serbian officials would collect taxes and that Serbian judges would determine Serbian cases. Furthermore, Serbia got favorable tariffs and trading privileges. Finally, Janissaries were excluded from owning land, and all Serbs who participated in the uprising were given amnesty. Miloš was more successful in securing gains for a number of reasons. First, he was more of a diplomat. Second, he was not facing the same international situation that Karadjordje had faced. During Karadjordje's struggle, the European powers were engaged in battle with Napoleon. By Obrenović's phase, Napoleon had been defeated, and the European powers, especially Russia, could turn their attention back to the Balkans.

ROLE OF THE SERBIAN ORTHODOX CHURCH IN THE NATIONAL MOVEMENT

During the revolution, only a minority of Serbs lived in the Pashalik of Belgrade. The remainder of the Serbian population was dispersed over Habsburg and other Ottoman lands. It was the less educated, less literate Serbs of the Pashalik of Belgrade who took up arms against the local Ottoman authorities and secured a degree of autonomy. But it was the more educated Serbs from the Habsburg lands, the *prečani* as they were called because they lived across (*preko*) the Sava River, who shaped the revolt into a national movement.

The Serbian Orthodox Church was central to the Serbian national movement. More a cultural and quasi-political institution than a religious one, it had preserved a Serbian identity through the centuries of Ottoman rule, and fostered the idea of political unity. The church's role resulted directly from the Ottoman millet system, which had allowed it to preserve autonomy and jurisdiction over legal and moral matters of its local population. Significant to later national aspirations, the church also served as a common point for Serbs who lived outside of the country's borders in Austrian or Ottoman territory, who despite their geopolitical division shared the Orthodox religion, allegiance to the Serbian Orthodox Church, and a common language written in the Cyrillic alphabet. The church perpetuated Serbian medieval history through a cult of Serbian royal saints and epic poetry. The church's monasteries were

The War between Serbia and Bulgaria: Serbian Artillery Crossing the Ploca Mountains. Engraving by J. Schonberg from the *Illustrated London News,* 16 January 1886. In November of 1885, Serbian prince Milan Obrenović launched a short, unsuccessful campaign to overturn the Bulgarian annexation of Rumelia. PRIVATE COLLECTION/BRIDGEMAN ART LIBRARY

educational and cultural centers for priests, some of whom would become leaders in the Serbian national movement.

Especially influential was the Metropolitanate of Karlovci in the Vojvodina (Serbian duchy), the area of southern Hungary to which many Serbs fled from the Ottomans. The greatest migration had occurred in 1690, when thousands migrated under the leadership of Patriarch Arsenius III Črnojević into Habsburg territory where they were granted lands by the Austrian emperor, Leopold I, and a measure of autonomy. Serbian society in the Vojvodina was organized around the church and included peasants and an influential middle class of merchants, artisans, clergy, and the military. This community became an important cultural center, and was influenced by Western ideas and the Enlightenment. Especially influential was the work

of two men, Dositej Obradović and Vuk Karadžić. Karadžić, the father of the Serbian language, codified the language and compiled a dictionary and grammar book, in addition to collecting traditional Serbian poetry and stories. Obradović was a monk who wrote Serbian literature in the vernacular. Both provided visions of the Serbian nation, albeit two very different ones; Obradović was influenced by Enlightenment thought, whereas Karadžić was inspired by Romanticism.

INTERNAL POLITICAL LIFE
After the revolution, Serbs were faced with establishing their own government and developing their economy, society, and culture, while concurrently trying to gain increasing independence from the Ottoman Porte. Two key questions dominated Serbian internal political life for much of the century

after the Serbian Revolution. The first was the rivalry between the Karadjordjević and Obrenović dynasties, which was rooted in the personal conflict between Karadjordje and Miloš. After winning the Second Uprising, Miloš began to encounter opposition from within, especially from supporters of Karadjordje. When Karadjordje returned to Serbia in 1817, Miloš had him killed and his stuffed head presented to the sultan. The conflict between these two dynasties persisted throughout the nineteenth century, deepened as their members began to pursue different political policies, and manifested itself in the form of several regime overthrows by one or the other.

The second political question was the debate over what the political structure of Serbia should be. Even though Miloš had led the Serbs in their quest for liberation, he was by no means liberally minded, and was not ready to extend rule to his people. Instead, he ruled as a paternalistic despot who equated his own political and economic interests with those of the state. It has been said that he ran the country like an Ottoman pasha or sultan. The life of the average Serbian peasant did not immediately improve after the Serbian Revolution. Serbian peasants faced an even heavier tax burden than under the Ottomans, because of the needs of the new state apparatus and Miloš's practice of bribing Ottoman officials. They still had to engage in forced labor (a labor tax) because Miloš needed workers to build roads, bridges, and public buildings. Miloš used his position as leader to secure significant personal wealth, by confiscating former Ottoman land, establishing monopolies on livestock export and salt, and maintaining peasant taxes. Furthermore, Miloš saw the need to control the potential political threat of Serbian military leaders, *knezes,* and prosperous merchants, many of whom were looking to replace the departing *sipahis.* As a result, he aimed to secure hereditary succession. Miloš did enjoy authority and popularity, which derived largely from the role he had played in the revolution, but also because Serbian peasants were accustomed to patriarchal, despotic rule.

Through negotiation and bribery, Miloš gained the Porte's recognition of Serbia's full autonomy in 1830. He succeeded in large part also because of Russian support, one example of how the intervention of the Great European Powers often played an important role in Serbia's political development. The terms of the 1830 *hatti-sherif* (irrevocable imperial decree) recognized Miloš as prince of Serbia with the right of hereditary succession. It gave Serbia control over its own internal affairs, namely the administration and collection of taxes and regulation of church affairs. It forbade Ottomans to live in the countryside and confiscated Ottoman landed property. It also delimited the borders that Serbia was to have until the Congress of Berlin of 1878, bounded by the Danube River to the north, the Drina River to the west, and the Timok River to the east, with a southern border directly above the town of Niš. The *hatti-sherif* also established a council and an assembly, which Miloš refused to implement. This issue gave rise to the struggle between Prince Miloš as the absolute ruler and the notables, a struggle that was to dominate Serbian political life until the promulgation of the first Serbian constitution in 1869.

LIMITING ABSOLUTE RULE

Having strong personal rule was less in keeping with Serbian tradition than a decentralized system of local notables. The notables, who drew largely on western European ideas and terminology, began demanding a constitution to limit the arbitrary and absolute rule of the prince. In 1838 the sultan issued the so-called Turkish constitution, which was to form the basis for the Serbian government until the Serbian constitution of 1869. It stipulated that sovereignty was to reside in a council of seventeen members who were to be appointed for life by the prince. The prince and the council were to share legislative functions, and the council had to approve laws and taxes, although the prince had absolute veto. It also made ministers responsible to the council, and regulated the civil service, judicial system, and state administration. Miloš accepted the constitution because of pressure from domestic opponents and European consuls. In 1839 he was forced to abdicate by a coalition of six council members—three of whom were *prečani*—calling themselves the Defenders fo the Constitution. Miloš, who was exiled to Habsburg territory, was succeeded by his son Michael (Mihailo), who as a minor, governed through regency. In 1842 Michael was overthrown by supporters of the

Karadjordjević dynasty, who recognized Karadjordje's son Alexander as the legitimate successor.

The Constitution Defenders instituted oligarchic rule, and promoted legality, greater economic freedom, and the advancement of education. While they were not democratic, they opposed the regulation of national life by the state. This period was dominated by powerful ministers, most prominently Interior Minister Ilija Garašanin, as the prince was too weak to significantly shape the government. The ministers established a bureaucratic regime through which they hoped to modernize Serbia and give it a European-style government. Most of the posts had to be filled by Serbs born and educated outside of the Pashalik of Belgrade, especially by the *prečani*. As a result, a significant cultural rift existed between the foreign-educated bureaucrats and the peasantry, as the former felt superior and the latter were suspicious. As an increasing number of native-born Serbs were sent abroad to receive their education, however, they gradually replaced the *prečani* in the regime. One of the greatest achievements of the Constitution Defenders was the enactment of the civil code of 1844, which was adapted almost entirely from Austrian models. The rule of the Constitution Defenders and Prince Alexander came to an end at a meeting of the national assembly on St. Andrew's Day in 1858, when a combination of local and commercial opponents forced them and the Karadjordjević dynasty from power. Miloš Obrenović was brought back to the throne the following year.

At this point in its political development, Serbia had three centers of power—the ruler, the council, and the assembly; by 1859 the latter gained advisory powers and had to be called every three years. Two political parties also began to emerge, the Liberals, who favored the supremacy of the council, and the Conservatives, who favored the ruler and the council. In 1860 Michael Obrenović came to the throne for a second time upon the death of Miloš. Michael is considered to have been the most effective ruler of modern Serbia. While he was in exile, he had traveled and received a formal education, the first Serbian prince to do so. Michael reasserted the power of the monarchy, and working with Garašanin, a Conservative, sought to eliminate opposition by repressing the Liberal Party. Toward this end, he passed a censor-

ship law in 1861 and virtually dissolved the highest court in 1864. He also focused on territorial expansion and securing the complete withdrawal of the Ottomans from the city garrisons, which was completed in 1867. Furthermore, he established a national militia, made all males between the ages of twenty and fifty subject to military service, and created a war ministry and facilities for the training of soldiers. He made alliances with neighboring Balkan states against the Ottoman Empire, but these were often thwarted by divergent and competing national interests. In 1868 Michael was assassinated, and having no heirs was succeeded by his fourteen-year-old cousin, Milan.

Milan Obrenović ruled with a three-man regency that included Jovan Ristić. Ristić was largely responsible for pushing through the first Serbian constitution in 1869, which replaced the Turkish constitution of 1838. Drafted by a constitutional assembly without foreign interference, the constitution reinforced a strong executive by giving the prince the power to appoint one-fourth of the National Assembly and to dismiss it at will. But it reflected the contemporary European ideas of the Liberals as well. The National Assembly, to which all taxpaying males would elect representatives, was to meet annually and hold public debates. Furthermore, the state council was reduced to an administrative committee. The constitution also provided a general declaration of civil rights, including the equality of citizens, property rights, and freedom of speech and religion. Ultimately, no one was happy with the constitution, as the prince and the Conservatives felt that it went too far in providing for parliamentary rights, and the Liberals felt that it did not go far enough. Much of the next decade was spent in efforts on all sides to revise the constitution.

Serbia moved a step closer to independence when it was recognized as a principality in 1878 at the Congress of Berlin. This is the same year that the Radicals, the ideological heirs of the socialist Svetozar Marković, came on the Serbian political scene. Nikola Pašić, the leader of the Radicals, was among the first to be elected to the National Assembly in 1878. The Radical Party, which was formally founded with the Radical Program of 1881, was the party of the peasants, at least traditionally. It advocated amending the constitution to enfranchise all adult citizens and to give the National Assembly full legislative power. The Radicals also called for improvements in the economy and education. The party was highly disciplined and systematically organized, and its influence was reflected in its victory at the polls. Prince Milan, however, decided to work with the Progressive Party, which was overshadowed by the Radicals and never gained much of a following. In 1882 Serbia was proclaimed a kingdom and Milan, king.

The next twenty years of Serbian political life would be dominated by the domestic affairs and scandals of the Obrenović dynasty. Before abdicating in 1889, Milan called a constitutional assembly in 1888, which was dominated by the Radicals. The new constitution that they drafted (which was adopted in January 1889 [December 1888, old style]) was more democratic than the constitution of 1869, as it gave more power to the parliament, instituted universal suffrage for taxpayers and secret elections, and more clearly defined civil liberties. Milan appointed a three-member regency to rule when his twelve-year-old son, Alexander, ascended the throne. Alexander's reign was dominated by the Radicals, and is best remembered for the scandal surrounding his wife, Draga, who was ten years his senior and reputed to be barren and promiscuous. His rule came to an end in 1903, when he and Draga were brutally assassinated in their palace by a group of young officers who believed Alexander's rule to be detrimental to Serbia's future.

The coup d'état reinstated the Karadjordjević dynasty under the rule of Peter Karadjordjević. A new constitution was promulgated in 1903, which was actually a modified version of the constitution of 1889. It was a remarkably liberal document that established Serbia as a hereditary constitutional monarchy and declared that all Serbs were equal before the law. Under this constitution the National Assembly had real powers. It also provided for freedom of the press and religion, as well as an independent judiciary and the abolition of the death penalty. This constitution marked the beginning of a new political orientation for Serbia, characterized by the establishment of justice and freedom, as well as improvements to the economy and the modernization of the army. King Peter was fiercely patriotic, a Russophile, and a staunch sup-

porter of Pan-Serbianism. During his reign relations with Serbia's Balkan neighbors and Russia improved, while relations with Austria-Hungary deteriorated, culminating in the outbreak of war in 1914.

ECONOMY AND SOCIETY

While Serbia spent much of the nineteenth century establishing a modern nation-state, economic development lagged behind political modernization. The nineteenth century saw significant demographic changes in Serbia, both in population growth and composition. The population of the Pashalik of Belgrade in 1815 was around 450,000. The first census taken in 1834 reported 678,192 inhabitants. Between 1834 and 1859, the population nearly doubled to one million and further jumped to 2.5 million by 1899. This figure included the territory surrounding Niš that had been added to Serbia after the Treaty of Berlin in 1878 (10,300 square kilometers [4,000 square miles] and 303,097 inhabitants). On the eve of World War I, Serbia had approximately 4.5 million inhabitants. This steady increase in population was due in part to high rural birthrates and the immigration into Serbia of Serbs from Bosnia-Herzegovina and Macedonia, motivated by worsening economic and political situations. Furthermore, territories added to Serbia after the Treaty of Berlin and after the Balkan Wars (1912–1913), especially the incorporation of Old Serbia (the southern provinces that had been under Ottoman rule), significantly contributed to its population increase.

The Serbian population also became increasingly Serbian, especially in the towns. In 1815, 97 percent of Serbs lived in the countryside, while the towns were inhabited largely by the fifteen thousand Muslim Ottomans living in Serbia, two-thirds of whom were Bosnian Muslim Slavs who spoke the same language as the Serbs. The towns were Ottoman administrative and military centers, and the predominant presence of the Muslims was evident in the Ottoman public buildings, mosques, fountains, baths, covered markets, and fortresses. The next largest urban population consisted of the Gypsies. There were also a comparatively smaller number of Jews, Greeks, and Hellenized Vlachs, or "Cincars" (Anglicized as "Tsintsars"), who comprised the merchant class. Through the course of the century many Greek traders departed voluntarily, while the Turks and other Muslims were driven out, with the final expulsion from cities occurring in 1867. By the end of the century, the ethnic composition of Serbia was nearly 90 percent Serb.

Serbia, predominantly a nation of small land-owners, faced significant obstacles to economic and social development, as it lacked a substantial merchant class to lead commerce. It also lacked communications and transportation networks. In the early nineteenth century, the Serbian economy centered on stock raising, with agriculture beginning to develop more intensely in the 1830s. The first significant economic change after the revolution was the rapid rise of a Serbian merchant class. Increasingly, Serbian merchants began to replace Greek and Jewish ones through a process of steady urbanization. Serbia's foreign trade doubled between 1850 and 1876. Livestock was the country's major export, with Austria-Hungary the market for 90 percent of Serbian exports. In turn, 90 percent of Serbian imports came from the Monarchy. This arrangement increasingly forced Serbia into a position of economic dependency, which was solidified in 1881 when Prince Milan Obrenović, an Austrophile, signed a secret trade agreement with Austria-Hungary that effectively made Serbia a political and economic vassal of the Monarchy. When Serbia refused to renew this commercial agreement, a tariff war, known as the Pig War, broke out between the two countries, lasting from 1906 to 1911. During this time, Serbia's economy suffered, even though the war did encourage the development of certain sectors of the economy, such as the meat slaughtering industry. By the turn of the century, animal husbandry had declined and agricultural products became Serbia's main export. During the century, Serbian agricultural production had increased, especially in wheat. Nevertheless, primitive agricultural technology prevented Serbia from remaining competitive as it entered the twentieth century. Another economic change was the introduction of a money economy, which also led to the disintegration of the *zadruga* because peasants no longer needed to be self-sufficient.

Industry was very slow to develop in Serbia, consisting initially only of ironworks to support the army. The government did build roads and bridges, and communication received a boost with the arrival of the telegraph in 1855. However, only

Serbian women learning to use rifles. Ilustration from *Le Petit Journal*, November 1908. The illustrator highlights the degree of Serbian nationalist sentiment during the Bosnian crisis of 1908. PRIVATE COLLECTION/BRIDGEMAN ART LIBRARY/ROGER-VIOLLET, PARIS

toward the end of the 1880s did small factories arise. The development of railroads began in 1884, funded largely by French companies. In the late 1890s, industrial development was more rapid because of an increase in government concessions and an injection of foreign and domestic capital, largely due to the emerging banking system. Toward the end of the century, telephones and electric lights appeared in Belgrade. Despite Serbia's economic development and demographic growth, the country remained largely agricultural, with over 84 percent of the population engaged in agriculture in 1900. At the outbreak of World War I, Serbia was still a peasant society.

CULTURAL LIFE

Until the 1870s, it was largely the Serbs from the Habsburg lands who led Serbia's cultural modernization. At the beginning of the century, there were very few primary schools and a deficit of professionally trained teachers. Initially, Habsburg Serbs filled most of the teaching posts. In the 1830 *hatti-sherif*, Serbs gained the right to build schools without the Porte's approval. The first law on elementary schools was passed in 1833, but a lack of paper, books, and qualified teachers thwarted their development. Education also suffered from inadequate funding by the government. In the second half of the century, steady progress could be seen. For example, in 1875 there were 534 elementary schools attended by approximately 23,000 students. Two years later the number of schools rose to 558 and students to 47,000. A law in 1882 made six years of elementary education obligatory, although there was a great deal of noncompliance, which is demonstrated by the fact that five years later no village in Serbia had even five grades. The slow development in education is also demonstrated by the low rates of literacy in Serbia. In 1866 only 4 percent of the population was literate, and by 1884 the number had risen to 11 percent. A substantial gap existed between townspeople and villagers. Only 6.4 percent of villagers were literate, compared with 43.7 percent of townspeople. Literacy among women was markedly lower, with only 0.3 percent of women in villages and 12.4 percent in towns being literate.

This town and country divide became even more striking when the capital city of Belgrade underwent a rapid cultural modernization in the 1870s and 1880s, after the expulsion of the Ottomans. This change manifested essentially as a Europeanization in style and manners, thus expelling the once-dominant Ottoman and Serbian patriarchal influences. The people adapted bourgeois fashions from Vienna, Budapest, and Paris. Belgrade became almost the exclusive center of higher culture, where the majority of newspapers and books were published. The circulation of newspapers, which were the primary vehicles for spreading modern culture, sharply increased after freedom of the press was assured in the 1869 constitution. A number of cultural institutions arose in the capital in the latter half of the century. In the 1850s the National Library and National Museum were established, followed by the Royal Academy of Sciences in 1887. The Great School (Velika škola), the highest institution of learning in Serbia,

was established in 1863 and was transformed into the University of Belgrade in 1905. The Serbian National Theater, which was established in 1869, had tremendous cultural influence. Also, the Royal Serbian Academy was founded in 1887 with the purpose of advancing scholarship.

EXTERNAL POLITICS

During Miloš's reign, the Serbian government pursued a nonaggressive foreign policy aimed primarily at gaining full autonomy from the Ottoman Empire. When the promulgation of the 1869 constitution somewhat settled internal political affairs, the Serbian government began to pursue an expansionist foreign policy aimed at incorporating the numerous Serbs who still lived in the surrounding Ottoman and Habsburg lands into the Serbian principality. This plan to liberate Serbs from imperial domination and to unify them into a single state was known as the Greater Serbia plan. This idea was first articulated in 1844 by Garašanin in a document called "Nacertanije" (Outline). Here, Garašanin proposed that Serbia reestablish the boundaries of the Serbian medieval kingdom, including the lands of Bosnia, Herzegovina, Montenegro, and Macedonia and areas of southern Hungary, as well as secure an outlet to the Adriatic Sea. The need to acquire an outlet to the sea became even more apparent in light of the economic difficulties Serbia suffered during the Pig War. This expansionist policy inevitably led Serbia to clash with the neighboring Austrian and Ottoman Empires, as it called for the incorporation into Serbia of imperial lands.

In the early twentieth century, Serbia went to war against the Ottoman Empire, and came to the brink of war with Austria-Hungary on several occasions prior to the outbreak of war in 1914. The closest Serbia came to war with the Monarchy was in 1908 when Austria-Hungary annexed Bosnia-Herzegovina, which it had occupied since 1878. The Serbian government was forced to accept the annexation, because the Great Powers were not ready or willing to go to war over the annexation. But a group of soldiers and civilians who were dissatisfied with the outcome of this so-called Annexation Crisis organized two nationalist organizations, Narodna odbrana (The National Defense) and Ujedinjenje ili smrt (Union or Death). These underground organizations worked toward the shared goal of a Greater Serbia, both through cultural work and political agitation.

At the same time, Serbia formed alliances with the neighboring countries of Bulgaria, Greece, and Montenegro to create the Balkan League, aimed at driving the Ottoman Empire from the peninsula. The alliance declared war on the Ottoman Empire in 1912 and defeated it in 1913. In the Treaty of London, which ended this First Balkan War, Austria-Hungary and Italy provided for the creation of an independent Albania, which prevented Serbia from getting an outlet to the sea. In compensation, it gave Serbia substantial territory in Macedonia. Shortly thereafter, Bulgaria went to war against Serbia and Greece over competing claims in Macedonia, launching the Second Balkan War. Reinforced by Montenegro, Romania, and the Ottoman Empire, Serbia and Greece quickly defeated Bulgaria. The ensuing Treaty of Bucharest reaffirmed Serbian gains in Macedonia. As a result of the Balkan Wars, the Kingdom of Serbia almost doubled in size from 48,000 square kilometers (18,500 square miles) to 87,300 square kilometers (33,700 miles), and its population jumped from 2.9 million to 4.4 million. It had also regained the lands of Old Serbia, which included the historically significant province of Kosovo.

While Serbia's struggle against the Ottomans was resolved with its victories in the Balkan Wars, its conflict with Austria-Hungary only continued escalating in the first decade of the twentieth century and ultimately culminated in the outbreak of war in July 1914 when the Austrian government held the Serbian government responsible for the actions of the Union or Death organization in assassinating the heir to the Habsburg throne, Archduke Francis Ferdinand. This Austro-Serbian war quickly devolved into World War I.

See also **Austria-Hungary; Balkan Wars; Belgrade; Bosnia-Herzegovina; Karadjordje; Millet System; Nationalism; Ottoman Empire; Slavophiles.**

BIBLIOGRAPHY

Dragnich, Alex N. *Serbia through the Ages.* Boulder, Colo., 2004.

Jelavich, Barbara. *History of the Balkans.* Vol. 1: *Eighteenth and Nineteenth Centuries.* Cambridge, U.K., 1983.

Lampe, John R. *Yugoslavia as History: Twice There Was a Country.* 2nd ed. Cambridge, U.K., 2000.

Petrovich, Michael Boro. *A History of Modern Serbia, 1804–1918.* 2 vols. New York, 1976.

Stokes, Gale. *Politics as Development: The Emergence of Political Parties in Nineteenth-Century Serbia.* Durham, N.C., 1990.

Tomasevich, Jozo. *Peasants, Politics, and Economic Change in Yugoslavia.* Stanford, Calif., 1955. Reprint, New York, 1975.

Vucinich, Wayne S. *Serbia between East and West: The Events of 1903–1908.* Stanford, Calif., 1954. Reprint, New York, 1968.

JOVANA L. KNEŽEVIĆ

SERFS, EMANCIPATION OF. Emancipation of serfs in Russia is associated with the 3 March (19 February, old style) 1861 "All-Merciful Manifesto" of Alexander II, the emperor of Russia (1855–1881). It involved the legal abolition of serfdom (known in Russia as *krepostnoe pravo*) and the liberation of over twenty million serfs. Although Russian serfs were among the last European serfs to gain legal freedom, Russia's experience squares with the long process of peasant emancipation throughout Europe. The abolition of serfdom throughout Europe in the areas where it survived into the eighteenth century began with the French Revolution and ended in 1864 with the emancipation of Romanian serfs.

What in fact brought to an end the system of peasant bondage in Russia? Why and how did serfs gain their legal freedom? These questions have produced scholarly controversy. In general, historians underscore either economic or political factors allegedly responsible for serfdom's abolition. Economic explanations suggest that the 1861 act was a result of the so-called crisis of feudalism. In this view, the new "capitalist forms of production" clashed with the old "feudal economy" and caused peasant resistance. This clash produced what some historians call a "revolutionary situation," a fatal condition that eroded serfdom and finally ended it. Political explanations usually emphasize the defeat of Russia in the Crimean War (1853–1856), portrayed as the apotheosis of "Russia's backwardness." They also accentuate the role of the state bureaucracy in initiating the reform of 1861. In this interpretation, the defeat forced the Russian autocracy to recognize the necessity of reforms. In order to carry out military and industrial reforms, the government finally decided to free the vast bulk of Russia's population. In contrast to approaches that focus on a mid-nineteenth-century "crisis," long-term economic, social, and cultural developments in Russia since the late eighteenth century can be seen as bringing serfdom to an end.

DIMENSIONS OF RUSSIAN SERFDOM

What was actually abolished in 1861? In the main, serfdom was a system of relations between individual landlords who owned the land and serfs who dwelled on and worked it. Serfdom had legal, economic, political, social, sociopsychological, and cultural dimensions and endured in Russia for more than two centuries.

Serfdom emerged in Russia in the sixteenth century, when a similar institution had declined in most parts of northwestern Europe. Beginning with a series of late-sixteenth-century decrees, the state severely restricted peasants' mobility and subjugated them to landlords' authority. The 1649 Law Code (*Ulozhenie*) definitively bound millions of peasants to the land by banning them from leaving their place of residence without permission. During the seventeenth and eighteenth centuries, serfdom matured and reached its height. By the early nineteenth century it began a gradual decline. The 1861 manifesto finally ended the legal bondage of landlords' serfs. (Earlier acts of the 1810s freed serfs of the Baltic provinces.)

A most important feature of Russian serfdom was that it occurred in a society where peasants constituted about 85 percent of the population. Approximately half of Russia's peasants lived on lands owned by individual landlords and thus were serfs; the landlords composed only about 1 percent of the population. According to the tenth imperial census (1857), the 10,694,445 male serfs accounted for about 49 percent of all male peasants and 34 percent of the empire's male population. An average noble estate accommodated several hundred serfs, with individual holdings running from several dozens to tens of thousands of people. A few noble magnates possessed hundreds of thousands serfs, whereas some impoverished nobles had none.

As the overwhelming majority of the population, peasants were in several respects the essential social group in Russia, especially with regard to their economic role. Peasants' crucial contribution to the local and national economies went far beyond producing agricultural commodities and paying feudal dues. In addition to their agricultural pursuits, peasants and serfs traded goods of all kinds, possessed manufacturing establishments and workshops, and were involved in various entrepreneurial and commercial ventures. With the absence of a significant middle class in Russia, peasants' activities predominated in these economic spheres.

Their economic, cultural, and social significance enabled peasants, and specifically serfs, to establish and maintain a balance between the diverse and often opposing interests of the state, the landlord, and themselves. The economic importance of the serfs simultaneously induced the state to regulate lord–peasant relations and permitted peasants to establish limits on the landlords' and local officials' prerogatives. The obvious factor was that the Russian national economy could not function without a certain degree of more or less free peasant and serf activity.

Serfs' economic importance perhaps helps explain certain juridical ambiguities of Russian serfdom. The legislation that established serfdom simultaneously empowered peasants to sustain their everyday economic, social, or cultural needs. Russian law allowed serfs to engage in various trading, commercial, and entrepreneurial ventures both within and away from the ascribed place of residence. The 1649 Law Code restricted peasant mobility but also granted serfs the right to leave the village temporarily in order to seek employment or pursue other economic or social activities. Studies show that during the first half of the nineteenth century, about a quarter of peasants (including serfs) of the central Russian provinces temporarily migrated each year, thus exercising significant territorial mobility.

On the one hand, landlords sometimes bought, sold, and punished serfs; on the other, the state protected serfs against "unreasonable" corporal punishment, banned the sale and mortgage of serfs without land, and outlawed advertisements of such transactions. Nonetheless, Russian serfs were usually bought and sold with the land they populated, a legally sanctioned transaction that signified the transfer of estates or parts of estates to new landlords. The state's laws restricted feudal obligations of serfs, and forbade landlords to intervene in serf marriages and separate serf families. Worthy of note is that despite the initial legal prohibitions on complaining against their landlords, serfs in some cases sued the lords in state courts and succeeded in bringing to trial those who transgressed their rights, including their own lords. During the late eighteenth century, a few landlords were tried for causing the deaths of their peasants, deprived of noble status, and sentenced to hard labor in Siberia for life. Those lords who harshly mistreated their serfs were normally ostracized in society.

Neither the state nor the landlord had an interest in completely binding the peasant. In order to sustain the national economy and the economic requirements of the landlord, the state needed to provide the peasantry, as a demographically and economically predominant social group, with certain legal protections and freedoms for territorial mobility, as well as for economic and social pursuits. This legal aspect distinguished serfdom from American slavery and brought it close to European feudalism. Contrasting Russian serfdom with American slavery, some contemporary Americans noted that in Russia serfs could not be beaten to death or separated from their families and sold like any other piece of merchandise, practices endured by many American slaves.

Supplementing the legal limits on the landlord's authority provided by the state, Russian serfs themselves deployed a broad range of means to curtail the lord's influence. Living on their land for centuries, serfs created and maintained their customs, cultural values, and institutions. These provided for peasants' survival by keeping a balance between external forces and their own individual and communal interests and needs. Hallowed tradition and indigenous institutions enabled peasants to set limits on the landlords' and the state's power and authority.

Most peasants spent a considerable part of their lives in extended two- and three-generational families. Peasant marriages, performed according to local tradition and custom, received full legal sanction. The couple's parents or guardians usually agreed upon a marriage contract. Studies illustrate that landlords rarely intervened in marriage contracts and usually did not separate serf families, practices forbidden by a 1722 law. In most affairs of family life, including economic and social activities and decision-making, the family enjoyed a significant degree of freedom from the landlord.

Most Russian serf families lived in villages (settlements with households, small stores, mills, communal buildings, a church, and a cemetery). One or more of these villages constituted the peasant commune, the most important economic and social feature of serfdom. The authority of the commune over villagers varied, depending upon local custom and the arrangements with the landlord. The serf commune ordinarily regulated land use, collected taxes, and was a site for interactions between the village, the landlord, and the state. The 1861 law preserved the peasant commune as an official institution and retained most of its functions.

Regarding their feudal duties, serfs were supposed to perform work for landlords (corvée or *barshchina*) part of the time or pay money rent (*obrok*), depending on the local economy and arrangements. A 1797 decree banned landlords from requiring their serfs to work more than three days a week, as well as to work on Sundays and holidays. Those on money rent paid landlords between 30 and 50 percent of their annual income. As the market economy accelerated during the first half of the nineteenth century, many landlords shifted their serfs to money rent. In general, serfs who paid rent in money enjoyed greater freedom from the landlords for their independent pursuits.

Although the agricultural economy predominated in Russia, serfs, as well as other categories of peasants, were usually multi-occupational. The local economy and the serfs' occupations depended largely upon regional conditions. In the southern, southeastern, and western regions local economies were oriented mainly toward agriculture, specifically grain production. The economy of the northern and central regions usually combined various nonagricultural and agricultural activities. With the expansion of the free-market economy, this regional specialization became more pronounced. In certain regions agriculture became a seasonal occupation and nonagricultural pursuits largely dominated the peasant economy.

About half the serfs engaged in various non-agricultural activities were hired workers, whereas others were small traders, craftsmen, self-employed in services, and even, although rarely, rich merchants and entrepreneurs. Large numbers of peasants maintained cottage industries as a seasonal business for the entire family, producing not only for the local market but for national and international ones as well. Peasants sold their products to traveling traders and merchants (themselves often serf peasants) who resold them in various national and regional markets and fairs, and even abroad. About a quarter of serfs temporarily migrated each year in order to pursue their economic or social activities outside the village.

CHALLENGES TO SERFDOM'S FOUNDATIONS

These legal, institutional, social, and economic factors underlay the internal dynamics and changes within serfdom during the centuries of its existence. New economic, social, and cultural realities that emerged during the first half of the nineteenth century, in turn, challenged serfdom's foundations.

The expansion of the peasantry's economic and social activities in the nineteenth century had wide-ranging repercussions. Peasants' engagement in various crafts and trades acquainted them with national and local economies and with pertinent state and local laws and regulations. Through economic advancement and education, some serfs entered the upper social strata. Although the number of such fortunate individuals was small when compared to the total serf population, the phenomenon impressed contemporary observers. One mid-nineteenth-century commentator pointed out that self-made peasants were forging to the head of merchant communities and emerging as leaders in public affairs. Some scholars began to describe peasants as the most economically important social estate. The development of new favorable attitudes toward the peasant estate and the wide recognition of peasants as an important economic and social force had political consequences. Contemporaries, including high state officials, increasingly viewed serfdom as a social evil. This opinion was expressed in numerous mid-nineteenth-century publications and literary works that attacked serfdom.

The ideas of the Enlightenment and liberalism penetrated into Russia prior to and especially during the reign of Nicholas I (1825–1855). Russian public discourse of the first half of the nineteenth century stressed the ideas of freedom and equality. These ideas were not limited to only a few enlightened individuals, but penetrated the minds and discourses of common people. Over the first half of the century, perceptions of serfs about themselves and their serf status dramatically changed. The number of peasant refusals to perform feudal duties increased during the first half of the nineteenth century, as peasants refused to work or pay rent because they perceived themselves as "free persons."

The process of emancipation of serfs started long before the final 1861 decision. The series of laws that regulated relations between landlords and their peasants were direct state responses to peasant economic and social activities. Peasants' public actions also influenced the peasant-oriented legislation of the first half of the nineteenth century. Beginning in the early nineteenth century, new laws eased peasant entry into nonagricultural activities, in part by restricting the lord's authority over serfs. New decrees enabled serfs to engage in virtually all kinds of economic activities and regulated those activities. A series of laws progressively limited the power of the lords over peasants engaged in licensed commercial and business enterprises and introduced private property rights for serfs. These laws ultimately applied to many tens of thousands of serfs. The law of 1812 granted serfs the right to engage in entrepreneurial activities in their own names. This law gave peasants of all categories virtually complete freedom to take up economic activities "such as those given to merchants and townspeople." Serfs were granted significant immunities from interference by the lord. The law of 1827 restricted lords' authority over peasants who engaged in commerce. It forbade landlords to "divert" peasants who obtained trading licenses from their business activities.

Of special interest is the law of 1835. This law prohibited lords and other "local authorities" from recalling peasant-migrants temporarily employed outside the estate. The law of 1848 granted serfs the right to possess (buy, inherit, sell, and so on) private enterprises. The law of 1856 set free serfs who settled on their own lands. Laws that regulated seasonal migration provided peasants, including serfs, the right to travel for employment or conduct their own business and to prolong their stay without undue interference from their landlords. These laws, often ignored in scholarship, were of tremendous historical significance. They challenged the foundation of serfdom by reducing the power of the lord over peasants.

During the first half of the nineteenth century, the state took harsh measures against lords who violated the provisions that regulated their relations with serfs. Over a hundred noble estates were under state guardianship because of the landlord's mistreatment of serfs. In these cases serfs' feudal obligations and payments went directly to the state, not the landlord. These legal actions gradually undermined the position of the nobility by the mid-nineteenth century and influenced serfdom's decline.

By the mid-nineteenth century in Russia only a few radically minded conservatives, usually members of the landed gentry, still supported the institution of serfdom and staunchly opposed its abolition. The defeat in the Crimean War made the position of these advocates of serfdom shaky and simultaneously solidified the position of those who desired liberal reforms. The defeat served as the final impetus to end the outmoded institution.

THE EMANCIPATION'S CREATION, PROVISIONS, AND CONSEQUENCES

In 1857 Emperor Alexander II appointed a "secret committee" to draw up a new law on abolition of serfdom. The committee, however, consisted of conservative state bureaucrats who opposed emancipation. It worked out a plan for emancipation according to which peasants were to gain their freedom but receive no arable land. The procedures for freeing serfs outlined in this project were extremely complicated. The project was not accepted, and in 1858 the government established the Main Committee to carry out a new project of serf emancipation. The government also established provincial gentry committees to discuss emancipation at the local level.

In general, most nobles agreed with the government's emancipation effort. It is clear, however, that they wanted to carve out for themselves as many privileges as possible. For instance, lords from the

agricultural provinces, where agriculture dominated the economy and was the major source of wealth, wanted to retain land and free their serfs without land or with very small allotments, all suggestions similar to those outlined in the 1857 commission proposal. Nevertheless, as an active social force, serfs also exercised some influence on the process of lawmaking. They publicly expressed their attitudes on the emancipation project. State institutions studied peasant opinion about the reform. Most state reports emphasized the peasants' desire both to gain legal freedom and to retain their land.

In 1859 and 1860 materials on public opinion about emancipation, as well as the official opinions of the local gentry committees, went to the Editing Commission and finally to the Main Committee. After brief consideration by the State Council, Alexander II signed the 1861 act of emancipation. The act granted the status of "free rural inhabitants" to over twenty million serfs. According to the act, serfs could purchase, or in some cases receive free, much of the land they had used before 1861. Alexander's emancipation, one of the most important legal acts in the history of imperial Russia, would have far-reaching consequences.

The foregoing description of serfdom during its last decades suggests that the 1861 abolition of serfdom had perhaps brought serfs somewhat less new freedom than some contemporaries and many serfs expected. Clearly, before the 1861 decree serfs exercised some freedoms regarding their economic and social activities and decisions, as well as territorial mobility. And, after the law's introduction former serfs still remained subjects of their village communes. In order to leave the village they had to obtain permission from the commune or other local authorities rather than from the landlords. The law also retained most of the functions and authorities of the commune, and extended some feudal obligations of serfs for certain periods of time, an arrangement that kept peasants in home villages. Some evidence suggests that the number of peasants who seasonally migrated decreased somewhat during the first decade after the emancipation, a phenomenon caused by the terms of the emancipation law.

These provisions represented an effort to retain for the landlords some of the economic powers they formerly enjoyed over serfs as well as to protect as much as possible nobles' former privileges.

Emancipation of a serf. A mid-nineteenth-century engraving depicts a ceremony in which a serf is officially granted freedom.
©BETTMANN/CORBIS

Nevertheless, the serf emancipation as a whole was in large part an achievement of the liberal-minded intelligentsia and statesmen. Individuals, such as Nikolai Milyutin, Yuri Samarin, Grand Duke Konstantin Nikolayevich, and Grand Duchess Elena Pavlovna, who identified themselves as "liberals," participated in the emancipation and exercised an influence on its preparation. The law was a compromise between conservatives who completely opposed emancipation and liberals who were moved by their belief in freedom. Liberals influenced the emperor to speed up the passage and implementation of the new law.

The 1861 law emancipated serfs with land, unlike millions of former American slaves freed a few years later without land. Peasants received much of the land they had previously used, although this land was assigned to peasant communes rather than to individual peasants. The state compensated landlords for the land they lost, whereas former serfs had to pay the state redemption payments over a period of forty-nine years for land they received. In cases in which former serfs took only one-quarter of their previously owned land (the so-called pauper's allotment), they were exempt from redemption payments. In order to estimate a redemption payment for each specific case, the government prepared inventories of landholdings and feudal obligations of former serfs. Peasants and landlords had to sign the inventory and thus agree on a final settlement. In most cases the land price was estimated at up to twice as much as its market value before 1861, a practice that benefited the lords and burdened the peasants.

According to various studies, serfs received from 10 to 18 percent less and in the southern provinces from 25 to 40 percent less land than they used before 1861. Landlords, who accounted for 1 percent of the population, retained about 95 million *desyatinas* (265.5 million acres) of land, whereas former serfs (34 percent of the population) remained with 116 million *desyatinas* (313.2 million acres). Most scholars suggest that serfs received inadequate land, in allotments hardly sufficient to maintain their households. Some historians, however, point out that land had provided peasants with only a part of their incomes, the rest of which came from economic activities not associated with land. In many cases, particularly in the areas where nonagricultural economic activities prevailed, peasants preferred to take the minimum pauper's allotment so as to pay no redemptions. Overall, former serfs had paid off about 680 million rubles of indebtedness by 1905, when, because of revolutionary challenges to the state, the redemption payments were abolished. The land arrangement of the 1861 law, along with the rapid growth of the population and resulting unemployment in the countryside, contributed to agrarian problems during the late nineteenth and early twentieth centuries.

The emancipation's land settlement was met with unexpected responses among former serfs. The emancipation set off a series of revolts and disturbances that swept throughout the Russian countryside. Scholars estimate that about 1,889 disorders occurred in 1861. The complicated nature of the emancipation and lack of confidence in the local nobles and authorities provoked peasant riots. Peasants believed that the local gentry had deceived them by manipulating the terms of the emancipation legislation. Some peasants found that the price on land was highly overestimated and refused to sign or otherwise confirm landholding inventories, which would have signified their acceptance of the terms of emancipation. In addition to peasant disturbances, during the early 1860s student uprisings broke out in cities; liberal-minded students had expected more far-reaching political reforms. In Tver (central Russia) a provincial noble assembly called in vain for the convocation of a constituent assembly in order to create a national constitutional government in Russia. Although the government of Alexander II took harsh measures to deal with these and other disturbances and to restore order, it continued the reform efforts. Simultaneously, the dissatisfaction of many educated Russians with the emancipation terms spurred the development of the revolutionary movement in Russia.

The law of 1861 set in motion a transformation of the Russian Empire. The emancipation contributed to the decline of the noble class in Russia and the rise of the middle class during the late imperial period. With the accompanying reforms of the 1860s, the abolition of serfdom stimulated rapid capitalist development during the late nineteenth century. Although the emancipation did not meet the expectations of peasants and the liberal intelligentsia, it ended human bondage of some twenty million Russian serfs, a signal event in Russian history.

See also **Alexander II; Great Reforms (Russia); Peasants; Russia.**

BIBLIOGRAPHY

Blum, Jerome. *The End of the Old Order in Rural Europe.* Princeton, N.J., 1978.

Emmons, Terrence, ed. *Emancipation of the Russian Serfs.* New York, 1970.

Field, Daniel. *The End of Serfdom: Nobility and Bureaucracy in Russia, 1855–1861.* Cambridge, Mass., 1976.

Gorshkov, Boris B. "Serfs on the Move: Peasant Seasonal Migration in Pre-Reform Russia, 1800–61." *Kritika: Explorations in Russian and Eurasian History* 1, no. 4 (2000): 627–656.

Gorshkov, Boris B., trans and ed. *A Life under Russian Serfdom: Memoirs of Savva Dmitrievich Purlevskii, 1800–1868.* Budapest, 2005.

Hoch, Steven L. *Serfdom and Social Control in Russia: Petrovskoe, a Village in Tambov.* Chicago, 1986.

Moon, David. *The Abolition of Serfdom in Russia, 1762–1907.* London, 2001.

BORIS B. GORSHKOV

SEURAT, GEORGES (1859–1891),
French neo-impressionist painter.

The outline of Georges-Pierre Seurat's short life can be recounted quickly. Born to a middle-class family in Paris on 2 December 1859, in 1878 Seurat enrolled at the École des beaux-arts, and in 1882 he began to submit works to the annual state-sponsored Salon. The Salon jury admitted a drawing in 1883, but the next year rejected Seurat's more ambitious entry, *Une Baignade, Asnières* (1883–1884; Bathers at Asnières). In this canvas—exhibited at an alternative venue, the Salon des Indépendants—Seurat referred to academic tradition, naturalist observation, and impressionist light effects. Yet he also hinted at something new,

SEURAT'S SCIENCE AND CRAFT

Seurat's innovative technique is usually described as "scientific," in keeping with the vocabulary used by the artist and his contemporaries, who lived in an age greatly enamored of science. Pissarro, for example, drew a distinction between "romantic" and "scientific" impressionism, implying a welcome eclipse of the former by the latter. But reference to science can mask the elements of intuition and craft so central to Seurat's achievement. The shimmering effect of his paintings results from careful juxtapositions of light and dark shades and of warm and cool colors, hence his own coinage, *chromo-luminarisme*. It is a myth that Seurat restricted himself to the three primary colors, pairing dots of blue and yellow (for instance) to form green. Seurat studied the principles governing solar or prismatic light as explained by scientists Michel-Eugène Chevreul and Ogden Rood, but he adapted their theories to his own particular goals and materials.

Another myth about Seurat's technique claims that his surfaces are regular patterns of tiny dots or points. (In fact, the term *pointillism* comes from the language of craft, *point* being French for "stitch.") In some cases, a coarsely woven canvas support lends a texture to thin paint layers, but the individual marks vary widely from small dabs to long streaks, angled in all directions: Seurat once described his brushwork as *bayalé* (broom-swept). Only in comparison with the loose, gestural brushwork of his immediate predecessors, the impressionists, could Seurat's hand appear mechanical.

depicting his subjects, modern working-class or lower-middle-class men, as idealized, monumental forms.

LA GRANDE JATTE

"The subject: the island beneath a scorching sky, at four o'clock, boats slipping along its flanks, stirring with a fortuitous Sunday population enjoying fresh air among the trees" ("VIIIe exposition impressio-

niste," p. 261). The young critic Félix Fénéon thus described Seurat's painting with a specificity that echoes the artist's title: *Un dimanche après-midi à l'Ile de la Grande Jatte—1884* (Sunday afternoon on the island of La Grande Jatte—1884). This tiny island in the Seine, a popular weekend destination just beyond Paris's city limits, was the focus of Seurat's attention for two years (1884–1886). Extant studies (twenty-six drawings, twenty-six panels, and three canvases) reveal much about the artist's evolving aims and methods. In keeping with impressionist practice, he produced numerous painted sketches on small wooden panels measuring 16 by 25 centimeters (6 $\frac{1}{4}$ by 9 $\frac{7}{8}$ inches). Records of light effects at different times of day, experiments with alternate positions for shadows, trees, figures, boats—these on-site sketches served as research notes when Seurat entered the studio to work on his 2-by-3-meter (81-by-120-inch) canvas, which would synthesize many moments of observation and aspire to a new classicism.

Seurat explained to the critic Gustave Kahn in 1888: "I want to make modern people, in their essential traits, move about as they do on those [Greek] friezes, and place them on canvases organized by harmonies of color, by directions of the tones in harmony with the lines, and by the directions of the lines" (Kahn, pp. 142–143). Ostensibly describing his method, he also defined his subject. Seurat's figures are numerous but not diverse, most of them recognizably members of the lower-middle to middle class, perhaps including some artisans. While some have contended that the scene is a sociological sampling of Paris or an anarchist manifesto, it can also be interpreted as an allegorical ideal in which the artist presented many contrasts, but no conflicts.

THE DEBUT OF NEO-IMPRESSIONISM

La Grande Jatte was shown in the eighth and last impressionist exhibition, which opened on 15 May 1886. Among the best known of the seventeen participating artists were Mary Cassatt, Edgar Degas, Paul Gauguin, and Berthe Morisot. Camille Pissarro had argued strenuously for the inclusion of Seurat, a newcomer. The relegation of Seurat's works to a separate gallery within the exhibition only emphasized his difference—and his influence. Paul Signac, Pissarro, and Pissarro's son Lucien

Sunday Afternoon on the Island of La Grande Jatte. Painting by Georges Seurat, 1884–1886. ©BETTMANN/CORBIS

each declared their affinity for the new style, which Fénéon dubbed neo-impressionism, in major works of their own.

La Grande Jatte established Seurat's celebrity, drawing positive and negative attention from commentators who made comparisons with early Renaissance art, Egyptian art, wooden toys, puppets, tapestries, broadsides, and illustrations by the English artist Kate Greenaway (best known for her children's book drawings). Undeniably, Seurat's quest to renovate impressionism struck a chord among a younger generation of artists, especially those who would become known as the symbolists. These painters and writers admired Seurat for going beyond the optical surface, eliminating haphazard contingency, and giving form to timeless ideals. "To synthesize a landscape in a definitive aspect which perpetuates its sensation, that is what the Neo-Impressionists try to do," summarized Fénéon in 1887 ("Le néo-impressionisme,"

p. 140). Many subsequent modernist movements embraced this same goal.

SEURAT AFTER *LA GRANDE JATTE*

Seurat's third major canvas, *Les Poseuses* (1887–1888; The models), self-consciously features its predecessor, *La Grande Jatte,* as a picture within the picture, hanging on the wall behind three young women. Alluding to the mythological Three Graces, *Poseuses* takes on the traditional art-historical subject of the nude, but these are not the voluptuous goddesses of Titian (Tiziano Vecelli) or Pierre-Auguste Renoir. Instead, they are modern girls who have briefly discarded their fashionable clothes. The French title, like its English cognate, refers to the models' task of posing for the artist, but also to the women parading fully dressed in the painting behind them. *La Parade* (1887–1888), *Le Chahut* (1889–1890), and *Le Cirque* (1890–1891) amplify this theme.

Rather than emphasizing the provocative aspects of these popular urban entertainments, Seurat instead revealed the commercialization underlying the apparently uninhibited performance—just as he had pointed out the regimentation of leisure in *La Grande Jatte*.

SEURAT'S LEGACY

On 29 March 1891 Seurat died of an acute respiratory infection at the age of thirty-one. His contemporaries immediately began to ponder his legacy; Signac, for example, did so both in his own painting and in the influential book *From Eugène Delacroix to Neo-Impressionism* (1899). This text encouraged artists such as Georges Braque, Robert Delaunay, and Pablo Picasso to view Seurat as a pioneer who had liberated color from its descriptive role. In subject and form, Seurat's art embraces both contrast and harmony. He addressed his contemporaries, but cast an eye to the past and the future. In less than a decade, he changed the course of modern art, prompting critics to devise new vocabularies, painters to experiment with new techniques, and viewers to learn new ways of looking. Seurat's wholly original mode of aesthetic innovation draws upon the positivist, naturalist convictions of the nineteenth century while pointing toward the abstract, ironic attitudes of the twentieth.

See also **Impressionism; Romanticism; Turner, J. M. W.**

BIBLIOGRAPHY

Primary Sources

Fénéon, Félix. "VIIIe exposition impressioniste." *La Vogue* 1 (13 June 1886): 261.

———. "Le néo-impressionisme." *L'art moderne* 7 (1 May 1887): 140.

———. *Oeuvres plus que complètes.* Edited by Joan U. Halperin. 2 vols. Geneva, 1970.

Kahn, Gustave. "Exposition Paris de Chavannes." *La Revue indépendante* 6 (February 1888): 142–143.

Signac, Paul. *D'Eugène Delacroix au néo-impressionnisme.* Paris, 1899.

Secondary Sources

"The *Grande Jatte* at 100." Special issue, edited by Susan F. Rossen. *Art Institute of Chicago Museum Studies* 14, no. 2 (1988).

Herbert, Robert L., et al. *Georges Seurat, 1859–1891.* New York, 1991. Exhibition catalog.

Herbert, Robert L., Neil Harris, Douglas W. Druick, et al. *Seurat and the Making of "La Grande Jatte."* Chicago, 2004. Exhibition catalog.

Moffett, Charles S., et al. *The New Painting: Impressionism, 1874–1886.* San Francisco and Washington, D.C., 1986. Exhibition catalog.

BRITT SALVESEN

SEWING MACHINE. The sewing machine made its debut in a culture that, for more than a century, had considered the needle "the woman's tool par excellence." Sewing was far from exclusively female, but since the late seventeenth century women workers, in defiance of long-term historical trends, had successfully laid claim to the guilds within the garment trades that made clothing for women and children. The Enlightenment belief in "nature" as an ordering principle, and thus of gender as a "natural" division of labor, bolstered conceptions that sewing—and making fashion—were inherently feminine, shoring up seamstresses' claims while simultaneously rationalizing women's exclusion from other trades and deeming their work unskilled. During the Industrial Revolution garment-making expanded rapidly, governments across Europe abolished guilds, and clothing manufacturers mobilized "battalions" of workers for increasingly poorly paid labor—work, it was said, fit only for women. By the 1830s the numbers of independent seamstresses had waned and the needleworker had become the very image of poverty, of women's vulnerability, and, for many social critics, of the wrongs of market culture or industrial society.

Small wonder, then, that the sewing machine sparked the hopes and fears evinced in an 1845 exchange between a reader and Barthélemy Thimonnier (1793–1857) (often considered the inventor of the sewing machine) on the pages of a provincial French newspaper. As one historian remarks, the eighteenth century's faith in progress rested on science, the nineteenth century's on mechanization. Machines evoked contradictory images of newfound power and acute powerlessness. They raised the specter of vast increases in productivity but also of changes in the organization of work and in the social and moral order, both of which, as is shown in the exchange, were

To the Editor,
You have announced to the public in the most laudatory terms the invention of a machine for sewing, due to the learned meditations of Monsieur Thimonnier, tailor from Amplepuis. . . . Of all the troubles that afflict humanity in our time, perhaps none is greater than the inability of a woman abandoned to herself to earn a living through her labor. Every day the strong sex makes new incursions in the trades which, because of their character, would seem to be the exclusive domain of women.

If the condition of the countless women in cities who spend their lives sewing and who are incapable of doing other work is already the source of moral concern; if, every day, some of these poor creatures, disheartened by poverty, debase themselves, succumbing to the deceptive promises of debauchery and seduction; if those who have the courage to resist the vices suggested by poverty earn a wage we know to be insufficient and find themselves unemployed due to lack of work, what will happen when five in six of these women has lost her only means of existence to a mechanical stitcher?

—a subscriber

Source: *Journal de Villefranche*, 14 and 28 September 1845.

Your newspaper this month published a letter from one of your subscribers concerning the sewing machine that is attributed to me . . .

Why should we consider these machines to be hostile to the female sex? Why not say, instead, that these machines will expand the industrial domain of women, make their forces equal of those of men, and place them at the same level of intelligence?

The industrial world is changing as if by magic, and people believe that the fate of the most interesting half of humanity will depend, forever, on the needle.

Rather than proscribe inventions that are destined to raise the well being of all, let us cry for reform in women's education. Let us create trade schools for working women as well as working men. In that way perhaps we will abolish, or at least reduce commensurate with their respective needs, the shocking inequalities between brother and sister, in the inequality (disproportion) of their wages.

—B. Thimonnier

---

powerfully symbolized by gender. Many nineteenth-century writers considered machines and femininity to be incompatible and, in characteristically Romantic style, cast industry against nature or demonized automatons against icons of feminine traditionalism: distaff, needle, and spinning wheel.

In the 1840s, however, the sewing machine played very little role in industry. Expensive and cumbersome, it only made sense in trades, such as shoemaking, in which complex production processes could be broken down into specialized tasks and assigned to specific workers. Factories served to coordinate production and ensure that machines were used efficiently, but clothing manufacturers contracted most sewing work out to either well-established subcontractors or small "jobbing" tailors who employed their wives, children, or other workers. After 1870 sewing technology went in two directions, the first toward specialized

machines to be used in factories, and the second toward improving and disseminating a small machine to be used in work that was contracted out. Outwork, or homework, saved manufacturers capital investments, it allowed them to skirt factory legislation, and it tapped a labor force willing, for diverse reasons, to accept low wages. By the eve of the war the expansion of homework had produced an international outcry over "sweated labor."

The sewing machine role's in industry was inseparable from its pioneering role as one of the first consumer durables to be marketed, on credit, to a mass public. In the 1890s sewing-machine salesmen went directly into the European countryside, offering machines on credit payment plans. In some regions they helped clothing manufacturers recruit outworkers for their industry, waiving down payments on the machine and arguing that the work opportunities or higher productivity would more than compensate for the monthly bills. Workers and reformers charged that these practices exacerbated the dynamics of sweated labor. Sewing machines were also sold in the new centers of working-class consumerism in cities. The Dufayel department store on the plebeian boulevard Barbès in Paris featured a department full of sewing machines at the top of its central staircase, just below stained-glass windows engraved with the store's motto, "Saving, Confidence, Abundance, and Work."

Sewing-machine manufacturers, particularly the American firm Singer, poured money into advertising. The advertising imagery was extraordinarily varied, a reflection of the multiple markets for this machine (industrialists, tailors and seamstresses, working-class families, and middle-class women), of the tentative or experimental character of early advertising, and of the knot of anxieties and aspirations tangled around the topics of "work" and "femininity." The decorative metalwork of the machines was sometimes sculpted into odd shapes: squirrels (symbol of frugality) or cupids with drawn bows. In advertisements, magicians conjured machines out of thin air. Elephants clambered onto sewing-machine chairs as they would onto circus pedestals, and monkeys hurtled down roller coasters on sewing machines—caricatures of "dexterity" and speed. Allegorical "liberty" figures danced with machines in their arms. A Singer sewing machine with wings took flight over the Eiffel Tower. Advertisements drew on now-familiar tropes of nineteenth-century domesticity, juxtaposing depictions of sewing-machine factories belching smoke with those of women safely (and industriously) sewing at a machine at home. They also borrowed freely from the imagery of empire and the "civilizing mission"; Singer aimed to reach "every corner of the inhabitable world" and to emancipate all of womankind, whether "white, red, black, or yellow."

Did sewing machines change women's household work? Yes, but not in the ways one might predict. Historians know more about the transformation of industry than they do about the history of unpaid household labor. But research shows that labor-saving domestic technologies were very slow to make their way into European homes. Middle-class women in Europe usually hired servants to do their work, and most working-class and peasant families were too poor to afford specifically domestic appliances. While women routinely spent long hours mending their families' linens and garments, to actually fashion clothing required skills that women usually acquired in industry and only afterward turned to use in their homes. Yet the sewing machine was one of the first widely disseminated consumer durables—by 1914 an estimated one in three European households from Portugal to Russia owned sewing machines—largely because it could be used for wage earning as well as household chores. In a century when the garment industry employed so many women, the sewing machine was almost inescapably hybrid, joining industrial and domestic—an object of desire that literally had to earn its place in the home.

See also **Consumerism; Industrial Revolution, First; Industrial Revolution, Second.**

BIBLIOGRAPHY

Coffin, Judith G. *The Politics of Women's Work: The Paris Garment Trades, 1750–1915.* Princeton, N.J., 1996.

Crowston, Clare Haru. *Fabricating Women: The Seamstresses of Old Regime France, 1675–1791.* Durham, N.C., 2001. The best analysis of prerevolutionary developments.

Frader, Laura L., and Sonya O. Rose, eds. *Gender and Class in Modern Europe.* Ithaca, N.Y., 1996.

Giedion, S. *Mechanization Takes Command: A Contribution to Anonymous History.* New York, 1948.

Green, Nancy L. *Ready-to-Wear and Ready-to-Work: A Century of Industry and Immigrants in Paris and New York.* Durham, N.C., 1997.

Hausen, Karin. "Technical Progress and Women's Labour in the Nineteenth Century." In *The Social History of Politics: Critical Perspectives in West German Historical Writing since 1945,* edited by Georg G. Iggers. New York, 1986.

Liu, Tessie P. *The Weaver's Knot: The Contradictions of Class Struggle and Family Solidarity in Western France, 1750–1914.* Ithaca, N.Y., 1994. Particularly astute on dynamics within working families.

Scott, Joan Wallach. *Gender and the Politics of History.* New York, 1988.

Scott, Joan Wallach, and Louise Tilly. *Women, Work, and Family.* New York, 1978. Still a classic.

Valenze, Deborah. *The First Industrial Woman.* New York, 1995.

JUDY COFFIN

SEXUALITY. The long nineteenth century was a unique period in the history of sexuality. During that era, and in contradistinction to what had gone before and was to come after, sexed bodies were regarded as stable platforms that expressed the gender and sexuality natural to them. The notion of sexuality as a thing apart from sex did not emerge until near the end of the century; until 1890 or so male and female sex established the material evidence for the social identity of individuals and the "natural" reproductive force of sexual desire. Prior to 1800 or so, the flux of fluids and temperature characteristic of Hippocratic medicine kept the boundaries of sex indistinct, and by the twentieth century the discovery of genes, sex chromosomes, and hormones fragmented sexed bodies and opened the way for the medical manipulation of sex itself. It was thus uniquely in the nineteenth century that medical and popular opinion alike believed male and female bodies produced masculinity and femininity and the desire to procreate by natural design.

The great irony of this holistic notion of sexuality rooted in biological sex is the fact that this era also marked a dramatic acceleration in the development of personal individuality. New refinements in selfhood were driven by the explosion of market capitalism, the appearance of a modern consumer culture, and by a rapid expansion in literacy. These phenomena coincided with a huge growth in urban populations, the result of steady rural immigration, and with the first notable declines in birthrates. As more children survived the first year of life, parenting became more affectionate in nature, but also more intense; middle-class children in particular were more scrutinized and regulated than ever before. The intimate dynamics of nuclear-family life produced novel forms of sexual resistance and behavior, the diversity of urban life provided anonymity for individuals and relative safety for sexual minorities, and there were more young women living unsupervised lives as maids and factory workers than ever before. It was inevitable that the prevailing models of procreative male and female sexuality would be undermined eventually by the centripetal forces of modern individualism, although medical and moral authorities fought a long rear-guard battle to prevent this from happening.

MIDDLE-CLASS SEXUALITY

As many historians of sexuality have shown, the foundations of the sexual ideals and practices that predominated in the nineteenth century were established by the urban middle classes of the previous century. Sexual self-control and the restriction of sexual activity to marriage were adaptive strategies employed by businessmen, professionals, and prosperous artisans as a way of safeguarding longevity and protecting scarce family assets threatened by infidelities or illegitimate children. What has come to be thought of as "puritanical" or "Victorian" sexual ideals were simply useful tactics for individuals whose most effective mode of self and familial advance was the slow and legal accumulation of capital, including the biological capital of good health. Venereal disease was particularly feared by such respectable folk, who manufactured numerous exaggerations about its virulence, contagiousness, and heritability as a kind of protective class mythology. Eventually, middle-class sexual codes became obligatory standards for members of other social formations. Middle-class public health experts, purity crusaders, and reforming politicians investigated and publicized the living and working conditions of the poor and the blight of prostitution, with an eye to expanding the scope of public respectability and health. They equated moral and physical depravity in a way that made masturbation the cardinal sexual sin of the era. A youth unoccupied by work or useful routine could be drawn to solitary self-pleasuring and from there to a series of allied vices that ruined her health and carried the risk of madness or other immoral or antisocial behavior.

SEXUAL "OTHERS"

While the sexual practices of the European peasantry and the urban working classes were also driven by procreative concerns, these groups seldom had the luxury of privacy or the incentives for self-improvement of their social betters. Their sexual behavior was more relaxed, and marriages were often the result of pregnancy, not the other way around. The knowledge of contraceptive techniques—withdrawal was by far the most common, but also sponges, pessaries, and condoms—and the will to use them were less developed outside the middle classes. Accordingly, birthrates, but also mortality rates, remained higher for some time than those of the middle classes. It is likely that the gap in sexual knowledge and practices between the middle classes and their social inferiors, including colonial peoples, was greater in this era than at any previous or subsequent time. Though this gap narrowed by the turn of the century, it served to reinforce racial and sexual binaries such as civilized/savage, respectable/degenerate, and other categories that typified prevailing biomedical discourse in the nineteenth century.

The primary victims of these stereotypes were the prostitutes who populated the ports and metropolitan areas of Western societies. Prostitution was regulated by many European states and municipalities, ostensibly to protect the health and identity of male clients, but also to supervise the women by ensuring they practiced their trade in brothels and stayed away from respectable neighborhoods. A notable exception to this practice was the repeal of the regulatory Contagious Diseases Act in Great Britain by a coalition of reformers led by Josephine Butler in 1886. Such moments of liberal largesse were rare, however; the fear of venereal disease, which was still virtually impossible to treat safely, spread throughout middle- and upper-class society and became a virtual "syphilophobia" by the end of the century. It was in this domain that the sexual "double standard" was most acute, but the demonization of prostitutes and virtual exoneration of their male clientele was only the most extreme expression of gendered standards for sexual comportment in law and custom that flourished throughout Europe and North America. Thus, in countries governed by a Roman law tradition, women surprised in flagrante delicto lost all rights to children and property, while her husband could openly keep a mistress providing he did not keep her in the family domicile. No legal grounds for establishing paternity existed in France until after the turn of the century, and the bar for proving cause in divorce cases was set far higher for women everywhere in Europe. It is not surprising therefore that first-wave feminists such as Christabel Pankhurst in Britain and Nelly Roussel in France indicted European patriarchy near the end of the century on behalf of sexually vulnerable women, within marriage and without.

SEXOLOGY AND THE "PERVERSIONS"

The expansion of national competition and nationalist passions after 1870 put a new premium on the health and numbers of the population. Politicians and intellectuals gave medical specialists and public health establishments the responsibility for identifying obstacles and producing improvement. Anything that prevented "normal" procreative sexuality was particularly suspicious in this climate of opinion, including trafficking in contraceptive knowledge or devices, but also deviations from the heterosexual and procreative "norm." Thus, police authorities actively prosecuted purveyors of contraceptive information, and medical specialists set about identifying and studying the varieties of sexual behavior. Masturbation was condemned anew, but so were other nonreproductive practices, which were considered to be diversions, exaggerations, or weakenings of "normal" procreative desire. The "perversions" of masochism and sadism were exaggerations of common impulses; exhibitionism was an impotent manifestation of sexual enfeeblement; and fetishism and homosexuality were regarded as forms of desire focused on inappropriate objects. Though they often favored policies of legal tolerance, the inventors of these new pathologies, among others the Austrian Richard von Krafft-Ebing, the Briton Henry Havelock Ellis, and the Frenchman Alfred Binet, considered the perversions to be diseases that virtually defined the selfhood of the being afflicted with them. Thus, inverts (homosexuals), masochists, sadists, and fetishists fell along the extremes of a spectrum of sexual selfhood, the center of which was occupied by healthy *heterosexuals*, another term coined in this era.

Tolerance in sexological theory was not often reflected by tolerance in clinical or legal practice. A new wave of antihomosexual legislation and enforcement put urban homosexual communities on notice and kept other men and women from exposing their sexual tastes; psychiatrists throughout Europe collaborated with prosecutors to find legal justifications for imprisoning offenders who were medically sick and therefore technically irresponsible in most European legal codes. Some doctors, however, worked to reshape popular and medical perspectives on the perversions, particularly homosexuality. Several German-speaking sexologists signed a petition requesting the decriminalization of homosexuality, led by Magnus Hirschfeld, the founder of the world's first homosexual rights organization, the Scientific-Humanitarian Committee; Krafft-Ebing; and Sigmund Freud. In his *Three Essays on the Theory of Sexuality* of 1905, Freud attacked the received idea that inversion (homosexuality) was a symptom of biological degeneration. It was best understood, he wrote, as a complex and situational sexual orientation based on life experience that did not compromise any other aspect of a person's life. Despite the presence of such progressive voices, little progress was made before World War I in protecting the rights of homosexual or other sexual minorities.

Homosexuals and homosexual communities were not obviously visible to others. Lesbian couples in middle age could live together without scandal in most places, but male homosexuals usually concealed their identities with some care in this era. Some neighborhoods in urban centers attracted large numbers of homosexual men and supported clubs and public places that catered to a homosexual clientele. Men interested primarily in sociability could identify one another by means of various cues, but homosexual sex in this era took place between older and younger men, or between soldiers, sailors, or other normally heterosexual men and homosexual men who assumed a feminine or passive sex role. It is not easy to generalize, but it appears that in this era prior to the emergence of egalitarian masculine sexual relations, homosexual sexual practices were modeled on the active and passive model of traditional heterosexuality.

MARRIED LOVE

Though premarital promiscuity was far more common among urban and rural lower-class youth than within the middle classes, all young Europeans practiced some form of courtship and a period of engagement during which time some intimacy was tolerated. Some old customs survived into the modern era, including the "bundling" of rural fiancés and wedding night parties in the bedchamber of the newly married couple, but increasingly newlyweds were expected to have a domicile separate from kin and to be bound together as a romantic couple. The

almost complete lack of knowledge about sexuality and reproduction beyond the sort supplied by peers and servants guaranteed a large number of wedding night fiascos, but as expectations were not often high, disappointments did not carry consequences dangerous to the marriage. Still, journals and personal memoirs yield evidence of couples whose degree of sexual satisfaction encompassed everything from caresses to intromissive orgasm for both partners. Though prostitutes were held to possess the summa of sexual knowledge among women, many others discovered the pleasures of the conjugal bed empirically. Despite the clear evidence of marital sensuality at the peak of "Victorian" prudery, the degree of ignorance about varieties of sexual pleasure and relatively primitive notions of contraception meant that married couples who wished to limit births engaged in abstinence or forms of sexual contact that did not permit the fullest measure of sexual satisfaction for either partner.

There were no sexual handbooks for married couples until the very end of this period. The first such books, such as the post–World War I volume, *Married Love* (1918), by Marie Stopes, provoked a stream of letters to her that revealed men's complete ignorance about the barest essentials of female pleasure. The closest thing to sex manuals in this era were the limited editions of pornography, usually in expensive editions, that circulated in libertine circles, and a steady stream of birth control manuals that were often quite good on the basic biology of contraception but thin on matters of pleasure, and, in any case, usually just as much part of the illegal literary underground as pornography. Even the first volumes of specialized medical texts such as Krafft-Ebing's *Psychopathia Sexualis* maintained the clinical descriptions of sexual material in Latin. The steady decline in the birthrate throughout Europe suggests, nonetheless, a degree of sexual knowledge sufficient to prevent unwanted pregnancies.

CONCLUSION

The system of sexual identity and practice that emerged near the end of the nineteenth century was essentially an amended version of the two-sex model of sex and gender that had flourished since at least the eighteenth century. The male was the active and superior sexual agent to the passive and inferior female. The invention of technical terminology and slang for homosexuality and the other "perversions" did not directly challenge this model but adapted itself to the dominant model of masculine activity and feminine passivity. Even hermaphrodites, whose existence was acknowledged by doctors, midwives, and a few others, were placed resolutely on one side or the other of the sex and gender divide. The persistence of the two-sex model in medical science, theology, and popular culture placed definite constraints on the ability of men and women to imagine or practice kinds of sexual pleasure that contradicted it. This model tied sexual activity more directly to reproductive biology than any time in human history before or since; it tried in theory, though it surely failed in practice, to limit sexual pleasure to procreative, marital sexual relations. Sigmund Freud boldly suggested that only cowards actually confined themselves to these sexual prescriptions, but the consequences of violating them were far from trivial.

See also **Body; Homosexuality and Lesbianism; Masculinity; Pornography; Prostitution.**

BIBLIOGRAPHY

Corbin, Alain. *Women for Hire: Prostitution and Sexuality in France after 1850.* Translated by Alan Sheridan. Cambridge, Mass., 1990.

Dreger, Alice Domurat. *Hermaphrodites and the Medical Invention of Sex.* Cambridge, Mass., 1998.

Eder, Franz X., Lesley A. Hall, and Gert Hekma, eds. *Sexual Cultures in Europe.* 2 vols. Manchester, U.K., 1998.

Laqueur, Thomas. *Making Sex: Body and Gender from the Greeks to Freud.* Cambridge, Mass., 1990.

Mason, Michael. *The Making of Victorian Sexuality.* Oxford, U.K., and New York, 1994.

———. *The Making of Victorian Sexual Attitudes.* Oxford, U.K., and New York, 1994.

Nye, Robert A. *Sexuality.* Oxford, U.K., 1999.

Oosterhuis, Harry. *Stepchildren of Nature: Krafft-Ebing, Psychiatry, and the Making of Sexual Identity.* Chicago, 2000.

Rosario, Vernon A. *The Erotic Imagination: French Histories of Perversity.* Oxford, U.K., 1997.

Russett, Cynthia Eagle. *Sexual Science: The Victorian Construction of Womanhood.* Cambridge, Mass., 1989.

ROBERT A. NYE

SHAMIL (c. 1797–1871), Muslim religious leader.

Born in Gimrah, in the Avar region of Dagestan, the Muslim religious leader Shamil founded his Islamic state in the Northeast Caucasus region of Chechnya and Dagestan from 1834 to 1859. This area was then part of the Russian Empire and remains part of the Russian Federation in the early twenty-first century. Shamil, who had access to the long and distinguished history of Dagestani contributions to Islamic scholarship, established Islamic law (*sharia*) and promoted ascetic Islamic customs among the diverse peoples of the region. His forces fought a protracted guerilla war against the Russian empire until he was surrounded and captured at the mountain hideout of Gunib in 1859.

Because of their regular and victorious wars against both the Ottoman Empire and Iran, the Russians were increasingly in control of southern borderland regions such as the Crimea and the Caucasus from the eighteenth century on. Georgian monarch Erekle II requested Russian support in 1783 against the surrounding Turkish, Persian, and North Caucasus mountain population, and Georgia served throughout the nineteenth century as an important Russian base for the military, administrative, and cultural incorporation of the region into the empire. Shamil's resistance in the mountains to the north continued to occupy Russia's military forces, however. Like other regions distant from the traditional centers of historic Islam, Shamil drew on the radicalism of local Sufi orders and networks. The conflict was a chapter in the larger story of Christian-Islamic tension prompted by European colonial expansion, with the Orthodox Georgians and Russians cooperating in the struggle against Shamil. The forces of Shamil famously assaulted the Chavchavadze estate in Georgia in 1855 and abducted a Georgian princess, whom Shamil later exchanged for his own son taken by the Russians in 1839.

After Shamil's capture in 1859, the Russian military turned its forces to the Northeast Caucasus mountain range, decimated this area, and exiled approximately four hundred thousand mountain inhabitants across the Black Sea to Ottoman Turkey. Subsequently Shamil lived with family members under Russian surveillance in Kaluga. In 1870 he traveled to the Ottoman Empire on a hajj to the Islamic holy lands, and died in Medina in March 1871.

The North Caucasus mountain regions remained prone to rebellion and opposition to rule from both imperial St. Petersburg and socialist Moscow. During World War II, Joseph Stalin and forces of the People's Commissariat of Internal Affairs (NKVD) accused the Muslim peoples of the region, such as the Chechens, Ingush, and Balkars, of collaboration with the approaching Germans, leading to the exile in 1943 and 1944 of approximately five hundred thousand people to Central Asia. As in the nineteenth century, many of those exiled died en route.

Shamil and the mountain insurgency in the North Caucasus was an ongoing subject of fascination for Russian literary figures from Alexander Pushkin to Leo Tolstoy, and the region remains a source of exploration in contemporary Russian cinema. Shamil's tour of Russian cities, including his journey to St. Petersburg to meet the tsar, in 1859 was extensively covered in the Russian press, where his story was presented as one of cultural transformation in the face of the virtues and superiority of Russian and European culture. In the North Caucasus, Shamil is remembered differently. The memory of the history of empire and deportation continues to inspire opposition to Russian rule, most recently in the ongoing Chechen Wars, which began in 1994. Shamil Basayev, the Chechen rebel, military strongman, and perpetrator of hostage-taking episodes and other forms of terrorism, claims to be distantly related to the nineteenth-century Shamil.

See also **Colonialism; Imperialism; Russia.**

BIBLIOGRAPHY

Gammer, Moshe. *Muslim Resistance to the Tsar: Shamil and the Conquest of Chechnia and Daghestan.* London, 1994.

Jersild, Austin. *Orientalism and Empire: North Caucasus Mountain Peoples and the Georgian Frontier, 1845– 1917.* Montreal, 2002.

Kemper, Michael, Amri Shikhsaidov, and Natalya Tagirova. "The Library of Imam Shamil." *Princeton University Library Chronicle* 64, no. 1 (2002): 121–140.

Layton, Susan. *Russian Literature and Empire: Conquest of the Caucasus from Pushkin to Tolstoy.* Cambridge, U.K., 1994.

Sanders, Thomas, Ernest Tucker, and Gary Hamburg, eds. and trans. *Russian-Muslim Confrontation in the Caucasus: Alternative Visions of the Conflict between Imam Shamil and the Russians, 1830–1859.* New York, 2004.

Zelkina, Anna. *In Quest for God and Freedom: The Sufi Response to the Russian Advance in the North Caucasus.* London, 2000.

AUSTIN JERSILD

SHAW, GEORGE BERNARD (1856–1950), Irish-born playwright, novelist, and critic.

Bernard Shaw's fame and importance rest finally on two distinctions. First, he was by any external measure the most important British dramatist since William Shakespeare. His playwriting career began with *Widowers' Houses* (1892) and continued unchecked almost until his death; he wrote in all fifty plays, and by the 1930s he had become part of the established classical repertoire, his plays regularly revived (at the Old Vic, London's "home of Shakespeare," among other theaters) even as new ones continued to appear. In the early twenty-first century Shaw is the only English-speaking playwright other than Shakespeare to have a major theatrical organization (the Shaw Festival at Niagara-on-the-Lake in Canada) named after him and primarily dedicated to his work.

Second, his plays are unique in their yoking of high comedy to sociopolitical comment. The socialist polemics—expressed in his early batch of "Plays Unpleasant" like *Widowers' Houses,* which dealt with slum landlordism, and *Mrs. Warren's Profession* (1893), about prostitution—were what first attracted his contemporaries' attention, and led to him being tagged as a social realist. It was a misconception partly fueled by his work as a theater critic; from 1895 to 1898 he wrote brilliant reviews for *Saturday Review,* in which he attacked late-Victorian escapist drama (and elaborate Victorian staging of Shakespeare). Henrik Ibsen was his hero, but he praised Ibsen as a theatrical sociologist rather than as the skeptical dramatic poet he actually was. In his own dramatic practice, however, he wrote madcap intellectual farce whose concerns sometimes overlapped with those of Ibsen's prose dramas but whose style never did. Ibsen might be mistaken for a naturalist; Shaw, after his first couple of plays, never could. Much of his appeal, in both his dramatic and nondramatic writing, lies in the sheer wit and buoyancy of his prose. His rhythms challenge and delight audiences; "the ear" (as he himself said of Shakespeare) "is the key to him."

Like many of the major "English" dramatists (William Congreve, George Farquhar, Richard Sheridan, Oliver Goldsmith, Oscar Wilde) Shaw was Irish. He was born in Dublin, into a Protestant family, and lived there until 1876, when he moved to London. His Irishness remained part of his image; and "image" was an important part of his success. He was the first major English writer since Samuel Johnson to have talked and postured his way into lasting prominence. His brogue, his red hair, his teetotalism, his vegetarianism, his incredible energy, his literary combativeness (which concealed a less notorious personal kindness)—all contributed to a persona consciously created and known as "GBS." (Shaw was always "Bernard Shaw" on his title-pages and said that nothing enraged him more "than to be Georged in print," but he had no objection to the popular employment of all three of his initials.) He was a celebrity in literary London long before he was a financial success; indeed, he lived in poverty until the production of *The Devil's Disciple* in 1897. By his death, of course, he was, thanks to performing and publishing royalties plus the sales of his plays to the movies, one of the wealthiest writers in the world. (It is worth repeating his possibly acpocryphal remark to movie mogul Samuel Goldwyn: "The problem between us, Mr. Goldwyn, is that you are only interested in art and I am only interested in money.")

From the 1880s onward Shaw was a socialist, not a revolutionary (though he was much influenced by his reading of Karl Marx). He was a founder and leading light of the Fabian Society (a group promoting non-Marxist socialism by progressive legislation, not revolution); Vladimir Lenin famously called him "a good man fallen among Fabians." He believed in the perfectibility of human society and even of the human race; he believed in great men, whom he dramatized in his historical plays *The Man of Destiny* (about

Napoleon, 1895) and especially *Caesar and Cleopatra* (1899), and in great women (*Saint Joan*, 1923), all of whom he imbued with his own qualities of humorous clear-sightedness and—the nearest thing to tragedy in his work—personal loneliness. Their contemporaries misunderstand them and eventually turn against them.

His key play is *Man and Superman* (1902), in which he uses the ceaselessly voluble armchair revolutionary John Tanner—something of a self-portrait—to preach his own brand of benevolent Nietzscheanism, and then brings him up against the true embodiment of his vaunted "Life Force," his enchanting ward Ann Whitefield whose sexual predatoriness he has been mocking without ever realizing that he himself is her "marked-down prey." When, at the end of four long acts, she ensnares him, the implication is that their union will contribute to the eventual advent of Shaw's longed-for Superman. Tanner is Shaw's mischievous updating of Don Juan Tenorio: mischievous because, as we learn from the long dream-sequence *Don Juan in Hell*, this is a legendary lover who has forsworn physical love and whose passions are now of the brain rather than the senses. But whatever its philosophical underpinnings, the play endures as a love-comedy, even a sex-comedy. It is a variation on an age-old comic theme: the bringing together, despite the misgivings of one or both, of two young people who are obviously made for one another. Shaw's most popular play, *Pygmalion* (1912), is a romance in spite of itself; though he fitted out its published version with a narrative sequel, claiming that its hero and heroine never got married, nobody has ever believed him. For the play to turn into *My Fair Lady* (1956), one of the best of romantic musical comedies, was not much of a stretch.

Shaw's own sex life was curious. Though extremely susceptible to women, he kept his virginity until 1885, when—on his twenty-ninth birthday—he succumbed to a temperamental Irish widow, Mrs. Julia (Jenny) Patterson. Other affairs followed, but his marriage—to another Irishwoman, Charlotte Payne-Townshend—was, though apparently very happy, platonic. (The marriage lasted from 1898 until Charlotte's death in 1943.) In his plays sexlessness, even when the subject is love, becomes a matter not just of nineteenth-century reticence but of principle. In *Back to Methuselah* (1920) he looks forward to an ideal future in which the body has been superseded by "pure thought."

This has not been, in literary and critical circles, a popular idea, despite Shaw's popularity in the theater (where intellectual passion counts for more than is sometimes acknowledged, and where sexuality can be, by adroit actors and directors, smuggled in). His politics cannot be pigeon-holed as left or right, militant or pacifist. In *Major Barbara* (1905) he gives an armaments manufacturer the best arguments, but he was vilified for opposing World War I. He said that the nearest thing he had to a religion was a belief in "Creative Evolution," but his enthusiasm for "strong men" led in the 1930s to a disquieting enthusiasm for dictators. He condemned Adolf Hitler's anti-Semitism, but in terms that suggested that it was no more than an aberration. He could not, apparently, conceive of the real depths of human hatred and human evil; the men who condemn his Saint Joan may be misguided but they are acting from, in their own minds, the purest motives, and Shaw lets them state their own case in the purest form.

Though he claimed in the play's preface that *Saint Joan* was the noblest kind of tragedy—one without villains—he lacked the tragic vision (the closest he came to it, and that fleetingly, was in the abrupt mock-apocalyptic climax to *Heartbreak House*, 1917), and this has caused him to be underrated in a culture that considers comedy an inferior form. Most infuriating of all, even to some of his greatest admirers, is the sense he conveys—in plays, prefaces, and in politico-economic works from *The Intelligent Woman's Guide to Socialism and Capitalism* (1927) to *Everybody's Political What's What* (1944)—that he has all the answers, and that all society's problems would be solved if people would only listen to him. The pervading sweet reasonableness, laced with paradox, can be oppressive (though it has also gained him many disciples). He himself seems sometimes to have tired of it, as is suggested by the uncharacteristically despairing epilogue to *Too True to Be Good* (1931) in which a burglar turned preacher confesses that he must go on talking even if no one is listening.

Linked to this is an often-leveled charge that he parodied more humorously in *Fanny's First Play*

(1911) that all his characters are figures "set up to spout Shaw." This, though, is only true if we concede that he must have been myriad-minded; his figures may all speak in the same style (so do those of many other playwrights) but their opinions vary wildly—and he can make each of them sound perfectly convincing. This is one reason why actors have little difficulty in animating them. Shaw's themes, even those of his earliest plays, still ring bells; questions of war and peace, riches and poverty, how and what to believe, have not died out yet. And the entertainment value remains constant.

See also **Fabians; Great Britain; Ibsen, Henrik; Marx, Karl; Socialism.**

BIBLIOGRAPHY

Primary Works

Shaw, Bernard. *What I Really Wrote about the War.* London, 1930.

————. *Our Theatres in the Nineties.* 3 vols. London, 1932.

————. *Everybody's Political What's What.* London, 1944.

————. *Bernard Shaw: Collected Letters.* Edited by Dan H. Laurence. 4 vols. London, 1965–1988.

————. *The Bodley Head Bernard Shaw: Collected Plays with Their Prefaces.* 7 vols. London, 1970–1974.

————. *The Intelligent Woman's Guide to Socialism, Capitalism, Sovietism and Fascism.* Harmondsworth, U.K., 1982.

————. *Major Critical Essays (The Quintessence of Ibsenism, The Perfect Wagnerite, The Sanity of Art).* Harmondsworth, U.K., 1986.

Secondary Sources

Bentley, Eric. *Bernard Shaw.* London, 1950.

Evans, Judith. *The Politics and Plays of Bernard Shaw.* Jefferson, N.C., and London, 2003.

Gahan, Peter. *Shaw Shadows: Rereading the Texts of Bernard Shaw.* Gainesville, Fla., 2004.

Gibbs, A. M. *A Bernard Shaw Chronology.* Basingstoke, Hampshire, U.K., and New York, 2001.

Holroyd, Michael. *Bernard Shaw: The One-Volume Definitive Edition.* New York, 1998.

Mander, Raymond, and Joe Mitchenson. *Theatrical Companion to Shaw: A Pictorial Record of the First Performances of the Plays of George Bernard Shaw.* London, 1954.

Morgan, Margery M. *The Shavian Playground: An Exploration of the Art of George Bernard Shaw.* London, 1972.

ROBERT CUSHMAN

SHELLEY, MARY (1797–1851), author of one of the most famous and disturbing literary works of the Romantic period.

Mary Wollstonecraft Shelley was the daughter of Mary Wollstonecraft (1759–1797), a leading British feminist, and William Godwin (1756–1836), a radical philosopher. Eleven days after her birth on 30 August 1797, her mother died. Raised primarily by Godwin's second wife, Mary Jane Clairmont, who favored her own children, Mary grew up in a household where she felt abandoned and unloved, much like the creature in her novel *Frankenstein*. On 28 July 1814, at sixteen, she eloped to France with the married poet Percy Bysshe Shelley (1792–1822). She immediately became pregnant, gave birth prematurely to a baby girl on 22 February 1815 (who died two weeks later), became pregnant again, and gave birth to a son named William on 24 January 1816. Four months later, she left England with Percy and her stepsister Claire Clairmont (with whom Percy had a sexual relationship) to follow Claire's new lover Lord Byron (1788–1822) to Geneva. There, on 16 June 1816, Mary had the "waking dream" that gave birth to the most mythic literary work of the Romantic period, the novel *Frankenstein, or the Modern Prometheus*.

Frankenstein functions on several levels. Psychologically, it uncovers the pregnancy anxieties felt by Mary, an eighteen-year-old, twice pregnant, and unmarried young woman: her fear of not being able adequately to mother a child, especially an abnormal child. As she wrote out the novel, Mary, who by December was pregnant again, came to identify with Victor Frankenstein's creature, the abandoned and unloved child who desperately seeks inclusion in a loving family, but is everywhere rejected, turning his desires instead to revenge and murder. The novel also offers a searing critique of recent scientific and technological discoveries, most notably those by Humphry Davy (1778–1829), Erasmus Darwin (1731–1802), and Luigi Galvani (1737–1798), discoveries that might enable a man to have a baby without a woman. To produce a creature without giving it adequate maternal care will, in Shelley's view, produce only monsters, monsters capable of destroying their makers. (In the late twentieth and early twenty-first centuries

Mary Shelley. Portrait by Richard Rothwell, 1841. © ARCHIVO ICONOGRAFICO, S.A./CORBIS

Shelley's critique has been applied to research on cloning, stem-cell engineering, the development of nuclear warfare, and genetically modified foods.) The novel further explores the consequences of an unconstrained Romantic poetic and political imagination, of the utopian thought that led to the disasters of the French Revolution, the Terror, and Napoleon's campaigns, which Shelley had witnessed and recorded in her first joint publication with Percy, *History of a Six Weeks' Tour* (1817). Throughout *Frankenstein*, Shelley implies that if Victor Frankenstein had been able to love and care for his creature, he might have prevented the violence that destroyed those dearest to him.

After Percy's wife's suicide, Mary and Percy married on 30 December 1816; their daughter Clara Everina was born on 1 September 1817, just as Mary finished *Frankenstein* (published anonymously in March 1818). Mary, now living in Italy, began a second novel, *Castruccio, Prince of Lucca* (retitled and published as *Valperga* in 1823), a portrayal of masculine egotism and female self-sacrifice in twelfth-century Italy. After the deaths of her two children (Clara in September 1818, William in June 1819), Mary sank into a severe depression, fuelled in part by her anger both at Percy's parental irresponsibility and womanizing and at Godwin's unconcern. This depression produced the brilliant novella *Mathilda* (not published until 1959), the first literary account of father-daughter incest told from the viewpoint of a daughter who both adores and hates her father.

Mary's fourth child, Percy Florence, was born on 12 November 1819; *Valperga* was completed in 1821. Shortly after a miscarriage that almost killed her on 16 June 1822, Percy Bysshe Shelley drowned on 8 July. Mary never recovered from this loss, partly because she blamed herself for Percy's unhappiness in the last year of their marriage. She dedicated herself to giving Percy a posthumous literary life, collecting and editing his poetry, and writing his biography (in the form of lengthy introductions to his poems). Her next novel, *The Last Man* (1826), explores the myriad varieties of human loss and grief as a plague relentlessly annihilates the human species; this story resonates powerfully at the turn of the twenty-first century with the threat of AIDS, new viruses, and bioterrorism. Writing constantly, she produced three more novels (*The Adventures of Perkin Warbeck* [1830]; *Lodore* [1835]; *Falkner* [1837]—all of which deal with failed family relationships), numerous stories, encyclopedia entries, and a travel book, *Rambles in Germany and Italy in 1840, 1842, and 1843* (1843). Shelley was able to provide her son with an excellent education at Harrow and Cambridge University. Nursed by the devoted Percy Florence and his wife, Jane, she died of a brain tumor on 1 February 1851, now recognized as the author of one of the most famous novels ever written.

See also **Byron, George Gordon; Godwin, William; Shelley, Percy Bysshe; Wollstonecraft, Mary.**

BIBLIOGRAPHY

Baldick, Chris. *In Frankenstein's Shadow: Myth, Monstrosity, and Nineteenth-Century Writing.* Oxford, U.K., 1987.

Mellor, Anne K. *Mary Shelley: Her Life, Her Fiction, Her Monsters.* New York, 1988.

Schor, Esther, ed. *The Cambridge Companion to Mary Shelley.* Cambridge, U.K., 2003.

Seymour, Miranda. *Mary Shelley.* New York, 2000.

ANNE K. MELLOR

SHELLEY, PERCY BYSSHE (1792–1822), English poet.

Born on 4 August 1792, into a family of privilege and social standing, Percy Bysshe Shelley voiced the yearnings of the underclasses and revolutionized English poetry. He saw his father, Sir Timothy Shelley (1753–1844), a Sussex squire and a member of Parliament, as an unredeemable tyrant, and maintained a lifelong concern with throwing off oppression.

His schooling at Syon House Academy (1802–1804) extended the sense of oppression he associated with his father to include all of society. Similarly, during the six years he spent at Eton he loathed life and developed a sense of isolation and a fear of violence. Before going up to Oxford in 1810, Shelley wrote several tales and poems characterized by their appeal to the lurid. At Oxford he was free of Eton, but was dejected by the atmosphere of established privilege and intellectual mediocrity. His publication in 1811 of *The Necessity of Atheism* represented a direct challenge to authority, and he was expelled as a result.

Breaking with his father, Shelley moved to London, where he drifted into a close friendship with sixteen-year-old Harriet Westbrook, the daughter of a London tavern owner, and in 1811 eloped with her to Edinburgh. They took up residence in the Lakes, where Shelley was influenced by the writings of the dissenting philosopher and atheist William Godwin (1756–1836), and by the poet and man of letters Robert Southey (1774–1843), who helped Shelley connect religion and social criticism.

The most intense education in practical politics came during a six-week stay in Ireland in 1812. Self-education, he believed, would remove prejudice. A good life built on atheism, free love, republicanism, and vegetarianism informed Shelley's first major poem, "Queen Mab" (1813), a work more philosophic than poetic.

In 1814 Shelley began an affair with Mary Godwin, the daughter of William Godwin and Mary Wollstonecraft. In 1816 his wife, Harriet, with whom he had two children, committed suicide. Shelley and Godwin eloped to Switzerland that same year. Shelley went through months of introspection following the upheaval caused by his actions. His verse allegory *Alastor, or The Spirit of Solitude* (1816) issues from his probings. It is a psychological meditation leading to an ideal vision of beauty. On a return to Switzerland he developed the idea of the confrontation between a sensitive mind and brutal, unthinking matter in "Mont Blanc" (1817) and began a friendship with Lord Byron (George Gordon Byron; 1788–1824). Shelley wrote his longest poem, and the last of his youth, "The Revolt of Islam," in 1818. Believing that the essence of revolution is moral and social, Shelley rose to a new dimension of literary maturity.

In 1818 Shelley moved permanently to Italy, where he produced the bulk of his poetic works, many of which were first published in *Posthumous Poems* (1824). Awash in personal difficulties, he considered his relationship with Byron in "Lines Written in the Euganean Hills." In Venice with Byron he wrote "Julian and Maddalo," a major poem of psychological analysis. In Naples he wrote "Stanzas Written in Dejection, near Naples," in which he concludes that Christianity suppressed ancient connections to nature at the cost of human development. Contemplating the ancient artifacts in Rome, Shelley arrived at the belief that power and imperialism were destroyed by the forces of human love, freedom, and nature. "Prometheus Unbound" is the result of Shelley's intense concentration and speculation. In it he shows that the immanence of a moral and political revolution achieved through suffering leads to hope.

The most popular of Shelley's works, *The Cenci* (1820), embodies his reaction to a culture of hypocrisy. Perhaps the greatest political poem ever written, "The Mask of Anarchy" was completed in twelve days. In Pisa in 1820 Shelley wrote "A Philosophical View of Reform" and the "Ode to Liberty," showing how human freedom in culture arises inevitably. "The Ode to the West Wind," "To a Skylark," and "The Cloud" give expression to an escape into a purer world of creative possibilities. Composing "The Witch of Atlas" provided another release of frustrated emotion. "Epipsychidion," another flight, is an erotic love hymn, and a review of his emotional life at twenty-eight.

Shelley's best-known prose appears in *A Defense of Poetry* (1821), where he notes that poetry has a moral and political function to enhance freedom in society. In "Adonias," he attacks reviewers and gives tribute to contemporaneous poets. Shelley's revolutionary ideals moved him to write *Fragments Written for Hellas* supporting Greek independence. Steeped in Dante, Shelley wrote his last major poem, "The Triumph of Life," in 1822. The sparse style and lack of personal emotion distinguishes the poem from his earlier works. On 8 July 1822, Shelley's sailing boat went down in the Gulf of Spezzia less than a month from his thirtieth birthday, and he drowned.

Critical perceptions of Shelley have followed two paths since the nineteenth century: the poet of abstraction challenging the limits of poetry and language, or the working-class hero. Hailed as the most lyrical of poets, who seeks aesthetic value in bodiless consciousness, he is equally evaluated as the champion of poetry in the service of politics, culture, and society.

See also **Byron, George Gordon; Godwin, William; Romanticism; Shelley, Mary.**

BIBLIOGRAPHY

Clark, Timothy, and Jerrold E. Hogle, eds. *Evaluating Shelley.* Edinburgh, 1996.

Holmes, Richard. *Shelley: The Pursuit.* New York, 1975.

King-Hele, Desmond. *Shelley: His Thought and Work.* 3rd ed. Rutherford, N.J., 1984.

Sperry, Stuart M. *Shelley's Major Verse: The Narrative and Dramatic Poetry.* Cambridge, Mass., 1988.

RICHARD L. GILLIN

SHIMONOSEKI, TREATY OF. Concluded on 17 April 1895, the Treaty of Shimonoseki ended the First Sino-Japanese War (1894–1895) and confirmed Japan's status as a major Far Eastern power. From the beginning of Japan's systematic involvement with the West in the 1850s, the adoption of Western methods, particularly in military and naval spheres, was seen as the way to escape Western domination. At the same time, an emerging generation of diplomats and theorists argued that to survive in its new environment, Japan must develop its own imperium. An island state poor in raw materials, it needed secure sources of the imports on which its industrialization and prosperity depended. Commerce and colonization, underwritten by armed force, were the prerequisites of national identity and national greatness.

A restored imperial government initially sought control of the island of Taiwan, which lay across the southern sea route to Japan, and a sphere of influence in Korea, the strategic bridge to an Asian mainland that during the 1880s seemed increasingly open to Japanese penetration. These initiatives, however, brought Japan into direct conflict with a Chinese empire whose recent contacts with the West had been quite different. Commercial expansion and cultural imperialism produced a series of armed clashes at the same time that the Manchu government confronted major local revolts culminating in the Taiping Rebellion (1851–1864). Impoverished and disorganized, China was unable to undertake the large-scale systematic military reforms its experience showed were necessary for the state's welfare.

Seeking both the specific advantage of control over Korea and the general status of Asia's leading power, Japan forced a quarrel with China in 1894. Most of the fighting took place in Korea and southern Manchuria. Japan by now possessed a national conscript army organized and trained on German lines. The navy, originally linked closely to Britain and still prone to placing orders in British shipyards, had increasingly developed its own approaches to doctrine and training, regarding British methods as too unsystematic. The Chinese land forces, haphazardly recruited and poorly supplied, nevertheless put up a determined resistance, and Japan's inexperience in large-scale war initially resulted in numerous operational and logistical errors. At sea it was another story, with Japan winning a decisive victory at the Battle of the Yalu on 17 September 1894.

In November, a steadily improving Japanese army overran the major fortress of Port Arthur. The navy then transported several divisions south to the Shandong Peninsula. In January 1895 they captured the Chinese naval base at Weihaiwei. What remained of the Chinese fleet, which had taken shelter there after its Yalu debacle, was destroyed or surrendered.

Unsupported and isolated, China sought a peace that came at a high price. The Treaty of Shimonoseki conceded Korea's independence—an obvious preliminary to a Japanese takeover. It also gave Japan Taiwan and the nearby Pescadores, and as a strategic bonus the Liaodong Peninsula and the fortress of Port Arthur on the Manchurian mainland. For the Western powers, who had closely observed the course of the war, that was too much, too soon. France, Russia, and Germany combined to encourage Japan to reconsider its terms for the sake of regional peace. Under the gun, Japan turned over its Manchurian acquisitions to Russia, while the other European powers—Britain included—established lesser footholds along the north China coast, a region Japan considered in its sphere of vital interest.

Shimonoseki left Japan determined to pursue its imperial course, and even more determined that the Europeans would never again be in a position to dictate to Japan on matters of its vital interest. For China, Shimonoseki was a humiliation: a catalyst for the emergence of a nationally based revolutionary movement committed to establishing a westernized government able to protect China from invaders and domestic enemies alike. For both Asian states, Shimonoseki's consequences reverberated through the twentieth century.

See also **Imperialism; Japan; Russo-Japanese War.**

BIBLIOGRAPHY

Jansen, Marius, et al. "The Historiography of the Sino-Japanese War." *The International History Review* 1 (April 1979): 191–227.

Lone, Stewart. *Japan's First Modern War.* New York, 1994.

DENNIS SHOWALTER

SIBERIA. Siberia is Russia's subcontinent of northern Asia. Its 13.5 million square kilometers (5.2 million square miles) comprise one-eleventh of the global landmass, and its forests make up one-fifth of the world's total. Although two-thirds of Siberian soil is locked in permafrost, the Black Earth Zone of the southwestern Siberian steppe is well suited for agriculture.

Siberia was Russia's late-nineteenth-century frontier. Intellectuals of the period idealized it as a land of freedom and individualism comparable to the American West, an interpretation echoed by American scholars of the late twentieth century. But in contrast to the U.S. frontier, Siberia's was conditioned by the overgovernment and undergovernment that typified tsarist Russia as a whole. Russia's East was both far wilder and far tamer than the Wild West. The regional folk saying "God is high above and the tsar is far away" expressed one aspect of the Siberian experience, but in response the central government made efforts to ensure that its presence was felt.

CONQUEST AND SETTLEMENT

The Russian conquest of Siberia began in 1582 and continued for the next century. It was propelled by the demand for furs, the largest revenue source of the Muscovite tsardom, which closely regulated trade in the valuable commodity. The last sizable portions of territory, forming the Russian Far East, were annexed from China in the late 1850s in a new era of imperialism.

Siberia's original inhabitants were two hundred thousand hunter-gatherers and pastoral nomads. They spoke Finno-Ugric, Samoyedic, Turkic, Manchu-Tungus, Mongolian, Eskimo, or Paleosiberian languages and adhered to Islam, Buddhism, or—in the main—shamanism. Russian conquest succeeded for the same reasons Europeans prevailed over indigenous societies elsewhere: disease, guns, and exploitation. Reforms written by Governor-General Mikhail Speransky and enacted in 1822 curtailed the worst abuses by replacing forcible collection of tribute with taxation, but this proved equally burdensome. He also granted the various ethnicities internal autonomy, religious toleration, and statutory protection of their territories—although the latter could be circumvented by the central government, which retained ownership of the land.

In 1800 a mere 560,000 Russians inhabited Siberia, and by 1860 natural increase brought that to 2.3 million (alongside 648,000 natives). The Russians were the descendants of fugitive serfs, Old Believers fleeing religious persecution, mer-

chants seeking opportunity, or the Cossacks, priests, and peasants who had been ordered there by the state to man and supply fortresses. Most Siberian towns evolved from these garrisons.

The slowness of settlement was a result of serfdom, which limited peasant mobility, and the early imperial government's view of Siberia less as a frontier extension of Russia proper than as a colony subject to exploitation for its resource wealth: originally furs, then the gold, silver, copper, coal, and iron discovered in the eighteenth and nineteenth centuries.

Siberia was also a dumping ground for criminals, vagrants, and dissidents. By the mid-nineteenth century, seventeen to nineteen thousand exiles were being shipped there annually, and convicts made up at least 10 percent of the population before the peasant influx of the 1890s, when it dropped to 5 percent. Some exiles were aristocratic political prisoners such as the participants in the 1825 Decembrist revolt and their families, who brought the first breath of European culture to Siberian towns, just as later generations of exiled radicals contributed to intellectual life. But most were criminals, and because exile was unsupervised and escape from penal convoys common, Siberian communities were plagued by violent outlaw gangs.

THE TRANS-SIBERIAN RAILROAD AND TSARIST ATTEMPTS TO ASSERT CONTROL

Siberia was remote from the concerns of St. Petersburg until the reigns of Alexander III (r. 1881–1894) and Nicholas II (r. 1894–1917), who sensed risks to Russian dominion in northern Asia. Great Britain was Russia's colonial rival, and its navy posed a threat to the weakly defended Siberian coastline. Agitated by notions of the "Yellow Peril," policymakers feared the Chinese would flood into underpopulated Siberia. The autocracy doubted the loyalty of indigenous peoples, including the large numbers of Chinese, Koreans, and Japanese already resident in the Russian Far East, and suspected Siberia's regionalist intelligentsia, which envied the republican institutions of the American West. And, from 1861 to 1894, nine hundred thousand peasants, now emancipated but seeking to escape land hunger, illegally migrated to Siberia; the tsarist regime could not abide the spontaneity or afford the loss of tax revenues.

To assert control over this vast territory the tsarist state built the Trans-Siberian Railroad (1892–1905, with extensions 1907–1916), took charge of the peasant resettlement movement, and stimulated regional economic development. The 4,800-kilometer-long (3,000-mile-long) railroad, construction of which was orchestrated by Sergei Witte, minister of finance from 1892 to 1903, ran through the most habitable zones of southern Siberia. Under the leadership of the imperial minister, Anatoly Kulomzin, government surveyors divided 21 million acres of land along the route into 40-acre plots in communal villages and distributed them to peasant migrants who were also given travel aid and loans for supplies. The state built schools, churches, and silos, and provided medical and veterinary care. Infrastructure and scientific projects were also undertaken, from irrigation works and construction of river ports to geological exploration and subsidization of local industry.

In this epoch of transcontinental railroad construction, the autocracy strove to prevent the Siberian frontier from becoming like the American West. The government outlawed real estate speculation; capped the size of landholdings; retained ownership of forests and railroads; restricted individual, noncommunal peasant farming; and refused calls for elective forms of local government. In one significant respect the two nations were similar: the Russian state confiscated millions of acres of land used by the Kazakhs and other indigenous peoples who stood in the way of white settlement.

The results were mixed. Five million peasants migrated to Siberia, nearly doubling the population by 1914. Despite tensions between old and new settlers, the rural economy boomed, and peasants enjoyed a living standard higher than the Russian norm. Cities along the railroad line also grew rapidly, and the foundations were laid for Siberian industrialization. On the other hand, the projection of Russian military power via the Trans-Siberian threatened Japanese interests and helped precipitate the disastrous Russo-Japanese War (1904–1905). The newly arrived railroad workers, miners, and factory laborers, often employed in miserable conditions, were susceptible to the political agitation carried out by exiled radicals. In the Revolution of 1905 and at the Lena goldfields in 1912, their working-class discontents exploded in strikes and rebellions that called into question the strength of the tsarist regime's hold over Siberia.

See also **Russia; Russo-Japanese War; Vladivostok.**

BIBLIOGRAPHY

Aust, Martin. "Rossia Siberica: Russian-Siberian History Compared to Medieval Conquest and Modern Colonialism." *Review* (Fernand Braudel Center) 27, no. 3 (2004): 181–205.

Bassin, Mark. "Inventing Siberia: Visions of the Russian East in the Early Nineteenth Century." *American Historical Review* 96, no. 3 (1991): 763–794.

Forsyth, James. *A History of the Peoples of Siberia: Russia's North Asian Colony, 1581–1990.* Cambridge, U.K., 1992.

Lincoln, W. Bruce. *The Conquest of a Continent: Siberia and the Russians.* New York, 1994.

Marks, Steven G. *Road to Power: The Trans-Siberian Railroad and the Colonization of Asian Russia, 1850–1917.* Ithaca, N.Y., 1991.

———. "Conquering the Great East: Kulomzin, Peasant Resettlement, and the Creation of Modern Siberia." In *Rediscovering Russia in Asia,* edited by Stephen Kotkin and David Wolff, 23–39. Armonk, N.Y., 1995.

Stephan, John J. *The Russian Far East: A History.* Stanford, Calif., 1994.

Wood, Alan, ed. *The History of Siberia: From Russian Conquest to Revolution.* London, 1991.

STEVEN G. MARKS

SICILIAN FASCI. The most striking features of Sicilian history in liberal Italy (1861–1922) are the development of the Mafia, peasant unrest, and the great migration to America. These three phenomena coalesced with peculiar dramatic unity in the 1890s in an ill-fated peasant movement known as the Sicilian Fasci (Leagues).

Most Sicilian peasants were outsiders in liberal Italy. They lacked the right to vote because they were poor and illiterate. (Suffrage was limited to property holders and those who could read and write.) They lacked market opportunities because the main source of employment, wheat farming, was dominated by the owners of vast estates (*latifondi*). Sicily became a social tinderbox in the early 1890s, when the national government granted radical freedoms—the rights to strike and to emigrate—without enacting suffrage and land reform to make peasants stakeholders in society.

The leagues' rise occurred between 1892 and 1893, during Giovanni Giolitti's first tenure as prime minister, a brief period when government tolerated an independent labor movement in the south. A handful of charismatic Sicilian socialists—among them Bernardino Verro in Corleone (heartland of *latifondi* and the Mafia)—rapidly founded the leagues, a federation of scores of workers' and peasants' associations. Impatient with the caution of artisans and workers in the coastal cities, the socialists made a strategic turn to the peasantry in the agrotowns of Sicily's harsh interior in 1893, sparking a four-month strike over agrarian contracts on the *latifondi*—modern Italy's first great peasant strike. Corleone quickly became the strategic center of the peasant movement and the epicenter of the strike wave thanks to Verro's charisma and hardnosed choices, including alliances with mafiosi.

On the eve of the strike, Verro accepted overtures from a Mafia group in Corleone, I Fratuzzi (Little Brothers) and became a member in order to give the strike teeth and protect himself from harm. He then placed several mafiosi, including a *capomafia* (the president of I Fratuzzi), on the Corleone league's executive committee. Concurrently, Verro recruited prominent mafiosi, notably Vito Cascio Ferro and Nunzio Giaimo, to senior positions in leagues in other towns.

Attorney General Giuseppe Sensales captured the logic of the situation: "The leaders of the Leagues, in order to induce the landowners to yield, decided to strike. However, this expedient, which works whenever there are strike funds, war chests for supporting the strikers, could not deliver any results in Sicily, where the peasants lack such means. Therefore [the Leagues] tried to achieve their aim by means of *intimidation* and *material violence*. And so one witnessed arson, destruction of property, dispersion of manure, and similar crimes" (p. 313). These crimes were committed with impunity thanks to collusion with mafiosi and the attendant *omertà* (code of silence). More broadly, the alliance with mafiosi made the leagues' threats credible. A Sicilian proverb of the period states, "If he can take what you have, give him what he wants."

If local mafia groups gave the leagues sharper teeth, the leagues gave broader structure to the mafia, which before then had been a very loosely integrated phenomenon. Palermo police commissioner Lucchesi observed that "crime has reached alarming levels, and I firmly believe that this state of affairs derives indeed from the Leagues' baleful action, for the underworld and the mafia have thereby become regimented and thus more effective at imposing themselves and in assuring impunity for perpetrators" (quoted in Alcorn 1999, pp. 272–273).

Authorities in Sicily, disoriented by the unprecedented unrest and hamstrung by *omertà*, had persistent difficulty in figuring out the movement's true aims. After nerve-wracking twists and turns in the strike, government mediation produced a compromise settlement, which soon collapsed because of overbidding by the leagues, which demanded "written acts of submission" from landowners. Faced with a challenge to their status on top of wage concessions, landowners responded with a lockout, despite widespread vandalism. Many peasants, probably a majority in the strike centers, were left without tenancies when the planting season ended in late November. At the same time, Giolitti's government fell, finally overtaken by a festering bank scandal.

In mid-December, during the transition to Francesco Crispi's new strongman government, the leagues lost control of the peasant movement as wildfires of protest against the *dazio consumo*—a despised excise tax on food and drink, levied at points of entry to the agrotowns—emerged in towns surrounding Palermo. The chaotic rebellion spread to the *latifondo* zone and beyond in late December. In a fateful shift from conflict with landowners over agrarian contracts to direct conflict with the state over taxes, crowds burned down tax-collection stations, pillaged government offices, and stoned troops, who in several instances fired upon demonstrators, killing scores. In January 1894, Crispi, unable to devise a peaceful solution, imposed martial law in Sicily and suppressed the leagues. Mafioso Nunzio Giaimo attempted to launch an insurrection, but repression and reaction held sway. Crispi tried to compensate the peasantry in two ways. First he proposed a land reform bill that went nowhere in the parliament of property holders, then he attempted a conquest of Ethiopia in 1896, partly in the hope of satisfying the peasantry's land hunger through colonial emigration, but he suffered humiliating military defeat.

The peasantry, left to its own devices by the leagues' defeat and by Crispi's failures, turned to emigration. Among the first to leave Corleone for America were mafiosi involved with the leagues. Vito Cascio Ferro, perhaps the most prominent mafioso in the movement, managed to pressure authorities in Palermo to put him in charge of granting emigration permits in the district of Corleone. Revolutionary mafiosi became pioneers and intermediaries of emigration, which quickly accelerated through the mechanisms of chain migration and became a flood at the turn of the century.

See also **Crispi, Francesco; Giolitti, Giovanni; Mafia; Sicily.**

BIBLIOGRAPHY

Alcorn, John. *Social Strife in Sicily, 1892–1894: The Rise and Fall of Peasant Leagues on the Latifondo before the Great Emigration.* New York, 1999.

———. "Revolutionary Mafiosi: Voice and Exit in the 1890s." In *L'associazionismo a Corleone: Un'inchiesta storica e sociologica,* edited by Paolo Viola and Titti Morello. Palermo, 2004. Archival documents, transcribed and annotated, pp. 1–93.

Renda, Francesco. *I Fasci siciliani, 1892–94.* Turin, 1977.

Rizzo, Rosanna. "Bernardino Verro: Luci e ombre di un dirigente contadino." In *L'associazionismo a Corleone: Un'inchiesta storica e sociologica,* edited by Paolo Viola and Titti Morello. Palermo, 2004.

Romano, Salvatore Francesco. *Storia dei Fasci siciliani.* Bari, Italy, 1959.

Sensales, Giuseppe. "Appunti sui Fasci dei Lavoratori." 1893. In *Fasci dei lavoratori (Saggi e Documenti),* by Massimo S. Ganci, 291–381. Caltanissetta-Rome, 1977.

JOHN ALCORN

SICILY. For Sicily, the experience of modernization was a complex and contentious experience. The Risorgimento in Sicily was characterized first by the old noble elite's struggle for autonomy from the Bourbon government in Naples, a struggle inspired in part by that government's attempt after 1815 to centralize, modernize, and generally improve the island's administration. Inevitably, this attempt threatened the traditional autonomy of the old elite and increased their resentment at, and opposition to, rule from Naples. Thus, the nobility's participation in the Sicilian Risorgimento was in many ways a defensive and conservative strategy. At the same time, however, a newly independent and sometimes conflicting movement emerged among less traditional groups demanding progressive and liberal reforms linked to similar liberal groups in Naples and elsewhere on the Italian peninsula. Finally, the island's politics also included revolutionary and conspiratorial groups. Some of these were inspired by Giuseppe Mazzini (1805–1872) and sought to establish a national unitary republic for the whole Italian peninsula, including Sicily. Others opposed Mazzini's leadership, and some were clearly socialist and anarchist. These political divisions were made more complicated by substantial regional differences, above all by a split between western Sicily (dominated by Palermo and by the autonomist movement) and eastern Sicily (centered on Messina and, increasingly, Catania, and more liberal), by the differences between these large coastal cities and the isolated villages of the interior and in the south of the island. While these disagreements provoked some of the most vibrant political and cultural debates in all of Risorgimento Italy, this lack of unity weakened the political effectiveness of opposition movements in Sicily.

This difficult political situation persisted after national unification in 1860–1861. Giuseppe Garibaldi's (1807–1882) famous invasion of Sicily with a thousand volunteers ("*i mille*") in the spring of 1860 was successful in overthrowing Bourbon rule in the island, and by the autumn in the whole of the Kingdom of the Two Sicilies as well. By claiming Sicily for "Italy and Victor Emmanuel," he also endorsed a unitary solution, while helping to exclude the Mazzinians. None of this, however, did anything to resolve the political divisions within Sicily and these divisions, as before, undermined the ability of Sicily's political leaders to speak for or defend the island's interests within the new Italian kingdom.

ECONOMY AND SOCIETY

Sicily's economic problems were in part those of uneven economic development. These were, in turn, a product of the great physical variations within this small island and the difficulty of establishing effective internal communications. During the nineteenth century the market-gardening regions of the plain of Catania and the north and west coasts, producing citrus fruits, vines, and olives, saw a rapid commercialization that was linked to foreign demand and foreign investment. By contrast, the vast cereal-growing estates (*latifondi*) of the Sicilian uplands and interior saw little or no commercialization, and the growing problem of soil exhaustion and erosion probably led to a decline in yields. In this way, economic growth in the nineteenth century reinforced the existing distinction between the relative wealth and sophistication of the plains, foothills, and cities of the coastal regions and the barren arid uplands of the interior. Moreover, the potential wealth offered by the development of sulfur mining in the interior (and Sicily had a virtual world monopoly in this period) was never realized. The mines were exploited by foreigners (largely the English), who used the political weight of their governments to frustrate attempts to refine the sulfur in Sicily and instead exported it in a crude state, with more profit to themselves. The land around the sulfur mines was also devastated by pollution, thus increasing the scarcity of productive land in the interior.

To these economic problems was added the extreme poverty of the population. Although the Bourbon government had tried to improve the lot of the Sicilian peasantry, through education and especially through land reform, these reforms failed and may well have been counterproductive. Land reform (essentially an attempt to redistribute some of the nobility's vast landholdings and to parcel out former common land among the peasantry) probably increased land hunger. In the event, much of the land that was made available was taken over by a new gentry or middle class and they proved, if anything, less entrepreneurial and more exploitative than their noble predecessors. The desperate state of the Sicilian peasantry was then exacerbated by rapid population growth, which increased pressure on the land.

John Goodwin, the British consul at Palermo in the early nineteenth century, translated the following description of the peasants "up country" by his friend, Francesco Ferrara:

> three fourths of the peasants, sallow, sickly and deformed, vegetate rather than live. Born to no other ends but to moisten the clods with the sweat of their brows, they feed upon herbs, clothe themselves in rags, and sleep huddled up together in smoky huts, amidst the stench of a dunghill. In winter they are shivering with cold; in summer they are burning with fever.

From a mood of relative acquiescence in the eighteenth century, the largely landless Sicilian peasants became, in the nineteenth, increasingly angry and rebellious. A great deal of their resentment was focused on land, on bad land which was rented out to them at high prices by unscrupulous landlords, and on land which had once been "common" and was now "usurped" (illegally seized and enclosed) by the same people. There was also growing discontent at the system of contracts and loans that were so designed to keep them permanently in debt to the landlord. The result was an explosion of violence in the Sicilian countryside, with the growth of banditry, land seizures, and destruction of property and, during the political revolutions of 1820, 1848–1849, and 1860, murderous assaults on the landlords and their representatives. Thus, to the political conflicts and economic difficulties of Risorgimento Sicily must be added the grave and growing problem of social unrest and crime.

CONTINUITY AND CHANGE

Through its revolution in 1860 and Garibaldi's successful invasion, Sicily had played a crucial role in the unification of Italy. Thereafter, Sicily's new political rulers—mostly moderate liberals from northern and central Italy—were confident that they would be able to resolve the political, economic, and social problems that beset this part of their kingdom. However, few of them knew anything about the Italy south of Rome, and fewer still had ever been there. While those who ventured south after 1860 were pleased by a seemingly eternal summer and by the beauty of the landscape, they were also shocked by an encounter with an alien culture and language. This sense of difference was reinforced by outbreaks of peasant violence and crime and by a series of popular revolts in Sicily, notably the Palermo revolt of 1866. In the

Children in the Sicilian countryside. Photograph by Wilhelm von Gloeden c. 1900. Mount Etna appears in the background. ©ALINARI ARCHIVES/CORBIS

years after unification the Italian south as a whole failed to develop economically at the same speed as parts of the north. Government reports from Sicily to the capital spoke of the "exceptional criminal tendencies" and "barbarism" of the local inhabitants. The situation in Sicily, according to one general, "was really something out of the Middle Ages"; both Sicily and the southern mainland were compared disparagingly to Africa and the rural poor to Bedouins. In this way, a distinctly racial edge crept into official discourse on the South, where it has remained—more or less hidden—ever since.

Italian unification accentuated southern Italy's internal divisions and made any kind of generalization more problematic than before. To Sicily, Italian unification brought greater administrative centralization, bigger police forces, better educa-

tion, infrastructural improvements, free trade, and increased political representation. These changes affected the different regions and social classes of Sicily in different ways. Sicilian deputies were elected to a new national parliament, but the electorate was only 2 percent of the total population. Palermo suffered economically from a further loss of its administrative responsibility but Catania benefited greatly from the introduction of free trade and the construction of railways. In general, the areas of the economy based on export (market gardening and sulfur mining) expanded, while free trade damaged Sicily's grain producers. The nobility, for the most part, gradually ceded their position of political (if not cultural) predominance; a commercial trading elite became more powerful in cities like Catania, Messina, and Trapani; while the new rural middle-classes acquired still more land, this time from the church, and took hold of local government, using its responsibilities for public works, policing, and taxation to create an intricate web of patronage and clientelism in their communities. The peasants were left no better off than before, and indeed had new demands made on them through military conscription and increased taxation.

MAKING ITALIANS?

From 1860 onward the Sicilian countryside was the scene of repeated cycles of revolt and repression. Between 1862 and 1868 the government organized six large-scale military operations to restore law and order, to enforce conscription and the payment of taxes, and to capture bandits and military deserters. Yet these operations were a failure and were marked by a refusal of the population to cooperate with the military. By the early 1870s crime and disorder reemerged once again. During the 1890s, amid widespread political and social chaos, Sicilian peasants formed agricultural unions (*fasci*) and began to win concessions from their landlords. However, the prime minister of Italy, Francesco Crispi (1819–1901), himself a Sicilian and an ex-revolutionary, saw the peasant unions as a threat to the government's alliance with the landlords. The unions were broken up and repressed with military force. Partly as a result of this failure, the Sicilian peasantry began to leave the land and to seek new ways of sustaining their families through emigration overseas.

In the early 1860s, moreover, the government found a new way of explaining and resolving the crisis in Sicily. In a letter of 1865, the prefect of Palermo claimed to have uncovered a conspiracy between political extremists and professional criminals. It was, he argued, this "so-called mafia"—an organization with its own laws, customs, and codes of behavior—that was responsible for the failure of government policy. Initially, this discovery helped justify government repression. Fairly soon, however, the government was to find an even better use for the criminals. From the late 1860s onward, the Palermo police began to use them as "middlemen," as a locally effective means of containing crime and maintaining order. After a change of government in 1876 (the "parliamentary revolu-

tion," whereby the Left came to power in Italy), the mafia emerged as a permanent shadow over public life in Sicily. The mafia assumed responsibility for negotiating compliance with government orders and for ensuring the success of government candidates in local elections, and they became involved in commercial activities as well, such as organizing labor markets and so on. Organized crime also provided a crucial link in the web of corruption and clientelism that increasingly characterized politics in Sicily, which tied this area of the Italian periphery to the central government in Rome. The mafia also came to dominate the public's perception of Sicily and its problems. Yet the origins of the mafia were largely political; they are to be found in the complex struggles of nineteenth-century Sicily and in the failure of liberal policy in the 1860s.

See also **Crispi, Francesco; Emigration; Garibaldi, Giuseppe; Italy; Kingdom of the Two Sicilies; Mafia; Naples; Sicilian Fasci.**

BIBLIOGRAPHY

Aymard, Maurice, and Giuseppe Giarrizzo, eds. *La Sicilia.* Turin, 1987.

Blok, Anton. *The Mafia of a Sicilian Village, 1860–1960: A Study of Violent Peasant Entrepreneurs.* Oxford, U.K., 1974.

Fiume, Giovanna. "Bandits, Violence and the Organization of Power in Sicily in the Early Nineteenth Century." In *Society and Politics in the Age of the Risorgimento. Essays in Honour of Denis Mack Smith,* edited by John A. Davis and Paul Ginsborg. Cambridge, U.K., 1991.

Smith, Denis Mack. *A History of Sicily: Modern Sicily after 1713.* London, 1968.

Riall, Lucy. *Sicily and the Unification of Italy: Liberal Policy and Local Power, 1859–1866.* Oxford, U.K., and New York, 1998.

———. "Elites in Search of Authority: Political Power and Social Order in Nineteenth-Century Sicily." *History Workshop Journal* 55 (2003): 25–46.

LUCY RIALL

SIEMENS, WERNER VON (1816–1892), German engineer and businessman.

The brilliant inventor and scientist Werner Siemens (the "von" was added in 1888) was also a visionary entrepreneur. Revolutionary changes, including industrialization, marked all spheres of life during Siemens's era. Germany was transformed, especially in the second half of the century, from a still largely agrarian country into one of the world's leading industrial nations. Even as the political and economic conditions of the age provided a fertile environment for the successful expansion of the young company Siemens & Halske, the inventions of Werner von Siemens and the economic activity of the company he founded also shaped their age.

Werner von Siemens was born as the fourth of fourteen children on 13 December 1816 to a tenant farmer and his wife in Lenthe near Hanover. The formal schooling typical of the upper middle class was not accessible to his family, and Siemens left school without taking the final exams in 1834 in order to join the Prussian army and so gain access to engineering training. His future work in the electrical engineering field was given a solid basis by his three years at the artillery and engineering school in Berlin.

Rapid, reliable communication was important to the military. In 1847 Siemens constructed a pointer telegraph that was a great improvement on previous equipment. After this early success, Siemens and the master mechanic Johann Georg Halske founded the Siemens & Halske Telegraph Construction Company in Berlin in 1847. Siemens left the army in 1849 in order to devote himself to the company.

Siemens & Halske, which began operating internationally very soon after its foundation, advanced from a small precision-engineering workshop to one of the world's leading electrical firms within a few decades. Siemens & Halske received its first large and highly prestigious state contract, for the building of a telegraph line between Berlin and Frankfurt am Main, in 1848. When its relationship with the Prussian Telegraph Administration deteriorated, the young company turned its focus to foreign markets in order to survive. Business improved in 1851 when Siemens & Halske received a commission to build the Russian telegraph network. English contracts also supported the company's continued success. Siemens constantly sought worldwide recognition of his inventions and enterprises, showing that he had an international vision rare among his contemporaries.

Siemens devoted himself to scientific research while maintaining his firm's business. Probably his most important contribution to electrical engineering came in 1866 when he discovered the dynamo-electric principle, which paved the way for electricity to be used as a source of power. Before the dynamo machine appeared on the scene, the production of large currents was dependent on batteries that quickly ran down or on magneto-electric machines with permanent magnets of limited efficiency. Siemens immediately recognized the potential economic impact of his discovery and in 1867 registered patents in Germany and England to ensure that he would profit from its implementation. Heavy-current engineering developed at a breathtaking pace on the basis of Siemens's experiments: the first electric streetlights were installed in Berlin and the first electric railway was presented at the Berlin Trade Fair in 1879, the first electric elevator was built in Mannheim in 1880, and the world's first electric streetcar went into service in Berlin-Lichterfelde in 1881. *Elektrotechnik*, the expression for electrical engineering that was coined by Siemens, became synonymous with its inventor's name.

In addition to his technical innovations and daring business undertakings, Siemens adopted social initiatives that gave him a reputation as a progressive. He introduced the stocktaking bonus in 1866, far ahead of his time. With this system he gave the employees of Siemens & Halske a share of the jointly achieved profits in addition to their regular earnings. In 1872, more than a decade before the introduction of statutory requirements governing provisions for pensions and surviving dependants, he founded a company pensions scheme. He saw such measures as a means of reinforcing employees' loyalty to the company and described this mixture of paternalistic responsibility and entrepreneurial calculation as "healthy self-interest."

Siemens was also a politician, serving as a member of the Prussian state assembly from 1862 to 1866 as an elected representative of the German Progressive Party (Deutsche Fortschrittspartei). He became a member of the Reich Patent Office in 1877 to secure the continued protection of patents. The Electrical Engineering Society, which he helped found in 1879, encouraged technical universities to introduce electrical-engineering programs.

Siemens was a successful entrepreneur not only because he discovered fundamental technical principles but also because he considered the whole process from invention to marketable product and system solutions. Siemens was frequently honored for his services to both science and society during his lifetime and was raised to the nobility by Emperor Frederick III (r. 1888) in 1888. Although he officially retired from the business in 1890, Siemens still had an important influence on his company until his death on 6 December 1892.

See also **Engineers; Germany; Industrial Revolution, Second; Science and Technology.**

BIBLIOGRAPHY

Primary Sources

Matschoss, Conrad. *Werner von Siemens: Ein kurzgefasstes Lebensbild nebst einer Auswahl seiner Briefe.* 2 vols. Berlin, 1916.

Siemens, Werner von. *Scientific and Technical Papers of Werner von Siemens.* 2 vols. London, 1892 and 1895. Translation of *Wissenschaftliche und Technische Arbeiten,* 2 vols (1891).

———. *Recollections.* Translated by William Chatterton Coupland. London and Munich, 1983. Translation of *Lebenserinnerungen* (1955), new edition edited by Wilfried Feldenkirchen (2004).

Secondary Sources

Feldenkirchen, Wilfried. *Werner von Siemens: Inventor and International Entrepreneur.* Columbus, Ohio, 1994.

WILFRIED FELDENKIRCHEN

SIEYÈS, EMMANUEL-JOSEPH (1748–1836), French revolutionary politician and writer.

The Abbé Emmanuel-Joseph Sieyès is synonymous with the French Revolution. He advocated voting reform in the Estates-General, publishing his famous pamphlet, *What Is the Third Estate?*, in January 1789. Elected to the Third Estate, Sieyès made the transition from writer to politician, serving in the National Assembly and later in the Convention before entering the executive branch as a director in 1799. Unhappy with the constitution and the direction of the revolution, he plotted with a number of former and current politicians, including General Napoleon Bonaparte (later

Napoleon I, r. 1804–1814/15) to overthrow the Directory. Sieyès's active role in French politics came to an end shortly after the coup of 18 Brumaire 1799. Sieyès was ultimately more influential as a writer and political commentator than as a politician, and although he was well respected by his contemporaries, he was unable to carry that respect over to his political career.

Sieyès was born into a middle class family in Fréjus, on the Mediterranean. He entered the clergy and studied at the Sorbonne, but his interests extended far beyond the Catholic Church. He eschewed religious dogma and embraced the intellectual climate of the Enlightenment, accepting the general precepts of the social contract and representative government. The Royal Order in Council (5 July 1788) led to intense debate over the structure of the future Estates-General. Sieyès joined the discourse, producing his first pamphlet, *Essay on Privilege,* in which he attacked the feudal structure of the proposed legislative body.

His assault upon privilege continued in his most famous work, *What Is the Third Estate?* Elections for the Estates-General were a month away, and Sieyès's pamphlet challenged not only the prevailing social and political structure but the right of the nobility to be represented at all. He argued that the Third Estate constituted "nineteen-twentieths" of the nation and comprised the productive sectors of society. He went so far as to reject the Estates-General in favor of an elected national assembly.

Sieyès determined to effect change and was elected to the Estates-General. He was a popular figure in the Third Estate and was instrumental in the creation of the National Assembly at the end of June 1789. The triumph of his political ideas brought him to a position of intellectual prominence in the assembly. Although he eventually joined the Jacobin Club, Sieyès was not a radical. As a member of the clergy he was none too pleased with the Civil Constitution in 1790 but ultimately voted for it. He remained in the legislature when the National Assembly became the Convention. His moderate stance and reputation in drawing up the Constitution of 1791 allowed him to weather the radical revolution during 1793 and 1794, but he accomplished this only by supporting the Committee of Public Safety.

The fall of Robespierre on 9 Thermidor (27 July 1794) gave Sieyès the opportunity to reemerge as a leading intellectual figure. He did not advocate universal suffrage, and the former revolutionary dictatorship only reinvigorated his opposition to it. He also rejected the concept of a strong executive branch and through his participation in writing the Constitution of 1795 was able to put his opposition into effect. During the Directory, he was a member of the Council of Five Hundred. His frustration with the ineffectiveness of the government led him to support the coup of Prairial (1799) and enter the executive as a director.

Although he became part of the executive, Sieyès was concerned about the Jacobinization of the legislature and had never been comfortable with the political system of the Directory. He plotted its demise in favor of a new constitutional government of his own design. Sieyès hoped that the coup of 18 Brumaire could restore a sense of direction to the stale revolution, but in doing so it introduced Napoleon Bonaparte into the equation. Sieyès underestimated Bonaparte's ambitions and overestimated his own reputation. By the beginning of January 1800, Napoleon easily eclipsed Sieyès as author of the new constitution and head of government. Sieyès took a back seat as one of the three consuls but was relegated thereafter to the Senate, where he remained until 1815.

Sieyès never again achieved the level of success he had found through his writings of 1788 and 1789. He was never a radical and certainly not a consummate Jacobin, even during the year of the Terror. He argued against royal veto power in 1790 and 1791 and did not support universal suffrage but preferred the Enlightenment notion of the "responsible"—which is to say, the propertied—serving in government. He was wary of a strong executive, be it a monarchy or a revolutionary committee. He suffered, however, from intellectual arrogance and was never able to rectify his constitutional theories with practical realities.

See also **French Revolution; Napoleon.**

BIBLIOGRAPHY

Clapham, J. H. *The Abbé Sieyès: An Essay in the Politics of the French Revolution.* London, 1912.

Sewell, William Hamilton. *A Rhetoric of Bourgeois Revolution: The Abbé Sieyès and* What Is the Third Estate? Durham, N.C., 1994.

FREDERICK C. SCHNEID

SILVER AGE. The Russian term *Silver Age*, or *Serebrianyi vek*, is taken from a classification in Latin literature and refers to a period in Russian literature from the 1890s through the first two decades of the twentieth century. Scholars have used the term interchangeably with the word *modernism*, although the Silver Age differs from modernism by evoking a comparison with the Golden Age of Russian literature, dominated by the figure of Alexander Pushkin. Some scholars have questioned the appropriateness of the term *Silver Age* to refer to this extremely rich period in Russian literature, because it would seem to imply a decline from the artistic advancements of the Golden Age. Because of the decadent connotations of the term and the lack of agreement particularly among early-twentieth-century scholars in their usage of the term, the Slavic scholar Omry Ronen set out to expose "the fallacy of the Silver Age." Nevertheless, the term *Silver Age* has gained wide currency among Slavic scholars both in Russia and in the West. Although it is usually used to refer to turn-of-the-century and early-twentieth-century Russian literature, its usage has also expanded to include Russian art of the same period and, in particular, the World of Art (*Mir iskusstva*) group, whose members included Léon Bakst, Alexandre Benois, Sergei Diaghilev, and Konstantin Somov.

ONSET AND DEVELOPMENT OF THE PERIOD

The onset of the Silver Age in Russian literature can be identified with the emergence of the Russian symbolist movement at the turn of the century. Formed in reaction to realism and positivism, Russian symbolism was largely a poetic movement heavily influenced by the poetry of Charles Baudelaire and the French symbolists, as well as the philosophy of Friedrich Nietzsche and the Russian religious thinker Vladimir Soloviev. Scholars have generally tended to divide the movement into two distinct generations. The first generation, which included such figures as Konstantin Balmont, Valery Bryusov, Zinaida Gippius,

Dmitri Merezhkovsky, and Fyodor Sologub, emerged at the turn of the century and has been associated with decadence and "art for art's sake." The second generation, whose members included Alexander Blok, Andrei Bely, and Vyacheslav Ivanov, began publishing just prior to the failed Revolution of 1905, and has usually been considered to be more mystical in orientation and indebted to the philosophy of Soloviev and especially to his concept of the Divine Sophia. Scholars have begun to question this rather rigid division of the symbolists into decadents and mystics. For all their differences, both generations of writers envisioned themselves as prophets and demonstrated a growing sense of cultural catastrophe, conditioned not only by the events of 1905 but also by their reading of the Book of Revelation. And both generations exhibited a neo-Romantic tendency to blur the boundaries between life and art. This predisposition was epitomized in the British context by the figure of Oscar Wilde and has come to be known in Russian scholarship as life-creation (*zhiznetvorchestvo*).

ACMEISM

After the final crisis in Russian symbolism in 1910, the Russian symbolist movement ceased to exist, although individual symbolists continued to publish and to flourish. Two new poetic movements emerged around this time, acmeism and futurism. Important precursors to the acmeists were the poets Innokenty Annensky and Mikhail Kuzmin. Whereas the symbolists had privileged poetry's relationship to the world beyond and to music and had imagined the poet as a priest or prophet, the acmeists emphasized poetry's connection to this world and to Logos and imagined the artist first and foremost as a craftsperson. A much less unified movement than symbolism, acmeism, or adamism as it was also known, included among its ranks the renowned poets Anna Akhmatova, Nikolai Gumilev, and Osip Mandelstam. Each of these poets developed a unique style that makes it difficult to identify one dominant acmeist poetics. Similar to the Anglo-American imagist H. D., Akhmatova exhibited a predilection in her early years for terse poetic dialogues that interrogated the problem of love and romantic relationships. In contrast, the acmeist poet and theoretician Gumilev was heavily influenced by the poetry of Théophile

Gautier and embraced exotic and Eastern themes in his poetry. Mandelstam, who has been compared to T. S. Eliot and Ezra Pound, professed his "nostalgia for world culture" and developed a highly allusive poetics that paid homage to a wide range of poetic precursors both ancient and modern. In spite of the acmeists' emphasis on cultural tradition, they eschewed bourgeois values, frequenting the Stray Dog (*Brodyachaya sobaka*), a St. Petersburg café that was also a favorite haunt of the futurists.

FUTURISM

While the acmeists exhibited a reverence for the past and for cultural tradition, the Russian futurists declared it necessary "to throw Pushkin, [Fyodor] Dostoyevsky, [Leo] Tolstoy, etc. overboard from the Ship of Modernity" in their 1912 manifesto "A Slap in the Face of Public Taste" (*Poshchechina obshchestvennomu vkusu*). Although by and large Russian futurism developed independently from Italian futurism, it shared with the latter and other European avant-garde movements a fascination with the modern and a desire to *épater le bourgeois* (shock the bourgeoisie). A no more unified movement than acmeism, Russian futurism counted more than fifty poets among its ranks. Among its most prominent figures were David Burliuk, Elena Guro, Velimir Khlebnikov, Alexander Kruchenykh, Vladimir Mayakovsky, and the young Boris Pasternak, many of whom also distinguished themselves as visual artists. While urban themes were popular among the futurists, they also exhibited a fascination with primitivism. Like the acmeists, the futurists sought to reinvigorate poetic language, valorizing the power of the word. Some of the futurists even strove to create a transrational language (*zaumnyi yazyk*). Although the futurists expressed no more reverence for their symbolist precursors than they had for the great Russian writers of the previous century, they shared with the symbolists a willingness to acknowledge the mystical aspects of language, as well as a fascination with self-creation. In fashioning the self, however, the futurists were much more invested in shocking the public, and they frequently staged outrageous public performances and literary provocations.

Although many of the major figures of the Silver Age identified themselves with the main literary movements of the period, there were also a great number of talented writers who were not defined by any one artistic movement. Among these artists were the female poets Allegro (Poliksena Solovieva), Mirra Lokhvitskaya, and Sofia Parnok; the peasant poets Sergei Yesenin, and Nikolai Klyuev; the prose writers Ivan Bunin, Nadezhda Teffi, Alexei Remizov, and Vasily Rozanov; as well as the outstanding female poet Marina Tsvetayeva, who combined daring verbal pyrotechnics, similar to those of the futurists, with an interest in myth.

END OF THE PERIOD AND ONGOING INFLUENCE

After the October Revolution of 1917, many of the writers who made their artistic debut in the first decade and a half of the century found it difficult to continue living and working in Soviet Russia. In August 1921 Blok, who had emerged as the foremost modernist poet, died, and Gumilev was executed by the Bolsheviks for alleged counter-revolutionary activities, marking the end of Russia's Silver Age for many scholars. While some writers such as Akhmatova and Pasternak continued living and writing in Soviet Russia, others such as Yesenin, Mandelstam, Mayakovsky, and Tsvetayeva either committed suicide or died at the hands of the Soviets. Still others such as Nina Berberova, Bunin, Gippius, Ivanov, Vladislav Khodasevich, and Merezhkovsky managed to keep alive the artistic traditions of the Silver Age in exile.

In spite of its relatively short duration, the Silver Age was a vibrant period in Russian literature and culture. While Russia's Golden Age was dominated by the figure of Pushkin, the Silver Age was more heterogeneous. If there was any one poet within the Silver Age to assume the role of successor to the father of Russian literature, Pushkin, it would have to be Blok who frequently fashioned himself as a child of his generation and whose highly mythologized death from "lack of air" following the revolution conferred upon him the consecrated status of poetic son. But the richness of the Silver Age is exemplified by the fact that there were a number of talented poets who vied for the role of literary heir to Pushkin. Among the major contenders were Akhmatova, Mandelstam, Pasternak, and Tsvetayeva, poets who now enjoy a wide readership both in and outside Russia. Although the political situation throughout much of the Soviet period often made it difficult to access the works of many of the writers of the Silver Age, the onset of perestroika in the mid-1980s and the collapse of the Soviet Union in 1991 has resulted in a renewed interest in this period. In the early twenty-first century, the Silver Age is undergoing a critical reevaluation in Russia comparable to that experienced by the Golden Age in the early twentieth century.

See also **Blok, Alexander; Futurism; Pushkin, Alexander; Soloviev, Vladimir; Symbolism.**

BIBLIOGRAPHY

Azadovski, Konstantin. "Russia's Silver Age in Today's Russia." *Surfaces* 9, article 101.2 (15 December 2001). Available at http://www.pum.umontreal.ca/revues/surfaces/vol9/vol9TdM.html.

Bowlt, John E. *The Silver Age: Russian Art of the Early Twentieth Century and the "World of Art" Group.* Newtonville, Mass., 1979.

Elsworth, John, ed. *The Silver Age in Russian Literature: Selected Papers from the Fourth World Congress for Soviet and East European Studies, Harrogate, 1990.* New York, 1992.

Gasparov, Boris, Robert P. Hughes, and Irina Paperno, eds. *Cultural Mythologies of Russian Modernism: From the Golden Age to the Silver Age.* Berkeley, Calif., 1992.

Kalb, Judith E., and J. Alexander Ogden, eds., with the collaboration of I. G. Vishnevetsky. *Russian Writers of the Silver Age, 1890–1925.* Vol. 295 of *Dictionary of Literary Biography.* Detroit, Mich., 2004.

Makovskii, Sergei. *Na Parnase "Serebrianogo veka."* Munich, 1962. Reprint, Moscow, 2000.

Ronen, Omry. *The Fallacy of the Silver Age in Twentieth-Century Russian Literature.* Amsterdam, 1997.

Terras, Victor. *Poetry of the Silver Age: The Various Voices of Russian Modernism.* Translated by Alexander Landman. Dresden, Germany, 1998.

JENIFER PRESTO

SIMMEL, GEORG (1858–1918), German sociologist.

Georg Simmel is now primarily known as one of the founders of sociology and as a brilliant commentator on the emergence of modernity in nineteenth-century Europe. He was born into a Jewish middle class family in Berlin, a city where he spent most of his life and that he deeply loved. While very much appreciated by his contemporaries, Simmel had a notoriously difficult academic career.

At the University of Berlin, Simmel studied ethnography, history, philosophy, psychology, and art history. Both his first dissertation (1881) and his second dissertation to qualify as a lecturer (*Habilitation*; 1885) were on the philosophy of Immanuel Kant. From 1885 to 1914, when he finally succeeded in getting a full professorship at the somewhat marginal University of Strasbourg (in philosophy), Simmel worked as an unpaid lecturer at the University of Berlin. Although he was soon known all over Europe as well as in the United States, his colleagues at the University of Berlin kept blocking Simmel's academic career. One important reason for this was their anti-Semitism; other reasons were that Simmel refused to attach himself to a single academic discipline and that he had little taste for academic formalities. As an example of the latter, it is often mentioned that his books and articles typically lack references and footnotes.

Simmel wrote in a variety of fields and on a variety of topics, and altogether he produced more than twenty books and two hundred articles. The topics that he covered ranged from Rembrandt, Goethe, and Nietzsche to psychology, moral philosophy, and philosophy of history. One central theme in many of these writings is Simmel's fascination with the work of Immanuel Kant, especially his epistemology. Kant's notion that one should distinguish between the forms of the human mind and its contents plays a major role not only in Simmel's philosophy but also in his sociology and his approach to modern culture. Another important theme in Simmel's work is his emphasis on the individual and his belief that the true meaning of culture is to develop the individual.

Since his death, Simmel has mainly been cast as a sociologist, and his two works *The Philosophy of Money* (1900) and *Sociology* (1908) are today regarded as classics in the field of sociology. The most important of these is *Sociology,* which contains Simmel's famous program for sociology as well as a dazzling set of illustrations of what a sociological analysis may look like. *Sociology* is more than seven hundred pages long and covers the topics of faithfulness, fashion, adornment, the stranger, and much, much more.

In the introductory theoretical chapter to *Sociology,* Simmel states that sociology should deal with *interaction* and in particular with *the social forms* that these interactions create. The content of these forms has to be taken into account but is primarily studied by the other social sciences, such as economics, history, and psychology. As examples of forms of interaction, Simmel mentions conflict, sociability, and subordination and superordination. A concrete phenomenon usually consists of several forms of interactions.

One of the most famous chapters in *Sociology* is entitled "The Quantitative Determination of Groups"; Simmel here suggests that numbers may influence the social structure of groups. When a group, for example, goes from having two members (a dyad) to three members (a triad), it changes dramatically. A majority can now be formed, and one member may play the other two members against each other (*tertius gaudens*). Modern network analysis often includes Simmel among its founders.

The Philosophy of Money can be characterized as a mixture of philosophy, cultural analysis, and economic sociology. According to Simmel, money is closely related to the cultural temper of modern society, which he characterizes as relativistic and restless. Money equalizes all values and also sets things in perpetual motion. Sociological insights in *The Philosophy of Money* include the observation that trust is central to the modern economy and that money is only as valid as the political authority that vouches for its value.

Simmel's work is extremely rich in ideas and highly enjoyable to read. While Simmel had few disciples in the ordinary sense of the word, he nonetheless influenced many intellectuals. He was well aware of the special influence he had on other thinkers, and has famously characterized it in the following way:

> I know that I shall die without spiritual heirs (and that is good). The estate I leave is like cash distributed among many heirs, each of which puts his share to use in some trade that is compatible with *his* nature but which can no longer be recognized as coming from that estate.

See also **Durkheim, Émile; Modernism; Sociology; Weber, Max.**

BIBLIOGRAPHY

Frisby, David. *Georg Simmel*. London, 2002.

Frisby, David, ed. *Georg Simmel: Critical Assessments*. 3 vols. 1994, London.

Köhnke, Klaus Christian. *Der junge Simmel*. Frankfurt am Main, Germany, 1996.

Poggi, Gianfranco. *Money and the Modern Mind: Georg Simmel's Philosophy of Money*. Berkeley, Calif., 1993.

RICHARD SWEDBERG

SISMONDI, JEAN-CHARLES LEONARD DE (1773–1842), Swiss economist and historian.

Jean-Charles Leonard Simonde, who adopted the name de Sismondi, constituted a bridge between the old and the postrevolutionary Europe. Eccentric in life, interests, and politics, he crossed national, disciplinary, and political borders. A brilliant economist, Sismondi was also, at the same or different times, a venerated historian, amateur politician, literary scholar, novelist, agronomist, and constitutionalist.

Sismondi was convinced that his constitutional studies, which showed in essence that constitution and laws lie at the base of liberty and determine the character of a people and citizenship, had real impact on Europe's political ideas. *Recherches sur les constitutions des peuples libres* (Inquiries into the constitutions of free nations; begun in 1796 and published in the 1830s), informed the project of Napoleon's liberal constitution that Sismondi—a republican and an opponent of Napoleon's dictatorial rule—helped Benjamin Constant in drafting in 1815.

Sismondi's contemporaries saw him above all as a historian of civic patriotism and active participation. Inquiries into the constitutions of the Italian republics led him to study their history, which resulted in his most remarkable historical work, *Histoire des républiques italiennes au Moyen Age* (History of the Italian republics in the Middle Ages), a "sixteen-volume hymn to the liberties of the medieval commune." From the appearance of the first volumes in 1807 (the whole cycle took until 1818 to complete), *History* was acclaimed as the founding work of a new historiography and Romantic nationalism. This detailed study traces the development of the Italian communes during the Middle Ages, their flourishing during the Renaissance (understood as the rebirth of freedom), and their subsequent decadence under the Medicis' tyranny, with public morality in decline and the pursuit of wealth replacing political involvement. In those free self-governed civic republics Sismondi found the origins of liberalism, whose fundamental tenets were that liberty is gained and defended through struggle; that freedom from political tyranny is inseparable from freedom from social misery; and that creativity and genius flourish only among free people.

Among Italians, *History* achieved an instant cult status. At the time when the movement toward Risorgimento (Italian national unification) was beginning to search for a past usable as a model for national regeneration, this book conceived Italy's civilization in a unitary way, integrating culture and politics. By representing Italy's history as a history of freedom, it became a founding text for a Risorgimento ideology.

In the same period, Sismondi turned his attention to the literatures of southern Europe. His approach was consonant with Madame de Staël's (1766–1817) historical and relational notion of literature as a mirror of a nation's esprit. Published starting in 1813, *De la littérature du midi de l'Europe* (*Historical View of the Literature of the South of Europe*) subordinated theory and literary criticism to historical exposition and related literature to politics, institutions, and national character.

Sismondi the economist first rose to international fame in 1803 with *De la richesse commerciale; ou, Principes d'économie politique appliqués à la législation du commerce* (On commercial wealth; or, principles of political economy applied to the legislation of commerce). It was basically the first comprehensive exposition of the doctrine of Adam Smith in a language other than English; in addition, it was perceived as opposing Napoleon's "system" in politics and economy. Instantly famous, Sismondi was acclaimed as the faithful interpreter of Smith. But it would be the "second Sismondi," the heterodox, who would make a lasting impact on economic sciences.

After years devoted to other concerns, Sismondi returned to the mechanisms of economy in the years

1817 to 1819, after the "general glut" made him realize the extent of social misery among industrial workers. Unemployment, hunger, sixteen-hour workdays, child labor, urban crime, violence, and class conflict at an unprecedented level were signs of disequilibrium, itself an unavoidable consequence of an uncontrolled production of commodities driven exclusively by the desire to accumulate wealth. Thus came Sismondi's final "conversion" from laissez-faire to the economics for the common good, marked by his *Nouveaux principes d'économie politique; ou, De la richesse dans ses rapports avec la population* (1819; *New Principles of Political Economy; or, Of Wealth in Its Relation to Population*), a book that later both Karl Marx and Vladimir Lenin would consider his most important contribution to political economy. *New Principles* is a critique of the capitalist system and of the discipline of political economy. The system of liberal economy—free market, self-interest, invisible hand, competition, technological progress—is blamed for bringing about a society that hinders rather than promotes general happiness. In this system, where the pursuit of wealth takes precedence over people and the majority has no share in the accumulated wealth, limitless production has become a goal in itself.

Sismondi believed that political economy had been and could again become a science of public happiness, of society and of government. So he believed it was in Adam Smith's "true doctrine," concerned with social utility and collective welfare. But in the half-century following the publication of Smith's *Wealth of Nations* (1776), political economy degenerated into a science concerned exclusively with the creation of wealth.

Sismondi's posthumous fortunes changed several times. His historical and literary studies seemed entirely forgotten, while his economic analysis, inspired by moral principle, stirred a strong interest, though almost exclusively among Marxists (Marx himself argued with Sismondi through *Das Kapital*). From that period dates the representation of Sismondi's thought as petit bourgeois, utopian, and backward looking, for Lenin the bad inspiration of Russian populists and what György Lukács would later name "romantic anticapitalism." Some dissident thinkers, however, considered Sismondi as a founder of the future

Sozialpolitik, and there has always existed a consistent following of Sismondi the agronomist, the prophet of the Tuscan *mezzadria* sharecropping system, as a harmonious solution for all rural societies.

See also **Agricultural Revolution; Liberalism; Marx, Karl; Staël, Germaine de.**

BIBLIOGRAPHY

Salis, Jean-Rodolphe de. *Sismondi (1773–1842): La vie et l'oeuvre d'un cosmopolite philosophe.* Paris, 1932.

MARTA PETRUSEWICZ

SISTER REPUBLICS. The term *sister republics* denotes those states set up in the 1790s by the invading armies of Revolutionary France. The institutions of these republics were remodeled along the lines of republican France, usually to the point of direct imitation, and their governments were staffed by professed supporters of the new French regime, referred to as "Jacobins" in older historiography and more accurately as "patriots" at the time, because they seldom equated to the French Montagnard faction of the Terror period of 1793 to 1794, and, as foreigners, were often regarded as suspicious by that regime. The sister republics were all west European states, often with names taken from the classical past. They ranged from the Batavian Republic (the former Dutch Republic/United Provinces) in the north to the Parthenopean Republic (the mainland section of the Kingdom of Naples) in the south.

THE REVOLUTIONARY HERITAGE

The origins of this particular kind of specifically ideological expansion are found in two elements of the early phases of the French Revolutionary Wars, which began in 1792. At the outset of the war between Revolutionary France and the Holy Roman Empire, the French Revolutionary government had the stated aim of helping any people, anywhere, who wished to overthrow their existing rulers and to establish a regime based on the principles of the Declaration of the Rights of Man and of the Citizen, propounded in 1789. The French declared themselves ready to support revolts in this cause, by force. This doctrine—described by its proponents as "war on the castle and peace upon the cottage"—had been encouraged by many foreign politicians and agitators of revolutionary principles, who had taken refuge in Paris from 1789 onward, usually after being persecuted at home. The patriot "Anacharsis" Cloots, driven out of the Austrian Netherlands (now Belgium) for his part in the anti-Austrian Vonckist revolt of 1789, was the most vociferous among them, but they also included the Englishman Thomas Paine, the author of *Common Sense* and *The Rights of Man,* who had behaved in similar fashion in the early stages of the American Revolution, and Peter Ochs, a Swiss. Cloots did not see his homeland become a sister republic; it was annexed directly to France, a victim of another revolutionary doctrine, that of "natural frontiers," which placed the Austrian Netherlands on the wrong side of the Rhine to qualify as a sister republic. Paine was elected "deputy for the human race" by the National Assembly—and later jailed by the Terrorists as an enemy agent—but did not head an English sister republic. The agitation of these figures was crucial, however, in convincing the French government of 1792 to 1793, led by Jacques-Pierre Brissot and the Girondin faction, that the French would be welcomed elsewhere in western Europe as liberators. At this stage, only the future Terrorist, Maximilien Robespierre, refrained from enthusiasm for the creation of prospective sister republics, noting that "No one likes armed missionaries." Generally, he was proved more correct than Cloots or the Girondins.

THE POLITICAL LIVES OF THE SISTER REPUBLICS

The sister republics had three major failings: they were brought into being only as a result of war, with all its attendant horrors and disruptions; they were foreign in origin—and more specifically, too novel in character—to most of those who became their "citizens"; above all, their resources were quickly appropriated by the French armies, as the basis of the Revolution's military strategy of "living off the land." For ordinary people, the creation of a sister republic was the result of invasion, rape, and pillage, and their institutionalization brought heavy taxation and conscription—"the blood tax." Whatever innovations and improvements the governments of the sister republics managed to introduce during the 1790s, they had to labor under

French military occupation, and served as little more than milk cows for the armies of the country their rulers referred to as "the Great Nation."

It was for the last of these reasons that, despite the narrow support they attracted, the French could still be drawn to the concept of sister republics throughout the 1790s. The last such plan, in 1798, was for Ireland, which would have proved a useful "back door" for an invasion of Britain. In 1796 a French force had been sent to the southern coast of Ireland, but was driven back by bad weather. But when the Irish patriots, centered on the Society of United Irishmen led by Wolfe Tone, rose in 1798, they did so alone. This example is indicative of how French attitudes to potential sister republics had shifted in the light of the indigenous resistance they created: Early French optimism had given way to pragmatism that bordered on cynicism, in that France would commit troops only if Tone's organization initiated a reasonably successful rebellion, sustained by indigenous support. When the rebellion failed, the French held back.

A year later, the Parthenopean Republic in southern Italy collapsed in the face of widespread, popular, clerical-led resistance. Here, a peasant army (the so-called Army of the Holy Faith) drawn from Calabria and led by Cardinal Fabrizio Ruffo made common cause with the *lazzaroni,* the working classes of Naples, to destroy the republic without foreign troops. In Piedmont, in northwestern Italy, the short-lived republic of 1798 to 1799, set up during a disastrous French military retreat, was also assailed by huge peasant risings in support of the advancing Austro-Russian armies; after a brief flirtation with a revived Piedmontese "Consulate," the French opted for full, direct annexation. The year 1799 endures as "the black year" among progressive Italians, just as 1798 is a tragic landmark for Irish secularist republicans. For the French at the time, these were also lessons in caution, marking the sister republics as a phenomenon of a particular period of the French Revolution.

The Batavian Republic was the first sister republic to be created, in 1795. It was followed by the Cispadane, which was set up in late 1796 by Napoleon and was carved out of Papal and Austrian territory south of the river Po. The Cisalpine, centered on the Austrian-ruled Duchy of Milan—Lombardy—was created in June 1797, at which time the Cispadane was merged into it. Also created in 1797 were the Ligurian and Helvetic republics, followed by the Roman (1798) and the Parthenopean (1799). Plans for a sister republic in the Rhineland came to nothing, the same fate as the "Irish Republic" of 1798. All were artificial creations, ideologically, but some were built on more solid foundations than others. The Helvetic and Batavian republics had strong historical roots; Helvetica is still the official name of Switzerland in the Romansh language. They were created in established political units, both of which had real, if nonrevolutionary, republican traditions. The Dutch had seen a revolution of their own—the "patriot revolt"—in 1787 to 1788, many of whose supporters rallied to the new regime. The Helvetic Republic survived, essentially, because the French were trusted to keep its warring factions in balance. In contrast, Napoleon revived the Cisalpine Republic in 1802, simply because he needed its resources, and knew he could count on support there, if the only alternative was a return to Austrian, as opposed to native, rule. Where such alternatives did exist, support for the French was very weak. The Parthenopean Republic, whose territory, if hardly its regime, were of ancient origin as a state, was revived as the Napoleonic Kingdom of Naples in 1806, when Napoleon put his brother Joseph on the throne and then replaced him in 1808, with his sister Caroline and his brother-in-law, Joachim Murat, but only after the Bourbons had betrayed their alliance with Napoleon. The French never really controlled it effectively. It remained a territorial state after 1815, when the Bourbons were restored, until the unification of Italy in 1861. The Ligurian Republic comprised the territory of the Republic of St. George, centered on Genoa in northwestern Italy, one of the oldest states in Europe; the French simply purged the old, aristocratic rulers and changed the name in 1797, later absorbing it into France, in 1805. The Batavian Republic went the same way, although it took longer: set up in 1795, it became the Kingdom of Holland, under Napoleon's younger brother Louis in 1806; finally, in 1810, it was made into French departments. Unlike the Ligurian Republic, however, it regained full independence in 1814. Most of the others, however, were short lived and artificial in nature; they seldom had real popular support and were propped up only by French arms. Where their lives were prolonged, it was because they were "converted" by Napoleon into "satellite kingdoms" thus enduring until his fall in 1814. This was the case for the Cisalpine—later Italian—Republic, which became the Kingdom of Italy (in 1805), which was ruled by Napoleon through his viceroy, Eugène de Beauharnais. The Roman Republic of 1798 to 1799, formed from the core of the Papal States, was never resurrected, however; when the French returned in 1809, they simply annexed its erstwhile territories to France.

Imitation of Revolutionary France was manifest institutionally in the creation of elected assemblies, where possible; the introduction of legal codes and the metric system of weights and measures; and the reorganization of administration, both local and national, along French lines. Many patriots, however, also sought to adapt these institutions to their indigenous traditions. This was usually lost on the majority of the populace, but where the republics survived, as in Switzerland and the Netherlands, and came under the leadership of more moderate patriots—such as Hans Reinhard in the former and Rutger Jan Schimmelpenninck in the latter—the experience made a direct and lasting contribution to the future. A civil war between traditionalists and supporters of a unitary state on the French model broke out in Switzerland in 1801, leading to Napoleon's Act of Mediation (1803). Politically, this favored the traditionalists, supporters of a more federal system that guaranteed the autonomy of the nineteen cantons, and thus the power bases of the old elites; unitarists such as Ochs now fell from power. Nevertheless, many institutional reforms were retained: religious toleration, legal equality, and educational and financial reforms modeled on those of France survived, but were now the preserve of the cantons, not a central government. This important compromise helped perpetuate much of the essence of the original sister republic after 1803, and then after 1814.

The Batavian Republic witnessed a comparable if not exact process of evolution. The patriot movement of 1787 to 1788 soon reemerged to take the reins of government and oust the Regent elites and the House of Orange, when the French definitively occupied the Netherlands in 1795, but such unity as there was in their ranks was short lived. As in Switzerland, serious divisions soon emerged between supporters of a unitarist, proto-French state, and those who sought to retain the autonomy of the traditional provinces and cities, "the federalists." Also as in Switzerland, these divisions tended to coincide with differing views on the scope of the new electorate, unitarists being, in the main, democrats, and federalists—such as Schimmelpenninck—oligarchs. In contrast to the history of the Helvetic Republic, Dutch disputes were not settled quickly, and the whole period, 1795 to 1806, was marked by a series of brief or abortive constitutional settlements. This lurching between unitarism and federalism was perpetuated as much by the political shifts within the French Directory as by internal Dutch politics. Only after 1799, under Napoleon, did the federalists gain any lasting hold on office, but the unitarists had made little impact on the country, at the local level. In direct contrast to the Swiss experience, whereas the Batavian Republic paid lip service to a unitary constitution for much of the time, the provinces and cities did little or nothing to implement proto-French reforms in the law, education, or financial policy. When Napoleon deposed Schimmelpenninck and created the Kingdom of Holland in 1806, the emphasis toward greater centralization gained impetus, and it was under Louis that the centralized state really took shape. This was the model adopted by the House of Orange, on its restoration in 1813. The Batavian Republic opened up a fundamental debate about the character of the new regime, but left it unresolved during its lifetime.

The prolongation of the Cisalpine/Italian Republic as the Kingdom of Italy did not achieve popular support, but it did influence the political classes of northern Italy, and French political culture put down real, if complex and nuanced, roots. The first republic lasted for only twenty-two months and collapsed in popular revolts in the wake of the French retreat of 1799, but it saw the first written constitution in Italy—slavishly modeled by Napoleon on that of the French Directory—together with a national flag, many legal reforms, and the creation of internal free trade. It would have counted for little, had Napoleon not reconquered Italy in 1800, and reestablished the republic, renamed "Italian," officially in 1802 and de facto from 1801. It was in this period, under the vice presidency of Francesco Melzi d'Eril, a moderate reformer akin to Schimmelpenninck and Reinhard, that the new regime took root and won more widespread support among the traditional elites. In these years, formerly disparate, small polities were welded into a unitary state, with no compromises to traditional political or administrative norms, and French laws and institutions had time to implant themselves. The direct nature of Napoleonic—as opposed to French Revolutionary—influence in the Cisalpine/Italian Republic gave it a more authoritarian character than in the Helvetic and Batavian cases. It was among the most heavily taxed and conscripted parts of Napoleonic Europe; like Batavia and Helvetia, it always had large contingents of French troops quartered on it, to spare France itself the full cost of war.

THE PLACE OF THE SISTER REPUBLICS IN EUROPEAN HISTORY

The lasting legacy of the sister republics was twofold. In practical terms, the creation of the proto-French new regimes was meaningful only in the cases of Batavia, Helvetia, and the Cisalpine/Italy, as these were the only republics to survive for an appreciable length of time. In these cases, however, much was done to lay the foundations for the character of these countries in the nineteenth century; the moments of republican reform mattered mainly because they were followed by over a decade of Napoleonic retrenchment, but they also served later generations of liberal and radical activists as a nebulous alternative model to Napoleonic authoritarianism. In this, their legacy merges with those of the more ephemeral republics in southern Italy and even Ireland. These brief, embattled moments became symbols to later generations of the possibility of truly liberal, parliamentary politics "on home soil." The more embattled and short lived the republican experience, the more heroic the failure. The Italian liberal Benedetto Croce (1866–1952) spoke thus of the patriots of the Parthenopean Republic, who were driven into the sea by their own "fellow citizens": "Our sympathies are with the precursors of the new Italy...they are with the flowers of meridional intellect and against obscurantism." In the years after 1945, when they might so easily have been equated with Quisling-like collaboration, the patriots of the sister republics were actually resurrected by Dutch and Italian liberals, as beacons of humanity and progress, in the postwar quest for a "usable past." The contemporary reality is better understood by the lynching of Giuseppe Prina, the finance minister of the Republic/Kingdom of Italy, by a mob in Milan, in 1814.

See also **Directory; French Revolution; French Revolutionary Wars and Napoleonic Wars; Jacobins; Napoleonic Empire.**

BIBLIOGRAPHY

Blanning, T. C. W. *The Origins of the French Revolutionary Wars.* London, 1986.

————. *The French Revolutionary Wars, 1787–1802.* London, 1996.

Elliott, Marianne. *Wolfe Tone: Prophet of Irish Independence.* New Haven, Conn., 1989. The best account of the Irish patriots and of 1798.

Grab, Alexander. *Napoleon and the Transformation of Europe.* Basingstoke, U.K., 2003. Contains information on western European countries across the period.

Oechsli, Wihelm. *A History of Switzerland, 1499–1914.* Translated by Eden and Cedar Paul. Cambridge, U.K., 1922.

Schama, Simon. *Patriots and Liberators: Revolution in the Netherlands, 1780–1813.* London, 1977. The best study in English of the Batavian Republic.

Woolf, Stuart. *A History of Italy, 1700–1860: The Social Constraints of Political Change.* London, 1979. Still the best general guide to Italy in this period.

MICHAEL BROERS

SLAVERY. At the very time slavery died in Europe—with the exception of Russia—in the fifteenth century, it was revived in the Americas, primarily by Europeans seeking to cultivate export staples from the tropics and semitropics. In order to tap the economic potential of the Americas, Europeans developed a complicated trading system connecting Africa, Europe, and the Americas. Thus, with a few early exceptions of Indian slaves, slave labor in the Americas was performed by imported African slaves. The millions of Africans forcefully shipped across the Atlantic formed the labor force that first won over and then developed key areas of the Americas. They also helped to enrich various European colonial powers. In the years before 1807 African slaves formed the great majority of all the people crossing the Atlantic: something like three million Africans crossed the Atlantic in British slave ships. But in the same period only one million Europeans settled in the Americas. In many key respects it was the African who was the pioneer of settlement in critical regions of the Americas. Africa provided the answer to a problem Europeans had encountered from their early days of settlement: how best to tap the vast potential of land in the Americas. Their settlements and colonies were on such a scale (though initially they had barely a toehold on the continent) that white migrants (free and indentured) and handfuls of local Indians were rarely adequate to the task. Africa seemed to provide the answer.

COLONIAL SLAVERY

Even before Columbus's landfall in the Americas, Europeans were already familiar with African slaves. Their early maritime and trading ventures along the West African coast had yielded African slaves, along with other items of trade. African slaves were transferred to Portugal and Spain, and later to the new Iberian outposts on the Atlantic islands in the late fifteenth century. It was a logical step for settlers in the Americas in need of labor to turn to Africans, especially in the early development of sugar plantations. Effectively pioneered on Brazilian sugar plantations, African slavery was later transferred north, to the Caribbean islands (again for sugar cultivation) before slipping farther north to the tobacco plantations of the Chesapeake and, later still, to the rice plantations of the Carolinas. Sugar was the engine that drew Africans in growing numbers.

Slavery differed greatly from one colony to another. Different crops dictated different structures of slave life, and very different patterns of slave work. These ranged from the large, military-like slave gangs on the big sugar plantations in Brazil and Jamaica, to the smaller work groups (black and white together) on Virginia's tobacco plantations, to the task system commonplace on the Carolina rice plantations. African enslaved labor quickly moved into all corners of the local American economies. As settler communities matured and developed into sophisticated societies, slaves could be found everywhere: from the urban life of towns and ports, to cowhands on the expansive frontier;

Slaves in neck chains and their African guard, Zanzibar, 1896. By the early nineteenth century, the island of Zanzibar off the coast of Tanzania was the center of a thriving slave trade and the site of the infamous Great Slave Market. Pressure from European governments led to the official cessation of the trade in 1873, but in reality the practice continued until after World War I. ©HULTON-DEUTSCH COLLECTION/CORBIS

from enslaved sailors in the Atlantic maritime fleets, to skilled craftsmen and women across the rural and urban Americas. Yet from the beginning to the end, the prime purpose of slavery was to provide the brute manual labor in the fields: in sugar, tobacco, rice, and cotton, and a string of other slave-worked commodities.

ATLANTIC ECONOMY
Slavery greatly enhanced the material well-being of the West, and African slaves were integral to the emergence of a massive Atlantic-wide economy that saw Europe, Africa, and the Americas locked into an intimate economic and social interdependence. Goods from Europe, and Asian goods transshipped through Europe (all backed by growing European financial and trading systems) were shipped to Africa to be exchanged for slaves, who

were then traded throughout the American slave colonies. Slave-grown tropical staples were shipped back for processing and sale in Europe (and beyond). It was however a hugely complex human, geographic, and economic system (too complex to be described as merely "triangular").

The Atlantic slave system was made possible by a remarkable maritime system. Scholars know of some twenty-seven thousand slave voyages, with the consequent impact on port development on both sides of the Atlantic. There were, in addition, major economic and social ramifications throughout the broader hinterlands of the ports linked to the Atlantic slave system.

The millions of Africans who survived to landfall in the Americas (many did not, of course) had endured a unique oceanic trauma even before being turned over to the lifetime of American slavery. Africans arrived sick, virtually naked, and with no material possessions. Yet, within a generation, they had shaped a string of vibrant slave societies, which had all the basic ingredients—of family, communities, beliefs, and cultural patterns—that provided the framework for black life (enslaved and free) thereafter. Slave social life, rooted in an African past (itself varied of course) but transformed by the specific circumstances of local life, differed from place to place. Much depended on geography and work (between, say, sugar and tobacco) and on the nature of local white society. What emerged were very different slave societies, between Brazil, the Caribbean, and North America. And even then there were marked distinctions among slaves even within those broader regions—distinctions shaped in large measure by the kind of work the slaves undertook. Life was very different for a domestic slave compared to a slave working on a coffee plantation. But whatever the system or work, slaves were kept at their toils by a mix of force, incentives, and—especially in the fields—by crude violence.

RESISTANCE

Not surprisingly, what united slaves everywhere was the enslaved people's hostility to slavery itself. Slaves everywhere went out of their way to resist, or to render slavery more tolerable. Resistance ranged from running away, open resistance, and violence (which was inevitably punished by the most draconian of slave owners' brutality), to the smallest acts of passive resistance. Slaves did what they could to change their enslavement. Yet only once, in Saint Domingue/Haiti, was local slavery utterly destroyed by the slaves.

Slavery in the Americas was remarkably durable and persistent, and for most of its history, it was able to deflect criticisms and objections. There had been, from the early Spanish settlements, notable critiques of slavery; on ethical, Christian, and even economic grounds. But the simple and pervasive economic success of slavery rendered most criticisms irrelevant. Objections were simply overwhelmed by the sounds and sights of profitable trade and business. Yet all that began to change from the mid-eighteenth century onward.

ATTACKS ON THE ATLANTIC SLAVE TRADE

The Atlantic slave trade was at its height when convergent critical forces began to attack. The initial roots of abolition were French and Scottish Enlightenment writers (most influentially Montesquieu [Charles-Louis de Secondat, 1689–1755] and Adam Smith [1723–1790]). But, with the exception of France's Amis des Noirs, Europe lacked the popular abolition base seen in Britain and North America. These Enlightenment writers merged with a new theological voice (led initially by Quakers and other dissenters) to attack the Atlantic slave trade itself. Slaves were instrumental in this campaign to undermine slavery, notably through the major Caribbean slave uprising. The impact of news about slave revolts affected the course of abolition in Europe, especially the revolt in Haiti lead by Toussaint.

The upheavals in France in 1789, and their impact on the French islands produced the greatest slave convulsion in the Americas: the slave revolution in Saint Domingue (1791–1804) and the eventual emergence of an independent Haiti (in 1804). Shock waves from that revolution rippled throughout the Americas, but despite the fears and uncertainties slavery elsewhere held fast—in the short term. In 1807 Great Britain outlawed the Atlantic slave trade, and in 1808 the importation of slaves became illegal in the United States. These actions were intended to cut off supplies of fresh Africans to the American plantations. Yet, even after abolition, something like three million Africans were shipped into the Americas, primarily to Brazil and Cuba. In both those countries, and in the United States, slavery experienced a revival on the back of new slave-grown crops. Cuba wanted labor for its tobacco plantations, Brazil for coffee and tobacco, the United States for the cotton plantations of the South.

In the nineteenth century, slavery seemed anomalous. On the one hand, U.S. cotton slavery illustrated once again the economic returns to be made from slave labor. On the other, slavery was a much denounced and disliked institution. In North America the economic ramifications of cotton slavery were enormous. Cotton was the nation's largest export. Inevitably, the north was deeply involved, via banking, finance, and trade. Yet at the same time there was a growing chorus of northern

Female slaves in neck chains, Zanzibar. © Bojan Brecelj/Corbis

religious and ethical opposition. The British on the other hand developed a new role as the world's major abolitionist power. Having abolished their own slave system in 1833, the British henceforth embarked on a global abolitionist crusade, trying to persuade other European slaving nations, and those in the Americas (led by the United States) to see the errors of their ways and to abandon slavery. The power of the Royal Navy and pressure from the Foreign Office was able to impose abolition on swathes of Africa and other regions. But slavery remained stubbornly resistant in the United States, Brazil, and Cuba, largely because of its profitability. Slaves cultivated the coffee for which Brazil became a byword, and the tobacco that made Cuba's name, and in both countries slave numbers were augmented by illicit imports of Africans until the 1860s.

The nineteenth century was, in many respects, the classic period of U.S. slavery; that is, the years

most commonly associated with slavery. Yet it was only the latest transformation in a form of bondage that had characterized human settlement across the Americas for centuries. Equally, and like the earlier slave systems, cotton slavery was linked to the economies of the wider world. Cotton from the South fueled the Industrial Revolution in Britain, which in its turn helped to clothe the world in cheap cotton garments. Once again, key areas of economic development in Europe were intimately linked to slavery in the Americas.

AFRICA

Africa, the source of enslaved labor used throughout the Americas, was persistently damaged by this enforced drain of people. Moreover this hemorrhage of Africans continued long after the Atlantic slave trade had ended. African slaves were moved north across the Sahara and east through East African slave ports. At the same time indigenous slave systems were consolidated in the nineteenth century. One result of the external slave trade from Africa was the strengthening of slavery within Africa itself. It was a great irony that abolitionists found themselves tackling the problems of slavery in Africa after they had helped undermine slavery in the Americas. But in both places, on both sides of the Atlantic, the size and strength of slavery was directly linked to earlier European (and later American) economic dependence on slave labor.

Slavery had a slow and long drawn-out death across the Americas. It survived in Cuba until 1886, and in Brazil until 1888, but by then it had been ended elsewhere across the Americas. In some places slavery had simply faded away, devoid of support or friends and overtaken by new economic circumstances. Yet in two main areas where slavery had dominated the economy (in the West Indies and in the U.S. South) demands to end slavery had been resisted. Even in Brazil, where slavery slowly lost influence and importance, it retained a residual importance in some regions until the bitter end.

CONSEQUENCES

The consequences of African slavery were at once both obvious and hidden, but always potent. Demands for African slave labor had scattered millions of Africans and their locally born descendants across the face of the Americas. African sweat converted whole regions of the Americas into profitable cultivation. The cultures of Africa, though transformed in passing from Africa to the Americas, became a basic, and sometimes dominant, feature of American life. Slavery also bequeathed a malignant legacy to later generations (indeed to the modern world). African slavery in the Americas, quite unlike other slave systems in other societies, was a highly racialized system. To be enslaved was to be black: to be black was to be enslaved. Economic usage, legal custom, and perhaps more important, popular convention, rendered the African an item of trade. The African as a thing, an object, was basic to the whole system. The ideas and values that underpinned that transformation of black humanity to the level of nonhuman survived long after slavery itself.

See also **Colonialism; Colonies; Race and Racism; Toussaint Louverture.**

BIBLIOGRAPHY

Blackburn, Robin. *The Overthrow of Colonial Slavery, 1776–1848.* London, 1988.

Drescher, Seymour. *From Slavery to Freedom: Comparative Studies in the Rise and Fall of Atlantic Slavery.* Oxford, U.K., 1999.

Hochschild, Adam. *Bury the Chains: Prophets and Rebels in the Fight to Free an Empire's Slaves.* Boston, 2005.

Inikori, Joseph E. *Africans and the Industrial Revolution in England: A Study in International Trade and Development.* Cambridge, U.K., 2002.

JAMES WALVIN

SLAVOPHILES. In nineteenth-century Russia the term *Slavophiles* (originally a nickname) was not a designation of all sorts of "friends of the Slavs" but the name of a closely knit group of thinkers who criticized the Westernization of Russia and preached a return to the "truly Christian" and Slavic principles of the Russian life before the reforms of Peter the Great (r. 1682–1725). The creators of this current were Ivan Kireyevsky (1806–1856), a philosopher who developed a sophisticated Russian version of conservative Romanticism; and Alexei Khomiakov (1804–1860), a lay theologian who elaborated the concept of *sobornost,* that is, free unity and conciliarity (from the Russian words *sobor* [council] and *sobirat* [bring together, unite]), seen as the inner essence of the Orthodox Church, sharply distinguishing it from the Catholic "unity without freedom" and the Protestant "freedom without unity." The most original representative of the younger Slavophiles was Konstantin Aksakov (1817–1860), an extreme Romantic antilegalist who treated law and the state as alienated, artificial forms of social life, acceptable only as necessary evils.

BASIC TENETS

The Slavophile contribution to Russian thought consisted mostly (though not exclusively) of providing elaborate arguments for returning to the native roots: for replacing the Eurocentric model of development—accused of bringing about destructive rationalization and atomization of life— by the "Russian way," based upon the communitarian spirit of Orthodox Christianity. The Slavophiles drew a sharp contrast between the Orthodox Church, seen as the only legitimate incarnation of Christian universalism, and the Roman Catholic Church, deeply contaminated by the juridical rationalism of the ancient Rome. Despite its multiple weaknesses, caused by its subjugation to the Westernizing state, the Russian church had preserved the truly Christian values, such as organic togetherness, integrality of spirit, and an inborn capacity for communal life based upon cooperation in love, and not merely contracts between competing individuals. A social embodiment of these anti-individualistic values was the Russian peasant commune. Ivan Aksakov (1823–1886; brother of Konstantin Aksakov) described it as the basic cell of an ideal society, integrated by moral principles of unanimity and concord, eliminating the divisive egoism of private property and getting along without the "outer truth" of juridical compulsion.

From the all-European perspective Slavophilism was a variant of Romantic anticapitalism, setting against capitalist modernization the idealized version of a traditional "organic society." Its critique of rationalism, as the cause of social atomization, was similar to (and inspired by) German conservative Romanticism. At the same time, however, Russian Slavophilism differed from German romantic conservatism in its antielitist aspects, reflecting its critical attitude toward the Russian Westernized elites. Unlike the German romantics, the Slavophiles rejected not only bourgeois individualism but aristocratic individualism as well. Their Romantic traditionalism was more populist and (relatively) more egalitarian than the similar trends in western Europe.

The Slavophiles defined the Russian mission in history in universalistic terms: Russia was to regenerate itself through the conscious return to its own Orthodox roots (which would involve the overcoming of the fateful split between its Westernized elite and the "common people"). By doing so, Russia would become the spiritual leader of the Christian world, showing the West the salutary example of the realization of truly Christian values in social life.

The Slavophile antithesis of Russia and Europe was presented as the antithesis of two types of personality and two types of knowledge: integral and disintegrated personality; living, integral knowledge and abstract, logical thought. Kireyevsky

defined rationalism, characteristic of the West, as a disease destroying the wholeness of the human spirit. Rational knowledge transforms reality into an aggregate of isolated fragments or, at best, into a dialectical tissue of abstract, incorporeal notions—which was the case with the "panlogism" of Georg Wilhelm Friedrich Hegel. Only by bringing together all spiritual forces, through the religious concentration of spirit, can humans find in themselves the "inner root of knowledge" and attain through it "an integral vision of the mind."

To support these views, Kireyevsky referred to the criticism of Hegel in Friedrich von Schelling's "positive philosophy" of 1841. Kireyevsky added, however, that a genuinely Christian philosophy, radically overcoming the rationalist disease, would require a thorough examination of the mystical theology of the Eastern fathers of the church. In his essay "On the Necessity and Possibility of New Principles in Philosophy" (1856), Kireyevsky provided a detailed outline of this philosophical project. Other Slavophiles saw it as a conception of the Russian mission in the sphere of thought: a mission of reconciling the truth of philosophy with the truth of the Revelation.

The foundations of Slavophile ideology were elaborated in the 1840s. The opponents of Slavophilism, called Westernizers, set against Slavophile traditionalism the ideal of *individual* freedom and *autonomous* personality, seen as the final product and central value of European progress. The main figure among the Westernizers was the famous literary critic and Left Hegelian thinker Vissarion Belinsky (1811–1848), a tremendous influence within the emerging Russian intelligentsia. In contrast to the Slavophile concept of an "integral," preindividualized person, Belinsky conceived personality as a radical negation of unreflective submission to traditionalism and saw the essence of historical progress in the growing individualization of people and rationalization of society. The reforms of Peter the Great were for him not a national apostasy but a turning point in the transformation of the patriarchal Russian "people" (*narod*) into a modern European "nation" (*natsiya*).

Similar ideas were developed in the 1840s by another Left Hegelian Westernizer, Alexander Herzen (1812–1870). He lost his faith in Western progress, however, when he left Russia (in 1847) and saw the victory of the bourgeoisie in the European Revolutions of 1848. This led Herzen to create the doctrine of "Russian socialism," which tried to reconcile the Western ideal of individual freedom with the Slavophile communalism.

THE NEW PERIOD

The new period in the history of Slavophilism began with Russia's defeat in the Crimean War (1853–1856) and the Great Reforms of Alexander II (r. 1855–1881). The political "thaw" made it possible and necessary for the Slavophiles to pass from theory to political practice. In these new conditions Slavophilism was transformed, on the one hand, into Pan-Slavism and, on the other, into the right wing of gentry liberalism. Ivan Aksakov became the leader of the Pan-Slav movement; Yuri Samarin (1819–1876), an enthusiastic disciple of Khomiakov, took an active part in the emancipation of the serfs, defending the peasant commune as a bulwark against proletarianization and as a supplier of cheap labor for the estates of the gentry. In both cases the anticapitalist Romantic utopia was silently abandoned and replaced with more realistic political aims, involving an acceptance of a conservative variant of a capitalist modernization of Russia.

Another feature of Slavophile thought in the 1860s and the 1870s was its evolution in the direction of ethnonationalism. The main impulse for this was the Polish uprising of 1863. This event convinced Samarin and Ivan Aksakov that the survival of the Russian Empire required not only further restrictions of the rights of national and religious minorities but also a national mobilization of the Orthodox and Russian-speaking masses. Aksakov's journal began to support the policy of Russification in the Congress Kingdom of Poland and the restrictive measures toward the Jews. This chauvinistic tendency (reinforced by Pan-Slavic demands for the conquest of Constantinople and the establishment of a powerful, Russian-led Slavic federation) reached its climax after the assassination of Alexander II on 13 March (1 March, old style) 1881. It was powerfully opposed, however, by Vladimir Soloviev (1853–1900), a thinker who was to become the greatest religious philosopher of Russia. At the beginning of his intellectual

evolution he was close to Ivan Aksakov and greatly influenced by Kireyevsky's ideas, but in the early 1880s he broke with the epigones of Slavophilism, committing himself to relentless struggle against religious and ethnic nationalism. The intention to restore the universalistic values of Christianity and to implement them in social life aroused in him deep sympathy to Roman Catholicism and willingness to cooperate with the liberals.

IMPACT AND LEGACY

The impact of Slavophile ideas on Russian thought was, on the whole, very diverse and profound. The Slavophile critique of the West, taken up by the novelist Fyodor Dostoyevsky, set the tone for all currents of nineteenth-century Russian anti-Westernism. The beginning of the twentieth century was the time of the antipositivist upheaval in the Russian culture, ushering in the so-called religiophilosophical renaissance. Representative thinkers of that time, deeply influenced by Dostoyevsky and Soloviev, were quick to discover the significance of the Slavophile religious philosophy. In his 1912 monograph on Khomiakov, Nikolai Berdyayev (1874–1948) described classical Slavophilism as laying foundations for a distinctively Russian tradition in philosophy. Another former Marxist, Sergei Bulgakov (1871–1944), took up the tasks of modernizing Orthodox theology and used for this purpose Khomiakov's concept of *sobornost*.

In the Soviet Union Slavophile ideas were marginalized in historical studies and suppressed as a living tradition. In the late twentieth century Mikhail Gorbachev's perestroika showed, however, that a hidden interest in Slavophilism remained quite vivid. In postcommunist Russia Slavophile ideas are invoked in all discussions about Russian national identity (or "the Russian idea") and the special tasks of Russian philosophy.

See also **Romanticism; Russia; Westernizers.**

BIBLIOGRAPHY

Christoff, Peter K. *An Introduction to Nineteenth-Century Russian Slavophilism.* Vol. 1: *A. S. Xomjakov,* The Hague, 1961; Vol. 2: *I. V. Kireevskij,* The Hague, 1972; Vol. 3: *K. S. Aksakov,* Princeton, N.J., 1982; Vol. 4: *Iu. F. Samarin.* Boulder, Colo., 1991.

Gratieux, Albert. *A. S. Khomiakov et le mouvement slavo-phile.* 2 vols. Paris, 1939.

Scanlan, James P. "Interpretations and Uses of Slavophilism in Recent Russian Thought." In *Russian Thought after Communism,* edited by James P. Scanlan, 31–61. Armonk, N.Y., 1994.

Walicki, Andrzej. *The Slavophile Controversy: History of a Conservative Utopia in Nineteenth-Century Russian Thought.* Translated by Hilda Andrews-Rusiecka. Oxford, U.K., 1975.

ANDRZEJ WALICKI

SMALLPOX. Smallpox is an acute infectious disease caused by the variola virus. It appears in many forms, some which are very mild and others that are usually fatal. Although the disease has been eradicated since 1977, during the eighteenth century, smallpox became one of Europe's most feared diseases, usually appearing in cycles of between five to seven years. Symptoms include headache, high fever, and vomiting; after the fever subsides, red spots appear that become filled with pus. Scabs formed by the drying out of the pustules fall off between one and three weeks later, leaving permanent scars. Some survivors were left blind by the disease and nearly all were disfigured to some degree.

It is hard to say whether deaths from smallpox actually increased or merely became more visible following the retreat of plague from western Europe. Yet there is some evidence to suggest that epidemics—like those that ravaged Europe in the 1750s—became more common as commercial and agricultural revolutions united hitherto remote populations.

INOCULATION AND VACCINATION

More attention began to be paid to the best means of treating and preventing the disease. Early in the century, the practice of inoculation—the use of the dried crusts of smallpox pustules to induce a mild form of the disease—was introduced into Europe from the Middle East. The practice could confer lifelong immunity but it was risky and many of those inoculated died, either from smallpox or some other infection introduced by the inoculator's lancet.

The appeal of inoculation was understandably limited. Most enthusiasm was shown by the aristocracy, which dreaded scarring from smallpox as something that adversely affected marriage prospects and, hence, the continuation of their dynasties. Outside the royal courts the practice thrived only where it was actively promoted by private individuals, such as improving landlords and philanthropic doctors. Inoculation was never embraced by the state and there is little evidence that it contributed materially to the stabilization of mortality that occurred in many European countries during the eighteenth century.

The advent of vaccination, by contrast, made an enormous difference. Pioneered by an English doctor, Edward Jenner (1749–1823), vaccination was based on the observation that milkmaids who contracted cowpox in the course of their work were seldom afflicted by the more serious disease, smallpox. In 1796 Jenner designed an experiment to test this, inoculating a local boy with cowpox and then with smallpox; he found that no symptoms of smallpox appeared. Further experiments confirmed these findings, and Jenner's new technique of "vaccination" was rapidly accepted by many medical practitioners and statesmen, including the French emperor Napoleon I and Thomas Jefferson. Indeed, many European states were quick to promote vaccination as a way of preventing costly and unnecessary deaths, and it soon became compulsory among key groups such as soldiers and sailors. Within a decade or so after Jenner's discovery, some local authorities in Britain were demanding vaccination before administering poor relief, while states such as Bavaria made it compulsory for those entering apprenticeships.

Thereafter, compulsory vaccination spread to other sections of the population, but with some national differences. One might expect authoritarian states to have proceeded more rapidly than others, but this was not always the case. Britain, which was famed for its liberalism, was quicker to introduce vaccination than was autocratic Prussia, for instance. In 1840 Britain was the first country to ban inoculation, and in 1853 it passed an act making vaccination compulsory within three months of birth. Prussia felt no need to follow suit at that time because its provisions for voluntary vaccination were so extensive.

OPPOSITION TO VACCINATION

Yet vaccination had numerous detractors. Its supporters found it difficult to explain the fact that some of those who had been vaccinated were still susceptible to smallpox. Such cases were comparatively few but they were sufficient to raise doubts about the efficacy of the operation among the public; at least until the introduction of revaccination later in the century. Infection was another serious problem. Multiple incisions were made with lancets and lymph from a previously vaccinated child was rubbed into them. This arm-to-arm method carried with it the risk of infection with diseases like erysipelas—a problem that was overcome in the 1880s and 1890s with the widespread use of lymph harvested from cows and the addition of glycerine, which killed many bacterial infections.

As vaccination was promoted more aggressively by the state, rumors abounded that governments were seeking to poison the lower classes or to "brand" them like cattle. There were also protests against the fines imposed on those who refused to bring children for vaccination. Nor was opposition confined to the working class. Concerns were expressed generally about compulsory vaccination as an infringement of civil liberties, while in some countries, especially Germany, advocates of holistic medicine argued that vaccination was unnecessary and unnatural, as it violated the integrity of the human body.

Opposition to vaccination grew in the face of more concerted efforts to prevent the disease, in the wake of the dreadful epidemic that afflicted Europe in the early 1870s. The epidemic appears to have begun in France immediately before the war with Prussia, and it spread via French prisoners of war to Prussian civilians. Claiming the lives of around half a million people, the epidemic spurred newly unified Germany to introduce compulsory vaccination and revaccination in 1874. The act provoked considerable resistance, and petitions amounting to over thirty thousand signatures were sent to the Reichstag. Many in France also wished to move toward compulsion, especially in view of the fact that the Prussian army (in which vaccination had been compulsory since 1834) suffered fewer than three hundred deaths from smallpox by comparison with over twenty-three thousand among French troops. Yet political conditions in the new Third Republic prevented the passage of such legislation until 1902.

Despite widespread resistance to compulsion, anti-vaccinationists won few victories. Only in Britain did they enjoy some success and then because their demands were moderate—the introduction of opt-outs for those who refused vaccination on grounds of conscience. Most European countries experienced a marked decline in smallpox mortality between 1880 and 1914. The disease continued to be a major cause of death only in Russia, Spain, Italy, and Portugal, which had poorly developed systems of vaccination. Other countries experienced falls in mortality consistent with the dates at which legislation was enacted and the rigor with which it was enforced. For example, in 1910 Russia suffered 400,000 recorded deaths from smallpox and Spain 37,000, whereas France had 11,000 and Germany only 386. The disruption caused by World War I inevitably led to an increase in smallpox deaths throughout Europe, with the worst epidemics occurring in countries such as Russia and Italy. Many central and western European countries also experienced epidemics but they were able to prevent the widespread devastation that had followed the war between France and Prussia in 1870. In these countries, smallpox was increasingly perceived as an alien disease, associated either with immigrants from eastern Europe, or with "reservoirs" of infection in Europe's Asian and African colonies.

See also **Jenner, Edward; Public Health; Science and Technology.**

BIBLIOGRAPHY

Baldwin, Peter. *Contagion and the State in Europe, 1830–1930.* Cambridge, U.K., 1999.

Cliff, A. D., and Matthew R. Smallman-Raynor. *War Epidemics: An Historical Geography of Infectious Diseases in Military Conflict and Civil Strife, 1850–2000.* Oxford, U.K., 2004.

Harrison, Mark. *Disease and the Modern World: 1500 to the Present Day.* Cambridge, U.K., 2004.

Hopkins, Donald R. *The Greatest Killer: Smallpox in History.* Chicago, 2002.

Porter, D., and R. Porter. "The Politics of Prevention: Anti-Vaccinationism and Public Health in Nineteenth-Century England." *Medical History* 32 (1988): 231–252.

Razzell, Peter. *The Conquest of Smallpox: The Impact of Inoculation on Smallpox Mortality in Eighteenth Century Britain*. Sussex, U.K., 1977.

MARK HARRISON

SMILES, SAMUEL (1812–1904), Scottish author and social reformer.

Samuel Smiles is often regarded as the preeminent advocate of the Victorian gospel of work. In reality, his legacy is much more complex. His evolution from a young radical to an elderly conservative can be seen as a metaphor for understanding middle and working-class politics in Victorian Britain.

Smiles's early career was marked by the economic uncertainty common to many members of the lower middle and working classes. Born in Scotland to Samuel and Janet Smiles, he was educated under strict Calvinist principles, apprenticed to a medical practitioner, and received a medical degree from Edinburgh University. In 1838, failing to establish a successful medical practice, Smiles sold what little property he owned and left Scotland. After touring the Netherlands and Germany, he accepted the editorship of a radical newspaper, the *Leeds Times*. Although this position paid little, it provided an ideal platform for a young man determined to effect social change. Smiles penned a number of anonymous articles advocating causes like women's education, free trade, and parliamentary reform while attacking the aristocracy mercilessly, though with little apparent effect. He also involved himself heavily in radical organizations such as the Leeds Parliamentary Reform Association (LPRA), which sought to build middle and working-class cooperation to bring pressure for the political reform.

Smiles provided an alternative to Chartist notions of popular democracy and direct action. He hoped to establish a society in which educated men and women of all classes treated each other as equals, engaged in rational debate, and agitated nonviolently toward a just society. This was certainly a utopian, even romantic vision, and after the LPRA faltered, Smiles lost faith in it. He failed to establish an organization that linked members of the working and middle classes in cooperative effort, and came to fear that Chartism would end in violent disorder.

In 1845, Smiles cut his ties with the *Leeds Times*. Until 1871, when he suffered a debilitating stroke, Smiles worked as an administrator in the railway and insurance industries. These positions provided him economic security, and his experiences in them inevitably colored his outlook. Over time, it accorded more and more closely with that of laissez-faire political economists. Although Smiles never lost his sympathy for social improvement or reform, he saw the best hopes for it in individual action.

In another respect 1845 was important. In May, Smiles began giving a lecture on the topic of "self-help." He refined the lecture over the succeeding years, and in 1859 the book *Self-Help* was published to immediate success. It sold over 270,000 copies in Britain during Smiles's lifetime, was translated into numerous other languages, and is still in print in the early twenty-first century. The thesis of the book was simple: that hard work, thrift, and perseverance would lead to personal success and national progress. "The spirit of self-help is the root of all genuine growth in the individual; and, exhibited in the lives of many, it constitutes the true source of national vigour and strength." Smiles illustrated and developed this idea with readable biographies and catch-phrases. While some critics have incorrectly seen *Self-Help* as a justification for self-interest, it is more accurately viewed as a defense of middle and working-class improvement.

Smiles's other books include didactic works such as *Character* (1872), *Thrift* (1875), *Duty* (1880), and *Life and Labour* (1887). All of his books use the lives of individuals as exemplars for the idea that a practical education, perseverance, and self-control lead to moral improvement, happiness, and success. They are filled with anecdotes and aphorisms, some of which have entered the popular vocabulary. "If at first you don't succeed, try, try again" has been credited to him.

Smiles's industrial and business biographies, such as *Life of George Stephenson* (1857), *Lives of Engineers* (3 vols., 1861–1862), *Industrial Biography: Iron Workers and Tool* Makers (1863), *Lives of*

Boulton and Watt (1865), and *Josiah Wedgwood* (1895), are similar in structure and tone to his didactic books. They are also valuable sources for information concerning these subjects, although they must be used cautiously and reflect more than a touch of hero worship. Most of the material on which they are based was assembled from interviews. The remarkable size of his body of work testifies that Smiles practiced the values of hard work and perseverance that he preached.

Smiles dedicated himself to the cause of working-class improvement, but by the time of his death, his name had become anathema to many who incorrectly saw him as a defender of greed. Nevertheless, even many socialists read him closely and lived by his maxims. Robert Blatchford praised his defense of honest labor and working-class toil, and Smiles's work may best be seen today as an early precursor of the self-help and motivational genres that were to become so popular in the twentieth and early twenty-first centuries.

See also **Carlyle, Thomas; Chartism; Conservatism; Dickens, Charles.**

BIBLIOGRAPHY

Morris, R. J. "Samuel Smiles and the Genesis of Self-Help; The Retreat to a Petit Bourgeois Utopia." *Historical Journal* 24, no. 1 (March 1981): 89–109.

Travers, Timothy. *Samuel Smiles and the Victorian Work Ethic.* New York, 1987.

Tyrrell, Alex. "Samuel Smiles and the Woman Question in Early Victorian Britain." *Journal of British Studies* 39, no. 2. (April 2000): 185–216.

CHRISTOPHER J. PROM

SOCCER. *See* Football (Soccer).

SOCIALISM. Although there were theoretically significant antecedents in both the utopian tradition associated with Sir Thomas More (*Utopia*, 1516), in which the holding of property in common is a central tenet; in certain strands of the republican tradition, where agrarian laws proposed the limitation of private property in land in particular; and in minor currents of debate during the French Revolutionary period, notably associated with Gracchus Baboeuf (1760–1797); European socialism proper commences with three main thinkers and the schools associated with them. In Britain, the Welsh industrialist Robert Owen is regarded as the founder of socialism, with the term gaining circulation from the late 1820s onward. In France, Claude-Henri de Rouvroy, comte de Saint-Simon and Charles Fourier commenced two socialist movements of note at about the same time. These movements were marginalized from 1848 onward by the growing influence of Karl Marx over European socialist thought, which eventuated by World War I, and notably the Bolshevik Revolution of 1917, with the virtual eclipse of most other socialist alternatives. This article accordingly will survey the commencement and development of the main early socialist writers and offer an account of Marx's thought and the later Marxist movements, and some later non-Marxist socialists.

OWEN AND OWENISM

Robert Owen (1771–1858) rose from humble origins to international fame as the manager of the New Lanark cotton mills south of Glasgow, whose management he assumed in 1800. Here, while Owen reaped a fortune through fine cotton-spinning, he improved working and living conditions for the workforce substantially. From his first substantial publication, *A New View of Society* (1813), Owen insisted on the malleability of human character, and its improvability, contingent on the reduction in poverty and temptations to crime and immorality. With the post-Napoleonic War economic slump, he turned from proposing wider but similar factory reforms to the problem of poverty as such, now urging the relocation of the urban poor in cooperative "villages" of around two thousand people each in the countryside, where labor would alternate between agriculture and manufactures, and the results would be shared in common. Initially termed "the social system," as opposed, by 1820, to the "individual system" of competition and "buying cheap and selling dear," this scheme was widely referred to as "socialism" by 1830. Owen attempted a number of practical communitarian ventures, notably at New Harmony, Indiana, in the mid- and late 1820s, and at Tytherly or Queenwood, Hampshire, in Britain, in the early 1840s. In these communities it was assumed that some exchange of aggregate social produce for greater free time would probably be agreed, such that needs would not expand indefinitely. It was also widely contended that traditional mechanisms of social coercion, such as the police, would be obviated by the improved moral behavior of the population, and the collective control that small communities could exert over their members. Neither these nor similar ventures proved successful, however.

Nonetheless Owenism both spawned a substantial social movement and produced a considerable body of theoretical literature. Its chief success socially lay in the creation—chiefly in London and the industrial districts, between 1835 and 1845—of an interlinked set of branches, whose aim was to raise funds to found a community, but which built "Halls of Science" for social and educational activities and by the early 1840s enjoyed audiences of some fifty thousand weekly. Its intellectual successes were primarily the work of three writers: George Mudie, the editor of the first Owenite journal of importance, *The Economist* (1821–1822); John Gray, author of *A Lecture on Human Happiness* (1825), *The Social System* (1831), and other works; and an Irish landowner, William Thompson, whose *Inquiry Concerning the Distribution of Wealth* (1824) and *Labor Rewarded* (1827) were the most astute engagements in early British socialism with the dominant school of liberal laissez-faire political economy. A later writer of note was John Francis Bray, author of *Labour's Wrong and Labour's Remedy* (1839). Collectively these writers disputed the inevitable tendency of capitalism to distribute wealth fairly, particularly to the laboring class. They contended that the market mechanism was prone to cyclical instability and fluctuations caused by overproduction and underconsumption, and by the early 1830s forecast increasingly severe crises induced by mechanization in particular. Early efforts to calculate the percentage of the value of the product received by the laborer, begun by the London doctor Charles Hall, were continued by the Owenites, and became central to the account of surplus value offered by Marx. Politically, most Owenites proposed democratic management of communitarian experiments but deferred to Owen's paternalistic leadership during much of the movement's history.

A SOUVENIR FOR MAY DAY 1907

A Souvenir for May Day 1907. Pen and ink drawing by the ardent English socialist artist and writer Walter Crane. PRIVATE COLLECTION/BRIDGEMAN ART LIBRARY

Owen himself preferred to avoid mechanisms of election and political contest, and proposed in his most mature formulation for social and political reorganization (*The Book of the New Moral World*, seven parts, 1836–1844) the future division of society into age groups, with each individual passing through an identical scheme of being educated, working, supervising others, governing the community, and negotiating relations with other communities. Owenism was also notable for its championing of women's rights in Britain, notably through the efforts of William Thompson and Anna Wheeler, whose *Appeal on Behalf of One Half the Human Race* was published in 1824.

FOURIER AND FOURIERISM

Like Owen, the French writer Charles Fourier (1772–1837) proposed a communitarian solution to poverty and the increasing competitiveness of liberal capitalist society, whose anarchic elements he had witnessed growing up in an affluent Lyon mercantile family. Like Owen, too, Fourier proposed to reorganize social thought into a new "social science" based on the law of "passionate attraction," which he assumed governed all material relations in the universe as well as human affairs. Fourier's communitarian ideal, which he called the "Phalanx" from about 1800, was however based on a much more radical view of the human passions, whose repression he condemned utterly. Instead, he assumed the community could both harmonize and satisfy human passions in a manner that promoted happiness while abolishing poverty. Fourier's main writings were the *Theory of the Four Movements* (1808), the *Traité de l'association domestique-agricole* (1821; Treaty of the domestic-agricultural association, 2 vols.), *Le nouveau monde industriel et sociétaire* (1829; The new industrial world and its members), and *La fausse industrie* (1835–1836; The false industry). His radical theories on sexuality and marriage, or "enslaved monogamy," which he proposed to abolish, and his urging of the necessity for universal sexual gratification, with a "Court of Love" supervising sexual relations, were regarded as overly controversial by his disciples and were suppressed. Fourier's account of commerce, like Owen's, focused on converting all forms of unproductive into productive labor by pooling resources communally and abolishing idleness. The system of "attractive association" was to be applied to work in order to release individual creative potential, and monotony was to be avoided by a scheme of rotation of up to eight tasks daily. The Phalanx was not designed to be completely communistic, and the product was to be divided into three parts: capital receiving four-twelfths, labor five-twelfths, and talent three-twelfths. The Fourierist movement spawned a number of communities in France and Britain, and rather more in the United States, notably during the 1840s. Fourier's chief disciple in France in this period was Victor-Prosper Considerant (1809–1893), while in the United States Albert Brisbane (1809–1890) proved an indefatigable interpreter.

SAINT-SIMON AND SAINT-SIMONISM

While both Owenism and Fourierism were communitarian in orientation, the third main strand of early-nineteenth-century European socialism, Saint-Simonism, was oriented toward alterations in the nation-state as a whole. Founded by Claude-Henri de Rouvroy, comte de Saint-Simon (1760–1825), a French aristocrat, the initial system was not socialist as such, but instead focused on the need for industrial reorganization. Saint-Simon coined the term *industrialism* to describe the progressive development of the modern economic system and its supplanting of earlier forms of both social and political organization, notably feudalism. In *L'industrie* (1816–1818) society is divided into three leading classes: scientists, writers, and artists; proprietors; and toilers. In the future, spiritual power was to be exercised by the first; temporal power, or control of the state, by the second; and the right of election by all workers. All useful workers were termed "industrialists" by Saint-Simon, who saw the postrevolutionary era as one of significant transition from a feudal or governmental regime to an industrial or administrative regime, where regulation of the process of production assumed primacy over the traditional mechanisms of regulating social behavior through politics. For Saint-Simon the future regime was to be meritocratic in the extreme, with a growing harmony of interests assumed between managers and the workforce. Politically, nations would offer economic "plans," but their development would be independent of national parliaments. Saint-Simon also proposed, in *De la réorganisation de la société européenne* (1814; Concerning the reorganization of European society), the reduction in influence of the European nation-state through a transnational European parliament composed of two houses.

Saint-Simon's most notable followers included his secretary, Auguste Comte (1798–1857), whose system, styled "positivism," was influential in the later nineteenth century, and a group of overtly socialist disciples, such as Olinde Rodrigue, Barthélemy-Prosper Enfantin, Philippe Buchez, Saint-Amand Bazard, Gustave d'Eichtal, and Michel Chevalier, who by the early 1830s had extended Saint-Simon's influence widely, even to Thomas Carlyle (1795–1881) in Britain. Their leading manifesto, *The Doctrine of Saint-Simon* (1828–1829), urged greater equality for women, ease of divorce, expanded national education, and a remodeling of both the productive and banking systems. The Saint-Simonian philosophy of history, and assumption of the leading role to be played by the supervision of production by contrast to traditional forms of government, were taken up by Marx and Carlyle, among later writers.

Among other early French socialist writers of note, mention should be made of Étienne Cabet (1788–1856), whose *Voyage en Icarie* (1840) helped to produce a communitarian emigrant movement in the United States, and Louis Blanc (1811–1882), whose *Organisation du travail* (1840) helped influence debates about the relationship between the state and the economy following the Revolution of 1848, and who is regarded as among the founders of state socialism.

KARL MARX

Early German socialism prior to Marx produced several thinkers of note, particularly Wilhelm Weitling (1808–1871), author of *Mankind as It Is and as It Ought to Be* (1838) and *Guarantees of Harmony and Freedom* (1842), and Moses Hess (1812–1875). No German socialist writer, however, achieved the stature of Karl Marx (1818–1883). The son of a Jewish lawyer converted to Protestantism, Marx was born and raised in Trier, and attended university in Bonn and then Berlin, where he was deeply influenced by Georg Wilhelm Friedrich Hegel (1770–1831). Hegel's followers in the early 1840s were divided into the "Young" or "Left" Hegelians, who contended that the dialectical process of historical development implied the emergence of a successively progressive, democratic regime, and his more orthodox disciples, who supported the view that the existing Prussian state exemplified the highest development that reason or "spirit" could assume. Emigrating to the Rhineland in 1842, Marx fell under the influence of the philosopher Ludwig Feuerbach (1804–1872), whose materialist account of religion as the projection of individual fears and desires led him to reject the Hegelian system. In 1844 in Paris, Marx converted to communism while applying the Feuerbachian scheme of alienation to his reading of Adam Smith's *Wealth of Nations* (1776). The "Paris Manuscripts," unpublished until the 1930s, offered an account of the varieties of alienation undergone by the working classes, and assumed as a central critical standpoint Feuerbach's theory that the "species

being," or communal essence possessed by all, was eradicated by the egotistical and competitive nature of modern commercial society. Since alienated labor was for Marx founded in the institution of private property as such, only its abolition, or communism, would bring about the resumption of a "general human emancipation" and reinforcement of the sociable aspects of human nature.

Nonetheless this analysis was in turn superseded after Marx commenced an intellectual partnership with a young German merchant also recently converted to communism, Friedrich Engels (1820–1895), whose account of industrial conditions in Manchester, *The Condition of the Working Class in England in 1844*, was published in 1845. Following their collaboration Marx and Engels agreed that any new critical system must be based on an amalgamation of the three most highly developed trends in European thought in the period, German philosophy, especially the critique of religion; French politics, in its revolutionary form; and British political economy, which provided the most incisive account of the actual workings of civil society. In the winter of 1845–1846 Marx and Engels wrote the work later published (but again not until the 1930s) as "The German Ideology," in which they now set aside as abstract the materialism of Feuerbach, and substituted instead the theory known as the "materialist conception of history." While much of Marx's energies at this point were devoted to distancing himself from his opponents on the left, notably Bruno Bauer (1809–1882) and the "True Socialists," attacked in *The Holy Family* (1845); the French mutualist Pierre-Joseph Proudhon (1809–1865), the target of *The Poverty of Philosophy* (1846); and the German individualist, Max Stirner (Johann Kaspar Schmidt; 1806–1856), the subject of the longest section of the "German Ideology"; the latter text also sets forth in outline the chief elements of what would later be regarded as the Marxian system. These consist, firstly, of a historical account of the succession of forms of property ownership from the earliest period to the present, in which three early types of ownership (tribal; ancient communal and state ownership, where slavery exists and private property begins; and feudal property) are succeeded by the emergence of the modern capitalist system of production; secondly, of the insistence on analyzing society

Austrian leaflet c. 1900. Illustration by Friedrich Kaskeline. A leaflet for the Austrian Social Democratic Party features a rhinocerous labelled "capitalism" impeding the progress of a locomotive labelled "the working people," fuelled by the Social Democratic Party. © AUSTRIAN ARCHIVES/CORBIS

in terms of an economic "basis"—the mode of production or system of property ownership—from which is derived the system of social and political relations, law, religion, politics, and thought as well, which constitute the "superstructure" of society; and thirdly, of the description of the motive force of social development as the struggle between classes, with the contest between the wealthy bourgeoisie and the propertyless proletariat looming as the decisive moment of modern history.

In this account Marx and Engels thus finally disposed of the Hegelian idealist system as well as Feuerbach's nonhistorical materialism. Politically, they dismissed the existing state as merely an organizing committee for bourgeois industrial and commercial interests, assuming instead in a Saint-Simonian vein that the organization of production would take priority in the future society. In a famous passage that suggests that in communist society one might alternate between hunting, fishing, rearing cattle, and engaging in critical activity in the course of a day, there are also echoes of Fourier's scheme for rotation of tasks. Given the sparsity of references to such

themes in the later works of Marx and Engels, doubts have been cast on the seriousness with which they may have been intended.

Nonetheless the single most famous exposition of Marx and Engels's social, political, and economic program, the *Manifesto of the Communist Party* (1848), certainly brings forward the leading themes of the "German Ideology." Commissioned by the leading revolutionary socialist organization of the period, the Communist League, the *Manifesto* describes the rise and development of the industrial proletariat, its growing poverty, the successive series of cyclical capitalist crises that further enrich the bourgeoisie, and the final crisis—then anticipated—in which the proletariat would seize power; establish a temporary "dictatorship of the proletariat" that would centralize the means of credit, communication, transportation, and production; and set in motion the eventual creation of the final stage of social development, "communist society." Marx's political thought remained relatively little developed, though during the Paris Commune (1870–1871) he suggested (in *The Civil*

Wars in France) that the form of government elected there corresponded to his notions of the "dictatorship of the proletariat." He has however been criticized for underestimating the force of nationalism in modern history.

Forced into exile in Britain, where he remained, often in poverty, for the rest of his life, Marx devoted most of his subsequent years to the analysis of the inner workings of the capitalist system, first in the *Critique of Political Economy* (1859), but most famously in *Das Kapital*, the first volume of which appeared in 1867, which offers an account of the generation of "surplus value" by way of assessing how the capitalist exploits the labor-power of the proletariat. In exile Marx was also active politically in the International Workingmen's Association, founded in London in 1864 but eventually dissolved following constant infighting with its anarchist members, led by one of Marx's leading critics, Mikhail Bakunin (1814–1876), whose *State and Anarchy* (1873) lambasted Marx's supposed dictatorial tendencies. Engels's later writings include *Anti-Dühring* (1878), which moved the materialist conception of history closer to an orientation with the natural sciences, *The Origins of the Family, Private Property, and the State* (1884), and a popular pamphlet, *Socialism: Utopian and Scientific* (1880).

THE DEVELOPMENT OF LATE-NINETEENTH-CENTURY SOCIALISM

Between Marx's death and the Bolshevik Revolution of 1917 the most important working-class movement inspired by his ideas emerged in Germany. German Social Democracy made a number of substantial innovations to it, notably in proposing a nonviolent, electoral strategy as a strategy for achieving political power. Here Ferdinand Lassalle (1825–1864), its earliest leader, was chiefly instrumental in proposing a view of the state as a neutral agency capable of being utilized by a proletarian political party, though Marx rejected the party's program in the *Critique of the Gotha Programme* (1875). Lassalle's chief successor was Karl Kautsky (1854–1938), whose "revisionist" Marxism stressed both the need to await the ripening of material conditions and the possibility of using existing parliamentary institutions to introduce fundamental social and economic changes. Such views were supported by Eduard Bernstein (1850–1932), whose *Evolutionary Socialism* (1898) provided a

restatement of the gradualist case. Bernstein also stressed the need for revision of Marx's account of capitalist crises, by emphasizing the increasing propensity of large-scale capitalist enterprises to stabilize in quasi-monopolistic forms. In *How Is Scientific Socialism Possible* (1901), Bernstein also broke from the argument that communism emerged inevitably out of the development of capitalism, describing it instead in quasi-moralistic terms as an ideal to be achieved. Such views, however, met with vehement opposition from the more revolutionary wing of the Social Democratic Party, notably Rosa Luxemburg (1870–1919), whose *Social Reform or Revolution* (1899) insisted on the necessity for a revolutionary commencement of the socialist regime. Luxemburg also stressed the growing internationalization of capitalism in the late nineteenth century, and its connections with imperialism, a thesis developed by New Liberal writers such as John Atkinson Hobson (1858–1940) as well as Marx's greatest Russian disciple, Vladimir Lenin (Vladimir Ilich Ulyanov; 1870–1924), who also provided a new account of the necessity for a vanguard of professional revolutionaries to introduce communism.

OTHER VARIETIES OF LATER-NINETEENTH-CENTURY SOCIALISM

Although Marxism emerged ideologically as victorious over other competing forms of socialism in the early twentieth century, a much greater range of socialist doctrine and movement is evident in the later nineteenth century. Less powerful Marxist parties developed in other European nations in this period, and there were also a variety of contending forms of non-Marxian socialism. In France, the Parti Ouvrier emerged in 1875–1876 after the failure of the Commune and was led by Jules Guesde (1845–1922). In Britain, Henry Mayers Hyndman (1842–1921) founded the Democratic Federation in 1881, while William Morris (1834–1896) united the Romantic, creative, and aesthetic ideals of John Ruskin (1819–1900) to a more anti-authoritarian brand of socialist program described most successfully in his utopia, *News from Nowhere* (1890), and through his organization, the Socialist League. Morris also insisted on restricting heavy industry wherever possible and curbing the propensity toward centralization evident both in modern capitalist development and Marxian theory. A growing stress on the individual in British

Participants at the tenth convention of the Italian Socialist Party, 1908. ©ALINARI ARCHIVES/CORBIS

socialism was shared by Edward Carpenter (1844–1929), author of *Civilization: Its Cause and Cure* (1889). Considerably more influential from a literary standpoint was Herbert George Wells (1866–1946), whose early dystopian satires gave way to a positive program of socialistic reform, partially outlined initially in *A Modern Utopia* (1905), and which brought him to associate with the Fabian socialists, notably Beatrice Webb (1858–1943), Sidney Webb (1859–1947), and George Bernard Shaw (1856–1950). The hallmark of Fabian socialism lay in its emphasis on gradual, incremental permeation of the political establishment and its reliance on the creation of an administrative, bureaucratic elite to oversee the development of a social reform program.

Throughout the nineteenth century, socialism also combined in various European countries with Christian reform doctrines and movements of varying types, producing a notable movement

in Britain, linked to the cooperative movement between 1848 and 1854, and led by Frederick Denison Maurice (1805–1872). Land nationalization movements in various countries, such as that led in Britain by the naturalist Alfred Russel Wallace (1823–1913), also contributed to the popularization of socialist ideals. A semiauthoritarian socialism indebted in part to Saint-Simon was popularized by Thomas Carlyle, whose *Past and Present* (1843) also promoted a philomedievalism of considerable influence later in the century. Among liberals, too, a group of reformers usually termed "New Liberals" emerged in late-nineteenth-century Britain, notably the economist and social theorist John Atkinson Hobson, author of *The Evolution of Modern Capitalism* (1894), *Imperialism* (1902), and other works. Distinctive to Hobson's views was an extension of the Ruskinian humanist critique of political economy, and the proposed development of a dual-sphere economy in which state-production would not supersede but operate alongside private enterprise. The growing tendency toward collectivism in British liberalism in this period was lent credence by the sympathetic treatment of socialism offered by the leading liberal philosopher and political economist of the period, John Stuart Mill (1806–1873), whose opposition to Marxian revolutionary socialism was nonetheless tempered by the proposal that capitalism might reach a "stationary state" where economic development could give way to a more qualitative emphasis on education and cultural activity. The growing trend toward statist intervention in most late-nineteenth-century European economies, however, was indebted to other factors besides the popular success of socialist agitation, including evangelical and philanthropical movements of humanitarian reform and the desire of authoritarian leaders to avoid greater socialist successes by introducing their own welfare measures (as in the case of the German chancellor Otto von Bismarck).

See also **Blanc, Louis; Capitalism; Class and Social Relations; Cooperative Movements; Industrial Revolution, First; Industrial Revolution, Second; Labor Movements; Liberalism; Owen, Robert; Strikes; Utopian Socialism.**

BIBLIOGRAPHY

Avineri, Shlomo. *The Social and Political Thought of Karl Marx.* London, 1968.

Beecher, Jonathan. *Charles Fourier: The Visionary and His World.* Berkeley, Calif., 1986.

Butler, Eliza M. *The Saint-Simonian Religion in Germany: A Study of the Young German Movement.* Cambridge, U.K., 1926.

Carver, Terrell. *Marx's Social Theory.* New York, 1982.

Claeys, Gregory. *Machinery, Money, and the Millennium: From Moral Economy to Socialism, 1815–1860.* Princeton, N.J., 1987.

———. *Citizens and Saints: Politics and Anti-Politics in Early British Socialism.* New York, 1989.

Cohen, Gerald A. *Karl Marx's Theory of History: A Defence.* Oxford, U.K., 1978.

Cole, George D. H. *A History of Socialist Thought.* Vol. 1: *Socialist Thought: The Forerunners, 1789–1850.* London, 1959.

Davidson, Rondel Van. *Did We Think Victory Great?: The Life and Ideas of Victor Considerant.* Lanham, Md., 1988.

Guarneri, Carl. *The Utopian Alternative: Fourierism in Nineteenth-Century America.* Ithaca, N.Y., 1991.

Guttsman, W. L. *The German Social Democratic Party, 1875–1933: From Ghetto to Government.* Boston, 1981.

Hunt, Richard. *Marxism and Totalitarian Democracy, 1818–1850.* Pittsburgh, Pa., 1974.

Iggers, Georg G., trans. *The Doctrine of Saint-Simon: An Exposition: First Year, 1828–1829.* New York, 1972.

Johnson, Christopher H. *Utopian Communism in France: Cabet and the Icarians, 1839–1851.* Ithaca, N.Y., 1974.

Kolakowski, Leszek. *Main Currents of Marxism.* 3 vols. Oxford, U.K., 1978.

Lattek, Christine. *Revolutionary Refugees: German Socialism in Britain, 1840–1860.* New York, 2005.

Lichtheim, George. *Marxism: An Historical and Critical Study.* London, 1964.

———. *The Origins of Socialism.* New York, 1969.

Maguire, John. *Marx's Paris Writings: An Analysis.* New York, 1972.

Manuel, Frank. *The New World of Henri Saint-Simon.* Cambridge, Mass., 1956.

McLellan, David. *The Thought of Karl Marx: An Introduction.* New York, 1971.

———. *Marxism after Marx: An Introduction.* London, 1980.

Mészáros, István. *Marx's Theory of Alienation.* New York, 1970.

Morgan, Roger. *The German Social Democrats and the First International, 1864–1872.* Cambridge, U.K., 1965.

Ollman, Bertell. *Alienation: Marx's Conception of Man in Capitalist Society.* New York, 1976.

Parekh, Bhikhu. *Marx's Theory of Ideology.* London, 1982.

Reichard, Richard. *Crippled from Birth: German Social Democracy, 1844–1870.* Ames, Iowa, 1969.

Tucker, Robert. *Philosophy and Myth in Karl Marx.* Cambridge, U.K., 1961.

Wittke, Carl. *The Utopian Communist: A Biography of Wilhelm Weitling, Nineteenth-Century Reformer.* Baton Rouge, La., 1950.

GREGORY CLAEYS

SOCIALISM, CHRISTIAN. *Christian Socialism* was the name given to a variety of religious groups during the nineteenth century in western Europe who tried to apply Christian teachings to solve social and economic problems resulting from industrialization. Only in England, from the 1850s through the 1920s, did groups formally

use the name "Christian Socialists." Informally, observers at various times applied it to Christian social activists in France, Belgium, and Germany. In 1850 a number of Anglican Christians, that is, members of the Church of England, created the Society for Promoting Working Men's Associations along with its journal, *The Christian Socialist*. This marked the first widely known use of the term. This group was inspired, and led for a time, by F. D. Maurice, Charles Kingsley, John Ludlow, and Edward Vansittart Neale. At the time, the Anglican Church usually had little to say about the terrible conditions of workers, beyond advocating charity on the part of the wealthy. The Christian Socialists believed that Biblical teachings justified workers' associations and governmental regulation of labor. Taking the medieval guilds of independent artisans as their inspiration, they supported producers' cooperatives more than they did true labor unions. While strongly encouraging workers to form associations, they usually hoped that educated middle-class Christians would play a leading role in these groups. The goal of the workers' associations would be social solidarity in place of antagonism between workers and the upper class.

Neither these Anglican leaders nor any of the activists elsewhere called Christian Socialists advocated government ownership of private property. In this sense, they were never truly socialist in the Marxist sense. Nonetheless, the advocacy for workers' associations and government action appeared radical among Christians in the nineteenth century.

The Society for Promoting Working Men's Associations and its journal soon ended in the mid-1850s, but their ideas and example continued. In 1889 a small but influential group of Anglican clergy and laypeople organized the Christian Social Union and its journal, *The Church Socialist;* this organization lasted until 1919. A similar Church Socialist League was founded by Baptists and other "nonconformists," that is, Protestants outside of the Church of England, in 1886, although some Anglicans were active in it; its organizers had begun publishing *Christian Socialist* in 1883. These groups abandoned the nostalgia for workers' associations or producers' cooperatives modeled on medieval guilds. Instead, through the Labour Party, they

supported labor unions and workers' political action to gain unemployment insurance, pensions, and state-supported housing. The more radical, still largely Anglican, Church Socialist League, founded in 1906, which began publishing *The Church Socialist* in 1912, advocated this program most clearly. They helped create within the British Labour Party an openness to Christianity and a resistance to anticlericalism that had no counterpart among socialist parties in France, Germany, Italy, or elsewhere in continental Europe. The most famous leader of this tendency was Philip Snowden (1864–1937), a Methodist weaver's son and member of the Free Church Socialist League, founded in 1909, who became a cabinet member in Labour Party governments in the 1920s and 1930s.

Some French Catholics in the 1840s who supported democracy and aiding workers were called Christian Socialists. Their most important leader, Philippe Buchez, like many of the British Christian Socialists, called for the creation of associations in which workers could provide insurance, regulate their trades, and advocate for better conditions. This wave of activism ended in the harsh struggles between Left and Right in the years following the Revolution of 1848 in France.

The intellectual basis of Catholicism as a social doctrine that provided an alternative to socialism is best seen, for example, in Juan Donoso Cortés's *Essay on Catholicism, Liberalism, and Socialism,* published in 1851: "Liberalism cultivates only individuality, even isolation. Socialism ... reacts against the prospect of savage competition with ... regimentation and collectivism." Catholic Christianity, Donoso Cortés argued, offered a third way. Social solidarity on Christian principles could protect workers without destroying liberty. Most "social Catholics" in the mid-nineteenth century concerned about the plight of workers, however, were still more inclined toward providing charity than creating organizations of workers that took account of their economic grievances. The Society of St. Vincent de Paul and other organizations offered food, clothing, and education. Catholic groups of workers, such as those inspired by Adolph Kolping, a German priest, beginning in 1846, were to be social, religious, and nonpolitical. Wilhelm von Ketteler, bishop of Mainz, Germany, in his 1864 work titled *The Work-*

ers' *Question and Christianity,* went further and called for state recognition of workers' associations and the need for these groups to make political demands. Only gradually did social Catholics give up the dream of re-creating the supposedly harmonious craft guilds of the pre–French Revolutionary period. Arthur Verhaegen, a sponsor of the Society of St. Vincent de Paul, helped found a Catholic labor union federation in Ghent, Belgium, in 1891. As he declared, "Charity is not enough to guarantee what is right. Next to it one must have justice." Pope Leo XIII's encyclical *Rerum Novarum,* promulgated in 1891, called on Catholics to solve economic grievances. Without advocating labor unions specifically, the pope provided an intellectual basis for their support. Catholic labor unions were usually allied with Christian Democratic political parties, which also began in Belgium, the Netherlands, Germany, Italy, Austria, and France in the 1890s. The Christian unions in Germany were exceptional in including both Protestants and Catholics. In the Netherlands, conservative Calvinists, under the leadership of a future prime minister, Abraham Kuyper, and the Anti-Revolutionary Party, provided the only example of Protestant Christian Democracy and organized their own labor unions. While called Christian Socialists by their opponents on both left and right, that is, by Marxist socialists or anarchists and by conservative Catholics, Catholic labor activists almost never used this term themselves. Yet it was frequently used to attack them. Verhaegen, who was of aristocratic descent, was sometimes mocked as the "Red Baron" for his allegedly left-wing sympathies. Catholic unions, although much smaller than those of the socialists, ensured that Christian Democratic parties would not be exclusively middle class and rural. As a result, Christian Democracy joined socialism as the most important political movements in much of continental Europe in the twentieth century.

See also **Catholicism, Political; Socialism.**

BIBLIOGRAPHY

Primary Source

Fremantle, Anne, ed. *The Papal Encyclicals in Their Historical Context.* New York, 1956.

Nitti, Francesco. *Catholic Socialism.* 3rd ed. Translated from the 2nd Italian ed. by Mary Mackintosh. London, 1911.

Secondary Sources

Backstrom, Philip N. *Christian Socialism and Co-operation in Victorian England: Edward Vansittart Neale and the Co-operative Movement.* London, 1974.

Berenson, Edward. *Populist Religion and Left-Wing Politics in France, 1830–1852.* Princeton, N.J., 1984.

Brose, Eric Dorn. *Christian Labor and the Politics of Frustration in Imperial Germany.* Washington, D.C., 1985.

Jones, Peter d'A. *The Christian Socialist Revival, 1877–1914: Religion, Class, and Social Conscience in Late Victorian England.* Princeton, N.J., 1968.

Kalyvas, Stathis N. *The Rise of Christian Democracy in Europe.* Ithaca, N.Y., 1996.

Misner, Paul. *Social Catholicism in Europe: From the Onset of Industrialization to the First World War.* New York, 1991.

Reckitt, Maurice B., ed. *For Christ and the People: Studies of Four Socialist Priests and Prophets of the Church of England between 1870 and 1930.* London, 1968.

Strikwerda, Carl. "A Resurgent Religion: The Rise of Catholic Social Movements in Nineteenth-Century Belgian Cities." In *European Religion in the Age of the Great Cities, 1830–1930,* edited by Hugh McLeod, 61–89. London, 1995.

CARL J. STRIKWERDA

SOCIALIST REVOLUTIONARIES.

The Socialist Revolutionary Party (PSR) organized workers, peasants, and the intelligentsia to overthrow the tsar and bring socialism to early-twentieth-century Russia. Although the PSR adapted Marxist ideology to Russian circumstances, it differed from the Russian Social Democratic Labor Party in tactics and political program. The PSR was organized in 1901 and 1902, developed a program in 1906, experienced factional conflict between the revolutions of 1905 and 1917, and in February 1917 emerged as the leading mass political party only to be defeated by party schisms over policy issues and political maneuvering in the Soviet government.

EARLY ORGANIZATION

In mid-nineteenth-century Russia, most socialists were populists who hoped that Russia could skip capitalism and develop socialism based upon the peasant commune. Populism produced a political party, Land and Liberty, which subsequently split over tactical and political questions. After the terrorist faction, the People's Will, assassinated Tsar Alexander II in 1881, populist organizations were decimated by arrests. Coupled with the advance of capitalism, the repression of the terrorists forced a reconsideration of revolutionary theory and practice. As a result, three neopopulist groups emerged in the 1890s. Centered in Saratov, Voronezh, and Minsk, the neopopulists focused agitation on urban centers and generally retained the populist tactic of terrorism. In January 1901 the first SR newspaper, *Revolutionary Russia,* was published in Moscow.

In a series of meetings in 1901 and 1902, the neopopulists Grigory A. Gershuni (1870–1908), Yekaterina K. Breshko-Breshkovskaya (1844–1934), Mikhail R. Gots (1866–1906), and Victor M. Chernov (1876–1952) engineered the formation of the PSR. Final impetus for unification was drawn from the peasant risings in 1902, which justified a role for the peasantry in the coming revolution. Chernov, arrested as a student in Moscow, later exiled to Tambov and an émigré after 1899, was the chief architect of the draft program adopted at the first party congress in January 1906. Chernov's program synthesized populist ideology and Marxism. While retaining a role for the individual, Chernov called for the formation of a revolutionary political party, based on mass agitation and propaganda, comprising peasants, workers, and the revolutionary intelligentsia. The program supported civil rights and liberties, separation of church and state, rights for nationalities within a federation, four-tailed (free, equal, secret, and direct) suffrage, election of a constituent assembly, and the formation of a people's militia. The agrarian program called for socialization of the land based upon the "right to land" and self-administration. Workers were promised an eight-hour day, a minimum wage, legal unions, social insurance, and progressive taxation. The party's Fighting Organization, organized in 1901 to carry out terrorist activities, supported terror for the purpose of defending the party from state repression, avenging unjust persecution of political activists, and demonstrating individual honor and self-sacrifice of its membership. As part of a system of revolutionary activity, the PSR asserted, terror could disorganize the state and cause the masses to act. Indeed, the assassinations of the minister of the interior, V. K. Plehve, in July 1904 and Grand Duke Sergei Alexandrovich in February 1905 by the Fighting Organization persuaded many to join the PSR.

SRS AND OTHER REVOLUTIONARY GROUPS

The PSR differed from the Social Democrats and other Marxists in its theory of class, in the decision to adopt terrorism, and in its theory of revolution. Chernov and the PSR defended the revolutionary intelligentsia as an avant-garde born of ideas not socioeconomics. Marxists relegated the intelligentsia to the capitalist class, although they conceded that the intelligentsia could become professional revolutionaries and adopt the worldview of workers. The PSR also allowed for the development of socialism among the peasantry because both peasants and workers remained impoverished and therefore oppressed by capitalism. Chernov and the PSR remained convinced that the unity of workers and peasants was required in Russia for a successful socialist revolution. Marxists believed the peasantry to be reactionary not revolutionary. The tactic of terror evoked the most serious conflicts between Marxist theorists and the PSR. Karl Marx indicated that terror, an act of isolated individuals, actually separated the party from the masses and could never act as a catalyst for revolution. Disorganization of the government could be accomplished only by a broad mass organization, never by the action of individuals. Finally, Russian revolutionaries convinced of Russian backwardness and the weakness of the bourgeoisie struggled with the theory of revolution. Marx indicated that the stage of capitalism was a necessary precondition for the socialist revolution, thereby effectively postponing Russian socialism to the distant future. To correct this dilemma, Leon Trotsky (1879–1940), a Russian Marxist, argued that the bourgeois revolution had to be made permanent by the actions of the proletariat, or working class, who would carry out the revolutionary tasks assigned by Marx to the bourgeoisie and transform Russia into socialism. Chernov's revolutionary theory called for a transitional revolutionary dictatorship between the bourgeois and socialist revolutions accompanied by socialization of the land to win socialism in the countryside.

The organizational structure of the PSR was similar to that of other revolutionary political parties in Russia. A central committee remained the leading institution directing the actions of committees at district, village, city, regional, and provincial levels. Leaders were both elected and co-opted following traditional methods in existence at local levels. An organizational bureau established in 1906 coordinated communication between the center and the periphery and administered finances and distribution of illegal literature. The party congress, which met only twice before 1914, was to decide major tactical, program, and policy issues. To supplement the rare congresses, party councils were held to address crises in the party such as responses to elections and the Azef affair in 1909. The PSR was financed by personal donations, dues, and foreign fund-raising trips to the West. Both formal organization and funding hindered centralized operations especially after 1907.

FROM 1905 TO 1917: REVOLUTION AND DEFEAT

By 1905, the PSR had become a mass party with cadres in urban centers as well as village committees. After the October Manifesto (1905) and the promulgation of the Fundamental Laws (1906), which promised a parliamentary regime and civil liberties, the PSR voted to boycott elections to the First Duma or Russian parliament. The PSR participated in elections to the Second Duma and collaborated with other socialist parties in the elections to secure victories for revolutionary activists. In 1907 state repression ended the party's temporary renunciation of terror.

Factional conflict plagued the PSR from the onset. On the left the Maximalists adopted economic terror against industrialists and landowners. By 1906 their determination to use bribery, expropriation, and extortion led to their formal expulsion from the PSR. On the right, the People's Socialists left the party during the "days of freedom" (1905–1907) when it became possible to abandon illegal organization. After the legalization of associations in 1906, many revolutionaries remained reluctant to return to underground activity. Before World War I, Chernov had successfully defeated the call by some party members to abandon illegal activity and concentrate agitation in legally recognized associations.

The most dangerous controversy involved the admission of the Central Committee in 1909 that Evno Azef (1869–1918), a prominent figure in the party and a leader of the Fighting Organization, was a police spy. Despite earlier evidence that Azef might be guilty, the Central Committee had refused to investigate and continued to promote Azef into prominent positions. Many in the Central Committee rejected the continuation of terrorist tactics as a result. The Fighting Organization remained ineffective after the scandal despite attempts to revive it.

From 1907 to 1917, the PSR participated in legal and illegal revolutionary activity inside Russia. Cooperation and collaboration with Social Democrats produced a broad-based revolutionary culture before the outbreak of World War I in 1914. Socialists cooperated in a number of legal congresses and conferences called to assemble doctors, women, teachers, leaders of cooperatives, and other professionals inside Russia. These activities contributed to the PSR's popularity among the widest cross section of Russian revolutionary groups—workers, peasants, and the intelligentsia.

During World War I, factions again emerged among most revolutionary groups. Chernov adopted an internationalist stance, while other party leaders became "defensists" and sought to secure Russia against defeat especially after the tsar was overthrown in the February Revolution of 1917. The Provisional Government formed in February was considered to represent the bourgeoisie, while the soviets represented the working masses. After a crisis threatened to topple the Provisional Government, PSR members on the right decided to cooperate with liberals and other moderate socialists. The Left Socialist Revolutionaries rejected cooperation with the Provisional Government and remained with the Bolsheviks in the Soviets. As the war continued, political and economic instability deepened and the Left SRs supported the overthrow of the Provisional Government in October 1917. The SRs held a majority in the Constituent Assembly that met in January 1918. It was dissolved within days by the new Bolshevik-dominated Soviet government. In March 1918 the Left SRs abandoned the government when a separate peace was signed with Germany. During the civil war, many SRs openly opposed the Soviets. After the defeat of opposition forces, many fled into exile abroad while others joined the Soviet government and became members of the Communist Party. The PSR was officially disbanded inside Russia in 1922.

See also **Bolsheviks; Mensheviks; Populists.**

BIBLIOGRAPHY

Primary Sources

Breshko-Breshkovskaia, Ekaterina Konstantinovna. *Hidden Springs of the Russian Revolution: Personal Memoirs of Katerina Breshkovskaia.* Stanford, Calif., 1931.

Chernov, Viktor M. *Zapiski sotsialista-revoliutsionera.* Berlin, 1922. Reprint, with a new introduction by Constantine Brancovan. Cambridge, Mass., 1975.

Secondary Sources

Hildermeier, Manfred. *The Russian Socialist Revolutionary Party before the First World War.* New York, 2000. English translation of the 1978 classic study of the SRs before 1914.

Melancon, Michael. *Stormy Petrels: The Socialist Revolutionaries in Russia's Labor Organizations, 1905–1914.* Pittsburgh, Pa., 1988. Systematic archival study of local activities between the revolutions.

Perrie, Maureen. *The Agrarian Policy of the Russian Socialist-Revolutionary Party from Its Origins through the Revolution of 1905–1907.* Cambridge, U.K., 1976. Focuses on the peasantry and the SRs.

Radkey, Oliver H. *The Agrarian Foes of Bolshevism: Promise and Default of the Russian Socialist Revolutionaries, February to October 1917.* New York, 1958. First three chapters cover the period before 1917.

Rice, Christopher. *Russian Workers and the Socialist-Revolutionary Party through the Revolution of 1905–07.* New York, 1988. Focuses on the urban activity of the SRs.

ALICE K. PATE

SOCIOLOGY. Auguste Comte coined the word *sociology* in the 1830s, but the idea of sociology had been developing for more than a century. The French tradition in which Comte (1798–1857) wrote stretched back through Henri de Saint-Simon, the marquis de Condorcet, and Jean-Jacques Rousseau to the baron de Montesquieu. But sociology's roots could be traced equally to Giambattista Vico in Italy; Thomas Hobbes and John Locke in England; Adam Ferguson, Adam Smith, and the Scottish moralists; and Johann Gottfried von Herder and Georg Wilhelm Friedrich Hegel in Germany. In different ways, these figures all contributed to the rise of a notion of "society" and "social organization" as distinct from government. This idea was prominent in explorations of natural law, pivotal to histories of civil society, and influentially linked to the development of nationalism. Starting in the late eighteenth century, it took on new significance in reflections on social change and attempts to redesign government. The American and especially the French revolutions marked a sharp increase in self-conscious attempts to reorganize society. The latter also brought a conservative reaction, famously from Edmund Burke and Joseph-Marie de Maistre, which stressed the danger of interfering too sharply with the social order inherited from centuries of trial-and-error testing and tradition.

SOCIAL CHANGE AND SOCIAL ORDER

Sociology was from the outset marked by both an engagement with projects of social reform and an understanding of society as quasi natural, even organic—and by the tension between the two. This grew more pronounced during the nineteenth century. New inequalities; industrialization and the squalor associated with rapid urbanization; intensified fear of immigrants; crime; and challenges to idealized family life all brought forth privately organized ameliorative projects, incipient welfare states, and challenging social movements. Sociology took shape while trying to inform each. But at the same time, concern for social order—and attempts to reestablish it after revolutionary disruptions—was enduringly central. The most influential theories of the century were broadly evolutionary and "objectivist" in trying to treat society as a natural phenomenon; Max Weber's interpretive historical sociology marked the most distinguished exception.

Sociology grew in distinct national traditions. A core concern was the course of social transformation associated with urbanization and industrial capitalism and its implications for social solidarity. In Germany, this received classical formulation in Ferdinand Tönnies's distinction between *gemeinschaft* and *gesellschaft* (1887). The basic contrast between small-scale village communities featuring dense social networks, face-to-face relationships, and a shared self-understanding with not only cities but also the larger, more abstract, more formally organized society of which they were a part was widely influential. Émile Durkheim (1858–1917) addressed a similar theme with an 1893 contrast between "mechanical" solidarity based on similarity (informed by anthropological accounts of segmentary lineage societies) and "organic" solidarity structured through the exchanges and complementarity among differentiated groups and occupations in larger, more modern societies. Sir Henry Maine (1822–1888) in 1861 stressed the shift from inherited status to individually chosen contract. More generally, the rise of modern society was seen as producing a new level of individualism.

Alexis de Tocqueville (1805–1859) had coined the term *individualism* in his study titled *Democracy in America* (1835–1840), and like democracy itself it could be seen as a trend without always being praised. Tocqueville was not a professional sociologist but very much part of the intellectual history of the emerging field. His concerns for how a more egalitarian society that prized individual choice might be held together without turning to tyrannical central government not only reflected ancient questions of political philosophy but also informed the development of sociology. If political scientists commonly approached this question in terms of the best structures of government, sociologists addressed it in terms of the sources of social solidarity, which they saw variously in culture and structures of social relationships.

Perhaps the single most influential sociologist of the nineteenth century, Herbert Spencer (1820–1903), was also concerned with the distinctive character of modern society but, unlike Tocqueville, unambiguously in favor of its growing individualism. Spencer's American follower, William Graham Sumner, would link Spencer's concept of "survival of the fittest" to individualistic free-market doctrines in the notion of "social Darwinism." Spencer situated his major works of sociology within an attempt to achieve an integrated theory of all evolution, biological—and indeed geological and cosmic—as well as sociological. Perhaps partly for this reason, and also because it was resisted at the ancient universities, sociology did not develop much as an autonomous discipline in Britain, though social

reformers and social historians advanced sociological theories, and the social survey was an important factor in policy making and public debate.

The continental European pioneer of the social survey was Frédéric Le Play (1806–1882), whose studies of work and family life in the mid-nineteenth century pioneered empirical research. A Catholic conservative, Le Play was concerned not to promote social change but to defend the importance of the institutions that contained it and shaped social solidarity, including religion, parental authority, and social hierarchy. The effort to document social conditions—and social problems—was, however, taken up by a variety of activists and reformers. In Britain, Charles Booth and B. Seebohm Rowntree focused on the extent of urban poverty as well as the diversity of livelihoods of the people of London (building on similar efforts by less analytic social reformers such as Henry Mayhew).

SOCIOLOGY AS SCIENCE

In most of Europe, the project of a scientific sociology was developed with a strong emphasis on theory. Comte coined not only the term *sociology*, but also *positivism*, by which he meant a program of scientific work that would guide the reorganization of society. Positivism took shape both as a widely influential movement for administrative reform and as a proposed nontheological religion of society itself (which was practiced well into the twentieth century, most prominently in Latin America but also in Britain, where a Church of Humanity was active in London). Comte's positivism also informed an approach to sociology as a matter of systemic theoretical integration incorporating sound empirical knowledge but never reducible to empiricism. The idea of seeing society as a whole was as central as the idea that it moved through historical stages of development. This would remain pivotal for Durkheim in the late nineteenth and early twentieth centuries.

Karl Marx (1818–1883) was if anything even more concerned with systemic totality, but his primary unit of analysis was not society, but modes of production such as capitalism. Any particular existing state of society was, for Marx, a conjuncture of an underlying causal structure—more or less generalizable across cases—and a number of more specific historical conditions and inheritances. Germany could thus see its future in the capitalist industrialization of England—even if Germany was also marked by political disunity and more advanced philosophy. Marx's theory was influential but not always dominant in a socialist movement that informed much nineteenth- and early-twentieth-century sociology throughout Europe (and indeed America, where history was later rewritten to minimize this). The relation between reformist (or even revolutionary) activism and science was a hotly contested concern as sociology began to gain an institutional foothold in universities toward the end of the nineteenth century. As in much connected to the development of modern universities, Germany was here a pioneer.

Comtean positivism had decreed the primacy of objective science, but not so clearly achieved it. Sociologists throughout the nineteenth century struggled with this problem. In the English-language countries, the philosophy of John Stuart Mill and the example of Darwinian biology dominated. In France, Cartesian rationalism remained preeminent, but experimental science grew in significance. In Germany, the *Methoden-streit* drew distinctions between historical sciences, with their emphasis on particular courses of events, and universalizing sciences that abstracted from such particulars to discern general laws. Sociology was divided between the two perspectives.

These national differences also shaped the way in which sociology was counterposed to other fields in an ecology of emerging disciplines. In the English-language countries, the idea of the "social sciences" situated sociology most influentially in relationship to economics and politics, and often focused sociologists on a struggle against utilitarianism. In France, sociology figured among the "human sciences," shaped deeply by philosophy, which ruled the intellectual hierarchy and the first degree curriculum, but in most direct competition with psychology. In Germany (and to varying extents the Nordic countries and the Austro-Hungarian Empire), sociology was usually one of the "historical" or "cultural" sciences, though some sociologists would contest the grouping with projects of identifying more universal social laws, or at least forms.

In every national context, sociologists sought to claim scientific objectivity. This was not merely a matter of claiming freedom from bias, or even distinctive method, but also distinctive objects of analysis. The very existence of society, or the social, was contested. In France, Gabriel Tarde (1843–1904) sought to develop sociology in close relationship to psychology, with extensive use of criminal statistics to document his theories about the centrality of imitation to social life. It was against his theories, in large part, that Durkheim sought to distinguish sociology more sharply from psychology, and to stress the autonomy of social facts (partly in response to the Comtean dictum that each science must have its own distinctive level of reality to study). Gustav Le Bon (1841–1931) drew on both Tarde's and Durkheim's ideas of group psychology in studies of crowds and revolutions, but his studies failed to advance a systematic integration of the two. Tarde's influence largely faded, and Durkheim's heirs dominated.

In countries influenced by Germanic intellectual traditions, positivism was recast in terms of the *Methodenstreit* and strong engagements with economics and law. The Austrian Ludwig Gumplowicz (1838–1909) pioneered an analysis of history as the result of the operations of "blind natural law," which he thought centered on struggles between social groups, including races. This was developed more critically and systematically by Gustav Ratzenhofer (1842–1904) as a theory of social interests and the lawfulness of all human organization. Ratzenhofer spent most of his career in the Austrian army, writing in the 1890s a series of studies showing "sociological knowledge" to be the necessary underpinning of politics and indeed all other social sciences. His positivist account of how interests gained lawful expression in social processes later underpinned the work of many of the first university-based sociologists (including not least Albion Small and other founders of the "Chicago school").

None of the most important early academic sociologists in Germany held his main academic appointments as a sociologist or institutionalized a department. Tönnies (1855–1936) was affiliated with the University of Kiel for more than fifty years but only for eight as a full professor. Berlin—both the city and the university—was a more vital center for German sociology. Yet anti-Semitism helped to minimize the academic opportunities for Georg Simmel (1858–1918), who gained a chair only late in his life after an intervention from the more socially respectable and academically central Max Weber (1864–1920). Weber himself was prominent in history, law, and economics as well as sociology—an interdisciplinary tradition that would continue with his brother Alfred Weber (1868–1958) and Ernst Troeltsch (1865–1923), a founder of the sociology of religion. Simmel distinguished sociology as a neo-Kantian inquiry into social forms from the concrete manifestations of those forms in empirical specifics. But he was nonetheless interested in both sides of the universalizing/particularizing distinction, as his *Philosophy of Money* (1900) showed. Max Weber and Tönnies were more deeply historical in orientation but also engaged in developing conceptual frameworks that would make interpretation and analysis of historical patterns systematic and allow at least qualified generalization. Weber's specific notion of analyzing "ideal types" was designed to allow the integration of attention to subjective categories informing social action and objectification through study of how concrete cases related to more abstract formulations.

Sociology gained academic stature most prominently through the work of Weber, Simmel, Durkheim, and others who came to maturity in the 1890s. From then until World War I, they laid foundations for the new discipline and recruited many of those who would carry it forward as an autonomous field in the universities after the war: Karl Mannheim (1893–1947) extended the Weberian tradition; Leopold von Wiese (1876–1969) pursued the formal analytic approach of Simmel; and Marcel Mauss (1872–1950) was the most influential of the several Durkheimians (whose influence was at least as great in anthropology). Though Germany produced a number of influential sociologists, it was slow to institutionalize the discipline in departments. Durkheim achieved this in France, persuading the Sorbonne to include sociology in the name of his chair (alongside education), and founding both a school of followers and a significant journal, the *Année sociologique*. L. T. Hobhouse (1864–1929), though he was perhaps more a political philosopher than a sociologist and saw sociology less as a separate discipline than a theme to be pursued by many,

eventually founded a department at the London School of Economics (where Mannheim was later drawn to the faculty) and the *Sociological Review*. But while European thought was enormously influential, academic institutionalization and graduate training was more advanced in the United States.

World War I was a sharp blow to the generation of the 1890s, and to the broadly progressive orientation of late-nineteenth-century sociologists. Both history and human nature appeared more problematic, and the challenges of achieving social integration that had driven many of the earlier sociologists demanded reconceptualization as a much-longer-term research program. The Italian Vilfredo Pareto (1848–1923), who had previously published major contributions to economics, became perhaps the single most influential European sociologist of the years after World War I. For the rest of the twentieth century, the relationship between the rational and the irrational, important earlier to Weber, gained new centrality as a fundamental sociological problem.

See also **Comte, Auguste; Durkheim, Emile; Marx, Karl; Simmel, Georg; Spencer, Herbert; Tocqueville, Alexis de; Weber, Max.**

BIBLIOGRAPHY

Bottomore, Tom, and Robert A. Nisbet, eds. *A History of Sociological Analysis.* New York, 1978.

Coser, Lewis A. *Masters of Sociological Thought: Ideas in Historical and Social Context.* Edited by Robert K. Merton. 2nd ed. New York, 1977.

Hughes, H. Stuart. *Consciousness and Society: The Reorientation of European Social Thought, 1890–1930.* New York, 1958. Reprint, with a new introduction by Stanley Hoffman, New Brunswick, N.J., 2002.

Levine, Donald N. *Visions of the Sociological Tradition.* Chicago, 1995.

Nisbet, Robert A. *The Sociological Tradition.* New York, 1966.

CRAIG CALHOUN

SOLOVIEV, VLADIMIR (1853–1900), Russian philosopher.

Vladimir Soloviev was the son of the foremost historian of Russia, Sergei Soloviev (1820–1879), and a distant offspring of the Ukrainian philosopher Grigory Skovoroda (1722–1794). Raised in the intensive intellectual environment of his parents' Moscow salon, Soloviev began his studies in the natural sciences but shifted to history and philology. His first major work, his master's thesis titled *The Crisis of Western Philosophy* (1874), argued against the predominant trend of positivism—an item of faith for many of his fellow university students in the era of populism. Soloviev proposed that positivism, with its focus on phenomena, or external objects, had exhausted its potential, and suggested turning, instead, inward to "l'être en soi" (being-in-itself); he saw in Eduard von Hartmann's "philosophy of the unconscious" the first signs of the reassertion of metaphysics. His doctoral dissertation, *A Critique of Abstract Principles* (1880), continued this theme, arguing the inevitable interconnection of absolute and "abstract" (scientific or scholastic) principles; in ethics, epistemology, and aesthetics, Soloviev proposed "all-unity" as an ultimate goal, to be realized in practice as a "free theocracy."

Soloviev's thought is characterized by a merging of philosophy and religion. Soloviev had a brilliant grounding in Western, and particularly German, philosophy, and he considered the work of Immanuel Kant to be the single most important turning point in modern intellectual history. Beginning in 1878, a series of public lectures on the philosophy of religion posed the critical set of issues for his writings of the 1880s. The *Lectures on Godmanhood* (1881; more recently translated as *Lectures on Divine Humanity*) are among his most striking and original works. Soloviev advocated the Orthodox principle of the divinization of man as an antidote to society's having fallen away from higher principles—particularly following the French Revolution. It was also here that he introduced the notion of Sophia, the Divine Wisdom— "the idea that [God] had before him in his creativity, and which, consequently, He realizes" through the creation of the world. Religion was crucial to this phase of Soloviev's intellectual development, as he became increasingly engaged in problems of the church and ecumenism; he saw the Eastern (Orthodox) Church as endowed with a divinity that could usefully supplement the human focus of the Western church. *La Russie et l'église univer-*

selle (1889, published in French in avoidance of the Russian censors; *Russia and the Universal Church*, 1948) openly advocated a union of Orthodox and Catholic churches under the pope's aegis. A later essay, *Mohammed: His Life and Religious Teachings* (1896), extended these ecumenical concerns beyond the Christian world.

In the 1890s Soloviev wrote perhaps his most fundamental work—a system of moral philosophy titled *The Justification of the Good* (1897). Conceived in the spirit of Kant's critiques, *Justification* boldly posed the question, "Does our life have any kind of purpose?" Soloviev perceived morality as dependent upon such factors as asceticism, shame, pity, and virtue; ultimately, a morally justifiable life could be defined through its constant association with, and aspiration to, a higher, absolute Good. Reversing the order of Kant's first and second critiques, Soloviev believed that theoretical philosophy must follow from practical, or moral, reason.

In addition to his philosophical oeuvre, Soloviev was also a poet and a publicist. His poems were often conceived in a humorous vein. One of the most wonderful, "Three Meetings" (1898), describes the philosopher's three encounters with Sophia, the Divine Wisdom. The final episode, which occurred during his travels in Egypt in 1876, finds Soloviev in the desert, being chased by angry Bedouins who mistook him, clad in top hat and coattails, for an evil spirit. The poem "Panmongolism" (1894) foretold a new invasion from the East, bringing destruction to Russia. Soloviev's most famous public speech was given on the occasion of the assassination of Tsar Alexander II in 1881: while condemning the conspirators, Soloviev at the same time argued against capital punishment, thus angering many conservatives.

Of his journalistic endeavors, several are worth particular attention. "Beauty in Nature" (1889) sought to emancipate aesthetics from biological necessity: natural beauty was anchored in ontology, and expressed an absolute and objective idea. "The Meaning of Love" (1892–1894), consisting of five essays, similarly polemicized with the then-fashionable biological determinism, proposing that sexual love, far from being nature's trick for the propagation of the species, was in fact the highest form of human affect: only through sexual love could an individual truly feel another person to be as worthy as him- or herself. Soloviev proposed eventually extending the principle of love into the foundation for a universal harmony. In "The Enemy from the East," written on the occasion of the severe famine of 1891, Soloviev took an ecological line: erosion, deforestation, and the sands sweeping in from the eastern steppes were the "enemy" that Russia would have to face.

Soloviev wrote in a largely alien environment: the last third of the nineteenth century was a time when cultural and intellectual life was mostly dominated by the radical intelligentsia. His work resonates particularly with that of his great contemporaries, Leo Tolstoy and Fyodor Dostoyevsky; arguably, he presented in philosophical terms many of the ideas they expressed through literature. Soloviev's philosophy, poetry, and other writings became enormously influential for the writers and poets of Russia's Silver Age—the cultural explosion of the early twentieth century that formed a part of European modernism. Such writers and philosophers as Alexander Blok, Andrei Bely, and Sergei Bulgakov drew heavily on his ideas: for example, Soloviev's poem "Panmongolism" was a fundamental inspiration for Blok's "The Scythians" (1918). Soloviev concluded his life with the equally influential "Three Conversations on War, Progress, and the End of History," which was appended by a "Brief Tale of the Antichrist" (1899–1900). This apocalyptic work once again foretold the growing power of the East, while prophesying such developments as a "more or less democratic" United States of Europe in the twenty-first century. Soloviev died in 1900, from illness and general neglect of his physical well-being.

See also **Bely, Andrei; Blok, Alexander; History; Positivism.**

BIBLIOGRAPHY

Courten, Manon de. *History, Sophia, and the Russian Nation: A Reassessment of Vladimir Soloviev's Views on History and His Social Commitment.* Bern and New York, 2004.

Kornblatt, Judith Deutsch, and Richard F. Gustafson, eds. *Russian Religious Thought.* Madison, Wis., 1996.

Lopatin, L. M. "Filosofskoe mirovozzrenie V. S. Solovieva." In his *Filosofskie kharakteristiki i rechi.* Moscow, 1911. Reprint, Moscow, 1995.

Mochulsky, Konstantin. *Vladimir Soloviev: Zhizn' i uchenie.* 2nd ed. Paris, 1951.

Strémoukhoff, D. *Vladimir Soloviev and His Messianic Work.* Belmont, Mass., 1980. Translation of *Soloviev et son oeuvre messianique* (1935).

Trubetskoy, E. N. *Mirosozertsanie V. S. Solovieva.* 2 vols. Moscow, 1913.

Valliere, Paul. *Modern Russian Theology: Bukharev, Soloviev, Bulgakov; Orthodox Theology in a New Key.* Grand Rapids, Mich., 2000.

CATHERINE EVTUHOV

SOREL, GEORGES (1847–1922), French political and social philosopher.

Georges Eugène Sorel was best known for his condemnation of bourgeois society, his critical interpretations of Marxism, and his emphasis on the power of myth and direct action. While his concern for the moral decadence of European society and the prospects for moral renewal represent consistent themes in Sorel's work, many scholars have emphasized his shifting, sometimes inconsistent, political opinions. Some have claimed that Sorel's work was influential in the ideological development of both communism and fascism.

Sorel was born in Cherbourg in Normandy on 2 November 1847 to a bourgeois family. Upon graduating from the École Polytechnique with an engineering degree in 1866, he joined the French government's Department of Bridges and Roads. He retired in 1891 at the age of forty-four, after his mother died, leaving him a small legacy. He and his wife moved to the Parisian suburb of Boulogne-sur-Seine, where he spent the remainder of his life as an independent scholar.

Sorel's critique of European society revolved around the idea that Europe had become a morally decadent culture in which people were motivated only by the desire for individual economic and political gain. For Sorel, a moral society was one in which rewards were commensurate with effort and in which people acted virtuously out of a sense of duty and conviction. Sorel's moral concerns were evident in his first two books, both published in 1889. One of these was a textual interpretation of the Bible. The other was an analysis of the trial of Socrates, which concluded that, while Socrates may have been innocent of the specific charges leveled against him, his teachings did lead to a decline in respect for Athenian institutions and thus helped to bring about the downfall of Athenian democracy. Another essay, written in 1894, held the rise of Christianity responsible for the decline of the Roman Empire.

Sorel apparently discovered Marx around 1892, shortly after moving to Paris. The Marxism to which he was first exposed was the orthodox "Scientific Marxism" of Jules Guesde and Paul Lafargue, and his early Marxist writings, mostly book reviews and review essays, reflected this orientation. Beginning around 1897, however, as Sorel's knowledge of Marxism grew deeper, he became critical of several elements of Marxist orthodoxy, including its schematic conception of history, its determinism, its failure to pay sufficient attention to moral and legal issues, and its belief in the inevitability of a successful proletarian revolution.

For Sorel, the key question for Marxism was the question of the moral preparation of the proletariat. He thought the fall of capitalism could be expected to lead to a more just society only if the workers could acquire a superior level of moral culture. For a brief time (1897–1898), Sorel harbored the hope that participation in democratic institutions might be able to produce free producers of the future. Starting around 1898, as he came to see democratic institutions as hopelessly mediocre and corrupting, he began to look to Syndicalism with its ideology of direct action on the part of workers as the best chance for fostering the moral development of the proletariat. His most famous work is his sympathetic analysis of Syndicalism, *Réflexions sur la violence* (Reflections on violence), first published in 1908. This period also saw the publication of *Illusions du progrès* (1908; The illusions of progress), an animated critique of the idea of progress in Western culture, and of a book on the work of the French historian Ernest Renan.

It must be pointed out that Sorel was never involved in a practical way with the Syndicalist movement, nor did he have much influence on the ideology or strategies of Syndicalist leaders. Rather, Syndicalism and the enthusiasm generated by the Syndicalist idea of the general strike influenced Sorel to theorize about the morally rejuvenating power of myth and direct action. Sorel's ideas about the power of myth to stir people to heroic action are his best-known intellectual contribution and the reason he is sometimes seen as an intellectual precursor to both Soviet communism and fascism.

As Syndicalism's successes declined after 1907, Sorel became disillusioned with it and began searching for other sources of moral renewal. In the period from 1910 to 1914, he became associated with leaders of the Action Française, a conservative, nationalist group. Beginning around 1914, Sorel was frequently ill and began writing much less. As of 1918, Sorel began to express an interest in Vladimir Lenin and the Russian Revolution. His last book, published in 1921, was an appreciative analysis of pragmatism.

See also **Marx, Karl; Socialism; Syndicalism.**

BIBLIOGRAPHY

Primary Sources

Sorel, Georges. *Reflections on Violence.* Edited by Jeremy Jennings. Cambridge, U.K., and New York, 1999. Translation of *Réflexions sur la violence* (1908).

———. *From Georges Sorel: Essays in Socialism and Philosophy.* Edited by John L. Stanley. Translated by John and Charlotte Stanley. New Brunswick, N.J., 1987.

Secondary Sources

Meisel, James Hans. *The Genesis of Georges Sorel: An Account of His Formative Period, Followed by a Study of His Influence.* Westport, Conn., 1982.

ARTHUR L. GREIL

SOUTH AFRICA. South Africa's remoteness from the wider world came to an end as a consequence of European seaborne expansion. From the mid-1600s, its southernmost Cape region became a fully fledged Dutch colony. The Dutch maintained control until 1795, when Britain seized the strategically advantageous Cape Colony during its battle with revolutionary France for command of the world's trading oceans. By the early nineteenth century, Britain was drawing this large new colonial possession into its long-haul routes of international trade and its network of imperial administration.

Zulu tribesmen in South Africa, c. 1901 The Zulus of southern Africa fiercely resisted British occupation in the Zulu War of 1877–1879 but were ultimately defeated following the capture and exile of their king, Cetshwayo. ©CORBIS

What British rule inherited was an agricultural territory with a dominant Dutch-speaking Boer settler minority of some 20,000; an unfree black population of over 25,000 imported slaves; around 15,000 mostly dispossessed pastoral Khoikhoi inhabitants, the remnants of a hunter-gatherer San ("Bushmen") population that had largely been decimated; and away to the east, a great mass of Bantu-speaking African peasants, thousands of whom were already incorporated within colonial borders through Boer expansion. These and the majority who still enjoyed precolonial independence lived in politically and culturally discrete societies. While lacking any imaginative conviction of a unified or even common African identity, chiefdoms were increasing in size and consolidating their political authority.

Processes of colonization and land alienation in favor of white settlers were intensified under more efficient British administration. The penetration of British capital, the influx of large groups of British immigrants, and the expansion of inland transport and shipping stimulated trade and raised levels of agricultural commercialization. In the Cape's eastern hinterland, where frontier settlers were tussling with African farmers for land, British regiments tipped the balance in a series of bitter land or frontier wars, as Xhosa peasants had their land expropriated for incoming settlers.

Incorporation of the Cape Colony into the British Empire also brought fundamental changes to the political and social relations of what had largely been a slave-based Dutch colonial society. British imperial humanitarianism introduced reforms to end what were seen as abuses and to bolster free capitalist development. The institution of slavery was abolished by the 1830s, ending the growth of unfree labor and adding freed slaves to landless Khoikhoi as a rural wage labor supply. Formal discrimination against "free persons of color" was also repealed in the 1820s, and the brutality of labor relations between employers and their laboring underclass was tempered by governing regulation. These ameliorative measures provided greater civic freedom for blacks fully incorporated into colonial society, but did not alter their economic subjection.

The major impulse behind the creation of a more liberal colonial order in South Africa was a liberal ideology introduced by Christian missionaries whose activities were now sponsored generously by British evangelical humanitarians. A spectrum of Protestant and other mission stations attracted a tributary of Christian black adherents, some fleeing from white farms in search of refuge and independence, some attracted to the economic possibilities offered by mission education and agricultural training, and others seeking new identities through conversion for lives ruptured by colonialism. Through the nineteenth century, new Christianized African classes emerged from this culture of improvement, including a modernizing peasantry, clergymen, teachers, lawyers, and journalists. Models of colonial collaboration, by the 1890s a number were eventually rejecting western mission churches for independent African versions of Christianity.

The emerging cleavages in South Africa were not only between white and black. Although the Cape Colony developed a parliamentary system and a level of responsible government resting on a common qualified franchise that privileged European political power, its colonists failed to unify. With little mixing between the British and a still predominant Boer-Afrikaner population, whites became ethnically divided. Most Boers resented the intrusive, reformist reach of British power, with poorer stock farmers in the east also chafing at a shortage of affordable land in the early decades of the nineteenth century. In the 1830s, around 15,000 Boers trekked northward into the South African hinterland, in a migration that became known as the Great Trek. By greatly extending the grip of European control, the incursion of trekkers into the interior had a profound impact upon the formation of a modern South Africa.

After a series of land clashes with Tswana, Ndebele, Zulu, and other resisting African societies, migrant Boer groups achieved their political purpose of breaking with Britain and establishing their own republican territories. Trekker power

along the east coast in Natal proved short-lived, however, as Britain nabbed the region as a colony in 1842 to entrench its command of coastal merchant trade and control of the eastern sea route. Imperial settlement schemes were put in place to make the territory English. But on the interior highveld of South Africa, the independent agrarian Boer states of the Orange Free State and South African Republic (Transvaal) were established by the 1850s. Their establishment meant that the area of South Africa under European control and settlement roughly doubled between the 1830s and the 1850s.

Constituted as Calvinist states founded on European supremacy, for some decades these land-locked white republican polities remained rickety. Locked in endemic land and livestock conflicts with neighboring Basotho, Pedi, and other African chiefdoms, they were also unable to slip the economic leash of the influential British Cape, the largest, wealthiest, most thoroughly colonized, and most populated settler territory, containing well over 200,000 whites (representing more than twice the combined total of the three other European possessions) and around half a million blacks. The Cape's trading economy curled out from the main colonial harbors and merchant houses, pulling in wool, grain, wine, and other agricultural products, and transporting a large range of imported commodities to internal markets for white and black consumers. This intensifying and increasingly unified network of commercial transactions and human communication drew Boer maize producers and hunters, English artisans and rural traders, and African farm tenants and laborers into a new and expanding colonial society, even as settler society set on excluding black inhabitants from political power. In patriarchal Boer states, whites maintained an absolute monopoly of formal political authority, while settlers in British Natal enjoyed an effective monopoly. Even in the relatively more liberal racial order of the Cape Colony, the electoral weight of black voters was kept marginal by franchise property requirements.

By the middle of the nineteenth century, South Africa had been transformed into a dense patchwork of mostly small agrarian societies. In the case

A village in the Transvaal c. 1900. Indigenous Africans in the Transvaal came under the de facto control of the Boers with the establishment of the South African Republic in 1857. ©HULTON-DEUTSCH COLLECTION/CORBIS

of African peoples, some, like the Xhosa, had been conquered and partly incorporated. Other chiefdoms, like those of the Swazi, remained substantially independent. Yet, however uneven the impact of colonialism, black and white inhabitants were being laced together by the pulsating forces of settler expansionism and merchant capitalism, radiating out from northwestern Europe. In this part of sub-Saharan Africa, Britain looked to the Cape as the hinge of a future integrated state in South Africa, imposing colonial peace, efficient rule, and developing the fiscal strength to defend itself, eventually turning the region into a peaceful British Dominion or an African Canada, even though its modest economic prospects made it less attractive to British immigrants than other white settler territories of the empire.

Imperial expectations of a gradual rate of change in South Africa were unsettled after 1870, as abundant deposits of minerals were discovered in its interior. In 1867, diamonds were found in an area claimed by the Orange Free State. Once the enormous scale of the deposit had been confirmed, the British government moved smartly to frustrate Boer republican assertions and annexed the diamond fields in order to place the territory under the authority of the Cape. The impact of mining rapidly transformed the economy of the entire region.

By the early 1870s, over 20,000 new white immigrants, mostly British, had converged on the area of Kimberley, the diamond town. So had tens of thousands of African migrant laborers, drawn from virtually every peasant community within southern Africa. White commercial farmers as well

The Kimberley Mine, South Africa, 1872. The discovery of large deposits of diamonds in South Africa circa 1870 quickly led to the development of major mining operations. The largest of these were established near the Northern Cape town of Kimberley. ©BETTMANN/CORBIS

as wealthier black agriculturalists also exploited new opportunities triggered by the opening of major new markets for food and fuel. European imports soared, fostering mercantile integration and boosting railway and road construction between the main coastal ports and the interior. By 1880 there was a weekly steamship service between Britain and the Cape, as well as telegraph communication.

The rapid industrialization spawned by development of the diamond fields had profound consequences for the future of South African economy and society. Mining became characterized by huge concentrations of capital and growing mergers to cut competition, a monopoly thrust in which Cecil John Rhodes (1853–1902) figured prominently. Furthermore, the new industrialization of the labor force deepened the already marked colonial distinc-

tion between skilled white workers and unskilled black workers. In Kimberley, immigrant white workers carved out a privileged position, bolstered by political rights, higher wages, and freedom to live a family existence. Migrant African mineworkers were obliged to carry passes that controlled their urban movements, and were all accommodated in closed, all-male barracks, also known as compounds, which they could not leave for the duration of their labor contracts. This stark racial division at the outset of South African industrialization bore early traces of the urban segregationist structure that the country would develop, through racial institutions of labor control and the housing of cheap black migrant laborers in overcrowded, Spartan compounds.

For the British, diamonds made the construction of a stable, single political sphere more urgent.

South Africa needed the stability of a common infrastructure to encourage and secure investment flows, and to regulate and funnel supplies of migrant labor to where these were most needed. From the mid-1870s, a forceful imperial push to bring about a confederation of the various South African colonies and territories was launched by the British colonial secretary, Lord Carnarvon (1831–1890). This involved pressure on the Boer republics, and the breaking of what remained of independent African power, exemplified by the invasion and dismembering of Zululand at the end of the 1870s. But the confederation policy turned out to be a dismal failure, not least because Boer republicans were unwilling to relinquish their sovereignty. If anything, Britain's high-handedness, including its blundering annexation of a disorderly and indebted South African Republic in 1877, increased divisions and antagonisms in the region instead of smothering them. While they continued to assert their paramountcy over the subcontinent, the British were driven out of the Transvaal in 1881 and forced to assent to its renewed independence. If economic integration was proceeding apace, political unity still looked far off.

In the mid-1880s, the evolution of South Africa was altered once again by the advent of a further and much greater surge of heavy capitalist enterprise. Following the discovery of gold in the Transvaal's Witwatersrand, South Africa's supplies became pivotal to the underpinning of currencies and international trade during the balmy years of the Gold Standard. With Transvaal gold already amounting to over a quarter of total world production by 1898, mining followed the Kimberley model but on a far more massive scale, quickly surpassing the diamond fields in turning the South African interior into the largest industrial complex on the continent and the site of the world's biggest gold extraction.

By the end of the 1890s, there were over 100,000 migrant African mineworkers in urban compounds on the Rand, remitting wages to the countryside for agricultural investment in an effort to arrest declining levels of peasant subsistence through continuous land loss. The gold industry was also a magnet to tens of thousands of overseas immigrant miners, artisans, traders, industrialists, and financiers, mainly British, but including a mix of other European nationalities. From the beginning, the industrial revolution in which they participated produced heavy demands and difficulties. Deep-level mining required costly long-term investment and large quantities of cheap labor to ensure profitability. Companies acted in concert to reduce costs by creating a common pool of unskilled African migrants, eliminating wage competition, and driving down wages through the 1890s.

The mineral transformations also created a sharp contradiction between a foreign, fast-living capitalist enclave on the Rand and a mostly poor, intensely religious, agricultural Boer state run by landed patriarchs of limited administrative capacity. Politically, gold was a poisoned chalice. Its tax revenues strengthened the South African Republic. But its foreign or *uitlander* stake endangered ideals of a free and pure Boer existence on the highveld. Lastly, the new industrial growth of the Transvaal enabled it to begin prying itself free of British economic domination, and to expand its influence in ways that contested Britain's supremacy in South Africa, such as its refusal to join a customs union with British colonies, and its preference for Portuguese Mozambique as a foreign trade artery.

The result of British imperial pressure to bring the South African Republic to heel was war in 1899 when the Transvaal Boers, in alliance with those of the Orange Free State, opted for war to try to preserve the basis of their republican state. Fighting until the Boer states surrendered, the end of the Boer War in 1902 saw Britain extinguishing a Republican order in South Africa and turning the Boer territories into the Transvaal and Orange River Colonies under its direct rule. Although now a set of Crown colonies rather than a unified country, South Africa was under the ultimate authority of Alfred Milner (1854–1925), London's High Commissioner there from 1898 to 1905, and the chief engineer of British policy to Anglicize the ex-Republics by swamping them with British settlers. With that achieved, they could then be coaxed into joining the Cape and Natal in a loyal, self-governing imperial Dominion.

In some senses, Britain's designs failed. There was no mass British emigration after 1902, and Boers or Afrikaners continued to constitute some

The mayor of Cape Town and his wife lead a procession after the opening of the new Parliament of the Union of South Africa, 1910. BRITISH EMPIRE AND COMMONWEALTH MUSEUM, BRISTOL, UK/BRIDGEMAN ART LIBRARY

60 percent of the white settler population of South Africa. Nor was their nationalism snuffed out, thanks to war memory of harsh military conquest and concentration camp sacrifice. On the other hand, as part of its reconstruction program, the British administration was committed to introducing self-government to incorporated Afrikaner territories on terms agreed to at the 1902 peace agreement, that the franchise would be restricted to white men and that the position of white property rights would be upheld. This produced a chorus of protest from blacks who had mostly been vehemently pro-British during the war and had anticipated some kind of emancipatory outcome to postwar reconstruction. But the London government was much more concerned with securing compromises and resolving competing claims between Afrikaner and British colonies in order to reconcile former republicans to imperial interests, than to lose much sleep over black grievances at political exclusion.

After much economic and political bargaining between the various colonies to achieve white "conciliation," the Union of South Africa was established in 1910, comprising around 1.2 million whites and over 5 million blacks. The formation of a unitary state with parliamentary sovereignty and supreme central state authority over all local institutions ended the colonial problem of South Africa for British imperial authority. Its inaugural Afrikaner leaders, Louis Botha (1862–1919) and Jan Christian Smuts (1870–1950), both republican generals who had fought against Britain during the 1899–1902 war, were more than prepared to shed Boer republicanism and let bygones be bygones. The principal British imperial connection through South African gold, which by 1914 amounted to over a third of the world's supply, enhanced prospects of strong industrial progress, urban expansion, and demographic growth. Furthermore, a racially segregationist Union would consolidate white authority, provide the scaffolding for the construction of a national white South African identity, and ease the implementation of a common "native policy," especially in labor supply and control.

The Union's independent Dominion status did little to weaken its dependent links to Britain. In 1914 it went to war promptly as a region of the British Empire, notwithstanding political opposition from many nationalist Afrikaners.

See also **Africa; Boer War; Colonialism; Colonies; Imperialism; Rhodes, Cecil.**

BIBLIOGRAPHY

Keegan, Timothy. *Colonial South Africa and the Origins of the Racial Order.* Charlottesville, Va., 1996.

Marks, Shula, and Anthony Atmore, eds. *Economy and Society in Pre-Industrial South Africa.* London, 1980.

Marks, Shula, and Richard Rathbone, eds. *Industrialisation and Social Change in South Africa.* New York, 1982.

Ross, Robert. *A Concise History of South Africa.* Cambridge, U.K., 1999.

Saunders, Christopher, and Iain R. Smith. "Southern Africa, 1795–1910." In *The Oxford History of the British Empire,* edited by Wm. Roger Louis. Vol. 3: *The Nineteenth Century,* 597–623. Oxford, U.K., 1999.

Thompson, Leonard. *A History of South Africa,* Rev. ed. New Haven, Conn., 1994.

WILLIAM NASSON

SPAIN. Spanish life at the end of the eighteenth century was chronicled in the paintings, tapestries, and engravings of a great Spanish genius: Francisco José de Goya y Lucientes (1746–1828). Around 1790 the Aragonese artist depicted the vitality of village fiestas in colorful tapestries; he revealed sensual *majas* (beauties) in his paintings, while his engravings and drawings showed Spain's new collective passion for *tauromaquia* (bullfighting), which was just being accepted as an art form. A celebrated portraitist, Goya painted the aristocracy and later the revolutionary ambassadors. With a series of eighty prints, *Los Caprichos* (1799), he engraved "the inumerable foibles and follies to be found in any society." More important, like the painter Diego Velásquez (1599–1660), Goya recorded for history the misery of those on the bottom of Spanish society—the beggars and deformed—and also the misery of those above. The extent of the decay of the Spanish Bourbon dynasty is revealed in the faces depicted in *La familia de Carlos IV* (The

family of Charles IV; 1800). Because the French emperor Napoleon I (1769–1821) focused only on this dynastic decay, and ignored the vitality of the people, the drama of the War of Independence exploded on Spain.

Charles IV (r. 1788–1808) was never more than a mediocre monarch, because his only real passion in life was hunting. In 1792 Manuel de Godoy (1767–1851) became his all-powerful prime minister, thanks to his love affair with the queen and the king's complete lack of interest his responsibilities as sovereign. During the French Revolutionary Wars (1792–1802), Spain initially fought against France, but by 1796 Godoy had formed an alliance with France against Great Britain. A disaster in foreign affairs, Godoy's alliance with revolutionary France cost Spain the colonies of Santo Domingo, Trinidad, and Louisiana. During the Napoleonic Wars (1803–1815), after the destruction of the Spanish fleet at the hands of the British at Trafalgar in 1805, Spain was effectively cut off from its remaining colonies, which were left to fend for themselves, a situation that accelerated their move toward independence.

Finally, after Napoleon's victory over Prussia at Jena in 1806, Godoy negotiated with the French the Treaty of Fontainebleau (1807), which divided Britain's ally Portugal between France and Spain, and which should have made Godoy a crown prince. But the French general Andoche Junot's (1771–1813) army marched on Lisbon in 1807, and French forces occupied the fortresses of Navarre and Catalonia early in 1808. Godoy had clearly miscalculated—Spain's own independence was under threat. A palace plot tried to replace King Charles with his son Ferdinand (1788–1833), who proceeded to denounce his friends when it was uncovered. But, strangely, public opinion believed to have found in Ferdinand a popular hero and a martyr.

On 17 March 1808, as the French cavalry commander Marshal Joachim Murat (1767–1815) was marching on Madrid, a popular uprising in Aranjuez overthrew Charles and Godoy and proclaimed Ferdinand king of Spain (as Ferdinand VII; r. March–May 1808). Marshal Murat refused to recognize the new king and with a mixture of promises and threats was able to evacuate the entire royal family to Bayonne, where Napoleon was

Execution of the Defenders of Madrid, 3 May 1808. Goya's 1814 painting memorializes Spanish civilians who fought against Napoleon's forces during the Spanish War for Independence. SCALA/ART RESOURCE, NY

awaiting them. The French emperor then forced Ferdinand to abdicate in favor of Napoleon's own elder brother, Joseph Bonaparte (1768–1844), and interned the Spanish Bourbons. Once the populace of the city of Madrid learned that the Spanish royal family was leaving the country, a crowd rose up against Murat's cavalry on 2 May 1808—Spain's war of independence had begun.

PENINSULAR WAR (1808–1814)

Between 20 and 30 May 1808, Asturias, Aragon, and Galicia refused obedience to any authority who collaborated with the French armies. In the first days of June, Joseph Bonaparte was proclaimed king just as the French army in Catalonia was defeated in Bruch and again close to the Guadalquivir River. Resistance to the invader was profound and included all provinces and all social classes to various degrees. The Spanish people waged war as a personal affair, revenge through the knife. It is certain that since the Middle Ages, the Spanish people had conserved a peculiar taste for macabre spectacles. "The honest men are not more loyal to me than the rabble," said Joseph Bonaparte. In face of a superior enemy, Spain reaffirmed its cohesion.

The movement was not only anti-French. In fact it was a prolongation of the uprising of Aranjuez, an expression of popular discontent within the country. However, most Spaniards could not agree where to place their hopes. For some, collaboration with France was the best way to renew the works of the eighteenth century, while others placed their hopes in the exiled Ferdinand. For still others, the patriarchal absolutism of Ferdinand was the guaranty of Spanish tradition—in other words, the medieval *fueros* (traditional rights) and the intimate relation between religion and politics. An uneasy alliance between "liberal" and "Carlist" Spain existed against the forces of the invader in a profound contradiction.

The great *provocateur* in the conflict was the Catholic Church. The average guerrilla went into battle—with the "atheist" Frenchman—covered with religious symbols. During the siege of Saragossa, the townsfolk said, "The Virgen doesn't want to be French." But not all was unity: during the first days of the war, the insurgents showed an evident pleasure in killing former Spanish authorities. Joseph Bonaparte compared the Spanish revolt to the year II of the French Revolution. Despite Joseph's abolition of the hated Inquisition, liberals sympathetic to the French felt that popular combativeness, at the service of tradition and religion, could easily turn against them.

Paradoxically, the management of this mass movement fell back on a small minority from the days of "enlightened despotism" of Charles III (r. 1759–1788); men like José Moñino y Redondo, the conde de Floridablanca (1728–1808), and Gaspar Melchor de Jovellanos (1744–1811), who joined the *Junta Central de Resistencia.* They continued in this leading role when the Cortes (parliament) was convoked in Cádiz. Because elections were impossible, the parliament became an artificial creation without direct contact with the guerrillas who were fighting the French. As Karl Marx later wrote: "At the time of the Cortes, Spain was divided into two parts, . . . action without ideas; in the rest of Spain, ideas without action." But that did not stop its mostly liberal constituents (lawyers, intellectuals, businessmen, and "Americans"—that is, creoles) from promulgating the first written constitution in Spain's history. The Constitution of 1812, commonly known as *La Pepa,* guaranteed national sovereignty and the legitimacy of Ferdinand VII as king.

Another interesting aspect of the war is how Spain reverted to an *instinctive federalism,* a terminology first coined by Marcelino Menéndez Pelayo (1856–1912). The mayor of the town of Móstoles declared war directly on Napoleon. The La Junta General del Principado de Asturias negotiated directly with Britain. The constitution of

the Junta Central mentioned curious "federal" proposals. In fact, power in Spain had become atomized.

Militarily, the Peninsular War marked Britain's return to the European Continental theater. In 1808 Lieutenant General Arthur Wellesley (1769–1851), later the first Duke of Wellington, landed in Portugal in 1808 at the head of an expeditionary force and defeated the French forces there under General Junot. In a controversial agreement called the Convention of Sintra, the British commander agreed to repatriate the bulk of the French forces to France. Wellesley was immediately recalled to London and replaced with General John Moore (1761–1809). At the same time, in Andalusia, French forces under General Pierre-Antoine Dupont de l'Étang (1765–1840) were defeated by a Spanish army at Bailén, an event which prompted the emperor Napoleon to take direct command in Spain.

At the head of over two hundred thousand troops, Napoleon chased Moore across northern Spain to the Galician port city of La Coruña, where the British general was killed during the forced evacuation of his army. Satisfied that one of his marshals could handle the situation, Napoleon returned to France, and never returned to Spain. Shortly thereafter, Wellesley, now Viscount Wellington, returned to the Iberian peninsula to lead a new British force. Napoleon appointed Marshal André Masséna (1758–1817), known as the *enfant chéri de la victoire* (victory's dear child) as leader of French armies on the peninsula. Wellington's strategy was based on increasing the fortifications at Torres Vedras as a stronghold against French attack. Although Masséna spent over a month trying to break through the British lines, he failed and was recalled to France.

By 1811 Wellington had pushed the French forces out of Portugal, and began advancing into Spain. In 1812 Wellington won a crushing victory over the French and seized Salamanca. Napoleon's disastrous retreat from Russia in the winter of 1812 also worked in Wellington's favor; after losing his vast invasion force, the French emperor could not spare any fresh reinforcements for the peninsula. In 1813 Wellington routed the forces of King Joseph (Bonaparte) in the Battle of

Ferdinand VII Swearing in the Constitution. Nineteenth-century engraving. ©ARCHIVO ICONOGRAFICO, S.A./CORBIS

Vitoria on 21 June, and crossed into France in 1814. The Peninsular War ended when Ferdinand VII was released from captivity at the Chateau de Valencay and returned to Spain to assume the throne.

THE POLITICS OF THE NINETEENTH CENTURY

The second reign of Ferdinand VII (1814–1833) was characterized by a curious mixture of cowardice and ferocious brutality. Its main features were the failure of the democratic spirit of 1812, and a general decay that became more profound as the Spanish empire in the Americas finally fell apart.

Within weeks of reassuming the Spanish throne, Ferdinand revoked the Constitution of 1812. Meanwhile, the South American wars of independence began in earnest in 1817, partly because of the independence exercised by the *Juntas,* or governing councils set up during the Peninsular War. With the ensuing shortfall in tax revenue, Spain rapidly went bankrupt. Between 1820 and 1823 however, a celebrated intermezzo took place. In Cádiz, a colonial expeditionary force mutinied, and its colonel, Rafael del Riego y Nuñez (1785–1823) rode across Andalusia proclaiming the restoration of the Constitution of 1812. When that rebellion looked close to collapse, yet another broke out in Galicia. When General Francisco Ballesteros (1770–1833) surrounded the royal palace, the king, startled by events, accepted the restoration of the 1812 constitution. But the ultras (absolutist royalists) remained active in Madrid. The moderates fell from power, and in Urgell, an intransigeant, "apostolic" regency was formed. At the Congress of Verona, François-Auguste-René de Chateaubriand (1768–1848) asked the Holy Alliance (Austria, Prussia, and Russia) to intervene in Spain, and the "100,000 sons of St. Louis" (*Los cien mil hijos de San Luís*), the royal French army, invaded Spain to crush the constitutionalists. While most generals avoided combat, French soldiers under Louis-Antoine Bourbon, the duc d'Angoulême (1775–1844), reestablished Ferdinand on his throne as absolute monarch.

Most liberal historians call the period from 1823 until Ferdinand's death in 1833 the "ominous decade" (la década ominosa) for good reason. Despite a general amnesty, Riego and his followers were the first to be publicly hanged. In 1825 the most popular leader of the guerrillas, El Empecinado, was shot. In 1826 it was the turn of Bazán. In 1831 General José María Torrijos was executed, and Mariana Pineda was garroted because she had sewn a liberal flag. But the "Apostolic" Ultras were still not satisfied. Recognizing Ferdinand's cowardly nature, the Ultras began promoting the king's brother, Don Carlos (Carlos María Isidro de Borbón; 1788–1855). But in 1830, Ferdinand's third wife, María Cristina (1806–1878), gave birth to a daughter. Don Carlos's supporters applied the Salic Law, of Bourbonic tradition, against the child. In order to avoid disinheriting his own daughter, Ferdinand turned again to the liberals, who forced him to make some concessions. Power became less oppressive, and the economy started to pick up. But after 1824, and the Battle of Ayacucho, any hope of regaining Spain's lost American colonies vanished as sixteen new American republics gained their independence.

Carlist wars   At Ferdinand's death, María Cristina became regent in the name of her daughter Isabella II (1830–1904). At the same moment, Ferdinand's brother, Don Carlos, was proclaimed king by his followers, and the First Carlist War broke out. It lasted seven years and affected above all the northern regions of the country: Catalonia, Navarre, the Basque provinces, and Valencia. Its high point came in 1835. With most of Spain north of the Ebro River controlled by his troops, the Basque Carlist general Tomás de Zumalacárregui y de Imaz (1788–1835) then threatened to march on Madrid. His mysterious death deprived Don Carlos of his best general and sealed the fate of the rebellion. At the same time, in Madrid, the regent tried to govern with the Castilian conservatives known as Moderados, and the opposition increased. In 1836 the "sergeants" managed to force the restoration of the Constitution of Cádiz on the regent at the palace of La Granja. The following year, María Cristina managed to have it replaced with a more moderate document.

The First Carlist War ended in 1839—when General Baldomero Fernández Espartero (1793–1879) embraced the Carlist general Rafael Maroto (1780–1848) at Vergara—but its legacy still lasts. Far beyond dynastic troubles, the Carlist wars were symbolic of the conflict between bureaucratic centralization and traditional *foral* rights, guaranteed in Spain since the Middle Ages as *fueros*. Only after Espartero, later known as the Duke of Victory, staged a coup d'état against María Cristina and replaced her as regent did the First Carlist War come to an end.

Espartero's initial popularity was short-lived: governing with a clique, Espartero had rebellious generals shot and bombarded Barcelona after an uprising. From that moment, Espartero was better known as *Ayacucho*, a rather unkind reference to his colonial past. By 1843, when General Ramón Maria Narváez (1800–1868) returned from exile, popular discontent had reached a climax in the cities. Finally, Espartero left for exile in London, but not before bombarding Seville.

Having reached a majority of age, Isabella was used by the moderates against the progessives. Her prime minister, General Luís González Bravo (1811–1871) and later Narváez forged the instruments of state control: in 1844 the rural police force Guardia Civil was created; in 1845 a constitution was promulgated that gave broad power to the executive. In 1848 the brutish Narváez was only able to stop the generalized European revolution by resorting to bloody repression. In 1847, however, small groups of Carlist guerrilleros began to reappear.

The marriage of the queen became the center of an international controversy that was resolved by marrying her off to a homosexual cousin. The intrigues of her favorites became the preferred subject of the Madrid rumor mill. But there were other notable scandals: the fortune of a dubious banker and the corruption surrounding the minister Luis José Sartorius Tapia. A coup of progressives and moderates called the Vicalvarada brought yet another general, Leopoldo O'Donnell (1809–1867), to head the government, and allowed Espartero to return home.

This governing duo was short lived. The two generals were overwhelmed by the extent of a popular uprising in Andalusia and were conse-

Liberal Uprising in Madrid. A nineteenth-century engraving commemorates the July 1854 uprising against the increasingly repressive policies of the government under Isabella II. ©ARCHIVO ICONOGRAPHICO, S.A./CORBIS

quently fired by the queen. From 1856 to 1868, Narváez alternated power (*el turno*) with O'Donnell and his Liberal Union, as other political parties were being born: republicans under Emilio Castelar y Ripoll (1832–1899) and Nicolás Salmerón y Alonso (1832–1908), and a federal party set up under Francisco Pi y Margall (1824–1901). Further foreign incidents brought two more generals onto the stage: Francisco Serrano y Domínguez (1810–1885) and Juan Prim (1814–1870). In the space of four years, Prim undertook no less than seven *pronunciamientos*, or coups d'état. In 1867 O'Donnell died, and in 1868 Narváez died. The queen was unanimously considered unbearable because of her private life. González Bravo tried to put down the agitation and became hated as a consequence. The fleet, garrisons, and local councils proclaimed fundamental freedoms and universal male suffrage. Serrano, who was chosen as chief, defeated the queen's troops, and Isabella left for exile in France.

As provisional leaders, Serrano and Prim convoked the Cortes. The result was a brilliant parliament that voted a very democratic constitution, but under a monarchy. A new difficulty arose: the choice of a king. The choice fell on Amadeo Ferdinando Maria di Savoia (1845–1890; r. 1870–1873), son of the king of Italy. Unfortunately, the very day of Amadeo's arrival in Spain, Prim was assassinated (30 December 1870). Alone, the king was left in an impossible position. The split inside the radical party between Práxedes Sagasta (1825–1903) and Manuel Ruíz Zorrilla (1833–1895), the outbreak of yet another Carlist war (1873–1876), and social agitation, led the king to abdicate, and the first Spanish republic was proclaimed on 11 February 1873.

The republic's first president was Estanislao Figueras (1819–1882; r. 1873), followed by Francisco Pi y Margall (r. 1873). Soon after, the republic's federalism was replaced by cantonalism and the cantons then declared independence. Pi resigned to avoid bloodshed. Even Salmerón (r. 1873) did not wish to apply the death penalty. With Emilio Castelar y Ripoll's (r. 1873–1874) arrival in power, the republic was instantly transformed into a unitary and authoritarian state, but it was too late. On 3 January 1874, General Manuel Pavía y Lacy (1814–1896) rode his horse into the Cortes and dissolved the parliament. A provisional dictatorship prepared the restoration of the monarchy in the name of Alfonso XII, (1857–1885; r. 1874–1885) Isabella's son. The young prince arrived back home from Britain accompanied by Antonio Cánovas del Castillo (1828–1897).

Bourbon Restoration (1875–1917) The period known as the Bourbon Restoration was dominated by two large political parties, the conservatives and liberals, who took turns running the government. The two major parties were surrounded by strong oppositions: to the right the Carlists and to the left the Republicans. From 1875 to 1885, with the Second Carlist War ended, a cleverly written constitution was promulgated that assured power on the local level to the *caciques,* or chiefs, and the alternation of power between the two major parties on the national level. This system for exchanging power became known as *el turno,* and the personality most associated with this period is the ultraconservative Cánovas del Castillo. In 1885, however, King Alfonso XII died unexpectedly, and the queen, who was pregnant, became regent.

The queen regent María Cristina (1858–1929) ruled from 1885 until 1902 and was highly respected. Under the dominating personality of Sagasta, the major political parties entered into a sort of truce. In 1898 Spain's attempts to suppress the independence movements in Cuba and the Philippines failed when the U.S. battleship *Maine* exploded in Havana Harbor, and the United States declared war on Spain. Although it was revealed many years later that the explosion was the result of a spark in the coal bunker, the United States used the event as a pretext to seize Spain's last colonial possessions. Despite the gallant stand of the Spanish naval squadron under Admiral Pascual Cervera y Topete (1839–1909) in the Battle of Santiago de Cuba and the country's sound finances, the defeat of 1898 marked the catastrophic end of

an empire and was comparable in many ways to France's defeat by Prussia in 1870. The immediate consequence of the independence of the everfaithful colony Cuba was to arouse the intellectuals in the restless regions of Catalonia and the Basque provinces.

Under Alfonso XIII (1886–1941; r. 1886–1931) from 1902 to 1914, these tensions became even more accute. The social climate was seething after 1898 and the attempts to pacify Spanish Morocco. On 31 May 1906 Alfonso married Victoria Eugénie Julia Ena—then known as Princess Ena of Battenberg (1887–1969)—a granddaughter of Queen Victoria. As their coach wound its way back to the royal palace, an anarchist threw a bomb that exploded in the midst of the crowd. Although many were killed, both Alfonso and his wife escaped harm. A strong character, the king preferred power and intrigue, with the consequence that by 1920 Alfonso had managed to make himself as detested as his grandmother Isabella; like her, he had became unbearable for the Spanish people.

During the early part of his reign, the conservative politician Antonio Maura y Montaner (1853–1925) managed to make himself equally hated. Out of the Union General de Trabajadores, the Spanish Socialist Workers' Party, or PSOE (Partido Socialista Obrero Español), was created in 1888. Maura's liberal rival Sigismundo Moret y Prendergast (1838–1913) became involved in petty intrigues. The most serious problems occurred in Catalonia, where worker anarchism and regionalism supported by the middle classes was on the rise. In 1906 Solidaridad Catalana stood in the elections, and in 1909 the call-up for troops to serve in Morocco led to the *Semana Trágica* (tragic week) in Barcelona, when the brutal repression of a series of strikes by the government caused a general uprising that saw the burning of many churches and convents. Maura was replaced by José Canalejas y Méndez (1854–1912), who tried to resolve the Moroccan problem and limit the power of the clergy. In an effort to head off the centrifugal force at work, he gave the Catalans limited autonomy with a new institution, the Mancomunitat de Cataluña (commonwealth of Catalonia). But Canalejas also fell victim to an anarchist assassin. The Conde de Romanones and

García Prieto then alternated with Eduardo Dato Iradier (1856–1921; premier 1913–1915, 1917, 1920–1921), Maura's great rival for the leadership of the Conservative Party. With the outbreak of World War I, those who were pro-Allies clashed with those who were sympathetic to the Central Powers (Germany, Austria-Hungary, Bulgaria, and the Ottoman Empire). Spain was still divided between authoritarians and liberals, and right and left—black and red.

FUNDAMENTAL PROBLEMS

The recurring leitmotif of the nineteenth century in Spain was a fundamental weakness at the center of power that allowed conspiracies and intrigue to flourish. Democratic traditions simply did not take hold: the most popular constitutional texts (the constitutions of 1812 and 1869) were only briefly applied. The others (1834, 1837, 1845, 1856) were compromises imposed by circumstance. The constitution of 1876 proved more robust and lasted longer. Under this charter, universal male suffrage was introduced in 1890, and it managed to regulate political life until 1923.

In 1898, however, just as in 1640 and 1700, this constitution could not stop the centrifugal forces at work in the most economically advanced provinces, which were of course the same areas of the old Carlist rebellions: Catalonia and the Basque provinces. The economic background that had fueled the independence movements in Cuba, Puerto Rico, and the Philippines in 1898 accentuated Catalan and Basque opposition to Madrid's authority. Simply put, these more advanced regions were increasingly unwilling to subsidize with tax revenue the backward areas of Castile and Andalusia.

In Catalonia, Enric Prat de la Riba (1879–1917) became the founding father of the *Lliga* of Catalan regional conservatives, which dominated Catalan national aspirations for close to twenty years. Without any doubt, "the earth, the race and the language" clearly defined the rebirth of Catalan identity, which became known as *catalanismo*. After 1898 the intellectuals began using the term *nationality*. Between 1833 and 1850, the Catalan language recovered its place thanks to authors like Buenaventura Carles Aribau (1798–1862), and historic works made the region's glorious past fashionable again. Even the reconquest of the language led by Pompeu Fabra (1868–1948) stems from the desire for political autonomy. The wily art critic, essayist, and philospher Eugenio d'Ors (1881–1954) eulogized Catalonia's classical past with *Noucentisme,* a term he coined to characterize twentieth-century Catalan culture, and associated French monarchical fascism with *Mediterranisme.*

In the Basque provinces a disaffected Carlist, Sabino Arana (1865–1903), reestablished Basque nationalism as an opposition to the Castilian center. His book, *Bizkaia por su independencia: Las cuatro glorias patrias* (1895) recounts the history of four medieval battles where Basques reaffirmed their independence over the Leonese and the Castilians. Arana's book is considered the bible of Basque nationalism, and he is still regarded as the founding father of the Partido Nacionalista Vasco, or Basque Nationalist Party.

As the extent of the disaster of 1898 sank in, a group of literary figures emerged that revitalized Spanish cultural life. The Generation of 1898 included the Basque philosopher Miguel de Unamuno y Jugo (1864–1936), the Galician novelist Ramón Maria del Valle-Inclán (1866–1936), the dramatist and Nobel prize winner Jacinto Benavente y Martínez (1866–1954), and the Basque novelist Pío Baroja (1872–1956). In architecture, Antonio Gaudi y Cornet's (1852–1926) very personal style gave Barcelona its most striking landmarks since the Gothic era. The philosopher José Ortega y Gasset (1883–1955) studied in Germany and returned with the vitalty he found there. In painting, Pablo Picasso (1881–1973) came to the forefront. Obsessed with the so-called Spanish Problem, they restored Spain's cultural preeminence despite a century of wars, coups, and colonial disaster.

See also **Anarchism; Ferdinand VII; Generation of 1898; Liberalism; Portugal; Revolutions of 1820.**

BIBLIOGRAPHY

Aróstegui, Julio, Jordi Canal, and Emilio Calleja. *Carlismo y las guerras carlistas.* Madrid, 2003.

Balcells, Albert. *Historia del nacionalisme cátala: Dels origens al nostre temps.* Barcelona, 1992.

Carr, Raymond. *Modern Spain, 1875–1980.* New York, 1981.

Chandler, David. *The Campaigns of Napoleon.* New York, 1966.

D'Ors, Eugenio. *La historia del mundo en 500 palabras.* Madrid, 1943.

Gomez y Amador, Luís. *La odisea del almirante cevera y su escuadra: La batalla naval de Santiago de Cuba, 1898.* Madrid, 2001.

Kurlansky, Mark. *The Basque History of the World.* New York, 2000.

Madariaga, Salvador de. *Spain: A Modern History.* New York, 1958.

Marshall-Cornwall, James. *Masséna: L'enfant chéri de la victoire.* Paris, 1967.

Pascual, Pedro. *Curas y frailes guerrilleros en la guerra de independencia.* Saragossa, Spain, 2000.

Pérez Galdós, Benito. *Episodios nacionales.* 46 vols. n.p., 1979. Rigorously documented, these novellas are the best way to understand the complicated story of Spain from 1789–1898. There are four series. The first two deal with the Peninsular War and the reign of Ferdinand VII.

Priego López, Juan. *La guerra de independencia.* 6 vols. Zaragoza, 1989.

CHRISTOPHER JONES

SPENCER, HERBERT (1820–1902), English philosopher and social theorist and a founding sociologist.

Born on 27 April 1820 in Derby, England, Herbert Spencer was the eldest son of (William) George Spencer, headmaster of a school in Derby. When he was three his father turned, unsuccessfully, to lace manufacture in Nottinghamshire but returned to Derby and to private coaching in 1827. Derby at this time was a hothouse of radical scientific culture centering on the town's Philosophical Society, founded by Erasmus Darwin, and of which George Spencer was secretary. At the age of thirteen Spencer began a three-year private tutelage with his uncle, the Reverend Thomas Spencer, curate at Hinton Charterhouse, near Bath. He was influenced by his father's individualism and antiestablishment views and the Benthamite views of his uncle. In 1836, after a brief stint as an assistant in a Derby private school, Spencer took a job as a civil engineer on the London to Birmingham and Birmingham to Gloucester railways. Here he gained firsthand experience of entrepreneurial and competitive endeavor. In 1842 he submitted a series of letters on politics to *The Nonconformist,* a radical newspaper; these were later published as "On the Proper Sphere of Government." Spencer's interest in government responsibility and the rights of workers waned, however, as his conviction grew that to intervene in social inequity was to go against the process of evolution.

Spencer worked for five years as a subeditor on London's *Economist* financial paper, and then from 1853 he devoted himself to writing professionally on a wide range of topics from population expansion to progress, education, and scientific method. But by 1855 he was suffering from extreme nervous exhaustion and was unable to work for eighteen months, and thereafter for only three hours a day. He was rescued financially by the end of the decade by a patron from North America, Professor Edward L. Youmans, a popular lecturer on scientific subjects who offered to market his books in the United States by mass subscription—thus securing him a regular income for the rest of his life. Considered by G. K. Chesterton to be one of the "great cosmic systematisers," Spencer came to be ranked alongside Charles Darwin, John Stuart Mill, and T. H. Huxley, and, as a member of the exclusive scientific X Club, he was known as Xhaustive Spencer. He enjoyed an outstanding scholarly and popular reputation in Britain, Europe, and North America in an expansive range of intellectual areas. His nine-volume *System of Synthetic Philosophy* (1862–1893) was widely translated, and a popular abridgement of his ideas, *The Study of Sociology,* which he wrote for the Paris-based International Scientific Series in 1873, went through twenty-one editions by 1894. During the 1870s and 1880s he received numerous offers of academic and ceremonial honors, but rejected most of these, disapproving in principle. In 1882 Youmans persuaded him to go on a literary tour of American universities. On his deathbed in 1903 he was nominated as a candidate for the newly founded Nobel prize for literature. He died in Brighton, England, on 8 December 1903.

EVOLUTION AS CENTRAL THEME
The idea of evolution in the broadest sense underpins all Spencer's work, and he did more than

anyone to popularize the term during the course of the nineteenth century, urging its relevance beyond biology to social and political systems. In *First Principles,* the first volume of *A System of Synthetic Philosophy,* he defined evolution as "a change from an indefinite incoherent homogeneity, to a definite, coherent heterogeneity, through continuous differentiations and integrations" and outlined the principles underpinning his beliefs, in order of importance, as the various competing models of development and evolution; ideas of matter and motion derived from theoretical mechanics; and the German physiologist Karl Ernst von Baer's model of the progression from homogeneity to heterogeneity in the structure of cell. Spencer revived speculative thinking, bringing together biology and social theory, and continually stressing the necessity of biology in social studies. Through analogy he condensed the laws of society and laws of physiology, arguing that all living forms, including society, were moving inevitably toward higher forms.

His first book, *Social Statics; or, The Conditions Essential to Human Happiness,* appeared in 1851. The term *social statics,* borrowed from Auguste Comte, refers to the conditions of social order, and the work defended individual liberties, arguing for "the right to ignore the state" in aiming at the "equilibrium of a perfect society." For Spencer "equilibration" was the happy point at which the evolutionary process reached its limit. He urged that society not be separated from nature, and that evolution was a progressive, teleological process toward an equilibrium whereby individuals adapt until reaching a state of perfect harmony with their environment: equilibration. Spencer denounced the effects of charity: "a sad population of imbeciles would our schemers fill the world with, could their plans last ... the average effect of the laws of nature is to 'purify' society from those who are, in some respect or other, essentially faulty," and he stressed that progress was not an accident but a necessity, and that civilization was not a construct but a part of nature "all of a piece with the development of the embryo or the unfolding of a flower."

The following year, in "A Theory of Population, Deduced from the General Law of Animal Fertility," published in the *Westminster Review,* he argued that population pressure and scarcity of resources were the engine of progress, following, but giving a quite different spin to, Malthusian ideas on population. In this article Spencer came close to establishing the principles of natural selection and coined the tautologous and now ubiquitous term *the survival of the fittest,* which Darwin then incorporated into his work, adding it to the heading of chapter four in the fifth edition of *The Origin of Species.* Spencer argued that the process of adaptation must occur without any charitable or state intervention, for only a competitive free-for-all would ensure the survival of the fittest.

In addition to Thomas Robert Malthus, Spencer was influenced by Jean-Baptiste Lamarck's account of a process of organic change generated by use, practice, and adaptation to environment, and, like Larmarck, but unlike Darwin, he made individual effort central to the process of evolution. Emphasizing the influence of external agencies on the development of an organism, he defended individual rights on Lamarckian grounds, seeing all organisms as tending toward self-sufficiency and individuation, and society as the aggregate of mutually dependent individuals. Change in society had to be preceded by the change and development of individuals, of which the development of moral sense and feeling was one expression. For Spencer, all progressive development was governed by the mechanical principle of the "persistence of force." A member of the British Liberal Party, he opposed any state intervention, aggressively promoting, instead, laissez-faire capitalism as the social form most likely to allow individuals to exercise their powers fully in the service of the community. This formed part of his functionalist view of society, in which society was analogous to an organism of which the parts played different functions. The pressures of competition would, he believed, ensure optimum adaptation and hence progress. In "The Social Organism," also published in the *Westminster Review* (1860), he argued that "the changes going on around" and "social organization in its leading traits ... are consequent on general natural causes," and, especially in *The Man versus the State* (1884), he emphasized the importance of administration of justice, which he equated with freedom and the protection of rights.

In his second book, *The Principles of Psychology* (1855), Spencer argued that mind was the product of environmentally induced organic evolution, and life "the continuous adjustment of internal relations to external relations." In the words of his biographer Hector Macpherson he turned psychology from "a sterile science confined to academic circles" into a "valuable instrument of scientific research" (cited in Duncan, p. 519). Later that decade Spencer turned his attention to education, writing a series of articles that argued against rote learning in favor of "self-development," based on problem solving, healthy exercise, and natural science. The "impersonal agency of Nature" should replace "the personal agency of parents." He argued that "all breaches of the laws of health are physical sins" and that excessive education was detrimental to a woman's reproductive health.

SPENCER'S INFLUENCE

Spencer's ideas lent themselves to a biologization of racial and social hierarchies, which would underpin late-nineteenth-century "social Darwinism"— the selective application of Darwinian ideas to society. He was nowhere more influential than in North America where his ideas were taken up by economists and social philosophers such as Thorstein Veblen (1857–1929) and the apologists William Graham Sumner (1840–1910), professor of sociology at Yale University, and Simon Nelson Patten (1852–1922), director of the Wharton business school at the University of Pennsylvania, who urged the social and racial application of the idea of the "survival of the fittest."

Spencer's ideas rapidly appealed to the broader cultural imagination. The English novelist and poet Thomas Hardy referred to him as one of the key influences on his life. Spencer introduced his theory of evolution over four issues of the *Westminster Review* during George Eliot's time as assistant editor (1851–1853), and she began a lifelong connection with him. She resisted his increasingly conservative ideas on women, however, and was taken more by his *Data of Ethics* (1879), in which he argued that as the sources of pleasure outgrew those of pain, egoism would allow for sympathy and gratification through the "gratification of others." And, the New Women writers of the century's final close were drawn to his work, which met their future-orientated perspective and their fascination with the relation between biology and society; several of their heroines are keen readers of his work, notably Sarah Grand's Evadne, the central character of her best-selling *The Heavenly Twins* (1893), and Ménie Muriel Dowie's eponymous activist in *Gallia* (1895), both of whom make biology and reproduction central to their feminism. The novelists Leo Tolstoy, Arnold Bennett, and D. H. Lawrence also referred to his ideas, and Jack London's semiautobiographical character Martin Eden is an ardent Spencerian whose desire to know sends him "adventuring over the world," and who is kept up all night, and day, reading *First Principles*—"here was Spencer, organizing all knowledge for him, reducing everything to unity, elaborating ultimate realities. . . . All was law. It was in obedience to law that the bird flew, and it was in obedience to the same law that fermenting slime had writhed and squirmed and put out legs and wings and become a bird"—but who comes to know, "full well, from his Spencer, that man can never attain ultimate knowledge of anything."

See also **Bentham, Jeremy; Capitalism; Comte, Auguste; Darwin, Charles; Eliot, George; Evolution; Malthus, Thomas Robert; Mill, John Stuart; Sociology; Utilitarianism.**

BIBLIOGRAPHY

Andreski, Stanislav, ed. *Herbert Spencer: Structure, Function, and Evolution.* New York, 1971.

Duncan, David. *The Life and Letters of Herbert Spencer.* London, 1908. Reprint, London, 1996.

Gray, Tim S. "Herbert Spencer: Individualist or Organicist?" *Political Studies* 33 (1985): 236–253.

———. *The Political Philosophy of Herbert Spencer.* Aldershot, U.K., 1996.

Jones, Greta. *Social Darwinism and English Thought: The Interaction between Biological and Social Theory.* Brighton, U.K., 1980.

Macpherson, Hector. *Herbert Spencer: The Man and His Work.* London, 1900.

Paxton, Nancy L. *George Eliot and Herbert Spencer: Feminism, Evolutionism, and the Reconstruction of Gender.* Princeton, N.J., 1991.

Peel, J. D. Y. *Herbert Spencer: The Evolution of a Sociologist.* London, 1971.

Richardson, Angelique. *Love and Eugenics in the Late Nineteenth Century: Rational Reproduction and the New Woman.* Oxford, U.K., 2003.

Rylance, Rick. *Victorian Psychology and British Culture, 1850–1880*. Oxford, U.K., 2000.

Taylor, M. W. *Men versus the State: Herbert Spencer and Late Victorian Individualism*. Oxford, U.K., 1992.

Wiltshire, David. *The Social and Political Thought of Herbert Spencer*. Oxford, U.K., 1978.

ANGELIQUE RICHARDSON

SPERANSKY, MIKHAIL (1772–1839), Russian politician.

Mikhail Speransky was one of the most important Russian statesmen of the nineteenth century. Born on 12 January (1 January, old style) 1772 in Chertkutino, Vladimir Province, the son of a village priest, Speransky attended the Vladimir ecclesiastical seminary. In 1790 he was one of the first chosen to study at the new Alexander Nevsky Seminary in St. Petersburg. A brilliant student, he taught at the academy for a time after graduation until becoming secretary to Prince Alexei Kurakin in 1796, beginning a meteoric rise within the Russian bureaucracy. In 1798 he married Elizabeth Stephens, an English woman, with whom he had a daughter. After his wife's death in 1799, Speransky focused almost entirely on his work, leading an isolated life both socially and politically.

In 1801 Alexander I became emperor. Between 1801 and 1812, during the early—and generally considered to be liberal—years of Alexander's reign, Speransky's outstanding talents as a clear and compelling writer were increasingly in demand. In 1802 Speransky became the secretary of the minister of the interior, Prince Kochubei; in 1807 Alexander I made Speransky his personal assistant. In 1802 Speransky wrote his first important political work, "On the Fundamental Laws of the State," in which he argued that the powers of the monarchy needed to be limited by society, or, more specifically, by a self-aware and powerful nobility. In what is generally considered to be his most important reform program, the Plan of 1809, Speransky wrote that the spirit of the times called for a constitutional monarchy kept in check by public opinion. A legislative body, the State Duma, would assist in this process. These views made Speransky many high-placed enemies, and com-bined with his social isolation and somewhat difficult personality led to his exile in March 1812.

In exile first in Nizhny Novgorod, then in the more remote town of Perm, Speransky worked for his rehabilitation. His appointment as governor of Penza Province in 1816 began his second career. Reorganizing the Penza bureaucracy prepared Speransky for the task of reforming the Siberian administration, which he undertook after being appointed governor-general of Siberia in 1819. Speransky's Siberian reforms, enacted in 1822, integrated the region into the Russian Empire and rationalized the administration. In 1821 he was allowed to return to St. Petersburg, where he oversaw the Siberian reforms and made plans for reorganizing local administration that, while not enacted, influenced later projects.

After Alexander I's death, in December 1825, a group of high-ranking officers staged a revolt against the new emperor, Nicholas I. During the inquiry following the failure of the coup, several of the "Decembrist" officers stated that Speransky had influenced them. Speransky was one of the participants in and organizers of the trial against the Decembrists, and called for harsh penalties.

After this show of loyalty to Nicholas, Speransky headed the effort to codify Russian laws. During his exile, Speransky had been influenced by the historical school of law. This school originated in Germany and argued that each nation developed according to its own essence, which was embodied in historical legal institutions and practices. The historical approach provided a foundation for Speransky's codification of Russian law, based on organizing and publishing the laws and edicts issued since the prior codification of 1649. Forty-five volumes of the *Complete Collection of the Laws of the Russian Empire* were issued in 1830; the fifteen-volume *Digest of the Laws,* which contained laws currently in effect, was published between 1832 and 1839. While the *Complete Collection of Laws* gave the texts of nearly all laws and edicts issued between 1649 and 1825, the *Digest* organized laws currently in effect by topic. Speransky incorporated a significant number of the concepts he put forth in the Plan of 1809 into the *Digest*. The codification was one of the main accomplishments of Nicholas's reign. After the codification was complete, Speransky traveled abroad, acted as a member of the State Council, and lectured to the tsarevitch, the future Alexander II, on law. He was made a count of the Russian Empire in January 1839 and died in St. Petersburg on 23 February (11 February, old style) 1839.

See also **Alexander I; Law, Theories of; Nicholas I; Siberia.**

BIBLIOGRAPHY

Raeff, Marc. *Michael Speransky: Statesman of Imperial Russia.* 2nd ed. The Hague, Netherlands, 1969.

Whisenhunt, William Benton. *In Search of Legality: Mikhail M. Speranskii and the Codification of Russian Law.* Boulder, Colo., 2001.

Wortman, Richard S. *The Development of a Russian Legal Consciousness.* Chicago, 1976.

SUSAN SMITH-PETER

SPIRITUALISM. Modern spiritualism began in the spring of 1848, with the appearance of a pamphlet describing a series of uncanny tapping noises in the Fox family home, a tiny wood-frame house in Hydesville, New York. These "raps," which appeared to emanate from a variety of hard surfaces, always occurred in the presence of the two youngest Fox daughters, eleven-year-old Kate and fourteen-year-old Margaret. The Fox family quickly discovered that the force producing these raps could answer questions by tapping in a simple alphabetic code. Through this cumbersome method, the noise-producing force declared itself to be the disembodied soul of a murdered peddler. As word of this strange phenomenon spread, visitors flocked to the house.

Within a few weeks, Kate and Margaret discovered they could produce these noises anywhere, and on behalf of a vast array of different spirits. These raps were a telegraphic code through which any disembodied soul could send dispatches to loved ones still living. As word of this development spread, others followed the example of the Fox girls, discovering their own varied talents as mediums: trance speech, table-moving, and automatic writing emerged alongside raps as means of relaying spirit messages. The most gifted mediums, many of whom were women, became celebrities whose exploits were reported in a burgeoning spiritualist press. Soon, it was possible to speak of modern spiritualism, a fully-fledged movement founded on the belief that the living could enter into regular communication with the dead.

In the early 1850s, this new movement traversed the Atlantic. Visiting American mediums caused a sensation in Great Britain, inspiring a nationwide interest in these phenomena. In elite circles, celebrity mediums impressed their audiences with spectacular manifestations. Beginning in 1855, for example, the American-born Daniel Dunglas Home (1833–1886) became famous for his ability to produce luminous spirit hands, to divine intimate secrets about strangers and their deceased relatives, to cause musical instruments to play of their own accord, and to hold himself suspended in mid-air. Aristocrats and eminent writers like Charles Dickens, Anthony and Rose Trollope, William Makepeace Thackeray, Robert and Elizabeth Barrett Browning, John Ruskin, and Edward Bulwer-Lytton attended these gatherings. British spiritualism also flourished in humbler circumstances, where visionary communications tended to be more important than spectacular phenomena. Beginning in the mid-1850s, skilled workers formed spiritualist societies in industrial regions like Yorkshire, and in the burgeoning manufacturing cities of Manchester, Nottingham, Belfast, and Glasgow.

Spiritualism spread rapidly to the Continent as well. By 1853, séances had become a topic of fashionable discussion in France and Germany. As in Britain, these strange phenomena captured the interest of both elite and ordinary people. The author Victor Hugo received whole poems through an animated table, the French empress Eugénie (r. 1853–1871) figured among the glamorous guests at Home's séances, and the German philosopher Arthur Schopenhauer published an essay on "Spirit Sight." At the same time, pamphlets aimed at large audiences, containing instructions on how to produce the new phenomena and explanations of their significance, sold briskly.

Despite this initial burst of popularity, however, it took nearly a decade for organized spiritualism to emerge fully on the Continent—it began in the late 1850s in France, and in the 1870s traveled across the Rhine. By the 1880s, spiritualist circles were

Spirit photograph by Edouard Buguet c. 1870. The simultaneous development of spiritualism and the nascent medium of photography in the mid-nineteenth century led naturally to the widespread production of photographs purporting to show spirit manifestations such as this one by French photographer Edouard Buguet. Buguet was convicted of fraud in 1874, but many supporters were undeterred in their belief in Buguet and spiritualism. MARY EVANS PICTURE LIBRARY

utopian socialist Charles Fourier's belief in reincarnation—an idea Anglo-Saxon spiritualists found repellent. German spiritualists conceived of the movement from yet a different perspective: as a vehicle for social progress and as a new element in an ongoing debate between the philosophical schools of idealism and materialism.

As spiritualism became a fixture of the period's cultural and intellectual life, an increasing number of scientists turned their attention to the mysterious phenomena mediums produced. At first, these studies were isolated endeavors. In the early 1870s, for example, Sir William Crookes (1832–1919), discoverer of the element thallium, attempted to measure the "psychic force" Home seemed to exude in séances. Similarly, in 1878, Carl Friedrich Zöllner (1800–1860), founder of the discipline of astrophysics, published a study of the medium Henry Slade (d. 1905), in which he hypothesized that some phenomena were the work of beings from an invisible fourth dimension. By the early 1880s, many believed the subject had become pressing enough to demand a more systematic response. To accomplish this goal, the Cambridge philosopher Henry Sidgwick (1838–1900) founded the Society for Psychical Research, an organization devoted to the experimental study of the mysterious powers of mind mediums exhibited. This current of scientific inquiry, as explored by thinkers like Frederick Myers (1843–1901), Pierre-Marie-Felix Janet (1859–1947) and Theodore Flournoy (1854–1920), played a crucial role in the development of a new psychological conception of subjectivity—one that posited the existence of a complex and active "subliminal" or unconscious mind.

During this period, spiritualism appealed to a remarkably broad range of people—from famous writers and scientists to housewives and industrial workers. This striking breadth mirrored the breadth of the anxieties and aspirations the movement addressed. For some, communication with the beyond was simply an attractive form of consolation, a way to remain in reassuring contact with deceased loved ones. For others, especially those who became mediums, spiritualism could be a source of social power and mobility. Mediumship gave women an opportunity to speak publicly in ways that were otherwise unavailable to them. It also provided people of humble social origin—like Home, or

thriving from San Francisco to Moscow. On the Continent, the movement took very different forms than it did in Britain or the United States. In France, and later in Italy and Spain, for example, believers referred to their ideas and practices as "Spiritism." Spiritist groups, perhaps echoing the hierarchical structure of the Catholic Church, tended to be considerably more centralized than their Anglo-Saxon counterparts. They also espoused a distinctive cosmology based on French thought, which incorporated Auguste Comte's positivist vision of history as a sweeping march of progress, and the century, an era of uncertainty and transition, this prospect proved attractive indeed.

See also **Popular and Elite Culture; Science and Technology; Secularization.**

BIBLIOGRAPHY

Doyle, Arthur Conan. *The History of Spiritualism.* 2 vols. New York, 1926.

Monroe, John Warne. "*Cartes de visite* from the Other World: Spiritism and the Discourse of *Laïcisme* in the Early Third Republic." *French Historical Studies* 26, no. 1 (2003): 119–153.

Oppenheim, Janet. *The Other World: Spiritualism and Psychical Research in England, 1850–1914.* Cambridge, U.K., 1985.

Owen, Alex. *The Darkened Room: Women, Power and Spiritualism in Late Nineteenth Century England.* London, 1989.

Treitel, Corinna. *A Science for the Soul: Occultism and the Genesis of the German Modern.* Baltimore, Md., 2004.

Turner, Frank M. *Between Science and Religion: The Reaction to Scientific Naturalism in Late Victorian England.* New Haven, Conn., 1974.

JOHN WARNE MONROE

Caricature of William Crookes with his device for measuring psychic force. From *Spy* magazine, 1903. An eminent physicist, Crookes was initially involved with spiritualism as a skeptic attempting to uncover fraud among practitioners. He later became convinced of the possibility of communicating with the spirit world. MARY EVANS PICTURE LIBRARY

the Italian peasant Eusapia Palladino (1854–1918)—access to undreamt of status and fame. More broadly, spiritualism seemed to address what many considered to be a fundamental problem of the age: the ever-growing incompatibility of scientific and religious knowledge. Where scientific truth was based on material data, gathered through a careful process of experimentation, religious truth was based on faith—an emotional, intuitive sense of commitment and acceptance. Spiritualism seemed to resolve this conflict by giving religious knowledge an empirical foundation as solid as the one scientific knowledge enjoyed. For seekers in the nineteenth

SPORTS

SPORTS. Between the eighteenth and nineteenth centuries Europe developed into a fulcrum of invention in the arenas of sports and gymnastics where, over the course of a few decades, a new relationship to physical exercise took shape and spread, eventually reaching every nation and social stratum. The term *sport* itself did not enter into use in France and Germany until the mid-nineteenth century, despite the existence of games such as tennis, among others, as far back as the Middle Ages. Continental Europe invented other models for the development of bodily excellence in the form of gymnastics, and Europeans viewed sports as mere amusements; in England, by contrast, they represented a form of educational practice that took place through competitive spectacles.

THE INVENTION OF MODERN SPORTS AND GYMNASTICS (1789–1870)

Modern sports first emerged in England from two sources, one professional and linked to the lower classes, the other amateur and bourgeois. During this same period gymnastics, an alternative form of physical activity espousing a different set of values, was being developed in Continental Europe as a response to increasing nationalist pressures and a fear of degeneracy.

British sports In eighteenth-century England wealthy landowners developed a pastime culture that increasingly valued physical exercise and competition between players, for example, hunting with dogs. The need to further codify these activities soon followed, aided by parliamentarianism, which altered mind-sets by inscribing the use of rules and arbitration upon English moral consciousness. The first rules for golf date from 1744 in Scotland, cricket in 1727, and a basic seven-rule boxing game began in 1743. These "gentlemen farmers," however, also adopted the habit of opposing one another via surrogates, using their fastest and strongest employees on the field or in the ring. These gatherings enjoyed great success with the people, even more so because the rural areas in England already had long-standing traditions of competitive games. Distance races, boxing matches, drunk boxing, animal fights (involving dogs, bears, cocks, etc.), and horse races were all part of daily English rural life and festivals. At the end of the eighteenth century and the beginning of the nineteenth, the combination of this popular culture and principles of codification resulted in the development of previously unheard-of events in which impassioned crowds gathered to bet on winners, fueling a steady increase in the ranks of bookmakers serving masses of spectators numbering as high as twenty thousand people.

In the early nineteenth century the high stakes involved drove those rural players with the most talent to sell themselves to the highest bidders, constituting a market that for the first time ever allowed professional boxers, swimmers, and runners to make a living off their sporting activity. Victorian society's downplaying of violence, attested to for example in the banning of animal fights in 1835 and 1849, played into the public's taste for the spectacle of sporting events where proxy confrontations were still possible.

The consequences of this desire for more spectacle included the invention of the "handicap" for preserving the suspense at the finish line, and in 1845 (one hundred years after its invention) the use of chronometry. Event organizers strove for originality to attract audiences, including the first "world championship" boxing match between black and white fighters in 1810, which took place in front of twenty-five thousand spectators, and the promise made by one pool superintendent to showcase a record-breaking breath-holding event. Eventually, some of these professional teams were organized into federal groups such as the National Swimming Society, which was founded in 1837 by a London-based wine merchant. In a few years regional branches of the society were created, and this institution also established an annual event calendar, organized local and national championship swimming tournaments, and assumed responsibility for the record keeping of individual performance.

Just as these popular and spectacle-driven professional sports were in the process of development, however, a second orientation emerged in the public schools between 1820 and 1850. These prestigious establishments, including the University of Oxford, the University of Cambridge, Rugby School, and Eton College, brought together under one roof the children of the aristocracy, the rural gentry, and the urban bourgeoisie, all of whom shared the same beliefs in progress, capitalism, and the Protestant ethic. This rapprochement of the upper social strata gave birth to an ethos that laid the groundwork for amateur sports to emerge.

In the public schools physical exercise previously had been based on gymnastics, whereas after school the students engaged in competitive sports that were tolerated more than encouraged by school officials, who never managed to prohibit them completely. Beginning in the 1820s, however, these games gained in status and eventually became primary elements in the British elite educational system. For example, the director of Rugby School, Thomas Arnold, decided to regulate its football matches: rules concerning duration, refereeing, the codification of "hacking" (stopping the man who has the ball), and the management of the matches by the students themselves all ensued. The goal was to use games played in the open air to produce "muscular Christians," meaning individuals capable of controlling their passions (disciplinary, sexual) through henceforth institutionalized activities and, even further, to produce men of initiative at a moment in history when England remained the world's most important economic and colonial power.

With the Rugby model in mind, the other educational establishments each followed suit with its own particular sport, including swimming at Eton and rowing at Oxford and Cambridge, the latter two having competed against each other every year since 1829. These developments were greatly favored by the expansion of the rail network from 1850 on, which helped multiply the number of encounters between university teams.

After graduating, students interested in continuing to play their favorite sports formed the first sporting clubs. The product of the favored classes and exclusively masculine, these players considered themselves the ambassadors of a way of life that drove them to advocate aggressively in favor of the idea of sports as an activity for amateurs that relied on limited violence, eventually leading to the establishment of rules and institutional structures intended to guide the final development of sports as a whole. In 1863 the rules of the Football Association were instituted for these purposes, and the first England Cup Tournament was held the following year. In early 1869 officials from several swimming clubs gathered in London to codify laws for the foundation of the Metropolitan Swimming Association, which was created later that year. By 1870, therefore, two great approaches to sports in Great Britain, one professional and the other amateur, coexisted and contributed equally through their activities and their conflicts to the creation of a sporting culture on a nationwide scale that was virtually unknown in the rest of Europe.

European gymnastics From the end of the eighteenth century to the second half of the nineteenth, a significant portion of Europe, notably Germany, Belgium, France, and Switzerland, witnessed the appearance of exercise institutions such as fencing rooms, baths, and private gymnasiums, often started by former soldiers and educators seeking a profitable transition to civilian life. Formal schools of gymnastics and physical exercise also arose during this time, and their owners did not hesitate to publicize their methods in multiple languages and across national borders. For example, the Swiss Clias could be found in France, England,

the Netherlands, and Denmark, while the French Triat opened a renowned venue in Brussels.

These gymnasiums existed exclusively in urban settings and catered to an essentially bourgeois, educated adult clientele who were highly receptive to Rousseauian ideas and placed their beliefs in the recommendations of hygienists who began to emphasize the role of regular physical activity taken in controlled doses. A generalized anxiety concerning racial degeneracy believed to be occurring via numerous epidemics did the rest.

Although some of these gymnasiums and exercise facilities were specialized for female clients (Clias in Switzerland, Laisné in France), for the most part they were reserved exclusively for men. This network reached its apogee in the 1860s, at which point a new form of gymnastics with more nationalist and educational aims, rather than being activity- and hygiene-based, began to emerge. Thus in the first half of the nineteenth century there arose a series of competing systems that in the minds of many reflected the national identity of each nation and its unique memory of the Napoleonic Wars, such as in Germany, Sweden, France, and Denmark.

In general terms these gymnastics were based on collective forms of exercise, with or without equipment, that valued discipline, the cult of the group, respect for the leader, and the integration of the individual into the group. According to national differences, they reflected the influence of either state institutions, including the army (the case for example with the Amoros method in France) and the schools, or private institutions.

For example, the principles championed by Friedrich Ludwig Jahn (1778–1852) in the German states can be understood only as reactions to the Napoleonic invasions. Heavily influenced by the thought of Johann Gottlieb Fichte and his hatred of the French, Jahn systematized a patriotic gymnastics in the service of the *deutsche Volkstum* (German community) with increasingly racist overtones. Anyone who "loves, praises, excuses or cohorts with foreigners" was barred from entry into the gymnastic society. The term *gymnastics* itself was replaced by the more German word *Turnen,* and *Turner* soon became synonymous with being skilled in the values of a unified

Germany. Various symbols including dress, hairstyle, and other devices came to reinforce this ideology, which was in direct opposition to British sports. Despite the fears, and the prohibitions, generated by this project of unification, *Turnen* spread to all the great cities of Germany in the form of societies, in particular after the Revolution of 1848–1849, at which point the model was exported to other European countries including Switzerland (with Adolf Spiess), Austria-Hungary (with the Von Stephany brothers), Italy (with Rodolfo Obermann), and Greece (with Georgios Pagon). In Belgium the followers of Carl Euler ran up against the practices of the Swedish method, which was the product of the work of one of Jahn's contemporaries, Per Henrik Ling (1776–1839), who advocated within Sweden itself a conception less anchored in nationalism and more influenced by the desire to improve the health of his compatriots. This approach stemmed from his own past, insofar as he had a wounded arm that regained its mobility only through gymnastic activity. In 1813, in Stockholm, Ling had founded the Royal Central Gymnastic Institute, the first training facility for gymnastics teachers in Europe. Furthermore, Ling, followed by his son Lijalmar, formalized his system based on scientific principles, and in the middle of the nineteenth century their students exported the Swedish method to the rest of northern Europe and England, and its influence spread elsewhere in Europe as well.

THE ERA OF INSTITUTIONALIZATION (1870–1890)

Beginning in the 1870s, physical activity generally came to be viewed more and more as a way to promote health and improve individual performance in the professional, military, and scholarly domestic spheres. Furthermore, what passed for sports in England and for gymnastics in the rest of Europe could not be directly compared. Though both reflected similar trends toward rationalization and institutionalization, the development of the former reflected the English social structure, leading to the eventual imposition of the amateur ethic upon the practices of professionals, whereas in Germany or France sports reflected the sociopolitical consequences of the battles of Sadowa (1866) and Sedan (1870), which had marked Prussian supremacy and led to the unification of Germany.

In England, the conflict-ridden coexistence of amateur practices alongside professional ones spurred unprecedented growth in sporting culture itself, particularly in the great urban centers. The competition between these two ethics drove those responsible for directing the development of the biggest sports to increasingly delineate the conditions surrounding the matches in a more precise manner. The number of articles of rules for the same sporting activity increased by a factor of two or three between 1870 and 1890, leading to the need for negotiation because the same rules were not always followed across different regions and universities. Consensus at times proved impossible, as witnessed for example in the creation in 1871 of the Rugby Football Association, whose officials did not share the positions of the English Football Association, founded in 1863. Disagreements concerning the definition of what constitutes an amateur, given the inadequacy of a code based primarily on class considerations, also produced significant tensions within institutions. In 1869 the Metropolitan Swimming Association (MSA) laid out its twenty-three-point "Laws of Amateur Swimming," immediately provoking harsh reactions from professionals thereby excluded from their chosen field as well as numerous amateurs who rejected the imperialism of directors based in London. Competitor institutions soon appeared, including the Professional Swimming Association for the former and the Amateur Swimming Union for the latter, before the MSA prevailed under the guise of a new name, the Swimming Association of Great Britain (1873), and then as the Amateur Swimming Association (instead of *Union*), starting in 1886.

Such restructuring reinforced the process of regulation that was already taking place, and the university ethic of the gentlemen amateur finally managed to dominate in the 1880s. The authorities responsible for regulating swimming, cycling, and other sports in that decade were bound together by these strong ties. Not all federations, however, were as closed off as the highly elitist members of the Marylebone Cricket Club, the Amateur Rowing Association, and the Lawn Tennis Association. After the Football Association formally recognized professional players in 1885, football became the most incontestably popular sport in the country. The number of clubs multiplied and spread further into the worker population. In a country in which three-fourths of the population lived in cities by the end of the century, urban youths increasingly played football. In 1874 there was only one football club in Birmingham—by 1880 there were 150, and Liverpool alone counted 200 in 1890.

London, then the world's largest city, also became England's and Europe's main hotspot for sports. Tens of thousands of spectators crowded around sporting fields and on the banks of the Thames to watch football, cricket, and rowing matches. A specialized press evolved, reinforcing the element of spectacle even more, and sport-specific venues were built on this success. Although for football modest fields were laid out wherever space near a factory was available, the first large stadiums, such as Scotland's Hampden Park (begun in 1893), also appeared during this period. Nearly one thousand golf courses were built in the last quarter of the nineteenth century. In 1912 England possessed eight hundred baths, six hundred of which were in fact swimming pools where meets were held, and seemingly every fancy hotel had its tennis court. In this way, over the course of just three decades, a network of dedicated sporting installations was erected that Continent-dwellers would soon regard with envy.

This English phase of the institutionalization and codification of sports could be found in the rest of Europe with respect to gymnastics but with notable variations based on national traditions. The origin of this process, however, was very different on the Continent because it was directly linked to the rise of German influence in the 1860s. Gymnastics became even more a tool for military preparation and civic education than before, with the support of the political authorities of the Continental Great Powers, and closely tied to the schools and armies.

In Germany, the *Turnen* societies were combined into a national federation (the Deutsche Turnerschaft) in 1868. Although the powerful largely impeded the movement's formal politicization, it was evident nonetheless in its military aspirations and found conditions highly favorable to its expansion in the Austro-Hungarian Empire. By the end of the

nineteenth century these societies counted more than a million members among their ranks.

Denmark created the Danish Shooting Federation (De Danske Skytteforeninger) in 1861 to counter this rise in German influence, but the movement's greatest development no doubt occurred in France. When the Third Republic emerged out of the ashes of defeat at Sedan and the loss of Alsace-Lorraine, gymnastics came to be organized along patriotic and "revanchist" lines that were very different from both private gymnastics and the nascent sporting activities. In 1873 these societies came together to form a movement for national federation, which resulted in the formation of the Union of Gymnastic Societies (Union des Sociétés de Gymnastique de France). This union enjoyed close relations with the political elite and the French Masons. From 251 societies in 1882, at the moment when nationalism increased its appeal (for example, with the creation of the Patriot League, or *Ligue des Patriotes*), the number of member gymnastic societies, including groups devoted to shooting and military preparation, exceeded fifty-four hundred just prior to World War I, with the number of individual members growing to half a million.

Gymnastics also met the needs of identity formation by becoming a tool for community cohesion and the reinforcement of nationalist sentiment. Though most evident in Germany and France, it also developed definitive forms in Italy through a national federation (the Federazione Ginnastica d'Italia), founded in 1869, even as the fractures between north and south were weakening the country. Less prevalent in Spain and Portugal, the gymnastic societies would play a similar role for the minority groups of the Austro-Hungarian Empire as they did in France, Germany, and Italy. They were particularly dense indeed among the Alsatians on the German Empire's western perimeter, as well as, in the Austro-Hungarian Empire, among the Slovenes to the south, in the form of the Sokol movement, and among the Slavic communities for whom the movement increasingly represented a form of group expression. Of course at the moment in 1862 when the term *sokol* (falcon) was chosen in honor of the legendary Slovenian heroes, the group's ranks did not yet number more than a few hundred individuals. Twenty years later, under the agency of Miroslav Tyrš in particular, the first *slet* (festival) still attracted just 760 gymnasts, but this number grew to 2,473 by the second one in 1891, and eventually reached 12,000 people by the sixth one in 1912.

Unlike the athletes involved in most sports, gymnasts from most nations generally were drawn from the middle and lower classes composed of workers and farmers. Still, the sporting clubs themselves invariably functioned like mini-societies with systems for sanction, discipline, rewards, and punishments. Becoming a member often presupposed a form of cooptation involving specific rites of initiation, usually including a requirement for wearing membership insignias as well as other marks of distinction such as clothing (caps, outfits, and uniforms), badges, and the recitation of hymns. The similarities, however, end there. The sporting clubs were driven to organize their activities in order to increase performance and win. By the end of the nineteenth century the role of the coach had become distinguished from that of team captain, whereas the two could have been easily confused just a decade earlier. The horse-training model, often referred to in the 1850s, became less useful when the first physiological benchmarks came into use after 1890. The early development of a sporting culture in England no doubt explains at least some of the differences between the activities practiced there, as opposed to on the Continent. The former had become highly specialized into specific sports at a time when the latter were to remain largely polyvalent until 1914. The first training manuals appeared in England in the second half of the nineteenth century, whereas it would take another generation for this kind of literature to spread on the Continent.

For their part the gymnasts promoted forms of activity that were legitimate and compatible with the patriotic voluntarism from which they had emerged. Military ranks, salutes, chants, systematic sanctions, flags, and hymns all constituted a framework within which physical training could be conceived only in terms of morality in action. Unlike the sports clubs, the gymnastic societies focused less on individual achievement and more on socialization and belonging to a group. The sporting "championships" that appeared more or less throughout Europe in the 1880s were therefore quite different than gymnastic "festivals" and "competitions" where individual medals were rarely awarded, in favor of team effort, parades, and other forms of collective exhibition.

DIFFUSION, DEMOCRATIZATION, AND ADOPTION (1870–1914)

As the British sporting model assumed its ultimate form, it also spread beyond its initial home and in two generations had conquered the European countries in which Britain had its greatest economic and cultural influences, or where the Industrial Revolution provided fertile ground. Indeed what sports were played in Continental Europe during these years initially reflected the presence of British nationals.

Englishmen founded both the Belgian Regatta Society (1851) and Belgium's first football club (in Antwerp, 1880). The northern and western regions of Germany, where commercial exchange with England was greatest, witnessed the birth of its first sports clubs. In France, the first football teams were formed in localities with the largest concentration of British émigrés, primarily in Le Havre (1872) and Paris (1877). Tennis developed in the seaside resorts of the Atlantic and North Sea, often on private estates or resorts where British vacationers were residing. In Spain, football was introduced by the Irish schools in Valladolid and Salamanca, although it was a Swiss who founded the famous Barcelona Football Club in 1899. Yet the first Swiss football championship was won by the Geneva team, composed entirely of English players. At other times it was visitors from a given country returning from a stay in England, who had been won over by sports, and who attempted to institute them upon their return. This process was evident in Italy, and even more so in Greece, where the organization of the first modern Olympic Games in 1896 substantially accelerated it.

In most instances this first phase gave way to a process whereby foreign sports seeped into the local population's middle class, which was susceptible to British culture. The first teams without British players appeared between 1880 and 1900, at the same time as federations were created either for specific sporting activities (e.g., the Spanish Cycling Federation in 1889, the Federation of French Rowing Societies in 1893, the Italian Athletics Federation in 1898) or in the form of open-ended groups such as the Union of French Sporting and Athletic Societies (1889), the Union of Belgian Athletic Sports Societies (1895), the Danish Sports Federation (1896), and the Greek Union of Associations for Athletic Sports and Gymnastics (1897). All of these institutions defined and codified their activities according to English rules, including the strict imposition of the original amateur ethos.

The ground was thus prepared for the reception given to English sports on the Continent by the increasing popularity of athletics and biking. Indeed the fashion for horse racing had already spread to the great European cities and tourist destinations by the mid-nineteenth century. Although events in this case remained reserved primarily for elites, they paved the way for the arrival of modern sports. Biking witnessed remarkable growth after 1880 in Italy (Italian Cyclists Union in 1885), Belgium, France (French Cyclists Union in 1881), and in Greece (Greek Cyclists Union in 1895), following a number of crucial technological innovations including the attachment of the chain to the rear wheel in 1880 and the rubber tire in 1888. Lodged between bourgeois pastime and popular sport, cycling, along with football, became one of the era's primary avenues for the democratization of sports itself. Several million bicycles had already been industrially produced before 1914. As early as 1890 several large races had begun, followed by the popular Tour de France in 1903, the Tour of Italy in 1909, and the Tour of Flanders in 1913.

The adoption and democratization of modern sports between 1870 and 1914 on the Continent, however, reflected a dual heritage. On the one hand the influence of traditional games continued in many regional and national cultures, in Belgium and Switzerland, for example, where the advent of some new sports led to the disappearance of some traditional ones. On the other hand, in Scandinavia, Germany, and France those faithful to gymnastics carried out vehement attacks against those deemed to have given in to the seductions of the British model. This opposition assumed forms at once social (bourgeois sports versus popular gymnastics), ideological (sports valuing individual performance over gymnastics promoting collective and public display), and nationalist (English sports versus national gymnastics).

Despite these sizable divergences, the English model clearly prevailed throughout most European countries between 1900 and 1914, although its total dissemination and adoption remained extremely incomplete. The democratization of sports in Europe was easiest with respect to certain activities such as football, cycling, and boxing; by contrast, others sports such as tennis, golf, and cricket remained largely the domain of elites by 1914. Track and field events and swimming were varyingly democratized depending on the different national cultures they encountered, a process accompanied furthermore by the birth of a workers' sports movement developed in opposition to the dominant models of sports and gymnastics. Beginning in 1893 Germany workers' federations for gymnastics, cycling, swimming, and track and field were created, counting nearly 350,000 people in their ranks by 1914. Other countries followed suit, leading to the creation in 1913 of the International Socialist Physical Education Association joining together five European nations: Germany, Belgium, France, Great Britain, and Italy.

Before 1914, both sports and gymnastics evinced the same reticence to allow the participation of women, yet throughout the nineteenth century, in England at least, many women swam, played tennis, accompanied their husbands on biking excursions, and, for the more intrepid among them at the beginning of the twentieth century, began to form hockey and even football teams. On the Continent a few exclusively female gymnastic societies existed after 1880, inspired by the Swiss and German examples of the initiatives taken by Phokion Heinrich Clias and Adolf Spiess, respectively. For the most part, however, these institutions were as a rule created by and for men in the nineteenth century. In a context of governmental and church-dominated conservatism, they contributed to the reinforcement of an ideal of bourgeois masculinity. Therefore those women who did engage in physical activity exposed themselves to indifference at best, and, at worst, approbation and renunciation, above all considering the fact that the symbols these activities espoused (in cycling technical progress and the wearing of trousers, the violence of team sports, the sweat and strain of racing) were simply too manifestly "masculine." The ideals related to sporting achievement and gymnastic accomplishment were very far indeed from the feminine stereotypes that dominated Europe at the time, though relatively more rapid advances could be seen in England and, to a lesser extent, in northern Europe, Germany, and France.

International competitions in Europe considerably stimulated an accelerated and broader circulation of physical models, practices, techniques, and technologies after 1890. The first such competition began in 1871 as a rugby match between England and Scotland. Sporting competitions served to mobilize nationalist sentiments, and infused the spectacle of sports with new vigor, but also tension. Besides the year 1904 (St. Louis, Missouri), all the Olympic Games before World War I took place in Europe (Athens in 1896 and 1906, Paris in 1900, London in 1908, and Stockholm in 1912). It was also in these capitols that the first world championships were held as well. By 1914 sports had become irrevocably politicized. Players' and spectators' love of sports now competed with combative nationalism.

See also **Body; Cycling; Football (Soccer); Olympic Games; Popular and Elite Culture.**

BIBLIOGRAPHY

Arnaud, Pierre, and Jean Camy, eds. *La naissance du mouvement sportif associatif en France.* Lyon, France, 1986.

Birley, Derek. *Land of Sport and Glory: Sport and British Society, 1887–1910.* Manchester, U.K., 1995.

Defrance, Jacques. *L'excellence corporelle: La formation des activités physiques et sportives modernes, 1770–1914.* Paris, 1987.

Eisenberg, Christiane. *"English Sports" und deutsche Bürger: Eine Gesellschaftsgeschichte, 1800–1939.* Paderborn, Germany, 1999.

Guttmann, Allen. *Sports: The First Five Millennia.* Amherst, Mass., 2004.

Holt, Richard. *Sport and the British: A Modern History.* Oxford, U.K., 1989.

Jaccoud, Christophe, Laurent Tissot, and Yves Pedrazzini, eds. *Sports en Suisse: Traditions, transitions et transformations.* Lausanne, Switzerland, 2000.

Krüger, Arnd, and Angela Teja, eds. *La comune Eredità dello Sport in Europa.* Rome, 1997.

Krüger, Arnd, and Else Trangbaek, eds. *The History of Physical Education and Sport from European Perspectives.* Copenhagen, 1999.

Mason, Tony, ed. *Sport in Britain: A Social History.* Cambridge, U.K., 1989.

Meinander, Henrik, and J. A. Mangan, eds. *The Nordic World: Sport in Society.* London, 1998.

Riordan, James, and Arnd Krüger, eds. *Europe Cultures in Sport: Examining the Nations and Regions.* Bristol, U.K., 2003.

Ueberhorst, Horst. *Turner unterm Sternenbanner.* Munich, 1978.

THIERRY TERRET

STAËL, GERMAINE DE (1766–1817), French writer.

Madame de Staël was one of the best known female writers and intellectuals of the late eighteenth and early nineteenth centuries in France and across Europe. Born to Swiss Protestant parents in Paris on 22 April 1766 as Ann Louise Germaine Necker, she became a champion of the liberal revolutionary cause in France and later an ardent opponent of the Napoleonic regime. Her father was renowned French Finance Minister Jacques Necker, and through his service to the French monarchy and her mother Suzanne's salon in Paris, young Germaine Necker became intimately familiar from an early age with intellectual currents and political developments in France on the eve of the Revolution. In 1786, she was married to a Swedish diplomat living in Paris, Eric Staël von Holstein. Their relationship was not a particularly close one, and Germaine soon became involved in the types of amorous dalliances so characteristic of the contemporary European aristocracy.

At her own salon in Paris, Madame de Staël hosted many leading French thinkers and early revolutionaries, among them the abbé Sieyès, and her salon became a central hub of political discussion in the capital. During the Revolution, de Staël advocated a moderate liberal path for France, envisioning a constitutional monarchy adhering to the principle of equality under the law. Meanwhile, she attempted to advance the political career of her lover, Louis de Narbonne, who indeed became, albeit only briefly, the French Minister of War starting in December 1791.

Her moderate political position, her continued loyalty to the monarchy, and her status as a woman made Madame de Staël increasingly

Baroness Germaine de Stäel. Portrait by Jean-Baptiste Isabey, 1797. RÉUNION DES MUSÉES NATIONAUX/ART RESOURCE, NY

vulnerable as the Revolution embarked upon its more radical course in the 1790s, and she left Paris in September 1792. Spending much of the next four years at Coppet, her parents' estate near Geneva, Germaine continued to write and discuss political matters. She criticized the excesses of the Reign of Terror and its neglect of civil liberties and freedoms. During these same years, her liaison with Narbonne came to an end, and she became romantically involved with Benjamin Constant. Their stormy relationship endured for well more than a decade.

The most turbulent and dangerous years for de Staël, however, were those of Napoleon Bonaparte (r. 1804–1814/15). The early nineteenth century would see her greatest literary successes as well, namely the novels *Delphine* (1802) and most notably *Corinne, or Italy* (1807), both of which hinge upon independent-minded heroines who meet with misfortune and suffering. Although her writings were not always overtly critical of the French government, the Napoleonic regime found much to dislike in these and other works by Germaine de Staël, for her writings displayed the shortcomings of authoritarianism, exalted the cause of liberty, and pointed to the inequities of contemporary society in matters such as marriage and divorce. In 1803, Madame de Staël was ordered to leave Paris. She spent the next decade largely in exile, but this allowed an opportunity to travel to places such as Germany, Italy, and Russia, where she was often well received by courts and aristocrats for her literary fame and her outspoken opposition to Napoleon. Her observations about the places she visited were recorded in such works as *On Germany* (1813) and the posthumously published *Ten Years of Exile* (1820). These years also proved full of change and upheaval in de Staël's personal life. Her husband died in 1802, but she took much harder the news of her beloved father's death in 1804. Her relationship with Benjamin Constant finally came to an end largely due to de Staël's relationship with a young Swiss, John Rocca, with whom she became romantically involved in 1810 and secretly married in 1816. Less than three years after returning to Paris in 1814, Germaine de Staël suffered a stroke in February 1817, and died on Bastille Day, 14 July 1817.

Madame de Staël's ideas were to have a profound impact on literary and political developments in the nineteenth century. Her ambitious and wide-ranging writings in many ways helped to usher in Romanticism in France, the modern study of comparative literature, and even the age of nationalism—in particular, *Corinne* helped to enliven the Italian unification movement. Additionally, her numerous writings relating to the French Revolution and her vision of a society of civil liberties and freedoms provided one of the foundations for French liberalism.

See also **Constant, Benjamin; Feminism; France; Napoleon; Romanticism.**

BIBLIOGRAPHY

Primary Sources

Staël, Madame de. *An Extraordinary Woman: Selected Writings of Germaine de Staël.* Translated by Vivian Folkenflik. New York, 1987.

Secondary Sources

Balayé, Simone. *Madame de Staël: écrire, lutter, vivre.* Geneva, 1994.

Besser, Gretchen Rous. *Germaine de Staël Revisited.* New York, 1994.

ADAM C. STANLEY

STATISTICS. The invention of statistics involved the recognition of a distinct and widely applicable set of procedures based on mathematical probability for studying mass phenomena.

THEORETICAL DEBATES

Pierre-Simon Laplace (1749–1827) is generally considered one of the fathers of (inverse) probabilities, mainly applied to astrophysics. He exploited the previous works of Abraham de Moivre (1667–1754) and Jakob Bernoulli (1654–1705). The development of mathematical probability, although motivated by problems in insurance, the social sciences, and astronomy, was actually linked to the analysis of games of chance. But, instead of adopting the law of large numbers (according to which the larger the sample, the less the conclusion will be liable to error), Laplace further developed an intuition of Thomas Bayes (1701–1761), who replaced the ordinary assumption of equally likely causes with the principle of a priori probabilities, which holds that each of the different causes of an event may occur. A direct probability is the chance that a fair coin tossed ten times will yield six heads and four tails; the inverse probability is the probability that the coin is unfair once it is known that six heads and four tails appeared in ten tosses. This conclusion allowed Laplace to indicate, for example, the most likely causes (climate, biology, etc.) of the higher rate of male births in London than in Paris.

The application of probability to the social sciences centered around the work of the Belgian Adolphe Quetelet (1796–1874). As a follower of the large numbers law, he supported general censuses rather than sample studies, whose selection he considered arbitrary. He was reluctant to group together as homogenous data that which he believed were not. Social scientists were thus encouraged to gather as much data as possible. Quetelet's name is tightly bound to the notion of the average person, with the statistical average turned into an ideal social type, for example, the average height of the soldier, the average income, age, and so on of a criminal or a drunk. He used probabilities to estimate the propensity of the average person to commit a crime. Quetelet saw in the regularity of crime the proof that statistical-social laws are true when applied to the whole society, although they may be false for a single individual. This approach reflected the nineteenth-century positivistic ideal of a science able to manage society. The liberal notion of equality is also reflected in the average person: in principle no a priori distinctions are made between individuals, but their social attitudes, as "scientifically" proved, can prevent society from deviance. Deviations from the average (and normality, as Émile Durkheim added later [1895]) cancel themselves out when a large enough number of cases is considered. In this view, statistics confirmed the stability of bourgeois society (Quetelet was writing in the immediate aftermath of the 1848 revolution) while trying to identify regularities in the apparent chaos that accompanied the fall of the *ancien régime* and the onset of the Industrial Revolution.

The judgment of homogeneity, however, could be made either on external grounds or on internal evidence. One solution consisted in developing a test of homogeneity internal to data (accomplished, for example, by the German statistician Wilhelm Lexis (1837–1914); another solution was to develop a methodology that acted as a surrogate for experimental control in social sciences. The three main contributors to the latter approach were Francis Galton, Francis Ysidro Edgeworth, and Karl Pearson. Galton (1822–1911), a romantic English traveler with a medical background, is known principally for his *Hereditary Genius* (1869). Unlike Quetelet, Galton seemed more interested in the exceptional than in the average. In his approach, the homogeneity of data was the starting tool and not the aim, as in Quetelet; in fact, once a stable homogenous group had been identified, Galton raised the question of identifying deviation from the average. For example, he classified how well hundreds of people performed a particular talent as evaluated according to a pre-settled scale. On this ground he identified the probability that certain characteristics of peas could be reproduced according to hereditary laws, and he extended this conclusion to human beings.

Edgeworth (1845–1926) corrected Galton's approach using Laplace's analysis of inverse probability. Edgeworth divided a population into subgroups and tested their homogeneity. By doing so, he anticipated the modern t-test and variance analysis. Pearson (1857–1936) went beyond Edgeworth's conclusions by considering homogenous groups and corresponding curves to be mental constructs rather than real phenomena. Pearson's philosophy of science, as expressed in his *Grammar of Science* (1892), constituted the ground on which he developed his analysis of skew curves, which were outside the bounds of the "normal distribution" studied by his predecessors.

The social and political implications of this new generation's studies were important. Galton is generally considered the founder of eugenics, the evolutionary doctrine holding that the condition of human beings can be improved through a scientific process of breeding rather than through education. Galton concluded that the upper classes hold their rank based not on greater economic means but on superior biological characteristics. Pearson further developed this approach in what became a form of social Darwinism: on the ground of a "real scientific knowledge" the state had to promote efficient reproduction of individuals, beyond personal beliefs and market competition.

Beginning in the 1860s and particularly during the last quarter of the nineteenth century, however, increasing criticism of positivism led to attacks on social and statistical determinism. Individual free will was opposed to "social laws" and statistical averages; Lexis and Georg Friedrich Knapp (1842–1926) in Germany, their students, and most of the Russian statisticians criticized universal statistical laws. They identified national paths of economic and demographic growth, and, by the same token, they stressed the role of individual freedom in social dynamics. According to Knapp, because every individual is different from every other individual, the notion of variation should replace that of statistical error.

Tightly linked with national specificities, regional and monographic analysis enjoyed increasing success in the last quarter of the nineteenth century. These studies were mostly developed in Germany and Russia where federalism (in the former case) or local governments (the zemstvos, in the latter case) encouraged studies on local economic conditions.

From a theoretical point of view, however, these studies raised a serious problem: in the absence of regular homogenous censuses, academic statisticians were rather skeptical about inference from samples largely gathered by administrative (above all local) statistical offices. Classical histories of statistics have contended that the theory of sampling was roughly constructed by the Norwegian statistician Anders Kiaer (1838–1919) in the 1890s and fully developed by Jerzy Neyman (1894–1981) in 1934. But the practice and theory of sampling were first developed in Russia, where, starting in the 1870s, several statistical bureaus of local self-government organizations (the zemstvos) developed monographic studies on the local population. Most of these studies were "partial" in the sense that they covered only a part of the population. During the following years, the best method of selecting the sample was under discussion in the meetings of the Russian statisticians as well as in their main publications. The first solution considered was that of a completely random selection; unfortunately, this approach required the contemporary achievement of general censuses upon which the test of representativeness could be made. Starting in 1887 a majority of Russian statisticians supported a "reasoned" selection of the sampling based on the investigator's knowledge of the main characteristics of the local economy and society. In the following years and up through the outbreak of World War I, Alexander Chuprov (1874–1926), Pafnuty Chebyshev (1821–1894), and Andrei Markov (1856–1922) strongly contributed to the development of sampling and probability theory in general.

Nevertheless, not only in Russia, but throughout Europe, the use of statistics in local and monographic studies highlighted the difficulty of balancing the reliability of studies and the need to limit their costs. The trade-off between cost–benefit analysis and sampling significance expressed two different notions of the use of scientific knowledge in the public sphere.

STATISTICIANS AND BUREAUCRATS

Before the nineteenth century, state statistics were limited to state budgeting and demographic concerns. It was only with the increasing economic and social activity of administrations that calculus and statistics acquired major social, political, and organizational roles. The nineteenth century was a period of increasing enthusiasm for statistics as a tool for a scientific management of politics. The positivist ideal and the reformist attitude of most of the European governments contributed to this success. Statistics entered general newspapers, and statistical societies multiplied after the 1830s (an era of social reforms in several European countries) either as sections of broader associations (e.g., the Academy of Sciences in France, the British Association for the Advancement of Science) or as independent associations (e.g., the London or Birmingham Statistical Society, the American Statistical Association). These different outcomes were linked either to the scientific debate (statistics as an independent science or as a general method for other sciences) or had political origins. For example, in Russia, up to World War I, local statisticians were forbidden from gathering as a group and were obliged to find a place in the general meetings of naturalists' associations.

International conferences aimed to offer the image of an international "objective" and homogenous science, and as such, held out the promise of the "scientific." Statisticians complained about the "ignorance" of professional politicians and the differences in the organization of national statistics. In France the statistical apparatus was highly centralized, whereas in Britain, Germany, and Russia, local administrations on the one hand and academicians on the other hand played major roles in the organization of statistical enquiries. Statisticians soon claimed not a mere executive but also a decisional role. In most of the nineteenth-century societies, this problem was deepened by the fact that statisticians mostly came from a different social group than did top-rank bureaucrats and politicians. Statistical analysis thus became a forum for professional, social, and political debates. For example, French and British statisticians focused on health problems in the burgeoning cities, as well as the living and working conditions of workers, and called for social and political reforms. For their part, Russian statisticians stressed the need for agrarian reforms and recommended the redistribution of noble and state lands to the peasants. World War I pushed specialists' ambitions to their apogee, while the ensuing interwar period was marked by the success of administrative bureaucracies.

See also **Demography; Galton, Francis; Quetelet, Lambert Adolphe Jacques.**

BIBLIOGRAPHY

Beaud, Jean-Pierre, and Jean-Guy Prévost. "La forme est le fond: La structuration des appareils statistiques nationaux (1800–1945)." *Revue de synthèse* 118, no. 4 (1997): 419–456.

Blum, Alain, and Martine Mespoulet. *L'anarchie bureaucratique: Pouvoir et statistique sous Staline.* Paris, 2003.

Brian, Eric. *La mesure de l'Etat: Administrateurs et géomètres au XVIIIe siècle.* Paris, 1994.

Dale, Andrew I. *A History of Inverse Probability: From Thomas Bayes to Karl Pearson.* 2nd ed. New York, 1999.

Desrosières, Alain. *The Politics of Large Numbers: A History of Statistical Reasoning.* Translated by Camille Naish. Cambridge, Mass., 1998. Translation of *La politique des grands nombres: Histoire de la raison statistique.*

MacKenzie, Donald A. *Statistics in Britain, 1865–1930: The Social Construction of Scientific Knowledge.* Edinburgh, 1981.

Patriarca, Silvana. *Numbers and Nationhood: Writing Statistics in Nineteenth-Century Italy.* Cambridge, U.K., 1996.

Perrot, Jean-Claude. *Une histoire intellectuelle de l'économie politique.* Paris, 1992.

Porter, Theodore M. *The Rise of Statistical Thinking, 1820–1900.* Princeton, N.J., 1986.

Stanziani, Alessandro. *L'économie en révolution: Le cas russe, 1870–1930.* Paris, 1998.

Stigler, Stephen M. *The History of Statistics: The Measurement of Uncertainty before 1900.* Cambridge, Mass., 1986.

Tooze, J. Adam. *Statistics and the German State, 1900–1945: The Making of Modern Economic Knowledge.* Cambridge, U.K., 2001.

ALESSANDRO STANZIANI

STEIN, HEINRICH FRIEDRICH KARL VOM UND ZUM (1757–1831), Prussian politician and reformer.

In June 1807, on the eve of Prussia's capitulation to Napoleon in the disastrous Treaty of Tilsit,

Heinrich Friedrich Karl vom und zum Stein summarized his bold plan for political and social reform in Prussia:

> The nation, despite all of its flaws, possesses a noble pride, energy, valor, and willingness to sacrifice itself for fatherland and freedom....If the nation is to be ennobled, the oppressed part of it must be given freedom, independence, and property; and this oppressed part must be granted the protection of the laws. (Levinger, p. 55)

Although Stein served as Prussia's prime minister for just thirteen months, from October 1807 to November 1808, generations of German historians have lionized him as a champion of liberal nationalism. His two principal legislative accomplishments were the October Edict of 1807, which liberated Prussia's serfs, and the Municipal Ordinance of 1808, which established institutions for local self-government in Prussia's towns. Though these were important measures in their own right, Stein's post-humous renown in Germany has stemmed less from the long-term political significance of his reforms than from his symbolic appeal to Germans of a wide range of political affiliations. A staunch monarchist and impassioned German nationalist, Stein also campaigned vigorously for the establishment of parliamentary institutions in Prussia. An advocate for a reinvigorated aristocracy, Stein also sought to abolish the hereditary exclusivity of the nobility, and he championed the principle of equality before the law. Thus, Germans across the political spectrum—not just liberals and conservatives, but even communists and Nazis—have all found something to admire in Stein's legacy.

Stein is perhaps best characterized as an aristocratic liberal, like Montesquieu (Charles-Louis de Secondat; 1689–1755) or Alexis de Tocqueville (1805–1859) in France. His political views were shaped by his social origin in a family of imperial knights of the Holy Roman Empire, owning estates in the Rhineland, where constitutional traditions remained stronger than in absolutist Prussia. Stein attended the University of Göttingen and held a series of administrative positions in the Prussian province of Westphalia, in the Rhineland, from 1780 to 1804, beginning as an official in the Mining Commission and ultimately rising to the post of provincial governor. In 1804 Stein was named Prussia's minister of economic affairs, though King Frederick William III (r. 1797–1840) dismissed him for insubordination in January 1807—in part because of Stein's advocacy for a program of administrative reform that sought to rationalize sovereign authority by limiting the power of the king's cronies serving in the cabinet.

Prussia's catastrophic military defeat by France in 1806–1807 persuaded Frederick William to swallow his pride and recall Stein to service as Prussia's prime minister. Stein immediately persuaded the king to promulgate the October Edict, which declared that as of 1810, "there will be only free people" in Prussia. The October Edict not only abolished hereditary serfdom, but also eliminated certain traditional restrictions on the Prussian bourgeoisie and nobility. Commoners obtained the right to purchase estates owned by nobles; conversely, nobles received the right to practice bourgeois professions without penalty to their status. Unfortunately for Prussia's serfs, the decree neither abolished all of their compulsory labor obligations to their former masters nor granted them ownership of the lands they had farmed—so many peasants ended up living under worse material conditions after emancipation than before.

The Municipal Ordinance, promulgated at the end of Stein's ministry in November 1808, promoted local self-government in Prussia's towns by creating local assemblies and by extending voting rights to all property-owning adult males who practiced a "municipal trade." These elected assemblies became an important force in governing Prussia's towns, checking the power of local bureaucrats appointed by the state. Stein envisioned the town councils as the first step toward a comprehensive system of representative assemblies at the county, provincial, and national level. This more ambitious vision for parliamentary government in Prussia remained unfulfilled, however, in part because of the inherent difficulties in reconciling the principles of monarchical sovereignty and parliamentary representation, both of which Stein championed with equal fervor.

In November 1808, Napoleon forced Frederick William III to dismiss Stein after a French spy intercepted a letter linking Stein to a group advocating a rebellion against France. Stein lived in exile from then until the outbreak of Prussia's War of Liberation against Napoleon of 1813–1814, continuing to lobby for an alliance with Austria and Russia to overthrow the French conquerors. At the Congress of Vienna of 1814–1815, where Stein served on the Russian delegation, he campaigned unsuccessfully for a reinvigorated German empire under Austrian and Prussian leadership. In 1815 he retired to his estate at Cappenberg, Westphalia, working for much of the rest of his life on the publication of the *Monumenta Germaniae historica,* a massive collection of early German historical documents.

See also **Congress of Vienna; French Revolutionary Wars and Napoleonic Wars; Germany; Napoleonic Empire; Prussia; Restoration.**

BIBLIOGRAPHY

Levinger, Matthew. *Enlightened Nationalism: The Transformation of Prussian Political Culture, 1806–1848.* New York, 2000.

Meinecke, Friedrich. *The Age of German Liberation, 1795–1815.* Edited by Peter Paret. Translated by Peter Paret and Helmuth Fischer. Berkeley, Calif., 1977.

Ritter, Gerhard. *Freiherr vom Stein: Eine politische Biographie.* 2nd ed. Frankfurt, 1983.

MATTHEW LEVINGER

STENDHAL (MARIE-HENRI BEYLE)

(1783–1842), French novelist.

Stendhal was the pseudonym of Marie-Henri Beyle, a major author and minor bureaucrat, whose life spanned the turbulent period from the French Revolution to the July Monarchy, and whose writing helped mark the advent of both Romanticism and realism in French literature.

Born in 1783 in Grenoble, the young Beyle, an ardent republican, found himself at odds with his conservative bourgeois family from an early age. Arriving in Paris in 1799, on the eve of Napoleon's coup d'état of 18 Brumaire (9 November), he renounced his plans to study mathematics at the École Polytechnique in order to serve as a clerk at the Ministry of War, headed by his cousin Pierre Daru. Following Napoleon from his triumphant crossing of the Alps to his disastrous retreat from Moscow, he began to write in earnest when Waterloo left him unemployed. After a seven-year sojourn in Milan, he spent most of the 1820s in Paris, where he published his first novels. With a liberal government once again in power after the Revolution of 1830, he secured a post as consul to the small Italian city of Civitavecchia, which provided him with the leisure, and secure income, necessary for his writing. He died in 1842 in Paris from an attack of apoplexy.

Stendhal tried a number of genres and subjects before turning to the novel. A lifelong music lover, he wrote first about his favorite composers—*Vies de Haydn, de Mozart et de Métastase* (1815; *Lives of Haydn, Mozart, and Metastasio*), *Vie de Rossini* (1823; *Life of Rossini*)—borrowing heavily from Italian sources, as he did in his *Histoire de la peinture en Italie* (1817; *History of Painting in Italy*). Stendhal also tried his hand at political biography, authoring two histories of Napoleon—*Vie de Napoléon* (1817; *Life of Napoleon*) and *Mémoires sur Napoléon* (1837; *Memoirs of Napoleon*)—as well as at politically inflected travel writing—*Rome, Naples et Florence* (1817; *Rome, Naples, and Florence*) and *Promenades dans Rome* (1829; *Walks in Rome*). Throughout his early career, however, he longed to write plays and prepared for the task by falling in love with a series of actresses and going to the theater as much as possible. His *Racine et Shakespeare* (*Racine and Shakespeare*), published in two parts (1823 and 1825), called for a new kind of historical drama as a way to confront contemporary political divisions. His rejection of the strictures of French classicism in favor of a more realistic form of theatrical historical representation, modeled on the English master, served as a rallying cry for the young generation of French Romantics.

By the time Victor Hugo's historical drama *Hernani* (1830) consecrated many elements of his vision, however, Stendhal had shifted his ambitions from theater to the novel. Behind this shift lay a recognition that with the decline of aristocratic culture in the nineteenth century, the novel had replaced the comedy as the most potent tool for social critique. While his early novel *Armance* (1827) had focused on an aristocratic hero, *Le Rouge et le Noir* (1830; *The Red and the Black*), based on a true story, depicts the social ascent of a provincial miller's son, Julien

Sorel, through hypocrisy and seduction and his eventual demise on the scaffold just as he is about to secure an aristocratic title. Denounced by contemporaries as immoral, the novel would later be celebrated as a founding monument of literary realism because of its psychological penetration and analysis of the political and social faultlines of post-Revolutionary France. In his later masterpiece, *La Chartreuse de Parme* (1839; *The Charterhouse of Parma*), Stendhal projects his critique of French politics and society onto a fictionalized Italian court. Dictated in a mere fifty-two days, the novel depicts the fate of a hero, Fabrice del Dongo, bred on Romantic dreams who fails to master a more prosaic present. The modernity of Stendhal's fiction lies not only in the way it represents the psychological and social conflicts faced by modern subjects, but also in its excision of the kind of picturesque description favored by his contemporaries, Walter Scott and Honoré de Balzac.

Along with two unfinished novels—*Lamiel* and *Lucien Leuwen*—he left two unfinished autobiographies: *Vie de Henry Brulard* (*The Life of Henry Brulard*, published in 1890) and *Souvenirs d'égotisme* (*Memoirs of an Egoist*, published in 1892). Stendhal emerges from these latter texts as a figure at war with the conventions, hypocrisy, and stupidity of the world around him. Indeed, critics and admirers have distilled a "philosophy of revolt" (in the words of Michel Crouzet) from Stendhal's life and work, which they have labeled "Beylism." Stendhal knew that his unflinching honesty and spare style would fail to please his contemporaries. He continually looked forward to finding readers in 1880, 1935, or 2000, while dedicating his novels to the "Happy Few"—a select coterie of kindred souls that has never ceased to grow.

See also **Balzac, Honoré de; France; Hugo, Victor; Realism and Naturalism; Romanticism.**

BIBLIOGRAPHY

Barbéris, Pierre. *Sur Stendhal*. Paris, 1982

Brooks, Peter. *Reading for the Plot: Design and Intention in Narrative*. Cambridge, Mass., 1992.

Crouzet, Michel. *Nature et société chez Stendhal: la révolte romantique*. Lille, 1985.

Kelly, Dorothy. *Fictional Genders: Role and Representation in Nineteenth-Century French Narrative*. Lincoln, Neb., 1989.

Petrey, Sandy. *Realism and Revolution: Balzac, Stendhal, Zola and the Performances of History*. Ithaca, N.Y., 1988.

Samuels, Maurice. *The Spectacular Past: Popular History and the Novel in Nineteenth-Century France*. Ithaca, N.Y., 2004.

MAURICE SAMUELS

STEPHEN, LESLIE (1832–1904), English writer.

Known to many as the father of the novelist Virginia Woolf (1882–1941), Leslie Stephen was one of the two or three most eminent Victorian men of letters. A noted Alpinist, a writer, a literary critic, a historian of ideas, an eloquent apologist for agnosticism, and a biographer, he was also an editor, both of the *Cornhill Magazine* and of the monumental *Dictionary of National Biography*. Born of Evangelical parents, he was educated at Eton and Trinity Hall, Cambridge, where he remained as Tutor from 1854 to 1862, when, having lost his faith, he resigned his tutorship and two years later left Cambridge for London to launch his career as a writer. In his Cambridge years he established himself as a noted rowing coach, as a conqueror of such formidable Alpine peaks as the Schreckhorn, and, in 1863, having crossed the Atlantic to visit the battlefields of the U.S. Civil War.

Radical in politics and freethinking in religious matters, he was an outspoken member of like-minded young men who denounced the established Church of England and the Tory Party as obstacles to progress and campaigned for national education, parliamentary reform, and the disestablishment of the church. Married to Harriet (Minny) Thackeray in 1867, he earned his living by writing for the *Saturday Review*, the *Pall Mall Gazette*, and contributing literary articles to the *Cornhill Magazine* of which he became editor in 1871. In that same year he published a collection of his much admired Alpine essays, *The Playground of Europe*. As editor of the *Cornhill* he not only published such writers as Thomas Hardy, Henry James, R. L. Stevenson, and Matthew Arnold, but also contributed his own distinguished literary essays, ultimately published as *Hours in a Library* (1874–1879; 1892).

Meanwhile, for the *Fortnightly Review* and *Frasier's Magazine,* he was firing off deliberately infidel essays that appeared as *Essays in Freethinking and Plainspeaking* (1873), the final essay of which is a manifesto calling for liberation from religious dogma and proclaiming the exhilaration of free thought. More such essays appeared during the 1870s, some made poignantly eloquent by his grief at the sudden death of Minny in 1875. These essays eventually appeared in his unapologetic *Agnostic's Apology* (1893). His most significant work in this decade, however, was *History of English Thought in the Eighteenth Century* (1876), his masterpiece in intellectual history, notable for his pioneer assertion (in England) that the history of ideas could not be written without showing how the social context shaped and determined ideas, not vice versa. Ideas took hold or were let go when they fit or did not fit the needs of human beings, a theory, Darwinian in imagery, that could be called historical naturalism, as distinct from historical materialism, which it resembles. More exemplary of his theory is his long delayed sequel, *The English Utilitarians* (1900), and, especially luminous, his smaller masterpiece *English Literature and Society in the Eighteenth Century* (1904), a seedbed from which have sprouted a large number of specialized studies.

How can morality survive without theology? To show the independence of morality on theology, Stephen wrote *The Science of Ethics* (1882). Most philosophers have found it wanting as ethics, but in the late twentieth century it had a better press as Peter Allan Dale and others recognized that Stephen anticipates the work of Émile Durkheim and Max Weber in displaying the social roots of moral codes. Likewise, the human being can be truly seen only within the social context. This is his way of writing such biographies as *Life of Henry Fawcett* (1884) and *The Life of James Fitzjames Stephen* (1895), less so perhaps in his English Men of Letters lives of Johnson (1878), Pope (1880), Swift (1882), and George Eliot (1902). However, as the creator and editor of the *Dictionary of National Biography* from 1882 to 1891, he held both his writers and himself to an unmatched standard of concise and purposeful

articulation of fact and produced an invaluable resource, not supplanted for a century, and for which he was knighted in 1903.

After retirement he spent his final years writing the essays (some of his best in fact) contained in his *Studies of a Biographer* (1898–1902) and the lectures collected in *Social Rights and Duties* (1896), as well as major works mentioned above. Then came a sort of autobiography, a poignant and revealing document, written to assuage his grief at the death of his second wife, Julia, in 1895, read by his descendants and biographers, but not published until 1977 as *The Mausoleum Book.* Leslie Stephen died of cancer on 22 February 1904.

See also **Intellectuals.**

BIBLIOGRAPHY

Primary Sources

Stephen, Leslie. *Essays on Freethinking and Plainspeaking.* London, 1873, 1907.

———. *History of English Thought in the Eighteenth Century.* 2 vols. London, 1876, 1902.

———. *The Science of Ethics.* London, 1882.

———. *The English Utilitarians.* 3 vols. London, 1900.

———. *English Literature and Society in the Eighteenth Century.* London, 1904.

———. *Selected Letters of Leslie Stephen.* 2 vols. Edited by John W. Bicknell. London, 1996.

Secondary Sources

Annan, Noel. *Leslie Stephen: The Godless Victorian.* New York, 1984. Sets Stephen within the central issues and among the major voices of his era.

Bicknell, John W. "Leslie Stephen's *English Thought in the Eighteenth Century:* A Tract for the Times." *Victorian Studies* 6 (1962): 103–120.

Fenwick, Gillian. *Leslie Stephen's Life in Letters: A Bibliographical Study.* Aldershot, U.K., 1993. Invaluable for any serious study of Stephen.

Maitland, Frederic L. *The Life and Letters of Leslie Stephen.* London, 1906. The earliest and most intimate portrait.

JOHN W. BICKNELL

STEVENSON, ROBERT LOUIS

(1850–1894), Scottish novelist, poet, essayist, travel writer.

Robert Louis Balfour Stevenson was born in Edinburgh into a well-known family of lighthouse engineers. However, he did not follow the family tradition and, at the age of twenty-one, he began to write travel tales and essays. He quickly established himself as a writer of promise.

Troubled by ill health from early childhood, Stevenson sought a climate that would be conducive to the treatment of his respiratory ailment. He traveled in France and in 1876 he met the American Fanny Osbourne, a married woman with two children. She made a strong impression on Stevenson and, despite his poor health, he followed her to the United States when she returned there. His account of that life-threatening journey appeared as *The Amateur Emigrant* (1879) and *Across the Plains* (1892). Following Fanny's divorce, she and Stevenson married in San Francisco in May 1880. The couple spent some time after the marriage in the abandoned mining camp of Silverado. This period is detailed in *The Silverado Squatters* (1884). The Stevensons arrived in England in August 1880 and Stevenson's father bought Fanny a house in Bournemouth as a wedding present. Persistent health problems necessitated the couple spending the successive winters of 1881 and 1882 in the Swiss Alps at Davos.

Stevenson embarked on a spell of prolific output. "Thrawn Janet," "The Merry Men," the essays published in *Familiar Studies of Men and Books* (1881), *Virginibus Puerisque* (1881), and the tales collected in *New Arabian Nights* (1882) ensured his growing status as a writer. *Treasure Island* was serialized in *Young Folks* during 1881–1882 but it did not bring Stevenson immediate popular acclaim. That came in 1886 with *Kidnapped* and *Strange Case of Dr Jekyll and Mr Hyde*. These works established Stevenson's reputation alongside Rudyard Kipling and H. Rider Haggard as a writer of adventure fiction.

Strange Case of Dr Jekyll and Mr Hyde concerns the strange fate of the well-respected Dr. Henry Jekyll, a man of scientific curiosity who releases his terrible alter ego, Edward Hyde, by a chemical process. Hyde, a troglodytic figure, is the polar opposite of the genteel and refined Jekyll. Hyde commits two violent crimes against innocent citizens, a young girl and an elderly man.

Dr. Jekyll's transformation releases him from the obligations of profession and social class but it also compromises his close relationship with his exclusively male companions. In order to resist the temptation to become Hyde, Henry Jekyll commits suicide in his laboratory.

The novella was well received by its late-Victorian audience and was considered to be a moral tale. Publication of the novella coincided with a growing interest in the sciences and with the pioneering work of Jean-Martin Charcot and Sigmund Freud in their exploration of human personality and identity. It also chronicled the late-nineteenth-century obsession with regression and atavism (the recurrence in an organism of a trait typical of an ancestral form) that was linked to Charles Darwin's conclusions in *Origin of Species* (1859). The text has continued to generate critical comment and is frequently compared to Oscar Wilde's *The Picture of Dorian Gray* (1891) and to Bram Stoker's *Dracula* (1897). "Jekyll and Hyde" has entered into common usage to describe an individual of split personality.

Following the death of his father in 1887, Stevenson, his mother, Fanny, and his stepson Lloyd Osbourne set off for the United States. They stayed at Saranac Lake in the Adirondack Mountains. Stevenson conceived the outline of *The Master of Ballantrae*, subtitled "A Winter's Tale," while at Saranac. The novel conveys the bleak wilderness of the physical landscape in a metaphorical wasteland. There are striking resemblances to James Hogg's *The Private Memoirs and Confessions of a Justified Sinner* (1824), which also deals with the politico-religious division of Scotland in the aftermath of the Jacobite Uprising of 1745. *The Master of Ballantrae* was completed in Samoa and published in 1889.

Stevenson's American publishers, Scribner's, commissioned a book on the South Seas and the family sailed from San Francisco and visited the islands of the Marquesas, the Paumotus, Tahiti, and finally Hawaii. They sailed on a further voyage to the Gilbert Islands and on to Samoa, where Stevenson settled on the island of Upolu in 1889. He built the house at Vailima where he resided and wrote until his death.

Stevenson soon became embroiled in the local politics of Samoa, and his writing developed an aggressive rejection of the values of the Victorian imperial project. "The Beach of Falesá" (1892) and *The Ebb Tide* (1893) together constitute a critique of imperialism that stands comparison with Joseph Conrad's *Heart of Darkness* (1899). In this regard Stevenson offers his readers an alternative to the views of empire expressed by both Kipling and John Buchan.

Catriona, or *David Balfour*, as the novel was marketed in the United States, is the sequel to *Kidnapped* and was published in 1893. The novel explores the same theme of duality that fascinated Stevenson throughout his life and intertwines the often antagonistic cultural traditions of the Scottish Highlands and Lowlands.

Stevenson was working on *Weir of Hermiston* when he suffered a cerebral hemorrhage and died at Vailima on 3 December 1894. This unfinished novel examines the issues of ancestry and heredity, seduction, murder, and injustice and bears close similarity to Thomas Hardy's *Tess of the D'Urbervilles* (1891).

Since the 1980s, Stevenson has been reevaluated as a late-nineteenth-century writer. He is one of a very few writers to have succeeded in all of his chosen genres. In addition, he contributed essays that establish him as an intellectual, a deep-thinking theoretician on writing and on art in the broader sense.

See also **Conrad, Joseph; Great Britain; Imperialism; Wilde, Oscar.**

BIBLIOGRAPHY

Booth, Bradford A., and E. Mehew. *The Letters of Robert Louis Stevenson*. 8 vols. New Haven, Conn., and London, 1994–1995.

Brantlinger, Patrick. *Rule of Darkness: British Literature and Imperialism, 1830–1914*. Ithaca, N.Y., 1988.

McLynn, Frank. *Robert Louis Stevenson: A Biography*. London, 1993.

Menikoff, Barry. *Robert Louis Stevenson and "The Beach of Falesá": A Study in Victorian Publishing*. Edinburgh, 1984.

ERIC MASSIE

STOLYPIN, PETER (1862–1911), Russian politician.

Peter Arkadyevich Stolypin was born in 1862 into a noble family that held high state positions, owned numerous estates, and was related to the writer Mikhail Lermontov. Stolypin married Olga Borisovna Neidgart, whose family also had entrée at court, before graduating from the department of natural sciences, St. Petersburg University, where his thesis focused on tobacco growing in the Caucasus. Stolypin served as *uezd* (county) and then *guberniya* (provincial) marshal of nobility in Kovno and from 1902 to 1903 as governor of Grodno, giving him more familiarity with agriculture, peasants, and Jewish, Polish, and Lithuanian citizens of the Russian Empire. From 1903 to 1906 Stolypin served as governor of the Volga province of Saratov, hard hit by revolutionary upheavals. His stern approach to revolutionaries helped promote him in May 1906 to minister of internal affairs, a post that dealt with peasants, national minorities, governors, medical personnel, and medicines. In July 1906 Tsar Nicholas II additionally appointed Stolypin chairman of the Council of Ministers, a quasi–prime ministerial position, because other ministers sometimes acted independently.

Practical rather then theoretical, Stolypin grappled with five challenges during his five-and-a-half-year administration: crushing terrorism, implementing reforms, working with the new national legislature, managing restive national minorities, and pleasing the tsar.

In 1906 and 1907 terrorists killed over four thousand people, mainly police and officials, and injured two of Stolypin's six children in a bomb attack on his dacha. Stolypin repressed about seventeen hundred suspected revolutionaries through courts martial in 1906 and 1907 and thereafter exiled several hundred per year to Siberia without court trial. He also countered liberal Constitutional Democrats, who consorted with radicals and promoted a radical political and socioeconomic agenda. Nevertheless, he offered cabinet posts to moderate opposition leaders, allowed pharmacist-revolutionaries to be elected to the board of the million-ruble Pharmacists' Pension Fund to control the fund, and supported socialized pharmacy in areas where private pharmacies were lacking.

Simultaneously Stolypin attempted to implement some fifty reforms. Key changes targeted the peasantry who constituted over 80 percent of the population. Fundamental were Stolypin's land reforms. Partially drafted by Sergei Witte, Stolypin had independently become convinced of their necessity. The main reform sought to replace the semisocialistic form of agriculture, practiced by three-fourths of peasants, in which the village commune parceled the arable land to constituent families in separated strips that were sometimes reapportioned, with capitalistic farmsteads. Peasant families were to receive ownership of the strips, which were then to be consolidated into farmsteads to make agriculture more efficient, to channel marginal farmers into industry, and to stop peasant assaults on estate owners. Parliament passed the reforms in 1910 and 1911. A controversial and difficult plan, by World War I, 50 percent of strips were held in hereditary tenure but only 10 percent were consolidated. Other agricultural reforms included enticing peasants to farm in Siberia, providing agronomic assistance, and mainstreaming peasants more fully. Despite partial realization of the land reforms, 20 percent of peasants were estimated to be prosperous. The Peasant Land Bank and private banks facilitated peasant purchase of estates so that by 1916 peasants owned approximately 80 percent of farmland, some extracommunal.

Other reforms enlarged rights for religious dissidents, the Old Believers, and for Jews and provided insurance for factory workers. Stolypin aimed to make local administration more efficient and strengthen the central government's control over local administration by instituting vice-governors on the county level. He attempted to expand self-government, which existed for taxpayers in cities and for property owners, including peasants, on the provincial and county level of thirty-four provinces, by lowering voting requirements and instituting zemstvos on the *volost* (township) level. He advocated local self-government in the nine western border provinces, but with provisions to protect Russian and other peasants from Polish landowners. Fellow ministers defeated the project on county governors. Parliamentary debate delayed the project on *volost* zemstvos. A parliamentary crisis arose over the Polish provisions in the western zemstvo bill in the spring of 1911, torpedoing Stolypin's career.

The new parliament consisted of a lower house, the Duma, elected by workers, peasants, industrialists, nobles, and national minorities, and an upper State Council, half appointed and half elected by corporate groups. Deeming the first two Dumas dominated by radicals and not committed to constructive work, Stolypin supported their dissolution. He began implementing reforms through Article 87 of the Fundamental Laws, which permitted the government to inaugurate measures while the Duma was not in session if they were later submitted to the parliament. On 16 June (3 June, old style) 1907 Stolypin summarily issued a new electoral law, not sanctioned by the Fundamental Laws, in order to produce a Duma dominated by moderates. Though it generated outrage, the strategy worked. The Third Duma (1907–1912) passed constructive legislation, such as the bills on universal primary education, the land reform, and factory workers' insurance. It also attempted to gain greater control over the budget and interpellated (formally questioned) ministers on their policies. Moderate opposition Octobrists, who dominated the Duma, fell out with Stolypin in 1909 and 1911, prompting him to draw closer to the Nationalist Party. Though not fully democratic or representational, archival evidence documents that workers and peasants as well as elites participated in the Duma, and it and the State Council began to evolve into more equal partners of the government.

Stolypin considered Finns, Poles, Ukrainians, Georgians, and Armenians citizens of the empire and opposed their centrifugal tendencies. His efforts to contain Finnish struggles for greater autonomy, partly based on his interpretation of pronouncements and laws, and partly affected by Tsar Nicholas's dislike of the Finns, particularly alienated this minority.

On 14 September (1 September, old style) 1911, at the opera in Kiev, a former revolutionary, Dmitri Bogrov, shot Stolypin, who died four days later. Though Bogrov apparently acted alone, police negligence spawned conspiracy theories about complicity in high government echelons. Mysteries about the assassination have not been fully resolved.

See also **Nicholas II; Revolution of 1905 (Russia); Russia; Witte, Sergei.**

BIBLIOGRAPHY

Ascher, Abraham. *P. A. Stolypin: The Search for Stability in Late Imperial Russia.* Stanford, Calif., 2001.

Conroy, Mary Schaeffer. *Peter Arkad'evich Stolypin: Practical Politics in Late Tsarist Russia.* Boulder, Colo., 1976.

———. *In Health and in Sickness: Pharmacy, Pharmacists, and the Pharmaceutical Industry in Late Imperial, Early Soviet Russia.* Boulder, Colo., 1994. Discusses the relationship between the Ministry of Internal Affairs and Stolypin, on the one hand, and pharmacy and the pharmaceutical industry, on the other.

Conroy, Mary Schaeffer, ed. *Emerging Democracy in Late Imperial Russia.* Niwot, Colo., 1998.

Edelman, Robert. *Gentry Politics on the Eve of the Russian Revolution: The Nationalist Party, 1907–1917.* New Brunswick, N.J., 1980.

Fedorov, B. G. *Petr Arkad'evich Stolypin.* Moscow, 2002. Among numerous works in Russian, this includes extensive material on the Stolypin family.

Korros, Alexandra. *A Reluctant Parliament: Stolypin, Nationalism, and the Politics of the Russian Imperial State Council, 1906–1911.* Lanham, Md., 2002.

Szeftel, Marc. *The Russian Constitution of April 23, 1906: Political Institutions of the Duma Monarchy.* Brussels, 1976.

Waldron, Peter. *Between Two Revolutions: Stolypin and the Politics of Renewal in Russia.* DeKalb, Ill., 1998.

MARY SCHAEFFER CONROY

STRACHEY, LYTTON (1880–1932), English writer, member of the Bloomsbury Group.

Giles Lytton Strachey was the eleventh of thirteen children born to Sir Richard Strachey, engineer and Indian colonial servant, and Jane Grant, essayist and suffragist. Lytton Strachey was named after his godfather, the first earl of Lytton, viceroy of India. The large discrepancy in his parents' ages (thirty years) resulted in Lytton being much closer to his mother than his father. Lady Strachey also inspired Lytton's early interest in literature. Diagnosed a neurasthenic as a teen, Strachey suffered from poor health his entire life, yet managed to have a prolific career as a writer. He was schooled at Leamington College, Liverpool University College, and Trinity College, Cambridge. Strachey's intelligence, lanky frame, and high-pitched voice attracted the attention of his peers at Cambridge who elected him to the secret society of Apostles in 1902, joining classmates John Maynard Keynes and Leonard Woolf. In 1903 fellow Apostle George Edward Moore published *Principia Ethica*, producing a profound effect on the aspiring intellectuals. *Principia* identified love and friendship as "the highest of human goods" and became a rationalizing factor in loosening the repression of homosexual tendencies among the Apostles. A teenager at the time of Oscar Wilde's trials for homosexuality, the young Strachey had struggled with what he called his "unnatural" desires, but at Cambridge he experienced a liberating moment in his sexual development. Surrounded by those he regarded as fellow "Greek souls," Strachey became a vocal advocate of the physical and spiritual superiority of all-male love.

In 1905 Strachey completed his work at Cambridge with a thesis on the English colonial administrator Warren Hastings (1732–1818) but failed to receive a Trinity fellowship. He returned to his parents' home in Lancaster Gate and supported himself as a journalist—contributing book and drama reviews to *The Spectator* magazine, the *Nation*, and the *Athenaeum*—and published two collections of verse and an important work of literary criticism, *Landmarks in French Literature* (1912). He also spent his Thursday evenings in the decade before World War I at the Gordon Square home of Virginia and Vanessa Stephen. They joined such other members of what became known as the Bloomsbury Group as Keynes, Clive Bell, Roger Fry, and Leonard Woolf for drinks and conversations about philosophy, art, religion, and politics. Strachey first broached the taboo subject of sex by pointing at a stain on Vanessa's dress and asking, "Semen?" Years later, Virginia Woolf reminisced that Strachey, as the leader of the "Bloomsberries," tore down the barriers of sexual reticence that had plagued their parents' generation. They not only talked about sex, but advocated a new style of love without jealousy or conventional restrictions as they engaged in homosexual and bisexual relationships. The group expanded in number, and by the 1920s the fame of its individual members as writers, artists, and intellectuals sealed its reputation as a cultural circle.

During World War I, Strachey was a conscientious objector, but his impact on the larger public would be felt most strongly in 1918 with the publication of his best-selling work, *Eminent Victorians*. Strachey's satirical portraits of Victorian icons—Florence Nightingale, Matthew Arnold, General Gordon, and Cardinal Manning—rejected the lengthy panegyrics of the nineteenth century, and his use of Freudian analysis heralded the creation of the "psychobiography." His following works included *Queen Victoria* (1921), which was awarded the James Tait Black Memorial Prize, *Elizabeth and Essex* (1928), and *Portraits in Miniature* (1931).

On the surface, Strachey appeared defiant of convention, but in his diary he wrote repeatedly of his loneliness and unhappiness with his looks. Although unsuccessful in forming lasting attachments with other men (his lovers included his cousin, the artist Duncan Grant, and Colette's translator, Roger Senhouse), he did inspire lifelong devotion from one person. In 1915 Strachey met the young art student Dora Carrington and, despite her subsequent marriage to Ralph Partridge and Strachey's love affairs, the couple shared a home for the next seventeen years. After his death in 1932 from cancer, Carrington committed suicide, noting in her diary that she was unable to live without Strachey.

Although heralded in 1918 as a revolutionary biographer, Strachey temporarily faded into obscurity in the years following his death, and his work, along with that of the other "Bloomsberries," was attacked by Cambridge critics I. A. Richards (1893–1979) and F. R. Leavis (1895–1978) as elitist and apolitical. *Bloomsbury* itself became a widely used term connoting an insular, snobbish aestheticism. Strachey also endured intense criticism while still alive from contemporaries like Rupert Brooke and D. H. Lawrence, who regarded his homosexuality as a corrupting influence among the younger generations at Cambridge. His sexuality, more than his writings, has continued to be a topic of scholarly debate. Feminist scholars rediscovered Bloomsbury in the 1960s and especially applauded Strachey and Virginia Woolf as advocates of androgyny and sexual freedom. Some scholars, however, have questioned Strachey's feminist sympathies and have portrayed his relationship with Dora Carrington as that of patriarch and household drudge. Michael Holroyd's two-volume biography of Strachey in 1968 (revised in 1995) offers a complex picture of a literary and sexual rebel still struggling with Victorian mores and legal codes as well as his own insecurities. Since the 1990s Queer theorists have championed Strachey—with his effeminate style of dress, high voice, and penchant for Wildean satire—as a camp artist. Although Strachey once joked that politics were as exciting as a game of bridge, he supported his mother's and sisters' efforts for women's suffrage, protested World War I, and opposed censorship. He did prefer, however, what he called the "subtle attack" to undermine Victorian strictures on religious, artistic, social, and sexual matters. The term *Stracheyesque* continues to evoke a particular style of writing and behavior that is transgressive, ironic, and always amusing.

See also **Homosexuality and Lesbianism; Wilde, Oscar.**

BIBLIOGRAPHY

Holroyd, Michael. *Lytton Strachey: A Critical Biography.* 2 vols. London, 1967–1968. Rev. ed., 1 vol., 1995.

Holroyd, Michael, ed. *Lytton Strachey by Himself: A Self-Portrait.* London, 1971.

Rosenbaum, S. P., ed. *The Bloomsbury Group: A Collection of Memoirs, Commentary, and Criticism.* Toronto, 1975.

Taddeo, Julie Anne. *Lytton Strachey and the Search for Modern Sexual Identity: The Last Eminent Victorian.* New York, 2002.

JULIE ANNE TADDEO

STRAUSS, JOHANN (1825–1899), Austrian composer.

Johann Baptist Strauss was a composer, conductor, and violinist of Hungarian origins, the eldest son of Johann Strauss (1804–1849; hereafter referred to as Strauss Father), and the brother of Josef (1827–1870) and Eduard (1835–1916). Johann Strauss was known variously as Strauss Son, Johann II, and Johann the younger. Actively discouraged from becoming a professional musician by his father, who intended him for a secure, middle-class career in banking, the younger Strauss was encouraged in his covert musical studies by his mother, Anna (1801–1870), largely because of her husband's infidelity with Emilie Trampusch, which severely restricted the flow of income to his legitimate family. After Strauss Father failed in his attempt to secure an official injunction on public appearances by his son, Johann II made his public début as a composer and conductor, together with twenty-four musicians, at a *soirée dansante* on 15 October 1844 in Dommayer's Casino in the suburb of Hietzing. Yet, despite the unanimous plaudits from the press for the eighteen-year-old and his music—the newspaper *Der Wanderer*, for example, predicted that "Strauss's name will be worthily continued in his son"—it was only with Strauss Father's untimely death from scarlet fever in 1849 that he could advance his own musical standing in his native Vienna.

During the 1848 Revolution in Vienna Strauss Father overtly supported the established monarchy, while Strauss Son sided with the capital's revolutionary elements in opposing the unyielding autocracy of the Austrian chancellor Clemens von Metternich. The younger Strauss's actions rendered him persona non grata in court circles and, although he subsequently strove to remedy his faux pas by composing works in honor of the new emperor, Francis Joseph I (1830–1916), it was not until 1863 that he was finally granted the prestigious honorary title of "k. k. Hofballmusik-Direktor" (Director of Music for the Imperial-Royal Court Balls) in succession to his father.

The constant physical and mental demands on Strauss resulted in his suffering a severe nervous breakdown in 1853, a desperate situation that ushered his brother Josef into the family music "business" as interim conductor and composer. Josef subsequently abandoned his career as an architect and draftsman and, together with Johann, held sway over Vienna's dance-music scene from the late 1850s until his death in 1870, each brother competitively inspiring the other to new heights of musical creativity. From the early 1860s their brother Eduard also appeared at the head of the Strauss Orchestra as a successful conductor and composer of dances and marches; indeed, after Johann devoted his attentions to operetta composition in 1870, sole direction of the orchestra transferred to Eduard until he disbanded it in New York in 1901.

Johann Strauss combined an unfaltering rich melodic invention with a masterly skill at orchestration, fully exploiting these gifts through his abilities as an astute businessman and showman. As early as 1855 the Viennese *Morgen-Blatt* accurately called him "a true beachcomber of world history," and during his life he rarely failed to commemorate in music any significant social, cultural, technological, or political event in Vienna or elsewhere. Like his father, he recognized that an international reputation could only be secured by traveling with his music: besides numerous concert tours throughout Europe, he performed in the United States at Boston and New York (1872), while his eleven seasons before Russian audiences at Pavlovsk (1856–1865 and 1869) laid the foundations of his considerable fortune. His easy gift for melody, enhanced through brilliant instrumentation, is apparent in his more than 580 waltzes, polkas, quadrilles, marches, solo songs, and works for male chorus, throughout which he maintained a supremely high standard of creativity that won him universal praise from audiences, music critics, and fellow composers including Giuseppe Verdi, Richard Wagner, Johannes Brahms, and Richard Strauss. His continuing worldwide reputation results in large part from the extraordinary popularity of a cluster of "evergreens," including the waltzes *An der schönen, blauen Donau* (*By the Beautiful, Blue Danube*) op. 314 (1867), *Geschichten aus dem Wienerwald* (*Tales from the Vienna Woods*) op. 325 (1868), *Wein, Weib und Gesang!* (*Wine, Woman and Song!*) op. 333 (1869), *Rosen aus dem Süden* (*Roses from the South*) op. 388 (1880), *Frühlingsstimmen* (*Voices of Spring*) op. 410 (1883) and *Kaiser-Walzer* (*Emperor Waltz*) op. 437 (1889) and the polkas *Annen-Polka* op. 117 (1852), *Tritsch-Tratsch* (*Chit-Chat*) op. 214 (1858), *Unter Donner und Blitz* (*Thunder and Lightning*) op. 324 (1868) and *Pizzicato* (1869, composed jointly with Josef). The landmark recording by Marco Polo in the 1980s and 1990s of Johann's entire orchestral output on fifty-two CDs, however, has facilitated the rediscovery and reassessment of a great many unjustly neglected musical treasures by the thrice-married "Waltz King."

The success of Jacques Offenbach's stage works in Vienna during the 1850s and 1860s, and their author's exorbitant financial demands, prompted the city's theater directors to approach Strauss to mount a home-grown riposte. He was eventually persuaded to experiment with composing operetta by his first wife, the theatrically experienced mezzo-soprano Jetty Treffz (1818–1878). The first of his stage works to reach production was *Indigo und die vierzig Räuber* (1871; *Indigo and the Forty Thieves*, 1871), a composition the *Fremden-Blatt* considered "promises the most splendid expectations for the future." A further fourteen operettas, a grand opera *Ritter Pásmán* (1892; *Knight Pásmán*) and an incomplete full-length ballet score, *Aschenbrödel* (1901; *Cinderella*), followed in its wake, with Strauss scoring his greatest box-office successes with *Die Fledermaus* (1874; *The Bat*), *Eine Nacht in Venedig* (1883; *A Night in Venice*) and *Der Zigeunerbaron* (1885; *The Gypsy Baron*). Although history has adjudged Strauss the leading exponent of "Silver Age" Viennese operetta, he was generally a poor judge of librettos and felt encumbered and restricted by the process of composing to prescribed texts.

Together with his brother Josef, Strauss developed the classical Viennese waltz to the point where it became as much a feature of the concert hall as the dance floor. In an 1894 speech Strauss freely acknowledged the debt he owed to his father and to the latter's friend and rival, Joseph Lanner (1801–1843), for formalizing, developing, and expanding the structure of the Viennese waltz from its origins in the unsophisticated rural dances of Austria and Germany. His characteristic modesty nevertheless concealed the fact that, as early as 1854, he had himself been hailed as a reformer of the stereotypical waltz form, shaping it into characteristic tone-pictures. Johann Strauss the Younger's musical legacy continues to captivate the world, charming new audiences and ensuring that he remains the most celebrated and enduringly successful of nineteenth-century light-music composers.

See also **Music; Offenbach, Jacques; Romanticism; Vienna.**

BIBLIOGRAPHY

Kemp, Peter. *J. Strauss Jr.: Complete Orchestral Works; Works for Male Chorus and Orchestra.* Marco Polo 8.223201–8.223279 (1988–1996). Historical sociopolitical program texts accompanying a fifty-two CD series.

———. *The Strauss Family: Portrait of a Musical Dynasty.* Tunbridge Wells, U.K., 1985. Revised as *The Strauss Family.* London, 1989.

Mailer, Franz. *Josef Strauss: Genius against His Will.* Translated by Philip G. Povey. Oxford, U.K., 1985. Translation of *Joseph Strauss: Genie wider Willen.* Vienna and Munich, 1977.

———. *Johann Strauss (Sohn): Leben und Werk in Briefen und Dokumenten.* 10 vols. Tutzing, 1983–2005.

Schneidereit, Otto. *Johann Strauss und die Stadt an der schönen blauen Donau.* Berlin, 1972.

Traubner, Richard. "Vienna Gold." In *Operetta: A Theatrical History,* pp. 103–131. New York, 1983. Reprint, 2003.

Wechsberg, Joseph. *The Waltz Emperors.* London, 1973.

PETER KEMP

STRAVINSKY, IGOR (1882–1971), Russian composer.

The highly influential composer Igor Fyodorovich Stravinsky (1882–1971) was born in Oranienbaum (now Lomonosov) Russia, near St. Petersburg. He was raised in the latter city (then the capital of Russia), where his father, Fyodor, was a prominent operatic bass-baritone. Thus Igor grew up in an environment steeped in music and the theater. In 1902, while studying law, he approached composer Nikolai Rimsky-Korsakov (1844–1908) and at some point afterward studied privately with him. In the ensuing decades, Stravinsky—who adopted citizenship in France (1934) and the United States (1945)—was associated with many of the important tendencies in twentieth-century music, from forms of nationalism and primitivism, to neoclassicism, to serialism. The pastiche element of his neoclassic music has even been interpreted as a harbinger of postmodernism.

Stravinsky's creative output is often divided into three periods, which the composer later described as having been demarcated by two "crises." His first or "Russian" phase was an outgrowth of his formative influences. In relatively early works such as *Scherzo fantastique* and *Fireworks* (both completed 1908), he emulated the techniques of Rimsky-Korsakov and other composers admired in his milieu. Even *The Firebird* (1910)—the first of his ballets written for impresario Sergei Diaghilev (1872–1929) and the Ballets Russes—owed a debt to established fashions (including French impressionism). Changes are more evident with the next ballet, *Petrushka* (1911), which is infused with nascent modernism as evidenced by its formal, textural, and thematic juxtapositions. The following ballet, *The Rite of Spring* (1913), took these characteristics to new levels. Indeed, its Paris premiere was the scene of a famous audience riot that guaranteed the growing reputation of the composer.

Especially after *The Rite,* some listeners began to discuss Stravinsky's music in terms of primitivism, which composer Marc Blitzstein (1905–1964) described as "violent, rhythmic, blunt," and characterized by "short successive electric moments" (p. 334). Many contemporaries were particularly intrigued by Stravinsky's rhythmic innovations. In the Russian-era works and afterward, one finds sections of metric irregularity—that is, with a shifting sense of where the "downbeats" fall—as well as sections of superimposed patterns, each internally consistent but combined to form cycles of polyrhythmic activity.

The first of the composer's period-delimiting "crises" was precipitated by the outbreak of World War I in 1914 and exacerbated by the Russian Revolution of 1917. The result was what he described as his "loss of Russia and its language of words as well as of music" (Stravinsky and Craft, p. 23). During the years that followed, as he lived first in Switzerland (1914–1920) and then in France (1920–1939), his so-called second musical style developed: the neoclassic. Generally speaking, neoclassic music imitates that of the past—especially that of the baroque and high classical periods of the eighteenth century—but more by translating the older idioms into those of the present day than by exactly replicating the older styles. If the music was steeped in counterpoint and textures reminiscent of the baroque, the motto "Back to Bach" was often attached. Stravinsky's foray into neoclassicism has been associated with the composition of various works, including the ballet *Pulcinella* (1920), which Stravinsky himself later suggested as a turning point. The new style was confirmed with the Octet for Wind Instruments (1923); its zenith came in 1951, with the completion of *The Rake's Progress,* an opera that harkened back to Wolfgang Amadeus Mozart (1756–1791).

By the mid-1920s Stravinsky was publicly condemning musical modernism, and so emerged one of the great polemics of the era, which pitted him against Austrian composer Arnold Schoenberg (1874–1951). Arthur Lourié (1892–1966) promoted the polarization when he described Schoenberg and Stravinsky as thesis and antithesis in his article "Neogothic and Neoclassic." The former's style was characterized as one of extreme expressiveness, emotionalism, and egocentric individualism. The latter's neoclassic style, in contrast, was described as objective and "purely musical," born of intellectualism and a triumph over the "personal utterance." Although Lourié's allegiances were with Stravinsky and his style, similar characterizations were later inverted in meaning by Theodor Adorno (1903–1969), a philosopher and writer on musical modernism. In *Philosophie der neuen Musik* (1949; Philosophy of modern music), he too argued that Schoenberg and Stravinsky were at the polarized extremes of contemporary music. For Adorno, however, Stravinsky's suppression of expression and subjectivity was to be condemned.

Given the dichotomy described above, it came as a surprise to many that in Stravinsky's third compositional phase he adopted a method closely associated with Schoenberg: serialism. It must be stressed that serialism is neither a "style" nor a monolithic system. It is a pliable method whereby a composer establishes an ordering of musical elements—most commonly notes, or more precisely the intervals between the notes—that will become referential for a work. Those who appropriated the method adapted it to their idiomatic inclinations, as did Stravinsky, who fashioned many distinctive procedures. As for the "crisis" that brought about this new orientation, Stravinsky remarked later that it was a product of the intense period of over three years in which he was immersed in *The Rake's Progress.* That is, having exhausted himself in the consummation of three decades of work in neoclassicism, he needed a creative change. Other factors also played a role. After World War II serialism had been adopted by many of the composers deemed most "progressive," especially in parts of Europe. In 1951, when Stravinsky visited Europe for the first time in a dozen years, he became aware that he was no longer relevant to many younger composers.

Thus, some have argued that his new phase was largely a matter of wanting to remain *au courant*.

Another important influence came in the form of Robert Craft (b. 1923), a conductor and advocate of Stravinsky's music as well as that of Schoenberg and his pupil Anton Webern (1883–1945). Craft had joined the Stravinsky household in 1949, where he first served as an assistant to the composer and eventually became something of a surrogate son. Craft later affirmed that he had been a catalyst for the work the composer undertook in this period. As for the serial music itself, although some of it sounds quite different from music of Stravinsky's earlier periods, there are similarities. For example, the Septet (1953) once more harkens "back to Bach," with its passacaglia and gigue movements. On the other hand, *Requiem Canticles* (1966)—his last major work—has affinities with the Russian-era works.

At the time of his death in 1971, two months before his eighty-ninth birthday, Stravinsky was routinely described as the (Western) world's greatest—or at least most celebrated—twentieth-century composer. Decades later, his reputation and influence still loom large, as attested to by the growing number of books and articles devoted to him. It should be noted that Stravinsky's own writings are not always reliable guides to his life and views, partly due to the extent to which ghostwriters or credited collaborators shaped the results, and partly because the composer occasionally seemed to change biographical details to suit the times. However, the accuracy of recent research has been greatly abetted by the ability to consult materials from his estate, many of which are now housed at the Paul Sacher Foundation in Basel, Switzerland.

See also **Avant-Garde; Diaghilev, Sergei; Modernism; Music; Primitivism; Rimsky-Korsakov, Nikolai; Schoenberg, Arnold.**

BIBLIOGRAPHY

Primary Source

Stravinsky, Igor, and Robert Craft. *Themes and Episodes*. New York, 1966.

Secondary Sources

Adorno, Theodor. *Philosophie der neuen Musik*. Tübingen, Germany, 1949.

Blitzstein, Marc. "The Phenomenon of Stravinsky." *Musical Quarterly* vol. 21, no. 3 (1935): 330–347.

Craft, Robert. *Stravinsky: Glimpses of a Life*. New York, 1992.

Cross, Jonathan. *The Stravinsky Legacy*. Cambridge, U.K., and New York, 1998.

Cross, Jonathan, ed. *The Cambridge Companion to Stravinsky*. Cambridge, U.K., and New York, 2003.

Griffiths, Paul. *Stravinsky*. London, 1992.

Joseph, Charles M. *Stravinsky Inside Out*. New Haven, Conn., 2001.

Lourié, Arthur. "Neogothic and Neoclassic." *Modern Music* vol. 5, no. 3 (1928): 3–8.

Taruskin, Richard. *Stravinsky and the Russian Traditions: A Biography of the Works through Mavra*. Berkeley, Calif., 1996.

Walsh, Stephen. *Stravinsky: A Creative Spring: Russia and France, 1882–1934*. New York, 1999.

DAVID CARSON BERRY

STRIKES. The strike, the collective withholding of labor in pursuit of specific economic or political goals, became the most pervasive form of labor protest in nineteenth-century Europe. It derived its centrality from capitalist transformations in the nature of work and labor relations and the emergence of new political and legal frameworks for workplace bargaining and negotiation. The strike evolved after the early nineteenth century in complex relations with other forms of worker protest and organizations, especially trade unions and workers' political parties. From the 1860s to 1914, Europe witnessed unprecedented rates of industrial militancy in which the strike proved to be the principal means of interest articulation for wage earners in urban manufacturing and rural production: it became the most effective means of securing higher wages, defending workplace autonomies and skills, redressing perceived indignities suffered at the hands of factory foremen or company owners, and securing basic civil and political rights.

LABOR PROTEST IN THE EARLY NINETEENTH CENTURY

If understood strictly in terms of temporary work stoppages designed to force concessions from employers, strikes were not new to the nineteenth century. Rather, what was new was that strikes became distinct from other forms of popular protest during this period and evolved into a new form of industrial action and the most common means of worker self-assertion by the end of the century. As historians have shown, popular protest took many forms before the nineteenth century: food riots, tax revolts, resistance against conscription, battles over the rights to the forest and its resources, religious rebellions and pogroms, and charivaris, customs involving the collective "shaming" of someone deemed in violation of local moral or sexual codes. These protests tended to be local, temporary, hastily organized or spontaneous actions, often involving physical violence, and they drew upon the participation of men and women (and often children) and socially heterogeneous groups from the lower ranks of society. The most closely related form of labor action in the early nineteenth century was machine-breaking. From 1811 to 1816, textile workers in the hosiery and lace industries of the East Midlands, the woolen industry of the West Riding in Yorkshire, and the cotton industry of southern Lancashire and northern Cheshire began to destroy shearing machines, gig-mills, and power looms in order to protest declining wages and unemployment. Similar actions also took place in France: in Vienne in 1819, in Saint Étienne in 1830, and in Paris, Bordeaux, Toulouse, and Saint Étienne in 1831; and in the German states: in Solingen in 1826, in Krefeld in 1828, in Saxony in the 1830s, and during the massive Silesian weavers' rebellion in 1844. Machine-breaking also entered the English countryside during the "Captain Swing" rebellion of 1830, when agricultural workers in the South East, Hampshire and the West Country, the Midlands, and East Anglia protested declining wages by threatening landowners and local public officials and destroying threshing machines. Indeed, many early nineteenth-century strikes, particularly among textile workers, took on several aspects of these forms of protest: in France, for example, they usually involved sudden work stoppages, followed by the formation of a crowd outside the workshop or factory, marches from factory to factory in order to recruit other workers from the same industry, street demonstrations, often to the accompaniment of drums and flags, and sometimes window breaking at offending

workshops. Generally these protests, which served as public demonstrations of outrage and discontent, ended either with arrests by local authorities or the return of workers to the factory. By contrast, other workers, especially artisans, engaged in activity that bore the marks of the later nineteenth-century strike: the preplanned and calculated withdrawal of labor, often involving workers' organizations, in order to pressure employers for specific economic gains: higher wages, improved working conditions, shorter working hours, changes in hiring practices, and regulations over the trades. The turn to this form of protest was already visible in Britain in the 1820s, in France in the 1830s and 1840s, and in the German states in the late 1840s.

Historians once commonly explained this process as a transition from "preindustrial" to "modern" forms of labor protest. According to this perspective, the adoption of the calculated strike, supported by trade unions, was part of a "learning process" by which workers embraced more "rational" forms of interest articulation commensurate with "modern" changes in the manufacturing process and industrial bargaining. This kind of "modernization" approach has been challenged in a number of ways. Social historians have demonstrated the ways in which popular protest before and during the first half of the nineteenth century, including machine breaking, involved complex interactions between crowds and authorities and negotiations over basic questions of fairness and morality and thus constituted entirely "rational" responses to dearth, high prices, unemployment, and declining livelihoods. In addition, they have pointed not only to the persistence of these forms of protests, especially subsistence and food riots, well into the twentieth century; they have also demonstrated the conjunctural specificities, rather than historical continuities, of mass direct actions. Finally, labor historians have emphasized the ways in which the organized strike emerged alongside and often in conjunction with other forms of spontaneous direct action taken by workers. Understanding the growing centrality of the "modern" strike as a form of labor protest, therefore, requires thinking about its historically contingent economic and political conditions of emergence and possibility in the nineteenth century and what made it the preferred form of industrial action.

In this regard, it is important to note two critical changes of the late eighteenth and early nineteenth centuries: the transition to capitalist markets in goods and labor and new divisions of labor and schemes of subcontracting; and the general reconfiguration of the political and legal frameworks by which labor relations were governed. The latter involved the dismantling of the manufacturing guilds and manorial systems, the banning of artisans' organizations, and the legal recodification of labor relations as strictly economic matters between individual wage earners and employers. This explains both the economic and political aims, necessitated by state involvement in instituting economic changes, of strikes in the early nineteenth century. On the one hand, strikes in Britain and France from the 1810s to the 1840s were aimed at securing workplace gains. On the other, many strikes evolved into wider political mobilizations seeking state intervention into the economy to curb unbridled competition and the degradation of the trades as well as political change in the direction of popular sovereignty. This applies as much to the strikes of French workers from the 1830s to 1848, which advanced the cause of republican socialism, as it does to the first nationwide strike of the nineteenth century: the 1842 general strike in Britain. The latter, which was centered in Lancashire but extended to the industrial regions of Scotland and Wales, involved five hundred thousand workers calling for "a fair day's wage for a fair day's work" and for the fulfillment of the demands for democratic reform and the requirement of "liberty" contained in the People's Charter.

INDUSTRIAL TRANSFORMATION, MASS POLITICS, AND THE STRIKE

Past explanations for the subsequent rise of the strike as the foremost industrial action in late nineteenth-century Europe, which rested on theories of working-class misery or deprivation, social dislocation associated with rural inhabitants being thrust into an urban context, and the more or less straightforward responses of workers to cyclical changes in the economy, have largely been abandoned. Most historians now explain the preeminence of the strike in terms of a combination of factors, including transformations in the industrial economy, the evolving social-structural conditions of residence and community, and the rise of workers' organizations and mass politics toward the end of the nineteenth century. Indeed, the second half of the nineteenth century was marked by the dramatic expansion of strike activity that can be analyzed in two distinct phases: a first phase from the 1860s to the 1880s and a second phase from 1890 to 1914. The transition from the first to the second phases was marked by the increasing organization and standardization of the strike as a form of industrial and political action. But this transformation is best understood not in terms of inevitable learning processes or entailed and "more rational" responses to economic changes but in terms of contingent social struggles over the conditions of work and the political relations which sustained them in the late nineteenth century.

After the collapse of the revolutions and mobilizations of 1848 and the general period of conservative repression in the 1850s, labor militancy rose exponentially toward the end of the 1860s. In addition to the sudden expansion of capitalist economies, this period brought new laws permitting the formation of workers' organizations and, in some cases, guaranteeing the right to strike: this happened, for example, in France in 1864, in Germany in 1869, in Spain in 1868, and in the Netherlands in 1872. The result was a dramatic increase in the number of strikes in a favorable economic conjuncture from the late 1860s to the early 1870s. In Britain, the number of strikes jumped from 30 in 1870 to 343 in 1872; in France, they increased from 72 in 1869 to 151 in 1872; and in Germany, they rose from 98 in 1869 to 223 in 1873. Indeed, the period from 1868 to 1873 witnessed the first transnational strike wave involving thousands of workers across industrializing Europe. Perhaps the most distinctive feature of this early phase of labor militancy was the complex relationship between strike activity and workers' organizations, namely the skilled craft unions forming during this period. Many of the strikes, especially in the 1870s, involved unorganized workers. In France, for example, of the 1,695 documented strikes from 1870 to 1890, some 51 percent were not planned in advance, 41 percent were launched by nonunionized workers and usually led by elected strike committees; and fully 82 percent of the sudden strikes were led by women workers, who were systematically excluded from formal organizations. In Britain, most of the strikes in the 1870s were also led by unorganized workers; here the strike became an effective recruiting mechanism for the unions: membership in the Trades Union Congress grew from about 250,000 to 1.2 million from 1870 to 1874 as a result of the strikes.

This relationship between trade unions and strikes, in which strikes encouraged union membership, was also visible during the second phase of strike activity from the late 1880s to 1914, when industrial transformation and mass union and working-class political mobilization altered the conditions and scope of strike activity. This era was marked by the unprecedented increase in the scale of labor militancy and the frequency of strikes. Britain was buffeted by two massive waves of industrial militancy, from 1889 to 1890, when the great London dock strike of 1889 was accompanied by some 2,400 strikes, and from 1911 to 1913, when British workers launched a staggering 3,165 strikes, resulting in a total of sixty million workdays lost. In Germany, the massive miners' strikes in the Ruhr in 1889–1890 began a steady increase in the number of strikes, from less than two hundred per year to over twenty-five hundred per year from 1900 to 1914. France experienced sudden increases in 1890 and 1899–1900, after which strikes peaked in 1906; overall, the frequency of French strikes increased by four times between 1885–1890 and 1910–1914. In Italy, the northern industrial regions registered a rapid increase in strike activity between 1901 and 1905; and the northern countryside witnessed an exponential increase in the number of strikes among agricultural workers during the same period. Aside from new laws permitting association and strikes in countries such as France and Italy after 1880, this increase in industrial actions was related to several factors. First, the economic changes of the Second Industrial Revolution, which brought new workplace hierarchies, divisions of labor, and increasing mechanization to large industrial plants, challenged the position of skilled workers and introduced increasing numbers of

"semiskilled" and "unskilled" workers, including many women, to the disciplinary regimes of the factory or workshop. In this context, the insecurities of industrial employment and the grievances associated with workplace discipline combined with favorable economic conjunctures and the high demand for labor to encourage militancy. Second, the new mass or industrial unions, with national congresses, in northern and central Europe and the federations of syndicates and chambers of labor in France, Italy, and Spain provided vital resources for workers in their efforts to organize and sustain strikes. Third, social segregation in European cities and towns during this period led to the formation of working-class subcultures—whether in industrial Lancashire or the Wedding district of Berlin—which enabled workers to maintain strike solidarity. Finally, workers' political organizations and parties were integral to this strike activity: the mass social democratic parties of north-central Europe and the anarchosyndicalist organizations in southern Europe often lent their support or direction to workers' strikes.

Nevertheless, that support could also put the brakes on strike activity during this period, when the organization and codification of industrial relations prompted trade unions to impose control over strikers, and industrial bargaining involving employers' organizations and state officials led to the increasing standardization of labor conflict. Thus, as employers formed their own associations in order to combat the trade unions, governments attempted to implement measures and institutions for labor conciliation after 1890. New codes and institutions for industrial arbitration were introduced haltingly in Germany in 1891 and more vigorously in France in 1892, in Italy in 1893, and in Britain in 1896; combined with negotiations between unions and employers, they contributed to an increasing number of collective bargaining agreements in countries such as Britain. But in this context, many trade unions also increasingly turned to gradualist strategies of workplace negotiation, carefully guarded their "war chests," and imposed discipline on an often restless rank and file. This was particularly the case with the German labor movement, which became increasingly bureaucratized in the decade before 1914. But state intervention could also facilitate

Strikers in Ireland, 1913. Irish labor leader James Larkin, weaing an overcoat, is shown with striking workers during the 1913 general strike. ©Hulton-Deutsch Collection/Corbis

trade-union militancy and strike activity. In the case of France, for example, episodic state-directed efforts at conflict resolution increasingly encouraged workers to launch massive immediate strikes, rather than long-prepared and drawn-out strikes, because government officials feared large and disruptive disputes and were thus more likely to put pressure on employers to seek compromises with workers.

Indeed, perhaps the most distinctive feature of the strike in the late nineteenth century was its political dimensions. On the shop floor, workers often struck a factory not just for higher wages or safer working conditions but over issues related to control over the work process and the authority of foremen. In some cases, these actions, for example those of the knife grinders of Solingen or the public gas stokers in Paris, could shape the work

process and employer decisions about the introduction of new technologies. In a more formal political sense, the general strike became a weapon to secure not only workplace improvements but political change as well. The general or political strike became a much-debated strategy in the organized labor movements of Europe. The syndicalists in France, Italy, and Spain viewed the strike as *the* principal means of worker self-assertion and political activity, and the social democratic parties of northern and central Europe began debating the merits of the general strike, particularly in response to the outbreak of a war in Europe, in the context of the Second International. If the latter avoided an official endorsement of the general strike, individual parties put it to use for the purpose of securing basic democratic aims within their own countries. In this regard, workers launched general strikes in Belgium, Sweden, Norway, Finland, Italy, and Austria at various times from the 1880s to 1913 in attempts to secure universal suffrage or democratic reforms. Indeed, the strike waves throughout Europe during and in the immediate aftermath of World War I not only helped to bring down the monarchies of Russia, Austria-Hungary, and Germany; they also provided support for the new suffrage laws and state welfare commitments in nearly all European countries after 1918.

See also **Anarchosyndicalism; Captain Swing; Industrial Revolution, First; Industrial Revolution, Second; Labor Movements; Machine Breaking; Socialism; Syndicalism.**

BIBLIOGRAPHY

Crew, David. *Town in the Ruhr: A Social History of Bochum, 1860–1914.* New York, 1979.

Cronin, James E. *Industrial Conflict in Modern Britain.* London, 1979.

Geary, Dick. *European Labour Protest, 1848–1939.* New York, 1981.

Haimson, Leopold H., and Charles Tilly. *Strikes, Wars, and Revolutions in an International Perspective: Strike Waves in the Late Nineteenth and Early Twentieth Centuries.* New York, 1989.

Hanagan, Michael P. *The Logic of Solidarity: Artisans and Industrial Workers in Three French Towns, 1871–1914.* Urbana, Ill., 1980.

Mommsen, Wolfgang J., and Hans-Gerhard Husung, eds. *The Development of Trade Unionism in Great Britain and Germany, 1880–1914.* London, 1985.

Perrot, Michelle. *Workers on Strike: France, 1871–1890.* Translated by Chris Turner with the assistance of Erica Carter and Claire Laudet. New Haven, Conn., 1987. Translation of *Jeunesse de la grève: France 1871–1890.*

Shorter, Edward, and Charles Tilly. *Strikes in France, 1830–1968.* New York, 1974.

Tilly, Charles, Louise Tilly, and Richard Tilly. *The Rebellious Century, 1830–1930.* Cambridge, Mass., 1975.

DENNIS SWEENEY

STRINDBERG, AUGUST (1849–1912), Swedish playwright, novelist, and poet.

August Strindberg was born in Stockholm, the third child in a large bourgeois family. The son of a servant on one side—his mother had been a waitress and housekeeper before her marriage—and of a well-to-do patriarchal businessman on the other, Strindberg created an image of himself as a vacillating soul. A similar social ambivalence underlies his most famous stage play, *Miss Julie* (1888; *Fröken Julie*), the dramatic story of a noblewoman who is drawn into an amorous and disastrous affair with her father's lackey. Strindberg's self-reference to an "underclass" origin also dictated his sympathies for the Swedish working class, for whom he was to become somewhat of a figurehead.

Strindberg epitomizes a modern age of industrial growth, demographic shifts from countryside to city living, and extensive urban renewal. In an early poem titled "The Esplanade System," his alter ego defends the new era: "We tear down for air and light / isn't that sufficient for building a new site?" These lines also point to Strindberg's real breakthrough as a writer with the iconoclastic novel *The Red Room* (1879; *Röda rummet*), a realistic depiction of social, political, and cultural phenomena in contemporary Stockholm. His view of Swedish society became still more critical in *The New Kingdom* (1882; *Det nya riket*). Shortly after its publication he left Sweden, accompanied by his first wife, Siri von Essen.

For Scandinavian artists and writers of Strindberg's generation, a stay abroad was almost a given part of their development. Strindberg spent much of the 1880s in France, Switzerland, southern Germany, and Denmark and the 1890s in Berlin, Paris, and, rather briefly, with his new in-laws, the Uhl family, in Austria. After the publication of his collection of short stories *Getting Married* (1884; *Giftas*), Strindberg's first stay abroad was interrupted by the so-called *Giftas* trial when he was brought to court on charges of blasphemy. Though he was acquitted and celebrated by many as a brave challenger of religious and moral hypocrisy, the *Giftas* trial signaled an upcoming period of turmoil in Strindberg's life usually referred to as the Inferno Crisis. After his divorce from Siri and a brief second marriage, followed by a period of scientific experimentation and futile attempts at making gold, Strindberg's psychic upheaval culminated in the mid-1890s. Abandoning his atheistic position and naturalistic writing of the 1880s, he now embraced a religion inspired by Emanuel Swedenborg and Eastern mysticism and created a new form of drama patterned on the subconscious world of dreams and nightmares. Foremost among these post-Inferno works are *A Dreamplay* (1901; *Ett drömspel*) and the chamber plays *The Pelican* (1907; *Pelikanen*) and *The Ghost Sonata* (1907; *Spöksonaten*). Strindberg also realized a lifelong dream of having a stage of his own, the small Intima Theatre in Stockholm, which produced his works from 1907 until 1911, when it went bankrupt. After being used as office space for many years, the premises were renovated and reopened in 2004.

Strindberg's post-Inferno works also comprise a group of plays based on Swedish history and patterned after Shakespeare's Tudor cycle. Like his predecessor he took liberties with historical facts, telescoped time and space for dramatic expediency, and saw a providential force behind royal decrees and national events. However, the history plays express, above all, Strindberg's own temperament, in which conflict becomes the keynote in all human relations. This trait still manifested itself at the very end of his life, when he became embroiled in a media debate referred to as the Strindberg Feud, in which he took issue with a number of literary, social, and political ideas. He died a controversial figure and was denied the Nobel Prize in literature by a conservative Swedish Academy. Instead he received, in time for his sixtieth birthday, an "alternate Nobel" award consisting of a substantial monetary sum donated by the general Swedish public.

Strindberg's posthumous reputation is twofold: one national, the other international. In his native Sweden he is a literary giant best known for his realistic fiction, foremost his popular novel about life in the archipelago, *The People of Hemsö* (1887; *Hemsöborna*), dramatized, filmed, and televised numerous times. Abroad his claim to fame rests primarily on his plays, most notably *Miss Julie, The Father* (1887; *Fadren*), *Creditors* (1889; *Fodringsägare*), *The Dance of Death* (1898; *Dödsdansem*) *The Pelican,* and *The Ghost Sonata*. But more than anything Strindberg's foreign image has been that of a "bedeviled viking" and a bitter misogynist who depicts life between the sexes as perpetual warfare.

Strindbergian scholarship reflects this dichotomous assessment. Swedish research has tended to focus on biographical and psychological life-and-letters studies. Martin Lamm's biography from 1942 established an early code, with the Inferno Crisis as a watershed divider. Gunnar Brandell's dissertation *Strindbergs Infernokris* (1950; Strindberg's inferno crisis) confirms Lamm's perspective. It was not until 1979 that the Swedish literary critic and journalist Olof Lagercrantz challenged the importance given to the Inferno Crisis in depicting Strindberg's life and literary development. Ulf Olsson's postmodernist study *Levande död* (1996; Living dead) breaks with the long biographical tradition in Swedish Strindberg scholarship. But it still continues to be represented in the meticulously documented new national edition of Strindberg's collected works, which when completed will comprise some seventy-two volumes under the editorial leadership of Lars Dahlbäck.

After Strindberg was recognized by several writers elsewhere in Europe and in the United States (Eugene O'Neill, Tennessee Williams, James Joyce, Samuel Beckett, and Eugene Ionesco), non-Swedish examinations of him have focused on his role in such literary movements as expressionism and modernism. In Germany, Walter Baumgartner and Thomas Fechner-Smarsly's 2003 volume of essays on Strindberg and the media presents his works in an intermedia context, as does a 1999 study by Egil Törnqvist, *Ibsen, Strindberg and the Intimate Theatre: Studies in TV Presentations.* In addition to new translations of his works in a number of different languages, an English multivolume Strindberg bibliography by Michael Robinson is near completion (forthcoming in 2006–2007). Altogether, the sheer volume of Strindberg scholarship mirrors the literary output of a prolific writer whose work displays the largest vocabulary in Swedish literature and who was in fact the first Swedish author to be able to live exclusively by his pen.

See also **Chekhov, Anton; Ibsen, Henrik; Shaw, George Bernard.**

BIBLIOGRAPHY

Balzamo, Elena. *August Strindberg: Visage et destin.* Paris, 1999.

Baumgartner, Walter, and Thomas Fechner-Smarsly, eds. *August Strindberg: Der Dichter und die Medien.* Munich, 2003.

Johanneson, Eric O. *The Novels of August Strindberg*. Berkeley, Calif., 1968.

Johnson, Walter. *Strindberg and the Historical Drama*. Seattle, Wash., 1963.

Lagercrantz, Olof. *August Strindberg*. Translated by Anselm Hollo. New York, 1984.

Lamm, Martin. *August Strindberg*. Translated by Harry G. Carlson. New York, 1971.

Robinson, Michael. *Strindberg and Autobiography*. Norwich, U.K., 1986.

Sprinchorn, Evert. *Strindberg as Dramatist*. New Haven, Conn., and London, 1982.

Steene, Birgitta. *The Greatest Fire: A Study of August Strindberg*. Carbondale, Ill., 1968.

Törnqvist, Egil. *Strindbergian Drama: Themes and Structure*. Stockholm, 1982.

BIRGITTA STEENE

STRUVE, PETER (1870–1944), Russian political economist and political figure.

A remarkable political thinker, scholar, and activist, Peter Struve long remained shadowy in the narrative of late tsarism and the Russian Revolution, largely because of his refusal to fit into the ideological frameworks erected around those events. The admiring and definitive two-volume study by Richard Pipes revived and contextualized a complex life. Struve's political values from youth to age forty-four described an arc from early conservatism to Marxism into conservative liberalism and strident nationalism.

The Struves were of German origin. Peter Struve's grandfather was a noted astronomer, and his father a governor of Perm Province. Peter attended school and university in St. Petersburg. While still a schoolboy, he lost faith in the autocracy following the censoring of his idol, the Slavophile nationalist Ivan Aksakov, in the mid-1880s. At university in the 1890s Struve became a Marxist. Along with other intellectuals—the so-called Legal Marxists—Struve argued in uncensored publications against the contentions of the "Legal Populists" that industrial capitalism and the consequent rise of a proletariat offered the only solution to Russia's backwardness and that the proletariat could serve as the sole instrument of a struggle for democracy. Struve's wide connections in Russia, which included Vladimir Lenin, and in Europe and his brilliant editorial gifts led to his invitation to write the famous manifesto announcing the formation in 1898 of the Russian Social Democratic Labor Party—ancestor of both Bolshevism and Menshevism. The manifesto linked the immediate demands of democracy and freedom of speech, press, and assembly for the working class with "the struggle for its final liberation, against private property and capitalism—for socialism" (Pipes, 1970, vol. 1, p. 194). Struve later admitted that this document only partially reflected his own views at the time.

The party's first congress, in Minsk, was broken up by the police, and the delegates went on to other congresses. Struve, meanwhile, had become enamored of neo-Kantianism, a species of idealistic philosophy that could not square with historical materialism or economic determinism. Under its influence and that of the German Marxist Eduard Bernstein, Struve became a revisionist—rejecting revolution as the means of achieving worker's democracy. Arrested for his role in a demonstration, Struve spent most of 1901 in administrative exile in the provinces. His writings there caused a break with the Social Democratic leaders, though he remained vaguely a socialist until 1907. In 1902 Struve went abroad and began to edit *Osvobozhdenie* (Liberation), a journal of constitutional liberalism that was smuggled into Russia. Around the journal, the Union of Liberation was founded in 1903, in Switzerland. Relatively capacious, the union contained currents of liberalism, the new religious consciousness, and neo-idealism, along with echoes of populism. Initially Struve placed his hopes in the zemstvo movement—local self-government forces that were an early cradle of moderate constitutionalism. In time, he came around to Pavel Milyukov's program of a liberal party independent of the zemstvo with the goal of universal suffrage and social reforms. When such a party took shape as the Constitutional Democratic Party (known as the Kadets) late in 1905, Struve, now back in St. Petersburg, joined. By this time, he opposed popular violence, professional revolutionaries, land seizures, and class struggle in favor of order, social peace, and respect for the state.

Struve alternated political engagement with serious scholarship. A man of immense erudition and wide cultural tastes, he studied in Germany and Russia and received degrees from St. Petersburg, Moscow, and Kiev universities and taught at the St. Petersburg Polytechnical Institute, specializing in economic history and theory. While a deputy to the Second Duma in 1907, Struve made secret overtures to the tsarist minister Peter Stolypin on ways to collaborate. But Stolypin dissolved the Duma and Struve incurred the anger of his Kadet colleagues for, in effect, parlaying with the enemy. Moving steadily to the right, Struve not only broke completely with socialism but also criticized his own liberal party and the intelligentsia as a whole, and spoke up for nationalism and empire. His participation in the 1909 anthology *Vekhi* (Landmarks) won him more enemies. Its authors challenged what they took to be infirmities of the Russian intelligentsia: leftist materialism, religious skepticism, and ignorance of law, philosophy, and culture. Struve's *Patriotica* (1911), a collection of articles from the previous five years, took him a step further into conservative nationalism, containing as it did an extreme reverence for the "external power" of the Russian state and a consequent demeaning of other nationalities, especially Ukrainian. The war of 1914 only magnified Struve's glorification of Russia and the state. Shocked by the Bolshevik takeover in 1917, he joined the anti-Bolshevik forces and served as foreign minister in the White government of General Peter Wrangel in 1920. Upon its disappearance, Struve lived abroad, was arrested briefly by the Gestapo in Belgrade, and died in 1944 in Paris, then occupied by the Nazi regime, which he detested.

See also **Bolsheviks; Kadets; Mensheviks; Milyukov, Pavel.**

BIBLIOGRAPHY

Kindersley, Richard. *The First Russian Revisionists: A Study of "Legal Marxism" in Russia.* Oxford, U.K., 1962.

Leontovitsch, Victor. *Geschichte des Liberalismus in Russland.* Frankfurt am Main, Germany, 1957.

Pipes, Richard. *Struve: Liberal on the Left, 1870–1905.* Cambridge, Mass., 1970.

———. *Struve: Liberal on the Right, 1905–1944.* Cambridge, Mass., 1980.

Struve, Peter B. *Collected Works.* Edited by Richard Pipes. 15 vols. Ann Arbor, Mich., 1970.

RICHARD STITES

SUBWAYS. In the nineteenth century London, Paris, and Berlin transformed from merely big and famous cities into metropolises. At the end of the century underground transport systems had become one of the core features representing the world's leading cities; an integral part of the industrialization of the city, they had a great impact on urban life and served as visible proof of modernity.

ORIGINS

From the 1830s on surface railways carried more and more workers and other people to the city center while the number of people living in urban areas rose continuously. Although the railways improved their services to the big cities throughout the century, the city centers had not been penetrated by the mainline companies. All of the railway lines stopped at the periphery, and the scattered railway stations lacked connection. Passengers had to change at the terminus to horse-drawn buses, trams, or cabs to get to another station or to their next destination in the city. Soon, traffic on main roads in the city centers began to jam. Beginning in the 1890s newspaper articles described the intolerable conditions on the road. Contemporaries—mainly leading engineers, politicians, and journalists—regarded subway systems as the ultimate technological solution to overcoming these intensifying traffic problems. The first underground line in the world, the Metropolitan Railway in London opened in 1863 from Farringdon to Paddington, linking together the three major mainline railway termini at King's Cross, Euston, and Paddington. (The name *metro* is derived from Metropolitan Railway.) The Metropolitan Railway was operated by steam engines, which made travel rather uncomfortable due to unventilated tunnels filled with smoke and the carriages lit by smelly, dripping, and flickering lamps.

In the 1880s, electrical companies, train operators, and engineers in London, Paris, and Berlin had simultaneously developed plans for improved underground systems. They soon came up with two breakthroughs: electric traction improving travel conditions and advances in tunnel-boring enabling deep-level tunneling. The hitherto applied "cut-and-cover" method under the roads was costly, made the systems uneconomical, and caused

The London subway, photographed in the 1890s. ©BETTMANN/CORBIS

disruptions on the surface. The new methods in tunneling relied on the use of an iron cylindrical cutting shield and used cast iron segments that were bolted into immediately behind the cutting shield to replace the previous practice of labor-intensive brickwork. Electrical traction was shown to be feasible at the world's fair in 1879. The first electrical tramway powered by overhead wiring ran in 1881 in Berlin. But electrification did not take off on a larger scale before the 1890s. The first new electrified underground, the City and South London Railway, opened in 1890. This pioneering undertaking led to great interest not only among people connected with railways and kindred undertakings, but among the general public as well.

Its success encouraged other cities to carry on with their own plans, as local authorities elsewhere considered the underground to be an efficient solution for their traffic problems. Budapest (1896), Glasgow (1897), Vienna (1898), Paris (1900),

Berlin (1902: combined elevated railway and underground system), and Hamburg (1912) followed by imitating and improving on London's model. In 1913 London already had a network of around 210 kilometers (10 lines), in Paris there were 10 lines with an extension of 93 kilometers and Berlin could muster up 36 kilometers of subway lines. Although Glasgow, Vienna, and Hamburg tried to share the fame of an underground system in the nineteenth century, each only ever had one line, which hardly contributed to their transport efficiency at the time.

IMPACT

Historians still argue whether urban transport caused suburbanization or followed an already existing pattern. But underground systems must be regarded as one of the key factors in this process. At the beginning of the twentieth century, while already linking inner-city destinations such as train stations, underground lines began to reach newly developed suburbs. One of these new areas was Metro-Land in London. Starting in 1915, the Metropolitan Railway published its famous series of Metro-Land guides, intended to encourage London businessmen to buy new homes in order to enjoy the "quiet restfulness and comfort of a residence in pure air and rural surroundings." Indeed, the underground system generated centripetal and centrifugal forces. The faster links to the outskirts of the cities not only helped to develop suburbs but also intensified the concentration process in the inner cities. Contemporary critics already pointed to changes in the social structure. Not only did the underground systems encourage the middle and upper classes to leave the city, the star-shaped networks in London and Berlin underserved wide parts of the city.

For contemporaries these underground systems provided a superior form of urban public transport as they increased mobility and expressed civic pride, progress, and modernity. A new underground also represented the technological and aesthetical capacities of modern engineering. It is perhaps worth noting that while London and Berlin emphasized the commercial and technical aspects of their underground systems, aesthetics were more important for the Paris development. There, the municipal council only agreed to build artistically pleasing viaducts and employed the avant-garde architect Hector Guimard to design the entrances to the Métropolitain. The fluid, curvilinear lines that characterize Guimard's designs became synonymous with the art nouveau movement at the time.

Although the stations in London were impressive as well, the general manager attracted international attention primarily with new technologies. With the City and South London Railway the company introduced only one class, a system that was adopted by the other railways soon afterward. The most impressive innovations however were the hydraulic and, later, electric lifts for up to eighty passengers as well as escalators (1911), which saved the passengers the fatigue of climbing and descending stairs to and from the trains.

In Paris the municipal council was responsible for building the underground. Therefore it was planned as a whole system in a much more logical and comprehensive way than in London, where private enterprises (railway companies) developed a series of competing lines. In Berlin the situation was even more complicated: private enterprises (Siemens and AEG) had to negotiate with the government as well as with different municipal authorities. In London the different underground railway companies did finally team up to form the Underground group in 1908, producing a standard map including all lines and using a common sign (the still-known roundel) as a part of promoting the new cooperation. At the same time, the Underground group began the tradition of artistic poster design that contributed to the high profile of the Underground. Advertising was deliberately designed to have a universal appeal. Unlike the main line railways, the Underground could offer the lure of comfortable travel on equal terms to rich and poor alike.

The underground made a big difference in mobility patterns for urban city dwellers. Already before World War I, all social classes traveled daily by underground. In 1913 London's Underground transported 710 million passengers (all railways, but 474 million passengers were carried by local railways in 1911), Paris's Métropolitain 312 million, and Berlin's Hoch- und Untergrundbahnen 73 million. In London and Paris underground transport contributed more than 50 percent to all urban public transport, while Berlin lagged only about 6 percent behind. Passengers clearly benefited from these new transport systems, but the various underground companies also made big economic gains.

See also **Berlin; Cities and Towns; London; Paris; Railroads; Transportation and Communications.**

BIBLIOGRAPHY

Bagwell, Philip, and Peter Lyth. *Transport in Britain: From Canal Lock to Gridlock.* London and New York, 2002.

Bendikat, Elfi. *Öffentliche Nahverkehrspolitik in Berlin und Paris: 1890–1914: Strukturbedingungen, politische Konzeptionen und Realisierungsprobleme.* Berlin, 1999.

Green, Oliver. *The London Underground: An Illustrated History.* Shepperton, U.K., 1987.

———. *Underground Art: London Transport Posters, 1908 to the Present.* London, 1990.

Halliday, Stephen. *Underground to Everywhere: London's Underground Railway in the Life of the Capital.* Stroud, U.K., 2001.

Hallsted-Baumert, Sheila. *Métro-cité: Le chemin de fer métropolitain à la conquête de Paris, 1871–1945,* Paris, 1997.

Lemke, Ulrich, and Uwe Poppel. *Berliner U-Bahn.* 4th edition. Düsseldorf, 1996.

Reilly, Michael. "Promoting the Subway: New York's Experience in an International Context, 1890–1914." *The Journal of Transport History* 13 (1992): 95–114.

Wolmar, Christian. *The Subterranean Railway: How the London Underground Was Built and How It Changed the City Forever.* London, 2004.

BARBARA SCHMUCKI

SUEZ CANAL. A nineteenth-century engineering wonder that realized age-old dreams and modern ambitions, the Suez Canal reinforced Egypt's position at the junction of international trade and hastened Europe's scramble for empire. Linking the Red Sea to the Mediterranean, the Canal runs for approximately 100 miles (160 meters), with an average width of 90 feet; unlike the Panama Canal, it requires no locks to compensate for differences in sea level along its course.

The Canal was the brainchild of Ferdinand de Lesseps (1805–1894), a French diplomat and consul general in Egypt from 1832 to 1838. There he befriended Muhammad Said, son of Mehmet Ali (r. 1805–1848), the Ottoman viceroy of Egypt, who had gained substantial autonomy and set out to modernize the country. His successor Abbas Hilmi I (r. 1848–1854) undid much of Mehmet Ali's agenda, but Said, who ruled from 1854 to 1863, reopened western-style academies, rebuilt the Delta Barrages (a system of dams on the Nile), and granted foreign concessions to establish a telegraph network and to link Suez to Alexandria by rail.

Lesseps, who had resigned from the foreign service, approached his old friend with an audacious proposal—deemed implausible by many—to cut a maritime channel through the Isthmus of Suez. The two signed a hastily written contract in 1856 that granted Lesseps's Suez Canal Company a ninety-nine-year concession to construct and operate the waterway. The company could import supplies duty free, had the right to mobilize unpaid peasant labor (the corvée), and would exercise extra-territorial rights on a freshwater canal to be cut through to the Nile. This included the right to cultivate and reap profits from newly arable land. In addition to the return on its shares, Egypt would accrue 15 percent profits from shipping transit. The concession signed, Lesseps floated 400,000 shares on the international market at 500 francs per share. Lesseps's venture was troubled from the start. He scrambled to gather capital commitments even as construction began and wound up fronting a large proportion of the initial cost outlay from personal funds. Lesseps faced bitter opposition from the British government, which feared exposing India and losing commercial revenues at Alexandria, and indifference from his own. Formal approval from the various governments involved came only after construction had commenced in 1859. The Ottomans agreed reluctantly. In 1860 Said, who had originally purchased 64,000 shares, found himself stuck with 114,000 unsold shares. To pay for these he first issued treasury bonds, then borrowed from foreign banks.

By the time the Canal neared completion in 1869, four years behind schedule, Said had died. The new viceroy, Ismail (r. 1863–1879), inherited a boom economy—the blockade of Southern shipping during the U.S. Civil War caused Egyptian cotton prices to skyrocket—but also a mounting foreign debt. Egypt's arrears for unpaid Canal shares had grown from fifteen million to fifty-four million francs by 1862. Ismail dreamed of furthering Said's modernizing agenda. Unfortunately, by late 1864 cotton prices had stabilized; the following year they plummeted. To make matters worse, French arbitration of a dispute between Egypt and the Canal Company resulted in a judgment of eighty-four million francs against Egypt.

In November 1869 Ismail presided over the gala opening of the Canal. His party drew an array of foreign dignitaries: the French empress Eugénie (Lesseps's cousin, who had helped persuade Napoleon III to back the project), Francis Joseph I of Austria, the writers Henrik Ibsen and Émile Zola, and Thomas Cook, the founder of modern tourism. A grand flotilla embarked south from Port Said on the Canal's Mediterranean mouth. At Ismailia the guests were treated to a banquet, at

A ship passes through the Suez Canal. Photograph c. 1890s. ©MICHAEL MASLAN HISTORIC PHOTOGRAPHS/CORBIS

which Lesseps and Ismail were toasted with allusions to Columbus and Moses.

The moment proved illusory. As Ismail's debts mounted his European creditors called in their loans. In 1875 he sold Egypt's 44 percent Canal Company shares to the British government headed by Benjamin Disraeli for nearly four million pounds (by 1908 they were worth twenty-five million pounds). Britain suddenly became the Canal Company's major shareholder. The following year, when Ismail suspended repayment of other outstanding loans, a European debt commission assumed control of Egypt's budget; under the system of Dual Control British and French cabinet ministers oversaw tax collection and expenditures. In April 1879, facing growing nationalist pressure, Ismail dismissed the Europeans. Two months later, at Europe's behest, the Ottoman sultan replaced Ismail as viceroy of Egypt, with his son, Tawfik (r. 1879–1892). Tawfik found his

authority curbed by a nationalist government, but survived the British invasion of 1882, which initiated what would become a seventy-seven-year occupation.

The Suez Canal would remain a point of bitter contention between Britain, its European rivals, and Egyptian nationalists. Under the veiled protectorate of Sir Evelyn Baring, the Earl of Cromer, British agent and consul general from 1883 to 1907, Egyptian financial health was restored. In 1888 the major maritime powers signed the Convention of Constantinople, which guaranteed "free and open" passage through the waterway to all nations "in time of war as in time of peace." For Britain, however, the Canal came to represent the lifeline of empire and played a major role in the decision to prolong the Egyptian occupation indefinitely. By the mid-1880s some 3,500 ships passed through the Canal annually, the majority of them British.

In 1914, when the Ottoman Empire allied with the Central Powers, Britain declared a protectorate over Egypt. Its Suez bases became major staging grounds in two world wars. For Egyptians the Canal, once envisioned by Said as a passageway to independence, became a site of national humiliation, symbolic of foreign political and economic domination. Some twenty thousand peasants reportedly died building the Canal. The murder of Prime Minister Boutros Ghali in 1910 is attributable in part to his backing a proposal to extend the concession past 1969. When Gamal Abdel Nasser (1918–1970) nationalized the Canal Company in 1956 he invoked Lesseps as a symbol of foreign oppression. During the Suez War, Egypt mined the Canal and Egyptian partisans toppled the statue of Lesseps that stood by the customs house in Port Said. The pedestal remains empty to this day.

See also **Egypt; Great Britain; Imperialism; Lesseps, Ferdinand-Marie de; Transportation and Communications.**

BIBLIOGRAPHY

Karabell, Zachary. *Parting the Desert: The Creation of the Suez Canal.* New York, 2003.

Landes, David. *Bankers and Pashas: International Finance and Economic Imperialism in Egypt.* Cambridge, Mass., 1979.

Owen, Roger. *The Middle East in the World Economy: 1800–1914.* London, 1981.

Sayyid-Marsot, Afaf Lutfi. *Egypt and Cromer: A Study in Anglo-Egyptian Relations.* London, 1968.

JOEL GORDON

SUFFRAGISM.

SUFFRAGISM. Suffragism is the advocacy of extending the right to vote to a larger portion of the population. The term most often refers to the advocacy of women's right to vote.

SUFFRAGE IN EUROPE IN 1789

The word *suffrage* was used to mean "the right to vote" in both English and French by the late Middle Ages, and variants such as "universal suffrage" appeared in Enlightenment tracts at least as early as 1765, but the term *suffragism* to describe the advocacy of spreading the right to vote

JOHN STUART MILL'S SPEECH TO THE HOUSE OF COMMONS ON BEHALF OF WOMEN'S SUFFRAGE, 20 MAY 1867

Mr. J. Stuart Mill: I rise, Sir, to propose an extension of the suffrage which can excite no party or class feeling in this House; which can give no umbrage to the keenest asserter of the claims of property or of members; an extension which has not the smallest tendency to disturb what we have heard so much about lately, the balance of political power, which cannot afflict the most timid alarmist with revolutionary terrors, or offend the most jealous democrat as an infringement of popular rights. There is nothing to distract our attention from the simple, whether there is any adequate justification for continuing to exclude an entire half of the community, not only from admission, but from the capability of being ever admitted within the pale of the Constitution, though they may fulfill all the conditions legally and constitutionally sufficient in every case but theirs. Sir, within the limits of our Constitution this is a solitary case. There is no other example of an exclusion which is absolute. If the law denied a vote to all but the possessors of £5,000 a year, the poorest man in the nation might—and now and then would—acquire the suffrage; but neither birth, nor fortune, nor merit, nor exertion, nor intellect, nor even that great disposer of human affairs, accident, can ever enable any woman to have her voice counted in those national affairs which touch her and hers as nearly as any other person in the nation. . . .

Source: Hansard, *British Parliamentary Debates,* 20 May 1867 (vol. 187, pp. 817–818).

did not appear in English until 1888, long after the first campaigns that it described.

Although studies of the suffrage could cover such special instances as the electors of the Holy Roman Empire, the College of Cardinals, or diets in several states (the Icelandic *Althing* was founded in 960), the most noted instances of expansion of the right to vote in 1789 were in Great Britain (for the House of Commons) and in France (for the Estates General).

SUFFRAGE EXPANSION IN BRITAIN

In Britain the suffrage was restricted to men and was limited, on the basis of taxes paid, chiefly to freeholders (landowners), who paid forty shillings per year in taxes; in Ireland Catholics were excluded from voting. This limited the British franchise to fewer than 250,000 voters, or approximately 3 percent of the population. In France, voting for the Estates General in 1789 approached universal manhood suffrage, but most of the electorate (the 97 percent of the population in the Third Estate) voted indirectly, for representatives who later assembled to elect the delegates to the Estates General.

William Pitt the Elder (Lord Chatham) and his son, William Pitt the Younger, both called for electoral reform in the 1780s, and Charles Grey (later Earl Grey) spoke out vigorously in 1793, but anxieties of the revolutionary age delayed serious consideration for a generation.

Suffrage reforms that slowly expanded the right to vote became one of the dominant characteristics of British history in the nineteenth century. The Reform Act of 1832 expanded the franchise from an electorate of 435,000 to 653,000 by giving the ballot to householders with an annual lease of £10. The Reform Act of 1867 (also known as the Representation of the People Act) broadened the range of tax payments that earned a ballot, resulting in an electorate of nearly two million. A third Reform Act in 1884 brought the total number of eligible voters to 4.4 million in the general elections of 1886, in a total population of 27 million. Age, gender, tax payments, and status (especially for felons and the insane) still limited the vote.

The gradual pace of suffrage reform in Britain led to some of the strongest suffrage movements of the century. The most ardent British suffragists of the early nineteenth century were the members of the Chartist movement, whose democratic demands included universal manhood suffrage. The landmark statement of this suffragism was the People's Charter, drafted by Feargus O'Connor and the members of the Working Men's Association in 1838.

SUFFRAGE EXPANSION IN FRANCE

The Constituent Assembly of the French Revolution narrowed the franchise rather than maintaining the remarkable electorate that voted for the Estates General. The Constitution of 1791, the first in French history, established the category of "active citizens" entitled to vote. It limited the suffrage to men at age twenty-five if they paid a tax equal to three days' work, had a record of residency in the same place, swore loyalty to the constitution (the *serment civique*), and were not domestic servants.

This restricted franchise led to demands from radicals that France adopt a democratic franchise, and the revolutionary constitution of the French Republic in 1793 (also known as the "Constitution of the Year I") established the target of "universal suffrage." This constitution explicitly excluded women by using the term *homme* for voters, but it reduced the age qualification to twenty-one and the residency requirement to six months, and eliminated property and tax-paying qualifications. This essentially created universal manhood suffrage, although the constitution was suspended before it could establish this suffrage.

For most of the nineteenth century France experienced a political battle over the suffrage. Conservative governments, such as the Directory in the constitution of 1795, restored property qualifications for the vote. The restored monarchy of the early nineteenth century imposed very severe restrictions. Louis XVIII's constitutional charter of 1814 granted the suffrage to men at age thirty if they paid 300 francs in taxes; it also restored the indirect franchise used for the Estates General by allowing people to vote for representatives in departmental electoral colleges that actually chose the deputies. King Charles X increased the tax payment required to vote. After the Revolution of 1830, King Louis-Philippe reduced both the tax payment and the age for voting (to twenty-five) but retained the principle of a severely restricted franchise.

The Constitution of the Second Republic, drafted by the revolutionary government of 1848, reiterated the principle of universal suffrage as a central doctrine of European republicanism, and France became the first European country to practice it. Article 24 of the constitution stated simply, "The suffrage is direct and universal. The ballot is secret." Article 25 defined its limits: "All Frenchmen in possession of their civil rights (i.e., excluding criminals) are electors, without any qualification of taxation, at age twenty-one."

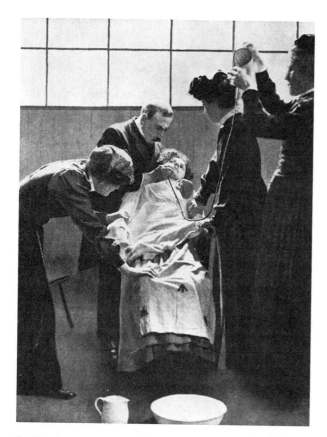

Suffragist being force-fed, London, 1912. Suffragists who were imprisoned for their activities sometimes attempted to stage hunger strikes and were subjected to force-feeding. ©BETTMANN/CORBIS

Whereas the British Reform Act of 1832 had increased the franchise by 49 percent, the Constitution of the Second Republic increased it forty-fold. The Third Republic's constitutional laws of 1875 perpetuated this standard of universal manhood suffrage and the image of France as the leader in European democratization. The republic, whose two predecessors had fallen to military leaders, did introduce one noteworthy new restriction of the suffrage: noncommissioned officers and men were disenfranchised while serving in the army.

SUFFRAGE VARIATIONS ACROSS NINETEENTH-CENTURY EUROPE

The conflict between the doctrine of "universal" suffrage and the conservative principle of restricting the franchise characterized the battles of nineteenth-century suffragism. Although voting rights were expanded in many regions, conserva-

tives typically prevented the adoption of effective universal suffrage. In Spain the century saw strife between a left that denounced monarchist absolutism and a right that feared republican anarchy; universal manhood suffrage was attempted only for the seven-year life of the Constitution of 1869. In the Netherlands, repeated demands for suffrage reform resulted in noteworthy reforms in 1887 and 1896, but these electoral laws fell far short of universal suffrage, allowing only seven hundred thousand to vote at the start of the twentieth century. The Danes promulgated a liberal constitution in 1849 and revised it in 1866, yet by 1914 still had not achieved universal manhood suffrage.

In Prussia conservatives developed a system, known as the "three-class suffrage," that promised universal suffrage yet subverted it. The Prussian electoral law of 1849 established universal manhood suffrage in elections to the *Landtag*, but it also divided voters into three classes, each class representing one-third of taxation of the total taxes collected. By this plutocratic version of universal suffrage, the few richest Prussians (who paid a third of the taxes) obtained an electoral weight far greater than the poorest (whose taxes totaled one-third); the weighted vote of the rich has been calculated at an electoral advantage of forty-one to two.

The Prussian response to suffragism was emulated by conservatives in other countries, often under the theory of "plural voting." Other German states directly copied the Prussian system (as Saxony did), but some countries developed elaborate variations. Belgium did not introduce universal manhood suffrage until 1893, and it came with a system of plural voting that gave multiple votes to some citizens on the basis of age, education, family size, and income. This idea of plural voting became the response of conservatives in some countries when women's suffrage became an issue: one conservative in France championed "familial suffrage," in which a husband or father would cast multiple votes for other members of his family.

Some conservative governments capitulated to the suffragist demand for universal suffrage by carefully limiting the effects of voting. Both Napoleon I and Napoleon III allowed universal suffrage in carefully controlled plebiscites that ratified government actions. The German chancellor Otto von Bismarck accepted universal manhood suffrage in elections for the lower house of both the North German Confederation (1867) and the German Empire (1871), but constructed a parliamentary system in which those elected could not control the government. Similar restraints limited the meaning of universal suffrage when adopted in Austria-Hungary (1907) and of the nearly universal suffrage employed to elect the First Duma in Russia (1906).

Universal suffrage was also criticized on the left for its failure to represent all opinions. The idea of a fairer franchise had been discussed as early as the debates in the French National Convention (1793), and it revived with a new respectability when John Stuart Mill advocated a system of proportional voting in which minorities would receive representation comparable to their share of the electorate. The utilitarianism system of proportional suffrage came to be known as "proportional representation" and it was championed by many democrats by the late nineteenth century. Forms of the proportional suffrage were adopted in several of the Swiss cantons in the second half of the century, then in elections at Hamburg in 1879, and for local contests in Serbia in 1888. Belgium became the first state to adopt this form of the suffrage in 1899, and before 1914 variants were being used in the Netherlands, Sweden, Finland, Portugal, and Bulgaria—but not in the Great Powers, although it was being seriously considered in France.

WOMEN'S SUFFRAGE

The widest use of the term *suffragism* in Europe before 1914 was to describe numerous movements for women's suffrage. The idea of the equal participation of women in civic affairs (*droit de cité*) had been proposed in 1787, on the eve of the French Revolution, by Marie-Jean de Caritat, marquis of Condorcet, but the male leaders of the revolutionary age showed no interest in the concept of women's suffrage. The revolution brought civil and political rights to Protestants (1791) and Jews (1791 and 1794), and to emancipated serfs and freed slaves (1789 and 1794), but explicitly denied equal rights to women, despite the active roles of women in the Revolution, from the *cahiers de doléances* through action in the streets.

Pioneering champions of women's rights in France (the term *feminists* was not coined until the end of the century) tried to convince the revolutionaries of 1848 to include women in "universal" suffrage. Leaders of women's clubs and press such as Eugénie Niboyet, Jeanne Deroin, and Pauline Roland tried tactics such as attempting to register to vote or running for office, to no avail. Deroin, who became the first French woman to run for office when she campaigned for the presidency of the Second Republic, wound up in jail, and the prominent male deputy who introduced women's suffrage in the revolutionary assembly, Victor Considerant, wound up in ridicule.

In Britain the Reform Act of 1832 expressly excluded women from voting. In 1866 Helen Taylor published an article calling for the enfranchisement of widows and spinsters, and British women soon petitioned Parliament to include equal rights in the coming reform of the suffrage. During the debate on the Reform Bill of 1867, John Stuart Mill asked the House of Commons to include women's suffrage on the same basis as men. Mill's amendment was defeated by a vote of 197–73 in a House of 658 members.

The refusal to grant women's suffrage in Britain and in France led to the growth of important suffragist movements in both countries in the late nineteenth century. Lydia Becker, Millicent Fawcett, and others soon created large and active suffrage movements in many of the cities of Britain, and in 1896 the seventeen largest of these societies agreed to join in forming a National Union of Women's Suffrage Societies under the leadership of Fawcett. By 1914 it had over five hundred member societies, and at one hundred thousand members it was by far the largest suffragist organization in Europe.

Suffragist societies were slower to develop in continental Europe, despite the historic role of France in proclaiming women's rights. Hubertine Auclert founded the first lasting women's suffrage organization in France, initially called Women's Rights and later called simply Women's Suffrage, in 1876. Despite her tireless campaigning, women's suffrage did not gain large-scale support until the founding of the French Union for Women's Suffrage (Union française pour le suffrage des femmes) by Jeanne Schmahl, Marguerite de Witt-Schlumberger, and Cécile Brunschwicg in 1909; by 1914 it had

London police arrest a women's suffrage advocate, May , 1914. ©Hulton-Deutsch Collection/Corbis

branches in seventy-five departments of France and twelve thousand members.

Other states were slow to develop suffragist campaigns. In Germany the women's rights movement preferred (as it had long done in France) to delay suffragism in order to concentrate on more moderate goals of civil rights, educational rights, and economic rights. Hedwig Dohm pressed for the vote, as Auclert had in France. Anita Augsburg, Marie Stritt, and other leaders agreed to join her in 1902 in founding the German Union for Women's Suffrage (Deutscher Verband für Frauenstimmrecht).

SUFFRAGISTS AND SUFFRAGETTES

In the early years of the twentieth century, suffragism turned toward greater militancy and even violence, especially in Britain. The foundation in 1903 of the Women's Social and Political Union,

led by Emmeline Pankhurst and her daughters, Christabel and Sylvia, provided the leadership for militant suffragists, who were soon branded "suffragettes" by the London press. The term was coined by the London *Daily Mail*, and it was intended to be a pejorative term, but militant suffragists embraced the name and applied it to one of their own publications. After 1905 some two thousand British suffragettes adopted a variety of violent tactics such as breaking shop windows, setting fire to (or flooding) postal boxes, tearing up the turf at golf courses, slashing famous paintings, and even arson. This did not win the vote, but as a consequence many women were imprisoned and treated to harsh forced feedings there when they attempted hunger strikes.

There were also suffragette demonstrations outside of England. In Ireland, Hanna Sheehy-

Skeffington led the Irish Women's Franchise League to emulate the WSPU after 1908; they broke windows in government buildings and set fire to the theater where the prime minister was scheduled to speak. In 1914 thirty-four Irish suffragettes were in prison. In France violence on behalf of women's suffrage was rarer. Auclert and Madeleine Pelletier both committed small acts of violence during the Parisian elections of 1908. Auclert broke into one poll and smashed the ballot box; Pelletier broke a window at another poll.

THE SUCCESS OF WOMEN'S SUFFRAGE TO 1914

In 1906 Finland, which had won a large degree of autonomy from Russia after the Russian Revolution of 1905, became the first European state to grant women's suffrage in national elections. In 1913 Norway became the first independent country to do so. When World War I began in 1914, none of the Great Powers had extended the national vote to women. Britain had, however, extended the right to vote in local elections in 1869, and women won a number of notable victories there. Eleanor Rathbone was elected to the city council of Liverpool, where she pioneered the debate on welfare. And in 1912 a loophole in Austrian legislation (which explicitly denied women's right to vote but did not mention women's right to stand for office) allowed a Czech writer, Bozena Vikova-Kuneticka, to become the first woman elected to Parliament in one of the Great Powers.

See also **Auclert, Hubertine; Chartism; Citizenship; Deroin, Jeanne; Fawcett, Millicent Garrett; Feminism; O'Connor, Feargus; Pankhurst, Emmeline, Christabel, and Sylvia; Pelletier, Madeleine; Roland, Pauline.**

BIBLIOGRAPHY

Daley, Caroline, and Melanie Nolan, eds. *Suffrage and Beyond: International Feminist Perspectives.* New York, 1994.

Droz, Jacques. *Réaction et suffrage universel en France et en Allemagne, 1848–1850.* Paris, 1963.

Gagel, Walter. *Die Wahlrechtsfrage in der Geschichte der deutschen liberalen Parteien, 1848–1918.* Düsseldorf, 1958.

Hause, Steven C., with Anne R. Kenney. *Women's Suffrage and Social Politics in the French Third Republic.* Princeton, N.J., 1984.

Hostettler, John. *Voting in Britain: A History of the Parliamentary Franchise.* Chichester, U.K., 2001.

Kahan, Alan S. *Liberalism in Nineteenth-Century Europe: The Political Culture of Limited Suffrage.* New York, 2003.

Liddington, Jill. *One Hand Tied behind Us: The Rise of the Women's Suffrage Movement.* London, 1978.

Rover, Constance. *Women's Suffrage and Party Politics in Britain, 1866–1914.* London, 1967.

STEVEN C. HAUSE

SUTTNER, BERTHA VON (1843–1914), Austrian peace activist.

Bertha Felice Sophie Kinsky was born 9 June 1843 in Prague into a venerable aristocratic family famed for three centuries of military credentials. Her seventy-five-year-old father, a third son, died before her birth, and her twenty-five-year-old mother was a commoner. In the rigid society of the Austro-Hungarian Empire, she was considered practically illegitimate, despite her arrival in the palatial family home on the Altstädter Ring. Raised by a mother who gambled their little money away in the world of casinos and watering places, Bertha, Countess Kinsky, broke free of her environment, used her skills in four languages as well as prodigious music education, and went out to earn her own living.

In 1873, thirty years old and unmarried, she became a governess in the Viennese home of the Baron von Suttner where she met and fell in love with the youngest son, Arthur Gundaccar von Suttner (1850–1902). The family's disapproval encouraged her to leave and Bertha Kinsky took a position in Paris with a Swedish manufacturer, Alfred Bernhard Nobel (1833–1896). While her employment lasted barely two weeks, she and Nobel remained fast friends through a rich and frequent correspondence. Bertha Kinsky returned to Vienna to elope with the young baron, who had telegraphed that he could not live without her. They moved to the Caucasus for about a decade to escape his family's opprobrium. There they struggled as language tutors, reading voraciously and launching careers as writers.

It was in this period of exile that von Suttner abandoned all ties to traditional religion, transformed by studies in Herbert Spencer (1820–1903), Ernst Heinrich Philipp August Haeckel (1834–1919), Charles Darwin (1809–1882), and Henry Thomas Buckle (1821–1862). Her ideas took shape—a thorough belief in rationality, in the possibility of positive evolution of both political and social relations, and the absolute necessity for world peace to be organized in order to undermine the forces of militaristic retrogression. She abandoned her military heritage to become one of the best-known peace activists in Europe before World War I.

In 1888 she anonymously published *Das Machinenzeitalter,* which attacked the exaggerated nationalism and militarism of the period, as well as outmoded ideas about education, human relations, love, women's position, and the uncritical acceptance of war as a phenomenon of nature. The book was widely reviewed and praised, but the work that made her famous, *Die Waffen nieder!* (Lay down your arms), published in 1889, earned her the sobriquet "the Harriet Beecher Stowe of the peace movement." A story of the imaginary Martha von Trilling, whose two husbands were killed in the mid-century wars, managed to do for the tiny peace movement what endless pamphlets, sermons, lectures, and meetings of societies had not done—command the public spotlight. The battlefield descriptions commanded reviewers' respect and some political admiration. Two printings were sold out by 1890 followed by translations into Swedish, French, and English that also sold out in 1891. Both expensive and popular editions followed over the next twenty-two years and by 1914, over a million copies circulated in sixteen languages (including Japanese and Russian). A film company completed a movie of the novel that was supposed to open in September 1914 in Vienna, where plans had been laid to hold the Universal Peace Congress. Obviously the Congress and film were canceled.

Von Suttner quickly found her soul mates in the emerging international peace movement whose Rome 1891 congress she attended. When the Universal Peace Congress voted to establish a permanent headquarters in Bern in 1892 (the Bureau international de la paix), von Suttner joined the council that set policies and organized pro-paganda. She founded the Austrian Peace Society and then helped create the German Peace Society, aided by her countryman, Alfred Hermann Fried (1864–1921). With her husband, she attacked the violent anti-Semitism of the Viennese mayor, Karl Lueger (1844–1910). Thereafter her lectures, articles, books, and interventions at conferences of pacifists and feminists made her an international celebrity. Her ties to Alfred Nobel convinced the skeptical millionaire inventor to support the peace movement. And she is famously credited with convincing Nobel to create the prizes, including the Peace Prize that he stipulated must be awarded by the Norwegian and not the Swedish committees. In 1905 she became the first woman to win the prize.

Following her husband's death (and the discovery of his liaison with a young female relative), von Suttner struggled to overcome her depression by a full career of lecturing, organizing, writing, correspondence, and participation in congresses. Her schedule took her to the United States; to The Hague during the 1899 and 1907 governmental conferences, where she used her aristocratic charm to lobby diplomats; to women's suffrage congresses whose cause she eventually incorporated into the peace argument. Von Suttner eventually moved to the position argued by most modern suffrage campaigners that women's participation in the public, political sector was essential and justified if modern society was to move toward an organized peace.

Despite charges of naivete, von Suttner's understanding of the dangers of a potential war were prophetic. She observed, in her Nobel acceptance speech, that "two eras of civilization [were] wrestling with each other" and a new one, representing "internationalization and unification," was threatening the old. But a belief that war was an anachronism did not mean it could not happen. Von Suttner died on 21 June 1914, a week before the shots at Sarajevo and fortunately avoided seeing the collapse that she had struggled to prevent.

See also **Nobel, Alfred; Pacifism.**

BIBLIOGRAPHY

Primary Sources

von Suttner, Bertha. *Das Maschinenzeitalter. Zukunftsvorlesungen über unsere Zeit von "Jemand."* Zurich, 1891.

———. *Lay Down Your Arms.* Translated by T. H. Holmes. London, 1892. Reprint, New York, 1972.

———. *Gesammelte Schriften.* 12 vols. Dresden, 1906.

———. *Memoirs of Bertha von Suttner: The Records of an Eventful Life.* 2 vols. London, 1910. Reprint, New York, 1972.

———. *Der Kampf um die Vermeidung des Weltkrieges: Randglossen aus zwei Jahrzehnten zu den Zeitereignissen vor der Katastrophe (1892–1900 und 1907–1914).* 2 vols. Zurich, 1917.

Secondary Sources

Abrams, Irwin. "Bertha von Suttner and the Nobel Peace Prize." *Journal of Central European Affairs* 22, no. 3 (1962): 286–307.

Braker, Regina. *Weapons of Women Writers: Bertha von Suttner's* Die Waffen nieder! *as Political Literature in the Tradition of Harriet Beecher Stowe's* Uncle Tom's Cabin. New York, 1995.

Hamann, Brigitte. *Bertha von Suttner: A Life for Peace.* Translated by Ann Dubsky. Syracuse, N.Y., 1996.

Kempf, Beatrix. *Suffragette for Peace: The Life of Bertha von Suttner.* Translated by R. W. Last. London, 1972.

Playne, Caroline E. *Bertha von Suttner and the Struggle to Avert the World War.* London, 1936.

SANDI E. COOPER

SWEDEN AND NORWAY.

The Sweden that entered the nineteenth century stood ruled unevenly by a despotic king and four cowering medieval "estates" bodies representing the clergy, nobility, peasantry, and the burgher class. Designed for a society innocent of the steam engine, this arrangement would not last.

LIBERALISM

The estates system was turned almost completely on its head in 1809 because of Gustav IV Adolph (r. 1792–1809), whose belligerence had almost led to an invasion of Sweden by Russia and France. His gamble forced the writing of a new, liberal constitution. This "instrument of government" guaranteed freedom of the press, speech, and worship; to achieve as much, and more, it also introduced the ombudsman, an agent to police the nation's administration. Its statutes moreover stipulated that noblemen surrender their exclusive, hereditary claims to state careers. More ambitiously still, the constitution forced the crown to accept a compromise between legislative and executive authority: members of the Riksdag, or Parliament of Estates—still intact, indeed stronger than ever—now enjoyed the right to veto legislation and the budget. Should the need arise they could impeach the king's councilors and ministers.

One after another these rights and liberties were withdrawn, however, provoking fury but no rebellion. Eventually Lars Johan Hierta, founder in 1830 of the newspaper *Aftonbladet* came to lead the campaign against censorship—against the 1812 *indragningsmakt,* or right to seizure, that held the press in check. His daily suffered fines and probations for its outspoken stands on issues. But however severe and numerous, punishments had the effect of inspiring rather than inhibiting cries for change. The imprisonment in 1838 of the journalist Magnus Crusenstolpe provoked rioting and casualties, martyrs for the cause of *yttrandefrihet* (freedom of speech).

King Charles XV (r. 1859–1872) understood the need for democracy and recognized, too, that his career depended on it. He immediately allowed public worship for creeds other than Lutheranism: hence the emergence of Baptists, Methodists (headed by the Scotsman George Scott [1804–1874]), Pentecostals, and other sects, although dutiful religious conviction was by and large waning. On 22 June 1866 this sovereign, agreed to relinquish much of the extensive executive power granted him by the constitution, allowing the creation of a bicameral, partially elected parliament to meet annually. An upper house would guard the interests of old noble families, and a lower house was to serve the aspirations of prosperous farmers and increasingly those of professionals like doctors, lawyers, and teachers. Appointees to this assembly were to be chosen by men at least twenty-one years of age with reasonable incomes—a franchise comprising a quarter of the adult male population. (Women would have to wait until 1919 for their right to vote.) Not until years later, however, between the world wars, would this system of representation function effectively and without prejudice. Be that as it may, the crown could no longer dictate, but had to negotiate its authority. Baron Louis De Geer, whose counsel as minister of justice had led to

Gudbrandsdalen, Norway, c. 1880. Old and new forms of transportation are juxtaposed in the village street. ©Michael Maslan Historic Photographs/Corbis

the Riksdag's transformation, in 1876 became Sweden's first prime minister. In 1883 a commoner, Carl Thyselius, took the office.

Given the hold of socialism on twentieth-century Sweden, one might think that this ideology developed comparatively early and quickly there, but like republicanism and capitalism it did not—this despite the influence of the revolutions of 1848 in France and elsewhere, which brought riots to Stockholm. Only in 1889 did Hjalmar Branting establish the Social Democratic Labor Party. At that time no legislation of significance regulated labor conditions for either adults or children. And employers owed their employees neither health insurance nor retirement pensions. This state of affairs also motivated the creation of the Confederation of Trade Unions in 1898. These socialists and syndicalists would make a difference, helping for example to assure working women a month of leave after childbirth.

AGRARIAN AND INDUSTRIAL CHANGE

Agriculture in nineteenth-century Sweden was on the whole traditional, never becoming especially advanced either in technique or technology. Often living hand to mouth, isolated, and without education, peasants—over half of whom were landowners—did not all know about enclosing their fields or rotating crops. It took many years for iron plows and harrows, not to mention harvesters, to become widely employed. Scania (Skåne) was the exception: here, Rutger Maclean (1742–1816) of Svaneholm, focused on profitability, selected seed for cultivation and applied fertilizer in abundance. This region's fields, some reclaimed from marshes, were blessed with fertile soil and ample sunshine. By 1900, however, although the country's overall productivity remained low, advances such as selective animal breeding and centrifugal cream separators for making butter were being employed in some areas.

In the last quarter of the century Swedes suffered the effects of their shortage of production, especially as the population had grown, invigorated by peace, the potato, and vaccination against traditional diseases. During this period, marked by a series of long, cold winters, farmers' plots gave surprisingly meager yields. Consequently—and because the cereal market had become increasingly international and competitive—many people began trying to make a life elsewhere, particularly around the Great Lakes of the United States. To a degree such emigration had taken place in the decades before 1850, but this had been the result of religious discrimination. In the 1880s alone nearly a half-million emigrants, mainly the landless young, opted to leave their homes, nation, and continent behind. Vilhelm Moberg (1898–1973) portrayed one family's migration from Småland to Minnesota in four heart-wrenching books, all enduring, popular classics. The author spoke from experience, for many of his own relatives had left (and were to leave) Sweden for the promise of land to call their own.

Like Denmark and Germany, Sweden experienced industrial mechanization in the second half of the nineteenth century. Helped by the abolishment of guilds in 1846 and a maturing system of private, speculative investment, Sweden's equivalents to Britain's Manchester and Sheffield began to develop in Norrköping and Eskilstuna. These textile and steel manufacturing centers eventually created large and effective "economies of scale." The nation had long been successfully engaged in iron production, despite competition from Russia, exporting the bulk to Britain along with timber in return for coffee, sugar, tobacco, and coal. Yet the majority of Swedes continued to work the land: in 1850 some 90 percent of them lived in villages; a half-century later the proportion was smaller but not by a considerable amount.

Industries of this sort depended on an improved and expanded infrastructure. By 1900 railways were common, and in subsequent years Sweden would construct an intricate, efficient network. Igniting this "revolution" in transportation, a twelve-mile track between Örebro and Ervalla opened in 1856. Soon train service also linked Gothenburg with Jonsered, and Malmö with Lund. In each of these cases a combination of public and private monies funded research, development, and production. The nation was becoming one, a phenomenon speeded by the introduction of the telegraph and telephone in 1853 and 1880 respectively.

EDUCATION

Improvements in education likewise deepened a sense of nationhood, of sharing as citizens. By 1900 Swedes boasted rates of literacy that were the envy of Europe. Each parish, supervised by an elected, lay board, was required by the School Law of 1842 to teach its children proficiency in reading, writing, and arithmetic with the help of a trained, professional corps of teachers. In 1882 it was mandated that students stay in school between ages seven and fourteen.

Like primary schools, secondary institutions of learning grew in number during the nineteenth century. They increasingly emphasized a new "modern" curriculum at the expense of the old classical canon of Greco-Roman language and culture. Students who excelled at this level stood a chance of admission to the Universities of Lund and Uppsala or to either the Technological or Medical Institute of Stockholm, each of which would in time be granted university status.

ART AND SCIENCE

Sweden enjoyed a legacy of ambitious, original scholarship, especially in science. The botanist Carl Linneaus's 1735 *System of Nature,* a taxonomy of plants (and living things generally) by genera and species, guides research in the field to this day. The centigrade scale for measuring temperature, devised in 1742, was the work of the astronomer Anders Celsius. In the nineteenth century Jöns Berzelius and Svante Arrhenius added to this record of distinction: the former, in 1818, authored a comprehensive if erratic periodic chemical table; the latter, in 1889, introduced the concept of "activation energy," helping to explain the reactions of molecules. In the tradition of Carl Wilhelm Scheele (1742–1786), these chemists led a vanguard that also included physicists: Johannes Rydberg's (1854–1919) work on electromagnetic radiation gave rise to a formula, while Anders Jonas Ångström's (1814–1874) name still graces a unit of measurement used in spectroscopy. Although not Swedish by birth, the Russian mathematician

A canal in Stockholm c. 1900. The city of Stockholm is situated on the archipelago between the Baltic Sea and Lake Mälaren, with a series of canals and other waterways separating various parts of the city. Here, a platform constructed in a canal is being used to wash clothing and bedding. ©PHOTO COLLECTION ALEXANDER ALLAND, SR./CORBIS

Sofia Kovalevskaya merits mention. A specialist in partial differential equations and the geometry of rotating solid objects, in 1884 she was appointed professor at the University of Stockholm, earning a chair five years later. (At the time only two other women in Europe enjoyed such rank.) With a view toward promoting such achievement, Stockholm's Alfred Nobel (1833–1896), the inventor of dynamite, willed his fortune (partly earned from petroleum exploration in the Caspian Sea) to fund annual international awards beginning in 1901 for triumphs in science, medicine, literature, and peace.

As in science so in art: Selma Lagerlöf (1858–1940) of Mårbacka, Värmland, and Stockholm's August Strindberg (1849–1912) produced some of the nineteenth century's richest and most varied literature. A restless sort, Strindberg wrote plays in multiple genres: historical works such as *Charles XII* (*Karl XII*, 1902), on the king who for his aggressive, military ambition earned himself the soubriquet "Alexander of the North"; realistic works such as *Miss Julie* (*Fröken Julie*, 1888), about a Midsummer Night tryst between lady and servant; and symbolist or expressionist works such as *Easter* and *Dance of Death* (*Påsk*, 1901; *Dödsdansen*, 1900). Thus while Strindberg normally wrote about the world he knew through experience, in the tradition of Viktor Rydberg, he also on occasion explored the fantastic and bizarre. Yet in all these plays lurks Strindberg's own turmoil, which makes the drama convincing and grave. The son of a well-to-do but failing merchant family, he was married and divorced three times, having children with each wife. A combination of socialist and anarchist, he loathed the bourgeoisie for its insipidity and materialism, evident in his novel *The Red Room* (*Röda rummet*, 1879) and his history of *Swedish People at Work and Play* (*Svenska folket i helg och söcken*, 1881–1882). For a commentary he wrote on Jesus, Strindberg was tried for blasphemy.

In him there was something of the painter Ernst Josephson, not to mention the Norwegian Edvard Munch, whose *Scream* (1893) with its churning, cavernous Oslofjord, begs the question of whether existence precedes our essence.

Trained as a schoolteacher, Lagerlöf wrote with less doubt and more joy than Strindberg. There is imagination and humor à la Gustav Fröding (1860–1911) in her oeuvre: witness the signature fairy tale *The Wonderful Adventures of Nils* (*Nils Holgerssons underbara resa genom Sverige*, 1906–1907). Inspired by Rudyard Kipling, the book consists of witty, graphic lessons in geography—seen through the eyes of a mischievous, elfish teenager riding a goose through the sky. Generally the book teaches love of nature, specifically an appreciation of Sweden's varied terrain and climate. While typically amusing and never caustic, Lagerlöf—who spent much of her life with a woman, Sophie Elkan (1853–1921)—also wrote critically. In *The Story of Gösta Berling* (*Gösta Berlings saga*, 1891), a novel about her home province, she explores the ruination of an estate by a dozen reckless cavaliers, outsiders without either feeling or respect for the land: ultimately a benign, knowledgeable countess (played by Greta Garbo in Mauritz Stiller's 1924 film adaptation) sets them straight, teaching their leader a lesson in responsibility.

Within the work of both Lagerlöf and Strindberg there is manifestly a touch of Esaias Tegnér's (1782–1846) "nationalism." The poet and bishop based much of his poetry on Old Norse legend, trumpeting Scandinavia's primacy—as did artists in all fields, music included. What the composer Edvard Grieg of Bergen, Norway, loved above all, however international his training in Leipzig, was the vernacular of the folk song. He cherished its history and melodious, narrative aspect, as evidenced in "Morning Mood" and "Mountain King" from his 1876 score for *Peer Gynt* (1867) by the playwright Henrik Ibsen. The play centers on an antihero and his transformation from an innocent youth of imagination to a worldly adult—a womanizer, thief, and slave trader—confused by his own ambition and hypocrisy. Its story actually suggests why nineteenth-century musicians, writers, and others found themselves inspired by national and local traditions. Memories of an allegedly simpler and ordered way of life

Emigrants leaving from Göteborg c. 1905. A ship carrying Swedish emigrants bound for North America prepares to leave the wharf in Göteborg. As with other parts of Europe, population pressures, poor agricultural conditions, and political unrest led large numbers of Scandinavians to emigrate during the period from 1840 to about 1910. ©CORBIS

offered refuge from a century that threatened to become the property of larger, global forces of change, symbolized by the locomotive.

THE UNION

The "union of Sweden and Norway, formed in 1814, ended on 7 June 1905. As of that date the houses of Bernadotte (King Oscar II; r. 1872–1907) and Oldenburg (King Håkon VII; r. 1905–1957) stood as equals—as separate constitutional monarchies. Sweden had acquired Norway from Denmark, as penalty for its defense of Napoleon I (r. 1804–1814/15). Norway, which protested the agreement, threatening war, eventually won considerable autonomy from Sweden. The king of Sweden enjoyed not an absolute but a suspensive veto on legislation passed by the parliament (Storting) in Oslo. Yet aware of how liberty was maturing elsewhere and roused by the nationalist Bjørnstjerne Bjørnson (1832–1910), Norwegians increasingly wanted their nation to themselves. Tempers began flaring over the appointment of a liaison between "master" and "subject" governments: Whose pre-

E U R O P E   1 7 8 9   T O   1 9 1 4

2287

rogative was it to select him? Soon too the dispute concerned Norway's wish to represent itself abroad, independently of Sweden. Without Norway and Finland, which had been lost to Russia in a series of battles in 1808–1809, Sweden could no longer, claim to be a *stormakt,* or "great power."

See also **Denmark; French Revolutionary Wars and Napoleonic Wars; Finland and the Baltic Provinces; Russia.**

BIBLIOGRAPHY

Barton, H. Arnold. *Sweden and Visions of Norway: Politics and Culture, 1814–1905.* Carbondale, Ill., 2003.

Derry, T. K. *A History of Modern Norway, 1814–1972.* Oxford, U.K., 1973.

Oakley, Stewart P. *A Short History of Sweden.* New York, 1966.

Stråth, Bo. *Union och demokrati: De förenade rikena Sverige-Norge, 1814–1905.* Stockholm, 2005.

JOHAN ÅHR

SWITZERLAND. In 1789 Switzerland was a loose confederation of small valleys—some independent, some not—and sovereign cities with surrounding territories. They called themselves "Republics" but not in the same sense that the word *republic* has in the early twenty-first century. For example, the Republic of Geneva was an aristocratic oligarchy of wealthy families, corrupt and undemocratic but, by the standards of eighteenth century Europe, "free." Independent, Protestant, and French-speaking, it published texts forbidden in Catholic France. Only a quarter of the population were "citizens" with full rights. The rest were either *habitants* (inhabitants) or *natifs* (native-born but without rights). All Swiss cities had similar constitutions.

At the eastern end of the sprawling confederation was Graubünden (the Gray Leagues), composed of several hundred sovereign village communities, which debated foreign and domestic affairs in village assemblies. South of the Alps lay the territories of Italian-speaking Switzerland around the valley of the river Ticino. Ticino before 1789 was a subject territory of the thirteen cantons of the so-called Old Confederation. In 1796, the Bern aristocrat Karl-Viktor von Bonstetten reported that Ticino suffered from bad government and that "in no corner of Europe, no matter how dismal, has torture raged so wildly as in Italian Switzerland," (Bonstetten, p. 140).

The European Romantics saw none of that. Nikolai Karamzin, in his *Letters of a Russian Traveler, 1789–1790,* expressed the early Romantic vision of Switzerland as a picturesque paradise: "What views! What scenes! . . . Happy Swiss! Dwelling in sweet nature's embrace, under beneficent laws of brotherly union, with simple ways, serving God." (Ely, p. 49). Switzerland, with its mountains and sturdy peasants, became a symbol of the perfect society. Friedrich Schiller's drama *Wilhelm Tell* (1804) immortalized this image of Swiss liberty, and Gioachino Rossini (1792–1868) turned the Schiller play into an opera, *Guillaume Tell* (1829), first performed in Paris on 3 August 1829. The Tell story has no historic basis but it became the "foundation myth" of modern Switzerland.

THE FRENCH REVOLUTION AND NAPOLEONIC ERA

In reality, Swiss peasants were far from "free." On 25 January 1798, French revolutionary troops crossed the borders of the Old Confederation to liberate them. The French imposed uniformity and centralization on a patchwork of ancient sovereignties. On 12 April 1798, "the One and Indivisible Helvetic Republic" was proclaimed. The Swiss were to be one people, in one unified state, governed from the center. The mountain communities of central Switzerland, however, refused. In September 1798, the tiny villages of Nidwald rose in revolt, proclaiming their ancient Catholic faith, their historic rights, and their hatred of new taxes imposed by what they saw as a puppet regime. By 1802 the protests had spread so widely that Napoleon had to intervene. On 19 February 1803, he imposed a modern, federal constitution on Switzerland, which restored the historic cantons but raised the former subject territories to full statehood.

The end of the Napoleonic Empire forced Switzerland to reorganize again. On 7 August 1815, the Swiss cantons (the name for the states in Swiss federalism) agreed on a new federal treaty.

Open-air assembly near Altdorf, Canton of Uri, Switzerland. Citizens gather to discuss public policy in this late-nineteenth-century photograph. ©Hulton-Deutsch Collection/Corbis

There were now twenty-two sovereign states in the confederation, but they differed in their political systems: nine cities (Bern, Lucerne, Freiburg, Solothurn, Schaffhausen, Zurich, Basel, Neuchâtel, and Geneva) had old-fashioned patrician or guild constitutions; eight mountain cantons (Uri, Schwyz, Obwald, Nidwald, Glarus, Zug, Appenzell Inner Rhodes, and Appenzell Outer Rhodes) had traditional communal systems in which the adult males met in the open air to vote on the laws; and five former subject territories (Aargau, Thurgau, Vaud, St. Gall, and Ticino) had modern representative, democratic constitutions. There was no central government, but a con-federal diet at which the cantons legislated for the confederation. At the Congress of Vienna in March 1815, the victorious Great Powers declared that the perpetual neutrality of Switzerland served the interests of Europe, and from that time on the Swiss Confederation has remained absolutely neutral.

1815 TO 1848
During the years 1815 to 1848, conservative regimes in Europe tried to suppress any hint of revolution. Switzerland with its "republics" posed a permanent threat to the reactionary system of European politics. Its various small states gave sanctuary to dangerous radicals, and its domestic radicals staged local revolutions. Prince Clemens von Metternich, the architect of European reaction, hated Switzerland. In 1845 he wrote, "Switzerland presents the most perfect image of a state in the process of social disintegration.... Switzerland stands alone today in Europe as a republic and serves troublemakers of every sort as a free haven," (Steinberg, p. 6).

The prince was particularly appalled by anti-Jesuit riots and by attacks on the Catholic Church. In 1841 the parliament in Protestant Aargau abolished monasteries and cloisters. Catholic Lucerne responded by entrusting the school system to the Jesuits, a provocative demonstration, which infuriated liberals in neighboring Aargau and Bern, who organized guerilla bands to try to overthrow the Lucerne conservative government. By 1847, civil war had broken out. A group of Catholic cantons formed a *Sonderbund* (special alliance), in violation of the federal constitution. The central government suppressed it by armed force. The fighting in the civil war lasted for twenty-six days and cost 150 soldiers on both sides their lives. The liberal victory outraged Metternich, and he would undoubtedly have intervened had revolution not broken out in 1848 all over Europe. He fled Vienna on 13 March 1848, and the Age of Metternich was over.

While European cities from Palermo to Warsaw saw violence and revolution, the Swiss transformed their constitution after their civil war into an American-style federal government. The U.S. Constitution of 1787 differed fundamentally from the Swiss Constitution of 1848 in two respects: the American system came from above, designed by the upper classes to protect their privileges and to maintain order against threats from below. The Swiss system grew from the bottom up and its main goal was to protect the rights of the sovereign communities. An American gets his or her citizenship from the U.S. government; a Swiss gets such rights from his or her "community of origin." The second difference lies in the peculiar Swiss dislike of one-person executives. At every level of Swiss government there are councils: communal councils, cantonal councils, and even a federal executive council. Thus the Swiss president is actually a committee (Federal Council) of seven persons elected not by the people but by the upper and lower houses of parliament meeting in joint session.

ECONOMIC DEVELOPMENT IN THE NINETEENTH CENTURY

Switzerland entered a more peaceful period in the nineteenth century, helped by the great economic boom between 1850 and 1873. From the early middle ages on, the Swiss were dedicated to commerce. In the late eighteenth century, the tiny city-republic of St. Gall (total population under eight thousand) had sixty substantial mercantile houses dealing in cotton, muslin, and embroidery. About one hundred thousand spinners, weavers, calico printers, and embroiderers worked for city companies on spinning wheels in their peasant cottages. In the 1850s and 1860s, railroads, water power, and machinery transformed Swiss manufacturing. By the 1880s, Basel, with 60,550 inhabitants, had become the richest city in Switzerland, the capital of a new industrial chemical industry. Watchmaking spread in French-speaking western Switzerland. Zurich specialized in cotton; St. Gall in embroidery. Throughout the nineteenth century, Switzerland was one-fifth richer than Belgium, France, and the Low Countries and was second only to the United Kingdom in gross national product per head. The *Nationalzeitung* described Basel as a place where "money is the surrogate for talent, diligence, honor, virtue." The same could have been said of every Swiss city.

On the eve of World War I, Switzerland was enjoying the fruits of a sustained economic boom. Population doubled between 1800 and 1910. The new, larger population had abandoned the small communities for the great cities. In 1850, only 6 percent of the Swiss lived in towns with more than ten thousand inhabitants; by 1914, 26 percent. By 1914, imports amounted to 1.92 million Swiss francs, or 46 percent of the net national product, and exports at 1.38 million Swiss francs represented 33 percent, a level of dependence on the international economy not reached again until the 1950s. Textiles made up 48 percent of exports in the years 1912 to 1913. Working wages were roughly twice as high in 1910 as they had been in 1875. The flourishing economy attracted foreign workers, a problem that reappeared after 1945. In 1914, 17 percent of the inhabitants of Switzerland were "foreign." The Federal Office of Statistics (FOS) calculated the number of foreigners in 1910 at approximately 552,000. It took fifty years to reach that level again.

DEMOCRATIZATION AND THE CONSTITUTION OF 1874

During the 1860s and 1870s, the new wealth, the new poverty, and the emergence of a new industrial working class led to demands for more rights. The

Liberals who made the settlement of 1848 were no democrats. They thought that persons without property had no independence and hence would degenerate into a mob. To their left, a radical movement grew up, and to their right, Catholics began to consider universal suffrage. Philipp Anton von Segesser (1817–1888), a Catholic nobleman from Lucerne, put it this way: "we of the conservative camp must put ourselves onto an entirely democratic basis. After the collapse of the old conditions nothing else can provide us with a future and a justification except pure democracy." Swiss politics moved toward ever more direct participation, which meant not just universal suffrage but popular referenda and initiatives (i.e., in which citizens propose legislation to parliament). As always, the cantons acted first. In December 1867, the radicals in Zurich succeeded in calling a constitutional convention, which gave the canton a new democratic constitution. It provided for direct election of all officials and agencies, the right to introduce legislation by popular initiative, and laws to protect workers. The movement spread, and on 19 April 1874, the Swiss approved a new constitution that included a provision for initiatives on national legislation and that strengthened the central government at the expense of the cantons. In 1891, Dr. Joseph Zemp, a Catholic from Lucerne, became the first Roman Catholic member of the Federal Council, the collective presidency. Old wounds from the religious wars had begun to heal.

SWITZERLAND ON THE EVE OF WORLD WAR I

By 1914, Switzerland had assumed its modern form: the home of a unique direct democracy, where local communities remained as important as the federal state, where parties shared power in collective, multi-party stability, and where every adult male served in the militia army and the country maintained armed neutrality. Tourists had replaced the Romantic poets; wealthy visitors enjoyed spectacular scenery and expensive hotels and bought Swiss watches, chocolate, and fine cutlery. Linguistic divisions remained a potential source of friction. Of the total population in 1910 of 3,375,300, the FOS calculated that 72.7 percent spoke German, 22.1 percent French, 3.9 percent Italian, and 1.2 percent Rhaeto-Romansch. World War I between Imperial Germany and the Third French Republic threw comfortable, stable Switzerland into a crisis. Suddenly, the Swiss divided across a linguistic line called the *Graben* (trench) between German speakers and French speakers, a division that continues to plague Swiss daily life into the twenty-first century.

The "long nineteenth century" had transformed the Helvetic Confederation, but it had preserved its peculiar variant of political liberty: "Swiss liberty," which expressed an idea of democracy from the bottom up. At the same time, this democracy represented groups more so than individuals. Neither the constitution of 1848 nor that of 1874 contained an American-style Bill of Rights. Switzerland in 1910 had a number of *enclaves* and *exclaves,* bits of territory that belong to one canton but that remain obstinately lodged in the territory of another, or bits of foreign states surrounded by Swiss territory. This oddity, the last remnant of the old Holy Roman Empire from which Switzerland emerged, guarantees the sovereignty and wishes of often very tiny communities. The passage from the Old Regime to modern society protected the rights of small communities to be different. It took seventy-one years, 1798 to 1869, for Canton Ticino to introduce the metric system. Nothing could be more Swiss than that.

See also **France; Germany; Italy.**

BIBLIOGRAPHY

Bonstetten, Karl Viktor von. *Lettere sopra i baliaggi italiani.* Locarno, 1984.

Bouvier, Nicolas, Gordon A. Craig, and Lionel Gossman. *Geneva, Zurich, Basel: History, Culture, and National Identity.* Princeton, N.J., 1994.

Ely, Christopher. *This Meager Nature: Landscape and National Identity in Imperial Russia.* Dekalb, Ill., 2002.

Gossman, Lionel. *Basel in the Age of Burckhardt: A Study in Unseasonable Ideas.* Chicago, 2000.

McPhee, John. *La Place de la Concorde Suisse.* New York, 1994.

Steinberg, Jonathan. *Why Switzerland?* Cambridge, U.K., 1996.

Zimmer, Oliver. *A Contested Nation. History, Memory and Nationalism in Switzerland, 1761–1891.* Cambridge, U.K., 2003.

JONATHAN STEINBERG

SYMBOLISM.

SYMBOLISM. Symbolism was an interdisciplinary movement in literature, art, music, and theater at the fin de siècle. The term *symbolism* is something of a misnomer, for it suggests that concrete images represented specific messages. On the contrary, symbolists often used words, images, or sounds in ways that were intentionally open ended and evocative. To avoid precision and a sense of deliberation in their work, symbolists experimented with innovative form. Poets used free verse as opposed to rhyme; artists either avoided naturalistic imagery, experimenting with line and color to stimulate emotions, or subverted naturalism by using it to create bizarre scenes and creatures that the senses have difficulty grasping. Symbolists were interested in the validity of the *au-delà* (the beyond): that which lies beyond the superficial appearance of things in the natural world. Lines from the poem "Correspondance" (1857) by Charles Baudelaire exemplified the connection between nature and the soul: "Nature is a temple of living pillars / where often words emerge, confused and dim / and man goes through this forest, with / familiar eyes of symbols always watching him."

ORIGINS AND CONTEXT

Symbolism was a movement of individuals who cultivated unique approaches and therefore has no unified stylistic tendency such as one might find, for example, in naturalism in literature or impressionism in art. Its beginning and end dates are imprecise. In literature, Baudelaire, Stéphane Mallarmé, Paul Verlaine, and Arthur Rimbaud are variously treated as precursors or "masters"; the same is true in art of Puvis de Chavannes, Gustave Moreau, Arnold Böcklin, and Dante Gabriel Rosetti. These artists of a slightly older generation were all active in the third quarter of the nineteenth century and in many ways continued the experiments of the Romantics of the first half of that century. Symbolism was built on the foundations of Romanticism, with its cult of the individual and its emphasis on the primacy of the imagination. Symbolism is generally thought of as a reaction against naturalism, a movement that had greater visibility in the third quarter of the nineteenth century than did late Romanticism. Naturalists such as the artist Jules Bastien-Lepage or the writer Émile Zola wished to express the details of contemporary life, especially among the poor. Many of them were influenced by a popular enthusiasm for science in the 1870s and 1880s; thus, these artists and writers were concerned with the relationship of the human figure to the natural world, including its environmental and hereditary circumstances. In an apparent paradox, Zola, along with other naturalists, believed that the way an artist depicted subject matter was influenced by his unique temperament; therefore, imagery contained subjective aspects that were tied to the life of the artist. This understanding of subjectivity drew on scientific inroads into the study of the unconscious in the nineteenth century.

Both in foregrounding subjectivity and in their concern with socially specific themes such as prostitution, disease, and the degrading aspects of the industrial present, symbolists shared many concerns with naturalists, although their treatment of them was less literal. A number of symbolists were consciously inspired by the science of their time; for them it confirmed the essential importance of the vital energies of the invisible. Impressionism, which was related to naturalism and concurrent with symbolism although peaking slightly earlier (c. 1875), was a form of naturalism that also emphasized the individual's response to subject matter: the optical and psychological sensation produced by a given scene upon one's vision and temperament. Impressionism and the neo-impressionist technique of Georges Seurat, with its exploration of physiological responses to line and color advocated by the aesthetician Charles Henri, were considered symbolist by critics of the movement. Further, the static form and quasi-geometric shapes found in neo-impressionist painting can be linked to a Platonic current within symbolism: the notion that the world that lies beyond appearances is one of ideals.

FROM DECADENCE TO SYMBOLISM

In the 1880s, naturalism began to be superseded by Decadence; an approach that is considered part of symbolism in the visual arts although treated as a separate manifestation in literature. Decadent work, such as the writing of Joris-Karl Huysmans, was fatalistic and morbid, filled with images of decay and dreadful sexuality, personified by the

Stephane Mallarmé. Painting by Edouard Manet, 1876. MUSÉE D'ORSAY, PARIS, FRANCE/BRIDGEMAN ART LIBRARY/LAUROS/GIRAUDON

femme fatale (fatal woman). Baudelaire's *Les Fleurs du mal* (1857; *Flowers of Evil*) and the writings of Edgar Allan Poe were precursors of these tendencies. The symbolist artists Gustav Klimt in Austria, Franz von Stuck in Germany, and Felicien Rops in Belgium and the graphic artist Aubrey Beardsley in Belgium all depicted the divisive and powerful women. The nascent feminist movement and fear of contracting syphilis from prostitutes were behind the iconic presence of such women in the art of the late nineteenth century. The antithesis of this symbol of division between the sexes was another symbolist trope: the androgyne represented the resolution of male and female into a harmonious entity.

Among the symbolist artists rooted in Decadence were the French artist Odilon Redon, who created morbid and fantastic works as early as the late 1870s, and the Norwegian Edward Munch. Munch had originally been a naturalist, concerned with themes of illness and death. In 1889 he visited Paris and discovered Decadent and symbolist poetry. His symbolist subject matter became intensely personal as he explored the dark human emotions of jealousy and despair, along with various neuroses. Like many symbolists, he believed his imagery to be informed by recent developments in science and, therefore, although not literal, to have a basis in truth. Like the German scientist Ernst Haeckel who advocated this doctrine, Munch was a monist, believing in a life force that pervaded all matter; death was but part of the transformation of energy that unified all of nature. He was also fascinated by the psychology of sexuality. Munch used these ideas to develop a series of twenty-two paintings between 1892 and 1902, originally titled *Love* and later called *The Frieze of Life*. In 1902, as the result of the termination of a traumatic relationship, Munch was shot but survived and experienced a series of breakdowns. What Munch identified as a "nerve crisis" exemplifies a kind of Romantic suffering shared by many of the symbolists. Whereas artists and writers of the Romantic generation were identified as melancholics, supposedly afflicted by a disordered temperament, those of the late nineteenth century were often thought of as neurasthenics, a pseudo-scientific disease of the time believed to be caused by stress to the nervous system, in their case through the hyperactivity of creative thought.

SYMBOLISM IN LITERATURE AND ART

Symbolism as a literary movement was first defined in 1886 in a manifesto, "Le Symbolisme," published by the symbolist writer Jean Moréas in *Le Figaro*. "Symbolist poetry," Moréas wrote, "attempts to clothe the Idea in a perceptible form." Among the symbolists who expressed the intangible and otherworldly through their imagery were Francis Vielé-Griffin, Stuart Merrill, Laurent Tailhade, Gustave Kahn, Jules Laforgue, Henri de Régnier, and René Ghil. In that same year, Mallarmé published his definition of symbolist poetry. Symbolism in the visual arts was defined by Albert Aurier in 1892 as "the painting of ideas." One year earlier, Aurier had already identified the painters Paul Gauguin and Vincent Van Gogh as symbolists. In the early twenty-first century Van Gogh is more commonly identified as an expressive naturalist, but Gauguin is still recognized as a leading symbolist. Gauguin began painting religious folk scenes in 1888, using what he termed a synthetist style. Synthetism refers both to the notion of combining memory and imagination in the selection of imagery and to formal issues, namely the use of flat planes of expressive non-naturalistic color and simplified form. In that same year, Mallarmé translated James Abbott McNeill Whistler's lecture, "Ten O'Clock," into French. Whistler was part of a movement in English art called aestheticism, which advocated artistic freedom over the reality of nature; it emphasized the importance of color and line as abstract arrangements or patterns that could stir the emotions in the way music could, and it may have influenced Gauguin and the synthetists; Whistler became identified by many in the circle of writers and artists around Mallarmé as a symbolist. Like Whistler, Gauguin and other symbolists found affinities for their explorations in music.

A virtual cult formed around the late Romantic composer Richard Wagner; many symbolist poets contributed to the journal *Revue Wagnérienne*, founded in 1885. Wagner emphasized sensation, emotion, and thought experienced as a totality. He established the influential concept of *Gesamtkunstwerk*, the ideal of unifying all the arts—music, poetry, painting, and architecture—into one synaesthetic experience. In 1889, Paul Sérusier inscribed Wagner's credo on the walls of an inn in southwestern France, which had just been decorated from ceiling to floor with paintings done in synthetist style by Gauguin and his followers. In the 1890s, a group of French symbolists called the nabis (prophets) appropriated synthetism in their depiction of religious or urban bourgeois subject matter, often with disturbing overtones related to contemporary psychology. They too would use this style in unified decorative schemes, including theatrical set designs. In 1890, the nabi theorist Maurice Denis defined a painting as "a flat surface covered with colors assembled in a certain order" (Denis, p. 540). Gauguin believed that the directness of synthetist style could be linked to similarities in the visual cultures of folk, tribal, and non-Western populations. He spent ten years in Tahiti and the Marquesas cultivating his self-identification as a "primitive" painter. The abstract tendencies inherent within synthetism would open the way to the early-twentieth-century abstraction of Wassily Kandinsky, Piet Mondrian, František Kupka, and Kazimir Malevich, all of whom were symbolists in their early years.

IRRATIONAL ASPECTS OF THE MIND

By the 1890s, the ideational realm of mysticism, religion, and the occult increasingly came to the fore among symbolists, reflecting a virtual religious revival in European culture. As divorced from material reality as such tendencies seem to be, many sought to reconcile scientific truths with the spiritual realm. The practice of hypnosis by psychologists seemed to validate psychic experience. Scientific confirmation of other irrational aspects of the mind, such as dreams or visions, also inspired the symbolists. The most influential occult doctrine, theosophy, made use of ideas that combined Eastern and Western religions with Darwinian evolution.

France led in the development of symbolism, but Belgium was another important early center. Many Belgian artists were represented at the Salons of the Rose + Cross, organized in Paris by Joséphin Péladan between 1892 and 1897. The artists who exhibited there painted in a traditional illusionistic style that emphasized the spiritual. Péladan requested submissions that evoked "the Catholic Ideal and Mysticism ... Legend, Myth, Allegory, the Dream, the Paraphrase of great poetry" (Péladan, pp. 33–34). Myth and legend were appreciated by the symbolists for their evocative potential. Péladan's example was followed in Brussels in the Salon d'Art Idéaliste. Belgium was also an important early center for symbolist poetry: both Émile Verhaeren and Albrecht Rodenbach worked here.

Avant-garde exhibiting societies were central to the spread of symbolism. Among them was the influential Brussels art society Les XX (1883–1893), which included many symbolists. In 1897 the Vienna Secession society built its own exhibition building and held twenty-three exhibitions between 1898 and 1905. The most famous of these was the Beethoven exhibition of 1902, which included decorative murals by Gustave Klimt. Other avant-garde secession movements, many of which favored the symbolists, quickly followed in Berlin, Munich, Dresden, Leipzig, Prague, and Krakow. Symbolist drama spread internationally as well and included productions at Paul Fort's Théâtre d'Art in France and the plays of Maurice Maeterlinck in Belgium and Henrik Ibsen in Norway.

By the first decade of the twentieth century, symbolism was already on the wane, to be replaced in art by experimental abstraction and a renewed emphasis on expressive figuration just before World War I. This late period was an eclectic one in literature; André Gide is an example of a former symbolist who turned toward sensual, lush, life-affirming themes that were part of the naturist movement. Yet symbolist tendencies were not yet over. The surrealist movement, which emerged after World War I, borrowed many ideas from the symbolists regarding the importance of dreams, the unconscious, and the evocative potential of imprecise or unexpected imagery.

See also **Fin de Siècle; Painting.**

BIBLIOGRAPHY

Burhan, Filiz Eda. *Vision and Visionaries: Nineteenth-Century Psychological Theory, the Occult Sciences and the Formation of a Symbolist Aesthetic in France.* Princeton, N.J., 1979.

Denis, Maurice. "Définition des néo-traditionisme." *Art et critique,* 12 August 1890, 540–542; and 30 August 1890, 556–558.

Dorra, Henri, ed. *Symbolist Art Theories: A Critical Anthology.* Berkeley, Calif., 1994.

Dowling, Linda C. *Language and Decadence in the Victorian Fin de Siecle.* Princeton, N.J., 1986.

Genova, Pamela Antonia. *Symbolist Journals: A Culture of Correspondence.* Burlington, Vt., 2002.

Gilman, Richard. *Decadence: The Strange Life of an Epithet.* New York, 1979.

Goldwater, Robert. *Symbolism.* New York, 1979.

Heller, Reinhold. *Munch: His Life and Work.* Chicago, 1984.

Henderson, Linda D. "Mysticism and Occultism." *Art Journal* 46 (1987): entire issue.

Hirsch, S., ed. "Symbolist Art and Literature." *Art Journal* 45 (1985): entire issue.

Lehman, A. G. *The Symbolist Aesthetic in France, 1885–1895.* Revised ed. Oxford, U.K., 1968.

Mathews, Patricia. *Passionate Discontent: Creativity, Gender and French Symbolist Art.* Chicago, 1999.

McIntosh, Christopher. *Eliphas Lévi and the French Occult Revival.* London, 1972.

Moréas, Jean. "Le Symbolisme." *Le Figaro* (18 September 1886).

Péladan, Joséphin. *Salon de la Rose + Cross, Rigle et Monitoire.* Paris, 1981.

Schorske, Carl E. *Fin-de-siècle Vienna: Politics and Culture.* New York, 1981.

Scott, David H. *Pictorialist Poetics: Poetry and the Visual Arts in 19th Century France.* Cambridge, U.K., 1988.

Shiff, Richard. *Cezanne and the End of Impressionism: A Study of the Theory, Technique, and Critical Evaluation of Modern Art.* Chicago, 1984.

BARBARA LARSON

SYMONDS, JOHN ADDINGTON

(1840–1893), English critic, historian, and poet.

From a contemporary perspective, the Victorian man of letters John Addington Symonds, best known for his monumental *Renaissance in Italy* (7 vols., 1875–1886), is chiefly distinguished as one of Western society's first gay militants. Homosexuality remained officially "unspeakable" throughout Symonds's life (unless mentioned in defamatory contexts). But, unlike even the near-transparent homosexual writers before him (e.g., Walt Whitman), from early in his career Symonds worked consciously to combat his culture's denial of homosexuality, striving to "speak" its presence—in himself, his society, and earlier history—to as large an audience as possible within the constraints of his time.

Symonds's emancipatory work took place in the midst of the double life typical of most homosexuals before the modern liberation movement. Outwardly a husband, father, and conventionally successful author, he privately struggled with his same-sex feelings and ultimately acquired a series of never entirely reciprocating male lovers. Writing became Symonds's primary means of understanding and communicating his homosexual concerns, in two ways. In his public work, Symonds often undertook subjects that allowed him to allude to homosexuality and sometimes directly represent it, from his early *Studies of the Greek Poets: Second Series* (1876) to his late *Walt Whitman: A Study* (1893). Symonds similarly played a crucial role in furthering frankness about Michelangelo, whose homosexual poems had been published accurately for the first time in 1863 after centuries of censorship. Symonds published a faithful English translation of Michelangelo's love poems to Tommaso Cavalieri in 1878 and discussed the subject relatively daringly in his bestselling 1893 biography of the artist.

Given the enforced social silencing of homosexuality in his time, however, Symonds's most assertive work inevitably remained private. From the early 1870s on he produced an unprecedented set of homosexual writings (including some of the frankest Victorian homosexual poetry) that were commercially unpublishable but that he determinedly issued as private pamphlets for circulation to interested others. Most influential were what were understood at the time to be the first polemical essays in defense of homosexuality in English (similar earlier work by Jeremy Bentham was still unknown): *A Problem in Greek Ethics* (written 1873, privately printed in 1883), and *A Problem in Modern Ethics* (1891), which focuses on later history and the new sexology and urges legal reform. The circulation of the latter especially helped create a confidential network of informed homosexuals in the 1890s who regarded Symonds as a liberationist leader, "the Gladstone of the affair," as the novelist Henry James, one affiliate, dubbed him in a 7 January 1893 letter.

The increasingly "open secret" of Symonds's activism led Havelock Ellis (1859–1939) to invite him to collaborate on *Sexual Inversion* (1897), the first published volume of what became *Studies in the Psychology of Sex*. Symonds died before the book's appearance, and his scandalized family had his name removed as coauthor after the first printing, but *A Problem in Greek Ethics* appeared in public for the first time as "Appendix A" and most of the book's male homosexual "cases" came from Symonds's sizable correspondence in response to *A Problem in Modern Ethics*. Symonds's major achievements of this kind, however, remained known to only a few acquaintances, though he left arrangements for their posthumous publication. These were his many letters to other homosexuals (including Sir Edmund Gosse, Edward Carpenter, and a skittish Whitman), the first surviving examples in history of extensive and candid homosexual correspondence, and his singular *Memoirs* (composed between 1889 and 1893 but not published until 1984), the first known homosexual autobiography and required reading for everyone interested in the history of sexuality.

Symonds's accomplishment must ultimately be seen in relation to the similar work of other nineteenth-century European homosexual thinkers, particularly Heinrich Hössli and Karl Heinrich Ulrichs. Furthermore, Symonds's liberation should not be overstated. He had inherited—particularly from his father, a respected and powerful Bristol physician who epitomized Victorian rectitude—the full panoply of official Victorian ideals, like "purity of conduct" and "respect for social law" (Symonds, 1984, pp. 127, 283), and he was never able to free himself completely from his culture's damning views; at one point in his *Memoirs,* for instance, Symonds calls his homosexuality a "besetting vice" (p. 283). Still, prompted by the new openings for homosexual expressiveness created by the individualist strains in Enlightenment and Romantic thought, Symonds persisted as no one before him in crafting a body of emancipatory homosexual writings aimed purposefully at "men constituted like me, [to] put on record the facts … so that [they] should feel that they are not alone" (pp. 266, 182–183). His achievement is all the more remarkable given the more openly menacing period in which he worked: 1885, just four years before Symonds began his *Memoirs,* saw the passage of the so-called Labouchere Amendment to the Criminal Law Amendments Act, whose new category of "gross indecency between men" made it easier to prosecute male homosexuals than ever before, and in 1895, two years after Symonds's death, Oscar Wilde (1854–1900) was convicted under the act and given the maximum sentence of two years at hard labor.

Symonds's work is further significant for the light it sheds on current issues in the new field of gay studies. For instance, in terms of the debate between "essentialists" and "constructionists" (i.e., between those who hold that sexual orientation is something "essential" to the person, constitutional and fundamentally unchangeable, and those who view it as a "cultural construction" and a personal choice assumed at will), Symonds is clearly the former. In his *Memoirs,* he reveals himself as attracted to other males from his earliest erotic recollections and as failing to "convert" to heterosexuality despite rigorous efforts. Furthermore, Symonds's flickerings of self-knowledge come not from the late-nineteenth-century sexology to which "constructionists" largely attribute the "modern invention" of homosexuality (a historical impossibility, since that field that did not

even exist in Symonds's youth) but from literature, particularly his readings of Plato, Renaissance poetry, and Whitman. Relatedly, though Symonds was familiar with the new sexological literature by the time he was writing his *Memoirs,* he uses its scientist terminology ("inversion," "homosexuality") reluctantly and sparingly in the text. Instead, Symonds's favorite terms for his orientation there are either earlier, affective, categorical language like "masculine love" (p. 99), or terminology derived from classical culture (e.g., "Greek love," p. 102), or extended descriptive phrases in everyday language that amount to de facto denotations of the subject, like "passion between males" or "a man's love for a man" (pp. 101, 266).

See also **Ellis, Havelock; Homosexuality and Lesbianism.**

BIBLIOGRAPHY

Primary Sources

James, Henry. *Henry James Letters.* 3 vols. Edited by Leon Edel. Cambridge, Mass., 1974–1984.

Ellis, Havelock, and John Addington Symonds. *Sexual Inversion.* London, 1897. Reprint, New York, 1975.

Schueller, Herbert M., and Robert L. Peters, eds. *The Letters of John Addington Symonds.* 3 vols. Detroit, Mich., 1967–1969.

Symonds, John Addington. *Memoirs.* Edited by Phyllis Grosskurth. New York, 1984.

Secondary Sources

Cady, Joseph. "'What Cannot Be': John Addington Symonds's *Memoirs* and Official Mappings of Victorian Homosexuality." *Victorian Newsletter* 81 (spring 1992): 47–51.

———. "John Addington Symonds." In *The Gay and Lesbian Literary Heritage,* edited by Claude J. Summers. New York, 1995.

Grosskurth, Phyllis. *The Woeful Victorian: A Biography of John Addington Symonds.* New York, 1964.

Robinson, Paul. *Gay Lives: Homosexual Autobiography from John Addington Symonds to Paul Monette.* Chicago, 1999.

JOSEPH CADY

SYNDICALISM. Syndicalism was a movement at the confluence of anarchism and early trade unionism. The term *syndicalism* comes from the

French *syndicalisme,* from *syndicat,* the common term for any group seeking to defend common interests. *Syndicat* came to mean "trade union," while *syndicalisme* came to mean the belief that workers could, through their unions, eschew socialist parties and electoral politics, defend and improve their conditions, gradually build their numbers, and eventually overthrow capitalism, replacing capitalist ownership with worker control through their own union organizations. The primary impulse for the ideology of syndicalism came from anarchists. Those hostile to syndicalism often referred to it as anarchosyndicalism, while those who favored it called it revolutionary syndicalism. Syndicalism first emerged in France during the 1880s and reached its apogee in the first decade of the twentieth century. Syndicalism developed in parallel fashion in Italy and Spain (and after World War I in a number of other countries).

ORIGINS OF SYNDICALISM IN FRANCE, 1884–1902

Syndicalism brought together the emerging forces of the labor movement with anarchists in the new Bourses du Travail (Labor Exchanges). In 1884 trade unions were legalized, and in 1886 the Paris Prefect of Police subsidized the first Bourse du Travail in order to control the crowds seeking work. Inspired by the Communard Jean Allemane and by the young anarchist journalist Fernand Pelloutier, Parisian workers insisted on their right to run the bourses themselves. They thus created a unique French institution, not only a place to look for jobs but also a space for political development. By 1907 there were 157 bourses across France.

In 1892 Pelloutier and Émile Pouget, also a journalist, helped create the Fédération des Bourses du Travail, which soon claimed four hundred thousand members. Pelloutier was secretary of the federation from 1895 until his death in 1901. The federation's Nantes Congress of 1894 was dominated by anarchists; the congress resolved that workers could achieve their own liberation through direct action, without participating in electoral politics. Henceforth the federation opposed republican and socialist parties that participated in electoral politics; it aimed to coordinate strikes and ultimately unleash the general strike that would bring down capitalism directly

and turn factories and workshops over to their workers. In 1895 a rival group founded the smaller Confédération Générale du Travail (CGT; General Confederation of Labor). A good many French workers began to turn toward syndicalism following the anarchist attacks of 1892–1894; "propaganda by the deed" seemed a dead end. In 1902 the two organizations merged under the name CGT with a program largely dictated by syndicalists, who controlled most of the top positions, though the secretary, Victor Griffuelhes, was also active in politics: he was linked to Edouard Vaillant's Blanquist Party as it turned toward socialist politics in the 1890s.

THE AMIENS CHARTER AND THE SHOWDOWN WITH GOVERNMENT, 1902–1914

In 1904 the CGT began preparing a great strike for the eight-hour day, scheduled for 1 May 1906. Many hoped this would be the general strike to bring down capitalism. But the strike was triggered prematurely when, on 10 March 1906, a gas explosion at Courrières killed between 1,060 and 1,300 miners. Across the country, 61,000 miners went on strike. Soon hundreds of thousands in all trades were striking.

Georges Clemenceau, then minister of the interior, covered the striking areas with troops— fifty thousand for Paris alone—and arrested seven hundred union leaders. Workers felt deserted by politicians: even the socialists had shown too much willingness to collaborate with the government. Labor would go it alone. The CGT Congress at Amiens in October 1906 voted overwhelmingly for a broad resolution that became known as the Amiens Charter. It was the most influential statement of the syndicalist ideal. It envisaged that the union movement should not only struggle for better conditions but also prepare "integral emancipation, which can be realized only by the expropriation of capitalist property" through a general strike. The union, "today the group of resistance, will be, in the future, the group of production and of distribution, the base of social reorganization." Direct, grassroots action, especially strikes, would in turn further strengthen unions, leading to the general strike. Through these unions, workers would replace owners, managers, and the whole capitalist structure with a democratic economic structure run by the workers themselves.

This was the key to syndicalist thought. Workers did not need and indeed should keep aloof from electoral politics, even from links to the Socialist Party. This view had long-lasting effects. Only the year before Amiens, the French socialists had unified into one party, the Section Française de l'Internationale Ouvrière (SFIO; French Section of the Workers' International). The Amiens Charter kept French unions independent of political parties and thus prevented the formation of a labor or social democratic party as in the United Kingdom and Germany. The charter also inspired some intellectuals, led by Georges Sorel, to the view that revolutionary violence would cleanse and purify society. Sorel believed that the general strike was only a myth to inspire workers. Such ideas, however, were extremely rare among workers themselves.

Clemenceau became prime minister after Amiens. During his three-year reign, troops brutally repressed many strikes, killing strikers and demonstrators on several occasions. The practical failure of direct action eroded the prestige of the hard-line syndicalists, and in July 1909 Griffuelhes was replaced as secretary of the CGT by Léon Jouhaux, a more pragmatic syndicalist, but repression continued to shift the balance of union power from syndicalists to moderates. By 1914 the CGT used the rhetoric of syndicalism only to cover the reality of pragmatic collective bargaining. When World War I began, far from declaring the general strike as many had once expected, the CGT cooperated with the government in the *union sacrée* (sacred union). Syndicalism ceased to be a major force in France, but it still had far to go in Italy and Spain.

SYNDICALISM IN ITALY

Syndicalism in Italy was a response to a new era in politics after the turn of the nineteenth century. Reformist socialists of the Partito Socialista Italiano (PSI; Italian Socialist Party) began cooperating with a progressive government. This policy worked well for workers in developed industrial areas but not for nonunionized labor, poor rural laborers in the south, or the unemployed, groups within which anarchists had developed significant support. From their ranks emerged syndicalists led by

Alceste de Ambris, who was involved in the first syndicalist newspaper, *Il sindacato operato* (The workers' union; first appeared 1905).

Expelled from the PSI and defeated when the reformists created the Confederazione Generale del Lavoro (CGL; General Confederation of Labor), the syndicalists, acting through a plethora of local organizations, encouraged major strikes among rural laborers and artisans. These reached a high point with a strike of 20,000 rural laborers in Parma in May and June 1908. The strike was defeated by the united front of employers. The syndicalists sought to regain support, setting up the Committee for Direct Action as a faction within the CGL in 1910. Antimilitarist ideas brought more workers to their movement after Italy declared war on the Ottoman Empire to make Libya an Italian colony in 1911. In November 1912 syndicalists split from the CGL and set up the Unione Sindacale Italiana (USI; Italian Syndicalist Union), which achieved a membership of one hundred thousand the following year.

By this point many political anarchists had joined the USI. Syndicalists found that however much their principles derived from anarchism, they were more interested in trade union issues, so the USI was torn between anarchist efforts to foment a revolution and unionist attempts to win battles with employers. In 1914 troops killed three workers at anarchist antimilitarist demonstrations, and anarchists called a general strike. The results took everyone by surprise. More than a million workers went on strike in what became known as "Red Week," June 1914. Although Benito Mussolini (the future dictator) in Milan, Alceste de Ambris in Parma, and Errico Malatesta in Ancona proved effective leaders in their areas, "Red Week" achieved only disillusionment. Nevertheless, it showed that syndicalism was a strong and growing force at the outbreak of World War I.

SYNDICALISM IN SPAIN

In the 1870s and 1880s Russian émigrés Mikhail Bakunin's and Peter Kropotkin's competing anarchist ideas inspired many in the nascent labor movement in Spain; those of Marx inspired others. The Marxists were at the core that in

1888 founded the Unión General de Trabajadores (UGT; General Union of Workers). It was not, however, until 1907 that, inspired by the Amiens Charter, Spanish anarchists and others founded the Solidaridad Obrera (SO; Workers' Solidarity) in Barcelona. Similar anarchist groups quickly sprang up across the country, and in November 1910 they coalesced as the Confederación Nacional del Trabajo (CNT; National Confederation of Labor).

The CNT aimed at unity with the UGT but became instead a competing trade-union central based on revolutionary syndicalism. In 1911, after its second congress, a general strike broke out. The government accused the CNT of fomenting the strike and declared the organization illegal. The CNT had only twenty-six thousand members, so it is more likely that many workers shared similar views than that the CNT actually caused the strike. But it was not until 1915 that the CNT was rebuilt. It played a major role after World War I, culminating in its major role on the Republican side in the Spanish civil war.

See also **Anarchism; Anarchosyndicalism; Labor Movements; Strikes.**

BIBLIOGRAPHY

Amdur, Kathryn E. *Syndicalist Legacy: Trade Unions and Politics in Two French Cities in the Era of World War I.* Urbana, Ill., 1986.

Ansell, Christopher K. *Schism and Solidarity in Social Movements: The Politics of Labor in the French Third Republic.* New York, 2001.

Levy, Carl. "Currents of Italian Syndicalism before 1926." *International Review of Social History* 45 (2000): 209–250.

Linden, Marcel van der, and Wayne Thorpe, eds. *Revolutionary Syndicalism: An International Perspective.* Aldershot, U.K., and Brookfield, Vt., 1990.

Milner, Susan. *The Dilemmas of Internationalism: French Syndicalism and the International Labour Movement, 1900–1914.* New York, 1990.

Mitchell, Barbara. *The Practical Revolutionaries: A New Interpretation of the French Anarchosyndicalists.* New York, 1987.

Papayanis, Nicholas. *Alphonse Merrheim: The Emergence of Reformism in Revolutionary Syndicalism, 1871–1925.* Dordrecht, Netherlands, and Boston, 1985.

Roberts, David D. *The Syndicalist Tradition and Italian Fascism.* Chapel Hill, N.C., 1979.

Sorel, Georges. *Reflections on Violence.* Translated by T. E. Hulme. New York, 1975.

Thorpe, Wayne. *The Workers Themselves: Revolutionary Syndicalism and International Labour, 1913–1923.* Boston, 1989.

Tucker, Kenneth H. *French Revolutionary Syndicalism and the Public Sphere.* New York, 1996.

Vandervort, Bruce. *Victor Griffuelhes and French Syndicalism, 1895–1922.* Baton Rouge, La., 1996.

CHARLES SOWERWINE

SYPHILIS. As is the case with many diseases that afflicted (and continue to afflict) European populations, the early names of syphilis reflected contemporary understandings of the origins of the disease. The disease has been traced back to French military campaigns in Italian lands, and more specifically to the Neapolitan excursions of Charles VIII (r. 1483–1498) in 1495. The subsequent demobilization of mercenaries facilitated the rapid spread of the disease throughout Europe. Dynastic loyalties influenced whether one referred to it as the "French" or "Neapolitan" disease. In the early sixteenth century a controversy arose as to whether the introduction of syphilis in Europe should be regarded as one of the major consequences of the Spanish conquest of the Americas; thus, occasionally, it was described as the "American" disease. Still others referred to syphilis simply as the "pox," conjuring up the physical manifestations of the disease that began on the genitals and that eventually spread over the entire body.

No matter how they named it, syphilis inspired fear and dread among sixteenth-century Europeans. They considered it worse than leprosy and the plague. Although they understood the link between sexual activity and infection, and developed therapies (a combination of mercury and the wood extract guaiac, applied either as an ointment or through friction) aimed at alleviating symptoms, Europeans often resorted to draconian measures. The city of Paris forbade the treatment of syphilis at the centrally located Hôtel Dieu; the stricken homeless population was driven out of Paris, and the poor were placed in barns located in outlying areas of the city. After the initial and rapid spread of syphilis in sixteenth-century Europe, rates of infection appear to have abated, which may account (in part) for a waning interest in the disease among medical authorities until the end of the eighteenth century. In this space created by medical neglect, charlatans and quacks arrived with their various remedies, eagerly embraced by Europeans searching for a quick and effective cure.

SYPHILIS IN NINETEENTH-CENTURY EUROPE

More surprising is the notable absence of syphilis in the medical advances that characterized nineteenth-century Europe. Apart from the important work of Philippe Ricord (1800–1889), who distinguished gonorrhea from syphilis, few doctors placed syphilis at the center of their research, and medical curricula largely ignored it. By contrast, syphilis figured prominently in a European social imagination—a veritable "bourgeois obsession"—that gave expression to a growing anxiety about the vexed relationship between individual liberty and social order. That obsession drew upon purported links between sex, prostitution, and the spread of syphilis. The prostitute, who lived outside the regulated contexts of marriage and family, and who separated sexual pleasure from the social functions of procreation, was seen as exercising an excessive and dangerous freedom. She lured unsuspecting single men away from the strictures of duty, risked the fortunes amassed by married men, and in doing so threatened the very institutions and values of society. In ways both figurative and material, syphilis embodied these dangers posed by the prostitute. It was she who spread the disease to unsuspecting men, in turn threatening the lives of innocent fiancées, moral wives and mothers, and future unborn generations.

The social imaginary of syphilis developed most precociously in France. Its influence was felt afar, made evident in the international recognition accorded to the work of the French social observer and hygienist Alexandre Parent-Duchâtelet (1790–1836). In his 1836 study *De la prostitution dans la ville de Paris* Parent-Duchâtelet set out in excruciating (although far from convincing) detail the characteristics of prostitutes that defined them a "race apart" and a veritable "counter society": their distaste for work, their love of luxury, and their unfortunate family origins. He also described

the peculiar regulation of prostitution adopted by French authorities. Recognizing the limitations of recourse to individual liberty or legislative pronouncement as effective strategies for addressing the problems posed by individual freedom, the French devised an extralegal regulatory system drawing on the cooperation of police and doctors. Prostitutes associated with "tolerated" houses were subject to weekly brothel medical examinations for syphilis. If infected, they were sent to Saint-Lazare, an institution that served as a prison and a hospital, and which combined curing and physical as well as moral discipline in the "treatment" of prostitutes supposedly suffering from syphilis. Prostitutes who were registered with the police authorities but who worked independently of tolerated houses were required to seek out the services of municipal dispensaries; they carried a card detailing their medical histories, while medical information pertaining to women associated with the tolerated houses was maintained by the brothel-keeper.

The British dealt with the problem of the relationship between syphilis and prostitution in slightly different ways. Defending (and defensive of) their time-honored commitment to individual liberty, British officials and social observers deplored the French toleration of brothels, which in their view recognized prostitution and thus perpetuated (rather than prevented) the demoralization of women. They also criticized the association of dispensaries and hospitals with prisons, because (in their view) it addressed the social problems involved in the spread of syphilis at the expense of depriving women of their civil rights. But prostitutes had been treated in British "lock hospitals" since the 1770s, and new hospitals were created during the first three decades of the nineteenth century. Like their French counterparts, these hospitals confined prostitutes to specific sections, restricted their mobility and access to visitors, required them to stay until "cured" or at least until no longer contagious, and wedded medical care to disciplinary and moralizing activities. Between 1864 and 1869 the government passed three Contagious Diseases Acts. Originally designed as exceptional legislation to deal with the problem of syphilis affecting soldiers in military districts in England and Ireland, the purview of the Acts was soon after extended to other areas. A rigorous and coercive regulation of syphilis in British colonial territories such as India and Hong Kong predated the passage of the CD Acts and persisted long after their repeal in the 1870s and 1880s. In those territories, the social anxieties conjured up by the interrelated problems of syphilis and prostitution dealt, above all, with the colonial prostitute and the threat she posed to the British soldier, settler, and "race."

TOWARD A NEW REGULATION OF SYPHILIS

The repeal of the CD Acts in England between 1870 and 1886 reflected the influence of the protest mounted against the regulation of prostitution and syphilis there by moral and Christian reformers such as Josephine Butler (1828–1906). Butler's criticisms gained attention in France as well, although French interest in reform was due in large part to the Republican ascendancy beginning in the 1870s and 1880s. French politicians, doctors, and social observers focused on the problem of regulating syphilis and prostitution as part of a larger criticism of the abuses perpetuated by the authoritarian Second Empire. They debated the relative merits of two alternatives: abolishing regulation altogether, and replacing it with new, more individualistic initiatives aimed at moral education and the promotion of early marriage, or elaborating a "neoregulationism" devoid of the abusive intrusions of police authority and carefully restricted to the medical question of diagnosing and treating syphilis. Neoregulationism emerged victorious.

The French medical community supported the alternative of neoregulationism. Indeed, that alternative owed much to the enhanced status of syphilis in French medicine at the end of the nineteenth century: the recognition of syphilology as a medical specialty and its inclusion in departments of dermatology, advances in understanding the different stages of syphilis and its connection to general paralysis, the "humanization" of syphilis treatment through its integration into general hospital care, and the creation of national leagues and international studies devoted to the problem of the disease. Many of these accomplishments became associated with the work of Alfred-Jean Fournier, "the new pope of syphilography." For all of Fournier's scientific preoccupation with syphilis, however,

Poster publicizing a syphilis sanitarium in Spain, early twentieth century. ©ARCHIVO ICONOGRAFICO,S.A./CORBIS

his work and the efforts of other neoregulationists more generally betray a deep reservoir of social anxiety that shaped the contours of interest in syphilis in fin-de-siècle France.

Fournier's articulation of the venereal peril was informed by an entirely new configuration of social concerns at the turn of the century, most importantly the influence of social Darwinism, worries about declining birth rates, and growing fears about the degeneration of the French "race." In the face of these threats, the specter of syphilis loomed even larger than it had in the 1830s and 1840s. Failing to distinguish between the possibility of hereditary and congenital syphilis, Fournier highlighted the deleterious consequences for babies born of sexual relations between prostitutes and their unsuspecting clients. Of more serious import, Fournier did not limit the effects of syphilis to sexual activity. Glassblowing, tattooing, and improperly cleaned medical instruments all provided conduits for the non-venereal transmission of syphilis, although both forms of the diseases contributed to the "peril." (The Russian venereologist Veniamin Tarnovsky [1839–1906] likewise distinguished between venereal and non-venereal syphilis, but in this case the distinction appears to have emphasized the dangers of illicit sexual relations—and social relations more generally—that characterized the industrial and urban centers of liberalizing Imperial Russia.) Despite their avowed commitment to reducing the role of police in the regulation of syphilis, Fournier and other neoregulationists retained their focus on the social threats posed by prostitutes, now with a new (and perhaps more insidious) twist: the objective was no longer to protect society by excluding or marginalizing the prostitute, but rather to "normalize" her, with the support of medical knowledge and according to the needs and dictates of society.

The twentieth century set the stage for many of the discoveries that we now associate with the scientific diagnosis and treatment of syphilis: the identification of its cause (*Treponema pallidum*) by Erich Hoffmann and Fritz Schaudinn in 1905,

the recognition of the diagnostic value of the Wassermann Test in 1906, and the introduction of penicillin in the 1950s. The benefits of these discoveries notwithstanding, an understanding of the problem of syphilis has continued to be refracted through the prism of social issues. Vichy France linked syphilis to the problem of Jews and "aliens"; in the early twenty-first century, syphilis conjures up the dangers of international tourism and promiscuity. In this regard, syphilis offers a telling instance of the difficulty encountered in separating the scientific understanding of disease from the elaboration of social values. As such, syphilis also represents the important and enduring role for historical scholarship in understanding the contours of disease and societal responses to it.

See also **Butler, Josephine; Prostitution; Public Health; Science and Technology; Sexuality.**

BIBLIOGRAPHY

Aisenberg, Andrew. "Syphilis and Prostitution: A Regulatory Couplet in Nineteenth-Century France." In *Sex, Sin, and Suffering: Venereal Disease and European Society, since 1870*, edited by Roger Davidson and Lesley A. Hall, 15–28. London and New York, 2001.

Corbin, Alain. *Women for Hire: Prostitution and Sexuality in France after 1850*. Translated by Alan Sheridan. Cambridge, Mass., 1990.

Engelstein, Laura. *The Keys to Happiness: Sex and the Search for Modernity in Fin-de-Siècle Russia*. Ithaca, N.Y., 1992.

Levine, Philippa. *Prostitution, Race, and Politics: Policing Venereal Disease in the British Empire*. New York, 2003.

Quétel, Claude. *The History of Syphilis*. Translated by Judith Braddock and Brian Pike. Baltimore, Md., 1990.

Walkowitz, Judith R. *Prostitution and Victorian Society: Women, Class, and the State*. Cambridge, U.K., and New York, 1980.

ANDREW AISENBERG

For Reference

Not to be taken from this room